Lecture Notes in Artificial Intelligence   8761

Subseries of Lecture Notes in Computer Science

Lecture Notes in Artificial Intelligence 8467

Subseries of Lecture Notes in Computer Science

LNAI Series Editors

Randy Goebel
University of Alberta, Edmonton, Canada
Yuzuru Tanaka
Hokkaido University, Sapporo, Japan
Wolfgang Wahlster
DFKI and Saarland University, Saarbrücken, Germany

LNAI Founding Series Editor

Joerg Siekmann
DFKI and Saarland University, Saarbrücken, Germany

Eduardo Fermé   João Leite (Eds.)

Logics in
Artificial Intelligence

14th European Conference, JELIA 2014
Funchal, Madeira, Portugal, September 24-26, 2014
Proceedings

 Springer

Volume Editors

Eduardo Fermé
University of Madeira
Funchal, Madeira, Portugal
E-mail: ferme@uma.pt

João Leite
CENTRIA, Universidade Nova de Lisboa
Caparica, Portugal
E-mail: jleite@fct.unl.pt

ISSN 0302-9743   e-ISSN 1611-3349
ISBN 978-3-319-11557-3   e-ISBN 978-3-319-11558-0
DOI 10.1007/978-3-319-11558-0
Springer Cham Heidelberg New York Dordrecht London

Library of Congress Control Number: 2014948692

LNCS Sublibrary: SL 7 – Artificial Intelligence

Typesetting: Camera-ready by author, data conversion by Scientific Publishing Services, Chennai, India

Printed on acid-free paper

Springer is part of Springer Science+Business Media (www.springer.com)

In her invited talk titled "Tools for the Investigation of Substructural and Paraconsistent Logics", Agata Ciabattoni (Vienna University of Technology, Austria), described her group's tools introducing sequent-style calculi for large classes of logics and using them to prove various results about these logics in a uniform and automated way. For the case studies of substructural and of paraconsistent logics the introduced calculi are used to prove standard completeness, decidability, and to provide new semantic foundations using non-deterministic matrices.

In his invited talk titled "How to Solve a Non-classical Planning Problem with a Classical Planner: the Power of Transformations", Hector Geffner (Universitat Pompeu Fabra in Barcelona, Spain) reviewed the inferences performed by classical planners that enable them to deal with large problems, and the transformations that have been developed for using these planners to deal with non-classical features such as soft goals, hidden goals to be recognized, planning with incomplete information and sensing, and multiagent nested beliefs.

In his invited talk titled "Towards Argument-based Persuasion Technologies", Anthony Hunter (University College London, United Kingdom), addressed persuasion systems, or systems that enter into dialogues with users to persuade them to undertake some action - mental or physical - or to not do some action, reviewing computational models of argument developed for modelling persuasion dialogues, in particular for handling their inherent uncertainty. Anthony Hunter's invited talk was generously supported by the European Network for Social Intelligence (SINTELNET).

We would like to thank the authors of all the submitted papers, the members of the Program Committee and the additional experts who helped during the reviewing process, for contributing and ensuring the high scientific quality of JELIA 2014.

We would also like to acknowledge the support of the University of Madeira, the Center for Artificial Intelligence (CENTRIA), the Portuguese Association for Artificial Intelligence (APPIA), Fundação para a Ciência e Tecnologia (FCT), the Artificial Intelligence Journal, DTIM, Springer, and EasyChair.

Finally, a word of gratitude to Maurício Reis and his local team for taking care of the local organization of the JELIA 2014.

July 2014   Eduardo Fermé
                                                        João Leite

Preface

These are the proceedings of the 14th European Conference on Logics in Artificial Intelligence (JELIA 2014) held during September 24–26, 2014 in Funchal, in the beautiful island of Madeira, Portugal, and organized by the University of Madeira and the Centre for Artificial Intelligence (CENTRIA) of the New University of Lisbon.

The European Conference on Logics in Artificial Intelligence (or Journées Européennes sur la Logique en Intelligence Artificielle - JELIA) began back in 1988, as a workshop, in response to the need for a European forum for the discussion of emerging work in this field. Since then, JELIA has been organised biennially, with proceedings published in the Springer-Verlag series Lecture Notes in Artificial Intelligence. Previous meetings took place in Roscoff, France (1988), Amsterdam, the Netherlands (1990), Berlin, Germany (1992), York, UK (1994), Évora, Portugal (1996), Dagstuhl, Germany (1998), Málaga, Spain (2000), Cosenza, Italy (2002), Lisbon, Portugal (2004), Liverpool, UK (2006), Dresden, Germany (2008), Helsinki, Finland (2010) and Toulouse, France (2012).

The aim of JELIA is to bring together active researchers interested in all aspects concerning the use of logics in artificial intelligence to discuss current research, results, problems, and applications of both theoretical and practical nature. JELIA strives to foster links and facilitate cross-fertilization of ideas among researchers from various disciplines, among researchers from academia and industry, and between theoreticians and practitioners.

The increasing interest in this forum, its international level with growing participation of researchers from outside Europe, and the overall technical quality, have turned JELIA into a major biennial forum for the discussion of logic-based approaches to artificial intelligence.

For the 2014 edition of JELIA, authors were invited to submit papers presenting original and unpublished research in all areas related to the use of logic in artificial intelligence.

There were 121 submissions, each reviewed by at least three Program Committee members. The committee decided to accept 32 full papers. An addition 12 submissions were accepted for a poster session and short presentation. T program also includes 4 invited talks - by Diego Calvanese, Agata Ciabatto Hector Geffner and Anthony Hunter - and is complemented by 5 system descr tions (3 full and 2 short).

In his invited talk titled "Query Answering over Description Logic Ont gies", Diego Calvanese (Free University of Bozen-Bolzano, Italy) overviewed main results and techniques developed in the last years for answering (unions conjunctive queries over DL ontologies, ranging from tableaux algorithms techniques based on automata on infinite trees for expressive DLs, to rewr based approaches for lightweight DLs.

Organization

Conference Chair

Eduardo Fermé   University of Madeira - CENTRIA, Portugal

Program Co-chairs

Eduardo Fermé   University of Madeira - CENTRIA, Portugal
João Leite   CENTRIA, New University of Lisbon, Portugal

Program Committee

Natasha Alechina   University of Nottingham, UK
José Júlio Alferes   CENTRIA, New University of Lisbon, Portugal
Leila Amgoud   IRIT-CNRS, University of Toulouse, France
Carlos Areces   National University of Córdoba, Argentina
Franz Baader   TU Dresden, Germany
Pietro Baroni   University of Brescia, Italy
Peter Baumgartner   NICTA, Australia
Salem Benferhat   CRIL-CNRS, University of Artois, Lens, France
Philippe Besnard   IRIT-CNRS, University of Toulouse, France
Alexander Bochman   Holon Institute of Technology, Israel
Richard Booth   University of Luxembourg, Luxembourg
Gerhard Brewka   University of Leipzig, Germany
Jan Broersen   Utrecht University, The Netherlands
Pedro Cabalar   University of Corunna, Spain
Walter Carnielli   State University of Campinas, Brazil
Carlos Damásio   CENTRIA, New University of Lisbon, Portugal
Mehdi Dastani   Utrecht University, The Netherlands
James Delgrande   Simon Fraser University, Canada
Marc Denecker   Catholic University of Leuven, Belgium
Didier Dubois   IRIT-CNRS, University of Toulouse, France
Paul Dunne   University of Liverpool, UK
Ulle Endriss   University of Amsterdam, The Netherlands
Wolfgang Faber   University of Huddersfield, UK
Luis Farinas Del Cerro   IRIT-CNRS, University of Toulouse, France
Michael Fink   Vienna University of Technology, Austria
Michael Fisher   University of Liverpool, UK
Laura Giordano   University of Eastern Piedmont, Italy

Lluis Godo	IIIA - CSIC, Spain
Valentin Goranko	Technical University of Denmark, Denmark
Andreas Herzig	IRIT-CNRS, University of Toulouse, France
Pascal Hitzler	Wright State University, USA
Tomi Janhunen	Aalto University, Finland
Tommi Junttila	Aalto University, Finland
Gabriele Kern-Isberner	TU Dortmund, Germany
Sébastien Konieczny	CRIL-CNRS, University of Artois, Lens, France
Roman Kontchakov	Birkbeck College, UK
Jérôme Lang	LAMSADE-CNRS, University of Paris-Dauphine, France
Joohyung Lee	Arizona State University, USA
Maurizio Lenzerini	University of Rome "La Sapienza", Italy
Nicola Leone	University of Calabria, Italy
Vladimir Lifschitz	University of Texas, USA
Emiliano Lorini	IRIT-CNRS, University of Toulouse, France
Carsten Lutz	University of Bremen, Germany
Ines Lynce	University of Lisbon, Portugal
Pierre Marquis	CRIL-CNRS, University of Artois, Lens, France
Jérôme Mengin	IRIT-CNRS, University of Toulouse, France
George Metcalfe	University of Bern, Switzerland
Thomas Meyer	CSIR Meraka Institute and University of KwaZulu-Natal, South Africa
Luís Moniz Pereira	CENTRIA, New University of Lisbon, Portugal
Angelo Montanari	University of Udine, Italy
Manuel Ojeda-Aciego	University of Malaga, Spain
Magdalena Ortiz	Vienna University of Technology, Austria
Jeff Z. Pan	University of Aberdeen, UK
David Pearce	Technical University of Madrid, Spain
André Platzer	Carnegie Mellon University, USA
Henri Prade	IRIT-CNRS, University of Toulouse, France
Mauricio Reis	University of Madeira, Portugal
Jussi Rintanen	Aalto University, Finland
Sebastian Rudolph	TU Dresden, Germany
Vladislav Ryzhikov	Free University of Bozen-Bolzano, Italy
Torsten Schaub	University of Potsdam, Germany
Steven Schockaert	Cardiff University, UK
Terrance Swift	CENTRIA, New University of Lisbon, Portugal
Michael Thielscher	The University of New South Wales, Australia
Mirek Truszczynski	University of Kentucky, USA
Wiebe Van Der Hoek	University of Liverpool, UK
Leon van der Torre	University of Luxembourg, Luxembourg
Toby Walsh	NICTA, Australia
Mary-Anne Williams	University of Technology, Australia
Frank Wolter	University of Liverpool, UK

Stefan Woltran   Vienna University of Technology, Austria
Michael Wooldridge   University of Oxford, UK
Michael Zakharyaschev   Birkbeck College, UK

Local Organising Committee Co-chairs

Eduardo Fermé   University of Madeira - CENTRIA, Portugal
Mauricio Reis   University of Madeira - CENTRIA, Portugal

Local Organizing Committee

Yuri Almeida   University of Madeira, Portugal
Maite Costa   University of Madeira, Portugal
José Serina   University of Madeira, Portugal
Tatiana Severim   University of Madeira, Portugal
Verónica Sousa   University of Madeira, Portugal

Additional Reviewers

Alsinet, Teresa   Ebtekar, Aram
Alviano, Mario   Fandinno, Jorge
Andres, Benjamin   Fichte, Johannes Klaus
Aucher, Guillaume   Garcia, Jhonatan
Baioletti, Marco   Gebser, Martin
Bartholomew, Michael   Gliozzi, Valentina
Baumann, Ringo   Gonçalves, Ricardo
Baumgartner, Alexander   Grandi, Umberto
Bernardini, Sara   Greco, Gianluigi
Blondeel, Marjon   Green, Todd
Bogaerts, Bart   Gutiérrez Basulto, Víctor
Botoeva, Elena   Hustadt, Ullrich
Burrieza, Alfredo   Inoue, Katsumi
Carral, David   Jansen, Joachim
Casini, Giovanni   Jensen, Martin Holm
Combi, Carlo   Jung, Jean Christoph
Dasseville, Ingmar   Klarman, Szymon
Dennis, Louise   Knobbout, Max
Devriendt, Jo   Kramdi, Seifeddine
Dodaro, Carmine   Lagniez, Jean Marie
Dovier, Agostino   Lam, Ho-Pun
Duijf, Hein   Linsbichler, Thomas
Dvorak, Wolfgang   Lippmann, Marcel

Lisitsa, Alexei
Ma, Yue
Mailly, Jean-Guy
Manna, Marco
Marchioni, Enrico
Markey, Nicolas
Martelli, Alberto
Mutharaju, Raghava
Muñoz-Velasco, Emilio
Nguyen, Hoang Nga
Nouioua, Farid
Oikarinen, Emilia
Ostrowski, Max
Pardo, Pere
Polberg, Sylwia
Porello, Daniele
Rajaratnam, David
Redl, Christoph
Ren, Yuan
Rens, Gavin
Ricca, Francesco
Ringeissen, Christophe
Rollon, Emma
Romero, Javier

Rümmele, Stefan
Salhi, Yakoub
Saptawijaya, Ari
Schmid, Ute
Schneider, Thomas
Sciavicco, Guido
Sengupta, Kunal
Stepanova, Daria
Strass, Hannes
Studer, Thomas
Testerink, Bas
Toman, David
Tsarkov, Dmitry
Uridia, Levan
Valverde, Agustin
Van Hertum, Pieter
Vesic, Srdjan
Wang, Cong
Wang, Yi
Wang, Yisong
Wang, Zhe
Zawadzki, Erik
Zhao, Yuting
Zhou, Yi

Table of Contents

Logics for Uncertain Reasoning

Non-Classical Logics

Answer-Set Programming

Belief Revision

Dealing with Inconsistency in ASP and DL

Reason about Actions and Causality

System Descriptions

Short System Descriptions

Short Papers

Query Answering over Description Logic Ontologies

Diego Calvanese

KRDB Research Centre for Knowledge and Data
Free University of Bozen-Bolzano
calvanese@inf.unibz.it

Abstract. Description Logics (DLs) provide the formal foundation for ontology languages, and they have been advocated as formalisms for modeling the domain of interest in various settings, including the Semantic Web, data and information integration, and ontology-based data access. An important requirement there is the ability to answer complex database-like queries, while taking into account both extensional and intensional domain knowledge. The task of answering queries has been investigated intensively in the last years for a variety of DLs, and considering both data complexity, i.e., the complexity measured in the size of the extensional information only, and combined complexity. On the one hand, it has been shown to be in general (exponentially) more difficult than the standard reasoning tasks of concept satisfiability and subsumption; on the other hand a broad range of techniques have been developed. We overview here some of the key techniques developed in the last years for query answering over DL ontologies, ranging from rewriting based approaches for lightweight DLs, to tableaux algorithms, and techniques based on automata on infinite trees for very expressive DLs. The associated results, accompanied by matching lower bounds, have contributed to shaping the computational complexity picture for ontology-based query answering.

1 Introduction

Description Logics [4] (DLs) are a class of logics that are particularly well suited for representing structured knowledge. They have been developed starting from the early 1980s in order to formalize early days knowledge representation formalisms, such as Semantic Networks and Frames, which lacked not only well understood computational properties, but despite their name even a formal semantics. Since then DLs have evolved into a large collection of variants that, in their various forms, subsume essentially all class-based representation formalisms used in Databases, Artificial Intelligence, and Software Engineering. DLs follow the quite common approach used in knowledge representation of modeling the domain of interest in terms of *concepts*, which denote sets of objects, and relations between objects belonging to certain concepts. We consider here "traditional" DLs, which are equipped only with binary relations, called *roles*, but many variants of DLs allowing for the use of relations of arbitrary arity have also been considered in the literature [47,15,14]. Starting from atomic concepts and roles, complex expressions can be constructed inductively by means of suitable concept and role forming operators. Such expressions are then used in an *ontology* to assert knowledge about the domain, both at the intensional level, in the *TBox* of the ontology, and at the extensional level, in the *ABox* of the ontology. Typically, the TBox consists of a set

E. Fermé and J. Leite (Eds.): JELIA 2014, LNAI 8761, pp. 1–17, 2014.

of inclusion assertions between concepts and between roles, where each such assertion states that the set of instances of one concept/role is included in the set of instance of another concept/role. The ABox instead contains facts about individual domain elements, asserting that some individual belongs to a concept, or that some pair of individuals is related by a role.

A distinguishing feature of DLs is the fact that quantification is restricted by the syntax of the logic (which is variable-free) to be *guarded*. A consequence is that DL concept expressions essentially can only be used to represent properties that are encoded by starting from an instance of the concept and following the roles in a *tree-like* navigation. Formally, this aspect is captured by the fact that DLs (in general) satisfy some form of *tree-model property*: if an ontology is satisfiable, then it admits a model that is constituted by a collection[1] of structures that are essentially[2] tree-shaped (when viewing objects as nodes, and relations between objects as edges connecting them). On the one hand, the tree-model property, which DLs share with modal logics and with many variants of program logics [50], accounts for many of the good computational properties of DLs, which, despite being first-order formalism, admit decidable and in many cases efficient inference. On the other hand, the restriction that is at the basis of the tree-model property brings about an intrinsic limitation in expressive power. This makes it impossible in DLs to express inter-relationships between objects that would correspond to following different navigation paths across the data. E.g., in a DL one could not express a concept denoting those individuals for which the house in which they live is located in the same city as the company in which they work. While this kind of restriction is considered acceptable when encoding knowledge at the intensional level in a TBox, it makes DLs not well-suited as a formalism for expressing queries, where in general one is interested in complex inter-relationships between objects.

For this reason, since the late 1990s, researchers have studied the setting where information needs expressed over knowledge encoded in an ontology are formulated not only in terms of concept or role expressions, but also in terms of more complex *queries* in the style of those used in databases [35,15]. In such a setting, where the presence of an ontology accounts for incomplete information, query answering is a form of logical implication, as opposed to model checking, which can be seen as the logical counterpart of query evaluation. For this reason, answering arbitrary (domain independent) FOL queries (corresponding to the core of SQL) over an ontology turns out to be immediately undecidable. Just consider evaluating the query $q(x) = A(x) \wedge \varphi$ over the ontology with an empty TBox and whose ABox just contains $A(c)$, where φ is an arbitrary FOL formula in which A does not appear; then c is in the answer to the query iff φ is valid.

This motivates why in the context of DLs, restricted classes of queries have been considered, which still allow for expressing sufficiently complex interrelationships between data, but do not incur in the computational problems caused by arbitrary FOL queries. A prominent such class of queries are *conjunctive queries* (CQs) [22], corresponding

---

[1] The ABox accounts for an arbitrary graph-shaped but finite portion of the model, and each object interpreting an individual of the ABox can be seen as the root of a possibly infinite tree originating from that object.

[2] Depending on the constructs of the DL, we might have to account for multiple role-labeled edges between nodes, or for special edges that point back to the ABox part.

to select-project-join SQL queries, and unions thereof (UCQs). Such queries account for the most common type of queries used in the relational setting, and also have found applications in other settings of incomplete information, such as data integration and data exchange [34,25]. DLs, as opposed to relational databases, allow one to represent knowledge in which the underlying data has a rather loose structure, such as the one encountered nowadays in graph databases. Indeed, in the setting of DLs, it became of interest to consider also more flexible mechanisms for querying such kind of data, as the one offered by variants of *regular path queries* [10,1], which allow one to retrieve pairs of objects connected by a path in the data that matches a regular expression over the set of roles (i.e., edge labels in the graph).

In the following, we discuss the challenges that arise when addressing the problem of answering queries over DL ontologies. Given the large amount of parameters that characterize the problem, and the variety of results that have been obtained in the area, our aim is not to be comprehensive, and we refer to [40,38] for recent overviews of query answering in ontologies. Instead, we aim at illustrating three different types of techniques that have been introduced in the literature, and that aimed at addressing different requirements for the problem of query answering over DL ontologies. After introducing in Section 2 some technical preliminaries on DLs and queries that are necessary for the subsequent development, we first illustrate in Section 3 a technique for efficient query answering in lightweight DLs that lends itself for an efficient implementation. Then, in Section 4 we present an adaptation of tableaux algorithms traditionally adopted for DL inference towards query answering in expressive DLs. The technique allows one to obtain optimal complexity bounds in terms of *data complexity*, i.e., when the complexity of the problem is measured in terms of the size of the ABox only. Finally, in Section 5, we present an approach based on automata on infinite trees, that leads to decidability and optimal complexity results (thought not in data complexity) for DLs and query languages that are among the most expressive ones for which decidability of query answering has been established so far.

2 Description Logic Ontologies and Queries

In DLs, the domain of interest is modeled by means of *concepts*, denoting classes of objects, and *roles* (i.e., binary relationships), denoting binary relations between objects.

Syntax of Description Logics. Arbitrary concepts and roles are obtained starting from atomic ones by applying suitable concept and role forming constructs, where the set of allowed constructs characterizes each specific DL. We introduce here the quite expressive DL $\mathcal{ALCOIQHb}_{reg}^{self}$, abbreviated simply as $\mathcal{DL}$, which is a super-language of the various DLs that we consider in this work[3]. Specifically, $\mathcal{DL}$ is an expressive DL in which concepts and roles are formed according to the following syntax:

$$C, C' \longrightarrow A \mid C \sqcap C' \mid \forall R.C \mid \neg C \mid \leqslant n\,S.C \mid \{a\} \mid \exists S.\mathsf{Self}$$
$$P \longrightarrow p \mid p^-$$
$$S, S' \longrightarrow P \mid S \cap S' \mid S \setminus S' \mid S \cup S'$$
$$R, R' \longrightarrow \mathsf{T} \mid S \mid R \cup R' \mid R \circ R' \mid R^* \mid id(C)$$

---

[3] $\mathcal{DL}$ is equivalent to the DL $\mathcal{ZOIQ}$ [20].

where A denotes an *atomic concept*, p an *atomic role*, S, S' simple roles, C, C' arbitrary *concepts*, and R, R' arbitrary *roles*, and a an individual. $\mathcal{DL}$ is obtained from the basic DL language $\mathcal{AL}$ (attributive language) [4], in which one can express concept intersection $C \sqcap C'$ and value restriction $\forall R.C$, by adding several concept and role forming constructs, each indicated by a letter or a sub/super-script in the name of the DL. Such constructs are negation $\neg C$ of arbitrary concepts (indicated by the letter $\mathcal{C}$ in $\mathcal{ALCOIQHb}_{reg}^{self}$), qualified number restrictions $\leqslant n\,S.C$ (indicated by $\mathcal{Q}$), nominals $\{a\}$ (indicated by $\mathcal{O}$), inverse roles p^- (indicated by $\mathcal{I}$), boolean combinations of atomic and inverse roles (indicated by b), the self-construct (indicated by the superscript ^{self}), and regular expressions over roles (indicated by the subscript $_{reg}$). We can also express the top concept $\top$ as an abbreviation for $A \sqcup \neg A$, for some concept A, the bottom concept $\bot$ as $\neg\top$, union $C_1 \sqcup C_2$ as $\neg(\neg C_1 \sqcap \neg C_2)$, and qualified existential quantification on roles $\exists R.C$ as $\neg\forall R.\neg C$. We observe that, in order to preserve decidability of inference, number restrictions are applied only to *simple* roles, i.e., atomic roles p, their inverses p^-, or boolean combinations thereof (see, e.g., [5,11] for the consequences of using more complex roles in number restrictions).

As in most DLs, a $\mathcal{DL}$ *ontology* is a pair $\mathcal{O} = \langle \mathcal{T}, \mathcal{A} \rangle$, where $\mathcal{T}$, the *TBox*, is a finite set of *intensional assertions*, and $\mathcal{A}$, the *ABox*, is a finite set of *extensional* (or, *membership*) *assertions*. Here we consider TBoxes consisting only of inclusion assertions between concepts and between simple roles[4]. An *inclusion assertion* has the form $C \sqsubseteq C'$, with C and C' arbitrary $\mathcal{DL}$ concepts, or $S \sqsubseteq S'$, with S and S' simple roles. Intuitively, it states that, in every model of the TBox, each instance of the left-hand side expression is also an instance of the right-hand side expression. We note that the letter $\mathcal{H}$ in the name of $\mathcal{ALCOIQHb}_{reg}^{self}$ accounts for the presence in the logic of role inclusions, by means of which one can express role *hierarchies*. The ABox consists of a set of extensional assertions, which are used to make statements about individuals. Each such assertion has the form $A(a)$, $p(a,b)$, $a \approx b$, or $a \not\approx b$, with A and p respectively an atomic concept and an atomic role occurring in $\mathcal{T}$, and a, b individuals.

Semantics of Description Logics. We now turn to the semantics of $\mathcal{DL}$, which is given in terms of interpretations. An *interpretation* $\mathcal{I} = (\Delta^{\mathcal{I}}, \cdot^{\mathcal{I}})$ consists of a non-empty interpretation domain $\Delta^{\mathcal{I}}$ and an interpretation function $\cdot^{\mathcal{I}}$, which assigns to each concept C a subset $C^{\mathcal{I}}$ of $\Delta^{\mathcal{I}}$, to each role R a binary relation $R^{\mathcal{I}}$ over $\Delta^{\mathcal{I}}$, and to each individual a an element $a^{\mathcal{I}} \in \Delta^{\mathcal{I}}$, in such a way that the conditions specified in Figure 1 are satisfied[5]. Unless stated otherwise, we don't make here the *unique name assumption*, i.e., we allow different individuals to be interpreted as the same domain element.

The semantics of a $\mathcal{DL}$ ontology $\mathcal{O} = \langle \mathcal{T}, \mathcal{A} \rangle$ is the set of *models* of $\mathcal{O}$, i.e., the set of interpretations satisfying all assertions in $\mathcal{T}$ and $\mathcal{A}$. It remains to specify when an interpretation satisfies an assertion. An interpretation $\mathcal{I}$ *satisfies* an inclusion assertion $C \sqsubseteq C'$ (resp., $R \sqsubseteq R'$), if $C^{\mathcal{I}} \subseteq C'^{\mathcal{I}}$ (resp., $R^{\mathcal{I}} \subseteq R'^{\mathcal{I}}$), a membership assertion

---

[4] The DLs underlying the Web Ontology Language OWL 2, standardized by the W3C [7], feature additional kinds of TBox assertions, which allow one to state, e.g., the symmetry, reflexivity, or transitivity of a role. We do not consider such kinds of assertions here.

[5] We have used "$\circ$" to denote concatenation of binary relations, and "*" to denote the reflexive-transitive closure of a binary relation.

$$A^{\mathcal{I}} \subseteq \Delta^{\mathcal{I}}$$
$$(C \sqcap C')^{\mathcal{I}} = C^{\mathcal{I}} \cap C'^{\mathcal{I}}$$
$$(\forall R.C)^{\mathcal{I}} = \{ o \mid \forall o'. (o, o') \in R^{\mathcal{I}} \to o' \in C^{\mathcal{I}} \}$$
$$\neg C^{\mathcal{I}} = \Delta^{\mathcal{I}} \setminus C^{\mathcal{I}}$$
$$(\leqslant n\, R.C)^{\mathcal{I}} = \{ o \mid \sharp\{ o' \in C^{\mathcal{I}} \mid (o, o') \in R^{\mathcal{I}} \} \leq n \}$$
$$\{a\}^{\mathcal{I}} = \{a^{\mathcal{I}}\}$$
$$\exists S.\mathrm{Self}^{\mathcal{I}} = \{ o \mid (o, o) \in S^{\mathcal{I}} \}$$

$$p^{\mathcal{I}} \subseteq \Delta^{\mathcal{I}} \times \Delta^{\mathcal{I}}$$
$$(p^-)^{\mathcal{I}} = \{(o, o') \mid (o', o) \in P^{\mathcal{I}}\}$$
$$(S \cap S')^{\mathcal{I}} = S^{\mathcal{I}} \cap S'^{\mathcal{I}}$$
$$(S \setminus S')^{\mathcal{I}} = S^{\mathcal{I}} \setminus S'^{\mathcal{I}}$$
$$(\top)^{\mathcal{I}} = \Delta^{\mathcal{I}} \times \Delta^{\mathcal{I}}$$
$$(R \cup R')^{\mathcal{I}} = R^{\mathcal{I}} \cup R'^{\mathcal{I}}$$
$$(R \circ R')^{\mathcal{I}} = R^{\mathcal{I}} \circ R'^{\mathcal{I}}$$
$$(R^*)^{\mathcal{I}} = (R^{\mathcal{I}})^*$$

Fig. 1. Interpretation of $\mathcal{DL}$ concepts and roles

$A(a)$ (resp., $p(a, b)$) if $a^{\mathcal{I}} \in A^{\mathcal{I}}$ (resp., $(a^{\mathcal{I}}, b^{\mathcal{I}}) \in p^{\mathcal{I}}$), an assertion of the form $a \approx b$ if $a^{\mathcal{I}} = b^{\mathcal{I}}$, and an assertion of the form $a \not\approx b$ if $a^{\mathcal{I}} \neq b^{\mathcal{I}}$.

The basic reasoning task in $\mathcal{DL}$ is that of *logical implication*, i.e., checking whether a TBox or ABox assertion is implied by an ontology, i.e., holds in every model of the ontology. All other ontology-level inference tasks, such as checking whether an ontology is satisfiable (i.e., admits a model), or whether a concept is satisfiable with respect to an ontology, can easily be reduced to logical implication. Like in many other expressive DLs, reasoning in $\mathcal{DL}$, is decidable in deterministic exponential time, and actually ExpTime-complete, see, e.g., [4].

We consider here various sub-languages of $\mathcal{DL}$. The logics $\mathcal{ALC}[\mathcal{O}][\mathcal{I}][\mathcal{Q}]\mathcal{H}[b_{reg}^{self}]$ are obtained from $\mathcal{DL}$ by possibly dropping some of the $\mathcal{O}$, $\mathcal{I}$, and $\mathcal{Q}$ constructs, or all of boolean combinations, regular expressions over roles, and the self-construct. Moreover, in the lightweight DL *DL-Lite$_{\mathcal{R}}$* [13], inclusion assertions have one of the forms:

$$B \sqsubseteq B' \qquad B \sqsubseteq \neg B' \qquad P \sqsubseteq P' \qquad P \sqsubseteq \neg P'$$

Here, roles P, P' are either an atomic role p or the inverse p^- of an atomic role, and *basic concepts* B, B' are constructed according to the following syntax:

$$B, B' \longrightarrow A \mid \exists P$$

where we use $\exists P$ as an abbreviation for $\exists P.\top$. Intuitively, a basic concept denotes either an atomic concept A, or the projection of a role p on its first component ($\exists p$) or second component ($\exists p^-$). Despite its simplicity, *DL-Lite* is able to capture the essential features of most conceptual modeling formalisms, such as UML Class Diagrams or Entity-Relationship schemata (see, e.g., [12]).

Queries. We introduce now *positive two-way regular path queries* (P2RPQs), which are a quite general class of queries that subsumes most of the query formalisms that have been considered in the context of query answering under incomplete information. A P2RPQ $q(\vec{x})$ has the form $\exists \vec{y}.\varphi$, where $\vec{x}$ and $\vec{y}$ are tuples of variables and φ is a formula built using $\wedge$ and $\vee$ from atoms of the form $C(v)$ and $R(v, v')$, where v, v' are variables from $\vec{x}$, from $\vec{y}$, or individuals, C is a (possibly complex) concept, and R is a (possibly complex) $\mathcal{DL}$ role. We call $\vec{x}$ the *answer* (or *distinguished*) *variables*, and $\vec{y}$

the *existential variables* of q. A Boolean query is one where $\vec{x}$ is the empty tuple $\langle\rangle$, i.e., all variables in the query are existential ones.

A P2RPQ consisting of a single role atom is a *two-way regular path query* (2RPQ), while one consisting of a conjunction of role atoms is a *conjunctive 2RPQ* (C2RPQ). When we do not allow for the use of inverse roles, we obtain the one-way variants of the above query languages, i.e., PRPQs/CRPQs/RPQs. When we further restrict P2RPQs so as to forbid the use of regular expressions in role atoms, we obtain the class of *positive queries* (PQs), and when we forbid also the use of disjunction, we obtain the well known class of *conjunctive queries* (CQs) [22,2]. A *unions of CQs* (UCQs) is a disjunction of CQs with the same answer variables. We observe that the possibility of using regular role expressions in the query atoms of (P/C)(2)RPQs significantly increases the expressive power of the query language, since it allows one to express complex navigations in the models of the given ontology, similar to those possible with (C)(2)RPQs studied in the setting of graph databases [26,16,17,18].

Given a P2RPQ $q(\vec{x}) = \exists \vec{y}.\varphi$ and an interpretation $\mathcal{I}$, let π be a total function from the variables and individuals occurring in q to $\Delta^{\mathcal{I}}$ such that $\pi(a) = a^{\mathcal{I}}$ for each individual a occurring in q. We write $\mathcal{I}, \pi \models C(v)$ if $\pi(v) \in C^{\mathcal{I}}$, and $\mathcal{I}, \pi \models R(v, v')$ if $(\pi(v), \pi(v')) \in R^{\mathcal{I}}$. Let γ be the Boolean expression obtained from φ by replacing each atom α in φ with *true*, if $\mathcal{I}, \pi \models \alpha$, and with *false* otherwise. If γ evaluates to *true*, we say that π is a *match for q in $\mathcal{I}$*, denoted $\mathcal{I}, \pi \models q$. When there is some match for q in $\mathcal{I}$, we also say that q can be *mapped to $\mathcal{I}$*.[6] The *answers* to $q(\vec{x})$ in $\mathcal{I}$, is the set $\mathrm{ans}(q, \mathcal{I}) = \{\pi(\vec{x}) \mid \mathcal{I}, \pi \models q\}$ of tuples of elements of $\Delta^{\mathcal{I}}$ to which the answer variables of q can be mapped by some match for q in $\mathcal{I}$. Given an ontology $\mathcal{O}$ and a query $q(\vec{x})$, a *certain answer* to q over $\mathcal{O}$ is a tuple $\vec{a}$ of individuals in $\mathcal{O}$ such that $\vec{a}^{\mathcal{I}} \in \mathrm{ans}(q, \mathcal{I})$, for every model $\mathcal{I}$ of $\mathcal{O}$. Note that, while an answer to a query over an interpretation $\mathcal{I}$ is a set of elements of $\Delta^{\mathcal{I}}$, a certain answer is a tuple of individuals appearing in $\mathcal{O}$. We denote with $\mathrm{cert}(q, \mathcal{O})$ the set of certain answers to q over $\mathcal{O}$.

For a Boolean query $q()$, we say that $\mathcal{I}$ *satisfies* $q()$, written $\mathcal{I} \models q()$, if there is some match for $q()$ in $\mathcal{I}$. We have that $\mathrm{cert}(q(), \mathcal{O})$ is either the empty tuple of individuals $\langle\rangle$ (representing *true*), when $\mathcal{I} \models q()$ for every model $\mathcal{I}$ of $\mathcal{O}$, or the empty set $\emptyset$ (representing *false*). In the former case, i.e., when $\mathrm{cert}(q, \mathcal{O}) = \{\langle\rangle\}$, we say that $\mathcal{O}$ *entails q*, denoted $\mathcal{O} \models q$.

Query evaluation consists in computing, given an ontology $\mathcal{O}$ and a P2RPQ $q(\vec{x})$, the set $\mathrm{cert}(q, \mathcal{O})$ of certain answers. The corresponding decision problem is the *recognition problem for query answering*, in which one wants to check whether a given a tuple $\vec{a}$ of individuals is in $\mathrm{cert}(q, \mathcal{O})$. When q is a Boolean query, the corresponding task is *query entailment*, which consists in verifying whether $\mathcal{O} \models q$. In fact, the recognition problem for query answering can be straightforwardly reduced to query entailment by considering the Boolean query obtained by substituting the distinguished variables of the query with the given tuple of individuals.

---

[6] When we view the query q as a relational structure in which the variables snd constants are the domain elements, then a match for q in an interpretation $\mathcal{I}$ is actually a *homomorphism* from q to $\mathcal{I}$ (cf. [22] for the case of CQs).

3 Query Answering by Rewriting in Lightweight DLs

We illustrate now the approach to query answering based on *query rewriting*, which was first introduced for answering UCQs over *DL-Lite* ontologies through the *PerfectRef* algorithm [13], and then extended to several other DLs [41,42,44,32], including also more expressive members of the *DL-Lite* family [3]. Such DLs share with *DL-Lite* some crucial properties that are necessary to make a rewriting based approach efficient. We illustrate now the approach for the case of UCQs over *DL-Lite$_R$* ontologies. We first recall that, in the case where the ontology is unsatisfiable, the answer to any UCQ is the set of all tuples of individuals appearing in the ontology. Therefore, we focus for now on the case where the ontology is satisfiable, and come back to satisfiability afterwards.

The key idea at the basis of the rewriting approach is to strictly separate the processing done with respect to the intensional level of the ontology (i.e., the TBox) from the processing done by taking into account the extensional level (i.e., the ABox, or data): (1) the query is processed and rewritten into a new query, based on the inclusion assertions in the TBox; (2) the TBox is discarded and the rewritten query is evaluated over the ABox, as if the ABox was a simple relational structure/database. More precisely, given a UCQ q over $\mathcal{O} = \langle \mathcal{T}, \mathcal{A} \rangle$, the *positive inclusion assertions* of $\mathcal{T}$, i.e., those inclusion assertions that contain no negation in the right-hand side, are compiled into q, thus obtaining a new query q'. Such new query q' is then evaluated over $\mathcal{A}$, thus essentially reducing query answering to query evaluation over a database instance. Since the size of q' does not depend on the ABox, the data complexity of the whole query answering algorithm is the same as the data complexity of evaluating q'. A crucial property for *DL-Lite* is that, in the case where q is a UCQ, the query q' is also a UCQ. Hence, the data complexity of the whole query answering algorithm is in AC^0, which is the complexity of evaluating a FOL query over a relational database.

Canonical Model. The rewriting based approach relies in an essential way on the *canonical model property*, which holds for *DL-Lite* and for the horn variants of many other DLs [33,24]. Such property ensures that every satisfiable ontology $\mathcal{O}$ admits a canonical model that is the least constrained model among all models of $\mathcal{O}$, and that can be homomorphically embedded in all other models. This in turn implies that the canonical model correctly represents *all* the models of $\mathcal{O}$ with respect to the problem of answering positive queries (and in particular, UCQs). In other words, for every UCQ q, we have that $\mathrm{cert}(q, \mathcal{O})$ is contained in the result of the evaluation of q over the canonical model[7]. Intuitively, the canonical model for a *DL-Lite* ontology $\mathcal{O} = \langle \mathcal{T}, \mathcal{A} \rangle$ contains the ABox $\mathcal{A}$, and in addition might contain existentially implied objects, whose existence is enforced by the TBox assertions with $\exists P$ in the right-hand side. For example, if the TBox contains an assertion *Student* $\sqsubseteq \exists$*attends*, expressing that every student should attend something (presumably a course), and the ABox contains the fact *Student(john)*, then the canonical model will contain a fact *attends(john, o_n)*, where o_n is a newly introduced object.

---

[7] Note that, since the domain of the canonical model contains the individuals of the ABox, hence the evaluation of a query over such model can indeed return a set of individuals.

$$
\begin{array}{rll}
A_1 \sqsubseteq A_2 & \ldots, A_2(x), \ldots & \leadsto & \ldots, A_1(x), \ldots \\
\exists p \sqsubseteq A & \ldots, A(x), \ldots & \leadsto & \ldots, p(x, \_), \ldots \\
\exists p^- \sqsubseteq & \ldots, A(x), \ldots & \leadsto & \ldots, p(\_, x), \ldots \\
A \sqsubseteq \exists p & \ldots, p(x, \_), \ldots & \leadsto & \ldots, A(x), \ldots \\
A \sqsubseteq \exists p^- & \ldots, p(\_, x), \ldots & \leadsto & \ldots, A(x), \ldots \\
\exists p_1 \sqsubseteq \exists p_2 & \ldots, p_2(x, \_), \ldots & \leadsto & \ldots, p_1(x, \_), \ldots \\
p_1 \sqsubseteq p_2 & \ldots, p_2(x, y), \ldots & \leadsto & \ldots, p_1(x, y), \ldots \\
\ldots
\end{array}
$$

Fig. 2. Rewriting of query atoms in $DL\text{-}Lite_\mathcal{R}$

First-Order Rewritability. We point out that the canonical model is in general infinite, hence it cannot be effectively computed in order to solve the query answering problem by actually evaluating the input query q over it. Instead, each CQ q_i in q is rewritten into a UCQ r_i in such a way that, whenever q_i has a match in some portion of the canonical model, then there will be a CQ among those in r_i that has a corresponding match in the ABox part of the canonical model. Informally, the rewriting algorithm initializes a set r of CQs with the CQs in the input query q, and processes each yet unprocessed query r_i in r by adding to r also all rewritings of r_i. For each atom α in r_i, it checks whether α can be rewritten by using one of the positive inclusions in the TBox, and if so, adds to r the CQ obtained from r_i by rewriting α. The rewriting of an atom uses a positive inclusion assertion as rewriting rule, applied from right to left, to compile away the knowledge represented by the positive inclusion itself. For example, using the inclusion $A_1 \sqsubseteq A_2$, an atom of the form $A_2(x)$ is rewritten to $A_1(x)$. Alternatively, we can consider this rewriting step as the application of standard resolution between the query and the inclusion $A_1 \sqsubseteq A_2$, viewed as the (implicitly universally quantified) formula $A_1(x) \to A_2(x)$. Other significant cases of rewritings of atoms are depicted in Figure 2, where each inclusion assertion in the left-most column accounts for rewriting the atom to the left of $\leadsto$ into the atom to the right of it. We have used "_" to denote a variable that occurs only once in the CQ (counting also occurrences in the head of the CQ). Besides rewriting atoms, a further processing step applied to r_i is to consider each pair of atoms α_1, α_2 occurring in the body of r_i that *unify*, and replace them with a single atom, also applying the most general unifier to the whole of r_i. In this way, variables that in r_i occur multiple times, might be replaced by an "_", and hence inclusion assertions might become applicable that were not so before the atom-unification step (cf. the rewriting rules in Figure 2 *requiring* the presence of "_").

The above presented rewriting technique realized through *PerfectRef*, allows us to establish that answering UCQs over satisfiable $DL\text{-}Lite_\mathcal{R}$ ontologies is *first-order rewritable*, i.e., the problem of computing certain answers over a satisfiable ontology can be reduced to the problem of evaluating a FOL query over the ABox of the ontology viewed as a database (with complete information). Specifically, let $\mathrm{rew}(q, \mathcal{T})$ denote the UCQ obtained as the result of applying *PerfectRef* to a UCQ q and $DL\text{-}Lite_\mathcal{R}$ TBox $\mathcal{T}$. Then, for every ABox $\mathcal{A}$ such that $\langle \mathcal{T}, \mathcal{A} \rangle$ is satisfiable, we have that

$$
\mathsf{cert}(q, \langle \mathcal{T}, \mathcal{A} \rangle) = \mathsf{ans}(\mathrm{rew}(q, \mathcal{T}), \mathcal{A})
$$

where ans(rew$(q, \mathcal{T}), \mathcal{A}$) denotes the evaluation of the UCQ rew$(q, \mathcal{T})$ over the ABox $\mathcal{A}$ viewed as a database (i.e., a first-order structure).

Ontology Satisfiability. The rewriting of a UCQ q with respect to a TBox $\mathcal{T}$ computed by *PerfectRef* depends only on the set of positive inclusion assertions in $\mathcal{T}$, while disjointness assertions (i.e., inclusion assertions containing a negated basic concept on the right-hand side) do not play any role in such a process. Indeed, the proof of correctness of *PerfectRef* [13], which is based on the canonical model property of *DL-Lite$_\mathcal{R}$*, shows that these kinds of assertions have to be considered only when verifying the ontology satisfiability. Once satisfiability is established, they can be ignored in the query rewriting phase. In fact, unsatisfiability of a *DL-Lite$_\mathcal{R}$* ontology is due to the presence of disjointness assertions and their interaction with positive inclusions. Such interaction can itself be captured by constructing a Boolean UCQ encoding the violation of disjointness assertions, rewriting such a UCQ with respect to the positive inclusions, and checking whether its evaluation over the ABox returns *true*. This in turn shows that also the problem of checking satisfiability of a *DL-Lite$_\mathcal{R}$* ontology is first-order rewritable [13].

Complexity of Query Evaluation. Summarizing the above results, and considering that evaluating a FOL query (and hence a UCQ) over a database is in AC^0 in data complexity, one obtains that answering UCQs over *DL-Lite$_\mathcal{R}$* ontologies has the same data complexity as evaluating UCQs in plain databases. By analyzing the overall rewriting-based query answering technique, and by exploiting a correspondence between the *DL-Lite* family and FOL with unary predicates [3], we are able obtain also tight complexity bounds in the size of the TBox (*schema complexity*) and of the overall input (*combined complexity*).

Theorem 1 ([13,3]). *Answering UCQs over DL-Lite$_\mathcal{R}$ ontologies is in AC^0 in data complexity, NLogSpace-complete in schema complexity, and NP-complete in combined complexity.*

While the above results sound very encouraging from the theoretical point of view, there still remain significant challenges to be addressed to make rewriting based techniques effective also in real world scenarios, where the TBox and/or the data underlying the ABox are very large, and/or queries have a large number of atoms. Indeed, also in the case where one admits rewritings expressed in languages different from UCQs (e.g., arbitrary FOL queries, or non-recursive Datalog), it has recently been shown that the smallest rewritings can grow exponentially with the size of the query [28]. This has led to an intensive and sustained effort aimed at developing techniques to improve query answering over ontologies, such as alternative rewriting techniques [42,46], techniques combining rewriting with partial materialization of the extensional level [31], and various optimization techniques that take into account also extensional constraints on the underlying data, or a mapping layer to relational data sources, i.e., the so-called *Ontology-Based Data Access* (OBDA) setting [43,45]

4 Data Complexity for Query Entailment in Expressive DLs

When a DL contains (explicit or implicit) forms of disjunction, there is no single model representing all possible models for the purpose of query answering. Hence, approaches that exploit the canonical model property, e.g., those based on query rewriting, are not directly applicable in this case. We illustrate now an alternative query answering technique that builds upon the *tableaux-based techniques* that have proved very successful for reasoning in expressive DLs [6,30,29,37].

Tableaux Algorithms for Ontology Reasoning. We illustrate first the idea underlying the use of tableaux algorithms for checking satisfiability of a DL ontology $\mathcal{O} = \langle \mathcal{T}, \mathcal{A} \rangle$, and show then how this approach can be adapted for query entailment. The tableaux algorithm tries to build a model of $\mathcal{O}$ by starting from the assertions in $\mathcal{A}$, and completing them according to what is required by $\mathcal{T}$. In doing so it builds non-deterministically a forest-shaped relational structure (hence, the algorithm actually maintains a set of structures), that we call here *completion forest*. The structure is forest-shaped, since each individual in the ABox $\mathcal{A}$ is the root of a tree generated by applying tableaux-style *expansion rules* to the facts in the completion forest. Essentially, each rule is associated to one of the constructs of the DL, has a precondition, expressed as one or more facts to which the rule is applied, and possibly comes with additional conditions related to applicability of the rule, or to blocking (necessary to ensure termination). As the result of the rule application, the set of facts in the completion forest is expanded, or more in general, changed, possibly by introducing new individuals. To deal, e.g., with incompleteness caused by the presence of disjunction, or with at-most restrictions that might require the identification of individuals, some of the rules are non-deterministic, and cause the generation of more than one new completion forest from the current one.

When no more rules can be applied, and no obvious contradiction (called a *clash*) is present in the current completion forest, the algorithm terminates, and the clash-free completion forest witnesses a model of the ontology $\mathcal{O}$ (soundness of the algorithm). Instead, when each of the non-deterministically generated completion forests contains a clash, it means that $\mathcal{O}$ does not admit any model, hence is unsatisfiable (completeness of the algorithm). In order to avoid infinite repetition of rule application, and hence ensure termination of the algorithm, suitable *blocking conditions* need to be applied. Intuitively, the nodes of a completion forest are labeled with sets of concepts, and a rule application is considered blocked for a node x if in the tree there is a predecessor of x labeled in a way that is "compatible" with x. The precise notion of "compatibility" between two nodes depends on the constructs of the considered DL, and might also involve looking at pairs of adjacent nodes, rather than at single nodes, see, e.g., [6].

Tableaux Algorithms for Query Entailment. As shown for the first time in [35] for the system CARIN, tableaux algorithms can be adapted to deal also with query entailment. We illustrate here the approach presented in [39] for entailment of a PQ q in an ontology $\mathcal{O}$ expressed in one of $\mathcal{ALCOIH}$, $\mathcal{ALCOQH}$, or $\mathcal{ALCIQH}$. As for the case of satisfiability, the technique makes use of completion forests, each of which is meant to capture a set of models of the ontology $\mathcal{O}$. Actually, at each step of the algorithm, each of the models of $\mathcal{O}$ is represented by one of the completion forests in the set maintained non-deterministically by the algorithm. More specifically, when a tableaux rule is applied to a completion forest F, each of the models represented by F is preserved in one of the completion forests generated as a result of the rule application. Therefore, checking whether $O \models q$ equals checking whether $F \models q$, for each completion forest F. The crux of the correctness of the technique lies in the fact that, for largely enough expanded F, one can check whether $F \models q$ effectively via a syntactic mapping of the variables in q to the nodes in F. Thus, to witness that $\mathcal{O} \not\models q$, it is sufficient to (non-deterministically) construct a large enough forest F to which q cannot be mapped.

As customary with tableaux-style algorithms, the algorithm makes use of suitable blocking conditions on the rules to ensure termination of forest expansion. The blocking conditions adopted for $\mathcal{ALCOIH}$, $\mathcal{ALCOQH}$, and $\mathcal{ALCIQH}$ are inspired by those in [35] for CARIN, but are able handle on the one hand nominals present in $\mathcal{ALCOIH}$ and $\mathcal{ALCOQH}$, and on the other hand the fact that $\mathcal{ALCIQH}$ does not have the *finite model property*. Lack of this property means that reasoning with respect to arbitrary models is different from reasoning with respect to finite models only, and implies that $\mathcal{O} \not\models q$ might hold, but this might be witnessed only by an infinite model. As a consequence, expansion forests cannot be considered themselves as models of $\mathcal{O}$, but rather are finite representations of possibly infinite structures obtained by unraveling the completion forest. A further complication comes from the fact that in the blocking conditions of the tableaux rules it is not sufficient anymore to consider single nodes (or pairs of adjacent nodes) as for satisfiability [6]. Instead, one needs to search in the completion forest for the repetition of subtrees, whose depth depends on the number of atoms in the query q. This leads to an additional exponential blowup in the computational complexity of the algorithm with respect to the tableaux algorithms for satisfiability in the same logics.

We also note that [39] presents a single algorithm for checking query entailment in $\mathcal{ALCOIH}$, $\mathcal{ALCOQH}$, and $\mathcal{ALCIQH}$, which includes tableaux rules for all of the constructs in the three logics. However, due to the subtle interaction between nominals, inverse roles, and number restrictions, termination of the algorithm is guaranteed only for TBoxes expressed in $\mathcal{ALCOIH}$, $\mathcal{ALCOQH}$, or $\mathcal{ALCIQH}$.

Complexity of Query Entailment. Interestingly, while the above described tableaux algorithm for checking $\mathcal{O} \models q$ is not computationally optimal in combined complexity, a careful analysis shows that the construction of completion forests, and the check whether q can be mapped to each such forest, can both be carried out by a non-deterministic algorithm that runs in polynomial time in the size of the ABox (and the number of individuals appearing in nominals). Hence, the overall algorithm is coNP in data complexity. This is also computationally optimal, since checking query entailment for CQs over an ontology whose TBox contains a single assertion of the form $A_1 \sqsubseteq A_2 \sqcup A_3$ is already coNP-hard in data complexity [14].

Theorem 2 ([39]). *Given an $\mathcal{ALCOIH}$, $\mathcal{ALCOQH}$, or $\mathcal{ALCIQH}$ ontology $\mathcal{O}$ and a PQ q, deciding whether $O \models q$ is:*

- *in coN3ExpTime in combined complexity.*
- *in coN2ExpTime in combined complexity for a fixed q (under the assumption that numbers appearing in number restrictions are encoded in unary).*
- *coNP-complete in data complexity.*

5 Query Entailment in Very Expressive DLs

We address now query entailment for the case where the ontology and/or the query may contain roles built as regular expressions over direct and inverse roles, or their Boolean combinations.

Automata Techniques for Reasoning over Ontologies. For many very expressive DLs, including those which allow for the use of regular expressions over roles, the standard reasoning task of checking concept satisfiability (possibly with respect to a TBox) is naturally solvable by tree-automata, thanks to the *tree model property* of such logics: each satisfiable concept C has a tree-shaped model [50,52] in which nodes are labeled with sets of concepts, and adjacent nodes in the tree are connected by one or more roles. Intuitively, such a tree-shaped model is obtained by unraveling an arbitrary model, introducing new nodes in the tree whenever the same node is encountered multiple times during the unraveling. Hence, one can construct a tree-automaton that accepts a tree representing a tree-shaped model, by naturally encoding in the transition function of the automaton the conditions that the DL constructs impose on adjacent nodes of the model/tree. Checking for the existence of a model amounts to checking for non-emptiness of the tree-automaton. A crucial observation is that, even for those logics that have the finite model property, the unraveling process produces an infinite tree, so that we need to resort to automata on *infinite* trees [48].

When also an ABox $\mathcal{A}$ is present this approach fails, since the assertions in $\mathcal{A}$ may arbitrarily connect individuals, and thus destroy the tree-structure. On the other hand, while a satisfiable $\mathcal{DL}$ ontology $\mathcal{O} = \langle \mathcal{A}, \mathcal{T} \rangle$ may lack a tree-shaped model, it always has a forest-shaped *canonical model*, in which the individuals in $\mathcal{A}$ can be arbitrarily connected, but each individual is the root of a tree-shaped model of $\mathcal{T}$. This property is usually sufficient to adapt algorithms for concept satisfiability so as to decide also ontology satisfiability. In particular, automata-based algorithms have been adapted, e.g., using the *pre-completion* technique [49], in which after a reasoning step on the ABox, automata are used to verify the existence of a tree-shaped model rooted at each ABox individual.

Automata Techniques for Query Entailment. However, a pre-completion based approach would not lend itself well for query entailment, where one needs to account also for the interaction between the variables in query atoms and the ABox individuals to which these variables have to be mapped. This holds especially in the case where the query itself might contain atoms that are regular expressions over roles, as in RPQs and their extensions. Therefore, we discuss here briefly a different approach to query entailment for very expressive DLs and queries, based on the idea of representing forest-shaped interpretations directly as trees in which the root is a dummy node, and all individuals appearing in the ABox and in nominals form the children of the root. From each of these first-level nodes, a possibly infinite tree departs. Adopting this kind of representation allows us to deal in a uniform way using tree automata both with the TBox and ABox constituting the ontology, and with the query [19,20,21].

Specifically, we illustrate an approach to check query entailment $\mathcal{O} \models q$, that is applicable when q is a P2RPQs and $\mathcal{O}$ is an ontology expressed in any sublanguage of

$\mathcal{DL}$ in which only two of the three constructs of nominals ($\mathcal{O}$), inverse roles ($\mathcal{I}$), and number restrictions ($\mathcal{Q}$) are present [20]. We use $\mathcal{DL}^-$ to denote such a logic. To decide whether $\mathcal{O} \models q$, it is sufficient to decide whether $\mathcal{O}$ has a tree-shaped (canonical) model in which q has no match. To check this using tree automata, we build an automaton $\mathbf{A}_{\mathcal{O} \not\models q}$ that accepts all trees that represent a model of $\mathcal{O}$ in which q has no match. Roughly speaking, $\mathbf{A}_{\mathcal{O} \not\models q}$ is obtained by intersecting two automata:

- $\mathbf{A}_{\mathcal{O}}$, which is a tree automaton that accepts the trees representing a model of $\mathcal{O}$. We make use of two-way alternating tree automata [51]: on the one hand, such automata can traverse a tree both downwards and upwards, which turns out to be convenient to deal with inverse roles; on the other hand, such automata are alternating, which means that they are equipped both with $\wedge$-transitions and with $\vee$-transitions, which allows one to naturally encode in the transition function of the automaton the structural conditions imposed by concept and role expressions.
- $\mathbf{A}_{\neg q}$, which accepts the trees representing an interpretation that admits no match for q. To obtain $\mathbf{A}_{\neg q}$, we first construct an automaton $\mathbf{A}_q$ that accepts a tree T if and only if q has a match in the interpretation represented by T. To construct $\mathbf{A}_q$, we need to treat the existential variables appearing in q as additional concept symbols, and represent them explicitly in the tree accepted by the automaton. Then, to construct $\mathbf{A}_{\neg q}$, we need to project away such additional symbols, before complementing the automaton, which results in an (inevitable) exponential blowup.

Hence, deciding query entailment reduces to checking whether $\mathbf{A}_{\mathcal{O} \not\models q}$ accepts the empty language.

The details of the constructions of the above described automata are quite involved. For the constructions, the proof of their correctness, and the computational complexity analysis, we refer to [21] for the case when $\mathcal{DL}^-$ does not include nominals (which corresponds to the DL $\mathcal{ZIQ}$ of [20]), and to [20] for the cases when $\mathcal{DL}^-$ includes nominals ($\mathcal{ZOI}$ and $\mathcal{ZOQ}$).

Theorem 3 ([19,21,20]). *Given an* $\mathcal{DL}^-$ *ontology* $\mathcal{O}$ *and a PQ* q, *deciding whether* $O \models q$ *is in* 2EXPTIME *in combined complexity (under the assumption that numbers appearing in number restrictions are encoded in unary).*

The above bound is tight, since query entailment is already 2EXPTIME-hard for the following cases:

- CQs over ontologies expressed in $\mathcal{ALCI}$ [36] or $\mathcal{ALCH}_{reg}$ [23];
- CRPQs or PQs over ontologies expressed in $\mathcal{ALC}$ [8].

Notice that the automata-theoretic approach above does not provide us any bound on data complexity (that is better than the one for combined complexity). In fact, it remains to be investigated whether in this approach it is possible to single out the contribution coming from the ABox and the nominals in the construction of the automata and the final emptiness check.

The above automata-based technique does also not work for the case of full $\mathcal{DL}$, i.e., when the logic contains both nominals, inverses, and number restrictions, since in such a case the tree model property fails, and tree automata do not seem suitable anymore as a technical tool. In fact, decidability of entailment for PQs over $\mathcal{ALCOIQ}$ ontologies has been established in [27] using model theoretic arguments, which do not provide any complexity upper bound. However, the problem is still open for logics including also regular expressions over roles (or alternatively, transitive roles also in the query, in line with what can be expressed in the Web Ontology Language OWL [7]).

Finally, we mention recent work that has considered the problem of query entailment also over lightweight DLs, for variants of queries containing regular expressions [9], and for their extension with nesting [8].

6 Conclusions

In this work, we have provided an overview of three prominent techniques that have been used in recent years to address the challenging problem of query answering and query entailment in DLs. Specifically, we have discussed: *(1)* a technique based on query rewriting suitable for UCQs over lightweight DLs, which provides optimal complexity bounds due to first-order rewritability; *(2)* a technique based on tableaux suitable for PQs over expressive DLs, which provides optimal bounds in data complexity, but not in combined complexity, and is not able to deal with regular expressions over roles in the ontology or the query; *(3)* a technique based on automata on infinite trees, which is able to deal with very expressive ontology and query languages containing regular expressions over roles, and provides optimal complexity bounds in combined complexity, but not in data complexity.

The research on query answering and query entailment is still very active, and the problem continues to provide challenges. On the one hand, from the theoretical point of view several decidability and complexity questions are still open. On the other hand, more work is required to implement query answering and query entailment algorithms for the more expressive ontology and query languages. And both for lightweight and for expressive languages, improvements in efficiency are needed, so at to make these techniques usable in real world scenarios.

Acknowledgments. This work has been partially supported by the EU IP project Optique (*Scalable End-user Access to Big Data*), grant agreement n. FP7-318338.

References

1. Abiteboul, S., Buneman, P., Suciu, D.: Data on the Web: From Relations to Semistructured Data and XML. Morgan Kaufmann (2000)
2. Abiteboul, S., Hull, R., Vianu, V.: Foundations of Databases. Addison Wesley Publ. Co. (1995)
3. Artale, A., Calvanese, D., Kontchakov, R., Zakharyaschev, M.: The DL-Lite family and relations. J. of Artificial Intelligence Research 36, 1–69 (2009)
4. Baader, F., Calvanese, D., McGuinness, D., Nardi, D., Patel-Schneider, P.F. (eds.): The Description Logic Handbook: Theory, Implementation and Applications. Cambridge University Press (2003)

5. Baader, F., Sattler, U.: Expressive number restrictions in description logics. J. of Logic and Computation 9(3), 319–350 (1999)
6. Baader, F., Sattler, U.: Tableau algorithms for description logics. In: Dyckhoff, R. (ed.) TABLEAUX 2000. LNCS (LNAI), vol. 1847, pp. 1–18. Springer, Heidelberg (2000)
7. Bao, J., et al.: OWL 2 Web Ontology Language document overview, W3C Recommendation, World Wide Web Consortium, 2nd edn. (December 2012), http://www.w3.org/TR/owl2-overview/
8. Bienvenu, M., Calvanese, D., Ortiz, M., Simkus, M.: Nested regular path queries in description logics. In: Proc. of the 14th Int. Conf. on the Principles of Knowledge Representation and Reasoning (KR 2014). AAAI Press (2014)
9. Bienvenu, M., Ortiz, M., Simkus, M.: Conjunctive regular path queries in lightweight description logics. In: Proc. of the 23rd Int. Joint Conf. on Artificial Intelligence, IJCAI 2013 (2013)
10. Buneman, P., Davidson, S., Hillebrand, G., Suciu, D.: A query language and optimization technique for unstructured data. In: Proc. of the ACM SIGMOD Int. Conf. on Management of Data, pp. 505–516 (1996)
11. Calvanese, D., De Giacomo, G.: Expressive description logics. In: Baader, et al. (eds.) [4], ch. 5, pp. 178–218
12. Calvanese, D., De Giacomo, G., Lembo, D., Lenzerini, M., Poggi, A., Rodriguez-Muro, M., Rosati, R.: Ontologies and databases: The DL-Lite approach. In: Tessaris, S., Franconi, E., Eiter, T., Gutierrez, C., Handschuh, S., Rousset, M.-C., Schmidt, R.A. (eds.) Reasoning Web. LNCS, vol. 5689, pp. 255–356. Springer, Heidelberg (2009)
13. Calvanese, D., De Giacomo, G., Lembo, D., Lenzerini, M., Rosati, R.: Tractable reasoning and efficient query answering in description logics: The DL-Lite family. J. of Automated Reasoning 39(3), 385–429 (2007)
14. Calvanese, D., De Giacomo, G., Lembo, D., Lenzerini, M., Rosati, R.: Data complexity of query answering in description logics. Artificial Intelligence 195, 335–360 (2013)
15. Calvanese, D., De Giacomo, G., Lenzerini, M.: On the decidability of query containment under constraints. In: Proc. of the 17th ACM SIGACT SIGMOD SIGART Symp. on Principles of Database Systems (PODS 1998), pp. 149–158 (1998)
16. Calvanese, D., De Giacomo, G., Lenzerini, M., Vardi, M.Y.: Containment of conjunctive regular path queries with inverse. In: Proc. of the 7th Int. Conf. on the Principles of Knowledge Representation and Reasoning (KR 2000), pp. 176–185 (2000)
17. Calvanese, D., De Giacomo, G., Lenzerini, M., Vardi, M.Y.: Rewriting of regular expressions and regular path queries. J. of Computer and System Sciences 64(3), 443–465 (2002)
18. Calvanese, D., De Giacomo, G., Lenzerini, M., Vardi, M.Y.: Reasoning on regular path queries. SIGMOD Record 32(4), 83–92 (2003)
19. Calvanese, D., Eiter, T., Ortiz, M.: Answering regular path queries in expressive description logics: An automata-theoretic approach. In: Proc. of the 22nd AAAI Conf. on Artificial Intelligence (AAAI 2007), pp. 391–396 (2007)
20. Calvanese, D., Eiter, T., Ortiz, M.: Regular path queries in expressive description logics with nominals. In: Proc. of the 21st Int. Joint Conf. on Artificial Intelligence (IJCAI 2009), pp. 714–720 (2009)
21. Calvanese, D., Ortiz, M., Eiter, T.: Answering regular path queries in expressive description logics via alternating tree-automata. Information and Computation 237, 12–55 (2014)
22. Chandra, A.K., Merlin, P.M.: Optimal implementation of conjunctive queries in relational data bases. In: Proc. of the 9th ACM Symp. on Theory of Computing (STOC 1977), pp. 77–90 (1977)
23. Eiter, T., Lutz, C., Ortiz, M., Šimkus, M.: Query answering in description logics with transitive roles. In: Proc. of the 21st Int. Joint Conf. on Artificial Intelligence (IJCAI 2009), pp. 759–764 (2009)

24. Eiter, T., Ortiz, M., Simkus, M., Tran, T.K., Xiao, G.: Query rewriting for Horn-SHIQ plus rules. In: Proc. of the 26th AAAI Conf. on Artificial Intelligence (AAAI 2012). AAAI Press (2012)

25. Fagin, R., Kolaitis, P.G., Miller, R.J., Popa, L.: Data exchange: Semantics and query answering. Theoretical Computer Science 336(1), 89–124 (2005)

26. Florescu, D., Levy, A., Suciu, D.: Query containment for conjunctive queries with regular expressions. In: Proc. of the 17th ACM SIGACT SIGMOD SIGART Symp. on Principles of Database Systems (PODS 1998), pp. 139–148 (1998)

27. Glimm, B., Rudolph, S.: Nominals, inverses, counting, and conjunctive queries or: Why infinity is your friend. J. of Artificial Intelligence Research 39, 429–481 (2010)

28. Gottlob, G., Kikot, S., Kontchakov, R., Podolskii, V.V., Schwentick, T., Zakharyaschev, M.: The price of query rewriting in ontology-based data access. Artificial Intelligence 213, 42–59 (2014)

29. Horrocks, I., Kutz, O., Sattler, U.: The even more irresistible $\mathcal{SROIQ}$. In: Proc. of the 10th Int. Conf. on the Principles of Knowledge Representation and Reasoning (KR 2006), pp. 57–67 (2006)

30. Horrocks, I., Sattler, U.: A tableau decision procedure for $\mathcal{SHOIQ}$. J. of Automated Reasoning 39(3), 249–276 (2007)

31. Kontchakov, R., Lutz, C., Toman, D., Wolter, F., Zakharyaschev, M.: The combined approach to query answering in DL-Lite. In: Proc. of the 12th Int. Conf. on the Principles of Knowledge Representation and Reasoning (KR 2010), pp. 247–257 (2010)

32. Krisnadhi, A., Lutz, C.: Data complexity in the $\mathcal{EL}$ family of description logics. In: Dershowitz, N., Voronkov, A. (eds.) LPAR 2007. LNCS (LNAI), vol. 4790, pp. 333–347. Springer, Heidelberg (2007)

33. Krötzsch, M., Rudolph, S., Hitzler, P.: Complexity boundaries for horn description logics. In: Proc. of the 22nd AAAI Conf. on Artificial Intelligence (AAAI 2007), pp. 452–457 (2007)

34. Lenzerini, M.: Data integration: A theoretical perspective. In: Proc. of the 21st ACM SIGACT SIGMOD SIGART Symp. on Principles of Database Systems (PODS 2002), pp. 233–246 (2002)

35. Levy, A.Y., Rousset, M.C.: Combining Horn rules and description logics in CARIN. Artificial Intelligence 104(1-2), 165–209 (1998)

36. Lutz, C.: Inverse roles make conjunctive queries hard. In: Proc. of the 20th Int. Workshop on Description Logic (DL 2007). CEUR Electronic Workshop Proceedings, vol. 250, pp. 100–111 (2007), http://ceur-ws.org/

37. Lutz, C., Milicic, M.: A tableau algorithm for description logics with concrete domains and general tboxes. J. of Automated Reasoning Special Issue on Automated Reasoning with Analytic Tableaux and Related Methods 38(1-3), 227–259 (2007)

38. Ortiz, M.: Ontology based query answering: The story so far. In: Proc. of the 7th Alberto Mendelzon Int. Workshop on Foundations of Data Management (AMW 2013). CEUR Electronic Workshop Proceedings, vol. 1087 (2013), http://ceur-ws.org/

39. Ortiz, M., Calvanese, D., Eiter, T.: Data complexity of query answering in expressive description logics via tableaux. J. of Automated Reasoning 41(1), 61–98 (2008)

40. Ortiz, M., Šimkus, M.: Reasoning and query answering in description logics. In: Eiter, T., Krennwallner, T. (eds.) Reasoning Web 2012. LNCS, vol. 7487, pp. 1–53. Springer, Heidelberg (2012)

41. Pérez-Urbina, H., Motik, B., Horrocks, I.: A comparison of query rewriting techniques for DL-lite. In: Proc. of the 22nd Int. Workshop on Description Logic (DL 2009). CEUR Electronic Workshop Proceedings, vol. 477 (2009), http://ceur-ws.org/

42. Pérez-Urbina, H., Motik, B., Horrocks, I.: Tractable query answering and rewriting under description logic constraints. J. of Applied Logic 8(2), 186–209 (2010)

43. Rodriguez-Muro, M., Calvanese, D.: High performance query answering over DL-Lite ontologies. In: Proc. of the 13th Int. Conf. on the Principles of Knowledge Representation and Reasoning (KR 2012), pp. 308–318 (2012)
44. Rosati, R.: On conjunctive query answering in $\mathcal{EL}$. In: Proc. of the 20th Int. Workshop on Description Logic (DL 2007). CEUR Electronic Workshop Proceedings, vol. 250, pp. 451–458 (2007), http://ceur-ws.org/
45. Rosati, R.: Prexto: Query rewriting under extensional constraints in DL-Lite. In: Simperl, E., Cimiano, P., Polleres, A., Corcho, O., Presutti, V. (eds.) ESWC 2012. LNCS, vol. 7295, pp. 360–374. Springer, Heidelberg (2012)
46. Rosati, R., Almatelli, A.: Improving query answering over DL-Lite ontologies. In: Proc. of the 12th Int. Conf. on the Principles of Knowledge Representation and Reasoning (KR 2010), pp. 290–300 (2010)
47. Schmolze, J.G.: Terminological knowledge representation systems supporting n-ary terms. In: Proc. of the 1st Int. Conf. on the Principles of Knowledge Representation and Reasoning (KR 1989), pp. 432–443 (1989)
48. Thomas, W.: Automata on infinite objects. In: van Leeuwen, J. (ed.) Handbook of Theoretical Computer Science, vol. B, ch. 4, pp. 133–192. Elsevier Science Publishers (1990)
49. Tobies, S.: Complexity Results and Practical Algorithms for Logics in Knowledge Representation. Ph.D. thesis, LuFG Theoretical Computer Science, RWTH-Aachen, Germany (2001)
50. Vardi, M.Y.: Why is modal logic so robustly decidable. In: DIMACS Series in Discrete Mathematics and Theoretical Computer Science, vol. 31, pp. 149–184. American Mathematical Society (1997)
51. Vardi, M.Y.: Reasoning about the past with two-way automata. In: Larsen, K.G., Skyum, S., Winskel, G. (eds.) ICALP 1998. LNCS, vol. 1443, pp. 628–641. Springer, Heidelberg (1998)
52. Vardi, M.Y., Wolper, P.: Automata-theoretic techniques for modal logics of programs. J. of Computer and System Sciences 32, 183–221 (1986)

Tools for the Investigation of Substructural and Paraconsistent Logics*

Agata Ciabattoni and Lara Spendier

Vienna University of Technology, Austria

Abstract. We present an overview of the methods in [10,7,13] and their implementation in the system **TINC**. This system introduces analytic calculi for large classes of substructural and paraconsistent logics, which it then uses to prove various results about the formalized logics.

1 Introduction

Logic is concerned with the study of reasoning and is the basis of applications in various fields. Classical logic is not adequate for all of them; for instance, it is ill-equipped to reason in presence of inconsistencies, inherently vague information, or about resources. Driven in part by the rising demand of practitioners, the last decades have witnessed an explosion of research on logics different from classical logic, and the definition of many new logics. These are often described in a declarative way within the framework due to Hilbert and Frege, which is however extremely cumbersome when it comes to finding or analyzing proofs. Moreover, a Hilbert-Frege system does not help answering useful questions about the formalized logic and its corresponding algebraic structure, such as 'Is the logic decidable?' or 'Is the logic standard[1] complete?'. Therefore providing an algorithmic presentation of logics, in particular in the form of *analytic calculi*, is essential both for understanding their mathematical properties and for developing potential applications. Analyticity is crucial as it means that proofs in these calculi proceed by a step-wise decomposition of the formulas to be proved.

Since the introduction of Gentzen's calculi *LK* and *LJ* for classical and intuitionistic logic, the *sequent calculus* has been one of the most popular frameworks for defining analytic calculi. Sequent calculi have been successfully used for studying important properties of their formalized logics such as decidability, complexity and interpolation; they have also proved useful for giving syntactic proofs of algebraic properties for which, in particular cases, semantic methods were not known, see e.g. [18]. These results all follow from the fundamental theorem of *cut-elimination*, which implies the redundancy of the cut rule and makes the calculi analytic. Despite the successful formalization of important logics, many natural and useful logics do not fit comfortably into the sequent framework. A huge range of extensions of the sequent calculus have been introduced

---

* Work supported by the FWF project START Y544-N23.

[1] That is complete with respect to algebras based on truth values in $[0, 1]$.

E. Fermé and J. Leite (Eds.): JELIA 2014, LNAI 8761, pp. 18–32, 2014.

in the last few decades to define analytic calculi for logics apparently lacking a (cut-free) sequent formalization.

In this paper we describe our tools (theory and implementation) for introducing analytic calculi for large classes of substructural and of paraconsistent logics and using them to prove various results about these logics.

The idea to use computer supported tools for the investigation of logics has already been around for more than two decades, see, e.g., [24]. In recent years, several tools following this spirit of "logic engineering" have been introduced. These aim at making theoretical results in logic more accessible to researchers and practitioners who might not have deep knowledge about the logical theory, e.g. [5,25,23]. An example of a "logic engineering" tool addressing the issue of finding analytic calculi is the system *MUltlog* [5] which introduces such calculi for the class of finite-valued logics.

Our system **TINC** (Tools for the Investigation of Non-Classical logics) is created along the lines of *MUltlog* to cover a wider range of logics. It introduces sequent-style calculi for large classes of propositional substructural, intermediate and paraconsistent logics, which it then uses: (i) to check whether a substructural logic is standard complete (and hence it is a fuzzy logic in the sense of [20,17]) and (ii) to extract non-deterministic finite-valued semantics for paraconsistent and related logics and provide a uniform decidability proof for them. **TINC** implements the theoretical results in [10,7,15,13], for which this paper provides an overview and a non-technical description.

2   The System TINC

The system **TINC**, available at http://www.logic.at/tinc, takes as input a logic specified via suitable Kripke models or Hilbert systems, returns (a paper written in LATEX containing) an analytic calculus and states certain properties of the logic. Currently, **TINC** includes the following tools which handle large classes of substructural, paraconsistent and intermediate logics:

AxiomCalc transforms any suitable axiomatic extension of Full Lambek calculus with exchange and weakening **FLew** (i.e., intuitionistic linear logic with weakening) into a cut-free sequent or hypersequent calculus. Moreover, the tool exploits the generated calculus by checking a sufficient condition for the standard completeness of the input logic.

Paralyzer (PARAconsistent logics anaLYZER) transforms large classes of Hilbert axioms defining paraconsistent (and related) logics into sequent calculus rules. Moreover, it extracts non-deterministic, finite-valued semantics from the obtained calculi which show the decidability of the logics and reveal whether the calculi are analytic. *Paralyzer* also provides an encoding of the introduced calculi for the proof-assistant *Isabelle* [27] that can be used for semi-automated proof search within the considered logics.

Framinator (FRAMe condItioNs Automatically TO Rules) transforms frame conditions expressed as classical first-order formulas within the class Π_2 of the arithmetical hierarchy (i.e. formulas of the form $\forall \overline{x} \exists \overline{y} P$, for P quantifier free) into cut-free labelled sequent calculi.

AxiomCalc implements in Prolog[2] the results in [10,7], *Paralyzer* in [13] and *Framinator* in [15]. The whole system consists of 34 files and around 5400 lines of code (including documentation). The general structure of the implementation is depicted in Figure 1 and is instantiated with specific methods for every tool.

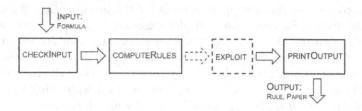

Fig. 1. Design of **TINC**

CHECKINPUT checks whether the syntactic form of the input formulas is correct. The core component COMPUTERULES implements the algorithm(s) to extract Gentzen-style rules out of the input formulas. The component EXPLOIT, which is not present in *Framinator*, implements methods that utilize the introduced calculus to reason about the logic and establish properties of it. PRINTOUTPUT contains everything that is related to presenting the results to the user.

The general idea behind the algorithm(s) implemented in COMPUTERULES is to start with a suitable analytic Gentzen-style calculus for a base logic and transform the Hilbert axioms or semantic conditions characterizing the logic at hand (i.e. the input formulas) into suitable rules.

Notation: henceforth we will use $\varphi, \psi, \alpha, \beta$ for (metavariables for) formulas. $\Gamma, \Delta, \Sigma, \Lambda$ will denote (metavariables for) multisets of formulas whereas Π will always stand for either a formula or the empty set.

Following [10] (and its generalization to display calculi in [16], and to labelled deductive systems in [15]) the key ingredients of the algorithm(s) are:

(1) the *invertibility* of the logical rules of the base calculus, and
(2) the following lemma, which allows formulas to change the side of the sequent by moving from the rule conclusion to the rule premise. For instance, its formulation for commutative (multiple-conclusion) sequent calculi is:

Lemma 1. *The sequent $\Gamma, \varphi \Rightarrow \psi, \Delta$ is interderivable with the rules (Γ' and Δ' are new metavariables):*

$$\frac{\Gamma' \Rightarrow \varphi, \Delta'}{\Gamma, \Gamma' \Rightarrow \psi, \Delta', \Delta} \qquad \text{and} \qquad \frac{\Gamma', \psi \Rightarrow \Delta'}{\Gamma, \Gamma', \varphi \Rightarrow \Delta', \Delta}$$

by using cut and the identity axiom $\alpha \Rightarrow \alpha$.

The transformation algorithm for substructural and for paraconsistent logics will be explained in the next sections which also contain examples of the corresponding tools *AxiomCalc* and *Paralyzer*.

---

[2] We used swi-prolog by Jan Wielemaker http://www.swi-prolog.org.

3   Substructural Logics

Substructural logics are obtained by dropping some of the structural rules from Gentzen's sequent calculus *LJ*. They encompass among many others classical, intuitionistic, intermediate, fuzzy, linear and relevant logics. Substructural logics are usually defined as axiomatic extensions of *full Lambek calculus* **FL**, that is non-commutative intuitionistic linear logic.

In this section we give an overview of the theoretical results in [10,12] and their use in the tool *AxiomCalc* focusing on substructural logics extending **FLew**, that is **FL** with the rules for exchange and weakening. Connectives in these logics are $\wedge$ (additive conjunction), $\cdot$ (multiplicative conjunction/fusion), $\vee$ (disjunction), $\rightarrow$ (implication) and the constants 1 and 0.

As usual, $\neg\varphi$ is used as an abbreviation for $\varphi \rightarrow 0$.

In the following we refer to [22,11,18] for all concepts of universal algebra and to [26] for sequent calculi.

3.1   From Axioms to Structural Rules

The algorithm in [10], which is the core of the implementation of *AxiomCalc*, transforms large classes of axioms into structural sequent and hypersequent rules.

Which axioms can we handle? The axioms that belong to the classes $\mathcal{N}_2$ and $\mathcal{P}_3$ of the substructural hierarchy – a syntactic classification of axioms over **FLew** (or, equivalently, of algebraic equations over integral and commutative residuated lattices) introduced in [10] for **FLe** (and in [12] for the non-commutative version). The hierarchy is based on the *polarity* of the connectives of the base sequent calculus for **FLew**; recall that a connective has *positive* (resp. *negative*) *polarity* if its left (resp. right) logical rule is invertible, i.e., the conclusion implies the premises, see [1]. The classes $\mathcal{P}_n$ and $\mathcal{N}_n$ contain axioms/equations with leading positive (1, $\vee$, $\cdot$) and negative connectives (0, $\rightarrow$, $\wedge$).

Definition 1 (Substructural Hierarchy [10]). *For $n \geq 0$, the sets $\mathcal{P}_n, \mathcal{N}_n$ of formulas are defined as follows ($\mathcal{P}_0$, $\mathcal{N}_0$ contain all atomic formulas):*

$$\mathcal{P}_{n+1} ::= \mathcal{N}_n \mid \mathcal{P}_{n+1} \cdot \mathcal{P}_{n+1} \mid \mathcal{P}_{n+1} \vee \mathcal{P}_{n+1} \mid 1$$
$$\mathcal{N}_{n+1} ::= \mathcal{P}_n \mid \mathcal{P}_{n+1} \rightarrow \mathcal{N}_{n+1} \mid \mathcal{N}_{n+1} \wedge \mathcal{N}_{n+1} \mid 0$$

Intuition: the different classes are defined by alternating connectives of different polarity. This accounts for the difficulty to deal with the corresponding axioms proof theoretically (and, as shown in [12], with the preservation under suitable order theoretic completions of the corresponding equations).

Example 1. Examples of Hilbert axioms within the classes $\mathcal{N}_2$ and $\mathcal{P}_3$ are

Class	Axiom	Name
$\mathcal{N}_2$	$\varphi \to \varphi \cdot \varphi$	contraction
	$\neg(\varphi \wedge \neg\varphi)$	weak contraction
	$\varphi \cdot \varphi \to \varphi \cdot \varphi \cdot \varphi$	3-contraction
$\mathcal{P}_2$	$\varphi \vee \neg\varphi$	excluded middle
	$(\varphi \to \psi) \vee (\psi \to \varphi)$	prelinearity
$\mathcal{P}_3$	$\neg\varphi \vee \neg\neg\varphi$	weak excluded middle
	$\neg(\varphi \cdot \psi) \vee (\varphi \wedge \psi \to \varphi \cdot \psi)$	weak nilpotent minimum

The procedure in [10] transforms each axiom within the class $\mathcal{N}_2$ into structural sequent calculus rules that preserve cut-elimination when added to the calculus *FLew* for **FLew** (see below). These rules are however not powerful enough to capture axioms beyond the class $\mathcal{N}_2$. Indeed, as shown in [10,12] they can only formalize properties that are already valid in intuitionistic logic ([10]) and among them only those whose corresponding algebraic equations are closed under the order theoretic completion known as Dedekind MacNeille[3], in the context of integral residuated lattices ([12]). These results ensure, for instance, that no structural sequent rule can capture the prelinearity axiom (see Example 1), which is present in all formalizations of Fuzzy Logic [20]. A structural rule for this axiom was introduced in [2] using the hypersequent calculus – a simple and natural generalization of Gentzen sequent calculus.

As proved in [10], and recalled below, the hypersequent calculus can indeed deal with all the axioms within the class $\mathcal{P}_3$.

Definition 2. *A hypersequent is a multiset of sequents written as $\Gamma_1 \Rightarrow \Delta_1 \mid \cdots \mid \Gamma_n \Rightarrow \Delta_n$ where each $\Gamma_i \Rightarrow \Delta_i$, $i = 1,\ldots,n$, is a sequent, called* component *of the hypersequent. If all components of a hypersequent contain at most one formula in the succedent, the hypersequent is called* single-conclusion, *and* multiple-conclusion *otherwise.*

The intuitive interpretation of the symbol "$\mid$" is disjunctive. This is reflected by the rules (EC) and (EW) (see Table 1), which are present in all hypersequent calculi. The base hypersequent calculus we use is *HFLew* (see Table 1). Its sequent version *FLew* is simply obtained by dropping the rules (EC) and (EW) and removing the side hypersequent G everywhere.

Definition 3. *Let r and r' be two (hyper)sequent calculus rules. We say that r and r' are* equivalent *in a (hyper)sequent calculus S if the set of sequents provable from the same (hyper)sequent assumptions in $S \cup \{r\}$ and in $S \cup \{r'\}$ coincide. The definition naturally extends to sets of rules.*

The algorithm in [10]: Following the idea sketched in Section 2, to transform axioms in the class $\mathcal{P}_3$ into equivalent structural (hyper)sequent rules we use

(1) the invertible logical rules of the base calculus $HFLew$, that are $(1,l)$, $(\vee, l)$, $(\cdot, l)$, $(0, r)$, $(\to, r)$ and $(\wedge, r)$, and
(2) the following version of Lemma 1:

---

[3] It is a generalization of Dedekind completion to ordered algebras, see e.g. [18].

$$\frac{}{G \mid \varphi \Rightarrow \varphi} \; (init) \qquad \frac{G \mid \Gamma \Rightarrow \Pi}{G \mid 1, \Gamma \Rightarrow \Pi} \; (1,l) \qquad \frac{G \mid \varphi, \psi, \Gamma \Rightarrow \Pi}{G \mid \varphi \cdot \psi, \Gamma \Rightarrow \Pi} \; (\cdot, l) \qquad \frac{G \mid \Gamma \Rightarrow \varphi \quad G \mid \Delta \Rightarrow \psi}{G \mid \Gamma, \Delta \Rightarrow \varphi \cdot \psi} \; (\cdot, r)$$

$$\frac{}{G \mid \Rightarrow 1} \; (1,r) \qquad \frac{G \mid \Gamma \Rightarrow \Pi}{G \mid \Gamma, \varphi \Rightarrow \Pi} \; (w,l) \qquad \frac{G \mid \varphi, \Gamma \Rightarrow \psi}{G \mid \Gamma \Rightarrow \varphi \to \psi} \; (\to, r) \qquad \frac{G \mid \Gamma \Rightarrow \varphi \quad G \mid \psi, \Delta \Rightarrow \Pi}{G \mid \Gamma, \varphi \to \psi, \Delta \Rightarrow \Pi} \; (\to, l)$$

$$\frac{G \mid \Gamma \Rightarrow}{G \mid \Gamma \Rightarrow 0} \; (0,r) \qquad \frac{G}{G \mid \Gamma \Rightarrow \Pi} \; (EW) \qquad \frac{G \mid \Gamma \Rightarrow \varphi_i}{G \mid \Gamma \Rightarrow \varphi_1 \vee \varphi_2} \; (\vee, r) \qquad \frac{G \mid \Gamma \Rightarrow \varphi \quad G \mid \varphi, \Delta \Rightarrow \Pi}{G \mid \Gamma, \Delta \Rightarrow \Pi} \; (cut)$$

$$\frac{G \mid \Gamma \Rightarrow}{G \mid \Gamma \Rightarrow \varphi} \; (w,r) \qquad \frac{G \mid \Gamma \Rightarrow \Pi \mid \Gamma \Rightarrow \Pi}{G \mid \Gamma \Rightarrow \Pi} \; (EC) \qquad \frac{G \mid \varphi, \Gamma \Rightarrow \Pi \quad G \mid \psi, \Gamma \Rightarrow \Pi}{G \mid \varphi \vee \psi, \Gamma \Rightarrow \Pi} \; (\vee, l)$$

Table 1. Hypersequent calculus *HFLew*

Lemma 2. *The hypersequent* $G \mid G' \mid \varphi_1, \ldots, \varphi_n \Rightarrow \psi$ *is equivalent to* $(\Gamma_1, \ldots, \Gamma_n, \Delta, \Pi$ *are new metavariables)*

$$\frac{G \mid \Gamma_1 \Rightarrow \varphi_1 \quad \cdots \quad G \mid \Gamma_n \Rightarrow \varphi_n}{G \mid G' \mid \Gamma_1, \ldots, \Gamma_n \Rightarrow \psi} \qquad \text{and} \qquad \frac{G \mid \psi, \Delta \Rightarrow \Pi}{G \mid G' \mid \varphi_1, \ldots, \varphi_n, \Delta \Rightarrow \Pi}$$

These two key ingredients are then integrated in the transformation procedure as follows. Given any axiom $\varphi \in \mathcal{N}_2$ or $\varphi \in \mathcal{P}_3$:

(i) We start with the sequent $\Rightarrow \varphi$ if $\varphi \in \mathcal{N}_2$ or with hypersequents $G \mid \Rightarrow \varphi_1 \mid \cdots \mid \Rightarrow \varphi_n$ if $\varphi \in \mathcal{P}_3$ (and hence its normal form is a conjunction of formulas of the form $\varphi_1 \vee \cdots \vee \varphi_n$ with $\varphi_1, \ldots, \varphi_n \in \mathcal{N}_2$). By utilizing the invertibility of the logical rules, we decompose φ as much as possible and obtain an equivalent set of (hyper)sequent rules R without premises. As an example, consider the axiom $\neg(\varphi \cdot \psi) \vee (\varphi \wedge \psi \to \varphi \cdot \psi) \in \mathcal{P}_3$, contained in the fuzzy logic **WNM** [17]:

$$G \mid \Rightarrow \neg(\varphi \cdot \psi) \mid \Rightarrow \varphi \wedge \psi \to \varphi \cdot \psi \quad \longrightarrow^{(i)} \quad G \mid \varphi, \psi \Rightarrow \mid \varphi \wedge \psi \Rightarrow \varphi \cdot \psi$$

(ii) We apply Lemma 2 to each $r \in R$ to change side of the sequents of those formulas that cannot be decomposed by logical rules in their current position; continuing our example we move $\varphi \wedge \psi$ and $\varphi \cdot \psi$ and get (Σ, Λ, Π are new metavariables)

$$\longrightarrow^{(ii)} \quad \frac{G \mid \Lambda \Rightarrow \varphi \wedge \psi \quad G \mid \Sigma, \varphi \cdot \psi \Rightarrow \Pi}{G \mid \varphi, \psi \Rightarrow \mid \Lambda, \Sigma \Rightarrow \Pi}$$

(iii) We utilize again the invertibility of the logical rules to decompose the compound formulas in the premises of each rule, resulting in a set of structural (hyper)sequent rules R_s. In our case R_s contains:

$$\longrightarrow^{(iii)} \quad \frac{G \mid \Lambda \Rightarrow \varphi \quad G \mid \Lambda \Rightarrow \psi \quad G \mid \Sigma, \varphi, \psi \Rightarrow \Pi}{G \mid \varphi, \psi \Rightarrow \mid \Lambda, \Sigma \Rightarrow \Pi}$$

(iv) The final step is a *completion procedure* that transforms each $r' \in R_s$ into an equivalent (hyper)sequent rule that preserves cut-elimination and the subformula property once it is added to the base calculus:

(iv.a) Using Lemma 2 we replace all the metavariables in the rule conclusions standing for formulas by new metavariables for multisets of formulas. Back to our example we get (Γ and Δ are new):

$$\longrightarrow^{(iv.a)} \frac{G \mid \Lambda \Rightarrow \varphi \quad G \mid \Lambda \Rightarrow \psi \quad G \mid \Sigma, \varphi, \psi \Rightarrow \Pi \quad G \mid \Gamma \Rightarrow \varphi \quad G \mid \Delta \Rightarrow \psi}{G \mid \Gamma, \Delta \Rightarrow \mid \Lambda, \Sigma \Rightarrow \Pi}$$

(iv.b) We remove all the metavariables that appear in the premises and not in the conclusion. When those variables appear on the left and on the right hand side of different premises we close the obtained rules under all possible applications of (*cut*). For the rule above we therefore get:

$$\frac{G \mid \Gamma, \Lambda, \Sigma \Rightarrow \Pi \quad G \mid \Sigma, \Lambda, \Lambda \Rightarrow \Pi \quad G \mid \Sigma, \Gamma, \Delta \Rightarrow \Pi \quad G \mid \Sigma, \Lambda, \Delta \Rightarrow \Pi}{G \mid \Gamma, \Delta \Rightarrow \mid \Lambda, \Sigma \Rightarrow \Pi} \quad (wnm)$$

Theorem 1 ([10]). *Given any axiom $\varphi \in \mathcal{N}_2$ ($\varphi \in \mathcal{P}_3$), the rules generated by the above algorithm are equivalent to φ in $FLew$ and they preserve cut elimination when added to the sequent calculus $FLew$ (hypersequent calculus $HFLew$).*

The above algorithm is implemented in the tool *AxiomCalc* that, given an input axiom, first determines the class in the hierarchy to which the axiom belongs and, if it is within $\mathcal{P}_3$, it automates the Steps (i)-(iv) above.

Example 2. Figure 2 below shows how to use *AxiomCalc* to define an analytic calculus for $FLew$ extended with the axiom $\varphi \cdot \varphi \rightarrow \varphi \cdot \varphi \cdot \varphi \in \mathcal{N}_2$.

3.2   An Application: Standard Completeness

The introduced calculi can be further utilized to check whether the corresponding logics are standard complete, i.e. complete for algebras with a real unit interval lattice reduct and hence whether they are fuzzy logics in the sense of [20,17]. The check is done using a sufficient condition for a hypersequent calculus to admit the elimination of the so-called density rule (below left is its Hilbert version and below right its hypersequent version in single-conclusion calculi):

$$\frac{(A \rightarrow p) \vee (p \rightarrow B) \vee C}{(A \rightarrow B) \vee C} \quad (density) \qquad \frac{G \mid \Gamma \Rightarrow p \mid \Sigma, p \Rightarrow \Pi}{G \mid \Gamma, \Sigma \Rightarrow \Pi} \quad (hdensity)$$

where p is a propositional variable not occurring in any instance of A, B, or C (Γ, Σ and Π). Ignoring C, *density* can intuitively be read contrapositively as saying (very roughly) "if $A > B$, then $A > p$ and $p > B$ for some p"; hence the name "density". The connection between the elimination of the density rule and standard completeness is as follows: as shown in [22], adding *density* to any axiomatic extension $\mathcal{L}$ of **FLew** with prelinearity (see Example 1) makes

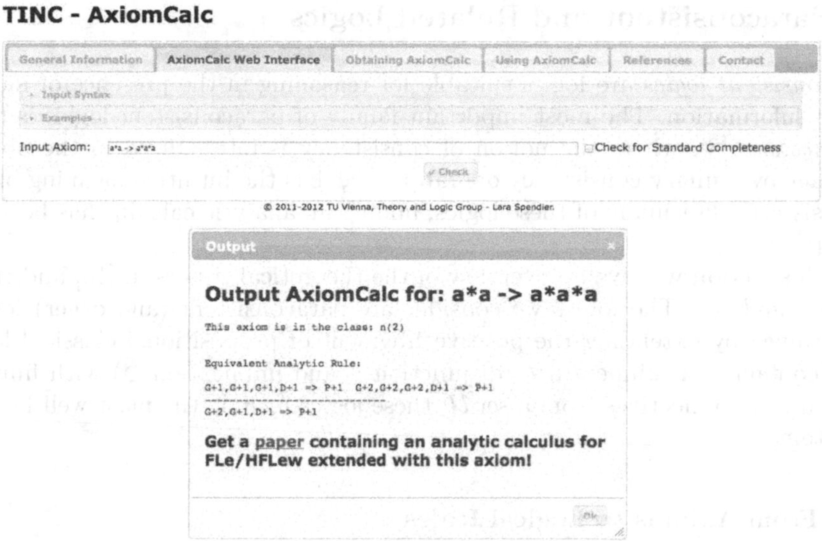

TINC - AxiomCalc

Fig. 2. Above: Main screen of *AxiomCalc* with the input axiom; below: Output

the corresponding logic *rational complete*, i.e., complete with respect to a corresponding class of (a) linearly and (b) densely ordered algebras; (a) is due to the prelinearity axiom, while (b) to the density rule. Hence by showing that the addition of *density* does not enlarge the set of provable formulas (i.e. *density* is an admissible or an eliminable rule) we get rational completeness for $\mathcal{L}$. Standard completeness with respect to algebras with lattice reduct [0, 1] can then be obtained in many cases by means of a Dedekind MacNeille-style completion.

A syntactic condition which guarantees the elimination of the density rule from a suitable hypersequent calculus was introduced in [7]. Using this result a uniform proof of standard completeness that applies to large classes of logics is as follows: let $\mathcal{L}$ be the logic obtained by extending **FLew** with prelinearity and with any (set of) axiom(s) within the class $\mathcal{P}_3$:

- We first introduce a hypersequent calculus $H\mathcal{L}$ for $\mathcal{L}$;
- If $H\mathcal{L}$ satisfies the sufficient condition in [7] then $\mathcal{L}$ is rational complete, and by [11] it is also standard complete being all algebraic equations corresponding to axioms within the class $\mathcal{P}_3$ closed under Dedekind-MacNeille completion when applied to subdirectly irreducible algebras.

This general approach contrasts with the logic-specific techniques usually employed to prove standard completeness, e.g. [19,17]. Moreover, it allows the discovery of new fuzzy logics in a completely automated way. The whole procedure is implemented in *AxiomCalc* and is started by ticking the checkbox "Check for Standard Completeness", see Figure 2 above.

4   Paraconsistent and Related Logics

Paraconsistent logics are logics suitable for reasoning in the presence of inconsistent information. The most important family of paraconsistent logics is that of *C-systems* [8], where the notion of consistency is internalized in the object language by a unary consistency operator $\circ$; $\circ\varphi$ has the intuitive meaning of "φ is consistent". For many of these logics, finding an analytic calculus has been an open problem.

In this section we give an overview of the theoretical results in [13] and their use in *Paralyzer*. The logics we consider are paraconsistent (and other) logics all obtained by extending the positive fragment of propositional classical logic $\mathbf{Cl}^+$ (containing conjunction $\wedge$, disjunction $\vee$ and implication $\supset$) with finitely many unary connectives from a set $\mathcal{U}$; these logics include the most well known C-systems.

4.1   From Axioms to Logical Rules

The algorithm in [13], which is the core of the implementation of the tool *Paralyzer*, transforms axioms into logical sequent rules.

Which axioms can we handle? All axioms belonging to the set of formulas **Ax** [13] that are (i) generated by the following grammar (where $\mathcal{G}$ is the initial variable and $\mathcal{U} = \{\star_1, \ldots, \star_n\}$):

$$\mathcal{G} = R_1 \mid R_2 \mid R_3 \qquad\qquad R_3 = (R_3 \diamond P_1) \mid (P_1 \diamond R_3) \mid \star \rhd p_1$$
$$R_1 = (R_1 \diamond P_1) \mid (P_1 \diamond R_1) \mid \star p_1 \qquad P_1 = (P_1 \diamond P_1) \mid \star p_1 \mid p_1 \mid p_2$$
$$R_2 = (R_2 \diamond P_2) \mid (P_2 \diamond R_2) \mid \star(p_1 \diamond p_2) \qquad P_2 = (P_2 \diamond P_2) \mid \star p_1 \mid p_1 \mid \star p_2 \mid p_2$$
$$\diamond = \wedge \mid \vee \mid \supset \qquad\qquad \star, \rhd = \star_1 \mid \cdots \mid \star_n$$

and (ii) satisfy the following technical condition: some subformula $\star p_1$ of a formula generated by R_1 (the subformulas $\star \rhd p_1$ or $\star(p_1 \diamond p_2)$ of a formula generated by R_3 or R_2, resp.) must not be contained in
(a) a positively[4] occurring (sub)formula of the form $\psi_1 \wedge \psi_2$, and
(b) a negatively occurring (sub)formula of the form $\psi_1 \vee \psi_2$ or $\psi_1 \supset \psi_2$.

Example 3. Examples of formulas in **Ax** are ($\diamond \in \{\vee, \wedge, \supset\}$ and $\neg, \circ \in \mathcal{U}$):

$(\mathbf{n_1})$ $p_1 \vee \neg p_1$	$(\mathbf{n_2})$ $p_1 \supset (\neg p_1 \supset p_2)$
$(\mathbf{c})$ $\neg\neg p_1 \supset p_1$	$(\mathbf{e})$ $p_1 \supset \neg\neg p_1$
$(\mathbf{n_\wedge^l})$ $\neg(p_1 \wedge p_2) \supset (\neg p_1 \vee \neg p_2)$	$(\mathbf{n_\wedge^r})$ $(\neg p_1 \vee \neg p_2) \supset \neg(p_1 \wedge p_2)$
$(\mathbf{n_\vee^l})$ $\neg(p_1 \vee p_2) \supset (\neg p_1 \wedge \neg p_2)$	$(\mathbf{n_\vee^r})$ $(\neg p_1 \wedge \neg p_2) \supset \neg(p_1 \vee p_2)$
$(\mathbf{n_\supset^l})$ $\neg(p_1 \supset p_2) \supset (p_1 \wedge \neg p_2)$	$(\mathbf{n_\supset^r})$ $(p_1 \wedge \neg p_2) \supset \neg(p_1 \supset p_2)$
$(\mathbf{b})$ $p_1 \supset (\neg p_1 \supset (\circ p_1 \supset p_2))$	$(\mathbf{r_\diamond})$ $\circ(p_1 \diamond p_2) \supset (\circ p_1 \vee \circ p_2)$
$(\mathbf{k})$ $\circ p_1 \vee (p_1 \wedge \neg p_1)$	$(\mathbf{i})$ $\neg \circ p_1 \supset (p_1 \wedge \neg p_1)$
$(\mathbf{o_\diamond^1})$ $\circ p_1 \supset \circ(p_1 \diamond p_2)$	$(\mathbf{o_\diamond^2})$ $\circ p_2 \supset \circ(p_1 \diamond p_2)$
$(\mathbf{a_\diamond})$ $(\circ p_1 \wedge \circ p_2) \supset \circ(p_1 \diamond p_2)$	$(\mathbf{a_\neg})$ $\circ p_1 \supset \circ \neg p_1$

---

[4] A subformula φ occurs *negatively* (*positively*, resp.) in ψ if there is an odd (even, resp.) number of implications $\supset$ in ψ having φ as a subformula of its antecedent.

Most C-systems (see, e.g., [8]) are obtained by employing suitable combinations of the above axioms which express various properties of negation and of the consistency operator $\circ$.

The algorithm in [13]: Following the idea sketched in Section 2, to transform the axioms within **Ax** into equivalent logical sequent rules we use:

(1) The invertible logical rules of the base sequent calculus LK^+ for $\mathbf{Cl}^+$, which is LK without negation (note that in LK^+ *all* rules for connectives are invertible), and

(2) Lemma 1.

The procedure to transform any $\varphi \in \mathbf{Ax}$ into equivalent rules (cf. Definition 3) then works as follows:

(i) Starting from $\Rightarrow \varphi$, by utilizing the invertibility of the logical rules of LK^+ as much as possible, φ is decomposed into its subformulas, thus obtaining an equivalent set of rules R without premises.

As an example, let $\varphi := p_1 \supset (\neg p_1 \supset (\circ p_1 \supset p_2))) \in \mathbf{Ax}$:

$$\Rightarrow p_1 \supset (\neg p_1 \supset (\circ p_1 \supset p_2)) \qquad \longrightarrow^{(i)} \overline{p_1 \Rightarrow \neg p_1 \supset (\circ p_1 \supset p_2)}$$

$$\longrightarrow^{(i)} \overline{p_1, \neg p_1 \Rightarrow \circ p_1 \supset p_2} \qquad \longrightarrow^{(i)} \overline{p_1, \neg p_1, \circ p_1 \Rightarrow p_2}$$

(ii) We remove all rules $r \subset R$ containing $p_i \Rightarrow p_i$ for $i \in \{1,2\}$ in their conclusion. Moreover, if a rule does not contain $\star(p_1 \diamond p_2)$ with $\star \in \mathcal{U}$ and $\diamond \in \{\vee, \wedge, \supset\}$, we can safely remove all variables p_2. In our example it gives:

$$\longrightarrow^{(ii)} \overline{p_1, \neg p_1, \circ p_1 \Rightarrow}$$

(iii) By using Lemma 1 all remaining formulas but one are moved to the premises of each rule, changing the side of the sequent. The formula that remains in the conclusion will be the one introduced by the rule and will be either of the form $\star p_1$ (when φ was generated by R_1), $\star \triangleright p_1$ or $\star(p_1 \diamond p_2)$, resp. (when φ was generated by R_3 or R_2, resp.) for any $\star, \triangleright \in \mathcal{U}$ and $\diamond \in \{\wedge, \vee, \supset\}$.

Continuing our example (using weakening and contraction of LK^+), we obtain

$$\longrightarrow^{(iii)} \frac{\Gamma \Rightarrow \Delta, p_1 \quad \Gamma \Rightarrow \Delta, \neg p_1}{\circ p_1, \Gamma \Rightarrow \Delta} \quad \text{or} \quad \longrightarrow^{(iii)} \frac{\Gamma \Rightarrow \Delta, p_1 \quad \Gamma \Rightarrow \Delta, \circ p_1}{\neg p_1, \Gamma \Rightarrow \Delta}$$

Theorem 2 ([13]). *Any axiom $\varphi \in \mathbf{Ax}$ can be transformed into sequent rules equivalent in LK^+ having the following form ($\star, \triangleright, \ast \in \mathcal{U}$ and $\diamond \in \{\wedge, \vee, \supset\}$):*

unary-one *rules*	binary *rules*	unary-two *rules*
$\dfrac{\mathcal{S}_1}{\Gamma, \star\varphi \Rightarrow \Delta}$	$\dfrac{\mathcal{S}_2}{\Gamma, \star(\varphi_1 \diamond \varphi_2) \Rightarrow \Delta}$	$\dfrac{\mathcal{S}_1}{\Gamma, \star \triangleright \varphi \Rightarrow \Delta}$
$\dfrac{\mathcal{S}_1}{\Gamma \Rightarrow \Delta, \star\varphi}$	$\dfrac{\mathcal{S}_2}{\Gamma \Rightarrow \Delta, \star(\varphi_1 \diamond \varphi_2)}$	$\dfrac{\mathcal{S}_1}{\Gamma \Rightarrow \Delta, \star \triangleright \varphi}$

where S_1 may contain premises of the form $\Gamma, \varphi \Rightarrow \Delta$; $\Gamma, *\varphi \Rightarrow \Delta$; $\Gamma \Rightarrow \Delta, \varphi$; and $\Gamma \Rightarrow \Delta, *\varphi$, while S_2 of the form $\Gamma, \varphi_i \Rightarrow \Delta$; $\Gamma, *\varphi_i \Rightarrow \Delta$; $\Gamma \Rightarrow \Delta, \varphi_i$, and $\Gamma \Rightarrow \Delta, *\varphi_i$ where $i \in \{1, 2\}$.

4.2 An Application: Non-deterministic Semantics

The introduced calculi, obtained by extending LK^+ with the special rules described in Theorem 2, are used to extract new semantics for the corresponding logics using *partial non-deterministic matrices (PNmatrices)*. These are a natural generalization of the standard multi-valued matrices, which allow the truth-value assigned to a complex formula to be chosen *non-deterministically* out of a given (possibly[5] empty) set of options.

Our semantics guarantee the decidability of the considered logics (Corollary 1) and are used to check whether the defined calculi satisfy a generalized notion of the subformula property (Theorem 4). Regarding the latter, note that the addition of the new logical sequent rules to LK^+ does not necessarily result in a cut-free system (or in a system satisfying some form of subformula property). In fact, checking whether this is the case requires a "global view" of the resulting calculus, which takes into account the way in which all the rules of the calculus mentioning the same connectives interact. This view is provided by our semantics and, as shown in [6], it amounts to checking only whether the resulting PNmatrix contains an empty set in the truth tables of the connectives.

Definition 4 ([6]). *A partial non-deterministic matrix (PNmatrix) $\mathcal{M}$ for a propositional language $\mathcal{L}$ consists of:*
(1) A set $\mathcal{V}_{\mathcal{M}}$ of truth values.
(2) A subset $\mathcal{D}_{\mathcal{M}} \subseteq \mathcal{V}_{\mathcal{M}}$ of designated truth values.
(3) A truth table $\diamond_{\mathcal{M}} : \mathcal{V}_{\mathcal{M}}^n \to P(\mathcal{V}_{\mathcal{M}})$ for every n-ary connective $\diamond$ of $\mathcal{L}$.

From sequent calculi to PNmatrices: Let G be sequent calculus obtained by adding to LK^+ any set R of unary-one, binary and unary-two rules with set $\mathcal{U}$ of unary connectives. The truth values $\mathcal{V}_{\mathcal{M}}$ of the PNmatrix for G are tuples over $\{0, 1\}$ of size "# of unary connectives in $\mathcal{U}$"+1; the tuples store the information about the value of a formula φ and also of $\star\varphi$ for each $\star \in \mathcal{U}$. The matrix is then constructed using the rules in R, which play different roles according to their type. More precisely,

- *unary-one* rules reduce the set $\mathcal{V}_{\mathcal{M}}$ of truth values,
- *unary-two* rules determine the truth tables of the unary connectives, and
- *binary* rules determine the truth tables of the binary connectives.

We show below how to construct a PNmatrix out of a concrete sequent calculus (see [6] for the general procedure and all technical details).

---

[5] The possibility of having empty spots in the matrices make PNmatrices a generalization of non-deterministic matrices Nmatrices [4].

Let $\mathcal{U} = \{\star\}$, and consider the sequent calculus LK^+ extended with the two rules (equivalent to the axioms $p_1 \supset (\star p_1 \supset p_2)$ and $\star \star p_1 \supset p_1$, respectively):

$$\frac{\Gamma \Rightarrow \Delta, \varphi}{\Gamma, \star\varphi \Rightarrow \Delta} \ (r_{uo}) \qquad \text{and} \qquad \frac{\Gamma, \varphi \Rightarrow \Delta}{\Gamma, \star \star \varphi \Rightarrow \Delta} \ (r_{ut})$$

We first construct the set of truth values $\mathcal{V}_\mathcal{M}$, starting with the set of all possible truth values of size 2 (i.e. $|\{\star\}| + 1$):

$$\{\langle 0, 0 \rangle, \langle 0, 1 \rangle, \langle 1, 0 \rangle, \langle 1, 1 \rangle\}$$

Note that a tuple $\langle x, y \rangle$ stands for $\langle \varphi : x, \star\varphi : y \rangle$, i.e., it says that x (resp. y) is the value of φ (resp. of $\star\varphi$).

As usual, we interpret formulas occurring on the right (left) hand side of a sequent as taking the value 1 (0). Hence the rule (r_{uo}) says that all tuples in which φ takes the value 1 (in the rule premise φ occurs on the right hand side) must also have that $\star\varphi$ takes the value 0. As $\langle 1, 1 \rangle$ does not satisfy this condition, the set of truth values is reduced to

$$\mathcal{V}_\mathcal{M} = \{\langle 0, 0 \rangle, \langle 0, 1 \rangle, \langle 1, 0 \rangle\}$$

The set of designated truth values $\mathcal{D}_\mathcal{M}$ contains all elements of $\mathcal{V}_\mathcal{M}$ where the first element is 1; in our case $\mathcal{D}_\mathcal{M} = \{\langle 1, 0 \rangle\}$.

The truth table of the unary connective $\star$ is determined in two steps:

First, we set up the basic truth table for $\star$ where we assign to every tuple $u \in \mathcal{V}_\mathcal{M}$ all tuples where φ coincides with $\star\varphi$ of u (see left table below), e.g. $u = \langle 0, 0 \rangle$ has $\langle 0, 0 \rangle, \langle 0, 1 \rangle$ as possible values.

Then, we have to consider the rule (r_{ut}) which says that for every tuple u in which φ takes the value 0 (in the rule premise, φ occurs on the left side) we delete the assigned tuples not having 0 for $\star \star \varphi$. E.g., for $u = \langle 0, 0 \rangle$ we delete the tuple $\langle 0, 1 \rangle$ as $\star\varphi$ takes 1 (we are in the truth table for the unary connective $\star$, and hence $\star\varphi$ corresponds to $\star \star \varphi$).

$\star$	
$\langle 0, 0 \rangle$	$\{\langle 0, 0 \rangle, \langle 0, 1 \rangle\}$
$\langle 0, 1 \rangle$	$\{\langle 1, 0 \rangle\}$
$\langle 1, 0 \rangle$	$\{\langle 0, 0 \rangle, \langle 0, 1 \rangle\}$

$\longrightarrow (r_{ut})$

$\star$	
$\langle 0, 0 \rangle$	$\{\langle 0, 0 \rangle\}$
$\langle 0, 1 \rangle$	$\{\langle 1, 0 \rangle\}$
$\langle 1, 0 \rangle$	$\{\langle 0, 0 \rangle, \langle 0, 1 \rangle\}$

Note that the PNmatrix for a calculus G can be automatically computed by the tool *Paralyzer* (see Example 4).

Theorem 3 ([13]). *Let G be the sequent calculus for the logic defined by extending* **Cl**$^+$ *with any $\varphi \in$* **Ax***, and $\mathcal{M}$ its associated PNmatrix, both obtained by the procedures sketched above. A sequent is provable in G iff it is valid[6] in $\mathcal{M}$.*

---

[6] That is it takes a designated truth value under all interpretations in $\mathcal{M}$.

As each logic characterized by a finite PNmatrix is decidable [6] we immediately have:

Corollary 1. *All logics extending* $\mathbf{Cl}^+$ *with axioms in* **Ax** *are decidable.*

The PNmatrix $\mathcal{M}$ is also used to check the analyticity of the corresponding calculus G:

Theorem 4 ([13]). $\mathcal{M}$ *does not contain empty sets in its truth tables iff whenever a sequent s is provable in G, s can be proved by using only its subformulas and their extensions with unary connectives from* $\mathcal{U}$.

Example 4. Consider the axioms $p_1 \vee \neg p_1$ and $\circ p_1 \supset \circ \neg p_1$, which are given as input (in a slightly adapted syntax) for *Paralyzer*, see Figure 3.

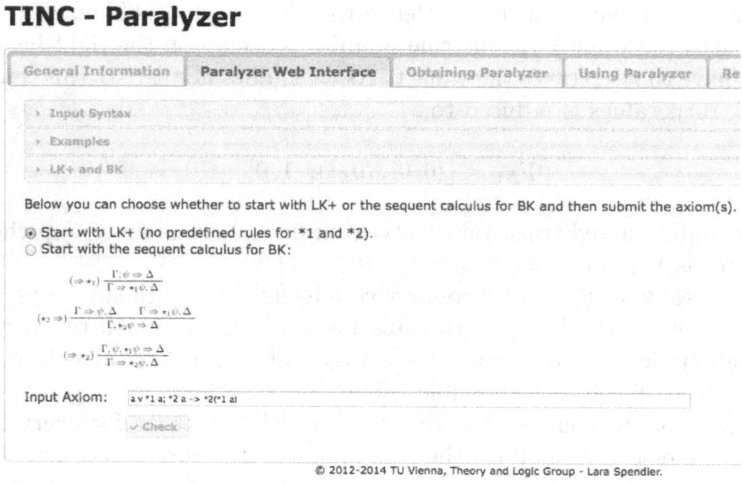

TINC - Paralyzer

Fig. 3. Main screen of *Paralyzer* with the input axioms. Note that the user can choose the base calculus between LK^+ (default option) and BK [3].

The computed rules and the associated PNmatrix are in Figure 4.

5   Future Research

The tools described in this paper provide automated support for the introduction of analytic calculi and the investigation of interesting properties (standard completeness, non-deterministic semantics and decidability) for many substructural and for many paraconsistent and related logics.

Many practical and theoretical issues are still to be addressed; among them extending our results to new logics including first-order logics. In the substructural case the main challenge is to find the right formalism (and method) to capture axioms beyond the level $\mathcal{P}_3$ of the substructural hierarchy.

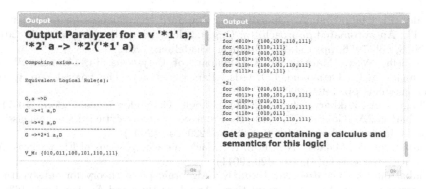

Fig. 4. Left: output containing the equivalent sequent rules and $\mathcal{V}_\mathcal{M}$ of the PNmatrix. Right: truth tables for the unary connectives.

For paraconsistent and related logics the introduction of analytic calculi could be easily adapted to capture e.g. paraconsistent logics extending intuitionistic logic, substructural paraconsistent logics or first-order logics; however the construction of the corresponding PNmatrices would require a deeper investigation. For the time being there is indeed no theory of PNmatrices for first-order logics, intuitionistic logics or substructural logics (that in fact lack even a theory of Nmatrices [4]). A step forward in this direction has been done in the recent work [14] that generalizes the results described in Section 4 to axioms in **Ax** with a possible nesting of unary connectives of any fixed depth. On a more practical level, the encoding into the proof-assistant *Isabelle* [27] of the calculi computed by *Paralyzer* allows us to find proofs of theorems in the considered logics in a semi-automated way. The definition of automated deduction procedures is currently under investigation; following [21], a possible approach is to search for suitable encodings of our calculi into SAT.

Finally, we plan to extend the system **TINC** with new tools that cover further classes of interesting logics, e.g. modal logics defined by Hilbert axioms.

References

1. Andreoli, J.-M.: Logic programming with focusing proofs in linear logic. Journal of Logic and Computation 2(3), 297–347 (1992)
2. Avron, A.: Hypersequents, logical consequence and intermediate logics for concurrency. Annals of Mathematics and Artificial Intelligence 4, 225–248 (1991)
3. Avron, A., Konikowska, B., Zamansky, A.: Cut-free sequent calculi for C-systems with generalized finite-valued semantics. Journal of Logic and Computation 21(3), 517–540 (2013)
4. Avron, A., Lev, I.: Non-deterministic multiple-valued structures. Journal of Logic and Computation 15(3), 241–261 (2005)
5. Baaz, M., Fermüller, C.G., Salzer, G., Zach, R.: MUltlog 1.0: Towards an expert system for many-valued logics. In: McRobbie, M.A., Slaney, J.K. (eds.) CADE 1996. LNCS, vol. 1104, pp. 226–230. Springer, Heidelberg (1996)
6. Baaz, M., Lahav, O., Zamansky, A.: Finite-valued semantics for canonical labelled calculi. Journal of Automated Reasoning 51(4), 401–430 (2013)

7. Baldi, P., Ciabattoni, A., Spendier, L.: Standard completeness for extensions of MTL: An automated approach. In: Ong, L., de Queiroz, R. (eds.) WoLLIC 2012. LNCS, vol. 7456, pp. 154–167. Springer, Heidelberg (2012)
8. Carnielli, W.A., Marcos, J.: A taxonomy of C-systems. In: Carnielli, W.A., Coniglio, M.E., Ottaviano, I.D. (eds.) Paraconsistency: The Logical Way to the Inconsistent, pp. 1–94 (2002)
9. Chagrov, A., Zakharyaschev, M.: Modal Logic. Clarendon Press, Oxford (1997)
10. Ciabattoni, A., Galatos, N., Terui, K.: From axioms to analytic rules in nonclassical logics. In: Proceedings of LICS 2008, pp. 229–240 (2008)
11. Ciabattoni, A., Galatos, N., Terui, K.: MacNeille Completions of FL-algebras. Algebra Universalis 66(4), 405–420 (2011)
12. Ciabattoni, A., Galatos, N., Terui, K.: Algebraic proof theory for substructural logics: cut-elimination and completions. Annals of Pure and Applied Logic 163(3), 266–290 (2012)
13. Ciabattoni, A., Lahav, O., Spendier, L., Zamansky, A.: Automated support for the investigation of paraconsistent and other logics. In: Artemov, S., Nerode, A. (eds.) LFCS 2013. LNCS, vol. 7734, pp. 119–133. Springer, Heidelberg (2013)
14. Ciabattoni, A., Lahav, O., Spendier, L., Zamansky, A.: Taming paraconsistent (and other) logics: An algorithmic approach (submitted 2014)
15. Ciabattoni, A., Maffezioli, P., Spendier, L.: Hypersequent and labelled calculi for intermediate logics. In: Galmiche, D., Larchey-Wendling, D. (eds.) TABLEAUX 2013. LNCS, vol. 8123, pp. 81–96. Springer, Heidelberg (2013)
16. Ciabattoni, A., Ramanayake, R.: Structural extensions of display calculi: A general recipe. In: Libkin, L., Kohlenbach, U., de Queiroz, R. (eds.) WoLLIC 2013. LNCS, vol. 8071, pp. 81–95. Springer, Heidelberg (2013)
17. Cintula, P., Hájek, P., Noguera, C. (eds.): Handbook of Mathematical Fuzzy Logic, vol. 1. Studies in Logic, Mathematical Logic and Foundations, vol. 37. College Publications (2011)
18. Galatos, N., Jipsen, P., Kowalski, T., Ono, H.: Residuated Lattices: An algebraic glimpse at substructural logics. Studies in Logics and the Foundations of Mathematics. Elsevier (2007)
19. Jenei, S., Montagna, F.: A proof of standard completeness for Esteva and Godo's MTL logic. Studia Logica 70(2), 183–192 (2002)
20. Hájek, P.: Metamathematics of Fuzzy Logic. Springer (1998)
21. Lahav, O., Zohar, Y.: SAT-based decision procedure for analytic pure sequent calculi. In: Demri, S., Kapur, D., Weidenbach, C. (eds.) IJCAR 2014. LNCS (LNAI), vol. 8562, pp. 76–90. Springer, Heidelberg (2014)
22. Metcalfe, G., Montagna, F.: Substructural fuzzy logics. Journal of Symbolic Logic 7(3), 834–864 (2007)
23. Nigam, V., Pimentel, E., Reis, G.: An extended framework for specifying and reasoning about proof systems. Journal of Logic and Computation (accepted)
24. Ohlbach, H.J.: Computer support for the development and investigation of logics. Logic Journal of the IGPL 4(1), 109–127 (1996)
25. Tishkovsky, D., Schmidt, R.A., Khodadadi, M.: The tableau prover generator MetTeL2. In: del Cerro, L.F., Herzig, A., Mengin, J. (eds.) JELIA 2012. LNCS, vol. 7519, pp. 492–495. Springer, Heidelberg (2012)
26. Troelstra, A.S., Schwichtenberg, H.: Basic Proof Theory. Cambridge University Press (2000)
27. Wenzel, M., Paulson, L.C., Nipkow, T.: The Isabelle Framework. In: Mohamed, O.A., Muñoz, C., Tahar, S. (eds.) TPHOLs 2008. LNCS, vol. 5170, pp. 33–38. Springer, Heidelberg (2008)

Non-classical Planning with a Classical Planner: The Power of Transformations

Hector Geffner

ICREA & Universitat Pompeu Fabra
Roc Boronat 138, 08018 Barcelona, Spain
hector.geffner@upf.edu
http://www.dtic.upf.edu/~hgeffner

Abstract. Planning is the model-based approach to autonomous behavior where a predictive model of actions and sensors is used to generate the behavior for achieving given goals. The main challenges in planning are computational as all models, whether featuring uncertainty and feedback or not, are intractable in the worst case when represented in compact form. Classical planning refers to the simplest form of planning where goals are to be achieved by applying deterministic actions to a fully known initial situation. In this invited paper, I review the inferences performed by classical planners that enable them to deal with large problems, and the transformations that have been developed for using these planners to deal with non-classical features such as soft goals, hidden goals to be recognized, planning with incomplete information and sensing, and multiagent nested beliefs.

1 Introduction

At the center of the problem of intelligent behavior is the problem of selecting the action to do next. In AI, three different approaches have been used to address this problem. In the *programming-based approach*, the controller that prescribes the action to do next is given by a programmer, usually in a suitable high-level language. In this approach, the problem is solved by the programmer in his head, and the solution is expressed as a high-level program in behavior-based languages, hierarchical task-networks, rules, or languages such as Golog [1,2]. In the *learning-based approach*, the controller is not given by a programmer but is induced from experience: the agent's own experience, in reinforcement learning, or the experience of a 'teacher' in supervised learning schemes [3]. Finally, in the *model-based approach*, the controller is not learned but is derived automatically from a model of the actions, sensors, and goals.

Planning is the model-based approach to action selection where different types of models are used to make precise the different types of agents, environments, and controllers [4,5]. Classical planning is the simplest form of planning, concerned with the achievement of goals in deterministic environments whose initial state is fully known. POMDP planning, on the other hand, allows for stochastic actions in partially observable environments. The main challenges in planning

E. Fermé and J. Leite (Eds.): JELIA 2014, LNAI 8761, pp. 33–47, 2014.

are computational, as all the models, whether accommodating feedback and uncertainty or not, are intractable in the worst case when models are represented in compact form.

In this paper, I review the inferences performed by classical planners that enable them to deal with large problems, and the transformations that have been developed for using these planners to deal with non-classical features such as soft goals, hidden goals to be recognized, planning with incomplete information and sensing, and multiagent nested beliefs.

2   Planning Models

A wide range of models used in planning can be understood as variations of a *basic state model* featuring

- a finite and discrete state space S,
- a *known initial state* $s_0 \in S$,
- a set $S_G \subseteq S$ of goal states,
- a set $A(s) \subseteq A$ of actions applicable in each state $s \in S$,
- a *deterministic* state transition function $f(a, s)$, $a \in A(s)$, and
- positive *action costs* $c(a, s)$.

This is the model underlying *classical planning* where it also normally assumed that action costs $c(a, s)$ do not depend on the state, and hence $c(a, s) = c(a)$. A solution or *plan* in this model is a sequence of applicable actions that map the initial state into a goal state. More precisely, a plan $\pi = a_0, \ldots, a_{n-1}$ must generate a state sequence $s_0, \ldots, s_n$ such that $a_i \in A(s_i)$, $s_{i+1} = f(a_i, s_i)$, and $s_n \in S_G$, for $i = 0, \ldots, n-1$. The cost of the plan is the sum of the action costs $c(a_i, s_i)$, and a plan is optimal if it has minimum cost over all plans.

A classical plan $a_0, \ldots, a_n$ represents an *open-loop controller* where the action to be done at time step i depends on the step index i. The solution of models that accommodate uncertainty and feedback, on the other hand, produce *closed-loop controllers* where the action to be done at step i depends on the actions and observations collected up to that point. These models can be obtained by relaxing some of the assumptions in the classical model.

In the model for *conformant planning*, the initial state s_0 is not known and it is replaced by a *set S_0* of possible initial states. Likewise, in non-deterministic conformant planning, the state transition function $f(a, s)$ is replaced by a non-deterministic transition function $F(a, s)$ that denotes the set of states that are possible after doing an action a in the state s. A *conformant plan* is an action sequence that must achieve the goal for any possible initial state and state transition.

In *contingent planning* or *partially observable planning*, a sensor model $O(a, s)$ is assumed that maps the current state s and last action a into a set of possible observation tokens that provide partial information about the true but possibly hidden state s. Contingent plans can be expressed in many forms, for example, as a function (policy) mapping *beliefs* into actions, where a belief represents a set of states that are deemed as possible. The initial belief state is given by the set of states S_0 that are initially possible, and the successor belief states can be obtained from the actions performed and the observations gathered, using the transition and sensor functions $F(\cdot, \cdot)$ and $O(\cdot, \cdot)$.

Partial Observable Markov Decision Processes (POMDPS) are contingent planning models where uncertainty about the initial situation, the next system state, and the possible token to be observed, are not represented by *sets* but by probability distributions. Beliefs in POMDPs are thus not sets of states but probability distributions over states. Markov Decision Processes are POMDPs where the states are fully observable.

Classical, conformant, contingent, MDP, and POMDP planners accept a compact description of the corresponding models and produce the solutions (controllers) automatically. On-line planners, on the other hand, produce the action to be done next in the current situation. The basic language for modeling classical planning problems is STRIPS, where a problem is a tuple $P = \langle F, I, O, G \rangle$ in which F is a set of atoms, $I \subseteq F$ and $G \subseteq F$ represent the initial and goal situations, and O is a set of actions a with preconditions, add, and delete effects, all part of F. The PDDL language provides a standard syntax for STRIPS and a number of extensions. Similar languages are used to describe the other planning models in compact form. In all cases, a problem involves a number of variables, boolean or not, and the states correspond to the possible valuations of such variables.

3   Classical Planning

A classical planning problem P can be mapped into a *path-finding* problem over a graph $\mathcal{S}(P)$ where the nodes are the states, the initial node and target nodes are the initial and goal states respectively, and a directed edge between two nodes denotes the existence of an action that maps one state into the other. Classical planning problems can thus be solved in theory by path-finding algorithms such as Dijkstra's, but not in practice, as the size of the graph is exponential in the number of problem variables. Current classical planners such as LAMA [6] thus appeal to *three ideas* for scaling up: automatically derived *heuristic functions* for guiding the search [7,8], the inference of implicit goals in the problems called *landmarks* [9], and a structural criterion for distinguishing the applicable actions that are more likely to be relevant called the *helpful actions* [10].

Heuristic functions have been used in AI since the 60s for making graph search goal-directed. An heuristic function $h(s)$ in planning provides a quick but approximate estimate of the cost of solving the problem from the state s. The new development in planning in the 90s was a way for deriving informed heuristic values effectively from STRIPS encodings. Basically, if $P(s)$ is the classical planning problem with initial state s, and $P^+(s)$ is the *delete-free relaxation* of $P(s)$; i.e., the STRIPS problem that results from dropping the "delete lists", the heuristic $h(s)$ is set to the cost of a *relaxed plan* for $P(s)$; namely a *plan for the relaxation* $P^+(s)$ [10]. While computing an optimal plan for the delete-free problem $P^+(s)$

remains NP-hard, computing one possibly non-optimal plan for $P^+(s)$ is easy. This is because delete-free problems are *fully decomposable*, and hence, a plan π that achieves p from s can be appended to a plan π' that achieves p' from s to yield a plan that achieves both p' and p.

As a result, a simple polynomial iterative procedure can be used to compute relaxed plans for achieving each of the atoms in the problem. Basically, an atom p is *reachable* in 0 steps with relaxed plan $\pi(p, s) = \{\}$ if $p \in s$ (p is true in s), while an atom p is *reachable* in $i + 1$ steps with relaxed plan $\pi(p_1, s), \ldots, \pi(p_n, s), a_p$ if p not reachable in i steps or less from s, and there is an action a_p that adds p with preconditions $p_1, \ldots, p_n$ reachable from s in no more than i steps.

It's simple to prove that the procedure terminates in a number of steps bounded by number of problem atoms (when there are no new reachable atoms), and that if an atom p is reachable, $\pi(p, s)$ is a relaxed plan for p from s; i.e. a plan for p in the relaxation $P^+(s)$. Also if an atom p is not reachable from s, there is no plan for p in the original problem $P(s)$. The heuristic $h_{FF}(s)$ used in the FF and LAMA planners is related to the number of *different* actions in the relaxed plans $\pi(G_i, s)$ for the problem goals G_i. The actions applicable in a state s that are regarded as *helpful* are the actions that are relevant to these relaxed plans; namely, those that add the precondition of an action in $\pi(G_i, s)$ or a goal G_i that is not true in s. Similarly, the *landmarks* in $P(s)$ are identified with the landmarks of the relaxation $P^+(s)$ which can be computed in low polynomial time; indeed, p is a landmark in $P^+(s)$ and hence in $P(s)$, iff the relaxed problem $P^+(s)$ has no plans once the actions that add the atom p are excluded.

State-of-the-art classical planners make use of these three notions, *heuristics*, *landmarks*, and *helpful actions* in different ways. For example, LAMA is a best-first search planner that uses *four queues* [11]: two of these queues are ordered by the h_{FF} heuristic and two are ordered by the number of unachieved landmarks. One queue for each heuristic is restricted to contain the children that result from the application of helpful actions, and the best first search alternates among the four queues. In this way, these planners tend to be robust and do not break down due to the number of atoms or actions in the problem. In the last few years, the SAT approach to classical planning [12], as pushed recently by Rintanen [13], has closed the performance gap with heuristic search planners quite considerably too.

4   Beyond Classical Planning

Classical planners work reasonably well by now, meaning that they can accept problems involving hundreds, and even thousand of actions and variables, often producing plans very quickly.[1] The sheer size of a problem is not an impediment in itself for solving it. The model underlying classical planning is simple but useful. Actions in planning can be activities or policies of any sort that can be characterized deterministically in terms of pre and postconditions. While non-deterministic effects are not accommodated, they can be handled sometimes in

---

[1] My focus is on satisficing planning, not optimal planning. Satisficing planners search for solutions that are good but not necessarily optimal.

a simple manner too. Some of the best planners in the MDP competitions held so far, for example, are not MDP solvers, but classical planners that *choose* one of the possible outcomes and replan from the current state when the system is observed off its expected trajectory [14].

For dealing with non-classical planning models in a more general way, two types of approaches have been pursued: a *top-down* approach, where *native solvers* are developed for more expressive models, and a *bottom-up* approach, where the power of classical planners is exploited by means of suitable *translations* [15]. MDP and POMDP planners are examples of native solvers for more expressive models. A limitation of these planners in comparison with classical planners is that *inference* is usually performed at the level of *states* and *belief states*, rather than at the level of *variables*. *Translation-based* approaches, on the other hand, leverage on classical planners for solving non-classical planning problems by introducing suitable transformations.

5   Translations and Transformations

Transformations have been developed for dealing with *soft goals, goal recognition, incomplete information and sensing,* and *multiagent nested beliefs.* The ideas underlying these transformations are reviewed below. Other features addressed in recent years using classical planners and transformations include *temporally extended goals* [16,17,18,19], *probabilistic conformant planning* [20], and *off-line contingent planning* [21,22].

5.1   Soft Goals and Rewards

Soft goals are used to express desirable outcomes that unlike standard hard goals are subject to a cost-utility tradeoff [23]. We consider STRIPS problems extended with positive *action costs* $c(a)$ for each action a, and non-negative *rewards* or *utilities* $u(p)$ for every atom p. The soft-goals of the problem are the atoms with positive utility. In the presence of soft goals, the target plans π are the ones that maximize the utility measure $u(\pi)$ given by the difference between the total utility obtained by the plan and its cost; i.e., $u(\pi) = \sum_{p:\pi\models p} u(p) - c(\pi)$ where $c(\pi)$ is the sum of the action costs in π, and the utility sum ranges over the soft goals p that are true at the end of the plan.

A plan π for a problem with soft goals is optimal when no other plan π' has utility $u(\pi')$ higher than $u(\pi)$. The International Planning Competition held in 2008 featured a *net-benefit optimal* track where the objective was to find $u(\pi)$ optimal plans [24]. Soft goal or net-benefit planning appears to be very different than classical planning as it involves two interrelated problems: deciding which soft goals to pursue and deciding how to achieve them. Indeed, most of the entries in the competition developed native planners for solving these two interrelated problems. More recently, it has been shown that problems P with soft goals can be compiled into *equivalent problems P' without soft goals* that can be solved by classical planners able to handle action costs only [25].

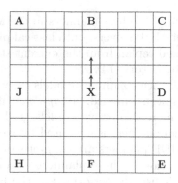

Fig. 1. Goal recognition: Where is the agent moving to?

The idea of the transformation is very simple. For soft-goals p associated with individual atoms, one adds new atoms p' that are made into *hard goals* in P' that are achievable in one of two ways: by the new actions *collect*(p) with precondition p and cost 0, or by the new actions *forgo*(p) with precondition $\bar{p}$, that stands for the negation of p, and cost equal to the utility $u(p)$ of p. Additional bookkeeping is needed in the translation so that these new actions can be done only after the actions in the original problem.

The two problems P and P' are equivalent in the sense that there is a correspondence between the plans for P and P', and corresponding plans are ranked in the same way. More specifically, for any plan π for P, there is a plan π' in P' that extends π with the *end* action and a set of *collect* and *forgo* actions whose cost is $c(\pi') = -u(\pi) + \alpha$ where α is a constant independent of both π and π'. Finding an optimal (maximum utility) plan π for P is therefore equivalent to finding an optimal (minimum cost) plan π' for P'. Interestingly, the cost-optimal planners that entered the optimal sequential track of the 2008 IPC, fed with the translations of the problems in the optimal net-benefit track, do significantly better than the net-benefit planners that entered the latter [25].

5.2 Plan and Goal Recognition

The need to recognize the goals and plans of an agent from observations of his behavior arises in a number of tasks. Goal recognition is like planning but in reverse: while in planning the goal is given and a plan is sought; in plan recognition, part of a plan is observed, and the agent goal is sought. Figure 1 shows a simple scenario of plan recognition where an agent is observed to move up twice from cell X. The question is which is the most likely destination among the possible targets A to J. Clearly, A, B and C appear to be more likely than D, E or F. The reason is that the agent is moving away from these other targets, while it's not moving away from A, B, or C. The second question is whether B can be regarded as more likely than A or C. It turns out that yes. If we adopt a Bayesian formulation, the probability of an hypothesis H given the observation Obs, $P(H|Obs)$ is given by the formula $P(H|Obs) = P(Obs|H)P(H)/P(Obs)$

where $P(Obs|H)$ represents how well the hypothesis H *predicts* the observation Obs, $P(H)$ stands for how likely is the hypothesis H a priori, and $P(Obs)$, which affects all hypotheses H equally, measures how surprising is the observation. In our problem, the hypotheses are about the possible destinations of the agent, and since there are no reasons to assume that one is more likely a priori than the others, Bayes rule yields that $P(H|Obs)$ should be proportional to the likelihood $P(Obs|H)$ that measures *how well H predicts Obs*. Going back to the figure, and assuming that the agent is reasonably 'rational' and hence wants to achieve his goals with least cost, it's clear that A, B, and C predict Obs better than D, E, F; and also that B predicts Obs better than A and C. This is because there is a single optimal plan for B that is compatible with Obs, but there are many optimal plans for A and for C, some of which are not compatible with Obs (as when the agent moves first left or right, rather than up). We say that a plan π is compatible with the observed action sequence Obs when the action sequence Obs is embedded in the action sequence π; i.e. when Obs is π but with certain actions in π omitted (not observed).

The reasoning above reduces goal recognition to Bayes' rule and how well each of the possible goals predicts the observed action sequence. Moreover, how well a goal G predicts the sequence Obs turns out to depend on considerations having to do with *costs*, and in particular, *two cost measures:* the cost of achieving G through a plan *compatible* with the observed action sequence Obs, and the cost of achieving G through a plan that is *not* compatible with Obs. We will denote the first cost as $c_P(G + Obs)$ and the second as $c_P(G + \overline{Obs})$, where P along with the observations Obs define the *plan recognition problem*. That is, P is like a classical planning problem but with the actual goal hidden and replaced by a set $\mathcal{G}$ of possible goals G, and a sequence of observed actions. The plan recognition problem is about inferring the probability distribution $P(G|Obs)$ over the possible goals $G \in \mathcal{G}$ where each possible goal G can be a (conjunctive) set of atoms.

The *cost differences* $\Delta(G, Obs) = c_P(G + \overline{Obs}) - c_P(G + Obs)$ for each of the possible goals G, which can range from $-\infty$ to $+\infty$, can be used to define the likelihoods $P(Obs|G)$, and hence, to obtain the goal posterior probabilities $P(G|Obs)$ when the goal priors $P(G)$ are given. Clearly, the higher the cost difference $\Delta(G, Obs)$, the better that G predicts Obs, and hence the higher the likelihood $P(Obs|G)$. The function used to map the Δ-costs into the $P(O|G)$ likelihoods is the sigmoid function, which follows from assuming that the agent is not perfectly rational [26]. The costs $c_P(G + \overline{Obs})$ and $c_P(G + Obs)$ can be computed by calling a classical planner over the two classical problems $P(G + \overline{Obs})$ and $P(G + Obs)$ that are obtained from P, the hypothetical goal G, and the observations. The result is that the goal posterior probabilities $P(G|Obs)$ can be computed through Bayes' rule and $2 \times |\mathcal{G}|$ calls to a classical planner.

5.3   Incomplete Information and Sensing

A (deterministic) *conformant problem* can be expressed as a tuple $P = \langle F, I, O, G \rangle$ where F stands for the fluents or atoms in the problem, O for the actions, I is a set of

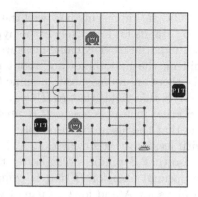

Fig. 2. Example of instances solved by on-line partially observable planner LW1 using linear translations and classical planners [27]. *Left: Minesweeper* instance where the star marks the first cell opened and empty cells have 0 counts. *Right: Wumpus* instance with 2 monsters and 2 pits. Positions of monsters, pits, and gold initially unknown.

clauses over F defining the initial situation, and G is a set of literals over F defining the (conjunctive) goal. The difference to classical problems is the uncertainty in the initial situation which is described by means of clauses. A clause is a disjunction of one or more literals, and a literal is an atom in F or its negation. We assume that the actions are not purely STRIPS but can feature conditional effects and negation; i.e., every action a is assumed to have a precondition given by a set of literals, and a set of *conditional effects* $a : C \to C'$ where C and C' are sets (conjunctions) of literals, meaning that the literals in C' become true after the action a if the literals in C were true when the action was done. The states associated with the problem P are valuations over the atoms in F, and the set of *possible initial states* are the states that satisfy the clauses in I.

A deterministic conformant problem P defines a conformant state model $\mathcal{S}(P)$ which is like the state model for a classical problem with one difference: there is no single initial state s_0 but a *set* of possible initial states S_0. A solution for P, namely a *conformant plan* for P, is an action sequence that simultaneously solves *all* the *classical state models* $\mathcal{S}'(P)$ that result from replacing the set of possible initial states S_0 in $\mathcal{S}(P)$ by each one of the states s_0 in S_0.

From a computational point of view, conformant planning can be formulated as a *path-finding problem* over a graph where the nodes in the graph do not represent the *states* of the problem as in classical planning but *belief states*, where a belief state is a set of states deemed possible at one point. An alternative approach, however, is to map deterministic conformant planning into classical ones [28]. The basic sound but incomplete translation removes the uncertainty in the problem by replacing each literal L in the conformant problem P by two literals KL and $K\neg L$, to be read as 'L is known to be true' and 'L is known to be false' respectively. If L is known to be true or known to be false in the initial situation, then the translation will contain respectively KL or $K\neg L$. On the other hand, if L is not known, then both KL and $K\neg L$ will be initially false.

The result is that there is no uncertainty in the initial situation of the translation which thus represents a classical planning problem.

More precisely, the basic translation K_0 is such that if $P = \langle F, I, O, G \rangle$ is a deterministic conformant problem, the translation $K_0(P)$ is the classical planning problem $K_0(P) = \langle F', I', O', G' \rangle$ where[2]

- $F' = \{KL, K\neg L \mid L \in F\}$
- $I' = \{KL \mid L$ is a unit clause in $I\}$
- $G' = \{KL \mid L \in G\}$
- $O' = O$ but with each precondition L for $a \in O$ replaced by KL, and each effect $a : C \to L$ replaced by $a : KC \to KL$ and $a : \neg K \neg C \to \neg K \neg L$.

The expressions KC and $\neg K \neg C$ for $C = \{L_1, L_2, \ldots\}$ are abbreviations for the conjunctions $\{KL_1, KL_2, \ldots\}$ and $\{\neg K \neg L_1, \neg K \neg L_2, \ldots\}$ respectively. Recall that in a classical planning problem, atoms that are not part of the initial situation are assumed to be initially false, so if KL is not part of I', KL will be initially false in $K_0(P)$.

The only subtlety in this translation is that each conditional effect $a : C \to L$ in P is mapped into *two* conditional effects in $K_0(P)$: a *support* effect $a : KC \to KL$ that ensures that L is known to be true when the condition C is known to be true, and a *cancellation* effect $a : \neg K \neg C \to \neg K \neg L$ that ensures that L is possible when the condition C is possible.

The translation $K_0(P)$ is *sound* as every classical plan that solves $K_0(P)$ is a conformant plan for P, but is *incomplete*, as not all conformant plans for P are classical plans for $K_0(P)$. The meaning of the KL literals follows a similar pattern: if a plan achieves KL in $K_0(P)$, then the same plan achieves L with certainty in P, yet a plan may achieve L with certainty in P without making the literal KL true in $K_0(P)$.

For completeness, the basic translation K_0 is extended into a general translation scheme $K_{T,M}$ where T and M are two parameters: a set of *tags* t and a set of *merges* m. A tag $t \in T$ is a set (conjunction) of literals L from P whose truth value in the initial situation is not known. The tags t are used to introduce a new class of literals KL/t in the classical problem $K_{T,M}(P)$ that represent the conditional statements: 'if t is initially true, then L is true'. Likewise, a merge m is a non-empty collection of tags t in T that stands for the Disjunctive Normal Form (DNF) formula $\bigvee_{t \in m} t$. A merge m is *valid* when one of the tags $t \in m$ must be true in I; i.e., when $I \models \bigvee_{t \in m} t$. A merge m for a literal L translates into a 'merge action' with effects that capture a simple form of reasoning by cases: $\bigwedge_{t \in m} KL/t \longrightarrow KL$.

The parametric translation scheme $K_{T,M}$ is the basic translation K_0 'conditioned' with the tags in T and extended with the actions that capture the merges in M. If $P = \langle F, I, O, G \rangle$ is a deterministic conformant problem, then $K_{T,M}(P)$ is the *classical planning problem* $K_{T,M}(P) = \langle F', I', O', G' \rangle$ where

---

[2] A conditional effect $a : C \to C'$ is assumed to be expressed as a collection of conditional effects $a : C \to L$, one for each literal L in C'. The symbol a stands for the action associated with these effects.

- $F' = \{KL/t, K\neg L/t \mid L \in F \text{ and } t \in T\}$,
- $I' = \{KL/t \mid I, t \models L\}$,
- $G' = \{KL \mid L \in G\}$,
- $O' = \{a : KC/t \to KL/t, \ a : \neg K\neg C/t \to \neg K\neg L/t \mid a : C \to L \text{ in } P\} \cup$
  $\{a_{m,L} : [\bigwedge_{t \in m} KL/t] \to KL \mid L \in P, m \in M\}$.

Two basic properties of the general translation scheme $K_{T,M}(P)$ are that it is always *sound* (provided that merges are valid), and for suitable choice of the sets of tags and merges T and M, it is *complete*. In particular, a complete instance of the general translation $K_{T,M}(P)$ results when the sets of tags T is the set S_0 of possible initial states of P, and $M = T$. While the resulting translation $K_{S0}(P)$ is exponential in the number of unknown atoms in the initial situation in the worst case, there is an alternative choice of tags and merges, called the $K_i(P)$ translation, that is exponential in the non-negative integer i, and that is *complete* for problems P that have a structural parameter $w(P)$, called the *width* of P, bounded by i. In problems defined over multivalued variables, this width stands for the maximum number of variables all of which are relevant to a variable appearing in an action precondition or goal [29]. It turns out that many conformant problems have a bounded and small width, and hence such problems can be efficiently solved by a classical planner after a low polynomial translation [28]. The conformant plans are then obtained from the classical plans by removing the 'merge' actions.

The translation-based approach, introduced initially for deterministic conformant planning, has been extended to deterministic planning with *sensing* [30,31]. Examples of problems solved by the on-line partially observable planner LW1 [27] that uses linear translations for both action selection and belief tracking are shown in Figure 2.

5.4   Finite-State Controllers

Finite-state controllers represent an action selection mechanism widely used in video-games and mobile robotics. In comparison to plans and POMDP policies, to be studied later, finite-state controllers have two advantages: they are often extremely compact, and they are general, applying not just to one problem but to many variations as well. As an illustration, Figure 3(a) depicts a simple problem over a 1×5 grid where a robot, initially at one of the two leftmost positions, must visit the rightmost position, marked B, and get back to A. Assuming that the robot can observe the mark in the current cell if any, and that the actions *Left* and *Right* deterministically move the robot one unit left and right respectively, the problem can be solved by planners that sense and POMDP planners. A solution to the problem, however, can also be expressed as the finite-state controller shown on the right. Starting in the controller state q_0, this controller selects the action *Right*, whether A or no mark ('−') is observed, until observing B. Then the controller selects the action *Left*, switches to state q_1, and remains in this state selecting the action *Left* as long as no mark is observed. Later, when a

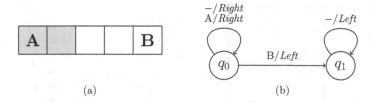

(a)   (b)

Fig. 3. (a) Agent initially in one of the two leftmost positions has to go to cell marked B and back to A. The marks are observable. (b) A 2-state controller that solves the problem and many variations of it. The circles are the controller states, and an edge $q \to q'$ labeled o/a means to perform action a when the observation is o in state q, switching then to state q'. The initial controller state is q_0.

mark is observed, no further actions are taken as the agent must be back at A, having achieved the goal.

The finite-state controller displayed in the figure has two appealing features: it is very compact (it involves two states only), and it is very general. Indeed, the problem can be changed in a number of ways and the controller would still work, driving the agent to the goal. For example, the *size of the grid* can be changed from 1×5 to $1 \times n$, the agent can be placed *initially* anywhere in the grid (except at B), and the actions can be made *non-deterministic* by adding 'noise' so that the agent can move one or two steps at a time. The controller would work for all these variations. This generality is well beyond the power of plans or policies that are normally tied to a particular state space.

The benefits of finite-state controllers, however, come at a price: unlike plans, they are usually not derived automatically but are written by hand; a task that is non-trivial even in the simplest cases. Recently, however, the problem of deriving compact and general finite-state controllers using planners has been considered [32]. Once again, this is achieved by using classical planners over suitable transformations. We sketch the main ideas below.

A finite-state controller $\mathcal{C}_N$ with N controller states $q_0, \ldots, q_{N-1}$ is fully characterized by the tuples (q, o, a, q') associated with the edges $q \xrightarrow{o/a} q'$ in the controller graph. These edges and hence, these tuples, prescribe the action a to do when the controller state is q and the observation is o, switching then to the controller state q' (which may be equal to q or not). A controller solves a problem P if starting in the distinguished controller state q_0, all the executions that are possible given the controller reach a goal state. The key question is how to find the tuples (q, o, a, q') that define such a controller. In [32], the problem P is transformed into a problem P' whose actions are associated with each one of the possible tuples (q, o, a, q'), and where extra fluents p_q and p_o for keeping track of the controller states and observations are introduced. The action $\langle t \rangle$ associated with the tuple $t = (q, o, a, q')$ behaves then very much like the action a but with two differences: first, the atoms p_q and p_o are added to the body of each conditional effect, so that the resulting action $\langle t \rangle$ behaves like the original

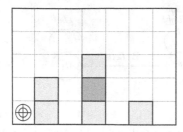
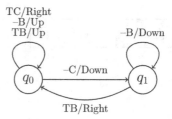

Fig. 4. *Left:* Problem where a visual-mark (on the lower left cell) must be placed on top of a green block whose location is not known, by moving the mark one cell at a time, and observing what's in the marked cell. *Right:* Finite-state controller obtained with a classical planner from translation. The controller solves the problem and *any variation* resulting from changes in either the *number* or *configuration* of blocks [32].

action a but only when the controller state is q and the observation is o; second, the action makes the atom p_q false and the atom $p_{q'}$ true, in accordance with the interpretation of the tuple (unless $q = q'$). Additional bookkeeping is required in the transformed problem P' to prevent plans from executing actions $\langle t \rangle$ and $\langle t' \rangle$ when $t = (q, o, a, q')$, $t' = (q, o, a', q'')$, and $a \neq a'$ or $q' \neq q''$. The reason is that no controller can include such pairs of tuples, as the action and new controller state are always a *function* of the current controller state and observation. Interestingly, the transformation from P into P' eliminates sensing by making the effects of the actions conditional on the current controller state and observation. The result is that while P is a partially observable problem, P' is a *conformant* problem, which as we have seen before, it can be transformed into a classical problem P''. The actions $\langle t \rangle$ that solve such classical problem encode the tuples that define the controller with up to N states that solves P.

As a further illustration of the power of these transformations, Figure 4, on the left, shows a problem inspired in the use of deictic representations where a visual-marker (the circle on the lower left) must be placed on top of a green block by moving it one cell at a time. The location of the green block is not known, and the observations are whether the cell currently marked contains a green block (G), a non-green block (B), or neither (C), and whether this cell is at the level of the table (T) or not (–). The *compact* and *general* controller shown on the right has been computed by running a *classical planner* over a translation obtained following the two steps above [32]. The controller solves the problem shown and any variation resulting from changes in either the *number* or *configuration* of blocks.

5.5   Planning with Other Agents in Mind

The muddy children puzzle is a common example used for illustrating the subtleties that arise when reasoning about the beliefs of other agents. In the problem, there are n children, k of whom have mud on their forehead. The children can see which other children are muddy but can't tell whether they are muddy or not.

The father comes and tells the children that at least one of them is muddy, and then asks the children whether they know whether they are muddy or not. It's possible to show that if the children are good reasoners, those who are muddy will know that they are muddy after the father repeats the question exactly k times [33]. When k is greater than 1, the puzzle is that the children arrive to this conclusion after expressing ignorance $k - 1$ times, and after (apparently) not learning anything new from the parent (they can all see at least one muddy child). A planning version of the problem can be constructed, for example, by asking one of the children to find out whether he is muddy or not by selecting another child X and asking him whether X knows whether he is muddy or not, with everyone listening to the response. The shortest plan in that case is to ask this question to the children seen to be muddy one by one.

The problem of characterizing the state of (nested) knowledge or beliefs in a setting where agents are able to act on the world, observe the world, and communicate their beliefs, has been studied in recent years in the area of dynamic epistemic logics [34,35]. Recently, an expressive and meaningful fragment of this logic has been identified where the methods for handling beliefs in the single agent setting are used to compute *linear plans* akin to multiagent conformant plans, using classical planners and a transformation that is quadratic in the number of possible initial states [36]. The planning version of the muddy children problem is an example of a problem that fits into this fragment. Similar methods have been developed also for computing join plans in a logical version of the multiagent planning models called Descentralized POMDPs [37].

6 Summary

Planning is the model-based approach to autonomous behavior where models come in many forms depending on the presence of uncertainty, the form of the feedback, and whether uncertainty is represented by means of sets or probability distributions. All forms of planning are intractable in the worst case when problems are represented in compact form, including the simplest form of planning, classical planning, where actions are deterministic and the initial state is fully known. In spite of this, significant progress has been achieved in classical planning in the last two decades for scaling up. Like in other AI models and solvers, the key is the exploitation of the problem structure by means of cost-effective forms of inference. In classical planning, this inference takes mainly the form of heuristics derived from the problem, landmarks that uncover implicit subgoals, and a structural criterion for distinguishing the applicable actions that are more likely to be relevant, called the helpful actions. Advances in classical planning have been exploited for dealing with non-classical problems by means of suitable transformations. Even if sound and complete translations are worst-case exponential, as in planning with incomplete information and sensing, compact polynomial but incomplete transformations have been shown to be very powerful as well. We have briefly reviewed transformations for dealing with soft goals, goal recognition, planning with incomplete information and sensing, and nested multiagent beliefs.

Acknowledgments. I have borrowed material from [15]. Some of the work reviewed has been done in collaboration with students and colleagues. I also thank João Leite and Eduardo Fermé for the invitation to talk at JELIA-2014.

References

1. Erol, K., Hendler, J., Nau, D.S.: HTN planning: Complexity and expressivity. In: Proc. 12th Nat. Conf. on Artificial Intelligence, pp. 1123–1123 (1994)
2. Levesque, H., Reiter, R., Lespérance, Y., Lin, F., Scherl, R.: GOLOG: A logic programming language for dynamic domains. J. of Logic Progr. 31, 59–83 (1997)
3. Sutton, R., Barto, A.: Introduction to Reinforcement Learning. MIT Press (1998)
4. Russell, S.J., Norvig, P.: Artificial Intelligence: A Modern Approach, 3rd edn. Prentice-Hall (2009)
5. Ghallab, M., Nau, D., Traverso, P.: Automated Planning: Theory and practice. Morgan Kaufmann (2004)
6. Richter, S., Westphal, M.: The LAMA planner: Guiding cost-based anytime planning with landmarks. Journal of Artificial Intelligence Research 39, 127–177 (2010)
7. McDermott, D.V.: Using regression-match graphs to control search in planning. Artificial Intelligence 109(1-2), 111–159 (1999)
8. Bonet, B., Geffner, H.: Planning as heuristic search. Artificial Intelligence 129(1-2), 5–33 (2001)
9. Hoffmann, J., Porteous, J., Sebastia, L.: Ordered landmarks in planning. Journal of Artificial Intelligence Research 22, 215–278 (2004)
10. Hoffmann, J., Nebel, B.: The FF planning system: Fast plan generation through heuristic search. Journal of Artificial Intelligence Research 14, 253–302 (2001)
11. Helmert, M.: The Fast Downward planning system. Journal of Artificial Intelligence Research 26, 191–246 (2006)
12. Kautz, H.A., Selman, B.: Pushing the envelope: Planning, propositional logic, and stochastic search. In: Proc. AAAI, pp. 1194–1201 (1996)
13. Rintanen, J.: Planning as satisfiability: Heuristics. Art. Int. 193, 45–86 (2012)
14. Yoon, S., Fern, A., Givan, R.: FF-replan: A baseline for probabilistic planning. In: Proc. 17th Int. Conf. on Automated Planning and Scheduling, pp. 352–359 (2007)
15. Geffner, H., Bonet, B.: A Concise Introduction to Models and Methods in Automated Planning. Morgan & Claypool (2013)
16. Cresswell, S., Coddington, A.M.: Compilation of LTL goal formulas into PDDL. In: Proc. 16th European Conf. on Artificial Intelligence, pp. 985–986 (2004)
17. Edelkamp, S.: On the compilation of plan constraints and preferences. In: Proc. 16th Int. Conf. on Automated Planning and Scheduling, pp. 374–377 (2006)
18. Albarghouthi, A., Baier, J.A., McIlraith, S.A.: On the use of planning technology for verification. In: Proc. ICAPS 2009 Workshop VV&PS (2009)
19. Patrizi, F., Lipovetzky, N., de Giacomo, G., Geffner, H.: Computing infinite plans for LTL goals using a classical planner. In: Proc. 22nd Int. Joint Conf. on Artificial Intelligence, pp. 2003–2008 (2011)
20. Taig, R., Brafman, R.: Compiling conformant probabilistic planning problems into classical planning. In: Proc. ICAPS (2013)
21. Brafman, R., Shani, G.: A multi-path compilation approach to contingent planning. In: Proc. AAAI (2012)
22. Palacios, H., Albore, A., Geffner, H.: Compiling contingent planning into classical planning: New translations and results. In: Proc. ICAPS Workshop on Models and Paradigms for Planning under Uncertainty (2014)

23. Smith, D.E.: Choosing objectives in over-subscription planning. In: Proc. 14th Int. Conf. on Automated Planning and Scheduling, pp. 393–401 (2004)
24. Helmert, M., Do, M.B., Refanidis, I.: 2008 IPC Deterministic planning competition. In: 6th IPC Booklet, ICAPS 2008 (2008)
25. Keyder, E., Geffner, H.: Soft goals can be compiled away. Journal of Artificial Intelligence Research 36, 547–556 (2009)
26. Ramírez, M., Geffner, H.: Probabilistic plan recognition using off-the-shelf classical planners. In: Proc. 24th Conf. on Artificial Intelligence, pp. 1121–1126 (2010)
27. Bonet, B., Geffner, H.: Flexible and scalable partially observable planning with linear translations. In: Proc. AAAI (2014)
28. Palacios, H., Geffner, H.: Compiling uncertainty away in conformant planning problems with bounded width. JAIR 35, 623–675 (2009)
29. Bonet, B., Geffner, H.: Width and complexity of belief tracking in non-deterministic conformant and contingent planning. In: Proc. 26th Conf. on Artificial Intelligence, pp. 1756–1762 (2012)
30. Albore, A., Palacios, H., Geffner, H.: A translation-based approach to contingent planning. In: Proc. 21st Int. Joint Conf. on Artificial Intelligence, pp. 1623–1628 (2009)
31. Maliah, S., Brafman, R., Karpas, E., Shani, G.: Partially observable online contingent planning using landmark heuristics. In: Proc. ICAPS (2014)
32. Bonet, B., Palacios, H., Geffner, H.: Automatic derivation of memoryless policies and finite-state controllers using classical planners. In: Proc. ICAPS (2009)
33. Fagin, R., Halpern, J., Moses, Y., Vardi, M.: Reasoning about Knowledge. MIT Press (1995)
34. van Ditmarsch, H., van der Hoek, W., Kooi, B.: Dynamic Epistemic Logic. Springer (2007)
35. van Ditmarsch, H., Kooi, B.: Semantic results for ontic and epistemic change. In: Logic and the Foundations of Game and Decision Theory (LOFT 7), pp. 87–117 (2008)
36. Kominis, F., Geffner, H.: Beliefs in multiagent planning: From one agent to many. In: Proc. ICAPS Workshop on Distributed and Multi-Agent Planning (2014)
37. Brafman, R., Shani, G., Zilberstein, S.: Qualitative planning under partial observability in multi-agent domains. In: Proc. AAAI (2013)

Opportunities for Argument-Centric Persuasion in Behaviour Change

Anthony Hunter

Department of Computer Science, University College London,
Gower Street, London WC1E 6BT, UK

Abstract. The aim of behaviour change is to help people overcome specific behavioural problems in their everyday life (e.g. helping people to decrease their calorie intake). In current persuasion technology for behaviour change, the emphasis is on helping people to explore their issues (e.g. through questionnaires or game playing) or to remember to follow a behaviour change plan (e.g. diaries and email reminders). So explicit argumentation with consideration of arguments and counterarguments are not supported with existing persuasion technologies. With recent developments in computational models of argument, there is the opportunity for argument-centric persuasion in behaviour change. In this paper, key requirements for this will be presented, together with some discussion of how computational models of argumentation can be harnessed.

1 Introduction

Persuasion is an activity that involves one party trying to induce another party to believe something or to do something. It is an important and multifaceted human facility. For some occupations, persuasion is paramount (for example in sales, marketing, advertising, politics, etc). However, we are all confronted with the need to persuade others on a regular basis in order to get our job done, or to get our needs or wishes met.

Psychological studies show how there are many factors that can have a substantial influence on whether persuasion will be successful. For any given situation, these factors may include what we may describe as rational criteria such as the merits of what we are being persuaded to believe or do, or the reliability of the information that is being presented to us. But often, seemingly irrational criteria may become important in the success of persuasion such as whether we like the person who is trying to persuade us, or what our peers may think of us [1]. When it comes to products and services, seemingly trivial factors such as the type of packaging, the colour of a vendor's logo, or a celebrity endorsement, can make a big difference. Sales, marketing, advertising, politics certainly exploit these seemingly irrational criteria.

As computing becomes involved in every sphere of life, so too is persuasion a target for applying computer-based solutions. Persuasion technologies have come out of developments in human-computer interaction research (see for example the influential work by Fogg [2]) with a particular emphasis on addressing the need

E. Fermé and J. Leite (Eds.): JELIA 2014, LNAI 8761, pp. 48–61, 2014.

for systems to help people make positive changes to their behaviour, particularly in healthcare and healthy life styles. Over the past 10 years, a wide variety of systems have been developed to help users to control body weight [3], to reduce fizzy drink consumption [4], to increase physical exercise [5], and to decrease stress-related illness [6].

Many of these persuasion technologies for behaviour change are based on some combination of questionnaires for finding out information from users, provision of information for directing the users to better behaviour, computer games to enable users to explore different scenarios concerning their behaviour, provision of diaries for getting users to record ongoing behaviour, and messages to remind the user to continue with the better behaviour. These systems tend to be heavily scripted multi-media solutions and they are often packaged as websites and/or apps for mobile devices.

Interestingly, argumentation is not central to the current manifestations of persuasion technologies. The arguments for good behaviour seem either to be assumed before the user accesses the persuasion technology (e.g. when using diaries, or receiving email reminders), or arguments are provided implicitly in the persuasion technology (e.g. through provision of information, or through game playing). So explicit argumentation with consideration of arguments and counterarguments are not supported with existing persuasion technologies.

This creates some interesting opportunities for artificial intelligence, using computational models of argument, to develop persuasion technologies for behaviour change where arguments are central. This leads to an opportunity for what we may call *argument-centric persuasion for behaviour change*. Computational models of argument are beginning to offer ways to formalize aspects of persuasion, and with some adaptation and development, they have the potential to be incorporated into valuable tools for changing behaviours.

In argument-centric persuasion technologies, a system enters into a dialogue with a user to persuade them to undertake some action. An action might be abstract such as believing something, or deciding something, or it might be a physical action such as buying something, or eating something, or taking some medicine, or it might be to not do some physical action such as not buying something, or not eating something, etc. The dialogue may involve steps where the system finds out more about the users beliefs, intentions and desires, and where the system offers arguments with the aim of changing the users beliefs, intentions and desires. The system also needs to handle objections or doubts by the user represented by counterarguments with the aim of providing a dialectically winning position. To illustrate how a dialogue can lead to the presentation of an appropriate context-sensitive argument consider the following example.

Example 1. The system moves are odd numbered, and the user moves are even numbered: (1) Do you need a snack? (2) Yes. (3) What is available? (4) Cup cake or salad. (5) Which do you prefer? (6) Cup cake. (7) Why? (8) I need a sugar rush from the cup cake. (9) Why? (10) I need a sugar rush in order to do some work. (11) The sugar rush from a cup cake is brief. So your need for a sugar rush does not imply you need a cup cake. Do you agree? (12) Yes.

In this paper, we will identify the requirements of argument-centric persuasion as applied to behaviour change, review some of the key features of computational models of argument, and then consider a simple case study to illustrate how we might address behaviour change by harnessing a computational model of argument.

2   Requirements for Argument-Centric Behaviour Change

There is increasing demand for tools to support behaviour change. Many people need help in changing their behaviour on every day matters in some respect such as promoting healthy life styles (eating more fruit and veg, exercise), weight management (e.g. addressing overweight, bulimia, anorexia), addiction management (gambling, alcohol, drugs, etc), treatment compliance (e.g. self-management of diabetes), personal financial (e.g. borrowing less, saving more), education (starting or continuing with a course, studying properly), encouraging citizenship (e.g. voting, recycling, contributing to charities), safe driving (e.g. not exceeding speed limits, not texting while driving), addressing anti-social behaviour (e.g. aggressive behaviour, vandalism), etc. Further applications may include automated systems for responding to antisocial behaviour online (e.g. racism, sexism, etc).

In these behaviour change applications, the following are key requirements for argument-centric persuasion technologies.

(Requirement 1) Goal orientation The system should aim to be successful in its persuasion dialogue. This means that the system should aim for a dialogue that concludes with the user being persuaded (as manifested for example by the user agreeing to an intended action).

(Requirement 2) Context sensitivity The system should ask the user questions in order to take account of the user's context and concerns. This may include the user's preferences, mood, desires, etc, at the time of the dialogue. By understanding the user, the system is more likely to identify arguments that will be successful in persuading the user.

(Requirement 3) Maintaining engagement The system should aim to minimize the chances that the user disengages from the dialogue. This means that the system should try to avoid the user becoming bored, irritated, etc, by the dialogue. So the system may have to trade a longer sequence of moves that would be more likely to be convincing (if the user remained engaged) for a shorter and more engaging sequence of moves.

(Requirement 4) Language sensitivity The system should use a language in the dialogue (for instance, complexity, vocabulary, style, etc) that is appropriate for the user in the current context. This may include consideration of the user's preferences, mood, desires, etc. It may also include the user's attitude to authority, expertise, etc. For instance, for persuading a teenager to desist from anti-social behaviour, using the language of his/her music or sports idols is more likely to be successful than the language of a school teacher.

(**Requirement 5**) **Argument quality** The system should present arguments and counterarguments that are informative, relevant, and believable, to the user. If the system presents uninformative, irrelevant, or unbelievable arguments (from the perspective of the user), the probability of successful persuasion is reduced, and it may alienate the user.

(**Requirement 6**) **Effort minimization** The system should aim to minimize the effort involved on the part of the user. This means that the user should not be asked unnecessary questions or presented unnecessary claims, or arguments/counterarguments, etc.

In argument-centric persuasion for behaviour change the system enters into a dialogue with the user. In the short-term, we may envisage that this dialogue involves limited kinds of interaction in order for the user to offer specific kinds of information to the system, or for the system to ask specific queries of the user. The allowed dialogues moves are specified for the particular application. The dialogues between the system and the user are restricted to the moves specified at the interface (i.e. the graphical user interface) at each step of the dialogue. The user can initiate a dialogue, and then the system manages the dialogue by asking queries of the user, where the allowed answers are given by a menu, and by positing arguments. For instance, for a weight management application that is intended to help the user decrease calorie consumption, the kinds of queries and posits that can be made by the system might be the following.

- Query for contextual information. For example, for the query, "How many cakes have you eaten today", the menu of answers could have "0", "1", "2", "3", "4", and "more than 4", and for the query, "Which of the following best describe how you feel today", the menu of answers could have "very hungry", "moderately hungry", "not hungry", and "full".
- Query for preferences over options. For example, for the query, "Which would you prefer to eat as a snack now", the menu of answers could have "Prefer cup cake to carrot", "Prefer carrot to cup cake", and "Indifferent between cup cake and carrot".
- Rebuttals with explanation. For example, suppose the user has chosen the reply "Prefer cup cake to carrot", the system could rebut this by saying "Remember your plan to lose weight therefore prefer carrot to cup cake".
- Undercuts with explanation. For example, suppose the user has chosen "Prefer cup cake to carrot" because "Cup cake gives a sugar rush and I need this to work late" (i.e. the user has selected "Cup cake gives a sugar rush and I need this to work late" from the menu of answers), the system could undercut this by saying "The sugar rush from a cup cake is brief, and so it will not help you to work late".

So we can adopt some intuitive requirements for argument-centric behaviour change, and we can impose some simple constraints on the mode of interaction between the user and the system in order to render the approach viable in the short-term. Obviously richer natural language interaction would be desirable, but it is less feasible in the short-term.

3   Computational Models of Argument

Computational models of argument reflect aspects of how humans use conflicting information by constructing and analyzing arguments. Formalizations of argumentation have been extensively studied, and some basic principles established. We can group much of this work in four levels as follows.

Dialectical level. Dialectics is concerned with determining which arguments win in some sense. In abstract argumentation, originally proposed in the seminal work by Dung [7], arguments and counterarguments can be represented by a graph. Each node node denotes an argument, and each arc denotes one argument attacking another argument. Dung then defined some principled ways to identify extensions of an argument graph. Each extension is a subset of arguments that together act as a coalition against attacks by other arguments. An argument in an extension is, in a sense, an acceptable argument.

Logical level. At the dialectic level, arguments are atomic. They are assumed to exist, but there is no mechanism for constructing them. Furthermore, they cannot be divided or combined. To address this, the logical level provides a way to construct arguments from knowledge. At the logical level, an argument is normally defined as a pair $\langle \Phi, \alpha \rangle$ where Φ is a minimal consistent subset of the knowledgebase (a set of formulae) that entails α (a formula). Here, Φ is called the support, and α is the claim, of the argument. Hence, starting with a set of formulae, arguments and counterarguments can be generated, where a counterargument (an argument that attacks another argument) either rebuts (i.e. negates the claim of the argument) or undercuts (i.e. negates the support of the argument). A range of options for structured argumentation at the logic level have been investigated (see [8,9,10,11] for tutorial reviews of some of the key proposals).

Dialogue level. Dialogical argumentation involves agents exchanging arguments in activities such as discussion, debate, persuasion, and negotiation. Dialogue games are now a common approach to characterizing argumentation-based agent dialogues (e.g. [12,13,14,15,16,17,18,19,20,21,22]). Dialogue games are normally made up of a set of communicative acts called moves, and a protocol specifying which moves can be made at each step of the dialogue. Dialogical argumentation can be viewed as incorporating logic-based argumentation, but in addition, dialogical argumentation involves representing and managing the locutions exchanged between the agents involved in the argumentation. The emphasis of the dialogical view is on the interactions between the agents, and on the process of building up, and analyzing, the set of arguments until the agents reach a conclusion.

Rhetorical level. Normally argumentation is undertaken with some wider context of goals for the agents involved, and so individual arguments are presented with some wider aim. For instance, if an agent is trying to persuade another agent to do something, then it is likely that some rhetorical device is harnessed and this will affect the nature of the arguments used (e.g. a politician may refer to investing in the future of the nation's children as a way of persuading colleagues to vote for an increase in taxation). Aspects of the rhetorical level include believability of arguments from the perspective of the audience [23], impact of arguments from the perspective of the audience [24], use of threats and rewards [25], appropriateness of advocates [26], and values of the audience [27,28,29].

There are a number of proposals that formalize aspects of persuasion. Most are aimed at providing protocols for dialogues (for a review see [30]). Forms of correctness (e.g. the dialogue system has the same extensions under particular dialectical semantics as using the agent's knowledgebases) have been shown for a variety of systems (e.g. [31,13,15,32]). However, strategies for persuasion, in particular taking into account beliefs of the opponent are under-developed.

There are a number of proposals for using probability theory in argumentation (e.g. [33,34,35,36,37,38,39]). For abstract argumentation, the epistemic approach involves assigning a probability value to each argument that denotes the degree to which it is believed [36,38,39]. An epistemic extension is then the set of arguments that have a probability value greater than 0.5. The justification approach involves a probability distribution over the subgraphs of the argument graph G [37,38]. The probability that a set of arguments Γ is an extension (according to a particular dialectical semantics S such as grounded, preferred, etc) is the sum of the probability assigned to each subgraph G' of G for which Γ is an extension of G' (according the dialectical semantics S).

Probabilistic models of the opponent have been used in some strategies [40,41] allowing the selection of moves for an agent based on what it believes the other agent believes. Utility theory has also been considered in argumentation (for example [42,43,44,45]) though none of these represents the uncertainty of moves made by each agent in argumentation. One approach that combines probability theory and utility theory (using decision theory) has been used in [46] to identify outcomes with maximum expected utility where outcomes are specified as particular arguments being included or excluded from extensions. Strategies in argumentation have also been analyzed using game theory [47,48,49], though these are more concerned with issues of manipulation, rather than persuasion.

So there is a range of formal systems for generating and comparing arguments and counterarguments, and for undertaking this within the context of a dialogue.

4   A Simple Case Study

In order to illustrate how we can adapt computational models of argument for argument-centric persuasion for behaviour change, we will consider a simple case study for helping a user to decrease his or her calorie intake for weight management. Background knowledge for this application could for example be compiled empirically by monitoring behavioural change sessions with counsellors [50].

Computational models of argument normally consider two or more agents who exchange moves according to some protocol (which specifies what moves are necessary or permissible at each stage of a dialogue). These agents are equal participants in the dialogue, and there is no restriction in the range of arguments and counterarguments that they can make. For behaviour change, we have an asymmetric situation where one agent (the system) provides the queries, the arguments and the counterarguments, and the other agent (the user) replies to queries. In order to allow the user to make a counterargument, the counterargument will also be generated by the system, and presented to the user in a query. The user either agrees or disagrees with it as a reply. For example, if the system has made an argument such as "You should eat salad because it is good for you", the user could be queried as to whether it subscribes to the counterargument "Do you refuse to eat salad because you think it is boring to eat?". As we will see later, the replies made by the user are restricted to those available by a menu of answers generated by the system.

So we require a set of statements that can be used in the dialogues. Each statement is atomic and cannot be divided into substatements. Each is represented by a sentence of English (a sy-sentence) as illustrated next.

s_0 = "User needs a meal" s_1 = "The best choice is a burger"

s_2 = "The best choice is fish" s_3 = "User needs to slim for fun run"

s_4 = "User needs to slim to be healthy" s_5 = "Fun run training uses lots of energy"

s_6 = "User needs occassional treats" s_7 = "User has eaten 10 burgers this week"

s_8 = "User wants a burger" s_9 = "User wants fish"

s_{10} = "Options are a burger or fish" s_{11} = "System has failed to persuade user"

s_{12} = "User agrees with argument a_1" s_{13} = "User disagrees with argument a_1"

s_{14} = "User agrees with argument a_2" s_{15} = "User disagrees with argument a_2"

s_{16} = "User agrees with argument a_5" s_{17} = "User disagrees with argument a_5"

s_{18} = "User agrees with argument a_4" s_{19} = "User disagrees with argument a_4"

We also require a set of queries. Each query is atomic and cannot be divided into subqueries. Each is represented by a sentence of English (a wh-sentence) as illustrated next.

q_0 = "Do you need a meal?"

q_1 = "What are the options?"

q_2 = "What do you prefer?"

q_3 = "Do you agree with argument a_1?"

q_4 = "Do you agree with argument a_2?"

q_5 = "Why do you disagree with argument a_1?"

q_6 = "Why do you disagree with argument a_2?"

q_7 = "Do you agree with argument a_5?"

q_8 = "Do you agree with argument a_4?"

In order to generate arguments, we require a logic. For our case study, we use a simple implicational logic. For this, we require a set of literals, and a set of rules of the form $\alpha_1 \wedge \ldots \wedge \alpha_m \to \beta_1 \wedge \ldots \wedge \beta_n$ where $\alpha_1, \ldots, \alpha_m$ and $\beta_1, \ldots, \beta_n$ are literals. Each literal is either a statement or an atom of the form $\mathrm{ok}(\mathrm{rule}_i)$ where the index i is a number. For our example, the following are rules.

$$s_3 \wedge ok(rule1) \rightarrow s_2 \wedge \neg s_1$$
$$s_4 \wedge ok(rule2) \rightarrow s_2 \wedge \neg s_1$$
$$s_5 \wedge ok(rule3) \rightarrow \neg ok(rule1)$$
$$s_6 \wedge ok(rule4) \rightarrow \neg ok(rule2)$$
$$s_7 \wedge ok(rule5) \rightarrow \neg ok(rule4)$$

Using the simple implicational logic, an argument is a tuple $\langle \Phi, \alpha \rangle$ where Φ contains one or more rules, and some literals, such that α can be obtained from Φ using modus ponens (but no other proof rule), and no subset of Φ entails α using modus ponens. An argument $\langle \Phi, \alpha \rangle$ attacks an argument $\langle \Psi, \beta \rangle$ iff there is a literal $\gamma \in \Psi$ such that $\{\alpha, \gamma\}$ is inconsistent according to classical logic. For our case study, the arguments and attacks are given in Figure 1.

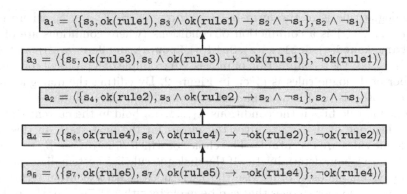

Fig. 1. The argument graph for the running example. Here there are two arguments for the goal of the persuasion (namely a_1 and a_2).

The system can make four types of dialogue move: (1) Ask(q) where q is a query; (2) Posit(a) where a is an argument; (3) Attack(a, a') where a and a' are arguments; and (4) Claim(s) where s is a statement. The user can only make one kind of move which is Reply(s) where s is a statement. An execution is a sequence of states where each state is a set of dialogue moves (as illustrated in Table 1).

The protocol is specified using a set dialogue rules. For each dialogue rule, the antecedent specifies when the rule can fire (i.e. the preconditions of the rule), and the consequent specifies the moves that follow from the firing of the rule (i.e. the postconditions of the rule).

For the conditions of dialogue rules, there are five types of predicate: Start which only holds in the initial state of the dialogue; Asked(q) which holds when the previous state has the move Ask(q); Replied(s) which holds if the previous state has the move Reply(s); Know(a) which holds if the system can use its knowledgebase together with the statements s which occur in moves Reply(s) in previous states to obtain the argument a; and Ucut(a, a') which holds it a is an argument that attacks argument a'.

Table 1. An execution of the dialogue rules for the running example

Step	Moves
0	$\{\texttt{Ask}(\texttt{q}_0)\}$
1	$\{\texttt{Reply}(\texttt{s}_0)\}$
2	$\{\texttt{Ask}(\texttt{q}_1)\}$
3	$\{\texttt{Reply}(\texttt{s}_{10})\}$
4	$\{\texttt{Ask}(\texttt{q}_2)\}$
5	$\{\texttt{Reply}(\texttt{s}_8)\}$
6	$\{\texttt{Posit}(\texttt{a}_2), \texttt{Ask}(\texttt{q}_4)\}$
7	$\{\texttt{Reply}(\texttt{s}_{14})\}$
8	$\{\texttt{Claim}(\texttt{s}_2)\}$

A dialogue rule is of the form $\alpha_1 \vee \ldots \vee \alpha_m \Rightarrow \beta_1 \vee \ldots \vee \beta_n$ where each $\alpha_i \in \{\alpha_1, \ldots, \alpha_m\}$ is a conjunction of conditions (where conditions are of the form $\texttt{Start}$, $\texttt{Asked}(\texttt{q})$, $\texttt{Replied}(\texttt{s})$, $\texttt{Said}(\texttt{s})$, $\texttt{Know}(\texttt{a})$, and $\texttt{Ucut}(\texttt{a}, \texttt{a}')$), and each β_i in $\{\beta_1, \ldots, \beta_n\}$ is a conjunction of moves. An example of a protocol containing a number of dialogue rules is given in Figure 2. By editing the dialogue rules, different protocols (and hence different state models) can be obtained.

A dialogue rule fires if the conditions $\alpha_1, \ldots, \alpha_m$ hold in the current state. If it fires, then one of $\beta_1, \ldots, \beta_n$ gives the moves for the next state. In this way, the dialogue rules are executable. The choice of which β_i in $\beta_1, \ldots, \beta_n$ to use for the next state is non-deterministic. If the dialogue rule is a system dialogue rule, then the system chooses, otherwise the user chooses. An execution terminates when there are no more moves that can be made by either the user or the system. The set of all executions for a protocol can be arranged as a state model as in Figure 3.

We now consider the user model (i.e. the model of the user which reflects the estimated uncertainty about what the user knows and believes). The first kind of uncertainty to consider is *perceptual uncertainty* which is the uncertainty about which arguments and attacks the user is aware of. The second kind of uncertainty is *epistemic uncertainty* which is uncertainty about which arguments and attacks the user believes.

From the system perspective, perceptual uncertainty concerns what arguments the user might start with. For instance, returning to Example 1, the system might not know if the user is aware of the fact the sugar rush from a cup cake is brief, and hence whether the user is aware of arguments based on it. We assume that once the system has told the user about an argument or attack, the user is aware of it, and hence that uncertainty falls to zero. Then from the system perspective, epistemic uncertainty concerns which arguments or attacks the user chooses to ignore because they do not believe them. Recent developments in probabilistic argumentation (e.g. [35,36,37,38,39] offer possibilities for capturing perceptual and epistemic uncertainty in user models. Furthermore, there are a number of possibilities for adapting recent proposals for strategies based on uncertain opponent models (e.g. [51,40,41,46]) that may provide appropriate strategies for argument-centric persuasion for behaviour change.

$$r_0 = \texttt{Start} \Rightarrow \texttt{Ask}(q_0)$$
$$r_1 = \texttt{Replied}(s_0) \Rightarrow \texttt{Ask}(q_1)$$
$$r_2 = \texttt{Replied}(s_{10}) \Rightarrow \texttt{Ask}(q_2)$$
$$r_3 = \texttt{Replied}(s_8) \Rightarrow (\texttt{Posit}(a_1) \wedge \texttt{Ask}(q_3)) \vee (\texttt{Posit}(a_2) \wedge \texttt{Ask}(q_4))$$
$$r_4 = \texttt{Replied}(s_9) \vee \texttt{Replied}(s_{12}) \vee \texttt{Replied}(s_{14}) \vee \texttt{Replied}(s_{16}) \Rightarrow \texttt{Claim}(s_2)$$
$$r_5 = \texttt{Replied}(s_{13}) \Rightarrow \texttt{Ask}(q_5)$$
$$r_6 = \texttt{Replied}(s_{15}) \Rightarrow \texttt{Ask}(q_6)$$
$$r_7 = \texttt{Replied}(s_5) \wedge \texttt{Know}(a_3) \wedge \texttt{Ucut}(a_3, a_1) \Rightarrow (\texttt{Posit}(a_3) \wedge \texttt{Attack}(a_3, a_1) \wedge \texttt{Claim}(s_1))$$
$$r_8 = \texttt{Replied}(s_6) \wedge \texttt{Know}(a_4) \wedge \texttt{Ucut}(a_4, a_3) \Rightarrow (\texttt{Posit}(a_4) \wedge \texttt{Attack}(a_4, a_1) \wedge \texttt{Ask}(q_8))$$
$$r_9 = \texttt{Replied}(s_{18}) \wedge \texttt{Know}(a_5) \wedge \texttt{Ucut}(a_5, a_4) \Rightarrow (\texttt{Posit}(a_5) \wedge \texttt{Attack}(a_5, a_4) \wedge \texttt{Ask}(q_7))$$
$$r_{10} = \texttt{Replied}(s_{17}) \Rightarrow \texttt{Claim}(s_{11})$$
$$r_{11} = \texttt{Asked}(q_0) \Rightarrow \texttt{Reply}(s_0)$$
$$r_{12} = \texttt{Asked}(q_1) \Rightarrow \texttt{Reply}(s_{10})$$
$$r_{13} = \texttt{Asked}(q_2) \Rightarrow \texttt{Reply}(s_8) \vee \texttt{Reply}(s_9)$$
$$r_{14} = \texttt{Asked}(q_3) \Rightarrow \texttt{Reply}(s_{12}) \vee \texttt{Reply}(s_{13})$$
$$r_{15} = \texttt{Asked}(q_4) \Rightarrow \texttt{Reply}(s_{14}) \vee \texttt{Reply}(s_{15})$$
$$r_{16} = \texttt{Asked}(q_5) \Rightarrow \texttt{Reply}(s_5)$$
$$r_{17} = \texttt{Asked}(q_6) \Rightarrow \texttt{Reply}(s_6)$$
$$r_{18} = \texttt{Asked}(q_7) \Rightarrow \texttt{Reply}(s_{16}) \vee \texttt{Reply}(s_{17})$$
$$r_{19} = \texttt{Asked}(q_8) \Rightarrow \texttt{Reply}(s_{18})$$

Fig. 2. Protocol for the running example. Rules r_0 to r_{10} are for the system for querying the user, for presenting arguments and counterarguments, and for making claims. Rules r_{11} to r_{19} are for the user to respond to queries. The first state is obtained using r_0.

Any dialogue that is generated by the protocol in this simple case study (i.e. Figure 3) involves few moves. However, for practical applications, the protocol would be substantially larger, and so some dialogues are potentially long. Long dialogues are much less likely to be followed by the user to the intended termination. Rather, the user will drop out, with the probability of dropping rising as the dialogue progresses. To address this problem, the user model can be used to determine what moves can be made by the system that are more likely to be successful with a smaller number of moves. This is a topic that hitherto has not been address in computational models of argument, though it does appear that it could be addressed using adaptation of probabilistic techniques for dialogical argumentation (as such as proposed in [40,41,46]).

In conclusion, we may be able to harness and adapt a number of established ideas in computational models of argument (at the dialectical, logical, and dialogue levels) to formalism the persuasion dialogues for behaviour change. Dialogue rules provide a flexible framework for specifying protocols. These can be easily changed whilst leaving the underlying algorithm for their execution unchanged. This idea of state-based execution of rules comes from a proposal for using executable logic for dialogical argumentation systems [52,53]. Development of intelligent strategies based on opponent modelling does require further research, but there are promising proposals that could be further developed.

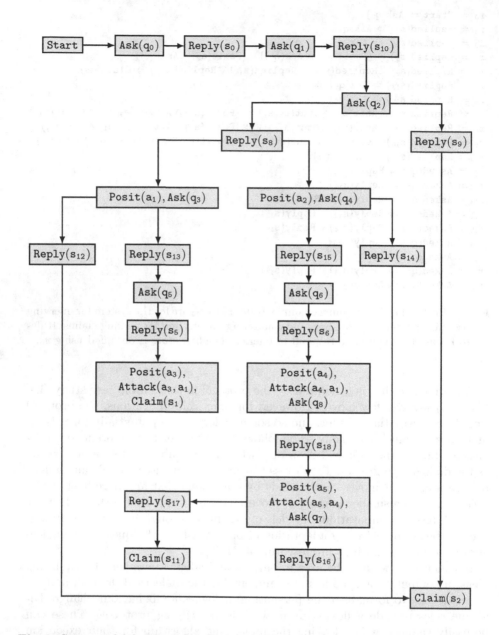

Fig. 3. State model for the protocol given in Figure 2. start gives the starting state. Each terminal state is a state without an exiting arc. Each state contains the moves that are made at that step of the dialogue. So multiple moves in a state means that multiple moves are made by the agent at that step in the dialogue. The Reply moves are made by the user. All other moves are made by the system.

5   Discussions

There are many situations where bringing about behaviour change is potentially of great benefit. By making argumentation central to the persuasion, we may be able to deliver technology that is more persuasive and more useful than existing approaches to persuasion technologies. This is a valuable opportunity for the application of computational models of argument. Computational models of argument offer theories for understanding argumentation, and technologies for participating in argumentation, for the dialectical, logical, and dialogical levels. With recent developments in user modelling (based on probabilistic argumentation), and strategies for argumentation, there is progress in the rhetorical level. Taken together, these offer a range of possibilities for designing and implementing argument-centric persuasion technology for behaviour change.

References

1. Cialdini, R.: Influence: The Psychology of Persuasion. HarperCollins (1984)
2. Fogg, B.: Persuasive computers. In: Proceedings of the SIGCHI Conference on Human Factors in Computings Systems, CHI, pp. 225–232 (1998)
3. Lehto, T., Oinas-Kukkonen, H.: Persuasive features in six weight loss websites: A qualitative evaluation. In: Ploug, T., Hasle, P., Oinas-Kukkonen, H. (eds.) PERSUASIVE 2010. LNCS, vol. 6137, pp. 162–173. Springer, Heidelberg (2010)
4. Langrial, S., Oinas-Kukkonen, H.: Less fizzy drinks: A multi-method study of persuasive reminders. In: Bang, M., Ragnemalm, E.L. (eds.) PERSUASIVE 2012. LNCS, vol. 7284, pp. 256–261. Springer, Heidelberg (2012)
5. Zwinderman, M.J., Shirzad, A., Ma, X., Bajracharya, P., Sandberg, H., Kaptein, M.C.: Phone row: A smartphone game designed to persuade people to engage in moderate-intensity physical activity. In: Bang, M., Ragnemalm, E.L. (eds.) PERSUASIVE 2012. LNCS, vol. 7284, pp. 55–66. Springer, Heidelberg (2012)
6. Kaipainen, K., Mattila, E., Kinnunen, M., Korhonen, I.: Facilitation of goal-setting and follow-up in internet intervention for health and wellness. In: Ploug, T., Hasle, P., Oinas-Kukkonen, H. (eds.) PERSUASIVE 2010. LNCS, vol. 6137, pp. 238–249. Springer, Heidelberg (2010)
7. Dung, P.: On the acceptability of arguments and its fundamental role in nonmonotonic reasoning, logic programming, and n-person games. Artificial Intelligence 77, 321–357 (1995)
8. Besnard, P., Hunter, A.: Constructing argument graphs with deductive arguments: A tutorial. Argument and Computation 5(1), 5–30 (2014)
9. Modgil, S., Prakken, H.: The aspic+ framework for structured argumentation: A tutorial. Argument and Computation 5(1), 31–62 (2014)
10. Toni, F.: A tutorial on assumption-based argumentation. Arument and Computation 5(1), 89–117 (2014)
11. Garcia, A., Simari, G.: Defeasible logic programming: Delp-servers, contextual queries, and explanations for answers. Argument and Computation 5(1), 63–88 (2014)
12. Amgoud, L., Maudet, N., Parsons, S.: Arguments, dialogue and negotiation. In: Fourteenth European Conference on Artifcial Intelligence (ECAI 2000), pp. 338–342. IOS Press (2000)

13. Black, E., Hunter, A.: An inquiry dialogue system. Autonomous Agents and Multi-Agent Systems 19(2), 173–209 (2009)
14. Dignum, F., Dunin-Keplicz, B., Verbrugge, R.: Dialogue in team formation. In: Dignum, F.P.M., Greaves, M. (eds.) Agent Communication. LNCS (LNAI), vol. 1916, pp. 264–280. Springer, Heidelberg (2000)
15. Fan, X., Toni, F.: Assumption-based argumentation dialogues. In: Proceedings of International Joint Conference on Artificial Intelligence (IJCAI 2011), pp. 198–203 (2011)
16. Hamblin, C.: Mathematical models of dialogue. Theoria 37, 567–583 (1971)
17. Mackenzie, J.: Question begging in non-cumulative systems. Journal of Philosophical Logic 8, 117–133 (1979)
18. McBurney, P., Parsons, S.: Games that agents play: A formal framework for dialogues between autonomous agents. Journal of Logic, Language and Information 11, 315–334 (2002)
19. McBurney, P., van Eijk, R., Parsons, S., Amgoud, L.: A dialogue-game protocol for agent purchase negotiations. Journal of Autonomous Agents and Multi-Agent Systems 7, 235–273 (2003)
20. Parsons, S., Wooldridge, M., Amgoud, L.: Properties and complexity of some formal inter-agent dialogues. J. of Logic and Comp. 13(3), 347–376 (2003)
21. Prakken, H.: Coherence and flexibility in dialogue games for argumentation. J. of Logic and Comp. 15(6), 1009–1040 (2005)
22. Walton, D., Krabbe, E.: Commitment in Dialogue: Basic Concepts of Interpersonal Reasoning. SUNY Press (1995)
23. Hunter, A.: Making argumentation more believable. In: Proceedings of AAAI 2004, pp. 269–274. MIT Press (2004)
24. Hunter, A.: Towards higher impact argumentation. In: Proceedings of AAAI 2004, pp. 275–280. MIT Press (2004)
25. Amgoud, L., Prade, H.: Formal handling of threats and rewards in a negotiation dialogue. In: Proceedings of AAMAS, pp. 529–536 (2005)
26. Hunter, A.: Reasoning about the appropriateness of proponents for arguments. In: Proceedings of AAAI, pp. 89–94 (2008)
27. Bench-Capon, T.: Persuasion in practical argument using value based argumentationframeworks. Journal of Logic and Computation 13(3), 429–448 (2003)
28. Bench-Capon, T., Doutre, S., Dunne, P.: Audiences in argumentation frameworks. Artificial Intelligence 171(1), 42–71 (2007)
29. Oren, N., Atkinson, K., Li, H.: Group persuasion through uncertain audience modelling. In: Proceedings of the International Comference on Computational Models of Argument (COMMA 2012), pp. 350–357 (2012)
30. Prakken, H.: Formal sytems for persuasion dialogue. Knowledge Engineering Review 21(2), 163–188 (2006)
31. Prakken, H.: Coherence and flexibility in dialogue games for argumentation. Journal of Logic and Computation 15(6), 1009–1040 (2005)
32. Caminada, M., Podlaszewski, M.: Grounded semantics as persuasion dialogue. In: Computational Models of Argument (COMMA 2012), pp. 478–485 (2012)
33. Haenni, R.: Cost-bounded argumentation. International Journal of Approximate Reasoning 26(2), 101–127 (2001)
34. Dung, P., Thang, P.: Towards (probabilistic) argumentation for jury-based dispute resolution. In: Computational Models of Argument (COMMA 2010), pp. 171–182. IOS Press (2010)

35. Li, H., Oren, N., Norman, T.J.: Probabilistic argumentation frameworks. In: Modgil, S., Oren, N., Toni, F. (eds.) TAFA 2011. LNCS (LNAI), vol. 7132, pp. 1–16. Springer, Heidelberg (2012)
36. Thimm, M.: A probabilistic semantics for abstract argumentation. In: Proceedings of the European Conference on Artificial Intelligence (ECAI 2012), pp. 750–755 (2012)
37. Hunter, A.: Some foundations for probabilistic argumentation. In: Proceedings of the International Comference on Computational Models of Argument (COMMA 2012), pp. 117–128 (2012)
38. Hunter, A.: A probabilistic approach to modelling uncertain logical arguments. International Journal of Approximate Reasoning 54(1), 47–81 (2013)
39. Hunter, A., Thimm, M.: Probabilistic argumentation with incomplete information. In: Proceedings of ECAI (in press, 2014)
40. Rienstra, T., Thimm, M., Oren, N.: Opponent models with uncertainty for strategic argumentation. In: Proceedings of IJCAI 2013. IJCAI/AAAI (2013)
41. Hunter, A.: Modelling uncertainty in persuasion. In: Liu, W., Subrahmanian, V.S., Wijsen, J. (eds.) SUM 2013. LNCS, vol. 8078, pp. 57–70. Springer, Heidelberg (2013)
42. Rahwan, I., Larson, K.: Pareto optimality in abstract argumentation. In: Proceedings of the Twenty-Third AAAI Conference on Artificial Intelligence (AAAI 2008). AAAI Press (2008)
43. Riveret, R., Prakken, H., Rotolo, A., Sartor, G.: Heuristics in argumentation: A game theory investigation. In: Computational Models of Argument (COMMA 2008). Frontiers in Artificial Intelligence and Applications, vol. 172, pp. 324–335. IOS Press (2008)
44. Matt, P.-A., Toni, F.: A game-theoretic measure of argument strength for abstract argumentation. In: Hölldobler, S., Lutz, C., Wansing, H. (eds.) JELIA 2008. LNCS (LNAI), vol. 5293, pp. 285–297. Springer, Heidelberg (2008)
45. Oren, N., Norman, T.J.: Arguing using opponent models. In: McBurney, P., Rahwan, I., Parsons, S., Maudet, N. (eds.) ArgMAS 2009. LNCS (LNAI), vol. 6057, pp. 160–174. Springer, Heidelberg (2010)
46. Hunter, A., Thimm, M.: Probabilistic argument graphs for argumentation lotteries. In: Computational Models of Argument (COMMA 2014). IOS Press (2014)
47. Rahwan, I., Larson, K.: Mechanism design for abstract argumentation. In: Proceedings of the 7th International Joint Conference on Autonomous Agents and Multiagent Systems (AAMAS 2008), pp. 1031–1038. IFAAMAS (2008)
48. Rahwan, I., Larson, K., Tohmé, F.: A characterisation of strategy-proofness for grounded argumentation semantics. In: Proceedings of the 21st International Joint Conference on Artificial Intelligence (IJCAI 2009), pp. 251–256 (2009)
49. Fan, X., Toni, F.: Mechanism design for argumentation-based persuasion. In: Computational Models of Argument (COMMA 2012), pp. 322–333 (2012)
50. Narita, T., Kitamura, Y.: Persuasive conversational agent with persuasion tactics. In: Ploug, T., Hasle, P., Oinas-Kukkonen, H. (eds.) PERSUASIVE 2010. LNCS, vol. 6137, pp. 15–26. Springer, Heidelberg (2010)
51. Hadjinikolis, C., Siantos, Y., Modgil, S., Black, E., McBurney, P.: Opponent modelling in persuasion dialogues. In: Proceedings of IJCAI (2013)
52. Black, E., Hunter, A.: Executable logic for dialogical argumentation. In: European Conf. on Artificial Intelligence (ECAI 2012), pp. 15–20. IOS Press (2012)
53. Hunter, A.: Analysis of dialogical argumentation via finite state machines. In: Liu, W., Subrahmanian, V.S., Wijsen, J. (eds.) SUM 2013. LNCS (LNAI), vol. 8078, pp. 1–14. Springer, Heidelberg (2013)

The Fuzzy Description Logic G-$\mathcal{FL}_0$ with Greatest Fixed-Point Semantics*

Stefan Borgwardt[1], José A. Leyva Galano[1], and Rafael Peñaloza[1,2]

[1] Theoretical Computer Science, TU Dresden, Germany
[2] Center for Advancing Electronics Dresden, Germany
{stefborg,penaloza}@tcs.inf.tu-dresden.de
jleyva1@gmail.com

Abstract. We study the fuzzy extension of the Description Logic $\mathcal{FL}_0$ with semantics based on the Gödel t-norm. We show that subsumption w.r.t. a finite set of primitive definitions, using greatest fixed-point semantics, can be characterized by a relation on weighted automata. We use this result to provide tight complexity bounds for reasoning in this logic, showing that it is PSPACE-complete. If the definitions do not contain cycles, subsumption becomes CO-NP-complete.

1 Introduction

Description logics (DLs) are used to describe the knowledge of an application domain in a formally well-defined manner [3]. The basic building blocks are *concepts* that intuitively describe a set of elements of the domain, and *roles*, which model binary relations over the domain. The expressivity of DLs is given by a set of *constructors* that are used to build complex concepts from so-called *concept names*, and is usually chosen to end up in decidable fragments of first-order predicate logic.

Knowledge about domain-specific terminology can be expressed by different kinds of axioms. For example, the *concept definition*

$$\mathsf{Father} \doteq \mathsf{Human} \sqcap \mathsf{Male} \sqcap \exists \mathsf{hasChild}.\top$$

is used to determine the extension of the concept name Father in terms of other concept names (Human, Male) and roles ($\mathsf{hasChild}$). In contrast, a *primitive* concept definition like

$$\mathsf{Human} \sqsubseteq \mathsf{Mammal} \sqcap \mathsf{Biped}$$

only bounds the interpretation of a concept name from above. Sometimes, one restricts (primitive) definitions to be *acyclic*, which means that the definition of a concept name cannot use itself (directly or indirectly via other definitions). In *general concept inclusions (GCIs)* such as

$$\forall \mathsf{hasParent}.\mathsf{Human} \sqsubseteq \mathsf{Human}$$

---

* Partially supported by the DFG under grant BA 1122/17-1, in the research training group 1763 (QuantLA), and the Cluster of Excellence 'Center for Advancing Electronics Dresden'.

E. Fermé and J. Leite (Eds.): JELIA 2014, LNAI 8761, pp. 62–76, 2014.

one can relate arbitrary complex expressions. These axioms are collected into so-called *TBoxes*, which can be either acyclic (containing acyclic definitions), cyclic (containing possibly cyclic definitions), or general (containing GCIs). To interpret cyclic TBoxes, several competing semantics have been proposed [19].

Different DLs vary in the choice of constructors allowed for building complex concepts. For example, the small DL $\mathcal{EL}$ uses the constructors *top* ($\top$), *conjunction* ($\sqcap$), and *existential restriction* ($\exists r.C$ for a role r and a concept C). We consider here mainly $\mathcal{FL}_0$, which has top, conjunctions, and *value restrictions* ($\forall r.C$). The DL $\mathcal{ALC}$ combines all the above constructors with *negation* ($\neg C$).

Fuzzy description logics have been introduced as extensions of classical DLs capable of representing and reasoning with vague or imprecise knowledge. The main idea behind these logics is to allow for a set of truth degrees, beyond the standard true and false; usually, the real interval $[0, 1]$ is considered. In this way, one can allow fuzzy concepts like Tall to assign an arbitrary degree of tallness to each individual, instead of simply classifying them into *tall* and *not tall*. Based on Mathematical Fuzzy Logic [13], a so-called *t-norm* defines the interpretation of conjunctions, and determines the semantics of the other constructors as well. The three main continuous t-norms are *Gödel* (G), *Łukasiewicz* (Ł), and *Product* (Π). The *Zadeh* semantics is another popular choice that is based on fuzzy set theory [25].

The area of fuzzy DLs recently experienced a shift, when it was shown that reasoning with GCIs easily becomes undecidable [1,7,9]. To guarantee decidability in fuzzy DLs, one can (i) restrict the semantics to consider finitely many truth degrees [8]; (ii) allow only acyclic or unfoldable TBoxes [5,22]; or (iii) restrict to Zadeh or Gödel semantics [6,17,20,21].

In the cases where the Gödel t-norm is used, the complexity of reasoning is typically the same as for its classical version, as shown for subsumption w.r.t. GCIs in G-$\mathcal{EL}$, which is polynomial [17,20], and G-$\mathcal{ALC}$, ExpTime-complete [6]. This latter result implies that subsumption in G-$\mathcal{FL}_0$ with general TBoxes is also ExpTime-complete since it is ExpTime-hard already in classical $\mathcal{FL}_0$ [2]. On the other hand, if TBoxes are restricted to contain only (cyclic) definitions, then deciding subsumption in classical $\mathcal{FL}_0$ under the greatest fixed-point semantics is known to be PSpace-complete [1]. For acyclic TBoxes, the complexity reduces to co-NP-complete [18]. In this paper, we analyze reasoning in the Gödel extension of this logic.

Consider the cyclic definition of a *tall person with only tall offspring* (Toto):

$$\text{Toto} \sqsubseteq \text{Person} \sqcap \text{Tall} \sqcap \forall \text{hasChild.Toto}$$

Choosing greatest fixed-point semantics is very natural in this setting, as it requires to always assign the largest possible degree for an individual to belong to Toto. Otherwise, Toto could simply assign degree 0 to all individuals, which is clearly not the intended meaning.

We show that the PSpace-upper bound for reasoning in the classical case also applies to this fuzzy DL. To prove this, we characterize the greatest fixed-point semantics of G-$\mathcal{FL}_0$ by means of $[0, 1]$-weighted automata. We then show that reasoning with these automata can be reduced to a linear number of inclusion tests between unweighted automata, which can be solved using only polynomial space [11]. For the case of acyclic TBoxes, our reduction yields acyclic automata and thus implies a CO-NP upper bound, again matching the complexity of reasoning in classical $\mathcal{FL}_0$.

2 Preliminaries

We first introduce some basic notions of lattice theory, which we use later to define the greatest fixed-point semantics in our fuzzy DL. For a more comprehensive overview on the topic, refer to [12]. Afterwards, we introduce fuzzy logics based on Gödel semantics, which are studied in more detail in [10,13,16].

2.1 Lattices, Operators, and Fixed-Points

A *lattice* is an algebraic structure $(L, \vee, \wedge)$ with two commutative, associative and idempotent binary operations $\vee$ (supremum) and $\wedge$ (infimum) that distribute over each other. It is *complete* if suprema and infima of arbitrary subsets $S \subseteq L$, denoted by $\bigvee_{x \in S} x$ and $\bigwedge_{x \in S} x$ respectively, exist. In this case, the lattice is *bounded* by the greatest element $\mathbf{1} := \bigvee_{x \in L} x$ and the least element $\mathbf{0} := \bigwedge_{x \in L} x$. Lattices induce a natural partial ordering on the elements of L where $x \leq y$ iff $x \wedge y = x$.

One common complete lattice used in fuzzy logics (see e.g. [10,13]) is the interval $[0, 1]$ with the usual order on the real numbers. Other complete lattices can be constructed as follows. Given a complete lattice L and a set S, the set L^S of all functions $f : S \to L$ is also a complete lattice, if infimum and supremum are defined component-wise. More precisely, for any two $f_1, f_2 \in L^S$, we define $f_1 \vee f_2$ for all $x \in S$ as $(f_1 \vee f_2)(x) := f_1(x) \vee f_2(x)$. If we similarly define the infimum, we obtain a lattice with the order $f_1 \leq f_2$ iff $f_1(x) \leq f_2(x)$ holds for all $x \in S$. It is easy to verify that infinite infima and suprema can then also be computed component-wise. We are particularly interested in operators on complete lattices L and their properties.

Definition 1 (fixed-point). *Let L be a complete lattice. A* fixed-point *of an operator $T : L \to L$ is an element $x \in L$ such that $T(x) = x$. It is the* greatest fixed-point *of T if for any fixed-point y of T we have $y \leq x$.*

The operator T is monotone *if for all $x, y \in L$, $x \leq y$ implies $T(x) \leq T(y)$. It is* downward ω-continuous *if for every decreasing chain $x_0 \geq x_1 \geq x_2 \geq \dots$ in L we have $T(\bigwedge_{i \geq 0} x_i) = \bigwedge_{i \geq 0} T(x_i)$.*

If it exists, the greatest fixed-point of T is unique and denoted by $\mathsf{gfp}(T)$.

It is easy to verify that every downward ω-continuous operator is also monotone. By a fundamental result from [24], every monotone operator T has a greatest fixed-point. If T is downward ω-continuous, then $\mathsf{gfp}(T)$ corresponds to the infimum of the decreasing chain $\mathbf{1} \geq T(\mathbf{1}) \geq T(T(\mathbf{1})) \geq \dots \geq T^i(\mathbf{1}) \geq \dots$ [15].

Proposition 2. *If L is a complete lattice and T a downward ω-continuous operator on L, then $\mathsf{gfp}(T) = \bigwedge_{i \geq 0} T^i(\mathbf{1})$.*

2.2 Gödel Fuzzy Logic

Our fuzzy DL is based on the well-known Gödel semantics for fuzzy logics, which is one of the main t-norm-based semantics used in Mathematical Fuzzy Logic [10,13] over the standard interval $[0,1]$. The *Gödel t-norm* is the binary minimum operator on $[0,1]$. For consistency, we use the lattice-theoretic notation $\wedge$ instead of min. An important property of this operator is that it preserves arbitrary infima and suprema on $[0,1]$, i.e. $\bigwedge_{i \in I}(x_i \wedge x) = \left(\bigwedge_{i \in I} x_i \right) \wedge x$ and $\bigvee_{i \in I}(x_i \wedge x) = \left(\bigvee_{i \in I} x_i \right) \wedge x$ for any index set I and elements $x, x_i \in [0,1]$ for all $i \in I$. In particular, this means that the Gödel t-norm is monotone in both arguments. The *residuum* of the Gödel t-norm is the binary operator $\Rightarrow_G$ on $[0,1]$ defined for all $x, y \in [0,1]$ by

$$x \Rightarrow_G y := \begin{cases} 1 & \text{if } x \leq y, \\ y & \text{otherwise.} \end{cases}$$

It is a fundamental property of a t-norm and its residuum that for all values $x, y, z \in [0,1]$, $x \wedge y \leq z$ iff $y \leq x \Rightarrow_G z$. As with the Gödel t-norm, its residuum preserves arbitrary infima in its second component. However, in the first component the order on $[0,1]$ is reversed.

Proposition 3. *For any index set I and values $x, x_i \in [0,1]$, $i \in I$, we have*

$$x \Rightarrow_G \left(\bigwedge_{i \in I} x_i \right) = \bigwedge_{i \in I} (x \Rightarrow_G x_i) \quad \text{and} \quad \left(\bigvee_{i \in I} x_i \right) \Rightarrow_G x = \bigwedge_{i \in I} (x_i \Rightarrow_G x).$$

This shows that the residuum is monotone in the second argument and antitone in the first argument. The following reformulation of nested residua in terms of infima will also prove useful.

Proposition 4. *For all values $x, x_1, \ldots, x_n \in [0,1]$, we have*

$$\big((x_1 \wedge \cdots \wedge x_n) \Rightarrow_G x \big) = \big(x_1 \Rightarrow_G \ldots (x_n \Rightarrow_G x) \ldots \big).$$

Proof. Both values are either x or 1, and they are 1 iff one of the operands x_i, $1 \leq i \leq n$, is smaller than or equal to x. $\qquad \square$

3 Fuzzy $\mathcal{FL}_0$

The fuzzy description logic G-$\mathcal{FL}_0$ has the same syntax as classical $\mathcal{FL}_0$. The difference lies in the interpretation of G-$\mathcal{FL}_0$-concepts.

Definition 5 (syntax). *Let N_C and N_R be two non-empty, disjoint sets of concept names and role names, respectively. Concepts are built from concept names using the constructors $\top$ (top), $C \sqcap D$ (conjunction), and $\forall r.C$ (value restriction for $r \in N_R$).*

A (primitive concept) definition is of the form $\langle A \sqsubseteq C \geq p \rangle$, where $A \in N_C$, C is a concept, and $p \in [0,1]$. A (cyclic) TBox is a finite set of definitions. Given a TBox $\mathcal{T}$, a concept name is defined if it appears on the left-hand side of a definition in $\mathcal{T}$, and primitive otherwise.

In contrast to the treatment of classical $\mathcal{FL}_0$ in [1], we permit several primitive definitions instead of only one (full) definition of the form $\langle A \doteq C_1 \sqcap \cdots \sqcap C_n \geq p \rangle$ for each concept name. This allows us to specify fuzzy degrees p_i for each of the conjuncts C_i independently. An *acyclic TBox* is a finite set of definitions without cyclic dependencies between the defined concept names.

We use the expression $\forall w.C$ with $w = r_1 r_2 \ldots r_n \in \mathsf{N}_\mathsf{R}^*$ to abbreviate the concept $\forall r_1. \forall r_2. \ldots \forall r_n.C$. We also allow $w = \varepsilon$, in which case $\forall w.C$ is simply C. We denote the set of concept names occurring in the TBox $\mathcal{T}$ by $\mathsf{N}_\mathsf{C}^\mathcal{T}$, the set of defined concept names in $\mathsf{N}_\mathsf{C}^\mathcal{T}$ by $\mathsf{N}_\mathsf{D}^\mathcal{T}$, and the set of primitive concept names in $\mathsf{N}_\mathsf{C}^\mathcal{T}$ by $\mathsf{N}_\mathsf{P}^\mathcal{T}$. Likewise, we collect all role names occurring in $\mathcal{T}$ into the set $\mathsf{N}_\mathsf{R}^\mathcal{T}$.

Definition 6 (semantics). *An* interpretation *is a pair* $\mathcal{I} = (\Delta^\mathcal{I}, \cdot^\mathcal{I})$, *where* $\Delta^\mathcal{I}$ *is a non-empty set, called the* domain *of* $\mathcal{I}$, *and the* interpretation function $\cdot^\mathcal{I}$ *maps every concept name* A *to a fuzzy set* $A^\mathcal{I} \colon \Delta^\mathcal{I} \to [0,1]$ *and every role name* r *to a fuzzy binary relation* $r^\mathcal{I} \colon \Delta^\mathcal{I} \times \Delta^\mathcal{I} \to [0,1]$. *This function is extended to concepts by setting* $\top^\mathcal{I}(x) := 1$, $(C \sqcap D)^\mathcal{I}(x) := C^\mathcal{I}(x) \wedge D^\mathcal{I}(x)$, *and* $(\forall r.C)^\mathcal{I}(x) := \bigwedge_{y \in \Delta^\mathcal{I}} (r^\mathcal{I}(x,y) \Rightarrow_\mathsf{G} C^\mathcal{I}(y))$ *for all* $x \in \Delta^\mathcal{I}$.

The interpretation $\mathcal{I}$ *satisfies (or is a* model of*) the definition* $\langle A \sqsubseteq C \geq p \rangle$ *if* $A^\mathcal{I}(x) \Rightarrow_\mathsf{G} C^\mathcal{I}(x) \geq p$ *holds for all* $x \in \Delta^\mathcal{I}$. *It satisfies (or is a* model of*) a TBox if it satisfies all its definitions.*

For an interpretation $\mathcal{I} = (\Delta, \cdot^\mathcal{I})$, $w = r_1 r_2 \ldots r_n \in \mathsf{N}_\mathsf{R}^*$, and elements $x_0, x_n \in \Delta$, we set $w^\mathcal{I}(x_0, x_n) := \bigvee_{x_1, \ldots, x_{n-1} \in \Delta} (r_1^\mathcal{I}(x_0, x_1) \wedge \cdots \wedge r_n^\mathcal{I}(x_{n-1}, x_n))$, and can thus treat $\forall w.C$ like an ordinary value restriction with

$$
\begin{aligned}
(\forall w.C)^\mathcal{I}(x_0) &:= \bigwedge_{x_n \in \Delta} (w^\mathcal{I}(x_0, x_n) \Rightarrow_\mathsf{G} C^\mathcal{I}(x_n)) \\
&= \bigwedge_{x_1, \ldots, x_n \in \Delta} \left((r_1^\mathcal{I}(x_0, x_1) \wedge \cdots \wedge r_n^\mathcal{I}(x_{n-1}, x_n)) \Rightarrow_\mathsf{G} C^\mathcal{I}(x_n) \right) \\
&= \bigwedge_{x_1, \ldots, x_n \in \Delta} \left(r_1^\mathcal{I}(x_0, x_1) \Rightarrow_\mathsf{G} \ldots (r_n^\mathcal{I}(x_{n-1}, x_n) \Rightarrow_\mathsf{G} C^\mathcal{I}(x_n)) \ldots \right) \\
&= (\forall r_1. \ldots \forall r_n.C)^\mathcal{I}(x_0)
\end{aligned}
$$

for all $x_0 \in \Delta$ (see Propositions 3 and 4).

It is convenient to consider TBoxes in normal form. The TBox $\mathcal{T}$ is in *normal form* if all definitions in $\mathcal{T}$ are of the form $\langle A \sqsubseteq \forall w.B \geq p \rangle$, where $A, B \in \mathsf{N}_\mathsf{C}$, $w \in \mathsf{N}_\mathsf{R}^*$, and $p \in [0,1]$, and there are no two definitions $\langle A \sqsubseteq \forall w.B \geq p \rangle$, $\langle A \sqsubseteq \forall w.B \geq p' \rangle$ with $p \neq p'$. Every TBox can be transformed into an equivalent TBox in normal form, as follows. First, we distribute the value restrictions over the conjunctions.

Lemma 7. *For every* $r \in \mathsf{N}_\mathsf{R}$, *concepts* C, D, *and interpretation* $\mathcal{I} = (\Delta, \cdot^\mathcal{I})$, *it holds that* $(\forall r.(C \sqcap D))^\mathcal{I} = (\forall r.C \sqcap \forall r.D)^\mathcal{I}$.

Proof. For every $x \in \Delta$, we have

$$
\begin{aligned}
(\forall r.(C \sqcap D))^{\mathcal{I}}(x) &= \bigwedge_{y \in \Delta} \left(r^{\mathcal{I}}(x,y) \Rightarrow_{\mathsf{G}} (C^{\mathcal{I}}(y) \wedge D^{\mathcal{I}}(y))\right) \\
&= \bigwedge_{y \in \Delta} \left((r^{\mathcal{I}}(x,y) \Rightarrow_{\mathsf{G}} C^{\mathcal{I}}(y)) \wedge (r^{\mathcal{I}}(x,y) \Rightarrow_{\mathsf{G}} D^{\mathcal{I}}(y))\right) \\
&= \left(\bigwedge_{y \in \Delta} (r^{\mathcal{I}}(x,y) \Rightarrow_{\mathsf{G}} C^{\mathcal{I}}(y))\right) \wedge \left(\bigwedge_{y \in \Delta} (r^{\mathcal{I}}(x,y) \Rightarrow_{\mathsf{G}} D^{\mathcal{I}}(y))\right) \\
&= (\forall r.C \sqcap \forall r.D)^{\mathcal{I}}(x)
\end{aligned}
$$

by Proposition 3. $\qquad\qquad\qquad\qquad\qquad\qquad\qquad\qquad\qquad\qquad\qquad\qquad\qquad$ □

Thus, we can equivalently write the right-hand sides of the definitions in $\mathcal{T}$ in the form $\forall w_1.B_1 \sqcap \cdots \sqcap \forall w_n.B_n$, where $w_i \in \mathsf{N}_\mathsf{R}^*$ and $B_i \in \mathsf{N}_\mathsf{C} \cup \{\top\}, 1 \le i \le n$. Since $\forall r.\top$ is equivalent to $\top$, we can remove all conjuncts of the form $\forall w.\top$ from this representation. After this transformation, all the definitions in the TBox are of the form $\langle A \sqsubseteq \forall w_1.B_1 \sqcap \cdots \sqcap \forall w_n.B_n \ge p \rangle$ with $B_i \in \mathsf{N}_\mathsf{C}, 1 \le i \le n$, or $\langle A \sqsubseteq \top \ge p \rangle$. The latter axioms are tautologies, and can hence be removed from the TBox without affecting the semantics.

It follows from Proposition 3 that an interpretation $\mathcal{I}$ satisfies the definition $\langle A \sqsubseteq \forall w_1.B_1 \sqcap \cdots \sqcap \forall w_n.B_n \ge p \rangle$ iff it satisfies $\langle A \sqsubseteq \forall w_i.B_i \ge p \rangle, 1 \le i \le n$. Thus, the former axiom can be equivalently replaced by the latter set of axioms.

After these steps, the TBox contains only axioms of the form $\langle A \sqsubseteq \forall w.B \ge p \rangle$ with $A, B \in \mathsf{N}_\mathsf{C}$, satisfying the first condition of the definition of normal form. Suppose now that $\mathcal{T}$ contains the axioms $\langle A \sqsubseteq \forall w.B \ge p \rangle$ and $\langle A \sqsubseteq \forall w.B \ge p' \rangle$ with $p > p'$. Then $\mathcal{T}$ is equivalent to the TBox $\mathcal{T} \setminus \{\langle A \sqsubseteq \forall w.B \ge p' \rangle\}$, i.e. the weaker axiom can be removed. It is clear that all of these transformations can be done in polynomial time in the size of the original TBox.

Concept definitions can be seen as a restriction of the interpretation of the defined concepts, depending on the interpretation of the primitive concepts. We use this intuition and consider *greatest fixed-point* semantics. The following construction is based on the classical notions from [1].

A *primitive interpretation* is a pair $\mathcal{J} = (\Delta, \cdot^{\mathcal{J}})$ as in Definition 6, except that $\cdot^{\mathcal{J}}$ is only defined on N_R and $\mathsf{N}_\mathsf{P}^{\mathcal{J}}$. Given such a $\mathcal{J}$, we use functions $f \in ([0,1]^\Delta)^{\mathsf{N}_\mathsf{D}^{\mathcal{J}}}$ to describe the interpretation of the remaining (defined) concept names. Recall that these functions form a complete lattice. In the following, we use the abbreviation $L_{\mathcal{J}}^{\mathcal{T}} := ([0,1]^\Delta)^{\mathsf{N}_\mathsf{D}^{\mathcal{J}}}$ for this lattice. Given a primitive interpretation $\mathcal{J}$ and a function $f \in L_{\mathcal{J}}^{\mathcal{T}}$, the *induced interpretation* $\mathcal{I}_{\mathcal{J},f}$ has the same domain as $\mathcal{J}$ and extends the interpretation function of $\mathcal{J}$ to the defined concepts names $A \in \mathsf{N}_\mathsf{D}^{\mathcal{J}}$ by taking $A^{\mathcal{I}_{\mathcal{J},f}} := f(A)$. The interpretation of the remaining concept names, i.e. those that do not occur in $\mathcal{T}$, is fixed to $\mathbf{0}$.

We can describe the effect that the axioms in $\mathcal{T}$ have on $L_{\mathcal{J}}^{\mathcal{T}}$ by the operator $T_{\mathcal{J}}^{\mathcal{T}} : L_{\mathcal{J}}^{\mathcal{T}} \to L_{\mathcal{J}}^{\mathcal{T}}$, which is defined as follows for all $f \in L_{\mathcal{J}}^{\mathcal{T}}$, $A \in \mathsf{N}_\mathsf{D}^{\mathcal{J}}$, and $x \in \Delta$:

$$
T_{\mathcal{J}}^{\mathcal{T}}(f)(A)(x) := \bigwedge_{\langle A \sqsubseteq C \ge p \rangle \in \mathcal{T}} (p \Rightarrow_{\mathsf{G}} C^{\mathcal{I}_{\mathcal{J},f}}(x)).
$$

This operator computes new values of the defined concept names according to the old interpretation $\mathcal{I}_{\mathcal{J},f}$ and their definitions in $\mathcal{T}$.

We are interested in using the greatest fixed-point of $T_{\mathcal{J}}^{\mathcal{T}}$, for some primitive interpretation $\mathcal{J}$, to define a new semantics for TBoxes $\mathcal{T}$ in G-$\mathcal{FL}_0$. Before being able to do this, we have to ensure that such a fixed-point exists.

Lemma 8. *Given a TBox $\mathcal{T}$ and a primitive interpretation $\mathcal{J} = (\Delta, \cdot^{\mathcal{J}})$, the operator $T_{\mathcal{J}}^{\mathcal{T}}$ on $L_{\mathcal{J}}^{\mathcal{T}}$ is downward ω-continuous.*

Proof. Consider a decreasing chain $f_0 \geq f_1 \geq f_2 \geq \ldots$ of functions in $L_{\mathcal{J}}^{\mathcal{T}}$. We use the abbreviations $f := \bigwedge_{i \geq 0} f_i$, $\mathcal{I} := \mathcal{I}_{\mathcal{J},f}$, and $\mathcal{I}_i := \mathcal{I}_{\mathcal{J},f_i}$ for all $i \geq 0$, and have to show that $T_{\mathcal{J}}^{\mathcal{T}}(f) = \bigwedge_{i \geq 0} T_{\mathcal{J}}^{\mathcal{T}}(f_i)$ holds.

First, we prove by induction on the structure of C that $C^{\mathcal{I}} = \bigwedge_{i \geq 0} C^{\mathcal{I}_i}$ holds for all concepts C built from $\mathsf{N}_R^{\mathcal{T}}$ and $\mathsf{N}_C^{\mathcal{T}}$, where $\bigwedge$ is defined as usual over the complete lattice $[0, 1]^{\Delta}$.

For $A \in \mathsf{N}_P^{\mathcal{T}}$, by the definition of $\mathcal{I}_{\mathcal{J},f}$ and $\mathcal{I}_{\mathcal{J},f_i}$ we have $A^{\mathcal{I}} = A^{\mathcal{J}} = A^{\mathcal{I}_i}$ for all $i \geq 0$, and thus $A^{\mathcal{I}} = A^{\mathcal{J}} = \bigwedge_{i \geq 0} A^{\mathcal{I}_i}$. For $A \in \mathsf{N}_D^{\mathcal{T}}$, we have

$$A^{\mathcal{I}} = f(A) = \Big(\bigwedge_{i \geq 0} f_i \Big)(A) = \bigwedge_{i \geq 0} f_i(A) = \bigwedge_{i \geq 0} A^{\mathcal{I}_i}$$

by the definition of $\mathcal{I}_{\mathcal{J},f}$ and $\mathcal{I}_{\mathcal{J},f_i}$ and the component-wise ordering on the complete lattice $L_{\mathcal{J}}^{\mathcal{T}}$.

For concepts of the form $C \sqcap D$, by the induction hypothesis and associativity of $\wedge$ we have

$$(C \sqcap D)^{\mathcal{I}} = C^{\mathcal{I}} \wedge D^{\mathcal{I}} = \Big(\bigwedge_{i \geq 0} C^{\mathcal{I}_i} \Big) \wedge \Big(\bigwedge_{i \geq 0} D^{\mathcal{I}_i} \Big) = \bigwedge_{i \geq 0} (C^{\mathcal{I}_i} \wedge D^{\mathcal{I}_i}) = \bigwedge_{i \geq 0} (C \sqcap D)^{\mathcal{I}_i}.$$

Consider now a value restriction $\forall r.C$. Using Proposition 3 we get for all $x \in \Delta$,

$$(\forall r.C)^{\mathcal{I}}(x) = \bigwedge_{y \in \Delta} (r^{\mathcal{I}}(x, y) \Rightarrow_G C^{\mathcal{I}}(y))$$

$$= \bigwedge_{y \in \Delta} \Big(r^{\mathcal{I}}(x, y) \Rightarrow_G \Big(\bigwedge_{i \geq 0} C^{\mathcal{I}_i}(y) \Big) \Big)$$

$$= \bigwedge_{y \in \Delta} \bigwedge_{i \geq 0} (r^{\mathcal{I}_i}(x, y) \Rightarrow_G C^{\mathcal{I}_i}(y)) = \Big(\bigwedge_{i \geq 0} (\forall r.C)^{\mathcal{I}_i} \Big)(x)$$

by the induction hypothesis and the component-wise ordering on $[0, 1]^{\Delta}$.

Using this, we can now prove the actual claim of the lemma. For all $A \in \mathsf{N}_D^{\mathcal{T}}$ and all $x \in \Delta$, we get, using again Proposition 3 and the previous claim,

$$T_{\mathcal{J}}^{\mathcal{T}}(f)(A)(x) = \bigwedge_{\langle A \sqsubseteq C \geq p \rangle \in \mathcal{T}} (p \Rightarrow_G C^{\mathcal{I}}(x))$$

$$= \bigwedge_{\langle A \sqsubseteq C \geq p \rangle \in \mathcal{T}} \Big(p \Rightarrow_G \Big(\bigwedge_{i \geq 0} C^{\mathcal{I}_i}(x) \Big) \Big)$$

$$= \bigwedge_{\langle A \sqsubseteq C \geq p \rangle \in \mathcal{T}} \bigwedge_{i \geq 0} (p \Rightarrow_{\mathsf{G}} C^{\mathcal{I}_i}(x)) = \Big(\bigwedge_{i \geq 0} T_{\mathcal{J}}^{\mathcal{T}}(f_i) \Big)(A)(x)$$

by the definition of $T_{\mathcal{J}}^{\mathcal{T}}$ and the component-wise ordering on $L_{\mathcal{J}}^{\mathcal{T}}$. $\qquad\square$

By Proposition 2, we know that $\mathsf{gfp}(T_{\mathcal{J}}^{\mathcal{T}})$ exists and is equal to $\bigwedge_{i \geq 0}(T_{\mathcal{J}}^{\mathcal{T}})^i(\mathbf{1})$, where $\mathbf{1}$ is the greatest element of the lattice $L_{\mathcal{J}}^{\mathcal{T}}$ that maps all defined concept names to $\top^{\mathcal{J}}$. In the following, we denote by $\mathsf{gfp}_{\mathcal{T}}(\mathcal{J})$ the interpretation $\mathcal{I}_{\mathcal{J},f}$ for $f := \mathsf{gfp}(T_{\mathcal{J}}^{\mathcal{T}})$. Note that $\mathcal{I} := \mathsf{gfp}_{\mathcal{T}}(\mathcal{J})$ is actually a model of $\mathcal{T}$ since for every $\langle A \sqsubseteq C \geq p \rangle \in \mathcal{T}$ and every $x \in \Delta$ we have

$$A^{\mathcal{I}}(x) = f(A)(x) = T_{\mathcal{J}}^{\mathcal{T}}(f)(A)(x) = \bigwedge_{\langle A \sqsubseteq C' \geq p' \rangle \in \mathcal{T}} (p' \Rightarrow_{\mathsf{G}} C'^{\mathcal{I}}(x)) \leq p \Rightarrow_{\mathsf{G}} C^{\mathcal{I}}(x),$$

and thus $p \wedge A^{\mathcal{I}}(x) \leq C^{\mathcal{I}}(x)$, which is equivalent to $p \leq A^{\mathcal{I}}(x) \Rightarrow_{\mathsf{G}} C^{\mathcal{I}}(x)$.

We can now define the reasoning problem in G-$\mathcal{FL}_0$ that we want to solve.

Definition 9 (gfp-subsumption). *An interpretation $\mathcal{I}$ is a gfp-model of a TBox $\mathcal{T}$ if there is a primitive interpretation $\mathcal{J}$ such that $\mathcal{I} = \mathsf{gfp}_{\mathcal{T}}(\mathcal{J})$. Given $A, B \in \mathsf{N_C}$ and $p \in [0,1]$, A is gfp-subsumed by B to degree p w.r.t. $\mathcal{T}$ (written $\mathcal{T} \models_{\mathsf{gfp}} \langle A \sqsubseteq B \geq p \rangle$), if for every gfp-model $\mathcal{I}$ of $\mathcal{T}$ and every $x \in \Delta^{\mathcal{I}}$ we have $A^{\mathcal{I}}(x) \Rightarrow_{\mathsf{G}} B^{\mathcal{I}}(x) \geq p$. The best gfp-subsumption degree of A and B w.r.t. $\mathcal{T}$ is the supremum over all p such that $\mathcal{T} \models_{\mathsf{gfp}} \langle A \sqsubseteq B \geq p \rangle$.*

Let now $\mathcal{T}$ be a TBox and $\mathcal{T}'$ the result of transforming $\mathcal{T}$ into normal form as described before. It is easy to verify that the operators $T_{\mathcal{J}}^{\mathcal{T}}$ and $T_{\mathcal{J}}^{\mathcal{T}'}$ coincide, and therefore the gfp-models of $\mathcal{T}$ are the same as those of $\mathcal{T}'$. To solve the problem of deciding gfp-subsumptions, it thus suffices to consider TBoxes in normal form.

4   Characterizing Subsumption Using Finite Automata

To decide gfp-subsumption between concept names, we employ an automata-based approach following [1]. However, here we use *weighted* automata.

Definition 10 (WWA). *A weighted automaton with word transitions (WWA) is a tuple $\mathcal{A} = (\Sigma, Q, q_0, \mathsf{wt}, q_f)$, where Σ is a finite alphabet of input symbols, Q is a finite set of states, $q_0 \in Q$ is the initial state, $\mathsf{wt} \colon Q \times \Sigma^* \times Q \to [0,1]$ is the transition weight function with the property that its support*

$$\mathsf{supp}(\mathsf{wt}) := \{(q, w, q') \in Q \times \Sigma^* \times Q \mid \mathsf{wt}(q, w, q') > 0\}$$

is finite, and $q_f \in Q$ is the final state.

A finite path in $\mathcal{A}$ is a sequence $\pi = q_0 w_1 q_1 w_2 \ldots w_n q_n$, where $q_i \in Q$ and $w_i \in \Sigma^*$ for all $i \in \{1, \ldots, n\}$, and $q_n = q_f$. Its label is the finite word $\ell(\pi) := w_1 w_2 \ldots w_n$. The weight of π is $\mathsf{wt}(\pi) := \bigwedge_{i=1}^n \mathsf{wt}(q_{i-1}, w_i, q_i)$. The set of all finite paths with label w in $\mathcal{A}$ is denoted $\mathsf{paths}(\mathcal{A}, w)$. The behavior $\|\mathcal{A}\| \colon \Sigma^* \to [0,1]$ of $\mathcal{A}$ is defined by $\|\mathcal{A}\|(w) := \bigvee_{\pi \in \mathsf{paths}(\mathcal{A}, w)} \mathsf{wt}(\pi)$ for $w \in \Sigma^*$.

If the image of the transition weight function is included in $\{0,1\}$, then we have a classical finite automaton with word transitions (WA). In this case, wt is usually described as a subset of $Q \times \Sigma^* \times Q$ and the behavior is characterized by the set $L(\mathcal{A})$, called the *language* of $\mathcal{A}$, of all words whose behavior is 1. The *inclusion problem* for WA is to decide, given two such automata $\mathcal{A}$ and $\mathcal{A}'$, whether $L(\mathcal{A}) \subseteq L(\mathcal{A}')$. This problem is known to be PSPACE-complete [11].

Our goal is to describe the restrictions imposed by a G-$\mathcal{FL}_0$ TBox $\mathcal{T}$ using a WWA. For the rest of this paper, we assume w.l.o.g. that $\mathcal{T}$ is in normal form.

Definition 11 (automata $\mathcal{A}_{A,B}^{\mathcal{T}}$). *For concept names $A, B \in N_C^{\mathcal{T}}$, the WWA $\mathcal{A}_{A,B}^{\mathcal{T}} = (N_R, N_C^{\mathcal{T}}, A, \mathsf{wt}_{\mathcal{T}}, B)$ is defined by the transition weight function*

$$\mathsf{wt}_{\mathcal{T}}(A', w, B') := \begin{cases} p & \text{if } \langle A' \sqsubseteq \forall w.B' \geq p \rangle \in \mathcal{T}, \\ 0 & \text{otherwise.} \end{cases}$$

For a TBox $\mathcal{T}$ and $A, A', B, B' \in N_C^{\mathcal{T}}$, the automata $\mathcal{A}_{A,B}^{\mathcal{T}}$ and $\mathcal{A}_{A',B'}^{\mathcal{T}}$ differ only in their initial and final states; their states and transition weight function are identical. Since $\mathcal{T}$ is in normal form, for any $A', B' \in N_C^{\mathcal{T}}$ and $w \in N_R^*$, there is at most one axiom $\langle A' \sqsubseteq \forall w.B' \geq p \rangle$ in $\mathcal{T}$, and hence the transition weight function is well-defined. This function has finite support since $\mathcal{T}$ is finite.

We now characterize the gfp-models of $\mathcal{T}$ by properties of the automata $\mathcal{A}_{A,B}^{\mathcal{T}}$.

Lemma 12. *For every gfp-model $\mathcal{I} = (\Delta, \cdot^{\mathcal{I}})$ of $\mathcal{T}$, $x \in \Delta$, and $A \in N_C^{\mathcal{T}}$,*

$$A^{\mathcal{I}}(x) = \bigwedge_{B \in N_P^{\mathcal{T}}} \bigwedge_{w \in N_R^*} (\|\mathcal{A}_{A,B}^{\mathcal{T}}\|(w) \Rightarrow_G (\forall w.B)^{\mathcal{I}}(x)).$$

Proof. If A is primitive, then the empty path $\pi = A \in \mathsf{paths}(\mathcal{A}_{A,A}^{\mathcal{T}}, \varepsilon)$ has weight $\mathsf{wt}_{\mathcal{T}}(\pi) = 1$, and hence $\|\mathcal{A}_{A,A}^{\mathcal{T}}\|(\varepsilon) = 1$. We also have $(\forall \varepsilon.A)^{\mathcal{I}}(x) = A^{\mathcal{I}}(x)$; thus, $A^{\mathcal{I}}(x) = (1 \Rightarrow_G A^{\mathcal{I}}(x)) \geq \bigwedge_{B \in N_P^{\mathcal{T}}} \bigwedge_{w \in N_R^*} (\|\mathcal{A}_{A,B}^{\mathcal{T}}\|(w) \Rightarrow_G (\forall w.B)^{\mathcal{I}}(x))$. Let now $B \in N_P^{\mathcal{T}}$ and $w \in N_R^*$ such that $A \neq B$ or $w \neq \varepsilon$. Since A is primitive, by Definition 11 any finite path π in $\mathcal{A}_{A,B}^{\mathcal{T}}$ with $\ell(\pi) = w$ must have weight 0; i.e. $\|\mathcal{A}_{A,B}^{\mathcal{T}}\|(w) = 0$, and thus $0 \Rightarrow_G (\forall w.B)^{\mathcal{I}}(x) = 1 \geq A^{\mathcal{I}}(x)$. This shows that the whole infimum is equal to $A^{\mathcal{I}}(x)$.

Consider now the case that $A \in N_D^{\mathcal{T}}$. Since $\mathcal{I}$ is a gfp-model of $\mathcal{T}$, there is a primitive interpretation $\mathcal{J}$ such that $\mathcal{I} = \mathsf{gfp}_{\mathcal{T}}(\mathcal{J})$; let $f := \mathsf{gfp}(T_{\mathcal{J}}^{\mathcal{T}})$. Thus, we have $A^{\mathcal{I}} = f(A) = T_{\mathcal{J}}^{\mathcal{T}}(f)(A) = \bigwedge_{i \geq 0} (T_{\mathcal{J}}^{\mathcal{T}})^i(1)(A)$ for all $A \in N_D^{\mathcal{T}}$.

[$\leq$] By Proposition 3 it suffices to show that for all $x \in \Delta$, $A \in N_D^{\mathcal{T}}$, $B \in N_P^{\mathcal{T}}$, and all finite non-empty paths π in $\mathcal{A}_{A,B}^{\mathcal{T}}$ it holds that

$$A^{\mathcal{I}}(x) \leq \mathsf{wt}_{\mathcal{T}}(\pi) \Rightarrow_G (\forall w.B)^{\mathcal{I}}(x), \tag{1}$$

where $w := \ell(\pi)$. This obviously holds for $\mathsf{wt}_{\mathcal{T}}(\pi) = 0$, and thus it remains to show this for paths with positive weight. Let $\pi = A w_1 A_1 w_2 \ldots w_n A_n$, where $A_i \in N_C^{\mathcal{T}}$ and $w_i \in N_R^*$ for all $i \in \{1, \ldots, n\}$ and $A_n = B$ is the only primitive concept name in this path. We prove (1) by induction on n. For $n = 1$, we have $\pi = A w_1 B$ and $\mathsf{wt}_\mathcal{T}(A, w_1, B) = \mathsf{wt}_\mathcal{T}(\pi) > 0$, and thus $\mathcal{T}$ contains the definition $\langle A \sqsubseteq \forall w_1.B \geq p \rangle$, with $p := \mathsf{wt}_\mathcal{T}(A, w_1, B)$. By the definition of $T_\mathcal{J}^\mathcal{T}$, we obtain

$$A^\mathcal{I}(x) = T_\mathcal{J}^\mathcal{T}(f)(A)(x) \leq p \Rightarrow_\mathsf{G} (\forall w_1.B)^\mathcal{I}(x) = \mathsf{wt}_\mathcal{T}(\pi) \Rightarrow_\mathsf{G} (\forall w.B)^\mathcal{I}(x).$$

For $n > 1$, consider the subpath $\pi' = A_1 w_2 \ldots w_n B$ in $\mathcal{A}_{A_1, B}^\mathcal{T}$ with the label $\ell(\pi') = w' := w_2 \ldots w_n$. For all $y \in \Delta$, the induction hypothesis yields that $A_1^\mathcal{I}(y) \leq \mathsf{wt}_\mathcal{T}(\pi') \Rightarrow_\mathsf{G} (\forall w'.B)^\mathcal{I}(y)$. Again, $p := \mathsf{wt}_\mathcal{T}(A, w_1, A_1) \geq \mathsf{wt}_\mathcal{T}(\pi) > 0$, and thus $\mathcal{T}$ contains the definition $\langle A \sqsubseteq \forall w_1.A_1 \geq p \rangle$. By the definitions of $T_\mathcal{J}^\mathcal{T}$, $\mathsf{wt}_\mathcal{T}(\pi)$, $w^\mathcal{I}$, and Propositions 3 and 4, we have

$$
\begin{aligned}
A^\mathcal{I}(x) &= T_\mathcal{J}^\mathcal{T}(f)(A)(x) \\
&\leq p \Rightarrow_\mathsf{G} (\forall w_1.A_1)^\mathcal{I}(x) \\
&= \bigwedge_{y \in \Delta} \left(p \Rightarrow_\mathsf{G} (w_1^\mathcal{I}(x, y) \Rightarrow_\mathsf{G} A_1^\mathcal{I}(y)) \right) \\
&\leq \bigwedge_{y \in \Delta} \left(p \Rightarrow_\mathsf{G} \left(w_1^\mathcal{I}(x, y) \Rightarrow_\mathsf{G} (\mathsf{wt}_\mathcal{T}(\pi') \Rightarrow_\mathsf{G} (\forall w'.B)^\mathcal{I}(y)) \right) \right) \\
&= (p \wedge \mathsf{wt}_\mathcal{T}(\pi')) \Rightarrow_\mathsf{G} \left(\bigwedge_{y \in \Delta} (w_1^\mathcal{I}(x, y) \Rightarrow_\mathsf{G} (\forall w'.B)^\mathcal{I}(y)) \right) \\
&= \mathsf{wt}_\mathcal{T}(\pi) \Rightarrow_\mathsf{G} (\forall w.B)^\mathcal{I}(x).
\end{aligned}
$$

[$\supseteq$] We show by induction on i that for all $x \in \Delta$, $A \in \mathsf{N}_\mathsf{D}^\mathcal{T}$, and $i \geq 0$, it holds

$$(T_\mathcal{J}^\mathcal{T})^i(1)(A)(x) \geq \bigwedge_{B \in \mathsf{N}_\mathsf{P}^\mathcal{T}} \bigwedge_{w \in \mathsf{N}_\mathsf{R}^*} (\|\mathcal{A}_{A,B}^\mathcal{T}\|(w) \Rightarrow_\mathsf{G} (\forall w.B)^\mathcal{I}(x)). \tag{2}$$

For $i = 0$, we have $(T_\mathcal{J}^\mathcal{T})^0(1)(A)(x) = 1(A)(x) = 1$, which obviously satisfies (2). For $i > 0$, by Proposition 3 we obtain

$$
\begin{aligned}
(T_\mathcal{J}^\mathcal{T})^i(1)(A)(x) &= T_\mathcal{J}^\mathcal{T}((T_\mathcal{J}^\mathcal{T})^{i-1}(1))(A)(x) \\
&= \bigwedge_{\langle A \sqsubseteq \forall w'.A' \geq p \rangle \in \mathcal{T}} (p \Rightarrow_\mathsf{G} (\forall w'.A')^{\mathcal{I}_{i-1}}(x)), \tag{3}
\end{aligned}
$$

where $\mathcal{I}_{i-1} := \mathcal{I}_{\mathcal{J}, (T_\mathcal{J}^\mathcal{T})^{i-1}(1)}$. Consider now any definition $\langle A \sqsubseteq \forall w'.A' \geq p \rangle \in \mathcal{T}$. Then $\pi' = A w' A'$ is a finite path in $\mathcal{A}_{A, A'}^\mathcal{T}$ with label w' and weight p.

If A' is a primitive concept name, then we have

$$p \Rightarrow_\mathsf{G} (\forall w'.A')^{\mathcal{I}_{i-1}}(x) \geq \|\mathcal{A}_{A,A'}^\mathcal{T}\|(w') \Rightarrow_\mathsf{G} (\forall w'.A')^\mathcal{I}(x)$$

by the definition of $\|\mathcal{A}_{A,A'}^\mathcal{T}\|(w')$ and the fact that the interpretation of $\forall w'.A'$ under $\mathcal{I}_{i-1}$ and $\mathcal{I}$ only depends on $\mathcal{J}$. If A' is defined, then we similarly get

$$
\begin{aligned}
&p \Rightarrow_\mathsf{G} (\forall w'.A')^{\mathcal{I}_{i-1}}(x) \\
&= \bigwedge_{y \in \Delta} \left(p \Rightarrow_\mathsf{G} (w'^\mathcal{J}(x, y) \Rightarrow_\mathsf{G} A'^{\mathcal{I}_{i-1}}(y)) \right)
\end{aligned}
$$

$$\geq \bigwedge_{y\in\Delta} \bigwedge_{B\in N_P^{\mathcal{T}}} \bigwedge_{w\in N_R^*} \left(p \Rightarrow_G \left(w'^{\mathcal{I}}(x,y) \Rightarrow_G \left(\|\mathcal{A}_{A',B}^{\mathcal{T}}\|(w) \Rightarrow_G (\forall w.B)^{\mathcal{I}}(y)\right)\right)\right)$$

$$= \bigwedge_{B\in N_P^{\mathcal{T}}} \bigwedge_{w\in N_R^*} \left(\left(p \wedge \|\mathcal{A}_{A',B}^{\mathcal{T}}\|(w)\right) \Rightarrow_G \left(\bigwedge_{y\in\Delta} \left(w'^{\mathcal{I}}(x,y) \Rightarrow_G (\forall w.B)^{\mathcal{I}}(y)\right)\right)\right)$$

$$= \bigwedge_{B\in N_P^{\mathcal{T}}} \bigwedge_{w\in N_R^*} \left(\left(\bigvee_{\pi\in\mathsf{paths}(\mathcal{A}_{A',B}^{\mathcal{T}},w)} (\mathsf{wt}_{\mathcal{T}}(\pi') \wedge \mathsf{wt}_{\mathcal{T}}(\pi))\right) \Rightarrow_G (\forall w'w.B)^{\mathcal{I}}(x)\right)$$

$$\geq \bigwedge_{B\in N_P^{\mathcal{T}}} \bigwedge_{w\in N_R^*} \left(\|\mathcal{A}_{A,B}^{\mathcal{T}}\|(w'w) \Rightarrow_G (\forall w'w.B)^{\mathcal{I}}(x)\right)$$

by the induction hypothesis, Propositions 3 and 4, and the definition of $\|\mathcal{A}_{A,B}^{\mathcal{T}}\|$.

In both cases, $p \Rightarrow_G (\forall w'.A')^{\mathcal{I}_{i-1}}(x)$ is an upper bound for the infimum in (2), and thus by (3) the same is true for $(T_{\mathcal{J}}^{\mathcal{T}})^i(1)(A)(x)$. $\qquad\square$

This allows us to prove gfp-subsumptions by comparing the behavior of WWA.

Lemma 13. Let $A, B \in N_C^{\mathcal{T}}$ and $p \in [0,1]$. Then $\mathcal{T} \models_{\mathsf{gfp}} \langle A \sqsubseteq B \geq p \rangle$ iff for all $C \in N_P^{\mathcal{T}}$ and $w \in N_R^*$ it holds that $p \wedge \|\mathcal{A}_{B,C}^{\mathcal{T}}\|(w) \leq \|\mathcal{A}_{A,C}^{\mathcal{T}}\|(w)$.

Proof. Assume that there exist $C \in N_P^{\mathcal{T}}$ and $w = r_1 \ldots r_n \in N_R^*$ such that $p \wedge \|\mathcal{A}_{B,C}^{\mathcal{T}}\|(w) > \|\mathcal{A}_{A,C}^{\mathcal{T}}\|(w)$. We define the primitive interpretation $\mathcal{J} = (\Delta, \cdot^{\mathcal{J}})$ where $\Delta := \{x_0, \ldots, x_n\}$, and for all $D \in N_P^{\mathcal{T}}$ and $r \in N_R$, the interpretation function is given by

$$D^{\mathcal{J}}(x) := \begin{cases} \|\mathcal{A}_{A,C}^{\mathcal{T}}\|(w) & \text{if } D = C \text{ and } x = x_n, \\ 1 & \text{otherwise; and} \end{cases}$$

$$r^{\mathcal{J}}(x,y) := \begin{cases} 1 & \text{if } x = x_{i-1}, y = x_i, \text{ and } r = r_i \text{ for some } i \in \{1, \ldots, n\}, \\ 0 & \text{otherwise.} \end{cases}$$

Consider now the gfp-model $\mathcal{I} := \mathsf{gfp}_{\mathcal{T}}(\mathcal{J})$ of $\mathcal{T}$. By construction, for all pairs $(w', D) \in N_R^* \times N_P^{\mathcal{T}} \setminus \{(w, C)\}$ we have $(\forall w'.D)^{\mathcal{I}}(x_0) = 1$. Moreover, we know that $(\forall w.C)^{\mathcal{I}}(x_0)$ is equal to $\|\mathcal{A}_{A,C}^{\mathcal{T}}\|(w)$, and thus strictly smaller than p and $\|\mathcal{A}_{B,C}^{\mathcal{T}}\|(w)$. By Lemma 12, all this implies that

$$A^{\mathcal{I}}(x_0) = \|\mathcal{A}_{A,C}^{\mathcal{T}}\|(w) \Rightarrow_G (\forall w.C)^{\mathcal{I}}(x_0) = 1 \text{ and}$$
$$B^{\mathcal{I}}(x_0) = \|\mathcal{A}_{B,C}^{\mathcal{T}}\|(w) \Rightarrow_G (\forall w.C)^{\mathcal{T}}(x_0) = (\forall w.C)^{\mathcal{I}}(x_0).$$

Thus $A^{\mathcal{I}}(x_0) \Rightarrow_G B^{\mathcal{I}}(x_0) = (\forall w.C)^{\mathcal{I}}(x_0) < p$, and $\mathcal{T} \not\models_{\mathsf{gfp}} \langle A \sqsubseteq B \geq p \rangle$.

Conversely, assume that there are a primitive interpretation $\mathcal{J} = (\Delta, \cdot^{\mathcal{J}})$ and an element $x \in \Delta$ such that $A^{\mathcal{I}}(x) \Rightarrow_G B^{\mathcal{I}}(x) < p$, where $\mathcal{I} := \mathsf{gfp}_{\mathcal{T}}(\mathcal{J})$. Thus, we have $p \wedge A^{\mathcal{I}}(x) > B^{\mathcal{I}}(x)$, which implies by Lemma 12 the existence of a $C \in N_P^{\mathcal{T}}$ and a $w \in N_R^*$ with $p \wedge A^{\mathcal{I}}(x) > \|\mathcal{A}_{B,C}^{\mathcal{T}}\|(w) \Rightarrow_G (\forall w.C)^{\mathcal{I}}(x)$. Again by Lemma 12, this shows that

$$p \wedge \|\mathcal{A}_{B,C}^{\mathcal{T}}\|(w) > A^{\mathcal{I}}(x) \Rightarrow_G (\forall w.C)^{\mathcal{I}}(x)$$
$$\geq \left(\|\mathcal{A}_{A,C}^{\mathcal{T}}\|(w) \Rightarrow_G (\forall w.C)^{\mathcal{I}}(x)\right) \Rightarrow_G (\forall w.C)^{\mathcal{I}}(x).$$

In particular, the latter value cannot be 1, and thus it is equal to $(\forall w.C)^{\mathcal{I}}(x)$. But this can only be the case if $\|\mathcal{A}_{A,C}^{\mathcal{T}}\|(w) \leq (\forall w.C)^{\mathcal{I}}(x)$. To summarize, we obtain $p \wedge \|\mathcal{A}_{B,C}^{\mathcal{T}}\|(w) > (\forall w.C)^{\mathcal{I}}(x) \geq \|\mathcal{A}_{A,C}^{\mathcal{T}}\|(w)$, as desired.   □

Denote by $\mathcal{V}_{\mathcal{T}} := \{0,1\} \cup \{p \in [0,1] \mid \langle A \sqsubseteq \forall w.B \geq p \rangle \in \mathcal{T}\}$ the set of all values appearing in $\mathcal{T}$, together with 0 and 1. Since $\mathsf{wt}_{\mathcal{T}}$ has finite support and takes only values from $\mathcal{V}_{\mathcal{T}}$, $p \wedge \|\mathcal{A}_{B,C}^{\mathcal{T}}\|(w) > \|\mathcal{A}_{A,C}^{\mathcal{T}}\|(w)$ holds iff $p' \wedge \|\mathcal{A}_{B,C}^{\mathcal{T}}\|(w) > \|\mathcal{A}_{A,C}^{\mathcal{T}}\|(w)$, where p' is the smallest element of $\mathcal{V}_{\mathcal{T}}$ such that $p' \geq p$. This shows that it suffices to be able to check gfp-subsumptions for the values in $\mathcal{V}_{\mathcal{T}}$. We now show how to do this by simulating $\mathcal{A}_{B,C}^{\mathcal{T}}$ and $\mathcal{A}_{A,C}^{\mathcal{T}}$ by polynomially many *unweighted* automata.

Definition 14 (automata $\mathcal{A}_{\geq p}$). *Given a WWA $\mathcal{A} = (\Sigma, Q, q_0, \mathsf{wt}, q_f)$ and a value $p \in [0,1]$, the WA $\mathcal{A}_{\geq p} = (\Sigma, Q, q_0, \mathsf{wt}_{\geq p}, q_f)$ is given by the transition relation $\mathsf{wt}_{\geq p} := \{(q, w, q') \in Q \times \Sigma^* \times Q \mid \mathsf{wt}(q, w, q') \geq p\}$.*

The language of this automaton has an obvious relation to the behavior of the original WWA.

Lemma 15. *Let $\mathcal{A}$ be a WWA over the alphabet Σ and $p \in [0,1]$. Then we have $L(\mathcal{A}_{\geq p}) = \{w \in \Sigma^* \mid \|\mathcal{A}\|(w) \geq p\}$.*

Proof. We have $w \in L(\mathcal{A}_{\geq p})$ iff there is a finite path $\pi = q_0 w_1 q_1 \ldots w_n q_n$ in $\mathcal{A}$ with label w such that $\mathsf{wt}(q_{i-1}, w_i, q_i) \geq p$ holds for all $i \in \{1, \ldots, n\}$. The latter condition is equivalent to the fact that $\mathsf{wt}(\pi) \geq p$. Thus, $w \in L(\mathcal{A}_{\geq p})$ implies that $\|\mathcal{A}\|(w) \geq p$. Conversely, since wt has finite support, there are only finitely many possible weights for any finite path in $\mathcal{A}$, and thus $\|\mathcal{A}\|(w) \geq p$ also implies that there exists a $\pi \in \mathsf{paths}(\mathcal{A}, w)$ with $\mathsf{wt}(\pi) \geq p$, and thus $w \in L(\mathcal{A}_{\geq p})$.   □

We thus obtain the following characterization of gfp-subsumption.

Lemma 16. *Let $A, B \in \mathsf{N}_{\mathsf{C}}^{\mathcal{T}}$ and $p \in \mathcal{V}_{\mathcal{T}}$. Then $\mathcal{T} \models_{\mathsf{gfp}} \langle A \sqsubseteq B \geq p \rangle$ iff for all $C \in \mathsf{N}_{\mathsf{P}}^{\mathcal{T}}$ and $p' \in \mathcal{V}_{\mathcal{T}}$ with $p' \leq p$ it holds that $L((\mathcal{A}_{B,C}^{\mathcal{T}})_{\geq p'}) \subseteq L((\mathcal{A}_{A,C}^{\mathcal{T}})_{\geq p'})$.*

Proof. Assume that we have $\mathcal{T} \models_{\mathsf{gfp}} \langle A \sqsubseteq B \geq p \rangle$ and consider any $C \in \mathsf{N}_{\mathsf{P}}^{\mathcal{T}}$, $w \in \mathsf{N}_{\mathsf{R}}^*$, and $p' \in \mathcal{V}_{\mathcal{T}} \cap [0,p]$ with $w \in L((\mathcal{A}_{B,C}^{\mathcal{T}})_{\geq p'})$. By Lemma 15, we obtain $\|\mathcal{A}_{B,C}^{\mathcal{T}}\|(w) \geq p'$, and by Lemma 13 we know that $\|\mathcal{A}_{A,C}^{\mathcal{T}}\| \geq p \wedge \|\mathcal{A}_{B,C}^{\mathcal{T}}\|(w) \geq p'$. Thus, $w \in L((\mathcal{A}_{A,C}^{\mathcal{T}})_{\geq p'})$.

Conversely, assume that $\mathcal{T} \models_{\mathsf{gfp}} \langle A \sqsubseteq B \geq p \rangle$ does not hold. Then by Lemma 13 there are $C \in \mathsf{N}_{\mathsf{P}}^{\mathcal{T}}$ and $w \in \mathsf{N}_{\mathsf{R}}^*$ such that $p \wedge \|\mathcal{A}_{B,C}^{\mathcal{T}}\|(w) > \|\mathcal{A}_{A,C}^{\mathcal{T}}\|(w)$. For the value $p' := p \wedge \|\mathcal{A}_{B,C}^{\mathcal{T}}\|(w) \in \mathcal{V}_{\mathcal{T}} \cap [0,p]$, we have $\|\mathcal{A}_{B,C}^{\mathcal{T}}\|(w) \geq p'$, but $\|\mathcal{A}_{A,C}^{\mathcal{T}}\|(w) < p'$, and thus $L((\mathcal{A}_{B,C}^{\mathcal{T}})_{\geq p'}) \nsubseteq L((\mathcal{A}_{A,C}^{\mathcal{T}})_{\geq p'})$ by Lemma 15.   □

Since the automata $(\mathcal{A}_{A,C}^{\mathcal{T}})_{\geq p'}$ correspond to those from [1] simulating subsumption in the (classical) TBoxes $\mathcal{T}_{\geq p'} := \{A' \sqsubseteq C' \mid \langle A' \sqsubseteq C' \geq q \rangle \in \mathcal{T}, q \geq p'\}$, we have shown that gfp-subsumption in G-$\mathcal{FL}_0$ can be reduced to polynomially many subsumption tests in $\mathcal{FL}_0$. The detour through WWA was necessary to account for the differences between the gfp-models of $\mathcal{T}$ and those of $\mathcal{T}_{\geq p'}$.

A direct consequence of this reduction is that gfp-subsumption between concept names in G-$\mathcal{FL}_0$ remains in the same complexity class as for classical $\mathcal{FL}_0$.

Theorem 17. *In G-$\mathcal{FL}_0$ with cyclic TBoxes, deciding gfp-subsumption between concept names is* PSPACE-*complete.*

Proof. By the reductions above, it suffices to decide the language inclusions $L((\mathcal{A}_{B,C}^{\mathcal{T}})_{\geq p}) \subseteq L((\mathcal{A}_{A,C}^{\mathcal{T}})_{\geq p})$ for all $C \in \mathsf{N}_{\mathsf{P}}^{\mathcal{T}}$ and $p \in \mathcal{V}_{\mathcal{T}}$. These polynomially many inclusion tests for WA can be done in polynomial space [11]. The problem is PSPACE-hard since gfp-subsumption in classical $\mathcal{FL}_0$ is PSPACE-hard [1]. $\square$

To compute the *best* gfp-subsumption degree between A and B, we have to check the above inclusions for increasing values $p \in \mathcal{V}_{\mathcal{T}}$. The largest p for which these checks succeed is the requested degree.

In the case of an acyclic TBox $\mathcal{T}$, it is easy to verify that the automata $(\mathcal{A}_{B,C}^{\mathcal{T}})_{\geq p}$ constructed above are in fact acyclic. Since inclusion between acyclic automata can be decided in CO-NP [11], we again obtain the same complexity as in the classical case.

Corollary 18. *In G-$\mathcal{FL}_0$ with acyclic TBoxes, deciding gfp-subsumption between concept names is* CO-NP-*complete.*

5 Conclusions

We have studied the complexity of reasoning in G-$\mathcal{FL}_0$ w.r.t. primitive concept definitions under greatest fixed-point semantics. Specifically, we have shown that gfp-subsumption between concept names can be reduced to a comparison of the behavior of weighted automata with word transitions. The latter can be solved by a polynomial number of inclusion tests on *unweighted* automata, and thus gfp-subsumption is PSPACE-complete for this logic, just as in the classical case. The same reduction yields CO-NP-completeness in the case of acyclic TBoxes.

In fuzzy DLs, reasoning is often restricted to so-called *witnessed* models [14]. Intuitively, they guarantee that the semantics of value restrictions can be computed as minima instead of possibly infinite infima. As our reduction does not make use of this property and the model constructed in the proof of Lemma 13 is witnessed, our results hold under both witnessed and general semantics.

These complexity results are consistent with previous work on extensions of description logics with Gödel semantics. Indeed, such extensions of $\mathcal{EL}$ [17,20] and $\mathcal{ALC}$ [6] have been shown to preserve the complexity of their classical counterpart. Since reasoning in both $\mathcal{FL}_0$ and in G-$\mathcal{ALC}$ w.r.t. general TBoxes is EXPTIME-complete, so is deciding subsumption in G-$\mathcal{FL}_0$ w.r.t. general TBoxes.

We expect our results to generalize easily to any other set of truth degrees that form a total order. However, the arguments used in this paper fail for arbitrary lattices, where incomparable truth degrees might exist [8,23]. Studying these two cases in detail is a task for future work. We also plan to consider fuzzy extensions of $\mathcal{FL}_0$ with semantics based on non-idempotent t-norms, such as the Łukasiewicz or product t-norms [13].

References

1. Baader, F.: Using automata theory for characterizing the semantics of terminological cycles. Annals of Mathematics and Artificial Intelligence 18(2), 175–219 (1996)
2. Baader, F., Brandt, S., Lutz, C.: Pushing the $\mathcal{EL}$ envelope. In: Kaelbling, L.P., Saffiotti, A. (eds.) Proc. of the 19th Int. Joint Conf. on Artificial Intelligence (IJCAI 2005), pp. 364–369. Professional Book Center (2005)
3. Baader, F., Calvanese, D., McGuinness, D.L., Nardi, D., Patel-Schneider, P.F. (eds.): The Description Logic Handbook: Theory, Implementation, and Applications, 2nd edn. Cambridge University Press (2007)
4. Baader, F., Peñaloza, R.: On the undecidability of fuzzy description logics with GCIs and product t-norm. In: Tinelli, C., Sofronie-Stokkermans, V. (eds.) FroCoS 2011. LNCS (LNAI), vol. 6989, pp. 55–70. Springer, Heidelberg (2011)
5. Bobillo, F., Straccia, U.: Fuzzy description logics with general t-norms and datatypes. Fuzzy Sets and Systems 160(23), 3382–3402 (2009)
6. Borgwardt, S., Distel, F., Peñaloza, R.: Decidable Gödel description logics without the finitely-valued model property. In: Proc. of the 14th Int. Conf. on Principles of Knowledge Representation and Reasoning (KR 2014). AAAI Press (to appear, 2014)
7. Borgwardt, S., Peñaloza, R.: Undecidability of fuzzy description logics. In: Brewka, G., Eiter, T., McIlraith, S.A. (eds.) Proc. of the 13th Int. Conf. on Principles of Knowledge Representation and Reasoning (KR 2012), pp. 232–242. AAAI Press (2012)
8. Borgwardt, S., Peñaloza, R.: The complexity of lattice-based fuzzy description logics. Journal on Data Semantics 2(1), 1–19 (2013)
9. Cerami, M., Straccia, U.: On the (un)decidability of fuzzy description logics under Łukasiewicz t-norm. Information Sciences 227, 1–21 (2013)
10. Cintula, P., Hájek, P., Noguera, C. (eds.): Handbook of Mathematical Fuzzy Logic, Studies in Logic, pp. 37–38. College Publications (2011)
11. Garey, M.R., Johnson, D.S.: Computers and Intractability: A Guide to the Theory of NP-Completeness. W. H. Freeman & Co., New York (1979)
12. Grätzer, G.: General Lattice Theory, 2nd edn. Birkhäuser (2003)
13. Hájek, P.: Metamathematics of Fuzzy Logic (Trends in Logic). Springer (2001)
14. Hájek, P.: Making fuzzy description logic more general. Fuzzy Sets and Systems 154(1), 1–15 (2005)
15. Kleene, S.C.: Introduction to Metamathematics. Van Nostrand, New York (1952)
16. Klement, E.P., Mesiar, R., Pap, E.: Triangular Norms. Trends in Logic, Studia Logica Library. Springer (2000)
17. Mailis, T., Stoilos, G., Simou, N., Stamou, G.B., Kollias, S.: Tractable reasoning with vague knowledge using fuzzy $\mathcal{EL}^{++}$. Journal of Intelligent Information Systems 39(2), 399–440 (2012)
18. Nebel, B.: Terminological reasoning is inherently intractable. Artificial Intelligence 43(2), 235–249 (1990)
19. Nebel, B.: Terminological cycles: Semantics and computational properties. In: Sowa, J. (ed.) Principles of Semantic Networks, pp. 331–362. Morgan Kaufmann (1991)
20. Stoilos, G., Stamou, G.B., Pan, J.Z.: Classifying fuzzy subsumption in fuzzy-$\mathcal{EL}+$. In: Baader, F., Lutz, C., Motik, B. (eds.) Proc. of the 2008 Int. Workshop on Description Logics (DL 2008). CEUR Workshop Proceedings, vol. 353 (2008)

21. Stoilos, G., Straccia, U., Stamou, G.B., Pan, J.Z.: General concept inclusions in fuzzy description logics. In: Brewka, G., Coradeschi, S., Perini, A., Traverso, P. (eds.) Proc. of the 17th Eur. Conf. on Artificial Intelligence (ECAI 2006), pp. 457–461. IOS Press (2006)
22. Straccia, U.: Reasoning within fuzzy description logics. Journal of Artificial Intelligence Research 14, 137–166 (2001)
23. Straccia, U.: Description logics over lattices. International Journal of Uncertainty, Fuzziness and Knowledge-Based Systems 14(1), 1–16 (2006)
24. Tarski, A.: A lattice-theoretical fixpoint theorem and its applications. Pacific Journal of Mathematics 5(2), 285–309 (1955)
25. Zadeh, L.A.: Fuzzy sets. Information and Control 8(3), 338–353 (1965)

Tight Complexity Bounds for Reasoning in the Description Logic $\mathcal{BEL}$

İsmail İlkan Ceylan[1,*] and Rafael Peñaloza[1,2,**]

[1] Theoretical Computer Science, TU Dresden, Germany
[2] Center for Advancing Electronics Dresden, Germany
{ceylan,penaloza}@tcs.inf.tu-dresden.de

Abstract. Recently, Bayesian extensions of Description Logics, and in particular the logic $\mathcal{BEL}$, were introduced as a means of representing certain knowledge that depends on an uncertain context. In this paper we introduce a novel structure, called *proof structure*, that encodes the contextual information required to deduce subsumption relations from a $\mathcal{BEL}$ knowledge base. Using this structure, we show that probabilistic reasoning in $\mathcal{BEL}$ can be reduced in polynomial time to standard Bayesian network inferences, thus obtaining tight complexity bounds for reasoning in $\mathcal{BEL}$.

1 Introduction

Description Logics (DLs) [2] are a family of knowledge representation formalisms that are characterized by their clear syntax, and formal, unambiguous semantics. DLs have been successfully employed for creating large knowledge bases, representing real application domains, prominently from the life sciences. Examples of such knowledge bases are SNOMED CT, GALEN, or the Gene Ontology.

A prominent missing feature of classical DLs is the capacity of specifying a *context* in which a portion of the knowledge holds. For instance, the behaviour of a system may depend on factors that are extrogenous to the domain, such as the weather conditions. For that reason, approaches for handling contexts in DLs have been studied; see e.g. [13,14]. Since the specific context in which the ontology is being applied (e.g., the weather) may be uncertain, it is important to adapt context-based reasoning to consider also a probabilistic distribution over the contexts. Recently, $\mathcal{BEL}$ [7] and other probabilistic extensions of DLs [8] were introduced to describe certain knowledge that depends on an uncertain context, which is described by a Bayesian network (BN). Using these logics, one can represent knowledge that holds e.g., when it rains. Interestingly, reasoning in $\mathcal{BEL}$ can be decoupled between the logical part, and BN inferences. However, despite the logical component of this logic being decidable in polynomial time, the best known algorithm for probabilistic reasoning in $\mathcal{BEL}$ runs in exponential time.

---

* Supported by DFG within the Research Training Group "RoSI" (GRK 1907).
** Partially supported by DFG within the Cluster of Excellence 'cfAED'.

E. Fermé and J. Leite (Eds.): JELIA 2014, LNAI 8761, pp. 77–91, 2014.

We use a novel structure, called the *proof structure*, to reduce probabilistic reasoning for a $\mathcal{BEL}$ knowledge base to probabilistic inferences in a BN. Briefly, a proof structure describes all contexts that entail the wanted consequence. The BN can then be used to compute the probability of these contexts, which yields the probability of the entailment. Since this reduction can be done in polynomial time, it provides tight upper bounds for the complexity of reasoning in $\mathcal{BEL}$.

2 $\mathcal{EL}$ and Proof Structures

$\mathcal{EL}$ is a light-weight DL that allows for polynomial-time reasoning. It is based on *concepts* and *roles*, corresponding to unary and binary predicates from first-order logic, respectively. $\mathcal{EL}$ concepts are built inductively from disjoint, countably infinite sets N_C and N_R of *concept names* and *role names*, and applying the syntax rule $C ::= A \mid \top \mid C \sqcap C \mid \exists r.C$, where $A \in N_C$ and $r \in N_R$.

The *semantics* of $\mathcal{EL}$ is given by *interpretations* $\mathcal{I} = (\Delta^{\mathcal{I}}, \cdot^{\mathcal{I}})$ where $\Delta^{\mathcal{I}}$ is a non-empty *domain* and $\cdot^{\mathcal{I}}$ is an *interpretation function* that maps every $A \in N_C$ to a set $A^{\mathcal{I}} \subseteq \Delta^{\mathcal{I}}$ and every role name r to a binary relation $r^{\mathcal{I}} \subseteq \Delta^{\mathcal{I}} \times \Delta^{\mathcal{I}}$. The interpretation function $\cdot^{\mathcal{I}}$ is extended to $\mathcal{EL}$ concepts by defining $\top^{\mathcal{I}} := \Delta^{\mathcal{I}}$, $(C \sqcap D)^{\mathcal{I}} := C^{\mathcal{I}} \cap D^{\mathcal{I}}$, and $(\exists r.C)^{\mathcal{I}} := \{d \in \Delta^{\mathcal{I}} \mid \exists e : (d,e) \in r^{\mathcal{I}} \wedge e \in C^{\mathcal{I}}\}$. The knowledge of a domain is represented through a set of axioms restricting the interpretation of the concepts.

Definition 1 (TBox). *A general concept inclusion (GCI) is an expression of the form $C \sqsubseteq D$, where C, D are concepts. A TBox $\mathcal{T}$ is a finite set of GCIs. The signature of $\mathcal{T}$ ($\mathsf{sig}(\mathcal{T})$) is the set of concept and role names appearing in $\mathcal{T}$. An interpretation $\mathcal{I}$ satisfies the GCI $C \sqsubseteq D$ iff $C^{\mathcal{I}} \subseteq D^{\mathcal{I}}$; $\mathcal{I}$ is a model of the TBox $\mathcal{T}$ iff it satisfies all the GCIs in $\mathcal{T}$.*

The main reasoning service in $\mathcal{EL}$ is deciding the subsumption relations between concepts based on their semantic definitions. A concept C is *subsumed by* D w.r.t. the TBox $\mathcal{T}$ ($\mathcal{T} \models C \sqsubseteq D$) iff $C^{\mathcal{I}} \subseteq D^{\mathcal{I}}$ for all models $\mathcal{I}$ of $\mathcal{T}$.

It has been shown that subsumption can be decided in $\mathcal{EL}$ by a completion algorithm in polynomial time [1]. This algorithm requires the TBox to be in *normal form*; i.e., where all axioms in the TBox are of one of the forms $A \sqsubseteq B \mid A \sqcap B \sqsubseteq C \mid A \sqsubseteq \exists r.B \mid \exists r.B \sqsubseteq A$. It is well known that every TBox can be transformed into an equivalent one in normal form of linear size [1,5]; for the rest of this paper, we assume that $\mathcal{T}$ is a TBox in normal form.

We are interested in deriving the subsumption relations in normal form that follow from $\mathcal{T}$; we call the set of all these subsumption relations the *normalised logical closure* of $\mathcal{T}$. This closure can be computed by an exhaustive application of the *deduction rules* from Table 1. Each rule maps a set of premises S to its consequence α; such a rule is *applicable* to a TBox $\mathcal{T}$ if $S \subseteq \mathcal{T}$ but $\alpha \notin \mathcal{T}$. In that case, its application adds α to $\mathcal{T}$. It is easy to see that these rules produce the normalised logical closure of the input TBox. Moreover, the deduction rules introduce only GCIs in normal form, and do not change the signature. Hence, if $n = |\mathsf{sig}(\mathcal{T})|$, the logical closure of $\mathcal{T}$ is found after at most n^3 rule applications.

Table 1. Deduction rules for $\mathcal{EL}$

$\mapsto$	Premises (S)	Result (α)	$\mapsto$	Premises (S)	Result (α)
1	$\langle A \sqsubseteq B \rangle, \langle B \sqsubseteq C \rangle$	$\langle A \sqsubseteq C \rangle$	7	$\langle A \sqsubseteq \exists r.B \rangle, \langle \exists r.B \sqsubseteq C \rangle$	$\langle A \sqsubseteq C \rangle$
2	$\langle A \sqsubseteq \exists r.B \rangle, \langle B \sqsubseteq C \rangle$	$\langle A \sqsubseteq \exists r.C \rangle$	8	$\langle A \sqcap B \sqsubseteq C \rangle, \langle C \sqsubseteq X \rangle$	$\langle A \sqcap B \sqsubseteq X \rangle$
3	$\langle A \sqsubseteq \exists r.B \rangle, \langle C \sqsubseteq A \rangle$	$\langle C \sqsubseteq \exists r.B \rangle$	9	$\langle A \sqcap B \sqsubseteq C \rangle, \langle X \sqsubseteq A \rangle$	$\langle X \sqcap B \sqsubseteq C \rangle$
4	$\langle \exists r.A \sqsubseteq B \rangle, \langle B \sqsubseteq C \rangle$	$\langle \exists r.A \sqsubseteq C \rangle$	10	$\langle A \sqcap B \sqsubseteq C \rangle, \langle X \sqsubseteq B \rangle$	$\langle A \sqcap X \sqsubseteq C \rangle$
5	$\langle \exists r.A \sqsubseteq B \rangle, \langle C \sqsubseteq A \rangle$	$\langle \exists r.C \sqsubseteq B \rangle$	11	$\langle X \sqcap X \sqsubseteq C \rangle$	$\langle X \sqsubseteq C \rangle$
6	$\langle \exists r.A \sqsubseteq B \rangle, \langle B \sqsubseteq \exists r.C \rangle$	$\langle A \sqsubseteq C \rangle$			

We will later associate a probability to the GCIs in the TBox $\mathcal{T}$, and will be interested in computing the probability of a subsumption. It will then be useful to be able not only to derive the GCI, but also *all* the sub-TBoxes of $\mathcal{T}$ from which it follows. Therefore, we store the traces of the deduction rules using a directed hypergraph. A *directed hypergraph* is a tuple $H = (V, E)$ where V is a non-empty set of *vertices* and E is a set of *directed hyper-edges* of the form $e = (S, v)$ where $S \subseteq V$ and $v \in V$. Given $S \subseteq V$ and $v \in V$, a *path from S to v in H* of *length* n is a sequence of hyper-edges $(S_1, v_1), (S_2, v_2), \dots, (S_n, v_n)$ where $v_n = v$ and $S_i \subseteq S \cup \{v_j \mid 0 < j < i\}$ for all $i, 1 \leq i \leq n$.

Given a TBox $\mathcal{T}$ in normal form, we build the hypergraph $H_\mathcal{T} = (V_\mathcal{T}, E_\mathcal{T})$, where $V_\mathcal{T}$ is the set of all GCIs in normal form that follow from $\mathcal{T}$ over the same signature and $E_\mathcal{T} = \{(S, \alpha) \mid S \mapsto \alpha, S \subseteq V_\mathcal{T}\}$, with $\mapsto$ the deduction relation defined in Table 1. We call this hypergraph the *proof structure* of $\mathcal{T}$. From the soundness and completeness of the deduction rules, we get the following lemma.

Lemma 2. *Let $\mathcal{T}$ be a TBox in normal form, $H_\mathcal{T} = (V_\mathcal{T}, E_\mathcal{T})$ its proof structure, $\mathcal{O} \subseteq \mathcal{T}$, and $C \sqsubseteq D \in V_\mathcal{T}$. There is a path from $\mathcal{O}$ to $C \sqsubseteq D$ in $H_\mathcal{T}$ iff $\mathcal{O} \models C \sqsubseteq D$.*

$H_\mathcal{T}$ is a compact representation of all the possible derivations of a GCI from the GCIs in $\mathcal{T}$ [3,4]. Traversing this hypergraph backwards from a GCI α being entailed by $\mathcal{T}$, one constructs all proofs for α; hence the name "proof structure." Since $|V_\mathcal{T}| \leq |\mathsf{sig}(\mathcal{T})|^3$, it suffices to consider paths of length at most $|\mathsf{sig}(\mathcal{T})|^3$.

Clearly, the proof structure $H_\mathcal{T}$ can be cyclic. To simplify the process of finding the causes of a GCI being entailed, we build an *unfolded* version of this hypergraph by making different copies of each node. In this case, nodes are pairs of axioms and labels, where the latter indicates to which level the nodes belong in the hypergraph. Given a set of axioms S, and $i \geq 0$, $S^i := \{(\alpha, i) \mid \alpha \in S\}$ denotes the i-labeled set of GCIs in S. Let $n := |\mathsf{sig}(\mathcal{T})|^3$, we define the sets $W_i, 0 \leq i \leq n$ inductively by setting $W_0 := \{(\alpha, 0) \mid \alpha \in \mathcal{T}\}$ and for all $i, 0 \leq i < n$

$$W_{i+1} := \{(\alpha, i+1) \mid S^i \subseteq W_i, S \mapsto \alpha\} \cup \{(\alpha, i+1) \mid (\alpha, i) \in W_i\}.$$

For each $i, 0 \leq i \leq n$, W_i contains all the GCIs that can be derived by at most i applications of the deduction rules from Table 1. The *unfolded proof structure* of $\mathcal{T}$ is the hypergraph $H_\mathcal{T}^u = (W_\mathcal{T}, F_\mathcal{T})$, where $W_\mathcal{T} := \bigcup_{i=0}^n W_i$ and $F_\mathcal{T} := \bigcup_{i=1}^n F_i$,

$$F_{i+1} := \{(S^i, (\alpha, i+1)) \mid S^i \subseteq W_i, S \mapsto \alpha\} \cup \{(\{(\alpha, i)\}, (\alpha, i+1)) \mid (\alpha, i) \in W_i\}.$$

Algorithm 1. Construction of the pruned proof structure

Input: TBox $\mathcal{T}$
Output: $H = (W, F)$ pruned proof structure for $\mathcal{T}$
1: $V_0 \leftarrow \mathcal{T}$, $E_0 \leftarrow \emptyset$, $i \leftarrow 0$
2: **do**
3:     $i \leftarrow i + 1$
4:     $V_i := V_{i-1} \cup \{\alpha \mid S \mapsto \alpha, S \subseteq V_{i-1}\}$
5:     $E_i = \{(S, \alpha) \mid S \mapsto \alpha, S \subseteq V_{i-1}\}$
6: **while** $V_i \neq V_{i-1}$ or $E_i \neq E_{i-1}$
7: $W := \{(\alpha, k) \mid \alpha \in V_k, 0 \leq k \leq i\}$
8: $E := \{(S, (\alpha, k)) \mid (S, \alpha) \in E_k, 0 \leq k \leq i\} \cup \{(\{(\alpha, k)\}, (\alpha, k+1)) \mid \alpha \in V_k, 0 \leq k < i\}$
9: **return** (W, E)

The following is a simple consequence of our constructions and Lemma 2.

Theorem 3. *Let $\mathcal{T}$ be a TBox, and $H_{\mathcal{T}} = (V_{\mathcal{T}}, E_{\mathcal{T}})$ and $H_{\mathcal{T}}^u = (W_{\mathcal{T}}, F_{\mathcal{T}})$ the proof structure and unfolded proof structure of $\mathcal{T}$, respectively. Then,*

1. *for all $C \sqsubseteq D \in V_{\mathcal{T}}$ and all $\mathcal{O} \subseteq \mathcal{T}$, $\mathcal{O} \models C \sqsubseteq D$ iff there is a path from $\{(\alpha, 0) \mid \alpha \in \mathcal{O}\}$ to $(C \sqsubseteq D, n)$ in $H_{\mathcal{T}}^u$, and*
2. *$(S, \alpha) \in E_{\mathcal{T}}$ iff $(S^{n-1}, (\alpha, n)) \in F_{\mathcal{T}}$.*

The unfolded proof structure of a TBox $\mathcal{T}$ is thus guaranteed to contain the information of all possible causes for a GCI to follow from $\mathcal{T}$. Moreover, this hypergraph is acyclic, and has polynomially many nodes, on the size of $\mathcal{T}$, by construction. Yet, this hypergraph may contain many redundant nodes. Indeed, it can be the case that all the simple paths in $H_{\mathcal{T}}$ starting from a subset of $\mathcal{T}$ are of length $k < n$. In that case, $W_i = W_{i+1}$ and $F_i = F_{i+1}$ hold for all $i \geq k$, modulo the second component. It thus suffices to consider the sub-hypergraph of $H_{\mathcal{T}}^u$ that contains only the nodes $\bigcup_{i=0}^{k} W_i$. Algorithm 1 describes a method for computing this pruned hypergraph. In the worst case, this algorithm will produce the whole unfolded proof structure of $\mathcal{T}$, but will stop the unfolding procedure earlier if possible. The **do-while** loop is executed at most $|\mathsf{sig}(\mathcal{T})|^3$ times, and each of these loops requires at most $|\mathsf{sig}(\mathcal{T})|^3$ steps.

Lemma 4. *Algorithm 1 terminates in time polynomial on the size of $\mathcal{T}$.*

We briefly illustrate the execution of Algorithm 1 on a simple TBox.

Example 5. Consider the $\mathcal{EL}$ TBox $\mathcal{T} = \{A \sqsubseteq B, B \sqsubseteq C, B \sqsubseteq D, C \sqsubseteq D\}$. The first levels of the unfolded proof structure of $\mathcal{T}$ are shown in Figure 1.[1] The first level V_0 of this hypergraph contains a representative for each axiom in $\mathcal{T}$. To construct the second level, we first copy all the GCIs in V_0 to V_1, and add a hyperedge joining the equivalent GCIs (represented by dashed lines in Figure 1). Then, we apply all possible deduction rules to the elements of V_0, and add a

---

[1] For the illustrations we drop the second component of the nodes, but visually make the level information explicit.

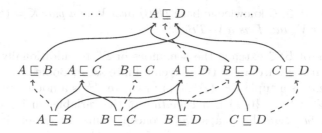

Fig. 1. The first levels of an unfolded proof structure and the paths to $\langle A \sqsubseteq D \rangle$

hyperedge from the premises at level V_0 to the conclusion at level V_1 (continuous lines). This procedure is repeated at each subsequent level. Notice that the set of GCIs at each level is monotonically increasing. Additionally, for each GCI, the in-degree of each representative monotonically increases throughout the levels.

In the next section, we recall $\mathcal{BEL}$, a probabilistic extension of $\mathcal{EL}$ based on Bayesian networks [7], and use the construction of the (unfolded) proof structure to provide tight complexity bounds for reasoning in this logic.

3   The Bayesian Description Logic $\mathcal{BEL}$

The probabilistic Description Logic $\mathcal{BEL}$ extends $\mathcal{EL}$ by associating every GCI in a TBox with a probabilistic context. The joint probability distribution of the contexts is encoded in a Bayesian network [12]. A *Bayesian network* (BN) is a pair $\mathcal{B} = (G, \Phi)$, where $G = (V, E)$ is a finite directed acyclic graph (DAG) whose nodes represent Boolean random variables,[2] and Φ contains, for every node $x \in V$, a conditional probability distribution $P_{\mathcal{B}}(x \mid \pi(x))$ of x given its parents $\pi(x)$. If V is the set of nodes in G, we say that $\mathcal{B}$ is a BN *over* V.

Intuitively, $G = (V, E)$ encodes a series of conditional independence assumptions between the random variables: every variable $x \in V$ is conditionally independent of its non-descendants given its parents. Thus, every BN $\mathcal{B}$ defines a unique joint probability distribution over V where $P_{\mathcal{B}}(V) = \prod_{x \in V} P_{\mathcal{B}}(x \mid \pi(x))$. As with classical DLs, the main building blocks in $\mathcal{BEL}$ are concepts, which are syntactically built as $\mathcal{EL}$ concepts. The domain knowledge is encoded by a generalization of TBoxes, where axioms are annotated with a context, defined by a set of literals belonging to a BN.

Definition 6 (KB). *Let V be a finite set of Boolean variables. A V-literal is an expression of the form x or $\neg x$, where $x \in V$; a V-context is a consistent set of V-literals.*

A V-restricted general concept inclusion (V-GCI) is of the form $\langle C \sqsubseteq D : \kappa \rangle$ where C and D are $\mathcal{BEL}$ concepts and κ is a V-context. A V-TBox is a finite

---

[2] In their general form, BNs allow for arbitrary discrete random variables. We restrict w.l.o.g. to Boolean variables for ease of presentation.

set of V-GCIs. A $\mathcal{BEL}$ *knowledge base (KB) over* V *is a pair* $\mathcal{K} = (\mathcal{B}, \mathcal{T})$ *where* $\mathcal{B}$ *is a BN over* V *and* $\mathcal{T}$ *is a* V*-TBox.*[3]

The semantics of $\mathcal{BEL}$ extends the semantics of $\mathcal{EL}$ by additionally evaluating the random variables from the BN. Given a finite set of Boolean variables V, a V-*interpretation* is a tuple $\mathcal{I} = (\Delta^{\mathcal{I}}, \cdot^{\mathcal{I}}, \mathcal{V}^{\mathcal{I}})$ where $\Delta^{\mathcal{I}}$ is a non-empty set called the *domain*, $\mathcal{V}^{\mathcal{I}} : V \to \{0, 1\}$ is a *valuation* of the variables in V, and $\cdot^{\mathcal{I}}$ is an *interpretation function* that maps every concept name A to a set $A^{\mathcal{I}} \subseteq \Delta^{\mathcal{I}}$ and every role name r to a binary relation $r^{\mathcal{I}} \subseteq \Delta^{\mathcal{I}} \times \Delta^{\mathcal{I}}$.

The interpretation function $\cdot^{\mathcal{I}}$ is extended to arbitrary $\mathcal{BEL}$ concepts as in $\mathcal{EL}$ and the valuation $\mathcal{V}^{\mathcal{I}}$ is extended to contexts by defining, for every $x \in V$, $\mathcal{V}^{\mathcal{I}}(\neg x) = 1 - \mathcal{V}^{\mathcal{I}}(x)$, and for every context κ, $\mathcal{V}^{\mathcal{I}}(\kappa) = \min_{\ell \in \kappa} \mathcal{V}^{\mathcal{I}}(\ell)$, where $\mathcal{V}^{\mathcal{I}}(\emptyset) := 1$. Intuitively, a context κ can be thought as a conjunction of literals, which is evaluated to 1 iff each literal is evaluated to 1.

The V-interpretation $\mathcal{I}$ is a *model* of the V-GCI $\langle C \sqsubseteq D : \kappa \rangle$, denoted as $\mathcal{I} \models \langle C \sqsubseteq D : \kappa \rangle$, iff (i) $\mathcal{V}^{\mathcal{I}}(\kappa) = 0$, or (ii) $C^{\mathcal{I}} \subseteq D^{\mathcal{I}}$. It is a *model* of the V-TBox $\mathcal{T}$ iff it is a model of all the V-GCIs in $\mathcal{T}$. The idea is that the restriction $C \sqsubseteq D$ is only required to hold whenever the context κ is satisfied. Thus, any interpretation that violates the context trivially satisfies the whole V-GCI.

Example 7. Let $V_0 = \{x, y, z\}$, and consider the V_0-TBox

$$\mathcal{T}_0 := \{\langle A \sqsubseteq C : \{x, y\}\rangle, \ \langle A \sqsubseteq B : \{\neg x\}\rangle, \ \langle B \sqsubseteq C : \{\neg x\}\rangle\}.$$

The V_0-interpretation $\mathcal{I}_0 = (\{d\}, \cdot^{\mathcal{I}_0}, \mathcal{V}_0)$ with $\mathcal{V}_0(\{x, \neg y, z\}) = 1$, $A^{\mathcal{I}_0} = \{d\}$, and $B^{\mathcal{I}_0} = C^{\mathcal{I}_0} = \emptyset$ is a model of $\mathcal{T}_0$, but is not a model of the V_0-GCI $\langle A \sqsubseteq B : \{x\}\rangle$, since $\mathcal{V}_0(\{x\}) = 1$ but $A^{\mathcal{I}_0} \not\subseteq B^{\mathcal{I}_0}$.

A V-TBox $\mathcal{T}$ is in *normal form* if for each V-GCI $\langle \alpha : \kappa \rangle \in \mathcal{T}$, α is an $\mathcal{EL}$ GCI in normal form. A $\mathcal{BEL}$ KB $\mathcal{K} = (\mathcal{T}, \mathcal{B})$ is in *normal form* if $\mathcal{T}$ is in normal form. As for $\mathcal{EL}$, every $\mathcal{BEL}$ KB can be transformed into an equivalent one in normal form in polynomial time [6]. Thus, we consider only $\mathcal{BEL}$ KBs in normal form in the following. The DL $\mathcal{EL}$ is a special case of $\mathcal{BEL}$ in which all V-GCIs are of the form $\langle C \sqsubseteq D : \emptyset \rangle$. Notice that every valuation satisfies the empty context $\emptyset$; thus, a V-interpretation $\mathcal{I}$ satisfies the V-GCI $\langle C \sqsubseteq D : \emptyset \rangle$ iff $C^{\mathcal{I}} \subseteq D^{\mathcal{I}}$. We say that $\mathcal{T}$ *entails* $\langle C \sqsubseteq D : \emptyset \rangle$ ($\mathcal{T} \models C \sqsubseteq D$), if every model of $\mathcal{T}$ is also a model of $\langle C \sqsubseteq D : \emptyset \rangle$. For a valuation $\mathcal{W}$ of the variables in V, we define the TBox containing all axioms that must be satisfied in any V-interpretation $\mathcal{I} = (\Delta^{\mathcal{I}}, \cdot^{\mathcal{I}}, \mathcal{V}^{\mathcal{I}})$ with $\mathcal{V}^{\mathcal{I}} = \mathcal{W}$.

Definition 8 (restriction). *Let* $\mathcal{K} = (\mathcal{B}, \mathcal{T})$ *be a* $\mathcal{BEL}$ *KB. The* restriction *of* $\mathcal{T}$ *to a valuation* $\mathcal{W}$ *of the variables in* V *is the* V-*TBox*

$$\mathcal{T}_{\mathcal{W}} := \{\langle C \sqsubseteq D : \emptyset \rangle \mid \langle C \sqsubseteq D : \kappa \rangle \in \mathcal{T}, \mathcal{W}(\kappa) = 1\}.$$

To handle the probabilistic knowledge provided by the BN, we extend the semantics of $\mathcal{BEL}$ through multiple-world interpretations. A V-interpretation describes

---

[3] Unless stated otherwise, we assume that $\mathcal{K}$ is over V in the rest of the paper.

a possible world; by assigning a probabilistic distribution over these interpretations, we describe the required probabilities, which should be consistent with the BN provided in the knowledge base.

Definition 9 (probabilistic model). *A probabilistic interpretation is a pair* $\mathcal{P} = (\mathfrak{I}, P_{\mathfrak{I}})$, *where* $\mathfrak{I}$ *is a set of V-interpretations and* $P_{\mathfrak{I}}$ *is a probability distribution over* $\mathfrak{I}$ *such that* $P_{\mathfrak{I}}(\mathcal{I}) > 0$ *only for finitely many interpretations* $\mathcal{I} \in \mathfrak{I}$. $\mathcal{P}$ *is a* model *of the TBox* $\mathcal{T}$ *if every* $\mathcal{I} \in \mathfrak{I}$ *is a model of* $\mathcal{T}$. $\mathcal{P}$ *is* consistent *with the BN* $\mathcal{B}$ *if for every possible valuation* $\mathcal{W}$ *of the variables in V it holds that*

$$\sum_{\mathcal{I} \in \mathfrak{I}, \mathcal{V}^{\mathcal{I}}=\mathcal{W}} P_{\mathfrak{I}}(\mathcal{I}) = P_{\mathcal{B}}(\mathcal{W}).$$

$\mathcal{P}$ *is a* model *of the KB* $(\mathcal{B}, \mathcal{T})$ *iff it is a model of* $\mathcal{T}$ *and consistent with* $\mathcal{B}$.

One simple consequence of this semantics is that probabilistic models preserve the probability distribution of $\mathcal{B}$ for contexts; the probability of a context κ is the sum of the probabilities of all valuations that extend κ.

3.1 Contextual Subsumption

Just as in classical DLs, we want to extract the information that is implicitly encoded in a $\mathcal{BEL}$ KB. In particular, we are interested in solving different reasoning tasks for this logic. One of the fundamental reasoning problems in $\mathcal{EL}$ is subsumption: is a concept C always interpreted as a subconcept of D? This problem is extended to also consider the contexts in $\mathcal{BEL}$.

Definition 10 (contextual subsumption). *Let* $\mathcal{K} = (\mathcal{T}, \mathcal{B})$ *be a* $\mathcal{BEL}$ *KB,* C, D *be two* $\mathcal{BEL}$ *concepts, and* κ *a V-context.* C *is* contextually subsumed *by* D *in* κ *w.r.t.* $\mathcal{K}$, *denoted* $\langle C \sqsubseteq_{\mathcal{K}} D : \kappa \rangle$, *if every probabilistic model of* $\mathcal{K}$ *is also a model of* $\{\langle C \sqsubseteq D : \kappa \rangle\}$.

Contextual subsumption depends only on the contexts, and not on their associated probabilities. It was shown in [7] that contextual subsumption is coNP-hard, even if considering only the empty context. To show that the problem is in fact coNP-complete, we use the following lemma also shown in [7].

Lemma 11. *Let* $\mathcal{K} = (\mathcal{B}, \mathcal{T})$ *be a KB. Then* $\langle C \sqsubseteq_{\mathcal{K}} D : \kappa \rangle$ *iff for every valuation* $\mathcal{W}$ *with* $\mathcal{W}(\kappa) = 1$, *it holds that* $\mathcal{T}_{\mathcal{W}} \models C \sqsubseteq D$.

Using this lemma, it is easy to see that contextual subsumption is in coNP: to decide that the subsumption does not hold, we simply guess a valuation $\mathcal{W}$ and verify in polynomial time that $\mathcal{W}(\kappa) = 1$ and $\mathcal{T}_{\mathcal{W}} \not\models C \sqsubseteq D$.

Corollary 12. *Contextual subsumption is coNP-complete.*

In $\mathcal{BEL}$ one might be interested in finding the probability with which such a consequence holds, or given a subsumption relation, computing the most probable context in which it holds. For the rest of this section, we formally define these reasoning tasks, and provide a method for solving them based on Bayesian networks inferences.

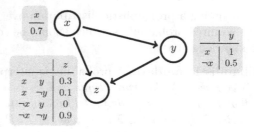

Fig. 2. A simple BN

3.2 Probabilistic Subsumption

We generalize subsumption between concepts to consider also the probabilities provided by the BN.

Definition 13 (p-subsumption). *Let $\mathcal{K} = (\mathcal{T}, \mathcal{B})$ be a $\mathcal{BEL}$ KB, C, D two $\mathcal{BEL}$ concepts, and κ a V-context. For a probabilistic interpretation $\mathcal{P} = (\mathfrak{I}, P_\mathfrak{I})$, we define $P(\langle C \sqsubseteq_\mathcal{P} D : \kappa\rangle) := \sum_{\mathcal{I} \in \mathfrak{I}, \mathcal{I} \models \langle C \sqsubseteq D : \kappa\rangle} P_\mathfrak{I}(\mathcal{I})$. The probability of the V-GCI $\langle C \sqsubseteq D : \kappa\rangle$ w.r.t. $\mathcal{K}$ is defined as*

$$P(\langle C \sqsubseteq_\mathcal{K} D : \kappa\rangle) := \inf_{\mathcal{P} \models \mathcal{K}} P(\langle C \sqsubseteq_\mathcal{P} D : \kappa\rangle).$$

We say that C is p-subsumed by D in κ, for $p \in (0, 1]$ if $P(\langle C \sqsubseteq_\mathcal{K} D : \kappa\rangle) \geq p$.

Proposition 14 ([7]). *Let $\mathcal{K} = (\mathcal{B}, \mathcal{T})$ be a KB. Then*

$$P(\langle C \sqsubseteq_\mathcal{K} D : \kappa\rangle) = 1 - P_\mathcal{B}(\kappa) + \sum_{\substack{\mathcal{T}_\mathcal{W} \models C \sqsubseteq D \\ \mathcal{W}(\kappa)=1}} P_\mathcal{B}(\mathcal{W}).$$

Example 15. Consider the KB $\mathcal{K}_0 = (\mathcal{B}_0, \mathcal{T}_0)$, where $\mathcal{B}_0$ is the BN from Figure 2 and $\mathcal{T}_0$ the V_0-TBox from Example 7. It follows that $P(\langle A \sqsubseteq_{\mathcal{K}_0} C : \{x, y\}\rangle) = 1$ from the first V-GCI in $\mathcal{T}$ and $P(\langle A \sqsubseteq_{\mathcal{K}_0} C : \{\neg x\}\rangle) = 1$ from the others since any model of $\mathcal{K}_0$ needs to satisfy the V-GCIs asserted in $\mathcal{T}$ by definition. Notice that $A \sqsubseteq C$ does not hold in context $\{x, \neg y\}$, but $P(\langle A \sqsubseteq_{\mathcal{K}_0} C : \{x, \neg y\}\rangle) = 1$. Since this describes all contexts, we conclude $P(\langle A \sqsubseteq_{\mathcal{K}_0} C : \emptyset\rangle) = 1$.

Deciding p-subsumption We show that deciding p-subsumption can be reduced to deciding the D-PR problem over a Bayesian network. Given a BN $\mathcal{B} = (G, \Phi)$ over V and a V-context κ, the *D-PR problem* consists on deciding whether $P_\mathcal{B}(\kappa) > p$. This problem is known to be PP-complete [9,22].

Let $\mathcal{K} = (\mathcal{T}, \mathcal{B})$ be an arbitrary but fixed $\mathcal{BEL}$ KB. From the labelled V-TBox $\mathcal{T}$, we construct the $\mathcal{EL}$ TBox $\mathcal{T}' := \{\alpha \mid \langle \alpha : \kappa\rangle \in \mathcal{T}\}$. $\mathcal{T}'$ contains the same axioms as $\mathcal{T}$, but ignores the contextual information encoded in their labels. Let now $H_\mathcal{T}^u$ be the (pruned) unraveled proof structure for $\mathcal{T}'$. By construction, $H_\mathcal{T}^u$ is a directed acyclic hypergraph. Our goal is to transform this hypergraph into a DAG and construct a BN, from which all the p-subsumption relations can be read through standard BN inferences. We explain this construction in two steps.

Algorithm 2. Construction of a DAG from a hypergraph

Input: $H = (V, E)$ directed acyclic hypergraph
Output: $G = (V', E')$ directed acyclic graph
1: $V' \leftarrow V, i, j \leftarrow 0$
2: **for** each $v \in V$ **do**
3:     $\mathfrak{S} \leftarrow \{S \mid (S, v) \in E\}, j \leftarrow i$
4:     **for** each $S \in \mathfrak{S}$ **do**
5:         $V' \leftarrow V' \cup \{\wedge_i\}, \ E' \leftarrow E' \cup \{(u, \wedge_i) \mid u \in S\}$
6:         **if** $i > j$ **then**
7:             $V' \leftarrow V' \cup \{\vee_i\}, \ E' \leftarrow E' \cup \{(\wedge_i, \vee_i)\}$
8:         $i \leftarrow i + 1$
9:     **if** $i = j + 1$ **then**   ▷ If the GCI has only one explanation
10:         $E' \leftarrow E' \cup \{(\wedge_j, v)\}$
11:     **else**
12:         $E' \leftarrow E' \cup \{(\vee_k, \vee_{k+1}) \mid j < k < i - 1\} \cup \{(\vee_{i-1}, v), (\wedge_j, \vee_{j+1})\}$
13: **return** $G = (V', E')$

From Hypergraph to DAG Hypergraphs generalize graphs by allowing edges to connect many vertices. These hyperedges can be seen as an encoding of a formula in disjunctive normal form. An edge (S, v) expresses that if all the elements in S can be reached, then v is also reachable; we see this as an implication: $\bigwedge_{w \in S} w \Rightarrow v$. Several edges sharing the same head $(S_1, v), (S_2, v), \ldots, (S_k, v)$ in the hypergraph can be described through the implication $\bigvee_{i=1}^{k}(\bigwedge_{w \in S_i} w) \Rightarrow v$. We can thus rewrite any directed acyclic hypergraph into a DAG by introducing auxiliary conjunctive and disjunctive nodes (see Figure 3); the proper semantics of these nodes will be guaranteed by the conditional probability distribution defined later. Since the space needed for describing the conditional probability tables in a BN is exponential on the number of parents of the node, we ensure that all the nodes in this DAG have at most two parent nodes.

Algorithm 2 constructs such a DAG from a directed hypergraph. The algorithm adds a new node $\wedge_i$ for each hyperedge (S, v) in the input hypergraph H, and connects it with all the nodes in S. If there are k hyperedges that lead to a single node v, it creates $k - 1$ nodes $\vee_i$. These are used to represent the binary disjunctions among all the hyperedges leading to v. The algorithm runs in polynomial time on the size of H, and if H is acyclic, the resulting graph G is acyclic too. Moreover, all the nodes $v \in V$ that existed in the input hypergraph have at most one parent node after the translation; every $\vee_i$ node has exactly two parents, and the number of parents of a node $\wedge_i$ is given by the set S from the hyperedge $(S, v) \in E$ that generated it. In particular, if the input hypergraph is the unraveled proof structure for a TBox $\mathcal{T}$, then the size of the generated graph G is polynomial on the size of $\mathcal{T}$, and each node has at most two parent nodes.

From DAG to BN The next step is to build a BN that preserves the probabilistic entailments of a $\mathcal{BEL}$ KB. Let $\mathcal{K} = (\mathcal{T}, \mathcal{B})$ be such a KB, with $\mathcal{B} = (G, \Phi)$, and let $G_{\mathcal{T}}$ be the DAG obtained from the unraveled proof structure of $\mathcal{T}$ using

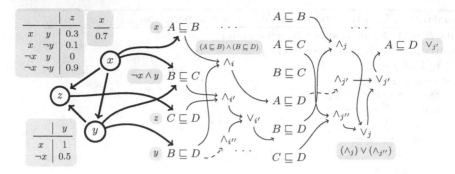

Fig. 3. A portion of the constructed BN

Algorithm 2. Recall that the nodes of $G_\mathcal{T}$ are either (i) pairs of the form (α, i), where α is a GCI in normal form built from the signature of $\mathcal{T}$, or (ii) an auxiliary disjunction ($\vee_i$) or conjunction ($\wedge_i$) node introduced by Algorithm 2. Moreover, $(\alpha, 0)$ is a node of $G_\mathcal{T}$ iff there is a context κ with $\langle \alpha : \kappa \rangle \in \mathcal{T}$. We assume w.l.o.g. that for node $(\alpha, 0)$ there is *exactly one* such context. If there were more than one, then we could extend the BN $\mathcal{B}$ with an additional variable which describes the disjunctions of these contexts, similarly to the construction of Algorithm 2. Similarly, we assume w.l.o.g. that each context κ appearing in $\mathcal{T}$ contains at most two literals, which is a restriction that can be easily removed by introducing auxiliary nodes as before. For a context κ, let $\mathsf{var}(\kappa)$ denote the set of all variables appearing in κ. We construct a new BN $\mathcal{B}_\mathcal{K}$ as follows.

Let $G = (V, E)$ and $G_\mathcal{T} = (V_\mathcal{T}, E_\mathcal{T})$. Construct the graph $G_\mathcal{K} = (V_\mathcal{K}, E_\mathcal{K})$, where $V_\mathcal{K} := V \cup V_\mathcal{T}$ and $E_\mathcal{K} := E \cup E_\mathcal{T} \cup \{(x, (\alpha, 0)) \mid \langle \alpha : \kappa \rangle \in \mathcal{T}, x \in \mathsf{var}(\kappa)\}$. Clearly, $G_\mathcal{K}$ is a DAG. We now need only to define the conditional probability tables for the nodes in $V_\mathcal{T}$ given their parents in $G_\mathcal{K}$; notice that the structure of the graph G remains unchanged for the construction of $G_\mathcal{K}$. For every node $(\alpha, 0) \in V_\mathcal{T}$, there is a κ such that $\langle \alpha : \kappa \rangle \in \mathcal{T}$; the parents of $(\alpha, 0)$ in $G_\mathcal{K}$ are then $\mathsf{var}(\kappa) \subseteq V$. The conditional probability of $(\alpha, 0)$ given its parents is defined, for every valuation $\mathcal{V}$ of $\mathsf{var}(\kappa)$ as $P_\mathcal{B}((\alpha, 0) = \mathsf{true} \mid \mathcal{V}) = \mathcal{V}(\kappa)$; that is, the probability of $(\alpha, 0)$ being true given a valuation of its parents is 1 if the valuation makes the context κ true; otherwise, it is 0. Each auxiliary node has at most two parents. The conditional probability of a conjunction node $\wedge_i$ being true is 1 iff all parents are true, and the conditional probability of a disjunction node $\vee_i$ being true is 1 iff at least one parent is true. Finally, every (α, i) with $i > 0$ has exactly one parent node v; (α, i) is true with probability 1 iff v is true.

Example 16. Consider the $\mathcal{BEL}$ KB $\mathcal{K} = (\mathcal{T}, \mathcal{B}_0)$ over $V = \{x, y, z\}$ where

$$\mathcal{T} = \{\langle A \sqsubseteq B : \{x\}\rangle, \langle B \sqsubseteq C : \{\neg x, y\}\rangle, \langle C \sqsubseteq D : \{z\}\rangle, \langle B \sqsubseteq D : \{y\}\rangle\}.$$

The BN obtained from this KB is depicted in Figure 3. The DAG obtained from the unraveled proof structure of $\mathcal{T}$ appears on the right, while the left part shows the original BN $\mathcal{B}_0$. The gray arrows depict the connection between these two DAGs, which is given by the labels in the V-GCIs in $\mathcal{T}$. The gray boxes denote the conditional probability of the different nodes given their parents.

Suppose that we are interested in $P(\langle A \sqsubseteq_\kappa D : \emptyset \rangle)$. From the unraveled proof structure, we can see that $A \sqsubseteq D$ can be deduced either using the axioms $A \sqsubseteq B$, $B \sqsubseteq C$, $C \sqsubseteq D$, or through the two axioms $A \sqsubseteq B$, $B \sqsubseteq D$. The probability of any of these combinations of axioms to appear is given by $\mathcal{B}_0$ and the contextual connection to the axioms at the lower level of the proof structure. Thus, to deduce $P(\langle A \sqsubseteq_\kappa D : \emptyset \rangle)$ we need only to compute the probability of the node $(A \sqsubseteq D, n)$, where n is the last level.

From the properties of proof structures and Theorem 3 we have that

$$P_{\mathcal{B}_\kappa}((\alpha, n) \mid \kappa) = \sum_{\mathcal{V}(\kappa)=1} P_{\mathcal{B}_\kappa}((\alpha, n) \mid \mathcal{V}) P_{\mathcal{B}_\kappa}(\mathcal{V}) = \sum_{\substack{\mathcal{T}_\mathcal{W} \models \alpha \\ \mathcal{W}(\kappa)=1}} P_{\mathcal{B}_\kappa}(\mathcal{W}).$$

which yields the following result.

Theorem 17. *Let* $\mathcal{K} = (\mathcal{T}, \mathcal{B})$ *be a* $\mathcal{BEL}$ *KB,* C, D *two* $\mathcal{BEL}$ *concepts,* κ *a* V-*context and* $n = |\mathsf{sig}(\mathcal{T})|^3$. *For a* V-*GCI* $\langle C \sqsubseteq D : \kappa \rangle$, *the following holds:* $P(\langle C \sqsubseteq_\kappa D : \kappa \rangle) = 1 - P_\mathcal{B}(\kappa) + P_{\mathcal{B}_\kappa}((C \sqsubseteq D, n) \mid \kappa)$.

This theorem states that we can reduce the problem of p-subsumption w.r.t. the $\mathcal{BEL}$ KB $\mathcal{K}$ to a probabilistic inference in the BN $\mathcal{B}_\kappa$. Notice that the size of $\mathcal{B}_\kappa$ is polynomial on the size of $\mathcal{K}$. This means that p-subsumption is at most as hard as deciding D-PR problems over the BN $\mathcal{B}_\kappa$ which is in PP [22]. Since p-subsumption is also PP-hard [7], we get the following.

Theorem 18. *Deciding* p-*subsumption is* PP-*complete in the size of the KB.*

3.3 Most Likely Context

Finding the most likely context for a consequence can be seen as the dual of computing the probability of this consequence. Intuitively, we are interested in finding the most likely explanation for an event; if a consequence holds, we want to find the context for which this consequence is most likely to occur.

Definition 19 (most likely context). *Let* $\mathcal{K} = (\mathcal{B}, \mathcal{T})$ *be a KB,* C, D *two* $\mathcal{BEL}$ *concepts. A* V-*context* κ *is a most likely context (mlc) for* $C \sqsubseteq D$ *if* (i) $\langle C \sqsubseteq_\kappa D : \kappa \rangle$ *and* (ii) *for all contexts* κ' *with* $\langle C \sqsubseteq_\kappa D : \kappa' \rangle$, $P_\mathcal{B}(\kappa) \geq P_\mathcal{B}(\kappa')$.

Computing all most likely contexts can be done in exponential time. Moreover, it is not possible to lower this bound since a GCI may have exponentially many mlcs. Here we are interested in finding one most likely context, or more precisely, on its associated decision problem: given a context κ, decide whether κ is an mlc for $C \sqsubseteq D$ w.r.t. $\mathcal{K}$. This problem is clearly in coNP^{PP}: to show that κ is not a mlc, we can guess a V-context κ', and check with a PP oracle that $\langle C \sqsubseteq_\kappa D : \kappa' \rangle$ and $P_\mathcal{B}(\kappa') > p$ hold, using the construction from Section 3.2.

To show that it is also coNP^{PP}-hard, we provide a reduction from D-MAP, which corresponds to finding a valuation that maximizes the probability of an event. Formally, the D-MAP problem consists of deciding, given a BN $\mathcal{B}$ over V, a set $Q \subseteq V$ a V-context κ, and $p > 0$, whether there exists a valuation λ of the variables in Q such that $P_\mathcal{B}(\kappa \cup \lambda) > p$.

Let $\mathcal{B} = ((V, E), \Phi)$ be a BN, κ a V-context, $Q = \{x_1, \ldots, x_k\} \subseteq V$, and $p > 0$. Define $V' = V \uplus \{x^+, x^- \mid x \in Q\} \uplus \{z\}$, where $\uplus$ denotes the disjoint union, and $E' = E \cup \{(x, x^+), (x, x^-) \mid x \in Q\}$. We construct $\mathcal{B}' = ((V', E'), \Phi')$ where Φ' contains $P_{\mathcal{B}'}(v \mid \pi(v)) = P_\mathcal{B}(v \mid \pi(x))$ for all $v \in V$, and $P_{\mathcal{B}'}(z) = p$, $P_{\mathcal{B}'}(x^+ \mid x) = 1$, $P_{\mathcal{B}'}(x^+ \mid \neg x) = 0$, $P_{\mathcal{B}'}(x^- \mid x) = 0$, and $P_{\mathcal{B}'}(x^- \mid \neg x) = 1$ for all $x \in Q$. Let now

$$\mathcal{T} = \{\langle A_{i-1} \sqsubseteq A_i : x_i^+ \rangle, \langle A_{i-1} \sqsubseteq A_i : x_i^- \rangle \mid 1 \leq i \leq k\} \cup$$
$$\{\langle A_k \sqsubseteq B : \kappa \rangle, \langle A_0 \sqsubseteq B : z \rangle\},$$

and $\mathcal{K} = (\mathcal{B}', \mathcal{T})$. It is easy to see that for any V'-context κ', if $\langle A_0 \sqsubseteq_\mathcal{K} B : \kappa \rangle$ and $z \notin \kappa'$, then $\kappa \subseteq \kappa'$ and for every $x \in Q, \{x^+, x^-\} \cap \kappa' \neq \emptyset$. Moreover, by construction $P_\mathcal{B}(z) = p$ and $P_\mathcal{B}(x^+, x^-) = 0$ for all $x \in Q$.

Theorem 20. *Let $\mathcal{B}$ be a BN over V, κ a V-context, $Q \subseteq V$, $p > 0$ and $\mathcal{K}$ the KB built as described above. There is a valuation λ of the variables in Q such that $P_\mathcal{B}(\lambda \cup \kappa) > p$ iff $\{z\}$ is not an mlc for $A_0 \sqsubseteq B$ w.r.t. $\mathcal{K}$.*

From this theorem, and the upper bound described above, we obtain a tight complexity bound for deciding a most likely context.

Corollary 21. *Deciding whether κ is a most likely context is coNP^{PP}-complete.*

If the context κ is a complete valuation, then the complexity of this problem reduces to NP-complete. This is an immediate result of applying the standard chain rule for exact inference, which is in PTIME, and reducing the *most probable explanation* (D-MPE) problem in BNs, which is NP-complete [23].

4   Related Work

The amount of work combining DLs with probabilities is too vast to enumerate here. We mention only the work that relates the closest to our approach, and refer the interested reader to a thorough, although slightly outdated survey [17].

An early attempt for combining BNs and DLs was P-CLASSIC [16], which extends CLASSIC through probability distributions over the interpretation domain. In the same line, in PR-OWL [10] the probabilistic component is interpreted by providing individuals with a probability distribution. As many others in the literature, these approaches differ from our multiple-world semantics, in which we consider a probability distribution over a set of classical DL interpretations.

Other probabilistic extensions of $\mathcal{EL}$ are [18] and [19]. The former introduces probabilities as a concept constructor, while in the latter the probabilities of axioms, which are always assumed to be independent, are implicitly encoded through a weighting function, which is interpreted with a log-linear model. Thus, both formalisms differ greatly from our approach.

DISPONTE [21] considers a multiple-world semantics. The main difference with our approach is that in DISPONTE, all probabilities are assumed to be independent, while we provide a joint probability distribution through the BN. Another minor difference is that $\mathcal{BEL}$ allows for classical consequences whereas DISPONTE does not. Closest to our approach is perhaps the Bayesian extension of DL-Lite called BDL-Lite [11]. Abstracting from the different logical component, BDL-Lite looks almost identical to $\mathcal{BEL}$. There is, however, a subtle but important difference. In our approach, an interpretation $\mathcal{I}$ satisfies a V-GCI $\langle C \sqsubseteq D : \kappa \rangle$ if $\mathcal{V}^{\mathcal{I}}(\kappa) = 1$ implies $C^{\mathcal{I}} \subseteq D^{\mathcal{I}}$. In [11], the authors employ a closed-world assumption over the contexts, where this implication is substituted for an equivalence; i.e., $\mathcal{V}^{\mathcal{I}}(\kappa) = 0$ also implies $C^{\mathcal{I}} \not\subseteq D^{\mathcal{I}}$. The use of such semantics can easily produce inconsistent KBs, which is impossible in $\mathcal{BEL}$.

5 Conclusions

We studied the probabilistic DL $\mathcal{BEL}$, which extends $\mathcal{EL}$ with uncertain contexts based on a BN. Given $\mathcal{BEL}$ KB $\mathcal{K}$, we construct in polynomial time a BN $\mathcal{B}_{\mathcal{K}}$ that encodes all the probabilistic and logical knowledge of $\mathcal{K}$ w.r.t. the signature of the KB. This construction is based on the proof structure, a hypergraph representation of all the traces of any consequence derivation. As a result, we obtain that (i) deciding p-subsumption in $\mathcal{BEL}$ can be reduced to exact inference in $\mathcal{B}_{\mathcal{K}}$ and (ii) one most likely context can be found by computing a valuation of a subset of the variables in $\mathcal{B}_{\mathcal{K}}$ that maximizes the probability of an event. These provide tight complexity bounds for both of the reasoning problems.

While the construction is polynomial on the input KB, the obtained DAG might not preserve all the desired properties of the original BN. For instance, it is known that the efficiency of the BN inference engines depends on the treewidth of the underlying DAG [20]; however, the proof structure used by our construction may increase the treewidth of the graph. One direction of future research will be to try to optimize the reduction by bounding the treewidth and reducing the ammount of nodes added to the graph.

Finally, it should be clear that our construction does not depend on the chosen DL $\mathcal{EL}$, but rather on the fact that a simple polynomial-time consequence-based method can be used to reason with it. It should thus be a simple task to generalize the approach to other consequence-based methods, e.g. [24]. It would also be interesting to generalize the probabilistic component to consider other kinds of probabilistic graphical models [15].

References

1. Baader, F., Brandt, S., Lutz, C.: Pushing the $\mathcal{EL}$ envelope. In: Proc. IJCAI 2005. Morgan Kaufmann (2005)
2. Baader, F., Calvanese, D., McGuinness, D.L., Nardi, D., Patel-Schneider, P.F. (eds.): The Description Logic Handbook: Theory, Implementation, and Applications, 2nd edn. Cambridge University Press (2007)
3. Baader, F., Peñaloza, R.: Automata-based axiom pinpointing. J. of Automated Reasoning 45(2), 91–129 (2010)
4. Baader, F., Peñaloza, R., Suntisrivaraporn, B.: Suntisrivaraporn, B.: Pinpointing in the description logic $\mathcal{EL}^+$. In: Hertzberg, J., Beetz, M., Englert, R. (eds.) KI 2007. LNCS (LNAI), vol. 4667, pp. 52–67. Springer, Heidelberg (2007)
5. Brandt, S.: Polynomial time reasoning in a description logic with existential restrictions, GCI axioms, and—what else? In: Proc. ECAI 2004, pp. 298–302. IOS Press (2004)
6. Ceylan, İ.İ.: Context-Sensitive Bayesian Description Logics. Master's thesis, Dresden University of Technology, Germany (2013)
7. Ceylan, İ.İ., Peñaloza, R.: The Bayesian Description Logic $\mathcal{BEL}$. In: Demri, S., Kapur, D., Weidenbach, C. (eds.) IJCAR 2014. LNCS (LNAI), vol. 8562, pp. 480–494. Springer, Heidelberg (2014)
8. Ceylan, İ.İ., Peñaloza, R.: Bayesian Description Logics. In: Bienvenu, M., Ortiz, M., Rosati, R., Simkus, M. (eds.) Proceedings of the 27th International Workshop on Description Logics (DL 2014). CEUR Workshop Proceedings, vol. 1193, pp. 447–458. CEUR-WS (2014)
9. Cooper, G.F.: The computational complexity of probabilistic inference using Bayesian belief networks (research note). Artif. Intel. 42(2-3), 393–405 (1990)
10. da Costa, P.C.G., Laskey, K.B., Laskey, K.J.: PR-OWL: A Bayesian ontology language for the semantic web. In: da Costa, P.C.G., d'Amato, C., Fanizzi, N., Laskey, K.B., Laskey, K.J., Lukasiewicz, T., Nickles, M., Pool, M. (eds.) URSW 2005 - 2007. LNCS (LNAI), vol. 5327, pp. 88–107. Springer, Heidelberg (2008)
11. d'Amato, C., Fanizzi, N., Lukasiewicz, T.: Tractable reasoning with Bayesian description logics. In: Greco, S., Lukasiewicz, T. (eds.) SUM 2008. LNCS (LNAI), vol. 5291, pp. 146–159. Springer, Heidelberg (2008)
12. Darwiche, A.: Modeling and Reasoning with Bayesian Networks. Cambridge University Press (2009)
13. Homola, M., Serafini, L.: Contextualized knowledge repositories for the semantic web. In: Web Semantics: Science, Services and Agents on the World Wide Web, vol. 12 (2012)
14. Klarman, S., Gutiérrez-Basulto, V.: $\mathcal{ALC}_{\mathcal{ALC}}$: A context description logic. In: Janhunen, T., Niemelä, I. (eds.) JELIA 2010. LNCS, vol. 6341, pp. 208–220. Springer, Heidelberg (2010)
15. Koller, D., Friedman, N.: Probabilistic Graphical Models - Principles and Techniques. MIT Press (2009)
16. Koller, D., Levy, A.Y., Pfeffer, A.: P-classic: A tractable probablistic description logic. In: Proc. 14th National Conference on Artificial Intelligence (AAAI 1997), pp. 390–397. AAAI Press (1997)
17. Lukasiewicz, T., Straccia, U.: Managing uncertainty and vagueness in description logics for the semantic web. J. of Web Semantics 6(4), 291–308 (2008)
18. Lutz, C., Schröder, L.: Probabilistic description logics for subjective uncertainty. In: Lin, F., Sattler, U., Truszczynski, M. (eds.) KR. AAAI Press (2010)

19. Niepert, M., Noessner, J., Stuckenschmidt, H.: Log-linear description logics. In: Walsh, T. (ed.) IJCAI, pp. 2153–2158. IJCAI/AAAI (2011)
20. Pan, H., McMichael, D., Lendjel, M.: Inference algorithms in Bayesian networks and the probanet system. Digital Signal Processing 8(4), 231–243 (1998)
21. Riguzzi, F., Bellodi, E., Lamma, E., Zese, R.: Epistemic and statistical probabilistic ontologies. In: Proc. 8th Int. Workshop on Uncertainty Reasoning for the Semantic Web (URSW 2012), vol. 900, pp. 3–14. CEUR-WS (2012)
22. Roth, D.: On the hardness of approximate reasoning. Artif. Intel. 82(1-2), 273–302 (1996)
23. Shimony, E.S.: Finding MAPs for belief networks is NP-hard. Artif. Intell. 68(2), 399–410 (1994)
24. Simancik, F., Kazakov, Y., Horrocks, I.: Consequence-based reasoning beyond horn ontologies. In: Proc. IJCAI 2011, pp. 1093–1098. IJCAI/AAAI (2011)

Relevant Closure:
A New Form of Defeasible Reasoning for Description Logics

Giovanni Casini, Thomas Meyer, Kodylan Moodley, and Riku Nortjé

Centre for Artificial Intelligence Research (CSIR Meraka and UKZN), South Africa
{gcasini,tmeyer,kmoodley,rnortje}@csir.co.za

Abstract. Among the various proposals for defeasible reasoning for description logics, Rational Closure, a procedure originally defined for propositional logic, turns out to have a number of desirable properties. Not only it is computationally feasible, but it can also be implemented using existing classical reasoners. One of its drawbacks is that it can be seen as too weak from the inferential point of view. To overcome this limitation we introduce in this paper two extensions of Rational Closure: Basic Relevant Closure and Minimal Relevant Closure. As the names suggest, both rely on defining a version of relevance. Our formalisation of relevance in this context is based on the notion of a justification (a minimal subset of sentences implying a given sentence). This is, to our knowledge, the first proposal for defining defeasibility in terms of justifications—a notion that is well-established in the area of ontology debugging. Both Basic and Minimal Relevant Closure increase the inferential power of Rational Closure, giving back intuitive conclusions that cannot be obtained from Rational Closure. We analyse the properties and present algorithms for both Basic and Minimal Relevant Closure, and provide experimental results for both Basic Relevant Closure and Minimal Relevant Closure, comparing it with Rational Closure.

1 Introduction

Description logics, or DLs [1], are central to many modern AI applications because they provide the logical foundations of formal ontologies. The past 20 years have witnessed many attempts to introduce defeasibility in a DL setting, ranging from preferential approaches [8,9,12,18,28] to circumscription [4,5,6,30], amongst others [2,15].

Preferential extensions of DLs based on the *KLM approach* [23,25] are particularly promising for two reasons. Firstly, it provides a formal analysis of defeasible properties, which plays a central role in assessing how intuitive the obtained results are. And secondly, it allows for decision problems to be reduced to classical entailment checking, sometimes without blowing up the computational complexity with respect to the underlying classical case. The main disadvantage of the KLM approach is that the its best known form of inferential closure, Rational Closure [25], can be seen as too weak from an inferential point of view. For example, it does not support the inheritance of defeasible properties. Suppose we know that mammalian and avian red blood cells are vertebrate red blood cells (MRBC ⊑ VRBC, ARBC ⊑ VRBC), that vertebrate red blood cells normally have a cell membrane (VRBC ⋤ ∃hasCM.⊤), that vertebrate red

E. Fermé and J. Leite (Eds.): JELIA 2014, LNAI 8761, pp. 92–106, 2014.

blood cells normally have a nucleus (VRBC ⊑̰ ∃hasN.⊤), but that mammalian red blood cells normally don't (MRBC ⊑̰ ¬∃hasN.⊤). Rational Closure allows us to conclude that avian vertebrate red blood cells normally have a cell membrane (ARBC ⊑̰ ∃hasCM.⊤), but not so for mammalian red blood cells (MRBC ⊑̰ ∃hasCM.⊤). Informally, the former can be concluded because avian red blood cells are a normal type of vertebrate red blood cell, while the latter can't because mammalian red blood cells are an abnormal type of vertebrate red blood cell.

In this paper we propose two new forms of defeasible reasoning to overcome this limitation. Both rely on the formalisation of a version of *relevance*. In resolving conflicts between sets of defeasible statements, we focus only on those that are *relevant* to the conflict, thereby ensuring that statements not involved in the conflict are guaranteed to be retained. For example, we regard VRBC ⊑̰ ∃hasCM.⊤ as *irrelevant* to the conflict between the three statements MRBC ⊑ VRBC, VRBC ⊑̰ ∃hasN.⊤, and MRBC ⊑̰ ¬∃hasN.⊤. As we shall see, this ensures that we can conclude, from both our new forms of defeasible reasoning, that MRBC ⊑̰ ∃hasCM.⊤.

The formal versions of relevance we employ are based on the notion of a *justification* – a minimal set of sentences responsible for a conflict [21]. We regard any sentence occurring in some justification as *potentially relevant* for resolving the conflict. All other sentences are deemed to be irrelevant to the conflict. Both Basic and Minimal Relevant Closure are based on the use of justifications. The difference between the two proposals is related to the way in which the relevant statements are chosen from among the potentially relevant ones.

Here we focus on the DL $\mathcal{ALC}$, although our definitions of Basic and Minimal Relevant Closure are applicable to any DL. The rest of the paper is structured as follows. First, we outline the DL $\mathcal{ALC}$ and how it can be extended to represent defeasible information. Then we discuss existing approaches to defeasible reasoning for DLs, with a focus on Rational Closure. This is followed by presentations of our proposals for Basic Relevant Closure and Minimal Relevant Closure. We then consider the formal properties of our proposals, after which we present experimental results, comparing both Basic Relevant Closure and Minimal Relevant Closure with Rational Closure. Finally, we discuss related work and conclude with some indications of future work.

2 $\mathcal{ALC}$ with Defeasible Subsumption

The language of the description logic $\mathcal{ALC}$ is built up from a finite set of *concept names* $\mathsf{N}_\mathscr{C}$ and a finite set of *role names* $\mathsf{N}_\mathscr{R}$. The set of complex concepts (denoted by $\mathcal{L}$) is built in the usual way according to the rule:

$$C ::= A \mid \top \mid \bot \mid \neg C \mid C \sqcap C \mid C \sqcup C \mid \exists r.C \mid \forall r.C$$

The semantics of $\mathcal{ALC}$ is the standard Tarskian semantics based on interpretations $\mathcal{I}$ of the form $\mathcal{I} := \langle \Delta^{\mathcal{I}}, \cdot^{\mathcal{I}} \rangle$, where the domain $\Delta^{\mathcal{I}}$ is a non-empty set and $\cdot^{\mathcal{I}}$ is an *interpretation function* mapping concept names A in $\mathsf{N}_\mathscr{C}$ to subsets $A^{\mathcal{I}}$ of $\Delta^{\mathcal{I}}$ and role names r in $\mathsf{N}_\mathscr{R}$ to binary relations $r^{\mathcal{I}}$ over $\Delta^{\mathcal{I}} \times \Delta^{\mathcal{I}}$.

Given $C, D \in \mathcal{L}$, $C \sqsubseteq D$ is a *(classical) subsumption*. An $\mathcal{ALC}$ *TBox* $\mathcal{T}$ is a finite set of classical subsumptions. An interpretation $\mathcal{I}$ *satisfies* $C \sqsubseteq D$ iff $C^{\mathcal{I}} \subseteq D^{\mathcal{I}}$.

Entailment of $C \sqsubseteq D$ by $\mathcal{T}$ is defined in the standard (Tarskian) way. For more details on DLs the reader is referred to the Description Logic Handbook [1].

For $\mathcal{ALC}$ with defeasible subsumption, or $\mathcal{ALC}(\underset{\sim}{\sqsubseteq})$, we also allow *defeasible subsumptions* of the form $C \underset{\sim}{\sqsubseteq} D$, collected in a defeasible TBox, or DBox (a finite set of defeasible subsumptions) . The semantics for $\mathcal{ALC}(\underset{\sim}{\sqsubseteq})$ is obtained by augmenting every classical interpretation with an ordering on its domain [8,18]. A ranked interpretation is a structure $\mathcal{R} = \langle \Delta^{\mathcal{R}}, \cdot^{\mathcal{R}}, \prec_{\mathcal{R}} \rangle$, where $\langle \Delta^{\mathcal{R}}, \cdot^{\mathcal{R}} \rangle$ is a DL interpretation and $\prec_{\mathcal{R}}$ is a modular ordering on $\Delta^{\mathcal{R}}$ satisfying the smoothness condition (for every $C \in \mathcal{L}$, if $C^{\mathcal{R}} \neq \emptyset$ then $\min_{\prec_{\mathcal{R}}}(C^{\mathcal{R}}) \neq \emptyset$), and where $\prec_{\mathcal{R}}$ is modular iff there is a ranking function $rk : X \longrightarrow \mathbb{N}$ s.t. for every $x, y \in \Delta^{\mathcal{R}}$, $x \prec_{\mathcal{R}} y$ iff $rk(x) < rk(y)$. A defeasible subsumption $C \underset{\sim}{\sqsubseteq} D$ is satisfied in $\mathcal{R}$ iff $\min_{\prec_{\mathcal{R}}}(C^{\mathcal{R}}) \subseteq D^{\mathcal{R}}$. Intuitively $C \underset{\sim}{\sqsubseteq} D$ is satisfied by $\mathcal{R}$ whenever the *most normal* Cs are also Ds. It is easy to see that every ranked interpretation $\mathcal{R}$ satisfies $C \sqsubseteq D$ iff $\mathcal{R}$ satisfies $C \sqcap \neg D \underset{\sim}{\sqsubseteq} \bot$. That is, classical information can "masquerade" as defeasible information.

3   Reasoning with Defeasible Knowledge Bases

From a KR perspective it is important to obtain an appropriate form of defeasible entailment for $\mathcal{ALC}(\underset{\sim}{\sqsubseteq})$. We shall deal with (defeasible) knowledge bases $\mathcal{K} = \langle \mathcal{T}, \mathcal{D} \rangle$, where $\mathcal{T}$ is a (classical) finite TBox and $\mathcal{D}$ a finite DBox. Given such a KB, the goal is to determine what (classical and defeasible) subsumption statements ought to follow from it. An obvious first attempt is to use the standard Tarskian notion of entailment applied to ranked interpretations: $\mathcal{K}$ *preferentially entails* $C \underset{\sim}{\sqsubseteq} D$ iff every ranked interpretation satisfying all elements of $\mathcal{K}$ also satisfies $C \underset{\sim}{\sqsubseteq} D$. However, it is known that this construction (known as Preferential Entailment) suffers from a number of drawbacks [25]. Firstly, it is *monotonic*—if $C \underset{\sim}{\sqsubseteq} D$ is in the Preferential Entailment of $\mathcal{K}$, then it is also in the Preferential Entailment of every $\mathcal{K}' = \langle \mathcal{T}', \mathcal{D}' \rangle$ such that $\mathcal{T} \subseteq \mathcal{T}'$ and $\mathcal{D} \subseteq \mathcal{D}'$. Secondly it is inferentially too weak—it does not support the inheritance of defeasible properties. An alternative to Preferential Entailment, first proposed by Lehmann et al. for the propositional case [25], and adapted to the DL case by Giordano et al. [17,16] and Britz et al. [9], is that of *Rational Closure*. It is inferentially stronger than Preferential Entailment, is not monotonic, and has (limited) support for the inheritance of defeasible properties. An elegant semantic description of Rational Closure was recently provided by Giordano et al. for both the propositional case [19] and for $\mathcal{ALC}(\underset{\sim}{\sqsubseteq})$ [17,16]. Our focus here is on an algorithm for Rational Closure for $\mathcal{ALC}(\underset{\sim}{\sqsubseteq})$, initially proposed by Casini and Straccia [12] and subsequently refined and implemented by Britz et al. [7]. A useful feature of the algorithm is that it reduces Rational Closure for $\mathcal{ALC}(\underset{\sim}{\sqsubseteq})$ to classical entailment checking for $\mathcal{ALC}$. Below we define Rational Closure and present the algorithm.

$C \in \mathcal{L}$ is said to be *exceptional* for a knowledge base $\mathcal{K}$ iff $\top \underset{\sim}{\sqsubseteq} \neg C$ is preferentially entailed by $\mathcal{K}$. Exceptionality checking can be reduced to classical entailment checking.

Proposition 1. *Britz et al. [7]: For a KB* $\mathcal{K} = \langle \mathcal{T}, \mathcal{D} \rangle$, *let* $\overline{\mathcal{D}} = \{\neg D \sqcup E \mid D \underset{\sim}{\sqsubseteq} E \in \mathcal{D}\}$. *For every* $C \in \mathcal{L}$, $\top \underset{\sim}{\sqsubseteq} \neg C$ *is preferentially entailed by* $\mathcal{K}$ *iff* $\mathcal{T} \models \bigsqcap \overline{\mathcal{D}} \sqsubseteq \neg C$.

Exceptionality is used to build up a sequence of *exceptionality sets* $E_0, E_1, \ldots$, and from this, an *exceptionality ranking* of concepts and defeasible subsumptions. Let

$\mathcal{E}_{\mathcal{T}}(\mathcal{D}) := \{C \mathrel{\reflectbox{$\sqsubseteq$}} D \in \mathcal{D} \mid \mathcal{T} \models \bigsqcap \overline{\mathcal{D}} \sqsubseteq \neg C\}$. Let $E_0 := \mathcal{D}$, and for $i > 0$, let $E_i := \mathcal{E}_{\mathcal{T}}(E_{i-1})$. It is easy to see that there is a smallest n such that $E_n = E_{n+1}$. The rank $r_{\mathcal{K}}(C)$ of $C \in \mathcal{L}$ is the smallest number r such that C is *not* exceptional for E_r. If C is exceptional for all E_i (for $i \geq 0$) then $r_{\mathcal{K}}(C) = \infty$. The rank $r_{\mathcal{K}}(C \mathrel{\reflectbox{$\sqsubseteq$}} D)$ of any $C \mathrel{\reflectbox{$\sqsubseteq$}} D$ is the rank $r_{\mathcal{K}}(C)$ of its antecedent C.

Definition 1. *Lehmann et al. [25], Britz et al. [9]: $C \mathrel{\reflectbox{$\sqsubseteq$}} D$ is in the Rational Closure of $\mathcal{K}$ iff $r_{\mathcal{K}}(C) < r_{\mathcal{K}}(C \sqcap \neg D)$ or $r_{\mathcal{K}}(C) = \infty$.*

Having defeasible subsumptions with infinite rank in the DBox is problematic from an algorithmic point of view because it does not allow for a clear separation of classical information (in the TBox $\mathcal{T}$) and defeasible information (in the DBox $\mathcal{D}$) in a knowledge base $\mathcal{K}$.

Definition 2. *A knowledge base $\mathcal{K} = \langle \mathcal{T}, \mathcal{D} \rangle$ is well-separated iff $r_{\mathcal{K}}(C \mathrel{\reflectbox{$\sqsubseteq$}} D) \neq \infty$ for every $C \mathrel{\reflectbox{$\sqsubseteq$}} D \in \mathcal{D}$.*

We will frequently assume knowledge bases to be well-separated. It is worth pointing out that this assumption is not a restriction of any kind, since every knowledge base can be converted into a well-separated one, as shown by Britz et al. [7].

Below we present a high-level version of the algorithm for Rational Closure implemented by Casini et al. [11]. It takes as input a *well-separated* KB $\mathcal{K} = \langle \mathcal{T}, \mathcal{D} \rangle$ and a query $C \mathrel{\reflectbox{$\sqsubseteq$}} D$, and returns **true** iff the query is in the Rational Closure of $\mathcal{K}$. It also assumes the existence of a *partition* procedure which computes the ranks of the subsumptions in $\mathcal{D}$ and partitions $\mathcal{D}$ into n equivalence classes according to rank: $i = 0, \ldots n$, $\mathcal{D}_i := \{C \mathrel{\reflectbox{$\sqsubseteq$}} D \mid r_{\mathcal{K}}(C) - i\}$. Note that, because $\mathcal{K}$ is well-separated, none of the elements of $\mathcal{D}$ will have infinite rank. The *partition* procedure performs at most a polynomial number of classical entailment checks to compute the ranks. The remaining part of the algorithm performs a linear number of classical entailment checks (in the size of $\mathcal{D}$).

Algorithm 1. Rational Closure

Input: A well-separated KB $\langle \mathcal{T}, \mathcal{D} \rangle$ and a query $C \mathrel{\reflectbox{$\sqsubseteq$}} D$
Output: **true** iff $C \mathrel{\reflectbox{$\sqsubseteq$}} D$ is in the Rational Closure of $\langle \mathcal{T}, \mathcal{D} \rangle$
1 $(\mathcal{D}_0, \ldots, \mathcal{D}_n, n) := partition(\mathcal{D})$;
2 $i := 0; \mathcal{D}' := \mathcal{D}$;
3 **while** $\mathcal{T} \models \bigsqcap \overline{\mathcal{D}'} \sqsubseteq \neg C$ **and** $\mathcal{D}' \neq \emptyset$ **do**
4   $\quad \lfloor \; \mathcal{D}' := \mathcal{D}' \setminus \mathcal{D}_i; i := i + 1;$
5 **return** $\mathcal{T} \models \overline{\mathcal{D}'} \sqcap C \sqsubseteq D$;

Informally, the algorithm keeps on removing defeasible subsumptions from $\mathcal{D}$, starting with the lowest rank, and proceeding rank by rank, until it finds the first DBox $\mathcal{D}'$ for which C is no longer exceptional. $C \mathrel{\reflectbox{$\sqsubseteq$}} D$ is then taken to be in the Rational Closure of $\mathcal{K}$ iff $\mathcal{T} \models \overline{\mathcal{D}'} \sqcap C \sqsubseteq D$. Observe that, since every classical subsumption $C \sqsubseteq D$ can be rewritten as a defeasible subsumption $C \sqcap \neg D \mathrel{\reflectbox{$\sqsubseteq$}} \bot$, Algorithm 1 is, indirectly, able to deal with classical queries (of the form $C \sqsubseteq D$) as well. The same holds for the other algorithms defined in this paper.

To see how the algorithm works, consider the following example, which we use as a running example in the rest of the paper.

Example 1. We know that both avian red blood cells and mammalian red blood cells are vertebrate red blood cells, and that vertebrate red blood cells normally have a cell membrane. We also know that vertebrate red blood cells normally have a nucleus, but that mammalian red blood cells normally don't. We can represent this information in the KB $\mathcal{K}^1 = \langle \mathcal{T}^1, \mathcal{D}^1 \rangle$ with $\mathcal{T}^1 = \{\text{ARBC} \sqsubseteq \text{VRBC}, \text{MRBC} \sqsubseteq \text{VRBC}\}$ and $\mathcal{D}^1 = \{\text{VRBC} \sqsubseteq \exists\text{hasCM}.\top, \text{VRBC} \sqsubseteq \exists\text{hasN}.\top, \text{MRBC} \sqsubseteq \neg\exists\text{hasN}.\top\}$.

We get $\mathcal{D}_0^1 = \{\text{VRBC} \sqsubseteq \exists\text{hasN}.\top, \text{VRBC} \sqsubseteq \exists\text{hasCM}.\top\}$, and $\mathcal{D}_1^1 = \{\text{MRBC} \sqsubseteq \neg\exists\text{hasN}.\top\}$. Given the query $\text{ARBC} \sqsubseteq \text{hasCM}.\top$, $\mathcal{D}' = \mathcal{D}^1$ in line 5, from which it follows that the query is in the Rational Closure of $\mathcal{K}^1$. Given the query $\text{MRBC} \sqsubseteq \text{hasCM}.\top$, however, we get $\mathcal{D}' = \mathcal{D}_1^1$ in line 5, and so this query is not in the Rational Closure of $\mathcal{K}^1$. An analysis of the latter query turns out to be very instructive for our purposes here. Observe that, to obtain $\mathcal{D}'$, the algorithm removes all elements of $\mathcal{D}_0^1 = \{\text{VRBC} \sqsubseteq \exists\text{hasN}.\top, \text{VRBC} \sqsubseteq \exists\text{hasCM}.\top\}$ from $\mathcal{D}^1$. Informally, the motivation for the removal of $\text{VRBC} \sqsubseteq \exists\text{hasN}.\top$ is easy to explain: together with $\text{MRBC} \sqsubseteq \text{VRBC}$ and $\text{MRBC} \sqsubseteq \neg\exists\text{hasN}.\top$ it is responsible for MRBC being exceptional. It is less clear, intuitively, why the defeasible subsumption $\text{VRBC} \sqsubseteq \exists\text{hasCM}.\top$ has to be removed. One could make the case that since it plays no part in the exceptionality of MRBC, it should be retained. As we shall discuss in the next section, this argument forms the basis of an approach to defeasible reasoning based on the *relevance* of defeasible subsumptions.

4   Relevant Closure

Here we outline our proposal for a version of defeasible reasoning based on relevance. The principle is an obvious abstraction of the argument outlined at the end of the previous section—identify those defeasible subsumptions deemed to be *relevant* w.r.t. a given query, and consider only these ones as being eligible for removal during the execution of the Rational Closure algorithm. More precisely, suppose we have identified $R \subseteq \mathcal{D}$ as the defeasible subsumptions relevant to the query $C \sqsubseteq D$. First we ensure that all elements of $\mathcal{D}$ that are *not* relevant to the query are *not* eligible for removal during execution of the Rational Closure algorithm. For $R \subseteq \mathcal{D}$ let $Rel^{\mathcal{K}}(R) := \langle R, R^- \rangle$, where $R^- = \mathcal{D} \setminus R$. That is, R^- is the set of all the defeasible subsumptions that are not eligible for removal since they are not relevant w.r.t. the query $C \sqsubseteq D$. Then we apply a variant of Algorithm 1 (the Rational Closure algorithm) to $\mathcal{K}$ in which the elements of R^- are not allowed to be eliminated. The basic algorithm for *Relevant Closure* is outlined below (Algorithm 2). Note that, as in the case of Algorithm 1, we assume that the knowledge base is well-separated. We say that a defeasible subsumption $C \sqsubseteq D$ is in the *Relevant Closure* of (a well-separated) $\mathcal{K}$ w.r.t. a set of relevant defeasible subsumptions R iff the Relevant Closure algorithm (Algorithm 2) returns **true**, with $\mathcal{K}$, $C \sqsubseteq D$, and $Rel^{\mathcal{K}}(R)$ as input.

For Example 1, an appropriate choice for R would be the set $\{\text{VRBC} \sqsubseteq \exists\text{hasN}.\top, \text{MRBC} \sqsubseteq \neg\exists\text{hasN}.\top\}$ since these are the two defeasible subsumptions responsible for MRBC being exceptional (w.r.t. $\mathcal{K}$). If $R = \{\text{VRBC} \sqsubseteq \exists\text{hasN}.\top, \text{MRBC} \sqsubseteq \neg\exists\text{hasN}.\top\}$

Algorithm 2. Relevant Closure

Input: A well-separated KB $\langle \mathcal{T}, \mathcal{D} \rangle$, a query $C \eqslantless D$, and the partition
$Rel^{\mathcal{K}}(R) = \langle R, R^{-} \rangle$
Output: **true** iff $C \eqslantless D$ is in the Relevant Closure of $\langle \mathcal{T}, \mathcal{D} \rangle$
1 $(\mathcal{D}_0, \ldots, \mathcal{D}_n, n) := partition(\mathcal{D})$;
2 $i := 0$; $R' := R$;
3 **while** $\mathcal{T} \models \bigsqcap \overline{R^-} \sqcap \bigsqcap \overline{R'} \sqsubseteq \neg C$ **and** $R' \neq \emptyset$ **do**
4 $\quad \lfloor \quad R' := R' \setminus (\mathcal{D}_i \cap R); i := i + 1$;
5 **return** $\mathcal{T} \models \bigsqcap \overline{R^-} \sqcap \bigsqcap \overline{R'} \sqcap C \sqsubseteq D$;

---

and $R^- = \{\text{VRBC} \eqslantless \exists \text{hasCM}.\top\}$ (that is, it is information not eligible for removal), it is easy to see that we can derive $\text{MRBC} \eqslantless \text{hasCM}.\top$, since $\{\text{ARBC} \sqsubseteq \text{VRBC}, \text{MRBC} \sqsubseteq \text{VRBC}\} \models (\neg \text{VRBC} \sqcup \text{hasCM}.\top) \sqcap (\neg \text{MRBC} \sqcap \neg \exists \text{hasN}.\top) \sqcap \text{MRBC} \sqsubseteq \text{hasCM}.\top$.

4.1 Basic Relevant Closure

The explanation above still leaves open the question of how to define relevance w.r.t. a query. The key insight in doing so, is to *associate relevance with the subsumptions responsible for making the antecedent of a query exceptional*. We shall refer to such sets of subsumptions as *justifications*.

Definition 3. *For* $\mathcal{K} = \langle \mathcal{T}, \mathcal{D} \rangle$, $\mathcal{J} \subseteq \mathcal{D}$, *and* $C \subset \mathcal{L}$, $\mathcal{J}$ *is a* C-*justification w.r.t.* $\mathcal{K}$ *iff* C *is exceptional for* $\langle \mathcal{T}, \mathcal{J} \rangle$ *(i.e.* $\top \eqslantless \neg C$ *is in the Preferential Entailment of* $\langle \mathcal{T}, \mathcal{J} \rangle$) *and for every* $\mathcal{J}' \subset \mathcal{J}$, C *is not exceptional for* $\mathcal{J}'$.

The choice of the term *justification* is not accidental, since it closely mirrors the notion of a justification for classical DLs, where a justification for a sentence α is a minimal set implying α [21]; it corresponds to the notion of *kernel*, used a lot in base-revision literature [20]. Given the correspondence between exceptionality and classical entailment in Proposition 1, the link is even closer.

Corollary 1. $\mathcal{J}$ *is a* C-*justification w.r.t.* $\mathcal{K} = \langle \mathcal{T}, \mathcal{D} \rangle$ *iff* $\mathcal{J} \subseteq \mathcal{D}$, $\mathcal{T} \models \overline{\mathcal{J}} \sqsubseteq \neg C$, *and for every* $\mathcal{J}' \subset \mathcal{J}$, $\mathcal{T} \not\models \overline{\mathcal{J}'} \sqsubseteq \neg C$.

This places us in a position to define our first relevance-based version of defeasible reasoning. We identify *relevance* for a query $C \eqslantless D$ with all subsumptions occurring in some C-justification for $\mathcal{K}$. For $C \in \mathcal{L}$, and a KB $\mathcal{K}$, let $\mathcal{J}^{\mathcal{K}}(C) = \{\mathcal{J} \mid \mathcal{J}$ is a C-justification w.r.t. $\mathcal{K}\}$.

Definition 4. $C \eqslantless D$ *is in the Basic Relevant Closure of* $\mathcal{K}$ *iff it is in the Relevant Closure of* $\mathcal{K}$ *w.r.t.* $\bigcup \mathcal{J}^{\mathcal{K}}(C)$.

For Example 1, $\mathcal{J} = \{\text{VRBC} \eqslantless \exists \text{hasN}.\top, \text{MRBC} \eqslantless \neg \exists \text{hasN}.\top\}$ is the one MRBC-justification for D^1, and $\text{MRBC} \eqslantless \text{hasCM}.\top$ is in the Basic Relevant Closure of $\mathcal{K}^1$ as seen above, since the axiom $\text{VRBC} \eqslantless \exists \text{hasCM}.\top$ is not in any MRBC-justification and is therefore deemed to be irrelevant w.r.t. the query.

To summarise, unlike Rational Closure, Basic Relevant Closure ensures that the defeasible property of having a cell membrane is inherited by mammalian red blood cells from vertebrate red blood cells, even though mammalian red blood cells are abnormal vertebrate red blood cells (in the sense of not having a nucleus).

4.2   Minimal Relevant Closure

Although Basic Relevant Closure is inferentially stronger than Rational Closure, it can still be viewed as inferentially too weak, since it views *all* subsumptions occurring in some C-justifications as relevant, and therefore eligible for removal. In particular, it does not make proper use of the *ranks* of the subsumptions in a DBox. In this section we strengthen the notion of relevance by identifying it with the subsumptions of lowest rank occurring in every C-justification (instead of all subsumptions occurring in some C-justification).

Definition 5. *For* $\mathcal{J} \subseteq \mathcal{D}$, *let* $\mathcal{J}^{\mathcal{K}}_{\min} := \{D \precsim E \mid r_{\mathcal{K}}(D) \leq r_{\mathcal{K}}(F) \text{ for every } F \precsim G \in \mathcal{J}\}$. *For* $C \in \mathcal{L}$, *let* $\mathcal{J}^{\mathcal{K}}_{\min}(C) := \bigcup_{\mathcal{J} \in \mathcal{J}^{\mathcal{K}}(C)} \mathcal{J}^{\mathcal{K}}_{\min}$.

The intuition can be explained as follows. To make an antecedent C non-exceptional w.r.t. $\mathcal{K}$, it is necessary to remove at least one element of every C-justification from $\mathcal{D}$. At the same time, the ranking of subsumptions provides guidance on which subsumptions ought to be removed first (subsumptions with lower ranks are removed first). Combining this, the subsumptions eligible for removal are taken to be precisely those that occur as the lowest ranked subsumptions in some C-justification.

Definition 6. $C \precsim D$ *is in the Minimal Relevant Closure of* $\mathcal{K}$ *iff it is in the Relevant Closure of* $\mathcal{K}$ *w.r.t.* $\bigcup \mathcal{J}^{\mathcal{D}}_{\min}(C)$.

To see how Minimal Relevant Closure differs from Basic Relevant Closure, we extend Example 1 as follows.

Example 2. In addition to the information in Example 1, we also know that mammalian sickle cells are mammalian red blood cells, that mammalian red blood cells normally have a bioconcave shape, but that mammalian sickle cells normally do not (they normally have a crescent shape). We represent this new information as $\mathcal{T}^2 = \{MSC \sqsubseteq MRBC\}$ and $\mathcal{D}^2 = \{MRBC \precsim \exists hasS.BC, MSC \precsim \neg\exists hasS.BC\}$.

To answer the query of whether mammalian sickle cells don't have a nucleus (that is, whether $MSC \precsim \neg\exists hasN.\top$) given a KB $\mathcal{K}^2 = \langle \mathcal{T}, \mathcal{D} \rangle$, with $\mathcal{T} = \mathcal{T}^1 \cup \mathcal{T}^2$ and $\mathcal{D} = \mathcal{D}^1 \cup \mathcal{D}^2$, note that there are two MSC-justifications for $\mathcal{K}$: $\mathcal{J}^1 = \{MRBC \precsim \neg\exists hasN.\top, VRBC \precsim \exists hasN.\top\}$, and $\mathcal{J}^2 = \{MRBC \precsim \exists hasS.BC, MSC \precsim \neg\exists hasS.BC\}$. Therefore $MSC \precsim \neg\exists hasN.\top$ is in the Basic Relevant Closure of $\mathcal{K}^2$ iff it is in the Relevant Closure of $\mathcal{K}$ w.r.t. R, where R consists of all of $\mathcal{D}$ except for the only irrelevant axiom $VRBC \precsim \exists hasCM.\top$ (the only axiom that does not appear in any MSC-justification). It turns out that $MSC \precsim \neg\exists hasN.\top$ is not in the Basic Relevant Closure of $\mathcal{K}^2$ since $MRBC \precsim \neg\exists hasN.\top$ is viewed as relevant w.r.t. the query.

To check if $MSC \precsim \neg\exists hasN.\top$ is in the Minimal Relevant Closure, note that $\mathcal{J}^1_{\min} = \{VRBC \precsim \exists hasN.\top\}$, and $\mathcal{J}^2_{\min} = \{MRBC \precsim \exists hasS.BC\}$. Thus, $MSC \precsim \neg\exists hasN.\top$ is in the Minimal Relevant Closure of $\mathcal{K}$ iff it is in the Relevant Closure of $\mathcal{K}$ w.r.t. R, where R consists of everything in $\mathcal{D}$ except for the defeasible subsumptions in the set $\{\mathsf{VRBC} \sqsubseteq \exists\mathsf{hasCM}.\top, \mathsf{MRBC} \sqsubseteq \neg\exists\mathsf{hasN}.\top, \mathsf{MSC} \sqsubseteq \neg\exists\mathsf{hasS}.\mathsf{BC}\}$. And this is the case, since $\mathsf{MRBC} \sqsubseteq \neg\exists\mathsf{hasN}.\top$ is now deemed to be *irrelevant* w.r.t. the query.

To summarise, unlike the case for Rational Closure and Basic Relevant Closure, using Minimal Relevant Closure we can conclude that mammalian sickle cells normally don't have a nucleus. The main reason is that, although Minimal Relevant Closure recognises that mammalian sickle cells are abnormal mammalian red blood cells, the information that mammalian red bloods cells do not have a nucleus is deemed to be irrelevant to this abnormality, which means that this defeasible property of mammalian red blood cells are inherited by mammalian sickle cells.

5 Properties of Relevant Closure

The previous sections contain a number of examples showing that both Basic and Minimal Relevant Closure provide better results than Rational Closure. The purpose of this section is to provide a more systematic evaluation. We commence by showing that Minimal Relevant Closure is inferentially stronger than Basic Relevant Closure which, in turn, is inferentially stronger than Rational Closure.

Proposition 2. *If $C \sqsubseteq D$ is in the Rational Closure of a knowledge base $\mathcal{K}$, then it is in the Basic Relevant Closure of $\mathcal{K}$ (the converse does not always hold). If $C \sqsubseteq D$ is in the Basic Relevant Closure of $\mathcal{K}$, then it is in the Minimal Relevant Closure of $\mathcal{K}$ (the converse does not always hold).*

It is known that Rational Closure and Preferential Entailment are equivalent w.r.t. the classical subsumptions they contain. The next result shows that this result extends to Basic and Minimal Relevant Closure as well.

Proposition 3. *$C \sqsubseteq D$ is in the Minimal Relevant Closure of a knowledge base $\mathcal{K}$, iff it is in the Basic Relevant Closure of $\mathcal{K}$, iff it is in the Rational Closure of $\mathcal{K}$ (iff it is in the Preferential Entailment of $\mathcal{K}$).*

One of the reasons Proposition 3 is important is that it ensures that Basic and Minimal Relevant Closure are proper generalisations of classical entailment: If $\mathcal{K} = \langle \mathcal{T}, \mathcal{D} \rangle$ is reduced to classical subsumptions—that is, if $\mathcal{K}$ is well-separated and $\mathcal{D} = \emptyset$—then Minimal and Basic Relevant Closure coincide with classical entailment.

From a practical point of view, one of the main advantages of both Basic and Minimal Relevant Closure is that, as for Rational Closure, their computation can be reduced to a sequence of classical entailment checks, thereby making it possible to employ existing optimised classical DL reasoners for this purpose. Below we provide high-level algorithms for both versions based on this principle.

The algorithm for Basic Relevant Closure takes as input a well-separated KB $\mathcal{K} = \langle \mathcal{T}, \mathcal{D} \rangle$, a query $C \sqsubseteq D$, and uses the *partition* procedure which partitions the elements of $\mathcal{D}$ according to ranks. It also assumes the existence of a *justifications* procedure which takes as input a DBox $\mathcal{K}$, a concept C, and returns the m C-justifications w.r.t. $\mathcal{K}$. It returns **true** iff the query is in the Basic Relevant Closure of $\mathcal{K}$.

Algorithm 3. Basic Relevant Closure

Input: A well-separated $\mathcal{K} = \langle \mathcal{T}, \mathcal{D} \rangle$ and a query $C \mathrel{\rlap{\raise{0.5ex}{$\sim$}}{\sqsubset}} D$
Output: **true** iff $C \mathrel{\rlap{\raise{0.5ex}{$\sim$}}{\sqsubset}} D$ is in the Basic Relevant Closure of $\mathcal{K}$
1 $(\mathcal{D}_0, \ldots, \mathcal{D}_n, n) := partition(\mathcal{D})$;
2 $(\mathcal{J}_1, \ldots, \mathcal{J}_m, m) := justifications(\mathcal{K}, C)$;
3 $\mathcal{J} := \bigcup_{j=1}^{j=m} \mathcal{J}_j$; $i := 0$; $\mathcal{D}' := \mathcal{D}$; $X := \emptyset$;
4 **while** $X \cap \mathcal{J}_j = \emptyset$ *for some* $j = 1, \ldots, m$ **and** $\mathcal{D}' \neq \emptyset$ **do**
5 $\quad\mid\quad \mathcal{D}' := \mathcal{D}' \setminus (\mathcal{J} \cap \mathcal{D}_i)$;
6 $\quad\mid\quad X := X \cup (\mathcal{J} \cap \mathcal{D}_i)$; $i := i + 1$;
7 **return** $\mathcal{T} \models \overline{\mathcal{D}'} \sqcap C \sqsubseteq D$;

In terms of computational complexity, the big difference between Algorithm 1 and Algorithm 3 is that the latter needs to compute all C-justifications which can involve an exponential number of classical entailment checks [21]. This is in contrast to Algorithm 1 which needs to perform at most a polynomial number of entailment checks. But, since entailment checking for $\mathcal{ALC}$ is EXPTIME-complete, computing the Basic Relevant Closure is EXPTIME-complete as well. From a practical perspective, Horridge [21] has shown that computing justifications is frequently feasible even for large ontologies. We address this issue again in the sections on experimental results and future work.

Next we provide a high-level algorithm for computing Minimal Relevant Closure. Like Algorithm 3, it takes as input a well-separated KB $\mathcal{K} = \langle \mathcal{T}, \mathcal{D} \rangle$ and a query

---

Algorithm 4. Minimal Relevant Closure

Input: A well-separated $\mathcal{K} = \langle \mathcal{T}, \mathcal{D} \rangle$ and a query $C \mathrel{\rlap{\raise{0.5ex}{$\sim$}}{\sqsubset}} D$
Output: **true** iff $C \mathrel{\rlap{\raise{0.5ex}{$\sim$}}{\sqsubset}} D$ is in the Minimal Relevant Closure of $\mathcal{K}$
1 $(\mathcal{D}_0, \ldots, \mathcal{D}_n, n) := partition(\mathcal{D})$;
2 $(\mathcal{J}_1, \ldots, \mathcal{J}_m, m) := justifications(\mathcal{K}, C)$;
3 **for** $j := 1$ *to* m **do**
4 $\quad\mid\quad k := min(\mathcal{D}_0, \ldots, \mathcal{D}_n, \mathcal{J}_j)$;
5 $\quad\mid\quad \mathcal{M}_j := \mathcal{J}_j \cap \mathcal{D}_k$;
6 $\mathcal{M} := \bigcup_{j=1}^{j=m} \mathcal{M}_j$; $i := 0$; $\mathcal{D}' := \mathcal{D}$; $X := \emptyset$;
7 **while** $X \cap \mathcal{M}_j = \emptyset$ *for some* $j = 1, \ldots, m$ **and** $\mathcal{D}' \neq \emptyset$ **do**
8 $\quad\mid\quad \mathcal{D}' := \mathcal{D}' \setminus (\mathcal{M} \cap \mathcal{D}_i)$;
9 $\quad\mid\quad X := X \cup (\mathcal{M} \cap \mathcal{D}_i)$; $i := i + 1$;
10 **return** $\mathcal{T} \models \overline{\mathcal{D}'} \sqcap C \sqsubseteq D$;

$C \mathrel{\rlap{\raise{0.5ex}{$\sim$}}{\sqsubset}} D$, uses the *partition* procedure which partitions the elements of $\mathcal{D}$ according to ranks, and uses the *justifications* procedure which takes as input $\mathcal{K}$, a concept C, and returns the m C-justifications w.r.t. $\mathcal{K}$. In addition, it assumes the existence of a *min* procedure which takes as input the partitioned version of $\mathcal{D}$ and any subset of $\mathcal{D}$, say Y, and returns the smallest j such that $Y \cap \mathcal{D}_j \neq \emptyset$.

Since the only real difference between Algorithm 3 and Algorithm 4 is the use of the *min* procedure, which does not involve any classical entailment check, it follows easily that computing the Minimal Relevant Closure is EXPTIME-complete as well.

To conclude this section we evaluate Basic and Minimal Relevant Closure against the KLM properties of Kraus et al. [23] for rational preferential consequence, translated to DLs.

$$(\text{Cons}) \; \top \not\sqsubset_{\approx} \bot \quad (\text{Ref}) \; C \sqsubset_{\approx} C$$

$$(\text{LLE}) \; \frac{\models C \equiv D, \; C \sqsubset_{\approx} E}{D \sqsubset_{\approx} E} \quad (\text{And}) \; \frac{C \sqsubset_{\approx} D, \; C \sqsubset_{\approx} E}{C \sqsubset_{\approx} D \sqcap E}$$

$$(\text{Or}) \; \frac{C \sqsubset_{\approx} E, \; D \sqsubset_{\approx} E}{C \sqcup D \sqsubset_{\approx} E} \quad (\text{RW}) \; \frac{C \sqsubset_{\approx} D, \; \models D \sqsubseteq E}{C \sqsubset_{\approx} E}$$

$$(\text{CM}) \; \frac{C \sqsubset_{\approx} D, \; C \sqsubset_{\approx} E}{C \sqcap D \sqsubset_{\approx} E} \quad (\text{RM}) \; \frac{C \sqsubset_{\approx} E, \; C \not\sqsubset_{\approx} \neg D}{C \sqcap D \sqsubset_{\approx} E}$$

With the exceptions of Cons, these have been discussed at length in the literature for both the propositional and the DL cases [23,25,24,18] and we shall not do so here. Semantically, Cons corresponds to the requirement that ranked interpretations have non-empty domains. Although these are actually properties of the defeasible subsumption relation $\sqsubset_{\approx}$, they can be viewed as properties of a closure operator as well. That is, we would say that Basic Relevant Closure satisfies the property Ref, for example, whenever $C \sqsubset_{\approx} C$ is in the Basic Relevant Closure of $\mathcal{D}$ for every DBox $\mathcal{D}$ and every $C \in \mathcal{L}$.

Proposition 4. *Both Basic Relevant Closure and Minimal Relevant Closure satisfy the properties Cons, Ref, LLE, And, and RW, and do not satisfy Or, CM, and RM.*

While Basic Relevant Closure and Minimal Relevant Closure are inferentially stronger than Rational Closure, and behave well in terms of the examples discussed, their failure to satisfy the formal properties Or, CM and RM is a drawback. We are currently investigating refinements of both Basic Relevant Closure and Minimal Relevant Closure that will satisfy these properties.

6 Experimental Results

In this section we report on preliminary experiments to determine the practical performance of Basic and Minimal Relevant Closure relative to Rational Closure. Our algorithms were implemented and applied to the generated dataset employed by Casini et al. [11]. The DBoxes are binned according to *percentage defeasibility* (ratio of the number of defeasible vs. classical subsumptions) in increments of 10 from 10 to 100, and vary uniformly in size between 150 and 5150 axioms. In addition to the generated DBoxes, we randomly generated a set of DBox queries using terms in their signatures. The task is then to check whether a query is in the Basic (resp. Minimal) Relevant Closure of the DBox and plot its performance relative to Rational Closure. The rankings of each DBox were precomputed because determining the ranking can be viewed as an offline process, and is not the central interest here. Experiments were performed on an Intel Core i7 machine with 4GB of memory allocated to the JVM (Java Virtual Machine). The underlying classical DL reasoning implementation used in our algorithm is Her-miT (http://www.hermit-reasoner.com). As a preliminary optimisation we prune away axioms from the rankings that are *irrelevant* to the query according to the notion of *entailment preserving modules* [14]

Results: Overall, the Basic and Minimal Relevant Closure took around one order of magnitude longer to compute than Rational Closure (see Figure 1).

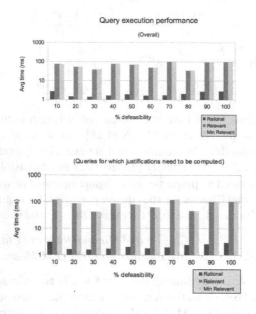

Fig. 1. Average query execution performance of Basic Relevant Closure (in red) vs. Rational Closure (in blue) over the dataset.

The reason for this discrepancy in performance is attributable to the relatively large number of classical entailment checks required to compute the justifications (see Figure 2) for Basic and Minimal Relevant Closure. Rational Closure, on the other hand, does not require to compute justifications and therefore in general is significantly faster. Another contributing factor to this is that HermiT is not optimised for entailment checks of the form found in Algorithms 3 and 4.

As expected, the performance of Basic (and Minimal) Relevant Closure drastically degrades when it has to compute a large number of justifications. We found that 8% of queries could not be computed in reasonable time. We introduced a timeout of 7000ms, which is one order of magnitude longer than that of the worst case query answering times for Rational Closure (700ms). The timeout accounts, to some extent, for the number of justifications being more or less constant. Despite this, we observe that an average query answering time of 100 milliseconds is promising as an initial result, especially since our algorithms are not highly optimised.

Since the practical feasibility of Basic and Minimal Relevant Closure relies on the justificatory structure of the DBoxes, we plan to investigate the prevalence of justifications

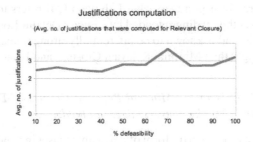

Fig. 2. Average number of justifications computed for query answering using Basic Relevant Closure

in real-world ontologies. This investigation could reveal the usefulness of these forms of reasoning in such contexts.

Finally, given the minor differences between the algorithms for Basic and Minimal Relevant Closure it is not surprising that the latter behaves very similarly to the former from a performance perspective.

7 Related Work

The semantic underpinnings of our work has its roots in the propositional approach to defeasible reasoning advocated by Lehmann and colleagues [23,25,24] and transported to the DL setting by Britz et al. [8,9] and Giordano et al. [18,17,16]. From an algorithmic perspective, Giordano et al. [18] present a tableau calculus for computing Preferential Entailment which relies on KLM-style rules. To our knowledge, this has not been implemented yet. Our work builds on that of Casini and Straccia [12] who describe an algorithm for computing (a slightly different version of) Rational Closure for $\mathcal{ALC}$, and Britz et al. [7], who refined the Casini-Straccia algorithm to correspond exactly to Rational Closure, and implemented the refined algorithm. Their accompanying experimental results showed that enriching DLs with defeasible subsumption is practically feasible.

Strongly related to our work as well is the approach to defeasible reasoning known as Lexicographic Closure, first proposed by Lehmann [24] for the propositional case, and extended to the DL case by Casini and Straccia [13]. Lukasiewicz [26] also proposed a method that, as a special case, corresponds to a version of Lexicographic Closure. Below we present a description of Lexicographic Closure for $\mathcal{ALC}(\sqsubseteq\!\!\!\sim)$ (space considerations prevent a more detailed description).

Let $\mathcal{K} = \langle \mathcal{T}, \mathcal{D} \rangle$ be a KB with $\mathcal{D}$ partitioned into $\mathcal{D}_0, \dots, \mathcal{D}_n$. For $\mathcal{D}' \subseteq \mathcal{D}$, let $k_i^{\mathcal{D}'} = |\mathcal{D}_i \cap \mathcal{D}'|$. Let $\prec$ be the lexicographic order on sequences of natural numbers of length $n + 2$. For $\mathcal{D}', \mathcal{D}'' \subseteq \mathcal{D}$, let $\mathcal{D}' \lhd \mathcal{D}''$ iff $[k_0^{\mathcal{D}'}, \dots, k_n^{\mathcal{D}'}, k_\infty^{\mathcal{D}'}] \prec [k_0^{\mathcal{D}''}, \dots, k_n^{\mathcal{D}''}, k_\infty^{\mathcal{D}''}]$. For $\mathcal{D}' \subseteq \mathcal{D}$ and $C \in \mathcal{L}$, $\mathcal{D}'$ is a *basis* for C w.r.t. $\mathcal{K}$ iff $\mathcal{T} \not\models \overline{\mathcal{D}'} \sqsubseteq \neg C$ and $\mathcal{D}'$ is maximal w.r.t. the ordering $\lhd$.

Definition 7. *For $C, D \in \mathcal{L}$, $C \sqsubseteq\!\!\!\sim D$ is in the Lexicographic Closure of $\mathcal{K} = \langle \mathcal{T}, \mathcal{D} \rangle$ iff for every basis $\mathcal{D}'$ for C w.r.t. $\mathcal{K}$, $\mathcal{T} \models \bigsqcap \overline{\mathcal{D}'} \sqcap C \sqsubseteq D$.*

Lexicographic Closure corresponds to what Lehmann [24] refers to *presumptive reasoning* and describes as the reading intended by Reiter's Default Logic [29]. It satisfies all the KLM properties, and is known to be inferentially stronger than Rational Closure. It turns out to be stronger than Minimal Relevant Closure (and Basic Relevant Closure) as well.

Proposition 5. *If $C \sqsubseteq D$ is in the Minimal Relevant Closure of $\mathcal{D}$, then it is in the Lexicographic Closure of $\mathcal{D}$. The converse does not hold.*

Lexicographic Closure is a powerful form of defeasible reasoning and is certainly worth further investigation in the context of DLs. At present, we are not aware of any implementation of Lexicographic Closure, though.

More generally, other proposals for defeasible reasoning include default-style rules in description logics [3,27], approaches based on circumscription for DLs [6,5,4,30], and approaches that combines an explicit knowledge operator with negation as failure [22,15]. To our knowledge, the formal properties of the consequence relation of these systems have not been investigated in detail, and none of them have been implemented.

8 Conclusion and Future Work

In this paper we proposed a new approach to defeasible reasoning for DLs based on the *relevance* of subsumptions to a query. We instantiated the approach with two versions of relevance-based defeasible reasoning—Basic Relevant Closure and Minimal Relevant Closure. We showed that both versions overcome some of the limitations of Rational Closure, the best known version of KLM-style defeasible reasoning. We presented experimental results based on an implementation of both Basic Relevant Closure and Minimal Relevant Closure, and compared it with existing results for Rational Closure. The results indicate that both Basic Relevant Closure and Minimal Relevant Closure are only slightly more expensive to compute than Rational Closure.

The relevance-based reasoning proposed in this paper is, to our knowledge, the first attempt to define a form of defeasible reasoning on the use of justifications—a notion on which the area of ontology debugging is based. An obvious extension to the current work is the investigation of relevance-based reasoning other than Basic and Minimal Relevant Closure. We are currently investigating a version that is inferentially stronger than Minimal Relevant Closure.

Here the focus was on defeasible reasoning for DBoxes without reference to ABox assertions. The incorporation of defeasible ABox reasoning into both forms of Relevant Closure presented here is similar to existing approaches for Rational Closure [17,16,10] and is left as future work.

Finally, there are two ways to deal with the computational burden associated with Relevant Closure in comparison with Rational Closure. Firstly, there is the option of optimised versions of the current implementations. Secondly, there is the possibility of developing efficient algorithms for approximating Basic or Minimal Relevant Closure, that are guaranteed to be at least as strong as Rational Closure, inferentially speaking. We are pursuing both options.

References

1. Baader, F., Calvanese, D., McGuinness, D., Nardi, D., Patel-Schneider, P.: The Description Logic Handbook: Theory, Implementation and Applications, 2nd edn. Cambridge University Press (2007)
2. Baader, F., Hollunder, B.: How to prefer more specific defaults in terminological default logic. In: Proceedings of IJCAI, pp. 669–674. Morgan Kaufmann Publishers (1993)
3. Baader, F., Hollunder, B.: Embedding defaults into terminological knowledge representation formalisms. Journal of Automated Reasoning, 306–317 (1995)
4. Bonatti, P., Faella, M., Sauro, L.: Defeasible inclusions in low-complexity DLs. JAIR 42, 719–764 (2011)
5. Bonatti, P., Faella, M., Sauro, L.: On the complexity of EL with defeasible inclusions. In: Proceedings of IJCAI, pp. 762–767 (2011)
6. Bonatti, P., Lutz, C., Wolter, F.: The complexity of circumscription in description logic. JAIR 35, 717–773 (2009)
7. Britz, K., Casini, G., Meyer, T., Moodley, K., Varzinczak, I.: Ordered interpretations and entailment for defeasible description logics. Technical report, CAIR, CSIR Meraka and UKZN, South Africa (2013)
8. Britz, K., Heidema, J., Meyer, T.: Semantic preferential subsumption. In: Lang, J., Brewka, G. (eds.) Proceedings of KR, pp. 476–484. AAAI Press/MIT Press (2008)
9. Britz, K., Meyer, T., Varzinczak, I.: Semantic foundation for preferential description logics. In: Wang, D., Reynolds, M. (eds.) AI 2011. LNCS (LNAI), vol. 7106, pp. 491–500. Springer, Heidelberg (2011)
10. Casini, G., Meyer, T., Moodley, K., Varzinczak, I.: Nonmonotonic reasoning in description logics: Rational closure for the Abox. In: Proceedings of DL, pp. 600–615 (2013)
11. Casini, G., Meyer, T., Moodley, K., Varzinczak, I.: Towards practical defeasible reasoning for description logics. In: Proceedings of DL, pp. 587–599 (2013)
12. Casini, G., Straccia, U.: Rational closure for defeasible description logics. In: Janhunen, T., Niemelä, I. (eds.) JELIA 2010. LNCS (LNAI), vol. 6341, pp. 77–90. Springer, Heidelberg (2010)
13. Casini, G., Straccia, U.: Lexicographic closure for defeasible description logics. In: Proc. of Australasian Ontology Workshop (2012)
14. Cuenca Grau, B., Horrocks, I., Kazakov, Y., Sattler, U.: Modular reuse of ontologies: Theory and practice. JAIR 31, 273–318 (2008)
15. Donini, F.M., Nardi, D., Rosati, R.: Description logics of minimal knowledge and negation as failure. TOCL 3(2), 177–225 (2002)
16. Giordano, L., Gliozzi, V., Olivetti, N.: Minimal model semantics and rational closure in description logics. In: Proceedings of DL (2013)
17. Giordano, L., Gliozzi, V., Olivetti, N., Pozzato, G.L.: Rational Closure in Description Logics of Typicality. In: IAF (2013)
18. Giordano, L., Olivetti, N., Gliozzi, V., Pozzato, G.L.: $\mathcal{ALC} + T$: A preferential extension of description logics. Fundamenta Informaticae 96(3), 341–372 (2009)
19. Giordano, L., Gliozzi, V., Olivetti, N., Pozzato, G.L.: A minimal model semantics for nonmonotonic reasoning. In: del Cerro, L.F., Herzig, A., Mengin, J. (eds.) JELIA 2012. LNCS, vol. 7519, pp. 228–241. Springer, Heidelberg (2012)
20. Hansson, S.O.: A Textbook of Belief Dynamics: Theory Change and Database Updating. Kluwer Academic Publishers (1999)
21. Horridge, M.: Justification based explanation in ontologies. The University of Manchester (2011)

22. Ke, P., Sattler, U.: Next Steps for Description Logics of Minimal Knowledge and Negation as Failure. In: Proceedings of DL (2008)
23. Kraus, S., Lehmann, D., Magidor, M.: Nonmonotonic reasoning, preferential models and cumulative logics. Artificial Intelligence 44, 167–207 (1990)
24. Lehmann, D.: Another perspective on default reasoning. Annals of Mathematics and Artificial Intelligence 15(1), 61–82 (1995)
25. Lehmann, D., Magidor, M.: What does a conditional knowledge base entail? Artificial Intelligence 55, 1–60 (1992)
26. Lukasiewicz, T.: Expressive probabilistic description logics. Artificial Intelligence 172(6-7), 852–883 (2008)
27. Padgham, L., Zhang, T.: A terminological logic with defaults: A definition and an application. In: Proceedings of IJCAI, pp. 662–668. Morgan Kaufmann (1994)
28. Quantz, J.: A preference semantics for defaults in terminological logics. In: Proceedings of KR, pp. 294–305 (1992)
29. Reiter, R.: A logic for default reasoning. Artificial Intelligence 13(1-2), 81–132 (1980)
30. Sengupta, K., Krisnadhi, A.A., Hitzler, P.: Local closed world semantics: Grounded circumscription for OWL. In: Aroyo, L., Welty, C., Alani, H., Taylor, J., Bernstein, A., Kagal, L., Noy, N., Blomqvist, E. (eds.) ISWC 2011, Part I. LNCS, vol. 7031, pp. 617–632. Springer, Heidelberg (2011)

Error-Tolerant Reasoning
in the Description Logic $\mathcal{EL}^\star$

Michel Ludwig and Rafael Peñaloza

Theoretical Computer Science, TU Dresden, Germany
Center for Advancing Electronics Dresden
{michel,penaloza}@tcs.inf.tu-dresden.de

Abstract. Developing and maintaining ontologies is an expensive and error-prone task. After an error is detected, users may have to wait for a long time before a corrected version of the ontology is available. In the meantime, one might still want to derive meaningful knowledge from the ontology, while avoiding the known errors. We study error-tolerant reasoning tasks in the description logic $\mathcal{EL}$. While these problems are intractable, we propose methods for improving the reasoning times by pre-compiling information about the known errors and using proof-theoretic techniques for computing justifications. A prototypical implementation shows that our approach is feasible for large ontologies used in practice.

1 Introduction

Description Logics (DLs) [3] are a family of knowledge representation formalisms that have been successfully used to model many application domains, specifically in the bio-medical areas. They are also the logical formalism underlying the standard ontology language for the semantic web OWL 2 [32]. As a consequence, more and larger ontologies are being built using these formalisms. Ontology engineering is expensive and error-prone; the combination of knowledge from multiple experts, and misunderstandings between them and the knowledge engineers may lead to subtle errors that are hard to detect. For example, several iterations of SNOMED CT [14,31] classified *amputation of finger* as a subclass of *amputation of hand* [7,8].

Since domain knowledge is needed for correcting an unwanted consequence, and its causes might not be obvious, it can take long before a corrected version of an ontology is released. For example, new versions of SNOMED are released every six months; one should then expect to wait at least that amount of time before an error is resolved. During that time, users should still be able to derive meaningful consequences from the ontology, while avoiding the known errors.

A related problem is *inconsistency-tolerant reasoning*, based on consistent query answering from databases [1,9], where the goal is to obtain meaningful consequences from an inconsistent ontology $\mathcal{O}$. Inconsistency is clearly an unwanted consequence from an ontology, but it is not the only one; for instance,

---

* Partially supported by DFG within the Cluster of Excellence 'cfAED'.

E. Fermé and J. Leite (Eds.): JELIA 2014, LNAI 8761, pp. 107–121, 2014.

while SNOMED is consistent, we would still like to avoid the erroneous subclass relationship between amputation of finger and amputation of hand. We generalize the idea of inconsistency-tolerant reasoning to *error-tolerant reasoning* in which other unwanted consequences, beyond inconsistency, are considered.

We focus mainly on two kinds of error-tolerant semantics; namely brave and cautious semantics. Intuitively, *cautious semantics* refer to consequences that follow from *all* the possible repairs of $\mathcal{O}$; this guarantees that, however the ontology is repaired, the consequence will still follow. For some consequences, one might only be interested in guaranteeing that it follows from *at least one* repair; this defines the *brave semantics*. As usual in inconsistency-tolerant reasoning, the *repairs* are maximal subontologies of $\mathcal{O}$ that do not entail the unwanted consequence. Notice that brave semantics are not closed under entailment; e.g., the conjunction of two brave consequences is not necessarily a brave consequence itself. However, brave consequences are still useful, e.g. to guarantee that a *wanted* consequence can still be derived from at least one repair (i.e., that it might still hold after the ontology is repaired) among other cases. We also consider the IAR semantics, proposed in [22] as a means to efficiently approximate cautious reasoning; see also [11, 30].

In this paper, we focus on subsumption between concepts w.r.t. a TBox in $\mathcal{EL}$, which is known to be polynomial [13]. As every $\mathcal{EL}$ TBox is consistent, considering inconsistency-tolerant semantics makes no sense in this setting. On the other hand, SNOMED CT and other large-scale ontologies are written in tractable extensions of this logic, and being able to handle errors written in them is a relevant problem for knowledge representation and ontology development.

We show that error-tolerant reasoning in $\mathcal{EL}$ is hard. More precisely, brave semantics is NP-complete, and cautious and IAR semantics are coNP-complete. These results are similar to the complexity of inconsistency-tolerant semantics in inexpressive logics [10, 30]. We also show that hardness does not depend only on the number of repairs: there exist errors with polynomially many repairs, for which error-tolerant reasoning requires super-polynomial time (unless P = NP).

To improve the time needed for error-tolerant reasoning, we propose to precompute the information on the causes of the error. We first annotate every axiom with the repairs to which it belongs. We then use a proof-theoretic approach, coupled with this annotated ontology, to derive error-tolerant consequences. We demonstrate the practical applicability of our approach for brave and cautious reasoning by applying a prototype-implementation on large ontologies used in practice. An extended version of this paper containing all proofs and details can be found in [25].

2   Preliminaries

We first briefly recall the DL $\mathcal{EL}$. Given two disjoint and countably infinite sets N_C and N_R of *concept-*, and *role-names*, respectively, concepts are constructed by $C ::= A \mid C \sqcap C \mid \exists r.C$, where $A \in N_C$ and $r \in N_R$. A *TBox* is a finite set of *general concept inclusions (GCIs)* of the form $C \sqsubseteq D$, where C, D are concepts.

Table 1. Syntax and semantics of $\mathcal{EL}$

Syntax	Semantics
$\top$	$\Delta^{\mathcal{I}}$
$C \sqcap D$	$C^{\mathcal{I}} \cap D^{\mathcal{I}}$
$\exists r.C$	$\{x \in \Delta^{\mathcal{I}} \mid \exists y \in \Delta^{\mathcal{I}} : (x,y) \in r^{\mathcal{I}} \wedge y \in C^{\mathcal{I}}\}$

The TBox is in *normal form* if all its GCIs are of the form $A \sqsubseteq \exists r.B$, $\exists r.A \sqsubseteq B$, or $A_1 \sqcap \ldots \sqcap A_n \sqsubseteq B$ with $n \geq 1$ and $A, A_1, \ldots, A_n, B \in \mathsf{N_C} \cup \{\top\}$.

The semantics of $\mathcal{EL}$ is defined through *interpretations* $\mathcal{I} = (\Delta^{\mathcal{I}}, \cdot^{\mathcal{I}})$, where $\Delta^{\mathcal{I}}$ is a non-empty *domain* and $\cdot^{\mathcal{I}}$ maps each $A \in \mathsf{N_C}$ to a set $A^{\mathcal{I}} \subseteq \Delta^{\mathcal{I}}$ and every $r \in \mathsf{N_R}$ to a binary relation $r^{\mathcal{I}}$ over $\Delta^{\mathcal{I}}$. This mapping is extended to arbitrary concepts as shown in Table 1. The interpretation $\mathcal{I}$ is a *model* of the TBox $\mathcal{T}$ if $C^{\mathcal{I}} \subseteq D^{\mathcal{I}}$ for every $C \sqsubseteq D \in \mathcal{T}$. The main reasoning problem is to decide *subsumption* [2,13]: C is *subsumed* by D w.r.t. $\mathcal{T}$ (denoted $C \sqsubseteq_{\mathcal{T}} D$) if $C^{\mathcal{I}} \subseteq D^{\mathcal{I}}$ holds for every model $\mathcal{I}$ of $\mathcal{T}$. $\mathcal{HL}$ is the sublogic of $\mathcal{EL}$ that does not allow existential restrictions; it is a syntactic variant of Horn logic: every Horn clause can be seen as an $\mathcal{HL}$ GCI. An $\mathcal{HL}$ TBox is a *core* TBox if all its axioms are of the form $A \sqsubseteq B$ with $A, B \in \mathsf{N_C}$.

Error-tolerant reasoning refers to the task of deriving meaningful consequences from a TBox that is known to contain errors. In the scope of this paper, an erroneous consequence refers to an error in a subsumption relation. If the TBox $\mathcal{T}$ entails an unwanted subsumption $C \sqsubseteq_{\mathcal{T}} D$, then we are interested in finding the ways in which this consequence can be avoided. To define error-tolerant reasoning formally, we need the notion of a repair.

Definition 1 (repair). *Let $\mathcal{T}$ be an $\mathcal{EL}$ TBox and $C \sqsubseteq_{\mathcal{T}} D$. A repair of $\mathcal{T}$ w.r.t. $C \sqsubseteq D$ is a maximal (w.r.t. set inclusion) subset $\mathcal{R} \subseteq \mathcal{T}$ such that $C \not\sqsubseteq_{\mathcal{R}} D$. The set of all repairs of $\mathcal{T}$ w.r.t. $C \sqsubseteq D$ is denoted by $\mathsf{Rep}_{\mathcal{T}}(C \sqsubseteq D)$.*

We will usually consider a fixed TBox $\mathcal{T}$, and hence say that $\mathcal{R}$ is a repair w.r.t. $C \sqsubseteq D$, or even simply a repair, if the consequence is clear from the context.

Example 2. The repairs of $\mathcal{T} = \{A \sqsubseteq \exists r.X, \exists r.X \sqsubseteq B, A \sqsubseteq Y, Y \sqsubseteq B, A \sqsubseteq B'\}$ w.r.t. the consequence $A \sqsubseteq B$ are the sets $\mathcal{R}_i := \mathcal{T} \setminus \mathcal{S}_i, 1 \leq i \leq 4$, where $\mathcal{S}_1 = \{A \sqsubseteq \exists r.X, A \sqsubseteq Y\}$, $\mathcal{S}_2 = \{A \sqsubseteq \exists r.X, Y \sqsubseteq B\}$, $\mathcal{S}_3 = \{\exists r.X \sqsubseteq B, A \sqsubseteq Y\}$, and $\mathcal{S}_4 = \{\exists r.X \sqsubseteq B, Y \sqsubseteq B\}$.

The number of repairs w.r.t. a consequence may be exponential, even for core TBoxes [28]. Each of these repairs is a potential way of avoiding the unwanted consequence; however, it is impossible to know *a priori* which is the best one to use for further reasoning tasks. One common approach is to be *cautious* and consider only those consequences that follow from *all* repairs. Alternatively, one can consider *brave* consequences: those that follow from at least one repair.

Definition 3 (cautious, brave). *Let $\mathcal{T}$ be an $\mathcal{EL}$ TBox, $C \sqsubseteq_{\mathcal{T}} D$, and C', D' be two $\mathcal{EL}$ concepts. C' is* brave *ly subsumed by D' w.r.t. $\mathcal{T}$ and $C \sqsubseteq D$ if there* is a repair $\mathcal{R} \in \mathsf{Rep}_{\mathcal{T}}(C \sqsubseteq D)$ such that $C' \sqsubseteq_{\mathcal{R}} D'$; C' is cautiously subsumed by D' w.r.t. $\mathcal{T}$ and $C \sqsubseteq D$ if for every repair $\mathcal{R} \in \mathsf{Rep}_{\mathcal{T}}(C \sqsubseteq D)$ it holds that $C' \sqsubseteq_{\mathcal{R}} D'$. If $\mathcal{T}$ or $C \sqsubseteq D$ are clear from the context, we usually omit them.

Example 4. Let $\mathcal{T}, \mathcal{R}_1, \ldots \mathcal{R}_4$ be as in Example 2. A is bravely but not cautiously subsumed by $Y \sqcap B'$ w.r.t. $\mathcal{T}$ and $A \sqsubseteq B$ since $A \sqsubseteq_{\mathcal{R}_2} Y \sqcap B'$ but $A \not\sqsubseteq_{\mathcal{R}_1} Y \sqcap B'$.

In the context of inconsistency-tolerant reasoning, other kinds of semantics which have better computational properties have been proposed [11, 22, 30]. Among these are the so-called IAR semantics, which consider the consequences that follow from the intersection of all repairs. Formally, C' is *IAR subsumed* by D' w.r.t. $\mathcal{T}$ and $C \sqsubseteq D$ if $C' \sqsubseteq_{\mathcal{Q}} D'$, where $\mathcal{Q} := \bigcap_{\mathcal{R} \in \mathsf{Rep}_{\mathcal{T}}(C \sqsubseteq D)} \mathcal{R}$.

Example 5. Let $\mathcal{T}$ and $\mathcal{R}_1, \ldots, \mathcal{R}_4$ be as in Example 2. Then A is IAR subsumed by B' w.r.t. $\mathcal{T}$ and $A \sqsubseteq B$ as $A \sqsubseteq B' \in \bigcap_{i=1}^{4} \mathcal{R}_i$.

A notion dual to repairs is that of MinAs, or justifications [7, 18]. A *MinA* for $C \sqsubseteq_{\mathcal{T}} D$ is a minimal (w.r.t. set inclusion) subset $\mathcal{M}$ of $\mathcal{T}$ such that $C \sqsubseteq_{\mathcal{M}} D$. We denote as $\mathsf{MinA}_{\mathcal{T}}(C \sqsubseteq D)$ the set of all MinAs for $C \sqsubseteq_{\mathcal{T}} D$. There is a close connection between repairs and MinAs for error-tolerant reasoning.

Theorem 6. *Let $\mathcal{T}$ be an $\mathcal{EL}$ TBox, C, C', D, D' concepts with $C \sqsubseteq_{\mathcal{T}} D$. Then*

1. *C' is cautiously subsumed by D' w.r.t. $\mathcal{T}$ and $C \sqsubseteq D$ iff for every repair $\mathcal{R} \in \mathsf{Rep}_{\mathcal{T}}(C \sqsubseteq D)$ there is an $\mathcal{M}' \in \mathsf{MinA}_{\mathcal{T}}(C' \sqsubseteq D')$ with $\mathcal{M}' \subseteq \mathcal{R}$; and*
2. *C' is bravely subsumed by D' w.r.t. $\mathcal{T}$ and $C \sqsubseteq D$ iff there is a repair $\mathcal{R} \in \mathsf{Rep}_{\mathcal{T}}(C \sqsubseteq D)$ and a MinA $\mathcal{M}' \in \mathsf{MinA}_{\mathcal{T}}(C' \sqsubseteq D')$ with $\mathcal{M}' \subseteq \mathcal{R}$.*

This theorem will be useful for developing a more efficient error-tolerant reasoning algorithm. Before describing this algorithm in detail, we study the complexity of this kind of reasoning.

3   Complexity

We show that deciding cautious and IAR subsumptions is intractable already for core TBoxes. Deciding brave subsumptions is intractable for $\mathcal{EL}$, but tractable for $\mathcal{HL}$. We first prove the latter claim using directed hypergraphs, which generalize graphs by connecting sets of nodes, rather than just nodes.

A *directed hypergraph* is a pair $\mathcal{G} = (\mathcal{V}, \mathcal{E})$, where $\mathcal{V}$ is a non-empty set of *nodes*, and $\mathcal{E}$ is a set of *directed hyperedges* $e = (S, S')$, with $S, S' \subseteq \mathcal{V}$. Given $S, T \subseteq \mathcal{V}$, a *path* from S to T in $\mathcal{G}$ is a set of hyperedges $\{(S_i, T_i) \in \mathcal{E} \mid 1 \leq i \leq n\}$ such that for every $1 \leq i \leq n$, $S_i \subseteq S \cup \bigcup_{j=1}^{n-1} T_j$, and $T \subseteq \bigcup_{i=1}^{n} T_i$ hold. The *reachability problem* in hypergraphs consists in deciding the existence of a path from S to T in $\mathcal{G}$. This problem is decidable in polynomial time on $|\mathcal{V}|$ [16].

Recall that $\mathcal{HL}$ concepts are conjunctions of concept names; we can represent $C = A_1 \sqcap \cdots \sqcap A_m$ as its set of conjuncts $S_C = \{A_1, \ldots, A_m\}$. Each GCI $C \sqsubseteq D$ yields a directed hyperedge (S_C, S_D) and every $\mathcal{HL}$-TBox $\mathcal{T}$ forms a directed hypergraph $\mathcal{G}_{\mathcal{T}}$. Then $C \sqsubseteq_{\mathcal{T}} D$ iff there is a path from S_C to S_D in $\mathcal{G}_{\mathcal{T}}$.

Theorem 7. *Brave subsumption in $\mathcal{HL}$ can be decided in polynomial time on the size of the TBox.*

Proof. Let $\mathcal{T}$ be an $\mathcal{HL}$ TBox, and C, C', D, D' be $\mathcal{HL}$ concepts. C' is bravely subsumed by D' w.r.t. $\mathcal{T}$ and $C \sqsubseteq D$ iff there is a path from $S_{C'}$ to $S_{D'}$ in $\mathcal{G}_{\mathcal{T}}$ that does not contain any path from S_C to S_D. If no such path exists, then (i) every path from $S_{C'}$ to $S_{D'}$ passes through S_D, and (ii) every path from $S_{C'}$ to S_D passes through S_C. We need to verify whether any of these two statements is violated. The existence of a path that does not pass through a given set is decidable in polynomial time.

However, for $\mathcal{EL}$ this problem is NP-complete. To prove this we adapt an idea from [27] for reducing the NP-hard *more minimal valuations* (MMV) problem [7, 15]: deciding, for a monotone Boolean formula φ and a set $\mathfrak{V}$ of minimal valuations satisfying φ, if there are other minimal valuations $V \notin \mathfrak{V}$ satisfying φ.

Theorem 8. *Brave subsumption in $\mathcal{EL}$ is NP-complete.*

We now show that the cautious and IAR semantics are intractable already for core TBoxes. This is a consequence of the intractability of the following problem.

Definition 9 (axiom relevance). *The* axiom relevance *problem consists in deciding, given a core TBox $\mathcal{T}$, $A \sqsubseteq B \in \mathcal{T}$, and $A_0 \sqsubseteq_{\mathcal{T}} B_0$, whether there is a repair $\mathcal{R}$ of $\mathcal{T}$ w.r.t. $A_0 \sqsubseteq B_0$ such that $A \sqsubseteq B \notin \mathcal{R}$.*

Lemma 10. *Axiom relevance is NP-hard.*

Proof. We reduce the NP-hard *path-via-node* problem [21]: given a directed graph $\mathcal{G} = (\mathcal{V}, \mathcal{E})$ and nodes $s, t, m \in \mathcal{V}$, decide if there is a simple path from s to t in $\mathcal{G}$ that goes through m. Given an instance of the path-via-node problem, we introduce a concept name A_v for every $v \in (\mathcal{V} \setminus \{m\}) \cup \{m_1, m_2\}$, and build the core TBox

$$\mathcal{T} := \{A_v \sqsubseteq A_w \mid (v, w) \in \mathcal{E}, v, w \neq m\} \cup \{A_v \sqsubseteq A_{m_1} \mid (v, m) \in \mathcal{E}, v \neq m\} \cup$$
$$\{A_{m_2} \sqsubseteq A_v \mid (m, v) \in \mathcal{E}, v \neq m\} \cup \{A_{m_1} \sqsubseteq A_{m_2}\}.$$

There is a simple path from s to t in $\mathcal{G}$ through m iff there is a repair $\mathcal{R}$ of $\mathcal{T}$ w.r.t. $A_s \sqsubseteq A_t$ with $A_{m_1} \sqsubseteq A_{m_2} \notin \mathcal{R}$.

Theorem 11. *Cautious subsumption and IAR subsumption w.r.t. core, $\mathcal{HL}$ or $\mathcal{EL}$ TBoxes are coNP-complete.*

Proof. If C is not cautiously subsumed by D, we can guess a set $\mathcal{R}$ and verify in polynomial time that $\mathcal{R}$ is a repair and $C \not\sqsubseteq_{\mathcal{R}} D$. If C is not IAR subsumed by D, we can guess a set $\mathcal{Q} \subseteq \mathcal{T}$, and for every GCI $C_i \sqsubseteq D_i \notin \mathcal{Q}$ a set $\mathcal{R}_i$ such that $C_i \sqsubseteq D_i \notin \mathcal{R}_i$. Verifying that each $\mathcal{R}_i$ is a repair and $C \not\sqsubseteq_{\mathcal{Q}} D$ is polynomial. Thus both problems are in coNP. To show hardness, for a GCI $C \sqsubseteq D \in \mathcal{T}$, there is a repair $\mathcal{R}$ such that $C \sqsubseteq D \notin \mathcal{R}$ iff $C \not\sqsubseteq_{\mathcal{R}} D$ iff C is neither cautiously nor IAR subsumed by D. By Lemma 10 both problems are coNP-hard.

Algorithm 1. Repairs entailing $C' \sqsubseteq D'$

Input: Unwanted consequence $C \sqsubseteq_{\mathcal{T}} D$, concepts C', D'
Output: $\mathfrak{R} \subseteq \mathsf{Rep}_{\mathcal{T}}(C \sqsubseteq D)$: repairs entailing $C' \sqsubseteq D'$
  $\mathfrak{R} \leftarrow \mathsf{Rep}_{\mathcal{T}}(C \sqsubseteq D)$
  for each $\mathcal{R} \in \mathsf{Rep}_{\mathcal{T}}(C \sqsubseteq D)$ **do**
    if $C' \not\sqsubseteq_{\mathcal{R}} D'$ **then**
      $\mathfrak{R} \leftarrow \mathfrak{R} \setminus \{\mathcal{R}\}$
  return $\mathfrak{R}$

The hardness of error-tolerant reasoning is usually attributed to the fact that there can exist exponentially many repairs for a given consequence. However, this argument is incomplete. For instance, brave reasoning remains polynomial in $\mathcal{HL}$, although consequences may have exponentially many repairs already in this logic. We show now that cautious and brave subsumption are also hard on the *number of repairs*; i.e., they are not what we call *repair-polynomial*.

Definition 12 (repair-polynomial). *An error-tolerant problem w.r.t. a TBox $\mathcal{T}$ and a consequence $C \sqsubseteq D$ is* repair-polynomial *if it can be solved by an algorithm that runs in polynomial time on the size of both $\mathcal{T}$ and $\mathsf{Rep}_{\mathcal{T}}(C \sqsubseteq D)$.*

Theorem 13. *Unless* P = NP, *cautious and brave subsumption of C' by D' w.r.t. $\mathcal{T}$ and $C \sqsubseteq D$ in $\mathcal{EL}$ are not repair-polynomial.*

The proof adapts the construction from Theorem 8 to reduce the problem of enumerating maximal valuations that falsify a formula to deciding cautious subsumption. The number of repairs obtained from the reduction is polynomial on the number of maximal valuations that falsify the formula. Since this enumeration cannot be solved in time polynomial on the number of maximal falsifiers, cautious reasoning can also not be performed in time polynomial on the number of repairs. An analogous argument is used for brave reasoning. All the details can be found in [25]. Thus, error-tolerant reasoning is hard even if only polynomially many repairs exist; i.e., there are cases where $|\mathsf{Rep}_{\mathcal{T}}(C \sqsubseteq D)|$ is polynomial on $|\mathcal{T}|$, but brave and cautious reasoning require super-polynomial time. The culprit for hardness is not the number of repairs *per se*, but rather the relationships among these repairs.

We now propose a method for improving the reasoning times, by precomputing the set of all repairs, and using this information effectively.

4 Precompiling Repairs

A naïve solution for deciding brave or cautious subsumptions would be to first enumerate all repairs and then check which of them entail the relation (the set $\mathfrak{R}$ in Algorithm 1). C' is then bravely or cautiously subsumed by D' iff $\mathfrak{R} \neq \emptyset$ or $\mathfrak{R} = \mathsf{Rep}_{\mathcal{T}}(C \sqsubseteq D)$, respectively. Each test $C' \sqsubseteq_{\mathcal{R}} D'$ requires polynomial time on $|\mathcal{R}| \leq |\mathcal{T}|$ [13], and exactly $|\mathsf{Rep}_{\mathcal{T}}(C \sqsubseteq D)|$ such tests are performed.

The **for** loop in the algorithm thus needs polynomial time on the sizes of $\mathcal{T}$ and $\mathsf{Rep}_\mathcal{T}(C \sqsubseteq D)$. From Theorem 13 it follows that the first step, namely the computation of all the repairs, must be expensive. In particular, these repairs cannot be enumerated in output-polynomial time; i.e., in time polynomial on the input *and the output* [17].

Corollary 14. *The set of repairs for an $\mathcal{EL}$ TBox $\mathcal{T}$ w.r.t. $C \sqsubseteq D$ cannot be enumerated in output polynomial time, unless* $\mathrm{P} = \mathrm{NP}$.

For any given error, one would usually try to decide whether several brave or cautious consequences hold. It thus makes sense to improve the execution time of each of these individual reasoning tasks by avoiding a repetition of the first, expensive, step.

The set of repairs can be computed in exponential time on the size of $\mathcal{T}$; this bound cannot be improved in general since (i) there might exist exponentially many such repairs, and (ii) they cannot be enumerated in output polynomial time. However, this set only needs to be computed once, when the error is found, and can then be used to improve the reasoning time for all subsequent subsumption relations. Once $\mathsf{Rep}_\mathcal{T}(C \sqsubseteq D)$ is known, Algorithm 1 computes $\mathfrak{R}$, and hence decides brave and cautious reasoning, in time polynomial on $|\mathcal{T}| \cdot |\mathsf{Rep}_\mathcal{T}(C \sqsubseteq D)|$. It is important to notice that this does not violate the result that cautious and brave reasoning are not repair-polynomial. The main difference is that this variant of Algorithm 1 does not need to compute the repairs; they are already given.

Clearly, Algorithm 1 does more than merely deciding cautious and brave consequences. Indeed, it computes the set of all repairs that entail $C' \sqsubseteq D'$. This information can be used to decide more complex reasoning tasks. For instance, one may be interested in knowing whether the consequence follows from *most*, or *at least k* repairs, to mention just two possible inferences. IAR semantics can also be decided in polynomial time on $\mathcal{T}$ and $\mathsf{Rep}_\mathcal{T}(C \sqsubseteq D)$: simply compute $\mathcal{Q} = \bigcap_{\mathcal{R} \in \mathsf{Rep}_\mathcal{T}(C \sqsubseteq D)} \mathcal{R}$, and test whether $C' \sqsubseteq_\mathcal{Q} D'$ holds. The first step needs polynomial time on $\mathsf{Rep}_\mathcal{T}(C \sqsubseteq D)$ while the second is polynomial on $\mathcal{Q} \subseteq \mathcal{T}$.

As we have seen, precompiling the set of repairs already yields an improvement on the time required for deciding error-tolerant subsumption relations. However, there are some obvious drawbacks to this idea. In particular, storing and maintaining a possibly exponential set of TBoxes can be a challenge for the knowledge engineer. Moreover, this method does not scale well for handling multiple errors that are found at different time points. When a new error is detected, the repairs of all the TBoxes need to be computed, potentially causing the introduction of redundant TBoxes that must later be removed. We improve on this solution by structuring all the repairs into a single labelled TBox.

Let $\mathsf{Rep}_\mathcal{T}(C \sqsubseteq D) = \{\mathcal{R}_1, \ldots, \mathcal{R}_n\}$. We label every GCI $E \sqsubseteq F \in \mathcal{T}$ with $\mathsf{lab}(E \sqsubseteq F) = \{i \mid E \sqsubseteq F \in \mathcal{R}_i\}$. Conversely, for every subset $I \subseteq \{1, \ldots, n\}$ we define the TBox $\mathcal{T}_I = \{E \sqsubseteq F \in \mathcal{T} \mid \mathsf{lab}(E \sqsubseteq F) = I\}$. A set I is a *component* if $\mathcal{T}_I \neq \emptyset$. Every axiom belongs to exactly one component and hence the number of components is bounded by $|\mathcal{T}|$. One can represent these components using only polynomial space and all repairs can be read from them via a directed acyclic

---

Algorithm 2. Decide cautious and brave subsumption

Input: Labelled TBox $\mathcal{T}$, concepts C', D'
  procedure IS-BRAVE($\mathcal{T}, C', D'$)
    for each $\mathcal{M} \in \mathsf{MinA}_{\mathcal{T}}(C' \sqsubseteq D')$ **do**
      if $\mathsf{lab}(\mathcal{M}) \neq \emptyset$ **then**
        return true
    return false
  procedure IS-CAUTIOUS($\mathcal{T}, C', D'$)
    $\nu \leftarrow \emptyset$
    for each $\mathcal{M} \in \mathsf{MinA}_{\mathcal{T}}(C' \sqsubseteq D')$ **do**
      $\nu \leftarrow \nu \cup \mathsf{lab}(\mathcal{M})$
      if $\nu = \{1, \ldots, n\}$ **then**
        return true
    return false

---

graph expressing dependencies between components. For simplicity we keep the representation as subsets of $\{1, \ldots, n\}$.

The labelled TBox has full information on the repairs, and on their relationship with each other. For $\mathcal{S} \subseteq \mathcal{T}$, $\mathsf{lab}(\mathcal{S}) := \bigcap_{E \sqsubseteq F \in \mathcal{S}} \mathsf{lab}(E \sqsubseteq F)$ yields all repairs containing $\mathcal{S}$. If $\mathcal{M}$ is a MinA for $C' \sqsubseteq D'$, $\mathsf{lab}(\mathcal{M})$ is a set of repairs entailing this subsumption. Moreover, $\nu(C' \sqsubseteq D') := \bigcup_{\mathcal{M} \in \mathsf{MinA}_{\mathcal{T}}(C' \sqsubseteq D')} \mathsf{lab}(\mathcal{M})$ is the set of all repairs entailing $C' \sqsubseteq D'$. Thus, C' is bravely subsumed by D' iff $\nu(C' \sqsubseteq D') \neq \emptyset$ and is cautiously subsumed iff $\nu(C' \sqsubseteq D') = \{1, \ldots, n\}$ (recall Theorem 6).

The set $\nu(C' \sqsubseteq D')$ corresponds to the so-called *boundary* for the subsumption $C' \sqsubseteq D'$ w.r.t. the labelled TBox $\mathcal{T}$ [4]. Several methods for computing the boundary exist. Since we are only interested in deciding whether this boundary is empty or equal to $\{1, \ldots, n\}$, we can optimize the algorithm to stop once this decision is made. This optimized method is described in Algorithm 2. The algorithm first computes all MinAs for $C' \sqsubseteq_{\mathcal{T}} D'$, and their labels iteratively. If one of this labels is not empty, then the subsumption is a brave consequence; the procedure IS-BRAVE then returns true. Alternatively, IS-CAUTIOUS accumulates the union of all these labels in a set ν until this set contains all repairs, at which point it returns true.

The main difference between Algorithm 1 and Algorithm 2 is that the former iterates over the set of repairs of the unwanted consequences, while the latter iterates over $\mathsf{MinA}_{\mathcal{T}}(C' \sqsubseteq D')$. Typically, consequences have a small number of MinAs, which only contain a few axioms, while repairs are usually large and numerous. Thus, although Algorithm 2 has the overhead of computing the MinAs for the wanted consequence, it then requires less and cheaper iterations. As confirmed by our experimental results, this approach does show an advantage in practice.

Using the labelled TBox, it is also possible to decide IAR semantics through one subsumption test, and hence in polynomial time on the size of $\mathcal{T}$, regardless of the number of repairs.

Table 2. Metrics of the ontologies used in the experiments

Ontology	#axioms	#conc. names	#role names
GALEN-OWL	45 499	23 136	404
NCI	159 805	104 087	92
SNOMED	369 194	310 013	58

Theorem 15. *Let* $n = |\mathsf{Rep}_{\mathcal{T}}(C \sqsubseteq D)|$. *Then* C' *is IAR-subsumed by* D' *iff* $C' \sqsubseteq_{\mathcal{T}_J} D'$, *where* $J = \{1, \ldots, n\}$.

This shows that precompiling all repairs into a labelled ontology can help reducing the overall complexity and execution time of reasoning. Next, we exploit the fact that the number of MinAs for consequences in ontologies used in practice is relatively small and compute them using a saturation-based approach.

5   Implementation and Experiments

We ran two separate series of experiments. The goal of the first series was to investigate the feasibility of error-tolerant reasoning in practice. We implemented a prototype tool in Java that checks whether a concept subsumption $C \sqsubseteq D$ is brave or cautious w.r.t. a given TBox $\mathcal{T}$ and a consequence $C' \sqsubseteq D'$. The tool uses Theorem 6 and the duality between MinAs and repairs, i.e. the repairs for $C' \sqsubseteq D'$ w.r.t $\mathcal{T}$ can be obtained from the MinAs for $C' \sqsubseteq D'$ w.r.t $\mathcal{T}$ by consecutively removing the minimal hitting sets [29] of the MinAs from $\mathcal{T}$. The tool first computes all the MinAs for both inclusions $C \sqsubseteq D$ and $C' \sqsubseteq D'$ w.r.t. $\mathcal{T}$, and then verifies whether some inclusions between the MinAs for $C \sqsubseteq D$ and $C' \sqsubseteq D'$ hold to check for brave or cautious subsumptions. Note that the inclusion conditions only depend on the MinAs for the wanted consequence $C \sqsubseteq D$ and the erroneous subsumption $C' \sqsubseteq D'$ and *not* on the repairs of $C' \sqsubseteq D'$. Consequently, the repairs for $C' \sqsubseteq D'$ do not have to be explicitly computed in our tool. For the computation of the MinAs we used a saturation-based approach based on a consequence-based calculus [19]. More details regarding the computation of MinAs can be found in [24].

We selected three ontologies that are expressed mainly in $\mathcal{EL}$ and are typically considered to pose different challenges to DL reasoners. These are the January 2009 international release of SNOMED CT, version 13.11d of the NCI thesaurus,[1] and the GALEN-OWL ontology.[2] All non-$\mathcal{EL}$ axioms (including axioms involving roles only, e.g. role inclusion axioms) were first removed from the ontologies. The number of axioms, concept names, and role names in the resulting ontologies is shown in Table 2.

For every ontology $\mathcal{T}$ we selected a number of inclusion chains of the form $A_1 \sqsubseteq_{\mathcal{T}} A_2 \sqsubseteq_{\mathcal{T}} A_3 \sqsubseteq_{\mathcal{T}} A_4$, which were then grouped into

---

[1] http://evs.nci.nih.gov/ftp1/NCI_Thesaurus
[2] http://owl.cs.manchester.ac.uk/research/co-ode/

Table 3. Experimental results obtained for checking brave and cautious subsumption

ontology	type	#succ. comp.	#brave	#cautious	avg. #MinAs	max #MinAs	avg. time (s)
GALEN	I	498 / 500	495	39	1.707 | 1.663	4 | 4	335.680
	II	500 / 500	268	48	2.068 | 1.388	6 | 2	331.823
NCI	I	26 / 26	26	2	1.269 | 1.154	2 | 3	13.465
	II	36 / 36	16	8	3.111 | 1.111	7 | 3	15.338
SNOMED	I	302 / 500	296	17	1.652 | 1.656	42 | 12	161.471
	II	314 / 500	154	34	3.908 | 1.879	54 | 54	150.566

- *Type I* inclusions, where $A_2 \sqsubseteq_\mathcal{T} A_4$ was set as the unwanted consequence, and
- *Type II* inclusions, where $A_2 \sqsubseteq_\mathcal{T} A_3$ was the unwanted consequence.

For the NCI and SNOMED CT ontologies we chose inclusions $A_2 \sqsubseteq A_4$ (for Type I) and $A_2 \sqsubseteq A_3$ (for Type II) that were *not* entailed by the consecutive version of the considered ontology, i.e. those that can be considered to be "mistakes" fixed in the consecutive release (the July 2009 international release of SNOMED CT and version 13.12e of the NCI Thesaurus). 500 inclusions of each type were found for SNOMED CT, but only 26 Type-I inclusions and 36 Type-II inclusions were detected in the case of NCI. For the GALEN-OWL ontology 500 inclusions chains of each type were chosen at random. For every Type-I chain, we then used our tool to check whether the inclusion $A_1 \sqsubseteq A_3$ is a brave or cautious consequence w.r.t. $A_2 \sqsubseteq A_4$. Similarly, for every Type-II inclusion we checked whether $A_1 \sqsubseteq A_4$ is a brave or cautious consequence w.r.t. $A_2 \sqsubseteq A_3$.

All experiments were conducted on a PC with an Intel Xeon E5-2640 CPU running at 2.50GHz. An execution timeout of 30 CPU minutes was imposed on each problem in this experiment series. The results obtained are shown in Table 3. The first two columns indicate the ontology that was used and the inclusion type. The next three columns show the number of successful computations within the time limit, and the number of brave and cautious subsumptions, respectively. The average and the maximal number of MinAs over the considered set of inclusions are shown in the next two columns. The left-hand side of each of these columns refers to the MinAs obtained for the consequence for which its brave or cautious entailment status should be checked, and the right-hand side refers to the unwanted consequence. The last column shows the average CPU time needed for the computations over each considered set of inclusions. All time values shown indicate total computation times.

The number of successful computations was the lowest for the experiments involving SNOMED, whereas no timeouts were incurred for NCI. Moreover, the highest average number of MinAs was found for Type-II inclusions for SNOMED with a maximal number of 54. GALEN-OWL required the longest computation times, which could be a consequence of the fact that the (full) GALEN ontology is generally seen as being difficult to classify by DL reasoners. The shortest computation times were reported for experiments involving NCI. It is important to notice, however, that the standard deviations of the computation times for GALEN and SNOMED were quite high. This indicates a large variation between problem instances; for example, some instances relating to GALEN required less than 9 seconds, and over one third of the experiments finished in sixty seconds or less. All the successful computations required at most 11 GiB of main memory.

In a second series of experiments we evaluated the advantages of performing precompilation when deciding several brave and cautious entailments w.r.t. an unwanted consequence. We therefore implemented a slightly improved version of Algorithm 1 which iterates over all the repairs for the unwanted consequence and determines whether a consequence that should be checked is brave or cautious by using the conditions from Definition 3. The implemented algorithm stops as quickly as possible, e.g. when a non-entailing repair has been found, we conclude immediately that the consequence is not cautious. The computation of the repairs is implemented by making use of the duality between MinAs and repairs (via the minimal hitting sets of the MinAs) as described above. The minimal hitting sets were computed using the Boolean algebraic algorithm from [23]. In the following we refer to this improved algorithm as the *naïve* approach. We used the reasoner ELK [20] to check whether a given inclusion follows from a repair. In particular, the incremental classification feature offered by ELK allowed us to further reduce reasoning times. When switching from a repair $\mathcal{R}$ to the next $\mathcal{R}'$, the knowledge about removed $(\mathcal{R} \setminus \mathcal{R}')$ and added axioms $(\mathcal{R}' \setminus \mathcal{R})$ was utilised by ELK to (potentially) avoid a complete reclassification.

Algorithm 2 was implemented in a straightforward way. The computation of the repairs for the unwanted consequence was implemented analogously to the naïve algorithm. Note that unlike with the naïve algorithm, all the MinAs for the wanted consequences had to be computed.

For comparing the performance of the naïve approach (Algorithm 1) against Algorithm 2 in practice, we selected 226 inclusions between concept names from SNOMED having more than 10 MinAs, with a maximum number of 223. For each inclusion $A \sqsubseteq B$ we randomly chose five inclusions $A'_i \sqsubseteq B'_i$ entailed by SNOMED, and tested whether $A'_i \sqsubseteq B'_i$ is a brave or cautious subsumption w.r.t. $A \sqsubseteq B$ for every $i \in \{1, \ldots, 5\}$ using the naïve approach and Algorithm 2. In this series of experiments we allowed each problem instance to run for at most 3600 CPU seconds, and 3 GiB of heap memory (with 16 GiB of main memory in total) were allocated to the Java VM. Each problem instance was run three times, and the best result was recorded.

The results obtained are depicted in Figure 1. The problem instances $A \sqsubseteq B$ are sorted ascendingly along the x-axis according to the number of repairs for $A \sqsubseteq B$. The required computation times for each problem instance (computing all repairs for the unwanted consequence and checking whether the five subsumptions are brave or cautious entailments w.r.t. the unwanted consequence) are shown along the y-axis on the left-hand side of the graph. If no corresponding y-value is shown for a given problem instance, the computation either timed out or ran out of memory in all three calls. The number of repairs for the unwanted consequences appears on the right-hand side.

One can see that a relatively small number of repairs can lead to several thousands (up to over 14 millions) of repairs. Also, if the number of repairs remains small, i.e. below 400, the naïve approach performs fairly well, even outperforming

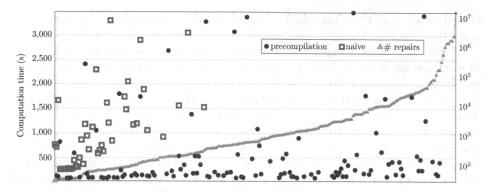

Fig. 1. Comparison of approaches for error-tolerant reasoning

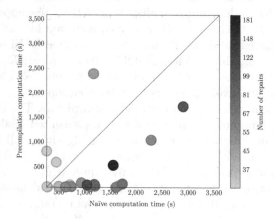

Fig. 2. Comparative performance according to the number of repairs

the precompilation approach on a few problem instances. For larger number of repairs, however, none of the computations for the naïve approach succeeded. The time required to perform reasoning with ELK outweighs the computation times of all the MinAs for the precompilation approach. In total 118 instances could be solved by at least one run of the precompilation approach, whereas only 42 computations finished when the naïve approach was used. Figure 2 shows the comparative behaviour of the two approaches over the 22 instances that succeeded in both methods. The tone of each point depicts the number of repairs of the unwanted consequence, as shown on the scale on the right. In the figure, points below the diagonal line correspond to instances where the precompilation approach performed better than the naïve approach. As it can be seen, the precompilation approach typically outperforms the naïve one, even in these simple cases, although there exist instances where the opposite behaviour is observed. However, there are also 20 instances where only the naïve approach succeeded. In our experiments the computation of the MinAs was typically the most time consuming part; the computation of the repairs once all the MinAs were available could be done fairly quickly.

6 Conclusions

We introduced error-tolerant reasoning inspired by inconsistency-tolerant semantics from DLs and consistent query answering over inconsistent databases. The main difference is that we allow for a general notion of *error* beyond inconsistency. We studied brave, cautious, and IAR reasoning, which depend on the class of repairs from which a consequence can be derived. Although we focused on subsumption w.r.t. $\mathcal{EL}$ TBoxes, these notions can be easily extended to any kind of monotonic consequences from a logical language.

Our results show that error-tolerant reasoning is hard in general for $\mathcal{EL}$, although brave reasoning remains polynomial for some of its sublogics. Interestingly, IAR semantics, introduced to regain tractability of inconsistency-tolerant query answering in light-weight DLs, is coNP-hard, even for the basic logic $\mathcal{HL}$ with core axioms. Moreover, the number of repairs is not the only culprit for hardness of these tasks: for both brave and cautious reasoning there is no polynomial-time algorithm on the size of $\mathcal{T}$ *and the number of repairs* that can solve these problems unless P = NP.

To overcome the complexity issues, we propose to compile the repairs into a labelled ontology. While the compilation step may require exponential time, after its execution IAR semantics can be decided in polynomial time, and brave and cautious semantics become repair-polynomial. Surprisingly, the idea of pre-computing the set of all repairs to improve the efficiency of reasoning seems to have been overlooked by the inconsistency-tolerant reasoning community.

To investigate the feasibility of error-tolerant reasoning in practice, we developed prototype tools based on computing all MinAs, and annotating axioms with the repairs they belong to. Our experiments show that despite their theoretical complexity, brave and cautious reasoning can be performed successfully in many practical cases, even for large ontologies. Our saturation-based procedure can detect a large number of MinAs for some consequences in a fairly short amount of time. We plan to study optimizations that can help us reduce the reasoning times further. A deeper analysis of our experimental results will be a first step in this direction. There is a close connection between error-tolerant reasoning and axiom-pinpointing [6, 7]; our labelled ontology method also relates to context-based reasoning [4]. Techniques developed for those areas, like e.g. automata-based pinpointing methods [5], could be useful in this setting.

It is known that for some inexpressive DLs, all MinAs can be enumerated in output-polynomial time [26,27]; the complexity of enumerating their repairs has not, to the best of our knowledge, been studied. We will investigate if enumerating repairs is also output-polynomial in those logics, and hence error-tolerant reasoning is repair-polynomial.

We will study the benefits of using labelled axioms for ontology contraction [12] and ontology evolution. Contraction operations can be simulated by modifying axiom labels, and minimal insertion operations add a labelled axiom. We will also extend our algorithms to more expressive logics. A full implementation and testing of these approaches is under development.

References

1. Arenas, M., Bertossi, L., Chomicki, J.: Consistent query answers in inconsistent databases. In: Proceedings of the 18th ACM SIGMOD-SIGACT-SIGART Symposium on Principles of Database Systems (PODS 1999), pp. 68–79. ACM (1999)
2. Baader, F.: Terminological cycles in a description logic with existential restrictions. In: Gottlob, G., Walsh, T. (eds.) Proceedings of the 18th International Joint Conference on Artificial Intelligence (IJCAI 2003), pp. 325–330. Morgan Kaufmann (2003)
3. Baader, F., Calvanese, D., McGuinness, D.L., Nardi, D., Patel-Schneider, P.F. (eds.): The Description Logic Handbook: Theory, Implementation, and Applications, 2nd edn. Cambridge University Press (2007)
4. Baader, F., Knechtel, M., Peñaloza, R.: Context-dependent views to axioms and consequences of semantic web ontologies. Journal of Web Semantics 12-13, 22–40 (2012), available at http://dx.doi.org/10.1016/j.websem.2011.11.006
5. Baader, F., Peñaloza, R.: Automata-based axiom pinpointing. Journal of Automated Reasoning 45(2), 91–129 (2010)
6. Baader, F., Peñaloza, R.: Axiom pinpointing in general tableaux. Journal of Logic and Computation 20(1), 5–34 (2010)
7. Baader, F., Peñaloza, R., Suntisrivaraporn, B.: Pinpointing in the description logic $\mathcal{EL}^+$. In: Hertzberg, J., Beetz, M., Englert, R. (eds.) KI 2007. LNCS (LNAI), vol. 4667, pp. 52–67. Springer, Heidelberg (2007)
8. Baader, F., Suntisrivaraporn, B.: Debugging SNOMED CT using axiom pinpointing in the description logic $\mathcal{EL}^+$. In: Proceedings of the 3rd Knowledge Representation in Medicine (KR-MED 2008): Representing and Sharing Knowledge Using SNOMED, vol. 410, CEUR-WS (2008)
9. Bertossi, L.: Database repairing and consistent query answering. Synthesis Lectures on Data Management 3(5), 1–121 (2011)
10. Bienvenu, M.: On the complexity of consistent query answering in the presence of simple ontologies. In: Proceedings of the 26th Natonal Conference on Artificial Intelligence, AAAI 2012 (2012)
11. Bienvenu, M., Rosati, R.: Tractable approximations of consistent query answering for robust ontology-based data access. In: Rossi, F. (ed.) Proceedings of the 23rd International Joint Conference on Artificial Intelligence (IJCAI 2013). AAAI Press (2013)
12. Booth, R., Meyer, T., Varzinczak, I.J.: First steps in $\mathcal{EL}$ contraction. In: Proceedings of the 2009 Workshop on Automated Reasoning About Context and Ontology Evolution, ARCOE 2009 (2009)
13. Brandt, S.: Polynomial time reasoning in a description logic with existential restrictions, GCI axioms, and - what else? In: de Mántaras, R.L., Saitta, L. (eds.) Proceedings of the 16th European Conference on Artificial Intelligence (ECAI 2004). pp. 298–302. IOS Press (2004)
14. Cote, R., Rothwell, D., Palotay, J., Beckett, R., Brochu, L.: The systematized nomenclature of human and veterinary medicine. Tech. rep., SNOMED International, Northfield, IL: College of American Pathologists (1993)
15. Eiter, T., Gottlob, G.: Identifying the minimal transversals of a hypergraph and related problems. Tech. Rep. CD-TR 91/16, Christian Doppler Laboratory for Expert Systems, TU Vienna (1991)
16. Gallo, G., Longo, G., Pallottino, S.: Directed hypergraphs and applications. Discrete Applied Mathematics 42(2), 177–201 (1993)

17. Johnson, D.S., Yannakakis, M., Papadimitriou, C.H.: On generating all maximal independent sets. Information Processing Letters 27(3), 119–123 (1988)
18. Kalyanpur, A., Parsia, B., Horridge, M., Sirin, E.: Finding all justifications of OWL DL entailments. In: Aberer, K., et al. (eds.) ASWC 2007 and ISWC 2007. LNCS, vol. 4825, pp. 267–280. Springer, Heidelberg (2007)
19. Kazakov, Y.: Consequence-driven reasoning for Horn SHIQ ontologies. In: Boutilier, C. (ed.) Proceedings of the 21st International Joint Conference on Artificial Intelligence (IJCAI 2009), pp. 2040–2045 (2009)
20. Kazakov, Y., Krötzsch, M., Simančík, F.: The incredible ELK: From polynomial procedures to efficient reasoning with $\mathcal{EL}$ ontologies. Journal of Automated Reasoning 53, 1–61 (2014)
21. Lapaugh, A.S., Papadimitriou, C.H.: The even-path problem for graphs and digraphs. Networks 14(4), 507–513 (1984), http://dx.doi.org/10.1002/net.3230140403
22. Lembo, D., Lenzerini, M., Rosati, R., Ruzzi, M., Savo, D.F.: Inconsistency-tolerant semantics for description logics. In: Hitzler, P., Lukasiewicz, T. (eds.) RR 2010. LNCS, vol. 6333, pp. 103–117. Springer, Heidelberg (2010)
23. Lin, L., Jiang, Y.: The computation of hitting sets: Review and new algorithms. Information Processing Letters 86(4), 177–184 (2003)
24. Ludwig, M.: Just: A tool for computing justifications w.r.t. $\mathcal{EL}$ ontologies. In: Proceedings of the 3rd International Workshop on OWL Reasoner Evaluation, ORE 2014 (2014)
25. Ludwig, M., Peñaloza, R.: Error-tolerant reasoning in the description logic $\mathcal{EL}$. LTCS-Report 14-11, Chair of Automata Theory, Institute of Theoretical Computer Science, Technische Universität Dresden, Dresden, Germany (2014), see http://lat.inf.tu-dresden.de/research/reports.html.
26. Peñaloza, R., Sertkaya, B.: Complexity of axiom pinpointing in the DL-Lite family of description logics. In: Coelho, H., Studer, R., Wooldridge, M. (eds.) Proceedings of the 19th European Conference on Artificial Intelligence (ECAI 2010). Frontiers in Artificial Intelligence and Applications, vol. 215, pp. 29–34. IOS Press (2010)
27. Peñaloza, R., Sertkaya, B.: On the complexity of axiom pinpointing in the $\mathcal{EL}$ family of description logics. In: Lin, F., Sattler, U., Truszczynski, M. (eds.) Proceedings of the Twelfth International Conference on Principles of Knowledge Representation and Reasoning (KR 2010). AAAI Press (2010)
28. Peñaloza, R.: Axiom-Pinpointing in Description Logics and Beyond. Ph.D. thesis, Dresden University of Technology, Germany (2009)
29. Reiter, R.: A theory of diagnosis from first principles. Artificial Intelligence 32(1), 57–95 (1987)
30. Rosati, R.: On the complexity of dealing with inconsistency in description logic ontologies. In: Walsh, T. (ed.) Proceedings of the 22nd International Joint Conference on Artificial Intelligence (IJCAI 2011), pp. 1057–1062. AAAI Press (2011)
31. Spackman, K.: Managing clinical terminology hierarchies using algorithmic calculation of subsumption: Experience with SNOMED-RT. Journal of the American Medical Informatics Association (2000); fall Symposium Special Issue
32. W3C OWL Working Group: OWL 2 web ontology language document overview. W3C Recommendation (2009), http://www.w3.org/TR/owl2-overview/

Sub-propositional Fragments of the Interval Temporal Logic of Allen's Relations*

Davide Bresolin, Emilio Muñoz-Velasco, and Guido Sciavicco

1 Department of Computer Science and Engineering
University of Bologna, Italy
davide.bresolin@unibo.it
2 Department of Applied Mathematics
University of Malaga, Spain
emilio@ctima.uma.es
3 Department of Information, Engineering and Communications
University of Murcia, Spain
guido@um.es

Abstract. Interval temporal logics provide a natural framework for temporal reasoning about interval structures over linearly ordered domains, where intervals are taken as the primitive ontological entities. The most influential propositional interval-based logic is probably Halpern and Shoham's Modal Logic of Time Intervals, a.k.a. HS. While most studies focused on the computational properties of the syntactic fragments that arise by considering only a subset of the set of modalities, the fragments that are obtained by weakening the propositional side have received very scarce attention. Here, we approach this problem by considering various sub-propositional fragments of HS, such as the so-called Horn, Krom, and core fragment. We prove that the Horn fragment of HS is undecidable on every interesting class of linearly ordered sets, and we briefly discuss the difficulties that arise when considering the other fragments.

1 Introduction

Most temporal logics proposed in the literature assume a point-based model of time, and they have been successfully applied in a variety of fields. However, a number of relevant application domains, such as planning and synthesis of controllers, are characterized by advanced features that are neglected or dealt with in an unsatisfactory way by point-based formalisms. Interval temporal logics provide a natural framework for temporal reasoning about interval structures over linearly (or partially) ordered domains. They take time intervals as the primitive ontological entities and define truth of formulas relative to time intervals, rather than time points; their modalities correspond to various relations between

---

* The authors acknowledge the support from the Italian GNCS Project *"Automata, games and temporal logics for verification and synthesis of safety-critical systems"* (D. Bresolin), the Spanish Project *TIN12-39353-C04-01* (E. Muñoz-Velasco), and the Spanish fellowship program *'Ramon y Cajal' RYC-2011-07821* (G. Sciavicco).

E. Fermé and J. Leite (Eds.): JELIA 2014, LNAI 8761, pp. 122–136, 2014.

pairs of intervals. Applications of interval-based reasoning systems range from hardware and real-time system verification to natural language processing, from constraint satisfaction to planning [1, 11, 20, 23].

The well-known logic HS [16] features a set of modalities that make it possible to express all Allen's interval relations [1]. HS is highly undecidable over most classes of linear orders, and this result motivated the search for (syntactic) HS fragments offering a good balance between expressiveness and decidability/complexity. The few decidable fragments that have been found present complexities that range from NP-complete (in very simple cases) to NEXPTIME-complete, to EXPSPACE-complete, to non-primitive recursive [5, 6, 8, 10, 17–19]. While the classification of fragments of HS in terms of the allowed modal operators can be considered almost completed, sub-propositional fragments of HS have received very scarce attention in the literature. Three propositional restrictions are often mentioned in the context of propositional, first-order, and modal logics, namely the *Horn*, *Krom*, and *core* fragments. They are all based on the *clausal* form of formulas, i.e., implications of the type $(\lambda_1 \wedge \ldots \wedge \lambda_n) \to (\lambda_{n+1} \vee \ldots \vee \lambda_{n+m})$ and define a particular fragment by limiting the applicability of Boolean operators and the number of literals in the clauses. In the case of modal logics, the restriction to Horn and core clauses can be separated into two cases, that basically differ from each other on the role played by existential modalities (diamonds). In the classical version, one may freely use both existential (diamond) and universal (box) modalities in *positive literals* [13, 14, 22], while in Artale's et. al. version [3] the use of existential modalities is restricted to obtain better computational properties. This duality does not affect the Krom fragment, since the existential modalities can be recovered using only boxes (preserving the satisfiability).

In this paper, we consider the five expressively different sub-propositional fragments of HS that emerge from the above discussion, and we prove that the Horn fragment of HS is undecidable under very weak assumptions of the underlying linear order (in fact, it is undecidable in any class of linear orders where full HS is). While inspired by existing work, our proof, which is the main contribution of this paper, necessarily differs from previous ones due to the limited expressive power of the Horn fragment. We conclude the paper by briefly discussing the reasons that make the Krom and core fragments more difficult to deal with.

2   HS: Syntax and Semantics

Let $\mathbb{D} = \langle D, < \rangle$ be a linearly ordered set. An *interval* over $\mathbb{D}$ is an ordered pair $[x, y]$, where $a, b \in D$ and $a < b$. In this paper, we assume the *strict semantics*, that is, we exclude point intervals and only consider strict intervals. The adoption of the strict semantics instead of the *non-strict semantics*, which includes point intervals, conforms to the definition of interval adopted by Allen in [1], but differs from the one given by Halpern and Shoham in [16]. It has at least two strong motivations: first, a number of representation paradoxes

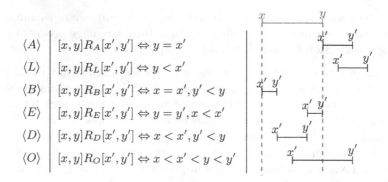

$\langle A \rangle$	$[x,y]R_A[x',y'] \Leftrightarrow y = x'$
$\langle L \rangle$	$[x,y]R_L[x',y'] \Leftrightarrow y < x'$
$\langle B \rangle$	$[x,y]R_B[x',y'] \Leftrightarrow x = x', y' < y$
$\langle E \rangle$	$[x,y]R_E[x',y'] \Leftrightarrow y = y', x < x'$
$\langle D \rangle$	$[x,y]R_D[x',y'] \Leftrightarrow x < x', y' < y$
$\langle O \rangle$	$[x,y]R_O[x',y'] \Leftrightarrow x < x' < y < y'$

Fig. 1. Allen's interval relations and the corresponding HS modalities

arise when the non-strict semantics is adopted, due to the presence of point intervals, as pointed out in [1]; second, when point intervals are included there seems to be no intuitive semantics for interval relations that makes them both pairwise disjoint and jointly exhaustive. It should be observed that, from the decidability/undecidability/complexity point of view, no differences have ever been found between the two semantic choices; there are no reasons to suspect that sub-propositional strict and non-strict HS restrictions might behave in a different way. If we exclude the identity relation, there are 12 different relations between two strict intervals in a linear order, often called *Allen's relations* [1]: the six relations R_A (adjacent to), R_L (later than), R_B (begins), R_E (ends), R_D (during), and R_O (overlaps), depicted in Fig. 1, and their inverses, that is, $R_{\overline{X}} = (R_X)^{-1}$, for each $X \in \{A, L, B, E, D, O\}$.

We interpret interval structures as Kripke structures, with Allen's relations playing the role of the accessibility relations. Thus, we associate a universal modality $[X]$ and an existential modality $\langle X \rangle$ with each Allen relation R_X. For each $X \in \{A, L, B, E, D, O\}$, the *transposes* of the modalities $[X]$ and $\langle X \rangle$ are the modalities $[\overline{X}]$ and $\langle \overline{X} \rangle$, corresponding to the inverse relation $R_{\overline{X}}$ of R_X. Halpern and Shoham's logic HS [16] is a multi-modal logic with formulas built from a finite, non-empty set $\mathcal{AP}$ of atomic propositions (also referred to as proposition letters), the classical propositional connectives, and a pair of modalities for each Allen relation:

$$\varphi ::= \bot \mid p \mid \neg\varphi \mid \varphi \vee \varphi \mid \varphi \wedge \varphi \mid \langle X \rangle\varphi \mid [X]\varphi \mid \langle \overline{X} \rangle\varphi \mid [\overline{X}]\varphi, \qquad (1)$$

where $p \in \mathcal{AP}$ and $X \in \{A, L, B, E, D, O\}$. The (strict) semantics of HS is given in terms of *interval models* $M = \langle \mathbb{I}(\mathbb{D}), V \rangle$, where $\mathbb{D}$ is a linear order, $\mathbb{I}(\mathbb{D})$ is the set of all (strict) intervals over $\mathbb{D}$, and V is a *valuation function* $V : \mathcal{AP} \mapsto 2^{\mathbb{I}(\mathbb{D})}$, which assigns to each atomic proposition $p \in \mathcal{AP}$ the set of intervals $V(p)$ on which p holds. The *truth* of a formula on a given interval $[x, y]$ in an interval model M is defined by structural induction on formulas as follows:

- $M, [x, y] \Vdash p$ if and only if $[x, y] \in V(p)$;
- Boolean connectives are dealt with in the standard way;

- $M, [x, y] \Vdash \langle X \rangle \psi$ if and only if there exists $[x', y']$ such that $[x, y] R_X [x', y']$ and $M, [x', y'] \Vdash \psi$;
- $M, [x, y] \Vdash [X] \psi$ if and only if for every $[x', y']$ such that $[x, y] R_X [x', y']$ we have that $M, [x', y'] \Vdash \psi$;
- $M, [x, y] \Vdash \langle \overline{X} \rangle \psi$ if and only if there exists $[x', y']$ such that $[x, y] R_{\overline{X}} [x', y']$ and $M, [x', y'] \Vdash \psi$;
- $M, [x, y] \Vdash [\overline{X}] \psi$ if and only if for every $[x', y']$ such that $[x, y] R_{\overline{X}} [x', y']$ we have that $M, [x', y'] \Vdash \psi$.

Formulas of HS can be interpreted over different classes of interval models, built from different classes of linear orders. Among others, we mention the following important classes of linear orders:

(i) the class of *all* linear orders Lin;

(ii) the class of *dense* linear orders Den, that is, those in which for every pair of distinct points there exists at least one point in between them (e.g., $\mathbb{Q}$ and $\mathbb{R}$);

(iii) the class of *strongly discrete* linear orders Dis, that is, those in which there is a finite number of elements between any two distinct elements;

(iv) the class of *weakly discrete* linear orders WDis, where every element, apart from the greatest element—if it exists—has an immediate successor, and every element, other than the least element—if it exists—has an immediate predecessor (this class includes, e.g., $\mathbb{Z} + \mathbb{Z}$);

(v) the class of *finite* linear orders Fin, that is, those having only finitely many points.

It is important to observe that all classes mentioned above, except Fin, share the common characteristic that possess at least one linear order with an infinitely ascending sequence of points (*infinite chain*).

3   Sub-propositional Fragments of HS

A *syntactical* fragment of HS can be defined by restricting the grammar (1) either by limiting the set of modalities that are included in the language, by limiting nesting of temporal modalities, or by restricting the application of boolean operators. While the first choice (limiting the set of modalities) has been extensively explored, the other two choices has received much scarcer attention. One of the very few examples is [9], where a NP-complete fragment of the temporal logic CDT (which includes HS) has been identified by limiting the nesting of temporal modalities. Here, we study restrictions of interval-based temporal logics along a different line: we limit the applicability of Boolean operators.

To enter into the details we need to start by defining the clausal form of HS-formulas. Clausal forms of modal logics, such as K, can be found, e.g., in [21]. In the context of temporal logics, such as Linear Temporal Logic (LTL), clausal forms [15] have been extensively explored for its applications in automated reasoning. No clausal forms for pure interval-based temporal logics have been proposed so far, to the best of our knowledge. We first introduce the notion of *positive temporal literals*, given by the following grammar:

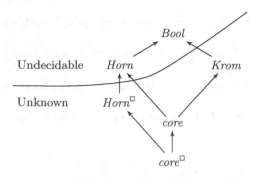

Fig. 2. Relative expressive power between sub-propositional restrictions and their decidability status for HS

$$\lambda ::= \bot \mid p \mid \langle X \rangle \bot \mid [X]\bot \mid \langle X \rangle p \mid [X]p \mid [U]p, \tag{2}$$

where $[X]$ and $\langle X \rangle$ HS modalities, and $[U]$ is the *universal* modality, that can be defined in HS in several ways, such as:

$$[U]\varphi = [\overline{A}][\overline{A}][A]\varphi \wedge [\overline{A}][A]\varphi \wedge [\overline{A}][A][A]\varphi. \tag{3}$$

An HS-formula is said to be in *clausal* form if and only if it can be written following the grammar:

$$\varphi ::= \lambda \mid \neg\lambda \mid [U](\neg\lambda_1 \vee \ldots \vee \neg\lambda_n \vee \lambda_{n+1} \vee \ldots \vee \lambda_{n+m}) \mid \varphi \wedge \varphi. \tag{4}$$

Every HS-formula can be transformed into an equi-satisfiable conjunction of HS-clauses; this transformation is rather standard.

Definition 1. *An* HS-*clause is said to be* Bool *if it can be obtained from (4); it is said to be* Horn *if* $m \leq 1$; *it is said to be* Krom *if* $n + m \leq 2$; *finally, it is said to be* core *if it is both* Bool *and* Horn, *that is, if* $n + m \leq 2$ *and* $m \leq 1$.

Here, we follow the classical definition of modal clauses [14, 15, 21, 22]. In [3], positive literals are defined restricting (2) by eliminating $\langle X \rangle \lambda$. As far as Bool and Krom clauses are concerned, this elimination does not weaken the expressive power; as a matter of fact, formulas of the type $\varphi = \langle X \rangle \psi$ can be recovered by introducing a new propositional letter p_φ, and by using the conjunction of clauses $\neg[X]p_\varphi \wedge [U](p_\varphi \vee \psi)$, which is clearly equi-satisfiable to φ. On the other hand, this is not necessarily true for Horn and core clauses. If we denote the latter fragments by $Horn^\square$ and $core^\square$, respectively, the relative expressive power for sub-propositional fragments of HS is as displayed in Fig. 2.

In this paper we prove that restricting to the Horn fragment of HS (HS$_{Horn}$) is not sufficient to recover decidability. The decidability/undecidability status of the Horn$^\square$, Krom, and core$^\square$ fragments is still an open problem. For the sake of comparison, we mention here that for LTL, whose satisfiability problem is PSPACE-complete [25], the complexity does not change neither when we restrict to the Horn fragment [12] nor to the Horn$^\square$ fragment (Chen and Lin's proof the use of diamond positive literal is not essential). In [3] it is proved that the core$^\square$ fragment of LTL is NP-hard and that the Krom fragment is NP, proving that all remaining restrictions of LTL are, in fact, NP-complete. Finally, only the Horn fragment of the modal logic K has been studied, and its complexity is the same as in the case of full K [22], that is, PSPACE-complete. Although the Krom and the core restrictions of modal and temporal logics have not received much attention in the literature, similar restrictions have been studied at least in the context of Description Logics, both in the atemporal case [2], and in the temporal one [4], justifying the interest in such sub-propositional limitations.

4   Undecidability of HS$_{Horn}$ in the Infinite Case

In this section, we assume that HS$_{Horn}$ is interpreted in any class of linearly ordered sets that possesses at least one linear order with an infinite chain, therefore solving the cases Lin, Den, Dis, and WDis. In the next section, we show how to modify the proof to deal with the case of Fin. Our construction adapts to the restricted applicability of Boolean operators the ideas from both the original undecidability proof for full HS [16], as well as the more recent undecidability proofs for fragments of HS [7]. It is based on a reduction of the *non-halting problem* of a deterministic Turing Machine on empty input [24].

A *Turing Machine* is defined as a tuple $\mathcal{A} = (Q, \Sigma, \Gamma, \delta, q_0, q_f)$, where Q is the set of states, q_0 (resp., q_f) is the initial (resp., final) state, Σ is the machine's alphabet that does not contain $\sqcup$ (blank), $\Gamma = \Sigma \cup \{\sqcup\}$ is the tape alphabet, and $\delta : Q \times \Gamma \to Q \times \Gamma \times \{L, R\}$ is the transition function (L, R represent the possible moves on the machine's tape: left, right). Even under the assumption that $\Sigma = \{0, 1\}$ and that the input is empty, both the halting and the non-halting problem for a deterministic Turing Machine are undecidable [24] (as a matter of fact, the former is R.E.-complete, while the latter is CO-R.E.-complete).

Our reduction is based on the idea of representing the *computation history* of $\mathcal{A}$. A *configuration* represents the status of $\mathcal{A}$ at a given moment of the computation, and includes the content of the tape, the position of the reading head, and the current state. Elements of the tape will be placed over *unit intervals* (or, simply, *units*), which we shall denote by u. We shall use the propositional symbol $*$ to separate successive configurations, $0, 1, \sqcup$ to represent tape cells *not* under the machine's head, and the propositional symbols q^c, with $q \in Q \setminus \{q_f\}$ and $c \in \{0, 1, \sqcup\}$, to represent the tape cell under the head and the current (non-final) state of the machine. Let $\mathcal{L}$ be the set $\{0, 1, \sqcup, *\} \cup \{q^c \mid q \in Q \setminus \{q_f\} \wedge c \in \{0, 1, \sqcup\}\} \cup \{q_f\}$, and consider the following group of formulas.

$$\phi_1 = \langle A \rangle u \wedge [U](u \to \langle A \rangle u) \qquad\qquad u\text{-}chain\ exists$$
$$\phi_2 = \langle A \rangle Start \wedge [U](Start \to \neg\langle \overline{A} \rangle u) \wedge [U](Start \to \neg\langle \overline{L} \rangle u) \quad no\ u\ in\ the\ past$$
$$\phi_3 = [U](u \to \neg\langle B \rangle u) \wedge [U](u \to \neg\langle E \rangle u) \qquad\qquad u\text{-}chain\ unique\ (1)$$
$$\phi_4 = [U](u \to \neg\langle D \rangle u) \wedge [U](u \to \neg\langle O \rangle u) \qquad\qquad u\text{-}chain\ unique\ (2)$$
$$\phi_5 = \bigwedge_{l \in \mathcal{L}} [U](l \to u) \qquad tape/state\ propositions\ and\ *\ are\ units$$
$$\phi_6 = \bigwedge_{l, l' \in \mathcal{L}, l \neq l'} [U](l \to \neg l') \qquad tape/state\ propositions\ and\ *\ are\ unique$$

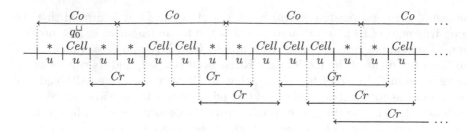

Fig. 3. Configurations

Lemma 1. *Suppose that $M, [x, y] \Vdash \phi_1 \wedge \ldots \wedge \phi_6$, then there exists an infinite sequence of points $y = y_0 < y_1 < \ldots$ such that:*

1. *for each $i \geq 0$, $M, [y_i, y_{i+1}] \Vdash u$;*
2. *no other interval $[z, t]$ satisfies u, unless $z > y_i$ for each $i \geq 0$;*
3. *for each interval $[z, t]$, if $M, [z, t] \Vdash l$ and $l \in \mathcal{L}$, then $M, [z, t] \Vdash u$;*
4. *for each $l_1, l_2 \in \mathcal{L}$ where $l_1 \neq l_2$, $M, [z, t] \Vdash l_1$ implies $M, [z, t] \not\Vdash l_2$.*

Proof. Since $M, [x, y] \Vdash \langle A \rangle u$, there exists $y' > y$ such that $[y, y']$ satisfies u; let us call $y_0 = y$ and $y_1 = y'$. From the fact that $M, [x, y] \Vdash [U](u \rightarrow \langle A \rangle u)$ we can easily conclude that the chain $y_0, y_1, \ldots$ exists (proving (1)). Consider now an interval $[z, t]$, such that $z \leq y_i$ for some y_i, $M, [z, t] \Vdash u$, but $[z, t] \neq [y_j, y_{j+1}]$ for each $j \geq 0$. We can assume w.l.o.g. that y_i is the smallest point of the chain such that $z \leq y_i$. Towards a contradiction, assume $z = y_i$; this means that $[z, t]$ is a u-interval that starts or is started by the u-interval $[y_i, y_{i+1}]$, which contradicts ϕ_3. Hence, $z < y_i$, and we can distinguish between the following cases. If $t > y_i$ then $[z, t]$ either contains, is finished by, or overlaps the u-interval $[y_j, y_{j+1}]$ in contradiction with ϕ_3 or ϕ_4. If $t \leq y_i$ and $y_i > y_0$ then $[z, t]$ is contained in the u-interval $[y_{j-1}, y_j]$, in contradiction with ϕ_4. Finally, if $y_i = y_0$ then $t \leq y_0$ and we have a contradiction with ϕ_2 (proving (2)). Thanks to ϕ_5 and ϕ_6, if some $l \in \mathcal{L}$ labels an interval, then it must be a u-interval (proving (3)), and such l is unique (proving (4)). □

Remark 1. Notice that Lemma 1 enables us to use a copy of $\mathbb{N}$, represented by the sequence $y_0, y_1, \ldots$, embedded into the (not necessarily discrete) linearly ordered set under consideration.

Configurations (denoted by Co) must be composed by unit intervals; there must be an infinite sequence of them; and each one must be started and finished by a unit labeled by $*$ (see Fig. 3). We use the proposition $Cell$ to characterize unit intervals containing a tape symbol (and not an $*$). Consider the following formulas:

$$\phi_7 = \langle A \rangle Co \wedge [U](Co \rightarrow \langle B \rangle *) \wedge [U](Co \rightarrow \langle E \rangle *) \qquad \textit{configuration structure}$$
$$\phi_8 = [U](Co \rightarrow \langle A \rangle Co) \qquad\qquad\qquad\qquad\qquad \textit{configuration sequence}$$

$\phi_9 = [U](Co \rightarrow [B]\neg Co) \wedge [U](Co \rightarrow [E]\neg Co)$ *configurations relations*

$\phi_{10} = [U](* \rightarrow \neg Cell) \wedge [U](Cell \rightarrow u) \wedge [U](((\langle \overline{D} \rangle Co \wedge u) \rightarrow Cell)$ *Cell iff* $\neg *$

Now, we have to make sure that the initial configuration is exactly as requested by the problem, that is, empty tape with the machine in the initial state q_0. This implies that the first Co must be a sequence of three unit intervals labeled respectively with $*$, $q_0^{\sqcup}$, and $*$. In order to encode exactly this situation, we make use of three new propositions N_1, N_2, and N_3.

$\phi_{11} = \langle A \rangle N_1 \wedge [U](N_1 \rightarrow \langle A \rangle N_2) \wedge [U](N_2 \rightarrow \langle A \rangle N_3)$ *Ns' position*

$\phi_{12} = [U](N_1 \rightarrow *) \wedge [U](N_2 \rightarrow q_0^{\sqcup}) \wedge [U](N_3 \rightarrow *)$ N_1, N_2, N_3's *content*

The length of successive configurations is controlled by the proposition Cr:

$\phi_{13} = [U](Cell \rightarrow \langle A \rangle Cr) \wedge [U](Cr \rightarrow \langle A \rangle Cell)$ *all cells forward-corr to cell*

$\phi_{14} = [U](Cell \wedge \langle A \rangle Cell \rightarrow \langle \overline{A} \rangle Cr)$ *all cells, but the last, back-corr to cell*

$\phi_{15} = [U](Cr \rightarrow [B]\neg Cr) \wedge [U](Cr \rightarrow [E]\neg Cr)$ *correspondences relations (1)*

$\phi_{16} = [U](Cr \rightarrow [D]\neg Cr) \wedge [U](Cr \rightarrow \langle \overline{A} \rangle Cell)$ *correspondences relations (2)*

$\phi_{17} = [U](Co \rightarrow [D]\neg Cr) \wedge [U](Co \rightarrow [E]\neg Cr)$ *config./corr. (1)*

$\phi_{18} = [U](Co \rightarrow [\overline{D}]\neg Cr) \wedge [U](Co \rightarrow [\overline{E}]\neg Cr)$ *config./corr. (2)*

Lemma 2. *Suppose that* $M, [x, y] \Vdash \phi_1 \wedge \ldots \wedge \phi_{18}$, *and consider the infinite sequence* $y_0, y_1, \ldots$, *where* $y = y_0$, *whose existence is guaranteed by Lemma 1. Then, there exists an infinite sequence of indexes* $k_0, k_1, \ldots$, *such that* $y_0 = y_{k_0}$ *and:*

1. $M, [y_0, y_1] \Vdash *$, $M, [y_1, y_2] \Vdash q_0^{\sqcup}$, *and* $M, [y_2, y_3] \Vdash *$;
2. *for each* $i \geq 0$, $M, [y_{k_i}, y_{k_{(i+1)}}] \Vdash Co$;
3. *for each* $i \geq 0$, $M, [y_{k_i}, y_{(k_i+1)}] \Vdash *$, $M, [y_{(k_{(i+1)}-1)}, y_{k_{(i+1)}}] \Vdash *$;
4. *for each* $i \geq 0$, $j \geq 1$, $M, [y_{(k_i+j)}, y_{(k_i+j+1)}] \Vdash Cell \wedge \neg *$;
5. *for each* $i \geq 0$, $j \geq 2$, $M, [y_{(k_i+j)}, y_{(k_{(i+1)}+j-1)}] \Vdash Cr$;
6. $k_1 - k_0 = 3$ *and, for every* $i > 1$, $0 \leq (k_i - k_{(i-1)}) - (k_{(i-1)} - k_{(i-2)}) \leq 1$;
7. *no other interval* $[z, t]$ *satisfies* Co *nor* Cr, *unless* $z > y_i$ *for each* $i \geq 0$.

Proof. Since $M, [x, y] \Vdash \phi_{11} \wedge \phi_{12}$, the first three units of the chain $y_0, y_1, \ldots$ are determined, and are, in this order, $*$, $q_0^{\sqcup}$, and $*$ (proving (1)).

Now, let us call $y_{k_0} = y_0$. The fact that a chain of Co-intervals starts at y_{k_0} is guaranteed by ϕ_7 and ϕ_8. We prove (2)–(6) by induction on the index i. For the base case, we need to prove that the Co-interval $[y_{k_0}, t]$ is such that $t = y_3$. Suppose, for the sake of contradiction, that $t < y_3$; in this case, we have a contradiction with ϕ_7 and with Lemma 1. If, on the other hand, $t > y_3$, then the Co-interval $[y_{k_0}, t]$ strictly contains $*$ by (1), and this is in contradiction with ϕ_{10}. Therefore, $t = y_3$, and we can set $y_{k_1} = y_3$. It remains to be shown that (5) holds for the base case. We know that $[y_{k_1}, t] = [y_3, t]$ is a Co-interval for some t, that $[y_3, y_4]$ is a $*$-interval, and that $[y_4, y_5]$ is a $Cell$-interval (by ϕ_7, ϕ_{10}). We also know that $[y_2, z]$ is a Cr-interval for some z by ϕ_{13}. We want to prove $z = y_4$. By ϕ_{13} we deduce that $z \geq y_4$. Suppose, by the sake of contradiction, that $z > y_4$. Let us analyze the content of $[y_5, y_6]$. If it is $*$, then $z \geq y_6$, and by ϕ_7 and ϕ_{10}, $[y_3, y_6]$ is a Co-interval, which either ends or is strictly contained in the Cr-interval $[y_2, z]$, a contradiction with ϕ_{18}. If it is $Cell$, by ϕ_{14}, $[s, y_4]$ must be a Cr-interval for some s. It happens that $s \geq y_2$ contradicts ϕ_{15} or ϕ_{16}, and that $s < y_2$ contradicts ϕ_{16} or Lemma 1. Therefore, s cannot be placed anywhere, and $z = y_4$. Thus (5) holds in the base case.

For the inductive case, assume (2)–(6) hold up to $i - 1$: we prove that (2)–(6) hold for i. By induction hypothesis, $[y_{k_{(i-1)}}, y_{k_i}]$ is a Co-interval for which (2)–(6) hold. By ϕ_8, $[y_{k_i}, t]$ is a Co-interval for some t. Assume that $(k_i - 1) - (k_{(i-1)} + 1) = n$, that is, assume that the Co-interval $[y_{k_{(i-1)}}, y_{k_i}]$ has precisely n (non-*) cells. Since $[y_{(k_i-1)}, y_{(k_i+n)}]$ is a Cr-interval by (5) applied on $i - 1$, then $[y_{(k_i+n)}, y_{(k_i+n+1)}]$ is a $Cell$-interval, and $[y_{(k_i+n+1)}, y_{(k_i+n+2)}]$ is either *-interval or a $Cell$-interval. In the first case, we let $y_{k_{(i+1)}} = y_{(k_i+n+2)}$ (proving (6) on i); in the second case, $[y_{(k_i+n+2)}, y_{(k_i+n+3)}]$ must be a *-interval (otherwise, we apply the same argument as in the base case, showing that there would be a Cr-interval whose starting point cannot be placed anywhere), and therefore we let $y_{k_{(i+1)}} = y_{(k_i+n+3)}$ (again, proving (6) on i). This argument also proves (2)–(4) for i. It remains to be proved that (5) holds the inductive case. To this end, we proceed, again, by induction on j, starting with the base case $j = 2$. By ϕ_{13}, $[y_{(k_i+2)}, z]$ is a Cr-interval. From ϕ_{17} we know $z > y_{k_{(i+1)}}$. Observe that $[y_{k_{(i+1)}}, t]$ is a Co-interval for some t; from ϕ_{18} we know that $z < t$. Towards a contradiction, assume $z > y_{k_{(i+1)}+1}$. Thanks to ϕ_{13}, the point z must start a cell, so that we can assume w.l.o.g. that $[y_{k_{(i+1)}+2}, y_{k_{(i+1)}+3}]$ is a cell. Then, by ϕ_{14}, $[s, y_{k_{(i+1)}+1}]$ must be a Cr-interval for some s, and by the same argument that we used before, we can prove that s cannot be placed anywhere. Thus, $z = y_{k_{(i+1)}+1}$ (proving (5)) in the base case. Now, it is easy to see that the inductive case proceeds in the same way; we can then conclude that (5) holds for each $j > 2$.

Finally, suppose that $M, [z, t] \Vdash Co$, $z \leq y_i$ for some i, and $[z, t] \neq [y_{k_i}, y_{k_{i+1}}]$ for each i. If $z < y_0$, then, by ϕ_7, z must start some u-interval, which is in contradiction with Lemma 1. Otherwise, $[z, t]$ is a Co-interval either contained, or started by, or ended by another Co-interval, which is in contradiction with ϕ_9. A similar reasoning applies for Cr-intervals (proving (7)).   □

The above two lemmas help us to set the underlying structure which we can now use to ensure the correct behaviour of $\mathcal{A}$. We are left with the problem of encoding the transition function δ. To this end, we enrich our language with a new set of propositional letters $\mathcal{L}^t = \{(l_1, l_2, l_3) \mid \forall i(1 \leq i \leq 3 \to l_i \in \mathcal{L})\}$ $(=\mathcal{L} \times \mathcal{L} \times \mathcal{L})$. Each proposition in $\mathcal{L}^t$ represents the content of three consecutive u-intervals; in this way, we have all information needed to encode δ at each step by reading only one proposition. We proceed as follows: first, the value of three successive cells is encoded in the correct triple from $\mathcal{L}^t$ and placed over a Cr-interval; second, this information is used to label the cells of the next configuration (see Fig 4) by taking into account the transition function δ. In the encoding of δ, we treat as special cases the situations in which: (i) the head is at the last cell of the segment of the tape currently shown and the head must be moved to the right and, (ii) the head is at the first cell of the tape and the head must be moved to the left. Consider the following formulas,

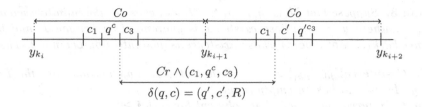

Fig. 4. An example of transition

where $c, c', c_1, c_2, c_3 \in \{0, 1, \sqcup, *\}$ and $q, q' \in Q$ (by a little abuse of notation, we assume that all symbols q_f^c are equal to q_f).

$$\phi_{19} = \bigwedge_{l_1, l_2, l_3 \in \mathcal{L}, l_2 \neq *} [U]((\langle \langle A \rangle l_1 \wedge l_2 \wedge \langle A \rangle l_3) \to \langle A \rangle (l_1, l_2, l_3)) \qquad \textit{info transfer}$$

$$\phi_{20} = \bigwedge_{l_1, l_2, l_3 \in \mathcal{L}} [U]((l_1, l_2, l_3) \to Cr) \qquad \textit{triple structure}$$

$$\phi_{21} = \bigwedge_{(c_1, c_2, c_3) \in \mathcal{L}^t} [U]((c_1, c_2, c_3) \to \langle A \rangle c_2) \qquad \textit{far from the head}$$

$$\phi_{22} = \bigwedge_{(c_1, q^c, c_3) \in \mathcal{L}^t}^{\delta(q,c) = (q', c', R)} [U]((c_1, q^c, c_3) \to \langle A \rangle c') \qquad \textit{rightwards (1)}$$

$$\phi_{23} = \bigwedge_{(q^c, c_2, c_3) \in \mathcal{L}^t, c_2 \neq *}^{\delta(q,c) = (q', c', R)} [U]((q^c, c_2, c_3) \to \langle A \rangle q'^{c_2}) \qquad \textit{rightwards (2)}$$

$$\phi_{24} = \bigwedge_{(c_1, c_2, q^c) \in \mathcal{L}^t}^{\delta(q,c) = (q', c', R)} [U]((c_1, c_2, q^c) \to \langle A \rangle c_2)) \qquad \textit{rightwards (3)}$$

$$\phi_{25} = \bigwedge_{(c_1, q^d, *) \in \mathcal{L}^t}^{\delta(q,c) = (q', c', R)} [U]((c_1, q^c, *) \to \langle A \rangle N^{q', c'}) \qquad \textit{last cell (1)}$$

$$\phi_{26} = \bigwedge_{N^{q', c'}} ([U](N^{q', c'} \to c') \wedge [U](N^{q', c'} \to \langle A \rangle q'^{\sqcup})) \qquad \textit{last cell (2)}$$

$$\phi_{27} = \bigwedge_{(c_1, q^c, c_3) \in \mathcal{L}^t, c_1 \neq *}^{\delta(q,c) = (q', c', L)} [U]((c_1, q^c, c_3) \to \langle A \rangle c') \qquad \textit{leftwards (1)}$$

$$\phi_{28} = \bigwedge_{(q^c, c_2, c_3) \in \mathcal{L}^t}^{\delta(q,c) = (q', c', L)} [U]((q^c, c_2, c_3) \to \langle A \rangle c_2) \qquad \textit{leftwards (2)}$$

$$\phi_{29} = \bigwedge_{(c_1, c_2, q^c) \in \mathcal{L}^t, c_2 \neq *}^{\delta(q,c) = (q', c', L)} [U]((c_1, c_2, q^c) \to \langle A \rangle q'^{c_2}) \qquad \textit{leftwards (3)}$$

$$\phi_{30} = \bigwedge_{(*, q^c, c_3) \in \mathcal{L}^t}^{\delta(q,c) = (q', c', L)} [U]((*, q^c, c_3) \to \langle A \rangle q'^{c'}) \qquad \textit{first cell (2)}$$

We can now prove that our construction works as designed. For a Turing Machine $\mathcal{A}$, we denote by C any $\mathcal{A}$-configuration, univocally determined by the content of the (interesting prefix of the) tape, the position of the reading head, and the state. An $\mathcal{A}$-configuration can be seen as the semantical counterpart of a *Co*-interval in our construction. An $\mathcal{A}$-configuration is said to be *initial* if its state is q_0, and *final* if its state is q_f and for any two $\mathcal{A}$-configurations C, C', we say that C' is the *successor* of C if and only if C' is obtained by C after exactly one application of δ. Finally, a *Co*-interval $[y_{k_i}, y_{k_{i+1}}]$ is said to be *coherent* if and only if the following two conditions apply: *(i)* there exists exactly one u-interval $[y_{(k_i+j)}, y_{(k_i+j+1)}]$ labeled by a symbol of the type q^d, where $q \in Q$ and $d \in \{0, 1, \sqcup\}$; *(ii)* every other interval $[y_{(k_i+h)}, y_{(k_i+h+1)}]$ labeled with *Cell* is also labeled by a symbol $d \in \{0, 1, \sqcup\}$. The following lemma allows us to determine the link between $\mathcal{A}$-configurations and *Co*-intervals.

Lemma 3. *Suppose that* $M, [x, y] \Vdash \phi_1 \wedge \ldots \wedge \phi_{30}$, *consider the infinite sequence* $y_0, y_1, \ldots,$ *where* $y = y_0$, *whose existence is guaranteed by Lemma 1, and the sequence* $k_0, k_1, \ldots$ *of indexes whose existence is guaranteed by Lemma 2. Then:*

1. *the Co-interval* $[y_{k_0}, y_{k_1}]$ *represents the initial $\mathcal{A}$-configuration when the Turing Machine $\mathcal{A}$ has an empty input;*
2. *the Co-interval* $[y_{k_{i+1}}, y_{k_{i+2}}]$ *is coherent for each* $i \geq 0$;
3. *the $\mathcal{A}$-configuration represented by the Co-interval* $[y_{k_i}, y_{k_{i+1}}]$ *is the successor of the $\mathcal{A}$-configuration represented by the Co-interval* $[y_{k_{i-1}}, y_{k_i}]$, *for each* $i > 0$.

Proof. The content of the interval $[y_{k_0}, y_{k_1}]$ is set as in Lemma 2, proving its coherence and its status of initial configuration (proving (1)). Points (2) and (3) must be proved together, and by induction; the base case is, as a matter of fact, a consequence of (1) (notice that at the base case, (3) is trivially satisfied). Consider, now, an index $i > 0$ and the $\mathcal{A}$-configuration C represented by the Co-interval $[y_{k_{i-1}}, y_{k_i}]$. Assume that the state in C is q, and that the head is reading $c \neq *$. There are several cases to be considered, depending on the movement required by δ, the relative position of the j-th cell ($j \geq 1$) currently read by the head (labeled, by hypothesis, with q^c), and the content c of its adjacent cell.

(a) $\delta(q, c) = (q', c', R)$ and the $(j+1)$-th unit is not $*$. By ϕ_{19} and ϕ_{20}, the unique Cr-interval $[y_{(k_{i-1}+j+1)}, y_{(k_i+j)}]$ is also labeled by (c_1, q^c, c_2) for some c_1, c_2. As a consequence, by ϕ_{22}, the j-th unit of $[y_{k_i}, y_{k_{i+1}}]$ is labeled by c'. Now, if $j > 1$, then the $(j-1)$-th unit is a cell, and, by ϕ_{19} and ϕ_{20}, the Cr-interval $[y_{(k_{i-1}+j)}, y_{(k_i+j-1)}]$ is labeled by (c_3, c_1, q^c) (for some c_3); therefore ϕ_{24} applies, meaning that the $(j-1)$-th unit of $[y_{k_{i+1}}, y_{k_{i+2}}]$ is labeled by c_1. Similarly, the value of the $(j+1)$-th cell (which cannot be $*$), is set by ϕ_{23}. Now, by the coherence of $[y_{k_{i-1}}, y_{k_i}]$ (inductive hypothesis), every unit strictly before the $(j-1)$-th (excluding the 0-th unit) is a cell, as well as every unit strictly after the $(j+1)$-th (excluding the last one). In the case of $j = 1$, it is clear by Lemma 2, that the first unit of $[y_{k_{i+1}}, y_{k_{i+2}}]$ is labeled by $*$, and the rest of the proof is similar to the case $j > 1$. Therefore, by ϕ_{19} and ϕ_{20}, their corresponding Cr-intervals are labeled by triples that do not include q^c for any c, and thanks to ϕ_{21} their corresponding units in the Co-interval $[y_{k_i}, y_{k_{i+1}}]$ are cells (and their content, which is preserved, cannot be q^c for any c). Thus, $[y_{k_i}, y_{k_{(i+1)}}]$ is a coherent $\mathcal{A}$-configuration, and its content is obtained by exactly one application of δ (proving (2) and (3) in this case).

(b) $\delta(q, c) = (q', c', R)$ and the $(j+1)$-th unit is $*$. The content of the j-th unit of the i-th Co-interval is determined by ϕ_{25} and ϕ_{26}. In particular, the j-th unit of the i-th Cr-interval is labeled by $N^{q', c'}$, which implies that it is also labeled by c' (and therefore it is a cell), and that the $(j+1)$-th cell must exist and must be labeled by $q'^\sqcup$. The content of the remaining cells, and therefore the coherence of the the i-th Co-interval can be then deduced by applying the same argument as before (proving (2) and (3) in this case).

(c) $\delta(q, c) = (q', c', L)$ and the $(j - 1)$-th unit is not $*$. In this case, one can proceed as in case *(a)*, only applying ϕ_{27}, ϕ_{28}, and ϕ_{29}.

(d) $\delta(q, c) = (q', c', L)$ and the $(j - 1)$-th unit is $*$. In this case, one can proceed as in case *(a)*. The requirement ϕ_{30} plays a major role here: by definition, when δ demands a movement leftwards while the head is on the first cell, the head should not move. □

The construction is now completed.

Theorem 1. *Let $\mathcal{A}$ be a deterministic Turing Machine. Then, $\mathcal{A}$ diverges on empty input if and only if the HS_{Horn}-formula*

$$NotHalts = \phi_1 \wedge \ldots \wedge \phi_{30} \wedge \neg\langle L\rangle q_f$$

is satisfiable on a model with an infinite chain.

Proof. If the formula $\phi_1 \wedge \ldots \wedge \phi_{30} \wedge \neg\langle L\rangle q_f$ is satisfiable, using Lemmas 1–3, we get the desired construction for proving that the Turing Machine $\mathcal{A}$ has an infinite computation on empty input. Conversely, if $\mathcal{A}$ does not halt on empty input, it is a straightforward exercise to prove the satisfiability of the formula *NotHalts*. □

Corollary 1. *The satisfiability problem for HS_{Horn} over* Lin, Dis, WDis, *and* Den *is undecidable.*

5 Undecidability of HS_{Horn} in the Finite Case

When we restrict our attention to the class Fin, the reduction of the non-halting problem for deterministic Turing machines can no longer be carried out, since we cannot represent an infinite computation on a structure with a finite number of points. Nevertheless, undecidability of HS_{Horn} can be proved by a reduction of the *halting* problem for deterministic Turing machines. In this case the formula must represent a finite computation reaching the final state q_f, and, thus, can be satisfied by a finite model. This can be achieved by very small changes in the formulas we used in the previous section, which we briefly summarize here.

First of all, the u-chain now becomes finite, and its encoding can be simplified by exploiting the strong discreteness of the model. Hence, formulas $\phi_1 - \phi_4$ must be replaced by the following two formulas:

$$\psi_1 = [\overline{A}]\bot \wedge \langle A\rangle u \wedge [U]((u \wedge \langle A\rangle\top) \to \langle A\rangle u) \qquad \textit{u-chain exists}$$
$$\psi_2 = [U](u \to [B]\bot) \qquad \textit{u is of length 1}$$

Similarly, the chain of Co-intervals must be finite, and hence ϕ_8 must be changed:

$$\psi_8 = [U]((Co \wedge \langle A\rangle\top) \to \langle A\rangle Co) \qquad \textit{configuration sequence}$$

The structure of Cr-intervals requires a little more attention: now, it is no longer true that every cell of each configuration starts a Cr-interval, but only those cells that are not in the last configuration. This can be achieved by adding a new proposition *Cont* and replacing ϕ_{13} with:

$$\psi_{13a} = [U]((Co \wedge \langle A \rangle \top) \to Cont) \qquad\qquad \text{mark the non-last } Co$$
$$\psi_{13b} = [U]((Cell \wedge \langle \overline{D} \rangle Cont) \to \langle A \rangle Cr) \qquad\qquad \text{forward-corr to cell}$$

All other formulas remains unchanged.

Theorem 2. *Let $\mathcal{A}$ be a deterministic Turing Machine. Then, $\mathcal{A}$ converges on empty input if and only if the* HS_{Horn}-*formula*

$$Halts = \psi_1 \wedge \psi_2 \wedge \phi_5 \wedge \ldots \wedge \phi_7 \wedge \psi_8 \wedge \phi_9 \wedge \ldots \wedge \phi_{12} \wedge \psi_{13a} \wedge \psi_{13b} \wedge \phi_{14} \wedge \ldots \wedge \phi_{30} \wedge \langle L \rangle q_f$$

is satisfiable on a finite model.

Corollary 2. *The satisfiability problem for* HS_{Horn} *over* Fin *is undecidable.*

6   Conclusions

Sub-propositional fragments of classical and modal logics, such as the Horn and Krom fragments, have been extensively studied. The generally high complexity of the (few) decidable interval-based temporal logics justifies a certain interest in exploring the sub-propositional fragments of HS in search of languages that present a better computational behaviour, and yet are, expressiveness-wise, suitable for some applications. In this paper we proved a first negative result in this sense, by showing that HS is still undecidable when its Horn fragment is considered. This result has been obtained under very weak assumptions on the class of models in which the logic is interpreted; as a matter of fact, we proved that HS_{Horn} is undecidable on every meaningful class of linearly ordered set (precisely as full HS is).

Despite this initial result, we believe that sub-propositional fragments of interval temporal logics deserves further study. On one hand, we plan to consider the Horn$^\square$ fragments of decidable interval logics such as $A\overline{A}$ and $B\overline{B}L\overline{L}$, to understand whether or not their satisfiability problem present a better computational behaviour; initial analysis in this sense suggest that this could be the case. On the other hand, the decidability of the satisfiability problem is still an open issue for HS_{Krom}, HS_{core}, as well as for $\mathsf{HS}_{Horn\square}$ and $\mathsf{HS}_{core\square}$ (the weaker definitions of the Horn and core fragments considered in [3]). In this respect, it is worth to observe that in our construction of the formula *NotHalts* only three clauses, namely ϕ_{10}, ϕ_{14}, and ϕ_{19}, are not core. We are pretty confident that the first two formulas, ϕ_{10} and ϕ_{14}, can be rewritten in the core fragment. The last one, though, presents more difficulties. In addition, the construction makes an extensive use of diamond modalities, and hence seems not be applicable to the fragments $\mathsf{HS}_{Horn\square}$ and $\mathsf{HS}_{core\square}$, suggesting that they may even be decidable.

References

1. Allen, J.F.: Maintaining knowledge about temporal intervals. Communications of the ACM 26(11), 832–843 (1983)

2. Artale, A., Calvanese, D., Kontchakov, R., Zakharyaschev, M.: DL-lite in the light of first-order logic. In: Proc. of the 22nd AAAI Conference on Artificial Intelligence, pp. 361–366 (2007)
3. Artale, A., Kontchakov, R., Ryzhikov, V., Zakharyaschev, M.: The complexity of clausal fragments of LTL. In: McMillan, K., Middeldorp, A., Voronkov, A. (eds.) LPAR-19 2013. LNCS, vol. 8312, pp. 35–52. Springer, Heidelberg (2013)
4. Artale, A., Ryzhikov, V., Kontchakov, R., Zakharyaschev, M.: A cookbook for temporal conceptual data modelling with description logics. ACM Transaction on Computational Logic (TOCL) (To appear)
5. Bresolin, D., Della Monica, D., Goranko, V., Montanari, A., Sciavicco, G.: Decidable and undecidable fragments of Halpern and Shoham's interval temporal logic: towards a complete classification. In: Cervesato, I., Veith, H., Voronkov, A. (eds.) LPAR 2008. LNCS (LNAI), vol. 5330, pp. 590–604. Springer, Heidelberg (2008)
6. Bresolin, D., Della Monica, D., Goranko, V., Montanari, A., Sciavicco, G.: The dark side of interval temporal logic: sharpening the undecidability border. In: Proc. of the 18th International Symposium on Temporal Representation and Reasoning (TIME), pp. 131–138. IEEE Comp. Society Press (2011)
7. Bresolin, D., Della Monica, D., Montanari, A., Sala, P., Sciavicco, G.: Interval temporal logics over strongly discrete linear orders: the complete picture. In: Proc. of the 4th International Symposium on Games, Automata, Logics, and Formal Verification (GANDALF). EPTCS, vol. 96, pp. 155–169 (2012)
8. Bresolin, D., Goranko, V., Montanari, A., Sala, P.: Tableau-based decision procedures for the logics of subinterval structures over dense orderings. Journal of Logic and Computation 20(1), 133–166 (2010)
9. Bresolin, D., Monica, D.D., Montanari, A., Sciavicco, G.: The light side of interval temporal logic: the Bernays-Schönfinkel fragment of CDT. Annals of Mathematics and Artificial Intelligence 71(1-3), 11–39 (2014)
10. Bresolin, D., Montanari, A., Sala, P., Sciavicco, G.: What's decidable about Halpern and Shoham's interval logic? the maximal fragment AB$\overline{\text{BL}}$. In: Proc. of the 26th IEEE Symposium on Logic in Computer Science (LICS), pp. 387–396. IEEE Computer Society (2011)
11. Chaochen, Z., Hansen, M.R.: Duration Calculus: A Formal Approach to Real-Time Systems. EATCS: Monographs in Theoretical Computer Science. Springer (2004)
12. Chen, C., Lin, I.: The computational complexity of satisfiability of temporal Horn formulas in propositional linear-time temporal logic. Information Processing Letters 3(45), 131–136 (1993)
13. Chen, C., Lin, I.: The computational complexity of the satisfiability of modal Horn clauses for modal propositional logics. Theoretical Computer Science 129(1), 95–121 (1994)
14. Fariñas Del Cerro, L., Penttonen, M.: A note on the complexity of the satisfiability of modal Horn clauses. Journal of Logic Programming 4(1), 1–10 (1987)
15. Fisher, M.: A resolution method for temporal logic. In: Proc. of the 12th International Joint Conference on Artificial Intelligence (IJCAI), pp. 99–104. Morgan Kaufman (1991)
16. Halpern, J., Shoham, Y.: A propositional modal logic of time intervals. Journal of the ACM 38(4), 935–962 (1991)
17. Marcinkowski, J., Michaliszyn, J.: The ultimate undecidability result for the Halpern-Shoham logic. In: Proc. of the 26th IEEE Symposium on Logic in Computer Science (LICS), pp. 377–386. IEEE Comp. Society Press (2011)

18. Montanari, A., Puppis, G., Sala, P.: Maximal decidable fragments of Halpern and Shoham's modal logic of intervals. In: Abramsky, S., Gavoille, C., Kirchner, C., Meyer auf der Heide, F., Spirakis, P.G. (eds.) ICALP 2010, Part II. LNCS, vol. 6199, pp. 345–356. Springer, Heidelberg (2010)
19. Montanari, A., Puppis, G., Sala, P., Sciavicco, G.: Decidability of the interval temporal logic $A\overline{BB}$ on natural numbers. In: Proc. of the 27th Symposium on Theoretical Aspects of Computer Science (STACS), pp. 597–608. Inria Nancy Grand Est & Loria (2010)
20. Moszkowski, B.: Reasoning about digital circuits. Tech. rep. stan-cs-83-970, Dept. of Computer Science, Stanford University, Stanford, CA (1983)
21. Nalon, C., Dixon, C.: Clausal resolution for normal modal logics. Journal of Algorithms 62(3-4), 117–134 (2007)
22. Nguyen, L.: On the complexity of fragments of modal logics. Advances in Modal Logic 5, 318–330 (2004)
23. Pratt-Hartmann, I.: Temporal prepositions and their logic. Artificial Intelligence 166(1-2), 1–36 (2005)
24. Sipser, M.: Introduction to the theory of computation. PWS Publishing Company (1997)
25. Sistla, A., Clarke, E.: The complexity of propositional linear temporal logic. Journal of the ACM 32, 733–749 (1985)

SAT Modulo Graphs: Acyclicity

Martin Gebser*, Tomi Janhunen, and Jussi Rintanen**

Helsinki Institute for Information Technology HIIT
Department of Information and Computer Science
Aalto University, FI-00076 AALTO, Finland

Abstract. Acyclicity is a recurring property of solutions to many important combinatorial problems. In this work we study embeddings of specialized acyclicity constraints in the satisfiability problem of the classical propositional logic (SAT). We propose an embedding of directed graphs in SAT, with arcs labelled with propositional variables, and an extended SAT problem in which all clauses have to be satisfied and the subgraph consisting of arcs labelled *true* is acyclic. We devise a constraint propagator for the acyclicity constraint and show how it can be incorporated in off-the-shelf SAT solvers. We show that all existing encodings of acyclicity constraints in SAT are either prohibitively large or do not sanction all inferences made by the constraint propagator. Our experiments demonstrate the advantages of our solver over other approaches for handling acyclicity.

1 Introduction

SAT, the satisfiability problem of the propositional logic, has emerged as a powerful framework for solving combinatorial problems in AI and other areas of computer science. For many applications the basic SAT problem is sufficient, including AI planning and related state-space search problems [13], but a number of important applications involves the expression of constraints that cannot be effectively encoded as sets of clauses. For this reason, various extensions of SAT have been proposed, including SAT + linear arithmetics in the SAT modulo Theories (SMT) framework [25,1]. Other instantiations of the SMT framework are possible, including bit vectors and arrays.

In this work, we consider extensions of SAT with graphs, initially focusing on satisfying an acyclicity constraint. Examples of combinatorial problems that involve acyclic graphs can be found in diverse areas. In machine learning, the structure learning problem for Bayesian networks is reducible to a MAXSAT problem and a main part of the reduction is about guaranteeing the acyclicity of resulting networks [4]. Acyclicity is implicit in inductive definitions (well-foundedness), and SAT solvers with efficient support for acyclicity constraints could be used in reasoning with logical languages that support inductive definitions [5]. Another closely related application is answer set programming, with which we have already experimented by using the technology presented in this paper [8]. Reasoning with physical networked systems – such as utility networks (power, water, communications) and transportation networks – often involves acyclicity and other graph constraints.

---

* Also affiliated with the University of Potsdam, Germany.
** Also affiliated with Griffith University, Brisbane, Australia.

E. Fermé and J. Leite (Eds.): JELIA 2014, LNAI 8761, pp. 137–151, 2014.

Reductions of acyclicity constraints to CNF SAT are known [4,21], but, as we will show later, they either have prohibitively large size or sanction weak inferences. This motivates looking into specialized propagators for acyclicity. We believe the same to hold for many other graph problems, suggesting a wider framework of *SAT modulo Graphs* which could be viewed as an instantiation of the SMT framework. In comparison to many SMT theories, reasoning with many graph properties has a low overhead, enabling a tighter integration with SAT solvers than what is generally possible. For example, it turns out that running full acyclicity tests in every search node of a SAT solver is in general very feasible. We use ACYC-SAT to denote our SAT modulo Graphs framework instantiated with the acyclicity constraint.

Acyclicity constraints are expressible in SMT with linear arithmetics and, in particular, the fragment known as *difference logic* [15], which extends propositional logic by simple difference constraints of the form $x - y \geq k$. However, when the full generality of such constraints is not needed, the approach proposed in this paper can provide a simpler and more efficient reasoning framework. Moreover, we anticipate future extensions of the framework to cover other types of graph-related constraints that are not naturally and efficiently expressible in SMT with linear arithmetics.

Our research makes a number of new contributions. First, we present a propagator for the acyclicity constraint and propose an implementation inside the CDCL algorithm for SAT. We believe that the simplicity and efficiency of this propagator provides a significant advantage over alternative ways of reasoning with acyclicity. Our experiments will illustrate that substantial performance advantage can be gained this way. Second, our contribution can be viewed as initiating the study of graph-based constraints in the SMT framework [25,1]. Earlier, SMT has been used most notably with theories for linear arithmetic and bit vectors. Concepts related to graphs, although important in many applications, have not been offered specialized support in the SMT framework.

The structure of the paper is as follows. First in Section 2 we propose an extension of the SAT problem for handling graphs and acyclicity constraints for them. In Section 3 we give some examples of the use of acyclicity constraints. Section 4 shows how a leading algorithm for solving the SAT problem can be extended with the acyclicity constraints. In Section 5 we present and evaluate alternatives to specialized acyclicity constraints, which is reduction of acyclicity to sets of clauses. Section 6 characterizes SAT modulo acyclicity in terms of a fragment of difference logic. In Section 7 we show that our implementation of acyclicity constraints generally and sometimes dramatically outperforms alternative approaches, including CNF encodings and difference logic solvers. Section 8 discusses related work and Section 9 concludes the paper.

2   Extending SAT with Acyclicity

We propose an extension of the standard SAT problem with acyclicity constraints. In addition to a set of clauses, the extended satisfiability problem includes a directed graph and a mapping from the arcs of the graph to propositional variables. A problem instance is satisfied if all clauses are satisfied, and there is no cycle in the graph such that for every arc in the cycle the corresponding propositional variable is true.

Definition 1. *An ACYC-SAT problem is a tuple $\langle X, C, N, A, l \rangle$ where*

1. *X is a finite set of propositional variables,*
2. *C is a set of clauses over X,*
3. *$G = \langle N, A \rangle$ is a directed graph with a finite set of nodes N and arcs $A \subseteq N \times N$, and*
4. *$l : A \to X$ is a labeling that assigns a propositional variable $l(n, n')$ to every arc (n, n') in the graph.*

Definition 2. *A solution to an ACYC-SAT problem $\langle X, C, N, A, l \rangle$ is a valuation $v :$ $X \to \{0, 1\}$ such that all clauses in C are true under v, and the subgraph $\langle N, A_1 \rangle$ of $\langle N, A \rangle$ such that $A_1 = \{(n, n') \in A \mid v(l(n, n')) = 1\}$ is acyclic, that is, there is no non-empty directed path in $\langle N, A_1 \rangle$ from any node back to itself.*

A number of other graph problems could be handled in the same framework, in some cases with small modifications to our algorithms, including s-t-reachability, a node being on a simple path between two other nodes, connectivity, and so on. These and other graph properties show up in main applications of SAT solving, including verification (model-checking), control and diagnosis of networked systems. Our experiments suggest that explicit support for them may substantially improve the effectiveness of SAT-based methods in these applications.

3 Examples

Acyclicity shows up explicitly or implicitly in many types of graph problems. As shown in Section 5, best known encodings of acyclicity as clausal constraints in SAT have a trade-off between size and propagation strength. Next we illustrate how acyclicity can benefit also encodings of problems that do not explicitly appeal to acyclicity.

Example 1 (Hamiltonian cycles). Encoding of Hamiltonian cycles for directed graphs uses propositional variables for every arc, marking the arc either *true* or *false*, and consists of the following constraints, which we will explain in more detail below.

- Every node has exactly one incoming arc.
- Every node has exactly one outgoing arc.
- There is no cycle in the graph formed by all incoming arcs of all nodes except one node (an arbitrarily chosen "starting node").

Given a directed graph $\langle N, A \rangle$ and a starting node $n_s \in N$, let a^n be propositional variables for arcs $(n, n_s) \in A$, expressing that (n, n_s) belongs to a Hamiltonian cycle, while arc variables $a^{n,n'}$ represent the same for arcs $(n, n') \in A$ to the remaining nodes $n' \in N \setminus \{n_s\}$. Then, given any arc $(n, n') \in A$, we use the following notation for the propositional variable expressing Hamiltonian cycle containment.

$$\alpha^{n,n'} = \begin{cases} a^n & \text{if} \quad n' = n_s \\ a^{n,n'} & \text{if} \quad n' \neq n_s \end{cases}$$

Moreover, for any node $y \in N$, let $x_1, \ldots, x_m$ and $z_1, \ldots, z_n$ denote the nodes x_i or z_j such that $(x_i, y) \in A$ or $(y, z_j) \in A$, respectively. Using the auxiliary propositions

$p^{y,0}, \ldots, p^{y,m}$ and $q^{y,0}, \ldots, q^{y,n}$ to represent that some incoming arc $(x_{i'}, y)$ or some outgoing arc $(y, z_{j'})$ with $i' \le i$ or $j' \le j$ belongs to a Hamiltonian cycle, the following formulas state that exactly one incoming and one outgoing arc must be picked for y.

$$\neg p^{y,0} \qquad \neg p^{y,i-1} \vee \neg \alpha^{x_i,y} \qquad p^{y,i-1} \vee \alpha^{x_i,y} \leftrightarrow p^{y,i} \qquad p^{y,m}$$

$$\neg q^{y,0} \qquad \neg q^{y,j-1} \vee \neg \alpha^{y,z_j} \qquad q^{y,j-1} \vee \alpha^{y,z_j} \leftrightarrow q^{y,j} \qquad q^{y,n}$$

Given such formulas for each node $y \in N$, models M such that the graph $\langle N, \{(n, n') \mid a^{n,n'} \in M\}\rangle$ is acyclic correspond to Hamiltonian cycles.   □

The size of the above encoding is linear in the number of both arcs and nodes.

Example 2 (s-t reachability). Our encoding of s-t reachability for undirected graphs uses propositional variables for marking each node as reachable or unreachable, and arc variables $a^{n,n'}$ as well as $a^{n',n}$ for every edge $\{n, n'\}$ in the graph. The encoding uses the following constraints.

- The starting node n_s is *reachable*.
- A node n' is *reachable* if and only if it is the starting node or there is another node n so that the variable $a^{n,n'}$ for the arc $n \to n'$ is true and n is *reachable*.
- The graph corresponding to the arc variables is acyclic.

Given an undirected graph $\langle N, E \rangle$, this approach can be formulated in terms of the clauses $r^{n'} \to \bigvee_{\{n,n'\} \in E} a^{n,n'}$ for each node $n' \in N \setminus \{n_s\}$, two clauses $a^{n,n'} \to r^n$ and $a^{n',n} \to r^{n'}$ per edge $\{n, n'\} \in E$, and the unit clause r^{n_t} asserting that the target node n_t must be reached. By requiring $G = \langle N, \{(n, n') \mid a^{n,n'} \in M\}\rangle$ to be acyclic for a model M, any path in G must trace back to the starting node n_s. In particular, this applies for the mandatory path to n_t.   □

Also this encoding is linear in the number of both edges and nodes. In many practical problems the degrees of nodes are bounded, small, or grow far slower than the number of nodes. In all of these cases the specialized acyclicity constraint leads to far smaller encodings than the use of clausal encodings (Section 5). Both encodings are easily adaptable to both directed and undirected graphs.

4   Acyclicity in SAT Solvers

The conflict-driven clause learning algorithm (CDCL) [16,18,17] is a leading systematic general-purpose algorithm for solving the SAT problem. The algorithm assigns truth-values to propositional variables, interleaved with calls to a propagator (inference rules), until an inconsistency (the empty clause) is inferred. The reasons for the inconsistency are analyzed, and a clause representing the assignments that led to the inconsistency is computed and added to the clause database (learned). Then the latest assignments are undone until the newly learned clause has exactly one unassigned variable, and the process of interleaved propagation and assignments resumes. Unsatisfiability is reported when learning the empty clause, and satisfiability is reported when all variables get assigned without obtaining a contradiction. The main propagation rule

```
 1:  PROCEDURE propagator(x);
 2:  let n_s → n_e be the arc corresponding to variable x;
 3:  traverse graph forwards from n_e, visiting nodes n
 4:     mark n;
 5:     IF n = n_s THEN
 6:        let x_1, ..., x_k be variables for arcs on path n_e ⟶ n_s;
 7:        initialize clause learning with ¬x ∨ ¬x_1 ∨ ··· ∨ ¬x_k;
 8:        RETURN reporting contradiction;
 9:  traverse graph backwards from n_s, visiting nodes n
10:     FOR EACH unassigned arc n' → n with n' marked DO
11:        let x' be the variable for arc n' → n;
12:        let P_1 be the set of variables for arcs on path n_e ⟶ n';
13:        let P_2 be the set of variables for arcs on path n ⟶ n_s;
14:        let c = ¬x ∨ ¬x' ∨ ⋁_{y∈P_1} ¬y ∨ ⋁_{y∈P_2} ¬y;
15:        push ¬x' in the propagation queue with c as the reason;
```

Fig. 1. Propagator for acyclicity that is based on two depth-first traversals, one forwards from the end node of the added arc, and the other backwards from the starting node of the arc

in CDCL and other systematic SAT algorithms is Unit Propagation (UP) which infers l from $l \vee l_1 \vee \cdots \vee l_k$ and complements $\overline{l_1}, \ldots, \overline{l_k}$, and detects inconsistencies when all literals in a clause are false. Next we describe a propagator for acyclicity when the presence of arcs in the graph is indicated by propositional variables assigned *true*.

4.1 Propagator for Acyclicity

We consider the arcs of a graph to be either *enabled*, *disabled*, or *possible*, if the corresponding propositional variable is respectively assigned *true*, *false*, or unassigned.

When a propositional variable for an arc (n_s, n_e) is set *true*, we can infer new facts. Assume that the graph contains a cycle $n_1, n_2, \ldots, n_k, n_1$ and all arcs except (n_i, n_{i+1}) for some $i \in \{1, \ldots, k-1\}$ (or (n_k, n_1)) are now enabled and (n_i, n_{i+1}) is possible. Hence we conclude that (n_i, n_{i+1}) (or (n_k, n_1)) should be disabled, and therefore the corresponding propositional variable must be *false*, because otherwise there would be a cycle in the graph.

The above reasoning can be implemented by two depth-first traversals of the graph, formalized as the procedure in Figure 1. The first traversal identifies all nodes that can be reached from n_e through a path of enabled arcs. The second traversal identifies all nodes from which n_s can be reached through enabled arcs. Now, any arc from the former set of nodes to the latter has to be disabled and the corresponding propositional variables set false. There may be 0 or more such arcs. During the first traversal we also detect whether we can reach n_s from n_e, detecting a new cycle. If this is the case, we act as if the clause set had a clause stating that at least one of the arcs has to be disabled, and then run the CDCL learning algorithm starting as if this clause had just been falsified.

When an arc is disabled, no reasoning is required.

The amount of graph traversal can be reduced by observing that any cycle must be completely contained in a *strongly connected component* (SCC) of the graph. Hence when detecting cycles or inferring new literals, it is unnecessary to follow any arc from one SCC to another. SCCs can be recognized as a preprocessing step in linear time [24], and each node could be labeled with the index of its SCC.

4.2   Integration in a CDCL Implementation

The integration of the acyclicity constraint in the CDCL algorithm is straightforward: whenever a propositional variable x corresponding to an arc is set *true*, call the procedure propagator(x) (from Section 4.1), possibly adding new literals in the propagation queue, and report inconsistency if a cycle has emerged.

When a cycle has emerged, the CDCL clause learning process is initiated with a clause consisting of the negations of the propositional variables involved in the detected cycle. We call this clause the *cycle clause*. The cycle clause itself does not need to be added in the clause database.

When an almost-cycle has emerged, the corresponding cycle clause is added in the clause database, and the negation of the remaining unassigned arc variable is added in the propagation queue with the new cycle clause as its reason.

4.3   Preprocessing with Logical Simplifications

The use of non-clausal constraints impacts the use of preprocessors designed for standard CNF SAT problems. Standard preprocessors only look at the clause set, and not being aware of the non-clausal acyclicity constraint render some preprocessing methods incorrect. For example, variable elimination methods [22] and eliminating pure literals are incorrect in this context. Both can be made correct by leaving the arc variables – the only class of variables involved in the acyclicity constraint – out of consideration.

Preprocessing techniques that are *monotone*, that is, their results remain correct even if the preprocessing is only applied to a subset of the clauses, are directly applicable in our setting. Examples of monotone preprocessing techniques are *unit propagation look-ahead* (also known as *failed literals*) and subsumption.

5   Comparison to Clausal Encodings

We compare the SAT algorithm extended with a built-in propagator for the acyclicity constraint to explicit encodings of the constraint we are aware of. Of particular interest are the *size* of the encodings, which determines how large or complicated graphs can be handled in practice, and the *propagation properties* of the encodings, which determine how well the encodings can prune search spaces. The following propagation properties are of interest.

INC	Is inconsistency (a cycle) detected with UP after all arcs forming a cycle are enabled?
BACK	For an enabled path $n_1, \ldots, n_k$, is arc (n_k, n_1) disabled by UP?

5.1 Explicit Enumeration of Cycles

The simplest encoding of acyclicity enumerates all possible cycles, and forbids enabling all arcs in each cycle. This leads to cycle clauses $\neg a_1 \vee \cdots \vee \neg a_n$ where $a_1, \ldots, a_n$ are variables for every arc in a cycle. The size of this encoding is in the worst case exponential in the number of nodes in the graph, and therefore in general impractical. We are not aware of prior uses of this encoding in any application. However, earlier works have – similarly to our propagator in Section 4.1 – generated some form of cycle clauses on-demand after detecting cycles by means external to the SAT solver [14].

This encoding propagates well. Every cycle is detected as soon as it emerges, so we have INC. When all but one arc in a potential cycle has been enabled, the remaining arc is disabled by unit propagation, so we have BACK.

5.2 Transitive Closure

In this encoding [21,4], variables $t^{x,y}$ indicate that (x, y) belongs to the transitive closure of the relation corresponding to the underlying graph, that is, there is a (non-empty) directed path from x to y in the graph. Variables $a^{x,y}$ for arcs (x, y) imply $t^{x,y}$, and transitivity is expressed by $a^{x,y} \wedge t^{y,z} \rightarrow t^{x,z}$. Cycles are forbidden by $a^{x,y} \rightarrow \neg t^{y,x}$. This encoding is $\mathcal{O}(NM)$ size (for N nodes and M arcs), with $\mathcal{O}(N^2)$ variables. The encoding satisfies both INC and BACK, but it is often impractical [21], especially for complete graphs with its prohibitive $\mathcal{O}(N^3)$ size.

5.3 Topological Sorting with Indices

In this encoding, each node n in the graph is (nondeterministically) assigned an integer index $I(n)$ (typically encoded as a binary number with $\log N$ propositional variables). For each arc (n_1, n_2) there is a formula saying that if the arc is enabled, then $I(n_1) < I(n_2)$. While this encoding is very compact, the need to nondeterministically choose the indexing makes its propagation properties weak: even when all arcs are enabled or disabled, the indexing still has to be chosen before anything can be inferred about acyclicity. Hence this encoding satisfies neither of the propagation properties.

5.4 Tree Reduction

In this encoding [2] (which can be viewed as an efficient specialization of a SAT encoding of linear arithmetic constraints by Tamura et al. [23]), first the leaves (nodes without children) are identified and "removed", and the process is repeated until for acyclic graphs all nodes are guaranteed to be "removed". Essentially, we are assigning each node n an index $I(n)$ that is the maximum length of a path from n to a leaf node. We have to consider paths up to length $N - 1$. The encoding states that for each node n, $I(n) = k$ iff for all children n_0 of n we have $I(n_0) < k$ and for at least one child n_0 we have $I(n_0) = k - 1$. Finally, unit clauses state that $I(n) < N$ for every node n.

The number of clauses needed for each node is proportional to N times the number of arcs going out from it. Hence the total number of clauses is at most the product of the number of nodes and the number of arcs.

Violation of the acyclicity requirement is detected by unit propagation. Hence we have INC. The number of unit propagation steps is bounded by the size of the encoding. However, this encoding does not have the BACK property because leaf nodes are not recognized before all their outgoing arcs have been disabled. Hence no unit propagation takes place, and there is nothing else that could recognize the potential cycle.

5.5 Summary of Encoding Properties

The properties of the above encodings are summarized as follows.

encoding	size	propagation
Enumerative	$\mathcal{O}(v^v)$	INC, BACK
Transitive Closure	$\mathcal{O}(ev)$	INC, BACK
Tree Reduction	$\mathcal{O}(ev)$	INC
Topological Sort	$\mathcal{O}(v \log v + e \log v)$	-

The most compact encodings have the weakest propagation properties. The only encodings that have both of the important properties have a quadratic or an exponential size and are therefore impractical for graphs larger than some tens or hundreds of nodes. In contrast, by using a specialized propagator for acyclicity both of the propagation properties are satisfied, with linear time and space worst-case complexities.

6   Relation to Difference Logic

In this section, we provide a detailed analysis of the relationship between ACYC-SAT and *integer difference logic* (IDL) [15]. This logic is an extension of propositional logic by simple difference constraints of the form $x - y \geq k$ where x and y are integer variables and k is a constant. To streamline the forthcoming analysis, we assume a clausal representation rather than full propositional syntax. Moreover, the expressive power of the language can be further constrained by assuming particular values for the constant k. For our purposes, setting $k = 1$ is obvious as this amounts to constraints of the form $x > y$. In what follows, we compare SAT modulo acyclicity with an IDL fragment, denoted by IDL(1), based on formulas of the form

$$l_1 \vee \ldots \vee l_m \vee (x_1 > y_1) \vee \ldots \vee (x_n > y_n) \tag{1}$$

where $l_1 \vee \ldots \vee l_m$ is a propositional clause and $x_1 > y_1, \ldots, x_n > y_n$ difference constraints. Such formulas can express disequality, since $x \neq y$ is equivalent to $(x > y) \vee (y > x)$. As we shall see, equality $x = y$ is not modularly expressible using formulas of the form (1). To this end, it is essential that difference constraints may not be negated, since the formula $\neg(x > y)$ is equivalent to $x \leq y$, i.e., one half of equality.

Next we will establish *linear*, *faithful*, and *modular* translations between IDL(1) and ACYC-SAT. By linearity we mean transformation in linear time. For faithfulness, we identify integer variables used in IDL with nodes in ACYC-SAT and insist on a relatively tight correspondence of models. Finally, modularity means that the translation is feasible one expression at a time. An *LFM-translation* from a logic to another possesses all the three properties of linearity, faithfulness and modularity, and, if such a translation exists, we take this as an indication that the former can be straightforwardly expressed in the latter. Analogous frameworks based on polynomial translations have been used when ranking non-monotonic logics and logic programs on the basis of expressive power [11,12].

Given a directed acyclic graph $G = \langle N, A \rangle$ and a node $n \in N$, we define the *elimination rank* of n in G, denoted by $\mathrm{er}_G(n)$, by setting $\mathrm{er}_G(n) = 0$ for any *root* node n and $\mathrm{er}_G(n) = i$ for any *non-root* node n that becomes a root once all nodes $n' \in N$ with $\mathrm{er}_G(n') < i$ have been eliminated from G.

Proposition 1. *There is an LFM-translation from ACYC-SAT to IDL(1).*

Proof sketch. An ACYC-SAT problem $\langle X, C, N, A, l \rangle$ conforming to Definition 1 can be linear-time translated into $\mathbf{T}_{\mathrm{IDL}}(C, A, l) = C \cup \{\neg l(x, y) \vee (x > y) \mid (x, y) \in A\}$. If v is a solution to the problem, a satisfying assignment v' for $\mathbf{T}_{\mathrm{IDL}}(C, A, l)$ is obtained by setting $v'(p) = v(p)$ for atomic propositions p and $v'(x) = \mathrm{er}_{\langle N, A' \rangle}(x)$ where $A' = \{(x, y) \in A \mid v(l(x, y)) = 1\}$. On the other hand, if v' is a satisfying assignment for $\mathbf{T}_{\mathrm{IDL}}(C, A, l)$, then a solution v can be extracted by setting $v(p) = v'(p)$ for atomic propositions p and $v(l(x, y)) = 1$ iff $v'(x) > v'(y)$ for $(x, y) \subset A$. The translation $\mathbf{T}_{\mathrm{IDL}}$ is modular since clauses in C and arcs in A can be translated one-by-one. $\square$

Proposition 2. *There is an LFM-translation from IDL(1) to ACYC-SAT.*

Proof sketch. Let S be a set of formulas of the form (1) based on sets of propositional and integer variables X and V, respectively. The linear-time translation into ACYC-SAT is $\langle X, C, V, A, l \rangle$ where A is the set of arcs (x, y) for which $x > y$ appears in S, l is a labeling which assigns a new atom $l(x, y)$ to every $(x, y) \in A$, and $C = \mathbf{T}_{\mathrm{ACYC}}(S)$ contains a clause $l_1 \vee \ldots \vee l_m \vee l(x_1, y_1) \vee \ldots \vee l(x_n, y_n)$ for each extended clause (1) in S. The correspondence between solutions v to $\langle X, C, V, A, l \rangle$ and assignments v satisfying S is the same as in Proposition 1. The translation $\mathbf{T}_{\mathrm{ACYC}}$ is also modular as extended clauses can be translated independently of each other. $\square$

The expressive power of extended clauses (1) can be increased by allowing difference constraints of the form $x - y \geq 0$, or equivalently, of the form $x \geq y$. As discussed above, this amounts to negating difference constraints in (1) but we rather preserve the positive form of difference constraints and allow $x \geq y$ in extended clauses.

Theorem 1 (Intranslatability). *There is no faithful and modular generalization of the translation $\mathbf{T}_{\mathrm{ACYC}}$ from IDL(1) to IDL(0,1).*

Proof. The constraint $x > y$ is translated by $\mathbf{T}_{\mathrm{ACYC}}$ into a unit clause $l(x, y)$ and an arc (x, y) labeled by $l(x, y)$. This constraint is inconsistent with $y \geq x$ in IDL(0,1). Let us then assume a faithful and modular generalization of $\mathbf{T}_{\mathrm{ACYC}}$, which means $\mathbf{T}_{\mathrm{ACYC}}(y \geq x)$ should be independent of the respective translations of any other extended clauses. It is clear by the faithfulness of $\mathbf{T}_{\mathrm{ACYC}}$ that $\mathbf{T}_{\mathrm{ACYC}}(y \geq x)$ must be consistent as $y \geq x$ is satisfiable in IDL(0,1). Let v satisfy $\mathbf{T}_{\mathrm{ACYC}}(y \geq x)$ modulo acyclicity. Since v should be excluded in the presence of $\mathbf{T}_{\mathrm{ACYC}}(x > y)$, i.e., the unit clause $l(x, y)$, and subject to the semantics of SAT modulo acyclicity, we have that

1. $v(l(x, y)) = 0$ or
2. $v(l(y, v_1) \wedge \ldots \wedge l(v_n, x)) = 1$ for new atoms labeling arcs $(y, v_1), \ldots, (v_n, x)$ that form a path in the graph where $n \geq 0$ and $v_1, \ldots, v_n$ are potential new (and necessarily local) integer variables used in the translation of $y \geq x$.

If $n = 0$, then the second item reduces to $v(l(y, x)) = 1$. Due to the second item and the acyclicity property enforced in ACYC-SAT, $v(l(x, y)) = 1$ is not feasible. Thus $v(l(x, y)) = 0$ is necessary and since v was arbitrary, the translation $\mathbf{T}_{\mathrm{ACYC}}(y \geq x)$ must entail $\neg l(x, y)$. This reflects the fact that $\neg(x > y)$ is equivalent to $y \geq x$.

The translation $\mathbf{T}_{\mathrm{ACYC}}(x \geq y)$ entails $\neg l(y, x)$ by symmetry. Together, translations $\mathbf{T}_{\mathrm{ACYC}}(y \geq x)$ and $\mathbf{T}_{\mathrm{ACYC}}(x \geq y)$ are consistent with $l(y, z)$ and $l(z, x)$, i.e., the modular translations $\mathbf{T}_{\mathrm{ACYC}}(y > z)$ and $\mathbf{T}_{\mathrm{ACYC}}(z > x)$. This is because z is different from x and y, $\mathbf{T}_{\mathrm{ACYC}}(y \geq x)$ can only refer to $l(x, y)$ and $l(y, x)$, and thus adding $l(y, z)$ and $l(z, x)$ as unit clauses cannot interfere with consistency. Moreover, the selected arcs (y, z) and (z, x) do not create a cycle. A contradiction, since the theory $\{y \geq x, x \geq y, y > z, z > x\}$ in IDL(0,1) is inconsistent. $\qquad \Box$

Theorem 1 shows formally that the expressive power of IDL(0,1) strictly exceeds that of IDL(1). This result, however, does not exclude the possibility for non-modular generalizations that, e.g., entirely embed difference constraints into clauses. But, on the other hand, achieving linearity may become a challenge due to interdependencies of integer variables. For instance, the transformation in [9] incurs a further logarithmic factor. To conclude the analysis in this section, we have identified a simple fragment of IDL that characterizes the expressive power of ACYC-SAT. This provides further insights into why an efficient implementation of the acyclicity extension can be expected.

7   Experimental Evaluation

We have implemented the acyclicity constraint propagator inside the MiniSAT solver, and then adapted it to the MiniSAT-based Glucose solver. We also extended the solvers' parsers with capabilities for reading graphs along with a SAT instance. All this is less than 500 lines of C++ code. Although our implementation does not try to amortize the costs of consecutive acyclicity tests, the propagator accounts only for a fraction of the total SAT solver runtime even with problem instances that intensively refer to graphs.

We empirically evaluated the performance of ACYC-SAT solvers on the Hamiltonian cycle problem as well as finding a directed acyclic graph, forest, or tree, subject to XOR-constraints over arcs. The problems and respective graph sizes in terms of nodes are indicated in the first two columns of Table 1. Per problem and graph size, we considered 100 (randomly generated) instances, that is, planar graphs in case of the Hamiltonian cycle problem or, otherwise, XOR-constraints to be fulfilled by a directed acyclic graph, forest, or tree, respectively. All experiments were run on a cluster of Linux machines, using a timeout of 3600 seconds per instance.

The evaluation includes our ACYC-SAT solvers Glucose-INC, Glucose-BACK, MiniSAT-INC, and MiniSAT-BACK, where the suffix INC indicates acyclicity propagation by detecting and denying cycles (using only the forwards traversal in Figure 1)

Table 1. Comparison between solvers for ACYC-SAT, SAT, ASP, and SMT on Hamiltonian cycle and directed acyclic graph problems

Problem	Size	Glucose-INC	Glucose-BACK	MiniSAT-INC	MiniSAT-BACK	Glucose-SAT	MiniSAT-SAT	Lingeling-SAT	Clasp-SAT	Clasp-ASP	Z3-SMT
Hamilton	100	0.21	0.07	**0.03**	0.04	224.14	275.00	2419.63	2600.90	0.95	2.45
	150	0.13	0.15	**0.10**	0.12	3440.00	3172.54	3536.02	—	20.16	50.64
Acyclic	25	0.08	0.05	0.05	**0.03**	2406.60	2934.30	1.61	1282.49	0.12	0.29
	50	2.34	**0.28**	1.64	0.29	3147.91	2988.30	17.09	—	0.76	7.61
	75	682.86	8.09	856.47	**4.76**	3241.00	3276.92	99.60	—	282.01	167.74
	100	2180.98	964.28	2172.01	**647.13**	3170.48	3176.70	2760.52	1984.10	831.33	2278.63
Forest	25	**0.59**	0.64	0.75	0.72	118.70	139.88	3.10	3.59	4.09	4.54
	50	**301.46**	304.44	466.56	498.00	1165.53	1438.49	667.24	1125.86	1039.26	1205.63
	75	**909.15**	1006.73	1011.05	920.43	2597.99	2708.27	1019.68	1470.12	1501.76	1755.28
	100	1349.29	1418.25	1271.86	**1269.47**	2882.20	2853.03	2131.73	2597.71	1632.94	2690.67
Tree	25	0.80	0.74	**0.67**	0.83	72.93	6.12	3.17	4.12	4.37	4.75
	50	**301.81**	315.83	564.05	544.43	815.09	1230.09	685.38	1126.76	1193.09	1208.36
	75	**947.61**	999.07	976.40	1025.02	2646.64	2749.26	1044.51	1633.95	1495.32	1726.56
	100	1348.91	1414.68	1330.81	**1224.28**	2882.36	2861.33	2239.12	2621.82	1995.19	2538.20

and BACK expresses that arc variables are also falsified to prevent cycles (using the entire propagator(x) routine in Figure 1). We compared our solvers to their base versions Glucose-SAT (3.0) and MiniSAT-SAT (2.2.0), run with plain SAT encodings based on Tree Reduction (cf. Section 5). Notably, for a graph with N nodes, the maximum length $l(n) = k$ from a node n to a leaf node is represented in terms of propositions for $l(n) < k, \ldots, l(n) < N - 1$, thus exploiting the order encoding approach [23]. Furthermore, we have included Lingeling (ats-57807c8-131016) as an example of a SAT solver with a good performance that is unrelated to MiniSAT and Glucose. These SAT solvers are complemented by the combined SAT and Answer Set Programming (ASP) solver Clasp (3.0.4), run as Clasp-SAT on SAT encodings or as Clasp-ASP on more compact ASP encodings of Tree Reduction of size $\mathcal{O}(e)$. The ASP formalism includes an (implicit) acyclicity test which enables more compact encodings than with SAT. Similarly, difference logic, supported by Z3-SMT (4.3.2), allows for compact encodings of acyclicity constraints as described in Section 6 (see [19] for relations to ASP).

Table 1 gives average runtimes taking timeouts as 3600 seconds, while indicating timeouts in all runs by "—" as well as the minimum average runtime per row in boldface. The advantage of our ACYC-SAT solvers clearly shows on the Hamiltonian cycle instances, where the requirement of exactly one incoming and outgoing arc per node along with the global acyclicity condition (excluding the incoming arc of a fixed starting node) permit a very compact encoding. Given that all instances are solved easily, the efforts of Glucose-BACK and MiniSAT-BACK to falsify arc variables result in small overhead compared to Glucose-INC and MiniSAT-INC which merely check acyclicity. In fact, the higher average runtime of Glucose-INC on instances with 100 nodes is due to a single outlier, taking longer than the other 99 instances together. On the other hand, all four plain SAT solvers suffer from less compact encodings, leading to significantly higher runtimes and plenty of timeouts. The latter can also be observed in comparison to Clasp-ASP and Z3-SMT, whose average runtimes are still two orders of magnitude higher than the ones of our ACYC-SAT solvers.

Considering the problem of finding a directed acyclic graph subject to XOR constraints, the extended propagation of Glucose-BACK and MiniSAT-BACK pays off and significantly reduces the amount of the search needed in comparison to Glucose-INC and MiniSAT-INC. Advantages over Clasp-ASP and Z3-SMT still amount to one order of magnitude in average runtime. In general, plain SAT solvers have again the most difficulties. The exceptionally good performance of Lingeling-SAT on instances up to size 75 is mostly due to its preprocessing and inprocessing techniques, not shared by the other three SAT solvers. Differences in SAT solver engines become also apparent when comparing Clasp-SAT which fails on instances with 50 or 75 nodes but solves more instances of size 100 than Lingeling-SAT. Finally, the problems of finding a forest or tree fulfilling XOR-constraints add further restrictions on directed acyclic graphs in question. Therefore, these problems are harder for our ACYC-SAT solvers, and side constraints seem to dominate over differences in acyclicity propagation. Nevertheless, the acyclicity extensions of both Glucose and MiniSAT still have a significant edge over the other solvers.

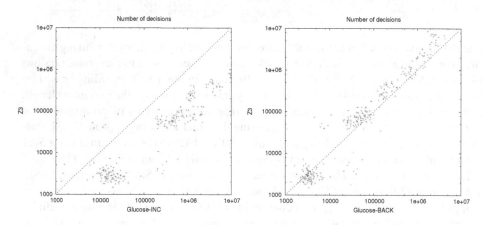

Fig. 2. Decisions for Z3 vs. Glucose-BACK and Glucose-INC on Acyclic instances from Table 1

8   Related Work

The way we integrate graph constraints in the SAT framework is highly analogous to the SMT framework [25,1]. Typical implementations of difference logic in SMT solvers [3,15,20] involve graph-based algorithms. Rather than finding values to integer variables and then checking the inequalities, the satisfiability of a set of difference constrains can be decided by checking the existence of a negative-weight loop in the corresponding weighted graph using standard algorithms. The SAT modulo Graphs framework proposed in this paper exploits graph algorithms in the implementation but also suggests using graphs explicitly as a core concept in modeling. Reasoning techniques proposed in [15] include a counterpart to our rule that infers that an arc that would complete a cycle must be disabled. Based on an experimental comparison between our solvers and Z3, we believe that Z3 performs similar inferences (but were not able to confirm this by inspecting its source code): numbers of decisions and conflicts in the search performed by Z3 are comparable to our Glucose-BACK solver, and significantly lower than with our Glucose-INC solver, as shown in Figure 2 which plots the numbers of decisions for these solvers and all of the Acyclic instances. Plots for conflicts are similar. Z3 runtimes are about 15 times higher than those of Glucose-BACK for small instances, and more for bigger ones, which must be due to the far higher overhead of difference logic.

Constraints on graphs have earlier been of some interest in the automated reasoning and constraint programming communities. The works closest to ours are the following. Hoffmann and van Beek have recently presented an acyclicity constraint specialized for the Bayesian network learning problem, in an unpublished work [10]. Dooms et al. [6,7] have proposed the CP(Graph) domain for constraint programming, in which variables have graphs as values and constraints express relations between different graphs.

9 Conclusion

We have presented a constraint propagator for a graph acyclicity constraint and its implementation in a SAT solver. In some important classes of SAT applications it is critical to express the acyclicity constraint compactly and to exploit it maximally to achieve efficient SAT solving. Such applications include Bayesian network learning, answer set programming, and reasoning about networked systems that are kept in an acyclic configuration, for example many electricity networks.

Our experiments show good scalability of our solvers in comparison to competing frameworks, including difference logic, and often dramatic improvements over acyclicity constraints encoded in the standard clausal SAT problem are apparent.

We are in the process of integrating acyclicity constraints in MAXSAT solvers, to be able to experiment with structure learning for Bayesian networks which is reducible to the weighted partial MAXSAT problem [4].

Future work includes addressing other important graph constraints, stemming from applications involving systems such as utility networks (power, water, telecommunications) and transportation. Graph constraints arising in these applications include reachability (one node is reachable from another), connectivity, and simple paths (a node is on a simple path between two given nodes). Similarly to acyclicity, these constraints do not appear to be expressible as clauses so that compactness (size less than quadratic) and strong propagations are both achieved, and unlike acyclicity, their expression in frameworks such as difference logic or ASP is not straightforward.

Acknowledgments. The support from the Finnish Center of Excellence in Computational Inference Research (COIN) funded by the Academy of Finland (under grant #251170) is gratefully acknowledged.

References

1. Audemard, G., Bertoli, P.G., Cimatti, A., Kornilowicz, A., Sebastiani, R.: A SAT based approach for solving formulas over Boolean and linear mathematical propositions. In: Voronkov, A. (ed.) CADE 2002. LNCS (LNAI), vol. 2392, pp. 195–210. Springer, Heidelberg (2002)

2. Corander, J., Janhunen, T., Rintanen, J., Nyman, H., Pensar, J.: Learning chordal Markov networks by constraint satisfaction. In: Burges, C.J.C., Bottou, L., Welling, M., Ghahramani, Z., Weinberger, K. (eds.) Advances in Neural Information Processing Systems 26, pp. 1349–1357 (2014)
3. Cotton, S., Maler, O.: Fast and flexible difference constraint propagation for DPLL(T). In: Biere, A., Gomes, C.P. (eds.) SAT 2006. LNCS, vol. 4121, pp. 170–183. Springer, Heidelberg (2006)
4. Cussens, J.: Bayesian network learning by compiling to weighted MAX-SAT. In: Proceedings of the Conference on Uncertainty in Artificial Intelligence, pp. 105–112. AUAI Press (2008)
5. Denecker, M., Ternovska, E.: A logic of nonmonotone inductive definitions. ACM Transactions on Computational Logic 9(2), 14:1–14:52 (2008)
6. Dooms, G., Deville, Y., Dupont, P.E.: Cp(graph): Introducing a graph computation domain in constraint programming. In: van Beek, P. (ed.) CP 2005. LNCS, vol. 3709, pp. 211–225. Springer, Heidelberg (2005)
7. Dooms, G., Katriel, I.: The minimum spanning tree constraint. In: Benhamou, F. (ed.) CP 2006. LNCS, vol. 4204, pp. 152–166. Springer, Heidelberg (2006)
8. Gebser, M., Janhunen, T., Rintanen, J.: Answer set programming as SAT modulo acyclicity. In: Proceedings of the 21st European Conference on Artificial Intelligence, ECAI 2014. IOS Press (2014)
9. Heljanko, K., Keinänen, M., Lange, M., Niemelä, I.: Solving parity games by a reduction to SAT. Journal for Computer and System Sciences 78(2), 430–440 (2012)
10. Hoffmann, H.F., van Beek, P.: A global acyclicity constraint for Bayesian network structure learning (September 2013) (unpublished manuscript in the Doctoral Program of the International Conference on Principles and Practice of Constraint Programming)
11. Janhunen, T.: Evaluating the effect of semi-normality on the expressiveness of defaults. Artificial Intelligence 144(1-2), 233–250 (2003)
12. Janhunen, T.: Some (in)translatability results for normal logic programs and propositional theories. Journal of Applied Non-Classical Logics 16(1-2), 35–86 (2006)
13. Kautz, H., Selman, B.: Pushing the envelope: planning, propositional logic, and stochastic search. In: Proceedings of the 13th National Conference on Artificial Intelligence and the 8th Innovative Applications of Artificial Intelligence Conference, pp. 1194–1201. AAAI Press (1996)
14. Lin, F., Zhao, Y.: ASSAT: Computing answer sets of a logic program by SAT solvers. Artificial Intelligence Journal 157(1), 115–137 (2004)
15. Mahfoudh, M., Niebert, P., Asarin, E., Maler, O.: A satisfiability checker for difference logic. In: Proceedings of SAT 2002 – Theory and Applications of Satisfiability Testing, vol. 2, pp. 222–230 (2002)
16. Marques-Silva, J.P., Sakallah, K.A.: GRASP: A new search algorithm for satisfiability. In: 1996 IEEE/ACM International Conference on Computer-Aided Design, ICCAD 1996. Digest of Technical Papers, pp. 220–227 (1996)
17. Mitchell, D.G.: A SAT solver primer. EATCS Bulletin 85, 112–133 (2005)
18. Moskewicz, M.W., Madigan, C.F., Zhao, Y., Zhang, L., Malik, S.: Chaff: engineering an efficient SAT solver. In: Proceedings of the 38th ACM/IEEE Design Automation Conference (DAC 2001), pp. 530–535. ACM Press (2001)
19. Niemelä, I.: Stable models and difference logic. Annals of Mathematics and Artificial Intelligence 53(1-4), 313–329 (2008)
20. Nieuwenhuis, R., Oliveras, A.: DPLL(T) with exhaustive theory propagation and its application to difference logic. In: Etessami, K., Rajamani, S.K. (eds.) CAV 2005. LNCS, vol. 3576, pp. 321–334. Springer, Heidelberg (2005)

21. Rintanen, J., Heljanko, K., Niemelä, I.: Parallel encodings of classical planning as satisfiability. In: Alferes, J.J., Leite, J. (eds.) JELIA 2004. LNCS (LNAI), vol. 3229, pp. 307–319. Springer, Heidelberg (2004)

22. Subbarayan, S., Pradhan, D.K.: NiVER: Non-increasing variable elimination resolution for preprocessing SAT instances. In: Hoos, H.H., Mitchell, D.G. (eds.) SAT 2004. LNCS, vol. 3542, pp. 276–291. Springer, Heidelberg (2005)

23. Tamura, N., Taga, A., Kitagawa, S., Banbara, M.: Compiling finite linear CSP into SAT. Constraints 14(2), 254–272 (2009)

24. Tarjan, R.E.: Depth first search and linear graph algorithms. SIAM Journal on Computing 1(2), 146–160 (1972)

25. Wolfman, S.A., Weld, D.S.: The LPSAT engine & its application to resource planning. In: Proceedings of the 16th International Joint Conference on Artificial Intelligence, pp. 310–315. Morgan Kaufmann Publishers (1999)

Enumerating Prime Implicants of Propositional Formulae in Conjunctive Normal Form

Said Jabbour[1], Joao Marques-Silva[2], Lakhdar Sais[1], and Yakoub Salhi[1]

[1] CRIL, Université d'Artois & CNRS, Lens, France
{jabbour,sais,salhi}@cril.fr
[2] CASL, University College Dublin, Ireland
jpms@ucd.ie

Abstract. In this paper, a new approach for enumerating the set prime implicants (PI) of a Boolean formula in conjunctive normal form (CNF) is proposed. It is based on an encoding of the input formula as a new one whose models correspond to the set of prime implicants of the original theory. This first PI enumeration approach is then enhanced by an original use of the boolean functions or gates usually involved in many CNF instances encoding real-world problems. Experimental evaluation on several classes of CNF instances shows the feasibility of our proposed framework.

1 Introduction

The problem of enumerating prime implicants (PIs) of Boolean functions is an important research topic from the early days of computer science. It was used in the context of boolean function minimization by Quine [29,28] and McCluskey [23]. This first application of the prime implicant canonical form is important as it allows to reduce digital circuit size and cost while improving the computing speed (e.g. [34]). In addition to digital circuit analysis and optimisation, PIs have found several other application domains including fault tree analysis [6,11], bioinformatics [1], databases [10], model based diagnosis [8], knowledge representation and reasoning [4]. The computation of prime implicants is also important in many subfields of artificial intelligence such us knowledge compilation [3,7], automated and non-monotonic reasoning [14], multi-agent systems [33].

Unfortunately, the problem of generating all prime implicants of a given propositional theory is a highly complex task. First, the number of prime implicants of a given theory can be exponential in the size of the theory, while finding just one prime implicant is an NP-hard task. Consequently, enumerating all PIs cannot be done in polynomial total time unless P=NP [16]. Despite this computational bottleneck, several techniques have been proposed in the literature. Many of these PI enumeration techniques are based on some adaptation of the well-known search paradigm, namely branch and bound/backtrack search procedures. Additionally, most of these techniques consider propositional formulae in conjunctive normal form (CNF), the standard representation of propositional knowledge bases. One can cite two related adaptations of the well-known DPLL

E. Fermé and J. Leite (Eds.): JELIA 2014, LNAI 8761, pp. 152–165, 2014.

procedure for prime implicants generation [5,32,30] or the modification of modern SAT solvers for computing one prime implicant [9]. Concurrently, almost simultaneously, a 0-1 integer linear programming (ILP) formulation [21,19] was proposed for computing minimum-size prime implicant improving the formulation given in [27]. In addition, a new algorithm for solving ILP was developed, built on top of a CDCL SAT solver. In [26], Palopoli et al. formulated two algorithms for PIs computation. The first one (called Enumerative Prime Implicants/Feasible Solutions - EPI/FS) search for a feasible solution of the linear program and then extract a prime implicant from it. The second variant, called EPI/OS, is obtained by simply adding a suitable minimization function to the ILP formulation.

In contrast to PI enumeration based on an adaptation of DPLL-like procedure (e.g. [5,32]) and ILP based formulations [21,27], in this paper, we first propose an original approach that rewrite the CNF formula Φ as a new CNF formula Φ' such that the prime implicants of Φ correspond the models of the new CNF Φ'. In this way, prime implicant enumeration is reduced to the problem of finding all models of a CNF formula. Such correspondence, allows us to benefit from the recent and continuous advances in practical SAT solving at least for finding one prime implicant. From the ILP formulation mentioned above [21,27], our PI enumeration encoding borrows only the idea of literal renaming. As such renaming substantially increases the number of variables and clauses, in our second contribution, an enhanced encoding is derived thanks to the structural knowledge recovered from the CNF formula. Indeed, by exploiting Boolean functions encoded in the formula, our new encoding allows significant reductions in the number of variables and clauses. Surprisingly, despite the numerous studies on this issue, to the best of our knowledge, there is no available PI enumeration tool. To compare our proposed approach, an additional PI enumeration algorithm is implemented, which is based on adapting previous work (see Section 5). More precisely, the CNF formula Φ is encoded as a partial MaxSAT formula Φ_P using a reformulation of the previous mentioned 0-1 ILP model. Thanks to the correspondence between minimal correction subsets (MCSs) of Φ_P and the prime implicants of Φ, we exploit the MCSs enumeration tool proposed recently in [22].

The paper is organized as follows. After some preliminary definitions and necessary notations, our SAT-based encoding of PI enumeration problem is provided in Section 3. Then, we describe in Section 4 our structure-based enhancement of PI enumeration. Then, an alternative approach for PIs generation is discussed in Section 5. An extensive experimental evaluation of our proposed approaches is provided (Section 6) before concluding.

2   Preliminary Definitions and Notations

We first introduce the satisfiability problem (SAT) and some necessary notations. SAT corresponds to the problem of deciding if a formula of propositional classical logic is consistent or not. It is one of the most studied NP-complete decision problem.

We consider the conjunctive normal form (CNF) representation for propositional formulas. A *CNF formula* Φ is a conjunction of clauses, where a *clause* is a disjunction of literals. A *literal* is a positive (p) or negated ($\neg p$) propositional variable. The two literals p and $\neg p$ are called *complementary*. We denote by $\bar{l}$ the complementary literal of l, i.e., if $l = p$ then $\bar{l} = \neg p$ and if $l = \neg p$ then $\bar{l} = p$. For a set of literals L, $\bar{L}$ is defined as $\{\bar{l} \mid l \in L\}$. A CNF formula can also be seen as a set of clauses, and a clause as a set of literals. Let us recall that any propositional formula can be translated to CNF using linear Tseitin's encoding [35]. We denote by $Var(\Phi)$ (respectively $Lit(\Phi)$) the set of propositional variables (respectively literals) occurring in Φ.

$\Phi|_x$ denotes the formula obtained from Φ by assigning x the truth-value *true*. Formally $\Phi|_x = \{c \mid c \in \Phi, \{x, \neg x\} \cap c = \emptyset\} \cup \{c \setminus \{\neg x\} \mid c \in \Phi, \neg x \in c\}$ (that is: the clauses containing x are therefore satisfied and removed; and those containing $\neg x$ are simplified). Φ^* denotes the formula Φ closed under unit propagation (UP closure), defined recursively as follows: (1) $\Phi^* = \Phi$ if Φ does not contain any unit clause, (2) $\Phi^* = \bot$ if Φ contains two unit-clauses $\{x\}$ and $\{\neg x\}$, (3) otherwise, $\Phi^* = (\Phi|_x)^*$ where x is the literal appearing in a unit clause of Φ. The set of unit propagated literals by applying UP closure on Φ is denoted $UP(\Phi)$.

An *interpretation* $\mathcal{B}$ of a propositional formula Φ is a function which associates a value $\mathcal{B}(p) \in \{0, 1\}$ (0 corresponds to *false* and 1 to *true*) to the variables $p \in Var(\Phi)$. An interpretation $\mathcal{B}$ of Φ is alternatively represented by a set of literals, i.e., $\mathcal{B} = \bigcup_{x \in Var(\Phi)} f(x)$, where $f(x) = x$ (respectively $f(x) = \neg x$), if $\mathcal{B}(x) = true$ (respectively $\mathcal{B}(x) = false$). A *model or an implicant* of a formula Φ is an interpretation $\mathcal{B}$ that satisfies the formula, noted $\mathcal{B} \vDash \Phi$. The *SAT problem* consists in deciding if a given formula admits a model or not.

An implicant $\mathcal{B}$ of Φ is called a *prime implicant* (in short PI), iff for all literals $l \in \mathcal{B}, \mathcal{B} \setminus \{l\} \nvDash \Phi$. We define $PI(\Phi)$ as the disjunction of all prime implicant of Φ. Obviously, $PI(\Phi)$ is logically equivalent to Φ, while its size might be exponential in the worst case.

3   SAT-Based Encoding of PI Enumeration Problem

In this section, we describe our SAT-based encoding of the prime implicant enumeration problem. The idea consists in reformulating the PI enumeration problem of a given CNF Φ as the model enumeration problem of a CNF Φ'.

Our encoding borrows the idea of literals renaming used in the ILP formulations proposed in [27,19,20]. Let Φ be a CNF formula. We associate to each element l of $Lit(\Phi)$ a propositional variable x_l. We define the CNF formula Φ^R as the formula obtained from Φ by renaming each literal l in $Lit(\Phi)$ by its corresponding propositional variable x_l, and by adding the following binary clauses:

$$\bigwedge_{p \in Var(\Phi)} \neg x_p \vee \neg x_{\neg p} \tag{1}$$

One can easily see that Φ and Φ^R are equisatisfiable.

Example 1. Let us consider the following CNF formula: $\Phi = (p \vee \neg q \vee r) \wedge (\neg p \vee \neg r) \wedge (q \vee \neg r)$. Then, we have $\Phi^R = (x_p \vee x_{\neg q} \vee x_r) \wedge (x_{\neg p} \vee x_{\neg r}) \wedge (x_q \vee x_{\neg r}) \wedge (\neg x_p \vee \neg x_{\neg p}) \wedge (\neg x_q \vee \neg x_{\neg q}) \wedge (\neg x_r \vee \neg x_{\neg r})$. As we can see, the formula Φ^R is a conjunction of two monotone CNF formulae.

We now propose a new constraint in order to establish a bijection between prime implicants of a CNF formula and the models of the resulting CNF formula. This additional formula $\mathcal{M}(\Phi^R)$ is defined as follows:

$$\mathcal{M}(\Phi^R) = \bigwedge_{l \in Lit(\Phi)} x_l \to \neg Cl(\Phi^R, x_l) \tag{2}$$

where $Cl(\Phi^R, x_l)$ corresponds to the restriction of Φ^R to the clauses containing x_l without the latter, i.e., $Cl(\Phi^R, x_l) \equiv \bigwedge_{c \in \Phi^R, x_l \in c} c \setminus \{x_l\}$.

For instance, if we consider again the formula Φ given in Example 1, $\mathcal{M}(\Phi^R)$ corresponds to the the the following formula: $(x_p \to \neg(x_{\neg q} \vee x_r)) \wedge (x_{\neg p} \to \neg x_{\neg r}) \wedge (x_q \to \neg x_{\neg r}) \wedge (x_{\neg q} \to \neg(x_p \vee x_r)) \wedge (x_r \to \neg(x_p \vee x_{\neg q})) \wedge (x_{\neg r} \to (x_q \wedge x_{\neg p}))$.

Theorem 1. *If $\mathcal{B}$ is a model of the formula $\Phi^R \wedge \mathcal{M}(\Phi^R)$, then the set of literals $I_\mathcal{B} = \{l \in Lit(\Phi) \mid \mathcal{B}(x_l) = 1\}$ is a prime implicant of Φ.*

Proof. Using the fact that Φ^R is nothing else than a renaming of the literals of Φ, we have $I_\mathcal{B}$ is an implicant of Φ. Assume now that $I_\mathcal{B}$ is not a prime implicant of Φ. Then, there exists $l_0 \in I$ such that $I_\mathcal{B} \setminus \{l_0\}$ is an implicant of Φ. Let $\mathcal{B}'$ be a Boolean interpretation of $\Phi^R \wedge \mathcal{M}(\Phi^R)$ defined as follows:

$$\mathcal{B}'(x_l) = \begin{cases} \mathcal{B}(x_l) & \text{if } l \neq l_0 \\ 0 & \text{otherwise} \end{cases}$$

Clearly, we have $\mathcal{B}'(x_{l_0}) = \mathcal{B}'(x_{\neg l_0}) = 0$. Indeed, $\mathcal{B}'(x_{l_0}) = 0$ (see the definition of $\mathcal{B}'$). Let us show that $\mathcal{B}'(x_{\neg l_0}) = 0$. By definition, we have $\mathcal{B}'(x_{\neg l_0}) = \mathcal{B}(x_{\neg l_0})$ because $\neg l_0 \neq l_0$. As $l_0 \in I_\mathcal{B}$, we have $\mathcal{B}(x_{l_0}) = 1$. Also, as $I_\mathcal{B}$ is an implicant of Φ, then it satisfies the binary clause $(\neg x_{l_0} \vee \neg x_{\neg l_0})$ (see formula (1). Consequently, we deduce that $\mathcal{B}(\neg x_{\neg l_0}) = 1$ i.e. $\mathcal{B}(x_{\neg l_0}) = 0$. Finally, $\mathcal{B}'(x_{\neg l_0}) = 0$. Using the formula $\mathcal{M}(\Phi^R)$, $\mathcal{B}(x_{l_0} \to \neg Cl(\Phi^R, x_{l_0})) = 1$ holds. Hence, we have $\mathcal{B}(Cl(\Phi^R, x_{l_0})) = 0$, since $\mathcal{B}(x_{l_0}) = 1$ because $l_0 \in I_\mathcal{B}$. Since $\mathcal{B}'$ is obtained from $\mathcal{B}$ by setting the truth value of x_{l_0} to 0 ($\mathcal{B}'(x_{l_0}) = 0$), then $\mathcal{B}(Cl(\Phi^R, x_{l_0})) = \mathcal{B}'(Cl(\Phi^R, x_{l_0})) = 0$. We then obtain that $\mathcal{B}'$ is not a model of Φ^R and we get a contradiction with $I_\mathcal{B} \setminus \{l_0\}$ is an implicant of Φ. Therefore, I is a prime implicant of Φ.

Theorem 2. *Let I be a prime implicant of Φ and $\mathcal{B}$ a Boolean interpretation of $\Phi^R \wedge \mathcal{M}(\Phi^R)$ defined as follows:*

$$\mathcal{B}(x_l) = \begin{cases} 1 & \text{if } l \in I \\ 0 & \text{otherwise} \end{cases}$$

Then, $\mathcal{B}$ is a model of $\Phi^R \wedge \mathcal{M}(\Phi^R)$.

Proof. Clearly, $\mathcal{B}$ is a model of Φ^R because I is a prime implicant of Φ. We now show that $\mathcal{B}$ is also a model of $\mathcal{M}(\Phi^R)$. Let l be a literal in $Lit(\Phi)$. If $\mathcal{B}(x_l) = 0$ then $\mathcal{B}(x_l \to \neg Cl(\Phi^R, x_l)) = 1$ holds. Otherwise, we have $\mathcal{B}(x_l) = 1$ and $l \in I$. If $\mathcal{B}(Cl(\Phi^R, x_l)) = 1$ then $I \setminus \{l\}$ is an implicant of Φ and we get a contradiction. Therefore, $\mathcal{B}(Cl(\Phi^R, x_l)) = 0$ holds. Consequently, $\mathcal{B}$ is a model of $\mathcal{M}(\Phi^R)$ and then of $\Phi^R \wedge \mathcal{M}(\Phi^R)$.

Corollary 1. *The number of prime implicants of Φ is equal to the number of models of $\Phi^R \wedge \mathcal{M}(\Phi^R)$.*

Proof. For all $\mathcal{B}_1$ and $\mathcal{B}_2$ two different models of $\Phi^R \wedge \mathcal{M}(\Phi^R)$, $I_{\mathcal{B}_1} \neq I_{\mathcal{B}_2}$ holds. Thus, using Theorem 1, we obtain that the number of prime implicants of Φ is greater than or equal to the number of models of $\Phi^R \wedge \mathcal{M}(\Phi^R)$. Moreover, using Theorem 2, the number of prime implicants of Φ is smaller than or equal to the number of models of $\Phi^R \wedge \mathcal{M}(\Phi^R)$. Therefore, the number of prime implicants of Φ is equal to the number of models of $\Phi^R \wedge \mathcal{M}(\Phi^R)$.

4   Structure-Based Enhancement of PI Enumeration

CNF formulae encoding real words problems usually involve a large fraction of clauses encoding different kind of boolean functions or gates. These Boolean functions result from the problem specification itself or introduced during the CNF transformation using the well-known Tseitin extension principle [35]. Tseitin's encoding consists in introducing fresh variables to represent sub-formulae in order to represent their truth values. For example, given a Boolean formula, containing the variables a and b, and v a fresh variable, one can add the definition $v \leftrightarrow a \vee b$ (called extension) to the formula while preserving satisfiability. Tseitin's extension principle is at the basis of the linear transformation of general Boolean formulae into CNF.

Boolean functions express strong relationships between variables, the goal of this section is to show how such variable dependencies can be exploited in the context of prime impliquant generation.

Let us first introduce some formal definitions and notations about Boolean functions or gates.

A *Boolean function or Gate* is an expression of the form $l' = f(l_1, \ldots, l_n)$, where $l', l_1, \ldots, l_n$ are literals and f is a logical connective among $\{\wedge, \vee, \Leftrightarrow\}$. It allows us to express that the truth value of l' is determined by $f(l_1, \ldots, l_n)$. According to f, a Boolean gate can be defined as a conjunction of clauses as follows:

1. $l' = \wedge(l_1, \ldots, l_n)$ represents the set of clauses $\{\neg l_1 \vee \cdots \vee \neg l_n \vee l', \neg l' \vee l_1, \ldots, \neg l' \vee l_n\}$;
2. $l' = \vee(l_1, \ldots, l_n)$ represents the set of clauses $\{\neg l' \vee l_1 \vee \cdots \vee l_n, \neg l_1 \vee l', \ldots, \neg l_n \vee l'\}$;
3. $l' =\Leftrightarrow (l_1, \ldots, l_n)$ represents the following equivalence chain (also called biconditional formula) $(l' \Leftrightarrow l_1 \Leftrightarrow, \ldots, \Leftrightarrow l_n)$.

Let us note that the Boolean functions using the connective $\wedge$ ($\wedge$-gates) and those using $\vee$ ($\vee$-gates) are dual. Indeed, any Boolean gate $l' = \wedge(l_1, \ldots, l_n)$ (resp. $l' = \vee(l_1, \ldots, l_n)$) is equivalent to $\neg l' = \vee(\neg l_1, \ldots, \neg l_n)$ (resp. $\neg l' = \wedge(\neg l_1, \ldots, \neg l_n)$). It is also important to note that for the third Boolean function (equivalence chain), its equivalent representation in CNF leads to a huge number of clauses (2^n clauses).

In general, we say that an expression $l' = f(l_1, \ldots, l_n)$ is a gate of a CNF formula Φ if it is a logical consequence of Φ. Unfortunately, this deduction problem is Co-NP Complete. However, several recent contributions addressed the issue of recovering Boolean functions from CNF formulae (e.g. [25,15,31,13,2]). In [25], a polynomial and syntactical approach, which recovers only Boolean functions implicitly present in the CNF formula. Another detection technique is proposed by Roy et al. in [31]. It operates by translating the gate matching problem into one of recognizing sub hypergraph isomorphism. This approach is clearly intractable. In [15], a new technique based on deduction restricted to unit propagation process is proposed. It extends the syntactical approach [25] and allows the detection of some hidden Boolean functions.

Given a formula CNF Φ, we can use two different methods for detecting Boolean functions encoded by the clauses of Φ.
The first detection method, called syntactical method, is a pattern matching approach that allows us to detect the Boolean functions that appear directly in the structure of the CNF formula [25].

Example 2. Let $\Phi \supseteq \{(y \vee \neg x_1 \vee \neg x_2 \vee \neg x_3), (\neg y \vee x_1), (\neg y \vee x_2), (\neg y \vee x_3)\}$.

In this example, we can detect syntactically the function $y - \wedge(x_1, x_2, x_3)$.

The second method is a semantic detection approach where the functions are detected using Unit Propagation (UP) [15]. Indeed, this method allows us to detect hidden Boolean functions linearly in the size of the CNF.

Example 3. Let $\Phi \supseteq \{(y \vee \neg x_1 \vee \neg x_2 \vee \neg x_3), (\neg y \vee x_1), (\neg x_1 \vee x_4), (\neg x_4 \vee x_2), (\neg x_2 \vee x_5), (\neg x_4 \vee \neg x_5 \vee x_3)\}$.

In this example, $UP(\Phi \wedge y) = \{x_1, x_4, x_2, x_5, x_3\}$ the set of unit propagated (UP) literals and we have the clause $c = (y \vee \neg x_1 \vee \neg x_2 \vee \neg x_3) \in \Phi$ which is such that $c \backslash \{y\} \subset \overline{UP(\Phi \wedge y)}$. So, we can discover the Boolean function $y = \wedge(x_1, x_2, x_3)$, that the above syntactical method does not help us to discover.

In our implementation, we exploit the semantic or UP-based approach proposed in [15]. Consequently, the boolean function of the form $l' = \Leftrightarrow (l_1, \ldots, l_n)$ is not considered in our experiments.

Let us now describe how these Boolean functions can be used to improve the PI enumeration CNF encoding.

Proposition 1. *Let Φ be a CNF formula and $l' = f(l_1, \ldots, l_n)$ a gate of Φ. then, for every prime implicant I, we have either $l' \in I$ or $\neg l' \in I$.*

Proof. Assume that there exists a prime implicant I such that both $l' \notin I$ and $\neg l' \notin I$ hold. Consider I' an extension of I which is obtained by assigning truth values to all the literals $l_1, \ldots, l_n$ and without assigning any truth value to l'. Thus, we have either $I'(f(l_1, \ldots, l_n)) = 0$ or $I'(f(l_1, \ldots, l_n)) = 1$. If $I'(f(l_1, \ldots, l_n)) = 0$ then $I' \cup \{l'\}$ is a counter-model of Φ and we get a contradiction. Otherwise, $I' \cup \{\neg l'\}$ is a counter-model of Φ and we also get contradiction.

Let Φ be a CNF formula and $\{l_1 = e_1, \ldots, l_n = e_n\}$ a set of its gates. Using Proposition 1, we know that it is not necessary to associate in our encoding fresh propositional variables (of the form x_l) to the literals in $S = \{l_1, \ldots, l_n, \neg l_1, \ldots, \neg l_n\}$. In this case, Φ^R is obtained by renaming only the literals in $Lit(\Phi) \setminus S$ and by redefining the formula (1) as follows:

$$\bigwedge_{p \in Var(\Phi) \setminus S} \neg x_p \vee \neg x_{\neg p} \tag{3}$$

We also redefine (2) as follows:

$$\mathcal{M}(\Phi^R) = \bigwedge_{l \in Lit(\Phi) \setminus S} x_l \to \neg Cl(\Phi^R, x_l) \tag{4}$$

Proposition 2. *Let Φ be a CNF formula and $l' = \wedge(l_1, \ldots, l_n)$ a gate of Φ. then, for every prime implicant I, we have either $\{l', l_1, \ldots, l_n\} \subseteq I$ or $\neg l' \in I$.*

Proof. In the same way as the proof of Proposition 1.

Using Proposition 2, one can reduce the formula $\mathcal{M}(\Phi^R)$. Indeed, given a Boolean gate $l' = \wedge(l_1, \ldots, l_n)$ of Φ, every formula of the form $x_l \to \neg Cl(\Phi^R, x_l)$ where $l \in \{l_1, \ldots, l_n\}$ can be reduced as follows:

$$(l' \vee (x_l \to \neg Cl(\Phi^R, x_l, l'))) \tag{5}$$

where $\neg Cl(\Phi^R, x_l, l')$ corresponds to the formula $\bigwedge_{c \in \Phi^R, \neg l' \notin c, x_l \in c} c \setminus \{x_l, l'\}$. This redefinition comes from the fact that if l' is in a prime implicant I then $l_1, \ldots, l_n$ are also in I. Thus, it is not necessary to reduce a model by removing literals in $\{l_1, \neg l_1, \ldots, l_n, \neg l_n\}$ when l' is true.

In the same way, we have also the following proposition:

Proposition 3. *Let Φ be a CNF formula and $l' = \Leftrightarrow (l_1, \ldots, l_n)$ a gate of Φ. then, for every prime implicant I and every $l \in \{l', l_1, \ldots, l_n\}$, we have either $l \in I$ or $\neg l \in I$.*

Using Proposition 3, we know that it is not necessary to associate in our encoding fresh propositional variables (of the form x_l) to the literals appearing in the equivalence chains. Other related well known XOR constraints of the form $(l_1 \oplus, \ldots, \oplus l_n)$ can be exploited in the same way. Their detection can be done using a pattern matching approach [25]. In this paper, the integration to our encoding of these specific Boolean functions is left as an interesting perspective.

5   Prime Implicant Enumeration: Alternative Approaches

As mentioned in the introduction, to the best of our knowledge, there is no available PI enumeration tool. To compare our proposed approach, we discuss an alternative that will be used in our comparative experimental evaluation (Section 6).

mcsls. One can envision a number of alternative approaches for enumerating prime implicants, by exploiting the 0-1 ILP model for computing a minimum size prime implicant [19]. Given a CNF formula Φ, let Φ_i denote the 0-1 ILP model associated with Φ:

$$minimize \sum_{l \in Lit(\Phi)} x_l \ subject\ to$$

$$\sum_{l \in c} x_l \geqslant 1 \quad for\ c \in \Phi \tag{6}$$

$$x_p + x_{\neg p} \leqslant 1 \quad for\ p \in Var(\Phi) \tag{7}$$

This model can be re-formulated as a partial MaxSAT formula [17] Φ_P. A simple observation is that *any* minimal correction subset (MCS) of Φ_P is a prime implicant of Φ. Therefore, a tool capable of enumerating the MCSes Φ_P can be used for enumerating the prime implicants of Φ. A number of approaches have been proposed in recent years for enumerating MCSes [18,24,22]. These either use MaxSAT [18,24] or dedicated algorithms [22], with recent results indicating that the dedicated algorithms outperform MaxSAT-based solutions.

6   Experiments

In this section, we present an experimental evaluation of our approach which consists in enumerating prime implicants of a CNF formula. As described above, our transformation allows to translate the problem of enumerating prime implicants of a formula Φ to that of enumerating models of a new formula Φ'. In this context, we use a modified version of MiniSAT [12] solver to enumerate the models of Φ'. Each time a model is found a prime implicant is extracted and the clause representing the negation of the model is added to seek for the next model until Φ' becomes unsatisfiable.

In order to evaluate the performances of our approach, we consider a comparison with the prime implicants enumerator (`mcsls` described in Section 5.

All the experimental results presented in this section have been obtained with a Quad-core Intel Xeon X5550 (2.66GHz, 32 GB RAM) cluster. Our experiments are conducted on benchmarks coming from 2012 MaxSAT Evaluation[1]. More precisely, we consider the enumeration of prime implicants of the hard parts of partial MaxSAT instances.

---

[1] MaxSAT Evaluations: http://www.maxsat.udl.cat

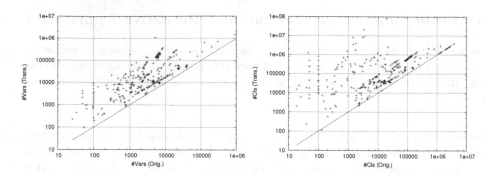

Fig. 1. Size of the Encoding With Boolean Gates

Let us first illustrate the size of our encoding enhanced with Boolean functions (or gates). In the scatter plot of Figure 1 (left hand side), each dot (x, y) represents the number of variables x of the original (Orig.) formula and the number of variables y of new formula (Trans.) respectively. As we can see, except for some few instances, the resulting encoding is, in general, of reasonable size (in many cases, the number of variables does not exceed ten times the original one). The same observation can be made on the number of clauses (see Figure 1 - right hand side).

Figure 2 shows the size of the encoding with and without using Boolean gates. As we can see, exploiting Boolean functions allows us to improve the encoding both in the number of variables and clauses. All the dots are below the diagonal.

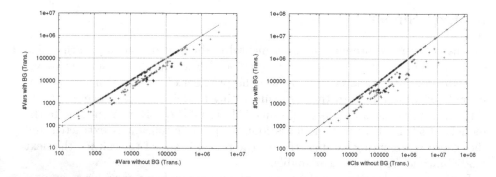

Fig. 2. Size of the Encoding With and Without Boolean Gates

On a representative sample of instances, Table 6 highlights some characteristics of the original formula and of those obtained using our encodings. In column 1, 2 and 3, we report respectively the name of the instance, its number of variables ($\#vars$) and clauses ($\#cls$). Columns 4 and 5 provide the increasing factor of the number of variables ($\times \#vars$) and clauses ($\times \#cls$) of the encoding without using Boolean Gates (*PI-Encoding*). In column 6, we provide the number of Boolean functions or Gates ($\#bg$) detected from the original instance. The two last columns show the increasing factor of the number of variables and clauses obtained using our enhanced encoding (with Boolean gates - *PI-Encoding + BG*).

We ran the two prime implicant enumerators, `primp` (our encoding *without Boolean gates*), `mcsls` (see Section 5) on the set of the 497 instances taken from the 2012 MaxSAT evaluation. In the first experiment, we limit the size of the output (number of prime implicants) to 10000 PIs and we compare the time needed for each approach to output this number of PIs or all PIs of the formula whenever it does not exceed 10000 PIs (with a time out of 1 hour). Figure 3, provides a comparison between `mcsls` and our `primp` approach. One can see that the majority of the dots are under the diagonal which illustrates the ability of `primp` to efficiently generate prime implicants compared to `mcsls`.

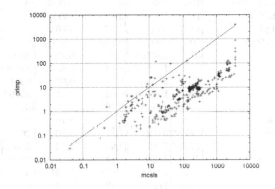

Fig. 3. mcls vs primp: CPU Time Needed to Compute $\leqslant$ 10000 PIs

For a deeper analysis, we ran `primp` and `mcsls` with a time limit fixed to 1 hour. We compare the number of prime implicants found by each PIs enumerator. In Figure 4, each dot (x, y) represents the number of prime implicants found by `mcsls` (x) and `primp` (y). This experiment confirms the efficiency of our approach. Indeed, the enumerator `primp` outperforms `mcsls`. Note that `primp` is able to generate 10 times more prime implicants than `mcsls` on several instances.

In our last experiment, we evaluate our encoding *enhanced with Boolean gates*. Figure 5, compares `primp` encoding (with and without Boolean gates) in terms of CPU time (in seconds) needed to generate the first 10000 PIs, under a time out of 1 hour. Note that the CPU time (seconds) includes the time needed for recovering Boolean gates from the CNF formula. The results demonstrate that exploiting Boolean functions makes significant improvements. Indeed, most of the dots are above the diagonal. Dots that are near the diagonal correspond to instances that involve a marginal number of Boolean functions.

Table 1. Size of the Encoding: Highlighting Results

Original Instance			PI-Encoding		PI-Encoding+BG		
instances	#vars	#cls	×(#vars)	×(#cls)	#bg	×(#vars)	×(#cls)
normalized-f20c10b_020_area_delay	4427	12489	3,89	6,46	2193	1,86	1,90
normalized-f20c10b_014_area_delay	5256	15392	4,12	6,89	2537	1,86	1,97
normalized-fir09_area_partials	5060	20159	6,11	22,60	4569	1,33	2,03
normalized-f20c10b_025_area_delay	16199	117003	16,81	11,41	8329	14,20	6,52
normalized-fir04_area_delay	741	1898	4,07	9,19	475	1,81	2,86
normalized-fir01_area_opers	194	289	3,62	7,91	86	2,07	3,45
normalized-f20c10b_003_area_delay	7343	22350	3,88	6,49	3292	1,80	1,80
normalized-fir05_area_partials	556	1526	4,91	28,42	338	2,96	11,59
normalized-fir10_area_partials	2091	7242	5,67	18,11	1618	2,21	4,63
normalized-m100_100_30_30.r	100	100	32,00	903,00	0	32,00	903,00
normalized-m50_100_70_70.r	100	50	37,00	4905,00	0	37,00	4905,00
normalized-max1024.pi	1317	936	5,97	49,08	0	5,97	49,08
normalized-m100_100_90_90.r	100	100	92,00	8103,00	0	92,00	8103,00
15tree801posib	39079	150154	6,46	6,79	35034	1,46	1,44
15tree201posib	38599	150827	6,64	6,89	34896	1,47	1,44
10tree515p	6738	25655	6,63	6,60	6241	1,42	1,40
15tree901p	38016	153438	6,92	7,01	35793	1,32	1,28
10tree315p	6666	25415	6,70	6,66	6147	1,44	1,42
normalized-s3-3-3-3pb	1124	2784	7,66	9,16	225	5,91	7,01
normalized-s3-3-3-2pb	1252	3112	7,71	9,20	267	5,94	7,04
normalized-hanoi4	1436	5388	4,94	4,13	550	2,81	2,28
normalized-ssa7552-159	2726	4323	2,51	3,79	2310	1,14	1,15
normalized-ii32e5	1044	12158	28,98	74,61	0	28,98	74,61
normalized-ii16b2	2152	17197	7,29	11,30	0	7,29	11,30
normalized-par32-2-c	2606	6509	7,56	8,89	372	6,92	8,12
normalized-ii32e3	660	5350	24,61	89,88	0	24,61	89,88
normalized-par32-4-c	2666	6659	7,57	8,90	372	6,95	8,14
normalized-ii32b2	522	2819	16,29	85,54	0	16,29	85,54
normalized-ii16b1	3456	26520	6,72	10,79	0	6,72	10,79
splitedReads_158.matrix	16983	41604	9,35	11,22	0	9,35	11,22
splitedReads_0.matrix	12962	41160	11,53	10,94	0	11,53	10,94
SU3_simp-genos.haps.72	6988	128835	30,75	6,14	1	30,75	6,14
simp-ibd_50.02	2763	41068	25,33	6,58	0	25,33	6,58
simp-ibd_50.04	3065	51631	29,10	6,69	0	29,10	6,69
simp-ibd_50.07	2917	45563	27,38	6,90	5	27,32	6,89
simp-test_chr10_JPT_75	474	3045	12,43	6,85	0	12,43	6,85
1knt_.5pti_.g.wcnf.t	2236	2120121	2,00	1,00	0	2,00	1,00
2knt_.5pti_.g.wcnf.t	2184	2019521	2,00	1,00	0	2,00	1,00
6ebx_.1era_.g.wcnf.t	1666	1187871	2,00	1,00	0	2,00	1,00
3ebx_.1era_.g.wcnf.t	2548	2767158	2,00	1,00	0	2,00	1,00

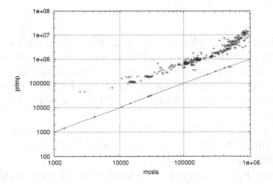

Fig. 4. mcsls vs primp : Number of Generated PIs in less than 1 hour

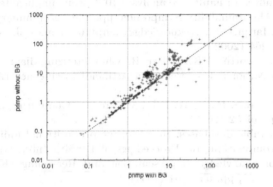

Fig. 5. primp with/without Boolean gates: CPU Time Needed to Compute ⩽ 10000 PIs

7   Conclusion and Future Works

In this paper, we propose a new approach for enumerating the set of prime implicants (PIs) of a Boolean formula in conjunctive normal form (CNF). It reformulates the original PI generation problem as a model generation problem of a new CNF formula. We also propose an essential interesting improvement of the encoding using Boolean functions recovered from the original formula. A comparative evaluation of our approach with an other alternative based PI generation method show significant improvements on several classes of CNF instances. This work open several issues for future research. We first plan to study how other interesting Boolean functions such as equivalence chain and XOR constraints can be recognized and integrated in our framework. Exploiting other structural properties (e.g. monotone literals) might lead to further improvements. To be exhaustive, we also plan to implement several other alternatives for computing prime implicants.

References

1. Acuña, V., Milreu, P.V., Cottret, L., Marchetti-Spaccamela, A., Stougie, L., Sagot, M.-F.: Algorithms and complexity of enumerating minimal precursor sets in genome-wide metabolic networks. Bioinformatics 28(19), 2474–2483 (2012)
2. Audemard, G., Saïs, L.: Circuit based encoding of CNF formula. In: Marques-Silva, J., Sakallah, K.A. (eds.) SAT 2007. LNCS, vol. 4501, pp. 16–21. Springer, Heidelberg (2007)
3. Boufkhad, Y., Gregoire, E., Marquis, P., Sais, L.: Tractable cover compilations. In: Proceedings of the Fifteenth International Joint Conference on Artificial Intelligence (IJCAI 1997), pp. 122–127 (1997)
4. Cadoli, M., Donini, F.M.: A survey on knowledge compilation. AI Commun. 10(3-4), 137–150 (1997)
5. Castell, T.: Computation of prime implicates and prime implicants by a variant of the Davis and Putnam procedure. In: ICTAI, pp. 428–429 (1996)
6. Coudert, O., Madre, J.: Fault tree analysis: 10^{20} prime implicants and beyond. In: Reliability and Maintainability Symposium, pp. 240–245 (January 1993)
7. Darwiche, A., Marquis, P.: A knowledge compilation map. J. Artif. Intell. Res. (JAIR) 17, 229–264 (2002)
8. de Kleer, J., Mackworth, A.K., Reiter, R.: Characterizing diagnoses. In: Proceedings of the 8th National Conference on Artificial Intelligence (AAAI 1990), pp. 324–330 (1990)
9. Déharbe, D., Fontaine, P., Berre, D.L., Mazure, B.: Computing prime implicants. In: FMCAD, pp. 46–52 (2013)
10. del Val, A.: Tractable databases: How to make propositional unit resolution complete through compilation. In: Proceedings of the 4th International Conference on Principles of Knowledge Representation and Reasoning (KR 1994), Bonn, Germany, May 24-27, pp. 551–561 (1994)
11. Dutuit, Y., Rauzy, A.: Exact and truncated computations of prime implicants of coherent and non-coherent fault trees within Aralia. Reliability Engineering and System Safety 58(2), 127–144 (1997)
12. Eén, N., Sörensson, N.: An extensible SAT-solver. In: Giunchiglia, E., Tacchella, A. (eds.) SAT 2003. LNCS, vol. 2919, pp. 502–518. Springer, Heidelberg (2004)
13. Fu, Z., Malik, S.: Extracting logic circuit structure from conjunctive normal form descriptions. In: 20th International Conference on VLSI Design (VLSI Design 2007), Sixth International Conference on Embedded Systems (ICES 2007), Bangalore, India, January 6-10, pp. 37–42 (2007)
14. Ginsberg, M.: A circumscriptive theorem prover. In: Reinfrank, M., Ginsberg, M.L., de Kleer, J., Sandewall, E. (eds.) Non-Monotonic Reasoning 1988. LNCS, vol. 346, pp. 100–114. Springer, Heidelberg (1988)
15. Grégoire, É., Ostrowski, R., Mazure, B., Saïs, L.: Automatic extraction of functional dependencies. In: Hoos, H.H., Mitchell, D.G. (eds.) SAT 2004. LNCS, vol. 3542, pp. 122–132. Springer, Heidelberg (2005)
16. Gurvich, V., Khachiyan, L.: On generating the irredundant conjunctive and disjunctive normal forms of monotone boolean functions. Discrete Applied Mathematics 96-97(1), 363–373 (1999)
17. Heras, F., Larrosa, J., de Givry, S., Schiex, T.: 2006 and 2007 Max-SAT evaluations: Contributed instances. JSAT 4(2-4), 239–250 (2008)
18. Liffiton, M.H., Sakallah, K.A.: Algorithms for computing minimal unsatisfiable subsets of constraints. J. Autom. Reasoning 40(1), 1–33 (2008)

19. Manquinho, V.M., Flores, P., Marques-Silva, J., Oliveira, A.L.: Prime implicant computation using satisfiability algorithms. In: Proc. of the IEEE International Conference on Tools with Artificial Intelligence, pp. 232–239 (1997)
20. Manquinho, V.M., Oliveira, A.L., Marques-Silva, J.: Models and algorithms for computing minimum-size prime implicants. In: Proc. International Workshop on Boolean Problems, IWBP 1998 (1998)
21. Marques-Silva, J.: On computing minimum size prime implicants. In: International Workshop on Logic Synthesis (1997)
22. Marques-Silva, J., Heras, F., Janota, M., Previti, A., Belov, A.: On computing minimal correction subsets. In: IJCAI (2013)
23. McCluskey Jr., E.J.: Minimization of boolean functions. Bell System Technical Journal 35(6), 1417–1444 (1956)
24. Morgado, A., Liffiton, M., Marques-Silva, J.: MaxSAT-based MCS enumeration. In: Biere, A., Nahir, A., Vos, T. (eds.) HVC. LNCS, vol. 7857, pp. 86–101. Springer, Heidelberg (2013)
25. Ostrowski, R., Grégoire, É., Mazure, B., Saïs, L.: Recovering and exploiting structural knowledge from CNF formulas. In: Van Hentenryck, P. (ed.) CP 2002. LNCS, vol. 2470, pp. 185–199. Springer, Heidelberg (2002)
26. Palopoli, L., Pirri, F., Pizzuti, C.: Algorithms for selective enumeration of prime implicants. Artificial Intelligence 111(1-2), 41–72 (1999)
27. Pizzuti, C.: Computing prime implicants by integer programming. In: Proceedings of the 8th International Conference on Tools with Artificial Intelligence, ICTAI, pp. 332–336. IEEE Computer Society, Washington, DC (1996)
28. Quine, W.: On cores and prime implicants of truth functions. American Mathematical Monthly, 755–760 (1959)
29. Quine, W.V.: The problem of simplifying truth functions. The American Mathematical Monthly 59(8), 521–531 (1952)
30. Ravi, K., Somenzi, F.: Minimal assignments for bounded model checking. In: Jensen, K., Podelski, A. (eds.) TACAS 2004. LNCS, vol. 2988, pp. 31–45. Springer, Heidelberg (2004)
31. Roy, J.A., Markov, I.L., Bertacco, V.: Restoring circuit structure from SAT instances. In: IWLS, Temecula Creek, CA, pp. 361–368 (June 2004)
32. Schrag, R.: Compilation for critically constrained knowledge bases. In: Proceedings of the Thirteenth National Conference on Artificial Intelligence and Eighth Innovative Applications of Artificial Intelligence Conference (AAAI 1996), pp. 510–515 (1996)
33. Slavkovik, M., Agotnes, T.: A judgment set similarity measure based on prime implicants. In: Proceedings of the 13th International Conference on Autonomous Agents and Multiagent Systems, AAMAS 2014 (to appear, 2014)
34. Tison, P.: Generalized consensus theory and applications to the minimization of boolean circuits. IEEE Transactions on Computers 16(4), 446–456 (1967)
35. Tseitin, G.: On the complexity of derivations in the propositional calculus. In: Slesenko, H. (ed.) Structures in Constructives Mathematics and Mathematical Logic, Part II, pp. 115–125 (1968)

Improving the Normalization of Weight Rules
in Answer Set Programs*

Jori Bomanson, Martin Gebser**, and Tomi Janhunen

Helsinki Institute for Information Technology HIIT
Department of Information and Computer Science
Aalto University, FI-00076 AALTO, Finland

Abstract. Cardinality and weight rules are important primitives in answer set programming. In this context, normalization means the translation of such rules back into normal rules, e.g., for the sake of boosting the search for answers sets. For instance, the normalization of cardinality rules can be based on Boolean circuits that effectively sort or select greatest elements amongst Boolean values. In this paper, we develop further constructions for the normalization of weight rules and adapt techniques that have been previously used to translate pseudo-Boolean constraints into the propositional satisfiability (SAT) problem. In particular, we consider mixed-radix numbers as an efficient way to represent and encode integer weights involved in a weight rule and propose a heuristic for selecting a suitable base. Moreover, we incorporate a scheme for structure sharing in the normalization procedure. In the experimental part, we study the effect of normalizing weight rules on compactness and search performance measured in terms of program size, search time, and number of conflicts.

1 Introduction

Cardinality and *weight* rules [38] are important primitives in answer set programming (ASP) [11]. They enable more compact problem encodings compared to *normal* rules, which formed the first syntax when the *stable model semantics* of rules was originally proposed [22]. Stable models are also called *answer sets*, and the basic intuition of ASP is to capture the solutions of the problem being solved as answer sets of a respective logic program. There are two mainstream approaches to computing answer sets for a logic program given as input. The first is represented by *native* answer set solvers [3,15,21,29,38], which have direct implementations of extended rule types in their data structures. The alternative, *translation-based* approach aims at transforming rules into other kinds of constraints and using off-the-shelf solver technology such as satisfiability (SAT) [9] solvers and their extensions for the actual search for answer sets (see, e.g., [23,26,28,32,34]). Regardless of the approach to compute answer sets, the *normalization* [10,26] of cardinality and weight rules becomes an interesting issue. In this context, this means translating extended rules back into normal rules, e.g., in order

---

* The support from the Finnish Centre of Excellence in Computational Inference Research (COIN) funded by the Academy of Finland (under grant #251170) is gratefully acknowledged.
** Also affiliated with the University of Potsdam, Germany

E. Fermé and J. Leite (Eds.): JELIA 2014, LNAI 8761, pp. 166–180, 2014.

to boost the search for answers sets. Normalization is also unavoidable if cardinality and weight constraints are not directly expressible in the language fragment supported by a back-end solver.

Intuitively, a cardinality rule with a *head* atom a, literals $l_1, \ldots, l_n$ in the *body*, and a bound $1 \leq k \leq n$ allows the derivation of a if at least k literals out of $l_1, \ldots, l_n$ can be satisfied by other rules. Existing approaches to normalize cardinality rules exploit translations based on *binary decision diagrams* [16] as well as *Boolean circuits* that effectively *sort* n Boolean values or *select* k greatest elements amongst them [5]. The normalization schemes developed in [26] and [10] introduce of the order of $k \times (n - k)$ or $n \times (\log_2 k)^2$ rules, respectively. The latter scheme is typically more compact and, as suggested by the experimental results in [10], also possibly faster when computing answer sets. Weight rules are similar to cardinality rules but each literal l_i in the body is assigned a positive (integer) weight w_i and, typically, we have that $k \ll \sum_{i=1}^{n} w_i$. The sum of the weights associated with satisfied literals matters when it comes to checking the bound $k \geq 0$ and deriving the head atom a. Literals with different weights bring about extra complexity and obvious asymmetry to the normalization of weight rules. Nevertheless, since cardinality rules form a special case of weight rules ($w_i = 1$ for each l_i), it is to be expected that normalization schemes developed for cardinality rules provide relevant primitives for the normalization of weight rules. Indeed, by introducing suitable auxiliary atoms, a number of rules polynomial in n, $\log_2 k$, and $\log_2(\sum_{i=1}^{n} w_i)$ will be sufficient.

The goal of this paper is to develop further constructions needed in the normalization of weight rules. A natural idea is to adapt techniques that have been previously used to translate pseudo-Boolean constraints into SAT. In particular, the sum of weights associated with satisfied literals is calculated stepwise as in the approach of [16]. In the purely binary case, this means summing up the bits constituting weights, so either 0 or 1, for satisfied literals, while propagating carry bits in increasing order of significance. This is also feasible with *merger* and *sorter* programs developed in [10], as they provide carry bits in a natural way. Since sorter programs consist of merger programs, we use the latter as basic primitives in this paper.

It is also possible to go beyond the base 2 and introduce *mixed-radix bases* to encode integer weights so that the number of digits to be summed gets smaller. In this paper, we propose a heuristic for selecting a suitable base rather than doing a complete search over all alternatives [12]. Moreover, to simplify the check for the bound k, we adopt the idea from [7] and initialize the weight sum calculation with a preselected *tare*. As a consequence, to perform the check it suffices to produce the most significant digit of the sum. Finally, we incorporate a mechanism for structure sharing in the normalization, which composes merger programs in a bottom-up fashion and shares structure whenever possible, while trying to maximize such possibilities.

The paper is organized as follows. Section 2 provides an account of the syntax and semantics of weight constraint programs, as well as a summary of principles for simplifying weight rules before normalization. The basic primitives for the normalization of weight rules, i.e., the merger programs discussed above, are introduced in Section 3, together with sorter programs built on top. The normalizations themselves are then developed in Section 4, where several schemes arise since mixed-radix bases and structure sharing are used. An experimental evaluation is carried out in Section 5, studying the effects of the new normalization schemes using the state-of-the-art ASP solver CLASP as back end. Related work and conclusions are discussed in Sections 6 and 7.

2 . Preliminaries

In what follows, we briefly introduce the syntactic fragments of ASP addressed in this paper, namely *normal logic programs* (NLPs) and *weight constraint programs* (WCPs). Afterwards, we introduce *mixed-radix notation* for encoding finite domain numbers.

Normal logic programs are defined as finite sets of *normal rules* of the form

$$a \leftarrow l_1, \ldots, l_n. \tag{1}$$

where a is a *propositional atom* (or an *atom* for short) and each l_i is a *literal*. Literals are either *positive* or *negative*, i.e., simply atoms 'b' or their *default negations* 'not c', respectively. Intuitively, the *head* atom a can be derived by the rule (1) whenever positive literals in the body are derivable by other rules in a program but none of the negative literals' atoms is derivable. A *weight rule* allows for a more versatile rule body:

$$a \leftarrow k \leq [l_1 = w_1, \ldots, l_n = w_n]. \tag{2}$$

Each body *literal* l_i in (2) is assigned a weight w_i. The weight w_i is charged if $l_i = b$ is positive and b can be derived or $l_i = $ not c is negative and c cannot be derived. The head a is derived if the sum of satisfied literals' weights is at least k. Also note that *cardinality rules* addressed in [10] are obtained as a special case of (2) when $w_i = 1$ for $1 \leq i \leq n$, and it is customary to omit weights then. Weight constraint programs P are defined as finite sets of normal and/or weight rules. A program P is called *positive* if no negative literals appear in the bodies of its rules.

To introduce the answer set semantics of WCPs, we write $\mathrm{At}(P)$ for the *signature* of a WCP P, i.e., a set of atoms to which all atoms occurring in P belong to. A positive literal $a \in \mathrm{At}(P)$ is *satisfied* in an *interpretation* $I \subseteq \mathrm{At}(P)$ of P, denoted $I \models a$, iff $a \in I$. A negative literal 'not a' is satisfied in I, denoted $I \models$ not a, iff $a \notin I$. The body of (1) is satisfied in I iff $I \models l_1, \ldots, I \models l_n$. Similarly, the body of (2), which contains the weighted literals $l_1 = w_1, \ldots, l_n = w_n$, is satisfied in I iff the *weight sum*

$$\sum_{1 \leq i \leq n,\, I \models l_i} w_i \geq k. \tag{3}$$

A rule (1), or alternatively (2), is satisfied in I iff the satisfaction of the body in I implies $a \in I$. An interpretation $I \subseteq \mathrm{At}(P)$ is a (*classical*) *model* of a program P, denoted $I \models P$, iff $I \models r$ for every rule $r \in P$. A model $M \models P$ is $\subseteq$-*minimal* iff there is no $M' \models P$ such that $M' \subset M$. Any positive program P is guaranteed to have a unique minimal model, the *least model* denoted by $\mathrm{LM}(P)$.

For a WCP P and an interpretation $M \subseteq \mathrm{At}(P)$, the *reduct* of P with respect to M, denoted by P^M, contains (i) a positive rule $a \leftarrow b_1, \ldots, b_n$ for each normal rule $a \leftarrow b_1, \ldots, b_n, $ not $c_1, \ldots, $ not c_m of P such that $M \not\models c_1, \ldots, M \not\models c_m$ [22] and (ii) a weight rule $a \leftarrow k' \leq [b_1 = w_1, \ldots, b_n = w_n]$ for each weight rule

$a \leftarrow k \leq [b_1 = w_1, \ldots, b_n = w_n, \text{not } c_1 = w_{n+1}, \ldots, \text{not } c_m = w_{n+m}]$ of P, where $k' = \max\{0, k - \sum_{1 \leq i \leq m, \, c_i \notin M} w_{n+i}\}$ is the new lower bound [38]. Given that P^M is positive by definition, an interpretation $M \subseteq \text{At}(P)$ of a WCP P is defined as a *stable model* of P iff $M = \text{LM}(P^M)$ [22,38]. The set of stable models, also called *answer sets*, of a WCP P is denoted by $\text{SM}(P)$.

Example 1. Consider a WCP P consisting of the following three rules:

$$a \leftarrow 5 \leq [b = 4, \text{not } c = 2]. \qquad b \leftarrow 1 \leq [\text{not } d = 1]. \qquad c \leftarrow 2 \leq [a = 1, c = 2].$$

Given $M_1 = \{a, b\}$, the reduct P^{M_1} consists of $a \leftarrow 3 \leq [b = 4]$, $b \leftarrow 0 \leq []$, and $c \leftarrow 2 \leq [a = 1, c = 2]$. As $\text{LM}(P^{M_1}) = \{a, b\} = M_1$, M_1 is a stable model of P. But $M_2 = \{a, b, c\}$ is not stable because $\text{LM}(P^{M_2}) = \{b\} \neq M_2$.   ∎

Since the body of a weight rule (2) can be satisfied by particular subsets of literals, it is to be expected that the normalization of the rule can become a complex operation in the worst case. Thus it makes sense to simplify weight rules before the actual normalization is performed. In the following, we provide a summary of useful principles in this respect. Some of them yield normal rules as by-product of simplification.

1. *Simplify weights*: if the weights $w_1, \ldots, w_n$ in (2) have a *greatest common divisor* (GCD) $d > 1$, replace them by $w_1/d, \ldots, w_n/d$ and the bound k by $\lceil k/d \rceil$.
2. *Normalize directly*: if the sum $s = \sum_{i=1}^{n} w_i \geq k$ but $s - w_i < k$ for each $1 \leq i \leq n$, all body literals are necessary to reach the bound, and (2) can be rewritten as a normal rule (1) by dropping the weights and the bound altogether.
3. *Remove inapplicable rules*: if $\sum_{i=1}^{n} w_i < k$, remove the rule (2) altogether.
4. *Remove dominating literals*: if the body of (2) contains a literal l_i with $w_i \geq k$, add a normal rule $a \leftarrow l_i$ and remove $l_i = w_i$ from the body.

Example 2. Let us reconsider the weight rules from Example 1. The weights of the first rule have the GCD $d = 2$, and the division yields $a \leftarrow 3 \leq [b = 2, \text{not } c = 1]$, which can be directly normalized as $a \leftarrow b, \text{not } c$. Similarly, the second rule can be directly normalized as $b \leftarrow \text{not } d$. The third rule has a dominating literal $c = 2$, which yields a normal rule $c \leftarrow c$. Such a tautological rule can be removed immediately. Since the remainder $c \leftarrow 2 \leq [a = 1]$ is inapplicable, only two normal rules $a \leftarrow b, \text{not } c$ and $b \leftarrow \text{not } d$ are left, and it is easy to see that $\{a, b\}$ is their unique stable model.   ∎

A *mixed-radix base* B is a sequence $b_1, \ldots, b_m$ of positive integers. Special cases of such include the binary and decimal bases, $\langle 2, 2, \ldots \rangle$ and $\langle 10, 10, \ldots \rangle$. In this paper, we deal with *finite-length* mixed-radix bases only and refer to them simply as *bases*. The *radices* $b_1, \ldots, b_m$ are indexed from the least significant, b_1, to the most significant, b_m, and we denote the integer at a given *radix position* i by $B(i) = b_i$. The length m is accessed with $|B|$. We define the ith *place value* of B as $\Pi(i) = \prod_{j=1}^{i-1} B(j)$. By w_B^i, we refer to the ith digit of an integer w in B. A *mixed-radix literal* H in base B is a sequence of sequences of literals $H = H_1, \ldots, H_{|B|}$, where each $H_i = h_{i,1}, \ldots, h_{i,n_i}$ captures the ith digit of the encoded value. Any such *literal digit* H_i represents a *unary* digit $v_M(H_i) \in \{0, \ldots, n_i\}$ given by the satisfied literals $h_{i,1}, \ldots, h_{i,j}$ for $0 \leq j \leq n_i$ in a model M. In turn, we write $v_M(H)$ for the value of H calculated

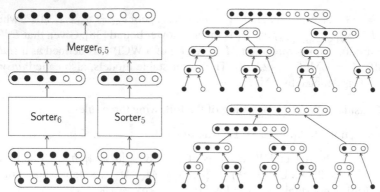

Fig. 1. A recursively constructed merge-sorter on the left, a corresponding unrolled merge-sorter on the top right, and an alternative merge-sorter on the bottom right. On the left and top right, inputs are split approximately in halves. On the bottom right, mergers are mainly laid-out for some power of two many inputs. Other splitting approaches are possible and investigated in Section 4.

as $\sum_{i=1}^{|B|} (v_M(H_i) \times \Pi(i))$. Finally, we distinguish *unique* mixed-radix literals with $n_i = B(i) - 1$ for $1 \leq i \leq |B|$, which represent each value uniquely, whereas *non-unique* mixed-radix literals can generally express a value by several combinations of digits. In the sequel, we make explicit when uniqueness is expected.

3   Merger and Sorter Programs

Sorting operations for, e.g., the normalization of cardinality rules are compactly implementable with the well known *merge-sorting* scheme, illustrated in Figure 1, where an input sequence of literals is recursively split in halves, sorted, and the intermediate results merged. Due to the ordered inputs, merging can be implemented in n^2 rules [7] without introducing any auxiliary atoms. A more efficient alternative that has been successfully applied in ASP [10] is Batcher's odd-even merger [8], which requires of the order of $n \times \log_2 n$ atoms and rules. Furthermore, the variety of options for primitives has been leveraged in practice by parametrizing the decision of when to apply which scheme [1]. For simplicity, we below abbreviate sequences of literals by capital letters. For instance, letting L be b, not c, we write $a \leftarrow 2 \leq [L, \text{not } d]$ as a shorthand for $a \leftarrow 2 \leq [b, \text{not } c, \text{not } d]$. The basic building blocks used in this work are mergers, and in the following we specify the behavior required by them. To this end, we rely on *visible strong equivalence* [10,27], denoted by $P \equiv_{vs} P'$ for two programs P and P'.

Definition 1. *Given three sequences $H_1 = h_1, \ldots, h_n$, $H_2 = h_{n+1}, \ldots, h_{n+m}$, and $S = s_1, \ldots, s_{n+m}$ of atoms, we call any NLP P a merger program, also referred to by $\mathsf{Merger}(H_1, H_2, S)$, if $P \cup Q \equiv_{vs} \{s_k \leftarrow k \leq [H_1, H_2]. \mid 1 \leq k \leq n + m\} \cup Q$ for $Q = \{h_i \leftarrow h_{i+1}. \mid 1 \leq i < n + m, i \neq n\}$.*

The role of Q in the above definition is to deny interpretations in which H_1 or H_2 is unordered and does not correspond to a unary digit, as presupposed for merging. In order to drop this restriction, a merge-sorter can be conceived as a binary tree with mergers as inner nodes and literals as leaves, as shown on the right in Figure 1. Starting from trivial sequences at the lowest level, successive merging then yields a sorted output.

Definition 2. *Given a sequence $L = l_1, \ldots, l_n$ of literals and a sequence $S = s_1, \ldots,$ s_n of atoms, we call any NLP P a* sorter program, *also referred to by* Sorter(L, S), *if $P \equiv_{vs} \{s_k \leftarrow k \leq [L]. \mid 1 \leq k \leq n\}$.*

Compared to a merger program, a sorter program does not build on preconditions and derives a unary digit representation for an arbitrary sequence of input literals.

4 Normalizing Weight Rules

In this section, we extend the translation of [7] to normalize WCPs into NLPs. To this end, we decompose normalization into parallel sorting tasks and a sequence of merging tasks. For the former subtasks, we generalize sorting to *weight sorting*.

Example 3. Let us consider a WCP P composed of the single rule

$$a \leftarrow 6 \leq [b = 2, c = 4, d = 3, e = 3, f = 1, g = 4].$$

The NLP realization of Sorter$_{17}(\langle b, b, c, c, c, c, d, d, d, e, e, e, f,$ $g, g, g, g\rangle, \langle s_1, \ldots, s_{17}\rangle)$ displayed in Figure 2, augmented with the rule $a \leftarrow s_6$, gives a plausible yet unnecessarily large normalization of P. This scheme, implemented via merge-sorting without simplifications by calling lp2normal2 -ws -r (cf. Section 5), results in 116 rules. Omitting the -r flag enables simplifications and reduces the number of rules to 53. For comparison, the translation described in the sequel leads to 16 rules only. While outcomes like this may seem to discourage unary weight sorting, it still permits compact constructions for rules with small weights and, in particular, cardinality rules.

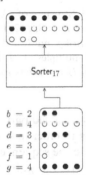

■ **Fig. 2:** Weight sorting

Returning to the general translation, we now describe the first constituent, addressing the calculation of a *digit-wise sum* of satisfied input weights in a chosen mixed-radix base B. Given a sequence $L = l_1, \ldots, l_n$ of literals and a sequence $W = w_1, \ldots, w_n$ of weights, we below write $L = W$ as a shorthand for $l_1 = w_1, \ldots, l_n = w_n$. Similarly, $L = W_B^i$ abbreviates $l_1 = (w_1)_B^i, \ldots, l_n = (w_n)_B^i$ for $1 \leq i \leq |B|$, associating the literals in L with the ith digits of their weights in B. Moreover, we refer to a program for weight sorting, such as Sorter$_{17}$ in Example 3, by WSorter.

Definition 3. *Given a sequence $L = W$ of weighted literals and a mixed-radix base B, a digit-wise sorter into the non-unique mixed-radix literal H is the program*

$$\text{WDigitwiseSorter}_B(L = W, H) = \bigcup_{i=1}^{|B|} \text{WSorter}(L = W_B^i, H_i). \qquad (4)$$

Equation (4) reveals the substeps of decomposing an input expression $L = W$ into digit-wise *bucket expressions* $L = W_B^i$, which are then subject to weight sorting. The result is a potentially non-unique mixed-radix literal H encoding the weight sum. An example of a digit-wise sorter is shown in Figure 3.

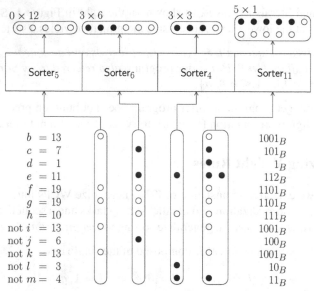

Fig. 3. Structure of a WDigitwiseSorter$_B$ program for the weighted literals displayed on the left in base $B = 3, 2, 2, 10$. Filled markers designate derivations stemming from the input literals c, d, e, not j, not l, and not m, satisfied in some interpretation M. From right to left, the sorters yield multiples of $\Pi(1) = 1$, $\Pi(2) = 3$, $\Pi(3) = 6$, and $\Pi(4) = 12$. The output mixed-radix literal H represents $v_M(H) = 0 \times 12 + 3 \times 6 + 3 \times 3 + 5 \times 1 = 7 + 1 + 11 + 6 + 3 + 4 = 32$.

The second part of the translation incorporates carries from less to more significant digits in order to derive the weight sum uniquely and accurately. In the following, we denote the sequence $s_d, s_{2d}, \ldots, s_{d\lfloor n/d \rfloor}$, involving every d^{th} element of a literal digit $S = s_1, \ldots, s_n$, by S/d.

Definition 4. *Given a mixed-radix literal $H = H_1, \ldots, H_{|B|}$ in base B, a carry merger into the sequence $S = S_1, \ldots, S_{|B|}$ of literal digits, where $S_1 = H_1$, is the program*

$$\text{WCarryMerger}_B(H, S) = \bigcup_{i=2}^{|B|} \text{Merger}(S_{i-1}/B(i-1), H_i, S_i). \qquad (5)$$

The intended purpose of the program in (5) is to produce the last digit $S_{|B|}$ of S, while $S_1, \ldots, S_{|B|-1}$ are intermediate results. The role of each merger is to combine carries from S_{i-1} with the unary input digit H_i at position i. To account for the significance gap $B(i-1)$ between S_{i-1} and H_i, the former is divided by $B(i-1)$ in order to extract the carry. An example carry merger is shown in Figure 4.

The digit-wise sorter and carry merger fit together to form a normal program to substitute for a weight rule. To this end, we follow the approach of [7] and first determine a tare t by which both sides of the inequality in (3) are offset. The benefit is that only the most significant digit in B of a weight sum is required for checking the lower bound k. This goal is met by the selection $t = (\lceil k/\Pi(|B|) \rceil \times \Pi(|B|)) - k$. Equipped with this choice for the tare t, we define the following program for weight rule normalization.

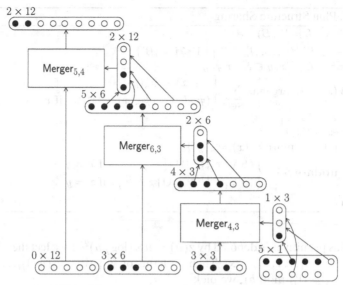

Fig. 4. Structure of a WCarryMerger$_B$ program for deriving a unique, most significant literal digit $S_{|B|}$ from digit-wise sums H_i in Figure 3. Each merger for $1 < i \leq |B|$ combines H_i with carries, extracted from an intermediate literal digit S_{i-1} by means of the division $S_{i-1}/B(i-1)$. For instance, in view of $B(1) = 3$, every third bit of $S_1 = H_1$ is used as carry for deriving S_2.

Definition 5. *Given a weight rule* $a \leftarrow k < [L = W]$ *and a mixed-radix base* B, *a weight sorting network is the program*

$$\text{WSortingNetwork}_{B,k}(L = W, a) = \text{WDigitwiseSorter}_B([L = W, \top = t], H)$$

$$\cup \ \text{WCarryMerger}_B(H, S) \qquad (6)$$

$$\cup \ \{a \leftarrow S_{|B|, \lceil k/\Pi(|B|)\rceil}.\ \}.$$

In the above, the symbol $\top$ stands for an arbitrary fact, and H and S for auxiliary (hidden) mixed-radix literals capturing the outputs of the utilized subprograms. In view of the tare t, the last rule in (6) merely propagates the truth value of a single output bit from the most significant literal digit $S_{|B|}$ to the original head atom a. Definition 5 readily leads to a weight rule normalization once a base B is picked, and we can then substitute a weight rule (2) with $\text{WSortingNetwork}_{B,k}([l_1 = w_1, \ldots, l_n = w_n], a)$.

The so far presented translation is an ASP variant of the *Global Polynomial Watchdog* [7] encoding, modified to use mixed-radix bases. In what follows, we describe two novel additions to the translation. We give a heuristic for base selection, which is different from the more or less exhaustive methods in [12,16]. Also, we provide a structure sharing approach to compress the digit-wise sorter component of the translation.

We perform mixed-radix *base selection* for a weight rule (2) by choosing radices one by one from the least to the most significant position. The choices are guided by heuristic estimates of the resulting translation size. In the following, we assume, for simplicity, that $\max\{w_1, \ldots, w_n\} \leq k \leq \sum_{j=1}^{n} w_j$, as guaranteed for example by the simplifications described in Section 2. Furthermore, the order of the size of sorters and

---

Algorithm 1. Plan Structure Sharing

1: **function** PLAN($L = W, B$)

2:     **let** $C \leftarrow \{[\, l_1^{(w_1)_B^i}, \ldots, l_n^{(w_n)_B^i} \,] \mid 1 \le i \le |B|\}$

3:     **while** $\exists S \in C : \exists x, y \in S : x \ne y$

4:         **let** $(x, y) \leftarrow \underset{x,y \in \bigcup C}{\arg\max} \sum_{S \in C} \begin{cases} \#_S(x) \times \#_S(y) & \text{if } x \ne y \\ (\#_S(x) \times (\#_S(x) - 1))/2 & \text{if } x = y \end{cases}$

5:         **let** $z \leftarrow [\, x, y \,]$

6:         **for each** $S \in C$

7:             **let** $j \leftarrow \min\{\#_S(x), \#_S(y)\}$

8:                 **update** $S \leftarrow \begin{cases} (S \setminus [\, x^j, y^j \,]) \cup [\, z^j \,] & \text{if } x \ne y \\ (S \setminus [\, x^{2\lfloor j/2 \rfloor} \,]) \cup [\, z^{\lfloor j/2 \rfloor} \,] & \text{if } x = y \end{cases}$

9:     **return** C

---

mergers used as primitives is denoted by $z(n) = n \times (\log_2 n)^2$. To select the ith radix b_i, we consider $B = b_1, \ldots, b_{i-1}, \infty$. Then, in terms of k_B^i, $W_B^i = (w_1)_B^i, \ldots, (w_n)_B^i$, and $s = \sum_{j=1}^{n} \left((w_j)_B^i \bmod b\right)$, we pick

$$b_i \leftarrow \underset{\substack{b \text{ is prime}, \, b \le \max \\ \{2, (w_1)_B^i, \ldots, (w_n)_B^i\}}}{\arg\max} \left(\begin{array}{l} z(s) + z\left(n/2 + \min\left\{\lceil s/b \rceil, \lfloor k_B^i/b \rfloor\right\} + 1\right) \\ + z(3/4 \times n) \times \log_2(1/(2 \times n \times b) \times \sum_{j=1}^{n}(w_j)_B^i) \end{array} \right).$$

The idea of the three addends is to generously estimate the size of primitives directly entailed by the choice of a prime b, the size of immediately following components, and the size of the entire remaining structure. Radices are picked until $\prod_{j=1}^{i} b_j > \max\{w_1, \ldots, w_n\}$, after which the selection finishes with the base $B = b_1, \ldots, b_{i-1}$, $\lceil (\sum_{j=1}^{n} w_j) / \prod_{j=1}^{i-1} b_j \rceil + 1$. In Section 5, we compare the effect of heuristically chosen mixed-radix bases with binary bases having $b_j = 2$ for $1 \le j < i$.

The digit-wise sorter in (4) consists of sorters that, when implemented via merge-sorting, form a *forest of mergers* on a common set of leaves. The mergers, i.e., inner nodes of the forest, produce sorted sequences based on bucket expressions. This paves the way for structure sharing. Namely, many of these mergers may coincide in terms of their output, and consequently parts of the combined subprograms that would otherwise be replicated can be reused instead. Respective savings are for instance achievable by structural hashing [16].

Our approach advances sharing, taking into account that there is a large degree of freedom in how a single merge-sorter is constructed. In fact, we may choose to split a sequence of input bits at various positions, not only in the middle, as shown on the right in Figure 1. Choices regarding such partitions generally lead to different amounts of reusable, coinciding structure. To this end, we propose Algorithm 1 to greedily expand opportunities for structure sharing. Thereby, we denote a *multiset* S on a set $X = \{x_1, \ldots, x_n\}$ of ground elements with respective *multiplicities* $i_1, \ldots, i_n$ by $[\, x_1^{i_1}, \ldots, x_n^{i_n} \,]$. The multiplicity i_j of $x_j \in X$ is referred to by $\#_S(x_j)$, and x_j is said to have i_j occurrenes in S. The superscript i_j can be omitted from $x_j^{i_j}$ if $i_j = 1$. Furthermore, we write $x \in S$ iff $x \in X$ and $\#_S(x) > 0$. At the beginning of the algorithm, the bucket expressions $L = W_B^i$ are gathered into a collection C of multi-sets, where the literals $L = l_1, \ldots, l_n$ form the common ground elements and the digits $W_B^i = (w_1)_B^i, \ldots, (w_n)_B^i$ give the multiplicities for $1 \leq i \leq |B|$. Then, iteratively, pairs (x, y) of elements with heuristically maximal joint occurrences in C are selected to form new multisets z replacing common occurrences of (x, y) in each $S \in C$. The introduced multisets z are in the sequel handled like regular ground elements, and the algorithm proceeds until every $S \in C$ consists of a single multiset. The resulting collection C will generally comprise nested multisets, which we interpret as a directed acyclic graph, intuitively consisting of a number of overlaid trees with the literals $l_1, \ldots, l_n$ as leaves, multisets z as roots, and inner nodes giving rise to mergers.

Example 4. Considering the weighted literals $a = 9, b = 3, c = 7, d = 2, e = 5, f = 4$ and the base $B = 2, 2, 9$, Algorithm 1 yields the following merge-sorter structure:

$$C \leftarrow \{[\,a, b, c, e\,], [\,b, c, d\,], [\,a^2, c, e, f\,]\},$$
$$C \leftarrow \{[\,[\,a, e\,], b, c\,], [\,b, c, d\,], [\,a, [\,a, e\,], c, f\,]\},$$
$$C \leftarrow \{[\,[\,a, e\,], [\,b, c\,]\,], [\,[\,b, c\,], d\,], [\,a, [\,a, e\,], c, f\,]\},$$
$$\vdots$$
$$C \leftarrow \{[\,[\,[\,a, e\,], [\,b, c\,]\,]\,], [\,[\,[\,b, c\,], d\,]\,], [\,[\,[\,a, [\,a, e\,]\,], [\,c, f\,]\,]\,]\}.\qquad\blacksquare$$

5 Experiments

The weight rule normalization techniques described in the previous section are implemented in the translation tool LP2NORMAL2 (v. 1.10).[1] In order to evaluate the effects of normalization, we ran LP2NORMAL2 together with the back-end ASP solver CLASP (v. 3.0.4) [21] on benchmarks stemming from five different domains: Bayesian network structure learning [14,25], chordal Markov network learning [13], the Fastfood logistics problem [10], and the Incremental scheduling and Nomystery planning tasks from the 4th ASP Competition [4]. The first two domains originally deal with optimization, and we devised satisfiable as well as unsatisfiable decision versions by picking the objective value of an optimum or its decrement (below indicated by the suffixes "Find" and "Prove") as upper bound on solution cost. The other three domains comprise genuine decision problems in which weight constraints restrict the cost of solutions. All experiments were run sequentially on a Linux machine with Intel Xeon E5-4650 CPUs, imposing a CPU time limit of 20 minutes and a memory limit of 3GB RAM per run.

Table 1 provides runtimes in seconds, numbers of constraints, and conflicts reported by CLASP, summing over all instances of a benchmark class and in total, for different weight rule implementations. In the native configuration, weight rules are not normalized but handled internally by CLASP [20]. Different translations by LP2NORMAL2 in the third to sixth column vary in the use of mixed-radix or binary bases as well as the exploitation of structure sharing. Furthermore, results for the Sequential Weight Counter (SWC) normalization scheme, used before in ASP [18] as well as SAT [24],

---

[1] Available with benchmarks at http://research.ics.aalto.fi/software/asp.

Table 1. Sums of runtimes, numbers of constraints, and conflicts encountered by CLASP

# Instances ↓ Benchmark	Native	Mixed		Binary		SWC
		Shared	Independent	Shared	Independent	
11 Bayes-Find	202	30	164	246	165	1,721
# Constraints	34,165	347,450	417,768	325,033	353,381	4,948,058
# Conflicts	12,277,288	181,957	822,390	1,056,764	868,056	616,930
11 Bayes-Prove	1,391	492	1,316	631	890	2,587
# Constraints	34,165	344,637	414,967	322,212	350,596	4,947,717
# Conflicts	52,773,713	1,393,935	3,293,955	1,933,103	3,165,312	1,459,105
11 Markov-Find	2,426	2,770	1,845	2,682	2,966	5,224
# Constraints	1,580,164	2,176,067	2,296,063	2,309,147	2,436,769	36,699,300
# Conflicts	1,771,663	1,276,599	1,092,467	1,130,776	1,178,797	318,771
11 Markov-Prove	2,251	3,294	3,428	3,255	3,229	5,402
# Constraints	1,580,164	2,182,157	2,302,171	2,307,991	2,435,603	36,694,525
# Conflicts	1,806,525	1,788,800	1,720,270	1,521,272	1,452,042	317,555
38 Fastfood	10,277	12,843	14,156	13,756	13,479	17,867
# Constraints	928,390	2,880,725	3,640,856	2,826,606	3,667,538	11,860,656
# Conflicts	122,423,130	47,566,085	42,794,938	44,148,615	49,035,512	8,940,612
12 Inc-Scheduling	257	1,340	1,330	1,481	1,581	
# Constraints	2,304,166	7,161,226	8,166,527	7,274,513	8,570,210	
# Conflicts	82,790	127,628	134,987	218,224	173,849	
15 Nomystery	4,907	4,236	3,332	4,290	3,512	4,739
# Constraints	845,321	1,678,580	2,330,329	1,725,458	2,459,603	5,115,156
# Conflicts	10,765,572	3,216,072	2,161,566	3,207,353	2,092,378	2,047,501
109 Summary	21,715	25,009	25,576	26,345	25,827	
# Constraints	7,306,535	16,770,842	19,568,681	17,090,960	20,273,700	
# Conflicts	201,900,681	55,551,076	52,020,573	53,216,107	57,965,946	
109 Summary	21,715	24,758	26,611	26,524	26,063	
without	7,306,535	17,279,805	21,632,440	17,665,922	22,358,451	
simplification	201,900,681	52,264,536	46,809,044	56,247,153	51,814,629	

are included for comparison. All normalization approaches make use of the weight rule simplifications described in Section 2. The last three rows, however, give accumulated results obtained without simplifications. The summaries exclude the SWC scheme, which works well on "small" weight rules but leads to significant size increases on large ones, as it exceeds the time and memory limits on Incremental scheduling instances.

Considering the benchmark classes in Table 1, normalization has a tremendous effect on the search performance of CLASP for the Bayesian network problems. Although the number of constraints increases roughly by a factor of 10, CLASP encounters about two orders of magnitude fewer conflicts on satisfiable as well as unsatisfiable instances (indicated by "Find" or "Prove"). In particular, we observe advantages due to using mixed-radix bases along with structure sharing. On the Markov network instances, the size increase but also the reduction of conflicts by applying the normalization schemes presented in Section 4 are modest. As a consequence, the runtimes stay roughly the same as with native weight rule handling by CLASP. Interestingly, the SWC scheme is able to significantly reduce the number of conflicts, yet the enormous size outweighs these gains. The Fastfood instances exhibit similar effects, that is, all normalization approaches lead to a reduction of conflicts, but the increased representation size inhibits runtime improvements. Unlike with the other problems, normalizations even deteriorate search in Incremental scheduling, and the additional atoms and constraints they introduce increase the number of conflicts. With the SWC scheme, the resulting problem size is even prohibitive here. These observations emphasize that the effects of normalization are problem-specific and that care is needed in deciding whether to normalize or not. In fact, normalizations turn again out to be helpful on Nomystery planning instances. Somewhat surprisingly, both with mixed-radix and binary bases, the omission of structure sharing leads to runtime improvements. Given the heuristic nature of structure sharing, it can bring about side-effects, so that it makes sense to keep such techniques optional.

In total, we conclude that the normalization approaches presented in Section 4 are practicable and at eye level with the native handling by CLASP. Although the problem size increases, the additional structure provided by the introduced atoms sometimes boosts search in terms of fewer conflicts, and the basic format of clausal constraints also makes them cheaper to propagate than weight rules handled natively. Advanced techniques like using mixed-radix instead of binary bases as well as structure sharing further improve the solving performance of CLASP on normalized inputs. Finally, taking into account that ASP grounders like GRINGO [19] do not themselves "clean up" ground rules before outputting them, the last three rows in Table 1 also indicate a benefit in terms of numbers of constraints due to simplifying weight rules a priori.

6 Related Work

Extended rule types were introduced in the late 90's [37], at the time when the paradigm of ASP itself was shaping up [30,33,35]. The treatment of weight rules varies from solver to solver. Native solvers like CLASP [20], DLV [17], IDP [41], SMODELS [38], and WASP2 [3] (where respective support is envisaged as future work) have internal data structures to handle weight rules. On the other hand, the CMODELS system [23] relies on translation [18] (to nested rules [31]). However, the systematic study of normalization approaches for extended rules was initiated with the LP2NORMAL system [26]. New schemes for the normalization of cardinality rules were introduced in [10], and this paper presents the respective generalizations to weight rules.

Weight rules are closely related to pseudo-Boolean constraints [36], and their normalization parallels translations of pseudo-Boolean constraints into plain SAT. The latter include adder circuits [16,40], binary decision diagrams [2,6,16,24,39], and sorting networks [7,16]. The normalization techniques presented in this paper can be understood as ASP adaptions and extensions of the *Global Polynomial Watchdog* [7] encoding of pseudo-Boolean constraints. Techniques for using mixed-radix bases [12,16] and structure sharing [2,16] have also been proposed in the context of SAT translation approaches. However, classical satisfiability equivalence between pseudo-Boolean constraints and their translations into SAT does not immediately carry forward to weight rules, for which other notions, such as *visible strong equivalence* [27], are needed to account for the stable model semantics. Boolean circuits based on monotone operators yield normalization schemes that preserve stable models in the sense of visible strong equivalence. In particular, this applies to the merger and sorter programs from [10].

7 Conclusions

We presented new ways to normalize weight rules, frequently arising in ASP applications. To this end, we exploit existing translations from pseudo-Boolean constraints into SAT and adapt them for the purpose of transforming weight rules. At the technical level, we use merger and sorter programs from [10] as basic primitives. The normalization schemes based on them combine a number ideas, viz. mixed-radix bases, structure sharing, and tares for simplified bound checking. Such a combination is novel both in the context of ASP as well as pseudo-Boolean satisfiability.

Normalization is an important task in translation-based ASP and, in particular, if a back-end solver does not support cardinality and weight constraints. Our preliminary experiments suggest that normalization does not deteriorate solver performance although the internal representations of logic programs are likely to grow. The decision versions of hard optimization problems exhibit that normalization can even boost the search for answer sets by offering suitable branch points for the underlying branch&bound algorithm. It is also clear that normalization pays off when a rule under consideration forms a corner case (cf. Section 2). For a broad-scale empirical assessment, we have submitted a number of systems exploiting normalization techniques developed in this paper to the 5th ASP Competition (ASPCOMP 2014).

As regards future work, there is a quest for selective normalization techniques that select a scheme on the fly or decide not to normalize, given the characteristics of a weight rule under consideration and suitable heuristics. The current implementation of LP2NORMAL2 already contains such an automatic mode.

References

1. Abío, I., Nieuwenhuis, R., Oliveras, A., Rodríguez-Carbonell, E.: A parametric approach for smaller and better encodings of cardinality constraints. In: Schulte, C. (ed.) CP 2013. LNCS, vol. 8124, pp. 80–96. Springer, Heidelberg (2013)
2. Abío, I., Nieuwenhuis, R., Oliveras, A., Rodríguez-Carbonell, E., Mayer-Eichberger, V.: A new look at BDDs for pseudo-Boolean constraints. Journal of Artificial Intelligence Research 45, 443–480 (2012)
3. Alviano, M., Dodaro, C., Ricca, F.: Preliminary report on WASP 2.0. In: NMR 2014 (2014)
4. Alviano, M., et al.: The fourth answer set programming competition: Preliminary report. In: Cabalar, P., Son, T.C. (eds.) LPNMR 2013. LNCS, vol. 8148, pp. 42–53. Springer, Heidelberg (2013)
5. Asín, R., Nieuwenhuis, R., Oliveras, A., Rodríguez-Carbonell, E.: Cardinality networks: A theoretical and empirical study. Constraints 16(2), 195–221 (2011)
6. Bailleux, O., Boufkhad, Y., Roussel, O.: A translation of pseudo Boolean constraints to SAT. Journal on Satisfiability, Boolean Modeling and Computation 2(1-4), 191–200 (2006)
7. Bailleux, O., Boufkhad, Y., Roussel, O.: New encodings of pseudo-Boolean constraints into CNF. In: Kullmann, O. (ed.) SAT 2009. LNCS, vol. 5584, pp. 181–194. Springer, Heidelberg (2009)

8. Batcher, K.: Sorting networks and their applications. In: AFIPS 1968, pp. 307–314. ACM (1968)
9. Biere, A., Heule, M., van Maaren, H., Walsh, T. (eds.): Handbook of Satisfiability. IOS (2009)
10. Bomanson, J., Janhunen, T.: Normalizing cardinality rules using merging and sorting constructions. In: Cabalar, P., Son, T.C. (eds.) LPNMR 2013. LNCS, vol. 8148, pp. 187–199. Springer, Heidelberg (2013)
11. Brewka, G., Eiter, T., Truszczyński, M.: Answer set programming at a glance. Communications of the ACM 54(12), 92–103 (2011)
12. Codish, M., Fekete, Y., Fuhs, C., Schneider-Kamp, P.: Optimal base encodings for pseudo-Boolean constraints. In: Abdulla, P.A., Leino, K.R.M. (eds.) TACAS 2011. LNCS, vol. 6605, pp. 189–204. Springer, Heidelberg (2011)
13. Corander, J., Janhunen, T., Rintanen, J., Nyman, H., Pensar, J.: Learning chordal Markov networks by constraint satisfaction. In: Advances in Neural Information Processing Systems 26, NIPS 2013, pp. 1349–1357 (2013)
14. Cussens, J.: Bayesian network learning with cutting planes. In: UAI 2011, pp. 153–160. AUAI (2011)
15. De Cat, B., Bogaerts, B., Bruynooghe, M., Denecker, M.: Predicate logic as a modelling language: The IDP system. CoRR abs/1401.6312 (2014)
16. Eén, N., Sörensson, N.: Translating pseudo-Boolean constraints into SAT. Journal on Satisfiability, Boolean Modeling and Computation 2(1-4), 1–26 (2006)
17. Faber, W., Pfeifer, G., Leone, N., Dell'Armi, T., Ielpa, G.: Design and implementation of aggregate functions in the DLV system. Theory and Practice of Logic Programming 8(5-6), 545–580 (2008)
18. Ferraris, P., Lifschitz, V.: Weight constraints as nested expressions. Theory and Practice of Logic Programming 5(1-2), 45–74 (2005)
19. Gebser, M., Kaminski, R., Kaufmann, B., Ostrowski, M., Schaub, T., Schneider, M.: Potassco: The Potsdam answer set solving collection. AI Communications 24(2), 107–124 (2011)
20. Gebser, M., Kaminski, R., Kaufmann, B., Schaub, T.: On the implementation of weight constraint rules in conflict-driven ASP solvers. In: Hill, P.M., Warren, D.S. (eds.) ICLP 2009. LNCS, vol. 5649, pp. 250–264. Springer, Heidelberg (2009)
21. Gebser, M., Kaufmann, B., Schaub, T.: Conflict-driven answer set solving: From theory to practice. Artificial Intelligence 187, 52–89 (2012)
22. Gelfond, M., Lifschitz, V.: The stable model semantics for logic programming. In: ICLP 1988, pp. 1070–1080. MIT (1988)
23. Giunchiglia, E., Lierler, Y., Maratea, M.: Answer set programming based on propositional satisfiability. Journal of Automated Reasoning 36(4), 345–377 (2006)
24. Hölldobler, S., Manthey, N., Steinke, P.: A compact encoding of pseudo-Boolean constraints into SAT. In: Glimm, B., Krüger, A. (eds.) KI 2012. LNCS, vol. 7526, pp. 107–118. Springer, Heidelberg (2012)
25. Jaakkola, T., Sontag, D., Globerson, A., Meila, M.: Learning Bayesian network structure using LP relaxations. In: AISTATS 2010, pp. 358–365. JMLR (2010)
26. Janhunen, T., Niemelä, I.: Compact translations of non-disjunctive answer set programs to propositional clauses. In: Balduccini, M., Son, T.C. (eds.) Gelfond Festschrift. LNCS (LNAI), vol. 6565, pp. 111–130. Springer, Heidelberg (2011)
27. Janhunen, T., Niemelä, I.: Applying visible strong equivalence in answer-set program transformations. In: Erdem, E., Lee, J., Lierler, Y., Pearce, D. (eds.) Lifschitz Festschrift. LNCS, vol. 7265, pp. 363–379. Springer, Heidelberg (2012)

28. Janhunen, T., Niemelä, I., Sevalnev, M.: Computing stable models via reductions to difference logic. In: Erdem, E., Lin, F., Schaub, T. (eds.) LPNMR 2009. LNCS, vol. 5753, pp. 142–154. Springer, Heidelberg (2009)

29. Leone, N., Pfeifer, G., Faber, W., Eiter, T., Gottlob, G., Perri, S., Scarcello, F.: The DLV system for knowledge representation and reasoning. ACM Transactions on Computational Logic 7(3), 499–562 (2006)

30. Lifschitz, V.: Answer set planning. In: ICLP 1999, pp. 23–37. MIT (1999)

31. Lifschitz, V., Tang, L., Turner, H.: Nested expressions in logic programs. Annals of Mathematics and Artificial Intelligence 25(3-4), 369–389 (1999)

32. Lin, F., Zhao, Y.: ASSAT: Computing answer sets of a logic program by SAT solvers. Artificial Intelligence 157(1-2), 115–137 (2004)

33. Marek, V., Truszczyński, M.: Stable models and an alternative logic programming paradigm. In: The Logic Programming Paradigm: A 25-Year Perspective, pp. 375–398. Springer (1999)

34. Nguyen, M., Janhunen, T., Niemelä, I.: Translating answer-set programs into bit-vector logic. In: Tompits, H., Abreu, S., Oetsch, J., Pührer, J., Seipel, D., Umeda, M., Wolf, A. (eds.) INAP/WLP 2011. LNCS (LNAI), vol. 7773, pp. 95–113. Springer, Heidelberg (2013)

35. Niemelä, I.: Logic programs with stable model semantics as a constraint programming paradigm. Annals of Mathematics and Artificial Intelligence 25(3-4), 241–273 (1999)

36. Roussel, O., Manquinho, V.: Pseudo-Boolean and cardinality constraints. In: Handbook of Satisfiability, pp. 695–733. IOS (2009)

37. Simons, P.: Extending the stable model semantics with more expressive rules. In: Gelfond, M., Leone, N., Pfeifer, G. (eds.) LPNMR 1999. LNCS (LNAI), vol. 1730, pp. 305–316. Springer, Heidelberg (1999)

38. Simons, P., Niemelä, I., Soininen, T.: Extending and implementing the stable model semantics. Artificial Intelligence 138(1-2), 181–234 (2002)

39. Tamura, N., Banbara, M., Soh, T.: PBSugar: Compiling pseudo-Boolean constraints to SAT with order encoding. In: PoS 2013 (2013)

40. Warners, J.: A linear-time transformation of linear inequalities into conjunctive normal form. Information Processing Letters 68(2), 63–69 (1998)

41. Wittocx, J., Denecker, M., Bruynooghe, M.: Constraint propagation for first-order logic and inductive definitions. ACM Transactions on Computational Logic 14(3), 17:1–17:45 (2013)

Logical Foundations of Possibilistic Keys

Henning Koehler[1], Uwe Leck[2], Sebastian Link[3], and Henri Prade[4]

[1] School of Engineering & Advanced Technology, Massey University, New Zealand
[2] University of Wisconsin-Superior, Superior, WI, U.S.A.
[3] Department of Computer Science, University of Auckland, New Zealand
[4] IRIT, CNRS and Université de Toulouse III, France
h.koehler@massey.ac.nz, uleck@uwsuper.edu,
s.link@auckland.ac.nz, prade@irit.fr

Abstract. Possibility theory is applied to introduce and reason about the fundamental notion of a key for uncertain data. Uncertainty is modeled qualitatively by assigning to tuples of data a degree of possibility with which they occur in a relation, and assigning to keys a degree of certainty which says to which tuples the key applies. The associated implication problem is characterized axiomatically and algorithmically. It is shown how sets of possibilistic keys can be visualized as possibilistic Armstrong relations, and how they can be discovered from given possibilistic relations. It is also shown how possibilistic keys can be used to clean dirty data by revising the belief in possibility degrees of tuples.

Keywords: Armstrong relation, Axiomatization, Database, Data cleaning, Data mining, Implication, Key, Possibility theory, Query processing, Uncertain Data.

1   Introduction

Background. The notion of a key is fundamental for understanding the structure and semantics of data. For relational databases, keys were already introduced in Codd's seminal paper [10]. Here, a key is a set of attributes that holds on a relation if there are no two different tuples in the relation that have matching values on all the attributes of the key. Keys uniquely identify tuples of data, and have therefore significant applications in data cleaning, integration, modeling, processing, and retrieval.

Motivation. Relational databases were developed for applications with certain data, such as accounting, inventory and payroll. Modern applications, such as information extraction, radio-frequency identification (RFID) and scientific data management, data cleaning and financial risk assessment produce large volumes of uncertain data. For instance, RFID is used to track movements of endangered species of animals, such as Grizzly Bears. For such an application it is desirable to associate degrees of possibility (p-degrees) with which tuples occur in a relation. Here, p-degrees represent the trust in the RFID readings, which can be derived from the strength, or precision of the devices that send and receive the signals. Table 1 shows a possibilistic relation (p-relation), where each tuple is associated with an element of a finite scale of p-degrees: $\alpha_1 > \ldots > \alpha_{k+1}$. The top degree α_1 is reserved for tuples that are 'fully possible', the bottom degree α_{k+1} for tuples that are 'impossible' to occur. Intermediate degrees can

E. Fermé and J. Leite (Eds.): JELIA 2014, LNAI 8761, pp. 181–195, 2014.

be used, such as 'quite possible' (α_2), 'medium possible' (α_3) and 'somewhat possible' (α_4) when some linguistic interpretation is preferred.

The p-degrees enable us to express keys with different degrees of certainty. For example, to express that it is 'somewhat possible' that the same grizzly is in different zones within an hour we declare the key {*time,rfid*} to be 'quite certain', stipulating that no two distinct tuples are at least 'medium possible' and have matching values on *time* and *rfid*. Similarly, to say that it is 'quite possible' that different grizzlies are in the same zone at the same time we declare the key {*zone,time*} to be 'somewhat certain', stipulating that no two distinct tuples are at least 'quite possible' and have matching values on *zone* and *time*. We apply possibility theory to establish possibilistic keys (PKs) as a fundamental notion to identify tuples of uncertain data.

Table 1. A Possibilistic Relation and Its Nested Chain of Possible Worlds

Possibilistic Relation

zone	time	rfid	object	p-degree
Z0	10am	H0	Grizzly	α_1
Z1	10am	H1	Grizzly	α_1
Z1	12pm	H2	Grizzly	α_1
Z3	1pm	H2	Grizzly	α_1
Z3	1pm	H3	Grizzly	α_2
Z3	3pm	H3	Grizzly	α_3
Z4	3pm	H3	Grizzly	α_4

Worlds of Possibilistic Relation

	zone	time	rfid	object
	Z0	10am	H0	Grizzly
	Z1	10am	H1	Grizzly
	Z1	12pm	H2	Grizzly
r_1	Z3	1pm	H2	Grizzly
r_2	Z3	1pm	H3	Grizzly
r_3	Z3	3pm	H3	Grizzly
r_4	Z4	3pm	H3	Grizzly

Contributions. (1) In Section 2 we point out the lack of qualitative approaches to constraints on uncertain data. (2) We define a semantics for keys on uncertain relations in Section 3. Here, uncertainty is modeled qualitatively by degrees of possibility. The degrees bring forward a nested chain of possible worlds, with each being a classical relation that has some possibility. Hence, the more possible the smaller a relation is, and the more keys can identify tuples uniquely. For example, the possible worlds of the p-relation from Table 1 are shown in Figure 1. The key {*time,rfid*} is satisfied by r_3 but not by r_4, and {*zone,time*} is satisfied by r_1 but not by r_2. (3) In Section 4 we establish axiomatic and linear-time algorithmic characterizations for the implication problem of PKs. (4) We show in Section 5 how to visualize PK sets as a single Armstrong p-relation. That is, for any given PK set Σ we compute a p-relation that satisfies any given PK φ if and only if φ is implied by Σ. While the problem of finding an Armstrong p-relation is precisely exponential, our output p-relation is always at most quadratic in the size of a minimum-sized Armstrong p-relation. (5) Using hypergraph transversals, we show in Section 5 how to discover the PKs that hold on a given p-relation. Visualization and discovery provide a communication framework for data engineers and domain experts to jointly acquire the set of PKs that are semantically meaningful for a given application. (6) In Section 6 we apply PKs to clean dirty data, and to query processing in Section 7. (7) In Section 8 we conclude and briefly discuss future work.

2 Related Work

The application of possibilistic logic to keys empowers applications to reason qualitatively about the uniqueness of tuples consisting of uncertain data. Data cleaning, data fusion and uncertain databases are thus primary impact areas. Section 6 illustrates how possibilistic keys can clean dirty data by revising the beliefs in p-degrees of tuples. Possibilistic keys are soft constraints that data shall satisfy after their integration from different sources. In this sense, data engineers can apply possibilistic keys as a means to impose solutions to the correlation problem, which aims to establish whether some information pertains to the same object or different ones [21]. For example, by declaring the key {*time,rfid*} on tuples that are at least medium possible, information about the same grizzly (*rfid*) at the same *time* is only recorded once in tuples that are at least medium possible (e.g. come from sufficiently trusted sources), while the key may be violated when tuples are present that are only somewhat possible.

Work on quantitative approaches to reason about uncertain data is huge, foremost probability theory [37]. The only study of keys on probabilistic databases we are aware of is [28], which is exclusively focused on query optimization. Qualitative approaches to uncertain data deal with either query languages or extensions of functional dependencies (FDs), with surveys found in [6,7] for example. Qualitative approaches to identify tuples of uncertain data have not been studied yet to the best of our knowledge. In particular, the notion of a possibilistic key is new. The only paper that considers schema design for uncertain databases is [35]. The authors develop an "FD theory for data models whose basic construct for uncertainty is alternatives" [35]. Their work is fundamentally different from our approach. Keys and FDs have also been included in description logic research [8,29,39], but have not been investigated yet for uncertain data.

Our contributions extend results on keys from classical relations, covered by the special case of two possibility degrees where $k = 1$. These include results on the implication problem [1,12], Armstrong relations [2,18,23,30] and the discovery of keys from relations [27,31], as well as data cleaning [4,9]. Keys have also been considered in other data models, including incomplete relations [24,38] and XML data [25,26]. Note that Armstrong relations are also an AI tool to acquire and reason about conditional independencies [20,32].

Possibilistic logic is a well-established tool for reasoning about uncertainty [13,16] with numerous applications in artificial intelligence [15], including approximate reasoning [40], non-monotonic reasoning [19], qualitative reasoning [36], belief revision [14,22,33], soft constraint satisfaction problems [5], decision-making under uncertainty [34], pattern classification and preferences [3]. Our results show that possibilistic logic is an AI framework that is suitable to extend the classical notion of a key from certain to uncertain data.

3 Possibilistic Keys

In this section we extend the classical relational model of data to model uncertain data qualitatively.

A relation schema, denoted by R, is a finite non-empty set of *attributes*. Each attribute $a \in R$ has a *domain dom*(a) of values. A *tuple* t over R is an element of the Cartesian product $\prod_{a \in R} dom(a)$ of the attributes' domains. For $X \subseteq R$ we denote by $t(X)$ the *projection* of t on X. A *relation* over R is a finite set r of tuples over R. As example we use the relation schema TRACKING with attributes *zone, time, rfid, object* from before. Tuples either belong or do not belong to a relation. For example, we cannot express that we have less confidence for the Grizzly identified by *rfid* value $H3$ to be in *zone* $Z3$ at $1pm$ than for the Grizzly identified by $H2$.

We model uncertain relations by assigning to each tuple some degree of possibility with which the tuple occurs in a relation. Formally, we have a *scale of possibility*, that is, a finite strict linear order $\mathcal{S} = (S, <)$ with $k + 1$ elements, denoted by $\alpha_1 > \cdots > \alpha_k > \alpha_{k+1}$. The elements $\alpha_i \in S$ are called *possibility degrees*, or p-degrees. The top p-degree α_1 is reserved for tuples that are 'fully possible' to occur in a relation, while the bottom p-degree α_{k+1} is reserved for tuples that are 'impossible' to occur. Humans like to use simple scales in everyday life to communicate, compare, or rank. Simple means to classify items qualitatively, rather than quantitatively by putting a precise value on it. Classical relations use two p-degrees, that is $k = 1$.

A *possibilistic relation schema* $(R, \mathcal{S})$, or p-relation schema, consists of a relation schema R and a possibility scale $\mathcal{S}$. A *possibilistic relation*, or p-relation, over $(R, \mathcal{S})$ consists of a relation r over R, and a function $Poss_r$ that assigns to each tuple $t \in r$ a p-degree $Poss_r(t) \in \mathcal{S}$. Table 1 shows a p-relation over (TRACKING, $\mathcal{S} = \{\alpha_1, \ldots, \alpha_5\}$).

P-relations enjoy a possible world semantics. For $i = 1, \ldots, k$ let r_i consist of all tuples in r that have p-degree at least α_i, that is, $r_i = \{t \in r \mid Poss_r(t) \geq \alpha_i\}$. Indeed, we have $r_1 \subseteq r_2 \subseteq \cdots \subseteq r_k$. The possibility distribution π_r for this linear chain of possible worlds is defined by $\pi_r(r_i) = \alpha_i$. Note that r_{k+1} is not a possible world, since its possibility $\pi(r_{k+1}) = \alpha_{k+1}$ means 'impossible'. Vice versa, the possibility $Poss_r(t)$ of a tuple $t \in r$ is the maximum possibility $\max\{\alpha_i \mid t \in r_i\}$ of a world to which t belongs. If $t \notin r_k$, then $Poss_r(t) = \alpha_{k+1}$. Every tuple that is 'fully possible' occurs in every possible world, and is therefore also 'fully certain'. Hence, relations are a special case of uncertain relations. Figure 1 shows the possible worlds $r_1 \subsetneq r_2 \subsetneq r_3 \subsetneq r_4$ of the p-relation of Table 1.

We introduce possibilistic keys, or PKs, as keys with some degree of certainty. As keys are fundamental to applications with certain data, PKs will serve a similar role for application with uncertain data. A *key* $K \subseteq R$ is satisfied by a relation r over R, denoted by $\models_r K$, if there are no distinct tuples $t, t' \in r$ with matching values on all the attributes in K. For example, the key $\{time, object\}$ is not satisfied by any relation $r_1, \ldots, r_4$. The key $\{zone, time\}$ is satisfied by r_1, but not by r_2. The key $\{zone, rfid\}$ is satisfied by r_2, but not by r_3. The key $\{time, rfid\}$ is satisfied by r_3, but not by r_4. The key $\{zone, time, rfid\}$ is satisfied by r_4.

The p-degrees of tuples result in degrees of certainty with which keys hold. Since $\{zone, time, rfid\}$ holds in every possible world, it is fully certain to hold on r. As $\{time, rfid\}$ is only violated in a somewhat possible world r_4, it is quite certain to hold on r. Since the smallest relation that violates $\{zone, rfid\}$ is the medium possible world r_3, it is medium certain to hold on r. As the smallest relation that violates $\{zone, time\}$

is the quite possible world r_2, it is somewhat certain to hold on r. Since $\{time, object\}$ is violated in the fully possible world r_1, it is not certain at all to hold on r.

Similar to a scale S of p-degrees for tuples we use a scale S^T of certainty degrees, or c-degrees, for keys. We use subscripted versions of the Greek letter β to denote c-degrees. Formally, the correspondence between p-degrees in S and the c-degrees in S^T can be defined by the mapping $\alpha_i \mapsto \beta_{k+2-i}$ for $i = 1, \ldots, k+1$. Hence, the certainty $C_r(K)$ with which the key K holds on the uncertain relation r is either the top degree β_1 if K is satisfied by r_k, or the minimum amongst the c-degrees β_{k+2-i} that correspond to possible worlds r_i in which K is violated, that is,

$$C_r(K) = \begin{cases} \beta_1 & , \text{if } r_k \text{ satisfies } K \\ \min\{\beta_{k+2-i} \mid \not\models_{r_i} K\} & , \text{otherwise} \end{cases}.$$

We can now define the semantics of possibilistic keys.

Definition 1. *Let (R, S) denote a p-relation schema. A possibilistic key (PK) over (R, S) is an expression (K, β) where $K \subseteq R$ and $\beta \in S^T$. A p-relation $(r, Poss_r)$ over (R, S) satisfies the PK (K, β) if and only if $C_r(K) \geq \beta$.* □

Example 1. The p-relation from Table 1 satisfies the PK set Σ consisting of

- $(\{zone, time, rfid\}, \beta_1)$,
- $(\{time, rfid\}, \beta_2)$,
- $(\{zone, rfid\}, \beta_3)$, and
- $(\{zone, time\}, \beta_4)$.

It violates the PK $(\{zone, rfid\}, \beta_2)$ since $C_r(\{zone, rfid\}) = \beta_3 < \beta_2$.

4   Reasoning Tools

First, we establish a strong correspondence between the implication of PKs and keys. Let $\Sigma \cup \{\varphi\}$ denote a set of PKs over (R, S). We say Σ implies φ, denoted by $\Sigma \models \varphi$, if every p-relation $(r, Poss_r)$ over (R, S) that satisfies every PK in Σ also satisfies φ. We use $\Sigma^* = \{\varphi \mid \Sigma \models \varphi\}$ to denote the *semantic closure* of Σ.

Example 2. Let Σ be as in Example 1, and $\varphi = (\{zone, rfid, object\}, \beta_2)$. Then Σ does not imply φ as the following p-relation witnesses:

zone	time	rfid	object	Poss. degree
Z0	10am	H0	Grizzly	α_1
Z0	3pm	H0	Grizzly	α_3

4.1   The Magic of β-Cuts

For a PK set Σ over (R, S) with $|S| = k+1$ and c-degree $\beta \in S^T$ where $\beta > \beta_{k+1}$, let $\Sigma_\beta = \{K \mid (K, \beta') \in \Sigma \text{ and } \beta' \geq \beta\}$ be the β-cut of Σ.

Theorem 1. *Let $\Sigma \cup \{(K, \beta)\}$ be a PK set over (R, S) where $\beta > \beta_{k+1}$. Then $\Sigma \models (K, \beta)$ if and only if $\Sigma_\beta \models K$.*

Proof. Suppose $(r, Poss_r)$ is some p-relation over $(R, \mathcal{S})$ that satisfies Σ, but violates (K, β). In particular, $C_r(K) < \beta$ implies that there is some relation r_i that violates K and where $\beta_{k+2-i} < \beta$. Let $K' \in \Sigma_\beta$, where $(K', \beta') \in \Sigma$. Since r satisfies $(K, \beta') \in \Sigma$ we have $C_r(K') \geq \beta' \geq \beta$. If r_i violated K', then $\beta > \beta_{k+2-i} \geq C_r(K') \geq \beta$, a contradiction. Hence, r_i satisfies Σ_β and violates K.

Let r' denote some relation that satisfies Σ_β and violates K, w.l.o.g. $r' = \{t, t'\}$. Let r be the p-relation over $(R, \mathcal{S})$ that consists of r' and where $Poss_{r'}(t) = \alpha_1$ and $Poss_{r'}(t') = \alpha_i$, such that $\beta_{k+1-i} = \beta$. Then r violates (K, β) since $C_r(K) = \beta_{k+2-i}$, as $r_i = r'$ is the smallest relation that violates K, and $\beta_{k+2-i} < \beta_{k+1-i} = \beta$. For $(K', \beta') \in \Sigma$ we distinguish two cases. If r_i satisfies K', then $C_r(K') = \beta_1 \geq \beta$. If r_i violates K', then $K' \notin \Sigma_\beta$, i.e., $\beta' < \beta = \beta_{k+1-i}$. Therefore, $\beta' \leq \beta_{k+2-i} = C_r(K')$ as $r_i = r'$ is the smallest relation that violates K'. We conclude that $C_r(K') \geq \beta'$. Consequently, $(r, Poss_r)$ is a p-relation that satisfies Σ and violates (K, β). □

Example 3. Let $\Sigma \cup \{\varphi\}$ be as in Example 2. Theorem 1 says that Σ_{β_2} does not imply $(\{zone, rfid, object\}, \beta_2)$. The possible world r_3 of the p-relation from Example 2:

zone	time	rfid	object
Z0	10am	H0	Grizzly
Z0	3pm	H0	Grizzly

satisfies the key $\{time, rfid\}$ that implies both keys in Σ_{β_2}. However, r_3 violates the key $\{zone, rfid, object\}$.

4.2   Axiomatic Characterization

We determine the semantic closure by applying *inference rules* of the form

$$\frac{\text{premise}}{\text{conclusion}} \text{ condition} .$$

For a set $\mathfrak{R}$ of inference rules let $\Sigma \vdash_\mathfrak{R} \varphi$ denote the *inference* of φ from Σ by $\mathfrak{R}$. That is, there is some sequence $\sigma_1, \ldots, \sigma_n$ such that $\sigma_n = \varphi$ and every σ_i is an element of Σ or is the conclusion that results from an application of an inference rule in $\mathfrak{R}$ to some premises in $\{\sigma_1, \ldots, \sigma_{i-1}\}$. Let $\Sigma_\mathfrak{R}^+ = \{\varphi \mid \Sigma \vdash_\mathfrak{R} \varphi\}$ be the *syntactic closure* of Σ under inferences by $\mathfrak{R}$. $\mathfrak{R}$ is *sound* (*complete*) if for every set Σ over every $(R, \mathcal{S})$ we have $\Sigma_\mathfrak{R}^+ \subseteq \Sigma^*$ ($\Sigma^* \subseteq \Sigma_\mathfrak{R}^+$). The (finite) set $\mathfrak{R}$ is a (finite) *axiomatization* if $\mathfrak{R}$ is both sound and complete.

For the set $\mathfrak{K}$ from Table 2 the attribute sets K, K' are subsets of a given R, and β, β' belong to a given $\mathcal{S}^T$. In particular, β_{k+1} denotes the bottom certainty degree.

Theorem 2. *The set $\mathfrak{K}$ forms a finite axiomatization for the implication problem of PKs.*

Proof. The soundness proof is straightforward and omitted. For completeness, we apply Theorem 1 and the fact that $\mathcal{K}'$ axiomatizes key implication. Let $(R, \mathcal{S})$ be a p-relation schema with $|\mathcal{S}| = k + 1$, and $\Sigma \cup \{(K, \beta)\}$ a PK set such that $\Sigma \models (K, \beta)$. We show that $\Sigma \vdash_\mathfrak{K} (K, \beta)$ holds.

For $\Sigma \models (K, \beta_{k+1})$ we have $\Sigma \vdash_\mathfrak{K} (K, \beta_{k+1})$ by applying $\mathcal{B}$. Let now $\beta < \beta_{k+1}$. From $\Sigma \models (K, \beta)$ we conclude $\Sigma_\beta \models K$ by Theorem 1. Since $\mathfrak{K}'$ is complete for key

Table 2. Axiomatization $\mathfrak{K}' = \{\mathcal{T}', \mathcal{S}'\}$ of Keys and $\mathfrak{K} = \{\mathcal{T}, \mathcal{S}, \mathcal{B}, \mathcal{W}\}$ of Possibilistic Keys

$\dfrac{}{\overline{R}}$ (top, $\mathcal{T}'$)	$\dfrac{}{\overline{(R,\beta)}}$ (top, $\mathcal{T}$)	$\dfrac{}{\overline{(K,\beta_{k+1})}}$ (bottom, $\mathcal{B}$)
$\dfrac{K}{K \cup K'}$ (superkey, $\mathcal{S}'$)	$\dfrac{(K,\beta)}{(K \cup K',\beta)}$ (superkey, $\mathcal{S}$)	$\dfrac{(K,\beta)}{(K,\beta')}\ \beta' \le \beta$ (weakening, $\mathcal{W}$)

implication, $\Sigma_\beta \vdash_{\mathfrak{K}'} K$ holds. Let $\Sigma_\beta^\beta = \{(K',\beta) \mid K' \in \Sigma_\beta\}$. Thus, the inference of K from Σ_β using $\mathcal{K}'$ can be turned into an inference of (K,β) from Σ_β^β by $\mathfrak{K}$, simply by adding β to each key in the inference. Hence, whenever $\mathcal{T}'$ or $\mathcal{S}'$ is applied, one applies instead $\mathcal{T}$ or $\mathcal{S}$, respectively. Consequently, $\Sigma_\beta^\beta \vdash_{\mathfrak{K}} (K,\beta)$. The definition of Σ_β^β ensures that every PK in Σ_β^β can be inferred from Σ by applying $\mathcal{W}$. Hence, $\Sigma_\beta^\beta \vdash_{\mathfrak{K}} (K,\beta)$ means that $\Sigma \vdash_{\mathfrak{K}} (K,\beta)$. $\qquad\square$

4.3 Algorithmic Characterization

While $\mathfrak{K}$ enables us to enumerate all PKs implied by a PK set Σ, in practice it often suffices to decide whether a given PK φ is implied by Σ. Enumerating all implied PKs and checking whether φ is among them is neither efficient nor makes good use of φ.

Theorem 3. *Let $\Sigma \cup \{(K,\beta)\}$ denote a set of PKs over $(R,\mathcal{S})$ with $|\mathcal{S}| = k+1$. Then Σ implies (K,β) if and only if $\beta = \beta_{k+1}$, or $K = R$, or there is some $(K',\beta') \in \Sigma$ such that $K' \subseteq K$ and $\beta' \ge \beta$.*

Proof. Theorem 1 shows for $i = 1,\ldots,k$ that Σ implies (K,β_i) if and only if Σ_β implies K. It is easy to observe from the axiomatization $\mathfrak{K}'$ of keys that Σ_β implies K if and only if $R = K$, or there is some $K' \in \Sigma_\beta$ such that $K' \subseteq K$ holds. As Σ implies (K,β_{k+1}), the theorem follows. $\qquad\square$

Corollary 1. *An instance $\Sigma \models \varphi$ of the implication problem can be decided in time $\mathcal{O}(\|\Sigma \cup \{\varphi\}\|)$ where $\|\Sigma\|$ denotes the total number of symbol occurrences in Σ.* $\qquad\square$

5 Acquisition Tools

New applications benefit from the ability of data engineers to acquire the PKs that are semantically meaningful in the domain of the application. For that purpose, data engineers communicate with domain experts. Now we establish two major tools that help data engineers to effectively communicate with domain experts. We follow the framework in Figure 1. Here, data engineers use our algorithm to visualize abstract PK sets Σ in form of some Armstrong p-relation r_Σ, which is then inspected jointly with domain experts. Domain experts may change r_Σ or supply entirely new data samples to the engineers. For that case we establish an algorithm that computes the set of PKs that hold in the data sample.

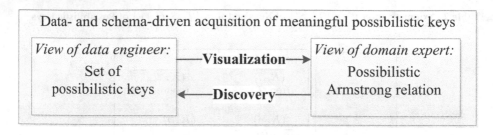

Fig. 1. Acquisition Framework for Possibilistic Keys

5.1 Structure and Computation of Visualizations

A p-relation $(r, Poss_r)$ over (R, S) is *Armstrong* for a PK set Σ if and only if for all PKs φ over (R, S), $(r, Poss_r)$ satisfies φ if and only if $\Sigma \models \varphi$. The maximum c-degree β by which a PK (K, β) is implied by Σ can 'simply be read-off' as the c-degree $C_r(K)$ of any Armstrong p-relation $(r, Poss_r)$ for Σ. Our first aim is to characterize the structure of Armstrong p-relations. We recall two notions from relational databases. The *agree set* of two tuples t, t' over R is the set $ag(t, t') = \{a \in R \mid t(a) = t'(a)\}$ of attributes on which t and t' have matching values. The agree set of a relation is the set $ag(r) = \{ag(t, t') \mid t, t' \in r \wedge t \neq t'\}$. Let Σ denote a set of keys over relation schema R. An *anti-key* of R with respect to Σ is a subset $A \subseteq R$ such that Σ does not imply the key A over R and for all $a \in R - A$, Σ implies the key $A \cup \{a\}$ over R. We denote by Σ^{-1} the set of all anti-keys of R with respect to Σ.

Theorem 4. *Let Σ denote a set of PKs, and let $(r, Poss_r)$ denote a p-relation over (R, S) with $|S| = k + 1$. Then $(r, Poss_r)$ is Armstrong for Σ if and only if for all $i = 1, \ldots, k$, the relation r_{k+1-i} is Armstrong for Σ_{β_i}. That is, for all $i = 1, \ldots, k$, $\Sigma_{\beta_i}^{-1} \subseteq ag(r_{k+1-i})$, and for all $K \in \Sigma_{\beta_i}$ and for all $X \in ag(r_{k+1-i})$, $K \not\subseteq X$.*

Proof. $(r, Poss_r)$ is Armstrong for Σ if and only if for all $i = 1, \ldots, k$, for all $K \subseteq R$, $\models_{(r, Poss_r)} (K, \beta_i)$ iff $\Sigma \models (K, \beta_i)$. However, $\models_{(r, Poss_r)} (K, \beta_i)$ iff $\models_{r_{k+1-i}} K$, and $\Sigma \models (K, \beta_i)$ iff $\Sigma_{\beta_i} \models K$. Therefore, $(r, Poss_r)$ is Armstrong for Σ if and only if for all $i = 1, \ldots, k$, r_{k+1-i} is an Armstrong relation for Σ_{β_i}. The second statement follows straight from the well-known result that a relation r is Armstrong for a set Σ of keys if and only if $\Sigma^{-1} \subseteq ag(r)$ and for all $K \in \Sigma$ and all $X \in ag(r)$, $K \not\subseteq X$ [11]. $\qquad\square$

Theorem 4 shows that Algorithm 1 computes an Armstrong p-relation for input Σ. The algorithm computes for $i = 1, \ldots, k$ the set $\Sigma_{\beta_i}^{-1}$ incrementally. Starting with a tuple of p-degree α_1, for $i = k, \ldots, 1$, each $A \in \Sigma_{\beta_i}^{-1}$ is realized as an agree set by introducing a tuple that agrees with the previous tuple on A and has p-degree α_{k+1-i}, as long as A did not already occur for some larger i.

Example 4. We apply Algorithm 1 to the set Σ from Example 1. Using the first letters of each attribute we obtain

Algorithm 1. Visualize

Input: $R, \{\beta_1, \ldots, \beta_k\}, \Sigma$
Output: Possibilistic Armstrong Relation $(r, Poss_r)$ for Σ
1: $\Sigma_0^{-1} \leftarrow \{R - \{a\} \mid a \in R\}$;
2: **for** $i = 1, \ldots, k$ **do**   ▷ Compute $\Sigma_{\beta_i}^{-1}$ incrementally
3:     $\Sigma_i \leftarrow \{K \mid (K, \beta_j) \in \Sigma$ and $j \leq i\}$,
4:     $\Sigma_i^{-1} \leftarrow$ ANTIKEYS$(R, \Sigma_i, \Sigma_{i-1}^{-1})$,
5: **end for**
6: **for all** $a \in R$ **do**
7:     $t_0(a) \leftarrow c_{a,0}$;   ▷ $c_{a,i}$ are fresh constants
8: **end for**
9: $j \leftarrow 0$; $r \leftarrow \{t_0\}$; $Poss_r(t_0) \leftarrow \alpha_1$; $\Sigma_0 \leftarrow \emptyset$;
10: **for** $i = k$ downto 1 **do**
11:     **for all** $A \in \Sigma_i^{-1} - \Sigma_0$ **do**
12:         $j \leftarrow j + 1$;
13:         **for all** $a \in R$ **do**   ▷ New tuple with agree set A
14:             **if** $a \in A$ **then** $t_j(a) \leftarrow t_{j-1}(a)$;
15:             **else** $t_j(a) \leftarrow c_{a,j}$;
16:             **end if**
17:         **end for**
18:         $Poss_r(t_j) \leftarrow \alpha_{k+1-i}$;   ▷ and p-degree α_{k+1-i}
19:         $r \leftarrow r \cup \{t_j\}$;
20:     **end for**
21:     $\Sigma_0 \leftarrow \Sigma_0 \cup \Sigma_i^{-1}$;
22: **end for**
23: **return** $(r, Poss_r)$;

Subroutine ANTIKEYS(R, Σ, Σ^{-1})
Input: R, Σ set of keys in Σ_i, Σ^{-1} set of anti-keys in Σ_{i-1}^{-1}
Output: Σ^{-1} set of anti-keys for Σ_{β_i}
24: **for all** $K \in \Sigma, A \in \Sigma^{-1}$ with $K \subseteq A$ **do**
25:     $\Sigma^{-1} \leftarrow (\Sigma^{-1} - \{A\}) \cup \bigcup_{a \in K}\{A - \{a\}\}$;
26: **end for**
27: $\Sigma^{-1} \leftarrow \{A \mid \forall B \in \Sigma^{-1} - \{A\}(A \not\subseteq B)\}$;
28: **return** Σ^{-1};

- $\Sigma_1 = \{ztr\}$ and $\Sigma_{\beta_1}^{-1} = \{zto, \underline{tro}, zro\}$
- $\Sigma_2 = \{tr\}$ and $\Sigma_{\beta_2}^{-1} = \{zto, \underline{zro}\}$
- $\Sigma_3 = \{zr\}$ and $\Sigma_{\beta_3}^{-1} = \{\underline{zto}, ro, zo\}$, and
- $\Sigma_4 = \{zt\}$ and $\Sigma_{\beta_4}^{-1} = \{\underline{to}, \underline{zo}, \underline{ro}\}$.

Anti-keys are underlined when they are realized as agree sets of tuples in the possibilistic Armstrong relation:

zone	time	rfid	object	Poss. degree
$c_{z,0}$	$c_{t,0}$	$c_{R,0}$	$c_{o,0}$	α_1
$c_{z,1}$	$c_{t,0}$	$c_{R,1}$	$c_{o,0}$	α_1
$c_{z,1}$	$c_{t,2}$	$c_{R,2}$	$c_{o,0}$	α_1
$c_{z,3}$	$c_{t,3}$	$c_{R,2}$	$c_{o,0}$	α_1
$c_{z,3}$	$c_{t,3}$	$c_{R,4}$	$c_{o,0}$	α_2
$c_{z,3}$	$c_{t,5}$	$c_{R,4}$	$c_{o,0}$	α_3
$c_{z,6}$	$c_{t,5}$	$c_{R,4}$	$c_{o,0}$	α_4

Fitting substitution yields the p-relation from Table 1.

Theorem 5. *Algorithm 1 computes an Armstrong p-relation for Σ whose size is at most quadratic in that of a minimum-sized Armstrong p-relation for Σ.*

Proof. The soundness of Algorithm 1 follows from Theorem 4, which also shows that for $\Sigma^{-1} = \bigcup_{i=1}^{k} \Sigma_i^{-1}$ we have $|\Sigma^{-1}| \leq ag(r) \leq \binom{|r|}{2}$. The inequalities establish the lower bound in $\frac{1}{2} \cdot \sqrt{1 + 8 \cdot |\Sigma^{-1}|} \leq |r| \leq |\Sigma^{-1}| + 1$. The upper bound follows from Algorithm 1. Hence, the p-relation computed by Algorithm 1 is at most quadratic in the size of a minimum-sized Armstrong p-relation for Σ. □

Finding Armstrong p-relations is precisely exponential. That means that there is an algorithm for computing an Armstrong p-relation whose running time is exponential in the size of Σ, and that there is some set Σ in which the number of tuples in each minimum-sized Armstrong p-relation for Σ is exponential thus, an exponential amount of time is required in this case simply to write down the p-relation.

Theorem 6. *Finding an Armstrong p-relation for a PK set Σ is precisely exponential in the size of Σ.*

Proof. Algorithm 1 computes an Armstrong p-relation for Σ in time at most exponential in its size. Some PK sets Σ have only Armstrong p-relations with exponentially many tuples in the size of Σ. For $R = \{a_1, \ldots, a_{2n}\}$, $\mathcal{S} = \{\alpha_1, \alpha_2\}$ and $\Sigma = \{(\{a_1, a_2\}, \beta_1), \ldots, (\{a_{2n-1}, a_{2n}\}, \beta_1)\}$ with size $2 \cdot n$, Σ^{-1} consists of the 2^n anti-keys $\bigcup_{j=1}^{n} X_j$ where $X_j \in \{a_{2j-1}, a_{2j}\}$. □

Armstrong p-relations for some other PK sets Σ' only require a number of tuples that is logarithmic in the size of Σ'. Such a set Σ' is given by the 2^n PKs $(\bigcup_{j=1}^{n} X_j, \beta_1)$ where $X_j \in \{a_{2j-1}, a_{2j}\}$. In fact, Algorithm 1 computes an Armstrong p-relation for Σ' with $n + 1$ tuples.

5.2 Discovery

Given a p-relation we may ask for which set Σ it is Armstrong. Algorithm 2 computes a cover Σ of the set of PKs satisfied by a given p-relation. A cover of some PK set Θ is a PK set Σ where $\Sigma^* = \Theta^*$. A *hypergraph* (V, E) consists of a vertex set V and a set E of subsets of V, called hyperedges. A set $T \subseteq V$ is a *transversal* of (V, E) if for all $H \in E, T \cap H \neq \emptyset$ holds. A transversal T of (V, E) is *minimal* if there is no transversal

T' of (V, E) such that $T' \subsetneq T$ [17]. Algorithm 2 computes the minimal transversals of the hypergraph that has the underlying attributes as vertex set and minimal disagree sets of tuples from world r_i as hyperedges. These form a cover of the set of keys that hold on r_i. The corresponding PKs thus hold with c-degree at least β_{k+1-i}. Using Theorem 3 we select PKs not implied by the other PKs as output.

Algorithm 2. Discover

Input: $(r, Poss_r)$ over $(R, \{\beta_1, \ldots, \beta_{k+1}\})$
Output: Cover Σ of PKs that are satisfied by $(r, Poss_r)$
 1: **for** $i = 1, \ldots, k$ **do**
 2:     $dis\text{-}ag(r_i) \leftarrow \min\{X \subseteq R \mid \exists t, t' \in r_i \forall a \in R(t(a) \neq t'(a) \leftrightarrow a \in X)\}$;
 3:     $\mathcal{H}_i \leftarrow (R, dis\text{-}ag(r_i))$;
 4:     $\Sigma_i \leftarrow \{(K, \beta_{k+1-i}) \mid K \in Tr(\mathcal{H}_i)\}$;
 5: **end for**
 6: $\Sigma \leftarrow \bigcup_{i=1}^k \Sigma_i$;
 7: $\Sigma \leftarrow \{(K, \beta) \in \Sigma \mid \neg\exists(K', \beta') \in \Sigma(K' \subseteq K \wedge \beta' > \beta)\}$;
 8: **return** Σ;

Example 5. We apply Algorithm 2 to the p-relation from Table 1. Using the first letters of each attribute we obtain

- $dis\text{-}ag(r_1) = \{zr, tr, zt\}$ and
  $\Sigma_1 = \{(zr, \beta_4), (tr, \beta_4), (zt, \beta_4)\}$
- $dis\text{-}ag(r_2) = \{zt, r\}$ and $\Sigma_2 = \{(zr, \beta_3), (tr, \beta_3)\}$
- $dis\text{-}ag(r_3) = \{t, r\}$ and $\Sigma_3 = \{(tr, \beta_2)\}$, and
- $dis\text{-}ag(r_4) = \{z, t, r\}$ and $\Sigma_3 = \{(ztr, \beta_1)\}$.

A cover Σ for the PKs that hold on the p-relation consists of (ztr, β_1), (tr, β_2), (zr, β_3), and (zt, β_4).

Theorem 7. *Algorithm 2 computes a cover of the set of PKs that are satisfied by the given p-relation r in time $\mathcal{O}(m + n^2)$ where $m := |R|^2 \times |r_k|^2 \times |dis\text{-}ag(r_k)|$ and $n := \prod_{X \in dis\text{-}ag(r_k)} |X|$.*

Proof. The soundness follows from the result that the keys of a relation are the minimal transversals of the disagree sets in the relation [11,31], and Theorem 3. The collection $dis\text{-}ag(r_i)$ is computed in time $\mathcal{O}(m)$. The set of all minimal transversals for the simple hypergraph $\mathcal{H}_i$ is computed in time $\mathcal{O}(n^2)$. Algorithm 2 can compute the minimal hypergraphs incrementally with additional disagree sets discovered from tuples with lower p-degrees. □

6   Data Cleaning

In this section we illustrate an application of possibilistic keys for data cleaning purposes. The classical data cleaning problem can be stated as follows: Given a relation r and a set Σ of keys, find a relation $r' \subseteq r$ of maximum cardinality such that r' satisfies Σ. For example, the relation r

		r			
zone	time	rfid	object	$Poss_r$	$Poss'_r$
Z3	1pm	H2	Grizzly	α_1	α_1
Z3	1pm	H3	Grizzly	α_1	α_2
Z3	3pm	H3	Grizzly	α_1	α_3
Z4	3pm	H3	Grizzly	α_1	α_4

violates the set $\Sigma = \{zt, zr, tr\}$ of keys. Solutions to the classical data cleaning problem would be the relations r_1 consisting of the first and third tuple, r_2 consisting of the first and last tuple, and r_3 consisting of the second and last tuple. Each solution requires us to remove at least two tuples from the relation. In this sense, classical data cleaning removes valuable information from the given relation.

We now introduce possibilistic data cleaning as a means to minimize the removal of tuples from a p-relation. For this purpose, we exploit the c-degrees of PKs to "reduce" the given p-degrees of tuples such that all PKs will be satisfied.

Given two p-relations $r_1 = (r', Poss_{r'})$ and $r_2 = (r, Poss_r)$ we say that r_1 is a *p-subrelation* of r_2, denoted by $r_1 \subseteq_p r_2$, if and only if $r'_i \subseteq r_i$ for $i = 1, \ldots, k$. The p-subset relationship is simply the partial order of functions induced by the ordering on p-degrees, that is, $r_1 \subseteq_p r_2$ if and only if $Poss_{r'}(t) \leq Poss_r(t)$ holds for all tuples t. The *p-cardinality* of the p-relation $(r, Poss_r)$ is the mapping $\mathcal{C} : \alpha_i \mapsto |r_i|$ for $i = 1, \ldots, k$. We compare p-cardinalities with respect to the lexicographical order, that is,

$$\mathcal{C}_1 <_L \mathcal{C}_2 :\Leftrightarrow \exists \alpha_i. \begin{array}{l} \mathcal{C}_1(\alpha_i) < \mathcal{C}_2(\alpha_i) \wedge \\ \mathcal{C}_1(\alpha_j) = \mathcal{C}_2(\alpha_j) \, \forall \alpha_j < \alpha_i \end{array}$$

The *possibilistic data cleaning problem* is: Given a p-relation r and set Σ of PKs, find a p-subrelation $r' \subseteq_p r$ of maximal p-cardinality so that Σ holds on r'.

A point that is perhaps controversial in our problem definition is the use of the lexicographic order $<_L$ in defining our target function to optimize. We chose this linearization of the natural partial order between p-cardinalities over other candidates for two reasons. Firstly, by maximizing $|r'_k| = |r'|$, the number of tuples completely "lost" during data cleaning is minimized. Secondly, it will allow us to develop more efficient algorithms for computing it.

For example, the p-relation $(r, Poss_r)$ violates the PK set

$$\Sigma = \{(zt, \beta_4), (zr, \beta_3), (tr, \beta_1)\}.$$

However, if we change the p-degree of the second tuple to α_2, the p-degree of the third tuple to α_3, and the p-degree of the last tuple to α_4, then the resulting p-relation $(r, Poss'_r)$ satisfies Σ. Note that none of the p-degrees had to be set to the bottom degree α_5. That is, every tuple in the cleaned p-relation $(r, Poss'_r)$ is at least somewhat possible to occur.

7   Query Processing

We demonstrate the benefit of PKs on query processing. Therefore, we add the attribute *p-degree* to the relation schema TRACKING with attributes *zone, time, rfid, object*.

Suppose we are interested in finding out which grizzly bears have been tracked in which zone, but we are only interested in answers that come from 'certain' or 'quite possible' tuples in the database. A user might enter the following SQL query:

zone	rfid	p-degree
Z0	H0	α_1
Z1	H1	α_1
Z1	H2	α_1
Z3	H2	α_1
Z3	H3	α_2

SELECT DISTINCT *zone*, *rfid*, *p-degree*
FROM TRACKING
WHERE *p-degree* $= \alpha_1$ OR *p-degree* $= \alpha_2$
ORDER BY *p-degree* ASC

which removes duplicate answers, and orders them with decreasing p-degree. When applied to the p-relation from Table 1, the query returns the answers on the right.

Firstly, our framework allows users to ask such queries - having available the p-degrees of tuples. Secondly, answers can be ordered according to the p-degree a huge benefit for users. Thirdly, the example shows how our framework can be embedded with standard technology, here SQL. Finally, recall our PK ($\{zone, rfid\}, \beta_3$) which holds on the set of tuples that have p-degree α_1 or α_2. Consequently, the query answers satisfy the key $\{zone, rfid\}$ and the DISTINCT clause becomes superfluous. A query optimizer, capable of reasoning about PKs, can remove the DISTINCT clause from the input query without affecting its output. This optimization saves response time when answering queries, as duplicate elimination is an expensive operation and therefore not executed by default in SQL databases. PKs, and the ability to reason about them, have therefore direct applications to query processing.

8   Conclusion and Future Work

Possibilistic keys have been introduced to efficiently identify tuples of uncertain data. Uncertainty is modeled qualitatively by applying the AI framework of possibilistic logic to the fundamental database concept of keys. Tools were established to efficiently reason about possibilistic keys, to visualize and discover them effectively. Together, these tools can be used by data engineers to acquire the possibilistic keys that are semantically meaningful for a given application domain. It was further illustrated how possibilistic keys can be used to clean dirty data and enhance query processing. The results show that possibilistic keys can benefit applications with uncertain data, very much in the same way that keys benefit applications with certain data. It is future work to implement our algorithms in the form of a design tool, to apply possibility theory to other classes of popular database concepts, and to find efficient solutions to the possibilistic data cleaning problem we introduced.

Acknowledgement. This research is supported by the Marsden fund council from Government funding, administered by the Royal Society of New Zealand.

References

1. Armstrong, W.W.: Dependency structures of data base relationships. In: IFIP Congress, pp. 580–583 (1974)
2. Beeri, C., Dowd, M., Fagin, R., Statman, R.: On the structure of Armstrong relations for functional dependencies. J. ACM 31(1), 30–46 (1984)

3. Benferhat, S., Dubois, D., Prade, H.: Towards a possibilistic logic handling of preferences. Appl. Intell. 14(3), 303–317 (2001)

4. Beskales, G., Ilyas, I.F., Golab, L.: Sampling the repairs of functional dependency violations under hard constraints. PVLDB 3(1) (2010)

5. Bistarelli, S., Codognet, P., Rossi, F.: Abstracting soft constraints: Framework, properties, examples. Artif. Intell. 139(2), 175–211 (2002)

6. Bosc, P., Dubois, D., Prade, H.: Fuzzy functional dependencies – an overview and a critical discussion. In: Proc. of the 3rd IEEE Inter. Conf. on Fuzzy Systems (FUZZ-IEEE 1994), Orlando, FL, June 26-29, pp. 325–330 (1994)

7. Bosc, P., Pivert, O.: On the impact of regular functional dependencies when moving to a possibilistic database framework. Fuzzy Sets and Systems 140(1), 207–227 (2003)

8. Calvanese, D., De Giacomo, G., Lenzerini, M.: Keys for free in description logics. In: Baader, F., Sattler, U. (eds.) Proceedings of the 2000 International Workshop on Description Logics (DL 2000), Aachen, Germany, August 17-19. CEUR Workshop Proceedings, vol. 33, pp. 79–88. CEUR-WS.org (2000)

9. Chu, X., Ilyas, I.F., Papotti, P.: Holistic data cleaning: Putting violations into context. In: Jensen, C.S., Jermaine, C.M., Zhou, X. (eds.) 29th IEEE International Conference on Data Engineering, ICDE 2013, Brisbane, Australia, April 8-12, pp. 458–469. IEEE Computer Society (2013)

10. Codd, E.F.: A relational model of data for large shared data banks. Commun. ACM 13(6), 377–387 (1970)

11. Demetrovics, J., Katona, G.O.H.: Extremal combinatorial problems of database models. In: Biskup, J., Demetrovics, J., Paredaens, J., Thalheim, B. (eds.) MFDBS 1987. LNCS, vol. 305, pp. 99–127. Springer, Heidelberg (1988)

12. Diederich, J., Milton, J.: New methods and fast algorithms for database normalization. ACM Trans. Database Syst. 13(3), 339–365 (1988)

13. Dubois, D., Lang, J., Prade, H.: Automated reasoning using possibilistic logic: Semantics, belief revision, and variable certainty weights. IEEE Trans. Knowl. Data Eng. 6(1), 64–71 (1994)

14. Dubois, D., Prade, H.: Epistemic entrenchment and possibilistic logic. Artif. Intell. 50(2), 223–239 (1991)

15. Dubois, D., Prade, H.: Fuzzy set and possibility theory-based methods in artificial intelligence. Artif. Intell. 148(1-2), 1–9 (2003)

16. Dubois, D., Prade, H., Schockaert, S.: Stable models in generalized possibilistic logic. In: Brewka, G., Eiter, T., McIlraith, S.A. (eds.) Principles of Knowledge Representation and Reasoning: Proceedings of the Thirteenth International Conference, KR 2012, Rome, Italy, June 10-14. AAAI Press (2012)

17. Eiter, T., Gottlob, G.: Identifying the minimal transversals of a hypergraph and related problems. SIAM J. Comput. 24(6), 1278–1304 (1995)

18. Fagin, R.: Horn clauses and database dependencies. J. ACM 29(4), 952–985 (1982)

19. Gärdenfors, P., Makinson, D.: Nonmonotonic inference based on expectations. Artif. Intell. 65(2), 197–245 (1994)

20. Geiger, D., Paz, A., Pearl, J.: Axioms and algorithms for inferences involving probabilistic independence. Inf. Comput. 91(1), 128–141 (1991)

21. Grabisch, M., Prade, H.: The correlation problem in sensor fusion in a possibilistic framework. Int. J. Intell. Syst. 16(11), 1273–1283 (2001)

22. Grove, A.: Two modellings for theory change. Journal of Philosophical Logic 17(2), 157–170 (1988)

23. Hartmann, S., Kirchberg, M., Link, S.: Design by example for SQL table definitions with functional dependencies. VLDB J 21(1), 121–144 (2012)

24. Hartmann, S., Leck, U., Link, S.: On Codd families of keys over incomplete relations. Comput. J. 54(7), 1166–1180 (2011)
25. Hartmann, S., Link, S.: Efficient reasoning about a robust XML key fragment. ACM Trans. Database Syst. 34(2) (2009)
26. Hartmann, S., Link, S.: Numerical constraints on XML data. Inf. Comput. 208(5), 521–544 (2010)
27. Heise, A., Quiane-Ruiz, J.-A., Abedjan, Z., Jentzsch, A., Naumann, F.: Scalable discovery of unique column combinations. PVLDB 7(4), 301–312 (2013)
28. Jha, A.K., Rastogi, V., Suciu, D.: Query evaluation with soft-key constraints. In: Lenzerini, M., Lembo, D. (eds.) Proceedings of the Twenty-Seventh ACM SIGMOD-SIGACT-SIGART Symposium on Principles of Database Systems, PODS 2008, Vancouver, BC, Canada, June 9-11, pp. 119–128. ACM (2008)
29. Lutz, C., Areces, C., Horrocks, I., Sattler, U.: Keys, nominals, and concrete domains. J. Artif. Intell. Res. (JAIR) 23, 667–726 (2005)
30. Mannila, H., Räihä, K.J.: Design by example: An application of Armstrong relations. J. Comput. Syst. Sci. 33(2), 126–141 (1986)
31. Mannila, H., Räihä, K.J.: Algorithms for inferring functional dependencies from relations. Data Knowl. Eng. 12(1), 83–99 (1994)
32. Niepert, M., Gyssens, M., Sayrafi, B., Gucht, D.V.: On the conditional independence implication problem: A lattice-theoretic approach. Artif. Intell. 202, 29–51 (2013)
33. Qi, G., Wang, K.: Conflict-based belief revision operators in possibilistic logic. In: Hoffmann, J., Selman, B. (eds.) Proceedings of the Twenty-Sixth AAAI Conference on Artificial Intelligence, Toronto, Ontario, Canada, July 22-26. AAAI Press (2012)
34. Sabbadin, R., Fargier, H., Lang, J.: Towards qualitative approaches to multi-stage decision making. Int. J. Approx. Reasoning 19(3-4), 441–471 (1998)
35. Sarma, A.D., Ullman, J.D., Widom, J.: Schema design for uncertain databases. In: Arenas, M., Bertossi, L.E. (eds.) Proceedings of the 3rd Alberto Mendelzon International Workshop on Foundations of Data Management, Arequipa, Peru, May 12-15. CEUR Workshop Proceedings, vol. 450. CEUR-WS.org (2009)
36. Shen, Q., Leitch, R.: Fuzzy qualitative simulation. IEEE Transactions on Systems, Man, and Cybernetics 23(4), 1038–1061 (1993)
37. Suciu, D., Olteanu, D., Ré, C., Koch, C.: Probabilistic Databases. Synthesis Lectures on Data Management. Morgan & Claypool Publishers (2011)
38. Thalheim, B.: On semantic issues connected with keys in relational databases permitting null values. Elektronische Informationsverarbeitung und Kybernetik 25(1/2), 11–20 (1989)
39. Toman, D., Weddell, G.E.: On keys and functional dependencies as first-class citizens in description logics. J. Autom. Reasoning 40(2-3), 117–132 (2008)
40. Zadeh, L.A.: Approximate reasoning based on fuzzy logic. In: Buchanan, B.G. (ed.) Proceedings of the Sixth International Joint Conference on Artificial Intelligence, IJCAI 1979, Tokyo, Japan, August 20-23, vol. 2, pp. 1004–1010. William Kaufmann (1979)

Possibilistic Boolean Games: Strategic Reasoning under Incomplete Information

Sofie De Clercq[1], Steven Schockaert[2], Martine De Cock[1,3], and Ann Nowé[4]

[1] Dept. of Applied Math., CS & Stats, Ghent University, Ghent, Belgium
{SofieR.DeClercq,Martine.DeCock}@ugent.be

[2] School of Computer Science & Informatics, Cardiff University, Cardiff, UK
S.Schockaert@cs.cardiff.ac.uk

[3] Center for Data Science, University of Washington Tacoma, USA
MDeCock@uw.edu

[4] Computational Modeling Lab, Vrije Universiteit Brussel, Brussels, Belgium
ANowe@vub.ac.be

Abstract. Boolean games offer a compact alternative to normal-form games, by encoding the goal of each agent as a propositional formula. In this paper, we show how this framework can be naturally extended to model situations in which agents are uncertain about other agents' goals. We first use uncertainty measures from possibility theory to semantically define (solution concepts to) Boolean games with incomplete information. Then we present a syntactic characterization of these semantics, which can readily be implemented, and we characterize the computational complexity.

1 Introduction

Boolean games (BGs) are games in which the agents' goals are formalized using propositional formulas [12]. The atomic propositional variables occurring in these goals are called the action variables, since each of them is controlled by one agent. Originally, BGs were introduced with binary preferences, i.e. the goal of an agent is a single propositional formula and the utility of an agent is 1 if its goal is satisfied and 0 otherwise [12]. Various suggestions have been made in the literature to overcome this limitation of expressiveness. One approach is the introduction of costs on the action variables [10]. Another suggestion is a generalization of the BG framework towards compact preference relations on the set of outcomes, e.g. by using a prioritized goal base per agent [4]. Recently, the limitation has also been overcome by replacing the classical two-valued logic for representing the goals by many-valued Łukasiewicz logic [13]. This extension allows many degrees to which a goal can be satisfied, as opposed to the sole distinction between satisfaction or non-satisfaction. In this paper, we consider a variant of BGs with prioritized goal bases. An agent is most eager to achieve the goal with the highest priority. If this goal cannot be achieved, the agent will settle with the satisfaction of the goal with the second-highest priority, etc.

Example 1. Bob and Alice are going out. Alice – agent 1 – controls action variable a, and Bob – agent 2 – controls b. Setting their action variable to true corresponds to attending a sports game; setting it to false corresponds to going to the theatre. Bob and

E. Fermé and J. Leite (Eds.): JELIA 2014, LNAI 8761, pp. 196–209, 2014.
© Springer International Publishing Switzerland 2014

Alice's first priority is to go out together. If they do not go out together, Bob prefers a sports game, whereas Alice prefers the theatre. This can be represented with a preference ordering over the outcomes per agent or with a pay-off matrix:

$(a, b) =_1 (\neg a, \neg b) >_1 (\neg a, b) >_1 (a, \neg b)$

$(a, b) =_2 (\neg a, \neg b) >_2 (\neg a, b) >_2 (a, \neg b)$

Bob \ Alice	a	$\neg a$
b	$(2, 2)$	$(1, 1)$
$\neg b$	$(0, 0)$	$(2, 2)$

There are 2 pure Nash equilibria – outcomes such that no one has an incentive to deviate: attending a sports game together and going to the theatre together.

Our aim in this paper is to propose an extension to the BG framework in which agents can be uncertain about other agents' goals. An important concern is that the resulting framework should still enable a compact and intuitive representation of games, as these are the main strengths of BGs. We therefore introduce a compact syntactic framework, which we prove to correspond to an intuitive semantic framework. Using our extended BG framework, we aim to determine rational behaviour for agents which are uncertain about the other agents' goals.

Although uncertainty in game theory has been studied extensively (see e.g. [14]), the literature on BGs with incomplete information is currently limited. Uncertainty can be either epistemic or stochastic of nature. The former is caused by incomplete knowledge about the game, whereas the latter is e.g. caused by actions which do not always have the same effect on the outcome. This paper concerns epistemic uncertainty. To the best of our knowledge, the existing work on BGs with uncertainty also falls in the category of epistemic uncertainty. However, in contrast to our work, the uncertainty is not related to the goals. Grant et al. [11] incorporate uncertainty in the BG framework by introducing a set of environment variables outside the control of any agent. Each agent has some (possibly incorrect) belief about the value of the environment variables. The focus of [11] is to manipulate the BGs by making announcements about the true value of some environment variables, in order to create a stable solution if there were none without the announcements. Ågotnes et al. [2] address uncertainty in BGs by extending the framework of BGs with a set of observable action variables for every agent, i.e. every agent can only observe the values assigned to a particular subset of action variables. As a result, agents are not able to distinguish between some strategy profiles, if these profiles only differ in action variables that are not observable to that agent. Three notions of verifiable equilibria are investigated, capturing respectively strategy profiles for which all agents know that they *might be* pure Nash equilibria (PNEs), strategy profiles for which all agents know that they *are* PNEs and strategy profiles for which it is common knowledge that they are PNEs, i.e. all agents know that they are PNEs and all agents know that all agents know that they are PNEs etc. The same authors have extended this framework to epistemic BGs [1], in which the logical language for describing goals is broadened to a multi-agent epistemic modal logic. Note, however, that agents are still completely aware of each others' goals in this framework.

In this paper, we study BGs with incomplete information, considering agents which have their own beliefs about the goals of other agents. Although probability theory is often used to model uncertainty in game theory [14], a possibilistic logic approach provides a simple and elegant mechanism for modeling partial ignorance, which is closely related to the notion of epistemic entrenchment [8]. Being based on ranking formulas (at the syntactic level) or possible worlds (at the semantic level), possibilistic logic has the advantage of staying close to classical logic. As a result, we will be able to introduce methods for solving possibilistic BGs that are entirely similar to methods for solving standard BGs.

Example 2. Consider again the scenario of Example 1, but assume that Bob and Alice are unaware of each other's goals. If Bob's knowledge of Alice's goal is correct, but Alice thinks that Bob does not want to join her to the theatre, then, based on their beliefs, attending a sports game together is a 'better' solution than going to the theatre together. Indeed, Alice believes that Bob will not agree to go to the theatre together, but they both believe that the other will agree to attend a sports game together.

The paper is structured as follows. First, we briefly recall possibility theory and BGs. In Section 3, we construct the framework of BGs with uncertainty, both from an intuitive semantic and a compact syntactic point of view. Moreover, we show that the proposed semantic and syntactic definitions are equivalent, and we characterise the complexity of the associated decision problems.

2   Preliminaries

In this section, we recall possibilistic logic and Boolean games. As usual, the logical language L_Φ associated with a finite set of atomic propositional variables (atoms) Φ contains the following formulas:

- every propositional variable of Φ,
- the logical constants $\bot$ and $\top$, and
- the formulas $\neg\varphi$, $\varphi \to \psi$, $\varphi \leftrightarrow \psi$, $\varphi \wedge \psi$ and $\varphi \vee \psi$ for every $\varphi, \psi \in L_\Phi$.

An interpretation of Φ is defined as a subset ω of Φ, with the convention that all atoms in ω are interpreted as true ($\top$) and all atoms in $\Phi \setminus \omega$ are interpreted as false ($\bot$). An interpretation can be extended to L_Φ in the usual way. If a formula $\varphi \in L_\Phi$ is true in an interpretation ω, we denote this as $\omega \models \varphi$.

2.1   Possibilistic Logic

Possibilistic logic (see e.g. [9] for a more comprehensive overview) is a popular tool to encode and reason about uncertain information in an intuitive and compact way.

Definition 1 (Possibility Distribution). *Let Ω be a finite universe. A possibility distribution on Ω is a mapping $\pi : \Omega \to [0,1]$.*

In possibilistic logic, given a logical language L_Φ, the set of interpretations of Φ is used as the universe of a possibility distribution. If $\pi(\omega) = 1$, ω is considered to be completely possible, whereas $\pi(\omega) = 0$ corresponds to ω being completely impossible. Available information encodes which worlds cannot be excluded based on available knowledge. Therefore, smaller possibility degrees are more specific, as they rule out more possible worlds. A possibility distribution such that $\pi(\omega) = 1$ for every $\omega \in \Omega$

thus corresponds to a state of complete ignorance. Note that a possibility distribution is not the same as a probability distribution, since we do not require that $\sum_{\omega \in \Omega} \pi(\omega) = 1$. An ordering $\leq$ on all possibility distributions on Ω can be defined as $\pi_1 \leq \pi_2$ iff it holds that $\pi_1(\omega) \leq \pi_2(\omega)$, $\forall \omega \in \Omega$, assuming the natural ordering on $[0, 1]$. We say that π_1 is at least as specific as π_2 when $\pi_1 \leq \pi_2$. The maximal elements w.r.t. $\leq$ are called the least specific possibility distributions. A possibility and necessity measure are induced by a possibility distribution in the following way.

Definition 2 (Possibility and Necessity Measure). *Given a possibility distribution π in a universe Ω, the possibility $\Pi(A)$ and necessity $N(A)$ that an event $A \subseteq \Omega$ occurs is defined as:*

$$\Pi(A) = \sup_{\omega \in A} \pi(\omega); \qquad N(A) = \inf_{\omega \notin A} (1 - \pi(\omega))$$

In possibilistic logic, we abbreviate $N(\{\omega \in \Omega \mid \omega \models \varphi\})$ as $N(\varphi)$ for a formula φ.

Definition 3 (Possibilistic Knowledge Base). *Let Φ be a set of atoms. A finite set $\{(\varphi_1, \alpha_1), \ldots, (\varphi_m, \alpha_m)\}$ of pairs of the form (φ_i, α_i), with $\varphi_i \in L_\Phi$ and $\alpha_i \in]0, 1]$, is a possibilistic knowledge base (KB). It encodes a possibility distribution, namely the least specific possibility distribution satisfying the constraints $N(\varphi_i) \geq \alpha_i$.*

The possibility distribution $\pi_\mathcal{K}$ encoded by a KB $\mathcal{K}$ is well-defined because there is a unique least specific possibility distribution which satisfies the constraints of $\mathcal{K}$ [7].

The necessity measure N satisfies the property $N(p \wedge q) = \min(N(p), N(q))$. The following inference rules are associated with possibilistic logic:

- $(\neg p \vee q, \alpha); (p \vee r, \beta) \vdash (q \vee r, \min(\alpha, \beta))$ (resolution rule),
- if p entails q classically, then $(p, \alpha) \vdash (q, \alpha)$ (formula weakening),
- for $\beta \leq \alpha$, $(p, \alpha) \vdash (p, \beta)$ (weight weakening),
- $(p, \alpha); (p, \beta) \vdash (p, \max(\alpha, \beta))$ (weight fusion).

The axioms consist of all propositional axioms with weight 1. These inference rules and axioms are sound and complete in the following sense [7]: it holds that $\mathcal{K} \vdash (\varphi, \alpha)$ iff $N(\varphi) \geq \alpha$ for the necessity measure N induced by $\pi_\mathcal{K}$. Another useful property is $\mathcal{K} \vdash (\varphi, \alpha)$ iff $\mathcal{K}_\alpha \vdash \varphi$ (in the classical sense) [9], with $\mathcal{K}_\alpha = \{\varphi \mid (\varphi, \beta) \in \mathcal{K}, \beta \geq \alpha\}$ the α-cut of $\mathcal{K}$.

2.2 Boolean Games

We use a generalization of the notion of Boolean games [5] by allowing agents to have non-dichotomous utilities. This approach is a variant of the BGs with prioritized goal bases considered in [4]. Our notation is based on [2].

Definition 4 (Boolean Game [4]). *A Boolean game (BG) is a tuple $G = (\Phi_1, \ldots, \Phi_n, \Gamma_1, \ldots, \Gamma_n)$. The set of agents $\{1, \ldots, n\}$ is denoted as N. For every $i \in N$, Φ_i is a finite set of propositional variables, disjoint with $\Phi_j, \forall j \neq i$. We denote $\Phi = \bigcup_{i \in N} \Phi_i$. For every $i \in N$, $\Gamma_i = \{\gamma_i^1; \ldots; \gamma_i^p\}$ is i's prioritized goal base. The formula $\gamma_i^j \in L_\Phi$ is agent i's goal of priority j. We assume that the number of priority levels p is fixed for all agents.*

The set Φ contains all action variables. Agent i can set the variables under its control, i.e. those in Φ_i, to true or false. Note that every variable is controlled by exactly one agent. By convention, priority numbers are ordered from high priority (level 1) to low priority (level p). Definition 4 corresponds to a particular case of generalized BGs [4], in which the preference relation is total for every agent. The results presented in this paper can easily be generalized to accommodate for partially ordered preference relations. However, as modeling preferences is not the focus of this paper, we prefer the simpler setting of Definition 4, for clarity.

Definition 5 (Strategy Profile [2]). *For each agent $i \in N$, an interpretation of Φ_i is called a strategy of i. An n-tuple $\boldsymbol{\nu} = (\nu_1, \ldots, \nu_n)$, with ν_i a strategy of agent i, is called a strategy profile or outcome of G.*

Because $\{\Phi_1, \ldots, \Phi_n\}$ is a partition of Φ and $\nu_i \subseteq \Phi_i, \forall i \in N$, we also (ab)use the set notation $\bigcup_{i \in N} \nu_i \subseteq \Phi$ for a strategy profile $\boldsymbol{\nu} = (\nu_1, \ldots, \nu_n)$. We denote the set of all strategy profiles as $\mathcal{V}$. With $\boldsymbol{\nu}_{-i}$ we denote the projection of the strategy profile $\boldsymbol{\nu} = (\nu_1, \ldots, \nu_n)$ on $\Phi_{-i} = \Phi \setminus \Phi_i$, i.e. $\boldsymbol{\nu}_{-i} = (\nu_1, \ldots, \nu_{i-1}, \nu_{i+1}, \ldots, \nu_n)$. If ν_i' is a strategy of agent i, then $(\boldsymbol{\nu}_{-i}, \nu_i')$ is a shorthand for $(\nu_1, \ldots, \nu_{i-1}, \nu_i', \nu_{i+1}, \ldots, \nu_n)$.

The utility for every agent i follows naturally from the satisfaction of its goals.

Definition 6 (Utility Function). *For each $i \in N$ and $\boldsymbol{\nu} \in \mathcal{V}$, the utility for $\boldsymbol{\nu}$ is defined as $u_i(\boldsymbol{\nu}) = p + 1 - \min\{k \mid 1 \leq k \leq p, \boldsymbol{\nu} \models \gamma_i^k\}$, with $\min \emptyset = p + 1$ by convention.*

Note that the specific utility values do not matter since the solution concepts that we will discuss in this paper are qualitative; only the preference ordering $\geq_i$ on $\mathcal{V}$ induced by the utility function u_i is relevant: $\boldsymbol{\nu} \geq_i \boldsymbol{\nu}'$ iff $u_i(\boldsymbol{\nu}) \geq u_i(\boldsymbol{\nu}'), \forall \boldsymbol{\nu}, \boldsymbol{\nu}' \in \mathcal{V}$. A common qualitative solution concept in game theory is the notion of pure Nash equilibrium.

Definition 7 (Pure Nash Equilibrium). *A strategy profile $\boldsymbol{\nu} = (\nu_1, \ldots, \nu_n)$ for a BG G is a pure Nash equilibrium (PNE) iff for every agent $i \in N$, ν_i is a best response (BR) to $\boldsymbol{\nu}_{-i}$, i.e. $u_i(\boldsymbol{\nu}) \geq u_i(\boldsymbol{\nu}_{-i}, \nu_i'), \forall \nu_i' \subseteq \Phi_i$.*

Example 1 (continued). Recall the scenario of Example 1. Alice and Bob's goal bases can be written as $\Gamma_1 = \{a \leftrightarrow b; \neg a\}$ and $\Gamma_2 = \{a \leftrightarrow b; b\}$. This encoding naturally captures the fact that e.g. Bob's first priority is to go out with Alice and his second priority is to attend a sports game. Both agents have utility 2 in the PNEs $\{a, b\}$ and $\emptyset$.

3 Boolean Games with Incomplete Information

3.1 Semantic Approach

Consider a set of agents N, controlling the action variables in $\Phi_1, \ldots, \Phi_n$, who are uncertain about each other's goals. Let us denote the set of possible goal bases with p levels as $\mathcal{G} = \{\{\gamma^1; \ldots; \gamma^p\} \mid \forall k \in \{1, \ldots, p\} : \gamma^k \in L_\Phi \text{ in conjunctive normal form and } (k \neq p \Rightarrow \gamma^k \models \gamma^{k+1})\}$. Note that any formula can be transformed into an equivalent formula in conjunctive normal form (CNF) and that any goal base $\{\gamma^1; \ldots; \gamma^p\}$ violating the condition $\gamma^k \models \gamma^{k+1}, \forall k \neq p$ can be transformed into a semantically equivalent goal base which does satisfy the property, namely $\{\gamma^1; \gamma^1 \vee \gamma^2; \ldots; \bigvee_{m=1}^{p} \gamma^m\}$.

Moreover, all agents have the same set of possible goal bases. Let us define $\mathcal{BG}(\Phi_1, \ldots, \Phi_n) = \{(\Phi_1, \ldots, \Phi_n, \Gamma_1, \ldots, \Gamma_n) \mid \Gamma_1, \ldots, \Gamma_n \in \mathcal{G}\}$ as the set of all possible BGs, given the considered partition of action variables. When the partition $\Phi_1, \ldots, \Phi_n$ is clear from the context, we abbreviate $\mathcal{BG}(\Phi_1, \ldots, \Phi_n)$ as $\mathcal{BG}$. The knowledge of an agent i about the goals of the other agents can be captured by a possibility distribution π_i over $\mathcal{BG}$, encoding i's beliefs about what is the actual game being played.

Example 2. Recall the scenario of Example 1. Suppose Bob has perfect knowledge of Alice's preferences, then $\pi_2 : \mathcal{BG} \to \{0,1\}$ maps every BG to 0, except the BGs with the preference orderings of Example 1, i.e. the actual game being played is the only one considered possible by Bob. Suppose Alice is certain that Bob wants to attend a sports game together, or attend the game on his own if attending it together is not possible. Then $\pi_1 : \mathcal{BG} \to \{0,1\}$ maps all BGs to 0, except those with the preference orderings

$$\{a,b\} =_1 \emptyset >_1 \{b\} >_1 \{a\}$$
$$\{a,b\} >_2 \{b\} >_2 \emptyset =_2 \{a\}$$

Bob \ Alice	a	$\neg a$
b	$(2,2)$	$(1,1)$
$\neg b$	$(0,0)$	$(0,2)$

Our first aim is to determine to which degree a specific strategy profile ν is necessarily/possibly a PNE according to agent i. Intuitively, it is possible to degree λ that a strategy profile ν is a PNE according to i iff there exists a BG $G \in \mathcal{BG}$ such that ν is a PNE in G and such that i considers it possible to degree λ that G is the real game being played, i.e.

$$\Pi_i(\{G \in \mathcal{BG} \mid \nu \text{ is a PNE in } G\}) = \lambda$$

Similarly, it is certain to degree λ that a strategy profile ν is a PNE according to i iff for every $G \in \mathcal{BG}$ such that ν is no PNE, it holds that i considers it possible to degree at most $1 - \lambda$ that G is the real game being played, i.e.

$$N_i(\{G \in \mathcal{BG} \mid \nu \text{ is a PNE in } G\}) = \lambda$$

Using the previously introduced degrees, we can define measures which offer a way to distinguish between multiple equilibria, motivated by Schellings' notion of focal points [15]. An equilibrium is a focal point if, for some reason other than its utility, it stands out from the other equilibria. In our case, the reason can be that agents have a higher certainty that the outcome is actually a PNE, using the degrees to which a strategy profile is necessarily a PNE. Note that there might not exist an outcome which every agent believes is necessarily a PNE, even when the (unknown) game being played has one or more PNEs. In such cases, the degree to which various strategy profiles are possibly a PNE could be used to guide decisions.

Definition 8. *Given the possibility measures Π_i for every i, the degree to which all agents find it possible that the strategy profile ν is a PNE is*

$$poss(\nu) = \min_{i \in N} \Pi_i(\{G \in \mathcal{BG} \mid \nu \text{ is a PNE in } G\})$$

Similarly, given the necessity measures N_i for every i, the degree to which all agents find it necessary that ν is a PNE is defined as

$$nec(\nu) = \min_{i \in N} N_i(\{G \in \mathcal{BG} \mid \nu \text{ is a PNE in } G\})$$

3.2   Syntactic Approach

While the concepts from Section 3.1 define useful notions w.r.t. the possibility or necessity that agents play best responses or that strategy profiles are PNEs, they cannot be applied in practice, since the number of BGs in $\mathcal{BG}$ is exponential. In this section, we present a syntactic counterpart which will allow for a more compact representation of the agents knowledge about the game being played.

Definition 9 (Goal-Knowledge Base). *Agent i's knowledge about the goals of agent j is encoded in a goal knowledge base $\mathcal{K}_i^j$ of i w.r.t. j containing formulas of the form $(\varphi \to g_j^k, \lambda)$, $(\varphi \leftarrow g_j^k, \lambda)$ or $(\varphi \leftrightarrow g_j^k, \lambda)$, where $1 \le k \le p$, $\varphi \in L_\Phi$, $\lambda \in \,]0, 1]$ and g_j^k a new atom, encoding j's goal of priority k. A goal-KB $\mathcal{K}_i^j$ is goal-consistent, i.e. for every $\varphi, \psi \in L_\Phi$ such that $(\varphi \to g_j^k, \lambda) \in \mathcal{K}_i^j$ and $(\psi \leftarrow g_j^k, \lambda) \in \mathcal{K}_i^j$, it holds that $\varphi \models \psi$ classically. Moreover, $\mathcal{K}_i^j$ contains $\{(g_j^k \to g_j^{k+1}, 1) \,|\, 1 \le k \le p-1\}$.*

A goal-KB $\mathcal{K}_i^j$ captures the knowledge of agent i about the goal base of agent j. In our examples, the formulas $\{(g_j^k \to g_j^{k+1}, 1) \,|\, 1 \le k \le p-1\}$, which belong to $\mathcal{K}_i^j$ by definition, are not explicitly mentioned. These formulas express that, if agent j's utility is at least $p + 1 - k$, it is at least $p - k$. Furthermore, the information that we like to express in $\mathcal{K}_i^j$ exists of necessary and/or sufficient conditions for the utility of agent j. For instance, agent i might believe that with certainty λ, φ is a sufficient condition for satisfying the goal with priority k, i.e. achieving a utility of at least $p + 1 - k$. This is encoded as $(\varphi \to g_j^k, \lambda) \in \mathcal{K}_i^j$. Similarly, agent i might believe with certainty λ that φ is a necessary condition for achieving the goal with priority k, i.e. $(\varphi \leftarrow g_j^k, \lambda) \in \mathcal{K}_i^j$. These types can be combined as $(\varphi \leftrightarrow g_j^k, \lambda) \in \mathcal{K}_i^j$. Note how adding the atoms g_j^k to the language allows us to explicitly encode what an agent knows about the goal of another agent. This is inspired by the approach from [16] for merging conflicting sources, where similarly additional atoms are introduced to encode knowledge about the unknown meaning of vague properties, in the form of necessary and sufficient conditions.

Example 4. Recall the scenario of Example 1. Suppose Bob has a good idea of what Alice's goal base looks like: $\mathcal{K}_2^1 = \{((a \leftrightarrow b) \leftrightarrow g_1^1, 0.9), (((a \leftrightarrow b) \vee \neg a) \leftrightarrow g_1^2, 0.6)\}$. He is very certain that Alice's first priority is to go out together and rather certain that she prefers the theatre in case they do not go out together. Although Alice is very certain that Bob will be pleased if they attend a sports game together, she is only a little certain whether Bob would be just as pleased if they attend the cultural event together. She knows Bob prefers to go a sports game as a second priority. Her knowledge of Bob's goal base can be captured by $\mathcal{K}_1^2 = \{((a \wedge b) \to g_2^1, 0.8), ((\neg a \wedge \neg b) \to g_2^1, 0.3), (b \to g_2^2, 1)\}$.

It is natural to assume that $\mathcal{K}_i^i = \{(g_i^k \leftrightarrow \bigvee_{m=1}^k \gamma_i^m, 1) \,|\, k \in \{1, \ldots, p\}\}$, i.e. every agent knows its own goal base and the corresponding utility. However, this assumption is not necessary for the results in this paper. By requiring goal-consistency, we ensure that the knowledge base $\mathcal{K}_i^j$ only encodes beliefs about the goal of agent j. Without this assumption, it could be possible to derive from $\mathcal{K}_i^j$ formulas of the form $\varphi \to \psi$, encoding dependencies between the action variables of other agents. Such dependencies could be useful for modeling suspected collusion, which we will not consider in this paper. However, we do not demand that the beliefs of an agent are correct, i.e. we do not assume that each agent considers the actual game possible.

Definition 10 (BG with Incomplete Information). *A Boolean game with incomplete information (BGI) is a tuple* $G = (\Phi_1, \ldots, \Phi_n, \Gamma_1, \ldots, \Gamma_n, \mathcal{K}_1, \ldots, \mathcal{K}_n)$ *with* $\Phi_1, \ldots,$ $\Phi_n, \Gamma_1, \ldots, \Gamma_n$ *as before and* $\mathcal{K}_i = \{\mathcal{K}_i^1, \ldots, \mathcal{K}_i^n\}$, *where* $\mathcal{K}_i^j$ *is a goal-KB of i w.r.t. j.*

Let us now consider how to compute the necessity and possibility that agent j plays a best response (BR) in the strategy profile ν according to agent i. First note that each $\nu \in \mathcal{V}$ corresponds unambiguously to a formula φ_ν in L_Φ in the following way:

$$\varphi_\nu = \bigwedge \{p \mid p \in \nu\} \wedge \bigwedge \{\neg p \mid p \in \Phi \setminus \nu\}$$

We also introduce the following notations:

$$\varphi_{\nu_{-j}} = \bigwedge \{p \mid p \in \nu \cap (\Phi \setminus \Phi_j)\} \wedge \bigwedge \{\neg p \mid p \in (\Phi \setminus \Phi_j) \setminus \nu\}$$

$$\varphi_{\nu_j} = \bigwedge \{p \mid p \in \nu_j \cap \Phi_j\} \wedge \bigwedge \{\neg p \mid p \in \Phi_j \setminus \nu_j\}$$

Note that $\varphi_{\nu_{-j}}$ is equivalent with $\bigvee \{\varphi_{(\nu_{-j}, \nu_j')} \mid \nu_j' \subseteq \Phi_j\}$.

Agent j plays a BR in the strategy profile ν iff for every alternative strategy $\nu_j' \subseteq \Phi_j$ it holds that $u_j(\nu) \geq u_j(\nu_{-j}, \nu_j')$. Essentially this boils down to the fact that, for some $k \in \{0, \ldots, p\}$, $u_j(\nu) \geq k$ and $\forall \nu_j' \subseteq \Phi_j : u_j(\nu_{-j}, \nu_j') \leq k$. Note that for $k = 0$, the first condition is always fulfilled. Similarly, for $k = p$, the second condition becomes trivial. Similarly, agent j plays no BR in ν iff there exists a $\nu_j' \subseteq \Phi_j$ such that $u_j(\nu) < u_j(\nu_{-j}, \nu_j')$. This means that, for all $k \in \{0, \ldots, p\}$, $u_j(\nu) < k$ or $\exists \nu_j' \subseteq \Phi_j : u_j(\nu_{-j}, \nu_j') > k$. The possibility of agent j playing a BR is dual to the necessity of agent j playing no BR. These insights motivate the following definition.

Definition 11. *Let $i, j \in N$ be two agents in a BGI G and let ν be a strategy profile of G. We denote $g_j^{p+1} = \top$ and $g_j^0 = \bot$ for every j. We say that j plays a BR in ν with necessity λ according to i, written $BR_i^n(j, \nu) = \lambda$, iff λ is the greatest value in $[0, 1]$ for which there exists some $k \in \{0, \ldots, p\}$ such that the following two conditions are satisfied:*

1. $\mathcal{K}_i^j \vdash (\varphi_\nu \to g_j^{k+1}, \lambda)$
2. $\mathcal{K}_i^j \vdash ((\varphi_{\nu_{-j}} \wedge \neg \varphi_{\nu_j}) \to \neg g_j^k, \lambda)$

Let λ^* be the smallest value greater than $1 - \lambda$ which occurs in $\mathcal{K}_i^j$. Agent i believes it is possible to degree λ that agent j plays a BR in ν, written $BR_i^p(j, \nu) = \lambda$, iff λ is the greatest value in $]0, 1]$ for which there exists some $k \in \{0, \ldots, p\}$ such that the following two conditions are satisfied:

1. $\mathcal{K}_i^j \nvdash (\varphi_\nu \to \neg g_j^{k+1}, \lambda^*)$
2. $\forall \nu_j' \subseteq \Phi_j : \mathcal{K}_i^j \nvdash (\varphi_{(\nu_{-j}, \nu_j')} \to g_j^k, \lambda^*)$

If no such λ exists, then $BR_i^p(j, \nu) = 0$.

Importantly, the syntax in Definition 11 allows to express the certainty or possibililty that an agent plays a BR, from the point of view of another agent. This forms an important base from which to define interesting solution concepts or measures in BGIs.

In this paper, we introduce the following measures that respectively reflect to what degree all agents believe it is necessary and possible that ν is a PNE.

Definition 12. *Let G be a BGI. For every strategy profile ν, we define the measures PNE^n and PNE^p as:*

$$PNE^n(\nu) = \min_{i \in N} \min_{j \in N} BR_i^n(j, \nu), \quad PNE^p(\nu) = \min_{i \in N} \min_{j \in N} BR_i^p(j, \nu)$$

If we assume that all agents know their own goal, then $BR_i^n(i, \nu) = BR_i^p(i, \nu) = 0$ if ν is not a PNE. Consequently, if ν is not a PNE, then we have $PNE^n(\nu) = PNE^p(\nu) = 0$. Note that the measures from Definition 12 induce a total ordering on $\mathcal{V}$, so there always exists a $\nu \in \mathcal{V}$ such that PNE^n or PNE^p is maximal.

Example 4 (continued). Let G be the BGI with the aforementioned goal-KBs and assume that Bob and Alice know their own goals. It can be computed that

	$\emptyset$	$\{a\}$	$\{b\}$	$\{a,b\}$
$\min_{j \in N} BR_1^n(j,.)$	0.3	0	0	0.8
$\min_{j \in N} BR_2^n(j,.)$	0.9	0	0	0.9
$PNE^n(.)$	0.3	0	0	0.8

The strategy profile $\{a, b\}$ has the highest value for PNE^n. Note that if Bob had the 'dual' beliefs of Alice, i.e. $\mathcal{K}_2^1 = \{((\neg a \wedge \neg b) \rightarrow g_1^1, 0.8), ((a \wedge b) \rightarrow g_1^1, 0.3), (\neg a \rightarrow g_1^2, 1)\}$, then $\emptyset$ and $\{a, b\}$ both had value 0.3 for PNE^n.

In [6], we showed that many solution concepts for BGs can be found by using a reduction to answer set programming. The concepts in this section, such as PNE^n, can be computed using a a straightforward generalization of the idea in [6].

3.3 Soundness and Completeness

In this section, we show that the solution concepts for BGIs that were introduced in Section 3.2 indeed correspond to their semantic counterparts from Section 3.1. The classical theory $\{\gamma_j^k \leftrightarrow g_j^k \mid k \in \{1, \ldots, p\}\}$ associated with the goal base $\Gamma_j = \{\gamma_j^1; \ldots; \gamma_j^p\} \in \mathcal{G}$ is denoted as T_j. A possibility distribution π_i^j on $\mathcal{G}$ can be associated with $\mathcal{K}_i^j$ in the following natural way, inspired by [3], with $\max \emptyset = 0$:

$$\pi_i^j(\Gamma_j) = 1 - \max\{\alpha_l \mid (\varphi_l, \alpha_l) \in \mathcal{K}_i^j, T_j \not\models \varphi_l\} \tag{1}$$

Intuitively, the higher the certainty of the formulas violated by Γ_j, the lower the possibility of Γ_j being the real goal base of agent j according to agent i. Note that if we make the reasonable assumption that an agent knows its own goals, then π_i^i maps all elements of $\mathcal{G}$ to 0 except the real goal base of i, which is mapped to 1. Given the BGI G and using the possibility distributions on $\mathcal{G}$ for every j, we can define a possibility distribution π_i^G on the set of possible BGs $\mathcal{BG}$:

$$\pi_i^G(G') = \min_{j \in N} \pi_i^j(\Gamma_j^{G'})$$

with $\Gamma_j^{G'}$ the goal base of agent j in the BG G'. This possibility distribution is the natural semantic counterpart of the BGI G. We now show that these possibility distributions π_i^G allow us to interpret the solution concepts that have been defined syntactically in Section 3.2 as instances of the semantically defined solution concepts from

Section 3.1. This is formalized in the following proposition and corollary. We use the notation $br_j(\nu, \Gamma_j)$ for the propositional variable corresponding to "agent j with goal base Γ_j plays a best response in ν".

Proposition 1. *For every $\nu \in \mathcal{V}$, $i, j \in N$ and $\lambda \in\,]0,1]$, it holds that*

$$BR_i^n(j, \nu) \geq \lambda \Leftrightarrow \forall \Gamma_j \in \mathcal{G} : \neg br_j(\nu, \Gamma_j) \Rightarrow \pi_i^j(\Gamma_j) \leq 1 - \lambda \qquad (2)$$

$$BR_i^p(j, \nu) \geq \lambda \Leftrightarrow \exists \Gamma_j \in \mathcal{G} : br_j(\nu, \Gamma_j) \wedge \pi_i^j(\Gamma_j) \geq \lambda \qquad (3)$$

Corollary 1. *Let us denote the possibility and necessity measure associated with π_i^G as Π_i^G and N_i^G. For every $\nu \in \mathcal{V}$ it holds that*

$$N_i^G(\{G' \in \mathcal{BG} \mid \nu \text{ is a PNE in } G'\}) = \min_{j \in N} BR_i^n(j, \nu) \qquad (4)$$

$$\Pi_i^G(\{G' \in \mathcal{BG} \mid \nu \text{ is a PNE in } G'\}) = \min_{j \in N} BR_i^p(j, \nu) \qquad (5)$$

Consequently, it holds that:

$$nec_G(\{G' \in \mathcal{BG} \mid \nu \text{ is a PNE in } G'\}) = PNE^n(\nu)$$

$$poss_G(\{G' \in \mathcal{BG} \mid \nu \text{ is a PNE in } G'\}) = PNE^p(\nu)$$

Before we prove Proposition 1 and Corollary 1, a lemma is stated which deals with the construction of specific goal bases in $\mathcal{G}$, given the knowledge about these goal bases.

Lemma 1. *Given a goal-KB $\mathcal{K}_i^j$, there exists a goal base $\Gamma_j \in \mathcal{G}$ such that $\pi_i^j(\Gamma_j) = 1$.*

Proof (Sketch). It is easily verified that the goal base $\Gamma_j = (\gamma_j^1; \ldots; \gamma_j^p)$ with γ_j^k the CNF of $\bigvee \{\varphi \mid \varphi \in L_\Phi, \exists \lambda > 0 : \mathcal{K}_i^j \vdash (\varphi \to g_j^k, \lambda)\}$ meets the condition $\pi_i^j(\Gamma_j) = 1$.

Note that the construction of Γ_j relies on the (constraint) syntax of the formulas in $\mathcal{K}_i^j$.

We now prove Proposition 1.

$\boxed{\Rightarrow \text{ of (2)}}$ We prove this by contraposition. Suppose there exists a $\Gamma_j \in \mathcal{G}$ such that j plays no BR in ν given Γ_j and $\pi_i^j(\Gamma_j) > 1 - \lambda$. Taking (1) into account, the latter implies that $\forall(\varphi_l, \alpha_l) \in \mathcal{K}_i^j : T_j \not\models \varphi_l \Rightarrow \alpha_l < \lambda$. By definition 11, $BR_i^n(j, \nu) \geq \lambda$ implies that there exists a $k' \in \{0, \ldots, p\}$ such that $\mathcal{K}_i^j \vdash (\varphi_\nu \to g_j^{k'+1}, \lambda)$ and $\mathcal{K}_i^j \vdash ((\varphi_{\nu_{-j}} \wedge \neg \varphi_{\nu_j}) \to \neg g_j^{k'}, \lambda)$. It follows that $T_j \models \varphi_\nu \to g_j^{k'+1}$ and $T_j \models (\varphi_{\nu_{-j}} \wedge \neg \varphi_{\nu_j}) \to \neg g_j^{k'}$. Consequently, by definition of T_j, if $k' \in \{1, \ldots, p - 1\}$, it holds that $T_j \models \varphi_\nu \to \gamma_j^{k'+1}$ and $T_j \models (\varphi_{\nu_{-j}} \wedge \neg \varphi_{\nu_j}) \to \neg \gamma_j^{k'}$. This means that j does play a BR in ν since the goal $\gamma_j^{k'+1}$ is satisfied in ν and for every alternative strategy of j, $\gamma_j^{k'}$ is not satisfied. If $k' = p$ or $k' = 0$ then j's utility is resp. 0 or p for every alternative strategy of j. In any case, agent j with goal base Γ_j plays a BR in ν.

$\boxed{\Leftarrow \text{ of (2)}}$ Suppose that $BR_i^n(j, \nu) < \lambda$, i.e. for every $k \in \{0, \ldots, p\}$ either $\mathcal{K}_i^j \not\vdash (\varphi_\nu \to g_j^{k+1}, \lambda)$ or $\mathcal{K}_i^j \not\vdash ((\varphi_{\nu_{-j}} \wedge \neg \varphi_{\nu_j}) \to \neg g_j^k, \lambda)$. Let k' be the greatest index for which $\mathcal{K}_i^j \nvdash (\varphi_\nu \to g_j^{k'}, \lambda)$. Note that $k' \geq 1$ since $g_j^0 = \bot$. Construct a goal base $\Gamma_j = (\gamma_j^1; \ldots; \gamma_j^p)$ with γ_j^k defined as the CNF of the formula

$$\bigvee\{\varphi \mid \varphi \in L_\Phi, \mathcal{K}_i^j \vdash (\varphi \to g_j^k, \lambda)\} \vee (\bigwedge\{\varphi \mid \varphi \in L_\Phi, \mathcal{K}_i^j \vdash (\varphi \leftarrow g_j^k, \lambda)\} \wedge \neg\varphi_\nu)$$

for $k \leq k'$, and γ_j^k defined as the CNF of the formula

$$\bigvee\{\varphi \mid \varphi \in L_\Phi, \mathcal{K}_i^j \vdash (\varphi \to g_j^k, \lambda)\} \vee (\bigwedge\{\varphi \mid \varphi \in L_\Phi, \varphi \neq \top, \mathcal{K}_i^j \vdash (\varphi \leftarrow g_j^k, \lambda)\})$$

for $k > k'$. One can straightforwardly check that $\Gamma_j \in \mathcal{G}$ and $\pi_i^j(\Gamma_j) > 1 - \lambda$ by checking that for every formula $(\varphi, \alpha) \in \mathcal{K}_i^j$ with $\alpha \geq \lambda$, it holds that $T_j \models \varphi$. Moreover, one can verify that j does not play a BR in ν with the constructed Γ_j (note that this would not be guaranteed by the goal base constructed in the proof of Lemma 1).

$\boxed{\Rightarrow \text{ of (3)}}$ Analogous to the proof of "$\Leftarrow$ of (2)".

$\boxed{\Leftarrow \text{ of (3)}}$ We prove directly that $\mathrm{BR}_i^p(j, \nu) \geq \lambda$, i.e. $\exists k \in \{0, \ldots, p\}$ such that $\mathcal{K}_i^j \nvdash (\varphi_\nu \to \neg g_j^{k+1}, \lambda^*)$ and $\forall \nu_j' : \mathcal{K}_i^j \nvdash (\varphi_{(\nu_{-j}, \nu_j')} \to g_j^k, \lambda^*)$. By assumption, there exists a Γ_j such that j plays a BR in ν and $\pi_i^j(\Gamma_j) \geq \lambda$. The former means that for some $k' \in \{0, \ldots, p\}$, $T_j \models \varphi_\nu \to \gamma_{k'+1}^j$ and $\forall \nu_j' : T_j \models \varphi_{(\nu_{-j}, \nu_j')} \to \neg\gamma_{k'}^j$. Since $T_j \models \gamma_l^j \leftrightarrow g_j^l$, it then holds that $T_j \models \varphi_\nu \to g_j^{k'+1}$. Since by definition $\varphi_\nu \nvDash \bot$, $T_j \nvDash \bot$ and $T_j \nvDash \neg\varphi_\nu$, it follows that $T_j \nvDash \varphi_\nu \to \neg g_j^{k'+1}$. The assumption that $\pi_i^j(\Gamma_j) \geq \lambda$ implies that $\forall(\varphi_l, \alpha_l) \in \mathcal{K}_i^j : T_j \nvDash \varphi_l \Rightarrow \alpha_l \leq 1 - \lambda$. It follows that $\mathcal{K}_i^j \nvdash (\varphi_\nu \to \neg g_j^{k'+1}, \lambda^*)$. Analogously, we can prove that $\forall \nu_j' : T_j \models \varphi_{(\nu_{-j}, \nu_j')} \to \neg\gamma_{k'}^j$ implies that $\forall \nu_j' : \mathcal{K}_i^j \nvdash (\varphi_{(\nu_{-j}, \nu_j')} \to g_j^{k'}, \lambda^*)$.

We now prove (4) of Corollary 1. The proof of (5) is analogous and the rest of Corollary 1 follows immediately.

$\boxed{\text{Proof of (4)}}$ By definition, $\min_{j \in N} \mathrm{BR}_i^n(j, \nu) \geq \lambda$ iff $\mathrm{BR}_i^n(j, \nu) \geq \lambda$ for every $j \in N$. We proved that the latter is equivalent with $\forall \Gamma_j \in \mathcal{G} : j$ no BR in $\nu \Rightarrow \pi_i^j(\Gamma_j) \leq 1 - \lambda$. We first prove that this implies that for all $G' \in \mathcal{BG}$ it holds that $\pi_i^G(G') \leq 1 - \lambda$ if ν is no PNE in G'. By definition, this means that $N_i^G(\{G' \in \mathcal{BG} \mid \nu \text{ is a PNE in } G'\}) \geq \lambda$. Take an arbitrary G' such that ν is no PNE in G'. Then there exists some j who plays no BR in ν if its goal base is $\Gamma_j^{G'}$. By assumption, this implies $\pi_i^j(\Gamma_j^{G'}) \leq 1 - \lambda$, which implies $\pi_i^G(G') \leq 1 - \lambda$ by definition. We now prove the opposite direction. Take an arbitrary j and Γ_j such that j plays no BR in ν with the goal base of j equal to Γ_j. Using Lemma 1, we can construct a $G' \in \mathcal{BG}$ such that $\Gamma_j^{G'} = \Gamma_j$ and $\pi_{j'}^i(\Gamma_{j'}^{G'}) = 1$ for every $j' \neq j$. Obviously ν is no PNE in G' since j plays no BR. By assumption and definition of N_i^G, it holds that $\pi_i^G(G') \leq 1 - \lambda$. Since $\pi_{j'}^i(\Gamma_{G'}^{j'}) = 1$ for every $j' \neq j$, it follows that $\pi_i^j(\Gamma_j) \leq 1 - \lambda$. Due to Proposition 1, we proved that $\mathrm{BR}_i^n(j, \nu) \geq \lambda$. Since j is arbitrary, it follows that $\min_{j \in N} \mathrm{BR}_i^n(j, \nu) \geq \lambda$.

Example 5. Recall the scenario of Example 2. We define the BGI G. Since Bob has perfect knowledge of Alice's preferences, his goal-KB can be modeled as $\mathcal{K}_2^1 = \mathcal{K}_1^1 = \{((a \leftrightarrow b) \leftrightarrow g_1^1, 1), (((a \leftrightarrow b) \vee \neg a) \leftrightarrow g_1^2, 1)\}$. Alice is certain that Bob wants to attend a sports game together, or attend the game on his own if attending it together is not possible. This can be captured by the goal-KB $\mathcal{K}_1^2 = \{((a \wedge b) \leftrightarrow g_2^1, 1), (b \leftrightarrow g_2^2, 1)\}$. It is easy to see that π_1^G and π_2^G correspond to the possibility distributions

π_1 and π_2 described in Example 2. Despite Alice's incorrect beliefs, Bob and Alice are both certain that attending a sports game together is a PNE, since $nec_G(\{G' \in \mathcal{BG} \mid \{a,b\}$ is a PNE in $G'\}) = PNE^n(\{a,b\}) = 1$. Contrary to Alice, Bob knows that going to the theatre together is a PNE as well.

An interesting question is how the agents' beliefs can influence the proposals they can make in e.g. bargaining protocols. Suppose for instance that Alice wants to make Bob a suggestion, then based on her beliefs, it would be rational to suggest to attend a sports game together. Bob would then rationally agree, based on his beliefs. However, if Bob were to make a proposal, he can choose between two rational suggestions: attending a sports game together or going to the theatre together. If he would do the latter, Alice would know that her beliefs are incorrect, assuming Bob behaves rationally. In future research, we will investigate these strategical interactions and how they allow agents to revise their beliefs. Other research possibilities lie in manipulating BGIs through communication, for instance through announcements, as investigated for BGs with environment variables [11]. Another option is to extend the BGI framework, allowing agents to also reason about the beliefs of other agents, although this is likely to lead to an increase in computational complexity.

4   Decision Problems

The decision problems associated with BGIs and the PNE^x measures are investigated.

Proposition 2. *Let G be a BGI and $\lambda \in \,]0,1]$. The following decision problems are Σ_2^P-complete:*

1. *Does there exist a strategy profile ν with $PNE^n(\nu) \geq \lambda$?*
2. *Does there exist a strategy profile ν with $PNE^p(\nu) \geq \lambda$?*

Proof. $\boxed{\text{Hardness of 1 and 2}}$ Both problems are Σ_2^P-hard since they contain the Σ_2^P-complete problem to decide whether a BG has a PNE as a special case. Indeed, when G is a BG, we can construct a BGI in which all agents have complete knowledge of each others goals. Then $PNE^n(\nu)$ and $PNE^p(\nu)$ coincide and take values in $\{0, 1\}$, depending on whether ν is a PNE or not. Consequently, G has a PNE iff there exists a ν with $PNE^n(\nu) = PNE^p(\nu) \geq \lambda$.

$\boxed{\text{Completeness of 1}}$ We can decide the problem by first guessing a strategy profile ν. Checking whether $PNE^n(\nu) \geq \lambda$ means checking whether $\mathrm{BR}_i^n(j, \nu) \geq \lambda$ for every $i, j \in N$. The latter involves checking possibilistic entailments, which can be done in constant time using an NP-oracle. Therefore, the decision problem is Σ_2^P-complete.

$\boxed{\text{Completeness of 2}}$ We can decide the problem by first guessing a strategy profile ν. Checking whether $PNE^p(\nu) \geq \lambda$ means checking whether $\mathrm{BR}_i^p(j, \nu) \geq \lambda$ for every $i, j \in N$. To see that the latter can be reduced to checking a polynomial number of possibilistic entailments, we need to rewrite the condition that $\forall \nu_j' \subseteq \Phi_j : \mathcal{K}_i^j \not\vdash (\varphi_{(\nu_{-j}, \nu_j')} \rightarrow g_j^k, \lambda^*)$. To this end, we define $\mathcal{K}^k$, for every $k \in \{1, \ldots, p\}$, as the KB $\mathcal{K}_i^j$ in which all formulas defining necessary and/or sufficient conditions for g_j^k are preserved; all formulas with necessary conditions for g_j^l ($l \geq k$) are translated into necessary conditions for g_j^k by replacing $(\varphi \rightarrow g_j^l, \alpha)$ by $(\varphi \rightarrow g_j^k, \alpha)$; all formulas with sufficient conditions for g_j^l ($l \leq k$) are translated into sufficient conditions for g_j^k by replacing $(\varphi \leftarrow g_j^l, \alpha)$ by $(\varphi \leftarrow g_j^k, \alpha)$; all other formulas are deleted. Then it holds

$$\forall \nu_j' \subseteq \Phi_j : \mathcal{K}_i^j \nvdash (\varphi_{(\boldsymbol{\nu}_{-j}, \nu_j')} \rightarrow g_j^k, \lambda^*)$$

$$\Leftrightarrow \forall \nu_j' \subseteq \Phi_j : \mathcal{K}^k \nvdash (\varphi_{(\boldsymbol{\nu}_{-j}, \nu_j')} \rightarrow g_j^k, \lambda^*)$$

$$\Leftrightarrow \forall \nu_j' \subseteq \Phi_j : \mathcal{K}_{1-\lambda}^k \nvdash \varphi_{(\boldsymbol{\nu}_{-j}, \nu_j')} \rightarrow g_j^k$$

$$\Leftrightarrow \forall \nu_j' \subseteq \Phi_j : \mathcal{K}_{1-\lambda}^k \text{ and } \varphi_{(\boldsymbol{\nu}_{-j}, \nu_j')} \text{ and } \neg g_j^k \text{ are consistent}$$

$$\Leftrightarrow \forall \nu_j' \subseteq \Phi_j : \mathcal{K}_{1-\lambda}'^k \text{ and } \varphi_{\nu_j'} \text{ are consistent}$$

where $\mathcal{K}_{1-\lambda}'^k$ is obtaind from $\mathcal{K}_{1-\lambda}^k$ by replacing each occurrence of g^k by $\bot$ and each occurrence of $p \in \Phi \backslash \Phi_j$ by its truth value ($\top$ or $\bot$) in $\boldsymbol{\nu}$. The last condition is equivalent with $\mathcal{K}_{1-\lambda}'^k$ being a tautology, which can be checked with a SAT-solver, i.e. in constant time with an NP-oracle.

The result of Proposition 2 shows that the complexity for the introduced measures does not increase compared to PNEs of BGs, since deciding whether a BG has a PNE is also Σ_2^P-complete. Moreover, given the experimental results reported in [6] for standard BGs, it seems plausible that a reduction to answer set programming would support an efficient computation of solutions for medium sized games.

5   Conclusion

We introduced the first BG framework that allows agents to be uncertain about the other agents' goals. We have argued that such a scenario can naturally be modeled by associating with each agent a possibility distribution over the universe of all possible games (given the considered partition of action variables). While this allows us to define a variety of solution concepts in a natural way, this semantic approach is not useful in practice, due to the exponential size of these possibility distributions. Therefore, we also proposed a syntactic counterpart, which avoids exponential representations by relying on standard possibilistic logic inference, and can be implemented by reduction to answer set programming. Our main result is that this syntactic characterization indeed corresponds to the intended semantic definitions. We furthermore showed that the computational complexity of reasoning with our Boolean games with incomplete information remains at the second level of the polynomial hierarchy. The present framework leads to several interesting avenues for future work. First, the approach could be generalized for taking into account prior beliefs about the likely behaviour of other players (e.g. for modeling collusion) and/or for modeling situations where agents may be uncertain about the actions that are being played by other agents. Moreover, it seems of interest to analyse the effect of adding communication to the framework, by allowing agents to strategically ask questions or make proposals to each other in order to reduce uncertainty or as part of a bargaining process.

References

1. Ågotnes, T., Harrenstein, P., van der Hoek, W., Wooldridge, M.: Boolean games with epistemic goals. In: Grossi, D., Roy, O., Huang, H. (eds.) LORI. LNCS, vol. 8196, pp. 1–14. Springer, Heidelberg (2013)
2. Ågotnes, T., Harrenstein, P., van der Hoek, W., Wooldridge, M.: Verifiable equilibria in Boolean games. In: Proc. IJCAI 2013, pp. 689–695 (2013)
3. Benferhat, S., Kaci, S.: Logical representation and fusion of prioritized information based on guaranteed possibility measures: Application to the distance-based merging of classical bases. Artificial Intelligence 148, 291–333 (2003)
4. Bonzon, E., Lagasquie-Schiex, M.-C., Lang, J.: Compact preference representation for Boolean games. In: Yang, Q., Webb, G. (eds.) PRICAI 2006. LNCS (LNAI), vol. 4099, pp. 41–50. Springer, Heidelberg (2006)
5. Bonzon, E., Lagasquie-Schiex, M.C., Lang, J., Zanuttini, B.: Boolean games revisited. In: Proc. ECAI 2006, pp. 265–269. ACM (2006)
6. De Clercq, S., Bauters, K., Schockaert, S., De Cock, M., Nowé, A.: Using answer set programming for solving Boolean games. In: Proc. KR 2014, pp. 602–605 (2014)
7. Dubois, D., Lang, J., Prade, H.: Possibilistic logic. In: Handbook of Logic for Artificial Intelligence and Logic Programming, vol. 3, pp. 439–513. Oxford University Press (1994)
8. Dubois, D., Prade, H.: Epistemic entrenchment and possibilistic logic. Artificial Intelligence 50(2), 223–239 (1991)
9. Dubois, D., Prade, H.: Possibilistic logic: a retrospective and prospective view. Fuzzy Sets and Systems 144, 3–23 (2004)
10. Dunne, P., van der Hoek, W., Kraus, S., Wooldridge, M.: Cooperative Boolean games. In: Proc. AAMAS 2008, vol. 2, pp. 1015–1022. IFAAMAS (2008)
11. Grant, J., Kraus, S., Wooldridge, M., Zuckerman, I.: Manipulating Boolean games through communication. In: Proc. IJCAI 2011, pp. 210–215 (2011)
12. Harrenstein, P., van der Hoek, W., Meyer, J.J., Witteveen, C.: Boolean games. In: Proc. TARK 2001, pp. 287–298. MKP Inc. (2001)
13. Marchioni, E., Wooldridge, M.: Łukasiewicz games. In: Proc. AAMAS 2014, pp. 837–844 (2014)
14. Osborne, M., Rubinstein, A.: A Course in Game Theory. MIT Press (1994)
15. Schelling, T.: The strategy of conflict. Oxford University Press (1960)
16. Schockaert, S., Prade, H.: Solving conflicts in information merging by a flexible interpretation of atomic propositions. Artificial Intelligence 175(11), 1815–1855 (2011)

LEG Networks for Ranking Functions

Christian Eichhorn and Gabriele Kern-Isberner

Lehrstuhl Informatik 1, Technische Universität Dortmund, Dortmund, Germany
{christian.eichhorn,gabriele.kern-isberner}@cs.tu-dortmund.de

Abstract. When using representations of plausibility for semantical frameworks, the storing capacity needed is usually exponentially in the number of variables. Therefore, network-based approaches that decompose the semantical space have proven to be fruitful in environments with probabilistic information. For applications where a more qualitative information is preferable to quantitative information, ordinal conditional functions (OCF) offer a convenient methodology. Here, Bayesian-like networks have been proposed for ranking functions, so called *OCF-networks*. These networks not only suffer from similar problems as Bayesian networks, in particular, allowing only restricted classes of conditional relationships, it also has been found recently that problems with admissibility may arise. In this paper we propose LEG networks for ranking functions, also carrying over an idea from probabilistics. OCF-LEG networks can be built for any conditional knowledge base and filled by local OCF that can be found by inductive reasoning. A global OCF is set up from the local ones, and it is shown that the global OCF is admissible with respect to the underlying knowledge base.

1 Introduction

Network-based approaches are very common in the field of probability theory, in particular, Bayesian networks [13] are used to (compactly) store the joint probability distribution of a set of variables under assumptions of conditional independence thus yielding the possibility to save only local probability information and calculate a global distribution by means of decomposition. For applications in which the information to be handled is a degree of plausibility or implausibility, *ordinal conditional functions* (OCF) [15], also known as *ranking functions*, offer a likewise satisfactory but essentially qualitative framework. It has been shown that Bayesian-style networks with local ranking tables instead of local tables of probabilities [6,3,8], so called *OCF-networks*, share the properties of local storing, decomposition and conditional independence with classical (that is, probabilistic) Bayesian networks. However, if an OCF-network has to be constructed from a knowledge base, the conditionals are restricted to a certain limited language; as an additional drawback, recent work [5] shows that the admissibility of the global ranking function with respect to the given knowledge base may be lost. The less well-known approach of networks of *local event groups* (LEG networks [10]) looks promising to overcome these deficiencies as there are algorithms to construct (especially the hypertree component of) a probabilistic LEG network from a knowledge base containing arbitrary conditionals [12].

In this paper we present an adaption of the LEG approach for ranking functions that is able to preserve the advantages of the probabilistic approach, i.e., decomposability,

E. Fermé and J. Leite (Eds.): JELIA 2014, LNAI 8761, pp. 210–223, 2014.

local representation of knowledge, and allowing general forms of knowledge bases, while still ensuring admissibility of the resulting global ranking function to the given knowledge bases. We prove that for LEGs that form hypertrees, the ranking variant of the consistency condition [10] is sufficient to guarantee that there is a global ranking function such that the local ranking functions of the LEGs which can be obtained by inductive reasoning like system Z [14] and c-representations [7], are marginal functions of this global function. Therefore, OCF-LEG networks provide a methodology to inductively compose an OCF for a knowledge base from local ranking functions. The LEG approach regards conditionals as undirected connections between variables and combines the variables jointly occurring in a conditional in the same hyperedge. This allows for generating the network component of OCF-LEG networks with arbitrary conditionals, which overcomes the language restriction of OCF-networks, replacing directed (usually viewed as cause-and-effect) connections between variables by unordered sets of variables that are connected by the respective conditionals. Doing so, also the strong acyclicity needed for OCF-networks is no longer necessary, while nonetheless acyclicity with respect to the hyperedges is needed, that is, we have to guarantee that the network is a hypertree. Nevertheless, OCF-LEG networks induce a conditional independence of neighbouring hyperedges in the network given their intersections, even without the strong assumptions needed for the Bayesian-style OCF-networks.

With this approach, an OCF-LEG network can be constructed inductively, generating both the local ranking functions as well as the network component from a (consistent) conditional knowledge base that can be divided into a set of local knowledge bases. These local computations reduce the number of affected conditionals as well as the number of affected variables significantly, both crucial factors of the computational complexity for either of the inductive approaches. Moreover, this switch from a global to a local perspective allows local inferences inside of the LEGs that coincide with global inferences, thanks to having full admissibility with respect to the given knowledge bases with this approach.

This paper is organised as follows: After the introduction in Section 1 and the formal preliminaries in Section 2 we briefly recall Spohn's ranking functions and two approaches to inductive reasoning, c-representations and System Z, in Section 3. Section 4 recalls OCF-networks as closest related work, and the necessary details for hypergraphs. In Section 5 we define OCF-LEG networks and prove their formal properties the algorithmic construction of which is the subject of Section 6. We conclude in Sect. 7.

2 Preliminaries

Let $\Sigma = \{V_1, \ldots, V_n\}$ be a finite set of propositional variables. We denote by $\mathfrak{L}$ the logical language of Σ under closure of conjunction ($\wedge$), disjunction ($\vee$) and negation ($\neg$) together with the symbol of tautology ($\top$) and contradiction ($\bot$). Let ϕ, ψ be formulas in $\mathfrak{L}$. We abbreviate conjunction by juxtaposition (that is, $\phi \wedge \psi$ is abbreviated as $\phi\psi$) and negation by overlining (that is, $\neg\phi$ is abbreviated as $\overline{\phi}$). A *literal* is a variable interpreted to *true* or *false*, we write v_i to denote the interpretation of V_i to *true*, $\overline{v}_i$ to denote the interpretation of V_i to *false* and $\dot{v}_i$ to denote a fixed interpretation of V_i. For a set $\mathbf{A} = \{A, B, C\} \subseteq \Sigma$, a denotes a complete conjunction $\mathbf{a} = \dot{a}\dot{b}\dot{c}$. For $\phi \in \mathfrak{L}$

we write $V_i \equiv \phi$ if $\dot{v}_i$ appears in ϕ. *Interpretations*, or *possible worlds*, are also defined in the usual way; the set of all possible worlds is denoted by Ω. We often use the 1-1 association between worlds and *complete conjunctions*, that is, conjunctions of literals where every variable $V_i \in \Sigma$ appears exactly once.

For a system $\{\Sigma_1, \ldots \Sigma_m\}$ of subsets $\Sigma_i \subseteq \Sigma$ for all $1 \le i \le m$, we denote by Ω_i the *local (possible) worlds*, that is, complete conjunctions of literals over Σ_i. To differentiate between possible worlds and local possible worlds we mark local possible worlds with a superscript such that $\omega^i \in \Omega_i$. To denote the projection of a possible world $\omega \in \Omega$ onto a subset Σ_i, we write $\Sigma_i(\omega) = \bigwedge_{\substack{V \in \Sigma_i \\ \omega \models \dot{v}}} \dot{v}$ with $\bigwedge_{\substack{V \in \Sigma_i \\ \omega \models \dot{v}}} \dot{v} \in \Omega_i$.

especially, $\varnothing(\omega) = \top$ for all $\omega \in \Omega$. A *conditional* $(\psi|\phi)$ represents the defeasible rule "if ϕ then *usually / normally* ψ" with the trivalent evaluation $[\![(\psi|\phi)]\!]_\omega = true$ iff $\omega \models \phi\psi$ (verification / acceptance), $[\![(\psi|\phi)]\!]_\omega = false$ iff $\omega \models \phi\overline{\psi}$ (falsification / refutation) and $[\![(\psi|\phi)]\!]_\omega = undefined$ iff $\omega \models \overline{\phi}$ (non-applicability) [4,7]. The language of all conditionals over $\mathfrak{L}$ is denoted by $(\mathfrak{L} \mid \mathfrak{L})$. A conditional $(\phi|\top)$ encodes a *plausible proposition*.

Let $\Gamma = \langle \mathcal{V}, \mathcal{E} \rangle$ be a directed, acyclic graph (DAG) with vertices $\mathcal{V} = \{V_1, \ldots, V_n\}$ and edges $\mathcal{E} \subseteq \mathcal{V} \times \mathcal{V}$. We define the *parents* of a vertex V, pa(V), as the direct predecessors of V (that is, pa$(V) = \{V'|(V', V) \in \mathcal{E}\}$) and the *descendants* of V, $desc(V)$, as the set of vertices V' for which there is a path from V to V' in $\mathcal{E}$. The set of *non-descendants* of V is the set of all vertices that are neither the parents nor the descendants of V, nor V itself, so $nd(V) = \mathcal{V} \setminus (desc(V) \cup \{V\} \cup \text{pa}(V))$.

3 OCF and Inductive Reasoning

An *ordinal conditional function* (OCF), also known as *ranking function* is a function that assigns to each world a rank of *disbelief* or *implausibility*, that is, the higher the rank of a world is, the less plausible this world is.

Definition 1 (Ranking function (OCF, [15])). *An ordinal conditional function (also called OCF or ranking function) κ is a function $\kappa : \Omega \to \mathbb{N}_0 \cup \{\infty\}$ such that the set $\{\omega \mid \kappa(\omega) = 0\}$ is not empty, i.e., there have to be worlds that are maximally plausible.*

The rank of a formula $\phi \in \mathfrak{L}$ is defined to be the minimal rank of all worlds that satisfy ϕ, $\kappa(\phi) = \min\{\kappa(\omega) | \omega \models \phi\}$, which implies $\kappa(\bot) = \infty$ and $\kappa(\top) = 0$. The rank of a conditional $(\psi|\phi) \in (\mathfrak{L}|\mathfrak{L})$ is defined by $\kappa(\psi|\phi) = \kappa(\phi\psi) - \kappa(\phi)$. With the rank ∞, ranking functions allow us to encode strict knowledge: Let $A \in \mathfrak{L}$ be a formula, then $\kappa(\overline{A}) = \infty$ states that $\overline{A}$ is maximally / absolutely disbelieved, and hence A is maximally / absolutely believed. The same holds for conditionals, where $(A|\top)$ encodes the conditional fact "normally, A holds", but if $\kappa(\overline{A}|\top) = \infty$, this becomes a strict fact.

Definition 2 (Marginal ranking function). *Let $\kappa : \Sigma \to \mathbb{N}_0 \cup \{\infty\}$ be a ranking function. The* marginal ranking function κ' *obtained from κ on $\Sigma' \subseteq \Sigma$ with corresponding models $\omega' \in \Omega'$ is defined by $\kappa'(\omega') := \kappa(\omega') = \min\{\kappa(\omega)|\omega \models \omega'\}$.*

Table 1. Car-start ranking function

ω	$hbfs$	$hbf\bar{s}$	$hb\bar{f}s$	$hb\bar{f}\bar{s}$	$h\bar{b}fs$	$h\bar{b}f\bar{s}$	$h\bar{b}\bar{f}s$	$h\bar{b}\bar{f}\bar{s}$
$\kappa(\omega)$	2	3	4	3	2	1	2	1

ω	$\bar{h}bfs$	$\bar{h}bf\bar{s}$	$\bar{h}b\bar{f}s$	$\bar{h}b\bar{f}\bar{s}$	$\bar{h}\bar{b}fs$	$\bar{h}\bar{b}f\bar{s}$	$\bar{h}\bar{b}\bar{f}s$	$\bar{h}\bar{b}\bar{f}\bar{s}$
$\kappa(\omega)$	0	1	2	1	2	1	2	1

Example 1 (Car start problem). As a running example we use the car start problem from [6,3] which deals with the question whether a given car will start (S): We know that a car usually will start (s) if the battery (B) is charged (b), otherwise it usually will not start ($\bar{s}$). We also know that a car usually will start (s) if the fuel tank (F) is sufficiently filled (f), otherwise it usually will not start. Additionally, we know that if the battery is charged and the fuel tank is empty, the car usually will not start and if the battery is discharged and the fuel tank is filled, the car usually will not start. If the headlights (H) have been left switched on overnight (h), the battery will usually be empty, the other way round if we have switched the headlights off ($\bar{h}$), the battery usually will remain charged. Usually, we will switch off the headlights overnight and usually, the fueltank is filled. This is formalised in the knowledge base

$$\Delta = \left\{ \begin{array}{l} (s|b), \quad (\bar{s}|\bar{b}), \quad (s|f), \quad (\bar{s}|\bar{f}), \quad (\bar{s}|b\bar{f}), \\ (\bar{s}|\bar{b}f), \quad (\bar{h}|\top), \quad (f|\top), \quad (b|h), \quad (b|\bar{h}) \end{array} \right\}. \tag{1}$$

Table 1 shows an OCF for this example. Here, the world where the headlights have been switched off, the battery is charged, the fuel-tank is full and the car starts is the most plausible world ($\kappa(\bar{h}bfs) = 0$), whereas the world where the headlights have been left switched on, the battery is charged, the fuel-tank is empty and the car starts is the most implausible one ($\kappa(hb\bar{f}s) = 4$).

Ranking functions are connected with knowledge bases by the notion of *admissibility*, ensuring that a ranking function accepts the conditionals given in the knowledge base.

Definition 3 (Acceptance / admissibility). *A ranking function κ accepts a conditional* $(\psi|\phi) \in (\mathcal{L}|\mathcal{L})$ *iff its verification is ranked more plausible than its refutation, in symbols* $\kappa \models (\psi|\phi)$, *if and only if* $\kappa(\phi\psi) < \kappa(\phi\bar{\psi})$. κ *is admissible with respect to* Δ *(accepts* Δ) *if and only if it accepts all conditionals in* Δ, *formally* $\kappa \models \Delta$ *iff* $\kappa \models (\psi_i|\phi_i)$ *for all* $1 \leq i \leq n$.

Example 2. In the running car-start example (Example 1), the ranking function of Table 1 accepts Δ as given in (1), for instance, we have $\kappa(b\bar{f}\bar{s}) = 1 < 2 = \kappa(b\bar{f}s)$ hence $\kappa \models (\bar{s}|b\bar{f})$.

Ranking functions induce a plausibility based preference relation on worlds: a world is κ-preferred to another if it is (strictly) more plausible with respect to κ, formally $\omega \leq_\kappa \omega'$ ($\omega <_\kappa \omega'$) if and only if $\kappa(\omega) \leq \kappa(\omega')$ ($\kappa(\omega) < \kappa(\omega')$) and by thus induce an inference relation based on preferential models (confer [11,15]). Since here we concentrate on the conceptual design of OCF-LEG networks, *inference* with OCFs will not be discussed further, cf., e.g., [9] for a discussion of (inductive) inference mechanisms using ranking semantics.

In this context, given a finite knowledge base, methods of inductive reasoning are able to generate a ranking function that accepts the knowledge base. We recall the approach of c-representations [7] which are part of a general principled framework for nonmonotonic reasoning and belief revision. C-representations make use of individual falsification impacts for the conditionals in the knowledge base which are chosen so as to ensure that the resulting ranking function is admissible with respect to the knowledge base.

Definition 4 (c-representation [7]). *A c-representation of a conditional knowledge base* $\Delta = \{(\psi_1|\phi_1), \ldots, (\psi_n|\phi_n)\} \subseteq (\mathfrak{L} \mid \mathfrak{L})$ *is an OCF of the form*

$$\kappa_\Delta^c(\omega) = \sum_{i=1, \omega \models A_i \overline{B}_i}^{n} \kappa_i^-, \qquad\qquad \kappa_i^- \in \mathbb{N}_0 \qquad\qquad (2)$$

where the values $\kappa_i^- \in \mathbb{N}_0$ *are impact values for falsifying conditionals and have to be chosen to make* κ_Δ^c Δ*-admissible, that is for all* $1 \leq i \leq n$ *it holds that* $\kappa_\Delta^c \models (B_i|A_i)$. *This is the case iff*

$$\kappa_i^- > \min_{\omega \models A_i B_i} \left\{ \sum_{i \neq j, \omega \models A_j \overline{B}_j} \kappa_j^- \right\} - \min_{\omega \models A_i \overline{B}_i} \left\{ \sum_{i \neq j, \omega \models A_j \overline{B}_j} \kappa_j^- \right\}. \qquad (3)$$

A minimal c-representation is obtained by choosing κ_i^- *minimally for all* $1 \leq i \leq n$.

Minimal c-representations rank worlds as plausible as possible while still maintaining the admissibility with respect to the knowledge base and following the schema (2) which ensures that each conditional in Δ has an impact that is independent of the respective possible world. Note that because of the inequalities, there is no unique solution for the system (3) for a knowledge base [7,1]; rather, c-representations provide a schema for inductive, model-based reasoning. Nonetheless, each c-representation licenses for high qualitative inference as, for example, shown in [9]. To include strict knowledge into the approach of c-representations, Definition 4 can be extended by allowing $\kappa_i^- = \infty$; however, we focus on conditionals as plausible rules here.

Example 3. We demonstrate c-representations with the running example (Example 1) enumerating the conditionals in the ordering of the knowledge base in (1), that is $r_1 = (s|b)$, $r_2 = (\overline{s}|\overline{b})$, and so forth. The verification/falsification behaviour of the knowledge base is shown in Table 2. This leads to the minimal falsification penalties, $\kappa_6^- = \kappa_9^- = 2$, $\kappa_3^- = \kappa_4^- = \kappa_8^- = 1$ and $\kappa_1^- = \kappa_2^- = \kappa_5^- = 0$. which yield the ranking function κ_Δ^c shown in Table 1.

Another approach to generate a ranking function that is admissible with respect to the given knowledge base is the well known System Z [14]. Both approaches induce inferences that satisfy all major postulates of nonmonotonic logics, however, system Z suffers from the so-called *drowning problem* [6] whereas c-representations do not.

Note that there are connections between ranking functions, possibilistics [2] and Dempster-Shafer theory [15], so techniques and results presented here may be relevant for those frameworks; a more thorough elaboration of this is left for future work.

Table 2. Verification/falsification behaviour for Example 3

ω	$h\,b\,f\,s$	$h\,b\,f\,\overline{s}$	$h\,b\,\overline{f}\,s$	$h\,b\,\overline{f}\,\overline{s}$
verifies	r_1,r_3,r_8	r_8	r_1	r_4,r_5
falsifies	r_7,r_9	r_1,r_3,r_7,r_9	r_4,r_5,r_7,r_8,r_9	r_1,r_8,r_7,r_9

ω	$h\,\overline{b}\,f\,s$	$h\,\overline{b}\,f\,\overline{s}$	$h\,\overline{b}\,\overline{f}\,s$	$h\,\overline{b}\,\overline{f}\,\overline{s}$
verifies	r_3,r_8,r_9	r_2,r_6,r_8,r_9	r_9	r_2,r_4,r_9
falsifies	r_2,r_6,r_7	r_3,r_7	r_2,r_4,r_8,r_7	r_8,r_7

ω	$\overline{h}\,b\,f\,s$	$\overline{h}\,b\,f\,\overline{s}$	$\overline{h}\,b\,\overline{f}\,s$	$\overline{h}\,b\,\overline{f}\,\overline{s}$
verifies	r_1,r_3,r_7,r_8,r_{10}	r_8,r_7,r_{10}	r_1,r_7,r_{10}	r_4,r_5,r_7,r_{10}
falsifies	—	r_1,r_3	r_4,r_5,r_8	r_1,r_8

ω	$\overline{h}\,\overline{b}\,f\,s$	$\overline{h}\,\overline{b}\,f\,\overline{s}$	$\overline{h}\,\overline{b}\,\overline{f}\,s$	$\overline{h}\,\overline{b}\,\overline{f}\,\overline{s}$
verifies	r_3,r_8,r_7	r_2,r_6,r_8,r_7	r_7	r_2,r_4,r_7
falsifies	r_2,r_6,r_{10}	r_3,r_{10}	r_2,r_4,r_8,r_{10}	r_8,r_{10}

4 Related Networks and Hypergraphs

To date, only few works have addressed how graph-based representations can be used for OCF. A prominent approach in this area are OCF-networks [6,3]. This network approach resembles Bayes networks by decomposing global to local information, with the difference that local and global belief are ranking values instead of probabilities. Similar to Bayes networks, OCF-networks provide a stratification of the global function into local ranking values defined by the structure of the graph. Like probabilities and following the definition of ranking functions, the local ranking values are normalised. The following definition summarises this approach.

Definition 5 (OCF-network). [6,3] *A directed acyclic graph (DAG) $\Gamma = \langle \Sigma, \mathcal{E} \rangle$ over a set of propositional atoms Σ is an* OCF-network *if each vertex $V \in \Sigma$ is annotated with a table of local rankings $\kappa_V(V \mid pa(V))$ with (local) ranking values specified for every configuration of V and $pa(V)$. According to the definition of ranking functions the local rankings must be normalised, i.e., $\min_{\dot{v}}\{\kappa(\dot{v} \mid pa(V))\} = 0$ for every configuration of $pa(V)$.*

The local ranking information in Γ can be used to define a global ranking function κ over Σ by applying the idea of stratification [6]: A function κ is *stratified* relative to an OCF-network Γ if and only if

$$\kappa(\omega) = \sum \kappa_V(V(\omega) \mid \mathrm{pa}(V)(\omega)), \qquad (4)$$

for every world ω. Although OCF-networks provide an efficient way of decomposing global ranking functions, this approach has some deficiencies with respect to general requirements of knowledge representation: Firstly, the algorithm to construct the graph component from knowledge bases [6] restricts the language of the conditionals to conditionals where the conclusion is a literal and the premise is a conjunction of literals (so called *single-elementary conditionals*). Even worse, recent work [5] shows that when the local ranking tables are computed from partitions of the knowledge base using methods of inductive reasoning it cannot be guaranteed that the global ranking function is admissible with respect to the global knowledge base. This occurs due to the weakness of the min-function inherent to the OCF framework and is independent from the used inductive approach.

Before we transfer the approach of LEG networks [10] from an epistemic state represented as (local) probability functions to an approach where the (local) beliefs are formalised as ranking functions, we recall the structure of hypertrees set up on subsets of a propositional alphabet underlying this approach. Hypertrees and the more general hypergraphs leave more room for flexible knowledge representation of conditionals than DAGs, in particular, they do not impose a rigid acyclic structure onto conditionals. We will see that using hypergraphs instead of DAGs overcomes the language restrictions and guarantees admissibility of the generated global ranking function with respect to the knowledge base used to set it up.

Definition 6 (Hypergraph, Hypertree [12,13]). *Let $\mathfrak{S}$ by a system of subsets of a propositional alphabet Σ such that $\bigcup_{\Sigma' \in \mathfrak{S}} \Sigma' = \Sigma$. Then $\langle \Sigma, \mathfrak{S} \rangle$ is a hypergraph. $\langle \Sigma, \mathfrak{S} \rangle$ is a hypertree if and only if there is an enumeration of $\mathfrak{S} = \{ \Sigma_1, \ldots, \Sigma_m \}$ such that for all $1 \leq i \leq m$, there is a $j < i$, such that*

$$\mathbb{S}_i = \Sigma_i \cap (\Sigma_1 \cup \ldots \cup \Sigma_{i-1}) \subseteq \Sigma_j. \tag{5}$$

(5) is called Running Intersection Property *(RIP). Note that $\mathbb{S}_1 = \varnothing$ and (5) is vacuous for the case $i = 1$. We call $S = \{ \mathbb{S}_1, \ldots, \mathbb{S}_m \}$ the* separators *of $\mathfrak{S}$ and define by $\mathcal{R} = \{ \mathbb{R}_1, \ldots, \mathbb{R}_m \}$ the set of* residues *with $\mathbb{R}_i = \Sigma_i \setminus \mathbb{S}_i, 1 \leq i \leq m$.*

Example 4. We illustrate Definition 6 with the car-start example (Example 1). We distribute our car-starting alphabet into the sets $\Sigma_1 = \{ H, B \}$ and $\Sigma_2 = \{ B, F, S \}$. This gives us the set of local worlds $\Omega_1 = \{ hb, h\overline{b}, \overline{h}b, \overline{h}\,\overline{b} \}$ for Σ_1 and the local worlds $\Omega_2 = \{ bfs, bf\overline{s}, b\overline{f}s, b\overline{f}\overline{s}, \overline{b}fs, \overline{b}f\overline{s}, \overline{b}\,\overline{f}s, \overline{b}\,\overline{f}\overline{s} \}$ for Σ_2. On these sets and for this enumeration, we obtain $\mathbb{S}_1 = \varnothing$, $\mathbb{R}_1 = \Sigma_1 \setminus \varnothing = \Sigma_1$, $\mathbb{S}_2 = \{ B \}$ and $\mathbb{R}_2 = \Sigma_2 \setminus \{ B \} = \{ F, S \}$. It is $\mathbb{S}_2 = \{ B \} \subseteq \{ H, B \} = \Sigma_1$, so the system $\{ \Sigma_1, \Sigma_2 \}$ satisfies the RIP, and therefore, $\langle \Sigma, \{ \Sigma_1, \Sigma_2 \} \rangle$ is a hypertree.

5   OCF-LEG Network

In the previous section we recalled hypergraphs which form the *network* part of OCF-LEG networks. Ranking functions as local or global OCFs have been characterised in Section 3. With these two components we define OCF-LEG networks analogous to probabilistic LEG networks [10]. LEG networks nicely combine the advantages of Markov and Bayes networks: They provide local undirected components (Markov but not Bayes) with a clear conditional semantics (Bayes but not Markov).

Definition 7 (OCF-LEG network). *Let $\Sigma_1, \ldots, \Sigma_m$ be a set of covering subsets over an alphabet Σ such that $\Sigma_i \subseteq \Sigma$, $1 \le i \le m$ and $\Sigma = \bigcup_{i=1}^{m} \Sigma_i$. Let $\kappa_1, \ldots, \kappa_m$ be ranking functions $\kappa_i : \Omega_i \to \mathbb{N}_0^\infty$, $1 \le i \le m$. We call a tuple $\langle \Sigma_i, \kappa_i \rangle$ of a subset $\Sigma_i \subseteq \Sigma$ with a ranking function κ_i on Ω_i a* local *event group (LEG). The system $\langle(\Sigma_1, \kappa_1), \ldots, (\Sigma_m, \kappa_m)\rangle$, abbreviated as $\langle(\Sigma_i, \kappa_i)\rangle_{i=1}^{m}$, is a ranking network of local event groups (OCF-LEG network) iff there is a global function κ on Ω with*

$$\kappa(\omega^i) = \kappa_i(\omega^i) \tag{6}$$

for all $\omega^i \in \Omega_i$ and all $1 \le i \le n$, that is, κ_i are the marginals of κ on Ω_i.

For a system $\langle(\Sigma_i, \kappa_i)\rangle_{i=1}^{m}$ to have a global ranking function as defined above, the following consistency condition (7) has to be fulfilled.

Proposition 1 (Consistency condition). *There is a global ordinal conditional function $\kappa : \Omega \to \mathbb{N}_0 \cup \{\infty\}$ for the system $\langle(\Sigma_i, \kappa_i)\rangle_{i=1}^{m}$ only if*

$$\kappa_i((\Sigma_i \cap \Sigma_j)(\omega)) = \kappa_j((\Sigma_i \cap \Sigma_j)(\omega)) \tag{7}$$

for all pairs $1 \le i, j < m$ and all worlds $\omega \in \Omega$.

Proof. If the ranking functions of the system $\langle(\Sigma_i, \kappa_i)\rangle_{i=1}^{m}$ would violate the consistency condition (7) then there would be a pair of $1 \le i, j \le m$ with the property $\kappa_i((\Sigma_i \cap \Sigma_j)(\omega)) \ne \kappa_j((\Sigma_i \cap \Sigma_j)(\omega))$. By Definition 7, a global OCF κ satisfies $\kappa(\omega^i) = \kappa_i(\omega^i)$ and hence the above would lead to $\kappa((\Sigma_i \cap \Sigma_j)(\omega)) \ne \kappa((\Sigma_i \cap \Sigma_j)(\omega))$ which is a direct contradiction. $\square$

On the other hand, Example 5 shows that the consistency condition (7) is not sufficient to guarantee the existence of a global OCF.

Example 5. Let $\Sigma = \{A, B, C\}$ with $\Sigma_1 = \{A, B\}$, $\Sigma_2 = \{A, C\}$ and $\Sigma_3 = \{B, C\}$. Let $\kappa_1(ab) = \kappa_1(a\bar{b}) = \kappa_1(\bar{a}\,\bar{b}) = 0$, $\kappa_1(\bar{a}b) = 1$, $\kappa_2(ac) = \kappa_2(\bar{a}c) = \kappa_2(\bar{a}\,\bar{c}) = 0$, $\kappa_2(a\bar{c}) = 1$, $\kappa_3(b\bar{c}) = \kappa_1(bc) = \kappa_1(\bar{b}\,\bar{c}) = 0$, $\kappa_3(bc) = 1$. The local κ_1, κ_2 and κ_3 satisfy the consistency condition (7) as can be checked easily. Assume there would be a global κ satisfying $\kappa(\omega^i) = \kappa_i(\omega^i)$ then $\kappa_2(a\bar{c}) = 1 = \kappa(a\bar{c}) = \min\{\kappa(ab\bar{c}), \kappa(a\bar{b}\bar{c})\}$ and $\kappa_1(ab) = 0 = \kappa(ab) = \min\{\kappa(abc), \kappa(ab\bar{c})\}$. The first equation implies that both $\kappa(ab\bar{c}) \ne 0$ and $\kappa(a\bar{b}\bar{c}) \ne 0$, so by the second we obtain that $\kappa(abc) = 0$. But then $\kappa(bc) = \min\{\kappa(abc), \kappa(\bar{a}bc)\} = 0 \ne 1 = \kappa_3(bc)$, and we see that according to Definition 7, κ can be no global OCF for $\langle(\Sigma_1, \kappa_1), (\Sigma_2, \kappa_2), (\Sigma_3, \kappa_3)\rangle$ in contradiction to the assumption. Hence even if κ_1, κ_2 and κ_3 satisfy the consistency condition, there is no global ranking function.

However, if in addition to (7), we presuppose that the system of subsets of Σ forms a hypertree on Σ, then the existence of a global ranking function can be ensured. This is captured formally with the following theorem.

Theorem 1. *Let $\Sigma_1, \ldots, \Sigma_m$ be a set of covering subsets $\Sigma_i \subseteq \Sigma$ with separators $\mathbb{S}_1, \ldots, \mathbb{S}_m$ for all $1 \le i \le m$ such that the RIP is satisfied, that is, $\langle \Sigma, \{\Sigma_1, \ldots, \Sigma_m\}\rangle$*

is a hypertree according to Definition 6. Let $\kappa_1, \ldots, \kappa_m$ be a set of OCFs on $\Omega_1, \ldots, \Omega_m$, respectively, that satisfy the consistency condition (7). Then the function

$$\kappa(\omega) = \sum_{i=1}^{m} \kappa_i(\Sigma_i(\omega)) - \sum_{i=1}^{m} \kappa_i(\mathbb{S}_i(\omega)) \tag{8}$$

is a global ranking function for the system $\langle(\Sigma_i, \kappa_i)\rangle_{i=1}^{m}$, that is, $\kappa(\omega^i) = \kappa_i(\omega^i)$ for all $\omega^i \in \Omega_i$, for all $1 \le i \le m$.

Since $\Sigma_i = \mathbb{R}_i \cup \mathbb{S}_i$ with residue $\mathbb{R}_i$, Equation. (8) is equivalent to

$$\kappa(\omega) = \sum_{i=1}^{m} \kappa_i(\mathbb{R}_i(\omega)|\mathbb{S}_i(\omega)). \tag{9}$$

Proof. First, we prove that the local ranking functions are marginals of the global one, i.e., $\kappa(\omega^h) = \kappa_h(\omega^h)$ for all $1 \le h \le m$ and all $\omega^h \in \Omega_h$. Let $\omega^h \in \Omega_h$ be arbitrary, but fixed.

With $\omega \models \omega^h$ and $\omega^h = \mathbf{r}_h\mathbf{s}_h$, where $\mathbf{r}_h$ is a configuration of the variables of $\mathbb{R}_h$ and $\mathbf{s}_h$ is a configuration of the variables in $\mathbb{S}_h$, the constraint of the min-term fixes the configuration of $\mathbb{S}_h$ to $\mathbf{s}_h$. $\langle(\Sigma_i, \kappa_i)\rangle_{i=1}^{m}$ is a hypertree on Σ, therefore the RIP guarantees that there are sets Σ_k, $k < h$ with $\mathbb{S}_h \subseteq \Sigma_k$, we choose such a set Σ_k. From the consistency condition (7) we obtain $\kappa_h(\mathbf{s}_h) = \kappa_k(\mathbf{s}_h)$. Additionally, $\Sigma_k = (\Sigma_k \setminus \mathbb{S}_h) \cup \mathbb{S}_h$ and hence for the local ranking function we have $\kappa_k(\Sigma_k(\omega)) - \kappa_h(\mathbf{s}_h) = \kappa_k((\Sigma_k \setminus \mathbb{S}_h)(\omega)|\mathbf{s}_h)$. Here, we set the propositional variables in $(\Sigma_k \setminus \mathbb{S}_h)$, which, in general, is not the residue $\mathbb{R}_k$, to a configuration $\widehat{\mathbf{r}}_k$, such that $\kappa_k(\widehat{\mathbf{r}}_k|\mathbf{s}_h) = 0$, which is equivalent to $\kappa_k(\widehat{\mathbf{r}}_k\mathbf{s}_h) - \kappa_h(\mathbf{s}_h) = 0$. This step fixes $\omega^k = \widehat{\mathbf{r}}_k\mathbf{s}_h$ and therefore the propositional variables in $\mathbb{S}_k$ to a configuration $\mathbf{s}_k$ such that $\omega^k \models \mathbf{s}_k$. We iterate this procedure, obtaining a sequence $(k_1, \ldots, k_p)$ of indices in $\{1, \ldots, m\}$ (with $k_1 = k$ and $k_p = 1$) such that $\mathbb{S}_h \subseteq \Sigma_{k_1}$, $\mathbb{S}_{k_1} \subseteq \Sigma_{k_2}, \ldots \mathbb{S}_{k_{p-1}} \subseteq \Sigma_1$, that is, $\Sigma_{k_1}, \ldots, \Sigma_{k_p}$ are the ancestors $(anc(\Sigma_h))$ of $\Sigma_h = \Sigma_{k_0}$. For each k_l, $l \ge 1$, a configuration ω^{k_l} of the variables in Σ_{k_l} is chosen that $\omega^{k_l} = \widehat{\mathbf{r}}_{k_l}\mathbf{s}_{k_{l-1}}$ with $\widehat{\mathbf{r}}_{k_l}$ referring to the variables in $\Sigma_{k_l} \setminus \mathbb{S}_{k_{l-1}}$ and $\kappa_{k_l}(\widehat{\mathbf{r}}_{k_l}|\mathbf{s}_{k_{l-1}}) = 0$, hence $\kappa_{k_l}(\omega^{k_l}) - \kappa_{k_l}(\mathbf{s}_{k_{l-1}}) = 0$. Since $\mathbb{S}_{k_{l-1}} \subseteq (\Sigma_{k_{l-1}} \cap \Sigma_{k_l})$ and due to (7), we have $\kappa_{k_{l-1}}(\mathbb{S}_{k_{l-1}}) = \kappa_{k_l}(\mathbb{S}_{k_{l-1}})$.

For the remaining Σ_i, from Σ_1 we move downwards through the hypertree (that is, in ascending order of the indices i), until we reach the first $\Sigma_j \notin anc(\Sigma_h)$. By the RIP, $\mathbb{S}_j$ is contained in one of the ancestors of Σ_h or Σ_h itself, and hence the outcomes of these variables have already been set to $\mathbf{s}_j$. We choose a configuration $\mathbf{r}_j$ of $\mathbb{R}_j$ such that $\kappa_j(\mathbf{r}_j|\mathbf{s}_j) = 0$, as above, hence $\kappa_j(\omega^j) - \kappa_j(\mathbf{s}_j) = 0$. We proceed downwards through the tree in this way, meeting all $\Sigma_j \notin anc(\Sigma_h) \cup \{\Sigma_h\}$, and choose configurations of $\omega^j = \mathbf{r}_j\mathbf{s}_j$ of the variables in all these Σ_j such that $\kappa_j(\mathbf{r}_j|\mathbf{s}_j) = 0$. In this way, we obtain a (global) world ω_0 with $\omega_0 \models \omega^h = \mathbf{r}_h\mathbf{s}_h$ for the selected Σ_h, $\omega_0 \models \omega^{k_l} = \widehat{\mathbf{r}}_{k_l}\mathbf{s}_{k_{l-1}}$ for its ancestors, and $\omega_0 \models \omega^j = \mathbf{r}_j\mathbf{s}_j$ for the remaining Σ_j, such that $\kappa_{k_l}(\omega^{k_l}) = \kappa_{k_{l-1}}(\mathbf{s}_{k_{l-1}})$, $1 \le l \le p$, and $\kappa_j(\omega^j) = \kappa_j(\mathbf{s}_j)$ for the remaining Σ_j. We rearrange the sum for $\kappa(\omega^h)$:

$$\kappa(\omega^h) = \min_{\omega \models \omega^h} \Big\{ \kappa_h(\omega^h) - \kappa_h(\mathbf{s}_h)$$

$$+ \sum_{l=1}^{p} \big(\kappa_{k_l}(\Sigma_i(\omega^{k_l})) - \kappa_{k_l}(\mathbf{s}_{k_l}) \big) + \sum_{\underset{\Sigma_i \notin (anc(\Sigma_h) \cup \{\Sigma_h\})}{i}} \big(\kappa_i(\omega^i) - \kappa_i(\mathbf{s}_i) \big) \Big\}$$

$$\leq \kappa_h(\omega^h) + \min_{\omega = \omega_0} \Big\{ \sum_{l=0}^{p-1} \underbrace{\big(\kappa_{k_{l+1}}(\omega^{k_{l+1}}) - \kappa_{k_l}(\mathbf{s}_{k_l}) \big)}_{=0} - \kappa_1(\top)$$

$$+ \sum_{\underset{\Sigma_i \notin (anc(\Sigma_h) \cup \{\Sigma_h\})}{i}} \underbrace{\big(\kappa_i(\omega^i) - \kappa_i(\mathbf{s}_i) \big)}_{=0} \Big\} = \kappa_h(\omega^h),$$

since $\kappa_1(\top) = 0$. Conversely, for each $\omega^h \in \Omega_h$ we have

$$\kappa(\omega^h) = \kappa_h(\omega^h) + \min_{\omega \models \omega^h} \Big\{ \sum_{l=0}^{p} \underbrace{\big(\kappa_{k_{l+1}}(\Sigma_{k_{l+1}}(\omega)) \kappa_{k_l}(\mathbb{S}_{k_l}(\omega)) \big)}_{\geq 0}$$

$$- \underbrace{\kappa_1(\top)}_{=0} + \sum_{\underset{\Sigma_i \notin (anc(\Sigma_h) \cup \{\Sigma_h\})}{i}} \underbrace{\big(\kappa_i(\Sigma_i(\omega)) - \kappa_i(\mathbb{S}_i(\omega)) \big)}_{\geq 0} \Big\}$$

It holds that $\kappa_{k_{l+1}}(\Sigma_{k_{l+1}}(\omega)) - \kappa_{k_l}(\mathbb{S}_{k_l}(\omega)) \geq 0$, since we have $\kappa_{k_l}(\mathbb{S}_{k_l}(\omega)) = \kappa_{k_{l+1}}(\mathbb{S}_{k_{l+1}}(\omega))$ and $\mathbb{S}_{k_l} \subseteq \Sigma_{k_{l+1}}$, hence $\kappa_{k_{l+1}}(\mathbb{S}_{k_l}(\omega)) \leq \kappa_{k_{l+1}}(\Sigma_{k_{l+1}}(\omega))$. Therefore we obtain $\kappa(\omega^h) \geq \kappa_h(\omega^h)$ and altogether, $\kappa(\omega^h) = \kappa_h(\omega^h)$, as required. As each local κ_h is a ranking function, it follows immediately that $\{\omega | \kappa(\omega) = 0\} \neq \varnothing$, i.e., κ is a ranking function. □

We illustrate Theorem 1 with the running example.

Example 6. We extend Example 4, so let $\Sigma_1 = \{H, B\}$ and $\Sigma_2 = \{B, F, S\}$ with $\mathbb{S}_1 = \varnothing, \mathbb{R}_1 = \Sigma_1, \mathbb{S}_2 = \{B\}$ and $\mathbb{R}_2 = \Sigma_2 \setminus \{B\} = \{F, S\}$. Clearly, the RIP holds with $\mathbb{S}_2 \subseteq \Sigma_1$. Let κ_1 and κ_2 be as shown in Table 3. These local ranking functions satisfy the consistency condition (7) on $\Sigma_1 \cap \Sigma_2 = \{B\}$: it is $\kappa_1(b) = 0 = \kappa_2(b)$ and $\kappa_1(\overline{b}) = 1 = \kappa_2(\overline{b})$. Table 4 illustrates the calculation of the global OCF κ according to Equation (8), which coincides with the one from Table 1. There we verify that κ is an OCF with $\kappa(\overline{h}bfs) = 0$, it is easily checked that κ coincides with κ_1 and κ_2.

Theorem 1 now ensures that the system $\langle \Sigma_i, \kappa_i \rangle_{i=1}^{m}$ forms an OCF-LEG network under the given preconditions.

Corollary 1. *Let* $\langle \Sigma, \langle \Sigma_i, \kappa_i \rangle_{i=1}^{m} \rangle$ *be a covering hypertree on an alphabet Σ with local OCFs κ_i, κ_j that satisfy the consistency condition (7) for all pairs $1 \leq i, j \leq m$. Then $\langle \Sigma_i, \kappa_i \rangle_{i=1}^{m}$ is an OCF-LEG network with a global ranking function κ according to Form. (8). Moreover, local inferences coincide with global ones, i.e., if ϕ, ψ are formulas all of which atoms are contained in the same Σ_i, then $\kappa \models (\psi | \phi)$ iff $\kappa_i \models (\psi | \phi)$.*

Furthermore, conditional independencies between parent and child subsets in the hypertree (given the connecting separator) can be observed which can be proved with techniques similar to those which are used for Theorem 1.

Table 3. Local OCFs for the car-start example

ω^1	$b\,h$	$b\,\overline{h}$	$\overline{b}\,h$	$\overline{b}\,\overline{h}$
$\kappa_1(\omega^1)$	2	0	1	1

ω^2	bfs	$bf\overline{s}$	$b\overline{f}s$	$b\overline{f}\,\overline{s}$	$\overline{b}fs$	$\overline{b}f\overline{s}$	$\overline{b}\,\overline{f}s$	$\overline{b}\,\overline{f}\,\overline{s}$
$\kappa_2(\omega^2)$	0	1	2	1	2	1	2	1

Table 4. Calculating a global OCF κ for Example 6

ω	$h\,bfs$	$h\,bf\overline{s}$	$h\,b\overline{f}s$	$h\,b\overline{f}\,\overline{s}$	$h\,\overline{b}fs$	$h\,\overline{b}f\overline{s}$	$h\,\overline{b}\,\overline{f}s$	$h\,\overline{b}\,\overline{f}\,\overline{s}$
$\kappa_1(\Sigma_1(\omega))$	2	2	2	2	1	1	1	1
$+\,\kappa_2(\Sigma_2(\omega))$	0	1	2	1	2	1	2	1
$-\,\kappa_2(\mathbb{S}_2(\omega))$	0	0	0	0	1	1	1	1
$=\quad\kappa(\omega)$	2	3	4	3	2	1	2	1

ω	$\overline{h}\,bfs$	$\overline{h}\,bf\overline{s}$	$\overline{h}\,b\overline{f}s$	$\overline{h}\,b\overline{f}\,\overline{s}$	$\overline{h}\,\overline{b}fs$	$\overline{h}\,\overline{b}f\overline{s}$	$\overline{h}\,\overline{b}\,\overline{f}s$	$\overline{h}\,\overline{b}\,\overline{f}\,\overline{s}$
$\kappa_1(\Sigma_1(\omega))$	0	0	0	0	1	1	1	1
$+\,\kappa_2(\Sigma_2(\omega))$	0	1	2	1	2	1	2	1
$-\,\kappa_2(\mathbb{S}_2(\omega))$	0	0	0	0	1	1	1	1
$=\quad\kappa(\omega)$	0	1	2	1	2	1	2	1

Proposition 2. *Let $\langle \Sigma_i, \kappa_i \rangle_{i=1}^m$ be an OCF-LEG network with a global ranking function according to formula (8). Let Σ_i be a child of Σ_j in the hypertree with appertaining separator $\mathbb{S}_i$ as defined in Definition 7. Then the sets $\Sigma_i \setminus \mathbb{S}_i$ and $\Sigma_j \setminus \mathbb{S}_i$ are conditionally independent given the separator $\mathbb{S}_i$, formally $(\Sigma_i \setminus \mathbb{S}_i) \perp\!\!\!\perp_\kappa (\Sigma_j \setminus \mathbb{S}_i) \mid \mathbb{S}_i$.*

6 Inductively Generating an OCF-LEG Network

In the previous section we showed that a global ranking function can be built up from local ranking functions on a hypertree structure. However, in application scenarios we assume it to be more likely that a user of a reasoning system may be able to specify general dependencies between events than that he specifies a hypertree of events with appropriate ranking functions. Therefore in this section we show how to use a given knowledge base for generating an OCF-LEG network by making use of ideas from [12,13].

Let $\Delta = \{(\psi_1|\phi_1), \dots, (\psi_n|\phi_n)\} \subseteq (\mathcal{L} \mid \mathcal{L})$ be a knowledge base. As a first step of the generation process, we set up $\mathfrak{S} = \{\Sigma', \Sigma'', \dots\}$ such that $\Sigma' = \{V \mid V \models (\psi|\phi)\}$ for each $(\psi|\phi) \in \Delta$, that is, every set Σ' is associated with a conditional $(\phi|\psi)$ by including all literals in the premise or conclusion of the conditional. Using the techniques from [12,13], we obtain a covering hypertree $\langle \Sigma, \mathcal{C} \rangle$ of $\mathfrak{S}$ such that $\mathcal{C} = \{\mathbb{C}_1, \dots, \mathbb{C}_m\}$ satisfies the RIP. We use $\mathcal{C}$ to cover Δ by subsets $\Delta_i \subseteq \Delta$ for every $\mathbb{C}_i \in \mathcal{C}$ such that for all $(\psi|\phi) \in \Delta$ we have $(\psi|\phi) \in \Delta_i$ if and only if $V \in \mathbb{C}_i$ for all $V \models \phi\psi$. Note that

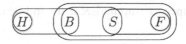

Fig. 1. Hypergraph of the car-start example (Ex. 7)

by this a conditional may be an element of several subsets. We illustrate this procedure by the introductory example:

Example 7. We use the running example (Example 1) to show the generation of a hypertree from a knowledge base. The variable set is $\Sigma = \{B, F, H, S\}$, together with the knowledge base we obtain the covering subsets $\{B, S\}, \{S, F\}, \{B, F, S\}, \{H\}, \{F\}$ and $\{B, H\}$ which is visualised by the hypergraph in Figure 1. Via the techniques of junction graph and cut-graph we obtain the cliques $\mathbb{C}_1 = \{H, B\}$ and $\mathbb{C}_2 = \{B, F, S\}$. $\mathbb{S}_2 = \mathbb{C}_1 \cap \mathbb{C}_2 = \{B\} \subseteq \mathbb{C}_1$, so the RIP is satisfied and so $\langle \Sigma, \{\mathbb{C}_1, \mathbb{C}_2\} \rangle$ is a hypertree. The knowledge base is divided into $\Delta_1 = \{(\overline{h}|\top), (\overline{b}|h), (b|\overline{h})\}$ because $H \in \mathbb{C}_1$ and $\{H, B\} \subseteq \mathbb{C}_1$ and $\Delta_2 = \{(s|b), (\overline{s}|\overline{b}), (s|f), (\overline{s}|\overline{f}), (\overline{s}|b\overline{f}), (\overline{s}|\overline{b}f), (f|\top)\}$, because $\{S, B\} \subseteq \mathbb{C}_2, \{S, F\} \subseteq \mathbb{C}_2$ and $\{B, F, S\} \subseteq \mathbb{C}_2$.

Note that this approach differs from the graph-generation approach of [6] in two major points: On the one hand, the approach in [6] generates a directed acyclic graph from the knowledge base, whereas here a (at this point, undirected) hypergraph is created[1]. On the other, the approach of [6] is restricted to a special subset of the language of conditionals, whereas this approach can be applied to sets of conditionals which are not restricted with respect to their logical language.

Now we generate the local ranking functions by means of inductive reasoning, that is, we instantiate an inductive reasoning approach with the sets Δ_i and the local alphabet Σ_i for each $1 \leq i \leq m$. We choose c-representations here, because they provide a versatile schema of Δ_i-models allowing for high-quality inference. We have to ensure that the system $\langle (\Sigma_i, \kappa_i) \rangle_{i=1}^m$ satisfies the consistency condition (7). The global ranking function is obtained from $\langle (\Sigma_i, \kappa_i) \rangle_{i=1}^m$ by Equation (8) and according to Theorem 1, $\langle (\Sigma_i, \kappa_i) \rangle_{i=1}^m$ is an OCF-LEG network.

Example 8. We continue Example 7 to illustrate this step in the OCF-LEG network generation. Here Δ is divided into the two subsets $\Delta_1 = \{(\overline{h}|\top), (\overline{b}|h), (b|\overline{h})\}$ and $\Delta_2 = \{(s|b), (\overline{s}|\overline{b}), (s|f), (\overline{s}|\overline{f}), (\overline{s}|b\overline{f}), (\overline{s}|\overline{b}f), (f|\top)\}$. We assume the conditionals in Δ_1 and Δ_2 to be enumerated in the presented ordering. For computing local minimal c-representations, let $\kappa_{1,i}^-$ denote the falsification impacts of Δ_1 and $\kappa_{2,i}^-$ denote the falsification impacts of Δ_2. According to Definition 4 and especially the system of inequations (3) we obtain $\kappa_{1,1}^- = 1, \kappa_{1,2}^- = 1$ and $\kappa_{1,3}^- = 1$ as falsification factors for the minimal c-representation of Δ_1 and $\kappa_{2,1}^- = 0, \kappa_{2,2}^- = 0, \kappa_{2,3}^- = 1, \kappa_{2,4}^- = 1, \kappa_{2,5}^- = 0, \kappa_{2,6}^- = 2$ and $\kappa_{2,7}^- = 1$ as falsification factors for the minimal c-representation of Δ_2. From these values, with Equation (2) we obtain the local OCFs from Example 6. The consistency condition (7) is satisfied, because $\Sigma_1 \cap \Sigma_2 = \{B\}$ and we have $\kappa_1(b) = 0 = \kappa_2(b)$ and $\kappa_1(\overline{b}) = 1 = \kappa_2(\overline{b})$. These c-representations are combined to the global OCF κ by Equation (8) according to Theorem 1 in Table 4.

---

[1] Note that OCF-networks [6,3,5] make use of the graph generation approach of [6].

The main results of the paper are summarised in the following theorem which follows directly from Theorem 1.

Theorem 2. *Let* $\Delta = \{(\psi_1|\phi_1), \ldots, (\psi_n|\phi_n)\} \subseteq (\mathfrak{L} \mid \mathfrak{L})$ *be a conditional knowledge base. Let* $\Delta_1, \ldots, \Delta_m$ *be a covering system of subsets of* Δ *which are based on a hypertree* $\langle \Sigma, \{\mathbb{C}_1, \ldots, \mathbb{C}_m\} \rangle$ *which is obtained by the procedure described above. Let* $\kappa_1, \ldots, \kappa_m$ *be ranking functions* $\kappa_i \models \Delta_i$ *resulting from an inductive reasoning approach on* Δ_i *for all* $1 \leq i \leq m$ *that satisfy the consistency condition (7). Let* κ *be the global ranking function obtained by Equation (8) on the system* $\langle (\Sigma_i, \kappa_i) \rangle_{i=1}^m$. *Then the global ranking function is admissible with respect to* Δ, *that is,* $\kappa \models \Delta$.

In contrast to OCF-networks, the procedure for generating OCF-LEG networks accepts arbitrary conditionals $(\psi|\phi) \in (\mathfrak{L}|\mathfrak{L})$ and thereby overcomes the language restriction of OCF-networks. Also, Theorem 2 shows that the generated global ranking function is admissible to the generating knowledge base, so this approach outperforms OCF-networks with respect to basic requirements of inductive reasoning. Note that we used the inductive reasoning approach c-representations as a proof of concept, only. The OCF-LEG formalism is independent from any inductive method, so also System Z [14] can be used. The time complexity of inductive semantical approaches depends on the size of the knowledge base and the size of the underlying propositional alphabet. The time complexity of System Z is $\mathcal{O}(|\Delta|^2)$ SAT instances [6]. Switching from a global to local views reduces the number of SAT instances from the global $|\Delta|$ to the sum of cardinalities of the local knowledge bases. Since we also switch from the global to (possibly quite smaller) local alphabets, the time-complexity of the SAT instances is reduced significantly. Therefore we expect an overall notably reduced computation time for the inductive generation of an OCF that is admissible with respect to Δ.

7   Conclusion

In this paper we introduced OCF-LEG networks as a qualitative variant of LEG networks. We showed that a hypertree with local ranking functions is an OCF-LEG network if the local OCFs satisfy the defined consistency condition, so that a global ranking function exists for which the local OCFs are marginals. Recalling the hypertree generation algorithm and combining it with c-representations as an approach for inductive reasoning we were able to present an algorithm which accepts any consistent knowledge base as input without any restrictions to the language of conditionals, as it is the case for OCF-networks. We proved that a global ranking function of an OCF-LEG network is always admissible to the generating knowledge base. As part of our ongoing work we plan to implement OCF-LEG networks, investigate ways to ensure the consistency condition to be satisfied and extend the OCF-LEG approach to weighted conditionals.

Acknowledgment. We thank the anonymous referees for their valuable hints that helped us improving the paper. This work was supported by Grant KI 1413/5 − 1 to Gabriele Kern-Isberner from the Deutsche Forschungsgemeinschaft (DFG) as part of the priority program "New Frameworks of Rationality" (SPP 1516). Christian Eichhorn is supported by this grant.

References

1. Beierle, C., Hermsen, R., Kern-Isberner, G.: Observations on the Minimality of Ranking Functions for Qualitative Conditional Knowledge Bases and their Computation. In: Proceedings of the 27th International FLAIRS Conference, FLAIRS'27 (2014)
2. Benferhat, S., Dubois, D., Garcia, L., Prade, H.: On the transformation between possibilistic logic bases and possibilistic causal networks. International Journal of Approximate Reasoning 9(2), 135–173 (2002)
3. Benferhat, S., Tabia, K.: Belief Change in OCF-Based Networks in Presence of Sequences of Observations and Interventions: Application to Alert Correlation. In: Zhang, B.-T., Orgun, M.A. (eds.) PRICAI 2010. LNCS, vol. 6230, pp. 14–26. Springer, Heidelberg (2010)
4. de Finetti, B.: Theory of Probability, vol. 1, 2. John Wiley and Sons, New York (1974)
5. Eichhorn, C., Kern-Isberner, G.: Using inductive reasoning for completing OCF-networks (2013) (submitted)
6. Goldszmidt, M., Pearl, J.: Qualitative probabilities for default reasoning, belief revision, and causal modeling. Artificial Intelligence 84(1-2), 57–112 (1996)
7. Kern-Isberner, G.: Conditionals in Nonmonotonic Reasoning and Belief Revision. LNCS (LNAI), vol. 2087. Springer, Heidelberg (2001)
8. Kern-Isberner, G., Eichhorn, C.: Intensional combination of rankings for OCF-networks. In: Boonthum-Denecke, C., Youngblood, M. (eds.) Proceedings of the 26th International FLAIRS Conference FLAIRS-2013, pp. 615–620. AAAI Press (2013)
9. Kern-Isberner, G., Eichhorn, C.: Structural inference from conditional knowledge bases. In: Unterhuber, M., Schurz, G. (eds.) Studia Logica Special Issue Logic and Probability: Reasoning in Uncertain Environments, vol. 102 (4), Springer Science+Business Media, Dordrecht (2014)
10. Lemmer, J.F.: Efficient minimum information updating for bayesian inferencing in expert systems. In: Proc. of the National Conference on Artificial Intelligence, AAAI 1982 (1982)
11. Makinson, D.: General patterns in nonmonotonic reasoning. In: Gabbay, D.M., Hogger, C.J., Robinson, J.A. (eds.) Handbook of Logic in Artificial Intelligence and Logic Programming, vol. 3, pp. 35–110. Oxford University Press, Inc., New York (1994)
12. Meyer, C.-H.: Korrektes Schließen bei unvollständiger Information: Anwendung des Prinzips der maximalen Entropie in einem probabilistischen Expertensystem. 41. Peter Lang Publishing, Inc. (1998)
13. Pearl, J.: Probabilistic reasoning in intelligent systems – networks of plausible inference. Morgan Kaufmann (1989)
14. Pearl, J.: System Z: A natural ordering of defaults with tractable applications to nonmonotonic reasoning. In: Proceedings of the 3rd Conference on Theoretical Aspects of Reasoning About Knowledge, TARK 1990, pp. 121–135. Morgan Kaufmann Publishers Inc., San Francisco (1990)
15. Spohn, W.: The Laws of Belief: Ranking Theory and Its Philosophical Applications. Oxford University Press (2012)

Logics for Approximating Implication Problems of Saturated Conditional Independence

Henning Koehler[1] and Sebastian Link[2]

[1] School of Engineering & Advanced Technology, Massey University, New Zealand
[2] Department of Computer Science, University of Auckland, New Zealand
h.koehler@massey.ac.nz, s.link@auckland.ac.nz

Abstract. Random variables are declared complete whenever they must not admit missing data. Intuitively, the larger the set of complete random variables the closer the implication of saturated conditional independence statements is approximated. Two different notions of implication are studied. In the classical notion, a statement is implied jointly by a set of statements, the fixed set of random variables and its subset of complete random variables. For the notion of pure implication the set of random variables is left undetermined. A first axiomatization for the classical notion is established that distinguishes purely implied from classically implied statements. Axiomatic, algorithmic and logical characterizations of pure implication are established. The latter appeal to applications in which the existence of random variables is uncertain, for example, when statements are integrated from different sources, when random variables are unknown or when they shall remain hidden.

Keywords: Approximation, Conditional Independence, Implication, Missing Data, Unknown Random Variable, $\mathcal{S}$-3 Logics.

1 Introduction

The concept of conditional independence (CI) is important for capturing structural aspects of probability distributions, for dealing with knowledge and uncertainty in artificial intelligence, and for learning and reasoning in intelligent systems [5,14,24]. Application areas include natural language processing, speech processing, computer vision, robotics, computational biology, and error-control coding [10,14,23]. Central to these applications is the implication problem, which is to decide for an arbitrary set V of random variables, and an arbitrary set $\Sigma \cup \{\varphi\}$ of CI statements over V, whether every probability model that satisfies every element in Σ also satisfies φ. Indeed, non-implied CI statements represent new opportunities to construct complex probability models with polynomially many parameters and to efficiently organize distributed probability computations [9]. An algorithm for deciding the implication problem can also test the consistency of independence and dependence statements collected from different sources; which is particularly important as these statements often introduce non-linear constraints resulting in unfeasible CSP instances [9,23]. While the

E. Fermé and J. Leite (Eds.): JELIA 2014, LNAI 8761, pp. 224–238, 2014.

decidability of the implication problem for CI statements relative to discrete probability measures remains open, it is not axiomatizable by a finite set of Horn rules [30] and already *coNP*-complete for stable CI statements [22]. The important subclass of saturated CI (SCI) statements, in which all given random variables occur, form a foundation for Markov networks [14]. In fact, graph separation and SCI statements enjoy the same axioms [9], and their implication problem is decidable in almost linear time [8]. The results have been carried over to the presence of missing data [20]. Here, conditional independence is not judged on conditions that carry missing data. The findings complement the recognized need to reveal missing data and to explain where they come from, e.g. [4,6,7,15,21,25,28,32]. In a simple health example, *m(etastatic cancer)* causes a *b(rain tumor)* resulting in a *c(oma)* or severe *h(eadaches)*. The independence between *ch* and *m*, given *b*, is formalized as the SCI statement $I(ch, m|b)$ over $V = \{b, c, h, m\}$. With missing data present, $I(ch, m|b)$ and $I(h, c|bm)$ together do not V-imply $I(cm, h|b)$ as the probability model M:

Probability model M					Probability model M'					
m	b	h	c	P	m	b	h	c	e	P
−	true	true	true	0.5	true	true	true	−	true	0.5
−	true	false	false	0.5	truc	true	false	−	false	0.5

Here, M satisfies $I(h, c|bm)$ as the condition bm involves missing data, represented by −. Random variables can be declared *complete* in which case − is not part of their domain [20]. The ability to specify a set $C \subseteq V$ of complete random variables provides us with a mechanism to not only control the occurrences of missing data, but also to approximate the classical implication of SCI statements, where no missing data occurs [20]. For example, if $m \in C$, then $I(ch, m|b)$ and $I(h, c|bm)$ together do (V, C)-imply $I(cm, h|b)$.

Most research on the implication problem of SCI statements assumes that the underlying set V of random variables is fixed. However, this assumption is impractical in an "open" world. For examples, not knowing all random variables should not prevent us from declaring some independence statements; and even if we know all random variables, we may not want to disclose all of them; or when independence statements are integrated from different sources. Instead, we may want to state that given b, m is independent from the set of remaining random variables, no matter what they are. This statement could be written as $I(m|b)$. The intriguing point is the difference between $I(h|b)$ and $I(cm|b)$ when V is left undetermined. For $C = \{m\}$, $I(cm|b)$ is C-implied by $I(m|b)$ and $I(c|bm)$, while $I(h|b)$ is not. In fact, the model M' above satisfies $I(m|b)$ and $I(c|bm)$, but does not satisfy $I(m|b)$. Note that $I(m|b)$ and $I(c|bm)$ together (V, C)-imply $I(h|b)$ for the fixed set $V = \{b, c, h, m\}$, but $I(m|b)$ and $I(c|bm)$ together do not C-imply $I(h|b)$ when the set of random variables is left undetermined.

The example illustrates the need to distinguish between classical and pure implication. The pure C-implication problem is to decide for every given finite set $\Sigma \cup \{\varphi\}$ of SCI statements and every given finite set C of complete random variables, whether every probability model π that i) involves at least the random variables in $\Sigma \cup \{\varphi\}$ and C, and ii) satisfies Σ, also satisfies φ.

Contribution. In Section 2 we show that the only existing axiomatization $\mathfrak{Z}_V$ for (V, C)-implication cannot distinguish between purely C-implied and (V, C)-implied SCI statements. That is, there are purely C-implied statements for which every inference by $\mathfrak{Z}_V$ applies the V-symmetry rule; giving incorrectly the impression that the pure C-implication of an SCI statement depends on V. In Section 3 we establish a finite axiomatization $\mathfrak{C}_V$ such that every purely C-implied statement can be inferred without the V-symmetry rule; and every (V, C)-implied statement can be inferred with only a single application of the V-symmetry rule, which occurs in the last step of the inference. In Section 4 we establish a finite axiomatization $\mathfrak{C}$ for pure C-implication. As $\mathfrak{C}$ results from $\mathfrak{C}_V$ by removal of the symmetry rule, the symmetry rule is only necessary to infer SCI statements that are (V, C)- but not C-implied. In Section 5, pure C-implication is characterized by (V, C)-implication where V involves random variables that do not occur in any of the given statements. This result is exploited in Section 6 to characterize pure C-implication logically by a propositional fragment in Cadoli and Schaerf's S-3 logics, and by multivalued database dependencies for missing data and by an almost linear-time algorithm in Section 7. Section 8 illustrates how our contribution complements related work. We conclude in Section 9.

2 Implication in Fixed Sets of Random Variables

The semantics of CI statements in the presence of missing data is summarized [20]. A definition is then given that embodies the ability of an axiomatization to separate (V, C)-implied SCI statements from purely C-implied ones. The existing axiomatization $\mathfrak{Z}_V$ for (V, C)-implication [20] does not have this ability.

We denote by $\mathfrak{V}$ a countably infinite set of distinct symbols $\{v_1, v_2, \ldots\}$ of *random variables*. A *domain mapping* is a mapping that associates a set, $dom(v_i)$, with each random variable v_i of a finite set $V \subseteq \mathfrak{V}$. This set is called the *domain* of v_i and each of its elements is a *data value* of v_i. We assume that each domain $dom(v_i)$ contains the element $-$, which we call the *marker*. Although we use the element $-$ like any other data value, we prefer to think of $-$ as a marker, denoting that no information is currently available about the data value of v_i. The interpretation of this marker as no information means that a data value does either not exist (known as a structural zero in statistics, and the null marker inapplicable in databases), or a data value exists but is currently unknown (known as a sampling zero in statistics, and the null marker applicable in databases). The disadvantage of using this interpretation is a loss in knowledge when representing data values known to not exist, or known to exist but currently unknown. One advantage of this interpretation is its simplicity. As another advantage one can represent missing data values, even if it is unknown whether they do not exist, or exist but are currently unknown. Strictly speaking, we shall call such random variables *incomplete* as their data values may be missing. *Complete random variables* were introduced in [20] to gain control over the occurrences of missing data values. If a random variable $v \in V$ is declared to be complete, then $- \notin dom(v)$. For a given V we use C to denote the set of random variables in V that are complete. Complete random variables were shown to provide an effective means to not just control the degree of uncertainty, but also to soundly approximate classical reasoning about saturated conditional probabilistic independence [20]. For $X = \{v_1, \ldots, v_k\} \subseteq V$ we say that $\mathbf{a}$ is an assignment of X, if $\mathbf{a} \in dom(v_1) \times \cdots \times dom(v_k)$. For an assignment $\mathbf{a}$ of X we write $\mathbf{a}(y)$ for the projection of $\mathbf{a}$ onto $Y \subseteq X$. We say that $\mathbf{a} = (\mathbf{a}_1, \ldots, \mathbf{a}_k)$ is X-complete, if $\mathbf{a}_i \neq -$ for all $i = 1, \ldots, k$.

A *probability model* over (V, C) is a pair (dom, P) where dom is a domain mapping that maps each $v \in V$ to a finite domain $dom(v)$, and $P : \prod_{v \in V} dom(v) \rightarrow [0, 1]$ is a probability distribution having the Cartesian product of these domains as its sample space. Note that $- \notin dom(v)$ whenever $v \in C$.

The expression $I(Y, Z|X)$ where X, Y and Z are disjoint subsets of V is called a *conditional independence* (CI) *statement* over (V, C). The set X is called the *condition* of $I(Y, Z|X)$. If $XYZ = V$, we call $I(Y, Z|X)$ a *saturated* CI (SCI) statement. Let (dom, P) be a probability model over (V, C). A CI statement $I(Y, Z|X)$ is said to *hold for* (dom, P) if for every complete assignment $\mathbf{x}$ of X, and for every assignment $\mathbf{y}, \mathbf{z}$ of Y and Z, respectively,

$$P(\mathbf{x}, \mathbf{y}, \mathbf{z}) \cdot P(\mathbf{x}) = P(\mathbf{x}, \mathbf{y}) \cdot P(\mathbf{x}, \mathbf{z}). \tag{1}$$

Equivalently, (dom, P) is said to *satisfy* $I(Y, Z|X)$ [20]. The satisfaction of $I(Y, Z|X)$ requires Equation 1 to hold for *complete* assignments $\mathbf{x}$ of X only. The reason is that the independence between $\mathbf{y}$ and $\mathbf{z}$ is conditional on $\mathbf{x}$. Indeed, in case there is *no information* about $\mathbf{x}$, then there should not be any requirement on the independence between $\mathbf{y}$ and $\mathbf{z}$.

The interactions of SCI statements have been formalized by the following notion of semantic implication. Let $\Sigma \cup \{\varphi\}$ be a set of SCI statements over (V, C). We say that Σ (V, C)-*implies* φ, denoted by $\Sigma \models_{(V,C)} \varphi$, if every probability model over (V, C) that satisfies every SCI statement $\sigma \in \Sigma$ also satisfies φ. The (V, C)-*implication problem* is the following problem.

PROBLEM:	(V, C)-implication problem
INPUT:	Set V of random variables
	Set $C \subseteq V$ of complete random variables
	Set $\Sigma \cup \{\varphi\}$ of SCI statements over V
OUTPUT:	Yes, if $\Sigma \models_{(V,C)} \varphi$; No, otherwise

For Σ we let $\Sigma^*_{(V,C)} = \{\varphi \mid \Sigma \models_{(V,C)} \varphi\}$ be the *semantic closure* of Σ, i.e., the set of all SCI statements (V, C)-implied by Σ. In order to determine the (V, C)-implied SCI statements we use a syntactic approach by applying inference rules. These inference rules have the form $\dfrac{\text{premises}}{\text{conclusion}}$ condition and inference rules without any premises are called *axioms*. An inference rule is called (V, C)-*sound*, if the premises of the rule (V, C)-imply the conclusion of the rule whenever the condition is satisfied. We let $\Sigma \vdash_{\mathfrak{R}} \varphi$ denote the *inference* of φ from Σ by the set $\mathfrak{R}$ of inference rules. That is, there is some sequence $\gamma = [\sigma_1, \ldots, \sigma_n]$ of SCI statements such that $\sigma_n = \varphi$ and every σ_i is an element of Σ or results from

Table 1. Axiomatization $3 = \{\mathcal{T}', \mathcal{S}', \mathcal{R}', \mathcal{W}'\}$ of (V, C)-implication

$\dfrac{}{I(\emptyset, V - X \mid X)}$ (saturated trivial independence, $\mathcal{T}'$)	$\dfrac{I(Y, Z \mid X)}{I(Z, Y \mid X)}$ (symmetry, $\mathcal{S}'$)
$\dfrac{I(YRS, ZT \mid X) \qquad I(RZ, ST \mid XY)}{I(Z, RSTY \mid X)}\, Y \subseteq C$ (restricted weak contraction, $\mathcal{R}'$)	$\dfrac{I(Y, ZT \mid X)}{I(Y, Z \mid XT)}$ (weak union, $\mathcal{W}'$)

Table 2. Axiomatization $3_V = \{\mathcal{T}, \mathcal{S}_V, \mathcal{R}, \mathcal{W}\}$ of (V, C)-implication

$\dfrac{}{I(\emptyset \mid X)}$ (saturated trivial independence, $\mathcal{T}$)	$\dfrac{I(Y \mid X)}{I(V - XY \mid X)}$ (V-symmetry, $\mathcal{S}_V$)
$\dfrac{I(YRS \mid X) \quad I(RZ \mid XY)}{I(Z - S \mid X)}\, Y \subseteq C$ (restricted weak contraction, $\mathcal{R}$)	$\dfrac{I(Y \mid X)}{I(Y - T \mid XT)}$ (weak union, $\mathcal{W}$)

an application of an inference rule in $\mathfrak{R}$ to some elements in $\{\sigma_1, \ldots, \sigma_{i-1}\}$. For Σ, let $\Sigma_{\mathfrak{R}}^+ = \{\varphi \mid \Sigma \vdash_{\mathfrak{R}} \varphi\}$ be its *syntactic closure* under inferences by $\mathfrak{R}$. A set $\mathfrak{R}$ of inference rules is said to be (V, C)-*sound* $((V, C)$-*complete*) for the (V, C)-implication of SCI statements, if for every V, every $C \subseteq V$, and for every set Σ of SCI statements over (V, C), we have $\Sigma_{\mathfrak{R}}^+ \subseteq \Sigma_{(V,C)}^*$ ($\Sigma_{(V,C)}^* \subseteq \Sigma_{\mathfrak{R}}^+$). The (finite) set $\mathfrak{R}$ is said to be a (finite) *axiomatization* for the (V, C)-implication of SCI statements if $\mathfrak{R}$ is both (V, C)-sound and (V, C)-complete.

Table 1 contains the set $3 = \{\mathcal{T}', \mathcal{S}', \mathcal{R}', \mathcal{W}'\}$ of inference rules that form a finite axiomatization for the (V, C)-implication of SCI statements [20].

Motivated by the introductory remarks we now write $I(Y|X)$ instead of writing $I(Y, V - XY|X)$ for an SCI statement over (V, C). It is first shown that the system $3_V = \{\mathcal{T}, \mathcal{S}, \mathcal{R}, \mathcal{W}\}$ from Table 2 forms a finite axiomatization for the (V, C)-implication of such SCI statements.

Proposition 1. 3_V *is a finite axiomatization for the (V, C)-implication of SCI statements.*

Proof. Let $V \subseteq \mathfrak{V}$ be a finite set of random variables and $C \subseteq V$. Let $\Sigma = \{I(Y_1|X_1), \ldots, I(Y_n|X_n)\}$ and $\varphi = I(Y|X)$ be a (set of) SCI statement(s) over (V, C). We can show by an induction over the inference length that $\Sigma \vdash_{3_V} \varphi$ if and only if $\Sigma' = \{I(Y_1, V - X_1Y_1|X_1), \ldots, I(Y_n, V - X_nY_n|X_n)\} \vdash_3 I(Y, V - XY|X)$. Hence, the (V, C)-soundness $((V, C)$-completeness) of 3_V follows from the (V, C)-soundness $((V, C)$-completeness) of 3 [20].

Example 1. Consider $\Sigma = \{I(m|b), I(c|bm)\}$, $\varphi = I(h|b)$ and $\varphi' = I(cm|b)$ as a (set of) SCI statement(s) over $(V = \{b, c, h, m\}, C = \{m\})$. Then $\Sigma \models_{(V,C)} \varphi$ and $\Sigma \models_{(V,C)} \varphi'$ as we can show, for example, by the following inference:

$$
\begin{array}{c}
 I(c|bm) \\
\hline
\mathcal{R}: \quad \dfrac{I(m|b) \quad \dfrac{\mathcal{S}_V: \; I(s|bm)}{I(h|b)}}{\mathcal{S}_V: \quad \quad I(cm|b)}\, m \in C \quad.
\end{array}
$$

However, since the V-symmetry rule is applied in each inference it is not clear whether φ or φ' is C-implied by Σ alone, that is, whether it is true that for all V', that include at least b, c, h, m, it holds that $\Sigma \models_{(V',C)} \varphi$ and $\Sigma \models_{(V',C)} \varphi'$, respectively. In fact, the introduction shows that Σ does not C-imply φ.

The last example motivates the following ability of an inference system: First infer all purely C-implied statements without any application of the symmetry rule, and subsequently, apply the V-symmetry rule once to some of these statements to infer all (V, C)-implied statements that do depend on V.

Definition 1. *Let $\mathfrak{S}_V$ denote a set of inference rules that is (V, C)-sound for the (V, C)-implication of SCI statements, and in which the V-symmetry rule $\mathcal{S}_V$ is the only inference rule dependent on V. We say that $\mathfrak{S}_V$ is conscious of pure C-implication, if for every V, every $C \subseteq V$, and every set $\Sigma \cup \{\varphi\}$ of SCI statements over (V, C) such that φ is (V, C)-implied by Σ there is some inference of φ from Σ by $\mathfrak{S}_V$ such that the V-symmetry rule $\mathcal{S}_V$ is applied at most once, and, if it is applied, then it is applied in the last step of the inference only.*

This raises the question if $\mathfrak{Z}_V$ is conscious of pure C-implication.

Theorem 1. $\mathfrak{Z}_V$ *is not conscious of pure C-implication.*

Proof. Let $V = \{b, c, h, m\}$, $C = \{m\}$ and $\Sigma = \{I(m|b), I(c|bm)\}$. One can show that $I(h|b) \notin \Sigma^+_{\{\mathcal{T},\mathcal{W},\mathcal{R}\}}$. Moreover, for all Y such that $h \in Y$, $I(Y|b) \notin \Sigma^+_{\{\mathcal{T},\mathcal{W},\mathcal{R}\}}$. However, $I(h|b) \in \Sigma^+_{\mathfrak{Z}_V}$ as shown in Example 1. Consequently, in any inference of $I(h|b)$ from Σ by $\mathfrak{Z}_V$ the V-symmetry rule $\mathcal{S}_V$ must be applied at least once, but is not just applied in the last step as $h \in V - \{b, c, m\}$.

As a consequence of Theorem 1 it is natural to ask whether there is any axiomatization that is conscious of pure C-implication.

3   Gaining Consciousness

Theorem 1 has shown that axiomatizations are, in general, not conscious of pure C-implication. We will now establish a finite conscious axiomatization for the (V, C)-implication of SCI statements. For this purpose, we consider two new (V, C)-sound inference rules:

$$
\dfrac{I(S\mid X) \quad I(RZ\mid XY)}{I(S \cap Z \mid X)}\ \substack{Y \subseteq C, \\ (RY) \cap S = \emptyset} \qquad\qquad \dfrac{I(YRS\mid X) \quad I(RZ\mid XY)}{I(RSYZ\mid X)}\ Y \subseteq C
$$

(restricted intersecting contraction, $\mathcal{A}$)   (restricted additive contraction, $\mathcal{I}$)

Theorem 2. *Let Σ be a set of SCI statements over V. For every inference γ from Σ by the system $\mathfrak{Z}_V = \{\mathcal{T}, \mathcal{S}_V, \mathcal{R}, \mathcal{W}\}$ there is an inference ξ from Σ by the system $\mathfrak{C}_V = \{\mathcal{T}, \mathcal{S}_V, \mathcal{R}, \mathcal{W}, \mathcal{A}, \mathcal{I}\}$ such that*
1. γ and ξ infer the same SCI statement,
2. $\mathcal{S}_V$ is applied at most once in ξ,
3. if $\mathcal{S}_V$ is applied in ξ, then as the last rule.

Example 2. Recall Example 1 where $V = \{b, c, h, m\}$, $C = \{m\}$, $\Sigma = \{I(m|b), I(c|bm)\}$, $\varphi = I(h|b)$ and $\varphi' = I(cm|b)$ While the inference of φ from Σ using $\mathfrak{Z}_V$ in Example 1 showed that $\Sigma \models_{(V,C)} \varphi$ and $\Sigma \models_{(V,C)} \varphi'$ hold, it did leave open the question whether Σ purely C-implies φ'. Indeed, no inference of φ' from Σ by $\mathfrak{Z}_V$ can provide this insight by Theorem 1. However, using $\mathfrak{C}_V$ we can obtain the following inference of φ' from Σ:

$$\frac{I(m|b) \qquad I(c|bm)}{\mathcal{A}: \qquad I(cm|b)} m \in C \ .$$

Indeed, the V-symmetry rule $\mathcal{S}_V$ is unnecessary to infer φ' from Σ.

Examples 1 and 2 indicate that the $C = \{m\}$-implication of $I(cm|b)$ by $\Sigma = \{I(m|b), I(c|bm)\}$ does not depend on the fixed set V of random variables. In what follows we will formalize the stronger notion of pure C-implication as motivated in the introduction. Theorem 2 shows that the set $\mathfrak{C} := \mathfrak{C}_V - \{\mathcal{S}_V\}$ of inference rules is nearly complete for the (V, C)-implication of SCI statements.

Theorem 3. *Let $\Sigma \cup \{I(Y|X)\}$ be a set of SCI statements over the set $V \supseteq C$ of random variables. Then $I(Y|X) \in \Sigma_{\mathfrak{C}_V}^+$ if and only if $I(Y|X) \in \Sigma_{\mathfrak{C}}^+$ or $I(V - XY|X) \in \Sigma_{\mathfrak{C}}^+$.*

Theorem 3 indicates that $\mathfrak{C}$ can infer every C-implied SCI statement that is independent from the set V of incomplete random variables. Another interpretation of Theorem 3 is the following. In using $\mathfrak{C}$ to infer (V, C)-implied statements, the fixation of V can be deferred until the last step of an inference.

4   Pure Implication

We formalize the notion of pure C-implication as motivated in the introduction. The set $\mathfrak{C}$ of inference rules is shown to form a finite axiomatization for pure C-implication. This enables us to distinguish between (V, C)-implied and purely C-implied statements. Pure C-implication can be applied whenever it is more convenient to use than (V, C)-implication. For example, when there is uncertainty about additional random variables that may be required in the future, when some variables are unknown, or when some variables shall remain hidden.

A *probability model* is a quadruple (V, C, dom, P) where $V = \{v_1, \ldots, v_n\} \subseteq \mathfrak{V}$ is a finite set of random variables, $C \subseteq V$, dom is a domain mapping that maps each v_i to a finite domain $dom(v_i)$, and $P : dom(v_1) \times \cdots \times dom(v_n) \to [0, 1]$ is a probability distribution having the Cartesian product of these domains as its sample space. Note that $- \notin dom(v_i)$ whenever $v_i \in C$. The expression $I(Y|X)$ where X and Y are finite, disjoint subsets of $\mathfrak{V}$ is called a *saturated conditional independence* (SCI) *statement*. We say that the SCI statement $I(Y|X)$ *holds* for (V, C, dom, P) if $XY \subseteq V$ and for every complete assignment $\mathbf{x}$ of X, every assignment $\mathbf{y}$ of Y, and every assignment $\mathbf{z}$ of $V - XY$, respectively,

$$P(\mathbf{x}, \mathbf{y}, \mathbf{z}) \cdot P(\mathbf{x}) = P(\mathbf{x}, \mathbf{y}) \cdot P(\mathbf{x}, \mathbf{z}).$$

Equivalently, (V, C, dom, P) is said to *satisfy* $I(Y|X)$. For an SCI statement $\sigma = I(Y|X)$ let $V_\sigma := XY$, and for a finite set Σ of SCI statements let $V_\Sigma := \bigcup_{\sigma \in \Sigma} V_\sigma$ denote the random variables that occur in it.

Definition 2. *Let $\Sigma \cup \{\varphi\}$ be a finite set of SCI statements, and C a finite set of complete random variables. We say that Σ purely C-implies φ, denoted by $\Sigma \models_C \varphi$, if and only if every probability model (V, C, dom, P) with $V_{\Sigma \cup \{\varphi\}} \subseteq V$ that satisfies every SCI statement $\sigma \in \Sigma$ also satisfies φ.*

In the definition of pure C-implication the set V of underlying random variables is left undetermined. The only requirement is that the SCI statements must apply to the probability model. The pure C-implication problem for SCI statements can be stated as follows.

PROBLEM:	Pure C-Implication Problem
INPUT:	Set $\Sigma \cup \{\varphi\}$ of SCI statements
	Finite set C of complete random variables
OUTPUT:	Yes, if $\Sigma \vdash_C \varphi$; No, otherwise

Pure C-implication is stronger than (V, C)-implication.

Proposition 2. *Let $\Sigma \cup \{\varphi\}$ be a finite set of SCI statements and C a finite set of complete random variables, such that $V_{\Sigma \cup \{\varphi\}} \cup C \subseteq V$. If $\Sigma \models_C \varphi$, then $\Sigma \models_{(V,C)} \varphi$, but the other direction may fail.*

Proof. The first statement follows directly from the definitions of pure C-implication and (V, C)-implication. For the other direction, let $V = \{b, c, h, m\}$, $C = \emptyset$, $\Sigma = \{I(ch|b)\}$ and let φ be $I(m|b)$. Clearly, Σ (V, C)-implies φ. However, Σ does not purely C-imply φ as the example from the introduction shows.   □

Soundness and completeness for pure C-implication are defined as their corresponding notions in the context of some fixed set V by dropping the reference to V. While saturated triviality axiom $\mathcal{T}$, weak union rule $\mathcal{W}$, and restricted weak contraction rule $\mathcal{R}$ are all C-sound, the V-symmetry rule $\mathcal{S}_V$ is (V, C)-sound but not C-sound.

Theorem 4. *The set $\mathfrak{C} = \{\mathcal{T}, \mathcal{W}, \mathcal{R}, \mathcal{A}, \mathcal{I}\}$ forms a finite axiomatization for the pure C-implication of SCI statements.*

Example 3. Recall Example 2 where $V = \{b, c, h, m\}$, $C = \{m\}$ and Σ consists of the two SCI statements $I(m|b)$ and $I(c|bm)$. The inference of $I(cm|b)$ from Σ by $\mathfrak{C}_V$ in Example 2 is actually an inference by $\mathfrak{C}$. Hence, $I(cm|b)$ is purely C-implied by Σ, as one would expect intuitively.

5   Classical and Pure Implication

Instances $\Sigma \models_C \varphi$ of the pure C-implication problem can be characterized by the instance $\Sigma \models_{(V,C)} \varphi$ of the (V,C)-implication problem for any set V of random variables that *properly* contains $V_{\Sigma \cup \{\varphi\}}$. Note that $C \subseteq V$ follows from the fact that we talk about (V,C)-implication.

Theorem 5. *Let $\Sigma \cup \{\varphi\}$ be a set of SCI statements. Then the following are equivalent:*

1. $\Sigma \models_C \varphi$
2. *for some $V \supseteq C$ such that $V_{\Sigma \cup \{\varphi\}} \subset V$, $\Sigma \models_{(V,C)} \varphi$*
3. *for all $V \supseteq C$ such that $V_{\Sigma \cup \{\varphi\}} \subset V$, $\Sigma \models_{(V,C)} \varphi$*

Proof. It is clear that *3.* entails *2.* Let $\varphi = I(Y|X)$, and let V be any finite set of random variables such that $V_{\Sigma \cup \{\varphi\}} \subset V$. If *2.* holds, then Theorem 3 and Theorem 4 show that *1.* holds or $\Sigma \vdash_{\mathfrak{c}} I(V - XY|X)$ holds. However, the latter condition cannot hold as $V - XY$ contains some random variable that does not occur in V_Σ. Hence, *2.* entails *1.* If *1.* holds, then Theorem 3 and Theorem 4 show that *3.* holds as well.   □

Example 4. For $C = \{m\}$, $\Sigma = \{I(m|b), I(c|bm)\}$ purely C-implies $I(cm|b)$ as, for instance, $\Sigma \models_{(V,C)} I(cm|b)$ for $V = \{b, c, h, m\}$. However, Σ does not purely C-imply $I(h|b)$ as for $V = \{b, c, h, m, e\}$, Σ does not (V,C)-imply $I(h|b)$ as witnessed in the introduction.

In the following we apply Theorem 5 to establish characterizations of pure C-implication in terms of logical formulae under $\mathcal{S}-3$ logic, database dependencies, and algorithmic solutions. For a finite set C of complete random variables, a finite set $\Sigma \cup \{\varphi\}$ of SCI statements we write $V_c = V_{\Sigma \cup \{\varphi\}} \cup C \cup \{v_0\}$ for some $v_0 \notin V_{\Sigma \cup \{\varphi\}}$, $\sigma_c = I(V_c - XY, Y|X)$ for $\sigma = I(Y|X) \in \Sigma \cup \{\varphi\}$ and $\Sigma_c = \{\sigma_c \mid \sigma \in \Sigma\}$. In particular, $\Sigma \models_C \varphi$ if and only if $\Sigma_c \models_{V_c,C} \varphi_c$.

6   Logical Characterization of Pure Implication

We recall $\mathcal{S}$-3 logics [16,27] and exploit them to establish a logical characterization of the pure C-implication problem. $\mathcal{S}$-3 logics were introduced as "a semantically well-founded logical framework for sound approximate reasoning, which is justifiable from the intuitive point of view, and to provide fast algorithms for dealing with it even when using expressive languages".

For a finite set L of propositional variables, let L^* denote the *propositional language* over L, generated from the unary connective $\neg$ (negation), and the binary connectives $\wedge$ (conjunction) and $\vee$ (disjunction). Elements of L^* are also called formulae of L, and usually denoted by φ', ψ' or their subscripted versions. Sets of formulae are denoted by Σ'. We omit parentheses if this does not cause ambiguity.

Let L^ℓ denote the set of all literals over L, i.e., $L^\ell = L \cup \{\neg v' \mid v' \in L\}$. Let $\mathcal{S} \subseteq L$. An $\mathcal{S}$-3 truth assignment of L is a total function $\omega : L^\ell \to \{\mathbb{F}, \mathbb{T}\}$

that maps every propositional variable $v' \in S$ and its negation $\neg v'$ into opposite truth values ($\omega(v') = \mathbb{T}$ if and only if $\omega(\neg v') = \mathbb{F}$), and that does not map both a propositional variable $v' \in L - S$ and its negation $\neg v'$ into *false* (we must not have $\omega(v') = \mathbb{F} = \omega(\neg v')$ for any $v' \in L - S$).

An S-3 truth assignment $\omega : L^\ell \to \{\mathbb{F}, \mathbb{T}\}$ of L can be lifted to a total function $\Omega : L^* \to \{\mathbb{F}, \mathbb{T}\}$. This lifting has been defined as follows [27]. An arbitrary formula φ' in L^* is firstly converted (in linear time in the size of the formula) into its corresponding formula φ'_N in *Negation Normal Form* (NNF) using the following rewriting rules: $\neg(\varphi' \wedge \psi') \mapsto (\neg\varphi' \vee \neg\psi')$, $\neg(\varphi' \vee \psi') \mapsto (\neg\varphi' \wedge \neg\psi')$, and $\neg(\neg\varphi') \mapsto \varphi'$. Therefore, negation in a formula in NNF occurs only at the literal level. The rules for assigning truth values to NNF formulae are as follows:

- $\Omega(\varphi') = \omega(\varphi')$, if $\varphi' \in L^\ell$,
- $\Omega(\varphi' \vee \psi') = \mathbb{T}$ if and only if $\Omega(\varphi') = \mathbb{T}$ or $\Omega(\psi') = \mathbb{T}$,
- $\Omega(\varphi' \wedge \psi') = \mathbb{T}$ if and only if $\Omega(\varphi') = \mathbb{T}$ and $\Omega(\psi') = \mathbb{T}$.

An S-3 truth assignment ω is a *model* of a set Σ' of L-formulae if and only if $\Omega(\sigma'_N) = \mathbb{T}$ holds for every $\sigma' \in \Sigma'$. We say that Σ' S-3 *implies* an L-formula φ', denoted by $\Sigma' \models^3_S \varphi'$, if and only if every S-3 truth assignment that is a model of Σ' is also a model of φ'.

Equivalences. Let $\phi : V_c \to L_c$ denote a bijection between a set V_c of random variables and the set $L_c = \{v' \mid v \in V\}$ of propositional variables. In particular, $\phi(C) = S \subseteq L_c$. We extend ϕ to a mapping Φ from the set of SCI statements over V_c to the set L^*_c. For an SCI statement $I(Y, Z \mid X)$ over V_c, let $\Phi(I(Y, Z \mid X))$ denote

$$\bigvee_{v \in X} \neg v' \vee \left(\bigwedge_{v \in Y} v'\right) \vee \left(\bigwedge_{v \in Z} v'\right).$$

Disjunctions over zero disjuncts are $\mathbb{F}$ and conjunctions over zero conjuncts are $\mathbb{T}$. We will denote $\Phi(\varphi_c) = \varphi'_c$ and $\Phi(\Sigma_c) = \{\Phi(\sigma_c) \mid \sigma \in \Sigma_c\} = \Sigma'_c$.

In our example, for $\varphi_c = I(ceh, m \mid b)$ we have $\varphi'_c = \neg b' \vee (c' \wedge e' \wedge h') \vee m'$, and for $\Sigma_c = \{I(cem, h \mid b)\}$ we have $\Sigma'_c = \{\neg b' \vee h' \vee (c' \wedge e' \wedge m')\}$.

It has been shown that for any set $\Sigma_c \cup \{\varphi_c\}$ of SCI statements over V_c there is a probability model $\pi = (dom, P)$ over (V_c, C) that satisfies Σ_c and violates φ_c if and only if there is an S-3 interpretation ω_π over L_c that is an S-3 model of Σ'_c but not an S-3 model of φ'_c [20]. For arbitrary probability models π it is not obvious how to define the S-3 interpretation ω_π. However, if Σ_c does not (V_c, C)-imply φ_c, then there is a special probability model $\pi = (dom, \{\mathbf{a}_1, \mathbf{a}_2\})$ over (V_c, C) that i) has two assignments $\mathbf{a}_1, \mathbf{a}_2\}$ of probability one half each, ii) satisfies all SCI statements in Σ_c and iii) violates φ_c. Given such π, let ω_π denote the following special S-3 interpretation of L_c [20]:

$$\omega_\pi(v') = \begin{cases} \mathbb{T}, & \text{if } \mathbf{a}_1(v) = \mathbf{a}_2(v) \\ \mathbb{F}, & \text{otherwise} \end{cases} \text{, and}$$

$$\omega_\pi(\neg v') = \begin{cases} \mathbb{T}, & \text{if } \mathbf{a}_1(v) = - = \mathbf{a}_2(v) \text{ or } \mathbf{a}_1(v) \neq \mathbf{a}_2(v) \\ \mathbb{F}, & \text{otherwise} \end{cases}.$$

From the results in [20] and Theorem 5 we obtain the following logical characterization of pure implication.

Theorem 6. *Let $\Sigma \cup \{\varphi\}$ be a finite set of SCI statements, C be a finite set of complete random variables, $L_c = \{v' \mid v \in V_{\Sigma \cup \{\varphi\}} \cup C \cup \{v_0\}\}$ and $\mathcal{S} = \{v' \mid v \in C\}$. Then $\Sigma \models_C \varphi$ if and only if $\Sigma'_c \models^3_{\mathcal{S}} \varphi'_c$.*

Proof. Theorem 5 shows that $\Sigma \models_C \varphi$ if and only if $\Sigma_c \models_{(V_c, C)} \varphi_c$ for $V_c = V_{\Sigma \cup \{\varphi\}} \cup C \cup \{v_0\}$. By [20, Thm.20], $\Sigma_c \models_{(V_c, C)} \varphi_c$ if and only if $\Sigma'_c \models^3_{\mathcal{S}} \varphi'_c$. □

Example 5. Recall that $\Sigma = \{I(m \mid b), I(c \mid bm)\}$ does not purely $C = \{m\}$-imply $\varphi = I(h \mid b)$ as the special probability model π defined by

m	b	h	c	e	P
true	true	true	−	true	0.5
true	true	false	−	false	0.5

satisfies Σ_c, but violates φ_c. Any special $\mathcal{S}$-3 interpretation where $\omega_\pi(m') = \mathbb{T} = \omega_\pi(c')$, $\omega_\pi(\neg b') = \omega_\pi(\neg m') = \omega_\pi(h') = \omega_\pi(e') = \mathbb{F}$ is an $\mathcal{S}$-3 model of $\Sigma'_c = \{\neg b' \vee m' \vee (c' \wedge e' \wedge h'), \neg b' \vee \neg m' \vee c' \vee (e' \wedge h')\}$, but not an $\mathcal{S}$-3 model of $\varphi'_c = \neg b' \vee h' \vee (c' \wedge e' \wedge m')$.

7 Database and Algorithmic Characterization

Let $\mathfrak{A} = \{\hat{v}_1, \hat{v}_2, \ldots\}$ be an infinite set of distinct symbols, called attributes. A *relation schema* is a finite non-empty subset R of $\mathfrak{A}$. Each attribute $\hat{v} \in R$ has an infinite domain $dom(\hat{v})$. In order to encompass missing data values the domain of each attribute contains the null marker $-$. The intention of $-$ is to mean "no information" [17]. A *tuple* over R is a function $t : R \to \bigcup_{\hat{v} \in R} dom(\hat{v})$ with $t(\hat{v}) \in dom(\hat{v})$ for all $\hat{v} \in R$. For $X \subseteq R$ let $t(X)$ denote the restriction of t to X. A *relation* r over R is a finite set of tuples over R. For a tuple t over R and a set $X \subseteq R$, t is said to be X-*total*, if for all $\hat{v} \in X$, $t(\hat{v}) \neq -$. A relation over R is X-total if every of its tuples is X-total. An R-total relation of R is said to be *total*. The industry-standard SQL allows its users to declare attributes NOT NULL. A null-free subschema (NFS) of R is a subset $R^s \subseteq R$. An R-relation satisfies an NFS R^s over R if it is R^s-total. A *multivalued dependency* (MVD) over R is a statement $X \twoheadrightarrow Y$ where X and Y are disjoint subsets of R [17]. The MVD $X \twoheadrightarrow Y$ over R is satisfied by a relation r over R if and only if for all $t_1, t_2 \in r$ the following holds: if t_1 and t_2 are X-total and $t_1(X) = t_2(X)$, then there is some $t \in r$ such that $t(XY) = t_1(XY)$ and $t(X(R - XY)) = t_2(X(R - XY))$. Thus, the relation r satisfies $X \twoheadrightarrow Y$ when every X-total value determines the set of values on Y independently of the set of values on $R - Y$. For a set $\hat{\Sigma} \cup \{\hat{\varphi}\}$ of MVDs over R, $\hat{\Sigma}$ (R, R^s)-implies $\hat{\varphi}$, denoted by $\hat{\Sigma} \models_{(R, R^s)} \hat{\varphi}$, if and only if every relation over R that satisfies the NFS R^s and all elements in $\hat{\Sigma}$ also satisfies $\hat{\varphi}$.

For a set $\Sigma_c \cup \{\varphi_c\}$ of SCI statements over V_c one may associate the set $\hat{\Sigma}_c \cup \{\hat{\varphi}_c\}$ of MVDs over $R_c := \{\hat{v} \mid v \in V_c\}$, where $\hat{\sigma}_c = X \twoheadrightarrow Y$ for $\sigma_c = I(Z, Y \mid X)$ and $\hat{\Sigma}_c = \{\hat{\sigma}_c \mid \sigma \in \Sigma_c\}$.

Theorem 7. *Let $\Sigma \cup \{\varphi\}$ be a finite set of SCI statement, and C a finite set of complete random variables. Then $\Sigma \models_C \varphi$ if and only if $\hat{\Sigma}_c \models_{(R_c, R_c^s)} \hat{\varphi}_c$, where $R_c = \{\hat{v} | v \in V_c\}$ and $R_c^s = \{\hat{v} | v \in C\}$.*

Proof. Theorem 5 shows that $\Sigma \models_C \varphi$ if and only if $\Sigma_c' \models_S^3 \varphi_c'$ for $S = \{v' | v \in C\}$. By [11, Cor. 6.9], $\Sigma_c' \models_S^3 \varphi_c'$ if and only if $\hat{\Sigma}_c \models_{(R_c, R_c^s)} \hat{\varphi}_c$.

[20, Cor. 28] shows that $\Sigma_c \models_{(V_c, C)} \varphi_c$ for $\varphi_c = I(Z, Y | X)$ iff $\Sigma_c[XC] \models_{(V_c, V_c)} \varphi_c$, that is, when no domain contains the marker. Here, $\Sigma_c[XC] := \{I(V, W | U) \mid I(V, W | U) \in \Sigma_c \wedge U \subseteq XC\}$. The *independence basis* $IDepB_{\Sigma_c[XC]}(X)$ consists of the minimal $Y \subseteq V_c - X$ such that $\Sigma_c[XC] \models_{(V_c, V_c)} I(Z, Y | X)$. By Theorem 6 and [11, Cor. 6.9], $\Sigma \models_C \varphi$ iff $\Sigma_c[\hat{X}C] \models_{(R_c, R_c)} \hat{\varphi}_c$, that is, every total relation over R_c that satisfies $\Sigma_c[\hat{X}C]$ also satisfies $\hat{\varphi}_c$. The latter problem has an efficient algorithmic solution [8].

Theorem 8. *Using the algorithm in [8], the pure implication problem $\Sigma \models_C I(Y | X)$ can be decided in time $\mathcal{O}(|\Sigma_c| + \min\{k_{\Sigma_c[XC]}, \log \bar{p}_{\Sigma_c[XC]}\} \times |\Sigma_c[XC]|)$. Herein, $|\Sigma_c|$ denotes the total number of random variables in Σ_c, $k_{\Sigma_c[XC]}$ denotes the cardinality of $\Sigma_c[XC]$, and $\bar{p}_{\Sigma_c[XC]}$ denotes the number of sets in $IDepB_{\Sigma_c[XC]}(X)$ that have non-empty intersection with Y.*

8 Related Work

Dawid [5] first investigated fundamental properties of conditional independence, leading to a claim that "rather than just being another useful tool in the statistician's kitbag, conditional independence offers a new language for the expression of statistical concepts and a framework for their study". Geiger and Pearl [9,24] have systematically investigated the implication problem for fragments of CI statements over different probability models. In particular, they have established an axiomatization of SCI statements by a finite set of Horn rules [9]. Studený [30] showed that no axiomatization by a finite set of Horn rules exists for general CI statements. Niepert et al. [22] established an axiomatization for stable CI statements, which subsume SCI statements, and showed that their associated implication problem is *coNP*-complete. Independently, database theory has investigated the concept of embedded multivalued dependencies (MVDs) whose implication problem is undecidable [12] and not axiomatizable by a finite set of Horn rules [29]. Studený also showed that the implication problem of embedded MVDs and that of CI statements do not coincide [30]. In contrast, the implication problems of MVDs, SCI statements and some fragement of Boolean propositional logic all coincide [9,26,31]. These findings have been established for the notion of implication over fixed sets of random variables and the idealized case where all data values are known. [3] differentiated between V-implication and pure implication for SCI statements in which all random variables are complete, applying ideas from database theory [1,18,2,19]. The equivalences between (V, C)-implication of SCI statements, S-3 implication of a propositional fragment, and implication

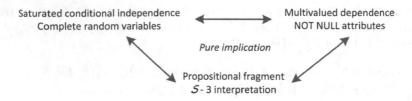

Fig. 1. Summary of equivalences between pure implication problems

of multivalued dependencies in the presence of NOT NULL constraints were established in [11,20]. The present article is the first to study pure C-implication of SCI statements. It subsumes two special cases from previous research, where i) all random variables are assumed to be complete [3], and ii) no random variable is assumed to be complete [13]. In particular, the equivalences summarized in Figure 1 complement the findings from [11,20] for implication in fixed universes.

9   Conclusion

Recently, probabilistic SCI statements were studied in a general framework in which occurrences of missing data are controlled by declaring members of a subset C of the set V of random variables to be complete. Axiomatic, algorithmic and logical characterizations of the associated implication problem were generalized from the idealized special case in which all random variables are complete, that is, where $C = V$. In this paper we investigated the difference between SCI statements (V, C)-implied jointly by a given set of SCI statements and a fixed set V, and those purely C-implied by a given set of SCI statements alone. It was shown that the only known axiomatization $\mathfrak{Z}_V$ for (V, C)-implication cannot separate (V, C)-implied from purely C-implied SCI statements. An axiomatization $\mathfrak{C}_V$ was established that can infer every purely C-implied SCI statement without applications of the V-symmetry rule $\mathcal{S}_V$, and infer every (V, C)-implied SCI statement with a single application of $\mathcal{S}_V$ in the last step of the inference only. The system $\mathfrak{C}$ that results from $\mathfrak{C}_V$ by removing $\mathcal{S}_V$ forms a finite axiomatization for the stronger notion of pure C-implication. The pure C-implication problem $\Sigma \models \varphi$ was characterized by the (V, C)-implication problem $\Sigma \models_{(V,C)} \varphi$ for sets $V \supseteq C$ that properly contain the random variables that occur in $\Sigma \cup \{\varphi\}$. This result enabled us to characterize pure C-implication logically and algorithmically as well. Our results clarify the role of the V-symmetry rule $\mathcal{S}_V$ as a pure means to infer (V, C)-implied SCI statements. The notion of pure C-implication is appealing when the existence of random variables is uncertain, for example, when independence statements are integrated from different sources, when random variables are unknown or shall remain hidden.

Acknowledgement. This research is supported by the Marsden fund council from Government funding, administered by the Royal Society of New Zealand.

References

1. Biskup, J.: Inferences of multivalued dependencies in fixed and undetermined universes. Theor. Comput. Sci. 10(1), 93–106 (1980)
2. Biskup, J., Link, S.: Appropriate inferences of data dependencies in relational databases. Ann. Math. Artif. Intell. 63(3-4), 213–255 (2012)
3. Biskup, J., Hartmann, S., Link, S.: Probabilistic conditional independence under schema certainty and uncertainty. In: Hüllermeier, E., Link, S., Fober, T., Seeger, B. (eds.) SUM 2012. LNCS, vol. 7520, pp. 365–378. Springer, Heidelberg (2012)
4. Chickering, D.M., Heckerman, D.: Efficient approximations for the marginal likelihood of Bayesian networks with hidden variables. Machine Learning 29(2-3), 181–212 (1997)
5. Dawid, A.P.: Conditional independence in statistical theory. Journal of the Royal Statistical Society. Series B (Methodological) 41(1), 1–31 (1979)
6. Dempster, A., Laird, N.M., Rubin, D.: Maximum likelihood from incomplete data via the EM algorithm. Journal of the Royal Statistical Society B 39, 1–39 (1977)
7. Friedman, N.: Learning belief networks in the presence of missing values and hidden variables. In: Fisher, D.H. (ed.) Proceedings of the Fourteenth International Conference on Machine Learning (ICML 1997), Nashville, Tennessee, USA, July 8-12, pp. 125–133. Morgan Kaufmann (1997)
8. Galil, Z.: An almost linear-time algorithm for computing a dependency basis in a relational database. J. ACM 29(1), 96–102 (1982)
9. Geiger, D., Pearl, J.: Logical and algorithmic properties of conditional independence and graphical models. The Annals of Statistics 21(4), 2001–2021 (1993)
10. Halpern, J.Y.: Reasoning about uncertainty. MIT Press (2005)
11. Hartmann, S., Link, S.: The implication problem of data dependencies over SQL table definitions: axiomatic, algorithmic and logical characterizations. ACM Trans. Database Syst. 37(2), Article 13 (2012)
12. Herrmann, C.: On the undecidability of implications between embedded multivalued database dependencies. Inf. Comput. 122(2), 221–235 (1995)
13. Koehler, H., Link, S.: Saturated conditional independence with fixed and undetermined sets of incomplete random variables. In: Zhang, N.L., Tian, J. (eds.) Proceedings of the Thirtieth Conference on Uncertainty in Artificial Intelligence, Quebec City, Quebec, Canada, July 23-27. AUAI Press (2013)
14. Koller, D., Friedman, N.: Probabilistic Graphical Models - Principles and Techniques. MIT Press (2009)
15. Lauritzen, S.: The EM algorithm for graphical association models with missing data. Computational Statistics and Data Analysis 19, 191–201 (1995)
16. Lenzerini, M., Schaerf, M.: The scientific legacy of Marco Cadoli in artificial intelligence. Intelligenza Artificiale 7(1), 1–5 (2013)
17. Lien, E.: On the equivalence of database models. J. ACM 29(2), 333–362 (1982)
18. Link, S.: Charting the completeness frontier of inference systems for multivalued dependencies. Acta Inf. 45(7-8), 565–591 (2008)
19. Link, S.: Characterizations of multivalued dependency implication over undetermined universes. J. Comput. Syst. Sci. 78(4), 1026–1044 (2012)
20. Link, S.: Sound approximate reasoning about saturated conditional probabilistic independence under controlled uncertainty. J. Applied Logic 11(3), 309–327 (2013)
21. Marlin, B.M., Zemel, R.S., Roweis, S.T., Slaney, M.: Recommender systems, missing data and statistical model estimation. In: Walsh, T. (ed.) Proceedings of the 22nd International Joint Conference on Artificial Intelligence, IJCAI 2011, Barcelona, Catalonia, Spain, July 16-22, pp. 2686–2691. IJCAI/AAAI (2011)

22. Niepert, M., Van Gucht, D., Gyssens, M.: Logical and algorithmic properties of stable conditional independence. Int. J. Approx. Reasoning 51(5), 531–543 (2010)
23. Niepert, M., Gyssens, M., Sayrafi, B., Gucht, D.V.: On the conditional independence implication problem: A lattice-theoretic approach. Artif. Intell. 202, 29–51 (2013)
24. Pearl, J.: Probabilistic Reasoning in Intelligent Systems: Networks of Plausible Inference. Morgan Kaufmann, San Francisco (1988)
25. Saar-Tsechansky, M., Provost, F.J.: Handling missing values when applying classification models. Journal of Machine Learning Research 8, 1623–1657 (2007)
26. Sagiv, Y., Delobel, C., Parker Jr., D.S., Fagin, R.: An equivalence between relational database dependencies and a fragment of propositional logic. J. ACM 28(3), 435–453 (1981)
27. Schaerf, M., Cadoli, M.: Tractable reasoning via approximation. Artif. Intell. 74, 249–310 (1995)
28. Singh, M.: Learning bayesian networks from incomplete data. In: Kuipers, B., Webber, B.L. (eds.) Proceedings of the Fourteenth National Conference on Artificial Intelligence and Ninth Innovative Applications of Artificial Intelligence Conference, AAAI 1997, IAAI 1997, Providence, Rhode Island, July 27-31, pp. 534–539. AAAI Press/The MIT Press (1997)
29. Stott Parker Jr., D., Parsaye-Ghomi, K.: Inferences involving embedded multivalued dependencies and transitive dependencies. In: Chen, P.P., Sprowls, R.C. (eds.) Proceedings of the 1980 ACM SIGMOD International Conference on Management of Data, Santa Monica, California, May 14-16, pp. 52–57. ACM Press (1980)
30. Studený, M.: Conditional independence relations have no finite complete characterization. In: Ámos Víšek, J. (ed.) Transactions of the 11th Prague Conference on Information Theory, Statistical Decision Functions and Random Processes, Prague, Czech Republic, August 27-31, 1990, pp. 377–396. Academia (1992)
31. Wong, S., Butz, C., Wu, D.: On the implication problem for probabilistic conditional independency. IEEE Trans. Systems, Man, and Cybernetics, Part A: Systems and Humans 30(6), 785–805 (2000)
32. Zhu, X., Zhang, S., Zhang, J., Zhang, C.: Cost-sensitive imputing missing values with ordering. In: Proceedings of the Twenty-Second AAAI Conference on Artificial Intelligence, Vancouver, British Columbia, Canada, July 22-26, pp. 1922–1923. AAAI Press (2007)

Finitary S5-Theories

Tran Cao Son[1], Enrico Pontelli[1], Chitta Baral[2], and Gregory Gelfond[2]

[1] Computer Science Department, New Mexico State University
{tson,epontell}@cs.nmsu.edu
[2] Department of Computer Science Engineering, Arizona State University
{chitta,gelfond.greg}@asu.edu

Abstract. The objective of this paper is to identify a class of epistemic logic theories with group knowledge operators which have the fundamental property of being characterized by a *finite* number of *finite* models (up to equivalence). We specifically focus on S5-theories. We call this class of epistemic logic theories as *finitary* S5-*theories*. Models of finitary S5-theories can be shown to be canonical in that they do not contain two worlds with the same interpretation. When the theory is *pure*, these models are minimal and differ from each other only in the actual world. The paper presents an algorithm for computing all models of a finitary S5-theory. Finitary S5-theories find applications in several contexts—in particular, the paper discusses their use in epistemic multi-agent planning.

1   Introduction and Motivation

Epistemic logics [2, 7, 8, 10] are a branch of modal logic that is concerned with representing and reasoning about the knowledge of collections of agents. These logics allow us to represent and reason about the knowledge of an agent about the world, its knowledge about other agents' knowledge, group's knowledge, common knowledge, etc. The models of an epistemic theory are commonly given by *pointed Kripke structures*. Each pointed Kripke structure consists of a set of elements named *worlds* (also known as *points*), a collection of binary relations between worlds (*accessibility relations*), a named valuation associated to each world, and an *actual world*—considered as the *"real state of the universe"*. Models of an epistemic theory can be potentially infinite. Indeed, one can easily create an infinite model of an epistemic theory from a finite one, by cloning its whole structure (including the accessibility relations, the worlds, etc.). *Bisimulation* (e.g., [2]) can be used to reduce the size of a model. It is possible to show that, given a theory that employs a single modal operator and has a finite signature, there are only finitely many models with the property that *(a)* all of them are finite and bisimulation-based minimal; and *(b)* any model of the theory is bisimilar (and, hence, equivalent) to one of those models. This is not true, however, for *multimodal* theories, i.e., theories with multiple modal operators.

In this paper, we study the questions of when a multimodal propositional epistemic theory can be characterized by *finitely many finite models* (up to equivalence), and how to compute these models. The motivation for these questions is twofold.

First, the question arises in the research on using epistemic theories in *Multi-Agent Systems (MAS)*, in particular, in the development of the *Dynamic Epistemic Logic (DEL)*

E. Fermé and J. Leite (Eds.): JELIA 2014, LNAI 8761, pp. 239–252, 2014.

[1, 3, 6, 11] for reasoning about effects of actions in MAS. This line of research has laid the foundations for the study of the epistemic planning problem in multi-agent environments [5, 12, 14]. Yet, the majority of the research in epistemic planning assumes that the set of *initial pointed Kripke structures* is given, and it is either finite [12, 14] or recursively enumerable [5]. This creates a gap between the rich literature in theoretical investigation of epistemic planning (e.g., formalization, complexity results) and the very modest developments in automated epistemic planning systems—that can benefit from the state-of-the-art techniques developed for planning systems in single-agent environments. In particular, there is a plethora of planners for single-agent environments, that perform exceptionally well in terms of scalability and efficiency;[1] the majority of them are heuristic forward-search planners. On the other hand, to the best of our knowledge, the systems described in [12, 14] are the only epistemic multi-agent planning prototypes available, that search for solutions using breath-first search and model checking.

The second research motivation comes from the observation that the **S5**-logic is the de-facto standard logic for reasoning and planning with sensing actions in presence of incomplete information for single-agent domains. The literature is scarce on methods for computing models of **S5** multimodal epistemic theories. Works such as [15, 16] are exceptions, and they focus on the least models of a modal theory. Several papers, instead, assume that such models are, *somehow*, given. For instance, after describing the muddy-children story, the authors of [7] present a model of the theory without detailing how should one construct such model and whether or not the theory has other "interesting" models.

These observations show that, in order to be able to use epistemic logic as a specification language in practical MAS applications, such as epistemic multi-agent planning, the issue of how to compute the set of models of a theory must be addressed.

In this paper, we address this question by identifying a class of *finitary **S5**-theories* with group and common knowledge operators, that can be characterized by finitely many finite models. We prove that each model of a finitary **S5**-theory is equivalent to one of these canonical models, and propose an effective algorithm for computing such set of canonical models. We discuss a representation of finitary **S5**-theories suitable for use with the algorithm. We also discuss the impact of these results in epistemic multi-agent planning.

2 Preliminary: Epistemic Logic

Let us consider the epistemic logic with a set $\mathcal{AG} = \{1, 2, \ldots, n\}$ of n agents; we will adopt the notation used in [2, 7]. The "physical" state of the world is described by a finite set $\mathcal{P}$ of *propositions*. The knowledge of the world of agent i is described by a modal operator $\mathbf{K}_i$; in particular, the knowledge of agents is encoded by *knowledge formulae* (or *formula*) in a logic extended with these operators, and defined as follows.

- *Atomic formulae:* an atomic formula is built using the propositions in $\mathcal{P}$ and the traditional propositional connectives $\vee$, $\wedge$, $\rightarrow$, $\neg$, etc. A *literal* is either an atom $f \in \mathcal{P}$ or its negation $\neg f$. $\top$ (resp. $\bot$) denotes *true* (resp. *false*).

---

[1] E.g., http://ipc.icaps-conference.org/ lists 27 participants in the 2011 International Planning Competition.

- *Knowledge formulae:* a knowledge formula is a formula in one of the following forms: *(i)* An atomic formula; *(ii)* A formula of the form $\mathbf{K}_i\varphi$, where φ is a knowledge formula; *(iii)* A formula of the form $\varphi_1 \vee \varphi_2$, $\varphi_1 \wedge \varphi_2$, $\varphi_1 \rightarrow \varphi_2$, or $\neg\varphi_1$, where φ_1, φ_2 are knowledge formulae; *(iv)* A formula of the form $\mathbf{E}_\alpha\varphi$ or $\mathbf{C}_\alpha\varphi$ where φ is a formula and $\emptyset \neq \alpha \subseteq \mathcal{AG}$.

Formulae of the form $\mathbf{E}_\alpha\varphi$ and $\mathbf{C}_\alpha\varphi$ are referred to as *group formulae*. Whenever $\alpha = \mathcal{AG}$, we simply write $\mathbf{E}\varphi$ and $\mathbf{C}\varphi$ to denote $\mathbf{E}_\alpha\varphi$ and $\mathbf{C}_\alpha\varphi$, respectively. When no confusion is possible, we will talk about formula instead of knowledge formula. Let us denote with $\mathcal{L}^{\mathcal{P}}_{\mathcal{AG}}$ the language of the knowledge formulae over $\mathcal{P}$ and $\mathcal{AG}$. An *epistemic theory* (or simply a *theory*) over the set of agents $\mathcal{AG}$ and propositions $\mathcal{P}$ is a set of knowledge formulae in $\mathcal{L}^{\mathcal{P}}_{\mathcal{AG}}$. To illustrate the language, we will use the well-known *Muddy Children* problem as a running example. For simplicity of the presentation, let us consider the case with two children.

> **[Muddy Children]** A father says to his two children that at least one of them has mud on the forehead. He then repeatedly asks "do you know whether you are dirty?" The first time the two children answer "no." The second time both answer "yes." The father and the children can see and hear each other, but no child can see his own forehead.

Let $\mathcal{AG} = \{1, 2\}$. Let m_i denote that child i is muddy. Some formulae in $\mathcal{L}^{\mathcal{P}}_{\mathcal{AG}}$ are: *(i)* m_i (i is muddy); *(ii)* $\mathbf{K}_1 m_1$ (child 1 knows he is muddy); *(iii)* $\mathbf{K}_1\mathbf{K}_2 m_2$ (child 1 knows that child 2 knows that he is muddy); and *(iv)* $\mathbf{C}_{\{1,2\}}(m_1 \vee m_2)$ (it is common knowledge among the children that at least one is muddy).

The semantics of knowledge formulae relies on the notion of Kripke structures.

Definition 1 (Kripke Structure). *A Kripke structure over $\mathcal{AG} = \{1, \ldots, n\}$ and $\mathcal{P}$ is a tuple $\langle S, \pi, \mathcal{K}_1, \ldots, \mathcal{K}_n \rangle$, where S is a set of points, π is a function that associates an interpretation of $\mathcal{P}$ to each element of S (i.e., $\pi : S \mapsto 2^{\mathcal{P}}$), and $\mathcal{K}_i \subseteq S \times S$ for $1 \leq i \leq n$. A pointed Kripke structure (or, pointed structure, for short) is a pair (M, s), where M is a Kripke structure and s, called the actual world, belongs to the set of points of M.*

For readability, we use $M[S]$, $M[\pi]$, and $M[i]$, to denote the components S, π, and $\mathcal{K}_i$ of M, respectively. Using this notation, $M[\pi](u)$ denotes the interpretation associated to the point u.

Definition 2 (Satisfaction Relation). *Given a formula φ and a pointed structure (M, s):*

- $(M, s) \models \varphi$ *if φ is an atomic formula and $M[\pi](s) \models \varphi$;*
- $(M, s) \models \mathbf{K}_i\varphi$ *if for each t such that $(s, t) \in \mathcal{K}_i$, $(M, t) \models \varphi$;*
- $(M, s) \models \neg\varphi$ *if $(M, s) \not\models \varphi$;*
- $(M, s) \models \varphi_1 \vee \varphi_2$ *if $(M, s) \models \varphi_1$ or $(M, s) \models \varphi_2$;*
- $(M, s) \models \varphi_1 \wedge \varphi_2$ *if $(M, s) \models \varphi_1$ and $(M, s) \models \varphi_2$;*
- $(M, s) \models \mathbf{E}_\alpha\varphi$ *if $(M, s) \models \mathbf{K}_i\varphi$ for every $i \in \alpha$;*
- $(M, s) \models \mathbf{C}_\alpha\varphi$ *if $(M, s) \models E^k_\alpha\varphi$ for every $k \geq 0$ where $E^0_\alpha\varphi = \varphi$ and $E^{k+1}_\alpha = E_\alpha(E^k_\alpha\varphi)$.*

$M \models \varphi$ denotes the fact that $(M, s) \models \varphi$ for each $s \in M[S]$, while $\models \varphi$ denotes the fact that $M \models \varphi$ for all Kripke structures M. We will often depict a Kripke structure

M as a directed labeled graph, with S as the set of nodes and with edges of the form (s, i, t) iff $(s, t) \in \mathcal{K}_i$. We say that u_n is reachable from u_1 if there is a sequence of edges $(u_1, i_1, u_2), (u_2, i_2, u_3), \ldots, (u_{n-1}, i_{n-1}, u_n)$ in M.

A Kripke structure denotes the possible "worlds" envisioned by the agents—and the presence of multiple worlds denotes uncertainty and presence of different knowledge. The relation $(s_1, s_2) \in \mathcal{K}_i$ indicates that the knowledge of agent i about the real state of the world is insufficient to distinguish between the state described by point s_1 and the one described by point s_2. For example, if $(s_1, s_2) \in \mathcal{K}_i$, $M[\pi](s_1) \models \varphi$ and $M[\pi](s_2) \models \neg\varphi$, everything else being the same, then this will indicate that agent i is uncertain about the truth of φ. Figure 1 displays a possible pointed structure for the

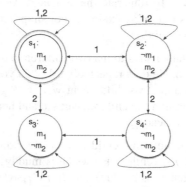

Fig. 1. A possible pointed structure for the Muddy Children Domain

Muddy Children Domain. In Figure 1, a circle represents a point. The name and interpretation of the points are written in the circle. Labeled edges between points denote the knowledge relations of the structure. A double circle identifies the actual world.

Various axioms are used to characterize epistemic logic systems. We will focus on the S5-logic that contains the following axioms for each agent i and formulae φ, ψ:

$$\models (\mathbf{K}_i\varphi \wedge \mathbf{K}_i(\varphi \Rightarrow \psi)) \Rightarrow \mathbf{K}_i\psi \tag{K}$$
$$\models \mathbf{K}_i\psi \Rightarrow \psi \tag{T}$$
$$\models \mathbf{K}_i\psi \Rightarrow \mathbf{K}_i\mathbf{K}_i\psi \tag{4}$$
$$\models \neg\mathbf{K}_i\psi \Rightarrow \mathbf{K}_i\neg\mathbf{K}_i\psi \tag{5}$$

A Kripke structure is said to be an S5-structure if it satisfies the properties **K**, **T**, **4**, and **5**. It can be shown that the relations $\mathcal{K}_i$ of S5-structures are reflexive, transitive, and symmetric. A theory plus the **K**, **T**, **4**, and **5** axioms is often referred to as an S5-*theory*. In the rest of this paper, we will consider only S5-theories. A theory T is said to be *satisfiable* (or *consistent*) if there exists a Kripke structure M and a point $s \in M[S]$ such that $(M, s) \models \psi$ for every $\psi \in T$. In this case, (M, s) is referred to as a *model* of T. Two pointed structures (M, s) and (M', s') are *equivalent* if, for every formula $\varphi \in \mathcal{L}_{AG}^{\mathcal{P}}$, $(M, s) \models \varphi$ iff $(M', s') \models \varphi$.

For simplicity of the presentation, we define

$$state(u) \equiv \bigwedge_{f \in \mathcal{P},\, M[\pi](u)(f)=\top} f \wedge \bigwedge_{f \in \mathcal{P},\, M[\pi](u)(f)=\bot} \neg f$$

for $u \in M[S]$. Intuitively, $state(u)$ is the formula representing the complete interpretation associated to the point u in the structure M, i.e., $M[\pi](u)$. We will often use $state(u)$ and $M[\pi](u)$ interchangeably. We say that (M, s) is *canonical* if $state(u) \not\equiv state(v)$ for every $u, v \in M[S]$, $u \neq v$. By $Mods_{S5}(T)$ we denote a set of S5-models of a theory T such that: *(a)* there are no two equivalent models in $Mods_{S5}(T)$; and *(b)* For each S5-model (M, s) of T, there exists a model (M', s') in $Mods_{S5}(T)$ such that (M, s) is equivalent to (M', s').

3   Finitary S5-Theories: Definition and Properties

In this section, we define the notion of *finitary S5-theories* and show that a finitary S5-theory can be characterized by finitely many finite models. We start with the specification of the types of formulae that we will consider. They are, in our observation, sufficiently expressive for use in the specification of the description of the actual world and the common knowledge among the agents. The allowed types of formulae are:

$$\varphi \tag{1}$$
$$\mathbf{C}(\mathbf{K}_i \varphi) \tag{2}$$
$$\mathbf{C}(\mathbf{K}_i \varphi \vee \mathbf{K}_i \neg \varphi) \tag{3}$$
$$\mathbf{C}(\neg \mathbf{K}_i \varphi \wedge \neg \mathbf{K}_i \neg \varphi) \tag{4}$$

where φ is an atomic formula. Intuitively, formulae of type (1) indicate properties that are true in the actual world; formulae of type (2)-(3) indicate that all agents know that agent i is aware of the truth value of φ; formulae of type (4) indicate that all agents know that agent i is not aware of whether φ is true or false. Since our focus is on S5-models of epistemic theories, it is easy to see that $\mathbf{C}(\mathbf{K}_i \varphi)$ can be simplified to $\mathbf{C}(\varphi)$. We say that a formula of the form (1)-(4) is in *disjunctive form* if its formula φ is a disjunction over literals from $\mathcal{P}$. A *complete clause* over $\mathcal{P}$ is a disjunction of the form $\bigvee_{p \in \mathcal{P}} p^*$ where p^* is either p or $\neg p$.

Example 1. In the muddy children story, the knowledge of the children after the father's announcement but before the children look at each other can be encoded by a theory T_0 consisting of the following formulae:

$$\mathbf{C}(\mathbf{K}_1(m_1 \vee m_2)) \qquad \mathbf{C}(\mathbf{K}_2(m_1 \vee m_2))$$
$$\mathbf{C}(\neg \mathbf{K}_1 m_1 \wedge \neg \mathbf{K}_1 \neg m_1) \qquad \mathbf{C}(\neg \mathbf{K}_1 m_2 \wedge \neg \mathbf{K}_1 \neg m_2)$$
$$\mathbf{C}(\neg \mathbf{K}_2 m_1 \wedge \neg \mathbf{K}_2 \neg m_1) \qquad \mathbf{C}(\neg \mathbf{K}_2 m_2 \wedge \neg \mathbf{K}_2 \neg m_2)$$

These formulae indicate that both children are aware that at least one of them is muddy (the formulas in the first row), but they are not aware of who among them is muddy; these items are all common knowledge.

If we take into account the fact that each child can see the other, and each child knows if the other one is muddy, then we need to add to T_0 the following formulae:

$$\mathbf{C}(\mathbf{K}_1 m_2 \vee \mathbf{K}_1 \neg m_2) \qquad \mathbf{C}(\mathbf{K}_2 m_1 \vee \mathbf{K}_2 \neg m_1)$$

Definition 3 (Primitive Finitary S5-Theory). *A theory T is said to be* primitive finitary **S5** *if*

- *Each formula in T is of the form (1)-(4); and*
- *For each complete clause φ over $\mathcal{P}$ and each agent i, T contains either* (i) $\mathbf{C}(\mathbf{K}_i\varphi)$ *or* (ii) $\mathbf{C}(\mathbf{K}_i\varphi \vee \mathbf{K}_i\neg\varphi)$ *or* (iii) $\mathbf{C}(\neg\mathbf{K}_i\varphi \wedge \neg\mathbf{K}_i\neg\varphi)$.

T *is said to be in* disjunctive form *if all statements in T are in disjunctive form.*

The second condition of the above definition deserves some discussion. It requires that T contains at least $|\mathcal{AG}| \times 2^{|\mathcal{P}|}$ formulae and could be unmanageable for large $\mathcal{P}$. This condition is introduced for simplicity of initial analysis of finitary S5-theories. This condition will be relaxed at the end of this section by replacing the requirement "T *contains*" with "T *entails.*" For example, the theory T_0 is not a primitive finitary S5-theory; T_0 is a finitary S5-theory (defined later) as it entails a primitive finitary S5-theory T_1.

Example 2. Let T_1 be the theory consisting of:

$$\mathbf{C}(\mathbf{K}_i(m_1 \vee m_2))$$
$$\mathbf{C}(\neg\mathbf{K}_i(m_1 \vee \neg m_2) \wedge \neg\mathbf{K}_i(\neg(m_1 \vee \neg m_2)))$$
$$\mathbf{C}(\neg\mathbf{K}_i(\neg m_1 \vee m_2) \wedge \neg\mathbf{K}_i(\neg(\neg m_1 \vee m_2)))$$
$$\mathbf{C}(\neg\mathbf{K}_i(\neg m_1 \vee \neg m_2) \wedge \neg\mathbf{K}_i(\neg(\neg m_1 \vee \neg m_2)))$$

where $i = 1, 2$. It is easy to see that T_1 is a primitive finitary S5-theory—and it is equivalent to T_0 from Example 1.

Primitive finitary S5-theories can represent interesting properties.

Example 3. Consider the statement *"it is common knowledge that none of the agents knows anything."* The statement can be represented by the theory

$$T_2 = \{\mathbf{C}(\neg\mathbf{K}_i\omega \wedge \neg\mathbf{K}_i\neg\omega) \mid i \in \mathcal{AG}, \omega \text{ is a complete clause over } \mathcal{P}\}.$$

We will show that a primitive finitary S5-theory can be characterized by finitely many finite S5-models. The proof of this property relies on a series of lemmas. We will next discuss these lemmas and provide proofs of the non-trivial ones. First, we observe that points that are unreachable from the actual world in a pointed structure can be removed.

Lemma 1. *Every* **S5**-*pointed structure* (M, s) *is equivalent to an* **S5**-*pointed structure* (M', s) *such that every* $u \in M'[S]$ *is reachable from s.*

The next lemma studies the properties of an S5-pointed structure satisfying a formula of the form (2) or (3).

Lemma 2. *Let* (M, s) *be an* **S5**-*pointed structure such that every* $u \in M[S]$ *is reachable from s. Let ψ be an atomic formula. Then,*

- $(M, s) \models \mathbf{C}(\psi)$ *iff* $M[\pi](u) \models \psi$ *for every* $u \in M[S]$.
- $(M, s) \models \mathbf{C}(\mathbf{K}_i\psi \vee \mathbf{K}_i\neg\psi)$ *iff for every pair* $(u, v) \in M[i]$ *it holds that* $M[\pi](u) \models \psi$ *iff* $M[\pi](v) \models \psi$.

Because $\mathbf{C}(\mathbf{K}_i\psi)$ implies $\mathbf{C}(\psi)$ in an S5-pointed structure (M, s) the first item of Lemma 2 shows that ψ is satisfied at every point in (M, s). The second item of Lemma 2 shows that every pair of points related by $\mathcal{K}_i$ either both satisfy or both do not satisfy the formula φ in an S5-pointed structure (M, s) satisfying a formula of the form (3).

The next lemma shows that an S5-pointed structure satisfying a formula of the form (4) must have at least one pair of points at which the value of the atomic formula mentioned in the formula differs. For a structure M and $u, v \in M[S]$, $M[\pi](u)(\psi) \neq M[\pi](v)(\psi)$ indicates that either $(M[\pi](u) \models \psi$ and $M[\pi](v) \not\models \psi)$ or $(M[\pi](u) \not\models \psi$ and $M[\pi](v) \models \psi)$, i.e., the value of ψ at u is different from the value of ψ at v.

Lemma 3. *Let (M, s) be an S5-pointed structure such that every $u \in M[S]$ is reachable from s. Let ψ be an atomic formula. Then, $(M, s) \models \mathbf{C}(\neg\mathbf{K}_i\psi \wedge \neg\mathbf{K}_i\neg\psi)$ iff for every $u \in M[S]$ there exists some $v \in M[S]$ such that $(u, v) \in M[i]$, and $M[\pi](u)(\psi) \neq M[\pi](v)(\psi)$.*

The proofs of Lemmas 1-3 follow from the definition of the satisfaction relation $\models$ between a pointed structure and a formula and the fact that $(M, s) \models \mathbf{C}(\psi)$ iff $(M, u) \models \psi$ for every u reachable from s. For this reason, they are omitted.

We will now focus on models of primitive finitary S5-theories. Let M be a Kripke structure. We define a relation $\sim$ among points of M as follows. For each $u, v \in M[S]$, $u \sim v$ iff $state(u) \equiv state(v)$. Thus, $u \sim v$ indicates that the interpretations associated to u and v are identical. It is easy to see that $\sim$ is an equivalence relation over $M[S]$. Let $\tilde{u}$ denote the equivalence class of u with respect to the relation $\sim$ (i.e., $\tilde{u} = [u]_\sim$).

Lemma 4. *Let (M, s) be an S5-model of a primitive finitary S5-theory such that every $u \in M[S]$ is reachable from s. Let φ be a complete clause and $i \in \mathcal{AG}$. Given $u \in M[S]$:*

- *If $(M, u) \models \mathbf{K}_i\varphi$ then $(M, s) \models \mathbf{C}(\mathbf{K}_i\varphi)$ or $(M, s) \models \mathbf{C}(\mathbf{K}_i\varphi \vee \mathbf{K}_i\neg\varphi)$;*
- *If $(M, u) \models \neg\mathbf{K}_i\varphi$ then $(M, s) \models \mathbf{C}(\neg\mathbf{K}_i\varphi \wedge \neg\mathbf{K}_i\neg\varphi)$.*

The proof of Lemma 4 makes use of Lemmas 2-3 and the fact that (M, s) is an S5-model of a primitive finitary S5-theory. The next lemma states a fundamental property of models of primitive finitary S5-theories.

Lemma 5. *Let (M, s) be an S5-model of a primitive finitary S5-theory such that every $u \in M[S]$ is reachable from s. Let $u, v \in M[S]$ such that $u \sim v$. Then, for every $i \in \mathcal{AG}$ and $x \in M[S]$ such that $(u, x) \in M[i]$ there exists $y \in M[S]$ such that $(v, y) \in M[i]$ and $x \sim y$.*

Proof. Let $K(p, i) = \{q \mid q \in M[S], (p, q) \in M[i]\}$—i.e., the set of points immediately related to p via $M[i]$. We consider two cases:

- **Case 1:** $K(u, i) \cap K(v, i) \neq \emptyset$. Since $M[i]$ is an equivalent relation, we can conclude that $K(u, i) = K(v, i)$ and the lemma is trivially proved (by taking $x = y$).
- **Case 2:** $K(u, i) \cap K(v, i) = \emptyset$. Let us assume that there exists some $x \in K(u, i)$ such that there exists no $y \in K(v, i)$ with $x \sim y$. This means that $(M, y) \models \neg state(x)$ for each $y \in K(v, i)$. In other words, $(M, v) \models \mathbf{K}_i(\neg state(x))$. As $\neg state(x)$ is a complete clause, this implies that (by Lemma 4):

$$(M, s) \models \mathbf{C}(\mathbf{K}_i \neg state(x)) \text{ or } (M, s) \models \mathbf{C}(\mathbf{K}_i \neg state(x) \vee \mathbf{K}_i state(x)) \quad (5)$$

On the other hand, $(M, u) \not\models \mathbf{K}_i(\neg state(x))$, since $x \in K(u, i)$ and $(M, x) \models state(x)$. This implies $(M, s) \models \mathbf{C}(\neg \mathbf{K}_i \neg state(x) \wedge \neg \mathbf{K}_i state(x))$ by Lemma 4. This contradicts (5), proving the lemma. $\qquad \square$

Lemma 5 shows that the points with the same interpretation have the same structure in an S5-model of a primitive finitary S5-theory, i.e., the accessibility relations associated to these points are identical. This indicates that we can group all such points into a single one, producing an equivalent model that is obviously finite. Let us show that this is indeed the case. Given a structure M, let $\widetilde{M}$ be the structure constructed as follows:

- $\widetilde{M}[S] = \{\tilde{u} \mid u \in M[S]\}$
- For every $u \in M[S]$ and $f \in \mathcal{P}$, $\widetilde{M}[\pi](\tilde{u})(f) = M[\pi](u)(f)$
- For each $i \in \mathcal{AG}$, $(\tilde{u}, \tilde{v}) \in \widetilde{M}[i]$ if there exists $(u', v') \in M[i]$ such that $u' \in \tilde{u}$ and $v' \in \tilde{v}$.

We call $(\widetilde{M}, \tilde{s})$ the *reduced pointed structure* of (M, s) and prove that it is an S5-pointed structure equivalent to (M, s):

Lemma 6. *Let (M, s) be an S5-model of a primitive finitary S5-theory T such that every $u \in M[S]$ is reachable from s. Furthermore, let $(\widetilde{M}, \tilde{s})$ be the reduced pointed structure of (M, s). Then, $(\widetilde{M}, \tilde{s})$ is a finite S5-model of T that is equivalent to (M, s).*

Proof. The proof of this lemma relies on Lemmas 2-3 and 5. We prove some representative properties.

- $(\widetilde{M}, \tilde{s})$ is S5. Reflexivity and symmetry are obvious. Let us prove transitivity: assume that $(\tilde{u}, \tilde{v}) \in \widetilde{M}[i]$ and $(\tilde{v}, \tilde{w}) \in \widetilde{M}[i]$. The former implies that there exists $(u_1, v_1) \in M[i]$ for some $u_1 \in \tilde{u}$ and $v_1 \in \tilde{v}$. The latter implies that there exists $(x_1, w_1) \in M[i]$ for some $x_1 \in \tilde{v}$ and $w_1 \in \tilde{w}$. Since $\sim$ is an equivalence relation, $v_1 \sim x_1$. Lemma 5 implies that there exists some $w_2 \sim w_1$ such that $(v_1, w_2) \in M[i]$ which implies that, by transitivity of $M[i]$, $(u_1, w_2) \in M[i]$, so $(\tilde{u}, \tilde{w}) \in \widetilde{M}[i]$, i.e., $\widetilde{M}[i]$ is transitive.
- $(\widetilde{M}, \tilde{s})$ is a model of T. We have that
  $(M, s) \models \mathbf{C}(\mathbf{K}_i \psi \vee \mathbf{K}_i \neg \psi)$ iff
  $\forall u, v \in M[S], (u, v) \in M[i]$ implies $M[\pi](u) \models \psi$ iff $M[\pi](v) \models \psi$ (by Lemma 2 w.r.t. (M, s)) iff
  $\forall \tilde{p}, \tilde{q} \in \widetilde{M}[S], u \in \tilde{p}$ and $v \in \tilde{q}, (\tilde{p}, \tilde{q}) \in \widetilde{M}[i]$ implies $\widetilde{M}[\pi](\tilde{p}) \models \psi$ iff $\widetilde{M}[\pi](\tilde{q}) \models \psi$ (construction of $(\widetilde{M}, \tilde{s})$) iff
  $(\widetilde{M}, \tilde{s}) \models \mathbf{C}(\mathbf{K}_i \psi \vee \mathbf{K}_i \neg \psi)$ (by Lemma 2 w.r.t. $(\widetilde{M}, \tilde{s})$).
  The proof for other statements is similar.
- $(\widetilde{M}, \tilde{s})$ is equivalent to (M, s). This is done by induction over the number of $\mathbf{K}$ operators in a formula. $\qquad \square$

Let

$$\mu Mods_{\mathbf{S5}}(T) = \left\{ (\widetilde{M}, \tilde{s}) \mid \begin{array}{l} (\widetilde{M}, \tilde{s}) \text{ is a reduced pointed structure} \\ \text{of a S5-model } (M, s) \text{ of } T \end{array} \right\}$$

Since each S5-model of T is equivalent to its reduced pointed structure, which has at most $2^{|\mathcal{P}|}$ points, we have the next theorem.

Theorem 1. *For a consistent primitive finitary S5-theory* T, $\mu Mods_{S5}(T)$ *is finite and such that each* (M, s) *in* $\mu Mods_{S5}(T)$ *is also finite.*

This theorem shows that primitive finitary S5-theories have the desired properties that we are looking for. The next theorem proves interesting properties of models of primitive finitary S5-theories which are useful for computing $\mu Mods_{S5}(T)$.

Theorem 2. *For a primitive finitary S5-theory* T, *every model* (M, s) *in* $\mu Mods_{S5}(T)$ *is canonical and* $|M[S]|$ *is minimal among all models of* T. *Furthermore, for every pair of models* (M, s) *and* (W, w) *in* $\mu Mods_{S5}(T)$, M *and* W *are identical, up to the names of the points.*

The first conclusion is trivial as each reduced pointed structure of a model of T is a canonical model of T. The next lemma proves the second conclusion.

Lemma 7. *Let* T *be a primitive finitary S5-theory,* (M, s) *and* (V, w) *in* $\mu Mods_{S5}(T)$, *and let* $i \in \mathcal{AG}$.
- *For each* $u \in M[S]$ *there exists some* $v \in V[S]$ *such that* $state(u) \equiv state(v)$.
- *If* $(u, p) \in M[i]$ *then there exists* $(v, q) \in V[i]$ *such that* $state(u) \equiv state(v)$ *and* $state(p) \equiv state(q)$.

Proof. (Sketch) The proof of the first property is similar to the proof of Lemma 5, with the minor modification that it refers to two structures and that both are models of T. In fact, if $u \in M[S]$ and there exists no $v \in V[S]$ such that $state(u) \equiv state(v)$ then $(V, w) \models \mathbf{C}(\mathbf{K}_k \neg state(u))$ and $(M, s) \not\models \mathbf{C}(\mathbf{K}_k \neg state(u))$ for $k \in \mathcal{AG}$, a contradiction. The proof of the second property uses a similar argument. □

To prove that the set of points of a model in $\mu Mods_{S5}(T)$ is minimal, we use the next lemma. We define:

$$F(T) = \{\varphi \mid \varphi \text{ appears in a formula of the form (2) of } T\}.$$

Lemma 8. *Let* (M, s) *be a canonical model of a primitive finitary S5-theory* T. *Then, the set* $M[S]$ *is exactly the set of interpretations of* $F(T)$ *and each* $u \in M[S]$ *is reachable.*

Proof. (Sketch) First, it follows directly from Lemma 2 and $\mathbf{C}(\mathbf{K}_i\psi) \models \mathbf{C}(\psi)$ in an S5-model that for each $u \in M[S]$, $state(u) \models \varphi$ for every $\varphi \in F(T)$. Second, because T is primitive finitary, if there is some interpretation I of $F(T)$ such that there exists no $u \in M[S]$ and $state(u) = I$ or there exists $u \in M[S]$ with $state(u) = I$ and u is not reachable from s then we can conclude that $(M, s) \models \mathbf{C}(\neg I)$, and because T is a primitive finitary, we have that $\neg I \in F(T)$. This implies that I cannot be an interpretation of $F(T)$, a contradiction. Both properties prove the lemma. □

We are now ready to define the notion of a *finitary S5-theory* that allows for Theorem 1 to extend to epistemic theories consisting of arbitrary formulae.

Definition 4 (Finitary S5-Theory). *An epistemic theory* T *is a finitary S5-theory if* $T \models H$ *and* H *is a primitive finitary S5-theory.* T *is pure if* T *contains only formulae of the form (1)-(4).*

We have that T_0 (Example 1) is a finitary **S5**-theory, since $T_0 \models T_1$ and T_1 is a primitive finitary **S5**-theory. Since a model of T is also a model of H if $T \models H$, the following theorem holds.

Theorem 3. *Every finitary* **S5**-*theory* T *has finitely many finite canonical models, up to equivalence. If* T *is pure then these models are minimal and their structures are identical up to the name of the points.*

4   Computing All Models of Finitary S5-Theories

In this section, we present an algorithm for computing $\mu Mods_{\mathbf{S5}}(T)$ for a primitive finitary **S5**-theory and discuss how this can be extended to arbitrary finitary **S5**-theories. Lemma 8 shows that $F(T)$ can be used to identify the set of points of canonical models of T. Applying this lemma to T_0 (Example 1), we know that for every canonical model (M, s) of T_0, $M[S] = \{s_1, s_2, s_3\}$ where $state(s_1) = m_1 \wedge m_2$, $state(s_2) = m_1 \wedge \neg m_2$, and $state(s_3) = \neg m_1 \wedge m_2$.

The next step is to determine the accessibility relations of $i \in \mathcal{AG}$. We will rely on Lemmas 2-3 and the following result:

Lemma 9. *Let* (M, s) *be a canonical model of a consistent primitive finitary* **S5**-*theory* T *and* $i \in \mathcal{AG}$. *Assume that for each complete clause* φ, *if* $T \not\models \mathbf{C}(\mathbf{K}_i \varphi)$ *then* $T \not\models \mathbf{C}(\mathbf{K}_i \varphi \vee \mathbf{K}_i \neg \varphi)$. *Then,* $(u, v) \in M[i]$ *for every pair* $u, v \in M[S]$.

Proof. The proof of this lemma is by contradiction and uses an idea similar to that used in the proof of Case 2 of Lemma 5. Since (M, s) is a canonical model, each $u \in M[S]$ is reachable from s. Assume that there exists a pair $u, v \in M[S]$ such that $(u, v) \notin M[i]$. We have that $(M, u) \models \mathbf{K}_i \neg state(v)$. As $\neg state(v)$ is a complete clause, by Lemma 4:

$$(M, s) \models \mathbf{C}(\mathbf{K}_i \neg state(v)) \quad \text{or} \ (M, s) \models \mathbf{C}(\mathbf{K}_i \neg state(v) \vee \mathbf{K}_i state(v)) \quad (6)$$

On the other hand, since $(u, v) \notin M[i]$ and M is a **S5**-structure, we have that $(M, v) \not\models \mathbf{K}_i \neg state(v)$. This, together with the assumption of the lemma, contradicts (6).   □

Algorithm 1[2] computes all canonical minimal models of a primitive finitary **S5**-theory. Its correctness follows from the properties of an **S5**-model of primitive finitary **S5**-theories discussed in Lemmas 2-3 and 7-9. This algorithm runs in polynomial time in the size of T, which, unfortunately, is exponential in the size of $\mathcal{P}$.

Note that, for the theory T_2 in Example 3, Algorithm 1 returns the set of pointed structures (M, s) such that $M[S]$ is the set of all interpretations of $\mathcal{P}$, $M[i]$ is a complete graph on $M[S]$, and $s \in M[S]$.

Fig. 2 shows one model of T_1 returned by Algorithm 1. Since $\mathbf{C}(\mathbf{K}_i(l_1 \vee l_2) \vee \mathbf{K}_i \neg (l_1 \vee l_2)) \notin T_1$ for every complete clause over $\{m_1, m_2\}$ that is different from $m_1 \vee m_2$, there is a link labeled i between every pair of worlds of the model. Since $I(T_1)$ is empty, $\mu Mods_{\mathbf{S5}}(T_1)$ contains three models, which differ from each other only in the actual world.

---

[2] We assume that the theory is consistent.

Algorithm 1. $Model(T)$

---

1. **Input**: A primitive finitary **S5**-theory T
2. **Output**: $\mu Mods_{\mathbf{S5}}(T)$
3. Compute $I(T) = \{\varphi \mid \varphi$ appears in some (1) of $T\}$
4. Compute $F(T) = \{\varphi \mid \varphi$ appears in some (2) of $T\}$
5. $\Sigma = \{u \mid u$ is an interpretation satisfying $F(T)\}$
6. Let $M[S] = \Sigma$, $M[\pi](u) = u$, and $M[i] = \{(u,v) \mid u,v \in \Sigma\}$
7. **for** each $\mathbf{C}(\mathbf{K}_i\varphi \vee \mathbf{K}_i\neg\varphi)$ in T **do**
8.   remove $(u,v) \in M[i]$ such that $M[\pi](u)(\varphi) \neq M[\pi](v)(\varphi)$
9. **end for**
10. **return** $\{(M,s) \mid s$ satisfies $I(T)\}$

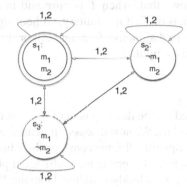

Fig. 2. A model of the theory T_1 in Example 2

The application of Algorithm 1 to an arbitrary finitary **S5**-theory T, where $T \models H$ for some primitive finitary **S5**-theory H, can be done in two steps: *(a)* Compute $\mu Mods_{\mathbf{S5}}(H)$; and *(b)* Eliminate models from $\mu Mods_{\mathbf{S5}}(H)$ which are not a model of T. Step *(b)* is necessary, since T can contain other formulae that are not entailed by H.[3] To accomplish *(a)*, the following tasks need to be performed: **(i)** Verify that T is finitary; **(ii)** Compute $I(T) = \{\psi \mid \psi$ is an atomic formula and $T \models \psi\}$ (Line 3) and $F(T) = \{\varphi \mid T \models \mathbf{C}(\varphi)\}$ (Line 4); **(iii)** Test for entailment (Line 7); **(iv)** Eliminate pointed structures that are not models of T (Line 10). Since these tasks are generally computational expensive, it it naturally to seek ways to improve performance. In the next section, we discuss a possible way to deal with **(iv)**. We will next show that when T is pure and in disjunctive form then the computation required in **(i)**-**(iii)** can be done in polynomial time in the size of T.

Given a pure theory T in disjunctive form, Task **(ii)** can be done as described in Lines 3 and 4 and does not require any additional computation. Given a pair (i, φ) of an agent i and a complete clause φ, we would like to efficiently determine whether $T \models \mathbf{C}(\mathbf{K}_i\varphi)$, $T \models \mathbf{C}(\mathbf{K}_i\varphi \vee \mathbf{K}_i\neg\varphi)$, or $T \models \mathbf{C}(\neg\mathbf{K}_i\varphi \wedge \neg\mathbf{K}_i\neg\varphi)$ hold. This task can be accomplished via a test for coverage defined as follows. We say that φ is *covered* by a set W of disjunctions over $\mathcal{P}$ if $\varphi \equiv \bigvee_{\psi \in W} \psi$. A pair (i, φ) is *covered* by T if

---

[3] A consequence of this elimination is that canonical models of a non-pure finitary **S5**-theory may not have the same structure and/or different set of worlds.

- T contains some statement $\mathbf{C}(\mathbf{K}_k\psi)$ (for some $k \in \mathcal{AG}$) such that $\psi \models \varphi$; or
- φ is covered by some consistent set of disjunctions
  $$W \subseteq \{\psi \mid \mathbf{C}(\mathbf{K}_i\psi \vee \mathbf{K}_i\neg\psi) \in T\}.$$

Intuitively, if (i, φ) is covered by T then it is common knowledge that i knows the truth value of φ. The first item implies that $T \models \mathbf{C}(\mathbf{K}_i\varphi)$, i.e., everyone knows φ. The second item states that everyone knows that i knows φ—because *(i)* φ is covered by a set of disjunctions that are known by i, *(ii)* this is common knowledge, and *(iii)* the axiom $\models (\mathbf{K}\psi_1 \vee \mathbf{K}\neg\psi_1) \wedge (\mathbf{K}\psi_2 \vee \mathbf{K}\neg\psi_2) \Rightarrow \mathbf{K}((\psi_1 \vee \psi_2) \vee \mathbf{K}\neg(\psi_1 \vee \psi_2))$. Thus, if φ is a complete clause and (i, φ) is not covered by T then $T \not\models \mathbf{C}(\mathbf{K}_i\varphi)$ and $T \not\models \mathbf{C}(\mathbf{K}_i\varphi \vee \mathbf{K}_i\neg\varphi)$. It is easy to see that checking whether (i, φ) is covered by T can be done in polynomial time in the size of T when T is pure and in disjunctive form.

The above discussion shows that, when T is pure and in disjunctive form, Algorithm 1 can compute all models of T, if it is finitary, without significant additional cost. For example, T_0 is pure and in disjunctive form and Algorithm 1 will return the same set of models as if T_1 is used as input.

5 Discussion

The previous sections focused on the development of the notion of a finitary **S5**-theory and the computation of its models. We now discuss a potential use of finitary **S5**-theories as a specification language. Specifically, we consider their use in the specification of the initial set of pointed structures for epistemic multi-agent planning. Let us consider a simple example concerning the Muddy Children Domain: "The father sees that his two children are muddy. The children can see each other, hear the father, and truthfully answer questions from the father but cannot talk to each other. They also know that none of the children knows whether he is muddy or not. How can the father inform his children that both of them are muddy without telling them the fact?" As we have mentioned earlier, previous works in epistemic multi-agent planning assume that the set of initial pointed structures is given, and these are assumed to be finite or enumerable. However, a way to specify the set of initial pointed structures is not offered. Clearly, finitary **S5**-theories can fill this need. Let us discuss some considerations in the use of finitary **S5**-theories as a specification language.

The definition of a finitary **S5**-theory, by Definitions 3-4, calls for the test of entailment (or the specification) of $|\mathcal{AG}| \times 2^{|\mathcal{P}|}$ formulae. Clearly, this is not desirable. To address this issue, let us observe that Algorithm 1 makes use of formulae of the form (4) implicitly (Line 6), by assuming that all but those complete clauses entailed by $F(T)$ are unknown to agent i and that is common knowledge. This means that we could reduce the task of specifying T by assuming that its set of statements of the form (4) is given implicitly, i.e., by representing the information that the agents do not know *implicitly*. This idea is similar to the use of the *Closed World Assumption* to represent incomplete information. This can be realized as follows. For a theory T and an agent $i \in \mathcal{AG}$, let

$$C(T, i) = \{\varphi \mid \varphi \text{ is a complete clause}, T \not\models \mathbf{C}(\mathbf{K}_i\varphi), T \not\models \mathbf{C}(\mathbf{K}_i\varphi \vee \mathbf{K}_i\neg\varphi)\}$$

Let $neg(T) = \bigcup_{i \in \mathcal{AG}} \{\mathbf{C}(\neg\mathbf{K}_i\varphi \wedge \neg\mathbf{K}_i\neg\varphi) \mid \varphi \in C(T, i)\}$. The *completion* of T is $comp(T) = T \cup neg(T)$.

Given an arbitrary theory T, $comp(T)$ is a finitary S5-theory; as such, it could be used as the specification of a finitary S5-theory. If $comp(T)$ is used and T is pure and in disjunctive form, then the specification (of T) only requires statements of the form (1)-(3). As such, finitary S5-theories can be used in a manner similar to how the conventional PDDL problem specification describes the initial states—for epistemic multi-agent planning. We expect that this can help bridging the gap between the development of epistemic multi-agent planning systems and the research in reasoning about the effects of actions in multi-agent domains mentioned earlier since several approaches to reasoning about actions and changes in multi-agent domains (e.g., [1, 3, 6, 11]) facilitate the implementation of a forward search planner in multi-agent domains.

We close the section with a brief discussion on other potential uses of finitary S5-theories. Finitary S5-theories are useful in applications where knowing that a property is true/false is insufficient, e.g., knowing that a theorem is correct is good but knowing the proof of the theorem (its witness) is necessary; knowing that a component of a system malfunctions is a good step in diagnosis but knowing why this is the case is better; knowing that a plan exists does not help if the sequence of actions is missing; etc.

6   Conclusion and Future Work

In this paper, we proposed the notion of *finitary* S5-*theories* and showed that a finitary S5-theory has finitely many finite S5-models. We proved that models of primitive finitary S5-theories share the same structure and have minimal size in terms of the number of worlds. We presented an algorithm for computing all canonical S5-models of a finitary S5-theory. We also argued that the algorithm runs in polynomial time in the size of a pure finitary S5-theory in disjunctive form. We proposed the use of completion of finitary S5-theories, enabling the implicit representation of negative knowledge, as a specification language in applications like epistemic multi-agent planning.

As future work, we plan to expand this research in four directions. First, we will experiment with the development of an epistemic multi-agent planner. Second, we will investigate possible ways to relax the conditions imposed on finitary S5-theories, while still maintaining its finiteness property. Third, we intend to investigate the relationships between the notion of completion of finitary S5-theory and the logic of only knowing for multi-agent systems developed by others (e.g., [13, 9]). Finally, we would like to identify situations in which the S5-requirements can be lifted.

Acknowledgments. The research has been partially supported by NSF grants HRD-1345232 and DGE-0947465. The authors would like to thank Guram Bezhanishvili and Nguyen L. A for the useful discussions and suggestions.

References

[1] Baltag, A., Moss, L.: Logics for epistemic programs. Synthese (2004)
[2] van Benthem, J.: Modal Logic for Open Minds. Center for the Study of Language and Information (2010)

[3] van Benthem, J., van Eijck, J., Kooi, B.P.: Logics of communication and change. Inf. Comput. 204(11), 1620–1662 (2006)

[4] Blackburn, P., Van Benthem, J., Wolter, F. (eds.): Handbook of Modal Logic. Elsevier (2007)

[5] Bolander, T., Andersen, M.: Epistemic Planning for Single and Multi-Agent Systems. Journal of Applied Non-Classical Logics 21(1) (2011)

[6] van Ditmarsch, H., van der Hoek, W., Kooi, B.: Dynamic Epistemic Logic. Springer (2007)

[7] Fagin, R., Halpern, J., Moses, Y., Vardi, M.: Reasoning about Knowledge. MIT Press (1995)

[8] Gabbay, D., Kurucz, A., Wolter, F., Zakharyaschev, M.: Many-Dimensional Modal Logics: Theory and Application. Elsevier (2003)

[9] Halpern, J.Y., Lakemeyer, G.: Multi-agent only knowing. In: Shoham, Y. (ed.) Proceedings of the Sixth Conference on Theoretical Aspects of Rationality and Knowledge, De Zeeuwse Stromen, The Netherlands, pp. 251–265. Morgan Kaufmann (1996)

[10] Halpern, J., Moses, Y.: A guide to completeness and complexity for modal logics of knowledge and belief. Artificial Intelligence 54, 319–379 (1992)

[11] Herzig, A., Lang, J., Marquis, P.: Action Progression and Revision in Multiagent Belief Structures. In: Sixth Workshop on Nonmonotonic Reasoning, Action, and Change, NRAC (2005)

[12] van der Hoek, W., Wooldridge, M.: Tractable multiagent planning for epistemic goals. In: Proceedings of The First International Joint Conference on Autonomous Agents & Multiagent Systems, AAMAS 2002, Bologna, Italy, pp. 1167–1174. ACM (2002)

[13] Lakemeyer, G., Levesque, H.J.: Only-knowing meets nonmonotonic modal logic. In: Brewka, G., Eiter, T., McIlraith, S.A. (eds.) Principles of Knowledge Representation and Reasoning: Proceedings of the Thirteenth International Conference, KR 2012, Rome, Italy, June 10-14. AAAI Press (2012)

[14] Löwe, B., Pacuit, E., Witzel, A.: DEL planning and some tractable cases. In: van Ditmarsch, H., Lang, J., Ju, S. (eds.) LORI 2011. LNCS, vol. 6953, pp. 179–192. Springer, Heidelberg (2011)

[15] Nguyen, L.A.: Constructing the least models for positive modal logic programs. Fundam. Inform. 42(1), 29–60 (2000)

[16] Nguyen, L.A.: Constructing finite least kripke models for positive logic programs in serial regular grammar logics. Logic Journal of the IGPL 16(2), 175–193 (2008)

Efficient Program Transformers
for Translating LCC to PDL

Pere Pardo, Enrique Sarrión-Morillo,
Fernando Soler-Toscano, and Fernando R. Velázquez-Quesada

Grupo de Lógica, Lenguaje e Información, Universidad de Sevilla, Sevilla, Spain
{ppardo1,esarrion,fsoler,frvelazquezquesada}@us.es

Abstract. This work proposes an alternative definition of the so-called program transformers, used to obtain reduction axioms in the Logic of Communication and Change. Our proposal uses an elegant matrix treatment of Brzozowski's equational method instead of Kleene's translation from finite automata to regular expressions. The two alternatives are shown to be equivalent, with Brzozowski's method having the advantage of being computationally more efficient.

Keywords: Logic of communication and change, propositional dynamic logic, action model, program transformer, reduction axiom.

1 Introduction

Dynamic Epistemic Logic [10,4] (*DEL*) encompasses several logical frameworks whose main aim is the study of different single- and multi-agent epistemic attitudes and the way they change due to diverse epistemic actions. These frameworks typically have two building blocks: a 'static' component using some semantic model to represent the notion to be studied (e.g., knowledge, belief), and a 'dynamic' component using model operations to represent actions that affect such notion (e.g., announcements, belief revision).[1]

Among the diverse existing *DEL* frameworks, the Logic of Communication and Change (LCC) of [5] stands as one of the most interesting. This framework, consisting of a propositional dynamic logic [12] (PDL) interpreted epistemically (its 'static' component) and the action models machinery [3,2] for representing actions (its 'dynamic' component), allows us to model not only diverse epistemic actions (e.g., public, private or secret announcements) but also factual changes.

A key feature of this logic is that it characterises an action model's execution via *reduction axioms*, i.e., via valid formulas that allow us to rewrite a formula with dynamic modalities as an equivalent one without them, thus reducing LCC to PDL and hence providing us with a compositional analysis for a wide range of

---

[1] This form of representing the dynamics is different from other approaches as, e.g., epistemic temporal logic [11,15] (*ETL*), in which the static model already describes not only the relevant notion but also all the possible ways it can change due to the chosen epistemic action(s). See [6] for a comparison between *DEL* and *ETL*.

E. Fermé and J. Leite (Eds.): JELIA 2014, LNAI 8761, pp. 253–266, 2014.

informational events. Among the reduction axioms, the following one is crucial, characterising the effect of an action model over epistemic PDL programs:

$$[\mathsf{U}, \mathsf{e}_i][\pi]\varphi \;\leftrightarrow\; \bigwedge_{j=0}^{n-1} [T_{ij}^{\mathsf{U}}(\pi)][\mathsf{U}, \mathsf{e}_j]\varphi$$

This axiom, presented in detail in what follows, is based on the correspondence between action models and finite automata observed in [7]; its main component, the so-called program transformer function T_{ij}^{U}, follows Kleene's translation from finite automata to regular expressions [13].

The present work proposes an alternative definition of a program transformer that uses a matrix treatment of Brzozowski's equational method for obtaining an expression representing the language accepted by a given finite automaton [8,9]. This alternative definition has the advantage of having a lower complexity, thus allowing more efficient implementations of any LCC-based method. The paper starts in Section 2 by recalling the LCC framework together with its reduction axioms and the definition of program transformers. Then Section 3 introduces this paper's proposal, used in Section 4 to define an alternative translation from LCC to PDL. Section 5 comments on the computational complexity of this approach, and Section 6 presents a summary and further research points.

2   Preliminaries: Logic of Communication and Change

Throughout this paper, let Var be a set of atoms and let Ag be a finite set of agents. In brief, LCC is an extension of (an epistemic interpretation of) PDL with formulas $[\mathsf{U}, \mathsf{e}]\varphi$ read as *"after any execution of* e *it holds that* φ*"*. Basic PDL modalities $[a]$ are read as *knowledge/belief* for each agent $a \in$ Ag; sequential composition $[a; b]$ is *nested knowledge/belief*; non-deterministic choice $[a \cup b]$ or $[B]$ is *group knowledge/belief*, and iteration $[B^*]$ and $[B^+]$ is *common knowledge* and resp. *belief* among the group of agents $B \subseteq$ Ag.

Definition 1 (Epistemic model). *An* epistemic model $M = (W, \langle R_a \rangle_{a \in \mathsf{Ag}}, V)$ *is a triple where* $W \neq \varnothing$ *is the set of worlds,* $R_a \subseteq (W \times W)$ *is an epistemic relation for each agent* $a \in$ Ag *and* $V :$ Var $\to \wp(W)$ *is an atomic evaluation.*

Definition 2 (Action model). *For a given language* $\mathcal{L}$ *built upon* Var *and* Ag, *an* $\mathcal{L}$ action model *is a tuple* $\mathsf{U} = (\mathsf{E}, \langle R_a \rangle_{a \in \mathsf{Ag}}, \mathsf{pre}, \mathsf{sub})$ *where* $\mathsf{E} = \{\mathsf{e}_0, \ldots, \mathsf{e}_{n-1}\}$ *is a finite set of actions,* $R_a \subseteq (\mathsf{E} \times \mathsf{E})$ *is a relation for each* $a \in$ Ag, $\mathsf{pre} : \mathsf{E} \to \mathcal{L}$ *is a map assigning a formula* $\mathsf{pre}(\mathsf{e})$ *to each action* $\mathsf{e} \in \mathsf{E}$, *and* $\mathsf{sub} : (\mathsf{E} \times \mathsf{Var}) \to \mathcal{L}$ *is a map assigning a formula* $p^{\mathsf{sub}(\mathsf{e})}$ *to each atom* $p \in$ Var *at each action* $\mathsf{e} \in \mathsf{E}$.

Just as relation R_a describes agent a's uncertainty about the situation, relation R_a describes the agent's uncertainty about the executed action: $\mathsf{e}\mathsf{R}_a\mathsf{f}$ indicates that if e is the action that is actually taking place, then from a's perspective the actual action might be f. In Definition 3, the language $\mathcal{L}_{\mathsf{LCC}}$ and an $\mathcal{L}_{\mathsf{LCC}}$ action model (an instance of the $\mathcal{L}$ action model of Definition 2) are defined simultaneously.

Definition 3 (Language $\mathcal{L}_{\mathsf{LCC}}$). *The language $\mathcal{L}_{\mathsf{LCC}}$ extends that of PDL with a clause $[\mathsf{U},\mathsf{e}]\varphi$ where U is an $\mathcal{L}_{\mathsf{LCC}}$ action model and e an action in it:*

$$\varphi ::= \top \mid p \mid \neg\varphi \mid \varphi_1 \wedge \varphi_2 \mid [\pi]\varphi \mid [\mathsf{U},\mathsf{e}]\varphi \qquad \pi ::= a \mid ?\varphi \mid \pi_1;\pi_2 \mid \pi_1 \cup \pi_2 \mid \pi^*$$

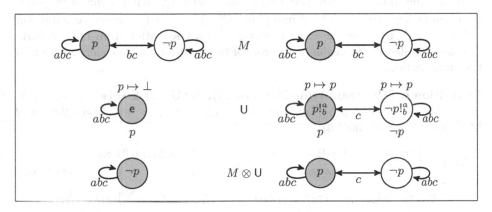

Fig. 1. An illustration of update execution for 3 agents $\mathsf{Ag} = \{a,b,c\}$ and an atom $\mathsf{Var} = \{p\}$. The actual state or action are depicted in gray; the relations $R_a, \mathsf{R}_a, \ldots$ are depicted as arrows, actions are depicted with preconditions below, and postconditions $p \mapsto p^{\mathsf{sub}(\cdot)}$ above. (top) An initial model M (drawn twice) where agents b,c know that agent a knows whether p; in fact agent a knows that p; (mid left) an action model U for a public switch from p to $\neg p$; (mid right) a private announcement by a to b about the truth-value of p; (bottom left) an updated model $M \otimes \mathsf{U}$ where it becomes common knowledge that $\neg p$; (bottom right) an updated model where only c is ignorant of p.

Definition 4 (Semantics of $\mathcal{L}_{\mathsf{LCC}}$). *Let $M = (W, \langle R_a \rangle_{a \in \mathsf{Ag}}, V)$ be an epistemic model. The function $[\![\cdot]\!]^M$, returning those worlds in W in which an $\mathcal{L}_{\mathsf{LCC}}$ formula holds and those pairs in $W \times W$ in which an $\mathcal{L}_{\mathsf{LCC}}$ program holds, is given by*

$$[\![\top]\!]^M = W \qquad\qquad\qquad [\![a]\!]^M = R_a$$
$$[\![p]\!]^M = V(p) \qquad\qquad\qquad [\![?\varphi]\!]^M = \mathsf{Id}_{[\![\varphi]\!]^M}$$
$$[\![\neg\varphi]\!]^M = W \setminus [\![\varphi]\!]^M \qquad\qquad [\![\pi_1;\pi_2]\!]^M = [\![\pi_1]\!]^M \circ [\![\pi_2]\!]^M$$
$$[\![\varphi_1 \wedge \varphi_2]\!]^M = [\![\varphi_1]\!]^M \cap [\![\varphi_2]\!]^M \qquad [\![\pi_1 \cup \pi_2]\!]^M = [\![\pi_1]\!]^M \cup [\![\pi_2]\!]^M$$
$$[\![[\pi]\varphi]\!]^M = \{w \in W \mid \forall v((w,v) \in [\![\pi]\!]^M \Rightarrow v \in [\![\varphi]\!]^M)\} \qquad [\![\pi^*]\!]^M = ([\![\pi]\!]^M)^*$$
$$[\![[\mathsf{U},\mathsf{e}]\varphi]\!]^M = \{w \in W \mid w \in [\![\mathsf{pre}(\mathsf{e})]\!]^M \Rightarrow (w,\mathsf{e}) \in [\![\varphi]\!]^{M \otimes \mathsf{U}}\}$$

where $\circ$ and $*$ are the composition and the reflexive transitive closure operator, respectively, and $M \otimes \mathsf{U}$ is the update execution defined next.

Definition 5 (Update execution). *Let M and U be an epistemic model and an action model, respectively, both over Var and Ag. The update execution of U on M is an epistemic model $(M \otimes \mathsf{U}) = (W^{M \otimes \mathsf{U}}, \langle R_a^{M \otimes \mathsf{U}} \rangle_{a \in \mathsf{Ag}}, V^{M \otimes \mathsf{U}})$ given by*

$$W^{M \otimes U} = \{ (w, e) \in W \times \mathsf{E} \mid w \in [\![\mathsf{pre}(e)]\!]^M \}$$
$$R_a^{M \otimes U} = \{ \langle (w, e), (v, f) \rangle \in W^{M \otimes U} \times W^{M \otimes U} \mid w R_a v \ and \ e R_a f \}$$
$$V^{M \otimes U}(p) = \{ (w, e) \in W^{M \otimes U} \mid w \in [\![p^{\mathsf{sub}(e)}]\!]^M \}$$

See Figure 1 for an illustration of different updates in an epistemic model.

In [5], the authors define program transformers T_{ij}^{U} that provide a mapping between LCC programs. These mappings $T_{ij}^{\mathsf{U}}(\pi)$ are used to generate reduction axioms (see Fig. 2) for the case $[\mathsf{U}, e][\pi]\varphi$, and a translation from LCC to PDL. A more detailed explanation of the role of the program transformers is given in the next section.

Definition 6 (Program transformers [5]). *Let* U *with* $\mathsf{E} = \{e_0, \ldots, e_{n-1}\}$ *be an action model. The* program transformer T_{ij}^{U} $(0 \leq i, j \leq n-1)$ *on the set of LCC programs is defined as:*

$$T_{ij}^{\mathsf{U}}(a) = \begin{cases} ?\mathsf{pre}(e_i); a & \text{if } e_i R_a e_j \\ ?\bot & \text{otherwise} \end{cases} \qquad T_{ij}^{\mathsf{U}}(?\varphi) = \begin{cases} ?(\mathsf{pre}(e_i) \wedge [\mathsf{U}, e_i]\varphi) & \text{if } i = j \\ ?\bot & \text{otherwise} \end{cases}$$

$$T_{ij}^{\mathsf{U}}(\pi_1; \pi_2) = \bigcup_{k=0}^{n-1}(T_{ik}^{\mathsf{U}}(\pi_1); T_{kj}^{\mathsf{U}}(\pi_2)) \qquad T_{ij}^{\mathsf{U}}(\pi_1 \cup \pi_2) = T_{ij}^{\mathsf{U}}(\pi_1) \cup T_{ij}^{\mathsf{U}}(\pi_2)$$

$$T_{ij}^{\mathsf{U}}(\pi^*) = K_{ijn}^{\mathsf{U}}(\pi)$$

where K_{ijn}^{U} *is inductively defined as follows:*

$$K_{ij0}^{\mathsf{U}}(\pi) = \begin{cases} ?\top \cup T_{ij}^{\mathsf{U}}(\pi) & \text{if } i = j \\ T_{ij}^{\mathsf{U}}(\pi) & \text{otherwise} \end{cases}$$

$$K_{ij(k+1)}^{\mathsf{U}}(\pi) = \begin{cases} (K_{kkk}^{\mathsf{U}}(\pi))^* & \text{if } i = k = j \\ (K_{kkk}^{\mathsf{U}}(\pi))^*; K_{kjk}^{\mathsf{U}}(\pi) & \text{if } i = k \neq j \\ K_{ikk}^{\mathsf{U}}(\pi); (K_{kkk}^{\mathsf{U}}(\pi))^* & \text{if } i \neq k = j \\ K_{ijk}^{\mathsf{U}}(\pi) \cup (K_{ikk}^{\mathsf{U}}(\pi); (K_{kkk}^{\mathsf{U}}(\pi))^*; K_{kjk}^{\mathsf{U}}(\pi)) & \text{if } i \neq k \neq j \end{cases}$$

$$(K) \ [\pi](\varphi \to \psi) \to ([\pi]\varphi \to [\pi]\psi) \qquad (top) \ [\mathsf{U}, e]\top \leftrightarrow \top$$
$$(test) \ [?\varphi_1]\varphi_2 \leftrightarrow (\varphi_1 \to \varphi_2) \qquad (atoms) \ [\mathsf{U}, e]p \leftrightarrow (\mathsf{pre}(e) \to p^{\mathsf{sub}(e)})$$
$$(seq.) \ [\pi_1; \pi_2]\varphi \leftrightarrow [\pi_1][\pi_2]\varphi \qquad (neg.) \ [\mathsf{U}, e]\neg\varphi \leftrightarrow (\mathsf{pre}(e) \to \neg[\mathsf{U}, e]\varphi)$$
$$(choice) \ [\pi_1 \cup \pi_2]\varphi \leftrightarrow [\pi_1]\varphi \wedge [\pi_2]\varphi \qquad (conj.) \ [\mathsf{U}, e](\varphi_1 \wedge \varphi_2) \leftrightarrow ([\mathsf{U}, e]\varphi_1 \wedge [\mathsf{U}, e]\varphi_2)$$
$$(mix) \ [\pi^*]\varphi \leftrightarrow \varphi \wedge [\pi][\pi^*]\varphi \qquad (prog.) \ [\mathsf{U}, e_i][\pi]\varphi \leftrightarrow \bigwedge_{j=0}^{n-1}[T_{ij}^{\mathsf{U}}(\pi)][\mathsf{U}, e_j]\varphi$$
$$(ind.) \ \varphi \wedge [\pi^*](\varphi \to [\pi]\varphi)) \to [\pi^*]\varphi \qquad (MP) \ \text{From} \vdash \varphi_1 \text{ and} \vdash \varphi_1 \to \varphi_2, \text{ infer} \vdash \varphi_2$$
$$(Nec_\pi) \ \text{From} \vdash \varphi, \text{ infer} \vdash [\pi]\varphi. \qquad (Nec_\mathsf{U}) \ \text{From} \vdash \varphi, \text{ infer} \vdash [\mathsf{U}, e]\varphi$$

Fig. 2. LCC calculus in [5] is that of PDL (left + MP + propositional calculus) plus reduction axioms for $[\mathsf{U}, e]$ (right)

3 A Matrix Calculus for Program Transformation

Intuitively, a reduction axiom for [U, e] characterises a situation *after* any update execution with U on e in terms of a situation *before* the update. For example, the axiom (*atoms*) states that an atom p will be the case *after* any update execution with U on e, i.e. $[U, e]p$, if and only if, *before* the update, the formula $p^{\mathrm{sub}(e)}$ holds whenever pre(e) holds, pre(e) $\rightarrow p^{\mathrm{sub}(e)}$. In the case of *(prog.)*, the axiom states that after any update execution with U on e_i every π-path will end in a φ-world, i.e. $[U, e_i][\pi]\varphi$, if and only if, before the update, every $T_{ij}^{U}(\pi)$-path ends in a world that will satisfy φ after any update execution with U on e_j where e_j is any action on U, $\bigwedge_{j=0}^{n-1}[T_{ij}^{U}(\pi)][U, e_j]\varphi$. Thus, the program transformer T_{ij}^{U} takes an LCC program π representing a path on $M \otimes U$ and returns an LCC program $T_{ij}^{U}(\pi)$ representing a 'matching' path on M, taking additional care that such path can be also reproduced in the action model U.

This paper proposes an alternative definition of program transformer that focuses mainly on the case for the Kleene closure operator. For every program π we define a matrix $\mu^{U}(\pi)$ whose cells are LCC programs. In this matrix, $\mu^{U}(\pi)[i, j]$ (the cell in the ith row and j^{th} column) corresponds to the transformation (i.e. the path in M) of π from e_i to e_j (i.e. the path in $M \otimes U$). The matrix $\mu^{U}(\pi)$ can be interpreted as the adjacency matrix of a labelled directed graph whose nodes are the actions in E and each edge from e_i to e_j is labelled with the transformation of π from e_i to e_j.

Example 1. The following graph will be used to illustrate the creation of the matrix $\mu^{U}(\pi^*)$ given $\mu^{U}(\pi)$. This is where our program transformers are substantially different from those in [5].

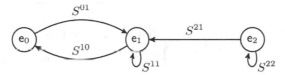

Suppose that the above graph represents the matrix $\mu^{U}(\pi)$, with labels S^{ij} representing the transformations of π from e_i to e_j (when there is no arrow between two -equal or different- nodes, it is assumed that the corresponding program is $?\bot$). In order to find the labels X^{ij} for the transformations of π^*, and thus the matrix $\mu^{U}(\pi^*)$, we follow an equational method first proposed by Brzozowski [8]. Observe, for example, how a π^*-path from e_1 to e_0 might start with S^{10} (an instance of π from e_1 to e_0) and then continue with X^{00} (an instance of π^* from e_0 to e_0), but it might also start with S^{11} (an instance of π from e_1 to e_1) and then continue with X^{10} (an instance of π^* from e_1 to e_0). In this case, these are the only two possibilities, and they can be represented by the following equation:

$$X^{10} = (S^{10}; X^{00}) \cup (S^{11}; X^{10}) \tag{1}$$

The equations for X^{00} and X^{20} can be obtained in a similar way:

$$X^{00} = ?\mathrm{pre}(e_0) \cup (S^{01}; X^{10}) \tag{2}$$

$$X^{20} = (S^{22}; X^{20}) \cup (S^{21}; X^{10}) \tag{3}$$

This yields an equation system of LCC programs with X^{00}, X^{10} and X^{20} as its only variables. Observe how, in (2), $?\mathsf{pre}(\mathsf{e}_0)$ indicates that a possible π^*-path from e_0 to e_0 is to do nothing, but the transformation should check whether e_0 is executable at the target state; hence the test $?\mathsf{pre}(\mathsf{e}_0)$.

To solve the above system we proceed by substitution using properties of Kleene algebra [14]. First, we can use (2) to replace X^{00} in (1):

$$
\begin{aligned}
X^{10} &= (S^{10}; (?\mathsf{pre}(\mathsf{e}_0) \cup (S^{01}; X^{10}))) \cup (S^{11}; X^{10}) \\
&= (S^{10}; ?\mathsf{pre}(\mathsf{e}_0)) \cup (S^{10}; S^{01}; X^{10}) \cup (S^{11}; X^{10}) \\
&= (S^{10}; ?\mathsf{pre}(\mathsf{e}_0)) \cup (((S^{10}; S^{01}) \cup S^{11}); X^{10}) \\
&= ((S^{10}; S^{01}) \cup S^{11})^*; S^{10}; ?\mathsf{pre}(\mathsf{e}_0)
\end{aligned}
\tag{4}
$$

The last equality in (4) uses Arden's Theorem [1]: $X = AX \cup B \Rightarrow X = A^*B$. After solving these equations, each X^{00}, X^{10} and X^{20} represents a transformed π^*-label from e_0, e_1 and e_2 to e_0, respectively; similar processes produce labels for π^*-paths to e_1 and e_2. The procedure is always the same, with a matrix calculus similar to that in Chapter 3 of [9] allowing us to calculate all X^{ij} in parallel and thus avoiding repeating the process for each destination node.

Formally, given an action model $\mathsf{U} = (\mathsf{E}, \mathsf{R}, \mathsf{pre}, \mathsf{sub})$ with $|\mathsf{E}| = n$, we define a function $\mu^{\mathsf{U}} : \Pi \to \mathcal{M}_{n \times n}$ where Π is the set of LCC programs and $\mathcal{M}_{n \times n}$ the class of n-square matrices. For each LCC program π, $\mu^{\mathsf{U}}(\pi)$ is a n-square matrix in which $\mu^{\mathsf{U}}(\pi)[i, j]$ is a transformation of π from e_i to e_j in the sense of the program transformers $T_{ij}^{\mathsf{U}}(\pi)$ of [5] (with $0 \le i, j \le n - 1$).

Definition 7. *The recursive definition of $\mu^{\mathsf{U}}(\pi)$ is as follows.*

– *Agents:*

$$
\mu^{\mathsf{U}}(a)[i, j] = \begin{cases} ?\mathsf{pre}(\mathsf{e}_i); a & \text{if } \mathsf{e}_i \mathsf{R}_a \mathsf{e}_j \\ ?\bot & \text{otherwise} \end{cases}
\tag{5}
$$

– *Test:*

$$
\mu^{\mathsf{U}}(?\varphi)[i, j] = \begin{cases} ?(\mathsf{pre}(\mathsf{e}_i) \wedge [\mathsf{U}, \mathsf{e}_i]\varphi) & \text{if } i = j \\ ?\bot & \text{otherwise} \end{cases}
\tag{6}
$$

– *Non-deterministic choice:*

$$
\mu^{\mathsf{U}}(\pi_1 \cup \pi_2)[i, j] = \bigoplus \{\mu^{\mathsf{U}}(\pi_1)[i, j], \ \mu^{\mathsf{U}}(\pi_2)[i, j]\}
\tag{7}
$$

$$
\text{where}^2 \ \bigoplus \Gamma = \begin{cases} \bigcup(\Gamma \setminus \{?\bot\}) & \text{if } \varnothing \neq \Gamma \neq \{?\bot\} \\ ?\bot & \text{otherwise} \end{cases}
\tag{8}
$$

– *Sequential composition:*

$$
\mu^{\mathsf{U}}(\pi_1; \pi_2)[i, j] = \bigoplus \{\mu^{\mathsf{U}}(\pi_1)[i, k] \odot \mu^{\mathsf{U}}(\pi_2)[k, j] \mid 0 \le k \le n - 1\}
\tag{9}
$$

---

^{2} Note that $\bigcup \Gamma$ is a generalised non-deterministic choice of the elements in Γ.

$$where\ \sigma \odot \rho = \begin{cases} \sigma; \rho & if\ \sigma \neq\ ?\bot \neq \rho \\ ?\bot & otherwise \end{cases} \tag{10}$$

- *Kleene closure:*

$$\mu^{\mathsf{U}}(\pi^*) = S_0^{\mathsf{U}}\left(\mu^{\mathsf{U}}(\pi)\ |\ A^{\mathsf{U}}\right) \tag{11}$$

where $\left(\mu^{\mathsf{U}}(\pi)\ |\ A^{\mathsf{U}}\right)$ *is an* $n \times 2n$ *matrix obtained by augmenting* $\mu^{\mathsf{U}}(\pi)$ *with* A^{U}, *an* $n \times n$ *matrix defined as*

$$A^{\mathsf{U}}[i,j] = \begin{cases} ?\mathsf{pre}(e_i) & if\ i = j \\ ?\bot & otherwise \end{cases} \tag{12}$$

Function $S_k^{\mathsf{U}}(M\ |\ A)$, *for* $0 \leq k < n$, *works over* $(M\ |\ A)$ *to get a matrix* $(M'\ |\ A')$ *and then calls* $S_{k+1}^{\mathsf{U}}(M'\ |\ A')$. *When* $k \geq n$, $S_k^{\mathsf{U}}(M\ |\ A)$ *returns the right part of the augmented matrix* $(M\ |\ A)$, *that is,* A. *Formally,*

$$S_k^{\mathsf{U}}(M\ |\ A) = \begin{cases} A & if\ k \geq n \\ S_{k+1}^{\mathsf{U}}(Subs_k(Ard_k(M\ |\ A))) & otherwise \end{cases} \tag{13}$$

with Ard_k *and* $Subs_k$ *functions from* $\mathcal{M}_{n \times 2n}$ *to* $\mathcal{M}_{n \times 2n}$ *that apply Arden's Theorem to row* k, *and a substitution to rows different than* k, *respectively, that is,*

$$Ard_k(N)[i,j] = \begin{cases} N[i,j] & if\ i \neq k \\ ?\bot & if\ i = k - j \\ N[i,j] & if\ i = k \neq j\ and\ N[k,k] = ?\bot \\ N[k,k]^* \odot N[i,j] & otherwise \end{cases} \tag{14}$$

$$Subs_k(N)[i,j] = \begin{cases} N[i,j] & if\ i = k \\ ?\bot & if\ i \neq k = j \\ \oplus\{N[i,k] \odot N[k,j], N[i,j]\} & otherwise \end{cases} \tag{15}$$

The following propositions prove the semantic equivalence of $\oplus\Gamma$ (8) and $\sigma \odot \rho$ (10) with standard PDL operators. Nevertheless, their syntactic definitions remove many useless $?\bot$ that appear during the transformation process, thus reducing the length of the transformed programs.

Proposition 1. *Given a set* Γ *of* LCC *programs,* $[\![\oplus\Gamma]\!]^M = [\![\bigcup\Gamma]\!]^M$ *for all epistemic models* M.

Proof. Take any epistemic model M. Equation (8) states that $\oplus\Gamma$ is a non-deterministic choice of the LCC programs in Γ that returns $\bigcup\Gamma \setminus \{?\bot\}$ when Γ is different from both $\varnothing$ and $\{?\bot\}$, and $?\bot$ otherwise. In the first case, $[\![\oplus\Gamma]\!]^M = [\![\bigcup\Gamma]\!]^M$ because $[\![\bigcup\Gamma]\!]^M = [\![\bigcup\Gamma \setminus \{?\bot\}]\!]^M$; in the second, $[\![\oplus\Gamma]\!]^M = [\![\bigcup\Gamma]\!]^M$ because $[\![\bigcup\varnothing]\!]^M = [\![\bigcup\{?\bot\}]\!]^M = [\![?\bot]\!]^M = \varnothing$.

Proposition 2. *If σ and ρ are two LCC programs, then $[\![\sigma;\rho]\!]^M = [\![\sigma \odot \rho]\!]^M$ for all epistemic models M.*

Proof. Take any epistemic model M. Equation (10) states that $\sigma \odot \rho$ differs from $\sigma;\rho$ only when either σ or else ρ is $?\perp$. But $[\![\sigma;?\perp]\!]^M = [\![?\perp;\sigma]\!]^M = [\![?\perp;?\perp]\!]^M = [\![?\perp]\!]^M = \varnothing$; hence, $[\![\sigma;\rho]\!]^M = [\![\sigma \odot \rho]\!]^M$.

Lemma 1. *Let $U = (E, R, pre, sub)$ be an action model with $e_i, e_j \in E$; let π be an LCC program. For any epistemic model M,*

$$[\![T_{ij}^U(\pi)]\!]^M = [\![\mu^U(\pi)[i,j]]\!]^M$$

Proof. By induction on the complexity of π. Let M be an epistemic model; then

(Base Cases: a and $?\varphi$) Trivial: the definitions are identical for a and $?\varphi$.

(Ind. Case $\pi_1 \cup \pi_2$) Suppose (Ind. Hyp.) the claim holds for π_1 and π_2. Then

$$
\begin{aligned}
[\![T_{ij}^U(\pi_1 \cup \pi_2)]\!]^M &= [\![T_{ij}^U(\pi_1) \cup T_{ij}^U(\pi_2)]\!]^M & \text{(Def. 6)}\\
&= [\![T_{ij}^U(\pi_1)]\!]^M \cup [\![T_{ij}^U(\pi_2)]\!]^M & \text{(Def. of } [\![\cdot]\!]^M)\\
&= [\![\mu^U(\pi_1)[i,j]]\!]^M \cup [\![\mu^U(\pi_2)[i,j]]\!]^M & \text{(Ind. Hyp.)}\\
&= \{\mu^U(\pi_1)[i,j] \cup \mu^U(\pi_2)[i,j]\}M & \text{(Def. of } [\![\cdot]\!]^M)\\
&= [\![\oplus\{\mu^U(\pi_1)[i,j], \mu^U(\pi_2)[i,j]\}]\!]^M & \text{(Prop. 1)}\\
&= [\![\mu^U(\pi_1 \cup \pi_2)[i,j]]\!]^M & \text{(Def. of } \mu^U(\pi_1 \cup \pi_2) \text{ in (7))}
\end{aligned}
$$

(Ind. Case $\pi_1;\pi_2$) Suppose (Ind. Hyp.) the claim holds for π_1 and π_2. Then

$$
\begin{aligned}
[\![T_{ij}^U(\pi_1;\pi_2)]\!]^M &= [\![\bigcup_{k=0}^{n-1}(T_{ik}^U(\pi_1); T_{kj}^U(\pi_2))]\!]^M & \text{(by Def. 6)}\\
&= \bigcup_{k=0}^{n-1} \left([\![T_{ik}^U(\pi_1)]\!]^M \circ [\![T_{kj}^U(\pi_2)]\!]^M\right) & \text{(by Def. of } [\![\cdot]\!]^M)\\
&= \bigcup_{k=0}^{n-1} \left([\![\mu^U(\pi_1)[i,k]]\!]^M \circ [\![\mu^U(\pi_2)[k,j]]\!]^M\right) & \text{(Ind. Hyp.)}\\
&= [\![\bigcup_{k=0}^{n-1}(\mu^U(\pi_1)[i,k]; \mu^U(\pi_2)[k,j])]\!]^M & \text{(by Def. of } [\![\cdot]\!]^M)\\
&= [\![\bigcup_{k=0}^{n-1}(\mu^U(\pi_1)[i,k] \odot \mu^U(\pi_2)[k,j])]\!]^M & \text{(Prop. 2)}\\
&= [\![\oplus\{\mu^U(\pi_1)[i,k] \odot \mu^U(\pi_2)[k,j] \mid 0 \le k \le n-1\}]\!]^M & \text{(Prop. 1)}\\
&= [\![\mu^U(\pi_1;\pi_2)[i,j]]\!]^M & \text{(by Def. of } \mu^U(\pi_1;\pi_2) \text{ in (9))}
\end{aligned}
$$

(Ind. Case π^*) Suppose (Ind. Hyp.) the claim holds for π and observe how $[\![\pi^*]\!]^M = [\![?\perp \cup (\pi;\pi^*)]\!]^M$ (which can be proved by PDL axioms). Now,

$$
\begin{aligned}
[\![T_{ij}^U(\pi^*)]\!]^M &= [\![T_{ij}^U(?\top \cup \pi;\pi^*)]\!]^M\\
&= [\![T_{ij}^U(?\top)]\!]^M \cup [\![\bigcup_{k=0}^{n-1}(T_{ik}^U(\pi); T_{kj}^U(\pi^*))]\!]^M & \text{(by Def. 6)}
\end{aligned}
$$

$$= [\![T_{ij}^{\mathsf{U}}(?\top)]\!]^M \cup \bigcup_{k=0}^{n-1} \left([\![T_{ik}^{\mathsf{U}}(\pi)]\!]^M \circ [\![T_{kj}^{\mathsf{U}}(\pi^*)]\!]^M\right) \quad \text{(by Def. of } [\![\cdot]\!]^M)$$

$$= [\![T_{ij}^{\mathsf{U}}(?\top)]\!]^M \cup \bigcup_{k=0}^{n-1} \left([\![\mu^{\mathsf{U}}(\pi)[i,k]]\!]^M \circ [\![T_{kj}^{\mathsf{U}}(\pi^*)]\!]^M\right) \quad \text{(Ind. Hyp.)}$$

The last equality produces n^2 relational equations. By abbreviating $[\![T_{ij}^{\mathsf{U}}(\pi^*)]\!]^M$ as X^{ij} for every $0 \le i, j \le n-1$, we get

$$X^{ij} = [\![T_{ij}^{\mathsf{U}}(?\top)]\!]^M \cup \bigcup_{k=0}^{n-1} \left([\![\mu^{\mathsf{U}}(\pi)[i,k]]\!]^M \circ X^{kj}\right) \tag{16}$$

Thus, it is enough to prove that $[\![\mu^{\mathsf{U}}(\pi^*)[i,j]]\!]^M$ is a solution for X^{ij}. This is shown in the following three propositions about the functions building $\mu^{\mathsf{U}}(\pi^*)$.

Proposition 3. *Take* $\Omega = (\mu^{\mathsf{U}}(\pi) \mid A^{\mathsf{U}})$ *(see (7)). Then,*

$$X^{ij} = [\![\Omega[i, j+n]]\!]^M \cup \bigcup_{k=0}^{n-1} \left([\![\Omega[i,k]]\!]^M \circ X^{kj}\right) \tag{17}$$

Proof. It will be shown that the right-hand side (r.h.s.) of (16) and (17) coincide. Their respective rightmost parts are equivalent since, for $0 \le k \le n-1$, $\Omega[i,k] = \mu^{\mathsf{U}}(\pi)[i,k]$ (recall that Ω is built by adding additional columns at the right of the n first columns of $\mu^{\mathsf{U}}(\pi)$, and the matrix's indexes start from 0). For the leftmost parts,

$$[\![T_{ij}^{\mathsf{U}}(?\top)]\!]^M = \begin{cases} [\![?(\mathsf{pre}(e_i) \wedge |\mathsf{U}, e_i|\top)]\!]^M & \text{if } i = j \\ [\![?\bot]\!]^M & \text{otherwise} \end{cases} \quad \text{(by Def. 6)}$$

$$= \begin{cases} [\![?\mathsf{pre}(e_i)]\!]^M & \text{if } i = j \\ [\![?\bot]\!]^M & \text{otherwise} \end{cases} \quad \text{(as } [\mathsf{U}, e_i]\top \text{ is trivially true)}$$

$$= [\![A^{\mathsf{U}}[i,j]]\!]^M = [\![\Omega[i, j+n]]\!]^M \quad \text{(by (12) and Def. of } \Omega)$$

Proposition 4. *For* $0 \le k \le n-1$, *if* N *is a matrix of size* $n \times 2n$ *with all cells in columns* $0, \dots, k-1$ *equal to* $?\bot$, *then* $Subs_k(Ard_k(N))$ *contains all cells in columns* $0, \dots, k$ *equal to* $?\bot$.

Proof. Start with $Ard_k(N)$. Observe in (14) that the only modified cells are in the kth row. Cell $Ard_k(N)[k,k]$ in the kth column is converted into $?\bot$. With respect to cells in columns from 0 to $k-1$, if they were $?\bot$, they continue being $?\bot$: those cells $N[i,j]$ do not change, if $N[k,k] = ?\bot$, or otherwise are converted by (14) into $N[k,k]^* \odot N[i,j]$ and, by (10), if $N[i,j] = ?\bot$, then $N[k,k]^* \odot N[i,j] = ?\bot$.

Now, call N' the output of $Ard_k(N)$ and observe $Subs_k(N')$'s definition (15): the only cells that change are in rows different to k. With respect to any such row i, the position in the kth column is made $?\bot$. For cells in previous columns, $j < k$, the last case in the definition returns $\oplus\{N'[i,k] \odot N'[k,j], N'[i,j]\}$. But as

N' is the result of $Ard_k(N)$, $N'[k,j]$ is $?\bot$ (because, as argued above, $Ard_k(N)$ works over the kth row and keeps the $?\bot$ in columns before k). Also, $N'[i,j] = ?\bot$, as columns $j < k$ are filled with $?\bot$. So $\oplus\{N'[i,k] \odot N'[k,j], N'[i,j]\}$ becomes $\oplus\{N'[i,k]\odot?\bot, ?\bot\}$ and, by (8) and (10), it is $?\bot$.

Proposition 5. *Given an $n \times 2n$ matrix N of* LCC *programs, the equations built using* (17), *with $\Omega = Subs_k(Ard_k(N))$, $0 \le k \le n - 1$, are correct transformations of the equations built in the same way with $\Omega = N$.*

Proof. As argued in the proof of Proposition 4, $Ard_k(N)$ works only on the kth row. If $N[k,k] = ?\bot$, nothing is done, so according to (17) the equations for X^{kj} $(0 \le j \le n - 1)$ do not change. Otherwise, the kth row of N changes: all cells $N[k,j]$ with $j \ne k$ become $N[k,k]^* \odot N[k,j]$, except $N[k,k]$ which becomes $?\bot$. Then, for every $0 \le j \le n - 1$, the equation for X^{kj} becomes (using index t instead of k and removing $[\![?\bot]\!]^M \circ X^{kj}$ from the union):

$$X^{kj} = [\![N[k,k]^* \odot N[k,j+n]]\!]^M \cup \bigcup_{\substack{0 \le t \le n-1 \\ t \ne k}} \left([\![N[k,k]^* \odot N[k,t]]\!]^M \circ X^{tj}\right)$$

By Proposition 2 and $[\![\cdot]\!]^M$'s definition, this can be rewritten as

$$X^{kj} = ([\![N[k,k]]\!]^M)^* \circ [\![N[k,j+n]]\!]^M \cup \\ \bigcup_{\substack{0 \le t \le n-1 \\ t \ne k}} \left(([\![N[k,k]]\!]^M)^* \circ [\![N[k,t]]\!]^M \circ X^{tj}\right) \tag{18}$$

which is an application of Arden's Theorem [1] to the corresponding equation for the original row in N:

$$X^{kj} = [\![N[k,j+n]]\!]^M \cup \bigcup_{0 \le t \le n-1} \left([\![N[k,t]]\!]^M \circ X^{tj}\right) \tag{19}$$

Arden's Theorem (which works on regular algebras, such as LCC programs) gives $X = A^* \circ B$ as a solution for $X = (A \circ X) \cup B$. In (19), X is X^{kj}, A is $[\![N[k,k]]\!]^M$, and B is the union of all terms in the r.h.s. of (19) except $[\![N[k,k]]\!]^M \circ X^{kj}$. Besides Arden's Theorem, from (19) to (18) we use $\circ$'s distribution over $\cup$.

Now denote by N' the output of $Ard_k(N)$. We move to $Subs_k(N')$ to show that the equations obtained from it with (17) are correct transformations of the equations built from N'. The only modified cells in $Subs_k(N')$ are in rows different to k, so it only affects equations for X^{ij} with $i \ne k$. According to (17), if $\Omega = N'$, these equations are (using t instead of k):

$$X^{ij} = [\![N'[i,j+n]]\!]^M \cup \bigcup_{t=0}^{n-1} \left([\![N'[i,t]]\!]^M \circ X^{tj}\right) \tag{20}$$

The same equation for $\Omega = Subs_k(N')$ becomes the following (we remove from the union the term $[\![?\bot]\!]^M \circ X^{kj}$, as it is equivalent to $\varnothing$):

$$X^{ij} = [\![\oplus\{N'[i,k] \odot N'[k,j+n], N'[i,j+n]\}]\!]^M \cup \\ \bigcup_{\substack{0 \le t \le n-1 \\ t \ne k}} \left([\![\oplus\{N'[i,k] \odot N'[k,t], N'[i,t]\}]\!]^M \circ X^{tj}\right) \tag{21}$$

By using Propositions 1 and 2 and the properties of $[\![\cdot]\!]^M$, equation (21) becomes

$$X^{ij} = ([\![N'[i,k]]\!]^M \circ [\![N'[k,j+n]]\!]^M) \cup [\![N'[i,j+n]]\!]^M \cup$$
$$\bigcup_{\substack{0 \le t \le n-1 \\ t \ne k}} \left((([\![N'[i,k]]\!]^M \circ [\![N'[k,t]]\!]^M) \cup [\![N'[i,t]]\!]^M) \circ X^{tj} \right) \qquad (22)$$

But note that in the equation for X^{kj}, which is the same at N' and $Subs_k(N')$, the kth row of N' is not changed by $Subs_k(N')$:

$$X^{kj} = [\![N'[k,j+n]]\!]^M \cup \bigcup_{\substack{0 \le t \le n-1 \\ t \ne k}} \left([\![N'[k,t]]\!]^M \circ X^{tj} \right) \qquad (23)$$

We have eliminated the term $[\![N'[k,k]]\!]^M \circ X^{kj}$ in (23) because $N' = Ard_k(N)$ and by (14), $N'[k,k] = ?\bot$, which produces $[\![N'[k,k]]\!]^M \circ X^{kj} = \varnothing$.

Observe that (22) can be obtained from (20) by replacing X^{kj} by the r.h.s. of (23) and applying the distribution of $\circ$ over $\cup$. So the modified equation (21) is equivalent to correct transformations of the original one (20).

The proof of the case π^* in Lemma 1 can be finished now. Take the set of relational equations given by (16). By (11), $\mu^{\cup}(\pi^*)$ operates by iterating calls to $S_k^{\cup}$ (with k from 0 to n) with $\Omega = (\mu^{\cup}(\pi) \mid A^{\cup})$ as the initial argument. Let M_{-1} be Ω and M_k the output of $S_k^{\cup}(M_{k-1})$. By Proposition 3, (17) gives equations equivalent to (16). By Proposition 5, the equations are correct for each successive M_k ($0 \le k \le n-1$). As the calls to $S_k^{\cup}$ are done iteratively with k from 0 to $n-1$, Proposition 4 guarantees that, in M_{n-1}, all cells in columns for 0 to $n-1$ are equal to $?\bot$. Thus, equations (17) for M_{n-1} are:

$$X^{ij} = [\![M_{n-1}[i,j+n]]\!]^M \qquad (24)$$

The rightmost union in (17) has disappeared ($M[i,k] = ?\bot$ for $0 \le k \le n-1$, and $[\![?\bot]\!]^M = \varnothing$). Now, by $S_k^{\cup}$'s definition in (13), $M_{n-1}[i,j+n] = M_n[i,j] = \mu^{\cup}(\pi^*)[i,j]$, so $X^{ij} = [\![\mu^{\cup}(\pi^*)[i,j]]\!]^M$. Then, since X^{ij} represents $[\![T_{ij}^{\cup}(\pi^*)]\!]^M$,

$$[\![T_{ij}^{\cup}(\pi^*)]\!]^M = [\![\mu^{\cup}(\pi^*)[i,j]]\!]^M$$

which completes the proof.

4   A New Translation and Axiom System for LCC

We can now define new translation functions t', r' as follows. Note that t' and r' are defined as the translation functions t, r for formulas φ and programs π proposed in [5],[3] with the only exception of formulas of the form $[\cup, e_i][\pi]\varphi$.

---

[3] Two minor mistakes for the cases $[\pi]\varphi$ and $[\cup, e]p$ are corrected here w.r.t. [5]; namely, these should respectively be $t([\cup, e]p) = t(pre(e)) \to t(p^{\text{sub}(e)})$ and $t([\cup, e_i][\pi]\varphi) = \bigwedge_{j=0}^{n-1} [r(T_{ij}^{\cup}(\pi))]t([\cup, e_j]\varphi)$.

$$
\begin{aligned}
t'(\top) &= \top & r'(a) &= a \\
t'(p) &= p & r'(B) &= B \\
t'(\neg\varphi) &= \neg t'(\varphi) & r'(?\varphi) &= ?t'(\varphi) \\
t'(\varphi_1 \wedge \varphi_2) &= t'(\varphi_1) \wedge t'(\varphi_2) & r'(\pi_1; \pi_2) &= r'(\pi_1); r'(\pi_2) \\
t'([\pi]\varphi) &= [r'(\pi)]t'(\varphi) & r'(\pi_1 \cup \pi_2) &= r'(\pi_1) \cup r'(\pi_2) \\
t'([\mathsf{U},\mathsf{e}]\top) &= \top & r'(\pi^*) &= (r'(\pi))^* \\
t'([\mathsf{U},\mathsf{e}]p) &= t'(\mathsf{pre}(\mathsf{e})) \rightarrow t'(p^{\mathsf{sub}(\mathsf{e})}) \\
t'([\mathsf{U},\mathsf{e}]\neg\varphi) &= t'(\mathsf{pre}(\mathsf{e})) \rightarrow \neg t'([\mathsf{U},\mathsf{e}]\varphi) \\
t'([\mathsf{U},\mathsf{e}](\varphi_1 \wedge \varphi_2)) &= t'([\mathsf{U},\mathsf{e}]\varphi) \wedge t'([\mathsf{U},\mathsf{e}]\varphi_2) \\
t'([\mathsf{U},\mathsf{e}_i][\pi]\varphi) &= \bigwedge_{\substack{0 \le j \le n-1 \\ \mu^{\mathsf{U}}(\pi)[i,j] \ne ?\bot}} [r'(\mu^{\mathsf{U}}(\pi)[i,j])]t'([\mathsf{U},\mathsf{e}_j]\varphi) \\
t'([\mathsf{U},\mathsf{e}][\mathsf{U}',\mathsf{e}']\varphi) &= t'([\mathsf{U},\mathsf{e}]t'([\mathsf{U}',\mathsf{e}']\varphi))
\end{aligned}
$$

Corollary 1. *The translation functions t', r' reduce the language of* LCC *to that of* PDL. *This translation is correct.*

Proof. The effective reduction from LCC to PDL is immediate by inspection. Its correctness follows from that in [5], with Lemma 1 for the case $[\mathsf{U},\mathsf{e}_i][\pi]\varphi$.

Definition 8. *We define a new axiom system for* LCC *by replacing the reduction axiom for* PDL *programs with the following*

$$
[\mathsf{U},\mathsf{e}_i][\pi]\varphi \quad \leftrightarrow \quad \bigwedge_{\substack{0 \le j \le n-1 \\ \mu^{\mathsf{U}}(\pi)[i,j] \ne ?\bot}} [\mu^{\mathsf{U}}(\pi)[i,j]][\mathsf{U},\mathsf{e}_j]\varphi \qquad (programs)
$$

Corollary 2. *The axiom system for* LCC *from Def. 8 is sound and complete.*

Proof. The only new axiom, that for PDL-programs, is sound by Lemma 1. For completeness, the proof system for PDL is complete, and every LCC formula is provably equivalent to a PDL formula using Corollary 1.

5   Complexity of the New Transformers

The original program transformers in [5] require exponential time due to the use of Kleene's method [13]. Moreover, the size of the transformed formulas of type π^* is also exponential because of the definition of K^{U}_{ijn} (Def. 6). We analyse now the complexity of computing $\mu^{\mathsf{U}}(\pi)$ for the different kinds of programs π. We assume typical data structures such as arrays (of dimensions 1 and 2) and hash tables with their usual properties.

Agents. According to (5), computing $\mu^{\mathsf{U}}(a)[i,j]$ requires to check whether $\mathsf{e}_i \mathsf{R}_a \mathsf{e}_j$ and, in the affirmative case, to obtain $?\mathsf{pre}(\mathsf{e}_i)$. The other operations can be clearly done in constant time: returning $?\mathsf{pre}(\mathsf{e}_i); a$ or $?\bot$. First, $\mathsf{e}_i \mathsf{R}_a \mathsf{e}_j$ can be checked in constant time if there is a bi-dimensional array M_a with $M_a[i,j]$ equal to 1 iff $\mathsf{e}_i \mathsf{R}_a \mathsf{e}_j$ and 0 otherwise. Also, $?\mathsf{pre}(\mathsf{e}_i)$ can be returned in constant time if there is an array P with $P[i] = \mathsf{pre}(\mathsf{e}_i)$. So $\mu^{\mathsf{U}}(a)[i,j]$ is computed in $\mathcal{O}(1)$. Then, the whole matrix $\mu^{\mathsf{U}}(a)$ can be computed in $\mathcal{O}(n^2)$.

Test. Computing $\mu^U(?\varphi)[i, j]$ (see (6)) requires again to access $\mathsf{pre}(e_i)$, which we argued to be in $\mathcal{O}(1)$. The other operations (checking whether $i = j$, or returning the corresponding value) are also clearly in $\mathcal{O}(1)$. So computing $\mu^U(?\varphi)[i, j]$ is again in $\mathcal{O}(1)$ and $\mu^U(?\varphi)$ in $\mathcal{O}(n^2)$.

Non-deterministic choice. Assume that $\mu^U(\pi_1)$ and $\mu^U(\pi_2)$ are given. Then, computing $\mu^U(\pi_1 \cup \pi_2)[i, j]$ (see (7)) requires a constant number of operations: access $\mu^U(\pi_1)[i, j]$ and $\mu^U(\pi_2)[i, j]$, check whether some of them is $?\bot$ and return the output. So computing the whole $\mu^U(\pi_1 \cup \pi_2)$ is again in $\mathcal{O}(n^2)$.

Sequential composition. Again, assume that $\mu^U(\pi_1)$ and $\mu^U(\pi_2)$ are given. Computing $\mu^U(\pi_1; \pi_2)[i, j]$ (see (9)) requires to get n values $\mu^U(\pi_1)[i, k] \odot \mu^U(\pi_2)[k, j]$. Each of these values can be computed in $\mathcal{O}(1)$, as the required operations are just to access both $\mu^U(\pi_1)[i, k]$ and $\mu^U(\pi_2)[k, j]$ and apply $\odot$. So the n values of $\mu^U(\pi_1)[i, k] \odot \mu^U(\pi_2)[k, j]$ are computed in $\mathcal{O}(n)$. Also, $\oplus$ must be applied to those values. It can be done by using a hash table where the different values are stored while they are being generated: new values are only inserted if they were not previously in. Assuming that the hash table is accessed in $\mathcal{O}(1)$, then $\mu^U(\pi_1; \pi_2)[i, j]$ is computed in $\mathcal{O}(n)$. So $\mu^U(\pi_1; \pi_2)$ is computed in $\mathcal{O}(n^3)$.

Kleene Closure. Again, we assume that $\mu^U(\pi)$ is given. Then, computing $\mu^U(\pi^*)$ requires first to build $(\mu^U(\pi) \mid \Lambda^U)$ and then n iterations of S_k^U (see (11)). Note that the size of $(\mu^U(\pi) \mid \Lambda^U)$ is $n \times 2n$ and to build each cell requires a constant number of operations. So building the initial matrix is in $\mathcal{O}(n^2)$. Now, each one of the n calls to S_k^U is in $\mathcal{O}(n^2)$: observe that Ard_k (see (14)) only changes the cells in row k and $Subs_k$ the cells in the other rows, and each cell can be modified in constant time. So the n calls to S_k^U are computed in $\mathcal{O}(n^3)$.

In previous paragraphs we have supposed that the matrices for subprograms were given. With that assumption, the greatest complexity to build $\mu^U(\pi)$ is in $\mathcal{O}(n^3)$. So, without the assumption, if g is the number of subprograms in π, building $\mu^U(\pi)$ from scratch is in $\mathcal{O}(g \cdot n^3)$.

6   Summary and Future Work

In this work, we presented an alternative definition of the program transformers used to obtain reduction axioms in LCC. The proposal uses a matrix treatment of Brzozowski's equational method in order to obtain a regular expression representing the language accepted by a finite automaton. While Brzozowski's method and that used in the original LCC paper [5] are equivalent, the first is computationally more efficient; moreover, the matrix treatment presented here is more synthetic, simple and elegant, thus allowing a simpler implementation.

Towards future work, some definitions used by program transformers (particularly the $\odot$ operation) can be modified to obtain even simpler expressions. For example, $\sigma \odot \rho$ might be defined as σ if $\sigma \neq ?\top = \rho$ and as ρ if $\sigma = ?\top$. Moreover, the algorithm implementing Ard_k and $Subs_k$ functions can be improved by disregarding the $N[i, j]$ elements with $j < k$ or $j > n + k$ (being $N[i, j]$ a $n \times 2n$ matrix), since those are necessarily equal to $?\bot$. These changes would provide a more efficient translation, although the order of complexity would not be lower.

Acknowledgements. We acknowledge support from the project FFI2011-15945-E (Ministerio de Economía y Competitividad, Spain). We would also like to express our gratitude to the anonymous referees, and to Barteld Kooi for a helpful discussion on the translation function.

References

1. Arden, D.N.: Delayed-logic and finite-state machines. In: SWCT (FOCS), pp. 133–151. IEEE Computer Society (1961)
2. Baltag, A., Moss, L.S.: Logics for epistemic programs. Synthese 139(2), 165–224 (2004)
3. Baltag, A., Moss, L.S., Solecki, S.: The logic of public announcements and common knowledge and private suspicions. In: Gilboa, I. (ed.) TARK, pp. 43–56. Morgan Kaufmann, San Francisco (1998)
4. van Benthem, J.: Logical Dynamics of Information and Interaction. Cambridge University Press (2011)
5. van Benthem, J., van Eijck, J., Kooi, B.: Logics of communication and change. Information and Computation 204(11), 1620–1662 (2006)
6. van Benthem, J., Gerbrandy, J., Hoshi, T., Pacuit, E.: Merging frameworks for interaction. Journal of Philosophical Logic 38(5), 491–526 (2009)
7. van Benthem, J., Kooi, B.: Reduction axioms for epistemic actions. In: Schmidt, R., Pratt-Hartmann, I., Reynolds, M., Wansing, H. (eds.) Advances in Modal Logic (Number UMCS-04-09-01 in Technical Report Series), pp. 197–211. Department of Computer Science, University of Manchester (2004)
8. Brzozowski, J.A.: Derivatives of regular expressions. Journal of the ACM 11(4), 481–494 (1964)
9. Conway, J.H.: Regular Algebra and Finite Machines. Chapman and Hall (1971)
10. van Ditmarsch, H., van der Hoek, W., Kooi, B.: Dynamic Epistemic Logic. Synthese Library Series, vol. 337. Springer (2007)
11. Fagin, R., Halpern, J.Y., Moses, Y., Vardi, M.Y.: Reasoning about knowledge. The MIT Press, Cambridge (1995)
12. Harel, D., Kozen, D., Tiuryn, J.: Dynamic Logic. MIT Press, Cambridge (2000)
13. Kleene, S.: Representation of events in nerve nets and finite automata. In: Shannon, C.E., McCarthy, J. (eds.) Automata Studies, pp. 3–41. Princeton University Press, Princeton (1956)
14. Kozen, D.: On kleene algebras and closed semirings. In: Rovan, B. (ed.) MFCS 1990. LNCS, vol. 452, pp. 26–47. Springer, Heidelberg (1990)
15. Parikh, R., Ramanujam, R.: A knowledge based semantics of messages. Journal of Logic, Language and Information 12(4), 453–467 (2003)

On the Expressiveness of the Interval Logic of Allen's Relations Over Finite and Discrete Linear Orders

Luca Aceto[1,2], Dario Della Monica[1], Anna Ingólfsdóttir[1],
Angelo Montanari[3], and Guido Sciavicco[4]

[1] ICE-TCS, School of Computer Science, Reykjavik University, Iceland
{luca,dariodm,annai}@ru.is
[2] Gran Sasso Science Institute, INFN, L'Aquila, Italy
[3] Dept. of Mathematics and Computer Science, University of Udine, Italy
angelo.montanari@uniud.it
[4] Dept. of Information Engineering and Communications, University of Murcia, Spain
guido@um.es

Abstract. Interval temporal logics take time intervals, instead of time instants, as their primitive temporal entities. One of the most studied interval temporal logics is Halpern and Shoham's modal logic of time intervals HS, which associates a modal operator with each binary relation between intervals over a linear order (the so-called Allen's interval relations). A complete classification of all HS fragments with respect to their relative expressive power has been recently given for the classes of all linear orders and of all dense linear orders. The cases of discrete and finite linear orders turn out to be much more involved. In this paper, we make a significant step towards solving the classification problem over those classes of linear orders. First, we illustrate various non-trivial temporal properties that can be expressed by HS fragments when interpreted over finite and discrete linear orders; then, we provide a complete set of definabilities for the HS modalities corresponding to the Allen's relations *meets*, *later*, *begins*, *finishes*, and *during*, as well as the ones corresponding to their inverse relations. The only missing cases are those of the relations *overlaps* and *overlapped by*.

1 Introduction

Interval reasoning naturally arises in various fields of computer science and artificial intelligence, ranging from hardware and real-time system verification to natural language processing, from constraint satisfaction to planning [4,5,16,24,25,27]. Interval temporal logics make it possible to reason about interval structures over linearly ordered domains, where time intervals, rather than time instants, are the primitive ontological entities. The distinctive features of interval temporal logics turn out to be useful in various application domains [8,13,23,24,27]. For instance, they allow one to model *telic statements*, that is, statements that express goals or accomplishments, e.g., the statement: 'The airplane flew from Venice to Toronto' [23]. Moreover, when we restrict ourselves to discrete linear orders, such as, for instance, $\mathbb{N}$ or $\mathbb{Z}$, some interval temporal logics are expressive enough to constrain the length of intervals, thus allowing one to specify safety properties involving quantitative conditions [23]. This is the case, for instance, with the well-known 'gas-burner' example [27]. Temporal logics with interval-

E. Fermé and J. Leite (Eds.): JELIA 2014, LNAI 8761, pp. 267–281, 2014.

based semantics have also been proposed as suitable formalisms for the specification and verification of hardware [24] and of real-time systems [27].

The variety of binary relations between intervals in a linear order was first studied by Allen [4], who investigated their use in systems for time management and planning. In [18], Halpern and Shoham introduced and systematically analyzed the (full) logic of Allen's relations, called HS in this paper, that features one modality for each Allen relation. In particular, they showed that HS is highly undecidable over most classes of linear orders. This result motivated the search for (syntactic) HS fragments offering a good balance between expressiveness and decidability/complexity [6,7,11,12,14,20,22,23]. A comparative analysis of the expressive power of HS fragments is far from being trivial, because some HS modalities are definable in terms of others, and thus syntactically different fragments may turn out to be equally expressive. Moreover, the definability of a specific modality in terms of other ones depends, in general, on the class of linear orders over which the logic is interpreted, and the classification of the relative expressive power of HS fragments with respect to a given class of linear orders cannot be directly transferred to another class. More precisely, while definabilities do transfer from a class $\mathcal{C}$ to all its proper sub-classes, there might be new definability relations that hold in some sub-class of $\mathcal{C}$, but not in $\mathcal{C}$ itself. Conversely, undefinabilities do transfer from a class to all its proper super-classes, but not vice versa. Proving a specific undefinability result amounts to providing a counterexample based on concrete linear orders from the considered class. As a matter of fact, different assumptions on the underlying linear orders give rise, in general, to different sets of definabilities [2,15].

Contribution. Many classes of linear orders are of practical interest, including the class of all (resp., dense, discrete, finite) linear orders, as well as the particular linear order on $\mathbb{R}$ (resp., $\mathbb{Q}$, $\mathbb{Z}$, and $\mathbb{N}$). A precise characterization of the expressive power of all HS fragments with respect to the class of all linear orders and that of all dense linear orders has been given in [15] and [2], respectively. The classification of HS fragments over the classes of discrete and finite linear orders presents a number of convoluted technical difficulties. In [14], which is an extended version of both [9] and [10], the authors focus on strongly discrete linear orders, by characterizing and classifying all *decidable* fragments of HS with respect to both complexity of the satisfiability problem and relative expressive power. In this paper, we make a significant step towards a complete classification of the expressiveness of all (*decidable* and *undecidable*) fragments of HS over finite and discrete linear orders, and in doing so we considerably extend the expressiveness results presented in [14]; in this respect, it is worth observing that, when considering all the HS fragments (thus not only the decidable ones) the undefinability results for the HS modalities presented in [14] must be generalized and extended. This generalization presents a number of technical difficulties, which are targeted here. Given the present contribution, the only missing piece of the expressiveness puzzle is that of the definabilities for the modality corresponding to the Allen relation *overlaps* (those for the inverse relation *overlapped by* would immediately follow by symmetry).

Structure of the Paper. In the next section, we introduce the logic HS. Then, in Section 3, we introduce the notion of definability of a modality in an HS fragment, and we present the main tool we use to prove our results. In order to provide the reader with

HS modalities	Allen's relations	Graphical representation

$$\langle A \rangle \quad [x,y]R_A[x',y'] \Leftrightarrow y = x'$$
$$\langle L \rangle \quad [x,y]R_L[x',y'] \Leftrightarrow y < x'$$
$$\langle B \rangle \quad [x,y]R_B[x',y'] \Leftrightarrow x = x', y' < y$$
$$\langle E \rangle \quad [x,y]R_E[x',y'] \Leftrightarrow y = y', x < x'$$
$$\langle D \rangle \quad [x,y]R_D[x',y'] \Leftrightarrow x < x', y' < y$$
$$\langle O \rangle \quad [x,y]R_O[x',y'] \Leftrightarrow x < x' < y < y'$$

Fig. 1. Allen's interval relations and the corresponding HS modalities

an idea of the expressive power of HS modalities, we also illustrate some meaningful temporal properties, like counting and boundedness properties, which can be expressed in HS fragments when interpreted over discrete linear orders. Then, as a warm-up, in Section 4 we present a first, simple expressiveness result, by providing the complete set of definabilities for the HS modalities $\langle A \rangle$, $\langle L \rangle$, $\langle \overline{A} \rangle$, and $\langle \overline{L} \rangle$, corresponding to Allen's relations *meets* and *later*, and their inverses *met by* and *before*, respectively. Section 5 contains our main technical result, that is, a complete set of definabilities for the HS modalities $\langle D \rangle$, $\langle E \rangle$, $\langle B \rangle$, $\langle \overline{D} \rangle$, $\langle \overline{E} \rangle$, and $\langle \overline{B} \rangle$, corresponding to Allen's relations *during*, *finishes*, and *begins*, and their inverses *contains*, *finished by*, and *begun by*, respectively. The proofs of the results in this section are rather difficult and much more technically involved than the ones in Section 4. Therefore, we limit ourselves to giving an overview of the proofs, and we refer the interested reader to [3] for the details.

2 Preliminaries

Let $\mathbb{D} = \langle D, < \rangle$ be a linearly ordered set. An *interval* over $\mathbb{D}$ is an ordered pair $[a, b]$, where $a, b \in D$ and $a \leq b$. An interval is called a *point interval* if $a = b$ and a *strict interval* if $a < b$. In this paper, we assume the *strict semantics*, that is, we exclude point intervals and only consider strict intervals. The adoption of the strict semantics, excluding point intervals, instead of the *non-strict semantics*, which includes them, conforms to the definition of interval adopted by Allen in [4]. If we exclude the identity relation, there are 12 different relations between two strict intervals in a linear order, often called *Allen's relations* [4]: the six relations R_A (adjacent to), R_L (later than), R_B (begins), R_E (ends), R_D (during), and R_O (overlaps), depicted in Fig. 1, and their inverses, that is, $R_{\overline{X}} = (R_X)^{-1}$, for each $X \in \{A, L, B, E, D, O\}$.

We interpret interval structures as Kripke structures, with Allen's relations playing the role of the accessibility relations. Thus, we associate a modality $\langle X \rangle$ with each Allen relation R_X. For each $X \in \{A, L, B, E, D, O\}$, the *transpose* of modality $\langle X \rangle$ is modality $\langle \overline{X} \rangle$, corresponding to the inverse relation $R_{\overline{X}}$ of R_X. Halpern and Shoham's logic HS [18] is a multi-modal logic with formulae built from a finite, non-empty set $\mathcal{AP}$ of atomic propositions (also referred to as proposition letters), the propositional connectives $\vee$ and $\neg$, and a modality for each Allen relation. With every subset $\{R_{X_1}, \ldots, R_{X_k}\}$ of these relations, we associate the fragment $X_1 X_2 \ldots X_k$ of HS, whose formulae are defined by the grammar: $\varphi ::= p \mid \neg\varphi \mid \varphi \vee \varphi \mid \langle X_1 \rangle \varphi \mid \ldots \mid \langle X_k \rangle \varphi$, where $p \in \mathcal{AP}$. The other propositional connectives and constants (e.g., $\wedge$, $\rightarrow$, and $\top$), as well as the dual modalities (e.g., $[A]\varphi \equiv \neg\langle A \rangle \neg\varphi$), can be derived in the standard way. We define the *modal depth* of a formula as the largest nesting of modal operators in it. For a fragment $\mathcal{F} = X_1 X_2 \ldots X_k$ and a modality $\langle X \rangle$, we write $\langle X \rangle \in \mathcal{F}$ if $X \in \{X_1, \ldots, X_k\}$. Given two fragments $\mathcal{F}_1$ and $\mathcal{F}_2$, we write $\mathcal{F}_1 \subseteq \mathcal{F}_2$ if $\langle X \rangle \in \mathcal{F}_1$ implies $\langle X \rangle \in \mathcal{F}_2$, for every modality $\langle X \rangle$. Finally, for a fragment $\mathcal{F} = X_1 X_2 \ldots X_k$ and a formula φ, we write $\varphi \in \mathcal{F}$ or, equivalently, we say that φ is an $\mathcal{F}$-formula, meaning that φ belongs to the language of $\mathcal{F}$.

The (strict) semantics of HS is given in terms of *interval models* $M = \langle \mathbb{I}(\mathbb{D}), V \rangle$, where $\mathbb{D}$ is a linear order, $\mathbb{I}(\mathbb{D})$ is the set of all (strict) intervals over $\mathbb{D}$, and V is a *valuation function* $V : \mathcal{AP} \mapsto 2^{\mathbb{I}(\mathbb{D})}$, which assigns to each atomic proposition $p \in \mathcal{AP}$ the set of intervals $V(p)$ on which p holds. The *truth* of a formula on a given interval $[x, y]$ in an interval model M is defined by structural induction on formulae as follows:

- $M, [x, y] \Vdash p$ if and only if $[x, y] \in V(p)$, for each $p \in \mathcal{AP}$;
- $M, [x, y] \Vdash \neg\psi$ if and only if it is not the case that $M, [x, y] \Vdash \psi$;
- $M, [x, y] \Vdash \varphi \vee \psi$ if and only if $M, [x, y] \Vdash \varphi$ or $M, [x, y] \Vdash \psi$;
- $M, [x, y] \Vdash \langle X \rangle \psi$ if and only if there exists $[x', y']$ such that $[x, y] R_X [x', y']$ and $M, [x', y'] \Vdash \psi$, for each modality $\langle X \rangle$.

Formulae of HS can be interpreted over a class of interval models (built on a given class of linear orders). Among others, we mention the following classes of (interval models built on important classes of) linear orders: *(i)* the class of *all* linear orders Lin; *(ii)* the class of (all) *dense* linear orders Den, that is, those in which for every pair of distinct points there exists at least one point in between them (e.g., $\mathbb{Q}$ and $\mathbb{R}$); *(iii)* the class of (all) *discrete* linear orders Dis, that is, those in which every element, apart from the greatest element, if it exists, has an immediate successor, and every element, other than the least element, if it exists, has an immediate predecessor (e.g., $\mathbb{N}$, $\mathbb{Z}$, and $\mathbb{Z} + \mathbb{Z}$); *(iv)* the class of (all) *finite* linear orders Fin, that is, those having only finitely many points. A formula ϕ of HS is *valid* over a class $\mathcal{C}$ of linear orders, denoted by $\Vdash_{\mathcal{C}} \phi$, if it is true on every interval in every interval model belonging to $\mathcal{C}$. Two formulae ϕ and ψ are *equivalent* relative to the class $\mathcal{C}$ of linear orders, denoted by $\phi \equiv_{\mathcal{C}} \psi$, if $\Vdash_{\mathcal{C}} \phi \leftrightarrow \psi$.

3   Definability and Expressivenesss

Definition 1 (Definability). *A modality $\langle X \rangle$ of HS is definable in an HS fragment $\mathcal{F}$ relative to a class $\mathcal{C}$ of linear orders, denoted $\langle X \rangle \lhd_{\mathcal{C}} \mathcal{F}$, if $\langle X \rangle p \equiv_{\mathcal{C}} \psi$ for some $\mathcal{F}$-formula ψ over the atomic proposition p, for any $p \in \mathcal{AP}$. Then, the equivalence $\langle X \rangle p \equiv_{\mathcal{C}} \psi$ is called a definability equation for $\langle X \rangle$ in $\mathcal{F}$ relative to $\mathcal{C}$. We write $\langle X \rangle \ntriangleleft_{\mathcal{C}} \mathcal{F}$ if it is not the case that $\langle X \rangle \lhd_{\mathcal{C}} \mathcal{F}$.*

As we have already noted, smaller classes of linear orders inherit the definabilities holding for larger classes: if $\mathcal{C}_1$ and $\mathcal{C}_2$ are classes of linear orders such that $\mathcal{C}_1 \subset \mathcal{C}_2$, then all definabilities holding for $\mathcal{C}_2$ are also valid for $\mathcal{C}_1$. However, more definabilities can possibly hold for $\mathcal{C}_1$. On the other hand, undefinability results for $\mathcal{C}_1$ hold also for

C_2. In the rest of the paper, we omit the class of linear orders when it is clear from the context (e.g., we will simply write $\langle X \rangle p \equiv \psi$ and $\langle X \rangle \lhd \mathcal{F}$ for $\langle X \rangle p \equiv_C \psi$ and $\langle X \rangle \lhd_C \mathcal{F}$, respectively).

It is known from [18] that, when the strict semantics is assumed, all HS modalities are definable in the fragment containing modalities $\langle A \rangle$, $\langle B \rangle$, and $\langle E \rangle$, and their transposes $\langle \overline{A} \rangle$, $\langle \overline{B} \rangle$, and $\langle \overline{E} \rangle$, while in the non-strict semantics, the four modalities $\langle B \rangle$, $\langle E \rangle$, $\langle \overline{B} \rangle$, and $\langle \overline{E} \rangle$ suffice, as shown in [26]. Given two HS fragments $\mathcal{F}_1$ and $\mathcal{F}_2$, we say that $\mathcal{F}_2$ is *at least as expressive as* $\mathcal{F}_1$, denoted $\mathcal{F}_1 \preceq \mathcal{F}_2$, if each operator $\langle X \rangle \in \mathcal{F}_1$ is definable in $\mathcal{F}_2$, and that $\mathcal{F}_1$ is *strictly less expressive than* $\mathcal{F}_2$, denoted $\mathcal{F}_1 \prec \mathcal{F}_2$, if $\mathcal{F}_1 \preceq \mathcal{F}_2$ holds but $\mathcal{F}_2 \preceq \mathcal{F}_1$ does not. The notions of *expressively equivalent* fragments and *expressively incomparable* fragments can be defined likewise.

Definition 2 (Optimal definability). *A definability $\langle X \rangle \lhd \mathcal{F}$ is optimal if $\langle X \rangle \ntrianglelefteq \mathcal{F}'$ for each fragment $\mathcal{F}'$ such that $\mathcal{F}' \prec \mathcal{F}$.*

3.1 Proof Techniques to Disprove Definability

In order to show non-definability of a given modality in a certain fragment, we use the standard notion of *N-bisimulation* [17,19,21], suitably adapted to our setting.

Definition 3. *Let $\mathcal{F}$ be an HS-fragment. An $\mathcal{F}_N$-bisimulation between two models $M = \langle \mathbb{I}(\mathbb{D}), V \rangle$ and $M' = \langle \mathbb{I}(\mathbb{D}'), V' \rangle$ over a set of proposition letters $\mathcal{AP}$ is a sequence of N relations $Z_N, \ldots, Z_1 \subseteq \mathbb{I}(\mathbb{D}) \times \mathbb{I}(\mathbb{D}')$ such that: (i) for every $([x, y], [x', y']) \subset Z_h$, with $N \geq h \geq 1$, $M, [x, y] \Vdash p$ if and only if $M', [x', y'] \Vdash p$, for all $p \in \mathcal{AP}$ (local condition); (ii) for every $([x, y], [x', y']) \in Z_h$, with $N \geq h > 1$, if $[x, y] R_X [v, w]$ for some $[v, w] \in \mathbb{I}(\mathbb{D})$ and some $\langle X \rangle \in \mathcal{F}$, then there exists $([v, w], [v', w']) \in Z_{h-1}$ such that $[x', y'] R_X [v', w']$ (forward condition); (iii) for every $([x, y], [x', y']) \in Z_h$, with $N \geq h > 1$, if $[x', y'] R_X [v', w']$ for some $[v', w'] \in \mathbb{I}(\mathbb{D}')$ and some $\langle X \rangle \in \mathcal{F}$, then there exists $([v, w], [v', w']) \in Z_{h-1}$ such that $[x, y] R_X [v, w]$ (backward condition).*

Given an $\mathcal{F}_N$-bisimulation, the truth of $\mathcal{F}$-formulae of modal depth at most $h - 1$ is invariant for pairs of intervals belonging to Z_h, with $N \geq h \geq 1$ (see, e.g., [17]). Thus, to prove that a modality $\langle X \rangle$ is not definable in $\mathcal{F}$, it suffices to provide, for every natural number N, a pair of models M and M', and an $\mathcal{F}_N$-bisimulation between them for which there exists a pair $([x, y], [x', y']) \in Z_N$ such that $M, [x, y] \Vdash \langle X \rangle p$ and $M', [x', y'] \Vdash \neg \langle X \rangle p$, for some $p \in \mathcal{AP}$ (in this case, we say that the $\mathcal{F}_N$-bisimulation *violates* $\langle X \rangle$). To convince oneself that this is enough to ensure that $\langle X \rangle$ is not definable by any $\mathcal{F}$-formula of any modal depth, assume, towards a contradiction, that ϕ is an $\mathcal{F}$-formula of modal depth n such that $\langle X \rangle p \equiv \phi$. Since, for each N, there is an $\mathcal{F}_N$-bisimulation that violates $\langle X \rangle$, there exists, in particular, one such bisimulation for $N = n + 1$. Let $([x, y], [x', y']) \in Z_N$ be the pair of intervals that *violates* $\langle X \rangle$, that is, $M, [x, y] \Vdash \langle X \rangle p$ and $M', [x', y'] \Vdash \neg \langle X \rangle p$. Then, the truth value of ϕ over $[x, y]$ (in M) and $[x', y']$ (in M') is the same, and this is in contradiction with the fact that $M, [x, y] \Vdash \langle X \rangle p$ and $M', [x', y'] \Vdash \neg \langle X \rangle p$. A result obtained following this argument applies to all classes of linear orders that contain (as their elements) both structures on which M and M' are based. Notice that, in some cases, it is convenient to define $\mathcal{F}_N$-bisimulations between a model M and itself.

It is worth pointing out that the standard notion of $\mathcal{F}$-*bisimulation* can be recovered as a special case of $\mathcal{F}_N$-bisimulation. Formally, an $\mathcal{F}$-bisimulation can be thought of as an $\mathcal{F}_N$-bisimulation with $N = 2$ and $Z_1 = Z_2$. In the following, as is customary, we will treat $\mathcal{F}$-bisimulations as relations instead of sequences of two equal relations: if the sequence Z_2, Z_1 is an $\mathcal{F}$-bisimulation, with $Z_1 = Z_2 = Z$, then we will simply refer to it as to the relation Z. It is important to notice that showing that two intervals are related by an $\mathcal{F}$-bisimulation (i.e., they are $\mathcal{F}$-*bisimilar*) is stronger than showing that they are related by a relation Z_N, which belongs to a sequence $Z_N, \ldots, Z_1$ corresponding to an $\mathcal{F}_N$-bisimulation (i.e., the intervals are $\mathcal{F}_N$-*bisimilar*). Indeed, while in the latter case we are only guaranteed invariance of $\mathcal{F}$-formulae of modal depth at most $N - 1$, in the former case the truth of $\mathcal{F}$-formulae of any (possibly unbounded) modal depth is preserved. This means that undefinability results obtained using $\mathcal{F}$-bisimulations are not restricted to the finitary logics we consider in this paper, but also apply to extensions with infinite disjunctions and with fixed-point operators.

Since $\mathcal{F}$-bisimulations are notationally easier to deal with than $\mathcal{F}_N$-bisimulations, it is in principle more convenient to use the former, rather than the latter, when proving an undefinability result. However, while in few cases (see Section 4) a proof based on $\mathcal{F}$-bisimulations is possible, this is not generally the case, because some modalities that cannot be defined in fragments of HS can be expressed in their infinitary versions. In those cases (see Section 5), we resort to a proof via $\mathcal{F}_N$-bisimulations.

For a given modality $\langle X \rangle$ and a given class $\mathcal{C}$ of linear orders, we shall identify a set of definabilities for $\langle X \rangle$, and we shall prove its *soundness*, by showing that each definability equation is valid in $\mathcal{C}$, and its *completeness*, by arguing that each definability is optimal and that there are no other optimal definabilities for $\langle X \rangle$ in $\mathcal{C}$. Completeness is proved by computing all maximal fragments $\mathcal{F}$ that cannot define $\langle X \rangle$ (in the attempt of defining $\langle X \rangle$ in $\mathcal{F}$, we can obviously use the set of known definabilities). For each modality, such fragments are listed in the last column of Fig. 2. Depending on the number of known definabilities, such a task can be time-consuming and error-prone, so an automated procedure has been implemented to serve the purpose [1]. Then, for each such $\mathcal{F}$ and each $N \in \mathbb{N}$, we provide an $\mathcal{F}_N$-bisimulation that violates $\langle X \rangle$. Notice that all the classes of linear orders we consider are (left/right) *symmetric*, namely, if a class $\mathcal{C}$ contains a linear order $\mathbb{D} = \langle D, \prec \rangle$, then it also contains (a linear order isomorphic to) its dual linear order $\mathbb{D}^d = \langle D, \succ \rangle$, where $\succ$ is the inverse of $\prec$. This implies that the definabilities for $\langle \overline{L} \rangle$, $\langle \overline{A} \rangle$, $\langle B \rangle$, and $\langle \overline{B} \rangle$ can be immediately deduced (and shown to be sound and optimal) from those for $\langle L \rangle$, $\langle A \rangle$, $\langle E \rangle$, and $\langle \overline{E} \rangle$, respectively.

Fig. 2 depicts the complete sets of optimal definabilities holding in Dis and Fin for the modalities $\langle L \rangle$, $\langle A \rangle$, $\langle D \rangle$, $\langle \overline{D} \rangle$, $\langle E \rangle$, and $\langle \overline{E} \rangle$ (recall that those for $\langle \overline{L} \rangle$, $\langle \overline{A} \rangle$, $\langle B \rangle$, and $\langle \overline{B} \rangle$ follow by symmetry). Section 4 and Section 5 are devoted to proving completeness of such sets. For all the modalities, but $\langle A \rangle$ and $\langle \overline{A} \rangle$, soundness is an immediate consequence of the corresponding soundness in Lin, shown in [15]. For lack of space, we omit the proofs of the soundness of the definabilities for $\langle A \rangle$ and $\langle \overline{A} \rangle$, which anyway are quite straightforward. Finally, while it is known from [18] that $\langle O \rangle \lhd \overline{B}E$ (resp., $\langle \overline{O} \rangle \lhd B\overline{E}$), it is still an open problem whether this is the only optimal definability for $\langle O \rangle$ (resp., $\langle \overline{O} \rangle$) in Dis and in Fin.

Modalities	Equations	Definabilities	Maximal fragments not defining it
$\langle L\rangle$	$\langle L\rangle p \equiv \langle A\rangle\langle A\rangle p$	$\langle L\rangle \lhd A$	BDOALBEDO BEDOĀLEDO
$\langle A\rangle$	$\langle A\rangle p \equiv \varphi(p) \vee \langle E\rangle\varphi(p)^{*}$	$\langle A\rangle \lhd \overline{BE}$	LBDOALBEDO LBEDOĀLEDO
	$^{*}\varphi(p) := [E]\bot \wedge \langle B\rangle([E][E]\bot \wedge\langle E\rangle(p \vee \langle B\rangle p))$		
$\langle D\rangle$	$\langle D\rangle p \equiv \langle B\rangle\langle E\rangle p$	$\langle D\rangle \lhd BE$	ALBOALBEDO ALEOĀLBEDO
$\langle \overline{D}\rangle$	$\langle \overline{D}\rangle p \equiv \langle \overline{B}\rangle\langle \overline{E}\rangle p$	$\langle D\rangle \lhd \overline{BE}$	ALBEDOALBO ALBEDOĀLEO
$\langle E\rangle$	no definabilities		ALBDOALBEDO
$\langle \overline{E}\rangle$	no definabilities		ALBEDOALBDO

Fig. 2. Optimal definabilities in Dis and Fin. The last column contains the maximal fragments not defining the modality under consideration.

3.2 Expressing Properties of a Model in HS Fragments

We give here a short account of meaningful temporal properties, such as counting and (un)boundedness ones, which can be expressed in HS fragments, when they are interpreted over discrete linear orders. The outcomes of such an analysis are summarized in Fig. 3 (other properties can obviously be expressed as Boolean combinations of those displayed). They demonstrate the expressiveness capabilities of HS modalities, which are of interest by themselves. As an example, constraining the length of intervals is a desirable ability of any formalism for representing and reasoning about temporal knowledge over a discrete domain. In fact, most HS fragments have many chances to succeed in practical applications, and thus it is definitely worth carrying out a taxonomic study of their expressiveness. As we already pointed out, such a study presents various intricacies. For instance, in some fragments, assuming the discreteness of the linear order suffices to constrain the length of intervals (this is the case with the fragment E); other fragments rely on additional assumptions (this is the case with the fragment DO, which requires the linear order to be right-unbounded). This gives evidence of how expressiveness results can be affected by the specific class of linear orders under consideration.

Counting Properties. When the linear order is assumed to be discrete, some HS fragments are powerful enough to constrain (to some extent) the *length* of an interval, that is, the number of its points minus one. Let $\sim\,\in\,\{<,\leq,=,\geq,>\}$. For every $k \in \mathbb{N}$, we define $\ell_{\sim k}$ as a (pre-interpreted) atomic proposition which is true over all and only those intervals whose length is $\sim$-related to k. Moreover, for a modality $\langle X\rangle$, we denote by $\langle X\rangle^{k}\varphi$ the formula $\langle X\rangle \ldots \langle X\rangle\varphi$, with k occurrences of $\langle X\rangle$ before φ. Limiting ourselves to a few examples, we highlight here the ability of some of the HS modalities to express $\ell_{\sim k}$, for any k. It is well known that the fragments E and B can express $\ell_{\sim k}$, for every k and $\sim$ (see, e.g., [18]). As an example, the formulae $\langle E\rangle^{k}\top$ and $[E]^{k}\bot$ are equivalent to $\ell_{>k}$ and $\ell_{\leq k}$, respectively. The fragment D features limited counting properties, as, for every k, $\langle D\rangle^{k}\top \wedge [D]^{k+1}\bot$ is true over intervals whose length is either $2 \cdot k + 1$ or $2 \cdot (k + 1)$ (notice that, as a particular instance, $[D]\bot$ is true over

Counting properties		Right Unboundedness ($\exists_r$)
$\ell_{>k}$	$\equiv \langle E \rangle^k \top$	$\langle \overline{B} \rangle \top, \quad \langle A \rangle \top$
$\ell_{=k}$	$\equiv \langle E \rangle^{k-1} \top \wedge [E]^k \bot$	$(\ddagger) \quad \langle O \rangle \top, \quad [B]\langle L \rangle \top$
$\ell_{>2 \cdot k}$	$\equiv \langle D \rangle^k \top$	$(\S) \quad \langle \overline{D} \rangle \top, \quad \langle \overline{E} \rangle \langle O \rangle \top$
$\ell_{\leq 2 \cdot k}$	$\equiv [D]^k \bot$	$(\ddagger,\S) \quad [\overline{O}]\langle L \rangle \top$
$\ell_{>1}$	$\equiv^\dagger \langle O \rangle \top$	$(\flat) \quad [D]\langle L \rangle \top$
$\ell_{>2 \cdot k+1}$	$\equiv^\dagger \langle D \rangle^k \langle O \rangle \top$	
$\ell_{=2 \cdot (k+1)}$	$\equiv^\dagger \langle D \rangle^k \langle O \rangle \top \wedge [D]^{k+1} \bot$	

$\dagger$: only on right-unbounded domains; $\ddagger$: only on intervals longer than 1;
$\S$: only on left-unbounded domains; $\flat$: only on intervals longer than 2.

Fig. 3. Expressiveness of HS modalities over discrete linear orders

intervals whose length is either 1 or 2). In a sense, it is not able to discriminate the parity of an interval. The counting capabilities of the fragment O are limited as well: it allows one to discriminate between *unit intervals* (intervals whose length is 1) and *non-unit intervals* (which are longer than 1), provided that the underlying linear order is right-unbounded, like $\mathbb{Z}$ or $\mathbb{N}$ ($\langle \overline{O} \rangle$ possesses the same capability, provided that the underlying linear order is left-unbounded, like $\mathbb{Z}$ or $\mathbb{Z}^-$). However, quite interestingly, by pairing $\langle D \rangle$ and $\langle O \rangle$, or, symmetrically, $\langle D \rangle$ and $\langle \overline{O} \rangle$, it is possible to express $\ell_{\sim k}$ for every k and $\sim$ over right-unbounded linear order (left-unbounded linear orders if $\langle O \rangle$ is replaced by $\langle \overline{O} \rangle$): it suffices to first use $\langle D \rangle$ to narrow the length down to k or $k + 1$, and then $\langle O \rangle$ (or $\langle \overline{O} \rangle$) to discriminate the parity.

(Un)boundedness Properties. Let us denote by $\exists_r$ (resp., $\exists_l$) a (pre-interpreted) atomic proposition that is true over all and only the intervals that have a point to their right (resp., left). Various combinations of HS operators can express $\exists_r$. Once again, while in some cases we need to assume only the discreteness of the underlying linear order, there are cases where the validity of the definability relies on additional assumptions. For example, to impose that the current interval has a point to the right within the fragment O, we can use $\langle O \rangle \top$ only on non-unit intervals (otherwise, $\langle O \rangle$ has no effect). Analogously, it is possible to express $\exists_l$, possibly under analogous assumptions.

4   The Easy Cases

In this section, we prove the completeness of the set of definabilities for the modalities $\langle L \rangle$, $\langle \overline{L} \rangle$, $\langle A \rangle$, and $\langle \overline{A} \rangle$, thus strengthening a similar result presented in [14, Theorem 1].

Theorem 1. *The sets of optimal definabilities for $\langle L \rangle$ and $\langle A \rangle$ (listed in Fig. 2), as well as (by symmetry) those for $\langle \overline{L} \rangle$ and $\langle \overline{A} \rangle$, are complete for the classes* Dis *and* Fin.

Proof. The results for $\langle L \rangle$ (and, symmetrically, for $\langle \overline{L} \rangle$) immediately follow from [15], as the completeness proof for $\langle L \rangle$ presented there used a bisimulation between models based on finite linear orders. Notice that $\langle L \rangle \lhd \overline{B}E$ holds in Dis and Fin, as it does in

Lin. However, such a definability, which is optimal in Lin, is not optimal in Dis and Fin (and thus it is not listed in Fig. 2), due to the fact that $\langle A \rangle \lhd \overline{BE}$ (which is not a sound definability in Lin) holds over Dis. As a pleasing consequence, we can extend Venema's result from [26] concerning the expressive completeness of the fragment $BE\overline{BE}$ in the non-strict semantics to the strict one under the discreteness assumption.

According to Fig. 2, $\langle A \rangle$ is definable in terms of $\overline{BE}$, implying that the maximal fragments not defining $\langle A \rangle$ are, as shown in the last column of Fig. 2, $LBDO\overline{ALBEDO}$ and $LBEDO\overline{ALEDO}$. Thus, proving that $\langle A \rangle \lhd \overline{BE}$ is the only optimal definability amounts to providing two bisimulations, namely an $LBDO\overline{ALBEDO}$- and an $LBEDO\overline{ALEDO}$-bisimulation that violate $\langle A \rangle$. As for the first one, we consider two models M and M', both based on the finite linear order $\{0, 1, 2\}$. We set $V(p) = \{[1, 2]\}$, $V'(p) = \emptyset$, and $Z = \{([0, 1], [0, 1]), ([0, 2], [0, 2])\}$. It is easy to verify that Z is an $LBDO\overline{ALBEDO}$-bisimulation that violates $\langle A \rangle$, as $M, [0, 1] \Vdash \langle A \rangle p$ and $M', [0, 1] \Vdash \neg \langle A \rangle p$. As for the second one, models and valuations are defined as before, but we take now $Z = \{([0, 1], [0, 1])\}$. Once again, it is easy to see that Z is an $LBEDO\overline{ALEDO}$-bisimulation that violates $\langle A \rangle$, as $M, [0, 1] \Vdash \langle A \rangle p$ and $M', [0, 1] \Vdash \neg \langle A \rangle p$. Since the result is based on a finite linear order, it holds for both Dis and Fin.   □

5 The Hard Cases

In this section, we provide the completeness result for the modalities $\langle D \rangle$ and $\langle \overline{D} \rangle$ (Theorem 2), as well as for $\langle E \rangle$, $\langle \overline{E} \rangle$, $\langle B \rangle$, and $\langle \overline{B} \rangle$ (Theorem 3). Because of the technical complexity of the proofs, we only provide proof sketches that explain the main ideas behind them at a very intuitive level, and refer the interested reader to [3] for the details.

In the following, we let $\mathbb{N}^{>c} = \{x \in \mathbb{N} \mid x > c\}$ and $\mathbb{Z}^{<-c} = \{x \in \mathbb{Z} \mid x < -c\}$, for each $c \geq 0$. Moreover, $\mathbb{N}^+$ and $\mathbb{Z}^-$ denote the sets $\mathbb{N}^{>0}$ and $\mathbb{Z}^{<-0}$, respectively. As a preliminary step, we introduce the notion of *equivalence up to* a given threshold, denoted by $\simeq_h^g$, which is used in both proofs to "simulate density", in a sense that will be made clear later on. It is a series of equivalence relations over $\mathbb{Z}$ up to a certain threshold, which is given by the value of the suitably defined *threshold function* g on h.

Definition 4 ($\simeq_h^g$). *For any given function* $g : \mathbb{D} \to \mathbb{N}$, *called* threshold function, *where* $\mathbb{D}$ *can be any prefix of* $\mathbb{N}^+$, *that is,* $\mathbb{D} = \{1, \ldots, N\}$ *for some* $N \in \mathbb{N}$, *and for every* $h \in \mathbb{D}$, *we define the relation of* equivalence up to $g(h)$, *denoted* $\simeq_h^g$, *as follows. For every pair of integers* $n_1, n_2 \in \mathbb{Z}$, $n_1 \simeq_h^g n_2$ *if and only if one of the following holds: (i)* $n_1 = n_2$, *(ii)* $n_1, n_2 > g(h)$, *or (iii)* $n_1, n_2 < -g(h)$.

Theorem 2. *The sets of optimal definabilities for* $\langle D \rangle$ *and* $\langle \overline{D} \rangle$ *(listed in Fig. 2) are complete for the classes* Dis *and* Fin.

In order to prove the above theorem, we proceed as follows. According to Fig. 2, $\langle D \rangle$ is definable in terms of BE; thus there are two maximal fragments not defining it, namely, $ALBO\overline{ALBEDO}$ and $ALEO\overline{ALBEDO}$. First, we observe that it is possible to define $\langle D \rangle$ in infinitary extensions of AB or $\overline{A}E$, using, respectively, the following formulae of unbounded modal depth:

$$\langle D \rangle p \equiv \begin{cases} \bigvee_{k \in \mathbb{N}} (\ell_{=k} \wedge \bigvee_{i < k-1} (\langle B \rangle (\ell_{=i} \wedge \langle A \rangle (\ell_{<k-i} \wedge p)))), \\ \bigvee_{k \in \mathbb{N}} (\ell_{=k} \wedge \bigvee_{i < k-1} (\langle E \rangle (\ell_{=i} \wedge \langle \overline{A} \rangle (\ell_{<k-i} \wedge p)))), \end{cases}$$

where length constraints of the form $\ell_{=k}$ and $\ell_{<k}$ can be expressed using either $\langle B \rangle$ or $\langle E \rangle$ (see Section 3.2). It immediately follows that there exists no $\overline{\mathsf{ALBOALBEDO}}$-bisimulation (resp., $\overline{\mathsf{ALEOALBEDO}}$-bisimulation) that violates $\langle D \rangle$, and thus we have to resort to $\overline{\mathsf{ALBOALBEDO}}_N$-bisimulations (resp., $\overline{\mathsf{ALEOALBEDO}}_N$-bisimulations). Besides, since the two fragments $\overline{\mathsf{ALBOALBEDO}}$ and $\overline{\mathsf{ALEOALBEDO}}$ are symmetric, that is, they are indistinguishable over symmetric classes of linear orders, providing an $\overline{\mathsf{ALBOALBEDO}}_N$-bisimulation that violates $\langle D \rangle$ suffices to prove the result. In what follows, we build such an $\overline{\mathsf{ALBOALBEDO}}_N$-bisimulation.

To this end, we first define the function $f : \{1, \dots, N\} \to \mathbb{N}$ as $f(h) = h + 1$. Then, we consider a bijection ξ from $\mathbb{Z} \times \mathbb{N}^+$ to $\mathbb{Z}^{<-k}$ such that $\xi(x, y) \leq x - k$ for each $(x, y) \in \mathbb{Z} \times \mathbb{N}^+$, and where $k = 2 \cdot f(N) + 4$. It is not difficult to convince oneself of the existence of such a function. Now, we define the function $\eta : \mathbb{Z} \to \mathbb{N}^+$ as:

$$\eta(x) = \begin{cases} \bar{y} + \bar{x} - x & \text{if } x = \xi(\bar{x}, \bar{y}) \text{ for some } \bar{x}, \bar{y} \\ k - 2 & \text{otherwise} \end{cases}$$

Notice that if $x = \xi(\bar{x}, \bar{y})$, then $\eta(x) \geq k + 1$ holds, because $\xi(\bar{x}, \bar{y}) = x \leq \bar{x} - k$ and $\bar{y} \geq 1$. Thus, for each x, we have $\eta(x) \geq k - 2$.

Proposition 1. *There exist two integers x and $x + 1$ such that $\eta(x) \geq \eta(x + 1) + 3$.*

Let $\delta(x, y) = y - x - \eta(x)$, for each interval $[x, y] \in \mathbb{I}(\mathbb{Z})$. The following lemma will be useful in the proof of Lemma 2.

Lemma 1. *The following statements hold.*
a) *For each interval $[x, y]$ and each $i \in \mathbb{Z}$, with $-f(N) - 1 \leq i \leq f(N) + 1$, there exist x' and x'' such that $x - x' = |i|$ and $\delta(x'', x) = i$.*
b) *For each interval $[x, y]$ and each $i \in \mathbb{Z}$, with $-f(N) - 1 \leq i \leq f(N) + 1$, there exists $x' < x$ such that $\delta(x', y) = i$.*

We let $M = \langle \mathbb{I}(\mathbb{Z}), V \rangle$, where the valuation V is as follows: $[x, y] \in V(p) \Leftrightarrow \delta(x, y) \geq 0$. Notice that M is parametric in N because k, used in the definitions of ξ and η, depends on N. Notice also that the length of p-intervals is at least $k - 2$.

We introduce here a sequence of relations $Z_N, \dots, Z_1$. In Lemma 2, we will show that it is an $\overline{\mathsf{ALBOALBEDO}}_N$-bisimulation that violates $\langle D \rangle$. To this end, it is convenient to define the equivalence relations $\equiv_\ell^h$ and $\equiv_\delta^h$, for each $h \in \{1, \dots, N\}$, as

$$[x, y] \equiv_\ell^h [w, z] \text{ if and only if } y - x \simeq_h^f z - w$$
$$[x, y] \equiv_\delta^h [w, z] \text{ if and only if } \delta(x, y) \simeq_h^f \delta(w, z),$$

where $\simeq_h^f$ is an equivalence up to $f(h)$. Intuitively, $\equiv_\ell^h$ relates pairs of intervals whose lengths coincide or are both larger than $f(h)$; $\equiv_\delta^h$ relates intervals $[x, y]$ and $[w, z]$ such that $\delta(x, y) = \delta(w, z)$ or $\min\{\delta(x, y), \delta(w, z)\} > f(h)$ or $\max\{\delta(x, y), \delta(w, z)\} < -f(h)$. Everything is set for the definition of the sequence of relations $\{Z_h\}_{1 \leq h \leq N}$.

Definition 5. *For each $h \in \{1, \dots, N\}$, the hth component Z_h of the sequence of relations $Z_N, \dots, Z_1$ is defined as:*
$$[x, y] Z_h [w, z] \Leftrightarrow [x, y] \equiv_\ell^h [w, z] \text{ and } [x, y] \equiv_\delta^h [w, z].$$

Since $\equiv_\ell^h$ and $\equiv_\delta^h$ are equivalence relations, so is Z_h, for each h.

Lemma 2. *The sequence of relations $Z_N, \dots, Z_1$ is an $\overline{\mathsf{ALBOALBEDO}}_N$-bisimulation that violates $\langle D \rangle$.*

Proof (sketch). We first show that $Z_N, \ldots, Z_1$ is an $\overline{\text{ALBOALBEDO}}_N$-bisimulation. The local condition is trivially fulfilled, as $[x, w] Z_h [w, z]$ implies $[x, w] \equiv_\delta^h [w, z]$, which, in turn, implies $\delta(x, y) \geq 0$ if and only if $\delta(w, z) \geq 0$, and thus $M, [x, y] \Vdash p$ if and only if $M, [w, z] \Vdash p$. To prove that the forward and the backward conditions are fulfilled as well, the intuitive idea is to show that, for each pair $([x, y], [w, z])$ of Z_h-related intervals and each modality $\langle X \rangle$ featured by the fragment $\overline{\text{ALBOALBEDO}}$, the set of equivalence classes (with respect to the relation Z_{h-1}) reachable from $[x, y]$ using $\langle X \rangle$ is equal to the set of equivalence classes reachable from $[w, z]$ using $\langle X \rangle$. The more difficult cases are the ones corresponding to the modalities $\langle \overline{A} \rangle$ and $\langle \overline{E} \rangle$. To cope with the former, it suffices to observe that from Lemma 1a it immediately follows that every equivalence class is reachable from any interval $[x', y']$, using the modality $\langle \overline{A} \rangle$. Similarly, Lemma 1b can be used to deal with the modality $\langle \overline{E} \rangle$.

To conclude the proof, consider $[x, y] = [0, k-3]$ and $[w, z]$, where $z = w + \eta(w) - 1$ and w is such that $\eta(w) \geq \eta(w + 1) + 3$ (the existence of such w is guaranteed by Proposition 1). We show that $([x, y], [w, z]) \in Z_N$, $M, [x, y] \Vdash \neg \langle D \rangle p$, and $M, [w, z] \Vdash \langle D \rangle p$. It is easy to see that both $[x, y] \equiv_\delta^h [w, z]$ and $[x, y] \equiv_\ell^h [w, z]$ hold. Thus, we have that $([x, y], [w, z]) \in Z_N$. Moreover, since $y - x < k - 2$, it is clear, from the definition of V, that none of its sub-interval satisfies p (because p-intervals are long at least $k - 2$), and thus $M, [x, y] \Vdash \neg \langle D \rangle p$ holds. Contrarily, $[w, z]$ is such that $M, [w, z] \Vdash \langle D \rangle p$ because the interval $[w+1, z-1]$ satisfies p. To see the latter, observe that $\delta(w + 1, z - 1) = z - 1 - w - 1 - \eta(w + 1) = \eta(w) - \eta(w + 1) - 3 \geq 0$. $\square$

The above proof makes use of a model based on $\mathbb{Z}$, and thus it proves the result for the class Dis. The whole construction can be adapted to deal with the class Fin as well, by using a finite, "large enough" portion of $\mathbb{Z}$, and then by taking special care of the intervals that are "close" to the borders. Moreover, by observing that $\langle D \rangle$ and $\langle \overline{D} \rangle$ behave in a very similar way when interpreted over classes of finite linear orders, it is possible to use the same idea to prove the result for the modality $\langle \overline{D} \rangle$ as well.

Theorem 3. *There are no definabilities for $\langle E \rangle$ and $\langle \overline{E} \rangle$ (as shown in Fig. 2), as well as for their transposes $\langle B \rangle$ and $\langle \overline{B} \rangle$, in the classes Dis and Fin.*

Proof (sketch). We only give the sketch of the proof for the operators $\langle E \rangle$ and $\langle \overline{E} \rangle$. The result for $\langle B \rangle$ and $\langle \overline{B} \rangle$ follows from a symmetric argument. According to Fig. 2, there are no definabilities for $\langle E \rangle$ when the underlying structure is discrete, and therefore $\overline{\text{ALBDOALBEDO}}$ is the only maximal fragment not defining it. This is also true on Lin and Den, but on Dis and Fin it is simply harder to prove. An indication of such a difficulty comes from the analysis of the proofs presented in [15], where the density of the models involved plays a major role. Similarly to the case of Theorem 2, $\langle E \rangle$ is definable in an infinitary extension of the language AB by the formula $\langle E \rangle p \equiv \bigvee_{k \in \mathbb{N}} (\ell_{=k} \wedge \bigvee_{i<k}(\langle B \rangle(\ell_{=i} \wedge \langle A \rangle(\ell_{=k-i} \wedge p))))$, since, as stated in Section 3.2, $\langle B \rangle$ can express $\ell_{=k}$, for every $k \in \mathbb{N}$. Thus, there exists no $\overline{\text{ALBOALBEDO}}$-bisimulation that violates $\langle E \rangle$, and we need to find an $\overline{\text{ALBDOALBEDO}}_N$-bisimulation.

Let $\mathbb{D}$ be a finite domain, e.g., an arbitrarily large prefix of $\mathbb{N}$. We define a model M based on it and an $\overline{\text{ALBDOALBEDO}}_N$-bisimulation between M and itself that violates $\langle E \rangle$. Given $N \in \mathbb{N}$, we make use of $h \leq N$ to refer to the hth component of the N-bisimulation, also called in the following the hth *step* of the N-bisimulation.

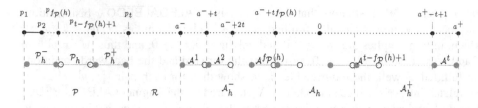

Fig. 4. A graphical account of the $\mathsf{ALBDO\overline{ALBEDO}}_N$-bisimulation that violates $\langle E \rangle$

Building the $\mathsf{ALBDO\overline{ALBEDO}}_N$-bisimulation relies on a very technical construction that allows us to "simulate density" over discrete models up to a certain threshold. To this end, we will use monotonically increasing threshold functions, which are parametric in h and which characterize a notion of "long interval", relative to a generic *step* h of the N-bisimulation. Since such functions are monotonic, intervals that are "long" at the step h of the N-bisimulation always contain intervals that are still "long" at the step $h - 1$, despite being obviously shorter of the containing interval. We will also use suitably defined equivalences up to a threshold (given by the aforementioned threshold functions) to recognize when two intervals are "long enough" to be indistinguishable by modal formulae in the fragment $\mathsf{ALBDO\overline{ALBEDO}}$ whose modal depth is less than $h \leq N$.

Now, we define the function $f(h) = h + 1$, which will be used as threshold function, and the function $f_{\mathcal{P}}(h) = \sum_{i=1}^{h} f(i)$. Notice that both functions are monotonically increasing. Moreover, we let $t = 2(f_{\mathcal{P}}(1) + N + 4)$, $a^+ = \frac{t^2}{2} - 1$, and $a^- = -\frac{t^2}{2}$.

Finally, we consider a partition of $\mathbb{D}$ as in Fig. 5. Three subsets, from left to right, are clearly identified: $\mathcal{P} = \{p_1, \ldots, p_t\}$, $\mathcal{R} = \{x \in \mathbb{D} \mid p_t < x < a^-\}$, and $\mathcal{A} = \{x \in \mathbb{D} \mid a^- \leq x \leq a^+\}$, where we let $p_t = a^- - t$ and, for each $i < t$, $p_i = p_{i+1} - 1$. For each h, we define further partitions of the subsets $\mathcal{P}$ and $\mathcal{A}$, as follows:

$$\mathcal{P} = \bigcup \begin{cases} \mathcal{P}_h^- = \{x \mid p_1 \leq x \leq p_{f_{\mathcal{P}}(h)}\} \\ \mathcal{P}_h^+ = \{x \mid p_{t-f_{\mathcal{P}}(h)+1} \leq x \leq p_t\} \\ \mathcal{P}_h = \{x \mid p_{f_{\mathcal{P}}(h)} < x < p_{t-f_{\mathcal{P}}(h)+1}\}, \end{cases}$$
$$\mathcal{A}^i = \{x \in \mathbb{D} \mid a^- + (i-1) \cdot t \leq x < a^- + i \cdot t\},$$
$$\mathcal{A} = \bigcup \begin{cases} \mathcal{A}_h^- = \bigcup_{i=1}^{f_{\mathcal{P}}(h)} \mathcal{A}^i \\ \mathcal{A}_h^+ = \bigcup_{i=t-f_{\mathcal{P}}(h)+1}^{t} \mathcal{A}^i \\ \mathcal{A}_h = \mathcal{A} \setminus (\mathcal{A}_h^- \cup \mathcal{A}_h^+) = \bigcup_{i=f_{\mathcal{P}}(h)+1}^{t-f_{\mathcal{P}}(h)} \mathcal{A}^i. \end{cases}$$

Roughly speaking, we can say that stepping from $h+1$ to h, the sets $\mathcal{P}_{h+1}^-$, $\mathcal{P}_{h+1}^+$, $\mathcal{A}_{h+1}^-$, and $\mathcal{A}_{h+1}^+$ shrink, while the sets $\mathcal{P}_{h+1}$ and $\mathcal{A}_{h+1}$ expand. Now, let M be a model based on $\mathbb{D}$ described as above. The valuation V of M uses the function $\mathcal{V} : \mathcal{A} \to \mathcal{P}$:

$$\mathcal{V}(y) = \begin{cases} p_1 + i & \text{if } y = a^- + i, \text{ for each } 0 \leq i < t \\ \mathcal{V}(y - t) & \text{if } a^- + t \leq y \leq a^+, \end{cases}$$
$$V(p) = \{[x, y] \mid y \in \mathcal{A} \text{ implies } x \leq \mathcal{V}(y)\}.$$

In order to define an $\mathsf{ALBDO\overline{ALBEDO}}_N$-bisimulation, we first define a sequence Z_N, $\ldots, Z_1$, which is common to both cases $\langle E \rangle$ and $\langle \overline{E} \rangle$, and then we show how to adjust it to obtain our results. To characterize the generic hth component Z_h of the sequence $Z_N, \ldots, Z_1$ we make use of an equivalence relation $\equiv_h$, parameterized by h, which is defined as follows. Let us denote by x (resp., w) the nth element of $\mathcal{A}_i$ (resp., the mth element of $\mathcal{A}_j$), that is, $x = a_n^i$ and $w = a_m^j$. Then, we have:

$$x \equiv_h w \text{ iff } \begin{cases} x = w \text{ or} \\ x, w \in \mathcal{P}_h \text{ or} \\ x, w \in \mathcal{A} \text{ and} \begin{cases} i = j \vee x, w \in \mathcal{A}_h, \text{ and} \\ m = n \vee f_{\mathcal{P}}(h) < m, n < t - f_{\mathcal{P}}(h) + 1. \end{cases} \end{cases}$$

We can now define Z_h as follows: for each $1 \leq h \leq N$, $([x, y], [w, z]) \in Z_h$ if and only if: (a) $x \equiv_h w$ and $y \equiv_h z$, (b) $y - x \simeq_h^f z - w$, (c) if $x, w \in \mathcal{P}$ and $y, z \in \mathcal{A}$, then $\mathcal{V}(y) - x \simeq_h^f \mathcal{V}(z) - w$, and (d) if $x \in \mathcal{A}^i$ and $y \in \mathcal{A}^j$ for some $i, j \in \{1, \ldots, t\}$, then $w \in \mathcal{A}^k$ and $z \in \mathcal{A}^\ell$ for some $k, \ell \in \{1, \ldots, t\}$ such that $j - i \simeq_h^f \ell - k$. As a last step, we define a new sequence of relations $Z_N^E, \ldots, Z_1^E$ such that $Z_N^E \cup Z_N, \ldots, Z_1^E \cup Z_1$ is an ALBDOALBEDO$_N$-bisimulation (the proof is technically involved, so details are omitted—see [3] for a fully-detailed account). Consider a point $a = a_m^i$ such that $i = m = \frac{t}{2}$, that is, a is the $\frac{t}{2}$th point of the $\frac{t}{2}$th sub-group of $\mathcal{A}$. It holds that $\mathcal{V}(a) = p_m = p_{\frac{t}{2}}$. Now, for each $1 \leq h \leq N$, let $Z_h^E = \{([\mathcal{V}(a) - (N-h+1), a], [\mathcal{V}(a) - (N-h), a])\}$. It is possible to see that $M, [\mathcal{V}(a) - 1, a] \Vdash \langle E \rangle p$, $M, [\mathcal{V}(a), a] \Vdash \neg \langle E \rangle p$, and $([\mathcal{V}(a) - 1, a], [\mathcal{V}(a), a]) \in Z_N^E$. Thus, $Z_N^E \cup Z_N, \ldots, Z_1^E \cup Z_1$ is an ALBDOALBEDO$_N$-bisimulation that violates $\langle E \rangle$.

To deal with the modality $\langle \overline{E} \rangle$, a new sequence $Z_N^{\overline{E}}, \ldots, Z_1^{\overline{E}}$ can be defined, following a similar technique, so that $Z_N^{\overline{E}} \cup Z_N, \ldots, Z_1^{\overline{E}} \cup Z_1$ is an ALBEDOALBDO$_N$-bisimulation that violates $\langle \overline{E} \rangle$. Since the proof only uses a finite linear order, the result holds for both Dis and Fin.   ⊓

6 Conclusions

In this paper we studied the expressiveness of fragments of the interval temporal logic HS interpreted over both discrete and finite linear orders. A complete classification of all such fragments with respect to their relative expressive power has been recently given for the classes of all linear orders and all dense linear orders. The cases of discrete and finite linear orders turn out to be much more involved. We provided a complete set of definabilities for the modalities corresponding to the Allen's relations *meets, later, begins, finishes,* and *during,* plus their transposes. We leave open the problem of identifying the complete set of definabilities for the modalities corresponding to the Allen relation *overlaps* and to its inverse *overlapped by.*

Acknowledgements. The authors acknowledge the support from the Spanish fellowship program *'Ramon y Cajal'* RYC-2011-07821 (G. Sciavicco), the project *Processes and Modal Logics* (project nr. 100048021) of the Icelandic Research Fund (L. Aceto, D. Della Monica, and A. Ingólfsdóttir), the project *Decidability and Expressiveness for Interval Temporal Logics* (project nr. 130802-051) of the Icelandic Research Fund (D. Della Monica), and the Italian GNCS project *Automata, games, and temporal logics for planning and synthesis of controllers in safety-critical systems* (A. Montanari).

References

1. Aceto, L., Della Monica, D., Ingólfsdóttir, A., Montanari, A., Sciavicco, G.: An algorithm for enumerating maximal models of Horn theories with an application to modal logics. In: McMillan, K., Middeldorp, A., Voronkov, A. (eds.) LPAR-19 2013. LNCS, vol. 8312, pp. 1–17. Springer, Heidelberg (2013)
2. Aceto, L., Della Monica, D., Ingólfsdóttir, A., Montanari, A., Sciavicco, G.: A complete classification of the expressiveness of interval logics of Allen's relations over dense linear orders. In: Proc. of the 20th TIME, pp. 65–72. IEEE Computer Society (2013)
3. Aceto, L., Della Monica, D., Ingólfsdóttir, A., Montanari, A., Sciavicco, G.: On the expressiveness of the interval logic of Allen's relations over finite and discrete linear orders (extended version) (2014), http://www.di.unisa.it/dottorandi/dario.dellamonica/temp/expr_disc_ext.%pdf
4. Allen, J.F.: Maintaining knowledge about temporal intervals. Communications of the ACM 26(11), 832–843 (1983)
5. Allen, J.F.: Towards a general theory of action and time. Artificial Intelligence 23(2), 123–154 (1984)
6. Bresolin, D., Della Monica, D., Goranko, V., Montanari, A., Sciavicco, G.: Decidable and undecidable fragments of Halpern and Shoham's interval temporal logic: Towards a complete classification. In: Cervesato, I., Veith, H., Voronkov, A. (eds.) LPAR 2008. LNCS (LNAI), vol. 5330, pp. 590–604. Springer, Heidelberg (2008)
7. Bresolin, D., Della Monica, D., Goranko, V., Montanari, A., Sciavicco, G.: The dark side of interval temporal logic: Sharpening the undecidability border. In: Proc. of the 18th TIME, pp. 131–138 (2011)
8. Bresolin, D., Della Monica, D., Goranko, V., Montanari, A., Sciavicco, G.: Metric propositional neighborhood interval logics on natural numbers. Software and Systems Modeling 12(2), 245–264 (2013)
9. Bresolin, D., Della Monica, D., Montanari, A., Sala, P., Sciavicco, G.: Interval Temporal Logics over finite linear orders: the complete picture. In: Proc. of the 20th ECAI, pp. 199–204 (2012)
10. Bresolin, D., Della Monica, D., Montanari, A., Sala, P., Sciavicco, G.: Interval Temporal Logics over strongly discrete linear orders: the complete picture. In: Proc. of the 3rd GandALF, pp. 155–168 (2012)
11. Bresolin, D., Goranko, V., Montanari, A., Sala, P.: Tableau-based decision procedures for the logics of subinterval structures over dense orderings. Journal of Logic and Computation 20(1), 133–166 (2010)
12. Bresolin, D., Montanari, A., Sala, P., Sciavicco, G.: What's decidable about Halpern and Shoham's interval logic? The maximal fragment $A\overline{B}\overline{B}\overline{L}$. In: Proc. of the 26th LICS, pp. 387–396 (2011)
13. Bresolin, D., Sala, P., Sciavicco, G.: On Begins, Meets, and Before. International Journal on Foundations of Computer Science 23(3), 559–583 (2012)
14. Bresolin, D., Della Monica, D., Montanari, A., Sala, P., Sciavicco, G.: Interval temporal logics over strongly discrete linear orders: Expressiveness and complexity. Theoretical Computer Science (2014) (online first since April 2014)
15. Della Monica, D., Goranko, V., Montanari, A., Sciavicco, G.: Expressiveness of the interval logics of Allen's relations on the class of all linear orders: Complete classification. In: Proc. of the 22nd IJCAI, pp. 845–850 (July 2011)
16. Della Monica, D., Goranko, V., Montanari, A., Sciavicco, G.: Interval temporal logics: a journey. Bulletin of the European Association for Theoretical Computer Science 105, 73–99 (2011)

17. Goranko, V., Otto, M.: Model theory of modal logic. In: Blackburn, P., van Benthem, J.F.A.K., Wolter, F. (eds.) Handbook of Modal Logic, pp. 249–329. Elsevier (2007)
18. Halpern, J., Shoham, Y.: A propositional modal logic of time intervals. Journal of the ACM 38(4), 935–962 (1991)
19. Hennessy, M., Milner, R.: Algebraic laws for nondeterminism and concurrency. Journal of the ACM 32(1), 137–161 (1985)
20. Marcinkowski, J., Michaliszyn, J.: The ultimate undecidability result for the Halpern-Shoham logic. In: Proc. of the 26th LICS, pp. 377–386. IEEE Computer Society (2011)
21. Milner, R.: A Calculus of Communicating Systems. Springer (1980)
22. Montanari, A., Puppis, G., Sala, P.: Maximal decidable fragments of Halpern and Shoham's modal logic of intervals. In: Abramsky, S., Gavoille, C., Kirchner, C., Meyer auf der Heide, F., Spirakis, P.G. (eds.) ICALP 2010. LNCS, vol. 6199, pp. 345–356. Springer, Heidelberg (2010)
23. Montanari, A., Puppis, G., Sala, P., Sciavicco, G.: Decidability of the interval temporal logic $A\overline{BB}$ over the natural numbers. In: Proc. of the 27th STACS, pp. 597–608 (2010)
24. Moszkowski, B.: Reasoning about digital circuits. Tech. rep. stan-cs-83-970, Dept. of Computer Science, Stanford University (1983)
25. Pratt-Hartmann, I.: Temporal prepositions and their logic. Artificial Intelligence 166(1-2), 1–36 (2005)
26. Venema, Y.: Expressiveness and completeness of an interval tense logic. Notre Dame Journal of Formal Logic 31(4), 529–547 (1990)
27. Zhou, C., Hansen, M.R.: Duration Calculus: A formal approach to real-time systems. EATCS Monographs in Theoretical Computer Science. Springer (2004)

Only-Knowing à la Halpern-Moses
for Non-omniscient Rational Agents:
A Preliminary Report

Dimitris Askounis[1], Costas D. Koutras[2], Christos Moyzes[3], and Yorgos Zikos[3]

[1] Decision Support Systems Lab
School of Electrical and Comp. Engineering
National Technical University of Athens
9, Iroon Polytechniou Street, 15773 Athens, Greece
askous@epu.ntua.gr
[2] Department of Informatics and Telecommunications
University of Peloponnese
end of Karaiskaki Street, 22 100 Tripolis, Greece
ckoutras@uop.gr
[3] Graduate Programme in Logic, Algorithms and Computation (MPLA)
Department of Mathematics, University of Athens
Panepistimiopolis, 157 84 Ilissia, Greece
cmoyzes@yahoo.gr, zikos@sch.gr

Abstract. We investigate the minimal knowledge approach of Halpern-Moses *'only knowing'* in the context of two syntactic variants of stable belief sets that aim in avoiding the unreasonably perfect omniscient agent modelled in R. Stalnaker's original definition of a stable epistemic state. The *'only knowing'* approach of J. Halpern and Y. Moses provides equivalent characterizations of *'honest'* formulas and characterizes the epistemic state of an agent that has been told only a finite number of facts. The formal account of what it means for an agent to *'only know a'* is actually based on 'minimal' epistemic states and is closely related to ground modal nonmonotonic logics. We examine here the behaviour of the HM-*'only knowing'* approach in the realm of the weak variants of stable epistemic states introduced recently by relaxing the positive or negative introspection context rules of Stalnaker's definition, in a way reminiscent of the work done in modal epistemic logic in response to the *'logical omniscience'* problem. We define the *'honest'* formulas - formulas which can be meaningfully *'only known'* - and characterize them in several ways, including model-theoretic characterizations using impossible worlds. As expected, the generalized *'only knowing'* approach lacks the simplicity and elegance shared by the approaches based on Stalnaker's stable sets (actually based on **S5**) but it is more realistic and can be handily fine-tuned.

Keywords: Only-knowing, minimal knowledge, modal nonmonotonic logic.

1   Introduction

The notion of *'only knowing'* introduced by J. Halpern and Y. Moses in [13] aims in characterizing *'the state of an agent that has been told only a finite number of facts'*

E. Fermé and J. Leite (Eds.): JELIA 2014, LNAI 8761, pp. 282–296, 2014.

[12, p. 79]. The idea is to obtain a meta-level formal account of the epistemic state asserting *the agent's knowledge contains no more than the information conveyed by some epistemic formula a* (intuitively, the conjunction of the finite knowledge base), which in turn, implies a description of the situation in which the agent '*only knows a*'.

The HM-'*only knowing*' approach is intuitively clear, mathematically interesting and pioneered a stream of research on '*minimal knowledge*' logics which are '*of essential importance for knowledge representation and inference*' [33]. The single-agent approach of [13] is based on the notion of *Stalnaker stable sets* and is essentially an S5-centered approach. Syntactically, it amounts in attempting to single out the '*propositionally minimum*' stable belief set which contains a (if it exists); semantically - and equivalently- it attempts to maximize the set of 'possibilities' (in terms of epistemically alternative states) in the relevant possible-worlds model. A subsequent paper by J. Halpern ([12]) generalized '*only knowing*' in the multi-agent setting, elaborating on the question '*what counts as a possibility in the multi-agent case*' and clarifying that '*only knowing*' can be also (and perhaps more meaningfully) understood in the context of **KD45** situations (rather that **S5** universal models). Of particular importance in this approach is the logical characterization of the '**honest**' formulas, the formulas that can actually represent '*all the agent knows*'. The idea of 'minimal knowledge' has been further investigated in AI; relevant results include the work of G. Schwarz and M. Truszczyński [30], the recent approach of D. Pearce and L. Uridia [29], the results of W. van der Hoek, J. Jaspars and E. Thijsse [33,16] and the work of Donini, Nardi and Rosati on the relation of 'minimal knowledge' to ground modal nonmonotonic logics [6]. Of related interest is the Only-Knowing approach of H. Levesque [25], which has been also extended to the multi-agent setting by J. Halpern, G. Lakemeyer and V. Belle [14,2] and has been also recently related to the McDermott & Doyle family of modal nonmonotonic logics [24].

The original, single-agent HM-'*only knowing*' approach is strongly based on the influential notion of stable belief sets, introduced by R. Stalnaker in the early '80s [32] as a formal representation of the epistemic state of an ideally rational agent, with full introspective capabilities. Assuming a propositional language, endowed with a modal operator $\Box\varphi$, interpreted as 'φ is believed', a set of formulas S is a stable set if it is 'stable' under classical inference and epistemic introspection:

(i) $Cn_{\mathbf{PC}}(S) \subseteq S$

(ii) $\varphi \in S$ implies $\Box\varphi \in S$

(iii) $\varphi \notin S$ implies $\neg\Box\varphi \in S$

This notion proved to be of major importance in modal nonmonotonic logics. The syntactic definition of stable sets is very natural and intuitive and it quickly became clear that they possess interesting properties while they do also admit simple and elegant semantic characterizations: they can be represented as the theories of universal (S5) Kripke models, or alternatively, as the set of beliefs of an agent residing in a **KD45** situation (see [28, Chapt.8], [11]). It is not hard to see however, that Stalnaker's stable sets model an extremely perfect reasoner in a way reminiscent of the '*logical omniscience*' problem in classical epistemic logic. Actually, the situation in Stalnaker's stable sets is a bit more uncomfortable: all tautologies are known and a stable set is a theory maximally consistent with provability in **S5**. This raises some important philosophical and technical questions in modal nonmonotonic reasoning, observed in [11] and partly addressed in the work of Marek, Schwarz and Truszczyński [27].

The *'logical omniscience'* problem in epistemic logic is about the many different facets of the unreasonably idealized nature of the account of knowledge and belief encoded in normal modal epistemic logics (see [10, Section 6], [15]). Two (out of several) of the most striking appearances of the *logical omniscience* problem are that (because of axiom **K**) the consequences of knowledge must be knowledge - an unrealistic assumption - and that (because of the **Rule of Necessitation**) all valid formulas are known, even if *'it would take more symbols than there are atoms in the universe to write down'* [7, p. 407]. There exist several ways to deal with *logical omniscience*: syntactically, one has to leave the realm of normal modal logics and drop at least axiom **K** and/or Rule **RN**. Model-theoretically, this means that one should consider either *impossible-worlds models* or *Scott-Montague semantics* (see Section 2)[1].

In previous work [23,21] we have followed a similar approach for defining syntactic variants of Stalnaker stable sets, aiming to describe the epistemic state of less idealized, non-omniscient agents. By varying the *context rules* for positive and negative introspection we have derived three alternative notions of stable epistemic state. For the first one (the RM-stable sets) we have proved an exact matching with a regular modal logic that can be plausibly considered as the regular counterpart to **S5** and a representation theorem with respect to possible worlds models allowing also for 'impossible' ('queer') worlds where nothing is known and everything is epistemically possible. For all three alternatives to Stalnaker stable sets, we have obtained representation theorems with respect to Scott-Montague possible-words models [23,21].

In this paper, we employ these alternative non-omniscient epistemic states to define an 'only knowing' approach for minimal knowledge à la Halpern & Moses, in a less idealized setting. We prove that such a project is feasible by defining appropriate notions of 'honesty' for our weak stable sets. Of course, as it has been shown in [21], leaving the 'perfect' setting of the **S5** Stalnaker stable sets and moving to the 'wild' world of (say) 'regular' RM-stable sets, implies leaving behind many of the mathematically elegant (but philosophically controversial) properties of Stalnaker stability. However, as we show in this paper, the situation can be technically controlled through the device of formulas like $\Box\top$, $\neg\Box\top$, $\Box\bot$, $\neg\Box\bot$ that allow us to 'navigate' through *possible* and *impossible* worlds, 'full' or empty neighborhoods. On the other hand, the philosophical discussion on the meaning (if any) of impossible worlds readily emerges; see Section 4.

2 Background Material

In this Section we briefly review the Modal Logic basics and establish notation and terminology. For the basics of Modal Logic the reader is referred to the books [3,5,17] and for the essentials of modal nonmonotonic logics to [28].

---

[1] In [15] various approaches for dealing with *'logical omniscience'* are considered: syntactic approaches, accounts of *awareness*, *algorithmic knowledge* and impossible worlds.

Modal Logic. The language of propositional logic is $\mathcal{L}$. We denote by $\mathcal{L}_\Box$ a modal propositional language whose operator $\Box\varphi$ has the reading 'φ is believed'. Sentence symbols include $\top$ (for *truth*) and $\bot$ (for *falsity*). Some of the important axioms in epistemic/doxastic logic are: **K**. $(\Box\varphi \wedge \Box(\varphi \supset \psi)) \supset \Box\psi$, **T**. $\Box\varphi \supset \varphi$ (*axiom of true, justified knowledge*), **D**. $\Box\varphi \supset \neg\Box\neg\varphi$ or $\neg(\Box\varphi \wedge \Box\neg\varphi)$ (*consistent belief*), **4**. $\Box\varphi \supset \Box\Box\varphi$ (*positive introspection*), **5**. $\neg\Box\varphi \supset \Box\neg\Box\varphi$ (*negative introspection*), **w5**. $(\varphi \wedge \neg\Box\varphi) \supset \Box\neg\Box\varphi$ (*negative introspection limited to true facts*), **p5**. $(\neg\Box\varphi \wedge \neg\Box\neg\varphi) \supset \Box\neg\Box\varphi$ (*negative introspection limited to possible facts*). The axiom **p5** has been investigated in [22] and provides inspiration for the context rules employed in [23,21]. **Modal logics** are sets of modal formulas containing classical propositional logic (i.e. containing all tautologies in the augmented language $\mathcal{L}_\Box$) and closed under rules **MP**. $\frac{\varphi,\varphi\supset\psi}{\psi}$ and **US** (Uniform Substitution). The smallest modal logic is denoted as **PC** (propositional calculus in the augmented language).

Normal Modal Logics. *Normal* are called those modal logics, which contain all instances of axiom **K** and are closed under rule

$$\textbf{RN. } \frac{\varphi}{\Box\varphi}$$

By $\textbf{KA}_1 \ldots \textbf{A}_n$ we denote the normal modal logic axiomatized by axioms $\textbf{A}_1$ to $\textbf{A}_n$. Well-known epistemic logics comprise **KT45** (**S5**) (a *strong logic of knowledge*) and **KD45** (a *logic of consistent belief*). Throughout our analysis in [23,21] we use the notion of strong provability from a theory I. In the case of a normal modal logic Λ we write $I \vdash^{RN}_\Lambda \varphi$ iff there is a Hilbert-style proof, where each step of the proof is a formula, which is a tautology in $\mathcal{L}_\Box$, or an instance of **K**, or an instance of an axiom of Λ, or a member of I, or a result of applying **MP** or **RN** to formulas of previous steps.

Relational Possible-Worlds Models. Normal modal logics are interpreted over relational (Kripke) models: a *Kripke model* $\mathfrak{M} = \langle W, R, V \rangle$ consists of a set of possible worlds W and a binary relation between them $R \subseteq W \times W$: whenever wRv, we say that world w '*sees*' world v. The valuation V determines which propositional variables are true inside each possible world. Within a world w, the propositional connectives ($\neg$, $\supset$, $\wedge$, $\vee$) are interpreted classically, while $\Box\varphi$ is true at w iff it is true in every world '*seen*' by w, notation: $(\mathfrak{M}, w \Vdash \Box\varphi$ iff $(\forall v \in W)(wRv \Rightarrow \mathfrak{M}, v \Vdash \varphi))$. A logic Λ is *determined* by a class of models iff it is *sound* and *complete* with respect to this class; it is known that **S5** is determined by the class of Kripke models with a *universal* relation, while **KD45** is determined by the class of models consisting of a world which '*sees*' a '*cluster*' (i.e. universally connected subset) of worlds and which does not necessarily 'see' itself; every model of this class has the form $\langle \{w\} \cup W, (\{w\} \cup W) \times W, V \rangle$.

Logical Omniscience. Normal modal epistemic logics suffer from the so-called *logical omniscience* problem, which can be partly attributed to axiom **K** and rule **RN**. Because of the latter, all tautologies are known. Also, because of the axiom **K**, logical consequences of knowledge constitute knowledge, something unreasonable in realistic situations. Note however that axiom **K** and axioms as simple as **N**.$\Box\top$ are unavoidable in Kripke models and ubiquitous in normal modal logics. See [10, Section 6] for more details on the *logical omniscience* problem.

Non-normal Modal Logics. A first step towards solving the logical omniscience problem is by defining **regular modal logics** which contain **K**, but substitute rule **RN** for rule

$$\mathbf{RM}. \quad \frac{\varphi \supset \psi}{\Box\varphi \supset \Box\psi}$$

We denote by $\mathbf{KA_1 \ldots A_{nR}}$ the regular modal logic axiomatized by axioms $\mathbf{A_1}$ to $\mathbf{A_n}$. In this case (of a regular modal logic Λ) we use again a notion of strong provability, where the application of **RN** in any step of the proof is replaced by **RM**, and we write $I \vdash^{\mathrm{RM}}_{\Lambda} \varphi$. There exist classes of logic weaker than regular, namely the monotonic and classical systems of modal logic (see [5, Part III]).

Impossible Worlds. Regular modal logics are interpreted on a strange species of possible world models; we will call them **q-models** here ($\mathfrak{M} = \langle W, N, R, V \rangle$) (see [31] for details). We now have two kinds of worlds: *normal* worlds (N), which behave in the way we described above and *non-normal* (also called *queer* or *impossible*) worlds ($W \setminus N$), where nothing is known/believed ($\Box\varphi$ is *never* true there) and everything is consistent to our state of affairs ($\neg\Box\neg\varphi$ is *always* true there). Within a world w, the propositional connectives are interpreted classically and $\Box\varphi$ is true at w iff $w \in N$ and $(\forall v \in W)(wRv \Rightarrow \mathfrak{M}, v \Vdash \varphi))$. Note that, by definition, the validity of $\Box\top$ eliminates all queer worlds, while the validity of $\neg\Box\top$ eliminates all normal worlds.

Scott-Montague Possible Worlds Models. Impossible worlds do not avoid the effect of **K**: to be able to eliminate **K** we have to resort to the semantics introduced independently by D. Scott and R. Montague, also called *neighborhood* semantics (*minimal models* in [5]). Neighborhood structures are very flexible and they are considered to be the standard semantic tool used to reason about non-normal modal logics. In this kind of models, which we will call **n-models** for brevity, each world does not 'see' other worlds but it is associated to a '*neighborhood*' of sets of possible worlds: an n-model is a triple $\mathfrak{N} = \langle W, E, V \rangle$, where W is any set of worlds, E is any function assigning to any world, its sets of 'neighboring' worlds (i.e. $E : W \to \mathcal{P}(\mathcal{P}(W))$) and V is again a valuation. The interpretation of any formula is exactly as in Kripke models, except of the formulas of the form $\Box\varphi$; such a formula is true at w iff the set of worlds where φ holds, belong to the possible neighborhoods of w: $\overline{V}(\varphi) = \{v \in W \mid \mathfrak{N}, v \Vdash \varphi\} \in E(w)$.

The directed graph $\mathfrak{F} = \langle W, R \rangle$, underlying a (Kripke, q-, or n-) model, is called a *frame*. The **theory of a** (Kripke, q- or n-) **model** $\mathfrak{M}$ (denoted as $Th(\mathfrak{M})$) is the set of all formulas being true in every world of $\mathfrak{M}$. Having a q-model, we can define a provably pointwise equivalent n-model.

Definition 1 ([31]). *Let* $\mathfrak{M} = \langle W, N, R, V \rangle$ *be a q-model and* $\mathfrak{N}_{\mathfrak{M}} = \langle W, E, V \rangle$ *the n-model, where* $E(w) = \{X \subseteq W \mid R_w \subseteq X\}^2$, *if* $w \in N$, *and* $E(w) = \varnothing$, *if* $w \in W \setminus N$. $\mathfrak{N}_{\mathfrak{M}}$ *is called the equivalent n-model produced by* $\mathfrak{M}$.

---

[2] $R_w = \{v \in W \mid wRv\}$.

Regular Modal Logic S5$'_R$. In previous work [21,23], we have investigated the regular modal logic S5$'_R$, where S5$'_R$ = KT4$_T$B$_T$R axiomatized by[3]:

4$_T$. $\Box\varphi \supset \Box(\Box\top \supset \Box\varphi)$

B$_T$. $(\varphi \wedge \Box\top) \supset \Box\neg\Box\neg\varphi$

5$_T$. $(\neg\Box\varphi \wedge \Box\top) \supset \Box\neg\Box\varphi$

In particular, we have investigated the proof theory of S5$'_R$ with a notion of strong provability from premises. The property of q-models which is relevant for S5$'_R$ is:

$$(\mathsf{U_q}) \quad (\forall w \in N)(\forall v \in W)wRv$$

We will call the q-models satisfying $\mathsf{U_q}$ **universal**. The following characterization of S5$'_R$ has been derived.

Proposition 1 ([21,23]). *S5$'_R$ is strongly complete with respect to all q-frames, for which* $(\mathsf{U_q})$ *holds.*

Context-Dependent Introspection Rules and Stable Belief Sets. Working as in [21,23], we consider the following context-dependent versions of the modal rules mentioned up to this point: assuming a set S of modal formulas, we denote the rules

$$\text{RN}_c. \quad \frac{\varphi \subseteq S}{\Box\varphi \in S} \qquad \text{NI}_c. \quad \frac{\varphi \notin S}{\neg\Box\varphi \in S}$$

$$\text{RM}_c. \quad \frac{\varphi \supset \psi \in S}{\Box\varphi \supset \Box\psi \in S} \qquad \text{RE}_c. \quad \frac{\varphi \equiv \psi \in S}{\Box\varphi \equiv \Box\psi \in S}$$

Stalnaker stable sets [32] are closed under propositional reasoning (i), under rule RN$_c$ (ii) and rule NI$_c$ (iii). The following theorem gathers some of their useful properties; see [28] for a proof.

Theorem 1. *1. A Stalnaker stable set is uniquely determined by its objective (non modal) part.*

2. If a set S is stable, then it is closed under strong S5 provability [4]. In particular, it contains every instance of K, T, 4, and 5.

3. A set S is stable iff it is the theory of a Kripke model with a universal accessibility relation.

4. A set S is stable iff it is the set of formulas believed in a world w of a KD45-model, i.e. S is stable iff there is a KD45-model $\mathfrak{M} = \langle W, R, V \rangle$ and $(\exists w \in W)S = \{\varphi \in \mathcal{L}_\Box \mid \mathfrak{M}, w \Vdash \Box\varphi\}$.

---

[3] We warn the reader that the names we have given to the axioms are not established in the literature and the same holds for the logic S5$'_R$. The first of these axioms appears in [31] under a different name.

[4] i.e. $S = \{\varphi \in \mathcal{L}_\Box \mid S \vdash_{\text{S5}} \varphi\}$.

3   Only-knowing

A stable set is intended to capture the epistemic state of a rational agent with full intro-spective capabilities. Being interested in the knowledge of an agent if '*all she knows is* α' it is only natural to consider the minimum among all stable sets that contain α. How-ever, different Stalnaker stable sets cannot strictly include one another. Based on the fact that stable sets are uniquely determined by their propositional part, J. Y. Halpern and Y. Moses in [13] suggest that we consider the stable set with the minimum propositional part among those that include α (when it exists); they then show it is equal to the theory of the largest S5 model, among those whose theory contains α. The existence of such sets or theories depends on the *honesty* of formula α. In [13], several intuitive notions of honesty are provided, and proven equivalent in order to support the robustness of this approach to only-knowing. Not every formula can be 'only known': the archetypical HM-dishonest formula is $\Box p \vee \Box q$; there can be no 'minimal' epistemic state containing this formula. In this Section, we provide respective notions for 'only knowing' in the context of our versions of stable sets introduced in [21,23]. The original definitions are:

Definition 2. *A formula* α *is **HM-honest$_S$** iff there exists a stable set* S^α *containing* α *such that* $S^\alpha \cap \mathcal{L} \subseteq S \cap \mathcal{L}$ *for all stable sets* S *that contain* α.

Definition 3. *Let* $\mathfrak{M}_\alpha$ *be the union of all S5 models* $\mathfrak{M}$ *such that* $\alpha \in Th(\mathfrak{M})$. *A formula* α *is **HM-honest$_M$** iff* $\alpha \in Th(\mathfrak{M}_\alpha)$.

Definition 4. *A formula* α *is **HM-honest$_K$** iff whenever* $\Box\alpha \supset \Box\varphi_1 \vee ... \vee \Box\varphi_n$ *is* **S5**-*valid, where* $\varphi_1, ..., \varphi_n \in \mathcal{L}$, *then* $\Box\alpha \supset \varphi_j$ *is* **S5**-*valid for some* $1 \leq j \leq n$.

along with a definition of honesty (**HM-honest$_D$**) of algorithmic nature.

3.1   Only-Knowing with RM-stable Sets

The first variant of a stable belief set is defined by substituting $\mathbf{RM_c}$ for $\mathbf{RN_c}$ in Stalnaker's definition.

Definition 5 ([23]). *A theory* $S \subseteq \mathcal{L}_\Box$ *is called* RM-stable *iff*

  (i) $\mathbf{PC} \subseteq S$ *and* S *is closed under* $\mathbf{MP}$
  (ii) S *is closed under rule* $\mathbf{RM_c}$. $\dfrac{\varphi \supset \psi \in S}{\Box\varphi \supset \Box\psi \in S}$
  (iii) S *is closed under rule* $\mathbf{NI_c}$. $\dfrac{\varphi \notin S}{\neg\Box\varphi \in S}$

RM-stable sets seem peculiar when compared to Stalnaker stable sets. Yet, they appear more familiar to eyes acquainted with regular modal logics. In particular, RM-stable sets are not uniquely determined by their 'objective' part; rather, they are completely 'governed' by a set of formulas of modal depth 1, involving the formulas that character-ize the normal and the 'queer' worlds. The following 'disjunction' properties are very useful.

Theorem 2 ([21]). *Let* $S \subseteq \mathcal{L}_\Box$ *be a consistent RM-stable set. Then for any formulas* $\varphi_i, \psi_j, \theta$:

(i) $\Box\varphi_1 \vee ... \vee \Box\varphi_k \vee \theta \in S$ iff $(\theta \in S)$ or $(\neg\Box\top \supset \theta \in S$ and $\varphi_i \in S$ for some $i \in \{1, ..., k\})$

(ii) $\neg\Box\varphi_1 \vee ... \vee \neg\Box\varphi_k \vee \theta \in S$ iff $(\Box\top \supset \theta \in S)$ or $(\varphi_i \notin S$ for some $i \in \{1, ..., k\})$

(iii) $\Box\varphi_1 \vee ... \vee \Box\varphi_k \vee \neg\Box\psi_1 \vee ... \vee \neg\Box\psi_m \vee \theta \in S$ iff $(\Box\top \supset \theta \in S)$ or $(\varphi_i \in S$ for some $i \in \{1, ..., k\})$ or $(\psi_i \notin S$ for some $i \in \{1, ..., m\})$

Theorem 3. *An RM-stable set S is uniquely determined by its formulas in $S \cap Q$, where*

$$Q = \mathcal{L} \cup \{\Box\top \supset \varphi \mid \varphi \in \mathcal{L}\} \cup \{\neg\Box\top \supset \varphi \mid \varphi \in \mathcal{L}\}$$

PROOF. So let S_1, S_2 be two RM-stable sets and $S_1 \cap Q = S_2 \cap Q$. For an arbitrary formula φ we prove $\varphi \in S_1 \Leftrightarrow \varphi \in S_2$ by induction on the modal depth of φ. Let φ be of modal depth n. By propositional reasoning, we know that $\varphi \equiv \varphi_1 \wedge ... \wedge \varphi_k$ where each φ_i is of the form $\Box a_1 \vee ... \vee \Box a_m \vee \neg\Box b_1 \vee ... \vee \neg\Box b_l \vee \psi$, $m, l \geq 0$, the a_i's and b_i's are formulas of smaller modal depth and ψ is a purely propositional formula. Also, for any RM-stable set S, $\varphi \in S \Leftrightarrow \varphi_1 \in S \& ... \& \varphi_k \in S$.
Base Cases: $n = 0$. If φ is propositional the claim is evident.
$n = 1$. We have that $a_1, ..., a_m, b_1, ..., b_l, \psi$ are propositional.
(i) φ_i is $\Box a_1 \vee ... \vee \Box a_m \vee \psi$. By Theorem 2 (i) $\varphi_i \in S_1 \Leftrightarrow (\psi \in S_1)$ or $(\neg\Box\top \rightarrow \psi \in S_1$ and $a_j \in S_1$ for some $j \in \{1, ..., m\}) \Leftrightarrow (\psi \in S_2)$ or $(\neg\Box\top \rightarrow \psi \in S_2$ and $a_j \in S_2$ for some $j \in \{1, ..., m\}) \Leftrightarrow \varphi_i \in S_2$
(ii) φ_i is $\neg\Box b_1 \vee ... \vee \neg\Box b_l \vee \psi$. By Theorem 2 (ii) $\varphi_i \in S_1 \Leftrightarrow (\Box\top \rightarrow \psi \in S_1)$ or $(b_j \notin S_1$ for some $j \in \{1, ..., l\}\}) \Leftrightarrow (\Box\top \rightarrow \psi \in S_2)$ or $(b_j \notin S_2) \Leftrightarrow \varphi_i \in S_2$
(iii) φ_i is $\Box a_1 \vee ... \vee \Box a_m \vee \neg\Box b_1 \vee ... \vee \neg\Box b_l \vee \psi$. By Theorem 2 (iii) $\varphi_i \in S_1 \Leftrightarrow (\Box\top \rightarrow \psi \in S_1)$ or $(a_j \in S_1$ for some $j \in \{1, ..., m\})$ or $(b_j \notin S_1$ for some $j \in \{1, ..., l\}) \Leftrightarrow (\Box\top \rightarrow \psi \in S_2)$ or $(a_j \in S_2$ for some $j \in \{1, ..., m\})$ or $(b_j \notin S_2$ for some $j \in \{1, ..., l\}) \Leftrightarrow \varphi_i \in S_2$
Induction Step: Essentially the same, we can now use the induction hypothesis instead of the initial assumptions. ∎

The RM-stable sets stand to $\mathbf{S5'_R}$ in very much the same way Stalnaker stable sets stand to $\mathbf{S5}$. The following representation theorem is also very useful.

Theorem 4 ([23]). *Let $S \subseteq \mathcal{L}_\Box$ be a consistent theory. S is RM-stable iff there is a q-model $\mathfrak{M} = \langle W, N, R, V \rangle$ satisfying property $(\mathsf{U_q})$ s.t. $Th(\mathfrak{M}) = S$. (Figure 1)*

Proviso. We explicitly state that for the purposes of the rest of this section, **we refer to consistent RM-stable sets that do not contain** $\neg\Box\top$. The second requirement is due to technical reasons having to do with our third notion of 'honesty', based on a kind of *disjunction property*.
The first notion of 'honesty' we introduce is based on our formal representation of the agent's epistemic state as an RM-stable set. We seek to define the 'minimal' epistemic state for a, assuming the agent 'only knows a'. It is now recognized [33] that minimality-via-stability depends on the background logic, and so is the case for our notion of RM-stability.

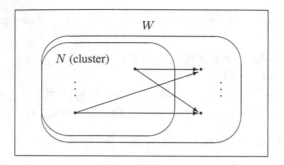

Fig. 1. The $S5'_R$ 'universal' q-model

Definition 6. *Consider an RM-stable set S and set Q as*

$$Q = \mathcal{L} \cup \{\Box\top \supset \varphi \mid \varphi \in \mathcal{L}\} \cup \{\neg\Box\top \supset \varphi \mid \varphi \in \mathcal{L}\}$$

*A formula α is **RM-honest$_S$** iff there exists an RM-stable set S^α containing α such that $S^\alpha \cap Q \subseteq S \cap Q$ for all RM-stable sets S that contain α.*

The second notion of 'honesty' (a form of '*information order*' [33]) involves possible (and, in our case, also impossible) worlds, and requires that an agent 'only knowing α' has the maximum set of '*possibilities*'. In our case, 'maximum' means the union of all models; as noted in [30], we seek for an inclusion-maximal preferred model, and the formulas true in the maximum model are to be considered as autoepistemic consequences of α. We need only consider the q-models in which each world is a truth assignment, and it is not the case that there exist multiple copies of the same world (assignment) in the 'normal' and the 'queer' part of the model. Having that in mind, the **union** of the q-models consists of a *normal part* (the union of the normal parts) and a *queer part* (the union of the queer parts of the models).

Definition 7. *Let $\mathfrak{M}_\alpha$ be the union of all universal q-models $\mathfrak{M}$ such that $\alpha \in Th(\mathfrak{M})$. A formula α is **RM-honest$_M$** iff $\alpha \in Th(\mathfrak{M}_\alpha)$.*

We are now ready to prove that the two definitions of RM-honesty coincide.

Theorem 5. *Let $\alpha \in \mathcal{L}_\Box$.*

1. α is RM-honest$_S$ $\iff$ α is RM-honest$_M$
2. $S^\alpha = Th(\mathfrak{M}_\alpha)$

PROOF. First, we show that $Th(\mathfrak{M}_\alpha) \cap Q \subseteq S \cap Q$ for all RM-stable sets S such that $\alpha \in S$. Let $\theta \in Th(\mathfrak{M}_\alpha) \cap Q$ and S be such a set. By Theorem 4 there exists a universal q-model $\mathfrak{M}$ such that $Th(\mathfrak{M}) = S$

– *Case 1:* $\theta \in \mathcal{L}$. θ is true for all worlds/valuations of $\mathfrak{M}_a$, which include those of $\mathfrak{M}$. Hence $\theta \in Th(\mathfrak{M}) \cap \mathcal{L} \subseteq S \cap Q$.

- *Case 2*: $\theta = \Box\top \supset \varphi$, for some $\varphi \in \mathcal{L}$. Then φ is true for all the normal words of $\mathfrak{M}_\alpha$, which include those of $\mathfrak{M}$. Hence $\theta \in Th(\mathfrak{M}) \cap \{\Box\top \supset \varphi | \varphi \in \mathcal{L}\} \subseteq S \cap Q$.

- *Case 3*: $\theta = \neg\Box\top \supset \varphi$, for some $\varphi \in \mathcal{L}$. Essentially, the same argument. φ is true for all the queer words of $\mathfrak{M}_\alpha$, which include those of $\mathfrak{M}$. Hence

$$\theta \in Th(\mathfrak{M}) \cap \{\neg\Box\top \supset \varphi | \varphi \in \mathcal{L}\} \subseteq S \cap Q$$

($\Rightarrow$) Since $Th(\mathfrak{M}_\alpha)$ is an RM-stable set (Theorem 4), and the RM-stable set with that property is unique (Theorem 3), it follows that $Th(\mathfrak{M}_\alpha) = S^\alpha$ and so $\alpha \in Th(\mathfrak{M}_\alpha)$.

($\Leftarrow$) It suffices to define $S^\alpha = Th(\mathfrak{M}_\alpha)$.   ∎

The following syntactic definition of RM-honesty relies on the properties of $\mathbf{S5'_R}$.

Definition 8. *A formula α is* **RM-honest$_K$** *iff whenever* $(\Box\top \supset \Box\alpha) \supset [\Box((\Box\top \supset \varphi_1) \wedge (\neg\Box\top \supset \psi_1))] \vee ... \vee [\Box((\Box\top \supset \varphi_n) \wedge (\neg\Box\top \supset \psi_n))] \vee \neg\Box\top$ *is* $\mathbf{S5'_R}$*-valid, where $\varphi_1, ..., \varphi_n, \psi_1, ..., \psi_n \in \mathcal{L}$, then* $(\Box\top \supset \Box\alpha) \supset (\Box\top \supset \varphi_j) \wedge (\neg\Box\top \supset \psi_j)$ *is* $\mathbf{S5'_R}$*-valid for some $1 \leq j \leq n$.*

With the following theorem all three notions of honesty provided are proven equivalent.

Theorem 6. *Let $\alpha \in \mathcal{L}_\Box$.*

1. α is RM-honest$_S$ $\Longrightarrow$ α is RM-honest$_K$

2. α is RM-honest$_K$ $\Longrightarrow$ α is RM-honest$_M$

PROOF. (1) Suppose a formula $(\Box\top \supset \Box\alpha) \supset [\Box((\Box\top \supset \varphi_1) \wedge (\neg\Box\top \supset \psi_1))] \vee ... \vee [\Box((\Box\top \supset \varphi_n) \wedge (\neg\Box\top \supset \psi_n))] \vee \neg\Box\top$ is $\mathbf{S5'_R}$-valid, thus, every RM-stable set containing α must also contain $\Box\top \supset \Box\alpha$ and consequently $[\Box((\Box\top \supset \varphi_1) \wedge (\neg\Box\top \supset \psi_1))] \vee ... \vee [\Box((\Box\top \supset \varphi_n) \wedge (\neg\Box\top \supset \psi_n))] \vee \neg\Box\top$. By Theorem 2 (iii) it must also contain $(\Box\top \supset \varphi_j) \wedge (\neg\Box\top \supset \psi_j)$ for some j. Given that α is RM-honest$_S$, S^α is an RM-stable set containing α, so let $(\Box\top \supset \varphi_j) \wedge (\neg\Box\top \supset \psi_j) \in S^\alpha$. Obviously $(\Box\top \supset \varphi_j) \in S^\alpha$ and $(\neg\Box\top \supset \psi_j) \in S^\alpha$. These formulas belong to $S^\alpha \cap Q$ so by definition of RM-honest$_S$ they exist in every RM-stable set containing α. It follows that $(\Box\top \supset \Box\alpha) \supset (\Box\top \supset \varphi_j) \wedge (\neg\Box\top \supset \psi_j)$ is $\mathbf{S5'_R}$-valid.

(2) α involves a finite number of primitive propositions, say $p_1, ..., p_n$. We need only consider models, whose worlds/valuations are the ones available for $p_1, ..., p_n$, so there are at most a finite number of q-models. Now suppose α is not RM-honest$_M$, that is there is no maximum model of α, only a finite number of maximals, say $\mathfrak{M}_1, ..., \mathfrak{M}_k$. With a finite number of primitive propositions we can fully describe each world with a formula (its valuation conjuncted with $\Box\top$ or $\neg\Box\top$ for being normal or queer, respectively). Since these models are different, each $\mathfrak{M}_i$ has a world w_i, described by the formula g_i, not existing in $\mathfrak{M}_{i+1(modk)}$. It is obvious that $\neg g_i \in Th(\mathfrak{M}_{i+1(modk)})$. Also $\neg g_i$ is of the form $\neg(P \wedge \Box\top)$ or $\neg(P \wedge \neg\Box\top)$, P propositional (conjunction of literals), so $\neg g_i \in Q$ and consequently $\neg g_i \equiv (\Box\top \supset \neg g_i) \wedge (\neg\Box\top \supset \neg g_i) \in Th(\mathfrak{M}')$ for any $\mathfrak{M}' \subseteq \mathfrak{M}_{i+1(modk)}$. These $\mathfrak{M}'$ over all i cover all q-models in which α is valid, so we have that $(\Box\top \supset \Box\alpha) \supset [\Box((\Box\top \supset \varphi_1) \wedge (\neg\Box\top \supset \psi_1))] \vee ... \vee [\Box((\Box\top \supset \varphi_n) \wedge (\neg\Box\top \supset \psi_n))] \vee \neg\Box\top$ is an $\mathbf{S5'_R}$-valid formula. Since α is RM-honest$_K$ we have that $(\Box\top \supset \Box\alpha) \supset (\Box\top \supset \neg g_i) \wedge (\neg\Box\top \supset \neg g_i)$ is $\mathbf{S5'_R}$-valid for some $i \in \{1, ..., k\}$. But $\mathfrak{M}_i, w_i \models a \wedge g_i \wedge (\Box\top \vee \neg\Box\top)$. A contradiction.   ∎

A natural question is whether RM-honesty implies HM-honesty or vice versa. The archetypical HM-dishonest formula $\Box p \vee \Box q$ is RM-dishonest too; if there was a maximum universal q-model for which $\Box p \vee \Box q$ was valid, that q-model would have zero queer worlds i.e. it would be an S5 model. However, as the following two examples show, neither of the aforementioned implications hold.

Proposition 2. *RM-honesty $\not\Rightarrow$ HM-honesty.*

PROOF. We prove that $\Box\Box\top \supset (\Box p \vee \Box q)$ is RM-honest but HM-dishonest. Consider the largest universal q-model possible, that is its normal and queer parts each, are a copy of all possible truth assignments. The formula $\Box\Box\top \supset (\Box p \vee \Box q)$ is valid in this maximum model, because $\neg\Box\Box\top$ is valid. Therefore the formula in question is RM-honest. On the other hand, assume the formula is HM-honest i.e. there exists a minimum (wrt to propositional formulas) stable set S than contains it. $\Box\Box\top$ is also contained in all stable sets, because $\top$ is contained in all stable sets. Consequently $(\Box p \vee \Box q) \in S$ and S is minimum i.e. $(\Box p \vee \Box q)$ is HM-honest. We derive a contradiction. ∎

Proposition 3. *HM-honesty $\not\Rightarrow$ RM-honesty.*

PROOF. We prove that $\Box\top \supset (\Box(\neg\Box\top \supset p) \vee \Box(\neg\Box\top \supset q))$ is HM-honest but RM-dishonest. Consider the largest S5 model possible, that is its worlds are all possible truth assignments. The formula in question is valid in this maximum model therefore it is HM-honest. Next, consider universal q-models $\mathfrak{M}_1, \mathfrak{M}_2$ such that $\mathfrak{M}_1, \mathfrak{M}_2$ contain some normal world, say w, the queer part of $\mathfrak{M}_1$ consists of all valuations that make p true, and the queer part of $\mathfrak{M}_2$ consists of all valuations that make q true. It is easy to see that $\Box\top \supset (\Box(\neg\Box\top \supset p) \vee \Box(\neg\Box\top \supset q))$ is valid in both models but not in $\mathfrak{M}_1 \cup \mathfrak{M}_2$. ∎

3.2 Only-Knowing with REp-Stable Sets

The following definition introduces another notion of stability.

Definition 9 ([21,23]). *S is called* REp-stable *iff*

(i) **PC** $\subseteq S$ *and S is closed under* **MP**

(ii) $\Box\top \in S$

(iii) S *is closed under rule* $\text{RE}_\mathbf{c}$. $\dfrac{\varphi \equiv \psi \in S}{\Box\varphi \equiv \Box\psi \in S}$

(iii) S *is closed under* $\text{NI}_{\mathbf{c-p}}$. $\dfrac{\varphi \notin S \quad \text{and} \quad \neg\varphi \notin S}{\neg\Box\varphi \in S}$

The following theorems are useful for understanding the structure of REp-stable sets.

Theorem 7 ([21]). *Let $S \subseteq \mathcal{L}_\Box$ be a consistent theory. S is REp-stable iff there is an n-model $\mathfrak{N} = \langle W, E, V \rangle$ s.t. $Th(\mathfrak{N}) = S$ and $(\forall w \in W)(E(w) = \{W\}$ or $E(w) = \{\varnothing, W\})$.*

Theorem 8 ([21]). *Let S be an REp-stable set. Then S is uniquely determined by its formulas in $S \cap Q$, where*

$$Q = \mathcal{L} \cup \{\Box\bot \supset \varphi \mid \varphi \in \mathcal{L}\} \cup \{\neg\Box\bot \supset \varphi \mid \varphi \in \mathcal{L}\}$$

Having proven Theorem 8 we can see a pattern emerging when we try to extend our results for REp-stable sets. Syntactically, we know which part of these stable sets uniquely determines them. Semantically, our representation theorem 7, show us that the models involved also have two kinds of worlds, which can be distinguished by some formula ($\Box\top$ in the case of RM-stable sets, $\Box\bot$ in the case of REp-stable sets). Thus we can repeat the definitions and proofs of the previous section, with only a few changes. The exception is the ones involving the validity in some logic, as we have no corresponding characterization for REp-stable sets. Finally, we only require our REp-stable sets to be consistent.

Definition 10. *Consider an REp-stable set S and Q as in Theorem 8. A formula α is **REp-honest$_S$** iff there exists an REp-stable set S^α containing α such that $S^\alpha \cap Q \subseteq S \cap Q$ for all REp-stable sets S that contain α.*

Definition 11. *Let $\mathfrak{M}_\alpha$ be the union of all n-models $\mathfrak{M}$ as in Theorem 7 such that $\alpha \in Th(\mathfrak{M})$. A formula α is **REp-honest$_M$** iff $\alpha \in Th(\mathfrak{M}_\alpha)$.*

Theorem 9. *Let $\alpha \in \mathcal{L}_\Box$.*
(i) α is REp-honest$_S$ $\iff$ α is REp-honest$_M$.
(ii) $S^\alpha = Th(\mathfrak{M}_\alpha)$.

PROOF. First, we show that $Th(\mathfrak{M}_\alpha) \cap Q \subseteq S \cap Q$ for all REp-stable sets S such that $\alpha \in S$. Let $\theta \in Th(\mathfrak{M}_\alpha) \cap Q$ and S be such a set. There exists an n-model $\mathfrak{M}$ as in Theorem 7, such that $Th(\mathfrak{M}) = S$.

- *Case 1*: $\theta \in \mathcal{L}$. θ is true for all worlds/valuations of $\mathfrak{M}_\alpha$, which include those of $\mathfrak{M}$. Hence $\theta \subset Th(\mathfrak{M}) \cap \mathcal{L} \subseteq S \cap Q$

- *Case 2*: $\theta = \Box\bot \supset \varphi$, for some $\varphi \in \mathcal{L}$. Then φ is true for all words w of $\mathfrak{M}_\alpha$, such that $E(w) = \{W, \varnothing\}$, which include those of $\mathfrak{M}$. Hence $\theta \in Th(\mathfrak{M}) \cap \{\Box\bot \supset \varphi | \varphi \in \mathcal{L}\} \subseteq S \cap Q$

- *Case 3*: $\theta = \neg\Box\bot \supset \varphi$, for some $\varphi \in \mathcal{L}$. Essentially, the same argument. φ is true for all words w of $\mathfrak{M}_\alpha$ such that $E(w) = W$, which include those of $\mathfrak{M}$. Hence $\theta \in Th(\mathfrak{M}) \cap \{\neg\Box\bot \supset \varphi | \varphi \in \mathcal{L}\} \subseteq S \cap Q$

($\Rightarrow$) Since $Th(\mathfrak{M}_\alpha)$ is an REp-stable set (Theorem 7), and the REp-stable with that property is unique (Theorem 8), it follows that $Th(\mathfrak{M}_\alpha) = S^\alpha$ and so $\alpha \in Th(\mathfrak{M}_\alpha)$.
($\Leftarrow$) It suffices to define $S^\alpha = Th(\mathfrak{M}_\alpha)$. ∎

4 Conclusions

In this paper, we have provided results which exhibit that it is completely feasible to transfer the enterprise of '*minimal knowledge*' approaches to the area of *non-normal* (in particular, *regular*) *modal logics*. We have defined notions of 'honesty' and HM-'only knowing' in the realm of stable epistemic states strongly connected to non-normal modal logics with impossible worlds or Scott-Montague semantics. Other approaches to 'honesty' and 'only knowing' exist: see [16,33,20]. However, we claim that our work further contributes in two important directions, with a philosophical and a technical interest. We bring 'impossible' worlds in the field of 'minimal knowledge' logics. This is, of course, something that requires justification. Given the intuitive appeal of relational, possible-worlds, epistemic semantics (where an *alternative* epistemic state implies *epistemic indistinguishability*), it is difficult to explain at the first place what does a 'queer' world represent. However, despite the (empiricist) philosophical objections against the 'impossible', it goes back to Hegel[5] that '... *one of the fundamental prejudices of logic as hitherto understood .. is that the contradictory cannot be imagined or thought* ...'. It is also conceivable that impossible worlds represent contradictory states of affairs in applications of Epistemic Logic in CS, where a processor can receive highly contradictory information from trusted sources.

Even more interesting, is the implicit adoption of the proof-theoretic machinery of regular (and other non-normal) modal logics in our investigations for modal nonmonotonic reasoning. Modal NMR has been dominated hitherto by the McDermott and Doyle paradigm, seeking for solutions T of the equation

$$T = Cn_\Lambda(I \cup \{\neg\Box\varphi \mid \varphi \notin T\})$$

parameterized by the underlying monotonic modal logic Λ. The strong provability notion involved in this approach, in particular Rule **RN**, actually suffices for providing stable solutions in this equation and importing **S5** in the agent's expansion, independently of the logic Λ adopted. It was found by Marek, Schwarz and Truszczyński that there exist whole intervals in the lattice of (monotonic) modal logics that generate the same nonmonotonic logic [27] and actually, those intervals often include *subnormal* modal logics (containing the minimum set of axioms needed, the rest is left to rule **RN**) unknown hitherto to modal logicians. It seems quite natural then to consider notions of strong provability not involving **RN** and ask to what kind of logics do they lead. It is however necessary to define and investigate the geography of candidate expansions, that is, the nature and behaviour of the epistemic states that will replace the Stalnaker stable sets. We have made the first steps in this direction, firstly by identifying variants of stable belief sets - in relation to regular logics with strong provability from premises - and now, by transferring the HM-'only knowing' approach to the 'wild' world of RM-stable and REp-stable belief sets. In a related direction, it should be noted that there exist recent proposals for dealing with *logical omniscience* [1,18] and it very much worth considering whether (and how) some of these ideas may be grafted into modal nonmonotonic logics.

Obviously, much remains to be done in this direction and we do hope that interesting results will emerge.

Acknowledgments. We wish to thank the anonymous JELIA 2014 referees for their constructive comments, important suggestions and useful pointers to similar results, whose relation with our approach is certainly worth investigating.

---

[5] See the '*Stanford Encyclopedia of Philosophy*' entry on 'Impossible Worlds'.

References

1. Ågotnes, T., Alechina, N.: The dynamics of syntactic knowledge. Journal of Logic and Computation 17(1), 83–116 (2007)
2. Belle, V., Lakemeyer, G.: Multi-agent only-knowing revisited. In: Lin, et al. (eds.) [26]
3. Blackburn, P., de Rijke, M., Venema, Y.: Modal Logic. Cambridge Tracts in Theoretical Computer Science, vol. 53. Cambridge University Press (2001)
4. Brewka, G., Eiter, T., McIlraith, S.A. (eds.): Principles of Knowledge Representation and Reasoning: Proceedings of the Thirteenth International Conference, KR 2012, Rome, Italy, June 10-14, 2012. AAAI Press (2012)
5. Chellas, B.F.: Modal Logic, an Introduction. Cambridge University Press (1980)
6. Donini, F.M., Nardi, D., Rosati, R.: Ground nonmonotonic modal logics. Journal of Logic and Computation 7(4), 523–548 (1997)
7. Fitting, M.C.: Basic Modal Logic. In: Gabbay, et al. (eds.) [8], vol. 1, pp. 368–448 (1993)
8. Gabbay, D.M., Hogger, C.J., Robinson, J.A. (eds.): Handbook of Logic in Artificial Intelligence and Logic Programming. Oxford University Press (1993)
9. Gabbay, D.M., Woods, J.: Logic and the Modalities in the Twentieth Century. Handbook of the History of Logic, vol. 7. North-Holland (2006)
10. Gochet, P., Gribomont, P.: Epistemic logic. In: Gabbay, Woods (eds.) [9], vol. 7, pp. 99–195 (2006)
11. Halpern, J.: A critical reexamination of default logic, autoepistemic logic and only-knowing. Computational Intelligence 13(1), 144–163 (1993); A preliminary version appears in Mundici, D., Gottlob, G., Leitsch, A. (eds.): KGC 1993. LNCS, vol. 713, pp. 144–163. Springer, Heidelberg (1993)
12. Halpern, J.: A theory of knowledge and ignorance for many agents. Journal of Logic and Computation 7(1), 79–108 (1997)
13. Halpern, J., Moses, Y.: Towards a theory of knowledge and ignorance: Preliminary report in Apt, K. (ed.) Logics and Models of Concurrent Systems. Springer (1985)
14. Halpern, J.Y., Lakemeyer, G.: Multi-agent only knowing. Journal of Logic and Computation 11(1), 41–70 (2001)
15. Halpern, J.Y., Pucella, R.: Dealing with logical omniscience: Expressiveness and pragmatics. Artificial Intelligence 175(1), 220–235 (2011)
16. van der Hock, W., Jaspars, J., Thijsse, E.: Honesty in partial logic. Studia Logica 56(3), 323–360 (1996)
17. Hughes, G.E., Cresswell, M.J.: A New Introduction to Modal Logic. Routledge (1996)
18. Jago, M.: Logics for Resource-Bounded Agents. PhD thesis, University of Nottingham (2006)
19. Janhunen, T., Niemelä, I. (eds.): JELIA 2010. LNCS, vol. 6341. Springer, Heidelberg (2010)
20. Jaspars, J.: A generalization of stability and its application to circumscription of positive introspective knowledge. In: Schönfeld, W., Börger, E., Kleine Büning, H., Richter, M.M. (eds.) CSL 1990. LNCS, vol. 533, pp. 289–299. Springer, Heidelberg (1991)
21. Koutras, C.D., Moyzes, C., Zikos, Y.: Syntactic reconstructions of stable belief sets. Technical report, Graduate Programme in Algorithms and Computation (2014)
22. Koutras, C.D., Zikos, Y.: On a modal epistemic axiom emerging from McDermott-Doyle logics. Fundamenta Informaticae 96(1-2), 111–125 (2009)
23. Koutras, C.D., Zikos, Y.: Stable belief sets revisited. In: Janhunen, Niemelä (eds.) [19], pp. 221–233
24. Lakemeyer, G., Levesque, H.J.: Only-knowing meets nonmonotonic modal logic. In: Brewka, et al. (eds.) [4]
25. Levesque, H.J.: All I Know: A study in autoepistemic logic. Artificial Intelligence 42(2-3), 263–309 (1990)

26. Lin, F., Sattler, U., Truszczynski, M. (eds.): Principles of Knowledge Representation and Reasoning: Proceedings of the Twelfth International Conference, KR 2010, Toronto, Ontario, Canada, May 9-13. AAAI Press (2010)

27. Marek, V.W., Schwarz, G.F., Truszczyński, M.: Modal non-monotonic logics: Ranges,characterization, computation. Journal of the ACM 40, 963–990 (1993)

28. Marek, V.W., Truszczyński, M.: Nonmonotonic Logic: Context-dependent Reasoning. Springer (1993)

29. Pearce, D., Uridia, L.: An approach to minimal belief via objective belief. In: Walsh (ed.) [34], pp. 1045–1050

30. Schwarz, G.F., Truszczyński, M.: Minimal knowledge problem: a new approach. Artificial Intelligence 67, 113–141 (1994)

31. Segerberg, K.: An essay in Clasical Modal Logic. Filosofiska Studies, Uppsala (1971)

32. Stalnaker, R.: A note on non-monotonic modal logic. Artificial Intelligence 64, 183–196 (1993) (Revised version of the unpublished note originally circulated in 1980)

33. van der Hoek, W., Jaspars, J., Thijsse, E.: Persistence and minimality in epistemic logic. Annals of Mathematics and Artificial Intelligence 27(1-4), 25–47 (1999)

34. Walsh, T. (ed.): Proceedings of the 22nd International Joint Conference on Artificial Intelligence, IJCAI 2011, Barcelona, Catalonia, Spain, July 16-22. IJCAI/AAAI (2011)

A Complexity Assessment for Queries Involving Sufficient and Necessary Causes[*]

Pedro Cabalar[1], Jorge Fandiño[1], and Michael Fink[2]

[1] Department of Computer Science
University of Corunna, Spain
{cabalar,jorge.fandino}@udc.es
[2] Vienna University of Technology,
Institute for Information Systems
Vienna, Austria
fink@kr.tuwien.ac.at

Abstract. In this work, we revisit a recently proposed multi-valued semantics for logic programs where each true atom in a stable model is associated with a set of expressions (or causal justifications) involving rule labels. For positive programs, these causal justifications correspond to the possible alternative proofs of the atom that further satisfy some kind of minimality or lack of redundancy. This information can be queried for different purposes such as debugging, program design, diagnosis or causal explanation. Unfortunately, in the worst case, the number of causal justifications for an atom can be exponential with respect to the program size, so that computing the complete causal model may become intractable in the general case. However, we may instead just be interested in querying whether some particular set of rules are involved in the atom derivation, either as a *sufficient cause* (they provide one of the alternative proofs) or as a *necessary cause* (they are mandatorily used in all proofs). In this paper, we formally define sufficient and necessary causation for this setting and provide precise complexity characterizations of the associated decision problems, showing that they remain within the first two levels of the polynomial hierarchy.

1 Introduction

An important challenge in Knowledge Representation (KR) and Reasoning is not only deriving conclusions from a given theory or knowledge base, but also providing *explanations* for their derivation. This is particularly interesting in KR areas related to causal reasoning. For instance, in diagnosis scenarios, when discrepancies between observations and predictions are found, we may be interested not only in exhibiting a set of malfunctioning components, but also the way in which these breakdowns have eventually caused each discrepancy. Another example is legal reasoning, where determining a legal responsibility usually involves finding out which agent (or agents) have eventually caused a given result – checking whether the agent is involved in the explanation for

---

[*] This research was partially supported by Spanish MEC project TIN2009-14562-C05-04, by Xunta de Galicia, Spain, grant GPC2014/070 and program INCITE 2011, Inditex-University of Corunna 2013 grants, as well as by the Austrian Science Fund (FWF) project P24090.

E. Fermé and J. Leite (Eds.): JELIA 2014, LNAI 8761, pp. 297–310, 2014.

that result is as important as the result occurrence itself. There are, however, different degrees in which a set of events or actions A may be "involved" in the explanation for some effect B. In some cases, A may *suffice* to explain B. In other cases, A alone cannot guarantee B, but is indispensable in any explanation for the latter, i.e., it is *necessary* for B. Let us illustrate these ideas with an example.

Example 1. An *alarm* is connected to three switches as depicted in Figure 1(a). Each switch is operated by a different person and, at a given moment, they all accidentally close the switches. We want to analyse the responsibility for firing a false alarm.

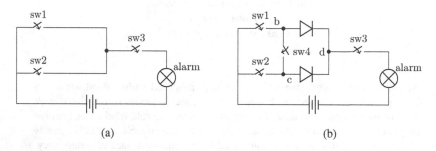

(a)   (b)

Fig. 1. A pair of circuits connecting switches and an alarm

Analysing the circuit, we find two explanations for the alarm: moving down sw_1 and sw_3 together *suffices* to fire the alarm, and the same happens for sw_2 and sw_3. However, had sw_3 not been moved down, the alarm would have not been fired. That means that closing sw_3 is a *necessary cause* to fire the alarm, pointing out that the operator for that switch has, somehow, a higher degree of responsibility. Consider now the elaboration depicted in Figure 1(b) with a fourth switch and its corresponding person in charge, and suppose again that all persons close their respective switches. The set of events $\{sw_1, sw_3, sw_4\}$ obviously suffice to fire the alarm, since $\{sw_1, sw_3\}$ are still sufficient for that purpose. However, sw_4 is irrelevant, and so, it does not constitute an *actual cause*, whereas $\{sw_1, sw_3\}$ is a *sufficient cause* since nothing can be removed from it without ceasing to be a sufficient explanation.

Until now, we have made explanations in terms of actions, ignoring their connection to their effects through chains of intermediate events. Suppose that we want to reflect, for instance, the causal relation between the switch movements and the facts representing that there is current at wire points b, c or d in Figure 1(b). To this aim, we will need to represent each explanation not just as a set of events, but as an ordered arrangement of them instead. For instance, the final effect for sw_1 is that the current reaches point d and the complete explanation for that effect would be now the sequence $sw_1 \cdot b \cdot d$. This, together with the action of closing sw_3, is a sufficient cause for *alarm*. Similarly, the joint occurrence of $sw_2 \cdot c \cdot d$ and sw_3 constitutes a second, alternative sufficient cause. A useful way of depicting explanations is by means of directed graphs with vertices representing events and edges representing causal connections among them. Figure 2 shows three sufficient explanations G_1, G_2 and G_3 for *alarm* corresponding to the circuit in

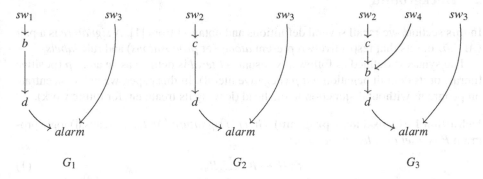

Fig. 2. Sufficient explanations for the alarm firing in Figure 1(b). G_1 and G_2 are causes.

Figure 1(b). The first two explanations G_1 and G_2 are sufficient causes, whereas G_3 is not a cause, since we can "remove" sw_4 and b and still get the sufficient explanation G_2.

In this paper, we provide a formal definition for the three[1] different types of causal relations introduced above, that is *sufficient explanation, sufficient cause* and *necessary cause*, and study how these causal assertions can be derived from a representation in the form of a labelled logic program. To this aim, we use a recently proposed causal approach [1] that provides a multi-valued extension of the stable model semantics [2]. In this approach, each true atom in a stable model is associated an expression involving rule labels, called its *causal justification*, that has a direct relation to sets of causal graphs as those in Figure 2. We summarise our contributions as follows.

- We formally define the concepts of *sufficient explanation, sufficient cause* and *necessary cause* for some atom (cf. Section 3).
- We show that the number of possible sufficient causes for an atom can be, in the worst case, exponential with respect to the program size. Despite this fact, proving exact complexity characterisations (cf. Section 4 and see Figure 3) of the associated decision problems, we establish that sufficient queries are not harder than traditional (brave or cautious) reasoning tasks under the stable model semantics.

	positive programs	with negation (brave)	with negation (cautions)
sufficient explanation	P	NP	coNP
sufficient cause	P	NP	coNP
necessary cause	coNP	Σ_2^P	coNP

Fig. 3. Completeness results for deciding different types of causation in causal logic programs

---

[1] We leave the study of *actual causation* (that is, events that are needed for some sufficient cause) for future work.

2   Background

In this section, we recall several definitions and notation from [1]. A *signature* is a pair $\langle At, Lb \rangle$ of sets that respectively represent *atoms* (or *propositions*) and rule *labels*.

The syntax is defined as follows. As usual, a *literal* is defined as an atom p (positive literal) or its default negation *not p* (negative literal). In this paper, we will concentrate on programs without disjunction in the head (leaving its treatment for future work).

Definition 1 (Causal logic program). *Given a signature $\langle At, Lb \rangle$, a (causal) logic program P is a set of rules of the form:*

$$t : H \leftarrow B_1, \dots, B_n, \tag{1}$$

where $t \in Lb \cup \{1\}$, H is an atom (the head*) and $B_1, \dots, B_n$ are literals (the* body*).*   □

For any rule R of the form (1) we define $label(R) \overset{\text{def}}{=} t$. We denote by $head(R) \overset{\text{def}}{=} H$ its *head*, and by $body(R) \overset{\text{def}}{=} \{B_1, \dots, B_n\}$ its *body*. When $n = 0$ we say that the rule is a *fact* and omit the symbol '$\leftarrow$.' When $t \in Lb$ we say that the rule is *labelled*; otherwise $t = 1$ and we omit both t and '$:$'. By these conventions, for instance, an unlabelled fact p is actually an abbreviation of $(1 : p \leftarrow)$. A logic program P is *positive* if it contains no default negation.

The semantics relies on assigning, to each atom, a causal term defined as follows.

Definition 2 (Causal values). *A (causal) term, t, over a set of labels Lb, is recursively defined as one of the following expressions $t ::= l \mid \prod S \mid \sum S \mid t_1 \cdot t_2 \mid (t_1)$ where $l \in Lb$, t_1, t_2 are, in turn, causal terms and S is a (possibly empty and possible infinite) set of causal terms. When S is finite and non-empty, $S = \{t_1, \dots, t_n\}$ we write $\prod S$ simply as $t_1 * \cdots * t_n$ and $\sum S$ as $t_1 + \cdots + t_n$. Causal values are the equivalence classes of causal terms under the axiomatic identities of distributive lattices plus those in Figure 4. The set of causal values is denoted by $\mathbf{V}_{Lb}$.*   □

Associativity	Absorption	Identity	Annihilator	Indempotence
$t \cdot (u{\cdot}w) = (t{\cdot}u) \cdot w$	$t = t + u \cdot t \cdot w$	$t = 1 \cdot t$	$0 = t \cdot 0$	$l \cdot l = l$
	$u \cdot t \cdot w = t * u \cdot t \cdot w$	$t = t \cdot 1$	$0 = 0 \cdot t$	

Addition distributivity	Product distributivity	Transitivity
$t \cdot (u{+}w) = (t{\cdot}u) + (t{\cdot}w)$	$c \cdot (d * e) = (c \cdot d) * (c \cdot e)$	$c \cdot d \cdot e = (c \cdot d) * (d \cdot e)$
$(t + u) \cdot w = (t{\cdot}w) + (u{\cdot}w)$	$(c * d) \cdot e = (c \cdot e) * (d \cdot e)$	with $d \neq 1$

Fig. 4. Properties of the '$\cdot$' operator (c, d, e are terms without '$+$' and l is a label)

We assume that '$\cdot$' has hieger priotity than '$*$', and its turn '$*$' has higher priority than '$+$'. When $S = \emptyset$, we denote, as usual $\prod S$ by 1 and $\sum S$ by 0. These values are the identities for the product and the addition, respectively. All three operations, '$*$', '$+$' and '$\cdot$' are associative. Furthermore, '$*$' and '$+$' are commutative and they hold the usual absorption and distributive laws with respect to infinite sums and products of any completely distributive lattice. The behaviour of the '$\cdot$' operator is more specific from this approach and is captured by the properties shown in Figure 4. Note that distributivity with respect to the product and transitivity are applicable to terms c, d, e without sums (this means that the empty sum, 0, is not allowed either) and idempotence is only applicable to atomic labels. As usual for lattices, we define an order relation $\leq$ as follows:

$$t \leq u \qquad \text{iff} \qquad (t * u = t) \qquad \text{iff} \qquad (t + u = u)$$

By the identity properties of $+$ and $*$, this immediately means that 1 is the top element and 0 the bottom element of this order relation.

Given a signature $\langle At, Lb \rangle$ a *causal interpretation* is a mapping $I : At \longrightarrow \mathbf{V}_{Lb}$ assigning a causal term to each atom. We denote the set of causal interpretations by $\mathbf{I}$. For interpretations I and J we say that $I \leq J$ whether $I(p) \leq J(p)$ for each atom $p \in At$. Hence, there is a $\leq$-bottom interpretation $\mathbf{0}$ (resp. a $\leq$-top interpretation $\mathbf{1}$) that maps each atom p to 0 (resp. 1). The value assigned to a negative literal *not p* by an interpretation I is defined as: $I(\textit{not } p) \overset{\text{def}}{=} 1$ if $I(p) = 0$; and $I(\textit{not } p) \overset{\text{def}}{=} 0$ otherwise.

We define next a simple variation of the standard Gelfond and Lifschitz' program reduct [2]. The *reduct* of program P with respect to a causal interpretation I, in symbols P^I, is the result of: (1) removing from P all rules R, s.t. $I(B) \neq 0$ for some negative literal $B \in body(R)$; and (2) removing all negative literals from the remaining rules.

Definition 3 (Causal model). *Given a positive causal logic program P, a causal interpretation I is a* causal stable model, *in symbols $I \models P$, if and only if I is the $\leq$-least interpretation such that*

$$\big(I(B_1) * \ldots * I(B_n) \big) \cdot t \leq I(H)$$

for each rule $R \in P$ of the form (1). *An interpretation I is a* causal stable model *of any program P iff I is a causal stable model of P^I.*   □

Definition 4 (Direct consequences). *Given a positive logic program P over signature $\langle At, Lb \rangle$, the operator of* direct consequences *is a function $T_P : \mathbf{I} \longrightarrow \mathbf{I}$ such that, for any causal interpretation I and any atom $p \in At$:*

$$T_P(I)(p) \overset{\text{def}}{=} \sum \big\{ \big(I(B_1) * \ldots * I(B_n) \big) \cdot t \mid (t : p \leftarrow B_1, \ldots, B_n) \in P \big\}$$

Theorem 1 (From Theorem 2 in [1]). *Let P be a (possibly infinite) positive logic program with n causal rules. Then, (i) $lfp(T_P)$ is the least model of the program P, and (ii) $lfp(T_P) = T_P \uparrow^{\omega} (\mathbf{0}) = T_P \uparrow^{n} (\mathbf{0})$.*   □

3   Query Language

In order to characterise the different types of causation, we must begin first by a formal description of causal explanations. In particular, an explanation will have the form of a particular kind of graph involving rule labels, as defined below.

Definition 5 (Explanation or Causal graph). *Given a set of labels Lb, an* explanation *or* causal graph *(c-graph) G is a transitively and reflexively closed directed graph with a set of vertices $V \subseteq Lb$ and a set of edges $E \subseteq V \times V$. The set of causal graphs is denoted by $\mathbf{C}_{Lb}$. A c-graph is* cyclic *if contains a (non-reflexive) cycle,* acyclic *otherwise.*   □

Imposing reflexivity is not essential, but is more convenient for obtaining simpler definitions. Transitivity, however, is crucial for defining an adequate ordering relation among
explanations with the simple use of the subgraph relation. To see why, let us consider
again the graphs G_2 and G_3 in Figure 2. As we explained in the introduction, G_3 is a
sufficient explanation for *alarm* but is not a sufficient *cause* because G_2 is also sufficient
and somehow "smaller." In fact, G_2 can be obtained by "removing" b and sw_4 from G_3
while respecting the rest of causal dependence relations. However, G_2 is not a subgraph
of G_3 since the edge (c,d) is not present in the latter. To capture this idea of being
smaller as a result of "removing parts" we must use instead the transitive closures: the
transitive closure of G_2 is indeed a subgraph of the transitive closure of G_3.

For any c-graph G we define an associated causal term $term(G)$ as follows:

$$term(G) \stackrel{\text{def}}{=} \prod \{ v_1 \cdot v_2 \mid (v_1, v_2) \text{ is an edge of } G \}$$

Definition 6 (sufficient explanation, sufficient cause, necessary cause). *Given an interpretation I and an atom p we say that a c-graph G is*

- *a sufficient explanation for p iff $term(G) \leq I(p)$*
- *a sufficient cause of p iff it is a subgraph-minimal sufficient explanation for p*
- *a necessary cause of p iff it is a subgraph of all sufficient causes of p and $I(p) \neq 0$.* □

Example 2 (Ex. 1 continued). A possible representation of the circuit in Figure 1(b) is
the logic program P_1 containing the following causal rules:

$$
\begin{array}{llll}
alarm: & alarm(T) & \leftarrow down(sw_3,T), current(c,T) & \qquad d: current(d,T) \leftarrow current(b,T) \\
b: & current(b,T) \leftarrow down(sw_1,T) & & \qquad d: current(d,T) \leftarrow current(c,T) \\
c: & current(c,T) \leftarrow down(sw_2,T) & & \qquad down(X,T) \leftarrow m(X,d,T) \\
& & & \qquad up(X,T) \leftarrow m(X,u,T)
\end{array}
$$

plus the corresponding inertia rules for atoms up and $down$ (we consider that the rest of
the fluents are non-inertial, and so, false by default):

$$up(X,T{+}1) \leftarrow up(X,T), not\, down(X,T{+}1) \qquad down(X,T{+}1) \leftarrow down(X,T), not\, up(X,T{+}1)$$

where X is any switch number $X \in \{1,2,3,4\}$ and T is a natural number representing a
time instant. Atoms $m(X,D,T)$ represent the action of moving switch X up 'u' or down
'd' at time instant T. Consider now a story where, initially, all switches are up, then sw_1
and sw_2 are closed in Situation 1, then sw_3 is closed at 3 and finally sw_4 closed at 4.
The following set of facts, added to P_1, captures this scenario:

$$
\begin{array}{llll}
& up(sw_s,0) & & \text{for } s \in \{1,2,3\} \\
sw_1: m(sw_1,d,1) & sw_2: m(sw_2,d,1) & sw_3: m(sw_3,d,3) & sw_4: m(sw_4,d,4)
\end{array}
$$

In the least model I of P_1, $I(alarm) = (sw_1 \cdot b \cdot d * sw_3) \cdot alarm + (sw_2 \cdot c \cdot d * sw_3) \cdot alarm$.
The correspondence between the left and right operands in the addition above with c-
graphs G_1 and G_2 in Figure 2 is easy to see. For instance $sw_1 \cdot b \cdot d$ corresponds to the
left branch of G_1, sw_3 to the right one and $alarm$ is its root. In fact, it can be shown, by
successive application of algebraic equivalences in Figure 4, that

$$term(G_1) = (sw_1 \cdot b \cdot d * sw_3) \cdot alarm \quad \text{and} \quad term(G_2) = (sw_2 \cdot c \cdot d * sw_3) \cdot alarm$$

In other words, $I(alarm) = term(G_1) + term(G_2)$ in the only causal stable model. Now, it is also easy to see, by idempotence of addition, that $term(G_1) + I(alarm) = I(alarm)$ which implies that $term(G_1) \leq I(alarm)$. According to Definition 6, this means that G_1 is, as we mentioned in the introduction, a sufficient explanation for $alarm$. Furthermore, no subgraph of G_1 is a sufficient explanation for p and consequently G_1 is also a sufficient cause of p. By a similar observation, G_2 is also a sufficient cause of p and it can be checked that, apart from G_1 and G_2, no other c-graph is a sufficient cause of p.   □

In the previous example, the causal term for $alarm$ obtained in the unique stable model of the program was equal to the sum of all terms associated with its sufficient causes. In fact, this constitutes a general property, as stated below.

Theorem 2. *Given an interpretation I and an atom p, the following holds:*

- $I(p) = \sum \{ \, term(G) \mid G \text{ is a sufficient cause of } p \, \}$, *and*
- *any c-graph G is a necessary cause of p (Def. 6) iff* $I(p) \leq term(G)$ *and* $I(p) \neq 0$. □

Finally, for a program with negation and its possible stable models, we define, as usual, cautious and brave versions of the three types of explanations defined before.

Definition 7. *Given a causal logic program P, an explanation of any type (sufficient explanation, sufficient cause or necessary cause) for an atom p is further said to be brave (resp. cautious) if it constitutes an explanation of that same type for p in some (resp. every) stable model of P.*   □

4 Complexity Assessment

The table in Figure 3 summarizes our complexity assessment (completeness results). Each row represents a query type – sufficient explanation, sufficient cause and necessary cause. The first column contains results for positive programs (unique stable model), whereas the second and the third columns respectively show the results for brave and cautions reasoning for programs with negation. Note that for sufficient queries the complexity is the same as for checking the truth of an atom in standard stable model semantics. Subesequently, we establish these results formally, starting with membership.

In order to check whether a c-graph G is, for instance, a brave (resp. cautious) sufficient cause of a given atom p for a program P we can begin computing the standard (non-causal) stable models of P. Since the causal reduct removes negations depending on whether negated atoms are 0 or different from 0 and there exists a one-to-one correspondence between causal stable models and standard stable models (see [1] for more details), we can build the reduct P^J using each non-causal stable model J and then proceed to compute its least causal model iterating the direct consequences operator for that reduct, T_{P^J}. Due to [1, Theorem 6], there is a 1-to-1 correspondence between least causal models obtained in this way and causal stable models of the program. Now it would remain to check whether $term(G) \leq I(p)$ in some (resp. every) causal stable model I. Unfortunately, comparing two arbitrary causal terms t and t' is not an easy task (in fact it is coNP-hard). A naive approach for that comparison would be rewriting t and t' in a normal form where '$\cdot$' and products are not in the scope of additions, something that can be always achieved by applying distributive laws of '$\cdot$' and '$*$' with respect to '$+$'. Once in that normal form, comparison is more or less straightforward ($\Sigma t_i \leq \Sigma t'_j$ iff for each term t_i there is some $t'_j \geq t_i$, and comparing terms just containing products and '$\cdot$' is a simple task). However, applying distributivity may easily blow up complexity. Consider the positive program P_2 consisting of the rules:

$$a : p_1 \qquad\qquad b : p_1 \qquad\qquad m_i : p_i \leftarrow p_{i-1}, q_{i-1} \qquad \text{for } i \in \{2,\ldots,n\}$$
$$c : q_1 \qquad\qquad d : q_1 \qquad\qquad n_i : q_i \leftarrow p_{i-1}, q_{i-1} \qquad \text{for } i \in \{2,\ldots,n\}$$

It is easy to see that the interpretations of atoms p_1 and q_1 in the least causal model I of P_2 are $a+b$ and $c+d$, respectively. The interpretation for p_2 corresponds to:

$$I(p_2) = (I(p_1) * I(q_1)) \cdot m_2 = ((a+b) * (c+d)) \cdot m_2$$
$$= (a*c) \cdot m_2 + (a*d) \cdot m_2 + (b*c) \cdot m_2 + (b*d) \cdot m_2$$

This addition cannot be further simplified. Thus, by Theorem 2, the four summands above are sufficient causes for p_2. Analogously, $I(q_2)$ can also be expressed as a sum of four sufficient causes – we just replace m_2 by n_2 in $I(p_2)$. But then, $I(p_3)$ corresponds to $(I(p_2) * I(q_2)) \cdot m_3$ and, applying distributivity, this yields a sum of 4×4 sufficient causes. In the general case, each atom p_n or q_n has $2^{2^{n-1}}$ sufficient causes so that expanding the complete causal value into this additive normal form becomes intractable.

Program P_2 also reveals another issue. Even if distributivity is not applied, the causal terms directly obtained by the T_{PJ} operator for p_2 and q_2 require 4 operators, the causal terms for p_3 and q_3 require 10, $I(p_3) = ((a+b) * (c+d)) \cdot m_2 * ((a+b) * (c+d)) \cdot n_2) \cdot m_3$ and, in general, the terms for p_n or q_n would require $2^n + 2^{n-1} - 2$ operators. However, an interesting observation is that subterm $(a_1 + b_1) * (c_1 + d_1)$ occurs twice in $I(p_3)$ above, and the same happens for $I(q_3)$. This subterm will occur four times in the causal terms for atoms p_4 and q_4. Avoiding repetitions will allow us computing the least model of T_{PJ} in polynomial time (and thus, using a polynomial number of operators to represent it).

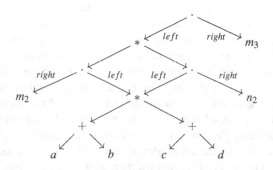

Fig. 5. The t-graph associated to $I(p_3)$ in program P_2

Definition 8 (Term and interpretation graph). *Given a set of labels Lb, a term graph (t-graph) $\tilde{T} = \langle V, E, f_V, f_E, v_r \rangle$ is a rooted, connected and labelled directed graph with a set of vertices V, edges E, root $v_r \in V$ and label functions $f_V : V \longrightarrow Lb \cup \{1, +, *, \cdot\}$ and $f_E : E \longrightarrow \{left, right\}$ such that*

1. *all leafs are labelled with* unitary causes *(a label in Lb or 1),*
2. *all non-leaf nodes are labelled with operators*
3. *for any vertex labelled with the application operator '·' there are exactly two outgoing edges labelled 'left' and 'right' being the target for the latter a leaf node. The rest of edges in the graph are unlabelled.* □

Each vertex in a t-graph $\tilde{T}$ represents a corresponding causal term as follows:

$$
\begin{aligned}
term_{\tilde{T}}(v) &= f_V(v) && \text{for any leaf } v \text{ in } \tilde{T} \\
term_{\tilde{T}}(v) &\stackrel{\text{def}}{=} \sum \{\, term(v') \mid (v, v') \in E \,\} && \text{if } f_V(v) = + \\
term_{\tilde{T}}(v) &\stackrel{\text{def}}{=} \prod \{\, term(v') \mid (v, v') \in E \,\} && \text{if } f_V(v) = * \\
term_{\tilde{T}}(v) &\stackrel{\text{def}}{=} term_{\tilde{T}}(u) \cdot term_{\tilde{T}}(w) && \text{if } f_V(v) = \cdot \text{ and } f_E(v, u) = left \\
& && \text{and } f_E(v, w) = right
\end{aligned}
$$

The term associated to a t-graph $\tilde{T}$ is the term associated with its root vertex v_r. As an example, Figure 5 represents the t-graph corresponding to $I(p_3)$ in the last example. We also extend these notions to interpretations. For an interpretation I, a *term interpretation* (t-interpretation) $\tilde{I}$ is just a function mapping each atom $p \in A$ to a t-graph $\tilde{T}$ such that $I(p) = term(\tilde{I}(p))$ for any atom p. We can now compute the least model of a positive program by iterating, a new direct consequences operator $\tilde{T}_P$ defined as $\tilde{T}_P(\tilde{I})(p) \stackrel{\text{def}}{=} \langle V_p, E_p, f_{V,p}, f_{E,p}, v_p \rangle$ where:

$$
\begin{aligned}
V_p &\stackrel{\text{def}}{=} \bigcup \{\, V_{\tilde{I}(R)} \cup \{v_p\} && \mid R \in P, head(R) = p \,\} \\
E_p &\stackrel{\text{def}}{=} \bigcup \{\, F_{\tilde{I}(R)} \cup \{(v_p, v_R)\} && \mid R \in P, head(R) = p \,\} \\
V_{\tilde{I}(R)} &\stackrel{\text{def}}{=} \bigcup \{\, V_{\tilde{I}(q)} && \mid q \in body(R) \,\} \cup \{\, v_R, w_R, v_l \,\} \\
E_{\tilde{I}(R)} &\stackrel{\text{def}}{=} \bigcup \{\, E_{\tilde{I}(q)} \cup \{(w_R, v_{\tilde{I}(q)})\} \mid q \in body(R) \,\} \cup \{\, (v_R, w_R)), (v_R, w_l) \,\}
\end{aligned}
$$

$$
f_{V,p}(v) \stackrel{\text{def}}{=} \begin{cases} + & \text{if } v = v_p \\ \cdot & \text{if } v = v_R \\ * & \text{if } v = w_R \\ label(R) & \text{if } v = w_l \\ f_{V,\tilde{I}(q)}(v) & \text{if } v \in V_{\tilde{I}(q)} \end{cases} \qquad f_{E,p}(e) \stackrel{\text{def}}{=} \begin{cases} left & \text{if } e = (v_R, w_l) \\ right & \text{if } e = (v_R, w_R) \\ f_{E,\tilde{I}(q)}(e) & \text{if } e \in E_{\tilde{I}(q)} \end{cases}
$$

and, for any atom q, $V_{\tilde{I}(q)}$, $E_{\tilde{I}(q)}$, $f_{V,\tilde{I}(q)}$, $f_{E,\tilde{I}(q)}$, $v_{\tilde{I}(q)}$ are respectively the set of vertices, edges, the label functions of vertices and edges and the root of the t-graph $\tilde{I}(q)$.

Theorem 3. *Let P be a positive logic program with n rules, and let I be its least model. Then $I(p) = term(\tilde{T}_P \uparrow^n (\tilde{0})(p))$ for all atoms p. Moreover, $\tilde{T}_P \uparrow^n (\tilde{0})(p)$ is computable in polynomial time with respect to the size of P.* □

Theorem 3 builds on a polynomial time computable procedure to obtain the least model of a positive program P. We exploit now the fact that the term associated to a c-graph has no sums to define a boolean function $sufficient(G, \tilde{T}, v, l)$ that can be recursively computed as follows:

(1) $\bigvee \{ sufficient(G, \tilde{T}, v_i, l) \mid (v, v_i) \in E \}$ if $f_V(v) = +$

(2) $\bigwedge \{ sufficient(G, \tilde{T}, v_i, l) \mid (v, v_i) \in E \}$ if $f_V(v) = *$

(3) $sufficient(G, \tilde{T}, v_l, l_r)$ if $f_V(v) = \cdot$, $f_E(v, v_l) = left$,
                                   $f_E(v, v_r) = right$, $f_V(v_r) = l_r$ and
                                   $(l_r, l) \in G$

(4) $true$ if $f_V(v) = l' \in Lb$, $l \neq 1$ and $(l', l) \in G$

(5) $sufficient(G, \tilde{T}, v_l, l)$ if $f_V(v) = \cdot$, $f_E(v, v_l) = left$,
                                   $f_E(v, v_r) = right$ and $f_V(v_r) = 1$

(6) $true$ if $f_V(v) = 1$ and $l = 1$

(7) $true$ if $f_V(v) = 1$, $l \neq 1$ and $(l, l) \in G$

(8) $true$ if $f_V(v) = l' \in Lb$, $l = 1$ and $(l', l') \in G$

(9) $false$ otherwise

$sufficient(G, \tilde{T}, v, l)$ computes whether, for a c-graph G, it holds that $term(G) \leq t \cdot l$ where t is the term associated with the subgraph of $\tilde{T}$ whose root is v. Note that cases 5-8 only perform the necessary simplifications when some vertex is 1. Then, if we define $sufficient(G, \tilde{T}) \stackrel{\text{def}}{=} sufficient(G, \tilde{T}, root(\tilde{T}), 1)$, the following result holds:

Theorem 4. *Given an interpretation I and a t-interpretation $\tilde{I}$, a causal graph G is a sufficient explanation for an atom p with respect to I iff $sufficient(G, \tilde{I}(p)) = true$.*   □

Corollary 1. *Given a positive causal logic program P, a causal graph G, and an atom p, deciding whether G is a sufficient explanation for p with respect to its least model is feasible in polynomial time.*   □

In order to decide whether an acyclic causal graph is a sufficient cause, we recall that the *transitive reduction* of a directed graph G is another graph that preserves the reachability relation of G with a minimal set of edges. Deciding whether a c-graph G is a sufficient cause of some atom p in the least model of a program P can be done by:

1. checking whether G is a sufficient explanation for p
2. computing the transitive reduction G^R of G
3. computing the set S^R of graphs obtained from G^R by removing one of its edges
4. computing the set S obtained from the transitive closures of all graphs in S^R
5. checking for every causal graph G' in S that it is not a sufficient explanantion for p.

Theorem 5. *Given a positive logic program P, an acyclic causal graph G, and an atom p, deciding whether G is a sufficient cause of p with respect to its least model is feasible in polynomial time.*   □

We consider now sufficient explanation and sufficient cause queries for programs with negation using the following nondeterministic procedure:

1. guessing a set of atoms J
2. checking whether J is the least classical model of the reduct P^J (ignoring labels)
3. checking whether G is a sufficient explanation for (resp. cause of) p w.r.t. P^J

This will succeed for some (resp. all) sets J iff G is a sufficient explanation for/cause of p with respect to some (resp. all) causal stable model(s) of P. Consequently we have the following membership results for brave (resp. cautions) sufficient explanations/causes:

Theorem 6. *Given a program P, deciding whether a c-graph G is a brave (resp. cautious) sufficient explanation is in NP (resp. in coNP). Deciding whether it is a sufficient cause of an atom p is in NP (resp in coNP) when it G is acyclic.*   □

In a similar way, we can decide whether G is a necessary cause as follows:

1. guess a set of atoms J and a causal graph G'
2. check whether J is the least classical model of the reduct of P^J (ignoring labels)
3. succeed if J does not contain p
4. check whether G' is a sufficient explanation of p w.r.t. P^J
5. check whether G is not a subgraph of G'

This procedure succeeds iff G is not a cautious necessary cause of p with respect to program P yielding the following result:

Theorem 7. *Given a causal logic program P, deciding whether a c-graph G is a cautious necessary cause of an atom p is in coNP.*   □

Finally, we can check brave necessary causation for an atom p by:

1. non-deterministically guessing a set of atoms J,
2. checking whether J is the least classical model of the reduct P^J (ignoring labels)
3. checking with an NP oracle (Theorem 7) whether G is necessary for p w.r.t. P^J

This will succeed iff G is necessary for p with respect to some stable model of program P. Hence, the problem can be decided non-deterministically in polynomial time with an NP-oracle ($NP^{NP} = \Sigma_2^P$):

Theorem 8. *Given a causal logic program P, deciding whether a c-graph G is a brave necessary cause of an atom p is in Σ_2^P.*   □

Turning to hardness, first note that any standard logic program is also an unlabelled causal logic program and an atom p is true in the former iff the empty c-graph (causal term 1) is a sufficient explanation (resp. a sufficient cause) for p. Therfore, the following result trivially follows:

Theorem 9. *Given a causal logic program P, deciding whether a c-graph G is a brave (resp. cautious) sufficient explanation or sufficient cause of some atom p is NP-complete (resp coNP-complete). Furthermore, P-hardness holds when P is positive.*   □

Let us next turn to the complexity results for necessary cause decision problems and show that they are tight too. First, we show that deciding whether a c-graph G is a brave necessary cause of some atom is Σ_2^P-hard by constructing a log-space reduction of deciding the truth of any quantified boolean formula of form $\varphi = \exists y_1, \ldots, y_n \forall x_1, \ldots, x_m \, \rho$, where $\rho = \psi_1 \vee \ldots \vee \psi_r$ and each $\psi_i = L_{i1} \wedge L_{i2} \wedge L_{i3}$ is a conjunction of three literals L_{ij} over atoms $y_1, \ldots, y_n, x_1, \ldots, x_m$, to a causal logic program P_φ as follows:

$$x_k : x_k \qquad\qquad\qquad \text{for each } k \in \{1,\ldots,m\}$$

$$t \; : t$$

$$x_k : \psi_i \leftarrow t \qquad\qquad \text{if } L_{ij} = x_k \text{ for each } i \in \{1,\ldots,r\}, \; j \in \{1,2,3\}$$

$$f \; : \psi_i \leftarrow x_k \qquad\qquad \text{if } L_{ij} = \bar{x}_k \text{ for each } i \in \{1,\ldots,r\}, \; j \in \{1,2,3\}$$

$$\rho \;\leftarrow \psi_1,\ldots,\; \psi_r$$

$$y_k \leftarrow not\; \bar{y}_k \qquad\qquad \text{for each } k \in \{1,\ldots,n\}$$

$$\bar{y}_k \leftarrow not\; y_k \qquad\qquad \text{for each } k \in \{1,\ldots,n\}$$

$$f \; : \psi_i \leftarrow y_k, t \qquad\quad \text{if } L_{ij} = y_k \text{ for each } i \in \{1,\ldots,r\}, \; j \in \{1,2,3\}$$

$$f \; : \psi_i \leftarrow \bar{y}_k, t \qquad\quad \text{if } L_{ij} = \bar{y}_k \text{ for each } i \in \{1,\ldots,r\}, \; j \in \{1,2,3\}$$

$$\psi_i \leftarrow \bar{y}_k \qquad\qquad\quad \text{if } L_{ij} = y_k \text{ for each } i \in \{1,\ldots,r\}, \; j \in \{1,2,3\}$$

$$\psi_i \leftarrow y_k \qquad\qquad\quad \text{if } L_{ij} = \bar{y}_k \text{ for each } i \in \{1,\ldots,r\}, \; j \in \{1,2,3\}$$

Obviously this transformation can be done using logarithmic space. Moreover, it can be shown that φ is true if and only if the c-graph G_{tf} formed by the edge (t,f) is a necessary cause of atom ρ. To wit, first observe that $I(\psi_i) = \sigma_I(L_{i1}) + \sigma_I(L_{i2}) + \sigma_I(L_{i3})$, for any causal stable model I of P_φ, and therefore

$$I(\rho) = \sum \{ \; \sigma_I(L_{1j_1}) * \ldots * \sigma_I(L_{rj_r}) \mid j_i \in \{1,2,3\} \; \}$$

where

$$\sigma_I(x_k) = t \cdot x_k \qquad \sigma_I(y_k) = t \cdot f \quad \text{if } I \models y_k \qquad \sigma_I(y_k) = 1 \quad \text{if } I \not\models y_k$$

$$\sigma_I(\bar{x}_k) = x_k \cdot f \qquad \sigma_I(\bar{y}_k) = t \cdot f \quad \text{if } I \not\models y_k \qquad \sigma_I(\bar{y}_k) = 1 \quad \text{if } I \models y_k$$

The value assigned to atom ρ corresponds to the conjunctive normal form of formula ρ, replacing $\bigwedge$ by Σ, $\vee$ by $*$ and L_{ij_i} by $\sigma_I(L_{ij_i})$. Clearly, $\forall x_1,\ldots,x_m \; \rho$ is true if and only if all disjunctions of its conjunctive normal form are valid. The latter is the case for a disjunction if it contains an existential variable y_k assigned to true or two complementary literals of an universal variable x_k. Intuitively, every causal stable model I encodes an assignment to the existential variables $y_1,\ldots,y_n$. If some y_k is assigned to true, then $\sigma_I(y_k) = t \cdot f$. Thus, with every disjunction $L_{1j_1} \vee \ldots \vee y_k \vee \ldots L_{rj_r}$ containing variable y_k, the value $\sigma_I(L_{1j_1}) * \ldots * t \cdot f * \ldots \sigma_I(L_{rj_r})$ is associated, which is obviously smaller than $t \cdot f$. The same also applies to every disjunction containing the literal $\bar{y}_k$ when y_k is assigned to false. Moreover, disjunctions of the form of $L_{1j_1} \vee \ldots \vee x_k \vee \ldots \vee \bar{x}_k \vee \ldots \vee L_{rj_r}$, i.e., containing complementary literals over an universal variable, are assigned a causal term $\sigma_I(L_{1j_1}) * \ldots * t \cdot x_k * \ldots * x_k \cdot f * \ldots * \sigma_I(L_{rj_r})$, which also is smaller than $t \cdot f$. As a consequence, formula φ is true if and only if there exists some causal stable model I (corresponding to an assignment on variables $y_1,\ldots,y_n$) such that $I(p) \leq t \cdot f$ (i.e., formula $\forall x_1,\ldots,x_m \; \rho$ is true under this assignment). The latter is equivalent to deciding whether the causal graph G_{tf} is a brave necessary cause of p (cf. Theorem 2).

Finally note that, for $n = 0$, i.e., when there are no existentially quantified variables, deciding whether φ is true is coNP-hard and P_φ becomes positive. Therefore:

Theorem 10. *Given a program P, a c-graph G, and an atom p, deciding whether there exists a causal stable model of P such that G is a necessary cause of p is Σ_2^P-complete (coNP-complete when P is positive).* $\qquad\square$

It is worth to mention that, concerning causal queries, natural problems usually involve acyclic causal graphs. Indeed, for sufficient causal queries we are imposing acyclicity, since otherwise the complexity raises from NP-complete to Σ_P^2-complete for brave reasoning and from polynomial to coNP-complete when the program is positive[2]. Note also that, at a first sight, the coNP result for cautious reasoning about necessary causes may seem surprising, as brave reasoning is Σ_P^2. The reason for this is that cautious reasoning ("for all models ...") and necessary causation ("for all sufficient causes ..."), are universal properties and, while these two sources of complexity are not independent, a witnessing (polynomially checkable) counter-example to their conjunction can be found.

5 Related Work and Conclusions

In this work, we have revisited a recent proposal for causal semantics in logic programming [1] that assigns a causal explanation to each true atom in a stable model, providing formal definitions for three different causal relationships: being a "sufficient explanation", being a "sufficient cause" and being a "necessary cause". We have shown that, while obtaining the complete causal explanation of an atom has exponential cost, querying whether some cause of p is of any of these three types remains within the first two levels of the polynomial hierarchy (see Figure 3). Although these results could be reasonable or sometimes even expected, their real significance is that they *affirm the adequacy* of the causal semantics proposed. In fact, this complexity study has led us to disregard a weaker approach previously considered in [3] where causal explanations did not guarantee transitivity, since this lack actually yielded higher complexity bounds.

The types of causation defined in the current paper are directly inspired by Hall's classification [4]. In that paper, a sufficient explanation is just called "being sufficient" whereas a sufficient cause is said to be "minimally sufficient." There are also other related works on explanations for logic programs as provided by approaches to debugging in ASP [5,6,7,8], approaches for justifications [9,10,11] or provenance and causality in datalog and databases [12,13,14]. Apart from establishing formal comparisons to these approaches, future work will be focused on three different directions. The next immediate step is implementing the query language to allow queries for positive programs and brave and cautious reasoning for programs with negation. A second line of research is completing the query language and the complexity assessment for *actual causation*. An *actual cause*, in the sense of Mackie [15] can be easily defined in this setting as any cause (or causal graph) that is stronger than (i.e., it is a subgraph of) some sufficient cause. This concept can be sometimes convenient since, in order to query if some graph is a sufficient cause, we must provide its complete description, including intermediate events, while for actual causation, we could just check if a partial description of that cause is involved in one of the sufficient explanations. Finally, our most challenging goal is incorporating this type of causal relationships as a new type of literals in program bodies. This would allow representing problems of the form "if sw_3 was a necessary cause for *alarm* then operator for sw_3 must be penalized" directly as logic program rules.

---

[2] We omit the proofs because of space limitations.

References

1. Cabalar, P., Fandinno, J., Fink, M.: Causal graph justifications of logic programs. In: Proc. of the 30th Intl. Conf. on Logic Programming (ICLP 2014) (to appear, 2014)
2. Gelfond, M., Lifschitz, V.: The stable model semantics for logic programming. In: Kowalski, R.A., Bowen, K.A. (eds.) Logic Programming: Proc. of the Fifth International Conference and Symposium, vol. 2, pp. 1070–1080. MIT Press, Cambridge (1988)
3. Cabalar, P., Fandinno, J.: An algebra of causal chains. In: Proc. of the 6th Workshop on Answer Set Programming and Other Computing Paradigms (ASPOCP 2013) (2013)
4. Hall, N.: Two concepts of causality, pp. 181–276 (2004)
5. Gebser, M., Pührer, J., Schaub, T., Tompits, H.: Meta-programming technique for debugging answer-set programs. In: Proc. of the 23rd Conf. on Artificial Inteligence (AAAI 2008), 448–453 (2008)
6. Pontelli, E., Son, T.C., El-Khatib, O.: Justifications for logic programs under answer set semantics. Theory and Practice of Logic Programming 9(1), 1–56 (2009)
7. Schulz, C., Sergot, M., Toni, F.: Argumentation-based answer set justification. In: Proc. of the 11th Intl. Symposium on Logical Formalizations of Commonsense Reasoning (Commonsense 2013) (2013)
8. Viegas Damásio, C., Analyti, A., Antoniou, G.: Justifications for logic programming. In: Cabalar, P., Son, T.C. (eds.) LPNMR 2013. LNCS, vol. 8148, pp. 530–542. Springer, Heidelberg (2013)
9. Pereira, L.M., Aparício, J.N., Alferes, J.J.: Derivation procedures for extended stable models. In: Mylopoulos, J., Reiter, R. (eds.) Proceedings of the 12th International Joint Conference on Artificial Intelligence, pp. 863–869. Morgan Kaufmann (1991)
10. Denecker, M., De Schreye, D.: Justification semantics: A unifiying framework for the semantics of logic programs. In: Proc. of the Logic Programming and Nonmonotonic Reasoning Workshop, pp. 365–379 (1993)
11. Vennekens, J.: Actual causation in cp-logic. TPLP 11(4-5), 647–662 (2011)
12. Green, T.J., Karvounarakis, G., Tannen, V.: Provenance semirings. In: Proceedings of the Twenty-sixth ACM SIGMOD-SIGACT-SIGART Symposium on Principles of Database Systems, pp. 31–40. ACM (2007)
13. Green, T.J.: Containment of conjunctive queries on annotated relations. Theory of Computing Systems 49(2), 429–459 (2011)
14. Meliou, A., Gatterbauer, W., Halpern, J.Y., Koch, C., Moore, K.F., Suciu, D.: Causality in databases. IEEE Data Eng. Bull. 33(EPFL-ARTICLE-165841), 59–67 (2010)
15. Mackie, J.L.: Causes and Conditions, vol. 2 (1965)

Inductive Learning of Answer Set Programs

Mark Law, Alessandra Russo*, and Krysia Broda

Department of Computing, Imperial College London, United Kingdom
{mark.law09,a.russo,k.broda}@imperial.ac.uk

Abstract. Existing work on Inductive Logic Programming (ILP) has focused mainly on the learning of definite programs or normal logic programs. In this paper, we aim to push the computational boundary to a wider class of programs: Answer Set Programs. We propose a new paradigm for ILP that integrates existing notions of brave and cautious semantics within a unifying learning framework whose inductive solutions are Answer Set Programs and examples are partial interpretations We present an algorithm that is sound and complete with respect to our new notion of inductive solutions. We demonstrate its applicability by discussing a prototype implementation, called ILASP (Inductive Learning of Answer Set Programs), and evaluate its use in the context of planning. In particular, we show how ILASP can be used to learn agent's knowledge about the environment. Solutions of the learned ASP program provide plans for the agent to travel through the given environment.

Keywords: Inductive Reasoning, Learning Answer Set Programs, Non-monotonic Inductive Logic Programming.

1 Introduction

For more than two decades, Inductive Logic Programming (ILP) [10] has been an area of much interest. Significant advances have been made both on new algorithms and systems (e.g. [15,8,1,11,12]) and proposals of new logical frameworks for inductive learning (e.g. [13,16]). In most of these approaches an inductive learning task is defined as the search for an hypothesis that, together with a given background knowledge, explains a set of observations (i.e. examples). Observations are usually grouped into positive (E^+) and negative (E^-) examples, and an *inductive solution* is defined as an hypothesis H that is consistent with the background knowledge B and that, together with B, entails the positive examples $(B \cup H \models e$ for every $e \in E^+)$ and does not entail the negative examples.

As stated in [16], this semantic view of inductive learning may be too "strong". When $B \cup H$ accepts more than one (minimal) model, it restricts solutions to be only those hypotheses H for which the given observations are true in the intersection of all models of $B \cup H$. Both Brave Induction [16] and Induction of Stable Models [13] applied induction to the stable model semantics [6] such that in situations when $B \cup H$ has more than one stable model, it is just necessary to guarantee that each example is true in at least one stable model of $B \cup H$.

---

* This research is partially funded by the 7th Framework EU-FET project 600792 "ALLOW Ensembles", and the EPSRC project EP/K033522/1 "Privacy Dynamics".

E. Fermé and J. Leite (Eds.): JELIA 2014, LNAI 8761, pp. 311–325, 2014.

Their notion of examples is, however, very specific: in [16] there is only one example defined as a conjunction of atoms, and in [13] examples are partial interpretations. When $B \cup H$ has multiple stable models, literals may be true in all models, some of, or none of them, and sometimes only a specified number of a particular set of literals should be true. Neither Brave Induction, nor Induction of Stable Models, is able to express through examples that a literal should be true in all/no stable models. To allow for hypotheses that are ASP programs, a more expressive notion of examples and inductive solution is therefore needed.

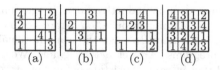

(a)   (b)   (c)   (d)

Fig. 1. (a) valid partial grid; (b/c) invalid partial grids; (d) valid complete grid

Consider a simplified version of a sudoku game where the grid includes only sixteen cells. Let us assume that basic definitions of *cell*, *same_row*, *same_col* and *same_block* (true only for two *different* cells in the same row/column/block) are given as background knowledge B expressed as an ASP program, and that the task is to learn an hypothesis H such that the Answer Sets of $B \cup H$ correspond to the valid sudoku grids. A possible hypothesis would be the ASP program:

```
1 { value(1, C), value(2, C), value(3, C), value(4, C) } 1 :- cell(C).
:- value(V, C1), value(V, C2), same_col(C1, C2).
:- value(V, C1), value(V, C2), same_row(C1, C2).
:- value(V, C1), value(V, C2), same_block(C1, C2).
```

To learn this program, single literal examples such as $value(1, cell(1, 1))$ would not be enough, as $value(1, cell(1, 1))$ being valid depends on the values of the other cells. Examples should therefore be (partial) grids, e.g. Figure 1(a), and the learned hypothesis, H, should be such that for every example E, $B \cup H$ has an Answer Set corresponding to a complete grid that extends E. It is not sufficient to consider *only* (positive) examples of what *should* be an Answer Set of $B \cup H$: no matter how many examples we give, the hypothesis $0\{value(1, C), value(2, C), value(3, C), value(4, C)\}4 \leftarrow cell(C)$ will always be in the solution space. Each valid sudoku board would be an Answer Set of this hypothesis; however, this is also true for invalid boards, such as those in Figure 1 (b) and (c). What is needed is the use of negative examples. In the sudoku game, negative examples would be invalid partial boards (e.g., Figure 1 (b) and (c)).

In Section 3 we propose a new paradigm for inductive learning, called *Learning from (partial) Answer Sets*. Our approach integrates notions of brave and cautious semantics within a unifying learning framework whose inductive solutions are ASP programs and both positive and negative examples are (partial) interpretations. Inductive solutions are ASP programs that together with a given background knowledge B have at least one Answer Set extending each positive example (this could be a different Answer Set for each example), and no Answer

Set which extends any negative example. The use of negative examples is what differentiates our approach from Brave Induction or Induction of Stable Models. In fact, neither of these two existing approaches would be able to learn the three constraints for the sudoku problem, but our approach can solve any Brave Induction or Induction of Stable Models task. In addition, in our framework negative examples drive the learning of constraints, or the learning of bounds on aggregates. In Section 4 we present our algorithm, *ILASP*, and argue its soundness and completeness with respect to our new notion of inductive learning. In Section 5 we investigate its applicability to a planning problem. We conclude the paper with a review of the related work and a discussion of future directions.

2 Background

We assume the following subset of the ASP language. A *literal* can be either an atom p or its *default negation* not p (often called *negation as failure*). A normal rule is of the form $h \leftarrow b_1, \ldots, b_n, \text{not } c_1, \ldots \text{not } c_m$ where h is called the *head*, $b_1, \ldots, b_n, \text{not } c_1, \ldots \text{not } c_m$ (collectively) is called the *body*, and all h, b_i, and c_j are atoms. A *constraint* is of the form $\leftarrow b_1, \ldots, b_n, \text{not } c_1, \ldots \text{not } c_m$. A *choice rule* is an expression of the form $l\{h_1, \ldots, h_m\}u \leftarrow b_1, \ldots, b_n, \text{not } c_1, \ldots \text{not } c_m$ where the head $l\{h_1, \ldots, h_m\}u$ is called an *aggregate*. In an aggregate l and u are integers and h_i, for $1 \leq i \leq m$, are atoms. A variable V occurring in a rule R is said to be *safe* if V occurs in at least one positive literal in the body of R; for example, X is not safe in the rules $p(X) \leftarrow q(Y), \text{ not } r(Y)$; or $p \leftarrow q, \text{ not } r(X)$.

An Answer Set Program P is a finite set of normal rules, constraints and choice rules. Given an ASP program P, the Herbrand Base of P, denoted as HB_P, is the set of all ground (variable free) atoms that can be formed from the predicates and constants that appear in P. When P includes only normal rules, a set $A \subseteq HB_P$ is an *Answer Set* of P iff it is the minimal model of the *reduct* P^A (constructed from the grounding of P by removing any rule whose body contains a literal not c_i where $c_i \in A$, and removing any negative literals in the remaining rules). An Answer Set satisfies a ground constraint $\leftarrow b_1, \ldots, b_n, \text{not } c_1, \ldots \text{not } c_m$ if $\{b_1, \ldots, b_n\} \not\subseteq A$ or $A \cap \{c_1, \ldots c_m\} \neq \emptyset$. Informally, given a ground choice rule $l\{h_1, \ldots, h_m\}u \leftarrow b_1, \ldots, b_n, \text{not } c_1, \ldots \text{not } c_m$ if the body is satisfied by A, then the rule has the effect of generating all Answer Sets in which $l \leq |A \cap \{h_1, \ldots, h_m\}| \leq u$. For a formal definition of the semantics of choice rules, the reader is referred to [5]. Throughout the paper we will denote with $AS(P)$ the set of all Answer Sets of P.

Definition 1. *A partial interpretation E is a pair $E = \langle E^{inc}, E^{exc} \rangle$ of sets of ground atoms, called the inclusions and exclusions respectively. An Answer Set A extends $\langle E^{inc}, E^{exc} \rangle$ if and only if $(E^{inc} \subseteq A) \wedge (E^{exc} \cap A = \emptyset)$.*

A partial interpretation E is *bravely* entailed by a program P if and only if there exists an Answer Set $A \in AS(P)$ such that A extends E. E is *cautiously* entailed by P if and only if every Answer Set $A \in AS(P)$ extends E.

3   Learning from Answer Sets

In this section we formalize our new paradigm of *Learning from (partial) Answer Sets*. We assume background knowledge and hypotheses to be ASP programs expressed using the ASP language defined in Section 2.

In an ILP task, the expressivity of the hypothesis space is defined by the *language bias* of the task, often characterised by mode declarations [11]. A language bias can be defined as a pair of sets of mode declarations $\langle M_h, M_b \rangle$, where M_h (resp. M_b) are called the *head* (resp. *body*) *mode declarations*. Each mode declaration $m_h \in M_h$ (resp. $m_b \in M_b$) is a literal whose abstracted arguments are either v or c. Informally, an atom is said to be *compatible* with a mode declaration m if each instance of v in m is replaced by a variable, and every c by a constant. Given a language bias $M = \langle M_h, M_b \rangle$, a rule of the form $h \leftarrow b_1, \ldots, b_n, not\ c_1, \ldots not\ c_m$ is in the search space S_M if and only if (i) h is empty; or h is an atom compatible with a mode declaration in M_h; or h is an aggregate $l\{h_1, \ldots h_k\}u$ such that $0 \leq l \leq u \leq k$ and $\forall i \in [1, k]$ h_i are compatible with mode declarations in M_h; (ii) $\forall i \in [1, n], \forall j \in [1, m]$ b_i and c_j are compatible with mode declarations in M_b, and finally (iii) all variables in the rule are safe. Each rule R in S_M is given a unique identifier R_{id}.

Example 1. Let M be the mode declarations $\langle\{value(c, v)\}, \{cell(v), value(v, v),$ $same\_block(v, v), same\_row(v, v), same\_col(v, v)\}\rangle$. Then the following are in S_M: $value(1, C) \leftarrow cell(C); 1\{value(1, C), value(2, C)\}2 \leftarrow cell(C); \leftarrow value(X, C1),$ $value(X, C2), same\_block(C1, C2);$ whereas the following are not: $value(C) \leftarrow$ $cell(C); cell(C) \leftarrow cell(C); \leftarrow value(1, C1), value(1, C2), same\_block(C1, C2).$[1]

Definition 2. *A Learning from Answer Sets task is a tuple $T = \langle B, S_M, E^+, E^- \rangle$ where B is the background knowledge, S_M is the search space defined by a language bias M, E^+ and E^- are sets of partial interpretations called, respectively, the positive and negative examples. An hypothesis H is an inductive solution of T (written $H \in ILP_{LAS}(T)$) if and only if:*

1. $H \subseteq S_M$
2. $\forall e^+ \in E^+$ $\exists A \in AS(B \cup H)$ *such that A extends e^+*
3. $\forall e^- \in E^-$ $\not\exists A \in AS(B \cup H)$ *such that A extends e^-*

Note that this definition combines properties of both the brave and cautious semantics: the positive examples must each be bravely entailed; whereas the negation of each negative example must be cautiously entailed.

Example 2. Let $B = \{p \leftarrow r\}$, $M = \langle\{q, r\}, \{p, r\}\rangle$, $E^+ = \{\langle\{p\}, \{q\}\rangle, \langle\{q\}, \{p\}\rangle\}$ and $E^- = \{\langle\emptyset, \{p, q\}\rangle, \langle\{p, q\}, \emptyset\rangle\}$. An inductive solution is the ASP program H given by $H = \{q \leftarrow not\ r; r \leftarrow not\ q\}$. The Answer Sets of $B \cup H$ are $\{p, r\}$ and $\{q\}$. The former extends the first positive example, the latter extends the second positive example and clearly neither of them extend any negative examples.

---

[1] Here, and in the rest of the paper, we use ; as a delimiter in sets of rules.

The following example shows that our learning setting, with the search space as defined in example 1, can learn the sudoku problem described in the introduction.

Example 3. Consider again the sudoku problem, with S_M as described in example 1, B containing the definitions of *same_row*, *same_col*, *same_block* and *cell*. Let the examples be as follows:

$$E^+ = \left\{ \begin{array}{l} \langle \{value(cell(1,1),1), \\ \quad value(cell(1,2),2), \\ \quad value(cell(1,3),3), \\ \quad value(cell(1,4),4), \\ \quad value(cell(2,3),2) \\ \quad \}, \emptyset \rangle \end{array} \right. \qquad E^- = \left\{ \begin{array}{l} \langle \{value(cell(1,1),1), \\ \quad value(cell(1,3),1)\}, \emptyset \rangle \\ \langle \{value(cell(1,1),1), \\ \quad value(cell(3,1),1)\}, \emptyset \rangle \\ \langle \{value(cell(1,1),1), \\ \quad value(cell(2,2),1)\}, \emptyset \rangle \end{array} \right.$$

Let $l\{value(C,1), value(C,2), value(C,3), value(C,4)\}u$ be denoted by $agg(l,u)$. The hypothesis $H_1 = \{agg(1,1) \leftarrow cell(C)\}$ is not an inductive solution, whereas $H_2 = \{agg(1,1) \leftarrow cell(C); \leftarrow value(V,C1), value(V,C2), same\_col(C1,C2); \leftarrow value(V,C1), value(V,C2), same\_row(C1,C2); \leftarrow value(V,C1), value(V,C2), same\_block(C1,C2)\}$ is an inductive solution. This shows that our learning task can incentivise the learning of constraints. With the examples as they are, if we take H_3 to be constructed from H_2 by replacing $agg(1,1)$ with $agg(0,1)$, then H_3 is still an inductive solution. Adding the negative example $\langle \emptyset, \{value(cell(1,1),1), value(cell(1,1),2), value(cell(1,1),3), value(cell(1,1),4), \}\rangle$, this is no longer the case. H_2 is an inductive solution, whereas H_3 is not. This shows that ILP_{LAS} is able to incentivise learning bounds on aggregates.

It is common practice in ILP to search for "optimal" hypotheses. This is usually defined in terms of the number of literals in the hypothesis. This does not apply well to hypotheses that include aggregates: the length of $1\{p,q\}1$ (exactly one of p and q is true) would be the same as the length of $0\{p,q\}2$ (none, either or both of p and q is true), but clearly they do not represent similar concepts. To calculate the length of an aggregate we convert it to disjunctive normal form, as this takes into account both the number of Answer Sets that the aggregate generates and the number of literals it uses. For example, $0\{p,q\}2$ is considered as $(p \wedge q) \vee (p \wedge \text{not } q) \vee (\text{not } p \wedge q) \vee (\text{not } p \wedge \text{not } q)$, which has length 8, whereas $1\{p,q\}1$ is considered as $(p \wedge \text{not } q) \vee (\text{not } p \wedge q)$, which has length 4.

Definition 3. *Given an hypothesis H, the length of the hypothesis, $|H|$, is the number of literals that appear in H^D, where H^D is constructed from H by converting all aggregates in H to disjunctive normal form.*

Given an ILP_{LAS} learning task $T = \langle B, S_M, E^+, E^- \rangle$, we denote with $ILP^*_{LAS}(T)$ the set of all optimal inductive solutions of T, where optimality is defined in terms of the length of the hypotheses. We will also denote with $ILP^n_{LAS}(T)$ the set of all inductive solutions of T which have length n.

4   Algorithm

In this section we describe our algorithm ILASP (Inductive Learning of Answer Set Programs) and state its soundness and completeness results. Due to space limitation, proofs have been omitted from the paper but they are available in [9].

Our algorithm works by encoding our ILP_{LAS} task into an ASP program. It makes use of two main concepts: *positive solutions* and *violating solutions*. Positive solutions are those hypotheses that, added to the background knowledge, have Answer Sets which extend each positive example. But some positive solutions may still cover negative examples; we call these the *violating solutions*. The underlying idea of our algorithm is to compute every violating solution of a given length, and then use these to generate a set of constraints which, when added to our task program, eliminate the violating solutions. Theorem 1 shows that the remaining positive solutions are indeed the inductive solutions of the given ILP_{LAS} task. ILASP uses the ASP solver clingo[4] to compute these solutions.

Definition 4. *Let $T = \langle B, S_M, E^+, E^- \rangle$ be an ILP_{LAS} task. An hypothesis $H \in positive\_solns(T)$ iff $H \subseteq S_M$ and $\forall e^+ \in E^+ \; \exists A \in AS(B \cup H)$ such that A extends e^+. A positive solution $H \in violating\_solns(T)$ iff $\exists e^- \in E^-$ $\exists A \in AS(B \cup H)$ such that A extends e^-. We write $positive\_solns^n(T)$ and $violating\_solns^n(T)$ to denote the positive and violating solutions of length n.*

Example 4. Consider the ILP_{LAS} task $T = \langle B, S_M, E^+, E^- \rangle$ where $B = \{q \leftarrow r\}$, $E^+ = \{\langle \{p\}, \emptyset \rangle, \langle \{q\}, \emptyset \rangle\}$, $E^- = \{\langle \{p, q\}, \emptyset \rangle\}$ and S_M is given by the following rules $\{p; \; r; \; p \leftarrow r; \quad p \leftarrow not\ r; \; r \leftarrow not\ p\}$[2]. The hypotheses $H_1 = \{p; \; r\}$, $H_2 = \{p \leftarrow r; \; r\}$ and $H_3 = \{p \leftarrow not\ r; \; r \leftarrow not\ p\}$ are among the positive solutions of T. Each of the first two hypotheses (together with the background knowledge) has one Answer Set: $\{p; q; r\}$. This extends the negative example in T, and so both hypotheses are violating solutions of T. Note that the positive solutions which are also violating solutions are not inductive solutions, whereas the third positive solution, which is not a violating solution is an inductive solution of T. This is a general property proven by Theorem 1.

Theorem 1. *Let $T = \langle B, S_M, E^+, E^- \rangle$ be an ILP_{LAS} learning task. Then $ILP_{LAS}(T) = positive\_solns(T) \setminus violating\_solns(T)$.*

One method to find all inductive solutions of an ILP_{LAS} learning task T would be to generate all *positive inductive solutions* of T, add each solution, in turn, to the background knowledge in T and solve the resulting program to check whether it accepts Answer Sets that extend any negative examples, i.e. whether it is a *violating solution* of T. As, in practice, this would be inefficient, we instead generate the violating solutions first and use these to constrain our search for positive solutions. Inspired by the technique in [2], we encode our ILP_{ASP} learning task as an ASP program whose Answer Sets will provide our positive solutions. But, differently from [2], our encoding uses a meta-level approach that

---

[2] In subsequent examples we will refer to these rules in S_M with their R_{id} a to e.

allows us to reason about multiple Answer Sets of $B \cup H$, as in our notion of positive solution there might be multiple positive examples that may be extended by different Answer Sets of $B \cup H$.

Specifically, our definition of a positive solution H requires that each positive example $e^+ \in E^+$ has an Answer Set of $B \cup H$ that extends it. We use the atom $e(A, e_{id}^+)$ to represent that a literal A is in the Answer Set that extends the positive example e^+ (with unique identifier e_{id}^+). For each $e^+ \in E^+$, the ground fact $ex(e_{id}^+)$. Each rule R in the background knowledge and in the given hypothesis space S_M, is rewritten in a meta-level form by replacing each atom A that appears in R with the atom $e(A, X)$ and adding $ex(X)$ to the body of the rule. In this way the evaluation of the rules (in $B \cup H$) can explicitly refer to specific Answer Sets that extend a specific positive example and guide the search accordingly. In the case of negative examples, for an hypothesis H to be a violating solution, it is only necessary that $B \cup H$ cover one negative example. We therefore use only the fact $ex(neg)$ to represent any negative example. We use a predicate $active(R_{id})$, added to the body of each rule $R \in S_M$, where R_{id} is a unique identifier for R. Rules not chosen for the hypothesis will have this condition evaluated to false (and the rule will be vacuously satisfied). Formally, given an Answer Set A, the function $meta^{-1}(A) = \{R \in S_M : active(R_{id}) \in A\}$.

Definition 5. *Let $T = \langle B, S_M, E^+, E^- \rangle$ be an ILP_{LAS} learning task and $n \in \mathbb{N}$. Let R_{id} be a unique identifier for each rule $R \in S_M$ and let e_{id}^+ be a unique identifier for each positive example $e^+ \in E^+$. The learning task T is represented as the ASP task program $T_{meta}^n = meta(B) \cup meta(S_M) \cup meta(E^+) \cup meta(E^-) \cup meta(Aux, n)$ where each of these five "meta" components are as follows:*

1. *$meta(B)$ is generated from B by replacing every atom A with the atom $e(A, X)$, and by adding the condition $ex(X)$ to the body of each rule.*
2. *$meta(S_M)$ is generated from S_M by replacing every atom A with the atom $e(A, X)$, and by adding the two conditions $active(R_{id})$ and $ex(X)$ to the body of the rule R that matches the correct rule identifier R_{id}.*
3. *$meta(E^+)$ includes for each $ex^+ = \langle \{li_1, \ldots, li_h\}, \{le_1, \ldots, le_k\} \rangle \in E^+$ the*
   rules: $\begin{cases} ex(ex_{id}^+); \quad \leftarrow not\ covered(ex_{id}^+); \\ covered(e_{id}^+) \leftarrow e(li_1, ex_{id}^+), \ldots, e(li_h, ex_{id}^+), \\ \qquad not\ e(le_1, ex_{id}^+), \ldots, not\ e(le_k, ex_{id}^+) \end{cases}$
4. *$meta(E^-)$ includes for each $e^- = \langle \{li_1, \ldots, li_h\}, \{le_1, \ldots, le_k\} \rangle \in E^-$ the rule:*
   $violating \leftarrow e(li_1, neg), \ldots, e(li_h, neg), not\ e(le_1, neg), \ldots, not\ e(le_k, neg)$
5. *$meta(Aux, n)$ includes the ground facts $length(R_{id}, |R|)$ for every rule $R \in S_M$ and the rule $n\ \#sum\{active(R) = X: length(R, X)\}n$ to impose that the total length of the (active) hypothesis has to be n.*

Example 5. Recall the task T in Example 4. T_{meta}^3 is as follows:

1. $meta(B) = \{e(q, X) \leftarrow e(r, X), ex(X)\}$
2. $meta(S_M) = \{e(p, X) \leftarrow active(a), ex(X); e(r, X) \leftarrow active(b), ex(X);$
   $e(p, X) \leftarrow e(r, X), active(c), ex(X); e(p, X) \leftarrow not\ e(r, X), active(d), ex(X);$
   $e(r, X) \leftarrow not\ e(p, X), active(e), ex(X)\}$

3. $meta(E^+) = \{covered(1) \leftarrow e(p, 1); covered(2) \leftarrow e(q, 2);$
   $\leftarrow not\ covered(1); \leftarrow not\ covered(2); ex(1); ex(2)\}$
4. $meta(E^-) = \{violating \leftarrow e(p, neg), e(q, neg)\}$
5. $meta(Aux, 3) = \{length(a, 1); length(b, 1); length(c, 2); length(d, 2);$
   $length(e, 2); 3\ \#sum\{active(R) = X : length(R, X)\}3\}$

Proposition 1. *Let* $T = \langle B, S_M, E^+, E^- \rangle$ *be an* ILP_{LAS} *task and* $n \in \mathcal{N}$*. Then* $H \in positive\_solns^n(T)$ *if and only if* $\exists A \in AS(T^n_{meta})$ *such that* $H = meta^{-1}(A)$*.*

But as stated in Theorem 1, to compute our inductive solution we need also to compute the violating solutions. The same ASP encoding described in Definition 5 can be used to generate all the violating solutions. Specifically, given a length n, the ASP program $T^n_{meta} \cup \{\leftarrow not\ violating;\ ex(neg)\}$ will have Answer Sets that include $active(R_{id})$ of hypotheses $R \in S_M$ that are violating solutions. This is captured by Proposition 2.

Proposition 2. *Let* $T = \langle B, S_M, E^+, E^- \rangle$ *be an* ILP_{LAS} *task and* $n \in \mathcal{N}$*. Let* P *be the ASP program* $T^n_{meta} \cup \{\leftarrow not\ violating;\ ex(neg)\}$*. Then* $H \in violating\_solns^n(T)$ *if and only if* $\exists A \in AS(P)$ *such that* $H = meta^{-1}(A)$*.*

The main idea of our learning algorithm, called ILASP, is to compute first all violating solutions of a given ILP_{LAS} learning task T by solving the ASP program $T^n_{meta} \cup \{\leftarrow not\ violating;\ ex(neg)\}$. Then to convert these solutions into constraints[3] and again to solve T^n_{meta}, augmented this time with these new constraints. The Answer Sets of this second step will provide all the inductive solutions of T. This is formally described in Algorithm 1.

Algorithm 1. ILASP

---

  procedure ILASP(T)
    $solutions = [\,]$
    for $n = 0$; $solutions.empty$; $n{+}{+}$ **do**
      $vs = AS(T^n_{meta} \cup \{\leftarrow not\ violating;\quad ex(neg)\})$
      $ps = AS(T^n_{meta} \cup \{constraint(meta^{-1}(V)) : V \in vs\})$
      $solutions = \{meta^{-1}(A) : A \in ps\}$
    end for
    return $solutions$
  end procedure

We denote with $ILP^n_{LAS}(T)$ the set of all inductive solutions of length n. Proposition 3 states that the Answer Sets of the ASP task program augmented with $constraint(H)$, for each violating solution H, correspond exactly to the inductive solutions of length n of the original learning task.

Proposition 3. *Let* $T = \langle B, S_M, E^+, E^- \rangle$ *be an* ILP_{LAS} *task and* $n \in \mathcal{N}$*. Let* $P = T^n_{meta} \cup \{constraint(V) : V \in violating\_solns^n(T)\}$*. Then a hypothesis* $H \in ILP^n_{LAS}(T)$ *if and only if* $\exists A \in AS(P)$ *such that* $H = meta^{-1}(A)$*.*

---

[3] $constraint(\{R_1, \ldots, R_h\})$ denotes the rule $\leftarrow active(R_{id1}), \ldots, active(R_{idh})$, where $R_{id1}, \ldots R_{idh}$ are the unique identifiers of rules $R_1, \ldots, R_h$ in H.

The following theorem states that $ILASP$ is sound and complete with respect to the notion of optimal[4] inductive solutions in $ILP^*_{LAS}(T)$. $ILASP(T)$ denotes the set of hypotheses computed by ILASP for a given ILP_{LAS} task T.

Theorem 2. *Let T be any ILP_{LAS} learning task such that there is at least one inductive solution. Then $ILASP(T) = ILP^*_{LAS}(T)$.*

Proof. At each step through the for loop (fix n to be any natural number): let H be an hypothesis of length n and $P = T^n_{meta} \cup \{\leftarrow \text{ not } violating;\ ex(neg)\}$. By Prop. 2, $H \in violating\_solns^n(T)$ iff $\exists A \in AS(P)$ st $H = meta^{-1}(A)$.

$\Rightarrow H \in violating\_solns^n(T)$ iff $\exists A \in vs$ st $H = meta^{-1}(A)$.

$\Rightarrow violating\_solns^n(T) = \{meta^{-1}(A) : A \in vs\}$

$ps = AS(T^n_{meta} \cup \{constraint(meta^{-1}(V)) : V \in vs\})$

$\Rightarrow ps = AS(T^n_{meta} \cup \{constraint(V) : V \in violating\_solns^n(T)\})$

$\Rightarrow H \in ILP^n_{LAS}(T)$ iff $\exists A \in ps$ st $H = meta^{-1}(A)$ by Proposition 3.

$\Rightarrow ILP^n_{LAS}(T) = \{meta^{-1}(A) : A \in ps\} = solutions$

As $ILASP(T)$ returns $ILP^n_{LAS}(T)$ for the first n for which it is non-empty, $ILASP(T) = ILP^*_{LAS}(T)$. $\qquad\square$

We are currently working to improve ILASP's scalability. In general there could be many violating solutions before the first inductive solution; for example, with the sudoku problem, the first positive solution is H_1 from example 3 which has length 17; however, the first inductive solution is not until H_2 at length 26. There are many thousands of violating solutions between lengths 17 and 26 (many of these are constructed by adding rules to H_1). By restricting the search space so that the only permitted aggregates are those of the form $agg(l, u)$ for some l and u (see example 3), our implementation was able to find the correct solution. In current work we are exploring techniques to make ILASP more efficient and more scalable. One possibility is to keep a set of full Answer Sets which extend negative examples. When we find a violating solution, we add an Answer Set to this set and rule out further solutions which accept this Answer Set. This set is likely to be much smaller than the set of violating solutions.

5 Application to a Planning Problem

In this section we apply our approach to a planning problem where an agent is in a room at a given position and attempts to get to a target position. Figure 2 gives a graphical representation of the room and the legend describes its main features. The challenge in this planning problem is that although the agent has complete knowledge of the grid map, it does not know the meaning of the various cell features. For instance, it knows which cells are locked, but not that to go through a locked cell it must first visit the key to that cell. The agent's goal is to learn the definition of valid move to allow it to reach the target position.

---

[4] Note that the optimality – hypotheses with shortest length – is guaranteed by the incremental property of our algorithm.

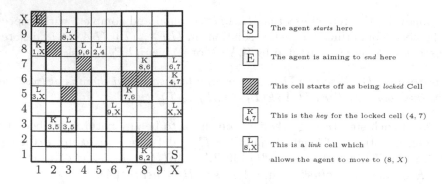

Fig. 2. Cells with diagonal lines are *locked* and the agent must visit the corresponding key before it can enter these cells. *Link* cells allow the agent to jump to the indicated destination cell. The thick black lines represent walls.

The planning problem is modelled as follows. At each step an oracle informs the agent on which cells it could move to next, called the *valid moves*. If the agent, using its current knowledge, infers valid moves that are different from that suggested by the oracle then the agent learns an updated hypothesis; otherwise it plans a path to the target position, using its current hypothesis, and selects as its next move the first move in the plan. By using ASP optimisation, the agent can even plan for the optimal (shortest) plan.[5] In what follows we show three scenarios illustrating three different learning outcomes. In the first scenario, the agent learns just the concept of valid move; in the second scenario, part of the existing background knowledge is removed and the agent has to also learn a new concept that does not appear in the examples or in the background knowledge, showing the ability of ILP_{LAS} to support predicate invention [11]. Finally, in the third scenario, the environment is non deterministic, causing the agent to learn a non deterministic notion of valid move.

Scenario 1: In this simplest scenario, the agent is given the grid map, encoded as facts, together with the history of the cells it has been at from the start and the notions of adjacent cells, visited cell and unlocked cell (given below).

```
unlocked(C, T) :- visited_cell(Key, T), key(C, Key).
unlocked(C, T) :- cell(C), not locked(C), time(T).
```

The task is for the agent to learn the rules:

```
valid_move(C1, T) :- agent_at(C2, T), not wall(C1, C2),
                     adjacent(C1, C2), unlocked(C1, T).
valid_move(C1, T) :- agent_at(C2, T), link(C2, C1), unlocked(C1, T).
```

We denote with VM_{oracle} the set of *valid_move*/2 facts that the oracle generates and with VM_{agent} the set of *valid_move*/2 facts that the agent infers at a given time using its current knowledge and hypothesis. When VM_{oracle} and VM_{agent} differ, the agent uses our *ILASP* algorithm to find a new hypothesis such that

---

[5] If the agent cannot generate, with its current knowledge, a plan to reach the target position, then optimality is defined in terms of exploration of the map.

VM_{agent} and VM_{oracle} are once again equal. The background knowledge consists of the definitions of *adjacent, unlocked, visited_cell* and of the history of the cells the agent has been at from the start. In this simple scenario the target program has only one Answer Set, thus only one positive example is necessary. In particular, at each learning step, the positive example is given by every valid move in VM_{oracle} that does not appear in VM_{agent}. These are the moves the agent did not realise were possible, hence it needs to learn. The negative examples are constructed from the moves that are in VM_{agent} but not in VM_{oracle}. These are the moves the agent wrongly thought were possible and that the new learned hypothesis should no longer cover. The first few sets of examples are shown in example 6. Note that the learning task does not take into account the complete history of the valid moves. So it is possible that the new hypothesis wrongly classifies as invalid a move made at an earlier step. If VM_{oracle} is still different to VM_{agent}, the examples are again updated and a new hypothesis is learned.

Example 6. At the first step $VM_{oracle} = \{(9,1),(10,2)\}$, but given the agent's initial hypothesis, $\emptyset$, $VM_{agent} = \emptyset$. The examples are therefore:

$$E^+ = \begin{cases} \langle\{valid\_move(cell(9,1),1), \\ \quad valid\_move(cell(10,2),1)\},\emptyset\rangle \end{cases} \qquad E^- = \emptyset$$

ILASP returns the hypothesis $valid\_move(C,T) \leftarrow unlocked(C,T)$. VM_{agent} and VM_{oracle} are still not equal as VM_{agent} now contains too many moves. The agent therefore extends its examples to:

$$E^+ = \begin{cases} \langle\{valid\_move(cell(9,1),1), \\ \quad valid\_move(cell(10,2),1) \\ \},\emptyset\rangle \end{cases} \quad E^- = \begin{cases} \langle\{valid\_move(cell(8,1),1)\},\emptyset\rangle, \\ \langle\{valid\_move(cell(7,1),1)\},\emptyset\rangle, \\ \quad \dots \end{cases}$$

The new hypothesis is $valid\_move(C,T) \leftarrow adjacent(C,C2), agent\_at(C2,T)$. VM_{agent} and VM_{oracle} are now equal, and so the agent makes it's first move (to $(9,1)$). VM_{oracle} and VM_{agent} are equal until the agent reaches $(8,1)$. VM_{agent} now has $(7,1)$ where VM_{oracle} does not. The previous example set is augmented with the new negative example $\langle\{valid\_move(cell(7,1),3)\},\emptyset\rangle$. As shown in Table 1, $ILASP$ is able to generate the correct solution in 6 learning steps; however, in this scenario it only had to learn a single predicate. Next we investigate what happens when $ILASP$ needs to learn an unseen predicate.

Scenario 2: This scenario differs from the previous one in that the agent is not given the definition of unlocked cell. The language bias of this learning task is therefore augmented with a new predicate, called *extra/2* added to both M_h and M_b. We expected the agent to learn the previous hypothesis along with the definition of *unlocked*; however, the agent learned the shorter hypothesis:

```
extra(C,T) :- agent_at(C1, V1), link(C1,C).
extra(C,T) :- adjacent(C,C1), agent_at(C1, T), not wall(C,C1).
valid_move(C, T) :- extra(C,T), not locked(C).
valid_move(C, T) :- extra(C,T), key(C1,C), visited_cell(C1,T).
```

So far, due to the deterministic environment the agent has learned programs with only one Answer Set. The next scenario explores a non-deterministic setting.

Table 1. Results for the first scenario. Each row shows the path the agent took while it believed a particular hypothesis $((1..3, 2)$ abbreviates $(1, 2), (2, 2), (3, 2))$.

Path	Hypotheses (With variables renamed for readability)
$(10, 1)$	
$(10, 1)$	$valid\_move(C, T) \leftarrow unlocked(C, T)$.
$(10..8, 1)$	$valid\_move(C, T) \leftarrow adjacent(C, C2), agent\_at(C2, T)$.
$(8, 1..4), (7..6, 4)$	$valid\_move(C, T) \leftarrow$ not $wall(C, C2), adjacent(C, C2), agent\_at(C2, T)$.
$(6, 4..7), (5, 7)$	$valid\_move(C, T) \leftarrow$ not $wall(C, C2), adjacent(C, C2), agent\_at(C2, T)$. $valid\_move(C, T) \leftarrow link(C, C2), agent\_at(C2, T)$.
$(5, 7..8), (2..3, 4),$ $(3, 3)$	$valid\_move(C, T) \leftarrow$ not $wall(C, C2), unlocked(C, T),$ $\qquad\qquad adjacent(C, C2), agent\_at(C2, T)$. $valid\_move(C, T) \leftarrow link(C, C2), agent\_at(C2, T)$.
$(3, 3), (2..3, 3),$ $(3, 5), \quad (2, 5..6),$ $(1, 6..7) \ (1, 8..5),$ $(3..1, 10)$	$valid\_move(C, T) \leftarrow$ not $wall(C, C2), unlocked(C, T),$ $\qquad\qquad adjacent(C, C2), agent\_at(C2, T)$. $valid\_move(C, T) \leftarrow link(C, C2), unlocked(C, T), agent\_at(C2, T)$.

Scenario 3: We now further complicate matters for our agent by removing the guarantee that the set of valid moves it has is always inferable given its history. The change to the scenario is that *link* is given an extra argument: the *flipped* destination cell (if the destination cell is (X, Y), the flipped cell is (Y, X)). Now whenever the agent lands on a link cell, the oracle decides (randomly) whether to give the destination cell, or the flipped cell as a valid move. In the first two scenarios we restricted the search space to hypotheses without aggregates, whereas here we allow aggregates, which extends the search space to include many more rules. As a consequence, to overcome the scalability issues discussed in the previous section, we needed to make a small addition to the background knowledge that combines the concepts of adjacent and wall into a new concept $joined(C1, C2) \leftarrow adjacent(C1, C2),$ not $wall$. In this scenario, in addition to the set of valid moves, the oracle also gives to the agent a second set of *potentially* valid moves (the union of all sets of valid moves the oracle could have given).

The fact that the environment is non-deterministic changes the learning task slightly. We can no longer encode every invalid move proposed by the agent at a particular time as a negative example. This is because, had the oracle made a different choice, the move *might* have been a valid one. If an invalid move appears in the set of *potentially valid* moves, then it is instead added to the exclusion set of the positive example at that time. This means that it cannot occur in the Answer Set extending this positive example, but could well appear in other Answer Sets of the program. The agent was able to learn the rules:

```
1 {valid_move(C, T); valid_move(FC, T)} 1 :-
    unlocked(C, T), link(C2, C, FC), agent_at(C2, T).
valid_move(C, T) :- unlocked(C, T), joined(C, C2), agent_at(C2, T).
```

6   Related Work

In this section we review the related work. We reformulate (but preserve the meaning of) some learning tasks to allow for easier comparison with our own.

The goal of traditional ILP has been to learn Prolog style logic programs. Usually this is restricted to learning definite programs (with no negation as failure). The learning task of these traditional ILP systems is equivalent to a Learning from Answer Sets task with a single positive example (and no negative examples) and with the search space restricted to definite logic programs. But learning more general ASP programs rather Prolog programs has the clear advantage that the ASP representation is completely declaratvie. In Prolog, we would have to learn a procedure for constructing valid sudoku boards, whereas in ASP we only learned the rules of sudoku.

Induction of Stable Models [13] extends the definition of ILP to the stable model semantics. An *Induction of Stable Models task* is a tuple $\langle B, S_M, E \rangle$ where B is the background knowledge, S_M is the search space and E is a set of partial interpretations. $H \in ILP_{sm}\langle B, M, E \rangle$ iff (i) $H \subseteq S_M$; and (ii) $\forall O \in E : \exists A \in AS(B \cup H)$ such that A extends O. This is a special case of ILP_{LAS}: with no negative examples. For any B, S_M, E: $ILP_{sm}\langle B, S_M, E \rangle = ILP_{LAS}\langle B, S_M, E, \emptyset \rangle$. However, negative examples are needed to learn Answer Set programs in practice, as otherwise there is no concept of what should not be in an Answer Set. In our planning, for instance, no negative examples would give the optimal solution $0\{valid\_move(C, T)\}1 \leftarrow cell(C), time(T)$ (at any time for each cell C, we may or may not be allowed to move to C). This does cover our positive examples, but it is not specific enough to be useful for planning.

Brave Induction[16] finds an hypothesis which covers a single observation O. A *Brave Induction task*, when defined in the context of ASP, is a tuple $\langle B, S_M, O \rangle$ where B is the background knowledge, S_M the search space and O is a set of atoms. $H \in ILP_b\langle B, M, O \rangle$ iff (i) $H \subseteq S_M$; and (ii) $\exists A \in AS(B \cup H)$ such that $O \subseteq A$. For any B, M, O, the Brave Induction task $ILP_b\langle B, M, O \rangle = ILP_{LAS}\langle B, M, \{\langle O, \emptyset \rangle\}, \emptyset \rangle$. ASPAL [2] uses ASP as a solver to compute a solution to a standard ILP Task. ASPAL's learning task, similarly to that of XHAIL [14], is between Brave Induction and Induction of Stable Models. It has a single positive example which is a partial interpretation. ASPAL's method of using an ASP solver to search for the inductive solutions to an ILP task inspired our own. Our method conducts the search in multiple stages however, as we not only require the brave entailment of the positive examples, but also the cautious entailment of the negation of our negative examples. The search spaces in ASPAL and XHAIL did not include aggregates or constraints.

In [3], De Raedt defines *Learning from Partial Interpretations*. Under ILP_{LFPI} an example E (a partial interpretation) is covered by a hypothesis H iff there is a model of $B \cup H$, which extends E. Unlike ILP_{LAS}, as this definition uses models, H covers an example E iff $B \cup H \cup E$ is consistent. Another approach is *Learning from Interpretation Transitions* [7]. The examples here are pairs of interpretations $\langle I, J \rangle$ such that J must equal $T_{B \cup H}(I)$. This task can be mapped to an ILP_{LAS} task by replacing every atom h in the head of rules in B and S_M or occuring in J with the new atom $tp(h)$, representing that $h \in T_{B \cup H}(I)$. Each $I_i \in \{I_1, \ldots, I_n\}$ would then be put in the background knowledge with a condition eg_i in the body (supported by a choice rule $1\{eg_1, \ldots, eg_n\}1$) and eg_i would be added to each J_i which then become the positive examples.

7   Conclusion and Future Work

We have presented a new paradigm for ILP that allows the learning of ASP programs. We have designed and implemented an algorithm which is able to compute inductive solutions, and have shown how it can be used in a planning problem.

There are two avenues of future work: improving the efficiency of our algorithm; and learning a larger subset of the language of ASP. In particular we believe that learning optimisation statements in ASP will facilitate many more applications, as most of ASP's applications involve optimisation.

References

1. Corapi, D., Russo, A., Lupu, E.: Inductive logic programming as abductive search. In: ICLP (Technical Communications), pp. 54–63 (2010)
2. Corapi, D., Russo, A., Lupu, E.: Inductive logic programming in answer set programming. In: Muggleton, S.H., Tamaddoni-Nezhad, A., Lisi, F.A. (eds.) ILP 2011. LNCS, vol. 7207, pp. 91–97. Springer, Heidelberg (2012)
3. De Raedt, L.: Logical settings for concept-learning. Artificial Intelligence 95(1), 187–201 (1997)
4. Gebser, M., Kaminski, R., Kaufmann, B., Ostrowski, M., Schaub, T., Schneider, M.: Potassco: The Potsdam answer set solving collection. AI Communications 24(2), 107–124 (2011)
5. Gebser, M., Kaminski, R., Kaufmann, B., Schaub, T.: Answer Set Solving in Practice. Synthesis Lectures on Artificial Intelligence and Machine Learning. Morgan and Claypool Publishers (2012)
6. Gelfond, M., Lifschitz, V.: The stable model semantics for logic programming. In: ICLP/SLP, vol. 88, pp. 1070–1080 (1988)
7. Inoue, K., Ribeiro, T., Sakama, C.: Learning from interpretation transition. Machine Learning 94(1), 51–79 (2014)
8. Kimber, T., Broda, K., Russo, A.: Induction on failure: learning connected horn theories. In: Erdem, E., Lin, F., Schaub, T. (eds.) LPNMR 2009. LNCS, vol. 5753, pp. 169–181. Springer, Heidelberg (2009)
9. Law, M., Russo, A., Broda, K.: Proofs for inductive learning of answer set programs, https://www.doc.ic.ac.uk/~ml1909/ILASP_Proofs.pdf
10. Muggleton, S.: Inductive logic programming. New Generation Computing 8(4), 295–318 (1991)
11. Muggleton, S., De Raedt, L., Poole, D., Bratko, I., Flach, P., Inoue, K., Srinivasan, A.: Ilp turns 20. Machine Learning 86(1), 3–23 (2012)
12. Muggleton, S., Lin, D.: Meta-interpretive learning of higher-order dyadic datalog: Predicate invention revisited. In: Proceedings of the Twenty-Third International Joint Conference on Artificial Intelligence, pp. 1551–1557. AAAI Press (2013)
13. Otero, R.: Induction of stable models. In: Rouveirol, C., Sebag, M. (eds.) ILP 2001. LNCS (LNAI), vol. 2157, pp. 193–205. Springer, Heidelberg (2001)

14. Ray, O.: Nonmonotonic abductive inductive learning. Journal of Applied Logic 7(3), 329–340 (2009)
15. Ray, O., Broda, K., Russo, A.: A hybrid abductive inductive proof procedure. Logic Journal of IGPL 12(5), 371–397 (2004)
16. Sakama, C., Inoue, K.: Brave induction: a logical framework for learning from incomplete information. Machine Learning 76(1), 3–35 (2009)

Stable Models of Fuzzy Propositional Formulas

Joohyung Lee and Yi Wang

School of Computing, Informatics, and Decision Systems Engineering
Arizona State University, Tempe, USA
{joolee,ywang485}@asu.edu

Abstract. We introduce the stable model semantics for fuzzy propositional formulas, which generalizes both fuzzy propositional logic and the stable model
semantics of Boolean propositional formulas. Combining the advantages of both
formalisms, the introduced language allows highly configurable default reasoning
involving fuzzy truth values. We show that several properties of Boolean stable
models are naturally extended to this formalism, and discuss how it is related to
other approaches to combining fuzzy logic and the stable model semantics.

1   Introduction

Answer set programming (ASP) [1] is a widely applied declarative programming
paradigm for the design and implementation of knowledge intensive applications. One
of the attractive features of ASP is its capability to model the nonmonotonic aspect of
knowledge. However, as its mathematical basis, the stable model semantics, is restricted
to Boolean values, it is too rigid to represent imprecise and vague information. Fuzzy
logic, as a form of many-valued logic, can handle vague information by interpreting
propositions with a truth degree in the interval of real numbers $[0, 1]$. The availability
of various fuzzy operators gives the user great flexibility in combining truth degrees.
However, the semantics of fuzzy logic is monotonic and is not flexible enough to handle
default reasoning as allowed in answer set programming.

Both the stable model semantics and fuzzy logic are generalizations of classical
propositional logic in different ways. While they do not subsume each other, it is clear
that many real-world problems require both their strengths. This led to the body of work
on combining fuzzy logic and the stable model semantics, known as fuzzy answer set
programming (e.g., [2–9]). However, most work considers simple rule forms and do not
allow connectives nested arbitrarily as in fuzzy logic.

Unlike existing work on fuzzy answer set semantics, in this paper, we extend the general stable model semantics from [10] to many-valued propositional formulas. The syntax of this language is the same as the syntax of fuzzy propositional logic. The semantics, on the other hand, distinguishes *stable* models from non-stable models. The language is a proper generalization of both fuzzy propositional logic and Boolean propositional formulas under the stable model semantics. This generalization is not simply a
pure theoretical pursuit, but has practical use in conveniently modeling defaults involving fuzzy truth values in dynamic domains. For example, consider modeling dynamics
of *trust* in social network. People trust each other in different degrees under some normal assumptions. If person A trusts person B, then A tends to trust person C whom
B trusts to a degree which is positively correlated to the degree to which A trusts B

E. Fermé and J. Leite (Eds.): JELIA 2014, LNAI 8761, pp. 326–339, 2014.
© Springer International Publishing Switzerland 2014

and the degree to which B trusts C. By default, the trust degrees would not change, but may decrease when a conflict arises between people. Modeling such a domain requires expressing defaults involving fuzzy truth values. We demonstrate that such examples can be conveniently modelled in our proposed language by taking advantage of its generality over the existing approaches to fuzzy ASP.

The paper is organized as follows. Section 2 reviews the syntax and the semantics of fuzzy propositional logic we discuss in the paper, as well as the stable model semantics of classical propositional formulas. Section 3 presents the stable model semantics of fuzzy propositional formulas along with examples, including the above trust example in the proposed language. Section 4 relates our fuzzy stable model semantics to the Boolean stable model semantics, and Section 5 relates it to other approaches to fuzzy ASP. Section 6 shows that several well-known properties of the Boolean stable model semantics can be easily extended to our fuzzy stable model semantics. Section 7 discusses other related work.

2 Preliminaries

2.1 Review: Stable Models of Classical Propositional Formulas

We review the definition of a stable model from [10] by limiting attention to the syntax of propositional formulas. Instead of defining stable models in terms of second-order logic as in [10], we express the same concept using auxiliary atoms that do not belong to the original signature. This slight reformulation will simplify our efforts in extending the stable model semantics to fuzzy propositional formulas without resorting to "second-order fuzzy logic."

Let σ be a classical propositional signature, let $\mathbf{p} = (p_1, \dots, p_n)$ be a list of distinct atoms belonging to σ, and let $\mathbf{q} = (q_1, \dots, q_n)$ be a list of new, distinct propositional atoms not belonging to σ. For two interpretations I and J of σ that agree on all atoms in $\sigma \setminus \mathbf{p}$, $I \cup J_{\mathbf{q}}^{\mathbf{p}}$ denotes the interpretation of $\sigma \cup \mathbf{q}$ that

- agrees with I on all atoms in σ, and
- for each atom $q_i \in \mathbf{q}$, $(I \cup J_{\mathbf{q}}^{\mathbf{p}})(q_i) = J(p_i)$.[1]

For any classical propositional formula F of signature σ, $F^*(\mathbf{q})$ is a classical propositional formula of signature $\sigma \cup \mathbf{q}$ that is defined recursively as follows:

- $p_i^* = q_i$ for each $p_i \in \mathbf{p}$;
- $F^* = F$ for any atom $F \notin \mathbf{p}$;
- $\bot^* = \bot$; $\top^* = \top$;
- $(\neg F)^* = \neg F$;
- $(F \wedge G)^* = F^* \wedge G^*$; $(F \vee G)^* = F^* \vee G^*$;
- $(F \rightarrow G)^* = (F^* \rightarrow G^*) \wedge (F \rightarrow G)$.

Let I and J be two interpretations of σ, and let $\mathbf{p}$ be a subset of σ. We say $J \leq^{\mathbf{p}} I$ if

---

[1] $I(p)$ denotes the truth value of p under I. We identify a list with a set if there is no confusion.

- J and I agree on all atoms not in $\mathbf{p}$, and
- for all $p \in \mathbf{p}$, if $J \models p$, then $I \models p$.

We say $J <^\mathbf{P} I$ if $J \leq^\mathbf{P} I$ and $J \neq I$.

Definition 1. *An interpretation I is a* stable model *of F relative to $\mathbf{p}$ (denoted $I \models$ SM$[F; \mathbf{p}]$)*

- *if $I \models F$, and*
- *there is no interpretation J such that $J <^\mathbf{P} I$ and $I \cup J_\mathbf{q}^\mathbf{P} \models F^*(\mathbf{q})$.*

Example 1. Consider a logic program

$$p \leftarrow not\ q, \quad q \leftarrow not\ p$$

which is understood as an alternative notation for propositional formula $F_1 = (\neg q \rightarrow p) \wedge (\neg p \rightarrow q)$. $F_1^*(u, v)$ is $(\neg q \rightarrow u) \wedge (\neg q \rightarrow p) \wedge (\neg p \rightarrow v) \wedge (\neg p \rightarrow q)$. We check that $I_1 = \{p\}$ (that is, p is TRUE and q is FALSE) [2] is a stable model of F_1 (relative to $\{p, q\}$): I_1 satisfies F_1, and $\emptyset$ is the only interpretation J such that $J <^{pq} I_1$. However, $I_1 \cup J_{uv}^{pq} = \{p\}$ does not satisfy $F_1^*(u, v)$ because it does not satisfy the first conjunctive term of $F_1^*(u, v)$. Similarly, we can check that $\{q\}$ is another stable model of F_1.

2.2 Review: Fuzzy Logic

Let σ be a fuzzy propositional signature, which is a set of symbols called *fuzzy atoms*. In addition, we assume the presence of a set $\mathbb{C}$ of fuzzy conjunction symbols, a set $\mathbb{D}$ of fuzzy disjunction symbols, a set $\mathbb{N}$ of fuzzy negation symbols, and a set $\mathbb{I}$ of fuzzy implication symbols.

A *fuzzy (propositional) formula* of σ is defined recursively as follows.

- every fuzzy atom $p \in \sigma$ is a fuzzy formula;
- every numeric constant $\bar{c}$ where c is a real number in $[0, 1]$ is a fuzzy formula;
- if F is a fuzzy formula, then $\neg F$ is a fuzzy formula, where $\neg \in \mathbb{N}$;
- if F and G are fuzzy formulas, then $F \otimes G$, $F \oplus G$ and $F \rightarrow G$ are fuzzy formulas, where $\otimes \in \mathbb{C}$, $\oplus \in \mathbb{D}$, and $\rightarrow \in \mathbb{I}$.

The models of a fuzzy formula are defined as follows [11]. The *fuzzy truth values* are the real numbers in the range $[0, 1]$. A *fuzzy interpretation I* of σ is a mapping from σ into $[0, 1]$.

The fuzzy operators are functions mapping one or a pair of truth values into a truth value. Among the operators, $\neg$ denotes a function from $[0, 1]$ into $[0, 1]$; $\otimes$, $\oplus$, and $\rightarrow$ denote functions from $[0, 1] \times [0, 1]$ into $[0, 1]$. The actual mapping performed by each operator can be defined in many different ways, but all of them satisfy the following conditions, which imply that the operators are generalizations of the corresponding classical propositional connectives:[3]

---

[2] We identify a propositional interpretation with the set of atoms that are true in it.

[3] We say that a function f of arity n is *increasing in its i-th argument* $(1 \leq i \leq n)$ if $f(arg_1, \dots, arg_i, \dots, arg_n) \leq f(arg_1, \dots, arg_i', \dots, arg_n)$ for all arguments such that $arg_i \leq arg_i'$; f is said to be *increasing* if it is increasing in all its arguments. The definition of *decreasing* is similar.

- a fuzzy negation $\neg$ is decreasing, and satisfies $\neg(0) = 1$ and $\neg(1) = 0$;
- a fuzzy conjunction $\otimes$ is increasing, commutative, associative, and $\otimes(1, x) = x$ for all $x \in [0, 1]$;
- a fuzzy disjunction $\oplus$ is increasing, commutative, associative, and $\oplus(0, x) = x$ for all $x \in [0, 1]$;
- a fuzzy implication $\rightarrow$ is decreasing in its first argument and increasing in its second argument; and $\rightarrow (1, x) = x$ and $\rightarrow (0, 0) = 1$ for all $x \in [0, 1]$.

Figure 1 lists some specific fuzzy operators that we use in this paper.

Symbol	Name	Definition
$\otimes_l$	Łukasiewicz t-norm	$\otimes_l(x, y) = max\,(x + y - 1, 0)$
$\oplus_l$	Łukasiewicz t-conorm	$\oplus_l(x, y) = min\,(x + y, 1)$
$\otimes_m$	minimum t-norm	$\otimes_m(x, y) = min\,(x, y)$
$\oplus_m$	maximum t-conorm	$\oplus_m(x, y) = max\,(x, y)$
$\otimes_p$	product t-norm	$\otimes_p(x, y) = x \cdot y$
$\oplus_p$	product t-conorm	$\oplus_p(x, y) = x + y - x \cdot y$
$\neg_s$	standard negator	$\neg_s(x) = 1 - x$
$\rightarrow_r$	the residual implicator of $\otimes_m$	$\rightarrow_r (x, y) = \begin{cases} 1 & \text{if } x \leq y \\ y & \text{otherwise} \end{cases}$
$\rightarrow_s$	the S-implicator induced by $\neg_s$ and $\oplus_m$	$\rightarrow_s (x, y) = max\,(1 - x, y)$

Fig. 1. Some t-norms, t-conorms, negator, and implicators

The *truth value* of a fuzzy formula F under I, denoted F^I, is defined recursively as follows:

- for any atom $p \in \sigma$, $p^I = I(p)$;
- for any numeric constant $\bar{c}$, $\bar{c}^I = c$;
- $(\neg F)^I = \neg(F^I)$;
- $(F \otimes G)^I = \otimes(F^I, G^I)$; $(F \oplus G)^I = \oplus(F^I, G^I)$; $(F \rightarrow G)^I = \rightarrow (F^I, G^I)$.

(For simplicity, we identify the symbols for the fuzzy operators with the truth value functions represented by them.)

Definition 2. *We say that a fuzzy interpretation I satisfies a fuzzy formula F w.r.t. a threshold $y \in [0, 1]$ if $F^I \geq y$, and denote it by $I \models_y F$. We call I a fuzzy y-model of F.*

We often omit the threshold y when it is 1.

3 Definition and Examples

We extend the notion of $J <^{\mathbf{p}} I$ in Section 2.1 as follows. For any two fuzzy interpretations J and I of the same signature σ and any subset $\mathbf{p}$ of σ, we say $J \leq^{\mathbf{p}} I$ if

- J and I agree on all fuzzy atoms not in $\mathbf{p}$, and
- for all $p \in \mathbf{p}$, $p^J \leq p^I$.

We say $J <^{\mathbf{P}} I$ if $J \leq^{\mathbf{P}} I$ and $J \neq I$.

As before, we assume a list $\mathbf{q} = (q_1, \ldots, q_n)$ of new, distinct fuzzy atoms that corresponds to $\mathbf{p} = (p_1, \ldots, p_n)$, and define $I \cup J_{\mathbf{q}}^{\mathbf{P}}$ in the same way. That is, when I and J agree on all atoms in $\sigma \setminus \mathbf{p}$, $I \cup J_{\mathbf{q}}^{\mathbf{P}}$ denotes the interpretation of $\sigma \cup \mathbf{q}$ that

- agrees with I on all atoms in σ, and
- for each $q_i \in \mathbf{q}$, $(I \cup J_{\mathbf{q}}^{\mathbf{P}})(q_i) = J(p_i)$.

The definition of F^* is also extended in a straightforward way: For any fuzzy formula F of signature σ, $F^*(\mathbf{q})$ is defined as follows.

- $p_i^* = q_i$ for each $p_i \in \mathbf{p}$;
- $F^* = F$ for any atom $F \notin \mathbf{p}$;
- $\bar{c}^* = \bar{c}$ for any numeric constant $\bar{c}$;
- $(\neg F)^* = \neg F$;
- $(F \otimes G)^* = F^* \otimes G^*$; $(F \oplus G)^* = F^* \oplus G^*$;
- $(F \rightarrow G)^* = (F^* \rightarrow G^*) \otimes_m (F \rightarrow G)$. [4]

Definition 3. *A fuzzy interpretation I is a fuzzy y-stable model of F relative to $\mathbf{p}$ (denoted $I \models_y SM[F; \mathbf{p}]$) if*

- *$I \models_y F$, and*
- *there is no fuzzy interpretation J such that $J <^{\mathbf{P}} I$ and $I \cup J_{\mathbf{q}}^{\mathbf{P}} \models_y F^*(\mathbf{q})$.*

We often omit the threshold y when it is 1, and omit $\mathbf{p}$ if it contains all atoms in σ.

Clearly, when $\mathbf{p}$ is empty, Definition 3 reduces to the definition of a fuzzy model in Definition 2 because there is no J such that $J <^\emptyset I$.

Also, Definition 3 is very similar to the definition of a stable model for classical propositional formulas in Definition 1. The main difference is that simply in the latter, atoms may have various degrees of truth, and accordingly the notion of $J <^{\mathbf{P}} I$ is more general. The precise relationship between the definitions is discussed in Section 4.

Example 2. Consider the fuzzy formula $F = \neg_s p \rightarrow_r q$ and the interpretation $I = \{(p, 0), (q, 0.6)\}$. $F^*(u, v)$ is

$$((\neg_s p)^* \rightarrow_r q^*) \otimes_m (\neg_s p \rightarrow_r q) = (\neg_s p \rightarrow_r v) \otimes_m (\neg_s p \rightarrow_r q).$$

$I \models_{0.6} SM[F; p, q]$. First, it is easy to see that $I \models_{0.6} F$, as

$$F^I =\rightarrow_r ((\neg_s p)^I, q^I) =\rightarrow_r (1 - p^I, q^I) =\rightarrow_r (1, 0.6) = 0.6.$$

Suppose there exists $J <^{pq} I$ such that $I \cup J_{uv}^{pq} \models_{0.6} F$, i.e.,

$$
\begin{aligned}
F^*(u, v)^{I \cup J_{uv}^{pq}} &= min \left(\rightarrow_r (\neg_s(p^I), v^{I \cup J_{uv}^{pq}}), \rightarrow_r (\neg_s(p^I), q^I) \right) \\
&= min \left(\rightarrow_r (1, q^J), 0.6 \right) \\
&= min \left(q^J, 0.6 \right) \geq 0.6.
\end{aligned}
$$

---

[4] Note the use of $\otimes_m$ here; the value of "conjunction" of $(F^* \rightarrow G^*)$ and $(F \rightarrow G)$ needs not be smaller than the value of $(F^* \rightarrow G^*)$ and the value of $(F \rightarrow G)$. It turns out that $\otimes_m$ is the only t-norm that satisfies this property.

So $q^J \geq 0.6$. This contradicts the assumption that $J <^{pq} I$. Therefore, such J does not exist, and I is a 0.6-stable model of F.

Example 3. p and $\neg_s\neg_s p$ have the same fuzzy models, but their stable models are different. This is similar to the fact that p and $\neg\neg p$ have different stable models according to the semantics from [10].

Clearly, any interpretation $I = \{(p, y)\}$, where y is any positive real number in $[0, 1]$, is a y-stable model of p relative to $\{p\}$. On the other hand, $I = \{(p, y)\}$ is not a y-stable model of $F = \neg_s\neg_s p$ relative to $\{p\}$. Formula $F^*(u)$ is $\neg_s\neg_s F$, and although $I \models_y F$, we have $I \cup J_u^p \models_y F^*(u)$ regardless of any J.

Example 4. Let $F_1 = p \rightarrow_s p$ and $F_2 = \neg_s p \oplus_m p$. Their fuzzy models are the same, but their stable models are not. This is similar to the relation between $p \rightarrow p$ and $\neg p \vee p$ in the Boolean stable model semantics. Indeed, observe that $F_1^*(u) = (p \rightarrow_s p) \otimes_m (u \rightarrow_s u)$ and $F_2^*(u) = \neg_s p \oplus_m u$.

The interpretation $I = \{(p, 1)\}$ is not a 1-stable model of F_1 relative to p, as witnessed by $J = \{(p, 0)\}$. However, I is a 1-stable model of F_2 relative to p: for any J,

$$F_2^*(u)^{I \cup J_u^p} = max\left(1 - p^I, p^J\right) = max\left(0, p^J\right) = p^J.$$

So, for $I \cup J_u^p$ to satisfy $F_2^*(u)$ to degree 1, p^J should be 1. Consequently, it is not possible to have $J <^p I$.

The following example illustrates how the commonsense law of inertia involving fuzzy truth values can be represented.

Example 5. Let σ be $\{p, np, q, nq\}$ and let F be $F_1 \otimes_m F_2$, where F_1 represents that p and np are complementary, i.e., the sum of their truth values is 1:

$$F_1 = \neg_s(p \otimes_l np) \otimes_m \neg_s\neg_s(p \oplus_l np).$$

F_2 represents that by default p has the truth value of q, and np has the truth value of nq:

$$F_2 = ((q \otimes_m \neg_s\neg_s p) \rightarrow_r p) \otimes_m ((nq \otimes_m \neg_s\neg_s np) \rightarrow_r np).$$

Let $\mathbf{p} = \{p, np\}$ and $\mathbf{u} = \{u, nu\}$. $F^*(\mathbf{u})$ is

$$\neg_s(p \otimes_l np) \otimes_m \neg_s\neg_s(p \oplus_l np)$$
$$\otimes_m((q \otimes_m \neg_s\neg_s p) \rightarrow_r u) \otimes_m ((q \otimes_m \neg_s\neg_s p) \rightarrow_r p)$$
$$\otimes_m((nq \otimes_m \neg_s\neg_s np) \rightarrow_r nu) \otimes_m ((nq \otimes_m \neg_s\neg_s np) \rightarrow_r np).$$

One can check that interpretation $I_1 = \{(p, x), (np, 1 - x), (q, x), (nq, 1 - x)\}$ (x is any value in $[0, 1]$) is a 1-stable model of F relative to (p, np); interpretation $I_2 = \{(p, y), (np, 1 - y), (q, x), (nq, 1 - x)\}$, where $y \neq x$, is not.

On the other hand, if we conjoin F with $(\overline{y} \rightarrow_r p) \otimes_m (\overline{1 - y} \rightarrow_r np)$, the default behavior is overridden: I_1 is not a 1-stable model of $F \otimes_m (\overline{y} \rightarrow_r p) \otimes_m (\overline{1 - y} \rightarrow_r np)$ relative to (p, np), but I_2 is.

This behavior is useful in expressing the commonsense law of inertia involving fuzzy values. Suppose q represents some fluent at time t, and p represents the fluent at time $t+1$. Then F states that, "by default, the fluent retains the previous value." The default value is overridden if there is an action that sets p to a different value.

Example 6. The trust example in the introduction can be formalized in the fuzzy stable model semantics as follows. Below x, y, z are schematic variables ranging over people, and t is a schematic variable ranging over time steps. $Trust(x, y, t)$ is a fuzzy atom representing that "x trusts y at time t." Similarly, $Distrust(x, y, t)$ is a fuzzy atom representing that "x distrusts y at time t."

The trust relation is reflexive:

$$F_1 = Trust(x, x, t).$$

The trust and distrust degrees are complementary, i.e., their sum is 1 (similar to Example 5):

$$F_2 = \neg_s(Trust(x, y, t) \otimes_l Distrust(x, y, t)),$$
$$F_3 = \neg_s\neg_s(Trust(x, y, t) \oplus_l Distrust(x, y, t)).$$

Initially, if x trusts y to degree d_1 and y trusts z to degree d_2, then x trusts z to degree $d_1 \times d_2$; further the initial distrust degree is 1 minus the initial trust degree.

$$F_4 = Trust(x, y, 0) \otimes_p Trust(y, z, 0) \rightarrow_r Trust(x, z, 0),$$
$$F_5 = \neg_s Trust(x, y, 0) \rightarrow_r Distrust(x, y, 0).$$

The inertia assumption (similar to Example 5):

$$F_6 = Trust(x, y, t) \otimes_m \neg_s\neg_s Trust(x, y, t+1) \rightarrow_r Trust(x, y, t+1),$$
$$F_7 = Distrust(x, y, t) \otimes_m \neg_s\neg_s Distrust(x, y, t+1) \rightarrow_r Distrust(x, y, t+1).$$

A conflict increases the distrust degree by the conflict degree:

$$F_8 = Conflict(x, y, t) \oplus_l Distrust(x, y, t) \rightarrow_r Distrust(x, y, t+1),$$
$$F_9 = \neg_s(Conflict(x, y, t) \oplus_l Distrust(x, y, t)) \rightarrow_r Trust(x, y, t+1).$$

Let F_{TW} be $F_1 \otimes_m F_2 \otimes_m \cdots \otimes_m F_9$. Suppose we have the formula $F_{Fact} = Fact_1 \otimes_m Fact_2$ that gives the initial trust degree.

$$Fact_1 = \overline{0.8} \rightarrow_r Trust(Alice, Bob, 0),$$
$$Fact_2 = \overline{0.7} \rightarrow_r Trust(Bob, Carol, 0).$$

Although there is no fact about how much *Alice* trusts *Carol*, any 1-stable model of $F_{TW} \otimes_m F_{Fact}$ assigns value 0.56 to the atom $Trust(Alice, Carol, 0)$. On the other hand, the 1-stable model assigns value 0 to $Trust(Alice, David, 0)$ due to the closed world assumption under the stable model semantics.

When we conjoin $F_{TW} \otimes F_{Fact}$ with $\overline{0.2} \rightarrow Conflict(Alice, Carol, 0)$, the 1-stable model of $F_{TW} \otimes_m F_{Fact} \otimes_m (\overline{0.2} \rightarrow Conflict(Alice, Carol, 0))$ manifests that the trust degree between *Alice* and *Carol* decreases to 0.36 at time 1. More generally, if we have more actions that change the trust degree in various ways, by specifying the entire history of actions, we can determine the evolution of the trust distribution among all the participants. Useful decisions can be made based on this information. For example, *Alice* may decide not to share her personal pictures to those whom she trusts less than degree 0.48.

Note that this example, like Example 5, uses nested connectives, such as $\neg_s\neg_s$, that are not available in previous fuzzy ASP semantics, such as [2, 3].

4   Relation to Boolean-Valued Stable Models

The Boolean stable model semantics in Section 2.1 can be embedded into the fuzzy stable model semantics as follows:

For any classical propositional formula F, define F^{fuzzy} to be the fuzzy propositional formula obtained from F by replacing $\perp$ with $\overline{0}$, $\top$ with $\overline{1}$, $\neg$ with $\neg_s$, $\wedge$ with $\otimes_m$, $\vee$ with $\oplus_m$, and $\rightarrow$ with $\rightarrow_s$. We identify the signature of F^{fuzzy} with the signature of F. Also, for any interpretation I, we define the corresponding fuzzy interpretation I^{fuzzy} as

- $I^{fuzzy}(p) = 1$ if $I(p) = \text{TRUE}$;
- $I^{fuzzy}(p) = 0$ otherwise.

The following theorem tells us that the Boolean-valued stable model semantics can be viewed as a special case of the fuzzy stable model semantics.

Theorem 1. *For any classical propositional formula F and any classical propositional interpretation I, I is a stable model of F relative to $\mathbf{p}$ iff I^{fuzzy} is a 1-stable model of F^{fuzzy} relative to $\mathbf{p}$.*

Example 7. Let F be the classical propositional formula $\neg p \rightarrow q$. F has only one stable model $I = \{q\}$. Clearly $I^{fuzzy} = \{(p, 0), (q, 1)\}$ is a 1-stable model of $F^{fuzzy} = \neg_s p \rightarrow_s q$.

Theorem 1 does not hold for an arbitrary choice of operators, as illustrated by the following example.

Example 8. Let F be the classical propositional formula $p \vee p$. Classical interpretation $I = \{p\}$ is a stable model of F. However, $I^{fuzzy} = \{(p, 1)\}$ is not a stable model of $F' = p \oplus_l p$ because there is $J = \{(p, 0.5)\}$ such that $I \cup J_q^p \models_1 q \oplus_l q$.

However, one direction of Theorem 1 holds for arbitrary choice of fuzzy operators.

Theorem 2. *For any classical propositional formula F, let F_1^{fuzzy} be the fuzzy formula obtained from F by replacing $\perp$ with $\overline{0}$, $\top$ with $\overline{1}$, $\neg$ with any fuzzy negation symbol, $\wedge$ with any fuzzy conjunction symbol, $\vee$ with any fuzzy disjunction symbol, and $\rightarrow$ with any fuzzy implication symbol. For any classical propositional interpretation I, if I^{fuzzy} is a 1-stable model of F_1^{fuzzy} relative to $\mathbf{p}$, then I is a stable model of F relative to $\mathbf{p}$.*

5   Relation to Other Approaches to Fuzzy ASP

5.1   Relation to Stable Models of Normal FASP Programs

A normal FASP program is a finite set of rules of the form

$$a \leftarrow b_1 \otimes \ldots \otimes b_m \otimes \neg b_{m+1} \otimes \ldots \otimes \neg b_n,$$

where $n \geq m \geq 0$, $a, b_1, \ldots, b_n$ are fuzzy atoms or numeric constants in $[0, 1]$, and $\otimes$ is any fuzzy conjunction. We identify the rule with the fuzzy implication

$$b_1 \otimes \ldots \otimes b_m \otimes \neg_s b_{m+1} \otimes \ldots \otimes \neg_s b_n \rightarrow_r a.$$

We say that a fuzzy interpretation I of signature σ *satisfies* a rule R if $R^I = 1$. I *satisfies* an FASP program Π if I satisfies every rule in Π.

According to [2], an interpretation I is a *fuzzy answer set* of a normal FASP program Π if I satisfies Π, and no interpretation J such that $J <^\sigma I$ satisfies the reduct of Π w.r.t. I, which is the program obtained from Π by replacing each negative literal $\neg b$ with the constant for $1 - b^I$.

Theorem 3. *For any normal FASP program* $\Pi = \{r_1, \ldots, r_n\}$, *let* F *be the fuzzy formula* $r_1 \otimes_m \ldots \otimes_m r_n$. *An interpretation* I *is a fuzzy answer set of* Π *in the sense of* [2] *if and only if* I *is a 1-stable model of* F.

Example 9. Let Π be the following program

$$p \leftarrow \neg q, \quad q \leftarrow \neg p.$$

The answer sets of Π according to [2] are $\{(p, x), (q, 1 - x)\}$, where x is any value in $[0, 1]$: the corresponding fuzzy formula F is $(\neg_s q \rightarrow_r p) \otimes_m (\neg_s p \rightarrow_r q)$; $F^*(u, v)$ is

$$F \otimes_m ((\neg_s q \rightarrow_r u) \otimes_m (\neg_s p \rightarrow_r v)).$$

One can check that the 1-stable models of F are also $\{(p, x), (q, 1 - x)\}$, where $x \in [0, 1]$.

5.2 Relation to Fuzzy Equilibrium Logic

Like the fuzzy stable model semantics introduced in this paper, fuzzy equilibrium logic [12] generalizes fuzzy ASP programs to arbitrary propositional formulas, but its definition is quite complex as it is based on a pair of intervals and considers strong negation as one of the primary connectives. Nonetheless we show that fuzzy equilibrium logic is essentially equivalent to the fuzzy stable model semantics where the threshold is restricted to 1 and all atoms are subject to minimization.

Review: Fuzzy Equilibrium Logic. We first review the definition of fuzzy equilibrium logic from [12]. The syntax is the same as the one we reviewed in Section 2.2 except that a new connective $\sim$ (strong negation) may appear in front of atoms.[5] For any fuzzy propositional signature σ, a (fuzzy N5) *valuation* is a mapping from $\{h, t\} \times \sigma$ to subintervals of $[0, 1]$ such that $V(t, a) \subseteq V(h, a)$ for each atom $a \in \sigma$. For $V(w, a) = [u, v]$, where $w \in \{h, t\}$, we write $V^-(w, a)$ to denote the lower bound u and $V^+(w, a)$ to denote the upper bound v. The *truth value* of a fuzzy formula under V is defined as follows.

- $V(w, \overline{c}) = [c, c]$ for any numeric constant $\overline{c}$;
- $V(w, \sim a) = [1 - V^+(w, a), 1 - V^-(w, a)]$, where $\sim$ is the symbol for strong negation;
- $V(w, F \otimes G) = [V^-(w, F) \otimes V^-(w, G), \ V^+(w, F) \otimes V^+(w, G)]$;[6]

---

[5] The definition from [12] allows strong negation in front of any formulas. We restrict its occurrence only in front of atoms as usual in answer set programs.

[6] For readability, we write the infix notation $(x \odot y)$ in place of $\odot(x, y)$.

- $V(w, F \oplus G) = [V^-(w, F) \oplus V^-(w, G), \ V^+(w, F) \oplus V^+(w, G)]$;
- $V(h, \neg F) = [1 - V^-(t, F), \ 1 - V^-(h, F)]$;
- $V(t, \neg F) = [1 - V^-(t, F), \ 1 - V^-(t, F)]$;
- $V(h, F \rightarrow G) = [min(V^-(h, F) \rightarrow V^-(h, G), V^-(t, F) \rightarrow V^-(t, G)),$
$$V^-(h, F) \rightarrow V^+(h, G)];$$
- $V(t, F \rightarrow G) = [V^-(t, F) \rightarrow V^-(t, G), \ V^-(t, F) \rightarrow V^+(t, G)]$.

A valuation V is a (fuzzy N5) model of a formula F if $V^-(h, F) = 1$, which implies $V^+(h, F) = V^-(t, F) = V^+(t, F) = 1$. For two valuations V and V', we say $V' \preceq V$ if $V'(t, a) = V(t, a)$ and $V(h, a) \subseteq V'(h, a)$ for all atoms a. We say $V' \prec V$ if $V' \preceq V$ and $V' \neq V$. We say that a model V of F is h-*minimal* if there is no model V' of F such that $V' \prec V$. An h-minimal fuzzy N5 model V of F is a *fuzzy equilibrium model* of F if $V(h, a) = V(t, a)$ for all atoms a.

In the Absence of Strong Negation. We first establish the correspondence between fuzzy stable models and fuzzy equilibrium models in the absence of strong negation. As in [12], we assume that the fuzzy negation $\neg$ is $\neg_s$.

For any valuation V, we define a fuzzy interpretation I_V as $p^{I_V} = V^-(h, p)$ for each atom $p \in \sigma$.

Theorem 4. *Let F be a fuzzy propositional formula of σ that contains no strong negation.*

(a) *A valuation V of σ is a fuzzy equilibrium model of F iff $V^-(h, p) = V^-(t, p)$, $V^+(h, p) = V^+(t, p) = 1$ for all atoms p in σ and I_V is a 1-stable model of F relative to σ.*
(b) *An interpretation I of σ is a 1-stable model of F relative to σ iff $I = I_V$ for some fuzzy equilibrium model V of F.*

In the Presence of Strong Negation. In this section we extend the relationship between fuzzy equilibrium logic and our stable model semantics by allowing strong negation. This is done by simulating strong negation by new atoms in our semantics.

Let σ denote the signature. For a fuzzy formula F over σ that may contain strong negation, define F' over $\sigma \cup \{np \mid p \in \sigma\}$ as the formula obtained from F by replacing all strong negations of atom $\sim p$ with a new atom np. The transformation $nneg(F)$ ("no strong negation") is defined as $nneg(F) = F' \otimes_m \bigotimes_{m \atop p \in \sigma} \neg_s(p \otimes_l np)$.

For any valuation V of σ, we define the interpretation I_V of $\sigma \cup \{np \mid p \in \sigma\}$ as

$$\begin{cases} p^{I_V} = V^-(h, p) & \text{for each } p \in \sigma \text{ ;} \\ np^{I_V} = 1 - V^+(h, p) & \text{for each } np \notin \sigma \text{ .} \end{cases}$$

Theorem 5. *For any fuzzy formula F of signature σ that may contain strong negation,*

(a) *A valuation V of σ is a fuzzy equilibrium model of F iff $V(h, p) = V(t, p)$ for all atoms p in σ and I_V is a 1-stable model of $nneg(F)$ relative to $\sigma \cup \{np \mid p \in \sigma\}$.*
(b) *An interpretation I of $\sigma \cup \{np \mid p \in \sigma\}$ is a 1-stable model of $nneg(F)$ relative to $\sigma \cup \{np \mid p \in \sigma\}$ iff $I = I_V$ for some fuzzy equilibrium model V of F.*

Example 10. For fuzzy formula $F = (\overline{0.2} \to_r p) \otimes_m (\overline{0.3} \to_r np)$, formula $nneg(F)$ is

$$(\overline{0.2} \to_r p) \otimes_m (\overline{0.3} \to_r np) \otimes_m \neg_s(p \otimes_l np).$$

One can check that the valuation V defined as $V(w,p) = [0.2, 0.7]$ is the only equilibrium model of F, and the interpretation $I_V = \{(p, 0.2), (np, 0.3)\}$ is the only 1-stable model of $nneg(F)$.

This idea of eliminating strong negation in favor of new atoms was used in Example 5 and 6.

6   Properties of Fuzzy Stable Models

In this section, we show that several well-known properties of the Boolean stable model semantics can be naturally extended to the fuzzy stable model semantics.

6.1   Alternative Definition of F^*

Proposition 1. *For any fuzzy formulas F, G and any fuzzy interpretations I, J such that $J \leq^{\mathbf{P}} I$,*

- $I \cup J_{\mathbf{q}}^{\mathbf{P}} \models_y \neg F^*(\mathbf{q}) \otimes_m \neg F$ *iff* $I \cup J_{\mathbf{q}}^{\mathbf{P}} \models_y \neg F$.
- $I \cup J_{\mathbf{q}}^{\mathbf{P}} \models_y (F^* \otimes G^*)(\mathbf{q}) \otimes_m (F \otimes G)$ *iff* $I \cup J_{\mathbf{q}}^{\mathbf{P}} \models_y (F^* \otimes G^*)(\mathbf{q})$.
- $I \cup J_{\mathbf{q}}^{\mathbf{P}} \models_y (F^* \oplus G^*)(\mathbf{q}) \otimes_m (F \oplus G)$ *iff* $I \cup J_{\mathbf{q}}^{\mathbf{P}} \models_y (F^* \oplus G^*)(\mathbf{q})$.

This proposition tells us that F^* in Section 3 can be equivalently defined by treating the fuzzy operators in the uniform way without affecting stable models.

- $(\neg F)^* = \neg F^* \otimes_m \neg F$;
- $(F \odot G)^* = (F^* \odot G^*) \otimes_m (F \odot G)$ for any binary operator $\odot$.

6.2   Theorem on Constraints

In answer set programming, constraints—rules with $\bot$ in the head—play an important role in view of the fact that adding a constraint eliminates the stable models that "violate" the constraint. The following theorem is the counterpart of Theorem 3 from [10] for fuzzy propositional formulas.

Theorem 6. *For any fuzzy formulas F and G, I is a 1-stable model of $F \otimes \neg G$ (relative to $\mathbf{p}$) if and only if I is a 1-stable model of F (relative to $\mathbf{p}$) and $I \models_1 \neg G$.*

Example 11. Consider $F = (\neg_s p \to_r q) \otimes_m (\neg_s q \to_r p) \otimes_m \neg_s p$. Formula F has only one 1-stable model $I = \{(p, 0), (q, 1)\}$, which is the only 1-stable model of $(\neg_s p \to_r q) \otimes_m (\neg_s q \to_r p)$ that satisfies $\neg_s p$ to degree 1.

If we consider a more general y-stable model, then only one direction holds.

Theorem 7. *For any fuzzy formulas F and G, if I is a y-stable model of $F \otimes \neg G$ (relative to $\mathbf{p}$), then I is a y-stable model of F (relative to $\mathbf{p}$) and $I \models_y \neg G$.*

Example 12. The other direction, that is, "if I is a y-stable model of F and $I \models_y \neg G$, then I is a y-stable model of $F \otimes \neg G$," does not hold in general. For example, consider $F = G = p$ and $\otimes$ to be $\otimes_l$, and interpretation $I = \{(p, 0.4)\}$. Clearly I is a 0.4-stable model of p and $I \models_{0.4} \neg p$, but I is not a 0.4-stable model of $p \otimes_l \neg p$. In fact, I is not even a 0.4-model of the formula.

6.3   Theorem on Choice Formulas

In the Boolean stable model semantics, formulas of the form $p \vee \neg p$ are called *choice formulas*, and adding them to the program makes atoms p exempt from minimization. Choice formulas have been shown to be useful in composing a program in the "Generate-and-Test" method. This section shows their counterpart in the fuzzy stable model semantics.

For any fuzzy atom p, *Choice*(p) stands for $p \oplus_l \neg_s p$. For any list $\mathbf{p} = (p_1, \ldots p_n)$ of fuzzy atoms, *Choice*$(\mathbf{p})$ stands for *Choice*$(p_1) \otimes \ldots \otimes$ *Choice*(p_n), where $\otimes$ is any fuzzy conjunction.

The following proposition tells that choice formulas are tautological.

Proposition 2. *For any fuzzy interpretation I and any list $\mathbf{p}$ of fuzzy atoms, $I \models_1$ Choice$(\mathbf{p})$.*

Theorem 8 is an extension of Theorem 2 from [10].

Theorem 8. *(a) If I is a y-stable model of F relative to $\mathbf{p} \cup \mathbf{q}$, then I is a y-stable model of F relative to $\mathbf{p}$.*
(b) I is a 1-stable model of F relative to $\mathbf{p}$ iff I is a 1-stable model of $F \otimes$ Choice$(\mathbf{q})$ relative to $\mathbf{p} \cup \mathbf{q}$.

Theorem 8 (b) does not hold for arbitrary threshold y (i.e., if "$1-$" is replaced with "$y-$"). For example, consider $F = \neg_s \neg_s q$ and $I = \{(q, 0.5)\}$. Clearly I is a 0.5-model of F, and thus I is a 0.5-stable model of F relative to $\emptyset$. However, I is not a 0.5-stable model of $F \otimes_m$ *Choice*$(q) = \neg_s \neg_s q \otimes_m (q \oplus_l \neg_s q)$ relative to $\emptyset \cup \{q\}$, as witnessed by $J = \{(q, 0)\}$.

Since the 1-stable models of F relative to $\emptyset$ are the models of F, it follows from Theorem 8 (b) that the 1-*stable models* of $F \otimes$ *Choice*(σ) relative to σ are exactly the 1-*models* of F.

Corollary 1. *Let F be a fuzzy formula of a finite signature σ. I is a 1-model of F iff I is a 1-stable model of $F \otimes$ Choice(σ) relative to σ.*

Example 13. Consider the fuzzy formula $F = \neg_s p \rightarrow_r q$. Although any interpretation I that satisfies $1 - p^I \leq q^I$ is a 1-model of F, among them only $\{(p, 0), (q, 1)\}$ is a 1-stable model of F. However, we check that all 1-models of F are exactly the 1-stable models of $G = F \otimes_m$ *Choice*$(p) \otimes_m$ *Choice*(q): $G^*(u, v)$ is

$$(\neg_s p \rightarrow_r q) \otimes_m (\neg_s p \rightarrow_r v) \otimes_m (u \oplus_l \neg_s p) \otimes_m (v \oplus_l \neg_s q)$$

and for $K = I \cup J_{uv}^{pq}$,

$$G^*(u, v)^K = 1 \otimes_m ((1 - p^K) \rightarrow_r v^K) \otimes_m (u^K \oplus_l (1 - p^K)) \otimes_m (v^K \oplus_l (1 - q^K)).$$

So, for K to satisfy $G^*(u, v)$ to degree 1, u^K should be at least p^K and v^K should be at least q^K. So there does not exist $J <^{pq} I$ such that $I \cup J_{uv}^{pq} \models_1 G^*(u, v)$, from which it follows that I is a 1-stable model of G.

7   Other Related Work

Several approaches to incorporating fuzziness into the answer set programming framework have been proposed. In this paper, we have formally compared our approach to [12] and [2]. Most of them consider the specific syntax where each formula is of the rule form $h \leftarrow B$ where h is an atom and B is a formula [4–7]. Among them, [4–6] allow B to be any arbitrary formula corresponding to an increasing function whose arguments are the atoms appearing in the formula. [7] allows B to correspond to either an increasing function or a decreasing function. [9] considers the normal program syntax, i.e., each rule is of the form $l_0 \leftarrow l_1 \otimes \ldots \otimes l_m \otimes not\ l_{m+1} \otimes \ldots \otimes not\ l_n$, where each l_i is an atom or the strong negation of an atom. In terms of semantics, most of the previous works rely on the notion of immediate consequence operator and relate the fixpoint of this operator to the minimal model of a positive program[7]. Similar to the approach [2] has adopted, the answer set of a positive program is defined as its minimal model, while an answer set of a non-positive program is defined in terms of the minimal model of the reduct, which is a positive program obtained based on the normal program and the specific interpretation being checked. [8] has proposed a semantics based on the notion of unfounded set.

It is worth noting that some of the related works have discussed the so-called residuated programs [4–6, 9], where each rule $h \leftarrow B$ is assigned a weight θ, and a rule is satisfied by an interpretation I if $I(h \leftarrow B) \geq \theta$. According to [5], this class of programs is able to capture many other logic programming paradigms, such as possibilistic logic programming, hybrid probabilistic logic programming, generalized annotated logic programming. Furthermore, as shown in [5], a weighted rule $(h \leftarrow B, \theta)$ can be simulated by $h \leftarrow B \otimes \theta$, where $(\otimes, \leftarrow)$ forms an adjoint pair.

It is well known in the Boolean stable model semantics that strong negation can be represented in terms of new atoms [10]. Our adaptation in the fuzzy stable model semantics is similar to the method from [9], in which the consistency of an interpretation is guaranteed by imposing the extra restriction $I(\sim p) \leq \sim I(p)$ for all atom p. Strong negation and consistency have also been studied in [13, 14].

8   Conclusion

We introduced a stable model semantics for fuzzy propositional formulas, which generalizes both the Boolean stable model semantics and fuzzy propositional logic. The syntax is the same as the syntax of fuzzy propositional logic, but the semantics defines *stable models* instead of *models*. The formalism allows highly configurable default reasoning involving fuzzy truth values. Our semantics, when we restrict threshold to be 1 and assume all atoms to be subject to minimization, is essentially equivalent to fuzzy equilibrium logic, but is much simpler. To the best of our knowledge, our representation of the commonsense law of inertia involving fuzzy values is new. The representation uses nested fuzzy operators, which are not available in other fuzzy ASP semantics for a restricted syntax.

---

[7] We call a program positive if it does not contain any default negation.

We showed that several traditional results in answer set programming can be naturally extended to this formalism, and expect that more results can be carried over. Future work includes implementing this language using mixed integer programming solvers or bilevel programming solvers [15].

Acknowledgements. We are grateful to Joseph Babb, Michael Bartholomew, Enrico Marchioni, and the anonymous referees for their useful comments and discussions related to this paper. This work was partially supported by the National Science Foundation under Grant IIS-1319794 and by the South Korea IT R&D program MKE/KIAT 2010-TD-300404-001.

References

1. Lifschitz, V.: What is answer set programming? In: Proceedings of the AAAI Conference on Artificial Intelligence, pp. 1594–1597. MIT Press (2008)
2. Lukasiewicz, T.: Fuzzy description logic programs under the answer set semantics for the semantic web. In: Eiter, T., Franconi, E., Hodgson, R., Stephens, S. (eds.) RuleML, pp. 89–96. IEEE Computer Society (2006)
3. Janssen, J., Vermeir, D., Schockaert, S., Cock, M.D.: Reducing fuzzy answer set programming to model finding in fuzzy logics. TPLP 12(6), 811–842 (2012)
4. Vojtás, P.: Fuzzy logic programming. Fuzzy Sets and Systems 124(3), 361–370 (2001)
5. Viegas Damásio, C., Moniz Pereira, L.: Monotonic and residuated logic programs. In: Benferhat, S., Besnard, P. (eds.) ECSQARU 2001. LNCS (LNAI), vol. 2143, pp. 748–759. Springer, Heidelberg (2001)
6. Medina, J., Ojeda-Aciego, M., Vojtáš, P.: Multi-adjoint logic programming with continuous semantics. In: Eiter, T., Faber, W., Truszczyński, M. (eds.) LPNMR 2001. LNCS (LNAI), vol. 2173, pp. 351–364. Springer, Heidelberg (2001)
7. Viegas Damásio, C., Moniz Pereira, L.: Antitonic logic programs. In: Eiter, T., Faber, W., Truszczyński, M. (eds.) LPNMR 2001. LNCS (LNAI), vol. 2173, pp. 379–392. Springer, Heidelberg (2001)
8. Nieuwenborgh, D.V., Cock, M.D., Vermeir, D.: An introduction to fuzzy answer set programming. Ann. Math. Artif. Intell. 50(3-4), 363–388 (2007)
9. Madrid, N., Ojeda-Aciego, M.: Towards a fuzzy answer set semantics for residuated logic programs. In: Web Intelligence/IAT Workshops, pp. 260–264. IEEE (2008)
10. Ferraris, P., Lee, J., Lifschitz, V.: Stable models and circumscription. Artificial Intelligence 175, 236–263 (2011)
11. Hajek, P.: Mathematics of Fuzzy Logic. Kluwer (1998)
12. Schockaert, S., Janssen, J., Vermeir, D.: Fuzzy equilibrium logic: Declarative problem solving in continuous domains. ACM Trans. Comput. Log. 13(4), 33 (2012)
13. Madrid, N., Ojeda-Aciego, M.: Measuring inconsistency in fuzzy answer set semantics. IEEE T. Fuzzy Systems 19(4), 605–622 (2011)
14. Madrid, N., Ojeda-Aciego, M.: On coherence and consistence in fuzzy answer set semantics for residuated logic programs. In: Di Gesù, V., Pal, S.K., Petrosino, A. (eds.) WILF 2009. LNCS, vol. 5571, pp. 60–67. Springer, Heidelberg (2009)
15. Alviano, M., Peñaloza, R.: Fuzzy answer sets approximations. TPLP 13(4-5), 753–767 (2013)

A Free Logic for Stable Models with Partial Intensional Functions*

Pedro Cabalar[1], Luis Fariñas del Cerro[2], David Pearce[3], and Agustin Valverde[4]

[1] Department of Computer Science
University of Corunna, Spain
cabalar@udc.es
[2] University of Toulouse IRIT, CNRS, France
farinas@irit.fr
[3] Universidad Politécnica de Madrid, Spain
david.pearce@upm.es
[4] Universidad de Málaga, Spain
a_valverde@ctima.uma.es

Abstract. In this paper we provide a new logical characterisation of stable models with partial functions that consists in a free-logic extension of Quantified Equilibrium Logic (QEL). In so-called "free" logics, terms may denote objects that are outside the domain of quantification, something that can be immediately used to capture partial functions. We show that this feature can be naturally accommodated in the monotonic basis of QEL (the logic of Quantified Here-and-There, QHT) by allowing variable quantification domains that depend on the world where the formula is being interpreted. The paper provides two main contributions: (i) a correspondence with Cabalar's semantics for stable models with partial functions; and (ii) a Gentzen system for free QHT, the monotonic basis of free QEL.

1 Introduction: Functions in ASP

Answer Set Programming (ASP) [21,22,5] constitutes nowadays one of the most popular paradigms for practical Knowledge Representation (KR) and problem solving, being regularly present in mainstream conferences on KR and Artificial Intelligence (AI). This popularity can be attributed not only to its practical applicability, with available state-of-the-art solvers[1] and an increasing number of applications, but also to its robust formal basis, relying on the *stable model* semantics for logic programs [15]. Although stable models were originally defined for propositional logic programs, their logical characterisation in terms of *Equilibrium Logic* [23] paved the way for their extension to more general syntactic classes. In particular, the first-order extension of this logic, *Quantified*

---

* This research was partially supported by: European French-Spanish Lab IREP; MEC project TIN2012-39353-C04; Junta de Andalucía project TIC115; Xunta de Galicia, Spain, grant GPC2013/070; and Universidad de Málaga, Campus de Excelencia Internacional Andalucía Tech.

[1] See, for instance the report from the fourth ASP Competition [1].

E. Fermé and J. Leite (Eds.): JELIA 2014, LNAI 8761, pp. 340–354, 2014.

Equilibrium Logic (QEL) [24], allows the definition of stable models for any arbitrary first-order theory [13] and became a powerful theoretical tool for analysing fundamental properties such as strong equivalence [19], safety [9], interpolation [14] or synonymy [25], being in this way a salient, successful case of Logics in AI.

The extension of stable models to an arbitrary first-order syntax has brought into focus a feature traditionally excluded from ASP: the treatment of functions. Although most ASP solvers are propositional, their input language allows the use of variables that, in an initial *grounding* phase, are replaced by their possible ground instantiations, under the assumption (inherited from logic programming) of an Herbrand domain. Due to grounding limitations, ASP has traditionally forbidden the use of functions because the simple introduction of one function symbol makes the Herbrand universe infinite. This distinctive difference between ASP and Prolog has been overcome with `DLV-complex` [11], a tool that allows the grounding of ASP programs with arbitrarily nested Herbrand functions that satisfy a given property of being *finitely-ground* [10] (although checking that property is undecidable).

Apart from Herbrand functions, a less explored possibility that has recently attracted attention is the use of *evaluable* functions in ASP. While an Herbrand function is expected to act as a *syntactic constructor* for defining objects in the universe, such as a tuple or a list, an evaluable function is expected to behave with its usual mathematical meaning, that is, as an *operator*[2] that returns a value, as, for instance, the standard arithmetic operations for integer numbers. Dealing with evaluable functions may have two main advantages. First, from the KR perspective, the use of nested functions usually allows a more compact and natural reading, avoiding the introduction of auxiliary variables that may become a potential source of error. To give an example, saying that X is a patrilineal great grandfather of Y could be naturally represented as $X = father(father(father(Y)))$ whereas in predicate notation, we would need a rule body of the form $father(Y, Z), father(Z, T), father(T, X)$ whose meaning is not so easily recognisable at a first sight, apart from requiring two extra auxiliary variables. Second, evaluable functions can be computationally exploited both at the grounding phase, reducing the ground program size, and at the solving phase, avoiding an overload of constraints.

An immediate interpretation for evaluable functions in ASP was already provided by QEL, since this logic was not necessarily restricted to Herbrand functions. As shown in [20], QEL semantics for evaluable functions[3] can be exploited for a more efficient grounding on scenarios with functional dependences, if we replace propositional ASP solvers by a CSP tool as a backend. Unfortunately, the other potential advantage of using functions, namely, their adequacy for a flexible KR, is not achieved by this approach. In particular, functions in QEL are somehow asymmetrical with respect to predicates, since they do not allow

---

[2] This distinction between constructors and operators is, in fact, part of the motivation from the area of *Functional Logic Programming* [16].

[3] Although Lin and Wang's approach was independently established, its correspondence to QEL was proven in [7].

non-monotonic reasoning (NMR). A reasonable requirement for a functional semantics is that replacing all predicates by Boolean functions should have no particular effect on the results excepting the minor changes in notation – each atom $p(X)$ would be replaced by the expression $p(X) = true$. However, predicates in ASP are *intensional*: we can just provide the rules for which they hold, assuming that anything else is false. Furthermore, thanks to default negation, we can further specify default rules for a predicate that are applied in the absence of exceptions. As an example, a graph can be described by merely asserting a fact $edge(i, j)$ for each edge, while remaining atoms for that predicate will be false by default. Moreover, we can inductively define a reachability predicate with the pair of rules:

$$reach(X, Y) \leftarrow edge(X, Y) \qquad reach(X, Y) \leftarrow edge(X, Z), reach(Z, Y)$$

something that is well-known to be non-representable in classical first-order logic. Unfortunately, under QEL semantics, functions behave "classically" and *there is no way of defining a function default value* without resorting to predicate-based representations. In our example, if we replace predicates *edge* and *reach* by Boolean functions, the stable models we obtain correspond to the *classical* models of the original predicate-based theory.

1.1 Approaches to Intensional Functions

Although the idea of default values for functions is not new [8], Lifschitz suggested the name *intensional functions* [18] to refer to evaluable functions that allow NMR features analogous to those obtained with intensional predicates. There currently exist two different ways of understanding intensional functions. On the one hand, Bartholomew and Lee introduced a variant [3] (we will call BL semantics) that repairs some counterintuitive features of Lifschitz's approach. Like the latter, BL semantics exclusively deals with total functions defining their "stability" in terms of value *uniqueness* among values stemming from possible models. On the other hand, a previous definition[4] by Cabalar [7] considers instead a minimal-information criterion for partial functions. To understand the difference, take the example formula:

$$father(abel) = adam \tag{1}$$

assuming *abel* and *adam* are Herbrand-constants. Under Cabalar's semantics this formula has a unique stable model where *abel*'s father is *adam* and *adam*'s father, in turn, is left *undefined by default*. Notice how this interpretation is aligned to the idea of minimal information from predicate-based representations. If we just had a predicate fact $father(abel, adam)$ the unique stable model would satisfy $\neg \exists x \, father(adam, x)$ underlining that *adam*'s father is undefined. In this sense, Cabalar's semantics can be seen as a "conversion" of predicate-based ASP into

---

[4] As shown in [4], the recent approach by Balduccini [2] for logic programs with partial functions is actually equivalent to Cabalar's semantics.

functional notation whose main advantage is nesting functions: for instance, we can conclude that Abel's grandfather $father(father(abel)) = father(adam)$ is also undefined.

Under BL semantics, however, (1) has no stable models since the value of $father(adam)$ is not uniquely defined – in principle, with those two persons in the domain, the possibilities are $father(adam) = abel$ or $father(adam) = adam$ himself. In this way, the intuition behind BL intensional functions is clearly different from predicate-based ASP and relies on an idea of selecting a function value when there is *no other way* to vary that value. This idea was captured in [4] and [12] defining in the latter a *flexible* extension of QEL together with a Gentzen calculus for the "flexible" version of its monotonic basis, the so-called logic of *Quantified Here-and-There* (QHT).

Apart from their different understandings for functions, one important difference in the behaviour of BL and Cabalar's semantics has to do with the treatment of nested functions. In particular, Cabalar's semantics satisfies:

$$\varphi(f(x)) \equiv \exists y \ (f(x) = y \land \varphi(y)) \tag{2}$$

for any term $f(x)$ occurring in formula φ, where x is free in φ and y is not free in φ. As a result, nested functions can be safely "unfolded" until all atoms involving functions eventually have the form $f(t) = t'$ where t and t' are function-free terms. This syntactic form is called *c-plain* in [4] and there it was shown that both BL and Cabalar's semantics coincide for this form of theory, under the assumption of total functions.[5] Unfortunately, the unfolding transformation (2) is not safe in BL semantics and the question whether any theory can be equivalently reduced to c-plain form under BL is still unanswered.

1.2 Contribution of the Paper

Although, as explained above, Cabalar's semantics seems a promising alternative for interpreting intensional functions, there was no axiomatisation for this logic yet, and so its properties could only be proved at a semantic level. In this paper, we consider an equivalent reformulation of Cabalar's semantics in terms of a *free-logic* extension of Quantified Equilibrium Logic (QEL). The term "free" logic refers to a family of formalisms where syntactic terms may denote objects that are outside the domain of quantification, something that can be used to capture partial functions.[6] We show that this feature can be naturally accommodated in the monotonic basis of QEL (the logic of Quantified Here-and-There, QHT)

---

[5] In fact, as explained in [4], the difference total/partial between the two semantics is not essential. In Cabalar's semantics, any function can always be forced to be total by adding an axiom $\neg\neg\exists y \ f(x) = y$. In BL semantics, we can always define a special constant *none* to represent the fact that the function has no value. A comparison like *none* = *none* would become true, but under c-plain syntax, such comparisons never occur.

[6] A useful reference is [26] that presents various approaches to free logic over intuitionistic logic.

by allowing variable quantification domains that depend on the world where the formula is being interpreted. Apart from capturing Cabalar's semantics, this free-logic characterisation also opens new possibilities for interpreting partial intensional functions that will be explored in the future.

The main contributions of the paper are as follows. First, in Section 2 we describe the free quantified logic of here-and-there, **FHT**, the monotonic basis of free QEL. In Section 3 we then show that **FHT**-models are equivalent to the semantics of Cabalar's partial functions. And in Section 4 we present a Gentzen calculus for **FHT** with corresponding completeness theorems.

2   The Free (Quantified) Here-and-There logic

We consider a first-order language with signature $\Sigma = \langle C, F, P \cup \{=\}\rangle$, where C is the set of constants (or 0-ary functions), F is the set of function symbols and P is the set of predicate symbols. We assume that each predicate $p \in P$ has an associated *arity*, an integer denoting the number of arguments $arity(p) \geq 0$. Similarly, each function $f \in F$ is associated with an $arity(f) > 0$.

First-order formulas are built up in the usual way, with the same syntax of classical predicate calculus with equality $=$. Formally, we assume a countably infinite set of variables, the constant $\perp$, the connectives, '$\vee$', '$\wedge$', '$\rightarrow$', '$\exists$', '$\forall$' and auxiliary parentheses. Negation is defined by $\neg\varphi \overset{\text{def}}{=} \varphi \rightarrow \perp$ and double implication is denoted by $\varphi \leftrightarrow \psi \overset{\text{def}}{=} (\varphi \rightarrow \psi) \wedge (\psi \rightarrow \varphi)$. We use letters x, y, z and their capital versions to denote variables, τ to denote terms, c to denote constants and d objects in the domain. Overlined letters like $\overline{x}, \overline{\tau}, \overline{c}, \overline{d}, \dots$ represent tuples (in this case of variables, terms, constants, and objects respectively). An atom like $\tau = \tau'$ is called an *equality atom*, whereas an atom like $p(\tau_1, \dots, \tau_n)$ with $n \geq 0$ for any predicate p different from equality is called a*predicate atom*. We denote by $At(C, F, P)$, or At for short, the set of ground predicate atoms over the language. We also write $Terms(C, F)$ to stand for the set of ground terms formed with constants in C and functions in F.

We will be exclusively interested in closed formulas or sentences, that is, those where each variable is bound by some quantifier. For the sake of readability, however, we will sometimes allow free variables, but as an abbreviation for their universal quantification. A set of sentences is called a *theory*.

Kripke semantics for intermediate logics relies on the idea of possible worlds with an accessibility relation $\leq$ among them that, at least, satisfies reflexivity and transitivity. The simplest case of intermediate logic strictly below classical logic is known as the Logic of Here-and-There (**HT**) [17] where only two worlds are considered, h ("here") and t ("there"), so that $h \leq t$. Apart from being reflexive and transitive, the relation $\leq$ in intermediate logics must also satisfy an important property called *persistence* or *inheritance* so that any accessible world $w' \geq w$ must have at least as much information (true assertions) as the current one w. In the propositional case, this implies that the true atoms in w are a subset of those in w'. In the first-order case, this is naturally extrapolated so that the extent of any predicate $p(\overline{x})$ in w is a subset of its extent in w'. For instance, in

HT we could have $\{p(0), p(1)\}$ true in world h and $\{p(0), p(1), p(2), p(3)\}$ true in world t. When thinking of logic programs, it is somehow natural that all worlds share a common domain, normally the Herbrand Universe, that in our example would correspond to $\{0, 1, 2, 3\}$. When this happens, we say that the intermediate logic has a *static domain*. This was, in fact, the choice taken in the original definition of Quantified Here-and-There with Static domains [24], or **SQHT** for short, where worlds h and t shared the same universe. In a more general setting, however, each world w could have its own domain D_w provided that, for any accessible world $w' \geq w$, we guarantee that the domain has at least as many objects as in w, that is, $D_w \subseteq D_{w'}$. In our example a possible situation could be, for instance, $D_h = \{0, 1, 2\}$ and $D_t = \{0, 1, 2, 3\}$. This immediately introduces a way of representing the idea of *undefined elements*: for instance, 3 is undefined in world h but becomes defined in world t whereas 4 is undefined in both worlds. Using non-static domains has immediate consequences for quantification and functional terms, since there may exist elements that cannot be denoted in the current world, but that become denotable in an accessible world instead. To be more precise, we use the Meinongiam approach for free semantics in intuitionistic logic [6,26], in which an outer domain $D \supseteq D_t$ is considered. This is exactly the semantic structure we introduce next for defining the *Free logic of Quantified Here-and-There*, or **FHT** for short.

Given a function σ and a tuple of terms $\overline{\tau} = \tau_1, \ldots, \tau_n$ we write $\sigma(\overline{\tau})$ to stand for the tuple $\sigma(\tau_1), \ldots, \sigma(\tau_n)$.

Definition 1 (FHT-interpretation). *An **FHT**-interpretation M, is a tuple $M - \langle D_h, D_t, D, \equiv, I, \sigma \rangle$ verifying the following conditions.*

(F1) $D_h \subseteq D_t \subseteq D$ *are a triple of increasing domains.*
(F2) $\equiv$ *is an equivalence relation on D_t, such that:*
    (a) *There is no pair of elements $d \neq d'$ from D_h such that $d \equiv d'$;*
    (b) *For all $d \in D_t$, there exists $d' \in D_h$ such that $d \equiv d'$.*

$\sigma \colon \mathrm{Terms}(C \cup D, F) \to D$, *the interpretation for terms, is a mapping recursively defined and verifying:*

(F3) $\sigma(d) = d$ *if $d \in D$.*
(F4) *For any world $w \in \{h, t\}$, if $\sigma(\tau) \in D_w$ then $\sigma(\tau') \in D_w$ for each subterm τ' of τ.*
(F5) *If $d_i \equiv d_i'$ for every i, then $\sigma(f(d_1, \ldots, d_n)) \equiv \sigma(f(d_1', \ldots, d_n'))$.*

I is an interpretation for predicates that assigns to each predicate p with arity n at each world $w \in \{h, t\}$ a set of tuples of elements $I(p, w)$ following the rules:

(F6) $I(p, w) \subseteq D_w^n$
(F7) *if $d, d' \in D_t$, $d \equiv d'$, and $(\ldots, d, \ldots) \in I(p, t)$, then $(\ldots, d', \ldots) \in I(p, t)$*
(F8) $I(p, h) \subseteq I(p, t)$. $\square$

Condition (F1) is standard for dynamic domains in intermediate logics – as we explained before, they must contain an increasing set of elements to satisfy the inheritance condition. Condition (F2) is necessary for capturing Cabalar's treatment of the equality predicate. While in the h world, an equality atom $\tau_1 = \tau_2$ will just be interpreted by checking whether $\sigma(\tau_1)$ and $\sigma(\tau_2)$ coincide, in the t world we will use instead a separate equivalence relation '$\equiv$' among elements in D_t. In this way, two different elements $d \neq d'$ can be equivalent $d \equiv d'$ and so, they can be interpreted as "equal" in the t world. Given some $d \in D_t$, we write $[d]$ to represent its $\equiv$-equivalence class. However, (F2) specifies two strong restrictions: (a) says that if these two different elements $d \neq d'$ are in D_h they cannot become equivalent in D_t. Intuitively, this will mean that if we have two *defined* terms in h with a different value, they must remain defined and different (equality is false) in world t. On the other hand, (b) means that all the elements we use in $D_t \setminus D_h$ must have some "purpose" with respect to D_h. More formally, any $d \in D_t \setminus D_h$ must be equivalent to some element in $D_h \subseteq D_t$. This restriction allows us to capture an important condition in Cabalar's semantics: *if a function is defined in world h, its value is maintained in world t.* We will see an example of this, once the satisfaction of formulas is defined. Since the $\equiv$ relation must behave as a kind of equality, it must additionally satisfy (F5) and (F7), so that replacement of equivalent terms preserves function values and truth for predicates. Conditions (F4) and (F6) mean that evaluation of predicates and terms at world w is "fixed" to elements in that world w, even through subterms. Notice that the expanded language includes a constant for each object in D and that (F3) evaluates any object constant to itself; for simplicity we do not make a notational difference between the domain element and its name. (F8) is the usual condition of persistence for predicate atoms from here to there.

We define when a **FHT**-interpretation $M = \langle D_h, D_t, D, \equiv, I, \sigma \rangle$ *satisfies* a formula φ at world $w \in \{h, t\}$, written $M, w \models \varphi$, recursively as follows:

- $M, w \not\models \bot$
- $M, w \models p(\overline{\tau})$ iff $\sigma(\overline{\tau}) \in I(p, w)$.
- $M, h \models \tau_1 = \tau_2$ iff $\sigma(\tau_1) = \sigma(\tau_2) \in D_h$.
- $M, t \models \tau_1 = \tau_2$ iff $\sigma(\tau_1), \sigma(\tau_2) \in D_t$ and $\sigma(\tau_1) \equiv \sigma(\tau_2)$.
- $M, w \models \varphi \wedge \psi$ iff $M, w \models \varphi$ and $M, w \models \psi$,
- $M, w \models \varphi \vee \psi$ iff $M, w \models \varphi$ or $M, w \models \psi$,
- $M, h \models \varphi \rightarrow \psi$ iff $M, t \models \varphi \rightarrow \psi$ and $M, h \not\models \varphi$ or $M, h \models \psi$,
- $M, t \models \varphi \rightarrow \psi$ iff, $M, t \not\models \varphi$ or $M, t \models \psi$,
- $M, w \models \forall x \, \varphi(x)$ iff $M, w \models \varphi(d)$ for all $d \in D_w$.
- $M, w \models \exists x \, \varphi(x)$ iff $M, w \models \varphi(d)$ for some $d \in D_w$.

The concepts of validity, equivalence and semantic consequence are defined as usual. To understand how these definitions work for undefined functions, let us extend our Biblical genealogy example.

Example 1. Assume we have the Herbrand constants *adam, cain, abel* and take the following situation that is compatible with Cabalar's semantics. Suppose that $M, w \models father(abel) = adam$ in worlds $w \in \{h, t\}$, whereas $father(cain)$ is undefined in world h, $M, h \models \neg \exists x father(cain) = x$ taking value *adam* in world t, $M, t \models father(cain) = adam$. Besides, in both worlds, we still have

$father(adam)$ undefined. To represent this situation in **FHT** we would fix $D_h = \{abel, cain, adam\}$, $D_t = D_h \cup \{cf\}$ and $D = D_h \cup \{af\}$ with $cf \equiv adam$ where cf and af are unnamed elements that respectively stand for "Cain's father" and "Adam's father." Then $\sigma(father(abel)) = adam \in D_h$, $\sigma(father(cain)) = cf \in D_t \setminus D_h$ but $cf \equiv adam$ and, finally, $\sigma(father(adam)) = af \in D \setminus D_t$.   □

To define equilibrium models, we say that an interpretation $M = \langle D_h, D_t, D, \equiv, I, \sigma \rangle$ is *smaller than* $M' = \langle D'_h, D'_t, D', \equiv', I', \sigma' \rangle$, written $M \leq M'$, when $D \setminus D_t = D' \setminus D'_t$ (elements that represent functions undefined both here and there must coincide in both interpretations), $I(p, t) = I'(p, t)$ and $I(p, h) \subseteq I'(p, h)$ for every predicate p, and finally, for every τ, one of these three cases holds: (1) $\sigma(\tau) \notin D_t$ and $\sigma'(\tau) \notin D'_t$; or (2) $\sigma(\tau) = \sigma'(\tau) \in D_h \cap D'_h$; or (3) $\sigma(\tau) \in D_t \setminus D_h$, $\sigma'(\tau) \in D'_h \cap D_h$, $\sigma(\tau) \equiv \sigma'(\tau)$. Then a model M of a theory Γ is said to be an *equilibrium model* iff there is no other model $M' \neq M$, $M' \leq M$ of Γ.

3   Relation to Cabalar's Partial Functions

In this section we recall the basic definitions from Cabalar's extension [7] of **SQHT** for dealing with partial functions. The main idea of this semantics relies on keeping a static domain D, common for both worlds h and t, but the interpretation of terms may map now to a special object $u \notin D$ that stands for "undefined." Let us denote this variant as **SQHT$_u$** and recall[7] next its main semantic definitions.

Definition 2 (SQHT$_u$-interpretation). *A* **SQHT$_u$**-*interpretation is a tuple* $M = \langle D, I, \sigma_h, \sigma_t \rangle$ *where* σ_w *with* $w \in \{h, t\}$ *are functions* $\sigma_w : Terms(C \cup D, F) \to D \cup \{u\}$ *with* u *some new element* $u \notin D$ *(standing for "undefined") and satisfying:*

(U1) $\sigma_w(d) = d$ *for all* $d \in D$.
(U2) *The mappings* σ_w *are recursive and verify* $\sigma_w(f(\overline{\tau})) = u$ *if* $\sigma_w(\tau_i) = u$ *for some* τ_i *in* $\overline{\tau}$.
(U3) $\sigma_h(\tau) = \sigma_t(\tau)$ *or* $\sigma_h(\tau) = u$ *for all* $\tau \in Terms(C \cup D, F)$.

and I *is an interpretation for predicates satisfying:*

(U4) $I(p, w) \subseteq D^n$, *if* $arity(p) = n$, *and*
(U5) $I(p, h) \subseteq I(p, t)$.   □

An interpretation $M = \langle D, I, \sigma_h, \sigma_t \rangle$ is *total* iff $\sigma_h = \sigma_t$ and $I(p, h) = I(p, t)$ for every predicate p. We say that $M = \langle D, I, \sigma_h, \sigma_t \rangle$ is *smaller than* $M' = \langle D, I', \sigma'_h, \sigma'_t \rangle$, written $M \leq M'$, when $I(p, t) = I'(p, t)$ and $I(p, h) \subseteq I'(p, h)$ for every predicate p, $\sigma_t = \sigma'_t$, and $\sigma_h(\tau) = u$ or $\sigma_h(\tau) = \sigma'_h(\tau)$ for every term τ.

---

[7] For simplicity, we omit the distinction between Herbrand and non-Herbrand functions made in the original definition of [7].

Definition 3 (Equilibrium model). *A total* **SQHT$_u$** *interpretation M is an equilibrium model of a theory Γ iff $M, h \models \alpha$ for all $\alpha \in \Gamma$ and there is no strictly smaller $M' < M$ such that $M', h \models \alpha$ for all $\alpha \in \Gamma$.*

The satisfaction relation in **SQHT$_u$**, written $\models_u$, is defined as follows.

- $M, w \models_u p(\overline{\tau})$ iff $\sigma_w(\overline{\tau}) \in I(p, w)$;
- $M, w \models_u \tau_1 = \tau_2$ iff $\sigma_w(\tau_1) = \sigma_w(\tau_2) \neq u$;
- $\bot, \wedge$ and $\vee$ are interpreted as usual;
- $M, h \models_u \varphi \to \psi$ iff $M, t \models_u \varphi \to \psi$ and either $M, h \not\models_u \varphi$ or $M, h \models_u \psi$;
- $M, t \models_u \varphi \to \psi$ iff   either $M, t \not\models_u \varphi$ or $M, t \models_u \psi$;
- $M, w \models_u \forall x \, \varphi(x)$ iff $M, w \models_u \varphi(d)$ for all $d \in D$;
- $M, w \models_u \exists x \, \varphi(x)$ iff $M, w \models_u \varphi(d)$ for some $d \in D$.

To prove equivalence between **SQHT** and **FHT** we will use the next observation.

Proposition 1. *Let $\mathcal{L}_1$ and $\mathcal{L}_2$ be two different Kripke logics for a common syntax and set of worlds W, and let c be a correspondence assigning an $\mathcal{L}_2$ interpretation M^c to any $\mathcal{L}_1$ interpretation M. If c is such that, at any world $w \in W$, both M, w and M^c, w satisfy the same set of formulas, then $\mathcal{L}_2 \subseteq \mathcal{L}_1$.*

We provide next a pair of correspondences that satisfy the conditions in Proposition 1: mapping '$*$' from **SQHT** interpretations into **FHT** interpretations, and mapping '$\dagger$' in the opposite direction. In the sequel, if $\tau \in \text{Terms}(D \cup C, F)$, we write $\tau(d_1, \dots, d_n)$ to indicate that $d_1, \dots, d_n$ are the elements of D occurring in τ. Given an **FHT** interpretation $M = \langle D_h, D_t, D, \equiv, I, \sigma \rangle$ and assuming $u \notin D$, we define an **SQHT$_u$** interpretation $M^* = \langle D^*, I, \sigma_h^*, \sigma_t^* \rangle$ as:

- $D^* \overset{\text{def}}{=} D_t / \equiv$
- If $\tau([d_1], \dots, [d_n]) \in \text{Terms}(D^* \cup C, F)$ with $d_i \in D_h$ and $\sigma(\tau(d_1, \dots, d_n)) \in D_h$, then $\sigma_h^*(\tau([d_1], \dots, [d_n])) = [\sigma(\tau(d_1, \dots, d_n))]$; otherwise, $\sigma_h^*(\tau([d_1], \dots, [d_n])) = u$.
- If $\sigma(\tau(d_1, \dots, d_n)) \in D_t$, then $\sigma_t^*(\tau([d_1], \dots, [d_n])) = [\sigma(\tau(d_1, \dots, d_n))]$; otherwise, $\sigma_t^*(\tau([d_1], \dots, [d_n])) = u$.
- If $d_i \in D_h$ for every i, $([d_1], \dots, [d_n]) \in I^*(p, h)$ iff $(d_1, \dots, d_n) \in I(p, h)$.
- $I^*(p, t) = \{([d_1], \dots, [d_n]) \mid (d_1, \dots, d_n) \in I(p, t)\}$, if $n = arity(p)$.

The mappings σ_w are well defined, because if $d \equiv d'$ and $\tau(d)$ is a term containing d, then by condition (F5), $\sigma(\tau(d)) \equiv \sigma(\tau(d'))$. The interpretation I^* is also well defined by conditions (F2) and (F6).

As an example, consider $D_h = \{0, 1, 2\}$, $D_t = \{0, 1, 2, 3\}$ and $D = \mathbb{N}$. Any σ in an **FHT**-interpretation will assign $\sigma(i) = i$ for any natural number $i \in \mathbb{N}$. Then $\sigma_h^*(i) = i$ for $i \in \{0, 1, 2\}$ and $\sigma_h^*(i) = u$ for all the rest. Similarly $\sigma_t^*(i) = i$ for $i \in \{0, 1, 2, 3\}$ and $\sigma_t^*(i) = u$ otherwise.

Proposition 2. *If M is an **FHT**-interpretation, then M^* is a well-formed **SQHT**-interpretation.*   □

Theorem 1. *Let M be an* **FHT** *interpretation and α an arbitrary sentence. Then $M, w \models \alpha$ iff $M^*, w \models_u \alpha$ for any $w \in \{h, t\}$.* □

Given an **SQHT$_u$**-interpretation $M = \langle D, I, \sigma_h, \sigma_t \rangle$ we provide now the correspondence for the other direction, defining the associated **FHT**-interpretation $M^\dagger = (D_h, D_t, D^\dagger, \equiv, I^\dagger, \sigma)$ as follows:

- $D^\dagger = \text{Terms}(D \cup C, F)/\equiv_h$, where $\tau_1 \equiv_h \tau_2$ if either $\tau_1 = \tau_2$, or $\sigma_h(\tau_1) = \sigma_h(\tau_2) \neq u$.
- $D_h = \{[\tau] \mid \sigma_h(\tau) \neq u\}$
- $D_t = \{[\tau] \mid \sigma_t(\tau) \neq u\}$
- $[\tau_1] \equiv [\tau_2]$ iff $\sigma_t(\tau_1) = \sigma_t(\tau_2)$.
- $\sigma([\tau]) = [\tau]$, $\sigma(f([\tau_1], \ldots, [\tau_2])) = [f(\tau_1, \ldots, \tau_2)]$.
- $I^\dagger(p, w) = \{([\tau_1], \ldots, [\tau_n]) \mid (\sigma_w(\tau_1), \ldots, \sigma_w(\tau_n)) \in I(p, w)\}$, if $n = arity(p)$.

The mapping σ is well defined, because if $\sigma_h(\tau_1) = \sigma_h(\tau_i')$ for every i, then, by recursion, $\sigma_h(f(\tau_1, \ldots, \tau_n)) = \sigma_h(f(\tau_1', \ldots, \tau_n'))$. On the other hand, $\equiv$ is well defined: if $\sigma_h(\tau_1) = \sigma_h(\tau_2) \neq u$, then $\sigma_t(\tau_1) = \sigma_h(\tau_1) = \sigma_h(\tau_2) = \sigma_t(\tau_2)$.

Proposition 3. *Let $M = \langle D, I, \sigma_h, \sigma_t \rangle$ be an* **SQHT$_u$**-*interpretation. Then $M^\dagger = \langle D_h, D_t, D^\dagger, \equiv, I^\dagger, \sigma \rangle$ is a well-formed* **FHT**-*interpretation.* □

Theorem 2. *Let M be an* **SQHT$_u$**-*interpretation and α an arbitrary sentence. Then $M, w \models_u \alpha$ iff $M^\dagger, w \models \alpha$ for any $w \in \{h, t\}$.* □

4 Gentzen Calculus FHTG

In this section we introduce a Gentzen Calculus **FHTG** with multi-consequent sequents of the form $\Gamma \vdash \Delta$ where, Γ and Δ are sets of formulas (respectively understood as a conjunction and a disjunction). The soundness of the system is guaranteed if the rules preserve the following property: for a rule $\frac{\Gamma_0 \vdash \Delta_0}{\Gamma_1 \vdash \Delta_1}$ if M is a countermodel of $\Gamma_0 \vdash \Delta_0$ then it is also a countermodel of $\Gamma_1 \vdash \Delta_1$; and M is a countermodel of $\Gamma \vdash \Delta$ if $M \models \varphi$ for every $\varphi \in \Gamma$ and $M \not\models \psi$ for every $\psi \in \Delta$. We begin by introducing the axioms and the rules of the basic system.

Axioms: $\qquad\qquad \Gamma, \varphi \vdash \Delta, \varphi; \qquad \Gamma, \varphi, \neg\varphi \vdash \Delta;$

Rules for propositional connectives:

$$\frac{\Gamma, \alpha, \beta \vdash \Delta}{\Gamma, \alpha \wedge \beta \vdash \Delta} \text{ (L-}\wedge) \qquad\qquad \frac{\Gamma \vdash \Delta, \alpha \quad \Gamma \vdash \Delta, \beta}{\Gamma \vdash \Delta, \alpha \wedge \beta} \text{ (R-}\wedge)$$

$$\frac{\Gamma, \alpha \vdash \Delta \quad \Gamma, \beta \vdash \Delta}{\Gamma, \alpha \vee \beta \vdash \Delta} \text{(L-}\vee) \qquad\qquad \frac{\Gamma \vdash \Delta, \alpha, \beta}{\Gamma \vdash \Delta, \alpha \vee \beta} \text{(R-}\vee)$$

$$\frac{\Gamma, \neg\alpha \vdash \Delta \quad \Gamma \vdash \Delta, \alpha, \neg\beta \quad \Gamma, \beta \vdash \Delta}{\Gamma, \alpha \rightarrow \beta \vdash \Delta} \text{ (L-}\rightarrow) \qquad \frac{\Gamma, \alpha \vdash \Delta, \beta \quad \Gamma, \neg\beta \vdash \Delta, \neg\alpha}{\Gamma \vdash \Delta, \alpha \rightarrow \beta} \text{ (R-}\rightarrow)$$

$$\frac{\Gamma, \neg\alpha, \neg\beta \vdash \Delta}{\Gamma, \neg(\alpha \vee \beta) \vdash \Delta} \text{ (L-}\neg\vee) \qquad\qquad \frac{\Gamma \vdash \Delta, \neg\alpha \quad \Gamma \vdash \Delta, \neg\beta}{\Gamma \vdash \Delta, \neg(\alpha \vee \beta)} \text{ (R-}\neg\vee)$$

$$\dfrac{\Gamma, \neg\alpha \vdash \Delta \qquad \Gamma, \neg\beta \vdash \Delta}{\Gamma, \neg(\alpha \wedge \beta) \vdash \Delta}\ (\text{L-}\neg\wedge) \qquad\qquad \dfrac{\Gamma \vdash \Delta, \neg\alpha, \neg\beta}{\Gamma \vdash \Delta, \neg(\alpha \wedge \beta)}\ (\text{R-}\neg\wedge)$$

$$\dfrac{\Gamma, \neg\beta \vdash \Delta, \neg\alpha}{\Gamma, \neg(\alpha \to \beta) \vdash \Delta}\ (\text{L-}\neg\to) \qquad\qquad \dfrac{\Gamma, \neg\alpha \vdash \Delta \qquad \Gamma \vdash \Delta, \neg\beta}{\Gamma \vdash \Delta, \neg(\alpha \to \beta)}\ (\text{R-}\neg\to)$$

$$\dfrac{\Gamma \vdash \Delta, \neg\alpha}{\Gamma, \neg\neg\alpha \vdash \Delta}\ (\text{L-}\neg\neg) \qquad\qquad \dfrac{\Gamma, \neg\alpha \vdash \Delta}{\Gamma \vdash \Delta, \neg\neg\alpha}\ (\text{R-}\neg\neg)$$

Rules for quantified formulas: The Gentzen system works over the domain V, a denumerable set of variables (or parameters); that is, the introduction of quantifiers is always made from variables, not from terms of the original language. In the following rules, y is a *fresh* variable, i.e. a variable which does not occur free in $\Gamma \cup \Delta$ and $\tau \in Terms(C \cup V, F)$:

$$\dfrac{\Gamma, y = \tau, \varphi(y) \vdash \Delta}{\Gamma, \exists x \varphi(x) \vdash \Delta}(\text{R-}\exists), \qquad \dfrac{\Gamma, y = \tau \vdash \Delta, \varphi(y)}{\Gamma \vdash \Delta, \forall x \varphi(x)}(\text{L-}\forall),$$

The atoms $y = \tau$ in the left-hand side introduce the elements y of the domain D_h. In the following rules, y may be any variable in V (not necessarily fresh), but we also need to include the atom $y = \tau$ in the left-hand side.

$$\dfrac{\Gamma, y = \tau, \varphi(y), \forall x \varphi(x) \vdash \Delta}{\Gamma, y = \tau, \forall x \varphi(x) \vdash \Delta}(\text{R-}\forall), \qquad \dfrac{\Gamma, y = \tau \vdash \Delta, \varphi(y), \exists x \varphi(x)}{\Gamma, y = \tau \vdash \Delta, \exists x \varphi(x)}(\text{L-}\exists)$$

Substitution rules: If τ_1, τ_2 are terms in $Terms(C \cup V, F)$:

$$\dfrac{\Gamma, \tau_1 = \tau_2, \varphi(\tau_1) \vdash \Delta}{\Gamma, \tau_1 = \tau_2, \varphi(\tau_2) \vdash \Delta}; \quad \dfrac{\Gamma, \tau_1 = \tau_2 \vdash \Delta, \varphi(\tau_1)}{\Gamma, \tau_1 = \tau_2 \vdash \Delta, \varphi(\tau_2)};$$

$$\dfrac{\Gamma, \neg\varphi(\tau_1) \vdash \Delta, \neg(\tau_1 = \tau_2)}{\Gamma, \neg\varphi(\tau_2) \vdash \Delta, \neg(\tau_1 = \tau_2)}; \quad \dfrac{\Gamma \vdash \Delta, \neg(\tau_1 = \tau_2), \neg\varphi(\tau_1)}{\Gamma \vdash \Delta, \neg(\tau_1 = \tau_2), \neg\varphi(\tau_2)};$$

Strictness rule (left side): The property (F4) for interpretations establishes the strictness of the assignment mapping, i.e. if a term τ is defined, every subterm τ' is also defined. The syntactic rule for this property is the following one:

$$\dfrac{\Gamma, x = \tau, y = \tau' \vdash \Delta}{\Gamma, x = \tau \vdash \Delta} \tag{3}$$

The previous set of rules is basic for systems built to characterize free logics. The rest of the rules are specific for our system.

Additional rule for equality: By (F2)-a, two distinct elements in D_h cannot be equivalent in D_t. The property (F2)-a is syntactically characterized by the rule

$$\dfrac{\Gamma, x = y \vdash \Delta}{\Gamma, x = y \vdash \Delta, \neg(x = y)} \tag{4}$$

On the other hand, by the property (F2)-b, every element of D_t, must be equivalent to one from D_h. The atom $\neg(y = \tau)$ in the right-hand side introduces the element y of the domain D_t, but does not determine any relation with D_h. So, to comply with property (F2)-b, we need to modify the standard rules for negated quantified formulas and strictness.

Rules for negated quantified formulas: In the following rules, y, z are fresh variables and $\tau \in Terms(C \cup V, F)$:

$$\frac{\Gamma, z = \tau, \neg\varphi(y) \vdash \Delta, \neg(y = \tau)}{\Gamma, \neg\forall x\varphi(x) \vdash \Delta}\text{(R-}\neg\forall\text{)}, \qquad \frac{\Gamma, z = \tau \vdash \Delta, \neg\varphi(y), \neg(y = \tau)}{\Gamma \vdash \Delta, \neg\exists x\varphi(x)}\text{(L-}\neg\exists\text{)}$$

The literal $\neg(y = \tau)$ says that y is a new element of D_t equivalent to τ, and the presence of the atom $z = \tau$ in the left-hand side says that τ is an element of D_h, as required by property (F2)-b; if we drop the condition (F2)-b in our models, these atoms in the left-hand sides of these rules must be also dropped.

In the following rules, y may be any variable in V (not necessarily fresh).

$$\frac{\Gamma, \neg\varphi(y), \neg\exists x\varphi(x) \vdash \Delta, \neg(y = \tau)}{\Gamma, \neg\exists x\varphi(x) \vdash \Delta, \neg(y = \tau)}\text{(R-}\neg\exists\text{)}$$

$$\frac{\Gamma \vdash \Delta, \neg(y = \tau), \neg\varphi(y), \neg\forall x\varphi(x)}{\Gamma \vdash \Delta, \neg(y = \tau), \neg\forall x\varphi(x)}\text{(L-}\neg\forall\text{)}$$

Strictness rule (right side): Let τ' below be a subterm of τ and y, z fresh variables. We add the atom $z = \tau'$ in the left-hand side to comply with (F2)-b.

$$\frac{\Gamma, z = \tau' \vdash \Delta, \neg(x = \tau), \neg(y = \tau')}{\Gamma \vdash \Delta, \neg(x = \tau)} \tag{5}$$

Auxiliary parameters elimination: As we have said, the quantifier rules only work with variables and thus, to prove formulas involving terms, these terms must be assigned to variables. This is done by auxiliary parameters elimination rules we denote as (ParEl). In the following rules, α is either a predicate symbol or the equality, every τ_i is a term in $Terms(C \cup V, F)$, and $x, x_1, \ldots, x_n$ are variables.

$$\frac{\Gamma, \alpha(x_1, \ldots, x_n), x_1 = \tau_1, \ldots, x_n = \tau_n \vdash \Delta}{\Gamma, \alpha(\tau_1, \ldots, \tau_n) \vdash \Delta}$$

$$\frac{\Gamma, x_1 = \tau_1, \ldots, x_n = \tau_n \vdash \alpha(x_1, \ldots, x_n), \Delta \quad \Gamma \vdash \Delta, \exists x(x = \tau_i), i = 1..n}{\Gamma \vdash \alpha(\tau_1, \ldots, \tau_n), \Delta}$$

$$\frac{\Gamma \vdash \neg\alpha(x_1, \ldots, x_n), \neg(x_1 = \tau_1), \ldots, \neg(x_n = \tau_n), \Delta}{\Gamma \vdash \neg\alpha(\tau_1, \ldots, \tau_n), \Delta}$$

$$\frac{\Gamma\neg\alpha(x_1, \ldots, x_n) \vdash \neg(x_1 = \tau_1), \ldots, \neg(x_n = \tau_n), \Delta \quad \Gamma, \neg\exists x(x = \tau_i) \vdash \Delta, i = 1..n}{\Gamma, \neg\alpha(\tau_1, \ldots, \tau_n) \vdash \Delta}$$

Example 2. The inference $p(a) \vdash \exists x(x = a)$ is provable in FHT,

$$\frac{p(y), y = a \vdash y = a, \exists x(x = a) \quad \text{(Axiom)}}{\frac{p(y), y = a \vdash \exists x(x = a) \quad \text{(L-}\exists\text{)}}{p(a) \vdash \exists x(x = a) \quad \text{(ParEl)}}}$$

because the truth of the atom $p(a)$ in a model requires that a is defined. This is a consequence of the condition (F6), $I(p, h) \subseteq D_h$, and syntactically of the auxiliary parameters elimination rules. However, the inference $\neg p(a) \vdash \exists x (x = a)$ is not provable. If we try to construct a proof applying the rules upwards we can deduce how to build a counterexample.

$$\cfrac{\cfrac{y = y, \neg p(y) \vdash \neg(y = a), y = a, \exists x (x = a)}{y = y, \neg p(y) \vdash \neg(y = a), \exists x (x = a)} \qquad \neg \exists x (x = a) \vdash \exists x (x = a)}{\neg p(a) \vdash \exists x (x = a)}$$

In the first step, we apply the parameter elimination rule; we would need to add the atom $y = y$ because y is a fresh variable and we need to define it as an element of D_h. In the second step we apply R-$\exists$; note that we would need the presence of the atom $y = y$ in the left-hand side to apply this rule. The sequent in the left branch is not open and it can not be generated from other sequents (the rule R-$\exists$ has been applied using the unique parameter in the sequent). Moreover, it is easy to construct a countermodel of this sequent,

$$D_h = \{y\}, \quad D_t = \{y, a\}, \quad y \equiv a, \quad I(p, h) = I(p, t) = \varnothing$$

which also is a countermodel of $\neg p(a) \vdash \exists x (x = a)$.

Theorem 3 (Soundness). *If Γ and Δ are lists of formulas such that $\Gamma \vdash \Delta$ is deducible in* **FHTG**, *and $\mathcal{I}$ is a model of Γ, then $\mathcal{I}$ is a model of a formula $\psi \in \Delta$. In particular, if $\Gamma \vdash \varphi$, then $\Gamma \models \varphi$*

As usual, the soundness proof consists in verifying that every rule preserves the satisfiability of sequents.

Theorem 4 (Completeness). *If Γ and Δ are lists of formulas such that for every model $\mathcal{I}$ of Γ there exists $\psi \in \Delta$ such that $\mathcal{I}$ is a model of ψ, then $\Gamma \vdash \Delta$ is deducible in* **FHTG**. *In particular, if $\Gamma \models \varphi$, then $\Gamma \vdash \varphi$.*

5   Conclusions

We have provided an alternative characterisation of (the monotonic basis for) Cabalar's semantics for partial intensional functions based on free logic. This characterisation allows us to establish a Gentzen calculus that can be used, for instance, to check strong equivalence properties or make formal analysis for theories involving partial functions. With respect to Cabalar's original approach, the current free-logic variant is more flexible: it can be modified in various ways by relaxing some of the conditions we had to impose to capture Cabalar's approach. Another interesting topic is the comparison to Flexible QHT and its Gentzen calculus presented in [12] whose main differences rely on the treatment of equality. We will study a formal comparison and explore the possibility of capturing both Cabalar's and BL functions in the same formal framework.

References

1. Alviano, M., et al.: The fourth answer set programming competition: Preliminary report. In: Cabalar, P., Son, T.C. (eds.) LPNMR 2013. LNCS, vol. 8148, pp. 42–53. Springer, Heidelberg (2013)
2. Balduccini, M.: A "Conservative" approach to extending answer set programming with non-herbrand functions. In: Erdem, E., Lee, J., Lierler, Y., Pearce, D. (eds.) Correct Reasoning. LNCS, vol. 7265, pp. 24–39. Springer, Heidelberg (2012)
3. Bartholomew, M., Lee, J.: Stable models of formulas with intensional functions. In: Proceedings of International Conference on Principles of Knowledge Representation and Reasoning, KR 2012, pp. 2–12 (2012)
4. Bartholomew, M., Lee, J.: On the stable model semantics for intensional functions. In: Proceedings of International Conference on Logic Programming, ICLP 2013 (2013)
5. Brewka, G., Eiter, T., Truszczynski, M.: Answer set programming at a glance. Commun. ACM 54(12), 92–103 (2011)
6. Burge, T.: Truth and singular terms. Nous 8(4), 309–325 (1974)
7. Cabalar, P.: Functional answer set programming. Theory and Practice of Logic Programming 10(2-3), 203–233 (2011)
8. Cabalar, P., Lorenzo, D.: Logic programs with functions and default values. In: Alferes, J.J., Leite, J. (eds.) JELIA 2004. LNCS (LNAI), vol. 3229, pp. 294–306. Springer, Heidelberg (2004)
9. Cabalar, P., Pearce, D., Valverde, A.: A revised concept of safety for general answer set programs. In: Erdem, E., Lin, F., Schaub, T. (eds.) LPNMR 2009. LNCS, vol. 5753, pp. 58–70. Springer, Heidelberg (2009)
10. Calimeri, F., Cozza, S., Ianni, G., Leone, N.: Computable functions in ASP: Theory and implementation. In: Garcia de la Banda, M., Pontelli, E. (eds.) ICLP 2008. LNCS, vol. 5366, pp. 407–424. Springer, Heidelberg (2008)
11. Calimeri, F., Cozza, S., Ianni, G., Leone, N.: An ASP system with functions, lists, and sets. In: Erdem, E., Lin, F., Schaub, T. (eds.) LPNMR 2009. LNCS, vol. 5753, pp. 483–489. Springer, Heidelberg (2009)
12. Farinãs del Cerro, L., Pearce, D., Valverde, A.: FQHT: The logic of stable models for logic programs with intensional functions. In: Proceedings of International Joint Conference on Artificial Intelligence, IJCAI 2013 (2013)
13. Ferraris, P., Lee, J., Lifschitz, V.: A new perspective on stable models. In: Proc. of the International Joint Conference on Artificial Intelligence (IJCAI 2007), pp. 372–379 (2007)
14. Gabbay, D.M., Pearce, D., Valverde, A.: Interpolable formulas in equilibrium logic and answer set programming. Journal of Artificial Intelligence Research (JAIR) 42, 917–943 (2011)
15. Gelfond, M., Lifschitz, V.: The stable model semantics for logic programming. In: Proc. of the 5th Intl. Conf. on Logic Programming, pp. 1070–1080 (1988)
16. Hanus, M.: The integration of functions into logic programming: from theory to practice. Journal of Logic Programming 19, 20, 583–628 (1994)
17. Heyting, A.: Die formalen Regeln der intuitionistischen Logik. Sitzungsberichte der Preussischen Akademie der Wissenschaften, Physikalisch-mathematische Klasse, pp. 42–56 (1930)
18. Lifschitz, V.: Logic programs with intensional functions. In: Proceedings of International Conference on Principles of Knowledge Representation and Reasoning, KR 2012 (2012)

19. Lifschitz, V., Pearce, D.J., Valverde, A.: A characterization of strong equivalence for logic programs with variables. In: Baral, C., Brewka, G., Schlipf, J. (eds.) LPNMR 2007. LNCS (LNAI), vol. 4483, pp. 188–200. Springer, Heidelberg (2007)

20. Lin, F., Wang, Y.: Answer set programming with functions. In: Proc. of the 11th Intl. Conf. on Principles of Knowledge Representation and Reasoning, KR 2008 (2008)

21. Marek, V., Truszczyński, M.: Stable models and an alternative logic programming paradigm. In: The Logic Programming Paradigm: a 25-Year Perspective, pp. 169–181. Springer (1999)

22. Niemelä, I.: Logic programs with stable model semantics as a constraint programming paradigm. Annals of Mathematics and Artificial Intelligence 25, 241–273 (1999)

23. Pearce, D.: A new logical characterisation of stable models and answer sets. In: Dix, J., Przymusinski, T.C., Moniz Pereira, L. (eds.) NMELP 1996. LNCS, vol. 1216, Springer, Heidelberg (1997)

24. Pearce, D.J., Valverde, A.: Towards a first order equilibrium logic for nonmonotonic reasoning. In: Alferes, J.J., Leite, J. (eds.) JELIA 2004. LNCS (LNAI), vol. 3229, pp. 147–160. Springer, Heidelberg (2004)

25. Pearce, D., Valverde, A.: Synonymous theories and knowledge representations in answer set programming. Journal of Computer and System Sciences 78(1), 86–104 (2012)

26. Posy, C.J.: A free IPC is a natural logic: Strong completeness for some intuitionistic free logics. Topoi 1(1-2), 30–43 (1982)

Constructive Models for Contraction
with Intransitive Plausibility Indifference

Pavlos Peppas[1,2] and Mary-Anne Williams[1]

[1] The Centre for Quantum Computation and Intelligent Systems
Faculty of Engineering and Information Technology
University of Technology, Sydney, NSW 2007, Australia
pavlos.peppas@uts.edu.au, Mary-Anne@it.uts.edu.au
[2] Dept of Business Administration
University of Patras, Patras, 265 00, Greece

Abstract. Plausibility rankings play a central role in modeling Belief Change, and they take different forms depending on the type of belief change under consideration: preorders on possible worlds, epistemic entrenchments, etc. A common feature of all these structures is that plausibility indifference is assumed to be transitive. In a previous article, [7], we argued that this is not always the case, and we introduced new sets of postulates for revision and contraction (weaker variants of the classical AGM postulates), that are liberated from the indifference transitivity assumption. Herein we complete the task by making the necessary adjustments to the epistemic entrenchment and the partial meet models. In particular we lift the indifference transitivity assumption from both these two models, and we establish representation results connecting the weaker models with the weaker postulates for contraction introduced in [7].

1 Introduction

In the classical AGM framework for belief change, [2], constructive models are typically based on rankings representing *comparative plausibility*. These rankings take different forms depending on the type of belief change under consideration, ranging from *preorders on possible worlds* [4], to *epistemic entrenchments* [3], to *ordering on remainders* [1]. The essence however in all those forms is the same: given the agent's initial belief set and the new epistemic input, plausibility rankings are used to determine the most plausible objects (worlds, sentences, or remainders respectively) among the available alternatives. The selected objects are subsequently used to define the next belief set.

An underlying assumption employed in the AGM framework, is that *indifference of comparative plausibility is transitive*. Consider for example the *faithful preorders* introduced in [4]. Comparative plausibility is modeled as a total preorder $\preceq$ on possible worlds, with plausibility decreasing as one moves up in $\preceq$. Suppose that two distinct possible worlds w_1, w_2 are equally plausible (or implausible) relative to the agents' initial belief state. Let us denote this by $w_1 \sim w_2$. Formally, $w_1 \sim w_2$ iff $w_1 \not\prec w_2$ and $w_2 \not\prec w_1$, where $\prec$ denotes the strict part of $\preceq$. Suppose now that w_2 is equally plausible

E. Fermé and J. Leite (Eds.): JELIA 2014, LNAI 8761, pp. 355–367, 2014.
© Springer International Publishing Switzerland 2014

to a third world w_3; i.e. $w_2 \sim w_3$. Since comparative plausibility is modeled as a total preorder, we immediately conclude that $w_1 \sim w_3$.

Economists on the other hand are more cautious. It has long been acknowledged in the area of *preference modelling* that transitivity is not always a natural property for indifference of preference. The following quote from [5] illustrates the problem:

> *"Find a subject who prefers a cup of coffee with one cube of sugar to one with five cubes (this should not be difficult). Now prepare 401 cups of coffee with $(1 + i/100) \cdot x$ grams of sugar, $i = 0, 1, \cdots, 400$, where x is the weight of one cube of sugar. It is evident that he will be indifferent between cup i and cup $i + 1$, for any i, but by choice he is not indifferent between $i = 0$ and $i = 400$."*

The above example, along with further arguments in [5], support the view that rational agents tend to discriminate between two alternatives α, β only when their difference[1] exceeds a certain *threshold*. In a recent paper we have argued that, for similar reasons, plausibility indifference as used in the area of belief change, cannot always be assumed to be transitive. Consider for example the following adaptation of the *bald man paradox* reported in [7]:

> *"Suppose that our agent, Myrto, believes that her grandfather Speros, whom she never met, had a full head of hair. It is therefore reasonable to assume that the possible world w_{5000} in which her grandfather has 5000 hairs is more plausible to Myrto than the world w_{50} in which Speros has only 50 hairs. On the other hand, it is also reasonable to assume that Myrto is indifferent between worlds, like w_{4657} and w_{4656}, which differ only in that Speros has a single hair less in the latter. If indifference was transitive (as is the case in the AGM framework), with 4050 applications of transitivity we would derive that Myrto is indifferent between w_{5000} and w_{50}, which of course is not true."*

Considerations like these led us to commence in [7] a research program of rebuilding the AGM framework with the purpose of liberating it from the assumption of transitive plausibility indifference. More precisely, our plan was to lift plausibility indifference from all five major models of the AGM framework while preserving the representation results connecting the models between them; namely, from the postulates for belief revision, the postulates for belief contraction, the possible worlds model for revision, the partial meet model for contraction, and the epistemic entrenchment model for contraction. In [7] we did so for three models (i.e. the postulates for revision and contraction, as well as the possible worlds model). In this paper we complete the task by liberating the remaining two models (i.e the epistemic entrenchment model and the partial meet model).

More precisely, in [7] we altered Katsuno and Mendelzon's possible worlds constructive model for revision, by replacing total preorders with *semiorders*[2] We also weakened the AGM postulates for revision and contraction accordingly. Representation

---

[1] Or more accurately, the difference of their respective utilities.
[2] Semiorders were introduced in [5], as a weakening of preorders to cater for intransitive indifference.

results were provided proving the new postulates for revision to be sound and complete with respect to the semiorders-based construction. Finally the Levi and Harper Identities were shown to survive the weakening of the AGM postulates.

In this paper we complete the reconstruction of the AGM framework by making appropriate adjustments to the partial meet and the epistemic entrenchment models, to liberate them from transitive indifference. Moreover we establish representation results connecting the adjusted models with the new postulates for contraction introduced in [7].

The paper is structured as follows. In the next section we introduce the necessary notation and terminology. Section 3 gives some background on semiorders, while Section 4 reviews the new postulates and results presented in [7]. In Section 5 we introduce weaker axioms for epistemic entrenchment, and study the relationship between these weaker epistemic entrenchments (called *semi-entrenchments*) and semiorders on possible worlds. Section 6 contains our representation results connecting semi-entrenchments with the contraction functions introduced in [7]. In Section 7 we repeat the same exercise for the partial meet model. Finally, in the last section we discuss related works and make some concluding remarks.

2   Formal Preliminaries

Throughout this paper we work with a finite set of propositional variables P. We define L to be the propositional language generated from P (using the standard boolean connectives $\wedge, \vee, \rightarrow, \leftrightarrow, \neg$ and the special symbols $\top, \bot$) and governed by classical propositional logic.

For a set of sentences Γ of L, we denote by $Cn(\Gamma)$ the set of all logical consequences of Γ, i.e., $Cn(\Gamma) = \{x \in L : \Gamma \models x\}$. We shall often write $Cn(x_1, \ldots, x_n)$, for sentences $x_1, \ldots, x_n$, as an abbreviation of $Cn(\{x_1, \ldots, x_n\})$. For any two sentences x, y we shall write $x \equiv y$ iff $Cn(x) = Cn(y)$.

A theory K of L is any set of sentences of L closed under $\models$, i.e., $K = Cn(K)$. We shall denote the set of all theories of L by $\mathcal{T}$. We define a *possible world* r (or simply a *world*), to be a consistent set of literals such that for any propositional variables $x \in P$, either $x \in r$ or $\neg x \in r$. We will often identify a world r with the conjunction of its literals, leaving it to the context to resolve any ambiguity (for example in "$\neg r$", r is a sentence, whereas in "$r \cap \{x\}$", r is a set of literals). We denote the set of all possible worlds by $\mathcal{M}$.

For a set of sentences Γ of L, $[\Gamma]$ denotes the set of all possible worlds that entail Γ; i.e. $[\Gamma] = \{r \in \mathcal{M} : r \models \Gamma\}$. Often we use the notation $[x]$ for a sentence $x \in L$, as an abbreviation of $[\{x\}]$. For a theory K and a set of sentences Γ of L, we denote by $K + \Gamma$ the closure under $\models$ of $K \cup \Gamma$, i.e., $K + \Gamma = Cn(K \cup \Gamma)$. For a sentence $x \in L$ we often write $K + x$ as an abbreviation of $K + \{x\}$.

Finally, some definitions on binary relations. Let V be a nonempty set and R a binary relation over V. For any subset S of V, by $min(S, R)$ we denote the set $min(S, R) = \{w \in S : \text{for all } w' \in S, w'Rw \text{ entails } wRw'\}$. The elements in $min(S, R)$ are called *minimal in S* with respect to R (or simply *minimal in S*, when R is understood from the context). Observe that if R is irreflexive and anti-symmetric, the above definition of *min* is equivalent to: $min(S, R) = \{w \in S : \text{there is no } w' \in S, \text{ such that } w'Rw\}$.

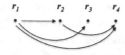

Fig. 1. Semiorder with Intransitive Indifference

In a similar fashion we define the set $max(S,R)$; i.e. $max(S,R) = \{w \in S$: for all $w' \in S, wRw'$ entails $w'Rw\}$. We call the elements of $max(S,R)$ the *maximal* elements of S with respect to R. Once again, if R is irreflexive and anti-symmetric, the above definition of *max* is equivalent to $max(S,R) = \{w \in S$: there is no $w' \in S$, such that $wRw'\}$.

We shall say that a binary R relation over V is a preorder iff R is *reflexive* and *transitive*. Moreover, R is said to be *total* iff for all $w, w' \in V$, wRw' or $w'Rw$.

3   Semiorders

Semiorders were introduced in [5] as a more natural alternative to total preorders for modelling preference. In this section we briefly review the main definition and results related to semiorders.

Given a finite set of choices V, a semiorder $\prec$ in V is defined as a binary relation over V that satisfies the following axioms, for any $r_1, r_2, r_3, r_4 \in V$:

(SO1) $r_1 \nprec r_1$.
(SO2)   If $r_1 \prec r_2 \prec r_3$ then $r_1 \prec r_4$ or $r_4 \prec r_3$.
(SO3)   If $r_1 \prec r_2$ and $r_3 \prec r_4$ then $r_1 \prec r_4$ or $r_3 \prec r_2$.

For any two choices $r_1, r_2 \in V$, we shall say that we are *indifferent* between r_1 and r_2, denoted $r_1 \sim r_2$, iff $r_1 \nprec r_2$ and $r_2 \nprec r_1$. It is not hard to verify that with semiorders, indifference is not in general transitive. Consider for example the semiorder $\prec$ depicted in Figure 1, where the arrows between alternatives indicate preference. It is easy to verify that $\prec$ satisfies (SO1) - (SO3). Moreover observe that $r_2 \sim r_3$, $r_3 \sim r_4$, and yet $r_2 \prec r_4$.

A central result on semiorders that sheds light to their inner workings, relates to their numerical representation. It has been shown, [10], [8], that every semiorder $\prec$ in V can be mapped to a *utility function* $u : V \mapsto \mathbb{R}$ such that for all $r_1, r_2 \in V$, $r_1 \prec r_2$ iff $u(r_2) - u(r_1) \geqslant 1$, and $r_1 \sim r_2$ iff $|u(r_2) - u(r_1)| < 1$. Intuitively this result says that the agent differentiates between two alternatives r_1 and r_2 iff the difference in their corresponding utilities exceeds a certain threshold (set to 1 in this case). For example, the semiorder $\prec$ of Figure 1 can be represented by the following utility function u: $u(r_1) = 0$, $u(r_2) = 1$, $u(r_3) = 1.5$, and $u(r_4) = 2$.

Other useful facts about semiorders are summarised in the following lemma reported in [7]:

Lemma 1. *Let V be a nonempty set, $\prec$ a semiorder in V, and S a nonempty subset of V. Then,* *(a)* $<$ is transitive.

(b) $min(S, <) \neq \emptyset$.

(c)   if $r \in S$ and $r \notin min(S, <)$, then there exists a $r' \in min(S, <)$ such that $r' < r$.

As noted earlier, in order to lift transitivity for plausibility indifference, in [7] we replaced total preorder with semiorders in Katsuno and Mendelzon's possible-worlds construction of a revision function [4]. More precisely, let K be a theory representing the initial belief set of a rational agent. We shall say that a semiorder $<$ in $\mathcal{M}$ is *faithful to K* iff the following conditions are satisfied:

(i)   If $r \in [K]$ then there is no $r' \in \mathcal{M}$ such that $r' < r$.

(ii)   If $r \in [K]$ and $r' \in (\mathcal{M} - [K])$ then $r < r'$.

Intuitively, a semiorder $<$ faithful to K represents a plausibility ranking on possible worlds: the more plausible a world r is, the lower it appears in the ranking. Hence in revising K by a sentence x, it is reasonable to assume that the resulting belief set $K * x$ is defined in terms of the most plausible x-worlds. This is precisely the construction proposed in [4] – except that total preorders instead of semiorders were used – and it is formally expressed by the following condition:

(AS) $[K * x] = min([x], <)$.

4   Weaker Postulates for Revision and Contraction

In the AGM framework, belief change is modelled as a function mapping a theory, representing the initial belief set, and a sentence, representing the epistemic input, to a new theory, that represents the next belief set. We shall call such functions *change functions*; i.e. a change function is any function from $\mathcal{T} \times L$ to $\mathcal{T}$. Depending on the constraints one places on change functions different types of belief change can be encoded. In particular, Alchourron, Gardenfors, and Makinson have introduced two sets of constraints on change functions, known as the *AGM postulates*, to model revision and contraction respectively (see [6]). As already mentioned, underlying these two sets of postulates is the assumption that plausibility indifference is transitive. In [7] we weakened the AGM postulates to lift the transitivity constraint. The resulting weaker postulates were numbered (A1) - (A10) for revision, and (B1) - (B10) for contraction. The postulates (A1) - (A10) are omitted due to space limitations (see [7] for details). The postulates (B1) - (B10) for contraction are listed below.

(B1) $K \div x$ is a theory.

(B2) $K \div x \subseteq K$.

(B3)   If $x \notin K$ then $K \div x = K$.

(B4)   If $\not\models x$ then $x \notin K \div x$.

(B5)   If $x \in K$ then $K \subseteq (K \div x) + x$.

(B6)   If $x \equiv y$ then $K \div x = K \div y$.

(B7) $(K \div x) \cap (K \div y) \subseteq K \div (x \wedge y)$.

(B8) $K \div (x \wedge y) \subseteq (K \div x) + (K \div y)$.

(B9)   If $K \div y \nsubseteq (K \div x) + \neg y$ then $K \div x \subseteq (K \div y) + \neg x$.

(B10)   If $x \vee y \in K \div x$, and $x \vee z \notin K \div x$ then $K \div (x \vee y) \subseteq K \div (x \vee z) + \neg(x \vee y)$.

The reader is referred to [7] for a discussion on these postulates. Herein, we shall only mention that the two sets of postulates are indeed weaker versions of the corresponding AGM postulates, and moreover they preserve the Levi and Harper Identities:

$$K \div x = (K * \neg x) \cap K \qquad \text{(Harper Identity)}$$
$$K * x = (K \div \neg x) + x \qquad \text{(Levi Identity)}$$

The following results have been established in [7]:

Theorem 1. *Let K be a theory, * a revision function satisfying (A1) - (A10), and $\div$ the function induced from * via the Harper Identity. Then $\div$ satisfies (B1) - (B10).*

Theorem 2. *Let K be a theory, $\div$ a contraction function satisfying (B1) - (B10), and * the function induced from $\div$ via the Levi Identity. Then * satisfies (A1) - (A10).*

In addition to the above theorems, another central representation result established in [7] is the connection between the new postulates (A1) - (A10) and the functions induced from semiorders via (AS):

Theorem 3. *Let K be a theory and * a revision function satisfying (A1) - (A10). Then there exists a semiorder $<$ faithful to K, that satisfies (AS).*

Theorem 4. *Let K be a theory and $<$ a semiorder faithful to K. The revision function * induced from $<$ via (AS), satisfies (A1) - (A10).*

5   Semi-entrenchments

An epistemic entrenchment is a total preorder $\leqslant$ on the sentences of L that was intro-duced in [3] to model the degree of resistance a belief exhibits to change; i.e. $x \leqslant y$ iff y's resistance to a change in its status is at least as strong as x's resistance. To capture the intended meaning of an epistemic entrenchment, the following axioms where proposed in [3]:

(EE1)   If $x \leqslant y$ and $y \leqslant z$ then $x \leqslant z$.

(EE2)   If $x \models y$ then $x \leqslant y$.

(EE3) $x \leqslant x \wedge y$ or $y \leqslant x \wedge y$.

(EE4)   When K is consistent, $x \notin K$ iff $x \leqslant y$ for all $y \in L$.

(EE5)   If $y \leqslant x$ for all $y \in L$, then $\models x$.

Given an epistemic entrenchment one can produce a contraction function that satis-fies the AGM postulates by means of the following condition:

(C$\div$) $y \in K \div x$ iff $y \in K$ and either $x < x \vee y$ or $\models x$.

It was shown in [3] that any binary relation $\leqslant$ over L satisfying (EE1) - (EE5) is a total preorder; hence indifference is transitive for epistemic entrenchments. In this section we shall weaken the axioms (EE1) - (EE5) to lift this constraint. Essentially we replace epistemic entrenchments $\leqslant$ with appropriately constrained semiorders $\prec$ over L. In particular, consider the following axioms, where x_1, x_2, x_3, x_4 are arbitrary sentences of L:

(C1)   If $x_1 \not\prec x_1$.
(C2)   If $x_1 \prec x_2 \prec x_3$, then $x_1 \prec x_4$ or $x_4 \prec x_3$.
(C3)   If $x_1 \prec x_2$ and $x_3 \prec x_4$, then $x_1 \prec x_4$ or $x_3 \prec x_2$.
(C4)   If $x_1 \prec x_2$ and $x_2 \models x_3$, then $x_1 \prec x_3$.
(C5)   If $x_1 \models x_2$ and $x_2 \prec x_3$, then $x_1 \prec x_3$.
(C6) $x_1 \prec x_2 \wedge x_3$ iff $x_1 \prec x_2$ and $x_1 \prec x_3$.
(C7)   If $x_1 \wedge x_2 \prec x_3$ then $x_1 \prec x_3$ or $x_2 \prec x_3$.
(C8)   Whenever K is consistent, $x_1 \notin K$ iff there is no $x_2 \in L$ such that $x_2 \prec x_1$.
(C9)   If $x_1 \notin K$ and $x_2 \in K$ then $x_1 \prec x_2$.
(C10)   If $\not\models x_1$ and $\models x_2$, then $x_1 \prec x_2$.

Axioms (C1) - (C3) state that $\prec$ is a semiorder (they are identical to (SO1) - (SO3)). We note that, by Lemma 1, (C1) - (C3) entail (EE1).[3] Axioms (C4) - (C5) are replacing (EE2). What necessitated the replacement of (EE2) is mainly the fact that $\prec$ corresponds to the *strict* part of $\leqslant$. For similar reasons, (EE3) was replaced by (C6) - (C7), (EE4) was replaced by (C8) - (C9), and (EE5) was replaced by (C10).

We define a *semi-entrenchment relative to a theory K* to be a binary relation $\prec$ over L that satisfies (C1) - (C10). We will prove that the change functions induced from semi-entrenchments are precisely those satisfying the postulates (B1) - (B10). This is the subject of the next section. In this section we will instead examine the relationship between semi-entrenchments and semiorders on possible worlds.

Let K be a theory of L. Condition (FC) below shows how to construct a semi-entrenchment $\prec$ relative to K, from a semiorder $<$ faithful to K; the reverse direction is served by condition (CF). In the conditions (FC) and (CF) below, x, y are sentences, and r, r' are possible worlds.

(FC) $x \prec y$ iff $\not\models x$ and for every $r' \in [\neg y]$ there is an $r \in [\neg x]$ such that $r < r'$.
(CF) $r < r'$ iff $\neg r \prec \neg r'$.

Theorem 5. *Let K be a theory of L. If $\prec$ is a semi-entrenchment relative to K, then the binary relation $<$ over M induced from $\prec$ via (CF) is a semiorder faithful to K. Conversely, if $<$ is a semiorder faithful to K, then the binary relation $\prec$ over L induced from $<$ via (FC) is a semi-entrenchment relative to K.*

Proof.
($\Rightarrow$)

Assume that $\prec$ is a semi-entrenchment relative to K, and $<$ is the binary relation over M induced from $\prec$ via (CF). Proving that $<$ is a semi-order is quite straightforward.

---

[3] Observe that although semiorders are transitive, the indifference relation induced by them is not (necessarily) transitive – see the example in Figure 1.

In particular, (SO1) follows immediately from (C1). For (SO2), let $r_1, r_2, r_3 \in \mathcal{M}$ be such that $r_1 \prec r_2 \prec r_3$. Then by (CF), $\neg r_1 \prec \neg r_2 \prec \neg r_3$. Consequently, by (C2), for any world $w \in \mathcal{M}$ we derive that $\neg r_1 \preccurlyeq \neg w$ or $\neg w \preccurlyeq \neg r_3$. This again entails via (CF) that $r_1 \prec w$ or $w \prec r_3$. Finally for (SO3), assume that $r_1, r_2, r_3, r_4 \in \mathcal{M}$ are such that $r_1 \prec r_2$ and $r_3 \prec r_4$. By (CF), it follows that $\neg r_1 \prec \neg r_2$ and $\neg r_3 \prec \neg r_4$. Then by (C3) we derive that $\neg r_1 \preccurlyeq \neg r_4$ or $\neg r_3 \preccurlyeq \neg r_2$, which again via (CF) entails $r_1 \prec r_4$ or $r_3 \prec r_2$ as desired.

To complete the proof of the first part of Theorem 5 we need to show that $\prec$ is also faithful to K. If K is inconsistent, then this is trivially true. Assume therefore that K is consistent. Let r be any world in $[K]$, and r' an arbitrary world in $\mathcal{M}$. From $r \in [K]$ it follows that $\neg r \notin K$. Then from (C8) it follows that $\neg r' \not\prec \neg r$, and consequently from (CF), $r' \not\prec r$. This proves condition (i) for faithfulness.

For condition (ii), consider any two worlds $r, r' \in \mathcal{M}$ such that $r \in [K]$ and $r' \notin [K]$. Clearly then, $\neg r \notin K$ and $\neg r' \in K$. Consequently from (C9), $\neg r \prec \neg r'$ and therefore by (CF), $r \prec r'$ as desired.

$(\Leftarrow)$

Assume that $\prec$ is a semiorder faithful to K and let $\preccurlyeq$ be the binary relation over L constructed from $\prec$ via (FC). We will prove that $\preccurlyeq$ satisfies (C1) - (C10).

For (C1), consider any sentence $x \in L$. If x is a tautology then by (FC), there is no $y \in L$ such that $x \preccurlyeq y$ and consequently, $x \not\preccurlyeq x$. Assume therefore that $\not\models x$. Then $[\neg x] \neq \varnothing$ and consequently from Lemma 1 we derive that $min([\neg x], \prec) \neq \varnothing$. Therefore there is a world $r \in [\neg x]$ such that $r' \not\prec r$ for all $r' \in [\neg x]$. This entails that $x \not\preccurlyeq x$ as desired.

For (C2), assume that for some $x_1, x_2, x_3 \in L$, $x_1 \preccurlyeq x_2 \preccurlyeq x_3$. Let y be an arbitrary sentence in L. From (FC) it follows immediately that x_1, x_2 are not tautologies. If $\models y$, then from $\not\models x_1$ and (FC) we derive immediately that $x_1 \preccurlyeq y$. Assume therefore that $\not\models y$, and suppose that $y \not\preccurlyeq x_3$. Consider now any world $r \in [\neg y]$. Since $y \not\preccurlyeq x_3$, it follows that there is a $r_3 \in [\neg x_3]$ such that $r \not\prec r_3$. On the other hand, from $x_2 \preccurlyeq x_3$ we derive that for some $r_2 \in [\neg x_2]$, $r_2 \prec r_3$. Similarly, from $x_1 \preccurlyeq x_2$ we derive that for some $r_1 \in [\neg x_1]$, $r_1 \prec r_2$. Then from $r \not\prec r_3$ and (SO2) we derive that $r_1 \prec r$. Since r was chosen as an arbitrary $\neg y$-world, from (FC) we derive $x_1 \preccurlyeq y$ as desired.

For (C3), assume that for some $x_1, x_2, x_3, x_4 \in L$, $x_1 \preccurlyeq x_2$ and $x_3 \preccurlyeq x_4$. Clearly then x_1, x_3 are not tautologies. Suppose now that $x_3 \not\preccurlyeq x_2$. We will show that $x_1 \preccurlyeq x_4$. From $x_3 \not\preccurlyeq x_2$ it follows that there is an $r_2 \in [\neg x_2]$ such that for all $r_3 \in [\neg x_3]$, $r_3 \not\prec r_2$. Moreover from $x_1 \preccurlyeq x_2$ we derive that for some $r_1 \in [\neg x_1]$, $r_1 \prec r_2$. Finally, from $x_3 \preccurlyeq x_4$ we have that for every $r_4 \in [\neg x_4]$ there is an $r'_3 \in [x_3]$ such that $r'_3 \prec r_4$. Since $r'_3 \not\prec r_2$, from (SO3) we derive that $r_1 \prec r_4$, for all $r_4 \in [\neg x_4]$. Hence $x_1 \preccurlyeq x_4$ as desired.

For (C4), assume that $x \models y$ and $z \prec x$. Then $\not\models z$, and for all $r' \in [\neg x]$ there is an $r \in [\neg z]$ such that $r \prec r'$. Moreover, from $x \models y$ we derive that $[\neg y] \subseteq [\neg x]$. Hence, clearly, for all $r' \in [\neg y]$ there is an $r \in [\neg z]$ such that $r \prec r'$. Consequently $z \preccurlyeq y$ as desired.

For (C5), assume that $x \models y$ and $y \prec z$. Then $\not\models y$. From $x \models y$ we derive that $[\neg y] \subseteq [\neg x]$; moreover, since $\not\models y$, $x \models y$ entails that $\not\models x$. On the other hand, from $y \prec z$ it follows that for all $r' \in [\neg z]$ there is an $r \in [\neg y]$ such that $r \prec r'$. Hence, since

$[\neg y] \subseteq [\neg x]$, for all $r' \in [\neg z]$ there is an $r \in [\neg x]$ such that $r \prec r'$. Consequently, since $\not\models x$, $x \prec z$ as desired.

For (C6), assume that for some $x, y, z \in L$, $x \prec y$ and $x \prec z$. Clearly by (FC), $\not\models x$. Let r' be any world in $[\neg(y \wedge z)]$. Then $r' \in [\neg y]$ or $r' \in [\neg z]$. In the first case, $x \prec y$ entails that there is an $r \in [\neg x]$ such that $r \prec r'$. Similarly in the later case, $x \prec z$ entails that for some $r \in [\neg x]$, $r \prec r'$. Hence from (FC) we derive that $x \prec y \wedge z$. This proves the right-to-left direction of (C6). For the converse, assume that $x \prec y \wedge z$. Then by (FC), $\not\models x$ and for any world $r' \in [\neg(y \wedge z)]$ there is an $r \in [\neg x]$ such that $r \prec r'$. Since $[\neg(y \wedge z)] = [\neg y] \cup [\neg z]$, from (FC) we then immediately derive that $x \prec y$ and $x \prec z$.

For (C7), assume that for some $x, y, z \in L$, $x \wedge y \prec z$. If at least one of x, y is a tautology, then (C7) follows directly from (C5) (which we have already shown that it holds). In particular, without loss of generality, assume that $\models x$. Then $y \models x \wedge y$, and since $x \wedge y \prec z$, from (C5) we derive that $y \prec z$ as desired. Assume therefore that $\not\models x$ and $\not\models y$, and suppose towards contradiction that $x \not\prec z$ and $y \not\prec z$. Then by (FC), there are $r_1, r_2 \in [\neg z]$ such that $r_3 \not\prec r_1$ for all $r_3 \in [\neg x]$, and $r_4 \not\prec r_2$ for all $r_4 \in [\neg y]$. On the other hand, since $x \wedge y \prec z$, by (FC) we derive that there exist $r_5, r_6 \in [\neg x] \cup [\neg y]$ such that $r_5 \prec r_1$ and $r_6 \prec r_2$. From (SO3) it then follows that $r_5 \prec r_2$ or $r_6 \prec r_1$. Let's take the first case where $r_5 \prec r_2$. Since we have shown that no $\neg y$-world can be smaller from r_2 (wrt $\prec$) it follows that $r_5 \notin [\neg y]$. However we have also assumed that $r_5 \prec r_1$, and since no $\neg x$-world can be smaller from r_1 (wrt $\prec$) it also follows that $r_5 \notin [\neg x]$. Clearly we have reached a contradiction, since $r_5 \in [\neg x] \cup [\neg y]$. With a totally symmetric arguments we also derive a contradiction for the second case where $r_6 \prec r_1$. This shows that $x \prec z$ or $y \prec z$ as desired.

For (C8), assume that K is consistent and let x be any sentence of L such that $x \notin K$. Suppose towards contradiction that there is a $y \in L$ such that $y \prec x$. Since $x \notin K$, it follows that $[\neg x] \cap [K] \neq \emptyset$. Let r' be any world in $[\neg x] \cap [K]$. From $y \prec x$ and (FC) we derive that there is an $r \in [\neg y]$ such that $r \prec r'$. This however contradicts our assumption that $\prec$ is faithful to K (since $r' \in [K]$). Hence we have proved the left-to-right direction of (C8). For the converse, assume that K is consistent and $x \in K$. Then $[K] \cap [\neg x] = \emptyset$. Moreover, since $\prec$ is faithful to K, we derive that $min(\mathcal{M}, \prec) = [K]$, and consequently, $min(\mathcal{M}, \prec) \cap [\neg x] = \emptyset$. Since L is built from finitely many propositional variables it follows that there is a $z \in L$ such that $[z] = [K]$. We will prove the right-to-left direction of (C8) by showing that $\neg z \prec x$. Clearly by construction, $[z] = min(\mathcal{M}, \prec)$. Moreover, since no $\neg x$-world is minimal wrt $\prec$, from Lemma 1.(c) we derive that for all $r' \in [\neg x]$ there is an $r \in [z]$ such that $r \prec r'$. Also observe that $\neg z$ is not a tautology, for otherwise $[K] = [z] = \emptyset$, which contradicts our assumption about the consistency of K. Hence by (FC) $\neg z \prec x$ as desired.

For (C9), let $x, y \in L$ be such that $x \notin K$ and $y \in K$. Then $[\neg x] \cap [K] \neq \emptyset$ and $[\neg y] \cap [K] = \emptyset$. Let r be any world in $[\neg x] \cap [K]$ and r' any world in $[\neg y]$. Since $\prec$ is faithful to K it follows that $r \prec r'$. Moreover, since $x \notin K$, it follows that $\not\models x$. Hence by (FC), $x \prec y$ as desired.

For (C10), let $x, y \in L$ be such that $\not\models x$ and $\models y$. Then $[\neg y] = \emptyset$ and consequently by (FC), $x \prec y$ as desired. ∎

The relationship between semi-entrenchments and faithful semiorders, as expressed with (FC) and (CF), can be strengthened even further. The next two theorems below show that (FC) and (CF) are interchangeable. The proofs are omitted due to space limitations:

Theorem 6. *Let K be a theory, $\prec$ a semi-entrenchment relative to K, and $<$ the binary relation over M induced from $\prec$ via (CF). Then the binary relation $<'$ over L induced from $<$ via (FC) is identical to $\prec$.*

Theorem 7. *Let K be a theory, $<$ a semiorder faithful to K, and $\prec$ the binary relation over L induced from $<$ via (FC). Then the binary relation $<'$ over M induced from $\prec$ via (CF) is identical to $<$.*

6   Semi-entrenchments and Belief Contraction

As alluded in the previous section, the functions induced from semi-entrenchments turn out to be precisely those satisfying the postulates (B1) - (B10). We prove this result utilising the (bidirectional) path already established in [7] and the previous section: i.e., the path from contraction functions to revision functions, to faithful semiorders, to semi-entrenchments.

Before using this path though we need to enhance it with Theorems 8, 9 below. The two theorems essentially show that the inter-definability of revision and contraction established in the AGM framework, survives the lifting of transitive indifference.

In particular, Theorem 8 below shows that if one starts with a contraction function $\div$ satisfying (B1) - (B10), then an application of the Levi Identity followed by an application of the Harper Identity will take her back to the original function $\div$. The reverse direction is treated by Theorem 9. Proofs of both theorems are omitted due to space limitations:

Theorem 8. *Let K be a theory, $\div$ a contraction function satisfying (B1) - (B10), and $*$ the change function induced from $\div$ via the Levi Identity. Moreover, let $\div'$ be the change function induced from $*$ via the Harper Identify. Then $\div = \div'$.*

Theorem 9. *Let K be a theory, $*$ a revision function satisfying (A1) - (A10), and $\div$ the change function induced from $*$ via the Harper Identity. Moreover, let $*'$ be the change function induced from $\div$ via the Levi Identify. Then $* = *'$.*

Turning now to the promised representation result (Theorem 10 below), let us first restate condition (C$\div$) using a semi-entenchment $\prec$ instead of an epistemic entrenchment $\leqslant$:

(EC) $y \in K \div x$ iff $y \in K$ and either $x \prec x \vee y$ or $\models x$.

Theorem 10. *Let K be a theory. If $\prec$ is a semi-entrenchment relative to K then the function $\div$ induced from $\prec$ via (EC) satisfies (B1) - (B10). Conversely, if $\div$ is a contraction function satisfying (B1) - (B10), then there exists a semi-entrenchment $\prec$ related to K that satisfies (EC).*

Proof.

($\Rightarrow$)

Let $\prec$ be a semi-entrenchment related to K and $\div$ the function induced from $\prec$ via (EC). Let $<$ be the binary relation induced from $\prec$ via (CF). Then by Theorem 5, $<$ is a semiorder faithful to K. Moreover, by Theorem 6, $\prec$ and $<$ are also related via (FC). Hence from the construction of $\div$ we derive that $y \in K \div x$ iff $y \in K$ and either $\models x$ or for every $r' \in [\neg x \wedge \neg y]$ there is an $r \in [\neg x]$ such that $r < r'$.

Next observe that whenever $x, y \in L$ are such that for every $r' \in [\neg x \wedge \neg y]$ there is an $r \in [\neg x]$ such that $r < r'$, it follows that $min([\neg x], <) \subseteq [y]$. The converse is also true. Combining the above it follows that

$$y \in K \div x \text{ iff } y \in K \text{ and either } \models x \text{ or } min([\neg x], <) \subseteq [y]$$

Let $*$ be the revision function induced from $<$. By Theorem 4 it follows that $*$ satisfies (A1) - (A10). Moreover, from the condition above and (AS) it follows that $y \in K \div x$ iff $y \in K$ and either $\models x$ or $y \in K * \neg x$. Consequently, by (A1) and (A2), we derive that $K \div x = (K * \neg x) \cap K$; i.e. $\div$ is related to $*$ via the Harper Identity. Therefore, since $*$ satisfies (A1) - (A10), it follows from Theorem 1 that $\div$ satisfies (B1) - (B10) as desired.

($\Leftarrow$)

Assume that $\div$ is a function satisfying (B1) - (B10), and let $*$ be the function induced from $\div$ via the Levi Identity. From Theorem 2 it follows that $*$ satisfies (A1) - (A10), and consequently there exists a semiorder $<$ faithful to K satisfying (AS) (Theorem 3). Let $\prec$ be the binary relation induced from $<$ via (FC). By Theorem 5, $\prec$ is a semi-entrenchment relative to K. Next we show that $\prec$ also satisfies (EC).

Starting with the left-to-right direction of (EC), consider any two sentence $x, y \in L$ and assume that $y \in K \div x$. Clearly then by (B2), $y \in K$. Hence, if $\models x$, then (the left-to-right direction of) (EC) is trivially true. Assume therefore that $\not\models x$. If $\models x \vee y$ then by (C10), $x \prec x \vee y$ and consequently (the left-to-right direction of) (EC) is again true. Assume therefore that $\not\models x \vee y$. From $y \in K \div x$ and the Levi Identity we derive that $y \in K * \neg x$ and consequently by (AS), $min([\neg x], <) \subseteq [y]$. This again entails that for any world $r' \in [\neg x \wedge \neg y]$ there exists a world $r \in [\neg x \wedge y]$ such that $r < r'$. Consequently by (FC), $x \vee \neg y \prec x \vee y$.[4] Since $x \models x \vee \neg y$, from (C5) we then derive that $x \prec x \vee y$ as desired. We have thus proved the left-to-right direction of (EC).

For the opposite direction assume that x, y are arbitrary sentences in L such that $y \in K$ and either $x \prec x \vee y$ or $\models x$. We will show that $y \in K \div x$.

If $\models x$ or if $x \notin K$ then (B1), (B2), (B3), and (B5) entail that $K \div x = K$, from which we trivially derive that $y \in K \div x$. Assume therefore that $x \in K$ and $\not\models x$. Hence $x \prec x \vee y$. From (FC) we then derive that for all $r' \in [\neg x \wedge \neg y]$ there is an $r \in [\neg x]$ such that $r < r'$. This again entails that $min([\neg x], <) \subseteq [y]$, and therefore by (AS), $y \in K * \neg x$. Let $\div'$ be the function induced from $*$ via the Harper Identity. Then, since

---

[4] To apply condition (FC) we need to establish that $\not\models x \vee \neg y$, or equivalently that $[\neg x \wedge y] \neq \varnothing$. This however follows from our previous assumptions. In particular, we have assumed that $\not\models x$, and therefore by Lemma 1, $min([\neg x], <) \neq \varnothing$. Let r_1 be any world in $min([\neg x], <)$. Since, as shown above, $min([\neg x], <) \subseteq [y]$, it follows that $r_1 \in [\neg x \wedge y]$, and therefore $[\neg x \wedge y] \neq \varnothing$ as desired.

$y \in K$, from $y \in K * \neg x$ we derive that $y \in K \div' x$. Consequently, from Theorem 8, we derive $y \in K \div x$ as desired. ∎

7   Semiorders in the Partial Meet Model

The only major model of the classical AGM framework we haven't considered yet is the *partial meet model* [1]. We do so in this section.

The partial meet model is a constructive model for contraction functions. Loosely speaking, the construction of a contraction function $\div$ via the partial meet model works as follows. Given an initial belief set K and a sentence x to be withdrawn from K, one considers all maximal subsets of K that fail to entail x. The "best" (i.e. most plausible) such subsets are then intersected to produce the next belief set $K \div x$. If the selection of the "best" subsets is based on a total preorder (over subsets of K), then the induced contraction functions coincide with those satisfying the AGM postulates for contraction.[5] Herein we shall replace the total preorders of the partial meet model with semiorders and prove soundness and completeness wrt the new postulates (B1) - (B10).

Let K be a theory and x a sentence in L. We shall say that a set of sentences H is a x-*remainder* (of K) iff H is a maximal subset of K that fails to entail x (i.e. $H \not\models x$). We shall denote the set of all x-remainders of K by $K \perp\!\!\!\perp x$; in the limiting case that x is a tautology, we define $K \perp\!\!\!\perp x = \{K\}$. The set of all remainders of K with respect to any $x \in L$ is denoted $\mathcal{R}_K$; i.e. $\mathcal{R}_K = \bigcup\{K \perp\!\!\!\perp x : x \in L\}$.

Consider now a semiorder $\ll$ over $\mathcal{R}_K$ representing the comparative plausibility of remainders. As discussed earlier, for a theory K and a sentence x, the partial meet model constructs $K \div x$ by interesting the "best" remainders in $K \perp\!\!\!\perp x$. This is formally expressed by condition (PM) below:

(PM) $K \div x = \bigcap max(K \perp\!\!\!\perp x, \ll)$

Our final representation result is Theorem 11 below, which shows that the functions induced from semiorders over remainders via (PM), are precisely those satisfying the axioms (B1) - (B10). The proof of the theorem is omitted due to space limitations.

Theorem 11. *Let K be a theory. For any semiorder $\ll$ in $\mathcal{R}_K$, the function $\div$ induced from $\ll$ via (PM) satisfies (B1) - (B10). Conversely, for any contraction function $\div$ satisfying (B1) - (B10), there exists a semiorder $\ll$ in $\mathcal{R}_K$ that satisfies (PM).*

8   Conclusion

Researchers in the *preference modelling* community have long argued in favor of *semi orders* over *total preorders* for modelling preference. The main advantage of semiorders is the intransitivity of indifference.

---

[5] It should be noted that the preorders used in the selection of the "best" remainder, do not need to be total for the partial meet model to match the AGM postulates for contraction; see Theorem 4.16 in [2]. However, as shown by Theorem 4.17 in [2], imposing totality has no effect on the properties of the induced contraction function. Hence we can assume the preorders of the partial meet model to be total without damaging the connection with the AGM postulates for contraction.

In a recent paper [7], we argued that for similar reasons, transitivity of plausibility indifference is also too strong an assumption in the context of Belief Change.[6] We therefore lifted this assumption from the AGM postulates for revision and contraction, as well as from the possible-models construction of Katsuno and Mendelzon. In this paper we completed the task by lifting transitive indifference from the remaining two major models of the AGM framework; namely, from the epistemic entrenchment model and the partial meet model. Moreover we established representation results connecting the weaker epistemic entrenchment and partial meet models, with the weaker axioms for contraction introduced in [7]. To aid us with the proofs of the main representation results, we established a number of auxiliary results connecting semiorders over worlds with semiorders over remainders, and with semi-entrenchments; these auxiliary results are also of interest in their own right.

We note that very recently, and for reasons other than those stated herein, Rott has also considered weaker versions of the AGM postulates for contraction, as well as of the partial meet and epistemic entrenchment models, [9]. However Rott's weakening is based on *interval orders* (on remainders) rather than semiorders. We recall that an interval order is a binary relation < satisfying (SO1) and (SO3), but not necessarily (SO2).

Acknowledgements. We are grateful to Abhaya Nayak, Maurice Pagnucco, Hans Rott, and the anonymous reviewers for many valuable comments on this work.

References

1. Alchourron, C., Gardenfors, P., Makinson, D.: On the logic of theory change: Partial meet functions for contraction and revision. Journal of Symbolic Logic 50, 510–530 (1985)
2. Gardenfors, P.: Knowledge in Flux. MIT Press (1988)
3. Gardenfors, P., Makinson, D.: Revisions of knowledge systems using epistemic entrench-ment. In: Proceedings of Theoretical Aspects of Reasoning about Knowledge, pp. 83–95. Morgan-Kaufmann (1988)
4. Katsuno, H., Mendelzon, A.: Propositional knowledge base revision and minimal change. Artificial Intelligence 52(3), 263–294 (1991)
5. Luce, R.D.: Semiorders and a theory of utility discrimination. Econometrica 24(2), 178–191 (1956)
6. Peppas, P.: Belief revision. In: Handbook of Knowledge Representation, pp. 317–359. Else-vier Science (2008)
7. Peppas, P., Williams, M.A.: Belief change and semiorders. In: Proceedings of the 14th Inter-national Conference on Principles of Knowledge Representation and Reasoning, KR 2014 (2014)
8. Rabinovitch, I.: The Scott-Suppes theorem on semiorders. Journal of Mathematical Psychol-ogy 1 (1977)
9. Rott, H.: Three floors for the theory of theory change. In: The Logica Yearbook 2013 (2014)
10. Scott, D., Suppes, P.: Foundational aspects of theories of measurement. Journal of Symbolic Logic 23(2) (1958)

---

[6] It is worth noting that *indifference* between two choices is different from *incomparability*. A study of this distinction in the context of Belief Revision is with pursuing.

Four Floors for the Theory of Theory Change:
The Case of Imperfect Discrimination

Hans Rott[*]

University of Regensburg, 93040 Regensburg, Germany
hans.rott@ur.de
http://www.uni-r.de/philosophie-rott

Abstract. The theory of theory change due to Alchourrón, Gärdenfors and Makinson ("AGM") has been widely known as being characterised by two packages of postulates. The basic package consists of six postulates and is very weak, the full package adds two further postulates and is very strong. Revisiting two classical constructions of theory contraction, viz., relational possible models contraction and entrenchment-based contraction on the one hand and tracing the idea of imperfect discrimination of plausibilities on the other, I argue that four intermediate levels can be distinguished that play important roles within the AGM theory.

Keywords: Theory change, belief contraction, possible models, entrenchment, interval orders, semiorders, exponentiated revision, AGM.

1 Introduction

The theory of theory change due to Alchourrón, Gärdenfors and Makinson ("AGM") has been widely known as being characterised by two packages of postulates. The basic package consists of six postulates and is very weak, the full package adds two further postulates and is very strong. In this paper, I will describe four intermediate levels within the AGM theory that, I believe, have not been sufficiently recognised so far. AGM created, to use this metaphor, a large hall building with a floor and a ceiling.[1] I argue that the space in between may be structured by fitting in four intermediate floors that house some important incarnations of the theory of theory change. The first and the second floor can be discerned within the original AGM modellings of the 1980s. The third floor is motivated by a concern with what is called "Disjunctive rationality" in nonmonotonic reasoning. This rationality requirement will lead us to a consideration of the idea of imperfect discrimination of differences in plausibility that can be modelled in two ways: first, by interval orders that are in fact characteristic of the third floor; second, by the more constrained semiorders which characterises the fourth floor, which is still significantly "below" the full theory of AGM.

Interval orders and semiorders make room for the idea of nontransitive "indifference" relations that are due to discrimination thresholds. The topic of imperfect discrimination

---

[*] I am grateful to Pavlos Peppas and Mary-Anne Williams for making available to me two versions of their (still unpublished) paper [20] and to three JELIA referees for helpful comments.
[1] For the historical development of the AGM theory, see Fermé and Hansson [4].

E. Fermé and J. Leite (Eds.): JELIA 2014, LNAI 8761, pp. 368–382, 2014.
© Springer International Publishing Switzerland 2014

originated in psychology in 1860 (G.Th. Fechner) and in economics in the late 1930s (N. Georgescu-Roegen, W.E. Armstrong). Seminal contributions to the understanding of interval orders and semiorders were made by Luce [16], Scott and Suppes [29], Roberts [21], Fishburn [5] and Mirkin [18]. For the theory of theory change, a choice-theoretic analysis of these orders is needed for which Jamison and Lau [12, 13] and Fishburn [6] are still the authoritative papers.[2] To the best of my knowledge, interval orders and semiorders have been recognised as relevant for the theory of theory change only recently, by Rott [26] and Peppas and Williams [20], respectively. The present paper, which is a sequel to [26], will complete and refine the insights gained in these papers.

2 Preparation

2.1 The Classical Theory of AGM

We will work with a propositional object language $\mathcal{L}$ that has the usual n-ary truth-functional operators $\perp$ and $\top$ ($n=0$), $\neg$ ($n=1$), $\vee$, $\wedge$, $\rightarrow$, and $\leftrightarrow$ ($n=2$). $\mathcal{L}$ is supposed to be governed by a Tarskian consequence operation Cn that includes classical propositional logic, is reflexive, idempotent, monotonic, compact, and satisfies the deduction theorem. We write $M \vdash \phi$ for $\phi \in Cn(M)$, $\phi \vdash \psi$ for $\psi \in Cn(\{\phi\})$, $\phi \dashv\vdash \psi$ for $Cn(\{\phi\}) = Cn(\{\psi\})$, $\vdash \phi$ for $\phi \in Cn(\emptyset)$, and $M \vdash N$ for $N \subseteq Cn(M)$. By K and variants like K', $K \dot{-} \phi$ etc., we denote *theories* in $\mathcal{L}$, i.e., subsets of $\mathcal{L}$ that are closed under Cn. W denotes the set of models for $\mathcal{L}$. $[\![\phi]\!]$ (or $[\![M]\!]$) is the set of models for $\mathcal{L}$ at which ϕ is (all elements of M are) true, $]\!]\phi[\![$ (or $]\!]M[\![$) is the set of models at which ϕ (at least one element of M) is false. For each model w, $\hat{w}$ denotes the set of sentences true at w.

Theories are infinite sets, but some theories can be be partitioned into finitely many equivalence classes with respect to Cn; such theories will be called *logically finite*. If K is logically finite, then $\bigwedge K$ denotes the conjunction of some representatives of the equivalence classes within K.[3] Every logically finite theory K has co-atoms, i.e., weakest non-tautological elements. The set of co-atoms of K is denoted by $Coat(K)$, and the set of co-atoms of K implied by ϕ is denoted by $Coat_K(\phi)$. There is a bijective mapping between the co-atoms and the non-models of K: if $\alpha \in Coat_K(\phi)$, then w_α, defined as the single element of $]\!]\alpha[\![$, is in $]\!]\phi[\![$; and conversely, if $w \in]\!]\phi[\![$, then α_w, defined as $\neg \bigwedge \hat{w}$, is in $Coat_K(\phi)$.[4]

We focus on the problem of *theory contraction*. Here the agent receives an input consisting in a sentence ϕ to be contracted from her theory K, and then performs an operation whose goal is to find a plausible outcome $K \dot{-} \phi$ that is a subset of the prior theory that does not imply ϕ.

The AGM theory has most prominently been characterised by a collection of rationality postulates that came in two packages. A set of six postulates constitutes the *basic*

---

[2] For further results, cf. Suppes, Krantz, Luce and Tversky [31, Ch. 16] and Aleskerov, Bouyssou and Monjardet [3, sections 2.5–2.6 and 3.6].

[3] Due to (K $\dot{-}$ 6) and a similar Extensionality axiom for entrenchment, it does not matter which representatives of the equivalence classes with respect to Cn figure in the big conjunctions, so there is no danger of failing well-definedness.

[4] We presuppose here that $\phi \in K$. Note that $Coat_K(\bigwedge K) = Coat(K)$.

theory, an extended set of eight postulates constitutes the *full theory*. These postulates have become famous as the "AGM postulates" (sometimes also called the "Gärdenfors postulates"):

(K÷1)	if K is a theory, then $K \dot{-} \phi$ is a theory	(Closure)
(K÷2)	$K \dot{-} \phi \subseteq K$	(Inclusion)
(K÷3)	if $\phi \notin K$, then $K \dot{-} \phi = K$	(Vacuity)
(K÷4)	if $\nvdash \phi$, then $\phi \notin K \dot{-} \phi$	(Success)
(K÷5)	$(K \dot{-} \phi) \cup \{\phi\} \vdash K$	(Recovery)
(K÷6)	if $\phi \dashv\vdash \psi$, then $K \dot{-} \phi = K \dot{-} \psi$	(Extensionality)
(K÷7)	$K \dot{-} \phi \cap K \dot{-} \psi \subseteq K \dot{-} (\phi \wedge \psi)$	(Conjunctive overlap)
(K÷8)	if $\phi \notin K \dot{-} (\phi \wedge \psi)$, then $K \dot{-} (\phi \wedge \psi) \subseteq K \dot{-} \phi$	(Conjunctive inclusion)

Justifications for these postulates are given in Gärdenfors [8, pp. 61–65]. Only the addition of the supplementary postulates (K÷7) and (K÷8) to the basic package made the theory really interesting. But the space between the basic and the full theory is huge and may be structured in various instructive ways. Two developments that both began around 1990 have helped to make this clear. First, theories of *non-monotonic reasoning* were introduced and rapidly developed in artificial intelligence research of the 1980s, and bridges to the theory of theory change were soon discovered [10]. Most of the widely discussed principles of non-monotonic reasoning translate into principles for theory change that lie *between* the basic and the full AGM theory. Second, the theory of theory change (as well as the theory of non-monotonic reasoning) was found to be amenable to a systematic interpretation in terms of *rational choice* [15, 23, 24, 28], and again, the most prominent principles of rational choice translate into principles for theory change that lie *between* the basic and the full AGM theory.

Even though the postulates (K÷1)–(K÷8) are perhaps the most widely known part of the AGM theory, it is not the postulates themselves that lend credibility and substance to the AGM theory. The success of the AGM program can be explained only by the fact that AGM at the same time developed three plausible constructive methods for theory change and that these methods satisfy their postulates: partial meet contraction, safe contraction and entrenchment-based contraction. The constructive methods served, as it were, as a semantics for the postulates.

We now briefly describe two methods of theory contraction. We restrict the following definitions to the contraction of K by a non-tautological ϕ (i.e., $\nvdash \phi$); for tautological sentences ϕ, $K \dot{-} \phi$ is usually put equal to K.

The *possible models contraction* of K by ϕ is based on a selection function (or choice function) σ which is applied to the set of possible models that do not satisfy ϕ. Intuitively, σ selects the most plausible of these models. In contrast to possible worlds, models are linguistically distinguishable: Any two models can be distinguished by some sentence that is true in one but not in the other. Grove [11] showed that the idea of possible models contraction is equivalent to AGM's idea of partial meet contraction.

Definition 1. *The possible models contraction generated by a selection function σ on W is defined as*

$$K \dot{-} \phi = \{\psi \in K : \psi \text{ is true throughout } \sigma(\,]\!]\phi[\![\,)\}$$

The possible models contraction $\doteq$ is relational *if it is generated by a selection function* σ *that is based on an acyclic binary relation* $\prec$ *on* W, *in such a way that for all* ϕ,

$$\sigma(\,]\!]\phi[\![\,) = \{w \in \,]\!]\phi[\![\, : w \prec v \text{ for no } v \in \,]\!]\phi[\![\,\}$$

The latter equation defines the *rationalisation* of σ by $\prec$; we also say that σ is based on *maximisation* with respect to $\prec$. Relations will play a central role in this paper, and much depends on their properties. We begin with purely *structural* properties that apply to relations of any kind.

Definition 2. *(i) A* strict partial order *is an irreflexive and transitive (and, thus, asymmetric) relation.*
(ii) An interval order *is a strict partial order that satisfies the*
    (Interval condition)   *If* $x < y$ *and* $u < v$, *then either* $x < v$ *or* $u < y$.
(iii) A semiorder *is an interval order that satisfies*
    (Semitransitivity)   *If* $x < y$ *and* $y < v$, *then either* $x < u$ *or* $u < v$.
(iv) A strict partial order *is* modular *(or* almost connected, virtually connected, *or* negatively transitive*) iff it satisfies*
    (Modularity)   *If* $x < y$, *then either* $x < u$ *or* $u < y$.

It is easy to check that for asymmetric relations, modularity implies both the Interval condition and Semitransitivity, and that for irreflexive relations, each of the Interval condition and Semitransitivity in turn implies transitivity. The Interval condition and Semitransitivity, however, are logically independent.

  Epistemic entrenchment-based contraction, or simply *entrenchment contraction*, is based on a binary relation $<$ over the sentences in the language $\mathcal{L}$. Here $\psi < \chi$ means that ψ is less "entrenched", or more easily given up, than χ.[5] We distinguish between three versions of the notion of entrenchment with increasing logical strength, introduced and motivated in [25], [22] and [9], respectively. They are relations over beliefs (expressible in $\mathcal{L}$), and the relevant properties make reference to the *contents* of beliefs.

Definition 3. *(i) A* basic entrenchment relation *is an irreflexive relation* $<$ *over* $\mathcal{L}$ *that satisfies*
    (Extensionality)   *If* $\phi < \psi$, $\phi \dashv\vdash \phi'$ *and* $\psi \dashv\vdash \psi'$, *then* $\phi' < \psi'$.
    (Choice easy)   *If* $\phi < \psi \wedge \chi$, *then* $\phi \wedge \psi < \chi$.
    (Choice hard)   *If* $\phi \wedge \psi < \chi$ *and* $\phi \wedge \chi < \psi$, *then* $\phi < \psi \wedge \chi$.
    (Maximality)   *If* $\nvdash \phi$, *then* $\phi < \top$.
(ii) A generalised *entrenchment relation is a basic entrenchment relation that satisfies*
    (Continuing up)   *If* $\phi < \psi$ *and* $\psi \vdash \chi$, *then* $\phi < \chi$.
    (Continuing down)   *If* $\phi < \psi$ *and* $\chi \vdash \phi$, *then* $\chi < \psi$.
(iii) A GM entrenchment relation *is a generalised entrenchment relation that is modular and satisfies*
    (K-Minimality)   *If* K *is consistent, then* ϕ *is in* K *if and only if* $\perp < \phi$.

---

[5] Each of $\prec$ and $<$ can be interpreted as a doxastic preference relation.

The two Choice conditions are the hallmark of the notion of entrenchment. Notice that basic entrenchment relations are not in general acyclic.[6] It is easily verified that basic entrenchment relations satisfy

(Conjunction down)   If $\phi \wedge \psi < \psi$, then $\phi < \psi$.

and that basic entrenchment relations satisfying Continuing down also satisfy[7]

(Conjunction up)   If $\phi < \psi$ and $\phi < \chi$, then $\phi < \psi \wedge \chi$.

Generalised entrenchment relations are transitive (and thus acyclic).[8]

Entrenchment-based contractions operate by directly comparing the entrenchment of certain elements of K.

Definition 4. *The entrenchment contraction generated by an entrenchment relation $<$ on $\mathcal{L}$ is defined as*

$$K \dot{-} \phi = \{\psi \in K : \phi < (\phi \vee \psi)\}.$$

This construction has been standard within the full AGM theory since Gärdenfors [8] and Gärdenfors and Makinson [9], but it can be used in the much more general context of the basic AGM theory [25]. Though being somewhat unintuitive at first sight, it can be justified by its perfect fit with the *re*construction of comparative entrenchments from a reasoner's contraction behaviour:

Definition 5. *Assuming that a contraction function $\dot{-}$ over K is given, the entrenchment relation $<$ over $\mathcal{L}$ revealed by $\dot{-}$ is given by*

$$\phi < \psi \text{ iff } \psi \in K \dot{-} (\phi \wedge \psi) \text{ and } \nvdash \phi.$$

2.2   Exponentiated Theory Change

In a finite context, we are able to represent an arbitrarily changed theory $K * \phi$ or $K \dot{-} \phi$, by a single sentence $\bigwedge(K * \phi)$ or $\bigwedge(K \dot{-} \phi)$, respectively.

Now let $*$ and $\dot{-}$ signify functions of belief change that take, for some given belief set K, an input sentence ϕ and return revised and contracted belief sets $K * \phi$ and $K \dot{-} \phi$, respectively. It is well known that the problem of theory revision is essentially equivalent to that of theory contraction, in virtue of the Levi identity, $K * \phi = \text{Cn}((K \dot{-} \neg \phi) \cup \{\phi\})$, and the Harper identity, $K \dot{-} \phi = K \cap K * \neg \phi$. We will now introduce a new kind of belief change operation and start with revisions.

Definition 6. *The* exponentiated revision functions $*^i$ and $*^{\leq i}$ *are given by simultaneous recursion:*

$$K *^1 \phi = K * \phi \qquad\qquad K *^{\leq 1} \phi = K * \phi$$
$$K *^{i+1} \phi = K * (\phi \wedge \neg \bigwedge(K *^{\leq i} \phi)) \qquad K *^{\leq(i+1)} \phi = (K *^{\leq i} \phi) \cap (K *^{i+1} \phi)$$

---

[6] See [25, pp. 268–269]. But they are asymmetric. Suppose for reductio that $\phi < \psi$ and $\psi < \phi$. Then by Extensionality and Choice easy, $\phi \wedge \psi \wedge \phi < \psi$ and $\phi \wedge \psi \wedge \psi < \phi$. Thus by Choice hard $\phi \wedge \psi < \phi \wedge \psi$, contradicting Irreflexivity.

[7] See [24, Observation 61(v)–(vi)].

[8] Suppose that $\phi < \psi$ and $\psi < \chi$. Then by Continuing down $\phi \wedge \chi < \psi$ and $\phi \wedge \psi < \chi$, and by Choice hard $\phi < \psi \wedge \chi$, and thus by Continuing up $\phi < \chi$. [22, Lemma 4(v)].

$*^1$ and $*^{\leq 1}$ are just identical to the AGM-style revision function that selects the best (i.e., maximal) models satisfying ϕ. $*^2$ proceeds by selecting the second-best models satisfying ϕ. $*^{\leq 2}$ proceeds by selecting of the union of the best and second-best such models. And so on. Thus $*^i$ selects the ith-best worlds satisfying the input sentence, and $*^{\leq i}$ takes the i best "layers" all together.[9] In a similar way, we propose

Definition 7. *The* exponentiated contraction functions $\dot{-}^i$ *and* $\dot{-}^{\leq i}$ *are given by simultaneous recursion:*

$$K \dot{-}^1 \phi = K \dot{-} \phi \qquad\qquad K \dot{-}^{\leq 1} \phi = K \dot{-} \phi$$
$$K \dot{-}^{i+1} \phi = K \dot{-} (\phi \vee \bigwedge (K \dot{-}^{\leq i} \phi)) \qquad K \dot{-}^{\leq (i+1)} \phi = (K \dot{-}^{\leq i} \phi) \cap (K \dot{-}^{i+1} \phi)$$

$\dot{-}^1$ and $\dot{-}^{\leq 1}$ are just identical to the AGM-style contraction function that adds to the models of K the best (maximal) models falsifying ϕ. $\dot{-}^2$ proceeds by adding the second-best models falsifying ϕ. $\dot{-}^{\leq 2}$ proceeds by selecting the union of the best and second-best such models. And so on. Exponentiated belief change is, I believe, a new variation on the classical AGM model that offers interesting perspectives for the qualitative modelling of iterated belief change. But this is not the topic of the present paper.

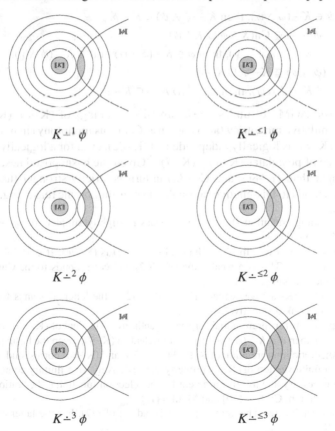

$$K \dot{-}^1 \phi \qquad\qquad K \dot{-}^{\leq 1} \phi$$

$$K \dot{-}^2 \phi \qquad\qquad K \dot{-}^{\leq 2} \phi$$

$$K \dot{-}^3 \phi \qquad\qquad K \dot{-}^{\leq 3} \phi$$

[9] Notice that it makes sense to speak of layers here even if the relations $\prec$ and $<$ are not modular, i.e., do not encode full comparability. For the sake of simplicity, however, the systems-of-spheres pictures below do presuppose full comparability.

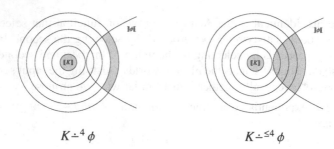

$$K \dot{-}^4 \phi \qquad\qquad K \dot{-}^{\leq 4} \phi$$

3   Four Intermediate Floors

3.1   Weakening the Full AGM Theory

All additional floors can be characterized by certain weakenings of the last postulate of AGM. Consider the following list.

(K$\dot{-}$8c)   If $\psi \in K \dot{-} (\phi \wedge \psi)$, then $K \dot{-} (\phi \wedge \psi) \subseteq K \dot{-} \phi$.

(K$\dot{-}$8r) $K \dot{-} (\phi \wedge \psi) \subseteq \mathrm{Cn}(K \dot{-} \phi \cup K \dot{-} \psi)$.

(K$\dot{-}$8p)   If $\phi \in K \dot{-} (\phi \wedge \psi \wedge \chi)$, then $\phi \in K \dot{-} (\phi \wedge \psi)$ or $\phi \in K \dot{-} (\phi \wedge \chi)$.

(K$\dot{-}$8d) $K \dot{-} (\phi \wedge \psi) \subseteq K \dot{-} \phi \cup K \dot{-} \psi$.

(K$\dot{-}$8s)   If $\phi \notin K \dot{-} (\phi \wedge \psi)$, then $K \dot{-}^{\leq 2} (\phi \wedge \psi) \subseteq K \dot{-} \phi$.[10]

Given the basic AGM postulates, these are all weakenings of (K$\dot{-}$8). (K$\dot{-}$8c) corresponds to Cumulative monotony (also known as Cautious monotony) in non-monotonic reasoning.[11] (K$\dot{-}$8r) is logically independent of (K$\dot{-}$8c), even for a logically finite K and in the presence of postulates (K$\dot{-}$1) – (K$\dot{-}$7).[12] Given the basic postulates, (K$\dot{-}$8p)[13] is strictly stronger than (K$\dot{-}$8r), and (K$\dot{-}$8d) in turn is strictly stronger than (K$\dot{-}$8p).[14] (K$\dot{-}$8d) corresponds to Disjunctive rationality in non-monotonic reasoning.[15] Given the

---

[10] The corresponding condition (K*8s) for revisions is slightly simpler: If $\neg\psi \notin K * \phi$, then $K *^{\leq 2} \phi \subseteq K * (\phi \wedge \psi)$.

[11] (K$\dot{-}$8c) plays a central role in [22]. The dual of (K$\dot{-}$8c) is (K$\dot{-}$7c): If $\psi \in K \dot{-} (\phi \wedge \psi)$, then $K \dot{-} \phi \subseteq K \dot{-} (\phi \wedge \psi)$. This is a weakening of (K$\dot{-}$7) and corresponds to the Cut condition in non-monotonic reasoning.

[12] Cf. [23, p. 1438]. (K$\dot{-}$8r) was called (K$\dot{-}$8vwd) in [24]; the letter 'r' stands for 'relational', 'vwd' for 'very weak disjunctive'.

[13] The letter 'p' stands for 'preferential' or 'partial antitony'. The dual of (K$\dot{-}$8p), viz. (K$\dot{-}$7p): If $\phi \in K \dot{-} (\phi \wedge \psi)$, then $\phi \in K \dot{-} (\phi \wedge \psi \wedge \chi)$, is equivalent to (K$\dot{-}$7), given the basic postulates. On the choice-theoretic interpretation of Rott [24], (K$\dot{-}$7p) and (K$\dot{-}$8p) correspond to Sen's property α and (a finite version of) Sen's property γ, respectively. In a finitary context, properties α and γ are necessary and jointly sufficient for the selection function to be "rationalisable" by a preference relation. Cf. Sen [30] and Moulin [19].

[14] For the former claim, see Theorem 2, parts (ii) and (v) of [27]. For the latter claim, see [26, pp. 199–200].

[15] See Rott [24, especially p. 104]. The condition (K$\dot{-}$8d) is equivalent with a seemingly stronger one: $K \dot{-} (\phi \wedge \psi) \subseteq K \dot{-} \phi$ or $K \dot{-} (\phi \wedge \psi) \subseteq K \dot{-} \psi$. This condition is called the Covering condition in [1] and Strong disjunctive rationality in [24].

basic postulates, (K÷8c) and (K÷8p) taken together imply (K÷8d); there is no analogous implication starting from (K÷8c) and (K÷8r).[16] (K÷8s) is logically independent of (K÷8d), even given (K÷8r) and (K÷8c).

We keep the ground floor and the top floor as established by AGM, and identify the following intermediate floors:

1st floor: basic AGM plus (K÷7) and (K÷8r)

2nd floor: basic AGM plus (K÷7), (K÷8c) and (K÷8r)

3rd floor: basic AGM plus (K÷7), (K÷8c) and (K÷8d)

4th floor: basic AGM plus (K÷7), (K÷8c), (K÷8d) and (K÷8s)

All these floors are above AGM's ground floor and below AGM's top floor, and floors with higher numbers are above the ones with lower numbers. "Being above" is metaphorical here for "being logically stronger".

In the remainder of this paper I will explain why these levels are particularly natural to add to the floor plan of AGM's edifice—at least as long as one focusses on logically finite theories.[17] On each of the four floors, the results pertaining to contractions based on possible models are restricted to the case of logically finite theories K; no such restriction applies to entrenchment-based contractions.

3.2   The Ground Floor

The ground floor is constituted by the basic AGM theory. It is known that possible models contractions satisfy the basic postulates (K÷1)–(K÷6), and that every contraction function satisfying these postulates can be represented as a possible models contraction [1, 11]. The same representation result is valid for the basic entrenchment contractions [25]. Notice that the contractions on the ground floor are relational, in a certain sense (Definition 4), with respect to entrenchment relations $<$ over the sentences of $\mathcal{L}$, but they are not in general relational (in the sense of Definition 1) with respect to the plausibility relations $<$ over the possible models for $\mathcal{L}$.

3.3   The 1st Floor

For a logically finite theory K, the relational possible models contractions satisfy the postulates (K÷1)–(K÷7) and (K÷8r), and every contraction function satisfying these postulates can be represented as a relational possible models contraction (apply Grove's [11] connection to [23, Corollary 2]).

For entrenchment-based contractions, (K÷7) corresponds exactly to Continuing down, while (K÷8r) corresponds exactly to the rather unintuitive

(EII⁻)   If $\phi \wedge \psi < \chi$ and $\nvdash \chi$, then there are ξ and ρ such that $\chi \dashv\vdash \xi \wedge \rho$ and $\phi \wedge \rho < \xi$ and $\psi \wedge \xi < \rho$.[18]

---

[16] See Theorem 2, parts (iv) and (v), of [27].

[17] (K÷8p) plays an auxiliary role in this architecture. It is interesting in itself only if (K÷8c) is not satisfied (or, what comes to much the same thing, only if the underlying doxastic preference relation is not transitive).

[18] See [24, Observation 68] and [27, Theorem 2 and Lemma 10]. "Correspondence" here means "correspondence via Definitions 4 and 5".

Given Extensionality and Maximality, EII$^-$ is a weakening of

(EII)   If $\phi \wedge \psi < \chi$, then either $\phi < \chi$ or $\psi < \chi$.[19]

The following lemma provides a slightly more accessible condition that is suitable for characterising the first floor:

Lemma 1. *Given the resources available on the first floor, EII$^-$ is equivalent to*

(EII^{coat}) If χ is a co-atom of K and $\phi \wedge \psi < \chi$, then either $\phi < \chi$ or $\psi < \chi$.

The proofs of all observations can be obtained from the author.[20]

3.4   The 2nd Floor

For a logically finite theory K, the transitively relational possible models contractions satisfy the postulates (K$\dot{-}$1)–(K$\dot{-}$7), (K$\dot{-}$8c) and (K$\dot{-}$8r), and every contraction function satisfying these postulates can be represented as a transitively relational possible models contraction (apply again Grove's [11] connection to [23, Corollary 2]).[21]

For entrenchment contractions, the new condition (K$\dot{-}$8c) corresponds exactly to Continuing up. So the second floor is inhabited by generalised entrenchment relations that satisfy EII$^-$. Since we have Continuing up available now, EII$^-$ can be simplified and strengthened to

(EII^{-o})   If $\phi \wedge \psi < \chi$ and $\nvdash \chi$, then there are ξ and ρ such that $\chi \dashv\vdash \xi \wedge \rho$ and $\phi < \xi$ and $\psi < \rho$.

It is on this second floor where the entrenchments of all elements of a logically finite theory are determined in a very natural way by the entrenchments of their co-atoms. We have the following useful result [27, Lemma 18(viii)]:

(Coat) $\phi < \psi$ iff for all β in $Coat_K(\psi)$ there is an α in $Coat_K(\phi)$ such that $\alpha < \beta$.

This has the following consequences:[22]

---

[19] To see this, put either $\xi = \chi$ and $\rho = \top$, or $\xi = \top$ and $\rho = \chi$.—Given Extensionality and Choice hard, EII follows from Modularity.

[20] On this first floor, we can link the reconstructive Definition 5 of entrenchment to the idea of maximisation in the possible models approach and get the following chain: $\phi < \psi$ iff $\psi \in K \dot{-} (\phi \wedge \psi)$; iff all $<$-maximal models in $]\!]\phi \wedge \psi[\![=]\!]\phi[\![\cup]\!]\psi[\![$ are in $[\![\psi]\!]$; iff for every w in $]\!]\psi[\![$ there is a v in $]\!]\phi \wedge \psi[\![$ such that $w < v$; iff for all β in $Coat_K(\psi)$ there is an α in $Coat_K(\phi \wedge \psi) = Coat_K(\phi) \cup Coat_K(\psi)$ such that $\alpha < \beta$. This not only connects the idea of entrenchment with the ordering of the models, but also determines the entrenchments within the whole of K through the entrenchments within the restricted set $Coat(K)$.

[21] Freund [7, Theorem 4.13] proved a very similar result for non-monotonic logics on logically finite languages. Just the route of approaching this result was different. For AGM reinterpreted via the Grove connection, all models are injective, then comes the relationality of selection functions (1st floor), and last comes their transitive relationality (2nd floor). In Freund's possible worlds models, everything is transitively relational (thus Preferential logic includes Cumulative monotony, the analogue of (K$\dot{-}$8c)), but injectiveness comes only at the end.

[22] Some of these observations were stated in [27, pp. 45–46].

Lemma 2. *Suppose that an arbitrary relation $<$ over a logically finite theory K satisfies the constraint (Coat). Then*

(i) $<$ *satisfies Extensionality, Choice easy, Continuing down, Continuing up and EII^{-o} over K.*

(ii) *If $<$ is acyclic or transitive over the set $Coat(K)$, then $<$ is acyclic and transitive, respectively, over the whole of K.*

(iii) *If $<$ is transitive over $Coat(K)$, then $<$ also satisfies Choice hard over K.*

(iv) *If $<$ satisfies the Interval condition or Semitransitivity over the set $Coat(K)$, then $<$ satisfies the Interval condition and Semitransitivity, respectively, over the whole of K.*

(v)   *If $\phi < \psi$, then none of the elements in $Coat_K(\psi)$ is $<$-minimal in $Coat_K(\phi \wedge \psi)$; if $<$ is transitive, then the converse holds as well.*[23]

3.5   The 3rd Floor

The new condition on the third floor is $(K \dot{-} 8d)$. A possible models contraction function over a logically finite theory K satisfies $(K \dot{-} 8d)$ if and only if the selection function σ on which it is based satisfies the following condition:[24]

(II^+) Either $\sigma(S) \subseteq \sigma(S \cup S')$ or $\sigma(S') \subseteq \sigma(S \cup S')$.

Condition (II^+) says that either all the best elements of S or all the best elements of S' are best elements of the union $S \cup S'$. One can now make the following

Observation 3. *Every choice function over the set of subsets of a finite domain rationalisable by an irreflexive relation that satisfies the Interval condition satisfies (II^+), and conversely every such choice function satisfying (II^+) can be rationalised by an irreflexive relation that satisfies the Interval condition.*[25]

So the possible models contractions living on the third floor are the ones that are based on interval orders. Given the importance of interval orders for the modelling of preferences with imperfect discrimination [3, 5, 18], the introduction of a third level to our floor plan appears to be justified.[26]

---

[23] Having in mind the dualities made use of already by Alchourrón and Makinson [2, pp. 190–191] and Grove [11], (v) in turn means: If $\phi < \psi$ then none of the models in $]\!]\psi[\![$ is minimal in $]\!]\phi \wedge \psi[\![$ (equivalently, all minimal models in $]\!]\phi \wedge \psi[\![$ are in $[\![\psi]\!]$); if $<$ is transitive, then the converse holds as well.

[24] See [24, Observations 25 and 26]. Notice that (II^+) guarantees that the rationalising acyclic preference relation $<$ is transitive. For suppose that $x < y$ and $y < u$ but not $x < u$. Then, by maximisation, $\sigma(\{x, y\}) = \{y\}$ and $\sigma(\{x, u\}) = \{x, u\}$, but $\sigma(\{x, y, u\}) = \{u\}$, contradicting (II^+).—The semantic condition corresponding to the weaker postulate $(K \dot{-} p)$ is: If $\sigma(S \cup S' \cup S'') \cap S = \emptyset$, then $\sigma(S \cup S') \cap S = \emptyset$ or $\sigma(S \cup S'') \cap S = \emptyset$. The semantic condition corresponding to $(K \dot{-} wd)$ which is equivalent to $(K \dot{-} p)$ (see [27, Theorem 2(ii)]) is: Either $\sigma(S) \cap S' \subseteq \sigma(S \cup S')$ or $\sigma(S') \cap S \subseteq \sigma(S \cup S')$. The constraint on relations rationalising such choice functions is: If $x < y$ and $u < v$, then either $x < v$ or $u < y$ or $x < u$ or $u < x$. Cf. [26, pp. 201–202].

[25] The proof of this observation is given in [26, p. 202].

[26] David Makinson [17, p. 97] seemed to favour living on the 3rd floor when he concluded, towards the end of his survey article on non-monotonic reasoning, that Disjunctive rationality

We read off (II$^+$) from the idea of Disjunctive rationality. It provides a simple characterisation of maximising choice based on interval orders (I have not seen it in the literature). The commonly quoted choice condition characterising choice based on an interval order is "Axiom 3" studied by Jamison and Lau [12, 13] and Fishburn [6]:

(JLF3)   Either $\sigma(S) \cap S' \subseteq \sigma(S')$ or $\sigma(S') \cap S \subseteq \sigma(S)$.

JLF3 is sometimes called "functional asymmetry" [3]. If a finitary choice function σ satisfies Sen's properties α and γ and Aizerman's property (cf. Moulin [19]), then JLF3 is equivalent with (II$^+$).

For entrenchment-based contractions, we have the following result:[27]

Observation 4. *(K$\dot{-}$8d) corresponds exactly to*

(EII$^+$)   If $\phi \wedge \psi < \chi \wedge \xi$ and $\nvdash \chi$ and $\nvdash \xi$, then either $\phi < \chi$ or $\psi < \xi$.

As the name indicates, EII$^+$ is a strengthening of EII (given Extensionality, Maximality and Irreflexivity): put $\xi = \chi$. EII$^+$ is almost as unintuitive as EII$^-$. Fortunately, the situation is improved by the above-mentioned fact that given (K$\dot{-}$1)–(K$\dot{-}$7) and (K$\dot{-}$8c), (K$\dot{-}$8p) is equivalent to (K$\dot{-}$8d). So we can substitute (K$\dot{-}$8p) for (K$\dot{-}$8d) in our characterisation of the 3rd floor, and (K$\dot{-}$8p) corresponds exactly to the much nicer condition EII for entrenchments.

Interestingly, instead of adding EII or EII$^+$ to reach the third floor, one may equivalently add the Interval condition for entrenchments:

Observation 5. *Given the resources of the first floor, EII or EII$^+$ are equivalent to the*

(Interval condition)   If $\phi < \psi$ and $\chi < \xi$, then either $\phi < \xi$ or $\chi < \psi$.

3.6   The 4th Floor

The new condition characteristic of the fourth floor is (K$\dot{-}$8s). It is unusual in that it refers to the exponentiated contraction $K \dot{-}^{\leq 2} \phi$. We pause a little in order to reassure us of its meaning. Restricting our attention to the principal case in which $\nvdash \phi$, what does it mean precisely, in terms of the possible models approach, that ψ is in $K \dot{-}^{\leq 2} \phi$? It means that ψ is in K and ϕ is true in the $\prec$-maximal models of $]\!]\phi[\![$ *and* it is true in the $\prec$-maximal models of $]\!]\phi[\![- \max_{\prec}( ]\!]\phi[\![ )$, i.e., those models that are dominated by, and only by, $\prec$-maximal $]\!]\phi[\![$-models. So ψ has to cover not only the maximally plausible models falsifying ϕ (as in Definition 1), but also the ϕ-falsifying models that are "just below" the maximal ones.

What does it mean, in terms of entrenchment, that ψ is in $K \dot{-}^{\leq 2} \phi$? We can reason as follows:

---

is desirable but Rational monotony is too strong to insist upon. Makinson mentions the Interval condition as sufficient for Disjunctive rationality and conjectures that it characterises Disjunctive rationality. Freund's [7, p. 244] Filtering condition, which is suitable for the characterisation of Disjunctive rationality in his framework, is weaker than the Interval condition.

[27] See [24, Observations 35–36 and 51] and [27, Theorem 2].

$\psi \in K \dot{-}^{\leq 2} \phi$ iff [by Def $\dot{-}^{\leq 2}$]

$\psi \in K \dot{-} \phi$ and $\psi \in K \dot{-}^2 \phi = K \dot{-} (\phi \vee \bigwedge(K \dot{-} \phi))$ iff [by Def 4]

$\psi \in K \dot{-} \phi$ and $\phi \vee \bigwedge(K \dot{-} \phi) < \phi \vee \bigwedge(K \dot{-} \phi) \vee \psi$ iff [by Def 4, Ext]

$\psi \in K$ and $\phi < \phi \vee \psi$ and $\phi \vee \bigwedge(K \dot{-} \phi) < \phi \vee \psi$ iff [by Cont down]

$\psi \in K$ and $\phi \vee \bigwedge(K \dot{-} \phi) < \phi \vee \psi$ iff [by Cont down and EII]

$\psi \in K$ and there is a $\chi \in K \dot{-} \phi$ such that $\phi \vee \chi < \phi \vee \psi$ iff [by Def 4]

$\psi \in K$ and there is a $\chi \in K$ such that $\phi < \phi \vee \chi$ and $\phi \vee \chi < \phi \vee \psi$.

So for ψ to be in $K \dot{-}^{\leq 2} \phi$, $\phi \vee \psi$ has to exceed in entrenchment not only ϕ (as in Definition 4), but also another sentence that is itself more entrenched than ϕ.[28]

For all logically finite theories K, a partial meet contraction function satisfies (K$\dot{-}$8s) if and only if the selection function σ on which it is based satisfies the following condition:

(IV$^-$)   If $S \subseteq S'$ and $\sigma(S') \cap S \neq \emptyset$, then $\sigma(S) \subseteq \sigma(S') \cup \sigma(S' \setminus \sigma(S'))$.

Condition (IV$^-$) says that if some of the best elements in a bigger set S' are contained in a subset S of S', then all the best elements of S are either best or second-best elements of S'. One can now make the following

Observation 6. *Every choice function over the set of subsets of a finite domain rationalisable by an irreflexive relation that satisfies Semitransitivity satisfies (IV$^-$), and conversely every such choice function satisfying (IV$^-$) can be rationalised by an irreflexive relation that satisfies Semitransitivity.*

So the possible models contractions living on the fourth floor are the ones that are based on semiorders. Given the importance of semiorders for the modelling of preferences with imperfect discrimination [3, 16, 21, 29], this justifies the introduction of a fourth level to our floor plan.

(IV$^-$) provides a simple and transparent characterisation of maximising choice based on semiorders. The commonly quoted choice condition characterising choice based on a semiorder, however, is "Axiom 5" studied by Jamison and Lau [12, 13] and Fishburn [6]. It can be written in this way:

(JLF5)   If $S \subseteq S'$, $S \cap \sigma(S') = \emptyset$ and $S'' \cap \sigma(S') \neq \emptyset$, then $\sigma(S'') \cap S \subseteq \sigma(S)$.

The conditions JLF3 and JLF5 provide the basis for the first axiomatisation of theory change determined by semiorders due to Peppas and Williams [20].[29] I believe to have improved upon this axiomatisation on two counts. First, JLF5 implies transitivity, and JLF5 is in fact the source of transitivity both in Fishburn's and in Peppas and Williams's papers. However, transitivity follows already from the Interval condition. So even if one is not willing to acknowledge the second floor, transitivity should be obtained already on the third floor, but JLF3 does not seem to be sufficient. Second, and more importantly,

---

[28] However, the final condition cannot further be reduced to

$\psi \in K$ and there is a $\chi \in K$ such that $\phi < \chi$ and $\chi < \phi \vee \psi$

Counterexample: Let $W = \{u, v, w, w'\}$, $u < v < w < w'$, $[\![p]\!] = \{v, w'\}$, $[\![q]\!] = \{v, w, w'\}$, $[\![r]\!] = \{u, w, w'\}$, and $K = \hat{w'}$. Then $p < r$ and $r < p \vee q$, but not $q \in K \dot{-}^{\leq 2} p$.

[29] Peppas and Williams's axiom B8 for belief contraction is (K$\dot{-}$8r); their axioms B9 and B10 correspond to JLF3 and JLF5, respectively.

it is very hard to gain an intuitive feeling for JLF5 or Peppas and Williams's analogue for belief revision theory. Exponentiated belief change, apart from being an interesting idea in itself, offers a much better intuitive grasp of the effects of semitransitivity.

For entrenchment contractions on the fourth floor, we finally have the following result:

Observation 7. $(K \dot{-} 8s)$ *corresponds exactly to*

(Semitransitivity)   *If $\phi < \psi$ and $\psi < \chi$, then either $\phi < \xi$ or $\xi < \chi$.*

3.7   The Top Floor

We will visit the top floor only briefly, because it is a very familiar venue. It houses the full AGM theory which we take here as an ideal limit of rational involvement in theory change. Terminologically, this is in line with the linguistic usage in non-monotonic logics common since Kraus, Lehmann and Magidor's [14] who called the analogue of $(K \dot{-} 8)$ "Rational monotony". In all classical AGM constructions for theory change, the top floor is reached by adding Modularity to the conditions one had before, thus making all models and sentences fully comparable and discriminable in terms of plausibility.[30] Modularity corresponds to Sen's property $\beta+$ which is stronger still than the choice conditions considered in the last sections. I call it (IV), using the numbering of [23]:

(IV)   If $S \subseteq S'$ and $\sigma(S') \cap S \neq \emptyset$, then $\sigma(S) \subseteq \sigma(S')$

4   Conclusion

The edifice of theory change built by AGM is like a big hall building that needs signposts to intermediate floors in order to become more habitable. I have shown that one can clearly and meaningfully identify four intermediate floors. At least the first and the second floor have been there all along, in the structure of AGM's original constructive models. The third floor, motivated by a concern for Disjunctive rationality, has directed our attention to the topic of imperfect discrimination of degrees of plausibility. A more constrained way of addressing this topic—by semiorders rather than interval orders—has led us to the fourth floor.

Bibliography

[1] Alchourrón, C.E., Gärdenfors, P., Makinson, D.: On the logic of theory change: Partial meet contraction and revision functions. Journal of Symbolic Logic 50, 510–530 (1985)

---

[30] In the full AGM theory of the 1980s, partial meet and entrenchment contractions were defined in terms of non-strict relations $\leq$ (and likewise $\trianglelefteq$). The corresponding strict relation needs to be defined as the converse of complement, i.e., by putting $x < y$ iff not $y \leq x$. A statement like $x \leq y$ in [1] or [9] thus has to be taken as meaning "x is less than or equal to or incomparable with y" rather than "x is less than or equal to y" (which explains the marginal role of connectivity and the starring role of transitivity in these papers).

[2] Alchourrón, C.E., Makinson, D.: Maps between some different kinds of contraction function: The finite case. Studia Logica 45, 187–198 (1986)

[3] Aleskerov, F., Bouyssou, D., Monjardet, B.: Utility Maximization, Choice and Preference, 2nd edn. Studies in Economic Theory, vol. 16. Springer, Berlin (2007)

[4] Fermé, E., Hansson, S.O.: AGM 25 years: Twenty-five years of research in belief change. Journal of Philosophical Logic 40(2), 295–331 (2011)

[5] Fishburn, P.C.: Intransitive indifference with unequal indifference intervals. Journal of Mathematical Psychology 7, 144–149 (1970)

[6] Fishburn, P.C.: Semiorders and choice functions. Econometrica 43, 975–977 (1975)

[7] Freund, M.: Injective models and disjunctive relations. Journal of Logic and Computation 3, 231–247 (1993)

[8] Gärdenfors, P.: Knowledge in Flux: Modeling the Dynamics of Epistemic States. Bradford Books. MIT Press, Cambridge (1988)

[9] Gärdenfors, P., Makinson, D.: Revisions of knowledge systems using epistemic entrenchment. In: Vardi, M. (ed.) Proceedings of the Second Conference on Theoretical Aspects of Reasoning About Knowledge (TARK 1988), pp. 83–95. Morgan Kaufmann, Los Altos (1988)

[10] Gärdenfors, P., Makinson, D.: Nonmonotonic inference based on expectations. Artificial Intelligence 65, 197–245 (1994)

[11] Grove, A.: Two modellings for theory change. Journal of Philosophical Logic 17, 157–170 (1988)

[12] Jamison, D.T., Lau, L.J.: Semiorders and the theory of choice. Econometrica 41, 901–912 (1973)

[13] Jamison, D.T., Lau, L.J.: Semiorders and the theory of choice: A correction. Econometrica 43, 979–980 (1975)

[14] Kraus, S., Lehmann, D., Magidor, M.: Nonmonotonic reasoning, preferential models and cumulative logics. Artificial Intelligence 44, 167–207 (1990)

[15] Lindström, S.: A semantic approach to nonmonotonic reasoning: Inference operations and choice. Tech. Rep. 1991:6, Department of Philosophy, University of Uppsala (1991), ultimately published as Tech. Rep. No.1994:10

[16] Luce, R.D.: Semiorders and a theory of utility discrimination. Econometrica 24, 178–191 (1956)

[17] Makinson, D.: General patterns in nonmonotonic reasoning. In: Gabbay, D.M., Hogger, C.J., Robinson, J.A. (eds.) Handbook of Logic in Artificial Intelligence and Logic Programming, vol. 3, pp. 35–110. Oxford University Press, Oxford (1994)

[18] Mirkin, B.G.: Description of some relations on the set of real-line intervals. Journal of Mathematical Psychology 9, 243–252 (1972)

[19] Moulin, H.: Choice functions over a finite set: A summary. Social Choice and Welfare 2, 147–160 (1985)

[20] Peppas, P., Williams, M.A.: Belief change and semiorders. In: Principles of Knowledge Representation and Reasoning: Proceedings of the Twelfth International Conference, KR 2014, Vienna, July 20-24 (2014)

[21] Roberts, F.: Indifference graphs. In: Harary, F. (ed.) Proof Techniques in Graph Theory, pp. 139–146. Academic Press, New York (1969)

[22] Rott, H.: Preferential belief change using generalized epistemic entrenchment. Journal of Logic, Language and Information 1, 45–78 (1992)

[23] Rott, H.: Belief contraction in the context of the general theory of rational choice. Journal of Symbolic Logic 58, 1426–1450 (1993)

[24] Rott, H.: Change, Choice and Inference: A Study in Belief Revision and Non-monotonic Reasoning. Oxford University Press, Oxford (2001)

[25] Rott, H.: Basic entrenchment. Studia Logica 73, 257–280 (2003)

[26] Rott, H.: Three floors for the theory of theory change. In: Punčochář, V., Dančák, M. (eds.) Logica Yearbook 2013, pp. 187–205. College Publications, London (2014)

[27] Rott, H., Hansson, S.O.: Safe contraction revisited. In: Hansson, S.O. (ed.) David Makinson on Classical Methods for Non-Classical Problems, pp. 35–70. Outstanding Contributions to Logic. Springer, Dordrecht (2014)

[28] Schlechta, K. (ed.): Nonmonotonic Logics. LNCS (LNAI), vol. 1187. Springer, Heidelberg (1997)

[29] Scott, D., Suppes, P.: Foundational aspects of theories of measurement. Journal of Symbolic Logic 23, 113–128 (1958)

[30] Sen, A.K.: Choice functions and revealed preference. Review of Economic Studies 38, 307–317 (1971), Reprinted in A.K.S., Choice, Welfare and Measurement, pp. 41–53. Blackwell, Oxford (1982)

[31] Suppes, P., Krantz, D.H., Luce, R.D., Tversky, A.: Foundations of Measurement. Geometrical, threshold and probabilistic representations, vol. 2. Academic Press, New York (1989)

Revisiting Postulates for Inconsistency Measures

Philippe Besnard

IRIT, CNRS, University of Toulouse, France
besnard@irit.fr

Abstract. Postulates for inconsistency measures are examined, the set of postulates due to Hunter and Konieczny being the starting point. Objections are raised against a few individual postulates. More general shortcomings are discussed and a new series of postulates is introduced.

1 Introduction

Many inconsistency measures over knowledge bases have been proposed [3,5,6,9,10,11,12,14,16]. The intuition is: the higher the amount of inconsistency in the knowledge base, the greater the number returned by the inconsistency measure (the range of an inconsistency measure is taken to be $R^+ \cup \{\infty\}$, so that the range is totally ordered and 0 is the least element).

An inconsistency measure is concerned with amount of inconsistency, it does *not* take into account other aspects whether subject matter of contradiction, source of information,... (of course, it is possible for example that a contradiction be more worrying than another —thus making more pressing *to act* [4] about it— but this has nothing to do with amount of inconsistency).

In a couple of influential papers [7] [8], Hunter and Konieczny have introduced postulates for inconsistency measures over knowledge bases. Such postulates are meant for inconsistency measures that account for a raw amount of inconsistency: e.g., an inconsistency measure I satisfying (Monotony) precludes I to be a ratio.

Hunter-Konieczny refer to a propositional language[1] $\mathcal{L}$ for classical logic $\vdash$. Finite sequences over $\mathcal{L}$ are called belief bases. $\mathcal{K}_{\mathcal{L}}$ is comprised of all belief bases over $\mathcal{L}$, in set-theoretic form (i.e., a member of $\mathcal{K}_{\mathcal{L}}$ is an ordinary set[2]).

According to Hunter and Konieczny, a function I over belief bases is an inconsistency measure if it satisfies the following properties, $\forall K, K' \in \mathcal{K}_{\mathcal{L}}, \forall \alpha, \beta \in \mathcal{L}$

- $I(K) = 0$ iff $K \nvdash \bot$ (Consistency Null)
- $I(K \cup K') \geq I(K)$ (Monotony)
- If α is free[3] for K then $I(K \cup \{\alpha\}) = I(K)$ (Free Formula Independence)
- If $\alpha \vdash \beta$ and $\alpha \nvdash \bot$ then $I(K \cup \{\alpha\}) \geq I(K \cup \{\beta\})$ (Dominance)

In this paper, we examine the HK set, namely (Consistency Null), (Monotony), (Free Formula Independence), and (Dominance), ignoring the lesser properties

---

[1] For simplicity, we use a language based on the complete set of connectives $\{\neg, \wedge, \vee\}$.
[2] In the conclusion, we mention the case of multisets.
[3] A formula φ is free for X iff $Y \cup \{\varphi\} \vdash \bot$ for no consistent subset Y of X.

E. Fermé and J. Leite (Eds.): JELIA 2014, LNAI 8761, pp. 383–396, 2014.
© Springer International Publishing Switzerland 2014

mentioned either by Hunter-Konieczny themselves [8] (e.g., MI-separability) or by Thimm [15] when he deals with probabilistic knowledge bases.

We start by arguing against (Free Formula Independence) and (Dominance) in Section 2. We browse in Section 3 several consequences of HK postulates, stressing the need for more general principles in each case. Section 4 is devoted to a major principle, replacement of equivalent subsets. Throughout Section 5, we introduce various postulates supplementing the original ones, ending with a new axiomatization. Section 6 can be viewed as a kind of rejoinder backing both (Free Formula Independence) and (Monotony) through the main new postulate.

2   Objections to HK Postulates

2.1   Objection to (Dominance)

In contrapositive form, (Dominance) says:

$$\text{For } \alpha \vdash \beta, \text{ if } I(K \cup \{\alpha\}) < I(K \cup \{\beta\}) \text{ then } \alpha \vdash \bot \tag{1}$$

although it makes sense that the left hand side holds without $\alpha \vdash \bot$. An example is as follows. Let $K = \{a \wedge b \wedge c \wedge \cdots \wedge z\}$. Take $\beta = \neg a \vee (\neg b \wedge \neg c \wedge \cdots \wedge \neg z)$ while $\alpha = \neg a$. We may hold $I(K \cup \{\alpha\}) < I(K \cup \{\beta\})$ on the following grounds:

- The inconsistency in $I(K \cup \{\alpha\})$ is $\neg a$ vs a.
- The inconsistency in $I(K \cup \{\beta\})$ is either as above (i.e., $\neg a$ vs a) or it is $\neg b \wedge \neg c \wedge \cdots \wedge \neg z$ vs $b \wedge c \wedge \cdots \wedge z$ that may be viewed as more inconsistent than the case $\neg a$ vs a, hence, $\{a \wedge b \wedge c \wedge \cdots \wedge z\} \cup \{\neg a \vee (\neg b \wedge \neg c \wedge \cdots \wedge \neg z)\}$ can be taken as more inconsistent overall than $\{a \wedge b \wedge c \wedge \cdots \wedge z\} \cup \{\neg a\}$ thereby violating (1) because $\alpha \not\vdash \bot$ here.

2.2   Objection to (Free Formula Independence)

Unfolding the definition of a free formula, (Free Formula Independence) is:

$$I(K \cup \{\alpha\}) = I(K) \text{ if } K' \cup \{\alpha\} \vdash \bot \text{ for no consistent subset } K' \text{ of } K \tag{2}$$

Consider $K = \{a \wedge c, b \wedge \neg c\}$ and $\alpha = \neg a \vee \neg b$ (no minimal inconsistent subset is a singleton set, unlike an example [8] against (Free Formula Independence)). Atoms a and b are compatible but $a \wedge b$ is contradicted by α, hence $K \cup \{\alpha\}$ may be regarded as more inconsistent than K: (2) is failed.

3   Consequences of HK Postulates

Proposition 1. *(Monotony) entails*

- *if* $I(K \cup \{\alpha \wedge \beta\}) = I(K \cup \{\alpha, \beta\})$ *then* $I(K \cup \{\alpha \wedge \beta\}) \geq I(K \cup \{\beta\})$

Proof. Assume $I(K \cup \{\alpha \wedge \beta\}) = I(K \cup \{\alpha, \beta\})$. According to (Monotony), $I(K \cup \{\alpha, \beta\}) \geq I(K \cup \{\beta\}$. Hence the result.

So, if I conforms with adjunction (roughly speaking, it means identifying $\{\alpha, \beta\}$ with $\{\alpha \wedge \beta\}$) then I respects the idea that adding a conjunct cannot make the amount of inconsistency decrease.

Notation. $\alpha \equiv \beta$ denotes that both $\alpha \vdash \beta$ and $\beta \vdash \alpha$ hold. Also, $\alpha \equiv \beta \vdash \gamma$ is an abbreviation for $\alpha \equiv \beta$ and $\beta \vdash \gamma$ (so, $\alpha \equiv \beta \nvdash \gamma$ means that $\alpha \equiv \beta$ and $\beta \nvdash \gamma$).

Proposition 2. *(Free Formula Independence) entails*

- *if $\alpha \equiv \top$ then $I(K \cup \{\alpha\}) = I(K)$*   (Tautology Independence)

Proof. A tautology is trivially a free formula for any K.

Unless $\beta \nvdash \bot$, there is however no guarantee that the following holds:

- *if $\alpha \equiv \top$ then $I(K \cup \{\alpha \wedge \beta\}) = I(K \cup \{\beta\})$*   ($\top$-conjunct Independence)

Proposition 3. *(Dominance) entails*

- *$I(K \cup \{\alpha_1, \ldots, \alpha_n\}) = I(K \cup \{\beta_1, \ldots, \beta_n\})$ if $\alpha_i \equiv \beta_i \nvdash \bot$ for $i = 1..n$* (Swap)

Proof. For $i = 1..n$, $\alpha_i \equiv \beta_i$ and (Dominance) can be applied in both directions. $I(K \cup \{\beta_1, \ldots, \beta_{i-1}, \alpha_i, \ldots, \alpha_n\}) = I(K \cup \{\beta_1, \ldots, \beta_i, \alpha_{i+1}, \ldots, \alpha_n\})$ for $i = 1..n$.

Proposition 3 fails to guarantee that I is independent of any consistent subset of the knowledge base being replaced by an equivalent (consistent) set of formulas:

- *if $K' \nvdash \bot$ and $K' \equiv K''$ then $I(K \cup K') = I(K \cup K'')$*   (Exchange)

Proposition 3 at least guarantees that any consistent formula of the knowledge base can be replaced by an equivalent formula without altering the result of the inconsistency measure. Of course, postulates for inconsistency measures are expected *not* to entail $I(K \cup \{\alpha\}) = I(K \cup \{\beta\})$ for $\alpha \equiv \beta$ such that $\alpha \vdash \bot$. However, some subcases are desirable such as $I(K \cup \{\alpha \vee \alpha\}) = I(K \cup \{\alpha\})$, $I(K \cup \{\alpha \wedge \beta\}) = I(K \cup \{\beta \wedge \alpha\})$, and so on, in full generality (even for $\alpha \vdash \bot$) but Proposition 3 fails to ensure any of these.

Proposition 4. *(Dominance) entails*

- *if $\alpha \wedge \beta \nvdash \bot$ then $I(K \cup \{\alpha \wedge \beta\}) \geq I(K \cup \{\beta\})$*

Proof. Applying (Dominance) to the valid entailment $\alpha \wedge \beta \vdash \beta$ yields the result.

Proposition 4 means that I respects the idea that adding a conjunct cannot make the amount of inconsistency decrease, in the case of a consistent conjunction (however, one really wonders why this is not guaranteed to hold in more cases?).

Proposition 5. *Due to (Dominance) and (Monotony)*

- *For $\alpha \in K$, if $\alpha \nvdash \bot$ and $\alpha \vdash \beta$ then $I(K \cup \{\beta\}) = I(K)$*

Proof. $I(K \cup \{\alpha\}) = I(K)$ as $\alpha \in K$. By (Dominance), $I(K \cup \{\alpha\}) \geq I(K \cup \{\beta\})$. Therefore, $I(K) \geq I(K \cup \{\beta\})$. The converse holds due to (Monotony).

Proposition 5 guarantees that a consequence of a consistent formula of the knowledge base can be added without altering the result of the inconsistency measure. What about a consequence of a consistent subset of the knowledge base? Indeed, Proposition 5 is a special case of

(A_n) For $\{\alpha_1,\ldots,\alpha_n\} \subseteq K$, if $\{\alpha_1,\ldots,\alpha_n\} \not\vdash \bot$ and $\{\alpha_1,\ldots,\alpha_n\} \vdash \beta$ then
$$I(K \cup \{\beta\}) = I(K)$$

That is, Proposition 5 guarantees (A_n) only for $n = 1$ but what is the rationale for stopping there?

Example 1. Let $K = \{\neg b, a \wedge b, b \wedge c\}$. Proposition 5 ensures that $I(K \cup \{a, c\}) = I(K \cup \{a\}) = I(K \cup \{c\}) = I(K)$. Although $a \wedge c$ behaves as a and c with respect to all contradictions in K (i.e., $a \wedge b$ vs $\neg b$ and $b \wedge c$ vs $\neg b$), HK postulates fail to ensure $I(K \cup \{a \wedge c\}) = I(K)$.

4   Two Postulates for Replacement of Equivalent Subsets

4.1   Replacing Consistent Equivalent Subsets: The Value of (Exchange)

To start with, (Exchange) is not a consequence of (Dominance) and (Monotony). An example is $K_1 = \{a \wedge c \wedge e, b \wedge d \wedge \neg e\}$ and $K_2 = \{a \wedge e, c \wedge e, b \wedge d \wedge \neg e\}$. By (Exchange), $I(K_1) = I(K_2)$ but HK postulates do not impose the equality. Next are a few results displaying properties of (Exchange).

Proposition 6. *The following items are pairwise equivalent:*

- *(Exchange)*
- *The family $(A_n)_{n \geq 1}$*
- *If $K' \not\vdash \bot$ and $K' \equiv K''$ then $I(K \cup K') = I((K \setminus K') \cup K'')$*
- *If $K' \not\vdash \bot$ and $K \cap K' = \emptyset$ and $K' \equiv K''$ then $I(K \cup K') = I(K \cup K'')$*
- *If $\{K_1,\ldots,K_n\}$ is a partition of $K \setminus K_0$ where $K_0 = \{\alpha \in K \mid \alpha \vdash \bot\}$ such that $K_i \not\vdash \bot$ and $K_i' \equiv K_i$ for $i = 1..n$ then $I(K) = I(K_0 \cup K_1' \cup \cdots \cup K_n')$*

Proof. Numbering the items (1)-(5) in the statement of Proposition 6, so that, e.g., (Exchange) is (1), we will begin by proving $(1) \Leftarrow (2) \Leftarrow (3)$. Thus, using the obvious fact $(3) \Leftarrow (1)$, the equivalence between each of $(1), (2), (3)$ will follow. Lastly, we will prove the equivalence of (4) with (1), and that of (5) with (3).

Assume (A_n) for all $n \geq 1$ and $K' \equiv K'' \not\vdash \bot$. (i) Let $K' = \{\alpha_1,\ldots,\alpha_m\}$. Define the sequence $\langle K_j' \rangle_{j \geq 0}$ where $K_0' = K \cup K''$ and $K_{j+1}' = K_j' \cup \{\alpha_{j+1}\}$. Clearly, $K'' \not\vdash \bot$ and $K'' \vdash \alpha_{j+1}$ and $K'' \subseteq K_j'$. Then, (A_n) can be applied to K_j' and this gives $I(K_j') = I(K_j' \cup \{\alpha_{j+1}\}) = I(K_{j+1}')$. Overall, $I(K_0') = I(K_m')$. So, $I(K \cup K'') = I(K \cup K' \cup K'')$. (ii) Let $K'' = \{\beta_1,\ldots,\beta_p\}$. Consider the sequence $\langle K_j'' \rangle_{j \geq 0}$ where $K_0'' = K \cup K'$ and $K_{j+1}'' = K_j'' \cup \{\beta_{j+1}\}$. Clearly, $K' \not\vdash \bot$ and $K' \vdash \beta_{j+1}$ and $K' \subseteq K_j''$. Hence, (A_n) can be applied to K_j'' and this gives $I(K_j'') = I(K_j'' \cup \{\beta_{j+1}\}) = I(K_{j+1}'')$. Overall, $I(K_0'') = I(K_p'')$. So, $I(K \cup K') = I(K \cup K' \cup K'')$. Combining the equalities, $I(K \cup K') = I(K \cup K'')$. That is, the family $(A_n)_{n \geq 1}$ entails (Exchange).

We now show that the family $(A_n)_{n \geq 1}$ is entailed by the third item in the statement of Proposition 6, denoted (Exchange'), which is:

If $K' \not\vdash \bot$ and $K' \equiv K''$ then $I(K \cup K') = I((K \setminus K') \cup K'')$.

Let $\{\alpha_1, \ldots, \alpha_n\} \subseteq K$ such that $\{\alpha_1, \ldots, \alpha_n\} \not\vdash \perp$ and $\{\alpha_1, \ldots, \alpha_n\} \vdash \beta$. So, $\{\alpha_1, \ldots, \alpha_n\} \equiv \{\alpha_1, \ldots, \alpha_n, \beta\}$. For $K' = \{\alpha_1, \ldots, \alpha_n\}$, $K'' = \{\alpha_1, \ldots, \alpha_n, \beta\}$ (Exchange') gives $I(K) = I((K \setminus \{\alpha_1, \ldots, \alpha_n\}) \cup \{\alpha_1, \ldots, \alpha_n, \beta\} = I(K \cup \{\beta\})$. By transitivity, we have thus shown that (Exchange) is entailed by (Exchange'). Since the converse is obvious, the equivalence between (Exchange), (Exchange') and the family $(A_n)_{n \geq 1}$ holds.

As to the fourth item in the statement of Proposition 6, it is trivially entailed by (Exchange), it clearly entails (Exchange'), so it is equivalent with (Exchange).

Consider now (Exchange''), the last item in the statement of Proposition 6:

If $\{K_1, \ldots, K_n\}$ is a partition of $K \setminus K_0$ where $K_0 = \{\alpha \in K \mid \alpha \vdash \perp\}$ such that $K_i \not\vdash \perp$ and $K_i' \equiv K_i$ for $i = 1..n$ then $I(K) = I(K_0 \cup K_1' \cup \cdots \cup K_n')$.

(i) Assume (Exchange'). We now prove (Exchange''). Let $\{K_1, \ldots, K_n\}$ be a partition of $K \setminus K_0$ satisfying the conditions of (Exchange''). Trivially, $I(K) = I(K_0 \cup K \setminus K_0) = I(K_0 \cup K_1 \cup \cdots \cup K_n)$. Then, $K_i \setminus K_n = K_i$ for $i = 1..n - 1$. Applying (Exchange') yields $I(K_0 \cup K_1 \cup \cdots \cup K_n) = I(K_0 \cup K_1 \cup \cdots \cup K_n')$ hence $I(K) = I(K_0 \cup K_1 \cup \cdots \cup K_n')$. Applying (Exchange') iteratively upon K_{n-1}, $K_{n-2}, \ldots, K_1$ gives $I(K) = I(K_0 \cup K_1' \cup \cdots \cup K_n')$.

(ii) Assume (Exchange''). We now prove (Exchange'). Let $K' \not\vdash \perp$ and $K'' \equiv K'$. Clearly, $(K \cup K')_0 = K_0$ and $(K \cup K') \setminus (K \cup K')_0 = (K \setminus K_0) \cup K'$. As each formula in $K \setminus K_0$ is consistent, $K \setminus K_0$ can be partitioned into $\{K_1, \ldots, K_n\}$ such that $K_i \not\vdash \perp$ for $i = 1..n$ (take $n = 0$ in the case that $K = K_0$). Then, $\{K_1 \setminus K', \ldots, K_n \setminus K', K'\}$ is a partition of $(K \setminus K_0) \cup K'$ satisfying the conditions in (Exchange''). Now, $I(K \cup K') = I(K_0 \cup (K_1 \setminus K') \cup \cdots \cup (K_n \setminus K') \cup K')$. Applying (Exchange'') with each K_i substituting itself and K'' substituting K', we obtain $I(K \cup K') = I(K_0 \cup (K_1 \setminus K') \cup \cdots \cup (K_n \setminus K') \cup K'')$. That is, $I(K \cup K') = I((K \setminus K') \cup K'')$.

Proposition 7. *(Exchange) entails (Swap).*

Proof. Taking advantage of transitivity of equality, it will be sufficient to prove $I(K \cup \{\beta_1, \ldots, \beta_{i-1}, \alpha_i, \ldots, \alpha_n\}) = I(K \cup \{\beta_1, \ldots, \beta_i, \alpha_{i+1}, \ldots, \alpha_n\})$ for $i = 1..n$. Due to $\alpha_i \equiv \beta_i$ and $\beta_i \not\vdash \perp$, it is the case that $\{\alpha_i\} \not\vdash \perp$ and $\{\alpha_i\} \equiv \{\alpha_i, \beta_i\}$. Therefore, (Exchange) can be applied to $K \cup \{\beta_1, \ldots, \beta_{i-1}, \alpha_{i+1}, \ldots, \alpha_n\}$ for $K' = \{\alpha_i\}$ and $K'' = \{\beta_i\}$. As a consequence, $I(K \cup \{\beta_1, \ldots, \beta_{i-1}, \alpha_i, \ldots, \alpha_n\})$ is equal to $I(K \cup \{\beta_1, \ldots, \beta_{i-1}, \alpha_{i+1}, \ldots, \alpha_n\} \cup \{\beta_i\})$ and the latter is exactly $I(K \cup \{\beta_1, \ldots, \beta_i, \alpha_{i+1}, \ldots, \alpha_n\})$.

That (Exchange) entails (Swap) is natural. More surprisingly, (Exchange) also entails (Tautology Independence) as the next result shows.

Proposition 8. *(Exchange) entails (Tautology Independence).*

Proof. The non-trivial case is $\alpha \notin K$. Apply (Exchange') for $K' = \{\alpha\}$ and $K'' = \emptyset$ so that $I(K \cup \{\alpha\}) = I((K \setminus \{\alpha\}) \cup \emptyset)$ ensues. So, $I(K \cup \{\alpha\}) = I(K)$.

4.2   The Value of an Adjunction Postulate

In keeping with the meaning of the conjunction connective in classical logic, consider a dedicated postulate in the form

- $I(K \cup \{\alpha, \beta\}) = I(K \cup \{\alpha \wedge \beta\})$ $\qquad$ (Adjunction Invariancy)

Proposition 9. *(Adjunction Invariancy) entails*

- $I(K \cup \{\alpha, \beta\}) = I((K \setminus \{\alpha, \beta\}) \cup \{\alpha \wedge \beta\})$ (Disjoint Adjunction Invariancy)
- $I(K) = I(\{\bigwedge K\})$ $\qquad$ (Full Adjunction Invariancy)
  where $\bigwedge K$ *denotes* $\alpha_1 \wedge \ldots \wedge \alpha_n$ *for any enumeration* $\alpha_1, \ldots, \alpha_n$ *of* K.

Proof. Let $K = \{\alpha_1, \ldots, \alpha_n\}$. Apply iteratively (Adjunction Invariancy) as $I(\{\alpha_1 \wedge \ldots \wedge \alpha_{i-1}, \alpha_i, \ldots, \alpha_n\}) = I(\{\alpha_1 \wedge \ldots \wedge \alpha_i, \alpha_{i+1}, \ldots, \alpha_n\})$ for $i = 2..n$.

Proposition 10. *Assuming* $I(\{\alpha \wedge (\beta \wedge \gamma)\}) = I(\{(\alpha \wedge \beta) \wedge \gamma\})$ *and* $I(\{\alpha \wedge \beta\}) = I(\{\beta \wedge \alpha\})$, *(Disjoint Adjunction Invariancy) and (Full Adjunction Invariancy) are equivalent.*

Proof. Assume (Full Adjunction Invariancy). $K \cup \{\alpha, \beta\} = (K \setminus \{\alpha, \beta\}) \cup \{\alpha, \beta\}$ yields $I(K \cup \{\alpha, \beta\}) = I((K \setminus \{\alpha, \beta\}) \cup \{\alpha, \beta\})$. By (Full Adjunction Invariancy), $I((K \setminus \{\alpha, \beta\}) \cup \{\alpha, \beta\}) = I(\{\bigwedge ((K \setminus \{\alpha, \beta\}) \cup \{\alpha, \beta\})\})$ and the latter can be written $I(\{\gamma_1 \wedge \ldots \wedge \gamma_n \wedge \alpha \wedge \beta\})$ for some enumeration $\gamma_1, \ldots, \gamma_n$ of $K \setminus \{\alpha, \beta\}$. I.e., $I(K \cup \{\alpha, \beta\}) = I(\{\gamma_1 \wedge \ldots \wedge \gamma_n \wedge \alpha \wedge \beta\})$. By (Full Adjunction Invariancy), $I((K \setminus \{\alpha, \beta\}) \cup \{\alpha \wedge \beta\}) = I(\{\bigwedge ((K \setminus \{\alpha, \beta\}) \cup \{\alpha \wedge \beta\})\})$ that can be written $I(\{\gamma_1 \wedge \ldots \wedge \gamma_n \wedge \alpha \wedge \beta\})$ for the same enumeration $\gamma_1, \ldots, \gamma_n$ of $K \setminus \{\alpha, \beta\}$. So, $I(K \cup \{\alpha, \beta\}) = I((K \setminus \{\alpha, \beta\}) \cup \{\alpha \wedge \beta\})$. As to the converse, it is trivial to use (Disjoint Adjunction Invariancy) iteratively to get (Full Adjunction Invariancy).

A counter-example to the purported equivalence of (Adjunction Invariancy) and (Full Adjunction Invariancy) is as follows. Let $K = \{a, b, \neg b \wedge \neg a\}$. Obviously, $I(K \cup \{a, b\}) = I(K)$ since $\{a, b\} \subseteq K$. (Full Adjunction Invariancy) gives $I(K) = I(\{\bigwedge_{\gamma \in K} \gamma\})$ i.e. $I(K \cup \{a, b\}) = I(\{\bigwedge_{\gamma \in K} \gamma\}) = I(\{a \wedge b \wedge \neg b \wedge \neg a\})$. A different case of applying (Full Adjunction Invariancy) gives $I(K \cup \{a \wedge b\}) = I(\{\bigwedge_{\gamma \in K \cup \{a \wedge b\}} \gamma\}) = I(\{a \wedge b \wedge \neg b \wedge \neg a \wedge a \wedge b\})$. However, HK postulates do not provide grounds to infer $I(\{a \wedge b \wedge \neg b \wedge \neg a\}) = I(\{a \wedge b \wedge \neg b \wedge \neg a \wedge a \wedge b\})$ hence (Adjunction Invariancy) may fail here.

(Adjunction Invariancy) offers a natural equivalence between (Monotony) and the principle which expresses that adding a conjunct cannot make the amount of inconsistency decrease:

Proposition 11. *Assuming (Consistency Null), (Adjunction Invariancy) yields that (Monotony) is equivalent with*

- $I(K \cup \{\alpha \wedge \beta\}) \geq I(K \cup \{\alpha\})$ $\qquad$ (Conjunction Dominance)

Proof. Assume (Monotony), an instance of which is $I(K \cup \{\alpha\}) \leq I(K \cup \{\alpha, \beta\})$. According to (Adjunction Invariancy), $I(K \cup \{\alpha, \beta\}) = I(K \cup \{\alpha \wedge \beta\})$. Hence,

$I(K \cup \{\alpha\}) \leq I(K \cup \{\alpha \wedge \beta\})$. That is, (Conjunction Dominance) holds. Assume (Conjunction Dominance). First, consider $K \neq \emptyset$. Let $\alpha \in K$. Due to (Conjunction Dominance), $I(K \cup \{\alpha\}) \leq I(K \cup \{\alpha \wedge \beta\})$. (Adjunction Invariancy) gives $I(K \cup \{\alpha, \beta\}) = I(K \cup \{\alpha \wedge \beta\})$. Hence, $I(K \cup \{\alpha\}) \leq I(K \cup \{\alpha, \beta\})$. I.e., $I(K) \leq I(K \cup \{\beta\})$ since $\alpha \in K$. For $K' \in \mathcal{K}_{\mathcal{L}}$, it is enough to iterate this finitely many times (one for every β in $K' \setminus K$) in order to obtain $I(K) \leq I(K \cup K')$. Now, consider $K = \emptyset$. By (Consistency Null), $I(K) = 0$ hence $I(K) \leq I(K \cup K')$.

(Free Formula Independence) yields (Tautology Independence) by Proposition 2 although a more general principle (e.g., ($\top$-conjunct Independence) or the like) ensuring that I is independent of tautologies is to be expected. The next result shows that (Adjunction Invariancy) is the way to get both postulates at once.

Proposition 12. *Assuming (Consistency Null), (Adjunction Invariancy) yields that (Tautology Independence) and ($\top$-conjunct Independence) are equivalent.*

Proof. For $\alpha \equiv \top$, (Adjunction Invariancy) and (Tautology Independence) give $I(K \cup \{\alpha \wedge \beta\}) = I(K \cup \{\alpha, \beta\}) = I(K \cup \{\beta\})$. As to the converse, let $\beta \in K$. Therefore, $I(K) = I(K \cup \{\beta\}) = I(K \cup \{\alpha \wedge \beta\}) = I(K \cup \{\alpha, \beta\}) = I(K \cup \{\alpha\})$. The case $K = \emptyset$ is settled by means of (Consistency Null).

Lastly, (Adjunction Invariancy) provides for free various principles related to (idempotence, commutativity, and associativity of) conjunction, as follows.

Proposition 13. *(Adjunction Invariancy) entails*

- $I(K \cup \{\alpha \wedge \alpha\}) - I(K \cup \{\alpha\})$
- $I(K \cup \{\alpha \wedge \beta\}) = I(K \cup \{\beta \wedge \alpha\})$
- $I(K \cup \{\alpha \wedge (\beta \wedge \gamma)\}) = I(K \cup \{(\alpha \wedge \beta) \wedge \gamma\})$

Proof. (i) $I(K \cup \{\alpha \wedge \alpha\}) = I(K \cup \{\alpha, \alpha\}) = I(K \cup \{\alpha\})$. (ii) $I(K \cup \{\alpha \wedge \beta\}) = I(K \cup \{\alpha, \beta\}) = I(K \cup \{\beta, \alpha\}) = I(K \cup \{\beta \wedge \alpha\})$. (iii) $I(K \cup \{\alpha \wedge (\beta \wedge \gamma)\}) = I(K \cup \{\alpha, \beta \wedge \gamma\}) = I(K \cup \{\alpha, \beta, \gamma\}) = I(K \cup \{\alpha \wedge \beta, \gamma\}) = I(K \cup \{(\alpha \wedge \beta) \wedge \gamma\})$.

(Adjunction Invariancy) and (Exchange) are two principles devoted to ensuring that replacing a subset of the knowledge base with an equivalent subset does not change the value given by the inconsistency measure. The contexts that these two principles require for the replacement to be safe differ:

1. For $K' \not\vdash \bot$, (Exchange) is more general than (Adjunction Invariancy) since (Exchange) guarantees $I(K \cup K') = I(K \cup K'')$ for every $K'' \equiv K'$ but (Adjunction Invariancy) ensures it only for $K'' = \{\bigwedge K'_i \mid \Upsilon = \{K'_1, .., K'_n\}\}$ where Υ ranges over the partitions of K'.
2. For $\alpha \vdash \bot$, (Adjunction Invariancy) is more general than (Exchange) because (Adjunction Invariancy) guarantees $I(K \cup \{\alpha, \beta\}) = I(K \cup \{\alpha \wedge \beta\})$ but (Exchange) does not guarantee it.

5   Revisiting HK Postulates

5.1   Sticking with (Consistency Null) and (Monotony)

(Consistency Null) or a like postulate is indispensable because there seems to be no way to have a sensible inconsistency measure that would not be able to always discriminate between consistency and inconsistency.

(Monotony) is to be kept since contradictions in classical logic (and basically all logics) are monotone [1] wrt. information: i.e., extra information cannot make a contradiction vanish.

However, we will not retain (Monotony) as an explicit postulate, because it ensues from the postulate to be introduced in Section 5.4.

5.2   Intended Postulates

In addition, both (Tautology Independence) and ($\top$-conjunct Independence) are due postulates. Even more generally, it would make no sense, when considering how inconsistent a theory is, to take into account any inessential difference in which a formula is written (for example, $\alpha \vee \beta$ instead of $\beta \vee \alpha$). Define α' to be a *prenormal form* of α if α' results from α by applying (possibly repeatedly) one or more of these principles: commutativity, associativity and distribution for $\wedge$ and $\vee$, De Morgan laws, double negation equivalence. Hence the next[4] postulate:

- If β is a prenormal form of α then $I(K \cup \{\alpha\}) = I(K \cup \{\beta\})$ (Rewriting)

As (Monotony) essentially means that extra information cannot make amount of inconsistency decrease, the same idea must apply to conjunction because $\alpha \wedge \beta$ cannot involve less information than α. Thus, another due postulate is:

- $I(K \cup \{\alpha \wedge \beta\}) \geq I(K \cup \{\alpha\})$ (Conjunction Dominance)

Indeed, it does not matter whether α or β or both are inconsistent: it definitely cannot be rational to hold that there is a case (even a single one) where extending K with a conjunction would result in *less* inconsistency than extending K with one of the conjuncts.

5.3   Taking Care of Disjunction

It is a delicate matter to assess how inconsistent a disjunction is, but bounds can be set. Indeed, a disjunction expresses two alternative possibilities, so that accrual across these would make little sense. That is, amount of inconsistency in $\alpha \vee \beta$ cannot exceed amount of inconsistency in either α or β, depending on which one involves a higher amount of inconsistency. Hence the next postulate.

---

[4] In sharp contrast to (Irrelevance of Syntax), i.e., $I(\{\alpha_1, \ldots, \alpha_n\}) = I(\{\beta_1, \ldots, \beta_n\})$ whenever $\alpha_i \equiv \beta_i$ for $i = 1..n$ (see [15]), that allows for destructive transformation from α to β when both are inconsistent, (Rewriting) takes care of inhibiting purely deductive transformations (the most important one is presumably from $\alpha \wedge \bot$ to $\bot$).

- $I(K \cup \{\alpha \vee \beta\}) \leq \max(I(K \cup \{\alpha\}), I(K \cup \{\beta\}))$ (Disjunct Maximality)

There are alternative formulations for (Disjunct Maximality), as follows.

Proposition 14. *Assuming $I(K \cup \{\alpha \vee \beta\}) = I(K \cup \{\beta \vee \alpha\})$, it is the case that (Disjunct Maximality) is equivalent with each of*

- *if $I(K \cup \{\alpha\}) \geq I(K \cup \{\beta\})$ then $I(K \cup \{\alpha\}) \geq I(K \cup \{\alpha \vee \beta\})$*

- $I(K \cup \{\alpha \vee \beta\}) \leq I(K \cup \{\alpha\})$ *or* $I(K \cup \{\alpha \vee \beta\}) \leq I(K \cup \{\beta\})$

Proof. Let us prove that (Disjunct Maximality) entails the first item. Assume $I(K \cup \{\alpha\}) \geq I(K \cup \{\beta\})$. I.e., $I(K \cup \{\alpha\}) = \max(I(K \cup \{\alpha\}), I(K \cup \{\beta\}))$. Using (Disjunct Maximality), $I(K \cup \{\alpha \vee \beta\}) \leq \max(I(K \cup \{\alpha\}), I(K \cup \{\beta\}))$, i.e. $I(K \cup \{\alpha\})) \geq I(K \cup \{\alpha \vee \beta\})$. As to the converse direction, assume that if $I(K \cup \{\alpha\}) \geq I(K \cup \{\beta\})$ then $I(K \cup \{\alpha\}) \geq I(K \cup \{\alpha \vee \beta\})$. Consider the case $\max(I(K \cup \{\alpha\}), I(K \cup \{\beta\})) = I(K \cup \{\alpha\})$. Hence, $I(K \cup \{\alpha\}) \geq I(K \cup \{\beta\})$. According to the assumption, it follows that $I(K \cup \{\alpha\}) \geq I(K \cup \{\alpha \vee \beta\})$. That is, $\max(I(K \cup \{\alpha\}), I(K \cup \{\beta\})) \geq I(K \cup \{\alpha \vee \beta\})$. Similarly, the case $\max(I(K \cup \{\alpha\}), I(K \cup \{\beta\})) = I(K \cup \{\beta\})$ gives $I(K \cup \{\beta\}) \geq I(K \cup \{\beta \vee \alpha\})$. Then, $I(K \cup \{\beta\}) \geq I(K \cup \{\alpha \vee \beta\})$ in view of the hypothesis in the statement of Proposition 14. That is, $\max(I(K \cup \{\alpha\}), I(K \cup \{\beta\})) \geq I(K \cup \{\alpha \vee \beta\})$. Combining both cases, (Disjunct Maximality) holds.

The equivalence of (Disjunct Maximality) with the last item is due to the fact that the codomain of I is totally ordered.

Although it is quite unclear how to weigh inconsistencies out of a disjunction, there is no reason to consider than both disjunct holding (whether tied together by a conjunction or not) might decrease amount of inconsistency, which justifies

- $I(K \cup \{\alpha \wedge \beta\}) \geq I(K \cup \{\alpha \vee \beta\})$ ($\wedge$-over-$\vee$ Dominance)

and its conjunction-free counterpart

- $I(K \cup \{\alpha, \beta\}) \geq I(K \cup \{\alpha \vee \beta\})$

Proposition 15. *Assuming $I(K \cup \{\alpha \wedge \beta\}) = I(K \cup \{\beta \wedge \alpha\})$, (Conjunction Dominance) and (Disjunct Maximality) entail ($\wedge$-over-$\vee$ Dominance).*

Proof. Given $I(K \cup \{\alpha \wedge \beta\}) = I(K \cup \{\beta \wedge \alpha\})$, (Conjunction Dominance) gives $I(K \cup \{\alpha \wedge \beta\}) \geq I(K \cup \{\alpha\})$ and $I(K \cup \{\alpha \wedge \beta\}) \geq I(K \cup \{\beta\})$. Therefore, $\max(I(K \cup \{\alpha\}), I(K \cup \{\beta\})) \leq I(K \cup \{\alpha \wedge \beta\})$. In view of (Disjunct Maximality), $I(K \cup \{\alpha \vee \beta\}) \leq \max(I(K \cup \{\alpha\}), I(K \cup \{\beta\}))$, and it accordingly follows that $I(K \cup \{\alpha \vee \beta\}) \leq I(K \cup \{\alpha \wedge \beta\})$ holds.

Proposition 16. *(Monotony) and (Disjunct Maximality) entail*

- $I(K \cup \{\alpha, \beta\}) \geq I(K \cup \{\alpha \vee \beta\})$

Proof. $I(K \cup \{\alpha\}) \leq I(K \cup \{\alpha, \beta\})$ and $I(K \cup \{\beta\}) \leq I(K \cup \{\alpha, \beta\})$ according to (Monotony). Consequently, $\max(I(K \cup \{\alpha\}), I(K \cup \{\beta\})) \leq I(K \cup \{\alpha, \beta\})$. Due to (Disjunct Maximality), $I(K \cup \{\alpha \vee \beta\}) \leq \max(I(K \cup \{\alpha\}), I(K \cup \{\beta\}))$. Therefore, $I(K \cup \{\alpha, \beta\}) \geq I(K \cup \{\alpha \vee \beta\})$.

5.4   A Schematic Postulate

The next postulate we introduce is to be presented in two steps.

1. (Monotony) expresses that adding information cannot result in a decrease of the amount of inconsistency in the knowledge base. Considering a notion of primitive conflicts that underlies amount of inconsistency, (Monotony) is a special case of a postulate stating that amount of inconsistency is monotone with respect to the set of primitive conflicts $C(K)$ of the knowledge base K:
   If $C(K) \subseteq C(K')$ then $I(K) \leq I(K')$.
   Clearly, I is to admit different postulates depending on what features are required for primitive conflicts (see Table 1).
2. Keep in mind that an inconsistency measure refers to logical content of the knowledge base, but does *not* depend upon other aspects whether subject matter of contradiction, source of information,... Amount of inconsistency is a *quantity* for which these other aspects are not taken into account. Now, what characterizes logical content is uniform substitutivity. A postulate stating that instantiating cannot make the amount of inconsistency decrease is:
   If $\sigma K = K'$ for some substitution σ then $I(K) \leq I(K')$.

   (Substitutivity Dominance)

Combining these two ideas, we obtain the following postulate

- If $C(\sigma K) \subseteq C(K')$ for some substitution σ then $I(K) \leq I(K')$

   (Subsumption Orientation)

Fact 1. *Every postulate of the form*

- $I(X) \leq I(Y)$ *for all* $X \in \mathcal{K}_{\mathcal{L}}$ *and* $Y \in \mathcal{K}_{\mathcal{L}}$ *such that condition* $C_{X,Y}$ *holds*

or of the form

- $I(X) = I(Y)$ *for all* $X \in \mathcal{K}_{\mathcal{L}}$ *and* $Y \in \mathcal{K}_{\mathcal{L}}$ *such that condition* $C_{X,Y}$ *holds*

is derived from (Subsumption Orientation) and from any property of C ensuring that condition C holds.

Individual properties of C ensuring condition C for a number of postulates, including all those previously mentioned in the paper, can be found in Table 1. (Variant Equality) in Table 1 is named after the notion of a variant [2]:

- If σ and σ' are substitutions s.t. $\sigma K = K'$ and $\sigma' K' = K$ then $I(K) = I(K')$

   (Variant Equality)

Also of interest is the following postulate, (Instance Low), which can be proven to be equivalent with (Variant Equality) together with (Monotony).

- If $\sigma K \subseteq K'$ for some substitution σ then $I(K) \leq I(K')$ (Instance Low)

Table 1. Conditions for postulates derived from (Subsumption Orientation)

Specific property for $\mathcal{C}$	Specific postulate entailed by (Subsumption Orientation)
No property needed	(Variant Equality)
No property needed	(Substitutivity Dominance)
$\mathcal{C}(K \cup \{\alpha\}) = \mathcal{C}(K)$ for $\alpha \equiv \top$	(Tautology Independence)
$\mathcal{C}(K \cup \{\alpha \wedge \beta\}) = \mathcal{C}(K \cup \{\beta\})$ for $\alpha \equiv \top$	($\top$-conjunct Independence)
$\mathcal{C}(K \cup \{\alpha\}) = \mathcal{C}(K \cup \{\alpha'\})$ for α' prenormal form of α	(Rewriting)
$\mathcal{C}(K) \subseteq \mathcal{C}(K \cup \{\alpha\})$	(Instance Low)
$\mathcal{C}(K) \subseteq \mathcal{C}(K \cup \{\alpha\})$	(Monotony)
$\mathcal{C}(K \cup \{\alpha \vee \beta\}) \subseteq \mathcal{C}(K \cup \{\alpha \wedge \beta\})$	($\wedge$-over-$\vee$ Dominance)
$\mathcal{C}(K \cup \{\alpha\}) \subseteq \mathcal{C}(K \cup \{\alpha \wedge \beta\})$	(Conjunction Dominance)
$\mathcal{C}(K \cup \{\alpha, \beta\}) = \mathcal{C}(K \cup \{\alpha \wedge \beta\})$	(Adjunction Invariancy)
$\mathcal{C}(K \cup \{\alpha \vee \beta\}) \subseteq \mathcal{C}(K \cup \{\alpha\})$ or $\mathcal{C}(K \cup \{\beta\})$	(Disjunct Maximality)
$\mathcal{C}(K \cup \{\alpha \vee \beta\}) \supseteq \mathcal{C}(K \cup \{\alpha\})$ or $\mathcal{C}(K \cup \{\beta\})$	(Disjunct Minimality)
$\mathcal{C}(K \cup K') = \mathcal{C}(K \cup K'')$ for $K'' \equiv K' \not\vdash \bot$	(Exchange)
$\mathcal{C}(K \cup \{\alpha_1, ..., \alpha_n\}) = \mathcal{C}(K \cup \{\beta_1, .., \beta_n\})$ if $\alpha_i \equiv \beta_i \not\vdash \bot$	(Swap)
$\mathcal{C}(K \cup \{\beta\}) \subseteq \mathcal{C}(K \cup \{\alpha\})$ for $\alpha \vdash \beta$ and $\alpha \not\vdash \bot$	(Dominance)
$\mathcal{C}(K \cup \{\alpha\}) = \mathcal{C}(K)$ for α free for K	(Free Formula Independence)

5.5 A New System of Postulates (Basic Version and Variants)

All the above actually suggests a new system of postulates, which consists simply of (Consistency Null) and (Subsumption Orientation). The system is actually parameterized by the properties imposed upon $\mathcal{C}$ in the latter. In the range thus induced by $\mathcal{C}$, a basic system emerges, which amounts to the following list:

Basic System

$I(K) = 0$ iff $K \not\vdash \bot$ (Consistency Null)

If α' is a prenormal form of α then $I(K \cup \{\alpha\}) = I(K \cup \{\alpha'\})$ (Rewriting)

If $\sigma K \subseteq K'$ for some substitution σ then $I(K) \leq I(K')$ (Instance Low)

$I(K \cup \{\alpha \vee \beta\}) \leq \max(I(K \cup \{\alpha\}), I(K \cup \{\beta\}))$ (Disjunct Maximality)

If $\alpha \equiv \top$ then $I(K) = I(K \cup \{\alpha\})$ (Tautology Independence)

If $\alpha \equiv \top$ then $I(K \cup \{\alpha \wedge \beta\}) = I(K \cup \{\beta\})$ ($\top$-conjunct Independence)

$I(K \cup \{\alpha\}) \leq I(K \cup \{\alpha \wedge \beta\})$ (Conjunction Dominance)

As was mentioned previously, (Variant Equality) and (Monotony) are implied by (Instance Low). They are then consequences of the basic system, and so are (Substitutivity Dominance) and ($\wedge$-over-$\vee$ Dominance). It is however the case for none of (Dominance), (Free Formula Independence), (Adjunction Invariancy), and (Exchange). It also happens that neither (Swap) nor (Disjunct Minimality) are consequences. Adding either one, or both, to the basic system results in minor variants.

However, adding (Free Formula Independence) yields a major variant devoted to inconsistency measures mainly based on minimal inconsistent subsets (see the next section). Adding (Adjunction Invariancy) and/or (Exchange) yields a major variant for inconsistency measures not based on minimal inconsistent subsets.

6   HK Postulates Identified as (Subsumption Orientation)

Time has come to make sense[5] of the HK choice of (Free Formula Independence) together with (Monotony), by means of Theorem 1 and Theorem 2.

Theorem 1. *Let C be such that for every $K \in \mathcal{K}_{\mathcal{L}}$ and for every $X \subseteq \mathcal{L}$ which is minimal inconsistent, $X \in C(K)$ iff $X \subseteq K$. If I satisfies both (Monotony) and (Free Formula Independence) then I satisfies (Subsumption Orientation) restricted to its non-substitution part, namely*

$$if\ C(K) \subseteq C(K')\ then\ I(K) \leq I(K').$$

Proof. Let $C(K) \subseteq C(K')$. Should K be a subset of K', (Monotony) yields $I(K) \leq I(K')$ as desired. So, let us turn to $K \not\subseteq K'$. Consider $\varphi \in K \setminus K'$. If φ were not free for K, there would exist a minimal inconsistent subset X of K such that $\varphi \in X$. Clearly, $X \not\subseteq K'$. The constraint imposed on C in the statement of the theorem would then yield both $X \in C(K)$ and $X \notin C(K')$, contradicting the assumption $C(K) \subseteq C(K')$. Hence, φ is free for K. In view of (Free Formula Independence), $I(K) = I(K \setminus \{\varphi\})$. The same reasoning applied to all the (finitely many) formulas in $K \setminus K'$ gives $I(K) = I(K \cap K')$. However, $K \cap K'$ is a subset of K' so that using (Monotony) yields $I(K \cap K') \leq I(K')$, hence $I(K) \leq I(K')$.

Define $\varXi = \{X \in \mathcal{K}_{\mathcal{L}} \mid \forall X' \subseteq X, X' \vdash \perp \Leftrightarrow X = X'\}$. Then, C is said to be *governed by minimal inconsistency* iff C satisfies the following property

$$if\ C(K) \cap \varXi \subseteq C(K') \cap \varXi\ then\ C(K) \subseteq C(K').$$

Please note that C being governed by minimal inconsistency does not mean that $C(K)$ is determined by the set of minimal inconsistent subsets of K. Intuitively, it only means that those Z in $C(K)$ which are not minimal inconsistent cannot override set-inclusion induced by minimal inconsistent subsets —i.e., no such Z can, individually or collectively, turn $C(K) \cap \varXi \subseteq C(K') \cap \varXi$ into $C(K) \not\subseteq C(K')$.

Theorem 2. *Let C be governed by minimal inconsistency and be such that for all $K \in \mathcal{K}_{\mathcal{L}}$ and all $X \subseteq \mathcal{L}$ which is minimal inconsistent, $X \in C(K)$ iff $X \subseteq K$. I satisfies (Monotony) and (Free Formula Independence) whenever I satisfies (Subsumption Orientation) restricted to its non-substitution part, namely*

$$if\ C(K) \subseteq C(K')\ then\ I(K) \leq I(K').$$

Proof. Trivially, if $X \subseteq K$ then $X \subseteq K \cup \{\alpha\}$. By the constraint imposed on C in the statement of the theorem, it follows that if $X \in C(K)$ then $X \in C(K \cup \{\alpha\})$. Since C is governed by minimal inconsistency, $C(K) \subseteq C(K \cup \{\alpha\})$ ensues and (Subsumption Orientation) yields (Monotony). Let α be a free formula for K. By definition, α is in no minimal inconsistent subset of $K \cup \{\alpha\}$. So, $X \subseteq K$ iff

---

[5] Although still not defending the choice of (Free Formula Independence).

$X \subseteq K \cup \{\alpha\}$ for all minimal inconsistent X. By the constraint imposed on $\mathcal{C}$ in the statement of the theorem, $X \in \mathcal{C}(K)$ iff $X \in \mathcal{C}(K \cup \{\alpha\})$ ensues for all minimal inconsistent X. In symbols, $\mathcal{C}(K) \cap \Xi = \mathcal{C}(K \cup \{\alpha\}) \cap \Xi$. Since $\mathcal{C}$ is governed by minimal inconsistency, it follows that $\mathcal{C}(K) = \mathcal{C}(K \cup \{\alpha\})$. Thus, (Free Formula Independence) holds, due to (Subsumption Orientation).

Therefore, Theorem 1 and Theorem 2 mean that, *if substitutivity is left aside*, (Subsumption Orientation) is equivalent with (Free Formula Independence) and (Monotony) when primitive conflicts are essentially minimal inconsistent subsets. So, these postulates form a natural pair *if it is assumed that* minimal inconsistent subsets must be the basis for inconsistency measuring.

7 Conclusion

We have proposed a new system of postulates for inconsistency measures, i.e.

- $I(K) = 0$ *iff K is consistent*   (Consistency Null)
- *If $\mathcal{C}(\sigma K) \subseteq \mathcal{C}(K')$ for some substitution σ then $I(K) \leq I(K')$*
                                                                         (Subsumption Orientation)
parameterized by the requirements imposed on $\mathcal{C}$.

The new system omits both (Dominance) and (Free Formula Independence), which we have argued against. We investigated various postulates, absent in the HK set, giving grounds to include them in the new system. We have shown that (Subsumption Orientation) not only accounts for the other postulates but also gives a justification for (Free Formula Independence) together with (Monotony), through focussing on minimal inconsistent subsets.

We do not hold that the new system, in its basic version or any variant, captures all desirable cases, we more simply claim for improving over the original HK set. In particular, we think that HK postulates suffer from over-commitment to minimal inconsistent subsets. Crucially, such a comment applies to *postulates* (because they would exclude all approaches that are not based upon minimal inconsistent subsets) but it does not apply to *measures* themselves: There can be excellent reasons to develop a specific inconsistency measure [9] [10] [13] ... based upon minimal inconsistent subsets.

For the class of inconsistency measures whose output does not depend on having a consistent subset replaced by an equivalent set of formulas, we have proposed (Exchange), *exclusive* of (Free Formula Independence) that only fits in the class of inconsistency measures based upon minimal inconsistent subsets.

As to future work, we must mention taking seriously belief bases as multisets. Perhaps the most insighful postulate in this respect is (Adjunction Invariancy) as there surely is some rationality in holding that $\{a \wedge b \wedge \neg a \wedge \neg b \wedge a \wedge b \wedge \neg a \wedge \neg b\}$ is more inconsistent than $\{a \wedge b \wedge \neg a \wedge \neg b\}$.

Acknowledgements. Many thanks to Hitoshi Omori for insightful discussions, to Sébastien Konieczny for helpful comments on a draft, and to the reviewers for constructive remarks.

References

1. Besnard, P.: Absurdity, contradictions, and logical formalisms. In: 22nd IEEE International Conference on Tools with Artificial Intelligence (ICTAI 2010), Arras, France, October 27-29, vol. 1, pp. 369–374. IEEE (2010)
2. Church, A.: Introduction to Mathematical Logic. Princeton University Press (1956)
3. Doder, D., Rašković, M., Marković, Z., Ognjanović, Z.: Measures of inconsistency and defaults. Journal of Approximate Reasoning 51(7), 832–845 (2011)
4. Gabbay, D., Hunter, A.: Making inconsistency respectable 2: Meta-level handling of inconsistent data. In: Moral, S., Kruse, R., Clarke, E. (eds.) ECSQARU 1993. LNCS, vol. 747, pp. 129–136. Springer, Heidelberg (1993)
5. Grant, J., Hunter, A.: Measuring inconsistency in knowledgebases. Journal of Intelligent Information Systems 27(2), 159–184 (2006)
6. Hunter, A.: Measuring inconsistency in knowledge via quasi-classical models. In: Dechter, R., Sutton, R. (eds.) 18th AAAI Conference on Artificial Intelligence (AAAI 2002), Edmonton, Alberta, Canada, July 28-August 1, pp. 68–73. AAAI Press/MIT Press (2002)
7. Hunter, A., Konieczny, S.: Measuring inconsistency through minimal inconsistent sets. In: Brewka, G., Lang, J. (eds.) 11th Conference on Principles of Knowledge Representation and Reasoning (KR 2008), Sydney, Australia, September 16-19, pp. 358–366. AAAI Press (2008)
8. Hunter, A., Konieczny, S.: On the measure of conflicts: Shapley inconsistency values. Artificial Intelligence 174(14), 1007–1026 (2010)
9. Jabbour, S., Raddaoui, B.: Measuring inconsistency through minimal proofs. In: van der Gaag, L.C. (ed.) ECSQARU 2013. LNCS, vol. 7958, pp. 290–301. Springer, Heidelberg (2013)
10. Knight, K.: Measuring inconsistency. Journal of Philosophical Logic 31(1), 77–98 (2002)
11. Ma, Y., Qi, G., Hitzler, P.: Computing inconsistency measure based on paraconsistent semantics. Logic and Computation 21(6), 1257–1281 (2011)
12. Mu, K., Liu, W., Jin, Z.: A general framework for measuring inconsistency through minimal inconsistent sets. Journal of Knowledge and Information Systems 27(1), 85–114 (2011)
13. Mu, K., Liu, W., Jin, Z.: Measuring the blame of each formula for inconsistent prioritized knowledge bases. Logic and Computation 22(3), 481–516 (2012)
14. Oller, C.: Measuring coherence using LP-models. Journal of Applied Logic 2(4), 451–455 (2004)
15. Thimm, M.: Inconsistency measures for probabilistic logics. Artificial Intelligence 197, 1–24 (2013)
16. Xiao, G., Ma, Y.: Inconsistency measurement based on variables in minimal unsatisfiable subsets. In: De Raedt, L., Bessière, C., Dubois, D., Doherty, P., Frasconi, P., Heintz, F., Lucas, P.J.F. (eds.) 20th European Conference on Artificial Intelligence (ECAI 2012), Montpellier, France, August 27-31, pp. 864–869. IOS Press (2012)

A Translation-Based Approach for Revision of Argumentation Frameworks

Sylvie Coste-Marquis, Sébastien Konieczny,
Jean-Guy Mailly, and Pierre Marquis

CRIL
Université d'Artois – CNRS
Lens, France
{coste,konieczny,mailly,marquis}@cril.fr

Abstract. In this paper, we investigate the revision issue for Dung argumentation frameworks. The main idea is that such frameworks can be translated into propositional formulae, allowing the use of propositional revision operators to perform a rational minimal change. Our translation-based approach to revising argumentation frameworks can take advantage of any propositional revision operator ∘. Via a translation, each propositional operator ∘ can be associated with some revision operators ⋆ suited to argumentation frameworks. Some rationality postulates for the ⋆ operators are presented. If the revision formulae are restricted to formulae about acceptance statuses, some ⋆ operators satisfy these postulates provided that the corresponding ∘ operator is AGM.

1 Introduction

In this paper, we investigate the revision issue for abstract argumentation frameworks à la Dung [17]. Such argumentation frameworks are directed graphs, where nodes correspond to arguments and arcs to attacks between arguments. In such frameworks, the status (acceptance) of each argument depends on the chosen acceptability semantics (grounded, preferred, stable – among others).

Change in argumentation frameworks is a very active topic in the argumentation community [9,8,11,3,6,2,10,7,13,15] In [16], a classification of the change operators is given. A change operator can be characterized by the nature of the constraint to enforce and the nature of the change to perform to reach the goal. In this work, we focus on two types of constraint and change: those concerning the *structure* of the argumentation graph, and those concerning the *acceptance statuses* of arguments.

We present a translation-based approach for revising argumentation systems. The aim is to characterize a set $F \star \varphi$ of argumentation systems which corresponds to the revision of the argumentation system F by the revision formula φ. Basically, given a semantics σ, we associate with F a propositional formula $f_\sigma(F)$ which represents it; given the revision formula φ, we take advantage of AGM revision operators ∘ in order to characterize the revision $F \star \varphi$ of F by φ. In a nutshell, the approach consists in revising using ∘ the representation of

E. Fermé and J. Leite (Eds.): JELIA 2014, LNAI 8761, pp. 397–411, 2014.

$f_\sigma(F)$ by a propositional formula induced by φ plus some additional constraints on the expected revision. The output is a propositional formula which characterizes the argumentation frameworks which can be interpreted as the revision of F by φ. This paper only presents propositional encodings for Dung's complete and stable semantics, but our revision method can be used with any other acceptability semantics σ, as soon as there is a propositional encoding for arguments acceptance given σ.

Some rationality postulates for the $\star$ operators are presented. We show that if the revision formulae are restricted to formulae about acceptance statuses, some $\star$ operators satisfy these postulates provided that the corresponding $\circ$ operator is AGM.

2   Background

Let us first define formally argumentation frameworks. We only consider the case of finite frameworks. The following notions come from [17].

Definition 1. *An* argumentation framework *(AF) is a pair $F = \langle A, R \rangle$ with A a finite set of abstract entities called* arguments *and R a binary relation on A called the* attack *relation.*

The intuitive meaning of an attack $(a, b) \in R$ is that a *defeats* b, so if a is accepted then b has to be rejected. An argument can be defended by another one against a third one: if $(a, b) \in R$ and $(b, c) \in R$, then a defends c against b. These two notions can be extended to sets: $S \subseteq A$ attacks (resp. defends) $a \in A$ if $\exists b \in S$ such that b attacks (resp. defends) a.

To compute the acceptance status of each argument, Dung defines several *acceptability semantics* which leads to sets of arguments (called *extensions*) which can be accepted together. A common point to these semantics is *conflict-freeness*: a set $S \subseteq A$ is *conflict-free* if and only if there is no $a, b \in S$ such that $(a, b) \in R$.

For instance, complete and stable semantics are defined as:

- A conflict-free set $S \subseteq A$ is a *complete extension* of F if and only if S contains every argument that S defends;
- A conflict-free set $S \subseteq A$ is a *stable extension* of F if and only if S attacks every argument that does not belong to S.

Given a semantics σ and a framework F, $Ext_\sigma(F)$ denotes the set of extensions of F. An argument a is skeptically accepted by F with respect to the semantics σ if and only if $\forall \varepsilon \in Ext_\sigma(F)$, $a \in \varepsilon$.

Let us also give a few preliminaries about belief revision. Intuitively, belief revision can be defined as the minimal change to enforce a new information in a logical belief base. It has been characterized in many settings, including the setting of deductively closed theories [1], and the setting of finite propositional belief bases [21]. These works give families of rationality postulates, which are logical properties that a rational revision operator is supposed to satisfy. Katsuno and Mendelzon [21] have proved that propositional revision operators can be characterized through the notion of faithful assignment:

Definition 2. *A faithful assignment is a mapping which associates a proposi-tional formula φ with a total pre-order $\leq_\varphi$ on interpretations such that:*

- *if $\omega \models \varphi$ and $\omega' \models \varphi$, then $\omega \approx_\varphi \omega'$;*
- *if $\omega \models \varphi$ and $\omega' \not\models \varphi$, then $\omega <_\varphi \omega'$;*
- *if $\varphi \equiv \psi$, then $\leq_\varphi = \leq_\psi$.*

Faithful assignments characterize well-behaved revision operators:[1]

Theorem 1. *A KM revision operator $\circ$ satisfies the rationality postulates from [21] if and only if there exists a faithful assignment which associates with every formula φ a total pre-order $\leq_\varphi$, and such that for every formula α:[2]*

$$Mod(\varphi \circ \alpha) = \min(Mod(\alpha), \leq_\varphi)$$

3   A Translation-Based Approach

In this section, we explain how to encode an argumentation framework into logical constraints, and which constraints must be added to take into account the main semantics of acceptability. Then we show that classical AGM revision operators can be used to revise an argumentation framework. This idea is rem-iniscent to the ones considered in [18,12] for other purposes (revising modal or non-classical formulae, and case-based reasoning).

3.1   A Propositional Encoding

Let us consider a finite set of arguments $A = \{a_1, \ldots, a_n\}$ and an argumentation framework $F = \langle A, R \rangle$.

Definition 3 (Propositional language based on A).
- *for $x \in A$, $acc(x)$ is a propositional variable meaning "the argument x is skeptically accepted by the framework F".*
- *for $x, y \in A$, $att(x, y)$ is a propositional variable meaning "the argument x attacks the argument y in the framework F".*
- *for $x \in A$, x is a propositional variable meaning "the argument x belongs to the extension of the framework F which is taken in consideration".*
- *$Prop_A = \{acc(x)|x \in A\} \cup \{att(x,y)|x,y \in A\} \cup \{x|x \in A\}$*
- *$\mathcal{L}_A$ is the propositional language built up from the set of variables $Prop_A$ and the connectives $\neg, \vee, \wedge$.*

---

[1] This result is a particular case of Grove's system of spheres [19].
[2] $Mod(\varphi)$ denotes the set of models of the propositional formula φ.
  Given a set S and a pre-order $\leq$ on S, $\min(S, \leq) = \{x \in S : \nexists y \in S, y \leq x$ and $x \not\leq y\}$.

An att-formula (resp. an acc-formula) is a formula from $\mathcal{L}_A$ which contains only variables from $\{att(x,y)|x,y \in A\}$ (resp. $\{acc(x)|x \in A\}$).

Clearly enough, the set of models over $\{att(x,y)|x,y \in A\}$ of an att-formula φ_{att} (called att-models) corresponds in a bijective way to a set of argumentation frameworks over A: (x,y) belongs to the attack relation R precisely when $att(x,y)$ is true in the model under consideration. It can be formalized through the definition of a mapping from a set of att litterals to an argumentation framework:

Definition 4 (Argumentation framework associated with a att-model).
Given a set A of arguments, any $m \subseteq \{att(x,y)|x,y \in A\}$ can be associated with an argumentation framework $arg(m) = \langle A, \{(x,y) \in A \times A|att(x,y) \in m\}\rangle$. This notion can be extended to the set of argumentation frameworks corresponding to a set of att-models: $arg(M) = \{arg(m)|m \in M\}$.

We also need the following notion of projection:

Definition 5 (att-projection of models and formulae). *Given a set A of arguments, any interpretation m over $\mathcal{L}_A$ can be projected on its att-part: $Proj_{att}(m) = m \cap \{att(x,y)|x,y \in A\}$. This notion can be extended to the projection of a formula $\varphi \in \mathcal{L}_A$: $Proj_{att}(\varphi) = \{Proj_{att}(m)|m \in Mod(\varphi)\}$.*

Then, a formula φ representing argumentation frameworks can be associated with these frameworks by combining these two mappings: $arg(Proj_{att}(\varphi))$.

The other way around, at a shallow level, any $F = \langle A, R\rangle$ can be represented by the formula over $\{att(x,y)|x,y \in A\}$

$$\bigwedge_{(x,y)\in R} att(x,y) \wedge \bigwedge_{(x,y)\notin R} \neg att(x,y)$$

but this translation does not take into account the semantics σ under which F must be interpreted. One clearly needs to consider σ in the encoding. We propose to do it as follows:

Definition 6 (σ-formula of F). *Given an argumentation framework $F = \langle A, R\rangle$ and a semantics σ, the σ-formula of F is*

$$f_\sigma(F) = \bigwedge_{(x,y)\in R} att(x,y) \wedge \bigwedge_{(x,y)\notin R} \neg att(x,y) \wedge th_\sigma(A)$$

where $th_\sigma(A)$ is a logical formula (the σ-theory of A) that encodes the semantics σ.

Now, the question is how to define $th_\sigma(A)$ for some usual semantics. To do so, we take advantage of the logical representation of σ-extensions as proposed in [4]. Let us begin with the stable semantics. It has been proved in [4] that the stable extensions of an argumentation framework $F = \langle\{a_1,\ldots,a_n\}, R\rangle$ are exactly the models of the propositional formula:

$$\bigwedge_{a_k\in A} (a_k \Leftrightarrow \bigwedge_{a_j:(a_j,a_k)\in R} \neg a_j)$$

It is interesting to note that an argument a_i is skeptically accepted by $F = \langle A, R \rangle$ if and only if every model of the previous formula contains a_i:

$$\models [\bigwedge_{a_k \in A} (a_k \Leftrightarrow \bigwedge_{a_j:(a_j,a_k) \in R} \neg a_j) \Rightarrow a_i]$$

or in a simpler way,

$$\forall a_1, \ldots, a_n, [\bigwedge_{a_k \in A} (a_k \Leftrightarrow \bigwedge_{a_j:(a_j,a_k) \in R} \neg a_j) \Rightarrow a_i] \text{ is valid.}$$

In this encoding, it is assumed that the argumentation framework is known. However, one can relax this assumption by taking advantage of the $att(x, y)$ variables:

$$acc(a_i) \Leftrightarrow \forall a_1, \ldots, a_n, [\bigwedge_{a_k \in A} (a_k \Leftrightarrow \bigwedge_{a_j \subset A} (att(a_j, a_k) \Rightarrow \neg a_j)) \Rightarrow a_i]$$

This formula encodes a way to compute the skeptically accepted arguments of any argumentation framework built on A given the stable semantics (it proves enough to condition the formula by the literals $att(a_j, a_k)$ corresponding to the attack relation of the given argumentation framework to recover the encoding from [4]).

Altogether, we get:

$$th_{st}(A) = \bigwedge_{a_i \in A} (acc(a_i) \Leftrightarrow \forall a_1, \ldots, a_n, (\bigwedge_{a_k \in A} (a_k \Leftrightarrow \bigwedge_{a_j \in A} (att(a_j, a_k) \Rightarrow \neg a_j)) \Rightarrow a_i))$$

It is well-known that a quantified Boolean formula (QBF) can be transformed into a classical propositional formula through the elimination of quantifications. We keep the notation of our encoding in QBF to keep reasonable the formula size, but it does not prevent from using KM revision operators (Section 3.2).

Example 1. *Let us illustrate these notions on F_1, given on Fig. 1.*

Fig. 1. The argumentation framework F_1

The stable theory of the set of arguments $A = \{a, b, c, d\}$ *is* $th_{st}(A) =$
$$acc(a) \Leftrightarrow \forall a, b, c, d, [[(a \Leftrightarrow (att(a,a) \Rightarrow \neg a) \wedge (att(b,a) \Rightarrow \neg b))$$
$$\wedge (att(c,a) \Rightarrow \neg c)) \wedge (att(d,a) \Rightarrow \neg d))$$
$$\wedge (b \Leftrightarrow (att(a,b) \Rightarrow \neg a) \wedge (att(b,b) \Rightarrow \neg b)$$
$$\wedge (att(c,b) \Rightarrow \neg c) \wedge (att(d,b) \Rightarrow \neg d))$$
$$\wedge (c \Leftrightarrow (att(a,c) \Rightarrow \neg a) \wedge (att(b,c) \Rightarrow \neg b)$$
$$\wedge (att(c,c) \Rightarrow \neg c) \wedge (att(d,c) \Rightarrow \neg d))$$
$$\wedge (d \Leftrightarrow (att(a,d) \Rightarrow \neg a) \wedge (att(b,d) \Rightarrow \neg b)$$
$$\wedge (att(c,d) \Rightarrow \neg c) \wedge (att(d,d) \Rightarrow \neg d))] \Rightarrow a]$$
$$\wedge \quad acc(b) \Leftrightarrow \forall a, b, c, d, [\ldots]$$
$$\wedge \quad acc(c) \Leftrightarrow \forall a, b, c, d, [\ldots]$$
$$\wedge \quad acc(d) \Leftrightarrow \forall a, b, c, d, [\ldots]$$
So the stable formula of F_1 *is given by*

$$th_{st}(A) \wedge \bigwedge_{(a,b) \in R} att(a,b) \wedge \bigwedge_{(a,b) \notin R} \neg att(a,b)$$

Propagating the values of att-variables allows to deduce the values of acc-variables $(acc(a) = acc(c) = true,$ *and* $acc(b) = acc(d) = false)$, *and so leads to the set of skeptically accepted arguments* $\{a, c\}$.

The complete-theory $th_{co}(A)$ of A can be defined in a similar way. First, let us recall the encoding of the complete extensions given in [4]:

$$\bigwedge_{a_k \in A} [(a_k \Rightarrow \bigwedge_{a_j : (a_j, a_k) \in R} \neg a_j) \wedge (a_k \Leftrightarrow \bigwedge_{a_j : (a_j, a_k) \in R} (\bigvee_{a_l : (a_l, a_j) \in R} a_l))]$$

Using a similar reasoning scheme, we get that:

$$th_{co}(A) = \bigwedge_{a_i \in A} [acc(a_i) \Leftrightarrow [\forall a_1, \ldots, a_n,$$
$$\bigwedge_{a_k \in A} [(a_k \Rightarrow \bigwedge_{a_j \in A} (att(a_j, a_k) \Rightarrow \neg a_j))$$
$$\wedge (a_k \Leftrightarrow \bigwedge_{a_j \in A} (att(a_j, a_k) \Rightarrow \bigvee_{a_l \in A} (att(a_l, a_j) \Rightarrow a_l)))]] \Rightarrow a_i]$$

3.2 Encoding Revision Operators with Logical Constraints

One can take advantage of the encodings presented in the previous section to define revision operators for argumentation frameworks, via the use of classical AGM operators. In particular, the KM revision operators $\circ$ defined for propositional logic [21] are suited to the language $\mathcal{L}_A$.

At a first glance, one can consider to revise $f_\sigma(F)$ by the revision formula φ. However, this is not sufficient. Indeed, if the revision formula φ does not correspond to any argumentation framework interpreted under the semantics σ (for instance, when $\varphi = acc(a) \wedge acc(b) \wedge att(a,b)$), then the revised formula will not correspond to any argumentation framework interpreted under σ. Indeed the success postulate $f_\sigma(F) \circ \varphi \models \varphi$ would force φ to be the case.

Such pathological scenarios must be avoided. A way to ensure it consists in revising $f_\sigma(F)$ by $\varphi \wedge th_\sigma(A)$ since the latter formula is logically consistent precisely when there exists at least one argumentation framework interpreted under σ which is compatible with φ.

Finally, the models of the revised formula $f_\sigma(F) \circ (\varphi \wedge th_\sigma(A))$, projected onto the $att(x, y)$ variables, characterize the revised argumentation frameworks.

Definition 7 (Translation-based revision). *Let* $\circ$ *be a KM revision operator. For any semantics* σ, *any argumentation framework* $F = \langle A, R \rangle$ *and any formula* $\varphi \in \mathcal{L}_A$, *the associated* translation-based revision operator $\star$ *is given by:*

$$F \star \varphi = arg(Proj_{att}(f_\sigma(F) \circ (\varphi \wedge th_\sigma(A))))$$

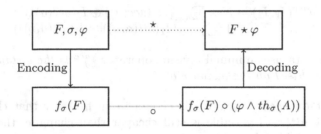

Fig. 2. Schematic explanation of the revision process

The decoding process is performed by the functions arg and $proj_{att}$ defined previously (Definition 4, Definition 5).

Let us instanciate this general definition of translation-based revision operators, using distances [3] between the interpretations over $\mathcal{L}_A$.

Definition 8 (Distance-based revision). *Let* d *be a distance between interpretations over* $\mathcal{L}_A$. *Given a formula* $\psi \in \mathcal{L}_A$, *the pre-order* $\leq_\psi$ *is defined by*

$$\omega \leq_\psi \omega' \text{ if and only if } d(\omega, Mod(\psi)) \leq d(\omega', Mod(\psi))$$

For any formulae $\psi, \alpha \in \mathcal{L}_A$, *the distance-based KM revision operator* $\circ_d$ *is defined by*

$$Mod(\psi \circ_d \alpha) = \min(Mod(\alpha), \leq_\psi)$$

Then, the distance-based AF revision operator $\star_d$ *is defined by*

$$F \star_d \varphi = arg(Proj_{att}(f_\sigma(F) \circ_d (\varphi \wedge th_\sigma(A))))$$

---

[3] We call a *distance* a function d such that (1) $d(x, y) = 0$ iff $x = y$; (2) $d(x, y) = d(y, x)$; (3) $d(x, z) \leq d(x, y) + d(y, z)$. In fact, we only need pseudo-distances: (3) is not required. Such a pseudo-distance d can be extended to a "distance" between an interpretation and a set of interpretations: $d(\omega, \Omega) = \min_{\omega' \in \Omega} d(\omega, \omega')$.

Depending on the revision operator ∘ used, the concept of minimal change in the argumentation framework can vary. A first option is to consider minimal change on the arguments statuses more important than minimal change on the attack relation.

To perform this kind of change, we can consider a weighted Dalal-like operator (see [14,21] for details about Dalal's revision operator) which ensures minimal change on the acc variables. This kind of revision operator is a particular distance-based revision operator:

Definition 9 (Arguments statuses minimal revision). *Let A be a set of arguments, let $N = |A|^2 + 1$. The acceptance-weighted distance d^{acc} between interpretations is defined by*[4]

$$d^{acc}(I_1, I_2) = N \times \sum_{a \in A}(I_1(acc(a)) \oplus I_2(acc(a))) \\ + \sum_{a,b \in A}(I_1(att(a,b)) \oplus I_2(att(a,b)))$$

The arguments statuses minimal revision operator $\star_d^{acc}$ is the distance-based revision operator based on the distance d^{acc}.

The weight on $acc(x)$ variables is chosen in such a way that changing the value of every $att(x,y)$ variable is still cheaper than changing the value of a single $acc(x)$ variable.

Conversely, we can define a Dalal-like revision operator which requires minimal change on the attack relation. Here the weights are chosen to ensure that changing the value of every $acc(x)$ variable is cheaper than changing the value of a single $att(x,y)$ variable:

Definition 10 (Attacks minimal revision). *Let A be a set of arguments, let $N = |A| + 1$. The attacks-weighted distance d^{att} between interpretations is defined by*

$$d^{att}(I_1, I_2) = \sum_{a \in A}(I_1(acc(a)) \oplus I_2(acc(a))) \\ + N \times \sum_{a,b \in A}(I_1(att(a,b)) \oplus I_2(att(a,b)))$$

The attacks minimal revision operator $\star_d^{att}$ is the distance-based revision operator based on the distance d^{att}.

Interestingly, the addition of new arguments is allowed.

Definition 11 (Open world revision). *Given $F = \langle A, R \rangle$ an AF, B a non-empty set of arguments such that $A \cap B = \emptyset$, $\varphi \in \mathcal{L}_{A \cup B}$ a formula and ∘ a KM revision operator. The associated open world revision operator $\star_B$ is defined as:*

$$F \star_B \varphi = arg(Proj_{att}(f_\sigma(F) \circ (\varphi \wedge th_\sigma(A \cup B))))$$

---

[4] The *exclusive or* $\oplus$ is the binary operation on Boolean variables defined by $x \oplus y \equiv (x \vee y) \wedge (\neg x \vee \neg y)$.

Here, new arguments and new attacks between them or between new and old arguments can be added.

More generally, one can constrain the revision process: some integrity constraints can be required for a particular application (because a given attack is known to hold for sure or because a given argument has to be skeptically accepted, and so cannot change during the revision):

Definition 12 (Constrained revision). *Given* $F = \langle A, R \rangle$ *an AF,* $\varphi, \mu \in \mathcal{L}_A$ *formulae and* $\circ$ *a KM revision operator. The associated* μ-*constrained revision operator is*

$$F \star_\mu \varphi = arg(Proj_{att}(f_\sigma(F) \circ (\varphi \wedge th_\sigma(A) \wedge \mu)))$$

Here are some examples of integrity constraints μ which can prove useful:

- $\bigwedge_{a \in A} \neg att(a, a)$ is useful when self-attacking arguments are not allowed [13];
- $\bigwedge_{(a,b) \in R} att(a, b) \wedge \bigwedge_{(a,b) \notin R} \neg att(a, b)$ is useful when attacks between former arguments must be preserved but attacks involving new arguments can be added [11].

Of course, the KM revision operator used to define $\star_B$ or $\star_\mu$ can take advantage of a weighted distance to ensure minimal change of arguments statuses or minimal change of the attack relation.

Depending on the situation, it can also be useful to consider a single argumentation framework as result of the revision process. This amounts to selecting one model of the projected formula. Several criteria can be used to do so; for space reasons, we will not detail them is this paper. Let us now illustrate two of the previously defined revision operators.

Example 2. *Let us revise the argumentation framework* F_1, *given on Fig.1, by the revision formula* $\varphi = acc(a) \wedge \neg att(a, b)$, *meaning that we want to change* F_1 *to have a skeptically accepted without a attacking b.*

F_1's single stable extension is $\{a, c\}$, *so a is already skeptically accepted, but* φ *is not satisfied because a attacks b. All possible results of attack minimal revision and argument minimal revision are given respectively on Fig.3(a) and Fig.3(b). F_2's stable extensions are* $\{\{a, c\}\{a, b, d\}\}$, *so a is the only skeptically accepted*

(a) F_2: Attack minimal revision of F_1 (b) F_3: Arguments statuses minimal revision of F_1

Fig. 3. Results of F_1 revisions

argument. With respect to acceptance statuses, the difference between F_1 and F_2 is 1, and there is also 1 attack different between them ((a, b) is removed).

The single stable extension of F_3 is $\{a, c\}$, so there is no difference between F_1 and F_3 with respect to acceptance statuses. The difference only concerns the attack relation $((a, b)$ is removed and (d, b) is added).

4   Rationality Postulates in the *acc* Case

In this section, we focus on constraints expressing an information about skeptically accepted arguments.

$Sc_\sigma(F)$ correspond to the *skeptical consequences* of the argumentation framework F with respect to the semantics σ. Formally, it is defined as $\{\bigcap_{\varepsilon \in Ext_\sigma(F)} \varepsilon\}$. We generalize this notion to $Sc_\sigma(S) = \bigcup_{F \in S} Sc_\sigma(F)$ where S is a set of argumentation frameworks. We call this set the skeptical consequences of S.

The satisfaction of *acc*-formulae can be defined with respect to a set of arguments. Let $\varepsilon \subseteq A$ and φ an *acc*-formula. The concept of *satisfaction* of φ by ε, noted $\varepsilon \hspace{-0.3em}\sim\hspace{-0.3em}\varphi$, is defined inductively as follows:

- If $\varphi = acc(a)$ with $a \in A$, then $\varepsilon \hspace{-0.3em}\sim\hspace{-0.3em}\varphi$ iff $a \in \varepsilon$,
- If $\varphi = (\varphi_1 \wedge \varphi_2)$, $\varepsilon \hspace{-0.3em}\sim\hspace{-0.3em}\varphi$ iff $\varepsilon \hspace{-0.3em}\sim\hspace{-0.3em}\varphi_1$ and $\varepsilon \hspace{-0.3em}\sim\hspace{-0.3em}\varphi_2$,
- If $\varphi = (\varphi_1 \vee \varphi_2)$, $\varepsilon \hspace{-0.3em}\sim\hspace{-0.3em}\varphi$ iff $\varepsilon \hspace{-0.3em}\sim\hspace{-0.3em}\varphi_1$ or $\varepsilon \hspace{-0.3em}\sim\hspace{-0.3em}\varphi_2$,
- If $\varphi = \neg\psi$, $\varepsilon \hspace{-0.3em}\sim\hspace{-0.3em}\varphi$ iff $\varepsilon \hspace{-0.3em}\not\sim\hspace{-0.3em}\psi$.

Then for any argumentation framework F, any set S of argumentation frameworks on A, and any semantics σ, we say that:

- φ is *skeptically accepted* w.r.t. F, noted $F \hspace{-0.3em}\sim_\sigma\hspace{-0.3em}\varphi$, if $\forall \varepsilon \in Sc_\sigma(F)$, $\varepsilon \hspace{-0.3em}\sim\hspace{-0.3em}\varphi$.
- φ is *rejected* w.r.t. F in the remaining case.
- φ is *skeptically accepted* w.r.t. S, noted $S \hspace{-0.3em}\sim_\sigma\hspace{-0.3em}\varphi$, if $\forall \varepsilon \in Sc_\sigma(S)$, $\varepsilon \hspace{-0.3em}\sim\hspace{-0.3em}\varphi$.
- φ is *rejected* w.r.t. S in the remaining case.

Each ε in the set $\mathcal{S}(\varphi) = \{\varepsilon \subseteq A | \varepsilon \hspace{-0.3em}\sim\hspace{-0.3em}\varphi\}$ is a possible set of skeptically accepted arguments with respect to a framework which accepts the formula φ.
A formula φ is said to be *acc-consistent* if and only if $\mathcal{S}(\varphi) \neq \emptyset$.
Two formulae φ and ψ are said to be *acc-equivalent*, noted $\varphi \equiv_{acc} \psi$, if and only if $\mathcal{S}(\varphi) = \mathcal{S}(\psi)$.
Let us now point out an adaptation of KM's postulates:

(AS1) $Sc_\sigma(F \star \varphi) \subseteq \mathcal{S}(\varphi)$
(AS2) If $Sc_\sigma(F) \cap \mathcal{S}(\varphi) \neq \emptyset$, then $Sc_\sigma(F \star \varphi) = Sc_\sigma(F) \cap \mathcal{S}(\varphi)$
(AS3) If φ is *acc*-consistent, then $Sc_\sigma(F \star \varphi) \neq \emptyset$
(AS4) If $\varphi \equiv_{acc} \psi$, then $Sc_\sigma(F \star \varphi) = Sc_\sigma(F \star \psi)$
(AS5) $Sc_\sigma(F \star \varphi) \cap \mathcal{S}(\psi) \subseteq Sc_\sigma(F \star (\varphi \wedge \psi))$
(AS6) If $Sc_\sigma(F \star \varphi) \cap \mathcal{S}(\psi) \neq \emptyset$, then $Sc_\sigma(F \star (\varphi \wedge \psi)) \subseteq Sc_\sigma(F \star \varphi) \cap \mathcal{S}(\psi)$

The first postulate is the *success* postulate: the result of the revision must satisfy the formula φ. **(AS2)** requires the skeptical consequences to stay the same ones if the input framework already satisfies φ. The third postulate states that revising a framework by a consistent formula cannot lead to an inconsistent result (such an inconsistent result is identified by an empty set of skeptical consequences). **(AS4)** states that revising by equivalent formulae leads to the same result. The last two postulates constrain the behavior of the revision operator when revising by a conjunction of formulae.

Similar postulates have been proposed in [13]. The main difference concerns the semantics of revision formulae. In [13], argumentation frameworks are revised by propositional formulae the satisfaction of which is defined with respect to the extensions. For instance, $a \vee b$ means "a or b must be in every extension" (and so, this formula is satisfied by a framework the extensions of which are $E = \{\{a\}, \{b\}\}$). Whereas here, formulae deal with the skeptical consequences of the framework, i.e. the intersection of the extensions. So the formula $acc(a) \vee acc(b)$ means "a must be in every extension or b must be in every extension", and is not satisfied by the set of extensions E.
More generally, the difference between our postulates and those expressed in [13] is the object of the constraint they give: in [13], the postulates give some constraint on the expected extensions of the output of the revision process, while the current postulates concern the set of skeptically accepted arguments.

The following proposition explains how to define a rational revision operator from any pseudo-distance between sets of arguments.

Proposition 1 *Given a pseudo-distance d between sets of arguments and an argumentation framework F, $\leq_F^d$ denotes the total pre-order between sets of arguments defined by: $\varepsilon_1 \leq_F^d \varepsilon_2$ iff $d(\varepsilon_1, Sc_\sigma(F)) \leq d(\varepsilon_2, Sc_\sigma(F))$.*
The pseudo-distance based revision operator $\star_d$ which satisfies

$$Sc_\sigma(F \star_d \varphi) = \min(\mathcal{S}(\varphi), \leq_F^d)$$

*satisfies the postulates **(AS1)** - **(AS6)**.*

Proof. **(AS1)** is satisfied from the definition of the operator.

If $Sc_\sigma(F) \cap \mathcal{S}(\varphi) \neq \emptyset$, then obviously $\forall \varepsilon \in Sc_\sigma(F) \cap \mathcal{S}(\varphi)$, $\varepsilon \in Sc_\sigma(F)$, and $d(\varepsilon, Sc_\sigma(F)) = 0$. Any ε' which is not in $Sc_\sigma(F) \cap \mathcal{S}(\varphi)$ either does not satisfy φ (and so does not belong to $\mathcal{S}(\varphi)$), or does not belong to $Sc_\sigma(F)$ (and so $d(\varepsilon', Sc_\sigma(F)) > 0$). So $\min(\mathcal{S}(\varphi), \leq_F^d) = Sc_\sigma(F) \cap \mathcal{S}(\varphi)$, which leads to **(AS2)**.
If φ is acc-consistent, $\mathcal{S}(\varphi) \neq \emptyset$, so $\min(\mathcal{S}(\varphi), \leq_F^d) \neq \emptyset$. So **(AS3)** holds.
$\varphi \equiv_{acc} \varphi$ can be rewritten $\mathcal{S}(\varphi) = \mathcal{S}(\psi)$, which leads to $\min(\mathcal{S}(\varphi), \leq_F^d) = \min(\mathcal{S}(\psi), \leq_F^d)$. It is enough to prove **(AS4)**.
If $Sc_\sigma(F \star \varphi) \cap \mathcal{S}(\psi) = \emptyset$, **(AS5)**-**(AS6)** are satisfied. We suppose now that $Sc_\sigma(F \star \varphi) \cap \mathcal{S}(\psi) \neq \emptyset$.
We first prove the inclusion $Sc_\sigma(F \star \varphi) \cap \mathcal{S}(\psi) \subseteq Sc_\sigma(F \star \varphi \wedge \psi)$. By *reductio ad absurdum*, suppose that $\exists \varepsilon \in Sc_\sigma(F \star \varphi) \cap \mathcal{S}(\varphi \wedge \psi)$ such that $\varepsilon \notin Sc_\sigma(F \star \varphi \wedge \psi)$, also written as $\varepsilon \in \min(\mathcal{S}(\varphi), \leq_F^d) \cap \mathcal{S}(\psi)$ and $\varepsilon \notin \min(\mathcal{S}(\varphi \wedge \psi), \leq_F^d)$. From the first part, we deduce $\varepsilon \in \mathcal{S}(\varphi \wedge \psi)$. However, ε is not a minimal element in this set with respect to $\leq_F^d$. Consequently, $\exists \varepsilon' \in \mathcal{S}(\varphi \wedge \psi)$ such that $\varepsilon' <_F^d \varepsilon$. From the definition of $\mathcal{S}(\varphi \wedge \psi)$, $\varepsilon' \in \mathcal{S}(\varphi)$ holds. This contradicts $\varepsilon \in \min(\mathcal{S}(\varphi), \leq_F^d)$. So $Sc_\sigma(F \star \varphi) \cap \mathcal{S}(\varphi \wedge \psi) \subseteq Sc_\sigma(F \star \varphi \wedge \psi)$, **(AS5)** holds.

If $Sc_\sigma(F \star \varphi) \cap S(\psi) \neq \emptyset$, let us suppose $\exists \varepsilon \in Sc_\sigma(F \star \varphi \wedge \psi)$ such that $\varepsilon \notin Sc_\sigma(F \star \varphi) \cap S(\psi)$. $\varepsilon \in \min(S(\varphi \wedge \psi), \leq_F^d) \Rightarrow \varepsilon \in S(\varphi \wedge \psi) \Rightarrow \varepsilon \in S(\psi)$ holds. From this and $\varepsilon \notin Sc_\sigma(F \star \varphi) \cap S(\psi)$, we deduce $\varepsilon \notin Sc_\sigma(F \star \varphi)$. Since we suppose that the intersection is non-empty, $\exists \varepsilon' \in Sc_\sigma(F \star \varphi) \cap S(\psi)$. In particular, ε' satisfies φ and ψ, i.e. $\varepsilon' \in S(\varphi) \cap S(\psi) = S(\varphi \wedge \psi)$. From $\varepsilon \in Sc_\sigma(F \star \varphi \wedge \psi) = \min(S(\varphi \wedge \psi), \leq_F^d)$ and $\leq_F^d$ is a total relation, $\varepsilon \leq_F^d \varepsilon'$. As $\varepsilon' \in Sc_\sigma(F \star \varphi) = \min(S(\varphi), \leq_F^d)$, $\varepsilon \in \min(S(\varphi), \leq_F^d)$. It is a contradiction. So $Sc_\sigma(F \star \varphi \wedge \psi) \subseteq Sc_\sigma(F \star \varphi) \cap S(\psi)$ holds.

The previous proposition gives a sufficient condition to prove that a pseudo-distance based revision operator satisfies the rationality postulates. From this proposition, we prove that the arguments statuses minimal revision operator (restricted to the *acc*-case) satisfies the postulates, through a reduction of this operator to a pseudo-distance based revision operator as described in Prop. 1.

Proposition 2 *The arguments statuses minimal revision operator satisfies the postulates (AS1)-(AS6).*

Proof. Let us show that the arguments statuses minimal revision operator is a pseudo-distance based revision operator. We define $Proj_{acc}$ as the counterpart of $Proj_{att}$ to project the formulae on their *acc*-part.
$F \star_D^{acc} \varphi = arg(Proj_{att}(f_\sigma(F) \circ_D^{acc} (\varphi \wedge th_\sigma(A))))$ leads to
$$Sc_\sigma(F \star_D^{acc} \varphi) = Proj_{acc}(f_\sigma(F) \circ_D^{acc} (\varphi \wedge th_\sigma(A)))$$
$$= Proj_{acc}(\min(Mod(\varphi \wedge th_\sigma(A)), \leq_F^{d_H^{acc}}))$$
Let us prove that projecting the minimal models of $\varphi \wedge th_\sigma(A)$ leads to the minimal sets of skeptically accepted arguments. The models of $\varphi \wedge th_\sigma(A)$ are the propositional representations of argumentation frameworks which satisfy φ, so it is obvious that the projection of the models on the *acc* variables allows to obtain a subset of $S(\varphi)$. Let us show that these sets of arguments are minimal with respect to $\leq_F^d$:
Given $m \in \min(Mod(\varphi \wedge th_\sigma(A)), \leq_F^{d_H^{acc}})$, we have $d_H^{acc}(m, Mod(f_\sigma(F))$ is minimal. $f_\sigma(F)$ has a single model m_F, so $d_H^{acc}(m, m_F)$ is minimal. In other words,

$$(|A|^2 + 1) \sum_{a \in A} (m(acc(a)) \oplus m_F(acc(a))) + \sum_{a,b \in A} (m(att(a,b)) \oplus m_F(att(a,b)))$$

is minimal. Let us suppose that the *acc* part of the distance is not minimal, i.e. there exists m' such that

$$(|A|^2+1) \sum_{a \in A} (m'(acc(a)) \oplus m_F(acc(a))) < (|A|^2+1) \sum_{a \in A} (m(acc(a)) \oplus m_F(acc(a)))$$

In the extreme case when $\sum_{a,b \in A}(m(att(a,b)) \oplus m_F(att(a,b))) = 0$ and $\sum_{a,b \in A}(m'(att(a,b)) \oplus m_F(att(a,b))) = |A|^2$,

$$(|A|^2 + 1) \sum_{a \in A} (m'(acc(a)) \oplus m_F(acc(a)))$$
$$+ \sum_{a,b \in A}(m'(att(a,b)) \oplus m_F(att(a,b)))$$
$$< (|A|^2 + 1) \sum_{a \in A}(m(acc(a)) \oplus m_F(acc(a)))$$
$$+ \sum_{a,b \in A}(m(att(a,b)) \oplus m_F(att(a,b)))$$

is ensured by the weight $|A|^2 + 1$ on the acc part. By *reductio ad absurdum*, we proved that the acc part of $d_H^{acc}(m, m_F)$ is minimal, i.e., $d_H(Proj_{acc}(m), Sc_\sigma(F))$ is minimal, with d_H the Hamming distance [20]. It implies

$$Sc_\sigma(F \star_D^{acc} \varphi) = Proj_{acc}(\min(Mod(\varphi' \wedge th_\sigma(A)), \leq_F^{d_F^{acc}}))$$
$$= \min(\mathcal{S}(\varphi), \leq_F^{d_H})$$

From Prop. 1, $\star_D^{acc}$ satisfies the postulates **(AS1)-(AS6)**.

5 Conclusion

In this paper, we studied a way to benefit from the well-known logical revision operators from Katsuno and Mendelzon's work ∘ to define revision operators ⋆ for abstract argumentation frameworks.

This approach is particularly interesting due to the ability of our revision operators to enforce both *structural* and *acceptability* constraints. Depending on the underlying operator ∘, the operator ⋆ ensures minimal change either on the acceptance statuses, or on the attack relation. Moreover, these operators can encode some change operators defined in some recent related works [11].

We have also stated some rationality postulates inspired by the classical AGM framework, and proved that under the constraint that revision formulae only deal with acceptability, a revision operator ⋆ based on an AGM operator ∘ satisfies our postulates.

As a future work, several possibilities are opened. First, this paper only presents the logical characterization of skeptical acceptance under the stable and complete semantics. It would be interesting to define a similar characterization of skeptical acceptance under other semantics, this can be done thanks to the encoding method defined in [4,22,23,5]. Another interesting result would be to define the credulous σ-theory for these semantics σ. We are also interested in enforcing the result of the revision to belong to a particular subclass of argumentation frameworks, as the acyclic argumentation frameworks.

Another point for further studies is the axiomatic characterization of revision operators. We proved that arguments statuses minimal revision satisfies some rationality postulates in the case of acceptability revision constraints, but it would be interesting to know if some other kinds of operators satisfy these postulates, and to know if some other kinds of revision constraints can be characterized.

At last, we plan to encode our revision operators into a SAT-based software. The propositional setting of our operators is particularly well-suited to SAT solvers, so this approach is very promising from a computational point of view.

Acknowledgments. We would like to thank the reviewers for their helpful comments and proposals. This work benefited from the support of the project AMANDE ANR-13-BS02-0004 of the French National Research Agency (ANR).

References

1. Alchourrón, C.E., Gärdenfors, P., Makinson, D.: On the logic of theory change: Partial meet contraction and revision functions. Journal of Symbolic Logic 50, 510–530 (1985)
2. Baumann, R.: What does it take to enforce an argument? minimal change in abstract argumentation. In: Proceedings of the European Conference on Artificial Intelligence (ECAI 2012), pp. 127–132 (2012)
3. Baumann, R., Brewka, G.: Expanding argumentation frameworks: Enforcing and monotonicity results. In: Proceedings of the Third International Conference on Computational Models of Argument (COMMA 2010), pp. 75–186 (2010)
4. Besnard, P., Doutre, S.: Checking the acceptability of a set of arguments. In: Proceedings of the 10th International Workshop on Non-Monotonic Reasoning (NMR 2004), pp. 59–64 (2004)
5. Besnard, P., Doutre, S., Herzig, A.: Encoding Argument Graphs in Logic. In: Laurent, A., Strauss, O., Bouchon-Meunier, B., Yager, R.R. (eds.) IPMU 2014, Part II. CCIS, vol. 443, pp. 345–354. Springer, Heidelberg (2014)
6. Bisquert, P., Cayrol, C., de Saint-Cyr, F.D., Lagasquie-Schiex, M.-C.: Change in argumentation systems: Exploring the interest of removing an argument. In: Benferhat, S., Grant, J. (eds.) SUM 2011. LNCS, vol. 6929, pp. 275–288. Springer, Heidelberg (2011)
7. Bisquert, P., Cayrol, C., de Saint-Cyr, F.D., Lagasquie-Schiex, M.-C.: Enforcement in argumentation is a kind of update. In: Liu, W., Subrahmanian, V.S., Wijsen, J. (eds.) SUM 2013. LNCS, vol. 8078, pp. 30–43. Springer, Heidelberg (2013)
8. Boella, G., Kaci, S., van der Torre, L.: Dynamics in argumentation with single extensions: Abstraction principles and the grounded extension. In: Sossai, C., Chemello, G. (eds.) ECSQARU 2009. LNCS, vol. 5590, pp. 107–118. Springer, Heidelberg (2009)
9. Boella, G., Kaci, S., van der Torre, L.: Dynamics in argumentation with single extensions: attack refinement and the grounded extension. In: Proceedings of the International Conference on Autonomous Agents and Multiagents Systems (AAMAS 2009), pp. 1213–1214 (2009)
10. Booth, R., Kaci, S., Rienstra, T., van der Torre, L.: A logical theory about dynamics in abstract argumentation. In: Liu, W., Subrahmanian, V.S., Wijsen, J. (eds.) SUM 2013. LNCS, vol. 8078, pp. 148–161. Springer, Heidelberg (2013)
11. Cayrol, C., de Saint-Cyr, F.D., Lagasquie-Schiex, M.C.: Change in abstract argumentation frameworks: Adding an argument. Journal of Artificial Intelligence Research 38, 49–84 (2010)
12. Cojan, J., Lieber, J.: Belief revision-based case-based reasoning. In: Richard, G. (ed.) ECAI 2012 Workshop Similarity and Analogy-Based Methods in AI, Montpellier, France, pp. 33–39 (2012)
13. Coste-Marquis, S., Konieczny, S., Mailly, J.G., Marquis, P.: On the revision of argumentation systems: Minimal change of arguments statuses. In: 14th International Conference on Principles of Knowledge Representation and Reasoning (KR 2014), Vienna, July 2014 (to appear)
14. Dalal, M.: Investigations into a theory of knowledge base revision: Preliminary report. In: Proceedings of the Seventh National Conference on Artificial Intelligence (AAAI 1988), pp. 475–479 (1988)
15. Doutre, S., Herzig, A., Perrussel, L.: A dynamic logic framework for abstract argumentation. In: Proceedings of the 14th International Conference on Principles of Knowledge Representation and Reasoning (KR 2014), pp. 62–71 (2014)

16. Doutre, S., Perrussel, L.: On Enforcing a Constraint in Argumentation. In: 11th European Workshop on Multi-Agent Systems, EUMAS 2013, Toulouse (2013)
17. Dung, P.M.: On the acceptability of arguments and its fundamental role in non-monotonic reasoning, logic programming, and n-person games. Artificial Intelligence 77(2), 321–357 (1995)
18. Gabbay, D., Rodrigues, O., Russo, A.: Revision by translation. In: Proceedings of the Seventh International Conference on Information Processing and Management of Uncertainty in Knowledge-Based Systems (IPMU 1998). Information, Uncertainty and Fusion, pp. 3–32 (1998)
19. Grove, A.: Two modellings for theory change. Journal of Philosophical Logic 17, 157–170 (1988)
20. Hamming, R.W.: Error detecting and error correcting codes. Bell System Technical Journal 29(2), 147–160 (1950)
21. Katsuno, H., Mendelzon, A.O.: Propositional knowledge base revision and minimal change. Artificial Intelligence 52, 263–294 (1991)
22. Nieves, J., Osorio, M., Corts, U.: Inferring preferred extensions by minimal models. In: Workshop on Argumentation and Non Monotonic Reasoning, Workshop at Logic Programming and Non-Monotonic Reasonning 2007 (LPNMR 2007), pp. 114–124 (2007)
23. Nofal, S., Atkinson, K., Dunne, P.: Algorithms for decision problems in argument systems under preferred semantics. Artificial Intelligence 207, 23–51 (2014)

Preserving Strong Equivalence while Forgetting

Matthias Knorr and José Julio Alferes

CENTRIA & Departamento de Informática, Faculdade Ciências e Tecnologia,
Universidade Nova de Lisboa, 2829-516 Caparica, Portugal

Abstract. A variety of proposals for forgetting in logic programs under different semantics have emerged that satisfy differing sets of properties considered desirable. Despite the achieved progress in devising approaches that capture an increasing number of these properties, the idea that the result of forgetting should preserve the meaning of the initial program for the remaining, non-forgotten, atoms, has not yet been captured. In particular, the existing proposals may not preserve dependency relations between such atoms that are given by the structure of the program. In logic programs, these relations are captured by strong equivalence, but, preserving strong equivalence of two different programs while forgetting does not suffice. Rather, strong equivalence relativized to the remaining atoms should be preserved between the original program and the one that results from forgetting. In this paper, we overcome this deficiency by formalizing the property that captures this maintenance of relations while forgetting, and at the same time a general semantic definition for such a forgetting for arbitrary logic programs. Then, we study forgetting for normal programs under the well-founded semantics, and for programs with double negation under the answer set semantics. In both cases, we focus on efficient syntax-based algorithms that only manipulate the rules in which changes are effectively necessary.

1   Introduction

Removing or hiding information that is no longer needed in a knowledge base, also known as *forgetting* or *variable elimination* [12], is important in Knowledge Representation and Reasoning (KRR). This is witnessed by the recent amount of work developed for different logical formalisms [20,9,16,13,21,2] and for Logic Programming (LP) in particular [6,15,14,1], and has been applied, e.g., in cognitive robotics, ontologies, and resolving conflicts.

For LP, these approaches are commonly introduced together with a number of desirable properties that justify design rationales and allow comparisons between different approaches. Yet, the property that the result of forgetting should preserve all the semantic dependencies contained in the original program, for all but the atom(s) to be forgotten, has not been considered.

Example 1. Consider a part of a taxonomy including professors, university staff, and persons with properties assigned to them, represented in rules:[1]

$$person(X) \leftarrow ustaff(X) \qquad ustaff(X) \leftarrow professor(X)$$

---

[1] As usual, rules with variables stand for the set of ground rules obtained by replacing the variables by constants in all possible ways.

E. Fermé and J. Leite (Eds.): JELIA 2014, LNAI 8761, pp. 412–425, 2014.
© Springer International Publishing Switzerland 2014

Consider that $professor(mary)$ is part of the program. Then, clearly, $person(mary)$ is derivable. Now suppose that we want to forget about the class university staff, e.g., because there are no longer specific properties attached to it. In this case, it should still be derivable that every professor is also a person, i.e., in the result of forgetting (all ground instances of) $ustaff(X)$ from this program, $person(mary)$ should still be derivable. This is indeed the case for most existing approaches of forgetting.

Now consider that university staff that are not professors must use the punch clock, and staff that do not have to use the punch clock have flexible schedules:

$$flexible(X) \leftarrow ustaff(X), not\, punchClock(X)$$
$$punchClock(X) \leftarrow ustaff(X), not\, professor(X)$$

Suppose that $professor(mary)$, $ustaff(peter)$ and $person(john)$ is the only information about these three individuals contained in the program. Then, we expect to derive that $flexible(mary)$ and $punchClock(peter)$ hold. Now suppose that we want to forget about $punchClock(X)$ from the program, then the derivation that professors have flexible schedules should not be lost. If we learn later that $john$ is a professor, then we would expect to be able to derive that he also has a flexible schedule, while $peter$ still does not. However, none of the existing proposals for forgetting in logic programs satisfies the desired behavior (see related work in Section 6).

Strong equivalence [10] has been introduced in LP to semantically capture the dependency relations between atoms expressed in logic programs, and has been used, e.g., in program optimization. Two programs P and Q are strongly equivalent if, for all programs R, $P \cup R$ and $Q \cup R$ are equivalent, i.e., they have the same models. However, preserving strong equivalence between programs to which the same forgetting is applied is not sufficient as it does not say much about how similar the output is to the original program [6,1]. Neither would considering strong equivalence between a program and its result of forgetting work, simply because, in general, this does not hold for all programs R: consider P with two rules $a \leftarrow not\, b$ and $b \leftarrow not\, c$, then adding just $c \leftarrow$ to P allows us to derive a, but adding $c \leftarrow$ and $b \leftarrow$ does not, and there is no program Q over a and c (and without b) that allows us to obtain the same result.

Instead, strong equivalence restricted to programs R over the remaining, non-forgotten, atoms should be preserved between the original program and the one that results from forgetting. Relativized strong equivalence (RSE) [5,17] was introduced to relax strong equivalence when certain internal atoms are no longer allowed to be part of R and thus captures our idea, yet no related notion of forgetting exists.

Most approaches for forgetting in LP also provide methods on how to obtain the result of forgetting, and often these methods rely on computing models and then determining a representation of the result of forgetting. Thus, the complexity of computing such a result usually corresponds to that of computing models in the considered class of logic programs, but additionally, the resulting program may be exponential in the size of the original program (see [14], and the syntactic transformation in [6]). We argue that computing the result of forgetting should in general not need to change any rules other than those containing the atoms to be forgotten. Therefore, we focus on syntax-based algorithms that manipulate precisely these rules without the need to compute any models. As argued in [6], such kind of algorithms are also of benefit for applications.

In this paper, we introduce a new property that formalizes the idea of preserving relativized strong equivalence while forgetting in LP and a new general definition of forgetting for logic programs that, besides our new property, also satisfies a number of other desired properties. We then study concrete cases of this new notion under the two most-widely used semantics for LP. Namely, we consider forgetting from normal logic programs under the well-founded semantics [7], and forgetting from programs with double negation under the answer set semantics [8]. It turns out, that such forgetting is not always possible in the latter case, so we subsequently study adequate restrictions under which our approach can still be applied. The construction of the resulting program, in both cases, is then achieved by applying syntactic transformations which do not require the computation of models. We can show that computing the resulting program is exponential in the number of rules that contain atoms to be forgotten and linear in the remaining. We argue that on average this is at least competitive when compared to computing models in P or NP (over the entire program), and certainly better than an algorithm that, in addition to computing models, creates a program exponential in the size of the entire given program.

2   Logic Programs

We start by recalling notions and notation of LPs. More precisely, we consider logic programs with double negation, a subset of extended logic programs [11].

A *logic program* P, is a finite set of rules r of the form

$$a \leftarrow b_1, ..., b_l, not\, c_1, ..., not\, c_m, not\, not\, d_1, ..., not\, not\, d_n$$

where a and all b_h, c_i, and d_j, for $1 \leq h \leq l$, $1 \leq i \leq m$, and $1 \leq j \leq n$, are propositional atoms over a signature Σ. Alternatively, a may be the special logical constant $\perp$ representing an empty head. Given such a rule r, we distinguish the *head* of r as $H(r) = a$, and the *body* of r, $B(r) = B^+(r) \cup not\, B^-(r) \cup not\, not\, B^{--}(r)$, where $B^+(r) = \{b_1, ..., b_l\}$, $B^-(r) = \{c_1, ..., c_m\}$, $B^{--}(r) = \{d_1, ..., d_n\}$, and, for a set A of atoms, $not\, A = \{not\, q: q \in A\}$ and $not\, not\, A = \{not\, not\, q: q \in A\}$.

Logic programs of this general form include a number of special kinds of rules: if $m = n = 0$, then we call r *positive*; if $l = m = n = 0$, then r is a *fact*; if $a = \perp$, then r is a *constraint*; and if $a \neq \perp$ and $n = 0$, we say r is *normal*. The classes of *positive* and *normal programs* are defined as a finite set of positive and normal rules, respectively.

We now recall the *answer set semantics* [8] by first defining the least model of positive programs and then relying on a generalization of the reduct to nested programs, a very general class of programs which admits double negation in the body [11].

Given a logic program P, B_P is the set of all atoms appearing in P. An *interpretation* for P is a set of atoms $I \in B_P$, and is meant to represent all the atoms considered true. A positive rule is *satisfied* in interpretation I if $B^+(r) \subseteq I$ implies $a \in I$. An interpretation I is a *model* of a positive program P if I satisfies all rules $r \in P$, and I is the *least model* of P if there is no model I' of P such that $I' \subset I$. The *reduct* of P w.r.t. an interpretation I is defined as $P^I = \{H(r) \leftarrow B^+(r) : r \in P, B^-(r) \cap I = \emptyset, B^{--}(r) \subseteq I\}$. Then, an interpretation I is an *answer set* of P iff I is the least model of P^I. A program is called *consistent* if it has (at least) one answer set, and the set of all answer sets of P is denoted by $M_{as}(P)$. Determining whether a (propositional) program has an answer set is NP-complete [4].[2]

We also consider the *well-founded semantics* [7] for normal programs. A *3-valued interpretation* I of a program P is defined as $I = I^+ \cup not\, I^-$ with $I^+ \cup I^- \subseteq B_P$ and $I^+ \cap I^- = \emptyset$; I^+ and I^- contain the atoms that are true and false in I, respectively; an atom p appearing neither in I^+ nor in I^- is undefined, and so is $not\, p$. The computation of the well-founded model requires a consequence operator T_P for three-valued interpretations that derives true information. For a normal program P and a three-valued interpretation I for P, we define $T_P(I) = \{H(r) : r \in P, B(r) \subseteq I\}$. The notion of unfounded set complements that by deriving false information. For a normal program P and a three-valued interpretation I for P, we say that $U \subseteq B_P$ is an *unfounded set* (of P) w.r.t. I if each atom $a \in U$ satisfies the following condition: for each rule $r \in P$ with $H(r) = a$ at least one of the following holds: (Ui) $not\, b_h \in I$ for some $b_h \in B^+(r)$, or $c_i \in I$ for some $c_i \in B^-(r)$; (Uii) $b_h \in U$ for some $b_h \in B^+(r)$. The *greatest unfounded set* $U_P(I)$ (of P) w.r.t. I always exists and leads to the definition of operator $W_P(I)$, by setting $W_P(I) = T_P(I) \cup not\, U_P(I)$. This operator W_P is monotonic, can be iterated by $W_P \uparrow 0 = \emptyset$, $W_P \uparrow (n+1) = W_P(W_P \uparrow n)$ for all n, and its least fixed point, which exactly corresponds to the *well-founded model* $M_{wf}(P)$, is obtained for some finite n for propositional normal programs as considered here. Determining $M_{wf}(P)$ of a (propositional) normal program is P-complete [4].

Finally, given a set of atoms V with $V \subseteq \Sigma$, two programs P_1 and P_2 are *strongly equivalent relative to V* under semantics S, denoted $P_1 \equiv_S^V P_2$, iff $M_S(P_1 \cup R) = M_S(P_2 \cup R)$ for all programs R over signature V. This notion is generalized from answer sets [17,5] to arbitrary semantics S and captures as special cases that P_1 and P_2 are *equivalent* and *strongly equivalent*, denoted $P_1 \equiv_S P_2$ and $P_1 \equiv_S^s P_2$, by considering $V = \emptyset$ and $V = \Sigma$, respectively.

3   Forgetting with Strong Persistence

In previous work [6,18,15,14,1], a number of desirable properties for forgetting in logic programs has been investigated under both answer set and well-founded semantics. Before we introduce our new property, we generalize several properties presented in [14] to arbitrary classes of logic programs and arbitrary semantics.

For that purpose, we define that, given interpretation I under semantics S and a set of atoms V, $I_{\|V}$ represents the part of I without elements from V. E.g., for the answer set semantics, $I_{\|V}$ represents $I \setminus V$ and for the well-founded semantics $I \setminus (V \cup not\, V)$. For sets of interpretations $\mathcal{I}$, we also define $\mathcal{I}_{\|V} = \{I_{\|V} : I \in \mathcal{I}\}$.

Now, let $\mathcal{C}$ be a class of logic programs over a signature Σ, P and P' programs in $\mathcal{C}$, S a semantics for $\mathcal{C}$, $V \subseteq B_P$, and $f(P, V)$ abstractly denote a program resulting from forgetting about V from P. Note that, in general $f(P, V)$ does not determine a syntactically unique program but rather one representative of a class of (strongly) equivalent programs (depending on the considered notion of forgetting, e.g., in most notions, a result $\{q \leftarrow\}$ would also represent $\{q \leftarrow; q \leftarrow q\}$). Some properties about $f(P, V)$ are:

---

[2] More precisely, this result coincides with the one first established for normal programs in [4].

(E) Existence w.r.t. $\mathcal{C}$: if P is in $\mathcal{C}$, then $f(P,V)$ is expressible in $\mathcal{C}$.
(IR) Irrelevance: $f(P,V) \equiv^s_S P'$ for some P' that does not contain any $v \in V$
(SE) Strong Equivalence: If $P \equiv^s_S P'$, then $f(P,V) \equiv^s_S f(P',V)$.
(CP) Consequence Persistence: $M_S(f(P,V)) = M_S(P)_{\|V}$.

There are three further properties presented in [14], but it is shown that two of them conflict with the others in the case of answer set semantics. Moreover, all three require an additional entailment relation over logic programs, defined over HT logic for answer set semantics in [14], which is non-standard since entailment in LP is usually considered only for (sets of) atoms. Since the choice of this entailment relation for each semantics affects whether these properties hold or not, we leave such a study for future work.

As motivated in the introduction, none of the existing definitions of forgetting ensures that the result of forgetting really semantically resembles the original program if we ignore the atom(s) to be forgotten. This is why we introduce a new property that can be considered a generalization of (CP), i.e., consequence persistence but under (relativized) strong equivalence, hence the name *strong persistence*.

(SP) Strong Persistence: $M_S(f(P,V) \cup R) = M_S(P \cup R)_{\|V}$ for all programs R over
    signature $\Sigma \setminus V$.

The definition of (SP) strongly resembles that of relativized strong equivalence. The only essential technical difference is that we have to omit the elements in V from the models of $P \cup R$. This also clarifies that, even though both notions are strongly related, they are not identical nor is one a special case of the other.

Given that none of the existing approaches on forgetting for logic programs satisfy (SP), we introduce a new general definition of forgetting in LP.

Definition 1. *Let $\mathcal{C}$ be a class of logic programs, and S a semantics for $\mathcal{C}$. A result of strong S-forgetting about $V \in B_P$ from $P \in \mathcal{C}$, denoted $F_S(P,V)$, is a program s.t.*

(1) all $v \in V$ do not appear in $F_S(P,V)$, and
(2) $M_S(F_S(P,V) \cup R) = M_S(P \cup R)_{\|V}$ for all programs R over signature $\Sigma \setminus V$.

Due to its generality, this notion of forgetting naturally satisfies (SP) for any class of programs and any semantics, but also several other of the previously introduced properties, namely (IR), (SE), and (CP).

Proposition 1. *Let $\mathcal{C}$ be a class of logic programs, and S a semantics for $\mathcal{C}$. Then strong S-forgetting satisfies (IR), (SE), (CP), and (SP).*

Whether our definition of forgetting also satisfies (E) depends on the concrete class of programs and semantics and, in the following sections, we answer this question for the well-founded semantics of normal programs, and the answer set semantics of programs with double negation.

4   Strong WF-Forgetting for Normal Programs

We first consider *strong wf-forgetting*, in which the considered class of logic programs is normal programs and the semantics the well-founded semantics. We start by providing an algorithm (Alg. 1) that computes a result that satisfies Def. 1 for the simpler case of forgetting a single atom p from a normal program P, denoted $F_{wf}(P, p)$. Here and in the following, we abuse notation, and represent the singleton set $\{p\}$ simply by p.

Before we discuss Alg. 1, we need to introduce one additional notion, namely that of a wf-dual w.r.t. a program P and an atom p, that is useful when substituting $not\, p$ in rules in P while forgetting about p from P. For that, given a literal l, the *complementary literal*, $\bar{l}$, is defined as $\bar{p} = not\, p$ and $\overline{not\, p} = p$.

Definition 2. *Let P be a normal program, $p \in B_P$, and R all the n rules in P of the form $p \leftarrow l_{j1}, \ldots, l_{jm_j}$ where $n \geq 1, 1 \leq j \leq n, m_j \geq 1$ for all j. The* wf-dual *w.r.t. P and p, denoted $\mathcal{D}_{wf}(P, p)$, is the set of all possible sets $\{\bar{l}_{1k_1}, \ldots, \bar{l}_{nk_n}\}$ with $1 \leq k_1 \leq m_1, \ldots, 1 \leq k_n \leq m_n$.*

The wf-dual w.r.t. P and p can be understood as a set of conjunctions that, building on the rules in P with head p and non-empty body, can be used to replace $not\, p$, but preserve its truth value. Consider P containing two rules $p \leftarrow s$ and $p \leftarrow not\, q, not\, r$. Then $\mathcal{D}_{wf}(P, p) = \{\{not\, s, q\}, \{not\, s, r\}\}$ and, e.g., $not\, p$ is true if one of the two conjuncts is true, false if both conjuncts are false, and undefined otherwise. This is what we apply in Alg. 1 whose details we explain next.

First, P' is initialized with P from which all rules whose head appears in the (positive) body are removed right away (line 1). This is known as elimination of tautologies TAUT [3]. Then, new rules are introduced by substituting occurrences of p in the bodies (of rules r) with the bodies of rules r_1 whose head is p, in a way similar to wGPPE [3] (lines 3-12). This includes a special case if $not\, p$ appears in the body of r_1 (lines 5-7). I.e., with such a rule alone, p would be undefined, which is why $not\, p$ is replaced with the negation of the rule head of r. Subsequently, all rules with p in the body can be removed (line 13). Next, new rules are introduced in which all $not\, p$ in rule bodies (apart from those with rule head p – line 14 – since those will be eliminated at the end) are substituted by the wf-duals (lines 14-28), unless one of the two special cases applies. Namely, either there is no rule with head p in which case $not\, p$ can simply be omitted in such a rule body (lines 15-16) or there is a fact for p, in which case none of the rules with $not\, p$ is considered any further for substitution (line 17). The application of the wf-duals again includes a special case to handle potential undefinedness due to the presence of $H(r)$ or p in the wf-dual (lines 20-22). Finally, rules containing p (in the head) or $not\, p$ in the body can be removed (line 29).

Example 2. Consider the following normal program P to illustrate Alg. 1:

$$r_1 : r \leftarrow p \qquad r_2 : q \leftarrow not\, p \qquad r_3 : p \leftarrow not\, p, t \qquad r_4 : p \leftarrow not\, s$$

The program $F_{wf}(P, p)$ returned by Alg. 1 is

$$r'_1 : r \leftarrow not\, r, t \qquad r'_2 : r \leftarrow not\, s \qquad r'_3 : q \leftarrow not\, q, s \qquad r'_4 : q \leftarrow not\, t, s$$

where r'_1 and r'_2 are obtained from r_1 in combination with r_3 (by lines 5-7) and r_4 (by lines 8-10), respectively, while r'_3 and r'_4 are obtained from r_2, the duals over r_3 and r_4, and lines 20-22 and 22-25 respectively. It can be verified that $M_{wf}(P') = M_{wf}(P)\|_{\{p\}} = \{r, not\, q, not\, s, not\, t\}$, i.e., (2) of Def. 1 holds for $R = \emptyset$. In fact,

input : Normal program P and $p \in B_P$
output: Normal program $P' = F_{wf}(P, p)$

```
1  P' := P \ {r ∈ P : H(r) ∩ B⁺(r) ≠ ∅};
2  R₁ := {r ∈ P' : H(r) = p};
3  for r ∈ P' s.t. p ∈ B(r) do
4  |   for r₁ ∈ R₁ do
5  |   |   if not p ∈ B(r₁) then
6  |   |   |   P' := P' ∪ {H(r) ← (B(r) \ {p}) ∪ ({not H(r)} ∪ (B(r₁) \ {not p}))};
7  |   |   end
8  |   |   else
9  |   |   |   P' := P' ∪ {H(r) ← (B(r) \ {p}) ∪ B(r₁)};
10 |   |   end
11 |   end
12 end
13 P' := P' \ {r ∈ P' : p ∈ B(r)};
14 R₂ := {r ∈ P' : not p ∈ B(r), H(r) ≠ p};
15 if R₁ = ∅ then
16 |   P' := P' ∪ {H(r) ← B(r)' : r ∈ R₂, B(r)' = B(r) \ {not p}};
17 else if {p ←} ⊄ R₁ then
18 |   for r ∈ R₂ do
19 |   |   for D ∈ 𝒟_{wf}(P, p) do
20 |   |   |   if (H(r) ∈ D) or (p ∈ D) then
21 |   |   |   |   P' := P' ∪ {H(r) ←
               (B(r) \ {not p}) ∪ ((D\{H(r), p}) ∪ {not H(r)})};
22 |   |   |   end
23 |   |   |   else
24 |   |   |   |   P' := P'∪{H(r) ← B(r)\{not p}∪D};
25 |   |   |   end
26 |   |   end
27 |   end
28 end
29 P' := P' \ (R₁ ∪ R₂);
```

Algorithm 1. Strong wf-forgetting for a single atom p

it holds for arbitrary programs R over $\Sigma \setminus \{p\}$, e.g., for $R = \{s \leftarrow r\}$, we have $M_{wf}(P' \cup R) = M_{wf}(P \cup R)_{\|\{p\}} = \{not\, t\}$.

Example 3. Consider only the rules and facts explicitly given in Ex. 1 as P. The result of $F_{wf}(P, V)$ with $V = \{punchClock(X) \mid X \in \{mary, peter, john\}\}$ contains precisely three instances of $flexible(X) \leftarrow ustaff(X), professor(X)$. Thus, $flexible(mary)$ is derivable right away, and if $professor(john)$ is added later, then $flexible(john)$ becomes derivable as well.

We can show that Alg. 1 always returns a result P' that corresponds to $F_{wf}(P, p)$.

Theorem 1. *Given a normal program P and $p \in B_P$, Alg. 1 computes $F_{wf}(P, p)$.*

Alg. 1 can be generalized to arbitrary sets $V \in B_P$ using the following property applicable to strong S-forgetting for arbitrary classes C of programs and semantics S for C.

Theorem 2. *Let C be a class of logic programs, S a semantics for C, $P \in C$, and $V_1, V_2 \subseteq B_P$. Then, for all $P' \in C$, P' is $F_S(P, V_1 \cup V_2)$ iff P' is $F_S(F_S(P, V_1), V_2)$.*

Thus, Alg. 1 allows us to compute strong wf-forgetting about one atom, and Thm. 2 ensures that we can forget a set of atoms by simply forgetting each atom one after the other in any chosen order. This also guarantees that **(E)** holds for strong wf-forgetting.

Proposition 2. *Strong wf-forgetting for normal programs satisfies* **(E)**.

The computational complexity of Alg. 1 is as follows.

Theorem 3. *Given a normal program P and $p \in B_P$, computing $F_{wf}(P, p)$ is in EX-PTIME in the number of rules containing occurrences of p and linear in the remaining rules.*

We would like to point out that this worst-case exponential is indeed limited to the wf-duals w.r.t. P and p, i.e., to the number of rules n_1 whose head is p and the number of body literals in these rules. In fact, any of the transformations in Alg. 1 (apart from the linear one in line 1) only affects rules in which p occurs. Since it is reasonable to assume that, in large programs, the atom to be forgotten does on average appear only in a small fraction of the rules, we argue that this considerably relativizes the high worst-case complexity, in the sense that an exponential on a small fraction of the input may be preferable to a polynomial over all rules as in [1].

5   Strong AS-Forgetting for Programs with Double Negation

We now present *strong as-forgetting* under the answer set semantics. Similar to [15,14], strong as-forgetting for normal programs does not satisfy **(E)**. Consider $p \leftarrow not\ q$ and $q \leftarrow not\ p$ whose answer sets are $\{p\}$ and $\{q\}$. The result of strong as-forgetting about q should have two answer sets $\{\}$ and $\{p\}$, and there is no normal program where an answer set is a subset of another. That is why we consider logic programs with double negation where one single rule $p \leftarrow not\ not\ p$ suffices as such result of forgetting.[3]

Unfortunately, due to such rules, strong as-forgetting under the answer set semantics for programs with double negation is not always possible.

Example 4. Consider the following program P from which we want to forget about p:

$$p \leftarrow not\ not\ p \qquad\qquad q \leftarrow p \qquad\qquad r \leftarrow not\ p$$

Strong as-forgetting requires to find a program over $\{q, r\}$ that satisfies condition (2) of Def. 1. Note first that P itself has two answer sets $\{p, q\}$ and $\{r\}$ and that adding either q or r as facts to P simply adds the atom to both answer sets, i.e., $P \cup \{q\}$ has two

---

[3] Applicability of ASP solvers to such programs is ensured by (linear) transformations cf. [6].

input : Program P with double negation
output: Program $P' = NF(P)$ in normal form

1   $P' := P \setminus \{r \in P : H(r) \cap B^+(r) \neq \emptyset\};$
2   $P' := P' \setminus \{r \in P : B^+(r) \cap B^-(r) \neq \emptyset\};$
3   $P' := P' \setminus \{r \in P : B^-(r) \cap B^{--}(r) \neq \emptyset\});$
4   $R' := \{r \in P' : B^+(r) \cap B^{--}(r) \neq \emptyset\};$
5   $P' := (P' \setminus R') \cup \{H(r) \leftarrow B(r)' : r \in R', B(r)' = B(r) \setminus \{not\,not\,q : q \in$
    $(B^+(r) \cap B^{--}(r))\}\};$
6   $R'' := \{r \in P' : H(r) \cap B^-(r) \neq \emptyset\};$
7   $P' := (P' \setminus R'') \cup \{\bot \leftarrow B(r) : r \in R''\};$
8   $R''' := \{r \in P' : H(r) = B^{--}(r), B^+(r) \cup B^-(r) = \emptyset\};$
9   **for** $r \in R'''$ **do**
10   **if** $\bot \leftarrow H(r)$ *or* $\bot \leftarrow not\,not\,H(r)$ **then**
11 | $P' := P' \setminus r;$
12   **end**
13   **if** $\bot \leftarrow not\,H(r)$ **then**
14 | $P' := (P' \setminus (r \cup \{\bot \leftarrow not\,H(r)\})) \cup \{H(r) \leftarrow\};$
15   **end**
16 **end**

Algorithm 2. Computing a normal form of P

answer sets $\{p, q\}$ and $\{q, r\}$ and $P \cup \{r\}$ has two answer sets $\{p, q, r\}$ and $\{r\}$. We thus require that $P' = F_{as}(P, p)$ has two answer sets $\{q\}$ and $\{r\}$, and that $P' \cup \{q\}$ and $P' \cup \{r\}$ also both have two answer sets, namely $\{q\}$ and $\{q, r\}$, and $\{r\}$ and $\{q, r\}$ respectively. Such a program P' does not exist over $\{q, r\}$ since (a) it is required to be symmetric in q and r, (b) we have to ensure that precisely only one of q and r is true in each answer set of P', but (c) adding either of the two explicitly, must not avoid the existence of an answer set that contains the other and in which both atoms are true.

In the following, we investigate conditions under which strong as-forgetting can still be applied focusing again on syntactic transformations (as in the previous section), in the sense that computing the result of forgetting about $V \in B_P$ in P only uses the rules r with $H(r) \in V$ to replace (possibly negated) occurrences of V in the bodies of rules.

    We start by introducing a normal form that simplifies the presentation and the cases to consider in such an algorithm, and, as a byproduct, reduces the size of the program. Formally, a logic program P with double negation is in *normal form* if: for every $p \in B_P$ and each rule $r \in P$, at most one of p, $not\,p$, and $not\,not\,p$ occurs in $B(r)$; if $H(r) = p$, then neither p nor $not\,p$ occur in $B(r)$; and if $r = p \leftarrow not\,not\,p$, then no constraint containing only p, $not\,p$, or $not\,not\,p$ in its body occurs in P. This normal form $NF(P)$ can be computed using Alg. 2 in linear time. It first applies some general program transformations including TAUT and CONTRA [3] (lines 1-7), and then handles the case that simplifies $p \leftarrow not\,not\,p$ in combination with constraints (lines 8-16). The algorithm is correct, and $NF(P)$ is strongly equivalent to the original program:

Proposition 3. *Let P be a logic program with double negation. Alg. 2 computes $NF(P)$, and P and $NF(P)$ are strongly equivalent.*

With such a normal form in place, we proceed to introduce a notion that indicates whether a certain atom p can be forgotten syntactically from a given program P.

Definition 3. *Let P be a logic program with double negation in normal form and $p \in B_P$. We call P p-forgettable if a) there is no $r \in P$ with $H(r) \cap B^{--}(r) \neq \emptyset$ or b) $p \leftarrow in P$, or c) there is no rule r with $H(r) \neq p$ and $p \in B^+(r) \cup B^-(r) \cup B^{--}(r)$.*

Case a) describes the kind of rule which in general conflicts with the existence of the result of strong as-forgetting (cf. also Ex. 4), while the cases b) and c) indicate exceptions under which rules described in a) are not problematic. Note that any normal logic program P is p-forgettable for any $p \in B_P$, and that rules matching case a) are allowed for all other atoms except the one to be forgotten.

Checking whether a program is p-forgettable is easy. So given a p-forgettable program P in normal form, we now introduce Alg. 3 for forgetting about a single atom p from P, denoted $F_{as}(P, p)$.

For that purpose, we introduce some further notation. First, we introduce a function N that applies a number of negation symbols to elements of a rule body by defining, for all $p \in B_P$ and for $x \in \{p, not\, p, not\, not\, p\}$, $N^0(x) = x$, $N^1(p) = not\, p$, $N^1(not\, p) = not\, not\, p$, and $N^1(not\, not\, p) = not\, p$, $N^2(p) = N^2(not\, not\, p) = not\, not\, p$ and $N^2(not\, p) = not\, p$, and $N^3 = N^1$. Also, for a rule body S, $N^i(S) = \{N^i(s) : s \in S\}$. We also adapt the notion of dual to strong as-forgetting.

Definition 4. *Let P be a logic program, $p \in B_P$, and R all $n \geq 1$ rules in P of the form $p \leftarrow l_{j1}, \ldots, l_{jm_j}$ where $1 \leq j \leq n$, $m_j \geq 1$ for all j. The as-dual w.r.t. P and p, denoted $\mathcal{D}_{as}(P, p)$, is the set of all possible sets $\{N^1(l_{1k_1}), \ldots, N^1(l_{nk_n})\}$, $1 \leq k_1 \leq m_1, \ldots, 1 \leq k_n \leq m_n$.*

Unlike the wf-dual, the as-dual contains only negated and double negated atoms.

We can now describe Alg. 3. First, P' and four disjoint sets of rules are initialized, in each of which p appears in the rules in a different form (lines 1-5). Then, the special case of existing a fact p is treated directly by introducing rules in which occurrences of p and $not\, not\, p$ in all rules in R_0 and R_2 (whose head is not p) are omitted (lines 6-9). Alternatively, if there is no fact p, then new rules are introduced by substituting all such occurrences of p and $not\, not\, p$ in a way similar to wGPPE [3] (lines 11-15), i.e., p and $not\, not\, p$ are adequately replaced by the rule bodies in R. Next, the replacement of $not\, p$ is treated, by simply canceling these if there is no rule with head p (lines 16-17) and using the as-dual otherwise (lines 18-24). Note that, unlike the previous section, no special case is necessary for handling potential occurrences of p of any form because P is p-forgettable and in normal form. Finally, all rules containing occurrences of p, $not\, p$, and $not\, not\, p$ are removed (line 26). Note that the steps introducing substitutions for p, $not\, p$, and $not\, not\, p$ in the bodies also handle constraints. Thus, it may happen that the result contains a rule $\bot \leftarrow$ which makes the resulting program permanently inconsistent and cannot be removed. This has similarly been observed in [14].

Example 5. Consider the following program P to illustrate Algs. 2 and 3.

$r_1 : q \leftarrow not\, p$ $r_3 : p \leftarrow r, not\, not\, r$ $r_5 : p \leftarrow not\, not\, p, not\, r, not\, not\, r$

$r_2 : p \leftarrow not\, t$ $r_4 : s \leftarrow not\, not\, p$

input : p-forgettable P in normal form and $p \in B_P$
output: Program $P' = F_{as}(P,p)$

1 $R := \{r \in P : H(r) = p\}$;
2 $R_0 := \{r \in P : p \in B(r)\}$;
3 $R_1 := \{r \in P : not\, p \in B(r)\}$;
4 $R_2 := \{r \in P : not\, not\, p \in B(r), H(r) \neq p\}$;
5 $P' := P$;
6 **if** $\{p \leftarrow\} \subseteq R$ **then**
7   **for** $r \in R_i$ s.t. $i = 0$ or $i = 2$ **do**
8        $P' := P' \cup \{H(r) \leftarrow (B(r) \setminus \{N^i(p)\})\}$;
9   **end**
10 **else**
11   **for** $r \in R_i$ s.t. $i = 0$ or $i = 2$ **do**
12   **for** $r_1 \in R$ **do**
13          $P' := P' \cup \{H(r) \leftarrow (B(r) \setminus \{N^i(p)\}) \cup N^i(B(r_1))\}$;
14   **end**
15   **end**
16   **if** $R = \emptyset$ **then**
17       $P' := P' \cup \{H(r) \leftarrow B(r)' : r \in R_1, B(r)' = B(r) \setminus \{not\, p\}\}$;
18   **else**
19   **for** $r \in R_1$ **do**
20   **for** $D_1 \in \mathcal{D}_{as}(P,p)$ **do**
21             $P' := P' \cup \{H(r) \leftarrow B(r) \setminus \{not\, p\} \cup D_1\}$;
22   **end**
23   **end**
24   **end**
25 **end**
26 $P' := P' \setminus (R \cup R_0 \cup R_1 \cup R_2)$;

Algorithm 3. Strong as-forgetting for a single atom p

Since P is clearly not in the normal form (r_3, r_5), we first apply Alg. 2 and obtain P'.

$$r_1 : q \leftarrow not\, p \qquad r_2 : p \leftarrow not\, t \qquad r'_3 : p \leftarrow r \qquad r_4 : s \leftarrow not\, not\, p$$

Rule r_3 is simplified to r'_3 according to lines 4-5 (of Alg. 2), and rule r_5 can simply be omitted due to line 3 (Alg. 2). Note that the resulting program is not only in the normal form, but also p-forgettable. It can then be verified that Alg. 3 returns the following program P'' when forgetting about p from P' (and thus from P).

$$r''_1 : q \leftarrow not\, not\, t, not\, r \qquad r''_2 : s \leftarrow not\, t \qquad r''_3 : s \leftarrow not\, not\, r$$

The rule r''_1 can be obtained from r_1 and the as-dual over r_2 and r'_3 (lines 18-24), while the rules r''_2 and r''_3 result from r_4 in combination with r_2 and r'_3, respectively (lines 11-15). It can be verified that $M_{as}(P'' \cup R) = M_{as}(P \cup R)$ holds for all R over $\Sigma \setminus \{p\}$. For example, for $R = \emptyset$, we obtain $M_{as}(P'') = M_{as}(P) = \{\{s\}\}$, and if we consider $R_1 = \{t \leftarrow not\, not\, t\}$, then $M_{as}(P \cup R_1) = M_{as}(P'' \cup R_1) = \{\{q, t\}, \{s\}\}$.

Example 6. Consider only the rules and facts explicitly given in Ex. 1 as P. The result of $F_{as}(P, V)$ with $V = \{punchClock(X) \mid X \in \{mary, peter, john\}\}$ contains precisely three instances of $flexible(X) \leftarrow ustaff(X), not\, not\, professor(X)$. Thus, again, $flexible(mary)$ is derivable right away, and if $professor(john)$ is added later, then $flexible(john)$ becomes derivable as well.

As expected, Alg. 3 always returns a result corresponding to $F_{as}(P, p)$.

Theorem 4. *Given a p-forgettable program P in normal form and $p \in B_P$, Alg. 3 computes $F_{as}(P, p)$.*

For the generalization to forgetting sets of atoms V, we can simply rely on Thm. 2 provided, of course, that the program is in normal form, which can easily be ensured by applying Alg. 2 after each step of forgetting, and that it is p-forgettable for each $p \in V$. If the latter is indeed the case, then we simply forget a set of atoms by forgetting one atom after the other. Note that Thm. 2 also allows us to forget atoms in any order. So, if one $p \in V$ is not p-forgettable immediately, then we may delay it and forget another atom q first which is q-forgettable at that time, thereby potentially modifying the program such that it becomes p-forgettable after q has been forgotten, by, e.g., reducing some rule to a fact for p or canceling a rule with head p and $p \in B^{--}(r)$. In this sense, whenever strong as-forgetting is applicable, then it ensures that **(E)** holds.

Proposition 4. *Strong as-forgetting for programs with double negation satisfies **(E)**.*

Under the same assumption, we can determine the complexity of strong as-forgetting.

Theorem 5. *Given a program P and $p \in B_P$, computing $F_{as}(P, p)$ is in EXPTIME in the number of rules containing occurrences of p and linear in the remaining rules.*

This result for computing $F_{as}(P, p)$ is identical to that of computing $F_{wf}(P, p)$ as obtained in Thm. 3. Indeed, the exponential can be traced to the as-duals, and an argument such as the one following Thm. 3 can be applied.

6   Related Work and Conclusions

We have proposed a new property for forgetting propositional variables, called strong persistence **(SP)**, that guarantees that the semantic dependencies between the extant propositional variables are kept. Since none of the existing approaches for forgetting in LP obeys this **(SP)**, we have introduced a new abstract definition of forgetting, which is closely related to **(SP)** and naturally satisfies a number of other properties previously studied in the literature. We have also studied this new notion of forgetting for the cases of well-founded semantics for normal programs and answer set semantics for programs with double negation, and focused on efficient syntax-based algorithms that effectively only touch the rules in which atoms to be forgotten appear.

Considering the related work, the only other forgetting for the well-founded semantics is [1] which does neither satisfy **(SP)** nor **(SE)**. Indeed, consider the following P which is a simplification of Ex. 1 (with obvious abbreviations):

$$flx(m) \leftarrow not\, pC(m) \qquad pC(m) \leftarrow not\, prof(m) \qquad prof(m)$$
$$flx(j) \leftarrow not\, pC(j) \qquad pC(j) \leftarrow not\, prof(j)$$

Even after forgetting about $\{pC(m), pC(j)\}$, $flx(m)$ should hold, and if $prof(j)$ is later added, then $flx(j)$ should hold as well. All three algorithms in [1] return only an instance of a rule with head $flx(X)$, viz., $flx(m) \leftarrow$. So, adding $prof(j)$ cannot yield the desired result. An advantage of [1] is that the size of the program always shrinks while forgetting. Also, computing the result is in PTIME, but over the entire program.

Regarding answer set semantics, several proposals exist, and we consider the same program P from above for comparison. The work in [19], which is based on syntactic transformations, returns only $prof(m)$ for strong forgetting, and, additionally, the facts $flx(m)$ and $flx(j)$ for weak forgetting. So neither of them satisfies **(SP)** nor actually **(SE)** or **(CP)**. The proposal in [6] satisfies **(CP)**, but not **(SE)**, nor **(SP)**, since in the considered example, $flx(m)$ would persist as a fact, but no rule with $flx(j)$ would be part of the result of forgetting, thus loosing the semantic relation that intuitively says that professors have flexible schedules. In [15], a correspondence based on strong equivalence via HT models [10] is established between a program and its result of forgetting, so **(SE)** is satisfied, but not **(CP)**. Also, the result is not always expressible as a logic program. The recent work in [14] further remedies that, thus satisfying both **(CP)** and **(SE)**, but not **(SP)**. In fact, since $flx(m)$ is part of the only answer set of P, its derivation persists, but, again, no rule with head $flx(j)$ is contained in the result of this forgetting. Finally, the three previous approaches have a worst case complexity of at least coNP on the entire program. But, as indicated for the syntactic transformation of [6] and for [14], the resulting program is in general of exponential size over the entire given program, whereas our approach is exponential only over the rules containing the atom(s) to be forgotten, and linear over the remainder, and does not require any additional model computation.

In terms of future work, we want to investigate the remaining properties presented in [14], including appropriate entailment relations for each semantics. The latter are most likely related to HT logics, which may also give rise to study the semantical relations, e.g., to the proposal in [14], which is based on this logic. Another topic to consider is the extension to other classes of programs and different semantics, e.g., disjunction in rules under answer set semantics, though we conjecture that efficient syntactic methods as investigated here cannot be used effectively for this class of programs and there is no clear counterpart for the well-founded semantics. Finally, we intend to implement our approach to allow testing its efficiency. In that regard, the normal programs resulting from forgetting under the well-founded semantics can be readily used, e.g., in XSB Prolog, while in the case of programs with double negation under answer set semantics, the applicability of ASP solvers to the results can be ensured based on (linear) transformations following ideas on N-acyclicity [6].

Acknowledgments. Matthias Knorr and José J. Alferes were partially supported by Fundação para a Ciência e a Tecnologia under project "ERRO – Efficient Reasoning with Rules and Ontologies" (PTDC/EIA-CCO/121823/2010) and Matthias Knorr also by FCT grant SFRH/BPD/86970/2012.

References

1. Alferes, J.J., Knorr, M., Wang, K.: Forgetting under the well-founded semantics. In: Cabalar, P., Son, T.C. (eds.) LPNMR 2013. LNCS, vol. 8148, pp. 36–41. Springer, Heidelberg (2013)
2. Antoniou, G., Eiter, T., Wang, K.: Forgetting for defeasible logic. In: Bjørner, N., Voronkov, A. (eds.) LPAR-18 2012. LNCS, vol. 7180, pp. 77–91. Springer, Heidelberg (2012)
3. Brass, S., Dix, J.: Semantics of (disjunctive) logic programs based on partial evaluation. J. Log. Program. 40(1), 1–46 (1999)
4. Dantsin, E., Eiter, T., Gottlob, G., Voronkov, A.: Complexity and expressive power of logic programming. ACM Comput. Surv. 33(3), 374–425 (2001)
5. Eiter, T., Fink, M., Woltran, S.: Semantical characterizations and complexity of equivalences in answer set programming. ACM Trans. Comput. Log. 8(3) (2007)
6. Eiter, T., Wang, K.: Semantic forgetting in answer set programming. Artif. Intell. 172(14), 1644–1672 (2008)
7. Gelder, A.V., Ross, K.A., Schlipf, J.S.: The well-founded semantics for general logic programs. J. ACM 38(3), 620–650 (1991)
8. Gelfond, M., Lifschitz, V.: Classical negation in logic programs and disjunctive databases. New Generation Comput. 9(3-4), 365–385 (1991)
9. Kontchakov, R., Wolter, F., Zakharyaschev, M.: Logic-based ontology comparison and module extraction, with an application to DL-Lite. Artif. Intell. 174(15), 1093–1141 (2010)
10. Lifschitz, V., Pearce, D., Valverde, A.: Strongly equivalent logic programs. ACM Trans. Comput. Log. 2(4), 526–541 (2001)
11. Lifschitz, V., Tang, L.R., Turner, H.: Nested expressions in logic programs. Ann. Math. Artif. Intell. 25(3-4), 369–389 (1999)
12. Lin, F., Reiter, R.: Forget it! In: Proceedings of the AAAI Fall Symposium on Relevance, pp. 154–159 (1994)
13. Lutz, C., Wolter, F.: Foundations for uniform interpolation and forgetting in expressive description logics. In: Walsh, T. (ed.) IJCAI 2011, Proceedings of the 22nd International Joint Conference on Artificial Intelligence, Barcelona, Catalonia, Spain, July 16-22, pp. 989–995. IJCAI/AAAI (2011)
14. Wang, Y., Wang, K., Zhang, M.: Forgetting for answer set programs revisited. In: Rossi, F. (ed.) IJCAI 2013, Proceedings of the 23rd International Joint Conference on Artificial Intelligence, Beijing, China, August 3-9, IJCAI/AAAI (2013)
15. Wang, Y., Zhang, Y., Zhou, Y., Zhang, M.: Forgetting in logic programs under strong equivalence. In: Brewka, G., Eiter, T., McIlraith, S.A. (eds.) Principles of Knowledge Representation and Reasoning: Proceedings of the Thirteenth International Conference, KR 2012, pp. 643–647. AAAI Press (2012)
16. Wang, Z., Wang, K., Topor, R.W., Pan, J.Z.: Forgetting for knowledge bases in DL-Lite. Ann. Math. Artif. Intell. 58(1-2), 117–151 (2010)
17. Woltran, S.: Characterizations for relativized notions of equivalence in answer set programming. In: Alferes, J.J., Leite, J. (eds.) JELIA 2004. LNCS (LNAI), vol. 3229, pp. 161–173. Springer, Heidelberg (2004)
18. Wong, K.S.: Forgetting in Logic Programs. Ph.D. thesis, The University of New South Wales (2009)
19. Zhang, Y., Foo, N.Y.: Solving logic program conflict through strong and weak forgettings. Artif. Intell. 170(8-9), 739–778 (2006)
20. Zhang, Y., Zhou, Y.: Knowledge forgetting: Properties and applications. Artif. Intell. 173(16-17), 1525–1537 (2009)
21. Zhou, Y., Zhang, Y.: Bounded forgetting. In: Burgard, W., Roth, D. (eds.) Proceedings of the Twenty-Fifth AAAI Conference on Artificial Intelligence, AAAI 2011, San Francisco, California, USA, August 7-11. AAAI Press (2011)

Computing Repairs for Inconsistent DL-programs over $\mathcal{EL}$ Ontologies

Thomas Eiter, Michael Fink, and Daria Stepanova

Institute of Information Systems
Vienna University of Technology
Favoritenstraße 9-11, A-1040 Vienna, Austria
{eiter,fink,dasha}@kr.tuwien.ac.at

Abstract. DL-programs couple nonmonotonic logic programs with DL-ontologies through queries in a loose way which may lead to inconsistency, i.e., lack of an answer set. Recently defined repair answer sets remedy this. In particular, for $DL\text{-}Lite_{\mathcal{A}}$ ontologies, the computation of deletion repair answer sets can effectively be reduced to constraint matching based on so-called support sets. Here we consider the problem for DL-programs over $\mathcal{EL}$ ontologies. This is more challenging than adopting a suitable notion of support sets and their computation. Compared to $DL\text{-}Lite_{\mathcal{A}}$, support sets may neither be small nor few, and completeness may need to be given up in favor of sound repair computation on incomplete support information. We provide such an algorithm and discuss partial support set computation, as well as a declarative implementation. Preliminary experiments show a very promising potential of the partial support set approach.

1 Introduction

Nonmonotonic Description Logic (DL-) programs [29] are a prominent proposal to combine rules and ontologies, following a loose coupling approach (see [21] for an overview of approaches). Due to a bidirectional information flow between rules and the ontology via special *DL-atoms*, they provide a powerful framework for expressing many advanced reasoning applications. However, the loose interaction between rules and the ontology can easily lead to inconsistency (lack of answer sets, i.e. models).

Example 1. Consider the DL-program $\Pi = \langle \mathcal{O}, \mathcal{P} \rangle$ in Figure 1 formalizing an access policy over an ontology $\mathcal{O} = \mathcal{T} \cup \mathcal{A}$ [4], whose taxonomy (TBox) $\mathcal{T}$ is given by (1)-(3), while (4)-(9) is a sample data part (ABox) $\mathcal{A}$. Besides facts (10), (11) and a simple rule (12), the rule part $\mathcal{P}$ contains defaults (13), (14) expressing that staff members are granted access to project files unless they are blacklisted, and a constraint (15), which forbids that owners of project information lack access to it. Both parts, $\mathcal{P}$ and $\mathcal{O}$, interact via DL-atoms, such as $\mathrm{DL}[Project \uplus projfile; StaffRequest](X)$. The latter specifies an update of $\mathcal{O}$, via operator $\uplus$, prior to querying it: i.e. additional assertions $Project(c)$ are considered for each individual c, such that $projfile(c)$ is true in an interpretation of $\mathcal{P}$, before all instances X of $StaffRequest$ are retrieved from $\mathcal{O}$. Inconsistency arises as *john*, the chief of project $p1$ and owner of its files, has no access to them.

As an inconsistent DL-program yields no information, a relevant issue is how to change it in order to gain consistency. In [9], different repair options were discussed

E. Fermé and J. Leite (Eds.): JELIA 2014, LNAI 8761, pp. 426–441, 2014.
© Springer International Publishing Switzerland 2014

$$\mathcal{O} = \begin{cases} (1)\ Blacklisted \sqsubseteq Staff \\ (2)\ StaffRequest \equiv \exists hasAction.Action \sqcap \exists hasSubject.Staff \sqcap \exists hasTarget.Project \\ (3)\ BlacklistedStaffRequest \equiv StaffRequest \sqcap \exists hasSubject.Blacklisted \\ (4)\ StaffRequest(r1) \quad (5)\ hasSubject(r1,john) \quad (6)\ Blacklisted(john) \\ (7)\ hasTarget(r1,p1) \quad (8)\ hasAction(r1,read) \quad (9)\ Action(read) \end{cases}$$

$$\mathcal{P} = \begin{cases} (10)\ projfile(p1); \quad (11)\ hasowner(p1,john); \\ (12)\ chief(Y) \leftarrow hasowner(X,Y), projfile(X); \\ (13)\ grant(X) \leftarrow DL[Project \uplus projfile; StaffRequest](X), not\ deny(X); \\ (14)\ deny(X) \leftarrow DL[Staff \uplus chief; BlacklistedStaffRequest](X), \\ (15)\ \bot \leftarrow hasowner(Y,Z), not\ grant(X), \\ \qquad DL[; hasTarget](X,Y), DL[; hasSubject](X,Z). \end{cases}$$

Fig. 1. DL-program Π over a policy ontology

and a theoretical framework for repairing inconsistent DL-programs was proposed, in which the ontology ABox (a likely source of errors) is changed such that the modified DL-program has answer sets, called *repair answer sets*. An algorithm to compute the latter was given in [9] as well, which however lacks practicality.

For *DL-Lite*$_{\mathcal{A}}$ ontologies, a more effective repair algorithm was given in [10]. It is based on support sets [8] for a DL-atom, which are portions of its input that together with the ABox determine the value of the DL-atom. The algorithm uses complete support families, i.e. stocks of support sets such that the value of each DL-atom under every interpretation can be decided without ontology access. Fortunately, for *DL-Lite*$_{\mathcal{A}}$ ontologies complete support families are small and easy to compute.

In this paper, we consider a similar approach for ontologies in $\mathcal{EL}$, which like *DL-Lite*$_{\mathcal{A}}$ is another prominent Description Logic that offers tractable reasoning. Despite limited expressivity, $\mathcal{EL}$ ontologies are still useful for many application domains, including biology, medicine, chemistry, policy, etc. Due to range restrictions and concept conjunctions on the left-hand side of inclusion axioms in $\mathcal{EL}$, a DL-atom accessing an $\mathcal{EL}$ ontology can have arbitrarily large and infinitely many support sets in general. While for acyclic TBoxes (which is a property often met in practice [13]) the latter is excluded, complete support set families can be still very large, and constructing as well as managing them might be impractical. This obstructs to a deployment of the approach in [10] to $\mathcal{EL}$ ontologies.

For this reason, we introduce here a more general algorithm for repair answer set computation that operates on incomplete (partial) support families. More specifically, our contributions and advances over previous works [8; 10] are summarized as follows:

– We generalize repair answer set computation to deal with partial support families, such that $\mathcal{EL}$ ontologies can be handled.
– Following [8], we formally define both ground and nonground support sets for $\mathcal{EL}$ ontologies and present techniques for their computation. In contrast to [8; 10], we take advantage of datalog rewritings of queries over an $\mathcal{EL}$ ontology (see also [15]).
– We provide a declarative realization of an algorithm dealing with partial support families for repair answer set computation within the DLVHEX system. For that,

$$\mathcal{T}_{norm} = \left\{ \begin{array}{l} (1*)\ \mathit{StaffRequest} \sqsubseteq \exists hasAction.Action \\ (2*)\ \mathit{StaffRequest} \sqsubseteq \exists hasSubject.Staff \\ (3*)\ \mathit{StaffRequest} \sqsubseteq \exists hasTarget.Project \\ (4*)\ \exists hasAction.Action \sqsubseteq C_{\exists hasA.A} \\ (5*)\ \exists hasSubject.Staff \sqsubseteq C_{\exists hasS.St} \\ (6*)\ \exists hasTarget.Project \sqsubseteq C_{\exists hasT.P} \\ (7*)\ C_{\exists hasA.A} \sqcap C_{\exists hasS.St} \sqsubseteq C_{\exists hasA.A \sqcap \exists hasS.St} \\ (8*)\ C_{\exists hasA.A \sqcap \exists hasS.St} \sqcap C_{\exists hasT.P} \sqsubseteq \mathit{StaffRequest} \end{array} \right\}$$

Fig. 2. Normalized TBox

we present some experimental results showing very promising potential of the approach.

As a practical result of this work, we have an implementation of inconsistency tolerant DL-programs over $\mathcal{EL}$-ontologies, which is the first of its kind.

2   Preliminaries

We first briefly recall DL-programs and repair answer sets; see [29; 9] for details.

Syntax. A DL-program is a pair $\Pi = \langle \mathcal{O}, \mathcal{P} \rangle$ of a finite ontology $\mathcal{O}$ and a finite set of rules $\mathcal{P}$ defined as follows.

- $\mathcal{O}$ is an *DL-knowledge base* (or *ontology*) over a signature $\Sigma_o = \langle \mathbf{I}, \mathbf{C}, \mathbf{R} \rangle$ with a set $\mathbf{I}$ of individuals, a set $\mathbf{C}$ of concept names and a set $\mathbf{R}$ of role names. We assume that $\mathcal{O} = \mathcal{T} \cup \mathcal{A}$ is a *consistent* $\mathcal{EL}$ KB [26] with *TBox* $\mathcal{T}$ and *ABox* $\mathcal{A}$, which are sets of axioms capturing taxonomic resp. factual knowledge. Concepts C and roles R obey the following syntax, where $A \in \mathbf{C}$ is an atomic concept and $U \in \mathbf{R}$ is an atomic role:

$$C \rightarrow A \quad B \rightarrow C \mid C \sqcap D \mid \exists R.C \quad R \rightarrow U$$

TBox axioms are of the form $B_1 \sqsubseteq B_2$ (inclusion axiom); ABox assertions are of the form $A(a)$ and $U(a,b)$, where $A \in \mathbf{C}$, $U \in \mathbf{R}$ and $a, b \in \mathbf{I}$; A TBox is *normalized*, if all of its axioms have one of the following forms:

$$A_1 \sqsubseteq A_2 \quad A_1 \sqcap A_2 \sqsubseteq A_3 \quad \exists R.A_1 \sqsubseteq A_2 \quad A_1 \sqsubseteq \exists R.A_2,$$

where A_1, A_2, A_3 are atomic concepts. E.g., the axioms (1) and (2) in Example 1 are in normal form, while axiom (3) is not. For any $\mathcal{EL}$ TBox, an equivalent TBox in normal form is constructable in linear time [26] (over an extended signature); Figure 2 shows a normalized form of the TBox in Example 1.

In the sequel, we use P as a generic predicate from $\mathbf{C} \cup \mathbf{R}$ (if distinction is immaterial).

- $\mathcal{P}$ consists of logic program rules r of the form

$$a_1 \vee \ldots \vee a_n \leftarrow b_1, \ldots, b_k, not\ b_{k+1}, \ldots, not\ b_m, \tag{1}$$

where $n + m > 0$, all a_i are lp-atoms, and each b_i is either an lp-atom or a DL-atom; here

- an *lp-atom* is a first-order atom $p(t)$ with predicate p from a set $\mathbf{P}$ of predicate names disjoint with $\mathbf{C}$ and $\mathbf{R}$, and constants from a set $\mathcal{C}$; we adopt $\mathcal{C} = \mathbf{I}$.

– a *DL-atom* $a(\mathbf{t})$ is of form $\mathrm{DL}[\lambda; Q](\mathbf{t})$, where

$$\lambda = S_1 \, op_1 \, p_1, \ldots, S_m \, op_m \, p_m, \quad m \geq 0, \tag{2}$$

s.t. for $1 \leq i \leq m$, $S_i \in \mathbf{C} \cup \mathbf{R}$, $op_i \in \{\uplus, \cup\!\!\!-\}$ is an *update operator*, [1] and $p_i \in \mathbf{P}$ is an *input predicate* of the same arity as S_i—intuitively, $op_i = \uplus$ (resp., $op_i = \cup\!\!\!-$) increases S_i (resp., $\neg S_i$) by the extension of p_i; $Q(\mathbf{t})$ is a *DL-query*, which is either of the form (i) $C(t)$, where C is a concept and t is a term; (ii) $R(t_1, t_2)$, where R is a role and t_1, t_2 are terms; or (iii) $\neg Q'(\mathbf{t})$ where $Q'(\mathbf{t})$ is from (i)-(ii).

If $n = 0$, the rule r is a *constraint*.

Example 2 (cont'd). The DL-atom $\mathrm{DL}[Project \uplus projfile; StaffRequest](X)$ contained in rule (12) of Example 1 first enriches the concept $Project$ in $\mathcal{O}$ by the extension of the predicate $projfile$ in $\mathcal{P}$ via $\uplus$, and then queries the concept $StaffRequest$.

Semantics. The semantics of a DL-program $\Pi = \langle \mathcal{O}, \mathcal{P} \rangle$ is in terms of its grounding $gr(\Pi) = \langle \mathcal{O}, gr(\mathcal{P}) \rangle$ over $\mathcal{C}$, i.e., $gr(\mathcal{P})$ contains all ground instances of rules r in $\mathcal{P}$ over $\mathcal{C}$. In the remainder, by default we assume that Π is ground.

A (Herbrand) *interpretation* of Π is a set $I \subseteq HB_\Pi$ of ground atoms, where HB_Π is the usual Herbrand base w.r.t. $\mathcal{C}$ and $\mathbf{P}$; I satisfies an lp-atom a, if $a \in I$ and a DL-atom a of the form (2) if

$$\mathcal{O} \cup \tau^I(a) \models Q(\mathbf{c}) \tag{3}$$

where $\tau^I(a) = \bigcup_{i=1}^m \Lambda_i(I)$, and $\Lambda_i(I) = \begin{cases} \{S_i(t) \mid p_i(t) \in I\}, & \text{for } op_i = \uplus; \\ \{\neg S_i(t) \mid p_i(t) \in I\}, & \text{for } op_i = \cup\!\!\!-. \end{cases}$

Satisfaction of a DL-rule r resp. set $\mathcal{P}$ of rules by I is then as usual, where I satisfies *not* b_j if I does not satisfy b_j; I satisfies Π, if it satisfies each $r \in \mathcal{P}$. We denote that I satisfies (is a *model* of) an object o (atom, rule, etc.) by $I \models^{\mathcal{O}} o$.

Example 3 (cont'd). Consider $I = \{projfile(p1), hasowner(p1, john), chief(john)\}$, which satisfies dl-atom $d = \mathrm{DL}[Project \uplus projfile; StaffRequest](r_1)$ of Example 1, as $\mathcal{O} \cup \tau^I(d) \models StaffRequest(r_1)$. However for $\mathcal{O}'$, given by $\mathcal{O}$ without (4) and (5), $\mathcal{O}' \cup \tau^I(d) \not\models StaffRequest(r_1)$ and thus I does not satisfy d under $\mathcal{O}'$.

An *(flp-)answer set* of $\Pi = \langle \mathcal{O}, \mathcal{P} \rangle$ is any interpretation I that is a $\subseteq$-minimal model of the *flp-reduct* Π_{FLP}^I, which maps $\mathcal{P}$ and $I \subseteq HB_\Pi$ to the rule set $\mathcal{P}_{FLP}^I = \{r_{FLP}^I \mid r \in gr(\mathcal{P})\}$, where $r_{FLP}^I = r$ if the body of r is satisfied, i.e., $I \models^{\mathcal{O}} b_i$, for all b_i, $1 \leq i \leq k$ and $I \not\models^{\mathcal{O}} b_j$, for all $k < j \leq m$; otherwise, r_{FLP}^I is void.

A DL-program Π is *inconsistent*, if it has no answer set. An interpretation I is an *(flp-)deletion repair answer set* of $\Pi = \langle \mathcal{T} \cup \mathcal{A}, \mathcal{P} \rangle$, if it is an *flp*-answer set of some $\Pi' = \langle \mathcal{T} \cup \mathcal{A}', \mathcal{P} \rangle$ where $\mathcal{A}' \subseteq \mathcal{A}$; any such $\mathcal{A}'$ is called a *deletion repair* of Π. Note that we consider arbitrary deletion repairs. One might resort to more refined notions of repair [9], e.g., $\subseteq$-maximal deletion repairs, however resulting in a complexity increase.

Example 4 (cont'd). Program Π is inconsistent; if we remove (6) from $\mathcal{A}$, then $I = \{projfile(p1), hasowner(p1, john), chief(john), grant(r1)\}$, becomes an answer set. Along with the facts (8) and (9) the *flp*-reduct $\mathcal{P}_{FLP}^I$ contains the ground rule (10),

---

[1] We disregard here for simplicity the less used constrains-operator $\cap$ and subsumption queries.

where X is substituted by $r1$. Then I is a deletion repair answer set with respect to the repair $\mathcal{A}' = \{Action(read), hasAction(r1, read), StaffRequest(r1), hasSubject (r1, john), hasTarget(r1, p1)\}$.

Shifting Lemma. To simplify matters and avoid dealing with the logic program predicates separately, we shall shift as in [10] the lp-input of DL-atoms to the ontology. Given a DL-atom $d = DL[\lambda; Q](t)$ and $P \circ p \in \lambda, \circ \in \{\uplus, \cup\}$, we call $P_p(c)$ an *input assertion for* d, where P_p is a fresh ontology predicate and $c \in \mathcal{C}$; $\mathcal{A}_d$ is the set of all such assertions. For a TBox $\mathcal{T}$ and a DL-atom d, we let $\mathcal{T}_d = \mathcal{T} \cup \{P_p \sqsubseteq P \mid P \uplus p \in \lambda\}$, and for an interpretation I, let $\mathcal{O}_d^I = \mathcal{T}_d \cup \mathcal{A} \cup \{P_p(t) \in \mathcal{A}_d \mid p(t) \in I\}$. We then have:

Proposition 1 ([10]). *For every* $\mathcal{O} = \mathcal{T} \cup \mathcal{A}$, *DL-atom* $d = DL[\lambda; Q](t)$ *and interpretation* I, *it holds that* $I \models^{\mathcal{O}} d$ *iff* $I \models^{\mathcal{O}_d^I} DL[\epsilon; Q](t)$ *iff* $\mathcal{O}_d^I \models Q(t)$.

Unlike $\mathcal{O} \cup \tau^I(d)$, in $\mathcal{O}_d^I$ there is a clear distinction between native assertions and input assertions for d w.r.t. I (via facts P_p and axioms $P_p \sqsubseteq P$), mirroring its lp-input.

3 Support Sets for DL-atoms

In this section, we provide a definition of support sets using the framework given in [8]. Intuitively, a *support set* for a DL-atom d is a portion of its input that determines the output values of d.

Definition 1 (Ground Support Sets). *Let* $d(c) = DL[\lambda; Q](c)$ *be a ground DL-atom of a DL-program* $\Pi = \langle \mathcal{O}, \mathcal{P} \rangle$. *Then a support set for* d *is a subset of the Herbrand Base* $S = \{p_i(t) \in HB_\Pi, P_i \uplus p_i \in \lambda\}$, *s.t. for all interpretations* $I, I' \supseteq S$, *it holds that* $I \models^{\mathcal{O}} d$ *iff* $I' \models^{\mathcal{O}} d$. *Moreover, S is positive (resp. negative), if for every interpretation* $I \supseteq S$ *it holds that* $I \models^{\mathcal{O}} d$ *(resp.* $I \not\models^{\mathcal{O}} d$).

In this work we exploit only positive support sets, i.e. portions of the ontology input, which ensure that the DL-atom will be true.

Example 5. Recall Π and $d(r1) = DL[Project \uplus projfile; StaffRequest](r1)$ from Example 1. A positive ground support set for $d(r1)$ is $S = \{projfile(p1)\}$. Indeed, for all interpretations $I \supseteq \{projfile(p1)\}$, it holds that $\mathcal{A} \cup \mathcal{T} \cup \lambda^I(d) \models StaffRequest(r1)$.

Intuitively, support sets reflect the relevant part of an external source (ontology in our case). Thus different ground support sets can be similar with respect to their structure. With this motivation in mind in [8] support sets were lifted to the nonground level. The definition of a nonground support set exploits source information in the form of so-called *conditional guards* (γ); we now adapt it to DL-programs.

Definition 2. *Let* Π *be a DL-program and let* $d(X) = DL[\lambda; Q](X)$ *be a DL-atom of* Π. *A positive nonground support set* S *for* $d(X)$ *is a pair* $\langle N, \gamma \rangle$, *where*

- $N \subseteq \{p_i(Y) \mid P_i \circ p_i \in \lambda, \circ \in \{\uplus, \cup\}\}$ *is a set of nonground atoms over the input signature* λ *of* d;
- $\gamma : \mathcal{C}^{|X|} \times grnd_{\mathcal{C}}(N) \rightarrow \{0, 1\}$ *is a Boolean function (called the guard), s.t. for all* $c \in \mathcal{C}^{|X|}$ *and* $N_{gr} \in grnd_{\mathcal{C}}(N)$ *it holds that* $\gamma(c, N_{gr}) = 1$ *only if* N_{gr} *is a ground support set for* $d(c)$.

In this definition, $grnd_C(N)$ is the support family, i.e. a set of support sets, constructed from N by replacing all variables with constants from C in all possible ways. Intuitively, the guard γ is an abstract function that checks a condition under which the ground atoms for predicates in N form a ground support set. A family **S** of support sets is said to be *complete* for a (non-ground) DL-atom $d(X)$ iff for every $c \in C^{|X|}$ and ground support set S of $d(c)$, there exists $S' = \langle N, \gamma \rangle \in \mathbf{S}$, such that $S \in grnd_c(N)$ and $\gamma(c, S) = 1$.

Example 6. The DL-atom $d(X) = \text{DL}[Project \uplus projfile; StaffRequest](X)$ has $S_1 = \langle projfile(Y), \gamma \rangle$ as a nonground support set, where $\gamma : C \times grnd_C(projfile(Y)) \rightarrow \{0, 1\}$ is such that $\gamma(c, projfile(c')) = 1$ only if the ABox $\mathcal{A}$ contains the assertions $hasAction(c, c_1)$, $Action(c_1)$, $hasSubject(c, c_2)$, $Staff(c_2)$, and $hasTarget(c, c')$, where c_1, c_2 are arbitrary constants from C.

Another nonground support set for $d(X)$ is $S_2 = \langle \emptyset, \gamma' \rangle$, where $\gamma' : C \times \emptyset \rightarrow \{0, 1\}$ is such that $\gamma'(c, \emptyset) = 1$ only if $StaffRequest(c) \in \mathcal{A}$.

The abstract definition of nonground support sets leaves room for flexible realization of the conditional guard γ. A natural one is by (unions of) conjunctive queries (UCQs) over the ontology ABox viewed as a database. In Example 6, the guard γ of S_1 takes as input a constant $c \in C$ and a ground instance of form $projfile(c')$, and returns 1 if the Boolean CQ $q(c) \leftarrow \exists X, X' \phi(X, X')$ evaluates to true, where $\phi(X, X') = hasAction(c, X) \wedge Action(X) \wedge hasSubject(c, X') \wedge Staff(X') \wedge hasTarget(c, c')$. The UCQ $q(c) \leftarrow \exists X, X' \phi(X, X') \vee \psi(X, X')$, where $\psi(X, X') - hasAction(c, X) \wedge Action(X) \wedge hasSubject(c, X') \wedge Blacklisted(X') \wedge hasTarget(c, X')$, is more general; even more general guards are possible (e.g. nonrecursive datalog programs).

3.1 Computing Support Sets for DL-atoms over $\mathcal{EL}$ Ontology

We now provide a method for support set construction that allows us to just work with ontology predicates when constructing nonground support sets.

As negation is not available nor expressible in $\mathcal{EL}$ ($\perp$ is unavailable), from now on we restrict our attention to DL-atoms $\text{DL}[\lambda; Q](c)$ with positive updates, i.e. $\circ \in \{\uplus\}$ for all $P \circ p \in \lambda$.

The discussion above reveals that for support set construction, it is natural to exploit (conjunctive) query answering methods in $\mathcal{EL}$ (e.g., [23; 19; 18; 25]). Most of them are based on rewriting the query and the TBox into a datalog program over the ABox; to construct guard functions that use a datalog rewriting of the TBox seems thus suggestive.

Suppose we are given a DL-program $\Pi = \langle \mathcal{O}, \mathcal{P} \rangle$, where $\mathcal{O} = \langle \mathcal{T}, \mathcal{A} \rangle$ is an $\mathcal{EL}$ ontology and a DL-atom $d(X) = \text{DL}[\lambda; Q](X)$. Our method for constructing nonground support sets for $d(X)$ consists of the following three steps.

Step 1. DL-query Rewriting over the TBox. The first step exploits the rewriting of the DL-query Q of $d(X)$ over the TBox $\mathcal{T}_d = \mathcal{T} \cup \{P_p \sqsubseteq P \mid P \uplus p \in \lambda\}$ into a set of datalog rules, see e.g. Figure 3. At the preprocessing stage, the normalization technique is first applied to the TBox $\mathcal{T}_d$. This technique restricts the syntactic form of TBoxes by decomposing complex axioms into syntactically simpler ones. For this purpose, a minimal required set of fresh concept symbols is introduced. Given a TBox

Table 1. $\mathcal{EL}$ TBox Rewriting

Axiom	Datalog rule
$A_1 \sqsubseteq A_2$	$A_2(X) \leftarrow A_1(X)$
$A_1 \sqcap A_2 \sqsubseteq A_3$	$A_3(X) \leftarrow A_1(X), A_2(X)$
$\exists R.A_2 \sqsubseteq A_1$	$A_2(X) \leftarrow R(X,Y), A_3(Y)$
$A_1 \sqsubseteq \exists R.A_2$	$R(X, o_{A_2}) \leftarrow A_1(X)$
	$A_2(o_{A_2}) \leftarrow A_1(X)$

$\mathcal{T}_d$, its normalized form $\mathcal{T}_{dnorm}$ is computed in linear time [1]. We then rewrite the part of the TBox, relevant for the query at hand, into a datalog program $Prog_{Q, \mathcal{T}_{dnorm}}$ using the translation given in Table 1, which is a variant of [22; 28]. When rewriting axioms of the form $A_1 \sqsubseteq \exists R.A_2$ (fourth axiom in Table 1) we introduce fresh constants (o_{A_2}) to represent "unknown" objects. A similar rewriting is exploited in the REQUIEM system (where function symbols are used instead of fresh constants). As a result we obtain:

Lemma 1. *For any data part, i.e., ABox $\mathcal{A}$, and any ground assertion $Q(c)$, deciding $Prog_{Q, \mathcal{T}_{dnorm}} \cup \mathcal{A} \models Q(c)$ is equivalent to checking $\mathcal{T}_{dnorm} \cup \mathcal{A} \models Q(c)$.*

Step 2. Query Unfolding. The second step proceeds with the standard unfolding of the rules of $Prog_{Q, \mathcal{T}_{dnorm}}$ w.r.t. the target DL-query Q. We start with the rule that has Q in the head and expand its body using other rules of the program $Prog_{Q, \mathcal{T}_{dnorm}}$. By applying this procedure exhaustively, we get a number of rules which correspond to the rewritings of the query Q over $\mathcal{T}_{dnorm}$. Note that it is not always possible to obtain all of the rewritings effectively, since in general there might be infinitely many of them (exponentially many for acyclic $\mathcal{T}$). We discuss possible restrictions in the next section.

Step 3. Support Set Extraction. The last step is devoted to the extraction of nonground support sets from the rewritings computed in Step 2. We select those that contain only predicates from $\mathcal{T}_d$ and obtain a set of rules r of the form

$$Q(\boldsymbol{X}) \leftarrow P_1(\boldsymbol{Y_1}), \dots P_k(\boldsymbol{Y_k}), P_{k+1 p_{k+1}}(\boldsymbol{Y_{k+1}}), \dots, P_{n p_n}(\boldsymbol{Y_n}), \qquad (4)$$

where each P_i is a native ontology predicate if $1 \leq i \leq k$, and a predicate mirroring lp-input of d otherwise. From such rules r we construct pairs $S = \langle N, \gamma \rangle$, where

- $N = \{p_i(\boldsymbol{Y_i}) \mid P_{i p_i}(\boldsymbol{Y_i}) \in B(r), k+1 \leq i \leq n\}$;
- $\gamma : \mathcal{C}^{|\boldsymbol{X}|} \times grnd_{\mathcal{C}}(N) \to \{0, 1\}$ is such that $\gamma(c, N_{gr}) = 1$ only if $Q(c)$ follows from $r \cup \mathcal{A}_d$, where $\mathcal{A}_d = \mathcal{A} \cup \{P_{i p_i}(t) \mid p_i(t) \in N_{gr}\}$.

Then the following holds.

Proposition 2. *Let $d(\boldsymbol{X}) = DL[\lambda; Q](\boldsymbol{X})$ be a DL-atom of a program $\Pi = \langle \mathcal{O}, \mathcal{P} \rangle$, where $\mathcal{O} = \langle \mathcal{T}, \mathcal{A} \rangle$, is an $\mathcal{EL}$ ontology. A set S, constructed using Step 1-Step 3 is a nonground support set for $d(\boldsymbol{X})$.*

Proof. Towards a contradiction assume that S is not a nonground support set for $d(\boldsymbol{X})$. This means that either (1) N is not a set of nonground predicates from λ or (2) the function γ of Definition 2 is not correct.

$$Prog_{Q,\mathcal{T}_{dnorm}} = \left\{ \begin{array}{l} (4')\ C_{\exists hasA.A}(X) \leftarrow hasAction(X,Y), Action(Y). \\ (5')\ C_{\exists hasS.St}(X) \leftarrow hasSubject(X,Y), Staff(Y). \\ (6')\ C_{\exists hasT.P}(X) \leftarrow hasTarget(X,Y), Project(Y). \\ (7')\ C_{\exists hasA.A \sqcap \exists hasS.St}(X) \leftarrow C_{\exists hasA.A}(X), C_{\exists hasS.St}(X). \\ (8')\ StaffRequest(X) \leftarrow C_{\exists hasA.A \sqcap \exists hasS.St}(X), C_{\exists hasT.P}(X). \\ (9)\ Project(X) \leftarrow Project_{projfile}(X). \end{array} \right\}$$

Fig. 3. DL-query Rewriting for $DL[Project \uplus projfile; StaffRequest](X)$ over $\mathcal{T}_{dnorm}$

The predicates of the form P_P in the TBox $\mathcal{T}_d$ are obtained from λ of $d(\boldsymbol{X})$ by construction and clearly so are the predicates $P_{j_{p_j}}$ of each rule r. Thus predicates in N are indeed nonground predicates from the input signature of $d(\boldsymbol{X})$.

Hence the function γ must be incorrect, i.e. some $\boldsymbol{c} \in \mathcal{C}^{|X|}$, and $N_{gr} \in grnd_C(N)$ must exist, s.t. $\gamma(\boldsymbol{c}, N_{gr}) = 1$ but N_{gr} is not a positive ground support set for $d(\boldsymbol{c})$. The latter means that some interpretation $I' \supseteq N_{gr}$ exists s.t. $I' \not\models^{\mathcal{O}} d(\boldsymbol{c})$. By Proposition 1 we have that $\mathcal{O}_d^{I'} \not\models Q(\boldsymbol{c})$, i.e. $\mathcal{T}_d \cup \mathcal{A}_d \cup \{P_{ip_i}(\boldsymbol{t}) \mid p_i(\boldsymbol{t}) \in I'\} \not\models Q(\boldsymbol{c})$. On the other hand, we know that $Q(\boldsymbol{c})$ follows from r and $\mathcal{A}_d \cup \{P_{ip_i}(\boldsymbol{t}) \mid p_i(\boldsymbol{t}) \in I'\}$. Since r is obtained by unfolding of the rules in $Prog_{Q,\mathcal{T}_{dnorm}}$, we know that $Q(\boldsymbol{c})$ also follows from $Prog_{Q,\mathcal{T}_{dnorm}} \cup \mathcal{A}_d$ and hence from $\mathcal{T}_{dnorm} \cup \mathcal{A}$ by construction of $Prog_{Q,\mathcal{T}_{dnorm}}$. Consequently, $\mathcal{T} \cup \mathcal{A}_d \models Q(\boldsymbol{c})$ must hold. $\qquad\square$

As shown above, when working with support sets we can restrict ourselves to the ontology predicates and operate only on them. More specifically, rules of the form (4) fully reflect nonground support sets as of Definition 2, and ground instantiations of such a rule over constants from $\mathcal{C}$ implicitly correspond to ground support sets.

According to novel results [15], complete support families can be computed for large classes of ontologies. However, in general there might be exponentially many unfoldings produced at Step 2. Thus, to cope with exponentiality, one might often want to apply reasonable restrictions on the support families.

4 Partial Support Family Computation

In this section we discuss restrictions on the size, structure and number of support sets, which is of interest for practical applications, and we analyze conditions under which all support sets from the restricted category form a complete support family.

In general, unlike for the $DL\text{-}Lite_A$ case, due to possible cyclic dependencies of the form $C \sqsubseteq \exists R.C$ allowed in $\mathcal{EL}$, the explanations of an instance query can be of infinite size and so are the support sets for DL-atoms accessing an $\mathcal{EL}$ ontology.

An analysis of a vast number of ontologies has revealed that in many realistic cases they do not contain (or imply) cyclic axioms [13]; we thus assume that the TBox of the ontology in a given DL-program is acyclic (i.e., does not entail inclusion axioms of form $C \sqsubseteq \exists R.C$). However, even under this restriction support sets can be large in general.

Example 7. If $\mathcal{T}$ implies the following chain of inclusions $\exists R_1.A_1 \sqsubseteq Q, \exists R_2.A_2 \sqsubseteq A_1, \exists R_3.A_3 \sqsubseteq A_2, \ldots, \exists R_n.A_n \sqsubseteq A_{n-1}$, then the set of ground support sets for

$$DL[R_1 \uplus p_1, R_2 \uplus p_2, \ldots, R_n \uplus p_n, A_n \uplus q; Q](c_1)$$

contains $\{p_1(c_1, c_2), p_2(c_2, c_3), p_3(c_3, c_4) \ldots p_n(c_{n-1}, c_n), q(c_n)\}$. Replacing A_i with nested range restrictions and conjunctions would yield support sets of exponential size.

This raises the question of reasonable restrictions on the form and size of support sets, and under which conditions such restrictions still yield complete support families.

Support set size. A natural approach for computing a partial support family is the restriction of the target support set size. We may put a certain bound on the size of support sets that we want to compute and proceed with unfolding of the rules of the datalog program. When a certain unfolding branch reaches the size limit, we stop its further expansion and choose a different branch.

Suppose the size is bounded by n. Under the following conditions on the TBox the set of all support sets of size at most n is complete:

– inclusions do not contain any existential restrictions on the left hand side and the number of conjuncts on the left hand side of all inclusions in the TBox is bounded by n.

– all existential restrictions of form $\exists R.A$ occurring on the left hand side of inclusions are such that A occurs in the TBox elsewhere only in simple atomic concept inclusions.

Number of Support Sets. Another restriction relevant in practice regards the number of support sets. In general, determining the exact number of support sets that is needed to form a complete family for a DL-atom is a hard problem. It is tightly related to counting minimal explanations for an abduction problem, which was analyzed in [16] for propositional theories under various restrictions; there it was shown that counting all smallest solutions (explanations) for an abduction problem over a Horn theory is $\#Opt_P[log_n]$-complete. Moreover, meaningful conditions such that a fixed number n of support sets suffices to obtain a complete family are non-obvious (bounded tree-width [14] might be useful, as for efficient datalog abduction); a careful analysis of real world ontologies is needed to ensure practical relevance. This remains for future research.

5   Algorithm for Repair Answer Set Computation

In this section, we present our algorithm *SoundRAnsSet* for computing deletion repair answer sets by exploiting support families for DL-atoms accessing an $\mathcal{EL}$ ontology.

Exploiting DLVHEX, DL-programs are evaluated via a rewriting $\hat{\Pi}$ of $gr(\Pi)$, where DL-atoms a are replaced by ordinary atoms e_a (*replacement atoms*), together with a guess on their truth by additional "choice" rules $e_a \vee ne_a$, where ne_a stands for the negation of e_a. We denote interpretations of $\hat{\Pi}$ by $\hat{I}$, and use $\hat{I}|_\Pi$ when referring to their restriction to the original language of Π.

The naive algorithm for repair answer set computation [9] cycles through all ABox candidates $\mathcal{A}'$ and checks whether under $\mathcal{A}'$ the guess for the replacement atoms coincides with their actual values. If $\mathcal{A}'$ fulfills this, an *unfoundedness check* is performed for this repair candidate. An alternative approach [10], specifically targeted at $DL\text{-}Lite_{\mathcal{A}}$ ontologies, aims at finding repairs using complete support families for DL-atoms. In our algorithm $SoundRAnsSet$ for $\mathcal{EL}$ ontologies (see Algorithm 1) we also exploit support families, but do not require that they are complete. If the families are complete (which may be known), then $SoundRAnsSet$ is guaranteed to be complete; otherwise, it may miss repair answer sets (an easy extension ensures completeness though).

We start (a) by computing a family $\mathbf{S}$ of nonground support sets for each DL-atom. Next the replacement program $\hat{\Pi}$ is created, whose answer sets $\hat{I}$ are computed one by one in (b). For $\hat{I}$, we first determine the sets D_p (resp. D_n) of DL-atoms that are guessed true (resp. false) in it and then use the function $Gr(\mathbf{S}, \hat{I}, \mathcal{A})$ which instantiates $\mathbf{S}$ for the DL-atoms in $D_p \cup D_n$ to relevant ground support sets, i.e., those compatible with $\hat{I}$.

In (d) we check whether some DL-atom in D_n has a support set S consisting just of input assertions; if so we move to the next answer set $\hat{I}$ of $\hat{\Pi}$. Otherwise, we (e) loop over all minimal hitting sets $H \subseteq \mathcal{A}$ of the support sets for DL-atoms in D_n, formed by ABox assertions only. For each H we check whether every atom in D_p has at least one support set disjoint from H. If yes (f), i.e. removing H from $\mathcal{A}$ does not affect the values of DL-atoms in D_p, then we evaluate in a *postcheck* the atoms from D_n over $\mathcal{T} \cup \mathcal{A} \backslash H$ w.r.t. $\hat{I}$. Otherwise, we evaluate the DL-atoms from D_n and D_p. A Boolean flag rep stores the evaluation result of a function $eval_n$(resp. $eval_p$). More specifically, given D_n (resp. D_p), $\hat{I}$ and $\mathcal{T} \cup \mathcal{A} \backslash H$, the function $eval_n$ (resp. $eval_p$) returns $true$, if all atoms in D_n (resp. D_p) evaluate to false (resp. true). If rep is $true$ and the foundedness check $flpFND(\hat{I}, \mathcal{A} \backslash H, \mathcal{P})$ succeeds, then in (g) $\hat{I}|_\Pi$ is output as repair answer set.

We remark that in many cases, the foundedness check might be trivial [7], if we would consider weak FLP-answer sets [9], it can be skipped.

Example 8 (cont'd). Consider Π from Example 1 with equivalence ($\equiv$) in axioms (2) and (3) substituted by $\sqsubseteq$. Let $\hat{I} = \{projfile(p1), hasowner(p1, john), chief(john), e_a, ne_b\}$ be returned at (b), where $a = DL[Project \uplus projfile; Staffrequest](r1)$ and $b = DL[Staff \uplus chief; BlacklistedStaffRequest](r1)$. At (c) we obtained

- $\mathbf{S}_{gr}^{\hat{I}}(a) = \{S_1, S_2\}$, where $S_1 = \{hasAction(r1, read), hasSubject(r1, john),$
  $Action(read), Staff(john), hasTarget(r1, p1), Project_{projfile}(p1)\}$ and
  $S_2 = \{StaffRequest(r1)\}$;
- $\mathbf{S}_{gr}^{\hat{I}}(b) = \{S_1', S_2'\}$ with $S_1' = \{StaffRequest(r1), hasSubject(r1, john),$
  $Blacklisted(john)\}$ and $S_2' = \{BlacklistedStaffRequest(r1)\}$.

At (e) we got a hitting set $H = \{StaffRequest(r1), BlacklistedStaffRequest(r1)\}$, which is disjoint with S_1. Thus we get to the if branch of (f) and check whether b is false under $\mathcal{A} \backslash \{StaffRequest(r1)\}$. This is not true, hence $rep = false$ and we pick a different hitting set H', e.g $\{Blacklisted(john), BlacklistedStaffRequest(r1)\}$. Proceeding with H', we get to (g), since at (f) $eval_n(b, \hat{I}, \mathcal{T} \cup \mathcal{A} \cap H) = true$.

Proposition 3. $SoundRAnsSet$ *is sound, it outputs only deletion repair answer sets.*

If the support families are complete, then the postchecks at (f) are redundant. In case the if-condition of (f) is satisfied, we set $rep = true$, otherwise $rep = false$.

Proposition 4. *If for all DL-atoms in Π the support families in $\mathbf{S}$ are complete, then $SoundRAnsSet$ is complete, i.e., it outputs every deletion repair answer set.*

Algorithm 1: *SoundRAnsSet*: compute deletion repair answer sets

    Input: $\Pi = \langle \mathcal{T} \cup \mathcal{A}, \mathcal{P} \rangle$
    Output: a set of deletion repair answer sets of Π

(a) compute a set **S** of nongr. supp. sets for the DL-atoms in Π

(b) **for** $\hat{I} \in AS(\hat{\Pi})$ **do**

(c) $D_p \leftarrow \{a \mid e_a \in \hat{I}\};\ D_n \in \{a \mid ne_a \in \hat{I}\};\ \mathbf{S}_{gr}^{\hat{I}} \leftarrow Gr(\mathbf{S}, \hat{I}, \mathcal{A})$;

(d)   **if** *every* $S \in \mathbf{S}_{gr}^{\hat{I}}(a')$ *for* $a' \in D_n$ *fulfills* $S \cap \mathcal{A} \neq \emptyset$ **then**

(e)   **for** *all min. hitting sets* $H \subseteq \mathcal{A}$ *of* $\bigcup_{a' \in D_n} \mathbf{S}_{gr}^{\hat{I}}(a')$ **do**

(f)   **if** *for every* $a \in D_p$ *some* $S \in \mathbf{S}_{gr}^{\hat{I}}(a)$ *exists s.t.* $S \cap H = \emptyset$;

             then $rep \leftarrow eval_n(D_n, \hat{I}, \mathcal{T} \cup \mathcal{A} \backslash H)$ **else**
             $rep \leftarrow eval_n(D_n, \hat{I}, \mathcal{T} \cup \mathcal{A} \backslash H) \wedge eval_p(D_p, \hat{I}, \mathcal{T} \cup \mathcal{A} \backslash H)$

(g)   **if** *rep and* $flpFND(\hat{I}, \langle \mathcal{T} \cup \mathcal{A} \backslash H, \mathcal{P} \rangle)$ **then** output $\hat{I}|_{\Pi}$

         end

     end

end

We easily can turn *SoundRAnsSet* into a complete algorithm, by modifying (e) to consider all hitting sets and not only minimal ones. In the worst case, this means a fallback to almost the naive algorithm (note that all hitting sets can be enumerated efficiently relative to their number).

6 Implementation and Experiments

We have implemented the algorithm within the DLVHEX evaluation framework,[2] thus providing a means to effectively compute some deletion repair answer sets for $\mathcal{EL}$. For support set computation we exploit the REQUIEM tool [22], which produces the rewritings of the target query using datalog rewriting techniques.

More specifically, we proceed as follows: first for each DL-atom we compute query rewritings of a certain size using REQUIEM. We then use a declarative approach for computing repair answer sets, in which support detection and minimal hitting set computation are accomplished by rules. To this end, for each DL-atom $a(\boldsymbol{X})$ fresh predicates $S_a(\boldsymbol{X}), S_a^{\mathcal{P}}(\boldsymbol{Y})$ and $S_a^{\mathcal{A},\mathcal{P}}(\boldsymbol{Y})$ are introduced, where $\boldsymbol{Y} = \boldsymbol{X}\boldsymbol{X}'$, which intuitively say that $a(\boldsymbol{X})$ has some support set, some support set with only logic program predicates, and some mixed support set, respectively (for simplicity we superficially use uniform variables). Furthermore, rules of the following form are added:

(1) $S_a(\boldsymbol{X}) \leftarrow S_a^{\mathcal{P}}(\boldsymbol{Y})$
(2) $S_a(\boldsymbol{X}) \leftarrow S_a^{\mathcal{A},\mathcal{P}}(\boldsymbol{Y})$

(3) $S_a^{\mathcal{P}}(\boldsymbol{Y}) \leftarrow rb(S_a^{p}(\boldsymbol{Y}))$
(4) $S_a^{\mathcal{A},\mathcal{P}}(\boldsymbol{Y}) \leftarrow rb(S_a^{\mathcal{A},\mathcal{P}}(\boldsymbol{Y})),$
               $nd(S^{\mathcal{A},\mathcal{P}}(\boldsymbol{Y}))$

(5) $\bot \leftarrow ne_a(\boldsymbol{X}), S_a^{\mathcal{P}}(\boldsymbol{Y})$
(6) $\bar{P}_{1a}(\boldsymbol{Y}) \vee \ldots \vee \bar{P}_{na}(\boldsymbol{Y}) \leftarrow ne_a(\boldsymbol{X}), S_a^{\mathcal{A},\mathcal{P}}(\boldsymbol{Y})$

(7) $eval_a(\boldsymbol{X}) \leftarrow e_a(\boldsymbol{X}), not\ C_a(\boldsymbol{X}), not\ S_a(\boldsymbol{X})$
(8) $eval_a(\boldsymbol{X}) \leftarrow ne_a(\boldsymbol{X}), not\ C_a(\boldsymbol{X})$

---

[2] http://www.kr.tuwien.ac.at/research/systems/dlvhex

Here $C_a(X)$ states that the support family for $a(X)$ is known to be complete; such information can be added by facts. The rules (1)-(4) derive information about support sets of $a(X)$ under a potential repair; $rb(S)$ stands for a rule body rendering of a support set S, and $nd(S) = not\ \bar{P}_{1a}(Y), \ldots, not\ \bar{P}_{na}(Y)$, where $\{P_{1a}(Y), \ldots, P_{na}(Y)\}$ is the ontology part of S and $\bar{P}_{ia}(Y)$ states that the assertion $P_{ia}(Y)$ is marked for deletion. The constraint (5) forbids $a(X)$, if guessed false, to have a matching support set with only input assertions; (6) means that if $a(X)$ has instead a matching mixed support set, then some assertion from its ontology part must be eliminated. The rule (7) says that if $a(X)$ is guessed true and completeness of its support family is not known, then an evaluation postcheck must be performed ($eval_a(X)$) if no matching support set is available; rule (8) is similar for $a(X)$ guessed false (mind rule (5)).

6.1 Experiments

We have conducted a preliminary experimental evaluation of our approach by considering inconsistent DL-programs over acyclic OWL 2 EL ontologies.

Experimental Setup. We have computed repair answer sets with complete and incomplete support families. The experiments were run on a Linux server with two 12-core AMD 6176 SE CPUs/128GB RAM using DLVHEX 2.3.0; a timeout of 300 secs was set for each run. As benchmarks, we used the following problems.

Access Policy Control. The first benchmark is a slight modification of Example 1 with an additional TBox axiom *Blacklisted* $\sqsubseteq$ *Unauthorized*. We have run experiments in two settings: (a) with complete support families and (b) with support families obtained under different restrictions, viz. bounded size and cardinality. We considered three ABoxes with 40, 100 and 1000 staff members, respectively, and generated facts of the form $hasowner(p_i, s_i)$, and such that $Staff(s_i), Project(p_i) \in \mathcal{A}$. For the setting where complete support families were computed, we used ABoxes with 100 and 1000 staff members, respectively. For the incomplete scenario we used an ABox with 40 staff members. In each data set, 30% of staff members are unauthorized and 20% are blacklisted. Instances vary on facts $hasowner(p_i, s_i)$. For each s_i, p_i s.t. $Staff(s_i)$, $Project(p_i) \in \mathcal{A}$, a fact $hasowner(p_i, s_i)$ is added to the program with probability $p/100$, where p ranges from 20 to 90 for the complete setting and from 5 to 35 for the incomplete one.

The total average running times (including support set computation and timeouts) for computing the first repair answer set for these settings are shown in Table 2. The number of timeouts per each run is reported in brackets. The columns for the incomplete case show the restriction on support sets we used in their generation, viz. size (resp. number) of support sets bounded by 2 resp. unlimited; the latter means that in fact all support sets were computed, but the system is not aware of the completeness.

We exploit partial completeness for the number restriction case, i.e. if no more support sets for an atom are computed and the number limit is not yet reached, then the support family for the considered atom is complete.

Open Street Map. For the second benchmark, we added rules on top of the ontology developed in the MyITS project,[3] which enhanced personalized route planning with

---

[3] http://www.kr.tuwien.ac.at/research/projects/myits/

Table 2. Policy benchmark results (30 runs per p; time in sec. (#timeouts) for 1st rep. AS)

p	Complete supp. family		p	Support set size restricted		Support set number restricted	
	$\mathcal{A}_{100}$	$\mathcal{A}_{1000}$		sizelim=2	sizelim=∞	numlim=2	numlim=∞
					$\mathcal{A}_{40}$		
20 (30)	2.28 (0)	13.89 (0)	5 (30)	21.09 (0)	4.35 (2)	2.70 (2)	4.30 (2)
30 (30)	2.27 (0)	13.93 (0)	10 (30)	26.62 (5)	5.50 (3)	6.64 (3)	5.49 (3)
40 (30)	2.28 (0)	14.02 (0)	15 (30)	30.20 (12)	7.53 (5)	3.25 (10)	7.56 (5)
50 (30)	2.29 (0)	14.33 (0)	20 (30)	48.99 (5)	5.21 (4)	3.07 (4)	5.38 (4)
60 (30)	2.28 (0)	14.59 (0)	25 (30)	37.37 (16)	26.41 (6)	4.48 (14)	26.39 (6)
70 (30)	2.29 (0)	15.08 (0)	30 (30)	19.33 (22)	38.75 (6)	6.74 (12)	40.41 (6)
80 (30)	2.30 (0)	15.59 (0)	35 (30)	16.32 (26)	49.41 (10)	5.23 (17)	51.47 (10)
90 (30)	2.30 (0)	16.23 (0)					

Table 3. OpenStreetMap benchmark results (30 runs per p; time in sec. (#timeouts) for 1st rep. AS)

p	Complete supp. family	Support set size restricted			Support set number restricted		
		sizelim=1	sizelim=2	sizelim=∞	numlim=1	numlim=2	numlim=∞
10 (30)	10.08 (0)	13.87 (0)	13.22 (0)	14.19 (0)	13.82 (0)	13.98 (0)	13.89 (0)
20 (30)	9.36 (0)	23.38 (0)	22.82 (0)	20.32 (1)	20.32 (1)	20.19 (1)	20.29 (1)
30 (30)	9.13 (0)	27.92 (1)	27.48 (1)	20.36 (3)	20.39 (3)	20.18 (3)	20.22 (3)
40 (30)	9.53 (0)	54.63 (3)	54.36 (3)	23.34 (10)	23.31 (10)	23.42 (10)	23.51 (10)
50 (30)	9.62 (0)	76.08 (1)	76.18 (1)	19.61 (13)	19.48 (13)	19.48 (13)	19.64 (13)

semantic information. The ontology contains 4601 axioms, where 406 axioms are in the TBox and 4195 are in the ABox. The fragment $\mathcal{O}$ relevant for our scenario and the rules P are shown in Figure 4. Intuitively, $\mathcal{O}$ states that building features located inside private areas are not publicly accessible and a covered bus stop is a bus stop with a roof. The rules P check that public stations do not lack public access, using CWA on private areas.

We used the method in [12] to extract data from the OpenStreetMap,[4] and we constructed an ABox $\mathcal{A}$ by extracting the sets of all bus stops (285) and leisure areas (682) of the Irish city Cork, as well as *isLocatedInside* relations between them (9) (i.e., bus stops located in leisure areas). As the data has been gathered by many volunteers, chances of inaccuracies may be high (e.g. imprecise gps data). As data about roofed bus stops and private areas is not available yet, we randomly made 80% of the bus stops roofed and 60% of leisure areas private. Finally, we added for each bs_i s.t. *isLocatedInside*$(bs_i, la_j) \in \mathcal{A}$ the fact $busstop(bs_i)$ to $\mathcal{P}$ with probability $p/100$. Some instances are inconsistent since in our data set there are roofed bus stops, located inside private areas.

The results for both complete and incomplete support families are shown in Table 3.

Discussion of Results. As expected, using complete support families works for both settings well in practice. For the policy benchmark, allowing up to 2 support sets is more effective than bounding the size by 2. This is due to exploitation of partial completeness for the case when the number of support sets is limited. Moreover, there are just few support sets for each DL-atom in this scenario; however almost all support sets have size larger than 2. Thus many random guesses on potential repair candidates need to be done, which is witnessed by jumps in the runtime for $p = 40$ to $p = 80$. If both size and number of support sets are unlimited, the obtained results are practically the same.

---

[4] http://www.openstreetmap.org/

$$\mathcal{O} = \left\{ \begin{array}{l} (1) \; BuildingFeature \sqcap \exists isLocatedInside.Private \sqsubseteq NoPublicAccess \\ (2) \; BusStop \sqcap Roofed \sqsubseteq CoveredBusStop \end{array} \right\}$$

$$\mathcal{P} = \left\{ \begin{array}{l} (9) \; publicstation(X) \leftarrow DL[BusStop \uplus busstop; \; CoveredBusStop](X); \\ \qquad \quad not \; DL[; \; Private](X); \\ (10) \perp \leftarrow DL[BuildingFeature \uplus publicstation; \; NoPublicAccess](X), \\ \qquad \quad publicstation(X). \end{array} \right\}$$

Fig. 4. DL-program Π over OpenStreetMap ontology

A similar behavior is observed for the OpenStreetMap scenario. Even if the ontology is big, runtimes do not differ significantly from the Policy example. This is due to liberal safety [6], which effectively restricts the reasoning only to relevant individuals. We can again see that bounding the number of support sets works better; however, there are no jumps for bounded support set size. This is because a considerable number of support sets has size at most 2, and they guide the repair search effectively.

7   Related Work and Conclusion

We considered computing repair answer sets of DL-programs over $\mathcal{EL}$ ontologies, for which we generalized the support set approach [10; 8] for $DL\text{-}Lite_A$ to work with incomplete families of supports sets; this advance is needed since in $\mathcal{EL}$ complete support families can be large or even infinite. We discussed how to generate support families, by exploiting query rewriting over ontologies to datalog [19; 23; 25], which is in contrast to [10; 8] where TBox classification is invoked. We presented an algorithm to compute deletion repair answer sets which trades answer completeness for scalability (a variant is complete); a declarative implementation shows very promising results.

As for related work, our DL-program repair is related to ABox cleaning [20; 24]. However, the latter differs in various aspects: it aims at restoring consistency of an *inconsistent* ontology by deleting $\subseteq$-minimal sets of assertions (i.e., computing $\subseteq$-maximal deletion repairs); we deal with inconsistency incurred on top of a consistent ontology, by arbitrary (non-monotonic) rules which access it with an interface. Furthermore, we must consider multiple ABoxes at once (via updates), and use $\mathcal{EL}$ instead of $DL\text{-}Lite$. Refining our algorithm to compute $\subseteq$-maximal deletion repairs is possible.

Our support sets are related to solutions of abduction problems for $\mathcal{EL}$ [2], and correspond in the ground case to support sets for query answering over first-order rewritable ontologies [3]; nonground computation naturally links to TBox classification [17]. Abduction had been studied for $DL\text{-}Lite$ in [5] and for datalog e.g. in [14; 16]. The use of incomplete support families for DL-atoms is related in spirit to approximate inconsistency-tolerant reasoning on DLs using restricted support sets [3]; however, we target repair computation while [3] targets inference from all repairs.

As for implementation, no comparable system exists. The DReW system [27] can evaluate DL-programs over $\mathcal{EL}$ ontologies after transforming the input to datalog, where DL-atoms are replaced by datalog rewritings; the latter amount to succinct representations of support sets. However, DReW can not handle inconsistencies and how to inject repairs efficiently is non-obvious (naive attempts fail).

It remains an issue for further research to identify classes of $\mathcal{EL}$ ontologies for which support sets have a benign structure and can be effectively computed, and on the other side to extend the work to other members of the $\mathcal{EL}$ family. To increase usability in practice, real world ontologies need to be analyzed to develop good heuristics and strategies for computing incomplete support families. Another possible research direction is computing specific types of repairs, e.g. by bounded deletion or addition [9].

References

1. Baader, F., Brandt, S., Lutz, C.: Pushing the $\mathcal{EL}$ envelope. In: Kaelbling, L.P., Saffiotti, A. (eds.) IJCAI, pp. 364–369. Prof. Book Center (2005)
2. Bienvenu, M.: Complexity of abduction in the $\mathcal{EL}$ family of lightweight description logics. In: KR Proc., pp. 220–230. AAAI Press (2008)
3. Bienvenu, M., Rosati, R.: New inconsistency-tolerant semantics for robust ontology-based data access. In: DL CEUR Workshop Proc., vol. 1014, pp. 53–64. CEUR-WS.org (2013)
4. Bonatti, P.A., Faella, M., Sauro, L.: $\mathcal{EL}$ with default attributes and overriding. In: Patel-Schneider, P.F., Pan, Y., Hitzler, P., Mika, P., Zhang, L., Pan, J.Z., Horrocks, I., Glimm, B. (eds.) ISWC 2010, Part I. LNCS, vol. 6496, pp. 64–79. Springer, Heidelberg (2010)
5. Borgida, A., Calvanese, D., Rodriguez-Muro, M.: Explanation in $DL\text{-}Lite$. In: DL CEUR Workshop Proc., vol. 353. CEUR-WS.org (2008)
6. Eiter, T., Fink, M., Krennwallner, T., Redl, C.: Liberal safety for answer set programs with external sources. In: AAAI, pp. 267-275. AAAI Press (2013)
7. Eiter, T., Fink, M., Krennwallner, T., Redl, C., Schüller, P.: Efficient HEX-program evaluation based on unfounded sets. J. of Artif. Intell. Res. 49, 269–321 (2014)
8. Eiter, T., Fink, M., Redl, C., Stepanova, D.: Exploiting support sets for answer set programs with external computations. In: AAAI (to appear, 2014)
9. Eiter, T., Fink, M., Stepanova, D.: Data repair of inconsistent DL-programs. In: IJCAI, pp. 869-876. IJCAI/AAAI (2013)
10. Eiter, T., Fink, M., Stepanova, D.: Towards practical deletion repair of inconsistent DL-programs. In: ECAI 2014 (to appear, 2014)
11. Eiter, T., Ianni, G., Lukasiewicz, T., Schindlauer, R., Tompits, H.: Combining answer set programming with description logics for the semantic web. Artif. Intell. 172(12-13), 1495–1539 (2008)
12. Eiter, T., Schneider, P., Simkus, M., Xiao, G.: Using *openstreetmap* data to create benchmarks for ontology-based query answering systems. In: ORE 2014 (to appear, 2014)
13. Gardiner, T., Tsarkov, D., Horrocks, I.: Framework for an automated comparison of description logic reasoners. In: Cruz, I., Decker, S., Allemang, D., Preist, C., Schwabe, D., Mika, P., Uschold, M., Aroyo, L.M. (eds.) ISWC 2006. LNCS, vol. 4273, pp. 654–667. Springer, Heidelberg (2006)
14. Gottlob, G., Pichler, R., Wei, F.: Efficient datalog abduction through bounded treewidth. In: AAAI, pp. 1626–1631. AAAI Press (2007)
15. Hansen, P., Lutz, C., Seylan, I., Wolter, F.: Query rewriting under $\mathcal{EL}$-TBoxes:efficient algorithms In: DL (to appear, 2014)
16. Hermann, M., Pichler, R.: Counting complexity of minimal cardinality and minimal weight abduction. In: Hölldobler, S., Lutz, C., Wansing, H. (eds.) JELIA 2008. LNCS (LNAI), vol. 5293, pp. 206–218. Springer, Heidelberg (2008)
17. Kazakov, Y., Krötzsch, M., Simancik, F.: The incredible ELK. J. of Autom. Reason, 1–61 (2013)
18. Kontchakov, R., Lutz, C., Toman, D., Wolter, F., Zakharyaschev, M.: The combined approach to query answering in $DL\text{-}Lite$. In: KR Proc., pp. 247–257. AAAI Press (2010)

19. Lutz, C., Toman, D., Wolter, F.: Conjunctive query answering in $\mathcal{EL}$ using a database system. In: OWLED. CEUR Workshop Proc., vol. 432. CEUR-WS.org (2008)
20. Masotti, G., Rosati, R., Ruzzi, M.: Practical abox cleaning in $DL\text{-}Lite$ (progress report). In: DL. CEUR Workshop Proc., vol. 745. CEUR-WS.org (2011)
21. Motik, B., Rosati, R.: Reconciling Description Logics and Rules. J. of the ACM 57(5), 1–62 (2010)
22. Pérez-Urbina, H., Motik, B., Horrocks, I.: Tractable query answering and rewriting under description logic constraints. J. of Applied Logic 8(2), 186–209 (2010)
23. Rosati, R.: On conjunctive query answering in $\mathcal{EL}$. In: DL CEUR Workshop Proc., vol. 250. CEUR-WS.org (2007)
24. Rosati, R., Ruzzi, M., Graziosi, M., Masotti, G.: Evaluation of techniques for inconsistency handling in OWL 2 QL ontologies. In: Cudré-Mauroux, P., et al. (eds.) ISWC 2012, Part II. LNCS, vol. 7650, pp. 337–349. Springer, Heidelberg (2012)
25. Stefanoni, G., Motik, B., Horrocks, I.: Small datalog query rewritings for $\mathcal{EL}$. In: DL CEUR Workshop Proc., vol. 846, CEUR-WS.org (2012)
26. Stuckenschmidt, H., Parent, C., Spaccapietra, S. (eds.): Modular Ontologies. LNCS, vol. 5445. Springer, Heidelberg (2009)
27. Xiao, G., Eiter, T., Heymans, S.: The DReW system for nonmonotonic DL-programs. In: CSWS 2012 and CWSC 2012, pp. 383–389. Springer, New York (2013)
28. Zhao, Y., Pan, J.Z., Ren, Y.: Implementing and evaluating a rule-based approach to querying regular $\mathcal{EL}$+ ontologies. In: HIS (3), pp. 493–498. IEEE Computer Society (2009)
29. Eiter, T., Ianni, G., Lukasiewicz, T., Schindlauer, R., Tompits, H.: Combining answer set programming with description logics for the Semantic Web. Artif. Intell. 172(12-13), 1495–1539 (2008)

A Prioritized Assertional-Based Revision for DL-Lite Knowledge Bases

Salem Benferhat[1], Zied Bouraoui[1], Odile Papini[2], and Eric Würbel[3]

[1] CRIL-CNRS UMR 8188, Univ Artois, France
{benferhat,bouraoui}@cril.univ-artois.fr
[2] LSIS-CNRS UMR 7296, Univ Aix Marseille, France
odile.papini@univ-amu.fr
[3] LSIS-CNRS UMR 7296, Univ Toulon, France
wurbel@univ-tln.fr

Abstract. *DL-Lite* is a powerful and tractable family of description logics. One of the fundamental issue in this area is the evolution or revision of knowledge bases. To this end, many approaches are recently developed for revising flat *DL-Lite* knowledge bases. This paper investigates "Prioritized Removed Sets Revision" (PRSR) in *DL-Lite* framework where the assertions or data are prioritized (for instance in case where the data are provided by multiple sources having different reliability levels). PRSR approach is based on inconsistency minimization in order to restore consistency where the minimality refers to the lexicographic criterion and not to the set inclusion one. We study different forms of incorporated information: an assertion, a positive inclusion axiom or a negative inclusion axiom. We show that under some conditions PRSR can be achieved in polynomial time. We give logical properties of the proposed operators in terms of satisfaction of Hansson's postulates rephrased in *DL-Lite* framework. We finally show how to use the notion of hitting sets for computing prioritized removed sets.

1 Introduction

In the last years, there has been an increasing use of ontologies in many application areas. Description Logics (DLs) have been recognized as a powerful formalism for both representing and reasoning about ontologies. A DL knowledge base is built upon two distinct components: A terminological base (called *TBox*), representing generic knowledge about the application domain, and an assertional base (called *ABox*), containing the assertional facts (i.e. individuals or constants) that instantiate terminological knowledge. Recently, a lot of attention was given to *DL-Lite* [8], a family of lightweight DLs specifically tailored for applications that use huge volumes of data, like Web applications, for which query answering is the most important reasoning task. *DL-Lite* guarantees a very low computational complexity of the reasoning process.

DLs knowledge base evolution gave rise to an increasing interest (e.g. [10,17]) and often concerns the situation where new information should be incorporated, while ensuring the consistency of the result. Such problem is well-known as a belief revision problem. It has been defined as knowledge change and has been characterized for instance by the well-known AGM postulates [1] for the revision of belief sets, or by the Hansson's postulates [11,13] for the revision of belief bases. Several works have

E. Fermé and J. Leite (Eds.): JELIA 2014, LNAI 8761, pp. 442–456, 2014.
© Springer International Publishing Switzerland 2014

been proposed for the revision of *DL-Lite* knowledge bases (e.g. [21,9,12]), and especially for the revision of the ABox, since *DL-Lite* has witnessed a well suitability for
Ontology-Based Data Access applications (OBDA). In such setting a TBox acts as being a schema used to reformulate raised queries in order to offer a better access to the
set of data stored in an ABox.

Recently, an assertional-based "Removed Sets Revision" (RSR) approach has been
proposed in [4] to revise *DL-Lite* knowledge bases. This approach is inspired from
belief base revision in propositional logic framework [23,16]. It is based on inconsistency minimization, and consists in determining the smallest subsets of assertions
which should be dropped from the current base in order to accept the new information
and restore consistency. Note that in this approach, the minimality is understood with
respect to cardinality and not with respect to set inclusion. The computation of the set
of minimal assertions responsible of conflicts can be performed in polynomial time.

In real word applications, data is often provided by several and potentially conflicting
sources. Their concatenation leads to a prioritized or a stratified ABox. This stratification generally results from two situations, as pointed out in [5]. The first one is when
each source provides its set of data without any priority between them, but there exists
a total pre-ordering between the sources, reflecting their reliability. The other situation
is when the sources are considered as equally reliable (i.e. having the same reliability
level), but there exists a preference ranking between the set of provided data according
to their level of certainty.

To illustrate this situation, let us give the following example, adapted from [9]. Let
K be a consistent knowledge base storing knowledge of an online newspaper collected
using RSS feeds or Web crawling. The terminological base of this newspapers is as
follows: wives are exactly those individuals who have husbands and some wives are
employed. The assertional base A comes from crawling three distinct Web sources A_1,
A_2 and A_3 where A_2 is more reliable than A_1 and A_1 is more reliable than A_3. A_1
says that Mary is a wife, A_2 says that Mary is employed and A_3 says that Mary's
husband is John. It is clear that connecting information issued from A_1, A_2 and A_3
gives a prioritized assertional base. Assume that we found out an information to be
incorporated into the knowledge base, which states that singles cannot be husbands.
One can easily check that this new information not conflicting with the old ones stored
in the knowledge base. Assume now that we found out another information saying that
John is now single. One can verifies that this new information conflicts with the previous
one. An important question addressed here is : "how one can we revise the knowledge
base, while taking into account priorities between the assertions?".

The role of priorities in belief revision is very important and it has been largely studied in the literature, in the case where knowledge bases are encoded in a propositional
logic setting (e.g. [6]). The notion of priorities in DLs is used in (e.g.[19]) to deal with
defaults terminology while assuming that the ABox is completely sure. In [18] priorities are used to deal with inconsistencies in DL knowledge bases. In [17] the notion of
priority has been used for ontology matching. Note that in [17] priorities are used on
the set of concepts name and not on formulas. However, as far as we know, revising of
prioritized assertional-based in *DL-Lite* knowledge bases has not been addressed so far.

This paper goes one step further in the definition of assertional-based RSR and investigates revision when priorities attached to assertions are available. This extension is based on the notion of Prioritized Removed Sets proposed in [3] for revising a set of prioritized propositional formulas. The minimality in revision with prioritized removed set refers to the lexicographic criterion and not to the set inclusion one. In this paper, we study revision for different forms of input: an ABox assertion or a TBox axiom. We define prioritized removed sets in *DL-Lite* framework. The main contribution of this work is to analyze the different scenarios of revision. In particular, we show that for some form of conflicts and some kinds of inputs, the revision process can be achieved in polynomial time. In the general case, we show that the number of prioritized removed sets is bounded and we propose an algorithm for computing them using the notion of hitting sets.

The rest of this paper is organized as follows. Section 2 gives brief preliminaries on *DL-Lite* logic. Section 3 investigates prioritized assertional-based removed sets revision within the framework of *DL-Lite* and gives the logical properties of the proposed operators. Section 4 provides algorithms for computing the prioritized removed sets through the use of hitting sets. We show that in particular cases revision process can be performed in a polynomial time. Section 5 concludes this paper.

2 Preliminaries

In this paper, we only consider $DL\text{-}Lite_R$, which underlies $OWL2\text{-}QL$. However, results of this work can be easily generalized for others DL-Lite logics (see [2] for more details about the *DL-Lite* family).

Syntax A *DL-Lite* knowledge base $\mathcal{K}=\langle \mathcal{T}, \mathcal{A} \rangle$ is built upon a set of atomic concepts (i.e. unary predicates), a set of atomic roles (i.e. binary predicates) and a set of individuals (i.e. constants). Complex concepts and roles are formed as follows:

$$B \longrightarrow A|\exists R \quad C \longrightarrow B|\neg B$$
$$R \longrightarrow P|P^- \quad E \longrightarrow R|\neg R$$

where A (*resp.* P) is an atomic concept (*resp.* role). B (*resp.* C) are called basic (*resp.* complex) concepts and roles R (*resp.* E) are called basic (*resp.* complex) roles. The TBox $\mathcal{T}$ consists of a finite set of *inclusion axioms between concepts* of the form: $B \sqsubseteq C$ and *inclusion axioms between roles* of the form: $R \sqsubseteq E$. The ABox $\mathcal{A}$ consists of a finite set of *membership assertions* on atomic concepts and on atomic roles of the form: $A(a_i)$, $P(a_i, a_j)$, where a_i and a_j are individuals. For the sake of simplicity, in the rest of this paper, when there is no ambiguity we simply use *DL-Lite* instead of $DL\text{-}Lite_R$.

Semantics The *DL-Lite* semantics is given by an interpretation $I = (\Delta, \cdot^I)$ which consists of a nonempty domain Δ and an interpretation function $\cdot^I$. The function $\cdot^I$ assigns to each individual a an element $a^I \in \Delta^I$, to each concept C a subset $C^I \subseteq \Delta^I$ and to each role R a binary relation $R^I \subseteq \Delta^I \times \Delta^I$ over Δ^I. Moreover, the interpretation function $\cdot^I$ is extended for all constructs of $DL\text{-}Lite_R$. For instance: $(\neg B)^I = \Delta^I \setminus B^I$, $(\exists R)^I = \{x \in \Delta^I | \exists y \in \Delta^I \ such that \ (x, y) \in R^I\}$ and $(P^-)^I = \{(y, x) \in \Delta^I \times$

$\Delta^I|(x, y) \in P^I\}$. Concerning the TBox, we say that I satisfies a concept (*resp.* role) inclusion axiom, denoted by $I \models B \sqsubseteq C$ (*resp.* $I \models R \sqsubseteq E$), iff $B^I \subseteq C^I$ (*resp.* $R^I \subseteq E^I$). Concerning the ABox, we say that I satisfies a concept (*resp.* role) membership assertion, denoted by $I \models A(a_i)$ (*resp.* $I \models P(a_i, a_j)$), iff $a_i^I \in A^I$ (*resp.* $(a_i^I, a_j^I) \in P^I$). Note that we only consider *DL-Lite* with unique name assumption. Finally, an interpretation I is said to satisfy a knowledge base $\mathcal{K} = \langle \mathcal{T}, \mathcal{A} \rangle$ iff I satisfies every axiom in $\mathcal{T}$ and every axiom in $\mathcal{A}$. Such interpretation is said to be a model of $\mathcal{K}$.

Incoherence and inconsistency Two kinds of inconsistency can be distinguished in DL-based knowledge bases: incoherence and inconsistency [4]. The former is considered as a kind of inconsistency in the TBox, i.e. the terminological part, of a knowledge base. The latter is the classical inconsistency for knowledge bases. Namely, a knowledge base is said to be inconsistent iff it does not admit any model and it is said to be incoherent if there exists at least a non-satisfiable concept, namely for each interpretation I which is a model of $\mathcal{T}$, we have $C^I = \emptyset$.

In *DL-Lite* a TBox $\mathcal{T} = \{PIs, NIs\}$ can be viewed as composed of positive inclusion axioms, denoted by (PIs), and negative inclusion axioms, denoted by (NIs). PIs are of the form $B_1 \sqsubseteq B_2$ or $R_1 \sqsubseteq R_2$ and NIs are of the form $B_1 \sqsubseteq \neg B_2$ or $R_1 \sqsubseteq \neg R_2$. The negative closure of $\mathcal{T}$, denoted by $cln(\mathcal{T})$, performs interaction between PIs and NIs. It represents the propagation of the NIs using both PIs and NIs in the TBox. $cln(\mathcal{T})$ is obtained by using the following rules repeatedly until reaching a fix point (see [8] for more details):

- all *NIs* in $\mathcal{T}$ are in $cln(\mathcal{T})$;
- if $B_1 \sqsubseteq B_2$ is in $\mathcal{T}$ and $B_2 \sqsubseteq \neg B_3$ or $B_3 \sqsubseteq \neg B_2$ is in $cln(\mathcal{T})$, then $B_1 \sqsubseteq \neg B_3$ is in $cln(\mathcal{T})$;
- if $R_1 \sqsubseteq R_2$ is in $\mathcal{T}$ and $\exists R_2 \sqsubseteq \neg B$ or $B \sqsubseteq \neg \exists R_2$ is in $cln(\mathcal{T})$, then $\exists R_1 \sqsubseteq \neg B$ is in $cln(\mathcal{T})$;
- if $R_1 \sqsubseteq R_2$ is in $\mathcal{T}$ and $\exists R_2^- \sqsubseteq \neg B$ or $B \sqsubseteq \neg \exists R_2^-$ is in $cln(\mathcal{T})$, then $\exists R_1^- \sqsubseteq \neg B$ is in $cln(\mathcal{T})$;
- if $R_1 \sqsubseteq R_2$ is in $\mathcal{T}$ and $R_2 \sqsubseteq \neg R_3$ or $R_3 \sqsubseteq \neg R_2$ is in $cln(\mathcal{T})$, then $R_1 \sqsubseteq \neg R_3$ is in $cln(\mathcal{T})$;
- if one of the assertions $\exists R \sqsubseteq \neg \exists R$, $\exists R^- \sqsubseteq \neg \exists R^-$ or $R \sqsubseteq \neg R$ is in $cln(\mathcal{T})$ then all three such assertions are in $cln(\mathcal{T})$.

An important property has been established in [8] for consistency checking in *DL-Lite*. Formally, $\mathcal{K}$ is consistent if and only if $\langle cln(\mathcal{T}), \mathcal{A} \rangle$ is consistent [8].

3   PRSR for DL-Lite Knowledge Bases

In this section, we investigate *DL-Lite* prioritized knowledge base revision using a lexicographical strategy based on inconsistency minimization, well-known as Prioritized Removed Sets Revision (PRSR) [3], and previously defined in a classical logic setting.

3.1 Conflict Sets

Let $\mathcal{L}$ be a *DL-Lite* description language, presented in section 2 and $\mathcal{K}=\langle \mathcal{T}, \mathcal{A}\rangle$ be a *DL-Lite* prioritized knowledge base expressed in $\mathcal{L}$. We assume $\mathcal{T}$ is coherent and not stratified. On contrast, the ABox is stratified i.e. partitioned into n strata, $\mathcal{A}=\mathcal{A}_1 \cup \cdots \cup \mathcal{A}_n$ such that the assertions in $\mathcal{A}_i$ have the same level of priority and have higher priority than the ones in $\mathcal{A}_j$ where $j > i$. We assume that $\mathcal{K}$ is consistent and let us denote by N a new consistent information to be accepted. The presence of this new information may lead to inconsistency according to the content of the TBox and the nature of the input information. Within the $DL\text{-}Lite_R$ language, N may be an assertions, a positive inclusion axiom (PI) or a negative inclusion axiom (NI). In some cases N may have a desirable interaction with $\mathcal{K}$. Clearly, according to [8], every *DL-Lite* knowledge base $\mathcal{K}$ with only PIs in its TBox is always satisfiable (consequence of Lemma 7 in [8]). However when the TBox $\mathcal{T}$ contains NI axioms then N may have an undesirable interaction with $\mathcal{K}$, which leads to inconsistency. In this case, a natural question for revising $\mathcal{K}$ is: which of the TBox axioms or ABox assertions should be removed first with respect to some ABox, since a TBox may be incoherent but never inconsistent. We remind the Calvanese *et al.* result [9].

Lemma 1. *Let* $\mathcal{K} = \langle \mathcal{T}, \mathcal{A}\rangle$ *be a DL-Lite knowledge base. If* $\mathcal{A} = \emptyset$ *then* $\mathcal{K}$ *is consistent. If* $\mathcal{K}$ *is inconsistent, then there exists a subset* $\mathcal{A}' \subseteq \mathcal{A}$ *with at most two elements, such that* $\mathcal{T} \cup \mathcal{A}'$ *is inconsistent.*

In this paper, revision leads to ignoring some assertions, namely we give a priority to the TBox over ABox. Furthermore we only focus on inconsistency and assume that $\mathcal{T}$ is coherent and not stratified. This is not a restriction. This particular case can be handled outside the revision problem considered in this paper. Recall that this choice is motivated by the fact that *DL-Lite* framework was especially tailored for Ontology-Based based Access setting, in which the TBox is needed to access to the data stored in the ABox. Let $\mathcal{K}$ be an inconsistent knowledge base, we define the notion of conflict as a minimal inconsistent subset of $\mathcal{A}$, more formally:

Definition 1. *Let* $\mathcal{K} = \langle \mathcal{T}, \mathcal{A}\rangle$ *be an inconsistent DL-Lite knowledge base. A conflict C is a set of membership assertions such that: i)* $C \subseteq \mathcal{A}$, *ii)* $\langle \mathcal{T}, C\rangle$ *is inconsistent, iii)* $\forall C', C' \subset C, \mathcal{T} \cup C'$ *is consistent.*

We denote by $\mathcal{C}(\mathcal{K})$ the collection of conflicts in $\mathcal{K}$. Since $\mathcal{K}$ is assumed to be finite, if $\mathcal{K}$ is inconsistent then $\mathcal{C}(\mathcal{K}) \neq \emptyset$ is also finite.

Within the *DL-Lite* framework, in order to restore consistency while keeping new information, the Prioritized Removed Sets Revision strategy removes exactly one assertion in each conflict, by choosing the minimum number of assertions from $\mathcal{A}_1$, then the minimum number of assertions in $\mathcal{A}_2$, and so on. Using lexicographic criterion instead of set inclusion one reduces the set of potential conflicts. Taking the stratification of the $ABox$ into account has not been considered before for revising or repairing *DL-Lite* knowledge bases (*e.g.* [15,7]).

We first define a lexicographic preference relation between subsets of the ABox.

Definition 2. *Let X and X' be two subsets of $\mathcal{A} = \mathcal{A}_1 \cup \ldots \cup \mathcal{A}_n$. X is strictly preferred to X', denoted by $X <_{lex} X'$ if and only if i) $\exists i, 1 \leq i \leq n$, $|X \cap \mathcal{A}_i| < |X' \cap \mathcal{A}_i|$, ii) $\forall j, 1 \leq j < i, |X \cap \mathcal{A}_j| = |X' \cap \mathcal{A}_j|$.*

Example 1. Let $\mathcal{A}$ be a stratified ABox $\mathcal{A} = \mathcal{A}_1 \cup \mathcal{A}_2 \cup \mathcal{A}_3$ where $\mathcal{A}_1 = \{B_1(a)\}$, $\mathcal{A}_2 = \{B_2(b)\}$ and $\mathcal{A}_3 = \{B_3(a), B_3(b)\}$. Let $X = \{B_3(a), B_3(b)\}$ and $X' = \{B_3(a), B_2(b)\}$ be two subsets of $\mathcal{A}$. We have $X <_{lex} X'$.

Definition 3. *let X and X' be two subsets of $\mathcal{A}$. X is at least equally preferred[1] to X', denoted by $X \leq_{lex} X'$ if and only if : i) $\exists i, 1 \leq i \leq n$, $|X \cap \mathcal{A}_i| \leq |X' \cap \mathcal{A}_i|$, ii) $\forall j, 1 \leq j < i, |X \cap \mathcal{A}_j| = |X' \cap \mathcal{A}_j|$.*

We now more formally present PRSR according to the nature of the input information.

3.2 Revision by a Membership Assertion

We first consider the case where N is a membership assertion. It corresponds to the revision by a fact or by an observation. In what follows, $\mathcal{K} \cup \{N\}$ denotes $\langle \mathcal{T}, \mathcal{A} \cup \{N\} \rangle$ where $\mathcal{A}$ is a prioritized ABox. The following definition introduces the concept of prioritized removed set.

Definition 4. *Let $\mathcal{K} = \langle \mathcal{T}, \mathcal{A} \rangle$ be a consistent stratified knowledge base and N be a membership assertion. A prioritized removed set, denoted by X, is a set of membership assertions such that i) $X \subseteq \mathcal{A}$, ii) $\langle \mathcal{T}, (\mathcal{A} \backslash X) \cup \{N\} \rangle$ is consistent, iii) $\forall X' \subseteq \mathcal{A}$, if $\langle \mathcal{T}, (\mathcal{A} \backslash X') \cup \{N\} \rangle$ is consistent then $X \leq_{lex} X'$.*

We denote by $\mathcal{PR}(\mathcal{K} \cup \{N\})$ the set of prioritized removed sets of $\mathcal{K} \cup \{N\}$. If $\mathcal{K} \cup \{N\}$ is consistent then $\mathcal{PR}(\mathcal{K} \cup \{N\}) = \emptyset$.

Proposition 1. *Let $\mathcal{K}$ be a consistent stratified knowledge base and N be a membership assertion. If $\mathcal{K} \cup \{N\}$ is inconsistent then $|\mathcal{PR}(\mathcal{K} \cup \{N\})| = 1$.*

Proof. Suppose that there are two prioritized removed sets X and X' such that $X \neq X'$. By Definition 4, $X \subseteq \mathcal{A}$, $X' \subseteq \mathcal{A}$, $X =_{lex} X'$ and $\forall C \in \mathcal{C}(\mathcal{K} \cup \{N\})$, $C \cap X \neq \emptyset$ and $C \cap X' \neq \emptyset$. Moreover $C \cap \{N\} \neq \emptyset$, therefore $|C \cap \mathcal{A}| = 3$ which contradicts lemma 1.   □

Definition 5. *Let $\mathcal{K} = \langle \mathcal{T}, \mathcal{A} \rangle$ be a consistent stratified knowledge base and N be a membership assertion. The revised knowledge base $\mathcal{K} \circ_{PRSR} N$ is defined by $\mathcal{K} \circ_{PRSR} N = \langle \mathcal{T}, \mathcal{A} \circ_{PRSR} N \rangle$ where $\mathcal{A} \circ_{PRSR} N = (\mathcal{A} \backslash X) \cup \{N\}$ with $X \in \mathcal{PR}(\mathcal{K} \cup \{N\})$.*

When N is a membership assertion and the ABox is prioritized, PRSR gives the same result as RSR[4] in the flat case (where all the assertions in the ABox have the same priority). More formally:

Proposition 2. *Let $\mathcal{K}$ be a consistent stratified knowledge base and N be a membership assertion. $\mathcal{K} \circ_{PRSR} N = \mathcal{K} \circ_{RSR} N$.*

---

[1] X is equally preferred to X', denoted by $X =_{lex} X'$, iff $X \leq_{lex} X'$ and $X' \leq_{lex} X$.

Proof (Sketch of proof). The proof is immediate. It follows from Proposition 1, since $|\mathcal{PR}(\mathcal{K} \cup \{N\})| = 1$. $\qquad\qquad\qquad\qquad\qquad\qquad\qquad\qquad\qquad\qquad\qquad\qquad\qquad\qquad$ □

Example 2. Let $\mathcal{K}=\langle \mathcal{T}, \mathcal{A} \rangle$ be a consistent stratified knowledge base such that $\mathcal{T}$ $=\{B_1 \sqsubseteq B_2, B_2 \sqsubseteq \neg B_3, B_3 \sqsubseteq \neg B_4\}$ and $\mathcal{A} = \mathcal{A}_1 \cup \mathcal{A}_2 \cup \mathcal{A}_3$, where $\mathcal{A}_1 = \{B_1(a)\}$ $\mathcal{A}_2 = \{B_3(b)\}$, $\mathcal{A}_3 = \{B_4(a)\}$. Let $N=B_3(a)$. Then $\mathcal{K} \cup \{N\}$ is inconsistent. By Definition 1, $\mathcal{C}(\mathcal{K} \cup \{N\}) = \{\{B_1(a), B_3(a)\}, \{B_3(a), B_4(a)\}\}$. Hence, by Definition 4, $\mathcal{PR}(\mathcal{K} \cup \{N\}) = \{\{B_1(a), B_4(a)\}\}$. Therefore $\mathcal{A} \circ_{PRSR} N = \{B_3(b), B_3(a)\}$.

As detailed in [4], computing the set of conflicts is polynomial. Moreover when the input is a membership assertion, as illustrated in the above example, Proposition 1 states that there is only one prioritized removed set, which is computed in polynomial time as shown in Section 4.

3.3   Revision by a Positive or a Negative Axiom

We now consider the case where the input N is a PI axiom or a NI axiom. In this case, $\mathcal{K} \cup \{N\}$ denotes $\langle \mathcal{T} \cup \{N\}, \mathcal{A} \rangle$.

Definition 6. *Let* $\mathcal{K}=\langle \mathcal{T}, \mathcal{A} \rangle$ *be a consistent stratified knowledge base, and N be a PI or a NI axiom. A prioritized removed set, denoted by X, is a set of assertions such that i)* $X \subseteq \mathcal{A}$, *ii)* $\langle \mathcal{T} \cup \{N\}, (\mathcal{A} \backslash X) \rangle$ *is consistent and iii)* $\forall X' \subseteq \mathcal{A}$, *if* $\langle \mathcal{T} \cup \{N\}, (\mathcal{A} \backslash X') \rangle$ *is consistent then* $X \leq_{lex} X'$.

Let us point out that Definition 6 is similar to Definition 4, except that new information is not added to the ABox but to the TBox. However, the revision process still considers the TBox as a stable knowledge. Therefore, in order to restore consistency, assertional elements should be removed. We denote again by $\mathcal{PR}(\mathcal{K} \cup \{N\})$ the set of prioritized removed sets of $\mathcal{K} \cup \{N\}$.

Example 3. Let $\mathcal{K}=\langle \mathcal{T}, \mathcal{A} \rangle$ be a consistent stratified knowledge base such that $\mathcal{T}=\{B_1 \sqsubseteq B_2, B_3 \sqsubseteq \neg B_4\}$ and $\mathcal{A} = \mathcal{A}_1 \cup \mathcal{A}_2 \cup \mathcal{A}_3$, where $\mathcal{A}_1 = \{B_1(a)\}$ $\mathcal{A}_2 = \{B_2(b)\}$, $\mathcal{A}_3 = \{B_3(a), B_3(b)\}$. Let $N=B_2 \sqsubseteq \neg B_3$. Then $\mathcal{K} \cup \{N\}$ is inconsistent. $\mathcal{C}(\mathcal{K} \cup \{N\}) = \{\{B_1(a), B_3(a)\}, \{B_2(b), B_3(b)\}\}$, the removed sets [4] are $X_1 = \{B_1(a), B_2(b)\}$, $X_2 = \{B_1(a), B_3(b)\}$, $X_3 = \{B_3(a), B_2(b)\}$, $X_4 = \{B_3(a), B_3(b)\}$ however there is only one prioritized removed set X_4 as illustrated in table 1.

Table 1. One prioritized removed set

$\mathcal{A}_i$	$\|X_1 \cap \mathcal{A}_i\|$	$\|X_2 \cap \mathcal{A}_i\|$	$\|X_3 \cap \mathcal{A}_i\|$	$\|X_4 \cap \mathcal{A}_i\|$
$\mathcal{A}_3$	0	1	1	2
$\mathcal{A}_2$	1	0	1	0
$\mathcal{A}_1$	1	1	0	0

If the stratification of $\mathcal{A}$ is $\mathcal{A}_1=\{B_1(a), B_3(a)\}$, $\mathcal{A}_2=\{B_2(b)\}$ and $\mathcal{A}_3 = \{B_3(b)\}$, then there are two prioritized removed sets X_2 and X_4 as illustrated in table 2.

Table 2. Two prioritized removed sets

$\mathcal{A}_i$	$|X_1 \cap \mathcal{A}_i|$	$|X_2 \cap \mathcal{A}_i|$	$|X_3 \cap \mathcal{A}_i|$	$|X_4 \cap \mathcal{A}_i|$
$\mathcal{A}_3$	0	1	0	1
$\mathcal{A}_2$	1	0	1	0
$\mathcal{A}_1$	1	1	1	1

When the input is a membership assertion, then there exists exactly one prioritized removed set. However, when the input information is a NI or a PI axiom there may exist one or several prioritized removed sets, as illustrated in the previous example. The following proposition provides the condition of the existence of exactly one prioritized removed set.

Proposition 3. *If for each $C \in \mathcal{C}(\mathcal{K} \cup \{N\})$, there exists i and j, $i \neq j$, such that $C \cap \mathcal{A}_i \neq \emptyset$ and $C \cap \mathcal{A}_j \neq \emptyset$, then $|\mathcal{PR}(\mathcal{K} \cup \{N\})| = 1$.*

Proof. Suppose that there are two prioritized removed sets, X and X', with $X \neq X'$. By Definition 6 $X \subseteq \mathcal{A}$, $X' \subseteq \mathcal{A}$, $X =_{lex} X'$ and $\forall C \in \mathcal{C}(\mathcal{K} \cup \{N\})$, $C \cap X \neq \emptyset$ and $C \cap X' \neq \emptyset$. If $|C \cap X| = 2$ (resp. $|C \cap X'| = 2$), then X (resp. X') is not a prioritized removed set. If $|C \cap X| = 1$ and $|C \cap X'| = 1$ then two cases hold. If $C \cap X \neq C \cap X'$, since there exists i and j, $i \neq j$, such that $C \cap \mathcal{A}_i \neq \emptyset$ and $C \cap \mathcal{A}_j \neq \emptyset$ which contradicts $X =_{lex} X'$. If $C \cap X = C \cap X'$ then $X = X'$ which contradicts the hypothesis. □

This situation holds when each stratum is consistent with $\mathcal{T} \cup \{N\}$, for example when the stratification comes from several experts with different degrees of reliability. In this case, as detailed in section 4, computing the unique prioritized removed set is polynomial. The following proposition gives the condition of existence of several prioritized removed sets.

Proposition 4. *If there exists $C \in \mathcal{C}(\mathcal{K} \cup \{N\})$ such that there exists i, $C \cap \mathcal{A}_i \neq \emptyset$ and for all j, $j \neq i$, $C \cap \mathcal{A}_j = \emptyset$, then $|\mathcal{PR}(\mathcal{K} \cup \{N\})| \geq 2$.*

Proof. Suppose there is only one prioritized removed set X. By Definition 6, $X \subseteq \mathcal{A}$ and $C \cap X \neq \emptyset$. If $|C \cap X| = 2$ then X is not a prioritized removed set. If $|C \cap X|=1$, since there exists i, such that $|C \cap \mathcal{A}_i|=2$ therefore there exists X and X' such that $C \cap X \neq \emptyset$ and $C \cap X' \neq \emptyset$ and $X =_{lex} X'$ which contradicts the hypothesis. □

There are several prioritized removed sets as soon as there are conflicts included in a stratum where each conflict may leads to two prioritized removed sets. Namely, let NC be the number of conflicts such that each one is included in a stratum, the number of prioritized removed sets is bounded by 2^{NC}. In such case, each prioritized removed set leads to a possible revised knowledge base: $\mathcal{K}_i=\langle \mathcal{T} \cup \{N\}, (\mathcal{A}\backslash X_i)\rangle$ with $X_i \in \mathcal{PR}(\mathcal{K} \cup \{N\})$. In the *DL-Lite* language, it is not possible to find a knowledge base which represents the disjunction of such possible revised knowledge base. If we want to keep the result of revision in *DL-Lite*, several options are possible. The first one is to consider the intersection of all possible revised knowledge bases however this option may be too cautious since it could remove too many assertions and contradicts in some sense the minimal change principle. Another option is to define a selection function, where the revised knowledge base is defined as follows.

Definition 7. *Let* $\mathcal{K}=\langle \mathcal{T}, \mathcal{A}\rangle$ *be a consistent stratified knowledge base and* N *be a PI or a NI axiom. Let* f *be a selection function, the revised knowledge base* $\mathcal{K} \circ_{PRSR} N$ *is such that* $\mathcal{K} \circ_{PRSR} N = \langle \mathcal{T} \cup \{N\}, \mathcal{A} \circ_{PRSR} N\rangle$, *where* $\mathcal{A} \circ_{PRSR} N = (\mathcal{A} \backslash f(\mathcal{PR}(\mathcal{K} \cup \{N\})))$.

When N is a NI or a PI axiom, PRSR generalizes RSR [4]. More formally:

Proposition 5. *Let* $\mathcal{K}=\langle \mathcal{T}, \mathcal{A}\rangle$ *be a consistent knowledge base,* N *be a PI or a NI axiom. If* $\mathcal{A}$ *is not stratified then* $\mathcal{K} \circ_{PRSR} N = \mathcal{K} \circ_{RSR} N$

Proof. If $\mathcal{A}$ is not stratified, i.e. there is only one stratum, conditions $i)$ and $ii)$ in Definition 6 do not change and condition $iii)$ becomes $\forall \subseteq \mathcal{A}$, if $\langle \mathcal{T} \cup \{N\}, (\mathcal{A} \backslash X')\rangle$ is consistent, then $|X \cap \mathcal{A}| < |X' \cap \mathcal{A}|$ since $X \subseteq \mathcal{A}$. It follows that $\forall \subseteq \mathcal{A}$ if $\langle \mathcal{T} \cup \{N\}, (\mathcal{A} \backslash X')\rangle$ is consistent then $|X| < |X'|$, which is the third condition in the definition of a removed set [4]. $\square$

3.4 Logical Properties

Revision within the framework of Description logics, in particular *DL-Lite*, requires belief bases, i.e. finite sets of formulas. Postulates have been proposed for characterizing belief bases revision in a propositional logic setting [11,13]. In [4] the Hansson's postulates are rephrased within DL-Lite framework.

Let $\mathcal{K}$, $\mathcal{K}'$ be *DL-Lite* knowledge bases, N and M be either membership assertions or positive or negative axioms, $\circ$ be a revision operator. $\mathcal{K} + N$ denotes the non closing expansion, i.e. $\mathcal{K} + N = \mathcal{K} \cup \{N\}$. The postulates are: **P1 (Success)** $N \in \mathcal{K} \circ N$. **P2 (Inclusion)** $\mathcal{K} \circ N \subseteq \mathcal{K} + N$. **P3 (Consistency)** $\mathcal{K} \circ N$ is consistent. **P4 (Vacuity)** If $\mathcal{K} \cup \{N\}$ is consistent then $\mathcal{K} \circ N = \mathcal{K} + \{N\}$. **P5 (Pre-expansion)** $(\mathcal{K} + N) \circ N = \mathcal{K} \circ N$. **P6 (Internal exchange)** If N, $M \in \mathcal{K}$ then $\mathcal{K} \circ N = \mathcal{K} \circ M$. **P7 (Core retainment)** If $M \in \mathcal{K}$ and $M \notin \mathcal{K} \circ N$ then there is at least one $\mathcal{K}'$ such that $\mathcal{K}' \subseteq \mathcal{K} + N$, and $\mathcal{K}'$ is consistent but $\mathcal{K}' \cup \{M\}$ is inconsistent. **P8 (Relevance)** If $M \in \mathcal{K}$ and $M \notin \mathcal{K} \circ N$ then there is at least one $\mathcal{K}'$ such that $\mathcal{K} \circ N \subseteq \mathcal{K}' \subseteq \mathcal{K} + N$, and $\mathcal{K}'$ is consistent but $K' \cup \{M\}$ is inconsistent.

Proposition 6. *Let* $\mathcal{K}$ *be a consistent stratified knowledge base. If* N *is a membership assertion then the revision operator* $\circ_{PRSR}$ *satisfies the postulates* **P1**- **P8**. *If* N *is a PI or a NI axiom then the revision operator* $\circ_{PRSR}$ *satisfies the postulates* **P1**- **P7**.

Proof (Sketch of proof). For both revision operators **P1-P6** follow from the definition of PRSR and **P7** follows from the existence of at least one prioritized removed set. On contrast **P8** requires the existence of only one prioritized removed set, which is the case when N is a membership assertion, but this is not the case in general when N is a PI or a NI axiom, except for the case stated in Proposition 3. $\square$

In the next section, we provide different algorithms for computing the prioritized removed sets depending on the nature of the input.

4   Computing Revision Operation

As stated before, when trying to revise a *DL-Lite* knowledge base we want to withdraw only ABox assertions in order to restore consistency, i.e. prioritized removed sets will only contain elements from the ABox. From the computational point of view, we have to distinguish several cases depending on the nature of the input N, the content of the knowledge base and the form of the conflicts.

4.1   Result of Revision by an Assertion

When new information is an assertion, thanks to Proposition 1, there exists only one prioritized removed set. The computation of this set amounts in picking in each conflict the assertion which is different from the input N. This operation follows from a simple and non costly adaptation of the algorithm given in [8] for checking the consistency of a *DL-Lite* knowledge base. The main difference is that in [8] the aim is only to check whether a *DL-Lite* knowledge base is consistent or not. Here, we do one step further, as we need to enumerate all assertional facts that conflict with the input. Computing these conflicting assertions with N first requires the negative closure $cln\,(\mathcal{T})$, computed using the rules given in Section 2 repetively until reaching a fixed point. We suppose that this is performed by a NegClosure function. We provide the algorithm ComputePRSR1, which computes the prioritized removed set $PR \in \mathcal{PR}(\mathcal{K} \cup \{N\})$.

Algorithm 1. ComputePRSR1

1: **function** ComputePRSR1 $(\mathcal{K} = \langle \mathcal{T}, \mathcal{A} \rangle, N)$
2:     $PR \leftarrow \emptyset$
3:     $cln\,(\mathcal{T}) \leftarrow$ NegClosure$(\mathcal{T})$
4:     **for all** $X \sqsubseteq \neg Y \in cln\,(\mathcal{T})$ **do**
5:         **for all** $\alpha \in \mathcal{A}$ **do**
6:             **if** $\langle X \sqsubseteq \neg Y, \{\alpha, N\} \rangle$ is inconsistent **then**
7:                 $PR \leftarrow PR \cup \{\alpha\}$
8:     **Return** PR

Generally, the computation of the conflicts proceeds with the evaluation over $\mathcal{A}$ of each NI axiom in $cln\,(\mathcal{T})$ in order to exhibit whether $\mathcal{A}$ contains assertions which contradict the NI axioms. Intuitively, for each $X \sqsubseteq \neg Y$ belonging to $cln\,(\mathcal{T})$, the evaluation of $X \sqsubseteq \neg Y$ over the $\mathcal{A}$ simply amounts to return all $(X(x), Y(x))$ such that $X(x)$ and $Y(x)$ belongs to $\mathcal{A}$. When N is an assertion, one can easily check that every conflict which contradicts a NI axiom is of the form $\{\alpha, N\}$ where $\alpha \in \mathcal{A}$. This means that there exists exactly one prioritized removed set. Hence, in this case the removed set computation can be performed in polynomial time.

Note that the algorithm ComputePRSR1 produces the same revision result as the algorithm proposed in [9], since revision with an ABox assertion is uniquely defined (theorem 13 in [9]).

4.2   PRSR Computation : Revision by an Axiom

We now detail the case where N is a PI or a NI axiom. According to Definition 6, computing $\mathcal{PR}(\mathcal{K} \cup \{N\})$ starts with the computation of $\mathcal{PR}((\mathcal{T} \cup \{N\}) \cup \mathcal{A}_1)$, then continues with the computation $\mathcal{PR}((\mathcal{T} \cup \{N\}) \cup (\mathcal{A}_1 \cup \mathcal{A}_2))$, and so on. A prioritized removed set is formed by picking in each conflict the least priority element. However, according to the form of conflicts, two situations hold as pointed out in Section 3.

The first one is when each conflict involves two elements having different levels of priority. From Proposition 3, we have shown that there exists only one prioritized removed set. We provide the algorithm COMPUTEPRSR2 which computes the prioritized removed set $PR \in \mathcal{PR}(\mathcal{K} \cup \{N\})$.

Algorithm 2. COMPUTEPRSR2

```
 1:  function COMPUTEPRSR2 (K = ⟨T, A⟩, N)
 2:      T' ← T ∪ {N}, K' = ⟨T', A⟩
 3:      cln (T') ← NEGCLOSURE(T')
 4:      PR ← ∅
 5:      i ← 1
 6:      while i ≤ n do
 7:          for all X ⊑ ¬Y ∈ cln (T') do
 8:              for all α ∈ A_i do
 9:                  j ← i + 1
10:                  while j ≤ n do
11:                      for all β ∈ A_j do
12:                          if ⟨X ⊑ ¬Y, {α, β}⟩ is inconsistent then
13:                              PR ← PR ∪ {β}
14:                              A_j ← A_j \ {β}
15:                      j ← j + 1
16:              i ← i + 1
17:      Return PR
```

The algorithm COMPUTEPRSR2 proceeds from a current layer to all the other less preferred layers and selects the assertions which conflict with the ones in the current layer. We increment from a layer to another in order to ensure the minimality of the prioritized removed set w.r.t. lexicographic ordering. Note that this algorithm is based on inconsistency checking and its computational complexity is polynomial.

We now describe the second case, where there exists at least a conflict involving two elements having the same priority level. In such situation there are several prioritized removed sets to be computed, as pointed out in Proposition 4. In order to compute them, we follow the idea proposed in [23], where removed sets in the flat case can be computed using the hitting set notion [20]. A hitting set is a set which intersects each set in a collection. A minimal hitting set, w.r.t. set inclusion, is called a kernel. Moreover, kernels which are minimal w.r.t. cardinality correspond to the definition of a removed set [23]. The same result has been established for the removed set revision of *DL-Lite* knowledge bases [4] where the computation of the kernels of $\mathcal{C}(\mathcal{K} \cup \{N\})$ is performed using Reiter's algorithm [20], modified in [22]. We recall this algorithm [4].

Definition 8. *A tree T is an HS-tree of $C(\mathcal{K} \cup \{N\})$ if and only if it is the smallest tree having the following properties:*

1. *Its root is labeled by an element from $C(\mathcal{K} \cup \{N\})$. If $C(\mathcal{K} \cup \{N\})$ is empty, its root labeled by ' $\sqrt{}$ '.*
2. *If m is a node from T, let $H(m)$ be the set of branch labels on the path going from the root to T to m. If m is labeled by ' $\sqrt{}$ ', it has no successor in T.*
3. *If m is labeled by a set $C \in C(\mathcal{K} \cup \{N\})$, then, for each $c \in C$, m has a successor node m_c in T, joined to m by a branch labeled by c. The label of m_c is a set $C' \in C(\mathcal{K} \cup \{N\})$ such that $C' \cap H(m_c) = \emptyset$, if such a set exist. Otherwise, m_c is labeled by ' $\sqrt{}$ '.*

The kernels correspond to the leaves labeled by $\sqrt{}$. For each such node m, $H(m)$ is a kernel of $C(\mathcal{K} \cup \{N\})$. We use the same pruning techniques as in [22].

Concerning prioritized removed sets, they are not necessarily minimal w.r.t. cardinality. But they are minimal w.r.t. lexicographic ordering ($\leq_{lex}$ for short). So, a naive algorithm for computing $\mathcal{PR}(\mathcal{K} \cup \{N\})$ is : (i) compute the kernels of $C(\mathcal{K} \cup \{N\})$. (ii) keep only minimal ones w.r.t. $\leq_{lex}$. However, we can improve the algorithm.

As we said before, a prioritized removed set is computed from one layer to another. The idea of the enhancement of the algorithm is as follows: First, compute the conflicts in the first layer, i.e. in $(\mathcal{T} \cup \{N\}) \cup \mathcal{A}_1$, then build the hitting set tree on this collection of conflicts. This tree allows for the computation of the kernels of $(\mathcal{T} \cup \{N\}) \cup \mathcal{A}_1$ minimal w.r.t. $\leq_{lex}$. From these kernels, continue the construction of the tree using conflicts in $(\mathcal{T} \cup \{N\}) \cup (\{A_1 \cup A_2\})$ if they exist, and so on until reaching a fixed point where no conflict will be generated. Now the kernels of the final hitting set tree using conflicts in $(\mathcal{T} \cup \{N\}) \cup (\{A_1 \cup A_2 \cup ... \cup A_n\})$ which are minimal w.r.t. $\leq_{lex}$ are the prioritized removed sets. The following algorithm COMPUTEPRSR3 computes $\mathcal{PR}(\mathcal{K} \cup \{N\})$ using hitting sets.

Algorithm 3. COMPUTEPRSR3

```
1: function COMPUTEPRSR3 (K=⟨T, A⟩, N)
2:     T' ← T ∪ {N}, K' = ⟨T', A⟩
3:     cln (T') ← NEGCLOSURE(T')
4:     PR(K') ← ∅
5:     C ← ∅, TREE← ∅, i ← 1
6:     while i ≤ n do
7:         for all X ⊑ ¬Y ∈ cln (T') do
8:             for all (α, β) s.t. α ∈ A₁, β ∈ A₁ ∪ ... ∪ Aᵢ do
9:                 if ⟨X ⊑ ¬Y, {α, β}⟩ is inconsistent then
10:                    C ← C ∪ {α, β}
11:            TREE← TREE.ADDFROMLEXKERNEL(HS(C))
12:            C ← ∅,
13:            i ← i + 1
14:     PR(K') ← LEXKERNEL(TREE)
15:     Return PR(K')
```

In this algorithm the function HS($\mathcal{C}$) takes as input the conflicts computed in each layer (if they exist) and builds the corresponding hitting sets tree (TREE), using the algorithm presented in Definition 8. From a layer to another, we resume the construction of (TREE) from its current kernels minimal w.r.t. $\leq_{lex}$. Namely, the function ADDFROMLEXKERNEL((HS($\mathcal{C}$)) builds the hitting set tree of a collection of conflicts $\mathcal{C}$ starting from the kernels branches of the current TREE which are minimal w.r.t. $\leq_{lex}$. Finally $\mathcal{PR}(\mathcal{K} \cup \{N\})$ corresponds to the kernels of TREE obtained using function LEXKERNEL(TREE)) which are minimal w.r.t. $\leq_{lex}$. Note that COMPUTEPRSR3 is a generalization of COMPUTEPRSR2, since when all conflicts involve elements from distinct layers, then the final tree will only contains one prioritized removed set. The following example illustrates this algorithm.

Example 4. Consider $\mathcal{K} = \langle \mathcal{T}, \mathcal{A} \rangle$, with $\mathcal{T} = \{A \sqsubseteq B, C \sqsubseteq B\}$ and $\mathcal{A} = \mathcal{A}_1 \cup \mathcal{A}_2 \cup \mathcal{A}_3 \cup \mathcal{A}_4$ where $\mathcal{A}_1 = \{A(a), D(a)\}$, $\mathcal{A}_2 = \{C(a), B(b)\}$, $\mathcal{A}_3 = \{D(b)\}$ and $\mathcal{A}_4 = \{D(c), C(c)\}$. We want to revise $\mathcal{K}$ with $N = B \sqsubseteq \neg D$. Then, We have $cln(\mathcal{T} \cup \{B \sqsubseteq \neg D\}) = \{B \sqsubseteq \neg D, A \sqsubseteq \neg D, C \sqsubseteq \neg D\}$. The conflicts obtained from $cln(\mathcal{T}') \cup \mathcal{A}_1$ are $\{A(a), D(a)\}$. The constructed tree using HS($\{A(a), D(a)\}$) will contain two branches labeled respectively by $A(a)$ and $D(a)$ which are kernels minimal w.r.t. $\leq_{lex}$ ($\leq_{lex}$ kernel). We continue with $cln(\mathcal{T}') \cup \mathcal{A}_1 \cup \mathcal{A}_2$ where $\{C(a), D(a)\}$ is a conflict. We resume the construction of the tree its current $\leq_{lex}$ kernel (branches labeled by $A(a)$ and $D(a)$) and we obtain three HS-tree: $\{A(a), C(a)\}$, $\{A(a), D(a)\}$ and $D(a)$ where only $D(a)$ is $\leq_{lex}$ kernel. Now, we increment to $cln(\mathcal{T}') \cup \mathcal{A}_1 \cup \mathcal{A}_2 \cup \mathcal{A}_3$ where $\{B(b), D(b)\}$ is a conflict and we continue the construction of the Tree from $D(a)$. We obtain $\{D(a), D(b)\}$ and $\{D(a), B(b)\}$ as HS-tree where only $\{D(a), D(b)\}$ is $\leq_{lex}$ kernel. Finally, We we have $\{D(c), C(c)\}$ as a conflict in $cln(\mathcal{T}') \cup \mathcal{A}_1 \cup \mathcal{A}_2 \cup \mathcal{A}_3 \cup \mathcal{A}_4$. We continue the construction of the tree from branch labeled by $\{D(a), D(b)\}$. We obtain two other branches labeled respectively by $\{D(a), D(b), C(c)\}$ and $\{D(a), D(b), D(c)\}$ which are two $\leq_{lex}$ kernels. Hence, $\mathcal{PR}(\mathcal{K} \cup \{N\}) = \{D(a), D(b), C(c)\}, \{D(a), D(b), D(c)\}$.

5   Conclusion

In this paper, we investigated Prioritized Removed Sets Revision of *DL-Lite* knowledge bases. We studied the revision operation for three forms of input, namely, an ABox assertion or a TBox axiom. We first defined the prioritized removed sets within the framework of *DL-Lite* as a lexicographic approach. We showed that when the input is an assertion then PRSR is computed in polynomial time. When the input is a PI or a NI axiom we provided the condition for the computation of PRSR in polynomial time. We showed that in the general case the number of prioritized removed sets is bounded and we proposed an algorithm for computing these sets using the notion of hitting sets. We finally gave logical properties of the proposed operators in terms of satisfaction of Hansson's postulates rephrased in our framework. In a near future we plan to investigate the iterated revision of *DL-Lite* knowledge bases. We also want focus on the extension of Removed Sets Fusion [14], defined in a propositional setting, to the merging of *DL-Lite* knowledge bases.

Acknowledgement. This work has received support from the french Agence Nationale de la Recherche, ASPIQ project reference ANR-12-BS02-0003.

References

1. Alchourrón, C.E., Gärdenfors, P., Makinson, D.: On the logic of theory change: Partial meet contraction and revision functions. J. Symb. Log. 50(2), 510–530 (1985)
2. Artale, A., Calvanese, D., Kontchakov, R., Zakharyaschev, M.: The dl-lite family and relations. J. Artif. Intell. Res (JAIR) 36, 1–69 (2009)
3. Benferhat, S., Ben-Naim, J., Papini, O., Würbel, E.: An answer set programming encoding of prioritized removed sets revision: application to gis. Appl. Intell. 32(1), 60–87 (2010)
4. Benferhat, S., Bouraoui, Z., Papini, O., Würbel, E.: Assertional-based removed sets revision of DL-Lite$_R$ knowledge bases. In: ISAIM (2014)
5. Benferhat, S., Dubois, D., Prade, H.: How to infer from inconsisent beliefs without revising. In: IJCAI, pp. 1449–1457 (1995)
6. Benferhat, S., Dubois, D., Prade, H., Williams, M. A.: A practical approach to revising prioritized knowledge bases. Studia Logica 70(1), 105–130 (2002)
7. Bienvenu, M., Rosati, R.: New inconsistency-tolerant semantics for robust ontology-based data access. In: Eiter, T., Glimm, B., Kazakov, Y., Krötzsch, M. (eds.) Description Logics. CEUR Workshop Proceedings, vol. 1014, pp. 53–64. CEUR-WS.org (2013)
8. Calvanese, D., Giacomo, G.D., Lembo, D., Lenzerini, M., Rosati, R.: Tractable reasoning and efficient query answering in description logics: The *dl-lite* family. J. Autom. Reasoning 39(3), 385–429 (2007)
9. Calvanese, D., Kharlamov, E., Nutt, W., Zheleznyakov, D.: Evolution of dl-lite knowledge bases. In: Patel-Schneider, P.F., Pan, Y., Hitzler, P., Mika, P., Zhang, L., Pan, J.Z., Horrocks, I., Glimm, B. (eds.) ISWC 2010, Part I. LNCS, vol. 6496, pp. 112–128. Springer, Heidelberg (2010)
10. Flouris, G., Plexousakis, D., Antoniou, G.: On applying the agm theory to dls and owl. In: Gil, Y., Motta, E., Benjamins, V.R., Musen, M.A. (eds.) ISWC 2005. LNCS, vol. 3729, pp. 216–231. Springer, Heidelberg (2005)
11. Fuhrmann, A.: An essay on contraction. CSLI Publications, Stanford (1997)
12. Gao, S., Qi, G., Wang, H.: A new operator for abox revision in dl-lite. In: Hoffmann, J., Selman, B. (eds.) AAAI. AAAI Press (2012)
13. Hansson, S.O.: Revision of belief sets and belief bases. Handbook of Defeasible Reasoning and Uncertainty Management Systems 3, 17–75 (1998)
14. Hué, J., Würbel, E., Papini, O.: Removed sets fusion: Performing off the shelf. In: Proc. of ECAI 2008 (FIAI 178), pp. 94–98 (2008)
15. Lembo, D., Lenzerini, M., Rosati, R., Ruzzi, M., Savo, D.F.: Inconsistency-tolerant semantics for description logics. In: Hitzler, P., Lukasiewicz, T. (eds.) RR 2010. LNCS, vol. 6333, pp. 103–117. Springer, Heidelberg (2010)
16. Papini, O.: A complete revision function in propositional calculus. In: ECAI, pp. 339–343 (1992)
17. Qi, G., Ji, Q., Haase, P.: A conflict-based operator for mapping revision. In: Bernstein, A., Karger, D.R., Heath, T., Feigenbaum, L., Maynard, D., Motta, E., Thirunarayan, K. (eds.) ISWC 2009. LNCS, vol. 5823, pp. 521–536. Springer, Heidelberg (2009)
18. Qi, G., Liu, W., Bell, D.A.: A revision-based approach to handling inconsistency in description logics. Artif. Intell. Rev. 26(1-2), 115–128 (2006)
19. Qi, G., Pan, J.: A stratfication-based approach for inconsistency handling in description logics. In: IWOD 2007, p. 83 (2007)

20. Reiter, R.: A theory of diagnosis from first principles. Artif. Intell. 32(1), 57–95 (1987)
21. Wang, Z., Wang, K., Topor, R.W.: A new approach to knowledge base revision in dl-lite. In: Fox, M., Poole, D. (eds.) AAAI. AAAI Press (2010)
22. Wilkerson, R.W., Greiner, R., Smith, B.A.: A correction to the algorithm in reiter's theory of diagnosis. Artificial Intelligence 41, 79–88 (1989)
23. Würbel, E., Jeansoulin, R., Papini, O.: Revision: An application in the framework of GIS. In: Cohn, A.G., Giunchiglia, F., Selman, B. (eds.) KR, pp. 505–515. Morgan Kaufmann (2000)

Modular Paracoherent Answer Sets*

Giovanni Amendola[1], Thomas Eiter[2], and Nicola Leone[1]

[1] Department of Mathematics and Computer Science, University of Calabria
Via P. Bucci, Cubo 30b, 87036 Rende (CS), Italy
amendola@mat.unical.it, leone@mat.unical.it
[2] Institute of Information Systems, Vienna University of Technology
Favoritenstraße 9-11, A-1040 Vienna, Austria
eiter@kr.tuwien.ac.at

Abstract. The answer set semantics may assign a logic program no model due to classic contradiction or cyclic negation. The latter can be remedied by resorting to a paracoherent semantics given by semi-equilibrium (SEQ) models, which are 3-valued interpretations that generalize the logical reconstruction of answer sets given by equilibrium models. While SEQ-models have interesting properties, they miss modularity in the rules, such that a natural modular (bottom up) evaluation of programs is hindered. We thus refine SEQ-models using splitting sets, the major tool for modularity in modeling and evaluating answer set programs. We consider canonical models that are independent of any particular splitting sequence from a class of splitting sequences, and present two such classes whose members are efficiently recognizable. Splitting SEQ-models does not make reasoning harder, except for deciding model existence in presence of constraints (without constraints, split SEQ-models always exist).

1 Introduction

As well-known, the answer set semantics [11] does not assign to every logic program a model. This can be either due to a logical contradiction, as emerging e.g. in the program $\{open \leftarrow not\ closed,\ \neg open \leftarrow\ \}$, or due to cyclic negation, as e.g. present in the program $\{shaves(joe, joe) \leftarrow not\ shaves(joe, joe)\}$, which is a paraphrase of Russell's paradox (where joe is the barber).

In order to avoid trivialization of reasoning from such programs, Inoue and Sakama [28] have introduced paraconsistent semantics for answer set programs. While dealing with explicit contradictions can be achieved with similar methods as for (non-)classical logic (cf. also [5,1,17]), dealing with cyclic negation turned out to be tricky. With the idea that atoms may also be possibly true (i.e., by belief), Inoue and Sakama defined a semi-stable semantics which for Russell's paradox above yields the model that $shaves(joe, joe)$ is possibly true, which seems reasonable. In fact, semi-stable semantics *approximates* answer set semantics and coincides with it whenever a program has some answer set; otherwise, it yields under Occam's razor models with a least set of atoms believed to be true. That is, the intrinsic *closed world assumption (CWA)* of logic programs is slightly relaxed for achieving stability of models.

* This work was partially supported by Regione Calabria under the EU Social Fund and project PIA KnowRex POR FESR 2007- 2013, and by the Italian Ministry of University and Research under PON project "Ba2Know (Business Analytics to Know) S.I.-LAB n. PON03PE_0001.

E. Fermé and J. Leite (Eds.): JELIA 2014, LNAI 8761, pp. 457–471, 2014.

In a similar vein, we can regard many semantics for non-monotonic logic programs that relax answer sets as *paracoherent semantics*, e.g. [3,9,18,22,23,25,27,29,31,32].[1] Ideally, such a relaxation meets for a program P the following desiderata [8]:

(D1) Every (consistent) answer set of P corresponds to a model (*answer set coverage*).

(D2) If P has some (consistent) answer set, then its models correspond to answer sets (*congruence*).

(D3) If P has a classical model, then P has a model (*classical coherence*).

In particular, (D3) intuitively says that in the extremal case, a relaxation should renounce to the selection principles imposed by the semantics on classical models (in particular, if a single classical model exists).

However, only few paracoherent semantics satisfy all three desiderata (cf. [8]). A recent one are semi-equilibrium (SEQ) models [8], which improve semi-stable models by avoiding some anomalies. SEQ-models are a relaxation of Pearce's well-known equilibrium models [19], which provide a logical reconstruction of answer sets alias stable models in terms of a non-monotonic version of Heyting's [12] logic of here and there. Roughly speaking, SEQ-models are 3-valued interpretations in which atoms can be true, false or believed to be true; the gap between believed and derivably true atoms is globally minimized by SEQ-models. Note that the distinction between believed and derivably true atoms in models is important; other approaches, e.g. CR-Prolog [3], make a distinction at the rule level.

While the SEQ-semantics has nice properties, it may select models that do not respect modular structure in the rules. To illustrate this, consider the following example.

Example 1. *Suppose we have a program that captures knowledge about friends of a person regarding visits to a party, where $go(X)$ informally means that X will go:*

$$P = \left\{ \begin{array}{l} go(John) \leftarrow not\ go(Mark); \\ go(Peter) \leftarrow go(John), not\ go(Bill); \\ go(Bill) \leftarrow go(Peter) \end{array} \right\}$$

Then P has no answer set; its semi-equilibrium models are $M_1 = (\emptyset, \{go(Mark)\})$, and $M_2 = (\{go(John)\}, \{go(John), go(Bill)\})$. Informally, a key difference between M_1 and M_2 concerns the beliefs on Mark and John. In M_2 Mark does not go, and, consequently, John will go (moreover, Bill is believed to go, and Peter will not go). In M_1, instead, we believe Mark will go, thus John will not go (likewise Peter and Bill).

None of the two models provides a fully coherent view (on the other hand, the program is incoherent, having no answer set). Nevertheless, M_2 appears preferable over M_1, since, according with a layering (stratification) principle, which is widely agreed in LP, one should prefer $go(John)$ rather than $go(Mark)$, as there is no way to derive $go(Mark)$ (which does not appear in the head of any rule of the program).

Modularity via rule dependency as in the example above is widely used in problem modeling and logic programs evaluation; in fact, program decomposition is crucial for efficient answer set computation. For the program P above, advanced answer set solvers

---

[1] Notably, Seipel's Evidential Stable Models for disjunctive LPs [29] coincide with SEQ-models.

like DLV and clasp immediately set $go(Mark)$ to false, as $go(Mark)$ does not occur in any rule head. In a customary bottom up computation along program components, answer sets are gradually extended until the whole program is covered, or incoherence is detected at some component (in our example for the last two rules). But rather than to abort the computation, we would like to switch to a paracoherent mode and continue with building semi-equilibrium models, as an approximation of answer sets.

In this general setting, we refine SEQ-models with the following contributions.

– Resorting to splitting sets [15], the major tool for modularity in modeling and evaluating answer set programs, we define *split SEQ-models* (Section 3), for which the program is evaluated in progressive layers according to a *splitting sequence* of the atoms. In the example above, the natural sequence $S = (\{go(Mark)\}, \{go(Mark), go(John)\}, \{go(Mark), go(John), go(Bill), go(Peter)\})$ will yield the expected result.

– In general, the resulting split SEQ-models depend on the particular splitting sequence S. We thus introduce *canonical splitting sequences*, with the property that the models are *independent* of any particular from a class of splitting sequences, and thus yield canonical models (Section 4). This is analogous to the *perfect models* of a (disjunctive) stratified program, which are independent of a concrete stratification [2,26]. For constraint-free programs P, the class derived from the strongly connected components (SCCs) of P warrants this property, as well as modularity property. For arbitrary programs, independence is held by a similar class derived from the maximal joined components (MJCs), merging SCCs involved in constraints.

– We characterize the computational complexity of split SEQ-model semantics, for canonical models and various classes of logic programs (Section 5). It appears that the refined semantics has the same complexity as SEQ semantics, except for the model existence problem, which gets harder in general. This provides useful insight for defining canonical models that satisfy all desiderata (D1)-(D3) for arbitrary programs, which we briefly discuss here (Section 7).

The refined semantics, and in particular the SCC-models semantics, lends for a modular use and bottom up evaluation of programs. Cautious merging of components, as done for MJC-models, aims at preserving independence of components and thus possible parallel evaluation. This makes the refined semantics attractive for incorporation into answer set evaluation frameworks, in order to add paracoherent features.

2 Preliminaries

We start with recalling answer set semantics and fixing notation, and then present the paracoherent semantics of semi-equilibrium models.

Answer Set Programs. Following the traditional grounding view [11], we concentrate on programs over a propositional signature Λ. A *disjunctive rule* r is of the form

$$a_1 \vee \cdots \vee a_l \leftarrow b_1, ..., b_m, not\ b_{m+1}, ..., not\ b_n, \tag{1}$$

where all a_i and b_j are atoms (from Λ) and $l \geq 0$, $n \geq m \geq 0$ and $l + n > 0$; *not* represents *negation-as-failure*. The set $H(r) = \{a_1, ..., a_l\}$ is the *head* of r, while $B^+(r) = \{b_1, ..., b_m\}$ and $B^-(r) = \{b_{m+1}, ..., b_n\}$ are the *positive body* and the *negative body* of r, respectively; the *body* of r is $B(r) = B^+(r) \cup B^-(r)$. We denote by $At(r) = H(r) \cup B(r)$ the set of all atoms occurring in r. For any set of atoms S, we let $not\ S = \{not\ a \mid a \in S\}$; rules of form (1) will also be written (in abuse of notation) $H(r) \leftarrow B^+(r), not\ B^-(r)$. A rule r is a *fact*, if $B(r) = \emptyset$ (we then omit $\leftarrow$); a *constraint*, if $H(r) = \emptyset$; *normal*, if $|H(r)| \leq 1$ and *positive*, if $B^-(r) = \emptyset$.

A *(disjunctive logic) program* P is a finite set of disjunctive rules. P is called *normal* [resp. *positive*] if each $r \in P$ is normal [resp. positive]. We let $At(P) = \bigcup_{r \in P} At(r)$.

Any set $I \subseteq \Lambda$ is an *interpretation*; it is a *model* of a program P (denoted $I \models P$) iff for each rule $r \in P$, $I \cap H(r) \neq \emptyset$ if $B^+(r) \subseteq I$ and $B^-(r) \cap I = \emptyset$ (denoted $I \models r$). A model M of P is *minimal*, iff no model $M' \subset M$ of P exists. We denote the by $MM(P)$ set of all minimal models of P and by $AS(P)$ the set of all *answer sets (or stable models)* of P, i.e., the set of all interpretations I such that $I \in MM(P^I)$, where P^I is the well-known *Gelfond-Lifschitz reduct* [11] of P w.r.t. I.

Semi-equilibrium Paracoherent Semantics. We call logic programs that lack answer sets due to cyclic dependency of atoms among each other by rules through negation *incoherent* (cf. Russel's paradox). The semi-equilibrium semantics [8] avoids incoherence by resorting to the view of answer sets in the *logic of here and there* (*HT-logic*) [19,20]. We focus here on formulas ϕ of the form

$$b_1 \wedge \ldots \wedge b_m \wedge \neg b_{m+1} \wedge \ldots \wedge \neg b_n \rightarrow a_1 \vee \ldots \vee a_l, \tag{2}$$

which correspond in an obvious way to rules of form (1). In *HT-logic*, *interpretations* are pairs (X, Y), $X \subseteq Y \subseteq \Lambda$, where X is the *here* world and Y the *there* world. Intuitively, the atoms in X are true (value **t**), atoms not in Y are false (**f**), and the atoms in $gap(X, Y) = Y \setminus X$ are believed to be true (**bt**). For any set A of HT-interpretations, we denote by $mc(A)$ the set of maximal canonical interpretations $(X, Y) \in A$, i.e., no $(X', Y') \in A$ exists such that $gap(X', Y') \subset gap(X, Y)$. We define (X, Y) to be an *HT-model* of the formula ϕ, denoted $(X, Y) \models \phi$, in a recursive way:

1. $(X, Y) \models a$ iff $a \in X$;
2. $(X, Y) \not\models \bot$; ($\bot$ is falsity)
3. $(X, Y) \models \phi \wedge \psi$ iff $(X, Y) \models \phi$ and $(X, Y) \models \psi$;
4. $(X, Y) \models \phi \vee \psi$ iff $(X, Y) \models \phi$ or $(X, Y) \models \psi$;
5. $(X, Y) \models \phi \rightarrow \psi$ iff (*i*) $(X, Y) \not\models \phi$ or $(X, Y) \models \psi$, and (*ii*) $Y \models \phi \rightarrow \psi$;[2]
6. $(X, Y) \models \neg\phi$ iff $(X, Y) \models \phi \rightarrow \bot$.

In particular, $(X, Y) \models \neg a$ iff $a \notin Y$, and $(X, Y) \models r$ for a rule r of form (2) iff either $\{a_1 \ldots, a_k\} \cap X \neq \emptyset$, $\{b_1, \ldots, b_m\} \not\subseteq Y$, or $\{b_{m+1}, \ldots, b_n\} \cap Y \neq \emptyset$. A HT-interpretation (X, Y) is an HT-model of a theory (i.e., a set of formulas) Θ, denoted $(X, Y) \models \Theta$ iff $(X, Y) \models \phi$ for each $\phi \in \Theta$. It is an *equilibrium (EQ) model* of Θ iff $X = Y$ and for every $X' \subset Y$ it holds that $(X', Y) \not\models \Theta$.

Example 2. *Consider the program* $P = \{a \leftarrow b;\ b \leftarrow not\ c;\ c \leftarrow not\ a\}$, *and the corresponding theory* $\Theta_P = \{b \rightarrow a;\ \neg c \rightarrow b;\ \neg a \rightarrow c\}$. *As easily checked,* $(\emptyset, ac)$, (a, ab), (a, abc), *and* (c, c) *are HT-models of* Θ_P; *the only equilibrium model is* (c, c).

As shown by Pearce [19], $M \subseteq At(P)$ fulfills $M \in AS(P)$ iff (M, M) is an EQ-model of Θ_P. Paracoherent answer sets emerge with minimal sets of believed atoms.

---

[2] Note that in condition 5.(*ii*) '$\models$' is the standard operator of classical propositional logic.

Definition 1 ([8]). *A semi-equilibrium (SEQ) model (or* paracoherent answer set*) of a program P is any HT-model* (X, Y) *of P s.t. (i)* $(X', Y) \not\models P$, *for all* $X' \subset X$ *(h-minimality) and (ii) no HT-model* (X', Y') *of P satisfies h-minimality and* $gap(X', Y') \subset gap(X, Y)$ *(gap-minimality).*

The set of all semi-equilibrium models of P is denoted by $SEQ(P)$.

Example 3. *Consider the program* $P = \{a \leftarrow b; \ b \leftarrow not\ a\}$. *Its HT-models are* $(\emptyset, a), (\emptyset, ab), (a, a), (a, ab), (b, ab)$ *and* (ab, ab). *Hence, there is no equilibrium model for P, while* $SEQ(P) = \{(\emptyset, a)\}$.

3   Split Semi-equilibrium Semantics

In this section, we introduce a refinement to the semi-equilibrium semantics. In fact we observe that sometimes gap minimization is too weak. Consider the following example.

Example 4. *Let* $P = \{c \leftarrow b, not\ c; \ b \leftarrow not\ a\}$; *then* $SEQ(P) = \{ \ (b, bc), (\emptyset, a)\}$. *Here* (b, bc) *is more appealing than* $(\emptyset, a)$ *because a is not derivable, as no rule has a in the head. Moreover, intuitively,* $P_1 = \{b \leftarrow not\ a\}$ *is a lower (coherent) part feeding into the upper part* $P_2 = \{c \leftarrow b, not\ c\}$.

To overcome this limitation, we introduce a refined paracoherent semantics, called *split semi-equilibrium semantics*. It coincides with the answer sets semantics in case of coherent programs, and selects a subset of the SEQ-models otherwise. The main results of this section are two model-theoretic characterizations which identify necessary and sufficient conditions for deciding whether a SEQ-model is selected.

Splitting Sets and Sequences. Splitting sets [15] allow us to divide a program P into a lower and a higher part which can be evaluated bottom up. More formally, a set $S \subset At(P)$ is a *splitting set* of P, if for every rule r in P such that $H(r) \cap S \neq \emptyset$ we have that $At(r) \subseteq S$. We denote by $b_S(P) - \{r \in | \ At(r) \subseteq S\}$ the *bottom* part of P, $t_S(P) = P \setminus b_S(P)$ the *top* part of P relative to S.

Splitting sets naturally lead to splitting sequences. A *splitting sequence* $S = (S_1, \ldots, S_n)$ of P is a sequence of splitting sets of P such that $S_i \subseteq S_j$ for each $i < j$.

Split Semi-equilibrium Models. We now introduce the notion of SEQ-*models related to a splitting set*. First given a splitting set S for a program P and an HT-interpretation (I, J) for $b_S(P)$, we let

$$P^S(I, J) = P \setminus b_S(P) \cup \{a \mid a \in I\} \cup \{\leftarrow not\ a \mid a \in J\} \cup \{\leftarrow a \mid a \in S \setminus J\}.$$

Informally, the bottom part of P w.r.t. S is replaced with rules and constraints which fix in any EQ-model of the remainder $(= t_S(P))$ the values of the atoms in S to (I, J).

Definition 2 (Semi-equilibrium models related to a splitting set). *Let S be a splitting set of a program P. Then the semi-equilibrium models of P related to S are defined as*

$$SEQ^S(P) = mc\left(\bigcup_{(I,J) \in SEQ(b_S(P))} SEQ(P^S(I, J)) \right). \tag{3}$$

Example 5 (cont'd). *For the splitting set* $S = \{a, b\}$ *of* P *in Example 4,* $b_S(P) = \{b \leftarrow not\ a\}$ *and* $SEQ(b_S(P)) = \{(b, b)\}$. *Hence,* $P^S(b, b) = \{c \leftarrow b, not\ c;\ b;\ \leftarrow a\}$ *and* $SEQ^S(P) = SEQ(P^S(b, b)) = \{(b, bc)\}$.

For any HT-model (X, Y) and splitting set S of a program P, we define the *restriction of* (X, Y) *to* S as $(X, Y)|_S = (X \cap S, Y \cap S)$.

Proposition 1. *Let* S *be a splitting set of a program* P. *If* $(X, Y) \in SEQ^S(P)$, *then* $(X, Y)|_S \in SEQ(b_S(P))$.

The following result shows that each semi-equilibrium model related to a given splitting set is always a semi-equilibrium model of the program.

Theorem 1 (Soundness). *Let* S *be a splitting set of a program* P. *If* $(X, Y) \in SEQ^S(P)$, *then* $(X, Y) \in SEQ(P)$.

The converse does not hold in general; in fact if we consider the program of Example 4 and the splitting set $S = \{a, b\}$ we have $SEQ^S(P) = \{(b, bc)\}$, while $SEQ(P) = \{(b, bc), (\emptyset, a)\}$. It is also clear that $SEQ^S(P)$ depends on the choice of S; in fact if $S = \emptyset$ then $SEQ^\emptyset(P) = SEQ(P)$.

Moreover for the validity of Theorem 1, the selection of maximal canonical HT-models is necessary. Indeed, for $P = \{a \leftarrow not\ b;\ b \leftarrow not\ a;\ c \leftarrow b, not\ c\}$ and the splitting set $S = \{a, b\}$, we have $SEQ(b_S(P)) = \{(a, a), (b, b)\}$; hence $SEQ(P^S(a, a)) \cup SEQ(P^S(b, b)) = \{(a, a), (b, bc)\}$, while $SEQ(P) = \{(a, a)\}$.

We have seen so far two necessary conditions for an HT-model to qualify as a semi-equilibrium model related to a given splitting set. These conditions are also sufficient.

Theorem 2 (Completeness). *Let* S *be a splitting set of a program* P. *If* $(X, Y) \in SEQ(P)$ *and* $(X, Y)|_S \in SEQ(b_S(P))$, *then* $(X, Y) \in SEQ^S(P)$.

Putting together the various results obtained so far we have proved the following semantic characterization for semi-equilibrium models related to a splitting set:

Theorem 3. *Let* S *be a splitting set of a program* P. *Then* $(X, Y) \in SEQ^S(P)$ *iff* $(X, Y) \in SEQ(P)$ *and* $(X, Y)|_S \in SEQ(b_S(P))$.

Now we generalize the use of splitting sets to compute the SEQ-models of a program via splitting sequences.

Definition 3 (Semi-equilibrium models related to a splitting sequence). *Given a splitting sequence* $S = (S_1, \ldots, S_n)$ *for a program* P, *we let* $S' = (S_2, \ldots, S_n)$ *and define the semi-equilibrium models of* P *related to the splitting sequence* $S = (S_1, \ldots, S_n)$ *as*

$$SEQ^S(P) = mc\left(\bigcup_{(I, J) \in SEQ(b_{S_1}(P))} SEQ^{S'}(P^{S_1}(I, J)) \right). \tag{4}$$

The SEQ-*models related to a splitting sequence* can be characterized similarly as those related to a splitting set. To ease presentation, for a program P and splitting sequence $S = (S_1, \ldots, S_n)$, we let $P_0 = P$ and $P_k = (P_{k-1})^{S_k}(I_k, J_k)$, where $(I_k, J_k) \in SEQ(b_{S_k}(P_{k-1}))$, $k = 1, \ldots, n$. We now state the main result of this section.

Theorem 4. *Let* $S = (S_1, ..., S_n)$ *be a splitting sequence of a program* P. *Then* $(X, Y) \in SEQ^S(P)$ *iff* $(X, Y) \in SEQ(P)$ *and* $(X, Y)|_{S_k} \in SEQ(b_{S_k}(P_{k-1}))$, *for* $k = 1, ..., n$.

Finally we observe that a classically consistent program does not necessarily have *split semi-equilibrium models* (but always *semi-equilibrium models*). In fact, if we consider $P = \{\leftarrow b; \ b \leftarrow not \ a\}$ and the splitting set $S = \{a\}$, we obtain $SEQ(b_S(P)) = \{(\emptyset, \emptyset)\}$ and so $SEQ^S(P) = \emptyset$. However (a, a) and $(\emptyset, a)$ are HT-models of P.

4 Canonical Semi-Equilibrium Models

The split semi-equilibrium semantics depends on the choice of the particular splitting sequence, which is not much desirable. We thus consider a way to obtain a refined split SEQ-semantics that is independent of a particular splitting sequence, but imposes conditions on sequences that come naturally with the program and can be easily tested.

Attractive for this purpose are the *strongly connected components* (SCCs) of a given program, which are at the heart of bottom up evaluation algorithms in ASP systems. In absence of constraints, we get the desired independence of a particular splitting sequence, such that we can then talk about the SCC-*models of a program*. Allowing for constraints will need a slight extension.

4.1 SCC-split Sequences and Models

Recall that the *dependency graph* of a program P is the directed graph $DG(P) = \langle V_{DG}, E_{DG} \rangle$, where $V_{DG} = At(P)$ and $E_{DG} = \{(a, b) \mid a \in H(r), b \in B(r) \cup (H(r) \setminus \{a\}), r \in P\}$. The SCCs of P, denoted $SCC(P)$, are the SCCs of $DG(P)$, and the supergraph of P is the graph $SG(P) = \langle V_{SG}, E_{SG} \rangle$, where $V_{SG} = SCC(P)$ and $E_{SG} = \{(C, C') \mid C \neq C' \in SCC(P), \exists a \in C, \exists b \in C'', (a, b) \in E_{DG}\}$. Note that $SG(P)$ is a directed acyclic graph (dag); recall that a *topological ordering* of a dag $G = \langle V, E \rangle$ is an ordering $v_1, v_2, ..., v_n$ of its vertices, denoted $\leq$, such that for every $(v_i, v_j) \subseteq E$ we have $i > j$. Such an ordering always exists, and the set $O(G)$ of all topological orderings of G is nonempty. Any such ordering of $SG(P)$ naturally induces a splitting sequence as follows.

Definition 4. *Let* P *be a program and let* $\leq = (C_1, ..., C_n)$ *be a topological ordering of* $SG(P)$. *Then the splitting sequence induced by* $\leq$ *is* $S_{\leq} = (S_1, ..., S_n)$, *where* $S_1 = C_1$ *and* $S_j = S_{j-1} \cup C_j$, *for* $j = 2, ..., n$.

We call any such $S_{\leq}$ a *SCC-splitting sequence*; note that $S_{\leq}$ is indeed a splitting sequence of P. We now have the following result.

Theorem 5. *Let* P *be a constraint-free program. For every* $\leq, \leq' \in O(SG(P))$, *we have* $SEQ^{S_{\leq}}(P) = SEQ^{S_{\leq'}}(P)$.

This result allows to define the SCC-*models of* P as $M^{SCC}(P) = SEQ^{S_{\leq}}(P)$ for an arbitrary topological ordering of $SG(P)$. We then obtain:

Proposition 2. *The SCC-models semantics, given by* $M^{SCC}(P)$ *for constraint-free* P, *satisfies (D1)-(D3).*

Example 6. *Consider* $P = \{a \leftarrow c, not\ a;\ a \leftarrow not\ b;\ c \leftarrow not\ d;\ b \leftarrow not\ e\};$ *its SCCs are* $C_1 = \{a\},\ C_2 = \{b\},\ C_3 = \{c\},\ C_4 = \{d\}$ *and* $C_5 = \{e\}$. *For* $\leq\ =$ $(C_4, C_5, C_3, C_2, C_1)$, *we obtain that* $SEQ^{S_\leq}(P) = SEQ^{(S_2, S_3, S_4, S_5)}(P^{S_1}(\emptyset, \emptyset)) =$ $SEQ^{(S_3, S_4, S_5)}(P_1^{S_2}(\emptyset, \emptyset)) = SEQ^{(S_4, S_5)}(P_2^{S_3}(c, c)) = SEQ^{(S_5)}(P_3^{S_4}(bc, bc)) = \{(bc,$ $abc)\};$ *hence* $M^{SCC}(P) = \{(bc, abc)\}$. *For* $\leq' = (C_5, C_2, C_4, C_3, C_1)$, *we obtain* $SEQ^{S_{\leq'}}(P) = \{(bc, abc)\}$, *in line with Theorem 5. Note that* $SEQ(P) = \{(bc, abc),$ $(b, bd), (ac, ace)\}$.

Finally, if we replace in Equation (4) SEQ, SEQ^S, and $SEQ^{S'}$ all by M^{SCC}, then the resulting equation holds; i.e., we can compute SCC-models modularly bottom up along an arbitrary splitting sequence (using always M^{SCC}).

4.2 MJC-split Sequences and Models

Theorem 5 fails if we allow constraints in P. E.g., the program $P = \{b;\ \leftarrow b, not\ a\}$ has the SCCs $\{a\}$ and $\{b\}$; hence $O(SG(P)) = \{(\{a\}, \{b\}), (\{b\}, \{a\})\}$. But the respective semi-equilibrium models are different: $SEQ^{(\{a\}, \{a,b\})}(P) = \emptyset$ and $SEQ^{(\{b\}, \{a,b\})}(P) = \{(b, ba)\}$. Note here that semi-equilibrium semantics is able to distinguish constraints $\leftarrow Body$ from rules $f \leftarrow Body, not\ f$; the latter can always be satisfied by believing f (and thus be viewed as soft constraints). On the other hand, Theorem 5 extends to the case without cross-component constraints, i.e., each constraint r is embedded in some SCC C_i ($B(r) \subseteq C_i \in SCC(P)$); otherwise, the order in which unrelated components appear in a splitting sequence may matter.

We thus consider merging SCCs of a program in such a way that independence of concrete topological orderings is preserved and merging is done only if deemed necessary. This is embodied by the *maximal joinable components* of a program, which lead to so called MJC-split sequences and models. Informally, relevant SCCs that are unordered (thus unproblematic in evaluation) are merged if they intersect with a constraint.

We start with introducing *related pairs* and *joinable pairs* of SCCs. We call (K_1, K_2) from $SCC(P)^2$ a *related pair*, if either $K_1 = K_2$ or some constraint $r \in P$ fulfills $At(r) \cap K_1 \neq \emptyset$ and $At(r) \cap K_2 \neq \emptyset$; by $C_{(K_1, K_2)}(P)$ we denote the set of all such constraints.

Definition 5. *A related pair* (K_1, K_2) *is a joinable pair iff* $K_1 = K_2$ *or some* $(C_1, \ldots, C_n)$ *in* $O(SG(P))$ *exists such that (i)* $K_1 = C_s$ *and* $K_2 = C_{s+1}$ *for some* $1 \leq s < n$, *(ii)* $(K_2, K_1) \notin E_{SG}$ *and (iii) there exists* $r \in C_{(K_1, K_2)}(P)$ *s.t.* $At(r) \subseteq C_1 \cup \ldots \cup C_{s+1}$.

We denote by $JP(P)$ the set of all *joinable pairs*. Intuitively item (i) states that in some topological ordering K_1 immediately precedes K_2; item (ii) states that no atom in K_2 directly depends on an atom from K_1. If this does not hold, joining K_1 and K_2 to achieve independence is not necessary as their ordering is fixed. Finally item (iii) requires that some constraint must access the two SCCs and appear in the evaluation in the bottom of the program computed so far.

Example 7. *For* $P = \{\leftarrow b, not\ a;\ \leftarrow b, not\ c;\ d \leftarrow not\ a;\ c \leftarrow not\ e;\ b \leftarrow c\}$, *we have* $SCC(P) = \{\{a\}, \{b\}, \{c\}, \{d\}, \{e\}\}$. *We observe that* $(\{c\}, \{b\})$ *is a related, but not a joinable pair, because* $(\{c\}, \{b\})$ *satisfies conditions (i) and (iii), but not (ii). On the other hand,* $(\{a\}, \{b\})$ *is a joinable pair.*

We now extend joinability from pairs to any number of SCCs.

Definition 6. *Let P be a program. Then* $K_1, ..., K_m \in SCC(P)$ *are joinable iff* $m = 2$ *and some* $K \in SCC(P)$ *exists such that* $(K_1, K), (K, K_2) \in JP(P)$, *or otherwise* K_i, K_j *are joinable for each* $i, j = 1, ..., m$. *We let* $JC(P) = \{\bigcup_{i=1}^{m} K_i \mid K_1, ..., K_m \in SCC(P)$ *are joinable*$\}$ *and call* $MJC(P) = \{J \in JC(P) \mid \forall J' \in JC(P) : J \not\subset J'\}$ *the set of all* maximal joined components *(MJCs) of P.*

Note that $(K_1, K_2) \in JP(P)$ implies that K_1 and K_2 are joinable.

Example 8. *In Ex. 7,* $(\{a\}, \{b\})$ *is the only nontrivial joinable pair; hence* $MJC(P) = \{\{a, b\}, \{c\}, \{d\}, \{e\}\}$.

As easily seen, $MJC(P)$ is a partitioning of $At(P)$ that results from merging SCCs. We define the *MJC graph* of P as $JG(P) = \langle V_{JG}, E_{JG} \rangle$, where $V_{JG} = MJC(P)$ and $E_{JG} = \{(J, J') \mid J \neq J' \in MJC(P), \exists a \in J, \exists b \in J', (a, b) \in E_{DG}\}$. Note that $JG(P)$ is like $SG(P)$ a dag, and hence admits a topological ordering; we denote by $O(JG(P))$ the set of all such orderings. We thus define

Definition 7. *Let P be a program and* $\leq = (J_1, ..., J_m)$ *be a topological ordering of* $JG(P)$. *Then the splitting sequence induced by* $\leq$ *is* $S_\leq = (S_1, ..., S_m)$, *where* $S_1 = J_1$ *and* $S_k = S_{k-1} \cup J_k$, *for* $k = 2, ..., m$.

The sequence $S_\leq$ is again indeed a splitting sequence, which we call a *MJC-splitting sequence*. We obtain a result analogous to Theorem 5, but in presence of constraints.

Theorem 6. *Let P be a program. For every* $\leq, \leq' \in O(JG(P))$, *we have* $SEQ^{S_\leq}(P) = SEQ^{S_{\leq'}}(P)$.

Similarly as SCC-models, we thus can define the MJC *models* of P as $M^{MJC}(P) = SEQ^{S_\leq}(P)$ for an arbitrary topological ordering $\leq$ of $JG(P)$.

Example 9 (cont'd). *Reconsider P in Example 7. Then for the ordering* $\leq = (\{a\}, \{d\}, \{e\}, \{c\}, \{b\})$ *we obtain* $SEQ^{S_\leq}(P) = \emptyset$, *while for* $\leq' = (\{e\}, \{c\}, \{b\}, \{a\}, \{d\})$ *we obtain* $SEQ^{S_{\leq'}}(P) = \{(bc, abc)\}$. *On the other hand,* $JG(P)$ *has the single topological ordering* $\leq = (\{e\}, \{c\}, \{a, b\}, \{d\})$, *and* $SEQ^{S_\leq}(P) = \{(bc, abc)\}$; *hence* $M^{MJC}(P) = \{(bc, abc)\}$. *Note that* $SEQ(P) = \{(bc, abc), (d, de)\}$.

The problem in Section 4.2 disappears when we use the MJCs. The program $P = \{\leftarrow b, not\ a;\ b\}$ there has the single MJC $J = \{a, b\}$, since the two SCCs $\{a\}$ and $\{b\}$ are related through the constraint $\leftarrow b, not\ a$ and thus joinable. As desired, we get (b, ab) as the (single) MJC-model of P.

Note that trivially, the MJC- and the SCC-semantics coincide for constraint-free programs (in fact, also in absence of cross-constraints). As for the desiderata, we note:

Proposition 3. *The MJC-models semantics, given by* $M^{MJC}(P)$ *for any program P, satisfies (D1)-(D2).*

Classical coherence (D3), however, is not ensured by MJC-models, due to lean component merging that fully preserves dependencies. To obtain a model, blurring strict dependencies can be necessary, where two aspects need to taken into account.

(A1) Inconsistency may still emerge from cross-component constraints.

Example 10. *The program $P = \{\leftarrow b, not\ a;\ b;\ b \leftarrow a\}$ has $MJC(P) = \{\{b\}, \{a\}\}$ as $\{b\}, \{a\}$ are not joinable. As the single MJC-splitting sequence, $(\{a\}, \{a, b\})$, admits no split SEQ-model, $M^{MJC}(P) = \emptyset$.*

This can be remedied by suitably merging components that intersect the same constraint.

(A2) A second, orthogonal aspect is dependence.

Example 11. *The program $P = \{\leftarrow b;\ b \leftarrow not\ a\}$ has no MJC-model, as the MJC-splitting sequence $S = (\{a\}, \{a, b\})$ admits no split SEQ-model; the culprit is a, which does not occur in the constraint.*

Clearly, the problem extends to dependence via an (arbitrarily long) chain of rules (e.g., change in Example 11 the rule to $b \leftarrow c_1$, $c_1 \leftarrow c_{i+1}$, $1 \le i < n$, $c_n \leftarrow not\ a$). Again, this can be remedied by merging components. Many merging policies to ensure (D3) are conceivable; however, such a policy should ideally not dismiss structure unless needed, and it should be efficiently computable; we defer further discussion to Section 7, as the next section will provide useful insight for it.

5   Complexity and Computation

In this section, we consider the computational complexity of the following major reasoning tasks for programs under split SEQ-semantics.

(MCH) Given a program P, a splitting sequence S and an HT-interpretation (X, Y), decide whether (X, Y) is a split semi-equilibrium model of P.

(INF) Given a program P, a splitting sequence S, an atom a and $v \in \{\mathbf{t}, \mathbf{f}, \mathbf{bt}\}$, decide if a is a brave [resp. cautious] SEQ^S-*consequence* of P with value v, denoted $P \models_S^{b,v} a$ [resp. $P \models_S^{c,v} a$], i.e., a has in some (all) $(X, Y) \in SEQ^S(P)$ value v.

(CON) Given a program P and a splitting sequence S, decide whether $SEQ^S(P) \ne \emptyset$.

We consider also SCC- and MJC-splitting sequences and several classes of programs, viz. normal, disjunctive, stratified, and headcycle-free programs.[3] Recall that a program P is *stratified*, if for each $r \in P$ and $C \in SCC(P)$ either $H(r) \cap C = \emptyset$ or $B^-(r) \cap C = \emptyset$; P is *headcycle-free (hcf)*, if $|H(r) \cap C| \le 1$ for each $r \in P$ and $C \in SCC(P')$, where $P' = \{a \leftarrow B^+(r) \mid r \in P,\ a \in H(r)\}$.

Positive programs are here of less interest, as $SEQ^S(P) = \{(M, M) \mid M \in MM(P)\}$ for each splitting sequence S. Furthermore, hcf-programs are under SEQ-semantics sensitive to body shifts; e.g., $P = \{a \vee b;\ a \leftarrow not\ a;\ b \leftarrow not\ b\}$ has the SEQ-models (a, ab) and (b, ab), while its shift $P_{\rightarrow} = \{a \leftarrow not\ b;\ b \leftarrow not\ a;\ a \leftarrow not\ a;\ b \leftarrow not\ b\}$ has the single SEQ-model $(\emptyset, ab)$.

Overview of Complexity Results. Our complexity results are summarized in Table 1. Briefly, they show that split SEQ-models have the same complexity as SEQ-models (i.e., structural information does not affect complexity) except on Problem CON, which is harder. The reason is that coherence (D3) no longer holds. In particular, this means

---

[3] Note that [8] did not consider stratified and hcf programs.

Table 1. Complexity of split SEQ-models (completeness results). The same results hold for canonical models (SCC-, MJC-split seq. S); diverging results for SEQ-models are in brackets.

Problem / Program P:	normal, strat. normal, headcycle-free	disj. strati- fied, disjunc- tive
(MCH) Model checking: $(X,Y) \in SEQ^S(P)$?	coNP	Π_2^p
(INF) Brave reasoning: $P \models_S^{b,v} a$?	Σ_2^p	Σ_3^p
Cautious reasoning: $P \models_S^{c,v} a$?	Π_2^p	Π_3^p
(CON) Existence: $SEQ^S(P) \neq \emptyset$?	Σ_2^p [NP]	Σ_3^p [NP]

that imposing a structural condition on building SEQ-models along SCCs may elimi- nate such models. Furthermore, it implies that no polynomial-time method μ exists that associates with P a splitting sequence $S = \mu(P)$, using a polynomial-time checkable criterion on P, such that (i) μ respects structure, i.e., $\mu(P) \neq (At(P))$ if $SEQ^S(P) \neq \emptyset$ for some $S \neq (At(P))$, and (ii) μ preserves consistency, i.e., $SEQ(P) \neq \emptyset$ implies $SEQ^S(P) \neq \emptyset$; this holds even if μ may be nondeterministic, i.e., can "guess" a suit- able S for P. In other words, the price for ensuring coherence with tractable (or NP) effort is to merge sometimes more components than necessary.

Problems MCH and INF do not become harder, as MCH reduces to polynomially many MCH instances without splitting. The hardness results for arbitrary splitting se- quences are inherited from respective results without splitting; we also provide results for stratified and hcf programs.

For SCC and MJC splitting sequences, we obtain analogous results; informally, the problems do not get easier as splitting can be blocked by irrelevant rules.

Details on the derivation of the results in Table 1 are omitted for space reasons and included in the extended version of this paper.

Constructing and Recognizing Canonical Splitting Sequences. It is well-known that $SCC(P)$ and $SG(P)$ are efficiently computable from P (using Tarjan's [30] algorithm even in linear time); hence, it is not hard to see that one can recognize a SCC-splitting sequence S in polynomial time, and that every such S can be (nondeterministically) generated in polynomial time (in fact, in linear time). We obtain similar tractability results for $MJC(P)$ and MJC-splitting sequences. To this end, we first note the fol- lowing useful proposition.

Proposition 4. *Let P be a program and let $K_1, K_2 \in SCC(P)$. Then K_1 and K_2 satisfy (i) and (ii) of Definition 5 iff they are disconnected in $SG(P)$, i.e., no path from K_1 to K_2 and vice versa exists.*

Theorem 7. *Given a program P, $MJC(P)$ and $JG(P)$ are computable in polynomial time (in time $O(cs \cdot \|P\|)$, where $cs = |\{r \in P \mid H(r) = \emptyset\}|$ and $\|P\|$ is the size of P).*

Proof (Sketch). For every constraint r, determine all $C_1, \ldots, C_k$ in $SCC(P)$ such that $C_i \cap B(r) \neq \emptyset$; suppose $C_1, \ldots, C_l, l \leq k$ are the maximal among them in $SG(P)$.

Using Proposition 4, it can be shown that the pairs (C_i, C_j), $1 \leq i \neq j \leq l$ are the joinable pairs witnessed by r (i.e., satisfying (iii)). One can compute $C_1, \ldots, C_l$ efficiently, e.g. using a stratified program P_r with the following rules:

1. $r_j \leftarrow$, for each $C_j \in V_{SG}$ such that $C_j \cap B(r) \neq \emptyset$;
2. $r_j \leftarrow r_i$ and $n\_max\_r_j \leftarrow r_i$, for each $(C_i, C_j) \in E_{SG}$;
3. $max\_r_j \leftarrow r_j$, not $n\_max\_r_j$, for each $C_i \in V_{SG}$.

The answer set of P_r yields $C_1, \ldots, C_l$, whose union $C_r = \bigcup_{i=1}^{l} C_i$ is contained in a (unique) MJC C (i.e., $C_r \subseteq C$). The set $MJC(P)$ is built by merging C_r and $C_{r'}$ s.t. $C_r \cap C_{r'} \neq \emptyset$ repeatedly. From $MJC(P)$ and $SG(P)$, computing $JG(P)$ is easy.

Each step: building $SCC(P)$, $SG(P)$ and P; evaluating P_r; computing C_r; merging the C_r's; and building $JG(P)$ from $MJC(P)$ and $SG(P)$ is feasible in linear time, except evaluating P_r, which takes $O(cs \cdot \|P\|)$ time; in total, this is $O(cs \cdot \|P\|)$ time. $\square$

6   Application: Inconsistency-Tolerant Query Answering

The standard answer set semantics may be regarded as appropriate when a knowledge base, i.e., logic program, is properly specified adopting the CWA principle to deal with incomplete information. Query answering over a knowledge base then resorts usually to brave or cautious inference from the answer sets of a knowledge base; let us focus on the latter here. However, if (unexpected) incoherence arises, then we lose all information and query answers are trivial. This, however, may not be satisfactory, especially if it is not possible to modify the knowledge base, which may be due to various reasons. Paracoherent semantics can be exploited to overcome this problem and to render query answering operational, without trivialization. In particular, SEQ-semantics is attractive as it builds on simple grounds and (1) brings in "unsupported" assumptions, (2) stays in model building close to answer sets, but distinguishes atoms that require such assumptions from atoms derivable without them, (3) keeps the CWA/LP spirit of minimal assumptions, and (4) easily lifts to extensions (nested programs, arbitrary formulas, aggregates, etc).

For instance, consider a variant of the Russell paraphrase from the Introduction [28]:

$$P = \{shaves(joe, X) \leftarrow not\ shaves(X, X);\ man(paul)\}.$$

While this program has no answer set, SEQ-semantics gives us the model

$(\{shave(joe, paul), man(paul)\}, \{shave(joe, paul), man(paul), shave(joe, joe)\})$;

here the incoherent rule $shaves(joe, joe) \leftarrow not\ shaves(joe, joe)$ obtained by grounding is isolated from rest of the program, avoiding the absence of solutions (a similar intuition is underlying the definition of CWA inhibition rule in [21], used for contradiction removal in a logic program), and allows us to derive, for instance, that $shave(joe, paul)$ and $man(paul)$ are true; furthermore, we can infer that $shave(joe, joe)$ can not be false. Such a capability seems very attractive in query answering.

Now reconsider the program in Example 1, and let us ask for query $go(John)$. Again answer set semantics yields only a trivial answer to the query. However the local incoherence is due to the second and the third rule, and the CWA implies that $go(Mark)$ is false; hence there is no reason to avoid the answer. Moreover split-SEQ semantics yields the unique model $(\{go(John)\}, \{go(John), go(Bill)\})$ and removes the SEQ-model ambiguity, as it makes stronger gap minimization through the bottom-up evaluation. In this way, the relaxation of CWA is minimized.

Notice that also the well-founded semantics (WFS) [31] avoids cyclic incoherence, but resorts to undefinedness that is cautiously propagated, such that reasoning by cases may be abandoned. For example, consider the program

$$P = \{a \leftarrow not\ b;\ b \leftarrow not\ a;\ c \leftarrow a;\ c \leftarrow b;\ d \leftarrow not\ d\}.$$

and ask the query c. The program is incoherent due to the last rule; under WFS, c is undefined (as a and b are, due to the first two rules), while split-SEQ semantics yields the models (ac, acd) and (bc, bcd), from which c is a cautious consequence as expected.

7 Discussion and Conclusion

Related Work. CR-Prolog [3] adds, roughly speaking, a subset-minimal set R of rules from a pool R' to program P such that $P \cup R$ is coherent, and accepts all answer sets of $P \cup R$. This is a (syntactic) inconsistency management strategy (possibly missing cases), not a logic-level semantic treatment of incoherence. Even for R' consisting of all atoms, it may disagree with SEQ-semantics, as adding facts is stronger than blocking negated atoms (admitting more answer sets).

To our knowledge, modularity aspects of paracoherent semantics have not been studied extensively. A noticeable exception is [9], which studied the applicability of splitting sets for several partial models semantics, among them the L-stable semantics. The latter is in spirit close to semi-equilibrium semantics but uses a different 3-valued logic. Unsurprisingly, it does not satisfy the splitting property. Huang et al. [13] showed that hybrid knowledge bases, which generalize logic programs, have modular paraconsistent semantics for stratified knowledge bases; however, the semantics aims at dealing with classical contradictions and not with incoherence in terms of instability through cyclic negation. Pereira and Pinto [24], using the layering notion, that is similar to SCC-split sequences, introduce Layered Models (LM) semantics which is an alternative semantics that extends the stable models semantics for normal logic programs. But LM are just a superset of stable models, and do not coincide with them on coherent programs, so the CWA is too relaxed. Finally, Faber et al. [10] introduced a notion of modularity for answer set semantics, based on syntactic relevance, which has paracoherent features. However, this notion was geared towards query answering rather than model building, and did not incorporate gap minimization at a semantic level.

Further Issues. By the results of Section 5, tractable merging policies that ensure classical coherence (D3) will sometimes merge more components than necessary. To deal with the issues (1) and (2) in Section 4.2, a parametric approach that gradually merges SCCs seems attractive. Let $D_k(C)$ denote the set of all descendants of C in $SG(P)$ within distance $k \geq 0$; then we may proceed as follows.

Create a graph G_k with a node v_r for each constraint r in P, which is labeled with the set of SCCs $\lambda(v_r) = cl_p(\bigcup\{D_k(C_i) \mid C_i \in SCC(P), C_i \cap B(r) \neq \emptyset\})$; here $cl_p(D)$ is a 'closure operation that for a set D of SCCs yields D plus all SCCs that are in $SG(P)$ on some path between two SCCs from D. Merge then nodes v_r and $v_{r'}$ (and their labels, using cl_p) such that $\lambda(v_r) \cap \lambda(v'_r) \neq \emptyset$ as long as possible. After that, add an edge from v to v', if $v \neq v'$ and $SG(P)$ has some edge (C_i, C_j) where $C_i \in \lambda(v)$ and $C_j \in \lambda(v')$. The resulting graph G_k is acyclic and distinct nodes have disjoint labels. Similar as for $JG(P)$, any topological ordering $\leq$ of G_k induces a splitting sequence $S_\leq$ (via the node labels); thanks to an analog of Theorem 6, one can define the M_k-models of P as $M_k(P) = SEQ^{S_\leq}(P)$ for an arbitrary $\leq$.

Clearly, $M_k(P) \subseteq M_{k+1}(P)$ holds for every $k \geq 0$, and $M_k(P) = SEQ(P)$ for large enough k; as $M^{MJC}(P) \subseteq M_0(P)$ holds, we have a hierarchy of models between $M^{MJC}(P)$ and $SEQ(P)$ which eventually establishes (D3); however, predicting the least k such that $M_k(P) \neq \emptyset$ is intractable.

Other relaxed notions of models (using different parameters for cross-constraints and direct dependency) are conceivable; we leave this for future study.

Summary and Outlook. We have studied a refinement of SEQ-semantics that respects modular structure, and we gave a semantics via splitting sets that is amenable to bottom up evaluation of programs.

The generic framework of Equilibrium Logic makes it easy to define SEQ-semantics via gap minimization for many extensions of the programs considered here, such as nested programs, programs with aggregates and external atoms, hybrid knowledge bases etc; programs with classical negation require to use more truth values [17]. It remains to consider modularity in these extensions and to define suitable refinements of SEQ-models. Particularly interesting are modular logic programs [14,6] where explicit (by module encapsulation) and implicit modularity (by splitting sets) occur at the same time.

Besides language extensions, another issue is generalizing the model selection. To this end, preference of gap minimization at higher over lower levels must be supported; however, this intuitively requires more guessing and hinders bottom up evaluation. Finally, efficient algorithms and an implementation are to be done, as well integration into an answer set building framework.

References

1. Alcântara, J., Damásio, C.V., Pereira, L.M.: A declarative characterization of disjunctive paraconsistent answer sets. In: Proc. ECAI 2004, pp. 951–952. IOS Press (2004)
2. Apt, K., Blair, H., Walker, A.: Towards a theory of declarative knowledge. In: Minker (ed.) [16], pp. 89–148
3. Balduccini, M., Gelfond, M.: Logic programs with consistency-restoring rules. In: McCarthy, J., Williams, M.A. (eds.) Int'l Symp. Logical Formalization of Commonsense Reasoning. AAAI 2003 Spring Symp. Series, pp. 9–18 (2003)
4. Ben-Eliyahu, R., Dechter, R.: Propositional semantics for disjunctive logic programs. Ann. Math. & Artif. Intell. 12, 53–87 (1994)
5. Blair, H.A., Subrahmanian, V.S.: Paraconsistent logic programming. Theor. Comput. Sci. 68(2), 135–154 (1989)
6. Dao-Tran, M., Eiter, T., Fink, M., Krennwallner, T.: Modular nonmonotonic logic programming revisited. In: Hill, P.M., Warren, D.S. (eds.) ICLP 2009. LNCS, vol. 5649, pp. 145–159. Springer, Heidelberg (2009)
7. Eiter, T., Gottlob, G.: On the computational cost of disjunctive logic programming: Propositional case. Ann. Math. & Artif. Intell. 15(3/4), 289–323 (1995)
8. Eiter, T., Fink, M., Moura, J.: Paracoherent answer set programming. In: Lin, F., Sattler, U., Truszczyński, M. (eds.) Proc. KR 2010, pp. 486–496. AAAI Press, Toronto (2010)
9. Eiter, T., Leone, N., Saccà, D.: On the partial semantics for disjunctive deductive databases. Ann. Math. & Artif. Intell. 19(1/2), 59–96 (1997)
10. Faber, W., Greco, G., Leone, N.: Magic sets and their application to data integration. J. Comput. Syst. Sci. 73(4), 584–609 (2007)

11. Gelfond, M., Lifschitz, V.: Classical negation in logic programs and disjunctive databases. New Generation Computing 9, 365–385 (1991)
12. Heyting, A.: Die formalen Regeln der intuitionistischen Logik. Sitzungsberichte der Preussischen Akademie der Wissenschaften 16(1), 42–56 (1930)
13. Huang, S., Li, Q., Hitzler, P.: Reasoning with inconsistencies in hybrid MKNF knowledge bases. Logic Journal of the IGPL 21(2), 263–290 (2013)
14. Janhunen, T., Oikarinen, E., Tompits, H., Woltran, S.: Modularity aspects of disjunctive stable models. J. Artif. Intell. Res. (JAIR) 35, 813–857 (2009)
15. Lifschitz, V., Turner, H.: Splitting a logic program. In: Proc. ICLP 1994, pp. 23–38. MIT-Press (1994)
16. Minker, J. (ed.): Foundations of Deductive Databases and Logic Programming. Morgan Kaufman, Washington, DC (1988)
17. Odintsov, S., Pearce, D.J.: Routley semantics for answer sets. In: Baral, C., Greco, G., Leone, N., Terracina, G. (eds.) LPNMR 2005. LNCS (LNAI), vol. 3662, pp. 343–355. Springer, Heidelberg (2005)
18. Osorio, M., Ramírez, J.R.A., Carballido, J.L.: Logical weak completions of paraconsistent logics. J. Log. Comput. 18(6), 913–940 (2008)
19. Pearce, D.: Equilibrium logic. Ann. Math. & Artif. Intell. 47(1-2), 3–41 (2006)
20. Pearce, D.J., Valverde, A.: Quantified equilibrium logic and foundations for answer set programs. In: Garcia de la Banda, M., Pontelli, E. (eds.) ICLP 2008. LNCS, vol. 5366, pp. 546–560. Springer, Heidelberg (2008)
21. Pereira, L.M., Alferes, J.J., Aparício, J.N.: Contradiction removal semantics with explicit negation. In: Masuch, M., Pólos, L. (eds.) Logic at Work 1992. LNCS, vol. 808, pp. 91–105. Springer (1992)
22. Pereira, L.M., Pinto, A.M.: Revised stable models - a semantics for logic programs. In: Bento, C., Cardoso, A., Dias, G. (eds.) EPIA 2005. LNCS (LNAI), vol. 3808, pp. 29–42. Springer, Heidelberg (2005)
23. Pereira, L.M., Pinto, A.M.: Approved models for normal logic programs. In: Dershowitz, N., Voronkov, A. (eds.) LPAR 2007. LNCS (LNAI), vol. 4790, pp. 454–468. Springer, Heidelberg (2007)
24. Pereira, L.M., Pinto, A.M.: Layered models top-down querying of normal logic programs. In: Gill, A., Swift, T. (eds.) PADL 2009. LNCS, vol. 5418, pp. 254–268. Springer, Heidelberg (2008)
25. Przymusinski, T.: Stable semantics for disjunctive programs. New Generation Computing 9, 401–424 (1991)
26. Przymusinski, T.C.: On the declarative semantics of deductive databases and logic programs. In: Minker (ed.) [16], pp. 193–216
27. Saccà, D., Zaniolo, C.: Partial models and three-valued stable models in logic programs with negation. In: Subrahmanian, V., et al. (eds.) Proc. LPNMR 1991, pp. 87–101. MIT Press (1991)
28. Sakama, C., Inoue, K.: Paraconsistent stable semantics for extended disjunctive programs. J. Log. Comput. 5(3), 265–285 (1995)
29. Seipel, D.: Partial evidential stable models for disjunctive deductive databases. In: Dix, J., Moniz Pereira, L., Przymusinski, T.C. (eds.) LPKR 1997. LNCS (LNAI), vol. 1471, pp. 66–84. Springer, Heidelberg (1998)
30. Tarjan, R.E.: Depth-first search and linear graph algorithms. SIAM J. Comput. 1(2), 146–160 (1972)
31. van Gelder, A., Ross, K., Schlipf, J.: The well-founded semantics for general logic programs. J. ACM 38(3), 620–650 (1991)
32. You, J.H., Yuan, L.: A three-valued semantics for deductive databases and logic programs. J. Comput. Syst. Sci. 49, 334–361 (1994)

Action Theories over Generalized Databases with Equality Constraints*

Fabio Patrizi and Stavros Vassos

Department of Computer, Control, and Management Engineering (DIAG)
Sapienza University of Rome
Rome, Italy
{patrizi,vassos}@dis.uniroma1.it

Abstract. In this work we focus on situation calculus action theories over *generalized databases with equality constraints*, here called GFDBs, which are able to finitely represent complete information over a possibly infinite number of objects. We contribute with the following: i) we show that GFDBs characterize the class of definitional KBs and that they are closed under progression; ii) we show that temporal projection queries are decidable for theories with an initial KB expressed as a GFDB, which we call GFDB-BATs; iii) we extend the notion of boundedness to allow for infinite objects in the extensions of fluents and prove that a wide class of generalized projection queries is decidable for GFDB-BAT under a restriction we call C-boundedness; iv) we show that checking whether C-boundedness holds for a given bound is decidable. The proposed action theories are to date the most expressive ones for which there are decidable methods for computing both progression and generalized projection.

Introduction

Situation calculus basic action theories (BATs) [13] are well-studied logical theories that consist of a first-order knowledge base (KB) which describes the initial state of a given domain, and a set of first-order axioms that specify how the properties of the domain change under the effects of named actions. Two important reasoning problems are studied in the context of variants of BATs: temporal *projection* and *progression*. Projection is about *predicting* whether a condition would hold in the resulting state if a series of actions were to be performed in the initial KB, while progression is about *updating* the KB by a new description that reflects the current state after actions have been performed.

If we think of a BAT as a database which also features some specified operations (or actions) that alter the data, solving the projection problem corresponds to answering a query over the state of the database after some of these operations are consecutively performed, while the progression problem is to provide a concrete representation of the resulting database state. It then becomes clear

---

* The authors acknowledge the support of the EU Project FP7-ICT 318338 (OP-TIQUE) and the Sapienza Award 2013 "Spiritlets" project.

E. Fermé and J. Leite (Eds.): JELIA 2014, LNAI 8761, pp. 472–485, 2014.
© Springer International Publishing Switzerland 2014

that these two problems are closely related. In particular, progression can be used as a way to solve the projection problem in the following way: first update the database according to the operations in question and then answer the query.

Nonetheless, this view is only helpful when the KB is a database. Solving projection and progression becomes very tricky in the general case when we have an unrestricted first-order specifications for the KB and the effects of actions. As far as progression is concerned, for the general case it has been shown that second-order logic may be required to capture the updated KB [9,15]; a list of some special cases where it becomes first-order is studied in [16]. Similarly, a few cases have been studied such that projection is decidable, namely *(i)* the case when the KB is a regular database as we discussed above [14], *(ii)* the case when the KB is an open-world database of a particular form, in which case a sound and sometimes complete method for projection is specified [12], *(iii)* the case of a modified version of the situation calculus built using a two-variable fragment of first-order logic [6] in which case projection is decidable, and, more recently, *(iv)* the case of bounded theories that require that in all models and in every situation there is a fixed upperbound on the number of positive atomic facts [3].

Notably, the case when the KB has the form of a *generalized database with constraints* [7], which allows to specify relations with possibly *infinitely many tuples*, has not been investigated. In this work we show that for a special type of BATs whose KB is a generalized database with equality constraints projection is decidable and a first-order progression can always be computed. We then look into richer forms of projection that may refer to more than one possible evolution of the initial KB, e.g., capturing invariants of the form "after execution of α condition ϕ always holds" and specify a condition that also ensures decidability. To the best of our knowledge these BATs are to date the most expressive ones with an infinite domain and possibly infinite extensions for fluents for which there are known decidable methods for computing both a first-order progression and generalized projection.

Situation Calculus Basic Action Theories (BATs)

The situation calculus as presented by Reiter [13] is a three-sorted first-order language $\mathcal{L}$ with equality (and some limited second-order features). The sorts are used to distinguish between actions, situations, and objects.

A *situation* represents a world history as a sequence of actions. S_0 is used to denote the initial situation and sequences of actions are built using the function symbol do, such that $do(a, s)$ denotes the successor situation resulting from performing action a in situation s. Actions need not be executable in all situations, and the predicate $Poss(a, s)$ states that action a is executable in situation s. We will typically use a to denote a variable of sort action and α to denote a term of sort action, and similarly s and σ for situations. A (relational) *fluent* is a predicate whose last argument is a situation, and thus whose value can change from situation to situation. We also assume a finite number of fluent and action symbols, $\mathcal{F}$ and $\mathcal{A}$, and an infinite number of constants $\mathcal{C}$.

Often we need to restrict our attention to sentences in $\mathcal{L}$ that refer to a particular situation. For example, the initial knowledge base (KB) is a finite set of sentences in $\mathcal{L}$ that do not mention any situation terms except for S_0. We define $\mathcal{L}_\sigma$ to be the subset of $\mathcal{L}$ that does not mention any other situation terms except for σ, does not mention $Poss$, and where σ is not used by any quantifier [9]. When a formula $\phi(\sigma)$ is in $\mathcal{L}_\sigma$ we say that it is *uniform in* σ [13].

We will be dealing with a specific kind of $\mathcal{L}$-theory, the so-called *basic action theory (BAT)* $\mathcal{D}$ which has the following form:[1]

$$\mathcal{D} = \mathcal{D}_{ap} \cup \mathcal{D}_{ss} \cup \mathcal{D}_{una} \cup \mathcal{D}_0 \cup \Sigma, \text{ where:}$$

1. $\mathcal{D}_{ap}$ is a set of action precondition axioms, one for each action function symbol $A_i \in \mathcal{A}$, of the form $Poss(A_i(\boldsymbol{x}), s) \equiv \Pi_i(\boldsymbol{x}, s)$, where $\Pi_i(\boldsymbol{x}, s)$ is in $\mathcal{L}_s$.
2. $\mathcal{D}_{ss}$ is a set of successor state axioms (SSAs), one per fluent symbol $F_i \in \mathcal{F}$, of the form $F_i(\boldsymbol{x}, do(a, s)) \equiv \Phi_i(\boldsymbol{x}, a, s)$, with $\Phi_i(\boldsymbol{x}, a, s) \in \mathcal{L}_s$. SSAs characterize the conditions under which F_i has a specific value at situation $do(a, s)$ as a function of situation s and action a.
3. $\mathcal{D}_{una}$ is the set of unique-names axioms for actions: $A_i(\boldsymbol{x}) \neq A_j(\boldsymbol{y})$, and $A_i(\boldsymbol{x}) = A_i(\boldsymbol{y}) \supset \boldsymbol{x} = \boldsymbol{y}$, for each pair of distinct symbols A_i and A_j in $\mathcal{A}$.
4. $\mathcal{D}_0$ is uniform in S_0 and describes the initial situation.
5. Σ is a set of foundational axioms which formally define legal situations and an ordering by means of symbol $\sqsubseteq$, also using a second-order inductive axiom.

Finally, we will typically restrict our attention to the case that distinct constants are always interpreted into different objects. This unique-names restriction can be captured by a set of axioms $\mathcal{E}$ consisting of the axioms of equality and the set of sentences $\{c_i \neq c_j | c_i, c_j \in \mathcal{C}, i \neq j\}$ [8].

Generalized Databases and Query Evaluation

A *generalized database* [7] is a first-order interpretation (finitely) represented as constraints on the tuples of relations. Generalized databases are obtained by including in each relation the (possibly infinite) set of tuples that satisfy the corresponding constraints. Various classes of constraints are considered. In this work we focus on equality constraints. Let us present basic definitions from [7] in the context of the situation calculus language $\mathcal{L}$ we specified.

Definition 1. *An* equality constraint *is a literal formula* $x\theta y$ *or* $x\theta c$, *where* $c \in \mathcal{C}$ *and* θ *is* $=$ *or* $\neq$. *A generalized k-tuple over variables* $x_1, \ldots, x_k$ *is a finite conjunction* ψ *of equality constraints whose variables are free and among* $x_1, \ldots, x_k$. *A generalized relation of arity k is a finite set* $R = \{\psi_1, \ldots, \psi_q\}$, *of generalized k-tuples over* $x_1, \ldots, x_k$. *The formula corresponding to a generalized relation R is the disjunction* $\psi_1 \vee \cdots \vee \psi_q$. *We will use* ϕ_R *to denote the quantifier-free formula corresponding to relation R.*

---

[1] For readability we often omit the leading universal quantifiers.

Generalized relations represent possibly infinite relations over the domain of sort objects of $\mathcal{L}$. In detail, let $R = \{\psi_1, \ldots, \psi_q\}$ be a generalized relation of arity k, and ϕ_R the formula corresponding to this relation. Then, R is associated with the k-ary relation $\{c \mid c \in \mathcal{C}^k, \mathcal{E} \models \phi_R(c)\}$. It is easy to see that any finite relation can be represented as a generalized relation, while infinite relations exist that are not captured by generalized ones.

The notion of generalized relation extends naturally to databases: a *generalized database* is a finite set of generalized relations. Differently from standard settings in databases, since generalized databases represent in general infinite relations, answers to queries are in general infinite and cannot be represented by means of finite relations. Nonetheless, it turns out that query answers over generalized databases can be represented as generalized relations with constraints, thus providing a closed representation system.

First observe that we can characterize the answer to a query by replacing the occurrences of relation atoms in the query by the formulas corresponding to the relations of the generalized database. Let $\varphi(x)$ be a first-order query over the relation symbols $R_1, \ldots, R_n$ and D a generalized database over the same relations. Let $\varphi[R_1/\phi_{R_1}, \ldots, R_n/\phi_{R_n}](x)$ be the first-order formula in $\mathcal{L}$ that is the result of replacing every occurrence of R_i in φ by ϕ_{R_i}. This formula, denoted here as $\varphi'(x)$, is then a finite representation of the answer to query φ over D.

The second trick is to observe that $\varphi'(x)$ can be represented as a finite set of generalized tuples that characterize the isomorphism types of regular tuples in the answer of the query. Kanellakis *et al.* [7] specify a procedure that first builds all the (finitely many) generalized tuples ψ over x using only the constants mentioned in $\varphi'(x)$, and then checks which of these are consistent with $\varphi'(x)$. The set of the ones that are consistent is a generalized relation that (finitely) represents the answer to $\varphi(x)$ over D.

Kanellakis *et al.* [7] also show that following this procedure the answer to a first-order query over a generalized database (with equality constraints) is computable in LOGSPACE data complexity. Thus, this constitutes a notable case of infinite databases for which an effective procedure exists to answer queries.

BATs with Generalized Fluent Databases (GFDBs)

Reiter [13] investigates the case where the initial knowledge base (KB) is a *definitional theory* with respect to the fluent atoms in S_0, i.e., with S_0 characterized as follows: $\bigwedge_{F_i \in \mathcal{F}} \forall x_i . F_i(x_i, S_0) \equiv \phi_i(x_i)$, where $\phi_i(x_i)$, called the *definition* for F_i, is an unrestricted first-order formula mentioning no situations. When the underlying language $\mathcal{L}$ includes only fluent predicates, as it is the case in this paper, a KB in such form is called a *definitional KBs*.

Definitional KBs in $\mathcal{L}$ capture *complete* information for fluents under the assumption of the unique-name axioms for constants and axioms for equality in $\mathcal{E}$. For example the following axiom states that there are exactly two atoms true for $In(x_1, x_2, S_0)$, namely $In(box, it_1, S_0)$ and $In(box, it_2, S_0)$:

$$\forall x \forall y (In(x, y, S_0) \equiv (x = box \wedge (y = it_1 \vee y = it_2))).$$

Nonetheless, the definition for a fluent can be any unrestricted first-order formula built over the constants in $\mathcal{C}$ and equality, for example it could have the following form that implies an infinity of ground atoms that are true in S_0:

$$\forall x \forall y (In(x, y, S_0) \equiv (x \neq box \wedge (y = it_1 \vee y = it_2))).$$

Note that this definition can be rewritten as a formula that corresponds to a generalized relation by distributing over the disjunction. Also, more complicated definitions that include quantification do not actually add to the expressiveness, as first-order theories of equality admit quantifier elimination [5].

We identify BATs over generalized databases as follows.

Definition 2. *A set $\mathcal{D}_0$ of first-order sentences uniform in S_0 is a generalized fluent database (GFDB) iff it has the form $\bigwedge_{F_i \in \mathcal{F}} \forall \boldsymbol{x_i}.F(\boldsymbol{x_i}, S_0) \equiv \phi_i(\boldsymbol{x_i})$, where $\phi_i(\boldsymbol{x_i})$ is a formula that corresponds to a generalized relation over $\boldsymbol{x}$, i.e., is a disjunction of conjunctions of equality constraints. A basic action theory $\mathcal{D}$ is a basic action theory over a generalized fluent database (BAT-GFDB) iff it also includes the set of axioms $\mathcal{E}$ and $\mathcal{D}_0$ is a generalized fluent database.*

Theorem 1. *Let ϕ be a definitional KB. There exists a GFDB ϕ' such that $\mathcal{E} \models \phi \equiv \phi'$.*

As discussed in the previous section for such KBs there is also a decidable LOGSPACE data complexity procedure for evaluating queries. Note also that equivalence of GFDBs can also be decided, formed as an appropriate query. With these tools available in the next sections we will proceed to show how solutions for progression and projection can be obtained for BAT-GFDBs. We close this section with a simple example of a GFDB-BAT.

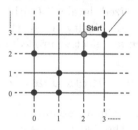

Fig. 1. Map of the *grid* domain

Example 1. Figure 1 shows a space where an agent can move only along specified lines. The agent starts in $(2, 3)$ and can initially move only vertically, i.e., to any position s.t. $x = 2$. After moving, the agent can change direction (at the next move) only if it has stopped at a crossing point (marked with solid circles). For instance, if the agent moves from $(2, 3)$ to $(2, 1)$, it cannot move next to, e.g., $(0, 1)$. Instead, if the agent stops in $(2, 2)$, it can then move along the x-axis to, e.g., $(10, 2)$. The crossing points are placed along the diagonal, i.e., points s.t. $x = y$, and at $(0, 2)$ and $(1, 0)$. A BAT describing this domain is as follows:

- Action types: $\mathcal{A} = \{moveTo(x, y)\}$
- Fluents: $\mathcal{F} = \{At(x, y, s), Dest(x, y, s), Cross(x, y, s)\}$
- $\mathcal{D}_0$: $At(x, y, S_0) \equiv x = 2 \wedge y = 3,\quad Dest(x, y, S_0) \equiv x = 2$

    $Cross(x, y, S_0) \equiv (x = y) \vee (x = 0 \wedge y = 2) \vee (x = 1 \wedge y = 0)$

- $\mathcal{D}_{ap}$: $Poss(moveTo(x, y), s) \equiv Dest(x, y, s)$

- $\mathcal{D}_{ss}$: $Cross(x, y, do(moveTo(x', y'), s)) \equiv Cross(x, y, s)$

    $At(x, y, do(moveTo(x', y'), s)) \equiv (x = x' \wedge y = y')$

    $Dest(x, y, do(moveTo(x', y'), s)) \equiv (Cross(x', y', s) \wedge (x = x' \vee y = y')) \vee$

    $\exists x'', y''.At(x'', y'', s) \wedge [(x' = x'' \wedge y' \neq y'' \wedge x = x') \vee$

    $(y' = y'' \wedge x' \neq x'' \wedge y = y') \vee (y' = y'' \wedge x' = x'' \wedge Dest(x, y, s))]$

Observe that the extension of fluent $Dest$ is initially infinite. Indeed, according to its definition, the fluent contains all possible tuples s.t. $x = 2$. Such tuples represent the infinitely many possible destinations available to the agent in S_0.

Progression of BAT-GFDBs

In order to do a one-step progression of the BAT $\mathcal{D}$ with respect to the ground action α we need to replace $\mathcal{D}_0$ in $\mathcal{D}$ by a suitable set $\mathcal{D}_\alpha$ of sentences uniform in $do(\alpha, S_0)$ so that the original theory $\mathcal{D}$ and the theory $(\mathcal{D} - \mathcal{D}_0) \cup \mathcal{D}_\alpha$ are equivalent with respect to how they describe the situation $do(\alpha, S_0)$ and the situations in the future of $do(\alpha, S_0)$.

Lin and Reiter [9] gave a model-theoretic definition for the progression $\mathcal{D}_\alpha$ of $\mathcal{D}_0$ wrt α and $\mathcal{D}$ that achieves this goal. Finding such a $\mathcal{D}_\alpha$ is a difficult task and it has been shown that second-order logic may be required in the general case [9,15]. Nonetheless, for the definitional KBs, and as a result also for the special case of generalized fluent databases, there is a very simple way to progress.

Theorem 2 ([9]). Let $\mathcal{D}_0$ be $\bigwedge_{F_i \in \mathcal{F}} \forall \boldsymbol{x_i}.F_i(\boldsymbol{x_i}, S_0) \equiv \phi_i(\boldsymbol{x_i})$, and for all $F_i \in \mathcal{F}$, let $\mathcal{D}_{ss}$ include an SSA of the form $F_i(\boldsymbol{x_i}, do(a, s)) \equiv \Phi_i(\boldsymbol{x_i}, \alpha, S_0)$. For each $F_i \in \mathcal{F}$, let $\Phi'_i(\boldsymbol{x_i}, \alpha, S_0)$ be the sentence obtained by replacing every occurrence of atoms $F_j(\boldsymbol{o}, S_0)$ in $\Phi_i(\boldsymbol{x_i}, \alpha, S_0)$ by $\phi_j(\boldsymbol{o})$, and $\mathcal{D}_\alpha$ be $\bigwedge_{F_i \in \mathcal{F}} \forall \boldsymbol{x_i}.F_i(\boldsymbol{x_i}, do(a, s)) \equiv \Phi'_i(\boldsymbol{x_i}, \alpha, S_0)$. Then, $\mathcal{D}_\alpha$ is a progression of $\mathcal{D}_0$ wrt α and the theory $\mathcal{D}$.

Observe that this is very similar to the first trick we discussed when we reviewed the work on generalized databases and query evaluation [7], where we replaced the occurrences of relation atoms in the query by the formulas corresponding to the relations of the generalized database. It is interesting to look into how this method works when $\mathcal{D}_0$ is a generalized fluent database, that will illustrate how the second trick can also be of use.

Note that since each $\Phi_i(\boldsymbol{x_i}, \alpha, S_0)$ in the SSAs is in general unrestricted, e.g., may include quantifiers, $\mathcal{D}_\alpha$ is not guaranteed to be in the form of a generalized fluent database even though $\mathcal{D}_0$ is. The point in using a form like the generalized fluent database is that it allows us to perform query evaluation using the methods and existing technologies in constraint databases instead of performing more general theorem proving. Therefore, we want progression to preserve the form of $\mathcal{D}_0$. The method of Theorem 2 does well in preserving the form of a *definitional KB* but does not preserve the form in the case of a generalized fluent database.

This is how the second trick becomes useful. The idea is to consider generalized tuples as the "base" formulas that we use to express any generalized fluent relation. This is similar to a regular database where we would update $\mathcal{D}_0$ into a $\mathcal{D}_\alpha$ such that for every fluent a finite list of tuples is specified. Theorem 1 then provides a way to transform, by means of quantifier elimination, the resulting $\mathcal{D}_\alpha$ of Theorem 2 into the form of a generalized fluent database.

Theorem 3. *Let $\mathcal{D}$ be a BAT over a generalized fluent database and α a ground action. Then there exists a first-order progression $\mathcal{D}_\alpha$ of $\mathcal{D}_0$ wrt α and $\mathcal{D}$ that is in the form of a generalized fluent database.*

As a consequence, we can *iteratively* progress a BAT-GFDB and express the state corresponding to any ground situation as a generalized fluent database.

Example 2. The following theory $\mathcal{D}_\alpha$ is the progression of the initial GFDB $\mathcal{D}_0$ of Example 1, wrt action $\alpha = moveTo(2, 2)$ (and theory $\mathcal{D}$):

$$At(x, y, do(\alpha, S_0)) \equiv x = 2 \wedge y = 2, \quad Dest(x, y, do(\alpha, S_0)) \equiv x = 2 \vee y = 2$$
$$Cross(x, y, do(\alpha, S_0)) \equiv (x = y) \vee (x = 0 \wedge y = 2) \vee (x = 1 \wedge y = 0)$$

Notice that, similarly to the initial situation, after executing α in S_0, the agent still has an infinite set of destinations available: all those s.t. $x = 2$ or $y = 2$.

Finally, since every definitional KB can be expressed as a GFDB, this analysis also illustrates a subtle detail about the way we understand progression. Both a progression $\mathcal{D}_\alpha$ according to Theorem 2 and a progression $\mathcal{D}'_\alpha$ according to Theorem 3 qualify as logically correct progressions of $\mathcal{D}_0$ and are logically equivalent (under the assumption of $\mathcal{E}$). Nonetheless, $\mathcal{D}_\alpha$ is more of a *logical specification of the changes* that need to be made due to action α and $\mathcal{D}'_\alpha$ more of a *materialized update* of these changes into a practical *normal form*.

Another way to look at it is that the progression procedure of Theorem 2 is purely syntactic (linear to the size of $\mathcal{D}_0$) and does not involve any form of evaluation; in a sense, the fluents are not updated to a new truth value but, rather, the new truth values are still specified with respect to the initial situation. Theorem proving is then needed in order to reason over the specification, even for a simple look-up query for a given atom. Even though this logical specification may in fact be beneficial in some cases, in practice we expect that materializing the update into a GFDB normal form (that explicitly lists the generalized tuples for each fluent) would offer similar advantages as updates do in regular databases.

Projection over BAT-GFDBs

The *(simple) projection problem* is the task of *predicting* whether a condition holds at a particular time in the future after a series of ground actions have been executed [13]. The following is a straightforward result.

Theorem 4. *Let $\mathcal{D}$ be a BAT-GFDB, $\alpha_1, \ldots, \alpha_n$ a sequence of ground actions, and $\phi(s)$ a first-order formula uniform in s. Then determining whether or not the following holds is decidable: $\mathcal{D} \models \phi(do(\alpha_n, \cdots do(\alpha_1, S_0)))$.*

This is not a new result and can be proven by means of regression and the fact that $\mathcal{E}$ is decidable. Our previous analysis also shows that simple projection queries over a BAT-GFDB can be decided by iteratively progressing $\mathcal{D}_0$ wrt $\alpha_1, \ldots, \alpha_n$ according to Th. 3 and then evaluating the query over the resulting GFDB following the method of [7]. Depending on the type of queries, and the frequency that actions occur, either approach may be preferred under conditions.

We now proceed to show a major result about the decidability of richer projection queries over BAT-GFDBs that may also quantify over future situations. A *generalized* version of the projection problem is when ϕ may refer to any number or combination of future situations. For instance, referring to Ex. 1, the formula $\forall s.do(moveTo(2,2), S_0) \sqsubseteq s \supset \exists xy.Dest(x, y, s)$ states that after executing action $moveTo(2,2)$ in the initial situation, the agent has an available destination in any future situation.

We consider the language $\mathcal{L}_p$ of *generalized projection queries* φ. $\mathcal{L}_p$ is defined on top of the language $\mathcal{L}_n$, whose formulas ψ are as follows: $\phi := x = c \mid x = y \mid F(\boldsymbol{x}, s) \mid F(\boldsymbol{x}, \sigma) \mid \neg \phi \mid \phi \wedge \phi \mid \exists x.\phi$, for F a fluent symbol, c a constant, and σ a ground situation term. $\mathcal{L}_p$ formulas are defined as: $\varphi := \phi \mid \neg \varphi \mid \varphi \wedge \varphi \mid \exists s.\sigma \sqsubseteq s \wedge \varphi$, where $\phi \in \mathcal{L}_n$ is any formula uniform in s or in a ground situation term σ, whose free variables (if any) are only of sort situation.

We also consider a class of BAT-GFDBs which we call C-bounded. To define it, let T_V be the (finite) set of all generalized tuples ψ that use equality constraints with (only variable) symbols from the finite set of variables V, and s.t. ψ does not contain multiple occurrences of some equality constraint. Notice that since generalized tuples are conjunctions (thus multiple occurrences of a conjunct do not change their semantics), T_V essentially contains all the possible generalized tuples one can build using symbols from V.

Definition 3. *Let $\mathcal{D}$ be a BAT-GFDB and B a natural number. A ground situation term σ is said to be* constant-bounded by B in $\mathcal{D}$ *(or simply C-bounded) iff for every fluent $F(\boldsymbol{x}, s) \in \mathcal{F}$, it is the case that $\mathcal{D} \models \bigvee_{\Psi \in 2^{T_V}} \exists \boldsymbol{y}.F(\boldsymbol{x}, \sigma) \equiv \bigvee_{\psi \in \Psi} \psi$, where: V is partitioned into X and Y, with X the set of variables occurring in $\boldsymbol{x}$, Y any set of variable symbols such that $|Y| = B$, and $\boldsymbol{y}$ are the free variables of ψ coming from Y. $\mathcal{D}$ is said to be* constant-bounded by a finite bound B, C-bounded by B *for short, iff every ground situation term of $\mathcal{D}$ that is executable is also C-bounded by B.*

Notice that Ψ above is a set of generalized tuples, thus the formula $\bigvee_{\psi \in \Psi} \psi$ is a generalized relation. Intuitively, Definition 3 requires that the definition of each fluent in σ is a generalized relation mentioning at most B distinct constants. An example of C-bounded BAT-GFDB is provided by the action theory of Ex. 1.

For this class of theories, we have the following result.

Theorem 5. *Given a BAT-GFDB $\mathcal{D}$ that is C-bounded by some B, and a generalized projection query sentence φ in $\mathcal{L}_p$, it is decidable to check whether $\mathcal{D} \models \varphi$.*

The rest of this section details the proof of this theorem.

Definition 4. *A (labelled) transition system over GFDBs (for a GFDB-BAT $\mathcal{D}$), GFDB-TS for short, is a tuple $T = (Q, q_0, \rightarrow, L)$, where:*

- Q *is the GFDB-TS's (nonempty) set of nodes[2];*
- $q_0 \in Q$ *is the GFDB-TS's initial node;*
- $\rightarrow \subseteq Q \times Act \times Q$ *is the GFDB-TS's transition relation, for Act the set of all ground action terms of $\mathcal{D}$; we interchange the notations $(q, \alpha, q') \in \rightarrow$ and $q \xrightarrow{\alpha} q'$;*
- L *is the GFDB-TS's labelling function, associating each node q with a generalized fluent database $L(q)$.*

We associate each ground situation term $\sigma = do([\alpha_1, \ldots, \alpha_n], S_0)$ with the node q_σ s.t. $q_0 \xrightarrow{\alpha_1} \cdots \xrightarrow{\alpha_{n-1}} q_\sigma$, if it exists.

In Def. 4, the label $L(q)$ of a generic node q is a GFDB, thus uniform in S_0 as required by the corresponding definition. Such GFDBs should be intuitively understood as defining the state of the situation obtained by executing, from S_0, the ground actions labeling a path from q_0 to q, while moving the "S_0 point of reference" to be the current situation.

Besides the standard semantics of $\mathcal{L}_p$ over action theories, we define an alternative semantics over GFDB-TSs.

Definition 5. *Given a GFDB-TS T, an $\mathcal{L}_p$ formula φ, and a node q of T, we define when T satisfies φ at node q, written $T, q \models \varphi$, as follows:*

- *for $\varphi = \phi \in \mathcal{L}_n$, $T, q \models \varphi$, iff*
  - *ϕ is uniform in s, i.e., of the form $\phi(s)$, and $\mathcal{E}, L(q) \models \phi(S_0)$, i.e., treated as a local query over node q; or*
  - *ϕ is uniform in σ, q_σ exists, and $T, q_\sigma \models \phi[\sigma/s]$, i.e., reduced to the previous case as a a unique base case;*
- *the semantics of the connectives $\neg, \wedge$ is as standard;*
- *$T, q \models \exists s.\sigma \sqsubseteq s \wedge \varphi$, for $\sigma = do([\alpha_1, \ldots, \alpha_n], S_0)$, if for some $\sigma' = do([\alpha_1, \ldots, \alpha_n, \ldots, \alpha_m], S_0)$ s.t. $m \geq n$, it is the case that $q_{\sigma'}$ is defined and $T, q_{\sigma'} \models \varphi[s/\sigma']$;*

When φ is a sentence, T is said to satisfy φ, written $T \models \varphi$ iff $T, q_0 \models \varphi$.

Every BAT-GFDB $\mathcal{D}$ induces an infinite GFDB-TS, as defined below.

---

[2] We use *node* instead of *state* to avoid confusion with the states associated with situations in action theories.

Definition 6. *The* induced GFDB-TS *of a BAT-GFDB* $\mathcal{D}$ *is the GFDB-TS* $T_{\mathcal{D}} = (Q, q_0, \rightarrow, L)$ *(over* $\mathcal{D}$*), s.t.:*

- Q *is the set of all* $\mathcal{D}$*'s ground situation terms;*
- $q_0 = S_0$;
- $q \xrightarrow{A(\mathbf{c})} q'$ *iff* $q' = do(A(\mathbf{c}), q)$;
- $L(q)$ *is a generalized database such that:*
  - *if* $q = q_0$ *then* $L(q) = \mathcal{D}_0$;
  - *if* $q \neq q_0$ *and there exists* q' *s.t.* $q' \xrightarrow{A(\mathbf{c})} q$, *then* $L(q')$ *is the progression of* $L(q)$ *wrt* $A(\mathbf{c})$ *and* $\mathcal{D}$, *where* $do(A(\mathbf{c}), q)$ *is replaced by* S_0.

Our first result shows that, as far as generalized projection queries are concerned, the induced GFDB-TS can be used as an alternative representation of $\mathcal{D}$.

Lemma 1. *Let* $\mathcal{D}$ *be a BAT-GFDB and* $T_{\mathcal{D}}$ *the corresponding induced GFDB-TS. Then, for any generalized projection query* φ *that is a sentence in* $\mathcal{L}_p$, *we have that* $\mathcal{D} \models \varphi$ *iff* $T_{\mathcal{D}} \models \varphi$.

Proof. By induction on the structure of φ.

Thus, one can check whether $\mathcal{D} \models \varphi$ using $T_{\mathcal{D}}$. Obviously, this does not imply decidability, as both the situation terms and the state space of $T_{\mathcal{D}}$ are in general infinite. We show next how to circumvent this problem when $\mathcal{D}$ is a BAT-GFDB C-bounded by a bound B.

Starting from $\mathcal{D}$ and φ, we construct a *finite* GFDB-TS $\hat{T}_{\mathcal{D}, \varphi}$ that is indistinguishable from $T_{\mathcal{D}}$, by φ. To this end, fix a finite set of constants $H \subseteq \mathcal{C}$, s.t. $\mathcal{C}_{\mathcal{D}} \cup \mathcal{C}_{\varphi} \subseteq H$ and $|H| \geq B \cdot |\mathcal{F}| + |\mathcal{C}_{\mathcal{D}} \cup \mathcal{C}_{\varphi}| + N_A$, where: $\mathcal{C}_{\mathcal{D}}$ and $\mathcal{C}_{\varphi}$ are the set of constants respectively occurring in $\mathcal{D}$ and φ, and N_A is the largest number of parameters in the action types of $\mathcal{D}$. The construction of $\hat{T}_{\mathcal{D}, \varphi}$ is shown in Algorithm 1, where $Progr(\mathcal{D}_0, A(\mathbf{c}))$ denotes the result of progressing an initial theory $\mathcal{D}_0$ w.r.t. a ground action $A(\mathbf{c})$, which we assume to be a GFDB (see Th. 3). The symbol $\equiv_{\mathcal{E}}$ represents logical equivalence between theories, under $\mathcal{E}$.

The procedure inductively builds a GD-TS for $\mathcal{D}$, by applying, at every step, all the executable actions obtained from the action types of $\mathcal{D}$ and the constants in H. Applying an action $A(\mathbf{h})$ consists in progressing (line 10) the labeling DB of the current node q (initially q_0) w.r.t. $A(\mathbf{h})$, provided it is executable according to the labeling $L(q)$ (line 9), then replacing, in the obtained progression, the situation term $do(A(\mathbf{h}), S_0)$ by S_0. If the obtained progression P is not logically equivalent (under $\mathcal{E}$) to any GFDB labeling some node of (the current) Q, then a fresh node q' is added to Q, with labeling $L(q) = P$ (lines 11–15); if instead some node q' exists with $L(q')$ logically equivalent to P, then q' is simply retrieved from Q (line 17), and no new node is added. In either case, a transition from q to q' under the executed action is added to $\rightarrow$ (line 15). Every time a fresh node is added to Q, it is stored in the set $Front$, containing the nodes of Q to be expanded. Initially, $Front = \{q_0\}$. The algorithm returns when $Front$ is empty.

Lemma 2. *Algorithm 1 terminates on any C-bounded BAT-GFDB* $\mathcal{D}$ *and generalized projection query* φ.

Algorithm 1. (Constructs $\hat{T}_{\mathcal{D},\varphi}$)

```
1: procedure BUILDÎ(D, φ)
2:     Q := {q₀};
3:     → := ∅;
4:     L(q₀) := D₀;
5:     Front := {q₀};
6:     while Front ≠ ∅ do
7:         for all q ∈ Front do
8:             Front := Front \ {q};
9:             for all A(h) s.t. A ∈ A, h ∈ H and E, L(q) ⊨ Poss(A(h), S₀) do
10:                 P := Progr(L(q), A(h))[do(S₀, A(h))/S₀];
11:                 if ¬∃q' ∈ Q s.t. P ≡ε L(q') then
12:                     let q' a fresh node;
13:                     Q := Q ∪ q';
14:                     L(q') := P;
15:                     Front := Front ∪ {q'};
16:                 else
17:                     let q' ∈ Q be s.t. L(q') ≡ε P;
18:                 end if
19:                 → := → ∪ (q, A(h), q');
20:             end for
21:         end for
22:     end while
23:     return (Q, q₀, →, L);
24: end procedure
```

Proof. Follows from the facts: H is finite; checking $\mathcal{E}, L(q) \models Poss(A(\boldsymbol{h}), S_0)$ is decidable as $L(q)$ is a GFDB; checking $P \equiv_{\mathcal{E}} L(q)$ is decidable, P and $L(q)$ being GFDBs; for a given (finite) set of fluents $\mathcal{F}$ and a finite set H of constants, there exist only finitely many equivalence classes of logically equivalent (under $\mathcal{E}$) GFDBs that can be defined using only constants from H.

The following result, together with Lemma 1, proves that one can use $\hat{T}_{\mathcal{D}\varphi}$, instead of the infinite $T_{\mathcal{D}}$, to check $\mathcal{D} \models \varphi$.

Lemma 3. *For any BAT-GFDB $\mathcal{D}$ C-bounded by some bound B and generalized projection query φ that is a sentence in $\mathcal{L}_p$, we have that: $T_{\mathcal{D}} \models \varphi$ iff $\hat{T}_{\mathcal{D},\varphi} \models \varphi$.*

Proof. (Sketch) Given two GFDBs $\mathcal{D}_0$ and $\mathcal{D}'_0$, and a set $C \subseteq \mathcal{C}$ of constants, write $\mathcal{D}_0 \approx_C \mathcal{D}'_0$, if there exists a bijection $\gamma : \mathcal{C}_{\mathcal{D}_0} \cup C \to \mathcal{C}_{\mathcal{D}'_0} \cup C$ that is the identity on C, s.t. for the theory $\mathcal{D}''_0$ obtained from $\mathcal{D}_0$ by renaming all of its constants c as $\gamma(c)$, it is the case that $\mathcal{D}''_0 \equiv_{\mathcal{E}} \mathcal{D}'_0$. (This intuitively means that $\mathcal{D}_0$ and $\mathcal{D}'_0$ are logically equivalent up to renaming of the constants not mentioned in C.) Then, let $T_{\mathcal{D}} = (Q, q_0, \to, L)$, $\hat{T}_{\mathcal{D},\varphi} = (\hat{Q}, \hat{q}_0, \hat{\to}, \hat{L})$, and $C_{\mathcal{D},\varphi} = \mathcal{C}_{\mathcal{D}} \cup \mathcal{C}_{\varphi}$. The proof is based on proving that (*) for any $q \in Q$ and $\hat{q} \in \hat{Q}$ s.t. $L(q) \approx_{C_{\mathcal{D},\varphi}} \hat{L}(\hat{q})$, $T_{\mathcal{D}}, q \models \varphi$ iff $\hat{T}_{\mathcal{D},\varphi}, \hat{q} \models \varphi$. Since $L(q_0) \approx_{C_{\mathcal{D},\varphi}} \hat{L}(\hat{q}_0)$ (see Algorithm 1), this implies that $T_D, q_0 \models \varphi$ iff $\hat{T}_{D,\varphi}, \hat{q}_0 \models \varphi$, i.e., $T_D \models \varphi$ iff $\hat{T}_{D,\varphi} \models \varphi$. The proof of (*), omitted for space reasons, is by induction on the structure of φ.

To complete the proof of Theorem 5, it remains to show that checking whether $\hat{T}_{D,\varphi} \models \varphi$ is decidable.

Lemma 4. *Given a C-bounded BAT-GFDB D and a generalized projection query φ that is a sentence in $\mathcal{L}_p$, checking whether $\hat{T}_{D,\varphi} \models \varphi$ is decidable.*

Proof. (Sketch) To perform the check, we use the following recursive procedure (the cases of boolean connectives $\neg$, $\wedge$ and $\vee$ are as standard):

```
 1: procedure CHECKT̂(q, φ)
 2:     if φ = ϕ ∈ Ln and ϕ is uniform in s then
 3:         return T̂D,φ, q ⊨ φ;
 4:     end if
 5:     if φ = ϕ ∈ Ln and ϕ is uniform in σ then
 6:         if qσ does not exist in Q then
 7:             return false;
 8:         else
 9:             return CHECKT̂(qσ, φ[σ/s]);
10:         end if
11:     end if
12:     if φ = ∃s.do([α1, . . . , αn], S0) ⊑ s ∧ ϕ then
```
13:        **for all** paths $q_0 \xrightarrow{\alpha_1} \cdots \xrightarrow{\alpha_n} q_{n+1} \xrightarrow{\alpha_{n+1}} \cdots \xrightarrow{\alpha_{m-1}} q_m$ s.t. in the suffix $q_{n+1} \xrightarrow{\alpha_{n+1}} \cdots \xrightarrow{\alpha_{m-1}} q_m$, no node occurs more than once **do**
```
14:            if CHECKT̂(qm, φ[s/σ']) == true, for σ' = do([α1, . . . , αm−1], S0) then
15:                return true;
16:            end if
17:        end for
18:        return false;
19:     end if
20: end procedure
```
(Termination and correctness proofs omitted for brevity.)

Lemmas 1, 2, 3 and 4 prove, together, Th. 5. By exploiting Th. 5 we can prove the following notable result.

Theorem 6. *Given a BAT-GFDB D and a natural number B, checking whether D is C-bounded by B is decidable.*

Proof. (Sketch) From D, a theory D', C-bounded by B by construction, can be derived that matches D up to the situations (if any) that violate C-boundedness, and s.t. the situations preceding a violation are marked with distinguished facts. This can be done because the formula $\varphi(s) = \bigvee_{\Psi \in 2^{T_V}} \exists y.F(x, s) \equiv \bigvee_{\psi \in \Psi} \psi$, which, for appropriate V, expresses that s is C-bounded by B, is regressable. We can then prove that $D \models \forall s.\varphi(s)$ iff $D' \models \forall s.\varphi'(s)$, with $\varphi'(s)$ expressing that situation s is not marked with any of the distinguished facts discussed above. Since D' is C-bounded, by Th. 5, $D' \models \varphi'$ is decidable. Thus, so is $D \models \varphi$.

Related Work

Our work relates definitional KBs and BATs over them to the work in databases and, in particular, constraint query languages (CQL). The representation of infinitely many tuples we use here shares a lot of similarities with the work in database theory about finitary representations of infinite query answers [1], and the more general approach of CQL of [7] that is our main inspiration.

Proper KBs [8] also generalize regular databases by allowing possibly infinite sets of positive or negative ground facts to be expressed, as well as tuples to be undefined (incomplete information). This provides enough expressive power to make theorem proving, in general, undecidable with proper KBs, even for queries about S_0. This is overcome in [8] by an approximate reasoning method which is always logically sound, but also complete only under specific conditions. The case of a KB as a generalized database with equality constraints, instead, is less expressive, as it captures only complete information, but effective, and logically correct methods exist for query answering, projection, and progression. In particular, wrt (possibly generalized) projection queries, our approach can deal with full first-order queries over S_0 and any projected ground future situation, as well as generalized projection queries of a particular form. In contrast, the approach of [8] can guarantee completeness only under some constraints on the first-order queries [11], that limit their expressivity.

The case of bounded action theories of [3] is the only one in the literature that investigates conditions under which generalized projection queries can be decided over BATs. They require a finite upperbound on the number of positive atomic facts for all models and situations, and look into queries that can be expressed over BATs using a first-order variant of the μ-calculus [4]. Our work extends this work in the case where fluents may have *infinite* extensions, concisely represented by means of equality constraints. We are able then to prove similar results for a wide class of general projection queries. Finally, the two-variable variant of situation calculus language in [6] allows richer forms of incomplete information in the initial KB, but is bound by the limitation of using only two variables, e.g., not being able to express reachability relations.

Conclusions and Future Work

In this paper we looked into situation calculus action theories over generalized fluent databases with equality constraints (GFDB), connecting the situation calculus with constraint query languages. We showed that GFDBs characterize the class of definitional KBs and that for action theories over such KBs (BAT-GFDBs), the KBs are *closed under progression*. We proved that simple projection queries over BAT-GFDBs are decidable in general. Also, extending the notion of *boundedness* proposed in [3], we introduced the notion of *C-boundedness* and showed that, under this, a wide class of generalized projection queries that include quantification over situations is decidable. Finally, we proved decidability of checking C-boundedness of a BAT-GFDB for some bound.

For future work we want to consider other constraints, in particular extending GFDBs to include linear orderings. We believe that this work can provide the ground for specifying action theories that capture topological properties and reason effectively over rich temporal aspects relating to projection and progression. We also intend to look into controlled ways to express incomplete information similar to the extensions of proper KBs in [10] and [2]. We believe that the latter can be used to include a practical form of incomplete information.

References

1. Chomicki, J., Imieliński, T.: Finite representation of infinite query answers. ACM Trans. Database Syst. 18(2), 181–223 (1993)
2. De Giacomo, G., Lespérance, Y., Levesque, H.J.: Efficient Reasoning in Proper Knowledge Bases with Unknown Individuals. In: Proc. of IJCAI 2011, pp. 827–832 (2011)
3. De Giacomo, G., Lespérance, Y., Patrizi, F.: Bounded Situation Calculus Action Theories and Decidable Verification. In: Proc of KR 2012 (2012)
4. Emerson, E.A.: Model Checking and the Mu-calculus. In: Descriptive Complexity and Finite Models, pp. 185–214 (1996)
5. Enderton, H., Enderton, H.B.: A Mathematical Introduction to Logic, 2nd edn. Academic Press (2001)
6. Gu, Y., Soutchanski, M.: Decidable Reasoning in a Modified Situation Calculus. In: Proc. of IJCAI 2007, pp. 1891–1897 (2007)
7. Kanellakis, P.C., Kuper, G.M., Revesz, P.Z.: Constraint Query Languages. Journal of Computer and System Sciences 51(1), 26–52 (1995)
8. Levesque, H.J.: A Completeness Result for Reasoning with Incomplete First-Order Knowledge Bases. In: Proc. of KR 1998 (1998)
9. Lin, F., Reiter, R.: How to Progress a Database. Artificial Intelligence 92(1-2), 131–167 (1997)
10. Liu, Y., Lakemeyer, G., Levesque, H.J.: A Logic of Limited Belief for Reasoning with Disjunctive Information. In: Proc. of KR 2004, pp. 587–597 (2004)
11. Liu, Y., Lakemeyer, G.: On the Expressiveness of Levesque's Normal Form. J. Artif. Int. Res. 31(1), 259–272 (2008)
12. Liu, Y., Levesque, H.J.: Tractable Reasoning with Incomplete First-Order Knowledge in Dynamic Systems with Context-Dependent Actions. In: Proc.of IJCAI 2005 (2005)
13. Reiter, R.: Knowledge in Action. Logical Foundations for Specifying and Implementing Dynamical Systems. MIT Press (2001)
14. Reiter, R.: The Projection Problem in the Situation Calculus: A Soundness and Completeness Result, with an Application to Database Updates. In: Proc. of AIPS 1992, pp. 198–203 (1992)
15. Vassos, S., Levesque, H.J.: How to progress a database III. Artificial Intelligence 195, 203–221 (2013)
16. Vassos, S., Patrizi, F.: A Classification of First-Order Progressable Action Theories in Situation Calculus. In: Proc. of IJCAI 2013 (2013)

A Dynamic View of Active Integrity Constraints

Guillaume Feuillade and Andreas Herzig

Université de Toulouse, IRIT-LILaC and CNRS, France

Abstract. Active integrity constraints have been introduced in the database community as a way to restore integrity. We view active integrity constraints as programs of Dynamic Logic of Propositional Assignments DL-PA and show how several semantics of database repair that were proposed in the literature can be characterised by DL-PA formulas. We moreover propose a new definition of repair. For all these definitions we provide DL-PA counterparts of decision problems such as the existence of a repair or the existence of a unique repair.

Keywords: Active integrity constraints, dynamic logic, propositional assignments.

1 Introduction

Updates under integrity constraints is an important and notoriously difficult issue in databases and AI. About ten years ago, active integrity constraints were proposed in the database literature as a 'more informed' way of maintaining database integrity [FGZ04, CTZ07, CT08, CGZ09, CT11, CF14]. There, an active integrity constraint is basically viewed as a couple $r = \langle C(r), R(r) \rangle$ where $C(r)$ is a formula and $R(r)$ is a set of update actions each of which is of the form either $p \leftarrow \top$ or $p \leftarrow \bot$, for some atomic formula p. The idea is that (1) when $C(r)$ is true then the constraint r is violated, and (2) a violated constraint can only be repaired by performing one or more of the update actions in $R(r)$.

In this paper we examine active integrity constraints in the framework of dynamic logic and argue that they should be viewed as a complex program: the sequential composition of the test of $C(r)$ and the nondeterministic choice of an action in $R(r)$. Repairing a database can then be done by means of a complex program that combines active integrity constraints. We use a simple yet powerful dialect of dynamic logic: Dynamic Logic of Propositional Assignments, abbreviated DL-PA [HLMT11, BHT13]. The latter is a simple instantiation of Propositional Dynamic Logic PDL [Har84, HKT00]: instead of PDL's abstract atomic programs, its atomic programs are update actions: assignments of propositional variables to either true or false, written $p \leftarrow \top$ and $p \leftarrow \bot$. Just as in PDL, these atomic programs can be combined by means of program operators: sequential and nondeterministic composition, finite iteration, and test. While DL-PA programs describe the evolution of the world, DL-PA formulas describe the state of the world. In particular, formulas of the form $\langle \pi \rangle \varphi$ express that φ is true after *some* possible execution of π, and $[\pi]\varphi$ expresses that φ is true after *every* possible execution of π. The models of DL-PA are considerably simpler than PDL's Kripke models: valuations of classical propositional logic are enough. The assignment $p \leftarrow \top$ inserts p, while the assignment $p \leftarrow \bot$ deletes p. It is shown in [HLMT11, BHT13] that every DL-PA formula can be reduced

E. Fermé and J. Leite (Eds.): JELIA 2014, LNAI 8761, pp. 486–499, 2014.

to an equivalent boolean formula. This will allow us to construct repaired databases syntactically.

Just as [CT11, CF14] we only consider ground constraints, i.e., we work with a propositional language.

The paper is organized as follows. After some preliminaries (Section 2) we recall DL-PA in Section 3. In Section 4 we recall static constraints and provide an embedding of the associated repairs that have been defined in the literature into DL-PA. In Section 5 we do the same for active integrity constraints. In Section 6 we propose a new definition in terms of **while** programs. Section 7 concludes.

2   Preliminaries

In this paper we consider propositional languages that are built from a countable set of propositional variables (alias atomic formulas) $\mathbb{P} = \{p, q, \ldots\}$. *Boolean formulas* are built from $\mathbb{P}$ by means of the boolean operators $\top$, $\bot$, $\neg$, and $\vee$ and are denoted by A, B, etc. The other boolean connectives $\wedge$, $\rightarrow$, and $\leftrightarrow$ are abbreviated in the usual way. A *literal* is an element of $\mathbb{P}$ or the negation of an element of $\mathbb{P}$ and a *clause* is a disjunction of literals. We define $\mathbb{P}_A$ to be the set of variables from $\mathbb{P}$ occurring in formula A. This extends to sets in the obvious way.

Valuations are subsets of $\mathbb{P}$ and are denoted by V, V_1, V_2, etc. The set of all valuations is therefore $\mathbb{V} = 2^{\mathbb{P}}$. It will sometimes be convenient to write $V(p) = \top$ instead of $p \in V$ and $V(p) = \bot$ instead of $p \notin V$. In the context of active integrity constraints a valuation is called a *database*.

A valuation determines the truth value of every boolean formula. The set of valuations where A is true is noted $\|A\|$. We sometimes write $V \models A$ when $A \in \|V\|$.

An *update action* is of the form $p \leftarrow \top$ and $p \leftarrow \bot$, for $p \in \mathbb{P}$. The former is the insertion of p and the latter is the deletion of p. We denote the set of all update actions by $\mathbb{U}$. We sometimes use X as a metavariable for $\top$ and $\bot$ and write $p \leftarrow \mathsf{X}$. For subsets P of $\mathbb{P}$ it will be convenient to write $P \leftarrow \top$ to denote the set of update actions $\{p \leftarrow \top : p \in P\}$, and likewise for $P \leftarrow \bot$. A set of update actions $U \subseteq \mathbb{U}$ is *consistent* if it does not contain both $p \leftarrow \top$ and $p \leftarrow \bot$, for some p.

The *update* of a valuation V by a set of update actions U is defined as:

$$V \circ U = (V \setminus \{p : p \leftarrow \bot \in U\}) \cup \{p : p \leftarrow \top \in U\}$$

So all the deletions are applied in parallel first, followed by the parallel application of all insertions. We could as well have chosen some other order of application. When U is consistent then all of them lead to the same result. In particular:

Proposition 1. *Let* $\{\alpha_1, \ldots, \alpha_n\}$ *be a consistent set of update actions. Let* $\langle k_1 \ldots k_n \rangle$ *be some permutation of* $\langle 1 \ldots n \rangle$. *Then* $V \circ \{\alpha_1, \ldots, \alpha_n\} = (\ldots (V \circ \{\alpha_{k_1}\}) \ldots) \circ \{\alpha_{k_n}\}$.

3   Dynamic Logic of Propositional Assignments

The first studies of assignments in the context of dynamic logic are due, among others, to Tiomkin and Makowski and van Eijck [TM85, vE00]. Dynamic Logic of Propositional Assignments DL-PA was introduced in [HLMT11] and was further studied in [BHT13]. Evidence for its widespread applicability was provided in several recent publications, including belief update and belief revision, argumentation, and planning [Her14, DHP14, HMNDBW14]. We briefly recall syntax and semantics.

3.1 Language

The language of DL-PA is defined by the following grammar:

$$\varphi ::= p \mid \top \mid \bot \mid \neg\varphi \mid \varphi \vee \varphi \mid \langle \pi \rangle \varphi$$
$$\pi ::= \alpha \mid \pi; \pi \mid \pi \cup \pi \mid \pi^* \mid \pi^- \mid \varphi?$$

where p ranges over the set of atomic formulas $\mathbb{P}$ and α ranges over the set of update actions $\mathbb{U}$. In DL-PA, update actions are called atomic assignments. The operators of sequential composition ("$;$"), nondeterministic composition ("$\cup$"), finite iteration ("$(.)^*$", the so-called Kleene star), and test ("$(.)?$") are familiar from PDL. The operator "$(.)^-$" is the converse operator. The formula $\langle \pi \rangle \varphi$ is read "there is an execution of π after which φ". The star-free fragment of DL-PA is the subset of the language made up of formulas without the Kleene star "$(.)^*$".

We define $\mathbb{P}_\varphi$ to be the set of variables from $\mathbb{P}$ occurring in formula φ, and we define $\mathbb{P}_\pi$ to be the set of variables from $\mathbb{P}$ occurring in program π. For example, $\mathbb{P}_{p \leftarrow q \cup p \leftarrow \neg q} = \{p, q\} = \mathbb{P}_{\langle p \leftarrow \bot \rangle q}$.

Several program abbreviations are familiar from PDL. First, **skip** abbreviates $\top?$ and **fail** abbreviates $\bot?$. Second, **if** φ **then** π_1 **else** π_2 is expressed by $(\varphi?; \pi_1) \cup (\neg\varphi?; \pi_2)$. Third, the loop **while** φ **do** π is expressed by $(\varphi?; \pi)^*; \neg\varphi?$. Let us moreover introduce assignments of literals to variables by means of the following two abbreviations:

$$p \leftarrow q = \textbf{if } q \textbf{ then } p \leftarrow \top \textbf{ else } p \leftarrow \bot \qquad p \leftarrow \neg q = \textbf{if } q \textbf{ then } p \leftarrow \bot \textbf{ else } p \leftarrow \top$$

The former assigns to p the truth value of q, while the latter assigns to p the truth value of $\neg q$. In particular, the program $p \leftarrow \neg p$ flips the truth value of p. Note that both abbreviations have constant length, namely 14. Finally and as usual in modal logic, $[\pi]\varphi$ abbreviates $\neg\langle \pi \rangle \neg\varphi$.

3.2 Semantics

DL-PA programs are interpreted by means of a relation between valuations. The atomic programs α update valuations just as singleton sets of update actions do (cf. the preceding section), and complex programs are interpreted just as in PDL by mutual recursion. Table 1 gives the interpretation of formulas and programs. where $\circ$ is relation composition and $(.)^{-1}$ is relation inverse.

A formula φ is DL-PA *valid* iff $\|\varphi\| = 2^\mathbb{P} = \mathbb{V}$. It is DL-PA *satisfiable* iff $\|\varphi\| \neq \emptyset$. For example, the formula $\langle p \leftarrow \bot \rangle \top$, $\langle p \leftarrow \top \rangle \varphi \leftrightarrow \neg\langle p \leftarrow \top \rangle \neg\varphi$, $\langle p \leftarrow \top \rangle p$, and $\langle p \leftarrow \bot \rangle \neg p$ are all valid.

Observe that if p does not occur in φ then formulas such as $\varphi \rightarrow \langle p \leftarrow \top \rangle \varphi$ and $\varphi \rightarrow \langle p \leftarrow \bot \rangle \varphi$ are valid. This is due to the following semantical property that is instrumental in the proof of several results in the rest of the paper.

Table 1. Interpretation of formulas and programs

$$\|p\| = \{V \; : \; p \in V\}$$
$$\|\top\| = \mathbb{V} = 2^{\mathbb{P}}$$
$$\|\bot\| = \emptyset$$
$$\|\neg\varphi\| = 2^{\mathbb{P}} \setminus \|\varphi\|$$
$$\|\varphi \vee \psi\| = \|\varphi\| \cup \|\psi\|$$
$$\|\langle\pi\rangle\varphi\| = \{V \; : \; \exists V_1 \text{ s.t. } \langle V, V_1\rangle \in \|\pi\| \text{ and } V_1 \in \|\varphi\|\}$$

$$\|\alpha\| = \{\langle V_1, V_2\rangle \; : \; V_2 = V_1 {\circ} \{\alpha\}\}$$
$$\|\pi ; \pi'\| = \|\pi\| \circ \|\pi'\|$$
$$\|\pi \cup \pi'\| = \|\pi\| \cup \|\pi'\|$$
$$\|\pi^*\| = (\|\pi\|)^*$$
$$\|\pi^-\| = (\|\pi\|)^{-1}$$
$$\|\varphi?\| = \{\langle V, V\rangle \; : \; V \in \|\varphi\|\}$$

Proposition 2. *Suppose* $\mathbb{P}_\varphi \cap P = \emptyset$, *i.e., none of the variables in P occurs in φ. Then* $V \cup P \in \|\varphi\|$ *iff* $V \setminus P \in \|\varphi\|$.

A distinguishing feature of DL-PA is that its dynamic operators can be eliminated (which is impossible in PDL). Just as for QBF, the resulting formula may be exponentially longer than the original formula.

Theorem 1 ([BHT13]). *For every* DL-PA *formula there is an equivalent boolean formula.*

Every assignment sequence $\alpha_1; \cdots; \alpha_n$ is a deterministic program that is always executable: for a given V, there is exactly one V' such that $\langle V, V'\rangle \in \|\alpha_1; \cdots; \alpha_n\|$. Moreover, when a set of update actions $\{\alpha_1, \ldots, \alpha_n\}$ is consistent then the order of the α_i in a sequential composition is irrelevant. The following can be viewed as a reformulation of Proposition 1 in terms of the DL-PA operator of sequential composition.

Proposition 3. *Let* $\{\alpha_1, \ldots, \alpha_n\}$ *be a consistent set of update actions. Let* $\langle k_1 \ldots k_n\rangle$ *be some permutation of* $\langle 1 \ldots n\rangle$. *Then* $V {\circ} \{\alpha_{k_1}, \ldots, \alpha_{k_n}\}$ *equals the single V' such that* $\langle V, V'\rangle \in \|\alpha_{k_1}; \cdots; \alpha_{k_n}\|$.

This entitles us to use sets of consistent update actions as programs: one may suppose that this stands for a sequential composition in some predefined order (based e.g. on the enumeration of the set of propositional variables).

4 Static Constraints and the Associated Repairs

In this section we consider the classical notion of database integrity that is defined in terms of *static integrity constraints* (or *static constraints* for short). In our propositional language they are nothing but boolean formulas. Two ways of repairing databases can be found in the literature on active integrity constraints [CT11]. Both consist in first finding an appropriate set of update actions U and then building the update $V \circ U$ of V by U as defined in Section 2. We relate them to well-known operations in belief revision and update [KM92], which allows us to reuse their embeddings into DL-PA [Her14].

4.1 Weak Repairs and Drastic Updates

Let V be a database and let C be a set of static constraints. A *weak repair* of V achieving C is a consistent set of update actions $U \subseteq \mathbb{U}$ such that $V \circ U \models \bigwedge C$ and such that U is *relevant* w.r.t. V. The latter means that $p \leftarrow \top \in U$ implies $p \notin V$ and $p \leftarrow \bot \in U$ implies $p \in V$.

Example 1. Let $V = \emptyset$ and let $C = \{p \lor q\}$. The weak repairs of V achieving C are all those subsets of the set of positive update actions $\{r \leftarrow \top : r \in \mathbb{P}\}$ that contain either $p \leftarrow \top$, or $q \leftarrow \top$, or both.

The example illustrates that weak repairs are indeed very weak. As the following result shows, if we consider what is true in all possible weak repairs then we obtain what is called a drastic update in the literature on belief revision and update.[1]

Proposition 4. *Let V be a database and let C be a set of static constraints. Then*

$$\{V \circ U : U \text{ is a weak repair of } V \text{ achieving } C\} = \left\| \bigwedge C \right\|.$$

Note that a weak repair may contain assignments of variables that do not occur in C. To remedy this we define a *relevant weak repair* to be a weak repair U such that if $p \leftarrow \top$ or $p \leftarrow \bot$ occurs in U then $p \in \mathbb{P}_C$.

This corresponds to a very basic update semantics that is sometimes called Winslett's standard semantics [Win90].

4.2 Repairs *Tout Court* and Their Relation to Winslett's PMA

A *repair* of V achieving C is a weak repair of V achieving C that is minimal w.r.t. set inclusion: there is no weak repair of V achieving C that is strictly contained in it.

Example 2. Let $V = \emptyset$ and $C = \{p \lor q\}$. There are exactly two repairs of V achieving C, viz. $\{p \leftarrow \top\}$ and $\{q \leftarrow \top\}$.

We are now going to relate repairs to Winslett's possible models approach PMA [Win88, Win90]. Remember that the update of a database V by a boolean formula A according to the PMA is the set of V' such that $V' \models A$ and such that the symmetric difference between V and V' is minimal w.r.t. set inclusion. Formally, symmetric difference is defined as $D(V, V') = \{p : V(p) \neq V'(p)\}$ and the PMA update of V by A is

$$V \diamond^{\text{pma}} A = \{V' : V' \models A \text{ and there is no } V'' \in \|A\| \text{ such that } D(V, V'') \subset D(V, V')\}$$

For example, $\emptyset \diamond^{\text{pma}} p \lor q = \{\{p\}, \{q\}\}$ and $\emptyset \diamond^{\text{pma}} (p \land q) \lor r = \{\{p, q\}, \{r\}\}$.

Proposition 5. *Let V be a database and let C be a set of static constraints. Then*

$$\{V \circ U : U \text{ is a repair of } V \text{ by } C\} = V \diamond^{\text{pma}} \left(\bigwedge C \right).$$

The above result justifies the term *PMA repair* that we are going to employ henceforth (because the mere term 'repairs' might lead to confusions).

---

[1] It is actually also a drastic revision because V is a complete database and update and revision coincide in that case [PNP+96].

4.3 Repairs and Weak Repairs in DL-PA

We now embed Winslett's standard semantics (and thereby relevant weak repairs) and the PMA (and thereby repairs *tout court*) into DL-PA. This was already done in [Her14], but our embeddings are slightly more elegant and are presented in a more uniform and streamlined way. We start with some auxiliary definitions.

To each propositional variable p we associate a *fresh* propositional variable $p^{\pm}$. Each proposition $p^{\pm}$ will register whether or not the proposition p has been modified along the update. This is necessary to ensure that every proposition is modified at most once during a repair. We extend the definition to sets of variables $P \subseteq \mathbb{P}$: $P^{\pm} = \{p^{\pm} \mid p \in P\}$.

First, we need a program that sets all the propositions in a given set P to $\perp$: $P \leftarrow \perp$ is the sequence of assignments $p \leftarrow \perp$ for all $p \in P$ (whose order does not matter, cf. Proposition 3). Therefore $\mathbb{P}_C{}^{\pm} \leftarrow \perp$ is going to initialise the relevant $p^{\pm}$ before the program containing toggle(p) below is executed.

Second, the following two DL-PA programs (1) modify a single proposition and store this and (2) undo that modification:

$$\text{toggle}(p) = \text{if } \neg p^{\pm} \text{ then } p \leftarrow \neg p; p^{\pm} \leftarrow \top \text{ else fail} = \neg p^{\pm}?; p \leftarrow \neg p; p^{\pm} \leftarrow \top$$
$$\text{undo}(p) = \text{if } p^{\pm} \text{ then } p \leftarrow \neg p; p^{\pm} \leftarrow \perp \text{ else fail} = p^{\pm}?; p \leftarrow \neg p; p^{\pm} \leftarrow \perp$$

The idea is that the variable $p^{\pm}$ keeps track of the modifications of p: we are going to ensure that it is true only once p has been modified during the current update. Then toggle(p) will flip the truth value of p if this value has not been modified yet and records the modification by setting $p^{\pm}$ to $\top$; if p has already been made true then toggle(p) fails. The program undo(p) undoes this.

Then a weak repair that is relevant w.r.t. C is achieved by the following DL-PA program:

$$\text{weakRepair}(C) = \mathbb{P}_C{}^{\pm} \leftarrow \perp; \left(\bigcup_{p \in \mathbb{P}_C} \text{toggle}(p) \right)^{*} ; \left(\bigwedge C \right)?$$

We note that since each variable can be updated at most once and since the order of the updates does not matter, this can be rewritten without the Kleene star as a sequence $(\text{toggle}(p_1) \cup \textbf{skip}); \dots ; (\text{toggle}(p_k) \cup \textbf{skip})$ where $p_1, \dots, p_k$ are the variables in $\mathbb{P}_C$.

We finally define the following DL-PA formula:

$$\text{Minimal}(C) = \neg \left\langle \left(\bigcup_{p \in \mathbb{P}_C} \text{undo}(p); \left(\bigcup_{p \in \mathbb{P}_C} \text{undo}(p) \right)^{*} \right) \right\rangle \bigwedge C$$

The program in this formula undoes a nonempty set of toggle(p) actions (and nondeterministically so, failing when there was no change at all). Therefore the formula Minimal(C) says that there is no execution of that program leading to a database closer to the actual database that satisfies the constraints. So the actual database corresponds to a minimal change of the initial database.[2]

---

[2] The difference with [Her14] is that our programs memorise that a variable has been flipped instead of storing its previous value.

Theorem 2. *Let C be a set of static constraints in the language of* $\mathbb{P}$ *and let* $V \subseteq \mathbb{P}$ *be a database (i.e., no* $p^{\pm}$ *occurs in either of them). Let U be a consistent set of update actions that is relevant w.r.t. V. Set* $V' = (V \circ U) \cup \{p^{\pm} : p \leftarrow \top \in U \text{ or } p \leftarrow \perp \in U\}$.

- *U is a relevant weak repair of V achieving C if and only if* $\langle V, V' \rangle \in \|\mathsf{weakRepair}(C)\|$.
- *U is a PMA repair of V achieving C iff* $\langle V, V' \rangle \in \|\mathsf{weakRepair}(C); \mathsf{Minimal}(C)?\|$.

Proof. For the first item, observe that $\langle V, V' \rangle \in \|\mathsf{weakRepair}(C)\|$ if and only if $V' \in \|C\|$ and the following holds for all variables $p \in \mathbb{P}$ (i.e., excluding the $p^{\pm}$): (a) $p^{\pm} \in V'$ iff $V(p) \neq V'(p)$ and (b) if $V(p) \neq V'(p)$ then $p \in \mathbb{P}_C$, i.e., only p's from C and the associated $p^{\pm}$ were modified.

For the second item, given some actual database V', define the initial database as

$$V = \{p \in \mathbb{P} : p \in V' \text{ and } p^{\pm} \notin V'\} \cup \{p \in \mathbb{P} : p \notin V' \text{ and } p^{\pm} \in V'\}.$$

Then $V' \in \|\mathsf{Minimal}(C)\|$ iff there is no $V'' \in \| \bigwedge C\|$ such that $D(V, V'') \subset D(V, V')$.[3]

5   Active Constraints and the Associated Repairs

Active integrity constraints were proposed about ten years ago [FGZ04], and various ways of repairing a database V by such constraints have been studied in the literature. We refer to [CT11] for an overview. Just as for static constraints, all definitions are based on the notion of *repair set*: an appropriate set of update actions U such that $V \circ U$ no longer violates the integrity constraints, where $V \circ U$ is the result of updating V with U as defined in Section 2 and is called the *repaired database*.

In the present section we recall syntax and semantics and show that they can be recast in DL-PA.

5.1   Active Integrity Constraints

An *active integrity constraint* (or *active constraint* for short), combines a static integrity constraint with a preferred repair action. Formally, an active constraint is a couple

$$r = \langle \mathsf{C}(r), \mathsf{R}(r) \rangle$$

where $\mathsf{C}(r)$ is a boolean formula and $\mathsf{R}(r)$ is a finite set of update actions that is consistent. As before, $\mathsf{C}(r)$ is a static integrity constraint that is violated when $\mathsf{C}(r)$ is false. If so then r is *applicable* and $\mathsf{R}(r)$ indicates how to get rid of the violation and achieve integrity. We view the elements of $\mathsf{R}(r)$ as *permitted* update actions: When $\mathsf{C}(r)$ is violated then each of the actions in $\mathsf{R}(r)$ gets a 'license to update'.[4] This is a rather imprecise description of the job the update actions in $\mathsf{R}(r)$ are expected to do, and in the literature various semantics are associated to a set of active constraints. For one of the most

---

[3]   Note that by definition of $\mathsf{toggle}(p)$, $p \in D(V, V')$ is equivalent to $p^{\pm} \in D(V, V')$ thus the inclusion $D(V, V'') \subset D(V, V')$ is not affected by the variables in $\mathbb{P}_C{}^{\pm}$.

[4]   The reading that is given in the literature is slightly different from ours: there, $\mathsf{R}(r)$ is called the set of preferred update actions.

prominent of them in terms of founded repairs, it turns out that the elements of $R(r)$ have to be viewed as *exclusive choices*: when some $\alpha \in R(r)$ is part of the repair set then no other β can be part of the repair set.

We say that an active constraint $r = \langle C(r), R(r) \rangle$ is *standard* if $C(r)$ is a clause and each update action in $R(r)$ produces one of the literals of $C(r)$: if $p \leftarrow \top \in R(r)$ then p has to be one of the literals of $C(r)$ and if $p \leftarrow \bot \in R(r)$ then $\neg p$ has to be one of the literals of $C(r)$.

Remark 1. The definition in the literature differs in several respects from ours here. First, $C(r)$ is not viewed as a static integrity constraint but as the negation of a static integrity constraint (r is violated when the first argument of r is true). Second, active constraints are noted $C(r) \rightarrow R(r)$, which makes them look like formulas. However, such formulas are non-standard because the right hand side of the implication is not a formula but a set of programs. So their semantics remains to be given: in the literature this is typically done by means of disjunctive logic programs under a non-monotonic semantics. Third, all active constraints have to be standard.

We denote finite sets of active constraints by η, η_1, etc. The set of static integrity constraints associated to such a set is defined as $C(\eta) = \{C(r) \ : \ r \in \eta\}$.

It remains to associate a semantics to active constraints. In the present and the following section we discuss the options and their properties.

5.2   Founded Weak Repairs and Founded Repairs

In the literature, founded repairs are considered to be a natural basic semantics of active constraints that is a good starting point for further refinements.

Given a set of active constraints η and a database V, a consistent set of update actions U is *founded* if for every $\alpha \in U$ there is an $r \in \eta$ such that (a) $\alpha \in R(r)$, (b) $V \circ U \models C(r)$, and (c) $V \circ (U \setminus \{\alpha\}) \not\models C(r)$. A set of update actions U is a *founded (weak) repair* of V by η if U is a (weak) repair of V achieving $C(\eta)$ and U is founded.

Remark 2. We have reformulated the original definition so that it applies to our more general definition of active constraint. Both are equivalent as far as standard active constraints are concerned.

Founded repairs do not necessarily exist [CT11, Example 2].

Example 3. Consider $\eta = \{\langle p, \{p \leftarrow \top\}\rangle, \langle p \vee q, \{q \leftarrow \top\}\rangle\}$. The set $\{p \leftarrow \top\}$ is a founded weak repair of $V_0 = \emptyset$ by η. It is the only such repair: the second update action in $\{p \leftarrow \top, q \leftarrow \top\}$ cannot be founded on the second active constraint of η.

In the next section, we propose an encoding of the notion of founded repairs in DL-PA.

Example 4 ([CT11], Example 3). Consider
$$\eta = \{\langle p \vee q, \{p \leftarrow \top\}\rangle, \langle \neg p \vee q, \{p \leftarrow \top\}\rangle, \langle p \vee \neg q, \{q \leftarrow \top\}\rangle\}.$$
The set $\{p \leftarrow \top, q \leftarrow \top\}$ is the only founded repair of $V_0 = \emptyset$ by η.

This illustrates *circularity of support*: each update action is individually founded because the others happen to be in the repair. Such repairs are considered to be unintended and the notion of *justified repair* was proposed to overcome the problem. Justified repairs can be encoded in DL-PA in a way similar to the encoding of founded repairs. We however do not work this out here.

5.3   Founded Repairs in DL-PA

We re-use the abbreviations weakRepair($C(\eta)$) and Minimal($C(\eta)$) that we have introduced in Section 4.3. Remember that in order to keep track of modifications we had supposed that we have at our disposal fresh variables $p^\pm$, one per variable $p \in \mathbb{P}$. We moreover need the following:

$$\mathsf{IsFounded}(\eta) = \bigwedge_{p \in \mathbb{P}_{C(\eta)}} \left(p^\pm \to \bigvee_{\substack{r \in \eta \\ p \leftarrow X \in R(r)}} \langle p \leftarrow \neg p \rangle \neg C(r) \right)$$

where X ranges over $\{\top, \bot\}$. The formula is true if and only if all current update actions (encoded in the current valuation by means of the fresh variables $p^\pm$) are founded.

Theorem 3. *Let η be a set of active integrity constraints in the language of $\mathbb{P}$ and let $V_0 \subseteq \mathbb{P}$ be a database (i.e., no $p^\pm$ occurs in either of them). Let U be a consistent set of update actions that is relevant w.r.t. V_0.*

- *U is a weak founded repair of V_0 by η iff*

$$\langle V_0, V_0 \circ U \rangle \in \|\mathsf{weakRepair}(C(\eta)); \mathsf{IsFounded}(\eta)?\|.$$

- *U is a founded repair of V_0 by η iff*

$$\langle V_0, V_0 \circ U \rangle \in \|\mathsf{weakRepair}(C(\eta)); \mathsf{IsFounded}(\eta)?; \mathsf{Minimal}(C(\eta))?\|.$$

Proof. Suppose V is some repaired database (containing variables $p^\pm$). Define the set of update actions

$$U_{V,\eta} = \{p \leftarrow \top \ : \ p^\pm \in V \text{ and } p \in V\} \cup \{p \leftarrow \bot \ : \ p^\pm \in V \text{ and } p \notin V\}.$$

Let us prove that $V \in \|\mathsf{weakRepair}(C(\eta)); \mathsf{IsFounded}(\eta)\|$? iff $U_{V,\eta}$ is a weak founded repair of V_0 by η. The latter means that for every $\alpha \in U_{V,\eta}$, the three conditions (a) $\alpha \in R(r)$, (b) $V_0 \circ U_{V,\eta} \models C(r)$, and (c) $V_0 \circ (U_{V,\eta} \setminus \{\alpha\}) \not\models C(r)$ are satisfied.

For the left-to-right direction consider some $p \leftarrow \top \in U_{V,\eta}$. Then $p^\pm \in V$. Condition (b) is satisfied from the definition weakRepair($C(\eta)$) and Theorem 2. Condition (a) is satisfied by the existence of a candidate rule in the definition of IsFounded(η); remark that we are guaranteed that the rule contains indeed $p \leftarrow \top$, as opposed to $p \leftarrow \bot$, because undoing the change on p changes $C(r)$ to false (so X has to be $\top$). Condition (c) is satisfied because $V_0 \circ (U \setminus \{p \leftarrow \top\}) \not\models C(r)$ is equivalent to $V_0 \circ U \models \neg \langle p \leftarrow \bot \rangle C(r)$.

For the right-to-left direction, Theorem 2 ensures that $U_{V,\eta}$ is a weak repair. To prove that $V \in \|\mathsf{IsFounded}(\eta)\|$, consider some $p^\pm \in V$. By definition, it entails $p \leftarrow X \in U_{V,\eta}$ for some $X \in \{\top, \bot\}$. Condition (a) ensures that there is a rule $r \in \eta$ with $p \leftarrow \top \in R(r)$. Condition (c) implies $V \models \neg \langle p \leftarrow \neg X \rangle C(r)$. This concludes.

6   A New Definition of Repair in DL-PA

We now propose two new definitions that take advantage of the resources of DL-PA. More precisely, we make use of **while** loops in order to iterate the application of active constraints. We start by discussing how databases can be repaired by applying active constraints in sequence. This will lead us to the definition of dynamic repair. We show that it is incomparable with both founded weak repairs and founded repairs.

6.1   Repairing a Database: A Dynamic View

Suppose there is only one active constraint r that is standard. Then it is clear how to proceed: either $V \models C(r)$ and there is nothing to do, or $V \not\models C(r)$ and we have to apply r. In the second case, each $\alpha_i \in R(r)$ provides a PMA repair of V achieving $C(r)$.[5] What about the case where $R(r)$ is empty? Well, then V cannot be repaired and we are stuck.

So far so good. The situation gets way more intricate when the set of active constraints η contains two or more elements that can interact.

Even for standard active constraints it might not be enough to apply only one of the update actions from $R(r)$: some of the active constraints might have to be applied several times in order to obtain integrity. The following example of an n-bit counter highlights this.

Example 5. Suppose we represent binary numbers up to $2^{n+1}-1$ by means of $n+1$ propositional variables: $\neg p_n \wedge \cdots \wedge \neg p_0$ represents the integer zero and $p_n \wedge \cdots \wedge p_0$ represents $2^{n+1}-1$. Let

$$r_1 = \langle p_0 \vee x_0 \vee \cdots \vee x_n, \{p_0 \leftarrow \top\} \rangle$$
$$r_{2_k} = \langle p_k \vee \neg p_{k-1} \vee \cdots \vee \neg p_0 \vee x_k, \{x_k \leftarrow \top\} \rangle, \quad \text{for } k \leq n$$
$$r_{3_k} = \langle p_k \vee \neg p_{k-1} \vee \cdots \vee \neg p_0 \vee \neg x_k, \{p_k \leftarrow \top, p_{k-1} \leftarrow \bot, \ldots, p_0 \leftarrow \bot\} \rangle, \quad \text{for } k \leq n$$
$$r_{4_k} = \langle \neg p_k \vee p_{k-1} \vee \cdots \vee p_0 \vee \neg x_k, \{x_k \leftarrow \bot\} \rangle, \quad \text{for } k \leq n$$

The idea is that when $\neg p_k \wedge p_{k-1} \wedge \cdots \wedge p_0$ is true, i.e., when the number $011\ldots1$ has to be incremented to $100\ldots0$, then x_k is made true by r_{2_k} and remains so unless $100\ldots0$ has been attained. This involves flipping the k digits in the conjunction $\neg p_k \wedge p_{k-1} \wedge \cdots \wedge p_0$: with active constraints this is done one-by-one by the rule r_{3_k}. Then x_k is set to false again by r_{4_k}. Let $\eta_n = \{r_1\} \cup \{r_{2_1}, \ldots, r_{2_n}\} \cup \{r_{3_1}, \ldots, r_{3_n}\} \cup \{r_{4_1}, \ldots, r_{4_n}\}$. Successive repairing steps implement an n-bit counter counting from the initial database $\emptyset$ to the database $\{p_n, \ldots, p_0\}$.

The computation takes $2^{n+1}-1$ steps, demonstrating that sometimes atomic repairs must be performed an exponential number of times: $V_0 = \emptyset$ can only be repaired by applying r_1 a number of times exponential in n.

Our example highlights the difference between dynamic repairs and founded repairs: in the latter an active constraint can only be used once.

---

[5] For our more general active constraints where there is no syntactical link between $C(r)$ and $R(r)$ we have to compute all possible minimal subsets $U \subseteq R(r)$ such that $V \models C(r)$. All of them are PMA repairs.

6.2 Dynamic Weak Repairs and Dynamic Repairs

We associate to every active constraint r the DL-PA programs

$$\pi_r = \neg C(r)?; \bigcup_{\alpha \in R(r)} \alpha \quad \text{and} \quad \pi_r^{\pm} = \neg C(r)?; \bigcup_{p \leftarrow X \in R(r)} (p \leftarrow X; p^{\pm} \leftarrow \top),$$

where we consider that $\bigcup_{\alpha \in R(r)} \alpha$ equals **fail** when $R(r)$ is empty. This matches the intuitive reading that we have given to active constraints in Section 5.1: the repair program π_r checks whether the static integrity constraint associated to r is violated and if so applies one of the update actions from $R(r)$. The program $\pi_r^{\pm}$ moreover stores that p has been changed. This is also supported by the following proposition, which tells us that applicability of an active constraint r is matched by the DL-PA notion of executability of the program π_r.

Proposition 6. *Let r be an active constraint and let V be a database. Then applicability of r at V is equivalent to both $V \models \langle \pi_r \rangle \top$ and $V \models \langle \pi_r \rangle^{\pm} \top$.*

Proof. It suffices to observe that when π is a nondeterministic composition of update actions then the equivalence $\varphi \leftrightarrow \langle \varphi?; \pi \rangle \top$ is DL-PA valid for every φ.

A *dynamic weak repair* of V by η is a set of update actions U such that U is relevant w.r.t. V and

$$\langle V, V \circ U \rangle \in \left\| \textbf{while} \; \neg C(\eta) \; \textbf{do} \; \Big(\bigcup_{r \in \eta} \pi_r \Big) \right\|.$$

Finally, U is a *dynamic repair* of V by η if U is a PMA repair of V by η that is dynamic.

Example 6 (Example 4, ctd.). Consider again
$$\eta = \{\langle p \vee q, \{p \leftarrow \top\}\rangle, \langle \neg p \vee q, \{p \leftarrow \top\}\rangle, \langle p \vee \neg q, \{q \leftarrow \top\}\rangle\}.$$
There is a single dynamic (weak) repair of $V_0 = \emptyset$ by η, viz. $\{p \leftarrow \top, q \leftarrow \top\}$.

Example 7 (Example 3, ctd.). Consider again $\eta = \{\langle p, \{p \leftarrow \top\}\rangle, \langle p \vee q, \{q \leftarrow \top\}\rangle\}$, whose only founded weak repair was $\{p \leftarrow \top\}$. There are two dynamic weak repairs of $V_0 = \emptyset$ by η, namely $\{p \leftarrow \top\}$ and $\{p \leftarrow \top, q \leftarrow \top\}$. Only the former is a dynamic repair.

The next example illustrates that dynamic weak repairs are not necessarily founded.

Example 8. Consider $\eta = \{\langle p \vee q, \{p \leftarrow \top, q \leftarrow \top\}\rangle, \langle p \vee r, \{p \leftarrow \top, r \leftarrow \top\}\rangle\}$. There are four dynamic weak repairs of $V_0 = \emptyset$ by η, namely $U_1 = \{p \leftarrow \top\}$, $U_2 = \{q \leftarrow \top, r \leftarrow \top\}$, $U_1' = \{p \leftarrow \top, q \leftarrow \top\}$, and $U_1'' = \{p \leftarrow \top, r \leftarrow \top\}$. Only U_1 and U_2 are dynamic repairs.

The next theorem characterises dynamic repairs in terms of DL-PA programs.

Theorem 4. *Let η be a set of active integrity constraints in the language of $\mathbb{P}$ and let $V_0 \subseteq \mathbb{P}$ be a database (i.e., no $p^{\pm}$ occurs in either of them). Let U be a consistent set of update actions that is relevant w.r.t. V_0. U is a dynamic repair of V_0 by η iff*

$$\langle V_0, V_0 \circ U \rangle \in \left\| \textbf{while} \; \neg C(\eta) \; \textbf{do} \; \Big(\bigcup_{r \in \eta} \pi_r^{\pm} \Big); \text{Minimal}\big(C(\eta)\big)? \right\|.$$

Other definitions of dynamic repairs are possible. We could e.g. stipulate that U is a dynamic repair of V if it is a dynamic weak repair that is minimal w.r.t. set inclusion, i.e., such that there is no dynamic weak repair U' of V such that $U' \subset U$. We have not explored this option in detail, but it seems that it can be captured in DL-PA as well.

7 Discussion and conclusion

We have shown how several definitions of database repair via active integrity constraints can be expressed in DL-PA, including a new proposal in terms of their iterated application. This allows us to claim that DL-PA is a nice integrated framework for database updates: it not only provides operators $p{\leftarrow}\top$ of insertion and $p{\leftarrow}\bot$ of deletion and more generally sets U of such assignments that can be applied to a database V; it also provides a means to reason about the repair of the resulting $V{\circ}U$ when some element of the set of integrity constraints is violated. For example, V' is a possible repair of the update of the database V by the deletion of p if and only if the couple $\langle V, V'\rangle$ belongs to the interpretation of the DL-PA program $p{\leftarrow}\bot; repair$, where $repair$ is one of the repair programs of theorems 2, 3, 4. Moreover, the set of candidate repaired databases is the interpretation of the DL-PA formula $\langle (p{\leftarrow}\bot; repair)^-\rangle\varphi_V$, where φ_V is a conjunction of literals describing V syntactically.

Beyond identifying possible repaired databases, our programs $repair$ also allow to solve decision problems. For example, we may check whether it is possible at all to repair V by model checking in DL-PA whether

$$V \models \langle repair\rangle\top.$$

We can also check whether there is a unique repair of V by model checking whether the set of databases V' such that $\langle V, V'\rangle \in \|repair\|$ is a singleton. This amounts to model check for each of the variables p occurring in the constraints whether

$$V \vdash [repair]p \vee [repair]\neg p.$$

We might as well wish to check possibility or unicity of the repairs independently of a specific database V. For example, we can check whether η can repair any database by checking whether the formula $\langle repair\rangle\top$ is DL-PA valid. A further interesting reasoning task is to check whether two sets of active constraints η_1 and η_2 are equivalent under a given semantics by checking whether $\|repair_{\eta_1}\| = \|repair_{\eta_2}\|$.

Our active integrity programs of the form $r = \langle C(r), R(r)\rangle$ generalise the condition $C(r)$ from disjunctions of clauses to arbitrary formulas (that could actually even be DL-PA formulas). This opens up two perspectives. First, our definition also covers revision programs [CT11]; we leave it to future work to establish the exact relationship. Second, we could further generalise the action $R(r)$ from a set of update actions to arbitrary DL-PA programs. Dynamic repairs would then still make sense, while it is not clear how founded and justified repairs would have to be defined.

It is known that deciding the existence of a repair is NP-complete for PMA repairs and for founded weak repairs, while it is Σ_P^2 complete for founded repairs [CT11]. We leave to future work the investigation of the complexity of dynamic repairs. What can already be said is that our repair programs $repair_\eta$ all have length polynomial in the size of η. Complexity results for the fragments of DL-PA containing the respective repair programs would therefore provide an upper complexity bound. These results remain to be established; they would parallel those for fragments of QBF. First steps are in [Her14].

Acknowledgements. Thanks are due to the reviewers for helpful comments.

References

[BHT13]   Balbiani, P., Herzig, A., Troquard, N.: Dynamic logic of propositional assignments: a well-behaved variant of PDL. In: Kupferman, O. (ed.) Logic in Computer Science (LICS). IEEE (2013)

[CF14]   Cruz-Filipe, L.: Optimizing computation of repairs from active integrity constraints. In: Beierle, C., Meghini, C. (eds.) FoIKS 2014. LNCS, vol. 8367, pp. 361–380. Springer, Heidelberg (2014)

[CGZ09]   Caroprese, L., Greco, S., Zumpano, E.: Active integrity constraints for database consistency maintenance. IEEE Trans. Knowl. Data Eng. 21(7), 1042–1058 (2009)

[CT08]   Caroprese, L., Truszczyński, M.: Declarative semantics for active integrity constraints. In: Garcia de la Banda, M., Pontelli, E. (eds.) ICLP 2008. LNCS, vol. 5366, pp. 269–283. Springer, Heidelberg (2008)

[CT11]   Caroprese, L., Truszczynski, M.: Active integrity constraints and revision programming. TPLP 11(6), 905–952 (2011)

[CTZ07]   Caroprese, L., Trubitsyna, I., Zumpano, E.: View updating through active integrity constraints. In: Dahl, V., Niemelä, I. (eds.) ICLP 2007. LNCS, vol. 4670, pp. 430–431. Springer, Heidelberg (2007)

[DHP14]   Doutre, S., Herzig, A., Perrussel, L.: A dynamic logic framework for abstract argumentation. In: International Conference on Principles of Knowledge Representation and Reasoning (KR), Vienna, Austria, pp. 143–152. AAAI Press (2014)

[FGZ04]   Flesca, S., Greco, S., Zumpano, E.: Active integrity constraints. In: Moggi, E., Warren, D.S. (eds.) PPDP, pp. 98–107. ACM (2004)

[Har84]   Harel, D.: Dynamic logic. In: Gabbay, D.M., Günthner, F. (eds.) Handbook of Philosophical Logic, vol. II, pp. 497–604. D. Reidel, Dordrecht (1984)

[Her14]   Herzig, A.: Belief change operations: A short history of nearly everything, told in dynamic logic of propositional assignments. In: Baral, C., De Giacomo, G. (eds.) Proc. KR 2014. AAAI Press (2014)

[HKT00]   Harel, D., Kozen, D., Tiuryn, J.: Dynamic Logic. MIT Press (2000)

[HLMT11]   Herzig, A., Lorini, E., Moisan, F., Troquard, N.: A dynamic logic of normative systems. In: Walsh, T. (ed.) International Joint Conference on Artificial Intelligence (IJCAI), Barcelona, pp. 228–233. IJCAI/AAAI (2011)

[HMNDBW14] Herzig, A., Menezes, V., De Barros, L.N., Wassermann, R.: On the revision of planning tasks. In: Schaub, T. (ed.) European Conference on Artificial Intelligence (ECAI) (August 2014)

[KM92]   Katsuno, H., Mendelzon, A.O.: On the difference between updating a knowledge base and revising it. In: Gärdenfors, P. (ed.) Belief Revision, pp. 183–203. Cambridge University Press (1992); preliminary version in Allen, J.A., Fikes, R., Sandewall, E. (eds.): Principles of Knowledge Representation and Reasoning: Proc. 2nd Int. Conf., pp. 387–394. Morgan Kaufmann Publishers (1991)

[PNP+96]   Peppas, P., Nayak, A.C., Pagnucco, M., Foo, N.Y., Kwok, R.B.H., Prokopenko, M.: Revision vs. update: Taking a closer look. In: Wahlster, W. (ed.) ECAI, pp. 95–99. John Wiley and Sons, Chichester (1996)

[TM85]   Tiomkin, M.L., Makowsky, J.A.: Propositional dynamic logic with local assignments. Theor. Comput. Sci. 36, 71–87 (1985)

[vE00]   van Eijck, J.: Making things happen. Studia Logica 66(1), 41–58 (2000)
[Win88]   Katsuno, H., Mendelzon, A.O.: On the difference between updating a knowl-
            edge base and revising it. In: Gärdenfors, P. (ed.) Belief Revision, pp. 183–203.
            Cambridge University Press (1992); Reasoning about action using a possible
            models approach. In: Proc. 7th Conf. on Artificial Intelligence (AAAI 1988),
            St. Paul, pp. 89–93 (1988)
[Win90]   Winslett, M.-A.: Updating Logical Databases. Cambridge Tracts in Theoretical
            Computer Science. Cambridge University Press (1990)

Similarity Orders from Causal Equations

Johannes Marti and Riccardo Pinosio

ILLC, University of Amsterdam

Abstract. The purpose of this paper is to demonstrate that, contrary to the received wisdom, causal reasoning can be formalized wholly within the framework of Lewis' conditional logic. To this aim we simulate causal reasoning based on structural equations in Lewis' order semantics. This reduction is based on a formalization of an intuitive idea for computing relative similarity between worlds. Worlds are the more similar the more they satisfy the same relevant propositions, where relevance is a comparative notion represented by a preorder. In the context of causal reasoning this relevance order on propositions depends on the causal structure of the problem domain.

Keywords: Causal reasoning, conditional logic, counterfactual conditionals, non-monotonic reasoning, similarity orders, structural equations.

1 Introduction

In this paper we show how causal reasoning based on systems of structural equations can be embedded into the framework of the similarity order semantics for conditional logic.

The order semantics for conditional logic was developed in [4] in order to analyze counterfactual conditionals. On this a approach a relative similarity order over possible worlds is taken as basic and counterfactual conditionals are evaluated by a minimization procedure in this similarity order. With this approach it has proven to be difficult to account for counterfactual conditionals which rely on causal dependencies in the problem domain [12]. The difficulty is to give an account of how to determine a relative similarity order that captures these causal dependencies [5].

In artificial intelligence the framework based on systems of structural equations has been very successful as a formalization of causal reasoning. Pearl's book [8] is the standard treatment of this approach. Here we also find a semantics for a restricted class of counterfactual conditionals. This semantics is not prone to the kind of counterexamples that have been proposed against the similarity approach.

Pearl already notices [8, Section 7.4] a close relation between the semantics for counterfactual conditionals on systems of structural equations and the semantics on similarity orders. In [10] Schulz brings the approach to counterfactual conditionals using structural equations closer to premise semantics for conditional logic [13,3], which is a framework essentially equivalent to the similarity approach [6]. In particular, by importing notions from premise semantics into

E. Fermé and J. Leite (Eds.): JELIA 2014, LNAI 8761, pp. 500–513, 2014.

the setting of structural equations, Schulz extends the class of conditionals that can be evaluated. However, it remained an open question how to construct a relative similarity order that captures precisely the causal dependencies encoded in a system of structural equations:

> While – as we have seen – we can understand Pearl's system as an instantiation of the similarity approach, so far we do not know the exact nature of the similarity relation that would give us Pearl's interpretation of would have conditionals. Of course, it would be nice to have a reformulation of Pearl's theory in terms of similarity. But the only thing we can say so far is that it looks as if the relevant similarity relation differs clearly from what has been proposed in premise semantics. [9, p. 113]

We show how to construct a relative similarity order between possible worlds from a system of structural equations such that the truth of counterfactual conditionals is preserved.

For our construction we introduce the notion of a relevance order. A relevance order is a preorder with a proposition associated to every element in the order. This notion is motivated by the premise semantics for conditional logic where a set of relevant propositions is associated to every world. In the definition of relevance orders we take, following previous work [7], the relevant propositions to be world-independent. Moreover, our notion of a relevance order makes precise the idea from [5] that relevance is a matter of degree. We thus order propositions by comparative relevance instead of just having a set of relevant propositions.

The paper has the following structure. In Section 2 we briefly review the language and order semantics of conditional logic. In Section 3 we review the framework of systems of structural equations. In Section 4 we introduce the notion of a relevance order. Section 5 contains the construction of relative similarity orders from systems of structural equations and proves the preservation of true conditionals. In Section 6 we show that the framework of relevance orders can also account for backtracking counterfactual conditionals.

2   Conditional Logic

In this section we present the syntax of conditional logic and review its semantics on relative similarity orders. The purpose is to fix the notation and clarify the setting. For an extensive technical treatment of conditional logic we refer to [14].

The language of conditional logic is the set of all formulas generated according to the following grammar:

$$\varphi ::= x \mid \varphi \wedge \varphi \mid \neg\varphi \mid \varphi \rightsquigarrow \varphi$$

where $x \in \mathsf{A}$ is an element from a fixed finite set $\mathsf{A} = \{x_0, x_1, \ldots, x_{n-1}\}$ of atomic sentences. The Boolean connectives $\vee$, $\rightarrow$ and $\leftrightarrow$ are defined in terms of $\neg$ and $\wedge$ in the usual way. Formulas of the form $\varphi \rightsquigarrow \psi$ are conditionals, where φ is the antecedent and ψ the consequent.

The semantics for conditional logic on relative similarity orders is based on a set W of worlds. We assume that the set of worlds W is the set of all Boolean valuations over the set of atomic sentences. This choice ensures the existence of enough possible worlds, which we need for the proof of our main result.

Definition 1. *A world* $w : A \to 2$ *is a function which assigns to every variable* x_k *with* $k < n$ *a binary value* $w_k = w(x_k)$. *We write* W *for the set of all worlds.*

The order semantics is based on preorders, which are just reflexive and transitive relations. If $\leq$ is preorder on a set V we also write $w < v$ for $w \leq v$ and not $v \leq w$. Given a set $U \subseteq V$ we use $\mathsf{Min}(\leq, U) \subseteq U$ for the set of minimal elements of U in $\leq$, that is

$$\mathsf{Min}(\leq, U) = \{m \in U \mid \text{if } u \leq m \text{ then } m \leq u \text{ for all } u \in U\}.$$

The semantic structures in the order semantics are relative similarity orders.

Definition 2. *A relative similarity order* $\leq$ *over* W *is a tertiary relation on* W *such that* $\leq_w$ *is preorder for every* $w \in W$.

We think of $v \leq_w u$ as meaning that the world v is more similar to the actual world w than the world u.

The standard semantics of the conditional on relative similarity orders is defined using minimization.

Definition 3. *The semantics of a conditional* $\varphi \rightsquigarrow \psi$ *on a relative similarity order* $\leq$ *is given by:*

$$w, \leq \models \varphi \rightsquigarrow \psi \quad \text{iff} \quad v, \leq \models \psi \text{ for all } v \in \mathsf{Min}(\leq_w, A), \text{ where}$$
$$A = \{v \in W \mid v, \leq \models \varphi\}$$

Intuitively, this clause says that $\varphi \rightsquigarrow \psi$ is true at a world w if ψ is true at all the φ-worlds that are maximally similar to w.

3   Causal Reasoning with Structural Equations

In this section we review causal reasoning based on functional causal models. We are working within the extended version of Pearl's framework [8] introduced by Schulz in [10]. These extensions allow for a more general approach to the evaluation of conditionals than [8].

Again we assume a fixed set of atomic binary variables $A = \{x_0, x_1, \ldots, x_{n-1}\}$ as given. These atomic variables represent the basic facts in the causal structure of the problem domain. We restrict our presentation to binary variables since these can be taken to be atomic sentences of conditional logic. However, the construction of this paper also works if the variables take values in any finite set. In that case one has to adapt the language of conditional logic by introducing atomic sentences expressing that a variable has a certain fixed value.

The causal structure of the problem domain is represented by a system of structural equations, which are called recursive causal models in [8, Definition 7.1.1] and dynamics in [10, Definition 1].

Definition 4. *A system of structural equations F is a set $F_{en} \subseteq A$ and a function $F_k : 2^k \to 2$ for every number k such that $x_k \in F_{en}$. We call F_{en} the endogenous variables of F and define the set of exogenous variables as $F_{ex} = A \setminus F_{en}$. If $F_{en} = A$ then we call F complete.*

If $F_k : 2^k \to 2$ is a constant function for every $k \in F_{en}$ then we call F constant. Every consistent conjunction of literals φ induces a constant system of equations $S(\varphi)$ such that $S(\varphi)_{en}$ is the set of all variables occurring in φ and $S(\varphi)_k$ is the constant function with value 1 if x_k occurs positively in φ and with value 0 otherwise.

We also call a system of structural equations just a system of equations. Intuitively, one thinks of a system of equations F as specifying, for every k such that $x_k \in F_{en}$, an equation

$$x_k = F_k(x_0, \ldots, x_{k-1}) \ .$$

This equation represents the causal dependence of the effect x_k on its causes, which are a subset of the variables $x_0, \ldots, x_{k-1}$. The following definition makes this subset of causes explicit.

Definition 5. *Let F be a system of structural equations. The variable $x_k \in F_{en}$ depends on the variable $x_l \in A$ if $x_k \in F_{en}$ and*

$$F_k(x_0, \ldots, x_{l-1}, 0, x_{l+1}, \ldots, x_{k-1}) \neq F_k(x_0, \ldots, x_{l-1}, 1, x_{l+1}, \ldots, x_{k-1})$$

for some assignment of binary values to $x_0, \ldots, x_{l-1}, x_{l+1}, \ldots, x_{k-1}$. Define the parent relation P on A such that $x_l P x_k$ if x_k depends on x_l.

The graph determined by the parent relation P on A is called the causal diagram of F. In our setting it follows by definition that this graph is acyclic since the equation F_k determining the value of x_k depends only on the previous variables $x_0, \ldots, x_{k-1}$. For this reason we can define the causal diagram of F as a poset.

Definition 6. *The causal diagram $G(F) = (A, \leq)$ associated to F is a poset over A where $\leq$ is the reflexive, transitive closure of the parent relation P.*

Our definition of a system of equations differs from Pearl's presentation in [8] where the equation defining the value of some variable can depend on the values of all other variables. Pearl then restricts his attention to recursive systems of equations, which are defined as those whose causal diagram is acyclic. One can show that any finite recursive system of equations can be put into the form of Definition 4; thus our setting is not more restrictive.

Our presentation allows us to exploit recursion on the natural numbers. If one uses the definition from [8] one has to resort to recursion over the parent relation, which is less familiar.

Example 1. Throughout this paper we use a slightly adapted version of an example from [11, p. 339]. In the example we consider five binary causal variables: r there is enough rain, f fertilizer is used, w the wheat crop is large, d there is high demand for wheat and p the wheat prize is high. The causal dependencies between these variables are that enough rain and the use of fertilizer causes the wheat crop to be large, and that a small wheat crop or a high demand for wheat causes the wheat prize to be high. This problem domain is represented by the following system of equations F, where we use Boolean formulas to specify binary functions:

$$w = r \wedge f$$
$$p = \neg w \vee d .$$

The causal diagram $G(F)$ of this system of equations is as follows:

If a world w satisfies all the causal laws represented by an equation in F then it is a solution to F. This motivates the following definition.

Definition 7. *A world w is a solution to a system of equations F if*

$$w_k = F(w_0, \ldots, w_{k-1}) \qquad \text{for all } k \text{ with } x_k \in F_{en} .$$

We write $[\![F]\!] \subseteq W$ for the the set of all solutions of F. We also use the notation $[\![x_k = G(x_0, \ldots, x_{k-1})]\!]$ for the set of solutions of the system of equations F with $F_{en} = \{x_k\}$ and $F_k = G$.

For a complete system of equations one can compute a unique solution by recursion on the natural numbers. This simplifies the presentation of [10] which relies on fixed points of logic programs.

Definition 8. *For a complete system of equations F define the world $\sigma(F) = w$ by a recursion on $k < n - 1$ such that $w_0 = F_0$ and $w_{k+1} = F_{k+1}(w_0, \ldots, w_k)$.*

The following proposition is proven by induction.

Proposition 1. *A system of equations F is complete if and only if it has a unique solution, which in this case is $\sigma(F)$.*

The following notion was introduced by [10].

Definition 9. *Let F be a system of equations. The basis $B^{F,w}$ of a world w is the complete system of equations for $B^{F,w}_{en} = \mathsf{A}$ where for $k < n$ we define*

$$B^{F,w}_k(x_0, \ldots, x_{k-1}) = \begin{cases} F_k(x_0, \ldots, x_{k-1}) & x_k \in F_{en} \text{ and } w_k = F_k(w_0, \ldots, w_{k-1}) \\ w(k) & \text{otherwise} . \end{cases}$$

The basis $B^{F,w}$ is a system of equations which differs minimally from F but has w as its unique solution. One can prove by a simple induction that:

Proposition 2. *The world w is the unique solution $\sigma(B^{F,w})$ of $B^{F,w}$.*

Intuitively, the basis $B^{F,w}$ keeps all the laws from F that are not violated at w and sets all other variables to their value in w by means of a constant equation.

The next definition captures intervention on a causal system by fixing the value of some variables on constant values. This corresponds to the definition of a submodel in [8].

Definition 10. *Let F and A be systems of equations such that A is constant. The intervention $F \mid A$ of F with A is defined to be the system of equations such that $(F \mid A)_{en} = F_{en} \cup A_{en}$ and for an k with $x_k \in F_{en} \cup A_{en}$*

$$(F \mid A)_k = \begin{cases} A_k & x_k \in A_{en} \\ F_k & x_k \in F_{en} \setminus A_{en} . \end{cases}$$

Note that $F \mid A$ is complete if F or A is complete.

We now define the semantics of the conditional on a system of equations.

Definition 11. *The semantics of a conditional $\varphi \rightsquigarrow \psi$, where φ is a consistent conjunction of literals, on a system of equations F is given by:*

$$w, F \models \varphi \rightsquigarrow \psi \quad \textit{iff} \quad \sigma(B^{F,w} \mid S(\varphi)), F \models \psi .$$

Note that this clause is well-defined because $B^{F,w} \mid S(\varphi)$ is complete since $B^{F,w}$ is complete.

Our definition of the semantics follows [10]. In the restricted case where φ contains only endogenous variables of F and w satisfies all the laws of F the above semantic clause for the conditional is equivalent to [8, Definition 7.1.5]. However, the semantics of [10] extends the semantics of [8] in two respects. First, the antecedent can contain variables that are exogenous in F. In [8] this is not possible because there interventions are only defined for endogenous variables. Second, conditionals can be evaluated at worlds which violate some of the laws represented in F. This works thanks to Schulz' notion of a basis, which deals with a violation of a law by an intervention. In [8] the world of evaluation only sets the values of exogenous variables in F. Hence it is implicitly assumed that it satisfies all the laws of F.

4   Relative Similarity Orders from Relevance Orders

In this section we introduce the notion of a relevance order and show how it can be used to construct a relative similarity order.

Definition 12. *A relevance order for a set of worlds W is a tuple $(D, \sqsubseteq, e)$ where D is a set whose elements we call descriptions, $\sqsubseteq$ is a preorder on D and $e : D \to \mathcal{P}W$ is a function mapping descriptions to sets of worlds.*

We keep the standard terminology and take propositions to be just sets of worlds. However, we treat the description $d \in D$ in a similar fashion as the proposition $e(d)$ determined by d. For instance we say that d is true at a world w if $w \in e(d)$.

The notion of a relevance order allows us to rank propositions according to how important it is to keep their truth value constant when switching to counterfactual worlds. Propositions which are low in the order are considered more important. For example, mathematical theorems would intuitively count as more relevant than physical laws, which in turn are more relevant than particular facts.

In Definition 12 propositions are not ordered directly as sets of worlds but by means of descriptions having those propositions as extensions. This simplifies later proofs, since one does not need to verify that distinct elements in the order are really distinct as sets of worlds.

We now show how to construct a relative similarity order between worlds from a relevance order. The following technical notion is needed.

Definition 13. *A proposition $U \subseteq W$ is v, u-separating if either $v \in U$ and $u \notin U$, or $v \notin U$ and $u \in U$. Given a relevance order $(D, \sqsubseteq, e)$ we say that a description $d \in D$ is v, u-separating if the proposition $e(d)$ is v, u-separating. We use $\mathsf{sep}(v, u) \subseteq D$ for the set of all v, u-separating descriptions. We use $\mathsf{sep}_w(v, u) \subseteq D$ for all the v, u-separating descriptions that are true at w.*

Now for the construction of the relative similarity order.

Definition 14. *The relative similarity order $(W, \leq)$ determined by a relevance order $(D, \sqsubseteq, e)$ for W is defined such that*

$$v \leq_w u \quad \textit{iff} \quad v \in e(d) \textit{ for all } d \in \mathsf{Min}(\sqsubseteq, \mathsf{sep}_w(v, u)) .$$

Similarity of worlds to w is determined only by the relevant propositions which are true at w. Thus, a world is the more similar to w the more of these proposition it makes true. When comparing two worlds for similarity to w, we consider only the most relevant propositions true at w which can distinguish between the two worlds. In the special case where $\sqsubseteq$ is a total preorder, meaning that any two elements are required to be comparable, our clause reduces to the discrimin ordering of [1].

We need to verify that Definition 13 actually yields a relative similarity order.

Proposition 3. *The relation $\leq_w$ from Definition 14 is reflexive and transitive for every world $w \in W$.*

Proof. Reflexivity holds because there are no v, v-separating descriptions.

For transitivity assume that $v \leq_w u$ and $u \leq_w z$. We show that $v \leq_w z$. So pick any $d \in \mathsf{Min}(\sqsubseteq, \mathsf{sep}_w(v, z))$ and assume for a contradiction that $v \notin e(d)$. Distinguish cases on whether $u \in e(d)$.

If $u \in e(d)$ then $d \in \mathsf{sep}_w(v, u)$ and because $v \leq_w u$ it follows that $v \in e(d)$. This contradicts the assumption $v \notin e(d)$.

If $u \notin e(d)$ we distinguish cases on whether $z \in e(d)$. If $z \in e(d)$ then $d \in \mathsf{sep}_w(u, z)$ and by $u \leq_w z$ we get that $u \in e(d)$, which is a contradiction. If $z \notin e(d)$ then contrary to our assumption d would not be v, z-separating.

With a proof similar to the one of Propositions 3 one can show that the relative similarity order determined by a relevance order satisfies the weak centering axiom $w \leq_w v$ and the triangularity axiom $v \leq_w u \wedge u \leq_v w \to v \leq_u w$. It is an open question what further axioms are enforced by this construction.

5   Relative Similarity Orders from System of Equations

This section contains the main technical result of this paper. We first define a ranking over propositions $R(F)$ and then prove that the semantics of the conditional in F is equivalent to its semantics on the relative similarity order determined by $R(F)$.

Definition 15. *For every system of equations F with causal diagram $G(F) = (A, \leq)$ define a ranking over descriptions $R(F) = (D, \sqsubseteq, e)$. The set D of descriptions is given by*

$$D \subseteq A \times (2 + \{\star\}),$$
$$D = \{(x_k, a) \mid x_k \in A, a \in 2\} \cup \{(x_k, \star) \mid x_k \in F_{en}\}.$$

The preorder $\sqsubseteq$ on D is defined such that

$$(x_k, a) \sqsubseteq (x_l, b) \quad \text{iff} \quad x_k < x_l \text{ in } G(F) \text{ or } (x_k = x_l \text{ and } (a = \star \text{ or } a = b)).$$

We leave it to the reader to check that this is indeed reflexive and transitive. The evaluation $e : D \to PW$ is given by

$$e(x_k, a) = [\![x_k = a]\!], \qquad\qquad x_k \in A, a \in 2$$
$$e(x_k, \star) = [\![x_k = F_k(x_0, \ldots, x_{k-1})]\!]. \qquad x_k \in F_{en}$$

One can obtain the ranking $R(F)$ from the causal diagram $G(F)$ by replacing all exogenous variables x_k with the antichain of two descriptions evaluating to $[\![x_k = 0]\!]$ and $[\![x_k = 1]\!]$ respectively, and all endogenous variables x_k with the following poset of descriptions, where the evaluations are displayed:

$$[\![x_k = 0]\!] \qquad [\![x_k = 1]\!]$$
$$\diagdown \qquad \diagup$$
$$[\![x_k = F_k(x_0, \ldots, x_{k-1})]\!]$$

Moreover a description in the subposet of a variable x_k is smaller than a description in the subposet of another variable x_l exactly if $x_k < x_l$ in $G(F)$.

Example 2. For the system of equations F from Example 1 we obtain the following relevance order $R(F)$:

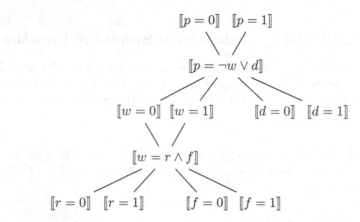

The idea behind the definition of $R(F)$ is that when evaluating counterfactual conditionals on a system of structural equations it is more important to keep the past than the future facts constant, and one rather gives a causal law up than any causes occurring in it. This order is reflected in the relevance ranking $R(F)$.

The following lemma states the crucial property of $R(F)$ which we exploit in the proof of Theorem 1.

Lemma 1. *Let F be a system of equations and consider two worlds w and v such that $w_l = v_l$ for all $l \neq k$ for some $k < n$. If $x_k \in F_{en}$ then any $d \in \mathsf{sep}(w, v)$ in $R(F)$ is an element in a suborder of $R(F)$ which has the following shape*

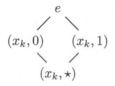

In other words: if $x_k \in F_{en}$ then any $d \in \mathsf{sep}(w, v)$ is either equal to $(x_k, 0)$, $(x_k, 1)$ or $(x_k, \star)$, or $(x_k, 0) \sqsubset d$ and $(x_k, 1) \sqsubset d$.

If $x_k \in F_{ex}$ then any $d \in \mathsf{sep}(w, v)$ in $R(F)$ is an element in a suborder of $R(F)$ which has the following shape

$$
\begin{array}{ccc}
 & e & \\
\diagup & & \diagdown \\
(x_k, 0) & & (x_k, 1)
\end{array}
$$

In other words: if $x_k \in F_{ex}$ then any $d \in \mathsf{sep}(w, v)$ is either equal to $(x_k, 0)$ or $(x_k, 1)$, or $(x_k, 0) \sqsubset d$ and $(x_k, 1) \sqsubset d$.

Proof. We show the case where $x_k \in F_{en}$ and leave the second similar case to the reader. We reason by contraposition.

First assume that $d = (x_l, a)$ where $x_l \neq x_k$ and $a \in 2$. Then certainly $d \notin \mathsf{sep}(w, v)$ because $\mathsf{e}(x_l, a) = [\![x_l = a]\!]$ and by assumption w and v agree on the value of x_l.

Now assume that $d = (x_l, \star)$ such that not $x_k \leq x_l$ in $G(F)$. First we have again by assumption that $w_l = v_l$ because $k \neq l$. Moreover F_l does not depend on x_k because otherwise x_k would be a parent of x_l and so $x_k \leq x_l$ in $G(F)$. So $F_l(w_0, \ldots, w_{l-1}) = F_l(v_0, \ldots, v_{l-1})$ again by the assumption that $w_m = v_m$ for all $m \neq k$. The facts that $w_l = v_l$ and that $F_l(w_0, \ldots, w_{l-1}) = F_l(v_0, \ldots, v_{l-1})$ entail that either both or none of w and v is in $[\![x_l = F_l(x_0, \ldots, x_{l-1})]\!] = \mathsf{e}(x_l, \star)$. Hence $d = (x_l, \star) \notin \mathsf{sep}(w, v)$. This concludes the proof.

We now prove our main result.

Theorem 1. *Let F and A be systems of equations such that A is constant. Denote by $\leq$ be the relative similarity order determined by $R(F)$. Then for every world $w \in W$:*

$$\mathsf{Min}(\leq_w, [\![A]\!]) = \{\sigma(B^{F,w} \mid A)\} \,.$$

Proof. Consider the world $s = \sigma(B^{F,w} \mid A)$ and take any world $z \in \mathsf{Min}(\leq_w, [\![A]\!])$. We show by an induction on $k < n$ that $z_k = s_k$.

It is sufficient to prove that $z_k = s_k$ on the assumption that $z_l = s_l$ for all $l < k$. This also covers the base case where $k = 0$ because then there are no $l < k$ and hence the assumption is trivially satisfied.

So pick any $k < n$ and assume that $z_l = s_l$ for all $l < k$. We want to show that $z_k = s_k$.

First consider the case where $m_k \in A_{en}$. In this case $v_k = A_k(s_0, \ldots, s_{k-1})$ by Definition 10 of $B^{F,w} \mid A$. Because $z \in \mathsf{Min}(\leq_w, [\![A]\!])$ and so $z \in [\![A]\!]$ we also have that $z_k = A_k(z_0, \ldots, z_{k-1})$. But $A_k(z_0, \ldots, z_{k-1}) = A_k(s_0, \ldots, s_{k-1})$ because A_k is a constant function.

In the other case where $x_k \notin A_{en}$ we have that $s_k = B_k^{F,w}(s_0, \ldots, s_{k-1})$. Again, we distinguish cases depending on the truth of $x_k \in F_{en}$ and $w_k = F_k(w_0, \ldots, w_{k-1})$.

If $x_k \in F_{en}$ and $w_k = F_k(w_0, \ldots, w_{k-1})$ then by Definition 9 of $B^{F,w}$ we have that $s_k = B_k^{F,w}(s_0, \ldots, s_{k-1}) = F_k(s_0, \ldots, s_{k-1})$. Assume for a contradiction that $z_k \neq F_k(s_0, \ldots, s_{k-1})$. By the induction hypothesis it follows that $z_k \neq F_k(z_0, \ldots, z_{k-1})$. We show that there is a world z' such that $z' \in [\![A]\!]$, $z' \leq_w z$ but not $z \leq_w z'$, which contradicts the assumption that $z \in \mathsf{Min}(\leq_w, [\![A]\!])$. The world z' is defined by setting $z'_l = z_l$ for all $l < n$ with $l \neq k$ and $z'_k = F_k(z'_0, \ldots, z'_{k-1})$. Since $x_k \notin A_{en}$, A is constant and $z \in [\![A]\!]$ it follows that $z' \in [\![A]\!]$. Now we have that $z', w \in [\![x_k = F_k(x_0, \ldots, x_{k-1})]\!]$ but $z \notin [\![x_k = F_k(x_0, \ldots, x_{k-1})]\!]$. Since $[\![x_k = F_k(x_0, \ldots, x_{k-1})]\!] = \mathsf{e}(x_k, \star)$ it follows by Lemma 1 that $(x_k, \star)$ is the only minimal z, z'-separating description that is true at w. So it follows by Definition 14 of $\leq_w$ that $z' \leq_w z$ but not $z \leq_w z'$.

In the other case we have that either $x_k \notin F_{en}$ or that $w_k \neq F_k(w_0, \ldots, w_{k-1})$. By Definition 9 it follows that $s_k = B^{F,w}(s_0, \ldots, s_{k-1}) = w_k$. Now assume for a contradiction that $s_k \neq z_k$. We again construct a z' such that $z' \in [\![A]\!]$, $z' \leq_w z$ but not $z \leq_w z'$ contradicting the assumption that $z \in \mathsf{Min}(\leq_w, [\![A]\!])$. The world

z' is defined by setting $z'_l = z_l$ for all $l < n$ with $l \neq k$ and $z'_k = w_k$. Since $x_k \notin A_{en}$, A is constant and $z \in [\![A]\!]$ it follows that $z' \in [\![A]\!]$. We now show that in $R(F)$ the description (x_k, w_k) is the only minimal z, z'-separating description that is true at w. For this we distinguish cases depending on whether $x_k \in F_{en}$.

First consider the case with $x_k \in F_{en}$. Then $w_k \neq F_k(w_0, \ldots, w_{k-1})$. We now consider the descriptions $(x_k, \star)$, (x_k, w_k) and (x_k, a) for $a \neq w_k$. We know that $w \notin [\![x_k = F_k(x_0, \ldots, x_{k-1})]\!] = \mathsf{e}(x_k, \star)$ and that $w \notin [\![x_k = a]\!] = \mathsf{e}(x_k, a)$. However, $[\![x_k = w_k]\!] = \mathsf{e}(x_k, w_k)$ is z, z'-separating and true at w. It follows by the first part of Lemma 1 that (x_k, w_k) is the only minimal z, z'-separating description that is true at w.

In the other case $x_k \notin F_{en}$ we only need to consider the descriptions (x_k, w_k) and (x_k, a) for $a \neq w_k$. By the same reasoning as in the previous case it follows that (x_k, w_k) is z, z'-separating and true at w and (x_k, a) fails to be true at w. So by the second part of Lemma 1 we get that (x_k, w_k) is the only minimal z, z'-separating description that is true at w.

From the fact that the only minimal z, z'-separating description true at w is (x_k, w_k) it follows that $z' \leq_w z$ but not $z \leq_w z'$ because $z' \in [\![x_k = w_k]\!]$ but $z \notin [\![x_k = w_k]\!]$. This concludes the proof of the theorem.

By unfolding Definition 3 and Definition 11 one now easily concludes that the truth of conditionals is preserved by construction of this paper.

Corollary 1. *Let F be systems of equations and denote by $\leq$ be the relative similarity order determined by $R(F)$. Consider a conditional $\varphi \rightsquigarrow \psi$ where φ is a consistent conjunction of literals. Then for every world $w \in W$*

$$w, F \models \varphi \rightsquigarrow \psi \quad \text{iff} \quad w, \leq\; \models \varphi \rightsquigarrow \psi.$$

6 Backtracking Counterfactual Conditionals

In this section we show that the framework of relevance orders is flexible enough to cope with backtracking counterfactual conditionals. A backtracking counterfactual conditional infers from an effect to a cause. This means that the antecedent of the conditional counterfactually assumes that a different effect than the one actually obtaining occurs, and the consequent reasons to a counterfactual cause. In Example 1, the conditional "if the wheat crop had been smaller last year, then there would have been either less rain or less fertilizer applied" is backtracking, since it reasons from the counterfactual effect of a smaller crop to the absence of one of the actual causes.

Backtracking does not arise in the evaluation of conditionals specified by the semantic clause in Definition 11. Take for instance the world $frwd\bar{p}$ as the actual world. One can check that according to Definition 11 the above backtracking conditional $\neg w \rightsquigarrow \neg r \vee \neg f$ turns out false at this world. The reason for this is that intervening with the antecedent of the conditional cancels the causal law leading from the consequent to the antecedent. The failure of backtracking also becomes obvious by inspecting the relevance order defined in Definition 15.

There a causal law is deemed as less relevant than the causes appearing in it. Thus counterfactual worlds which violate the causal law will be more similar to the actual world than those which violate the causes.

Backtracking conditionals, however, seem to play a role in communication. In [5, p. 457] Lewis argues that there is an ambiguity between interpreting counterfactual conditionals with a standard, non backtracking or with a backtracking resolution. In conversation, different contextual factors can trigger the backtracking interpretation of counterfactual conditionals. We show that the ambiguity between these two interpretations can be accounted for as a choice between different relevance orders. We now show how to modify the relevance order from Example 2 to allow for backtracking in the evaluation of the conditional $\neg w \rightsquigarrow \neg r \vee \neg f$.

The most obvious modification of the original order from Example 2 to allow for backtracking is to make the causal law $w = r \wedge f$ more relevant than the causal facts $r = 0$, $r = 1$, $f = 0$ and $f = 1$ occurring in it. Thus one obtains the following order:

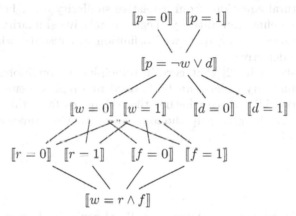

In the similarity order determined by this relevance order the conditional $\neg w \rightsquigarrow \neg r \vee \neg f$ is true at $u = frw\bar{d}\bar{p}$. In particular, one can verify that $\mathrm{Min}(\leq_u, [\![w = 0]\!])$ $= \{\bar{f}r\bar{w}\bar{d}p, f\bar{r}\bar{w}\bar{d}p\}$. Note that we have two non logically equivalent minimal worlds. For this reason, both $\neg w \rightsquigarrow r$ and $\neg w \rightsquigarrow \neg r$ are false at u, which means that conditional excluded middle fails. This situation could never arise in the case of non backtracking counterfactual conditionals, as one can see from Theorem 1.

The example shows that the approach presented here can be adapted to deal with backtracking counterfactual conditionals. The relevance order given in the example, however, admits backtracking only over one particular causal law, namely $\neg w \rightsquigarrow \neg r \vee \neg f$. By a stepwise swapping of causal laws with causes, one can precisely determine how many steps one can backtrack along which laws. The limit case, allowing all backtracking, is determined by a relevance order in which all causal laws are strictly more relevant than all particular facts that occur as causes or effects. Our theory does not determine how much backtracking is admissible, but leaves this choice to the modeler, depending on the application.

7   Conclusions and Further Work

In this paper we have presented a construction of relative similarity orders between possible worlds from systems of structural equations which preserves the truth of counterfactual conditionals. This shows that the framework of similarity orders can adequately model causal dependencies of a problem domain.

Our construction crucially depends on the notion of a relevance order over propositions. Relevance orders are a powerful tool to construct relative similarity orders, as they allow us to precisely control which propositions matter for the similarity of worlds. The treatment of backtracking in Section 6 gives an idea of the flexibility of the approach. It might thus be of interest to employ relevance orders in other settings where conditional logic is used. For instance, in belief revision they could be used to determine plausibility orders from rankings over evidence. A technical problem is to characterize the class of relative similarity orders which arise from relevance orders and to axiomatize its conditional logic.

A natural question is whether there is an inverse construction reading off a system of structural equations from a relative similarity order between worlds. One would thus define causality by means of relative similarity orders. This would be a semantic analog to Lewis' definition of causality, which is widely considered to be defective.

It has been shown in [2] that certain principles of conditional logic which are valid over similarity orders can be falsified by cyclic systems of equations. It might be worthwhile to see whether the techniques from this paper can be adapted to this case by giving up the assumption that relevance and similarity orders are transitive.

References

1. Coste-Marquis, S., Lang, J., Liberatore, P., Marquis, P.: Expressive power and succinctness of propositional languages for preference representation. In: Dubois, D., Welty, C.A., Williams, M.-A. (eds.) KR, pp. 203–212. AAAI Press (2004)
2. Halpern, J.Y.: From causal models to counterfactual structures. Review of Symbolic Logic 6(2), 305–322 (2013)
3. Kratzer, A.: Partition and revision: The semantics of counterfactuals. Journal of Philosophical Logic 10(2), 201–216 (1981)
4. Lewis, D.: Counterfactuals. Blackwell Publishers (1973)
5. Lewis, D.: Counterfactual dependence and time's arrow. Noûs 13(4), 455–476 (1979)
6. Lewis, D.: Ordering semantics and premise semantics for counterfactuals. Journal of Philosophical Logic 10(2), 217–234 (1981)
7. Marti, J., Pinosio, R.: Topological semantics for conditionals. In: Punčochář, V., Švarný, P. (eds.) The Logica Yearbook 2013. College Publications (to appear)
8. Pearl, J.: Causality: Models, Reasoning, and Inference. Cambridge University Press (2000)
9. Schulz, K.: Minimal Models in Semantics and Pragmatics: Free Choice, Exhaustivity, and Conditionals. PhD thesis, University of Amsterdam (2007)

10. Schulz, K.: "If you'd wiggled A, then B would've changed" - Causality and counterfactual conditionals. Synthese 179(2), 239–251 (2011)
11. Simon, H.A., Rescher, N.: Cause and counterfactual. Philosophy of Science 33(4), 323–340 (1966)
12. Tichý, P.: A counterexample to the Stalnaker-Lewis analysis of counterfactuals. Philosophical Studies 29(4), 271–273 (1976)
13. Veltman, F.: Prejudices, presuppositions, and the theory of counterfactuals. In: Groenendijk, J., Stokhof, M. (eds.) Amsterdam Papers in Formal Grammar, vol. 1, pp. 248–282. Centrale Interfaculteit, Universiteit van Amsterdam (1976)
14. Veltman, F.: Logics for Conditionals. PhD thesis, University of Amsterdam (1985)

Verification of Context-Sensitive Knowledge and Action Bases

Diego Calvanese[1], İsmail İlkan Ceylan[2], Marco Montali[1], and Ario Santoso[1]

[1] Free University of Bozen-Bolzano, Italy
lastname@inf.unibz.it
[2] Technische Universität Dresden, Germany
ceylan@tcs.inf.tu-dresden.de

Abstract. Knowledge and Action Bases (KABs) have been recently proposed as a formal framework to capture the dynamics of systems which manipulate Description Logic (DL) Knowledge Bases (KBs) through action execution. In this work, we enrich the KAB setting with contextual information, making use of different context dimensions. On the one hand, context is determined by the environment using context-changing actions that make use of the current state of the KB and the current context. On the other hand, it affects the set of TBox assertions that are relevant at each time point, and that have to be considered when processing queries posed over the KAB. Here we extend to our enriched setting the results on verification of rich temporal properties expressed in μ-calculus, which had been established for standard KABs. Specifically, we show that under a run-boundedness condition, verification stays decidable and does not incur in any additional cost in terms of worst-case complexity. We also show how to adapt syntactic conditions ensuring run-boundedness so as to account for contextual information, taking into account context-dependent activation of TBox assertions.

1 Introduction

Recent work in the areas of knowledge representation, databases, and business processes [15,26,4,10,19] has identified the need for integrating static and dynamic aspects in the design and maintenance of complex information systems. The *static* aspects are characterized on the one hand by the data manipulated by the system, and on the other hand by possibly complex domain knowledge that may vary during the evolution of the system. Instead, *dynamic* aspects are affected by the processes that operate over the system, by executing actions that manipulate the state of the system. In such a setting, in which new data may be imported into the system from the outside environment, the system becomes infinite-state in general, and the verification of temporal properties becomes more challenging: indeed, neither finite-state model checking [14] nor most of the current techniques for infinite-state model checking apply to this case.

Knowledge and action bases (KABs) [4] have been introduced recently as a mechanism for capturing systems in which knowledge, data, and processes are combined and treated as first-class citizens. In particular, KABs provide a mechanism to represent semantically rich information in terms of a description logic (DL) [1] knowledge base (KB) and a set of actions that manipulate such a KB over time. Additionally, actions

E. Fermé and J. Leite (Eds.): JELIA 2014, LNAI 8761, pp. 514–528, 2014.

allow one to import into the system fresh values from the outside, via service calls. In this setting, the problem of verification of rich temporal properties expressed over KABs in a first-order variant of the μ-calculus has been studied. Decidability has been established under the assumptions that in the properties first-order quantification across states is restricted, and that the system satisfies a so-called *run-boundedness* condition. Intuitively, these ensure that along each run the system cannot encounter (and hence manipulate) an unbounded number of distinct objects. In KABs, the intensional knowledge about the domain, expressed in terms of a DL TBox, is assumed to be fixed along the evolution of the system, i.e., independent of the actual state. However, this assumption is in general too restrictive, since specific knowledge might hold or be applicable only in specific, *context-dependent* circumstances. Ideally, one should be able to form statements that are known to be true in certain cases, but not necessarily in all.

Work on representing and formally reasoning over contexts dates back to work on generality in AI see [20]. Since then, there has been some effort in knowledge representation and in DLs to devise context-sensitive formalisms, ranging from multi-context systems [5] to many-dimensional logics [18]. An important aspect in modeling context is related to the choice of which kind of information is considered to be fixed and which context dependent. Specifically, for DLs, one can define the assertions in the TBox [2,13], the concepts [5], or both [24,18] as context-dependent. Each choice addresses different needs, and results in differences in the complexity of reasoning.

We follow here the approach of [2,13], and introduce *contextualized TBoxes*, in which each inclusion assertion is adorned with context information that determines under which circumstances the inclusion assertion is considered to hold. The relation among contexts is described by means of a lattice in [2] and by means of a directed acyclic graph in [13]. In our case, we represent context using a finite set of context dimensions, each characterized by a finite set of domain values that are organized in a tree structure. If for a context dimension d, a value v_2 is placed below v_1 in the tree (i.e., v_2 is a descendant of v_1), then the context associated to v_1 is considered to be more general than the one for v_2, and hence whenever context dimension d is in value v_2, it is also in value v_1.

Starting from this representation of contexts, we enrich KABs towards *context-sensitive KABs* (CKABs), by representing the intensional information about the domain using a contextualized TBox, in place of an ordinary one. Moreover, the action component of KABs, which specifies how the states of the system evolve, is extended in CKABs with *context changing actions*. Such actions determine values for context dimensions in the new state, based on the data and the context in the current state. In addition, also regular state-changing actions can query, besides the state, also the context, and hence be enabled or disabled according to the context. Notably, we show that verification of a very rich temporal logic, which can be used to query the system evolution, contexts, and data, is decidable for run-bounded CKABs. We also discuss how to recast the syntactic condition of *weak acyclicity* [4], which ensures run-boundedness, to the case of CKABs.

2 Preliminaries

2.1 *DL-Lite*$_\mathcal{A}$

For expressing knowledge bases, we use the lightweight Description Logic (DL) [1] *DL-Lite*$_\mathcal{A}$ [9,7]. The syntax for *concept* and *role* expressions in *DL-Lite*$_\mathcal{A}$ is as follows:

$$B \ ::= \ N \mid \exists R \qquad\qquad R \ ::= \ P \mid P^-$$

where N denotes a *concept name*, B a *basic concept*, P a *role name*, P^- an *inverse role*, and R a *basic role*. A *DL-Lite*$_\mathcal{A}$ *knowledge base* (KB) is a tuple $\mathcal{O} = \langle T, A \rangle$, where:

– T is a TBox, containing a finite set of assertion of the form:

$$B_1 \sqsubseteq B_2 \qquad R_1 \sqsubseteq R_2 \qquad B_1 \sqsubseteq \neg B_2 \qquad R_1 \sqsubseteq \neg R_2 \qquad \text{(funct } R)$$

From left to right, assertions of the first two columns respectively denote *positive inclusions* between basic concepts and basic roles; assertions of the third and fourth columns denote *negative inclusions* between basic concepts and basic roles; assertions of the last column denote *functionality* on roles.

– A is an Abox, i.e., a finite set of *ABox membership assertions* of the form $N(c_1)$ or $P(c_1, c_2)$, where c_1, c_2 denote individuals (constants).

We use the standard semantics of DLs based on FOL interpretations $\mathcal{I} = (\Delta^\mathcal{I}, \cdot^\mathcal{I})$ such that $c^\mathcal{I} \in \Delta^\mathcal{I}$, $N^\mathcal{I} \subseteq \Delta^\mathcal{I}$, and $P^\mathcal{I} \subseteq \Delta^\mathcal{I} \times \Delta^\mathcal{I}$. The semantics of the *DL-Lite*$_\mathcal{A}$ constructs and of TBox and ABox assertions, and the notions of *satisfaction* and of *model* are as usual (see, e.g., [9]). We also say that A is T-*consistent* if $\mathcal{O} = \langle T, A \rangle$ is satisfiable, i.e., admits at least one model.

Queries. We are interested to query the KB, i.e., retrieving relevant constants in the ABox based on the query. We denote with ADOM(A) the *set of constants appearing in A*. A *union of conjunctive queries* (UCQ) q over a KB $\mathcal{O} = \langle T, A \rangle$ is a FOL formula of the form $\bigvee_{1 \leq i \leq n} \exists \vec{y_i}.conj_i(\vec{x}, \vec{y_i})$ with free variables $\vec{x}$ and existentially quantified variables $\vec{y_1}, \ldots, \vec{y_n}$. Each $conj_i(\vec{x}, \vec{y_i})$ in q is a conjunction of atoms of the form $N(z)$, $P(z, z')$, where N and P respectively denote a concept and a role name occurring in T, and z, z' are constants in ADOM(A) or variables in $\vec{x}$ or $\vec{y_i}$, for some $1 \leq i \leq n$.

The *(certain) answers* of q over $\mathcal{O} = \langle T, A \rangle$ are defined as the set $ans(q, T, A)$ of substitutions σ which substitute the free variables of q with constants from ADOM(A) such that $q\sigma$ evaluates to true in every model of $\mathcal{O} = \langle T, A \rangle$. If q has no free variables, then it is called *boolean* and its certain answers are either true or false.

We also consider an extension of UCQs, namely *EQL-Lite*(UCQ) [8] (briefly, ECQs), that is, the FOL query language whose atoms are UCQs evaluated according to the certain answer semantics above. Formally, an *ECQ* over a TBox T is a possibly open formula of the form:

$$Q \ ::= \ [q] \mid \neg Q \mid Q_1 \wedge Q_2 \mid \exists x.Q$$

where q is a UCQ over T. The *certain answers* ANS(Q, T, A) *of an ECQ Q over* $\mathcal{O} = \langle T, A \rangle$ are obtained by first computing the certain answers over $\mathcal{O} = \langle T, A \rangle$ of each UCQs embedded in Q, then evaluating them through the first-order part of Q, and interpreting existential variables as ranging over ADOM(A). As stated in [8], the reformulation algorithm for answering query q over $DL\text{-}Lite_A$ KB $\mathcal{O} = \langle T, A \rangle$ which allows us to "compile away" the TBox (i.e., $ans(q, T, A) = ans(rew(q), \emptyset, A)$, where $rew(q)$ is a UCQ computed by the algorithm in [7]) can be extended to ECQs.

2.2 Knowledge and Action Bases

In the following, we make use of a countably infinite set Δ of *constants*, and a finite set $\mathcal{F}$ of *functions* representing *service calls*, which can be used to introduce fresh values from Δ into the system.

A *knowledge and action base* (KAB) is a tuple $\mathcal{K} = \langle T, A_0, \Gamma, \Pi \rangle$ where: *(i) T* is a $DL\text{-}Lite_A$ TBox capturing the domain of interest, *(ii)* A_0 is the initial $DL\text{-}Lite_A$ ABox, which intuitively represents the initial data of the system, *(iii)* Γ is a finite set of actions that characterize the evolution of the system, *(iv)* Π is a finite set of condition-action rules forming a process that intuitively specifies when and how an action can be executed. T and A_0 together form the *knowledge base* while Γ and Π form the *action base*.

An *action* $\alpha \in \Gamma$ represents the progression mechanism that changes the ABox in the current state and hence generates a new ABox for the successor state. Formally, an action $\alpha \in \Gamma$ is represented as $\alpha(p_1, \ldots, p_n) : \{e_1, \ldots, e_m\}$ where *(i)* α is the *action name*, *(ii)* $p_1, \ldots, p_n$ are the *input parameters*, and *(iii)* $\{e_1, \ldots, e_m\}$ is the set of *effects*. Each effect e_i is of the form $[q_i^+] \wedge Q_i^- \rightsquigarrow A_i$, where: (a) q_i^+ is an UCQ, and Q_i^- is an arbitrary ECQ whose free variables occur all among the free variables of q_i^+. (b) A_i is a set of facts (over the alphabet of T) which includes as terms: constants in ADOM(A_0), input parameters, free variables of q_i^+, and Skolem terms representing service calls formed by applying a function $f \in \mathcal{F}$ to one of the previous kinds of terms. Intuitively, q_i^+, together with Q_i^- acting as a filter, selects the values that instantiate the facts listed in A_i. Collectively, the instantiated facts produced from all the effects of α constitute the newly generated ABox, once the ground service calls are substituted with corresponding results. The *process* Π is formally defined as a finite set of *condition-action rules* of the form $Q(\vec{x}) \mapsto \alpha(\vec{x})$, where: *(i)* $\alpha \in \Gamma$ is an action, and *(ii)* $Q(\vec{x})$ is an ECQ over T, which has the parameters of α as free variables $\vec{x}$, and quantified variables or values in ADOM(A_0) as additional terms.

Notice that KABs are a pristine action specification framework, aimed at understanding the interaction between the static and dynamic components of systems evolving over time, towards general decidability results for verification. On top of KABs, several abstractions typical of reasoning about actions in AI can be built, see, e.g., [22].

KABs Execution Semantics. The execution semantics of a KAB is defined in terms of a possibly infinite-state transition system. Formally, given a KAB $\mathcal{K} = \langle T, A_0, \Gamma, \Pi \rangle$, we define its semantics by the *transition system* $\Upsilon_{\mathcal{K}} = \langle \Delta, T, \Sigma, s_0, abox, \Rightarrow \rangle$, where: *(i) T* is a $DL\text{-}Lite_A$ TBox; *(ii)* Σ is a (possibly infinite) set of states; *(iii)* $s_0 \in \Sigma$ is the initial state; *(iv)* $abox$ is a function that, given a state $s \in \Sigma$, returns an ABox associated to s; *(v)* $\Rightarrow \subseteq \Sigma \times \Sigma$ is a transition relation between pairs of states. Intuitively, the transitions system $\Upsilon_{\mathcal{K}}$ of KAB $\mathcal{K}$ captures all possible evolutions of the system by the actions in accordance with the process rules.

During the execution, an action can issue service calls. In this paper, we assume that the semantics of service calls is *deterministic*, i.e., along a run of the system, whenever a service is called with the same input parameters, it will return the same value. To enforce this semantics, the transition system remembers the results of previous service calls in a so-called service call map that is part of the system state. Formally, a *service call map* is defined as a partial function $m : \mathbb{SC} \to \Delta$, where $\mathbb{SC}$ is the set $\{f(v_1, \ldots, v_n) \mid f/n \in \mathcal{F} \text{ and } \{v_1, \ldots, v_n\} \subseteq \Delta\}$ of (skolem terms representing) *service calls*. Each state $s \in \Sigma$ of the transition system $\Upsilon_\mathcal{K}$ is a tuple $\langle A, m \rangle$, where A is an ABox and m is a service call map.

The semantics of an *action execution* is as follows: Given a state $s = \langle A, m \rangle$, let $\alpha \in \Gamma$ be an action of the form $\alpha(p_1, \ldots, p_n) : \{e_1, \ldots, e_m\}$ with $e_i = [q_i^+] \wedge Q_i^- \rightsquigarrow A_i$, and let σ be a *parameter substitution* for $p_1, \ldots, p_n$ with values taken from Δ. We say that α is executable in state s with parameter substitution σ, if there exists a condition-action rule $Q(\vec{x}) \mapsto \alpha(\vec{x}) \in \Pi$ s.t. $\mathrm{ANS}(Q\sigma, T, A)$ is true. The result of the application of α to an ABox A using a parameter substitution σ is captured by the following function:

$$\mathrm{DO}(T, A, \alpha\sigma) = \bigcup_{[q_i^+] \wedge Q_i^- \rightsquigarrow A_i \text{ in } \alpha} \bigcup_{\rho \in \mathrm{ANS}(([q_i^+] \wedge Q_i^-)\sigma, T, A)} A_i \sigma\rho$$

Intuitively, the result of the evaluation of α is obtained by combining the contribution of each effect of α, which in turn is obtained by grounding the facts A_i in the head of the effect with all the certain answers of the query $[q_i^+] \wedge Q_i^-$ over $\langle T, A \rangle$.

The result of $\mathrm{DO}(T, A, \alpha\sigma)$ is in general not a proper ABox, because it could contain (ground) Skolem terms, attesting that in order to produce the ABox, some service calls have to be issued. We denote by $\mathrm{CALLS}(\mathrm{DO}(T, A, \alpha\sigma))$ the set of such ground service calls, and by $\mathrm{EVALS}(T, A, \alpha\sigma)$ the set of substitutions that replace such calls with concrete values taken from Δ. Specifically, $\mathrm{EVALS}(T, A, \alpha\sigma)$ is defined as

$$\mathrm{EVALS}(T, A, \alpha\sigma) = \{\theta \mid \theta : \mathrm{CALLS}(\mathrm{DO}(T, A, \alpha\sigma)) \to \Delta \text{ is a total function}\}.$$

With all these notions in place, we can now recall the execution semantics of a KAB $\mathcal{K} = \langle T, A_0, \Gamma, \Pi \rangle$. To do so, we first introduce a transition relation $\mathrm{EXEC}_\mathcal{K}$ that connects pairs of ABoxes and service call maps due to action execution. In particular, $\langle\langle A, m \rangle, \alpha\sigma, \langle A', m' \rangle\rangle \in \mathrm{EXEC}_\mathcal{K}$ if the following holds: (i) α is *executable* in state $s = \langle A, m \rangle$ with parameter substitution σ; (ii) there exists $\theta \in \mathrm{EVALS}(T, A, \alpha\sigma)$ s.t. θ and m "agree" on the common values in their domains (in order to realize the deterministic service call semantics); (iii) $A' = \mathrm{DO}(T, A, \alpha\sigma)\theta$; (iv) $m' = m \cup \theta$ (i.e., updating the history of issued service calls).

The transition system $\Upsilon_\mathcal{K}$ of $\mathcal{K}$ is then defined as $\langle \Delta, T, \Sigma, s_0, abox, \Rightarrow \rangle$ where $s_0 = \langle A_0, \emptyset \rangle$, and Σ and $\Rightarrow$ are defined by simultaneous induction as the smallest sets satisfying the following properties: (i) $s_0 \in \Sigma$; (ii) if $\langle A, m \rangle \in \Sigma$, then for all actions $\alpha \in \Gamma$, for all substitutions σ for the parameters of α and for all $\langle A', m' \rangle$ s.t. $\langle\langle A, m \rangle, \alpha\sigma, \langle A', m' \rangle\rangle \in \mathrm{EXEC}_\mathcal{K}$ and A' is T-consistent, we have $\langle A', m' \rangle \in \Sigma$, $\langle A, m \rangle \Rightarrow \langle A', m' \rangle$. A *run* of $\Upsilon_\mathcal{K}$ is a (possibly infinite) sequence $s_0 s_1 \cdots$ of states of $\Upsilon_\mathcal{K}$ such that $s_i \Rightarrow s_{i+1}$, for all $i \geq 0$.

3 Contextualizing Knowledge Bases

Following [21], we formalize context as a mathematical object. Basically, we follow the approach in [24] of contextualizing knowledge bases by adopting the metaphor of considering context as a box [6,17]. Specifically, this means that the knowledge represented by the TBox (together with the ABox) in a certain context is affected by the values of parameters used to characterize the context itself.

Formally, to define the context, we fix a set of variables $\mathbb{C}_{dim} = \{d_1, \ldots, d_n\}$ called *context dimensions*. Each context dimension $d_i \in \mathbb{C}_{dim}$ comes with its own tree-shaped finite *value domain* $\langle Dom(d_i), \prec_{d_i}\rangle$, where $Dom(d_i)$ represents the finite set of domain values, and $\prec_{d_i}$ represents the predecessor relation forming the tree. We denote the domain value in the root of the tree with $\top_{d_i}$. Intuitively, $\top_{d_i}$ is the most general value in the tree-shaped value hierarchy of $Dom(d_i)$. We denote the fact that a context dimension d is in value v by $[d \rightsquigarrow v]$, and call this a *context dimension assignment*.

A *context* C over a set $\mathbb{C}_{dim}$ of context dimensions is defined as a set $\{[d_1 \rightsquigarrow v_1], \ldots, [d_n \rightsquigarrow v_n]\}$ of context dimension assignments such that for each context dimension $d \in \mathbb{C}_{dim}$, there exists exactly one assignment $[d \rightsquigarrow v] \in C$.

To predicate over contexts, we introduce a *context expression language* $\mathcal{L}_{cx}$ over $\mathbb{C}_{dim}$, which corresponds to propositional logic where the propositional letters are context dimension assignments over $\mathbb{C}_{dim}$. The syntax of $\mathcal{L}_{cx}$ is as follows:

$$\varphi_C ::= [d \rightsquigarrow v] \mid \varphi_C \wedge \varphi_C' \mid \neg\varphi_C$$

where $d \in \mathbb{C}_{dim}$, and $v \in Dom(d)$. We adopt the standard propositional logic semantics and the usual abbreviations. The notion of *satisfiability* and *model* are as usual. We call a formula expressed in $\mathcal{L}_{cx}$ a *context expression*.

Observe that a context $C = \{[d_1 \rightsquigarrow v_1], \ldots, [d_n \rightsquigarrow v_n]\}$, being a set of (atomic) formulas in $\mathcal{L}_{cx}$, can be considered as a propositional theory. The semantics of value domains in $\mathbb{C}_{dim}$ can also be characterized by a $\mathcal{L}_{cx}$ theory. Specifically, we define the theory $\Phi_{\mathbb{C}_{dim}}$ as the smallest set of context expressions satisfying the following conditions. For every context dimension $d \in \mathbb{C}_{dim}$, we have:

- For all values $v_1, v_2 \in Dom(d)$ s.t. $v_1 \prec_d v_2$, we have that $\Phi_{\mathbb{C}_{dim}}$ contains the expression $[d \rightsquigarrow v_1] \rightarrow [d \rightsquigarrow v_2]$. Intuitively, this states that the value v_2 is more general than v_1, and hence, whenever we have $[d \rightsquigarrow v_1]$ we can infer that $[d \rightsquigarrow v_2]$.
- For all values $v_1, v_2, v \in Dom(d)$ s.t. $v_1 \prec_d v$ and $v_2 \prec_d v$, we have that $\Phi_{\mathbb{C}_{dim}}$ contains the expression $[d \rightsquigarrow v_1] \rightarrow \neg[d \rightsquigarrow v_2]$. Intuitively, this expresses that sibling values v_1 and v_2 are disjoint.

Example 1. Consider an online retail enterprise (e.g., amazon.com) with many warehouses. A simple order processing scenario is as follows: (i) The customer submits the order. (ii) The central processing office receives the order. (iii) The *assembler* collects the ordered product. For each product that is not available in the central warehouse, the assembler makes a request to one of the warehouses having that product. (iv) The *wrapper* wraps the ordered product. (v) The *quality controller (QC)* checks the prepared order. (vi) The *delivery team* delivers the order to the delivery service. In this scenario we consider $\mathbb{C}_{dim} = \{\text{PP}, \text{S}\}$, where PP stands for *processing plan*, and S stands for *season*. $Dom(\text{PP}) = \{\text{WE}, \text{ME}, \text{RE}, \text{N}, \text{AP}\}$ (WE stands for *worker efficiency*, ME stands for *material efficiency*, RE stands for *resource efficiency*, N stands for *normal processing plan*, and AP stands for *any processing plan*.), where (i) WE $\prec_{\mathrm{PP}}$ RE, (ii) ME $\prec_{\mathrm{PP}}$ RE, (iii) RE $\prec_{\mathrm{PP}}$ AP, (iv) N $\prec_{\mathrm{PP}}$ AP, For example, WE $\prec_{\mathrm{PP}}$ RE means that *worker efficiency* is a form of *resource efficiency*. $Dom(\mathrm{S}) = \{\mathrm{WH}, \mathrm{PS}, \mathrm{LS}, \mathrm{NS}, \mathrm{AS}\}$ (WH stands for *winter holiday*, PS stands for *peak season*, LS stands for *low season*, NS stands for *normal season*, and AS stands for *any season*.), where (i) WH $\prec_{\mathrm{S}}$ PS, (ii) PS $\prec_{\mathrm{S}}$ AS, (iii) NS $\prec_{\mathrm{S}}$ AS, (iv) LS $\prec_{\mathrm{S}}$ AS.

Context-Sensitive Knowledge Bases. We define a *context-sensitive knowledge base* (CKB) $\mathcal{O}_{cx}$ over $\mathbb{C}_{dim}$ as a standard DL knowledge base in which the TBox assertions are contextualized. Formally, a *contextualized TBox* T_{cx} over $\mathbb{C}_{dim}$ is a finite set of assertions of the form $\langle t : \varphi \rangle$, where t is a TBox assertion and φ is a context expression over $\mathbb{C}_{dim}$. Intuitively, $\langle t : \varphi \rangle$ expresses that the TBox assertion t holds in all those contexts satisfying φ, taking into account the theory $\Phi_{\mathbb{C}_{dim}}$. Given a contextualized TBox T_{cx}, we denote with $\mathrm{VOC}(T_{cx})$ the set of all concept and role names appearing in T_{cx}, independently from the context.

Given a CKB $\mathcal{O}_{cx} = \langle T_{cx}, A \rangle$ and a context C, both over $\mathbb{C}_{dim}$, we define the *KB* $\mathcal{O}_{cx}$ *in context* C as the KB $\mathcal{O}_{cx}^C = \langle T_{cx}^C, A \rangle$, where $T_{cx}^C = \{t \mid \langle t : \varphi \rangle \in T_{cx} \text{ and } C \cup \Phi_{\mathbb{C}_{dim}} \models \varphi\}$.

Example 2. Continuing our example, in a normal situation, to guarantee a suitable service quality, *wrapper* and *assembler* must not be the *QC*. However, in the situation (context) where we have either *peak season* ([S $\rightsquigarrow$ PS]) or the company wants to promote *worker efficiency* ([PP $\rightsquigarrow$ WE]), the *wrapper* and the *assembler* act also as *QC*. This situation can be encoded as follows:

$\langle$Assembler $\sqsubseteq \neg$QC : [PP $\rightsquigarrow$ N] $\wedge$ [S $\rightsquigarrow$ NS]$\rangle$ $\langle$Assembler $\sqsubseteq$ QC : [PP $\rightsquigarrow$ WE] $\vee$ [S $\rightsquigarrow$ PS]$\rangle$
$\langle$Wrapper $\sqsubseteq \neg$QC : [PP $\rightsquigarrow$ N] $\wedge$ [S $\rightsquigarrow$ NS]$\rangle$ $\langle$Wrapper $\sqsubseteq$ QC : [PP $\rightsquigarrow$ WE] $\vee$ [S $\rightsquigarrow$ PS]$\rangle$

4   Context-Sensitive Knowledge and Action Bases

We now enhance KABs with context-related information, introducing in particular *context-sensitive knowledge and action bases* (CKABs), which consist of: *(i)* a context-sensitive knowledge base (CKB), which maintains the information of interest, *(ii)* an action base, which characterizes the system evolution, and *(iii)* context information that evolves over time, capturing changing circumstances. Differently from KABs, where the TBox is fixed a-priori and remains rigid during the evolution of the system, in CKABs the TBox changes depending on the current context. Alongside the evolution mechanism for data borrowed from KABs, CKABs include also a progression mechanism for the context itself, giving raise to a system in which data and context evolve simultaneously.

4.1   Formalization of CKABs

As for standard KABs, in addition to Δ and $\mathcal{F}$, we fix the set $\mathbb{C}_{dim} = \{d_1, \ldots, d_n\}$ of *context dimensions*. A CKAB is a tuple $\mathcal{K}_{cx} = \langle T_{cx}, A_0, \Gamma, \Pi, C_0, \Pi_C \rangle$ where:

- T_{cx} is a *DL-Lite$_A$ contextualized TBox* capturing the domain of interest.
- A_0 and Γ are as in a KAB.

- Π is a finite set of condition-action rules that extend those of KABs by including, in the precondition, a context expression. Such context expression implicitly selects those contexts in which the corresponding action can be executed. Specifically, each condition-action rule has the form $\langle Q(\vec{x}), \varphi_C \rangle \mapsto \alpha(\vec{x})$, where *(i)* $\alpha \in \Gamma$ is an action, *(ii)* $Q(\vec{x})$ is an ECQ over T_{cx} whose free variables $\vec{x}$ correspond exactly to the parameters of α, and *(iii)* φ_C is a context expression over $\mathbb{C}_{dim}$.
- C_0 is the initial context over $\mathbb{C}_{dim}$.
- Π_C is a finite set of context-evolution rules, each of which determines the configuration of the new context depending on the current context and data. Each *context-evolution rule* has the form $\langle Q, \varphi_C \rangle \mapsto C_{new}$, where: *(i)* Q is a boolean ECQ over T_{cx}, *(ii)* φ_C is a context expression, and *(iii)* C_{new} is a finite set of context dimension assignments such that for each context dimension $d \in \mathbb{C}_{dim}$, there exists *at most one* context dimension assignment $[d \rightsquigarrow v] \in C$. If a context variable is not assigned by C_{new}, it maintains the assignment of the previous state.

Example 3. In our running example, suppose the company has *warehouses* in a remote area (*remote warehouses*), each of which is expected to guarantee a certain *time to delivery* (TTD) for products. During the *low season*, the company is free to set the TTD for all its remote warehouses, which we model as a chgTTD() action. The execution of this action is controlled by the condition-action rule $\langle \exists w.\mathsf{RemWH}(w), [\mathsf{S} \rightsquigarrow \mathsf{LS}] \rangle \mapsto \mathsf{chgTTD}()$. Assuming that the company maintains the TTD for a remote warehouse in the relation hasTTD, the chgTTD() action can be specified as follows:

chgTTD() : { RemWH(x) $\wedge$ hasTTD(x, y) $\rightsquigarrow$ {RemWH(x), hasTTD(x, newTTD(x, y))}}

Intuitively, the unique effect in hasTTD updates the TTD of a remote warehouse x, by issuing a service call newTTD(x, y), which also takes into account the current TTD y of x.

Example 4. An example of context-evolution rule is $\langle \mathsf{true}, [\mathsf{S} \rightsquigarrow \mathsf{PS}] \rangle \mapsto [\mathsf{S} \rightsquigarrow \mathsf{NS}]$. It models the transition from *peak season* to *normal season*, independently from the data.

4.2   CKAB Execution Semantics

We are interested in verifying temporal properties over the evolution of CKABs, in particular "robust" properties that the system is required to guarantee independently from context changes. Towards this goal, we define the execution semantics of CKABs in terms of a possibly infinite-state transition system that simultaneously captures all possible evolutions of the system as well as all possible context changes.

Each state in the execution of a CKAB is a tuple $\langle id, A, m, C \rangle$, where id is a state identifier, A is an ABox maintaining the current data, m is a service call map accounting for the service call results obtained so far, and C is the current context. The context univocally selects which are the axioms of the contextual TBox that currently hold, in turn determining the current KB.

Formally, given a CKAB $\mathcal{K}_{cx} = \langle T_{cx}, A_0, \Gamma, \Pi, C_0, \Pi_C \rangle$, we define its semantics in terms of a *context-sensitive transition system* $\Upsilon_{\mathcal{K}_{cx}} = \langle \Delta, T_{cx}, \Sigma, s_0, abox, ctx, \Rightarrow \rangle$, where: *(i)* T_{cx} is a contextualized TBox; *(ii)* Σ is a set of states; *(iii)* $s_0 \in \Sigma$ is the initial state; *(iv)* $abox$ is a function that, given a state $s \in \Sigma$, returns the ABox associated to

s; *(v) ctx* is a function that, given a state $s \in \Sigma$, returns the context associated to s; *(vi)* $\Rightarrow \ \subseteq \Sigma \times \Sigma$ is a transition relation between pairs of states.

Starting from the initial state s_0, $\Upsilon_{\mathcal{K}_{cx}}$ accounts for all the possible (simultaneous) data and context transitions. To single out the dynamics of the system as opposed to those of the context, the transition system is built by repeatedly alternating between system and context transitions. Technically, we revise the notion of executability for KABs by taking into account context expressions, as well as the context evolution. Given an action $\alpha \in \Gamma$, we say that α is *executable* in state s with parameter substitution σ if there exists a condition-action rule $\langle Q(\vec{x}), \varphi_C \rangle \mapsto \alpha(\vec{x})$ in Π s.t. $\vec{x}\sigma \in \text{ANS}(Q, T_{cx}^{ctx(s)}, abox(s))$ and $ctx(s) \cup \Phi_{\mathbb{C}_{dim}} \models \varphi_C$.

We then introduce an *action transition relation* $\text{EXEC}_{\mathcal{K}_{cx}}$, where $\langle\langle A, m, C \rangle, \alpha\sigma, \langle A', m', C' \rangle\rangle \in \text{EXEC}_{\mathcal{K}_{cx}}$ if the following holds:

- Action α is *executable* in state $\langle A, m, C \rangle$ with parameter substitution σ.
- There exists $\theta \in \text{EVALS}(T_{cx}^C, A, \alpha\sigma)$ s.t. θ and m "agree" on the common values in their domains;
- $A' = \text{DO}(T_{cx}^C, A, \alpha\sigma)\theta$;
- $m' = m \cup \theta$;
- $C' = C$, i.e., the context does not change.

Alongside the action transition relation, we also define a *context transition relation* $\text{CEXEC}_{\mathcal{K}_{cx}}$, where $\langle\langle A, m, C \rangle, \langle A', m', C' \rangle\rangle \in \text{CEXEC}_{\mathcal{K}_{cx}}$ if the following holds:

- $A' = A$, i.e., the ABox does not change;
- $m' = m$, i.e., the service call map does not change;
- there exists a context rule $\langle Q, \varphi_C \rangle \mapsto C_{new}$ in Π_C s.t.: *(i)* $\text{ANS}(Q, T_{cx}^C, A)$ is true; *(ii)* $C \cup \Phi_{\mathbb{C}_{dim}} \models \varphi_C$; *(iii)* for every context dimension $d \in \mathbb{C}_{dim}$ s.t. $[d \rightsquigarrow v] \in C_{new}$, we have $[d \rightsquigarrow v] \in C'$; *(iv)* for every context dimension $d \in \mathbb{C}_{dim}$ s.t. $[d \rightsquigarrow v] \in C$, and there does not exist any v_2 s.t. $[d \rightsquigarrow v_2] \in C_{new}$, we have $[d \rightsquigarrow v] \in C'$.

Given these, we can now define how $\Upsilon_{\mathcal{K}_{cx}}$ is constructed, by suitably alternating the action and context transitions. In order to single out the states obtained by applying just an action transition and for which the context transition has not taken place yet, we introduce a special marker State(inter), which is an ABox assertion with a fresh concept name State and a fresh constant inter. When State(inter) is present, it means that the state has been produced by an action execution, and that the next transition will represent a context change. Such states can be considered as intermediate, in the sense that the overall change both of the ABox facts and of the context has not taken place yet.

Formally, given a CKAB $\mathcal{K}_{cx} = \langle T_{cx}, A_0, \Gamma, \Pi, C_0, \Pi_C \rangle$, the context-sensitive transition system $\Upsilon_{\mathcal{K}_{cx}} = \langle \Delta, T_{cx}, \Sigma, s_0, abox, ctx, \Rightarrow \rangle$ is defined as follows:

- $s_0 = \langle id_0, A_0, \emptyset, C_0 \rangle$;
- Σ and $\Rightarrow$ are defined by simultaneous induction as the smallest sets satisfying the following properties: *(i)* $s_0 \in \Sigma$; *(ii)* if $\langle id, A, m, C \rangle \in \Sigma$ and State(inter) $\notin A$, then for all actions $\alpha \in \Gamma$, for all substitutions σ for the parameters of α, and for all A', m' s.t. $\langle\langle A, m, C \rangle, \alpha\sigma, \langle A', m', C \rangle\rangle \in \text{EXEC}_{\mathcal{K}_{cx}}$, let

$$S = \{\langle id'', A', m', C' \rangle \mid id'' \text{ is a fresh identifier, and there is } \langle A', m', C \rangle$$
$$\text{such that } \langle\langle A', m', C \rangle, \langle A', m', C' \rangle\rangle \in \text{CEXEC}_{\mathcal{K}_{cx}}\}.$$

If for some $\langle id'', A', m', C' \rangle \in S$, we have that A' is $T_{cx}^{C'}$-consistent, then $s' \in \Sigma$ and $\langle id, A, m, C \rangle \Rightarrow s'$, where $s' = \langle id', A' \cup \{\text{State}(\text{inter})\}, m', C \rangle$ and id' is a fresh identifier. Moreover, in this case, for each $s'' = \langle id'', A', m', C' \rangle \in S$ such that A' is $T_{cx}^{C'}$-consistent, we have that $s'' \in \Sigma$ and $s' \Rightarrow s''$.

Notice that, if at some point in the above inductive construction, for no $\langle id'', A', m', C' \rangle \in S$ we have that A' is $T_{cx}^{C'}$-consistent, then neither the state s' nor any state in S becomes part of Σ.

5 Verifying Temporal Properties over CKAB

Given a CKAB $\mathcal{K}_{cx}$, we are interested in verifying whether the evolution of $\mathcal{K}_{cx}$, which is represented by $\Upsilon_{\mathcal{K}_{cx}}$, complies with some given temporal property. The challenge is that in general the transition system is infinite due to the presence of services calls, which can introduce arbitrary fresh values into the system.

5.1 Verification Formalism: Context-Sensitive FO-Variant of μ-Calculus

In order to specify temporal properties over CKABs, we use a first-order variant of μ-calculus [25,23], one of the most powerful temporal logics, which subsumes LTL, PSL, and CTL* [14]. In particular, we introduce the language $\mu\mathcal{L}_{\text{CTX}}$ of *context-sensitive temporal properties*, which is based on $\mu\mathcal{L}_A^{\text{EQL}}$ defined in [4]. Basically, we exploit ECQs to query the states, and support a first-order quantification across states, where the quantification ranges over the constants in the current active domain. Additionally, we augment ECQs with context expressions, which allows us to check also context information while querying states. Formally, $\mu\mathcal{L}_{\text{CTX}}$ is defined as follows:

$$\Phi := Q \mid \varphi_C \mid \neg\Phi \mid \Phi_1 \wedge \Phi_2 \mid \exists x.\Phi \mid \langle-\rangle\square\Phi \mid \square\square\Phi \mid Z \mid \mu Z.\Phi$$

where Q is a possibly open EQL query that can make use of the distinguished constants in $\text{ADOM}(A_0)$, φ_C is a context expression over $\mathcal{L}_{cx}$, and Z is a second order predicate variable (of arity 0). We adopt the usual abbreviations of FOL, and also $\square\Phi = \neg\langle-\rangle\neg\Phi$ and $\nu Z.\Phi = \neg\mu Z.\neg\Phi[Z/\neg Z]$. Hence $\langle-\rangle\langle-\rangle\Phi = \neg\square\square\neg\Phi$ and $\square\langle-\rangle\Phi = \neg\langle-\rangle\square\neg\Phi$.

Notice that $\langle-\rangle\square\Phi$ and $\square\square\Phi$ are used in $\mu\mathcal{L}_{\text{CTX}}$ to quantify over the successor states of the current state, obtained after a state-changing transition followed by a context-changing one. This allows one to separately control how the property quantifies over state and context changes. Furthermore, due to the fact that the diamond and box operators can be only used in pairs, the local queries that inspect the data and the context maintained by the states are never issued over intermediate states, but only over those resulting from the combination of an action and context transition.

The semantics of $\mu\mathcal{L}_{\text{CTX}}$ is defined over a transition system $\Upsilon = \langle \Delta, T_{cx}, \Sigma, s_0, abox, ctx, \Rightarrow \rangle$. Since $\mu\mathcal{L}_{\text{CTX}}$ contains formulae with both individual and predicate free variables, given a transition system Υ, we introduce an individual variable valuation v, i.e., a mapping from individual variables x to Δ, and a predicate variable valuation V, i.e., a mapping from predicate variables Z to subsets of Σ. The semantics of $\mu\mathcal{L}_{\text{CTX}}$ follows the standard μ-calculus semantics, except for the semantics of queries and of quantification. We assign meaning to $\mu\mathcal{L}_{\text{CTX}}$ formulae by associating to Υ and V an *extension function* $(\cdot)^{\Upsilon}_{v,V}$, which maps $\mu\mathcal{L}_{\text{CTX}}$ formulas to subsets of Σ. The extension function $(\cdot)^{\Upsilon}_{v,V}$ is defined inductively as follows:

$$(Q)^{\Upsilon}_{v,V} = \{s \in \Sigma \mid \text{ANS}(Qv, T^C_{cx}, abox(s)) = true\}$$
$$(\varphi_C)^{\Upsilon}_{v,V} = \{s \in \Sigma \mid ctx(s) \cup \Phi_{C_{dim}} \models \varphi_C\}$$
$$(\exists x.\Phi)^{\Upsilon}_{v,V} = \{s \in \Sigma \mid \exists d.d \in \text{ADOM}(abox(s)) \text{ and } s \in (\Phi)^{\Upsilon}_{v[x/d],V}\}$$
$$(Z)^{\Upsilon}_{v,V} = V(Z) \subseteq \Sigma$$
$$(\neg\Phi)^{\Upsilon}_{v,V} = \Sigma - (\Phi)^{\Upsilon}_{v,V}$$
$$(\Phi_1 \vee \Phi_2)^{\Upsilon}_{v,V} = (\Phi_1)^{\Upsilon}_{v,V} \cup (\Phi_2)^{\Upsilon}_{v,V}$$
$$(\langle -\rangle\Phi)^{\Upsilon}_{v,V} = \{s \in \Sigma \mid \exists s'. s \Rightarrow s' \text{ and } s' \in (\Phi)^{\Upsilon}_{v,V}\}$$
$$(\mu Z.\Phi)^{\Upsilon}_{v,V} = \bigcap\{\mathcal{E} \subseteq \Sigma \mid (\Phi)^{\Upsilon}_{v,V[Z/\mathcal{E}]} \subseteq \mathcal{E}\}$$

where Qv is the query obtained from Q by substituting its free variables according to v. For a closed formula Φ (for which $(\Phi)^{\Upsilon}_{v,V}$ does not depend on v or V), we denote with $(\Phi)^{\Upsilon}$ the extension of Φ in Υ, and we say that Φ holds in a state $s \in \Sigma$ if $s \in (\Phi)^{\Upsilon}$.

Model checking is the problem of checking whether $s_0 \in (\Phi)^{\Upsilon}$, denoted by $\Upsilon \models \Phi$. We are interested in *verification* of $\mu\mathcal{L}_{\text{CTX}}$ properties over CKABs, i.e., given a CKAB $\mathcal{K}_{cx}$, and a $\mu\mathcal{L}_{\text{CTX}}$ property Φ, check whether $\Upsilon_{\mathcal{K}_{cx}} \models \Phi$.

Example 5. In our running example, the property $\nu Z.(\forall x.\text{CustOrder}(x) \wedge [\text{S} \leadsto \text{PS}] \rightarrow \mu Y.(\text{Delivered}(x) \vee \boxminus\boxminus Y)) \wedge \boxminus\boxminus Z$ checks that every customer order placed during peak season will be eventually delivered, independently on how the context and the state evolve.

5.2   Decidability of Verification

In general, verification of temporal properties over CKABs is undecidable, even for properties as simple as reachability, which can be expressed in much weaker languages than $\mu\mathcal{L}_{\text{CTX}}$. This follows immediately from the fact that CKABs generalize KABs [4].

In order to establish decidability of verification, we need to pose restrictions on the form of CKABs. We adopt the semantic restriction of *run-boundedness* identified in [4], which intuitively imposes that along every run the number of distinct values cumulatively appearing in the ABoxes of the states in the run is bounded. Formally, given a CKAB $\mathcal{K}_{cx}$, a run $\tau = s_0 s_1 \cdots$ of $\Upsilon_{\mathcal{K}_{cx}}$ is *bounded* if there exists a finite bound b s.t. $\left| \bigcup_{s \text{ state of } \tau} \text{ADOM}(abox(s)) \right| < b$. We say that $\mathcal{K}_{cx}$ is *run-bounded* if there exists a bound b s.t. every run τ in $\Upsilon_{\mathcal{K}_{cx}}$ is bounded by b. The following result shows that the decidability of verification for run-bounded KABs can be lifted to CKABs as well.

Theorem 1. *Verification of $\mu\mathcal{L}_{\text{CTX}}$ properties over run-bounded CKABs is decidable, and can be reduced to finite-state model checking.*

Proof (sketch). For a run-bounded CKAB $\mathcal{K}_{cx}$, we construct a faithful finite-state abstraction for $\Upsilon_{\mathcal{K}_{cx}}$, that is, a finite-state transition system $\theta_{\mathcal{K}_{cx}}$ s.t., for every $\mu\mathcal{L}_{\text{CTX}}$ property Φ, we have that $\theta_{\mathcal{K}_{cx}} \models \Phi$ if and only if $\Upsilon_{\mathcal{K}_{cx}} \models \Phi$.

We observe that, thanks to run-boundedness, the number of distinct states appearing along each run of $\Upsilon_{\mathcal{K}_{cx}}$ is finite. Hence, the only source of infinity present in $\Upsilon_{\mathcal{K}_{cx}}$ is due to infinite branching. A distinctive feature of CKABs is that distinct states may differ not only in the ABox, but also in the TBox. However, the possible TBoxes that can be encountered during the system evolution depend only on the contexts, and not on the data contained in the ABoxes. Since contexts are propositional, only a finite number of distinct TBoxes will appear in $\Upsilon_{\mathcal{K}_{cx}}$. This, in turn, shows that infinite branching is only caused by the possibly infinite number of distinct values returned by the service calls. Hence, the source of infinity in CKABs is analogous to that of KABs, and we can adopt the same *pruning strategy* as for KABs [12]: we have shown that two successor states whose ABoxes are isomorphic w.r.t. values not present in $\text{ADOM}(A_0)$ cannot be distinguished by $\mu\mathcal{L}_A$ formulas, and therefore it is sufficient to keep only one of them in the faithful abstraction. The claim follows since $\mu\mathcal{L}_{\text{CTX}}$ is a fragment of $\mu\mathcal{L}_A$. $\square$

We close by observing that, due to the "alternating" nature between action and context transitions in $\Upsilon_{\mathcal{K}_{cx}}$, we can interpret $\Upsilon_{\mathcal{K}_{cx}}$ as a game structure in which the system is the "good" player and the context is the "bad" player. In this light, $\mu\mathcal{L}_{\text{CTX}}$ formulas that are in negation-normal form and only make use of temporal operators $\langle-\rangle[-]$ and $[-][-]$ can express properties that the system is required to guarantee independently on how the context evolves. Thanks to Theorem 1, and by observing that CKABs meet the so-called *genericity property* in the sense of [11], we can not only verify whether there exists a system strategy to enforce a property of this kind, but also effectively extract such strategy, following the metaphor of *synthesis via model checking*.

6   Weakly Acyclic CKABs

Even though run-boundedness guarantees decidability of $\mu\mathcal{L}_{\text{CTX}}$ verification over CK-ABs, it is a semantic property, which is undecidable to check [3]. To mitigate this problem, [3] provides a sufficient condition for run-boundedness. Such condition leverages on the notion of *weak-acyclicity* in data exchange [16], and is syntactically checked over a dependency graph that over-approximates the transfer of values from relation components to other relation components, according to the specification of the system actions.

Intuitively, weak-acyclicity checks for the presence of service calls that can feed themselves, either directly or indirectly, through a chain of other service calls. This cyclic dependency gives raise to runs in which infinitely many distinct service calls are issued, and possibly return infinitely many distinct values, thus making those runs unbounded.

In [4], the notion of weak-acyclicity has been suitably recast in the context of KABs, taking advantage from first-order rewritability of EQL queries over *DL-Lite* ontologies, and from the fact that KABs have a TBox that is fixed, i.e., independent of the state. The idea is to construct the dependency graph approximating the behavior of the KAB action component, by considering the contribution of the TBox.

The main difficulty in lifting weak-acyclicity to our setting, is that due to the presence of the context, the TBox changes over time. To tackle this issue, we observe that the current TBox is determined by the current context, and that each action α in a CKAB can be executed only in those contexts that match with the context expressions contained in the pre-conditions of condition-action rules having α in their head. Therefore, when analyzing the contribution of α to the dependency graph, we consider all the possible finitely many contexts in which α can be applied, and consider the application of α with all corresponding TBoxes.

Formally, given a CKAB $\mathcal{K}_{cx} = \langle T_{cx}, A_0, \Gamma, \Pi, C_0, \Pi_C \rangle$, we define its *dependency graph* $G = \langle V, E \rangle$ as follows.

The set V of nodes is created from the concepts and roles in $\text{VOC}(T_{cx})$, as the smallest set satisfying the following conditions: (a) for each concept N in $\text{VOC}(T_{cx})$, V contains one node $\langle N, 1 \rangle$; (b) for each role R in $\text{VOC}(T_{cx})$, V contains two nodes $\langle R, 1 \rangle$ and $\langle R, 2 \rangle$, respectively reflecting the first and second component of R.

The set E of edges is created based on the condition-action rules in Π and the actions in Γ. Each edge represents a possible data transfer from one node (i.e., concept/role component) to another node, due to some action effect. In particular, a *normal* edge represents a value transfer, whereas a *special* edge represents that the source node is part of the input for a service call whose result is stored in the target node. Specifically, E is the smallest set satisfying the following conditions (we consider the contribution of concepts, the case of role components is analogous):

1. E contains an ordinary edge $\langle N_1, 1 \rangle \to \langle N_2, 1 \rangle$ if there exist *(i)* an action $\alpha \in \Gamma$, *(ii)* an effect $[q^+] \wedge Q^- \rightsquigarrow A'$ in α, *(iii)* a condition-action rule $\langle Q(\vec{x}), \varphi_C \rangle \mapsto \alpha(\vec{x})$, and *(iv)* a variable x, s.t. $N_1(x)$ appears in $rew(q^+, T_{cx}^{C_\alpha})$ (i.e., in the perfect rewriting of q^+ w.r.t. $T_{cx}^{C_\alpha}$), and $N_2(x)$ appears in A'.

2. E contains a special edge $\langle N_1, 1 \rangle \overset{*}{\to} \langle N_2, 1 \rangle$ if there exist *(i)* an action $\alpha \in \Gamma$, *(ii)* an effect $[q^+] \wedge Q^- \rightsquigarrow A'$ in α, *(iii)* a condition-action rule $\langle Q(\vec{x}), \varphi_C \rangle \mapsto \alpha(\vec{x})$, and *(iv)* a variable x, s.t. $N_1(x)$ appears in $rew(q^+, T_{cx}^{C_\alpha})$, and $N_2(f(\ldots, x, \ldots))$ appears in A'.

A CKAB $\mathcal{K}_{cx}$ is *weakly acyclic* if its dependency graph has no cycle going through a special edge. Such a cycle witnesses that the same service call (in)directly feeds itself. The following result shows that such "context-aware" dependency graph can be effectively used as a sufficient condition for checking whether a CKAB is run-bounded.

Theorem 2. *Given a weakly acyclic CKAB $\mathcal{K}_{cx}$, we have that $\Upsilon_{\mathcal{K}_{cx}}$ is run-bounded.*

Proof (sketch). The proof is obtained by observing that the dependency graph construction for CKABs corresponds to that of standard KABs, imagining that the context is "compiled away", and that each (contextualized) action α of the CKAB under study is translated into a set of actions $\alpha_1, \ldots, \alpha_n$, each corresponding to the execution of α in one of the possible contexts in which α can be applied. Observe that n is finite and, in the worst case, it corresponds to the overall number of contexts that can be encountered in the system. In standard KABs, the contribution of each action to the dependency graph is obtained by compiling away the TBox and by considering the rewritten queries in the action effects. Hence, there is no difference between a normal KAB and a CKAB in which each of the aforementioned α_i is rewritten using the TBox obtained from the context to which α_i corresponds. This is exactly what the dependency graph construction provided above does. We can therefore recast Theorem 6.1 in [12] to obtain the claim. □

From Theorems 1 and 2, we finally obtain:

Corollary 1. *Verification of $\mu\mathcal{L}_{CTX}$ properties over weakly acyclic CKABs is decidable, and can be reduced to finite-state model checking.*

7 Conclusion

We have introduced context-sensitive KABs, which extend KABs with contextual information. In this enriched setting, we make use of context-sensitive temporal properties based on a FOL variant of μ-calculus, and establish decidability of verification for such logic over CKABs in which the data values encountered along each run are bounded.

In this work, we adopt a simplistic approach to deal with inconsistency, based on simply rejecting inconsistent states. This approach is particularly critical in the presence of contextual information, which could lead to an inconsistent state simply due to a context change. In this light, it is particularly interesting to merge the approach presented in this paper with the one in [12], where inconsistency is treated in a more sophisticated way, based on the notion of repairs.

Acknowledgments. This research has been partially supported by the EU IP project Optique (*Scalable End-user Access to Big Data*), grant agreement n. FP7-318338, and by DFG within the Research Training Group "RoSI" (GRK 1907).

References

1. Baader, F., Calvanese, D., McGuinness, D., Nardi, D., Patel-Schneider, P.F. (eds.): The Description Logic Handbook: Theory, Implementation and Applications. Cambridge University Press (2003)
2. Baader, F., Knechtel, M., Peñaloza, R.: Context-dependent views to axioms and consequences of semantic web ontologies. John Wiley & Sons 12–13, 22–40 (2012)
3. Bagheri Hariri, B., Calvanese, D., De Giacomo, G., Deutsch, A., Montali, M.: Verification of relational data-centric dynamic systems with external services. In: Proc. of the 32nd ACM SIGACT SIGMOD SIGAI Symp. on Principles of Database Systems (PODS), pp. 163–174 (2013)
4. Bagheri Hariri, B., Calvanese, D., Montali, M., De Giacomo, G., De Masellis, R., Felli, P.: Description logic knowledge and action bases. J. of Artificial Intelligence Research 46, 651–686 (2013)
5. Borgida, A., Serafini, L.: Distributed description logics: Assimilating information from peer sources. J. on Data Semantics 1, 153–184 (2003)
6. Bozzato, L., Ghidini, C., Serafini, L.: Comparing contextual and flat representations of knowledge: A concrete case about football data. In: Proc. of the 7th Int. Conf. on Knowledge Capture (K-CAP), pp. 9–16. ACM Press (2013)
7. Calvanese, D., De Giacomo, G., Lembo, D., Lenzerini, M., Poggi, A., Rodríguez-Muro, M., Rosati, R.: Ontologies and databases: The *DL-Lite* approach. In: Tessaris, S., Franconi, E., Eiter, T., Gutierrez, C., Handschuh, S., Rousset, M.-C., Schmidt, R.A. (eds.) Reasoning Web. LNCS, vol. 5689, pp. 255–356. Springer, Heidelberg (2009)
8. Calvanese, D., De Giacomo, G., Lembo, D., Lenzerini, M., Rosati, R.: EQL-Lite: Effective first-order query processing in description logics. In: Proc. of the 20th Int. Joint Conf. on Artificial Intelligence (IJCAI), pp. 274–279 (2007)

9. Calvanese, D., De Giacomo, G., Lembo, D., Lenzerini, M., Rosati, R.: Tractable reasoning and efficient query answering in description logics: The *DL-Lite* family. J. of Automated Reasoning 39(3), 385–429 (2007)
10. Calvanese, D., De Giacomo, G., Lembo, D., Montali, M., Santoso, A.: Ontology-based governance of data-aware processes. In: Krötzsch, M., Straccia, U. (eds.) RR 2012. LNCS, vol. 7497, pp. 25–41. Springer, Heidelberg (2012)
11. Calvanese, D., De Giacomo, G., Montali, M., Patrizi, F.: Verification and synthesis in description logic based dynamic systems. In: Faber, W., Lembo, D. (eds.) RR 2013. LNCS, vol. 7994, pp. 50–64. Springer, Heidelberg (2013)
12. Calvanese, D., Kharlamov, E., Montali, M., Santoso, A., Zheleznyakov, D.: Verification of inconsistency-aware knowledge and action bases. In: Proc. of the 23rd Int. Joint Conf. on Artificial Intelligence, IJCAI (2013)
13. Ceylan, İ.İ., Peñaloza, R.: The Bayesian description logic $\mathcal{BEL}$. In: Demri, S., Kapur, D., Weidenbach, C. (eds.) IJCAR 2014. LNCS, vol. 8562, pp. 480–494. Springer, Heidelberg (2014)
14. Clarke, E.M., Grumberg, O., Peled, D.A.: Model checking. The MIT Press, Cambridge (1999)
15. Deutsch, A., Hull, R., Patrizi, F., Vianu, V.: Automatic verification of data-centric business processes. In: Proc. of the 12th Int. Conf. on Database Theory (ICDT), pp. 252–267 (2009)
16. Fagin, R., Kolaitis, P.G., Miller, R.J., Popa, L.: Data exchange: Semantics and query answering. Theoretical Computer Science 336(1), 89–124 (2005)
17. Giunchiglia, F., Bouquet, P.: Introduction to contextual reasoning. an artificial intelligence perspective. In: Perspectives on Cognitive Science, pp. 138–159. NBU Press (1997)
18. Klarman, S., Gutiérrez-Basulto, V.: $\mathcal{ALC}_{\mathcal{ALC}}$: A context description logic. In: Janhunen, T., Niemelä, I. (eds.) JELIA 2010. LNCS, vol. 6341, pp. 208–220. Springer, Heidelberg (2010)
19. Limonad, L., De Leenheer, P., Linehan, M., Hull, R., Vaculín, R.: Ontology of dynamic entities. In: Atzeni, P., Cheung, D., Ram, S. (eds.) ER 2012. LNCS, vol. 7532, pp. 345–358. Springer, Heidelberg (2012)
20. McCarthy, J.: Generality in artificial intelligence. Commun. ACM 30(12), 1030–1035 (1987)
21. McCarthy, J.: Notes on formalizing context. In: Proc. of the 13th Int. Joint Conf. on Artificial Intelligence (IJCAI), pp. 555–560 (1993)
22. Montali, M., Calvanese, D., De Giacomo, G.: Verification of data-aware commitment-based multiagent systems. In: Proc. of the 13th Int. Conf. on Autonomous Agents and Multiagent Systems (AAMAS 2014), pp. 157–164 (2014)
23. Park, D.M.R.: Finiteness is Muineffable. Theoretical Computer Science 3(2), 173–181 (1976)
24. Serafini, L., Homola, M.: Contextualized knowledge repositories for the semantic web. J. of Web Semantics 12, 64–87 (2012)
25. Stirling, C.: Modal and Temporal Properties of Processes. Springer (2001)
26. Vianu, V.: Automatic verification of database-driven systems: A new frontier. In: Proc. of the 12th Int. Conf. on Database Theory (ICDT), pp. 1–13 (2009)

System ASPMT2SMT:
Computing ASPMT Theories by SMT Solvers

Michael Bartholomew and Joohyung Lee

School of Computing, Informatics, and Decision Systems Engineering
Arizona State University, Tempe, USA
{mjbartho,joolee}@asu.edu

Abstract. Answer Set Programming Modulo Theories (ASPMT) is an approach to combining answer set programming and satisfiability modulo theories based on the functional stable model semantics. It is shown that the tight fragment of ASPMT programs can be turned into SMT instances, thereby allowing SMT solvers to compute stable models of ASPMT programs. In this paper we present a compiler called ASPSMT2SMT, which implements this translation. The system uses ASP grounder GRINGO and SMT solver Z3. GRINGO partially grounds input programs while leaving some variables to be processed by Z3. We demonstrate that the system can effectively handle real number computations for reasoning about continuous changes.

1 Introduction

Answer Set Programming (ASP) is a widely used declarative computing paradigm. Its success is largely due to the expressivity of its modeling language and efficiency of ASP solvers thanks to intelligent grounding and efficient search methods that originated from propositional satisfiability (SAT) solvers. While grounding methods implemented in ASP solvers are highly optimized, ASP inherently suffers when variables range over large domains. Furthermore, real number computations are not supported by ASP solvers because grounding cannot be even applied. Thus reasoning about continuous changes even for a small interval requires loss of precision by discretizing the domain.

Satisfiability Modulo Theories (SMT) emerged as an enhancement of SAT, which can be also viewed as a special case of (decidable) first-order logic in which certain predicate and function symbols in background theories have fixed interpretations. Example background theories are the theory of real numbers, the theory of linear arithmetic, and difference logic.

A few approaches to loosely combining ASP and SMT/CSP exist [1,2,3], in which nonmonotonicity of the semantics is related to predicates in ASP but has nothing to do with functions in SMT/CSP. For instance, while

$$WaterLevel(t+1, tank, l) \leftarrow WaterLevel(t, tank, l), \; not \; \neg WaterLevel(t+1, tank, l)$$

(t is a variable ranging over steps; l is a variable for the water level) represents the default value of water level correctly (albeit grounding suffers when the variables range

E. Fermé and J. Leite (Eds.): JELIA 2014, LNAI 8761, pp. 529–542, 2014.
© Springer International Publishing Switzerland 2014

over a large numeric domain), rewriting it in the language of CLINGCON—a combination of ASP solver CLINGO and constraint solver GECODE—as

$$WaterLevel(t+1, tank) =^\$ l \;\leftarrow\; WaterLevel(t, tank) =^\$ l, \; not \; \neg(WaterLevel(t+1, tank) =^\$ l)$$

does not express the concept of defaults correctly.

In [4], it was observed that a tight integration of ASP and SMT requires a generalization of the stable model semantics in which default reasoning can be expressed via (non-Herbrand) functions as well as predicates. Based on the functional stable model semantics from [5], a new framework called "Answer Set Programming Modulo Theories (ASPMT)" was proposed, which is analogous to SMT. Just like SMT is a generalization of SAT and, at the same time, a special case of first-order logic with fixed background theories, ASPMT is a generalization of the traditional ASP and, at the same time, a special case of the functional stable model semantics in which certain background theories are assumed. Unlike SMT, ASPMT allows expressive nonmonotonic reasoning as allowed in ASP.

It is shown in [4], a fragment of ASPMT instances can be turned into SMT instances, so that SMT solvers can be used for computing stable models of ASPMT instances. In this paper, we report an implementation of this translation in the system called "ASPMT2SMT." The system first partially grounds the theory by replacing "ASP variables" with ground terms, leaving other "SMT variables" ungrounded. Then, it computes the completion of the theory. Under certain conditions guaranteed by the class of ASPMT theories considered, the remaining variables can then be eliminated. After performing this elimination, the ASPMT2SMT system then invokes the Z3 system to compute classical models, which correspond to the stable models of the original theory. We show that several examples involving both discrete changes as well as continuous changes can be naturally represented in the input language of ASPMT2SMT, and can be effectively computed.

The paper is organized as follows. In section 2, we first review the functional stable models semantics and as its special case, ASPMT, and then review the theorem on completion from [5]. In section 3, we describe the process of variable elimination used by the system. In section 4, we describe the architecture of the system as well as the syntax of the input language. Finally, in section 5, we present several experiments with and without continuous reasoning and compare the performance to ASP solver CLINGO when appropriate.

The system is available at http://reasoning.eas.asu.edu/aspmt.

2   Preliminaries

2.1   Review of the Functional Stable Model Semantics

We review the stable model semantics of intensional functions from [5]. Formulas are built the same as in first-order logic.

Similar to circumscription, for predicate symbols (constants or variables) u and c, expression $u \leq c$ is defined as shorthand for $\forall \mathbf{x}(u(\mathbf{x}) \rightarrow c(\mathbf{x}))$. Expression $u = c$ is defined as $\forall \mathbf{x}(u(\mathbf{x}) \leftrightarrow c(\mathbf{x}))$ if u and c are predicate symbols, and $\forall \mathbf{x}(u(\mathbf{x}) = c(\mathbf{x}))$ if they are function symbols. For lists of symbols $\mathbf{u} = (u_1, \ldots, u_n)$ and $\mathbf{c} = (c_1, \ldots, c_n)$, expression $\mathbf{u} \leq \mathbf{c}$ is defined as $(u_1 \leq c_1) \wedge \cdots \wedge (u_n \leq c_n)$, and similarly, expression $\mathbf{u} = \mathbf{c}$ is defined as $(u_1 = c_1) \wedge \cdots \wedge (u_n = c_n)$. Let $\mathbf{c}$ be a list of distinct predicate and function constants, and let $\widehat{\mathbf{c}}$ be a list of distinct predicate and function variables corresponding to $\mathbf{c}$. By $\mathbf{c}^{pred}$ ($\mathbf{c}^{func}$, respectively) we mean the list of all predicate constants (function constants, respectively) in $\mathbf{c}$, and by $\widehat{\mathbf{c}}^{pred}$ ($\widehat{\mathbf{c}}^{func}$, respectively) the list of the corresponding predicate variables (function variables, respectively) in $\widehat{\mathbf{c}}$.

For any formula F and any list of predicate and function constants $\mathbf{c}$, which we call *intensional* constants, expression $\mathrm{SM}[F; \mathbf{c}]$ is defined as

$$F \wedge \neg \exists \widehat{\mathbf{c}}(\widehat{\mathbf{c}} < \mathbf{c} \wedge F^*(\widehat{\mathbf{c}})),$$

where $\widehat{\mathbf{c}} < \mathbf{c}$ is shorthand for $(\widehat{\mathbf{c}}^{pred} \leq \mathbf{c}^{pred}) \wedge \neg(\widehat{\mathbf{c}} = \mathbf{c})$, and $F^*(\widehat{\mathbf{c}})$ is defined recursively as follows.

- When F is an atomic formula, F^* is $F' \wedge F$ where F' is obtained from F by replacing all intensional (function and predicate) constants $\mathbf{c}$ in it with the corresponding (function and predicate) variables from $\widehat{\mathbf{c}}$;
- $(G \wedge H)^* = G^* \wedge H^*$; $(G \vee H)^* = G^* \vee H^*$;
- $(G \rightarrow H)^* = (G^* \rightarrow H^*) \wedge (G \rightarrow H)$;
- $(\forall x G)^* = \forall x G^*$; $(\exists x F)^* = \exists x F^*$.

(We understand $\neg F$ as shorthand for $F \rightarrow \bot$; $\top$ as $\neg \bot$; and $F \leftrightarrow G$ as $(F \rightarrow G) \wedge (G \rightarrow F)$.)

When F is a sentence, the models of $\mathrm{SM}[F; \mathbf{c}]$ are called the *stable* models of F *relative to* $\mathbf{c}$. They are the models of F that are "stable" on $\mathbf{c}$. The definition can be easily extended to formulas of many-sorted signatures.

This definition of a stable model is a proper generalization of the one from [6], which views logic programs as a special case of first-order formulas.

We will often write $G \leftarrow F$, in a rule form as in logic programs, to denote the universal closure of $F \rightarrow G$. A finite set of formulas is identified with the conjunction of the formulas in the set.

By $\{c = v\}$, we abbreviate the formula $c = v \vee \neg(c = v)$ which, in the functional stable model semantics, can be intuitively understood as "by default, c is mapped to v".

2.2 ASPMT as a Special Case of the Functional Stable Model Semantics

We review the semantics of ASPMT described in [4]. Formally, an SMT instance is a formula in many-sorted first-order logic, where some designated function and predicate constants are constrained by some fixed background interpretation. SMT is the problem of determining whether such a formula has a model that expands the background interpretation [7].

The syntax of ASPMT is the same as that of SMT. Let σ^{bg} be the (many-sorted) signature of the background theory bg. An interpretation of σ^{bg} is called a *background interpretation* if it satisfies the background theory. For instance, in the theory of reals, we assume that σ^{bg} contains the set $\mathcal{R}$ of symbols for all real numbers, the set of arithmetic functions over real numbers, and the set $\{<,>,\leq,\geq,=\}$ of binary predicates over real numbers. Background interpretations interpret these symbols in the standard way.

Let σ be a signature that is disjoint from σ^{bg}. We refer to functions in σ^{bg} as interpreted functions and functions in σ as uninterpreted functions. We say that an interpretation I of σ satisfies F w.r.t. the background theory bg, denoted by $I \models_{bg} F$, if there is a background interpretation J of σ^{bg} that has the same universe as I, and $I \cup J$ satisfies F. For any ASPMT sentence F with background theory σ^{bg}, interpretation I is a *stable model* of F relative to $\mathbf{c}$ (w.r.t. background theory σ^{bg}) if $I \models_{bg} \text{SM}[F;\mathbf{c}]$. When $\mathbf{c}$ is empty, the stable models of F coincides with the models of F.

Consider the following running example from a Texas Action Group discussion[1].

> A car is on a road of length L. If the accelerator is activated, the car will speed up with constant acceleration A until the accelerator is released or the car reaches its maximum speed MS, whichever comes first. If the brake is activated, the car will slow down with acceleration $\neg A$ until the brake is released or the car stops, whichever comes first. Otherwise, the speed of the car remains constant. Give a formal representation of this domain, and write a program that uses your representation to generate a plan satisfying the following conditions: at duration 0, the car is at rest at one end of the road; at duration T, it should be at rest at the other end.

This problem is an instance of planning with continuous time, which requires real number computations.

The domain can be naturally represented in ASPMT as follows. Below s ranges over time steps, b is a boolean variable, x, y, a, c, d are all real variables, and A and MS are some specific numbers.

We represent that the actions *Accel* and *Decel* are exogenous and the duration of each time step is to be arbitrarily selected as

$$\{Accel(s) = b\}, \qquad \{Decel(s) = b\}, \qquad \{Duration(s) = x\}.$$

Both *Accel* and *Decel* cannot be performed at the same time:

$$\bot \leftarrow Accel(s) = \text{TRUE} \wedge Decel(s) = \text{TRUE}.$$

The effects of *Accel* and *Decel* on *Speed* are described as

$$Speed(s+1) = y \leftarrow Accel(s) = \text{TRUE} \wedge Speed(s) = x \wedge Duration(s) = d$$
$$\wedge (y = x + \text{A} \times d),$$
$$Speed(s+1) = y \leftarrow Decel(s) = \text{TRUE} \wedge Speed(s) = x \wedge Duration(s) = d$$
$$\wedge (y = x - \text{A} \times d).$$

The preconditions of *Accel* and *Decel* are described as

$$\bot \leftarrow Accel(s) = \text{TRUE} \wedge Speed(s) = x \wedge Duration(s) = d$$
$$\wedge (y = x + \text{A} \times d) \wedge (y > \text{MS}),$$
$$\bot \leftarrow Decel(s) = \text{TRUE} \wedge Speed(s) = x \wedge Duration(s) = d$$
$$\wedge (y = x - \text{A} \times d) \wedge (y < 0).$$

---

[1] http://www.cs.utexas.edu/users/vl/tag/continuous_problem

Speed is inertial:

$$\{Speed(s+1) = x\} \leftarrow Speed(s) = x.$$

The *Location* is defined in terms of *Speed* and *Duration* as

$$Location(s+1) = y \leftarrow Location(s) = x \wedge Speed(s) = a \wedge Speed(s+1) = c$$
$$\wedge \, Duration(s) = d \wedge y = x + ((a+c)/2) \times d.$$

2.3   Theorem on Completion

We review the theorem on completion from [4]. The *completion* turns "tight" ASPMT instances into equivalent SMT instances, so that SMT solvers can be used for computing this fragment of ASPMT.

We say that a formula F is in *Clark normal form* (relative to the list $\mathbf{c}$ of intensional constants) if it is a conjunction of sentences of the form

$$\forall \mathbf{x}(G \to p(\mathbf{x})) \tag{1}$$

and

$$\forall \mathbf{x}y(G \to f(\mathbf{x}) = y) \tag{2}$$

one for each intensional predicate p and each intensional function f, where $\mathbf{x}$ is a list of distinct object variables, y is a variable, and G is a formula that has no free variables other than those in $\mathbf{x}$ and y, and sentences of the form

$$\leftarrow G. \tag{3}$$

The *completion* of a formula F in Clark normal form (relative to $\mathbf{c}$) is obtained from F by replacing each conjunctive term (1) with

$$\forall \mathbf{x}(p(\mathbf{x}) \leftrightarrow G), \tag{4}$$

each conjunctive term (2) with

$$\forall \mathbf{x}y(f(\mathbf{x}) = y \leftrightarrow G), \tag{5}$$

and each conjunctive term (3) with $\neg G$.

An occurrence of a symbol or a subformula in a formula F is called *strictly positive* in F if that occurrence is not in the antecedent of any implication in F.

The *dependency graph* of a formula F relative to $\mathbf{c}$, denoted by $\mathrm{DG}_{\mathbf{c}}[F]$, is the directed graph that

- has all members of $\mathbf{c}$ as its vertices, and
- has an edge from c to d if, for some strictly positive occurrence of $G \to H$ in F, c has a strictly positive occurrence in H, and d has a strictly positive occurrence in G.

We say that F is *tight* on $\mathbf{c}$ if the dependency graph of F relative to $\mathbf{c}$ is acyclic.

Theorem 1 *([4, Theorem 2]) For any formula F in Clark normal form that is tight on* **c**, *an interpretation I that satisfies $\exists xy(x \neq y)$ is a model of* $\mathrm{SM}[F; \mathbf{c}]$ *iff I is a model of the completion of F relative to* **c**.

For example, the car example formalization contains the following implications for the function $Speed(1)$:

$Speed(1) = y \leftarrow Accel(0) = \mathrm{TRUE} \wedge Speed(0) = x \wedge Duration(0) = d \wedge (y = x + \mathrm{A} \times d)$
$Speed(1) = y \leftarrow Decel(0) = \mathrm{TRUE} \wedge Speed(0) = x \wedge Duration(0) = d \wedge (y = x - \mathrm{A} \times d)$
$Speed(1) = y \leftarrow Speed(0) = y \wedge \neg\neg(Speed(1) = y)$

$(\{c = v\} \leftarrow G$ is strongly equivalent to $c = v \leftarrow G \wedge \neg\neg(c = v))$ and the completion contains the following equivalence.

$$
\begin{aligned}
Speed(1) = y \leftrightarrow \\
\exists xd(\ (Accel(0) = \mathrm{TRUE} \wedge Speed(0) = x \wedge Duration(0) = d \wedge (y = x + \mathrm{A} \times d)) \\
\vee (Decel(0) = \mathrm{TRUE} \wedge Speed(0) = x \wedge Duration(0) = d \wedge (y = x - \mathrm{A} \times d)) \\
\vee Speed(0) = y\ )
\end{aligned}
\tag{6}
$$

3   Variable Elimination

Some SMT solvers do not support variables at all (e.g. iSAT) while others suffer in performance when handling variables (e.g. Z3). While we can partially ground the input theories, some variables have large (or infinite) domains and should not (or cannot) be grounded. Thus, we consider two types of variables: *ASP variables*—variables which are grounded by ASP grounders—and *SMT variables*—variables which should not be grounded. After eliminating ASP variables by grounding, we consider the problem of equivalently rewriting the completion of the partially ground ASPMT theory so that the result contains no variables.

To ensure that variable elimination can be performed, we impose some syntactic restrictions on ASPMT instances. We first impose that no SMT variable appears in the argument of an uninterpreted function.

We assume ASPMT2SMT programs comprised of rules of the form $H \leftarrow B$ where

- H is $\perp$ or an atom of the form $f(\mathbf{t}) = v$, where $f(\mathbf{t})$ is a term and v is a variable;
- B is a conjunction of atomic formulas possibly preceded with $\neg$.

We define the *variable dependency graph* of a conjunction of possibly negated atomic formulas $C_1 \wedge \cdots \wedge C_n$ as follows. The vertices are the variables occurring in $C_1 \wedge \cdots \wedge C_n$. There is a directed edge from v to u if there is a C_i that is $v = t$ or $t = v$ for some term t such that u appears in t. We say a variable v depends on a variable u if there is a directed path from v to u in the variable dependency graph. We say a rule $H \leftarrow B$ is *variable isolated* if every variable v in it occurs in an equality $t = v$ or $v = t$ that is not negated in B and the variable dependency graph of B is acyclic.

Example 1. The rule $f = x \leftarrow g = 2 \times x$ is not variable isolated because variable x does not occur in an equality $x = t$ or $t = x$ in the body. Instead, we write this as $f = x \leftarrow (g = y) \wedge (y = 2 \times x)$, which is variable isolated.

The rule $f = x \leftarrow (2 \times x = y) \wedge (2 \times y = x)$ is not variable isolated; although variable y occurs in an equality of the form $t = y$, the dependency graph is not acyclic.

The variable elimination is performed modularly so the process needs only to be described for a single equivalence. If an ASPMT program contains no variables in arguments of uninterpreted functions, any equivalence in the completion of the ASPMT program will be of the form

$$\forall v(f = v \leftrightarrow \exists \mathbf{x}(B_1(v, \mathbf{x}) \vee \cdots \vee B_k(v, \mathbf{x})))$$

where each B_i is a conjunction of possibly negated literals and has $v = t$ as a non-negated subformula, and the variable dependency graph of B is acyclic. In the following, the notation F_t^v denotes the formula obtained from F by replacing every occurrence of the variable v with the term t. We define the process of eliminating variables from such an equivalence E as follows.

1. Given an equivalence $E = \forall v(f = v \leftrightarrow \exists \mathbf{x}(B_1(v, \mathbf{x}) \vee \cdots \vee B_k(v, \mathbf{x})))$,
   $F := \forall v(f = v \rightarrow \exists \mathbf{x}(B_1(v, \mathbf{x}) \vee \cdots \vee B_k(v, \mathbf{x})))$;
   $G := \forall v(\exists \mathbf{x}(B_1(v, \mathbf{x}) \vee \cdots \vee B_k(v, \mathbf{x})) \rightarrow f = v)$.
2. Eliminate variables from F as follows:
   (a) $F := \exists \mathbf{x}(B_1(v, \mathbf{x})_f^v \vee \cdots \vee B_k(v, \mathbf{x})_f^v)$ and then equivalently,
       $F := \exists \mathbf{x}(B_1(v, \mathbf{x})_f^v) \vee \cdots \vee \exists \mathbf{x}(B_k(v, \mathbf{x})_f^v)$.
   (b) $F_i := \exists \mathbf{x}(B_i(v, \mathbf{x})_f^v)$.
   (c) Eliminate variables from F_i as follows:
       i. $D_i := B_i(v, \mathbf{x})_f^v$.
       ii. While there is a variable x still in D_i, select a conjunctive term $x = t$ or
           $t = x$ (such that no variable in t depends on x) in D_i, then $D_i := (D_i)_t^x$.
       iii. $F_i = D_i$ (drop the existential quantifier since there are no variables in D_i).
   (d) $F := F_1 \vee \cdots \vee F_k$.
3. Eliminate variables from G as follows:
   (a) $G := \forall v \mathbf{x}((B_1(v, \mathbf{x}) \vee \cdots \vee B_k(v, \mathbf{x})) \rightarrow f = v)$ and then equivalently,
       $G := \forall v \mathbf{x}(B_1(v, \mathbf{x}) \rightarrow f = v) \wedge \cdots \wedge \forall v \mathbf{x}(B_k(v, \mathbf{x}) \rightarrow f = v)$.
   (b) $G_i := \forall v \mathbf{x}(B_i(v, \mathbf{x}) \rightarrow f = v)$.
   (c) Eliminate variables from G_i as follows:
       i. $D_i := B_i(v, \mathbf{x}) \rightarrow f = v$.
       ii. While there is a variable x still in D_i, select a conjunctive term $x = t$ or
           $t = x$ (such that no variable in t depends on x) from the body of D_i, then
           $D_i := (D_i)_t^x$.
       iii. $G_i = D_i$ (drop the universal quantifier since there are no variables in D_i).
   (d) $G := G_1 \vee \cdots \vee G_k$.
4. $E := F \wedge G$.

The following proposition asserts the correctness of this method. Note that the absence of variables in arguments of uninterpreted functions can be achieved by grounding ASP variables and enforcing that no SMT variables occur in uninterpreted functions.

Proposition 1 *For any completion of a variable isolated ASPMT program with no variables in arguments of uninterpreted functions, applying variable elimination method repeatedly results in a classically equivalent formula that contains no variables.*

For example, given the equivalence (6), Step 2a) turns the implication from left to right into the formula

$$\exists xd(\quad (Accel(0) = \text{TRUE} \land Speed(0) = x \land Duration(0) = d \land (Speed(1) = x + \text{A} \times d))$$
$$\lor (Decel(0) = \text{TRUE} \land Speed(0) = x \land Duration(0) = d \land (Speed(1) = x - \text{A} \times d))$$
$$\lor (Speed(0) = Speed(1)))$$

And then step 2d) produces

$$(Accel(0) = \text{TRUE} \land Speed(1) = Speed(0) + \text{A} \times Duration(0)) \lor$$
$$(Decel(0) = \text{TRUE} \land Speed(1) = Speed(0) - \text{A} \times Duration(0)) \lor$$
$$(Speed(0) = Speed(1)).$$

4   ASPMT2SMT System

4.1   Syntax of Input Language

In addition to the syntactic restriction on ASPMT rules imposed in the previous section, the current version of system ASPMT2SMT assumes that the input program is **f**-*plain* [5], as well as "av-separated," which intuitively means that no variable occurring in an argument of an uninterpreted function is related to the value variable of another uninterpreted functions via equality.[2] For example, for the rule $f(x) = 1 \leftarrow g = y \land y = x$, variable x is an argument of f and is also related to the value variable y of g via equality $y = x$. The reason for this restriction is because the system sets the equalities $g = y$ and $y = x$ aside (so that GRINGO does not ground them), and ground the rule and then replace the equalities back to yield

$$f(1) = 1 \leftarrow g = y \land y = x$$
$$f(2) = 1 \leftarrow g = y \land y = x$$
$$\cdots$$

rather than the intended

$$f(1) = 1 \leftarrow g = y \land y = 1$$
$$f(2) = 1 \leftarrow g = y \land y = 2.$$
$$\cdots$$

It should also be noted that the only background theories considered in this version of the implementation are arithmetic over reals and integers.

System ASPMT2SMT uses a syntax similar to system CPLUS2ASP [8] for declarations and a syntax similar to system F2LP [9] for rules.

There are declarations of four kinds, `sorts`, `objects`, `constants`, and `variables`. The sort declarations specify user data types (note: these cannot be used for value sorts). The object declarations specify the elements of the user-declared data types. The constant declarations specify all of the (possibly boolean) function constants that appear in the theory. The variables declarations specify the user-declared data types associated with each variable. Declarations for the car example are shown below.

---

[2] See the system homepage for the precise description of this condition.

```
:- sorts
  step; astep.

:- objects
  0..st              :: step;              0..st-1               :: astep.

:- constants
  time(step)         :: real[0..t];        accel(astep)          :: boolean;
  duration(astep)    :: real[0..t];        decel(astep)          :: boolean;
  speed(step)        :: real[0..ms];       location(step)        :: real[0..1].

:- variables
  S                  :: astep;             B                     :: boolean.
```

Only propositional connectives are supported in this version of ASPMT2SMT and these are represented in the system as follows:

$\wedge$	$\vee$	$\neg$	$\rightarrow$	$\leftarrow$
&	|	not	->	<-

Comparison and arithmetic operators are represented as usual:

$<$	$\leq$	$\geq$	$>$	$=$	$\neq$	add	subtract	multiply	divide
<	<=	>=	>	=	!=	+	−	*	/

$a \mathrel{!=} b$ is understood as $\neg(a = b)$. To abbreviate the formula $A \vee \neg A$, which is useful for expressing defaults and inertia, we write $\{A\}$. The rest of the car example is shown below.

```
% Actions and durations are exogenous
{accel(S)=B}.
{decel(S)=B}.
{duration(S)=X}.

% no concurrent actions
<- accel(S)=true & decel(S)=true.

% effects of accel and decel
speed(S+1)=Y <- accel(S)=true & speed(S)=X & duration(S)=D & Y = X+ar*D.
speed(S+1)=Y <- decel(S)=true & speed(S)=X & duration(S)=D & Y = X-ar*D.

% preconditions of accel and decel
<- accel(S)=true & speed(S)=X & duration(S)=D & Y = X+ar*D & Y > ms.
<- decel(S)=true & speed(S)=X & duration(S)=D & Y = X-ar*D & Y < 0.

% inertia of speed
{speed(S+1)=X} <- speed(S)=X.

location(S+1)=Y <- location(S)=X & speed(S)=A &
    speed(S+1)=C & duration(S)=D & Y = X+(A+C)/2*D.
```

```
time(S+1)=Y <- time(S)=X & duration(S)=D & Y=X+D.

% problem instance
time(0)=0.        speed(0)=0.        location(0)=0.
<- location(st) = Z & Z != 1.
<- speed(st) = Z & Z != 0.
<- time(st) = Z & Z != t.
```

This description can be run by the command

```
$aspmt2smt car -c st=3 -c t=4 -c ms=4 -c ar=3 -c l=10
```

which yields the output

```
accel(0) = true  accel(1) = false  accel(2) = false
decel(0) = false  decel(1) = false  decel(2) = true
duration(0) = 1.1835034190  duration(1) = 1.6329931618
duration(2) = 1.1835034190  location(0) = 0.0
location(1) = 2.1010205144  location(2) = 7.8989794855
location(3) = 10.0  speed(0) = 0.0
speed(1) = 3.5505102572  speed(2) = 3.5505102572
speed(3) = 0.0  time(0) = 0.0  time(1) = 1.1835034190
time(2) = 2.8164965809  time(3) = 4.0
z3 time in milliseconds: 30
Total time in milliseconds: 71
```

4.2 Architecture

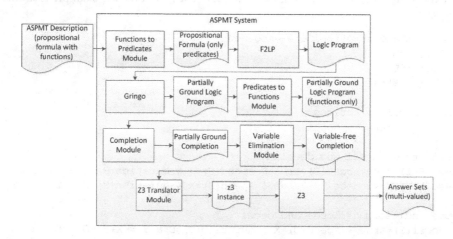

Fig. 1. ASPMT2SMT System Architecture

The architecture of ASPMT2SMT system is shown in Figure 1. The system first converts the ASPMT description to a propositional formula containing only predicates. In addition, this step substitutes auxiliary constants for SMT variables and necessary preprocessing for F2LP (v1.3) and GRINGO (v3.0.4) to enable partial grounding of ASP variables only. F2LP transforms the propositional formula into a logic program and then GRINGO performs partial grounding on only the ASP variables. The ASPMT2SMT system then converts the predicates back to functions and replaces the auxiliary constants with the original expressions. Then the system computes the completion of this partially ground logic program and performs variable elimination on that completion. Finally, the system converts this variable-free description into the language of Z3 and then relies on Z3 to produce models which correspond to stable models of the original ASPMT description.

For instance, consider the result of variable elimination on the portion of the completion related to $speed(1)$ of the running car example:

$$(Accel(0) = \text{TRUE} \land Speed(1) = Speed(0) + A \times Duration(0)) \lor$$
$$(Decel(0) = \text{TRUE} \land Speed(1) = Speed(0) - A \times Duration(0)) \lor$$
$$(Speed(0) = Speed(1)).$$

In the language of Z3, this is

```
(assert (or (or
   (and (= accel_0_ true) (= speed_1_ (+ speed_0_ (* duration_0_ a)))))
   (and (= decel_0_ true) (= speed_1_ (- speed_0_ (* duration_0_ a)))))
   (= speed_1_ speed_0_) ))
```

5 Experiments

The following experiments demonstrate the capability of the ASPMT2SMT system to perform nonmonotonic reasoning about continuous changes. In addition, this shows a significant performance increase compared to ASP solvers for domains in which only SMT variables have large domains. However, when ASP variables have large domains, similar scalability issues arise as comparable grounding still occurs.

All experiments were performed on an Intel Core 2 Duo 3.00 GHZ CPU with 4 GB RAM running Ubuntu 13.10. The domain descriptions of these examples can be found from the system homepage.

5.1 Leaking Bucket

Consider a leaking bucket with maximum capacity c that loses one unit of water every time step by default. The bucket can be refilled to its maximum capacity by the action $fill$. The initial capacity is 5 and the desired capacity is 10.

c	CLINGO v3.0.5 Run Time (Grounding + Solving)	ASPMT2SMT v0.9 Run Time (Preprocessing + solving)
10	0s (0s+0s)	.037s (.027s + .01s)
50	.02s (02s + 0s)	.089s (.079s + .01s)
100	.12s (.12s + 0s)	.180s (.170s + .01s)
500	8.69s (8.68s + .01s)	1.731s (1.661s + .07s)
1000	60.32s (60.29s+ .03s)	35.326s (35.206s + .12s)

We see that in this experiment, ASPMT2SMT does not yield significantly better results than CLINGO. The reason for this is that the scaling of this domain takes place in the number of time steps. Thus, since ASPMT2SMT uses GRINGO to generate fluents for each of these time steps, the ground descriptions given to CLINGO and Z3 are of similar size. Consequently, we see that the majority of the time taken for ASPMT2SMT is in preprocessing.

5.2 Car Example

k	CLINGO v3.0.5 Run Time (Grounding + Solving)	ASPMT2SMT v0.9 Run Time (Preprocessing + solving)
1	n/a	.084s (.054s + .03s)
5	n/a	.085s (.055s + .03s)
10	n/a	.085s (.055s + .03s)
50	n/a	.087s (.047s + .04s)
100	n/a	.088s (.048s + .04s)
1	.61s (.6s + .01s)	.060s (.050s + .01s)
2	48.81s (48.73s + .08s)	.07s (.050s + .02s)
3	> 30 minutes	.072s (.052s + .02s)
5	> 30 minutes	.068s (.048s + .02s)
10	> 30 minutes	.068s (.048s + .02s)
50	> 30 minutes	.068s (.048s + .02s)
100	> 30 minutes	.072s (.052s + .02s)

Recall the car example in Section 2.2. The first half of the experiments are done with the values $L = 10k$, $A = 3k$, $MS = 4k$, $T = 4k$, which yields solutions with irrational values and so cannot be solved by system CLINGO. The second half of the experiments are done with the values $L = 4k$, $A = k$, $MS = 4k$, $T = 4k$, which yields solutions with integral values and so can be solved by system CLINGO. In this example, only the SMT variables have increasing domains but the ASP variable domain remains the same.

Consequently, the ASPMT2SMT system scales very well compared to the ASP system which can only complete the two smallest size domains.

We also experimented with CLINGCON. Since CLINGCON does not allow intensional functions, we need to encode the example differently using auxiliary abnormality atoms to represent the notions of inertia and default behaviors. In the first set of experiments, CLINGCON performed better than ASPMT2SMT, but like CLINGO, the current version of CLINGCON cannot handle real numbers, so it is not applicable to the second set of experiments.

5.3 Space Shuttle Example

k	CLINGO v3.0.5 Run Time (Grounding + Solving)	ASPMT2SMT v0.9 Run Time (Preprocessing + solving)
1	0s (0s + 0s)	.048s (.038s + .01s)
5	.03s (.02s + .01s)	.047s (.037s + .01s)
10	.14s (.9s + .5s)	.053s (.043s + .01s)
50	7.83s (3.36s + 4.47s)	.050s (.040s + .01s)
100	39.65s (16.14s + 23.51s)	.051s (.041s + .01s)

The following example is from [10], which represents cumulative effects on continuous changes. A spacecraft is not affected by any external forces. It has two jets and the force that can be applied by each jet along each axis is at most $4k$. The initial position of the rocket is $(0,0,0)$ and its initial velocity is $(0,1,1)$. How can it get to $(0,3k,2k)$ within 2 seconds? Assume the mass is 2.

Again in this problem, the scaling lies only in the size of the value of the functions involved in the description. Consequently, we see no scaling issues in either ASPMT2SMT or CLINGCON.

5.4 Bouncing Ball Example

k	CLINGO v3.0.5 Run Time (Grounding + Solving)	ASPMT2SMT v0.9 Run Time (Preprocessing + solving)
1	n/a	.072s (.062s + .01s)
10	n/a	.072s (.062s + .01s)
100	n/a	.071s (.061s + .01s)
1000	n/a	.075s (.065s + .01s)
10000	n/a	.082s (.062s + .02s)

The following example is from [11]. A ball is held above the ground by an agent. The actions available to the agent are *drop* and *catch*. Dropping the ball causes the height of the ball to change continuously with time as defined by Newton's laws of motion. As the ball accelerates towards the ground it gains velocity. If the ball is not caught before it reaches the ground, it hits the ground with speed s and bounces up into the air with speed $r \times s$ where $r = .95$ is the rebound coefficient. The bouncing ball reaches a certain height and falls back towards the ground due to gravity. An agent is holding a ball at height $100k$. We want to have the ball hit the ground and caught at height 50.

Again, CLINGO and CLINGCON are unable to find solutions to this domain since solutions are not integral. Also, we see that ASPMT2SMT suffers no scaling issues here again due to the fact that in this problem the scaling lies only in the size of the value of the functions involved in the description.

6 Conclusion

We presented system ASPMT2SMT, which translates ASPMT instances into SMT instances, and uses SMT solvers to compute ASPMT. Unlike other ASP solvers, this system can compute effective real number computation by leveraging the effective SMT solvers. Future work includes extending the system to handle other background theories, and investigate a larger fragment of ASPMT instances that can be turned into SMT instances.

Acknowledgements. We are grateful to the anonymous referees for their useful comments. This work was partially supported by the National Science Foundation under Grant IIS-1319794 and by the South Korea IT R&D program MKE/KIAT 2010-TD-300404-001.

References

1. Gebser, M., Ostrowski, M., Schaub, T.: Constraint answer set solving. In: Hill, P.M., Warren, D.S. (eds.) ICLP 2009. LNCS, vol. 5649, pp. 235–249. Springer, Heidelberg (2009)
2. Balduccini, M.: Representing constraint satisfaction problems in answer set programming. In: Working Notes of the Workshop on Answer Set Programming and Other Computing Paradigms, ASPOCP (2009)

3. Janhunen, T., Liu, G., Niemelä, I.: Tight integration of non-ground answer set programming and satisfiability modulo theories. In: Working notes of the 1st Workshop on Grounding and Transformations for Theories with Variables (2011)

4. Bartholomew, M., Lee, J.: Functional stable model semantics and answer set programming modulo theories. In: Proceedings of International Joint Conference on Artificial Intelligence, IJCAI (2013)

5. Bartholomew, M., Lee, J.: Stable models of formulas with intensional functions. In: Proceedings of International Conference on Principles of Knowledge Representation and Reasoning (KR), pp. 2–12 (2012)

6. Ferraris, P., Lee, J., Lifschitz, V.: Stable models and circumscription. Artificial Intelligence 175, 236–263 (2011)

7. Barrett, C.W., Sebastiani, R., Seshia, S.A., Tinelli, C.: Satisfiability modulo theories. In: Biere, A., Heule, M., van Maaren, H., Walsh, T. (eds.) Handbook of Satisfiability. Frontiers in Artificial Intelligence and Applications, vol. 185, pp. 825–885. IOS Press (2009)

8. Babb, J., Lee, J.: Cplus2ASP: Computing action language $C+$ in answer set programming. In: Cabalar, P., Son, T.C. (eds.) LPNMR 2013. LNCS, vol. 8148, pp. 122–134. Springer, Heidelberg (2013)

9. Lee, J., Palla, R.: System F2LP – computing answer sets of first-order formulas. In: Erdem, E., Lin, F., Schaub, T. (eds.) LPNMR 2009. LNCS, vol. 5753, pp. 515–521. Springer, Heidelberg (2009)

10. Lee, J., Lifschitz, V.: Describing additive fluents in action language $C+$. In: Proceedings of International Joint Conference on Artificial Intelligence (IJCAI), pp. 1079–1084 (2003)

11. Chintabathina, S.: Towards answer set prolog based architectures for intelligent agents. In: AAAI 2008, pp. 1843–1844 (2008)

A Library of Anti-unification Algorithms

Alexander Baumgartner and Temur Kutsia

RISC, Johannes Kepler University, Linz, Austria

Abstract. Generalization problems arise in many branches of artificial intelligence: machine learning, analogical and case-based reasoning, cognitive modeling, knowledge discovery, etc. Anti-unification is a technique used often to solve generalization problems. In this paper we describe an open-source library of some newly developed anti-unification algorithms in various theories: for first- and second-order unranked terms, higher-order patterns, and nominal terms.

1 Introduction

Given concrete examples, find an expression which adopts all their common features and has them as particular instances: This is an informal formulation of the generalization problem that arises in many branches of artificial intelligence. For instance, in inductive logic programming, which combines logic programming with machine learning, generalization is one of the steps used to fit the theory being learned to example clauses. In cognitive modeling, analogical reasoning relies on exploring and generalizing common features of different domains. Proof abstraction and lemma generation, software code clone detection and procedure invention are some other examples that involve generalization.

Anti-unification is a technique used often to solve generalization problems. Given two terms t_1 and t_2, this technique requires finding a term t such that both t_1 and t_2 are instances of t under some substitutions. Interesting generalizations are the least general ones. Introduced in [21, 22] for the first-order syntactic case, anti-unification has been extended to more complex theories and is used in various applications. For some of those developments, one can see [2–4, 8–11, 14, 15, 17, 18, 20, 23]. First-order order-sorted equational anti-unification (for combinations of associative and commutative theories with or without unit element) has been implemented in Maude and is freely available [1].

The open-source library described in this paper implements anti-unification for unranked terms, higher-order patterns, and nominal terms. Theories over these expressions have applications in knowledge representation, reasoning, programming, etc. Generalization problems in these theories may arise, for instance, in proof generalization or analogical reasoning in higher-order or nominal logic, in learning or refactoring λ-Prolog and α-Prolog programs, in detection of similarities in XML documents or in pieces of software code, just to name a few. Therefore, the algorithms provided by the library can be a valuable ingredient for tools that need to solve such generalization problems.

To be more specific, the library contains Java implementation of the following algorithms:

E. Fermé and J. Leite (Eds.): JELIA 2014, LNAI 8761, pp. 543–557, 2014.

- first-order rigid unranked anti-unification from [16],
- second-order unranked anti-unification from [5],
- higher-order (pattern) anti-unification from [6] and
  - its subalgorithm for deciding α-equivalence,
- nominal anti-unification from [7] and
  - its subalgorithm for deciding equivariance.

The mentioned subalgorithms are needed to compute *least general* generalizations. All these algorithms can be accessed from the Web page of the SToUT project at RISC: http://www.risc.jku.at/projects/stout/. Each of them has a separate Web page with a convenient Web interface to try the algorithm online. There are also the link to the paper where the algorithm is described, a brief explanation of the syntax, and some examples. Besides using the Web interface, the user may try also a shell version of each algorithm, or download the sources, or embed the algorithm in her/his own project. A sample code of the latter option is also available from the Web.

In this paper, for each algorithm mentioned above we define the problem it solves, give some simple examples, indicate its Web address, and explain the Web interface. For some of them, we also explain how it can be embedded in users projects.

2   Structure of the Library

We describe the structure of the library in a bit more detail. It consists of four Java libraries for four anti-unification algorithms (urau.jar, urauc.jar, hoau.jar and nau.jar), which have the same structure. There is one main package which starts with the name at.jku.risc.stout, followed by a short abbreviation for the implemented algorithm (e.g. urau, urauc, hoau or nau). Under this main package there are three subpackages, namely algo, data and util. The data package has one subpackage of its own, which is called data.atom. The main package is irrelevant for using the library, as it only contains some test cases and the user interfaces. For instance, the applets which are used in the web frontend. Nevertheless, the source code might

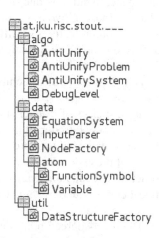

be interesting as those Java classes serve as reference implementations of the library.

As the name suggests, the package algo contains the algorithmic part of the library. There is a Java class named AntiUnify which serves as entry point of the respective anti-unification algorithm. The data package contains some Java classes which are needed to build the term structure. Furthermore, it includes the equation system which consists of some term pairs, and it offers a default implementation of an input parser, named InputParser. The Java class EquationSystem is implemented in a generic way, such that it can be used for different types of equation systems. In the util package there are some utility classes like DataStructureFactory which is used by the library to instantiate structures (e.g., lists, queues, maps, sets). The user of the library is free to choose an arbitrary implementation for all of those data structures, which might have some advantages on the performance of the provided algorithms. The package `data.atom` contains the atomic building blocks for constructing the terms.

3   Unranked First-Order Anti-unification

The problem of unranked anti-unification is formulated for terms defined over unranked alphabet. Hedge variables are used to fill in gaps in generalizations, while term variables abstract single subterms with different top function symbols. Unranked anti-unification is finitary, but it turned out that a minimal and complete algorithm may compute up to 3^n generalizations, where n is the size of the input. To deal with this problem, the notion of $\mathcal{R}_T$-*generalization* has been introduced in [16].

Definitions. Given pairwise disjoint countable sets of unranked function symbols $\mathcal{F}$ (symbols without fixed arity), term variables $\mathcal{V}_T$, and hedge variables $\mathcal{V}_H$, *terms* t and *hedges* $\tilde{s}$ are defined by the following grammar:

$$t ::= x \mid f(\tilde{s}) \quad s ::= t \mid X \quad \tilde{s} ::= s_1, \dots, s_n \quad \text{where } x \in \mathcal{V}_T, f \in \mathcal{F}, X \in \mathcal{V}_H, n \geqslant 0.$$

Substitutions map term variables $(x, y, \dots)$ to terms and hedge variables $(X, Y, \dots)$ to hedges. For instance, $\{x \mapsto f(a), X \mapsto (g(y, b), c), Y \mapsto ()\}$ is a substitution, where () is the empty hedge and a, b, c, f, g are unranked function symbols. Applying it to $f(x, X, Y)$ gives $f(f(a), g(y, b), c)$.

The set of positions (typically I, J) of a hedge $\tilde{s}$, denoted $pos(\tilde{s})$, is a prefix-closed set of strings of positive integers. For example, $pos(a, f(b, g(c)), d) = \{1, 2, 2\cdot1, 2\cdot2, 2\cdot2\cdot1, 3\}$. The symbol g stands at the position $2\cdot2$ and c occurs at the position $2\cdot2\cdot1$.

Two symbols $s_1, s_2 \in \mathcal{F} \cup \mathcal{V}_H \cup \mathcal{V}_C$ of a hedge are *horizontal consecutive* if their positions $I_{s_1}\cdot i_{s_1}$ and $I_{s_2}\cdot i_{s_2}$ are in the relation $I_{s_1} = I_{s_1}$ and $i_{s_1} + 1 = i_{s_2}$. They are in a *vertical chain* if their positions I_{s_1} and I_{s_2} are in the relation $I_{s_1}\cdot1 = I_{s_2}$ and $I_{s_1}\cdot2 \notin pos(\tilde{s})$. For example, in $(a, f(g(a, b)))$, the occurrence of a at position 1 and f at 2 are horizontal consecutive. The occurrence of f at 2 and g at $2\cdot1$ are in vertical chain.

Given two hedges $\tilde{s}$ and $\tilde{q}$, an *alignment* is a sequence of the form $f_1\langle I_1, J_1 \rangle \dots f_m\langle I_m, J_m \rangle$ such that $I_1 < \dots < I_m, J_1 < \dots < J_m$, and f_k is the symbol at position I_k in $\tilde{s}$ and at position J_k in $\tilde{q}$ for all $1 \leqslant k \leqslant m$. With $<$ we denote the (strict) lexicographic ordering on positions, e.g., $1\cdot2\cdot1 < 1\cdot2\cdot2$ and $1\cdot2\cdot1 < 1\cdot2\cdot1\cdot2$.

A *rigidity function* $\mathcal{R}$ is a function that returns a set of alignments for two hedges with all the positions in the alignments being singleton integers (allowing only top symbols). Typical examples of rigidity functions are those which return longest common subsequences or longest common substrings of the top symbols of the input hedges.

Given two variable-disjoint hedges $\tilde{s}, \tilde{q}$ and the rigidity function $\mathcal{R}$, we say that a hedge $\tilde{g}$ that generalizes both $\tilde{s}$ and $\tilde{q}$ is their $\mathcal{R}_T$-*generalization*, if either $\mathcal{R}(\tilde{s}, \tilde{q}) = \varnothing$ and $\tilde{g}$ is a hedge variable or a sequence of term variables, or there exists an alignment $f_1\langle i_1, j_1 \rangle \dots f_n\langle i_n, j_n \rangle \in \mathcal{R}(\tilde{s}, \tilde{q})$, such that:

1. If the sequence $\tilde{g}$ contains a pair of horizontal consecutive variables, then both of them are term variables.

2. If we remove all variables that occur as elements of $\tilde{g}$, we get a sequence of the form $f_1(\tilde{g}_1), \ldots, f_n(\tilde{g}_n)$.

3. For every $1 \leqslant k \leqslant n$, there exists a pair of sequences $\tilde{s}_k$ and $\tilde{q}_k$ such that $\tilde{s}|_{i_k} = f_k(\tilde{s}_k), \tilde{q}|_{j_k} = f_k(\tilde{q}_k)$ and $\tilde{g}_k$ is an $\mathcal{R}_\mathsf{T}$-generalization of $\tilde{s}_k$ and $\tilde{q}_k$.

The implemented anti-unification algorithm solves the following problem:

   Given: Two variable-disjoint hedges $\tilde{s}$ and $\tilde{q}$ and the rigidity function $\mathcal{R}$.
   Find: A complete set of $\mathcal{R}_\mathsf{T}$-generalizations for $\tilde{s}, \tilde{q}$ and $\mathcal{R}$.

For instance, $\{(g(a,a), X, f(g(a), g(Y))), (X, g(x,x), f(g(a), g(Z)))\}$ is the minimal complete set of $\mathcal{R}_\mathsf{T}$-generalization of the hedges $(g(a,a), g(b,b), f(g(a), g(a)))$ and $(g(a,a), f(g(a), g))$, where $\mathcal{R}$ computes longest common subsequences.

Web page. The implementation of unranked rigid anti-unification is available from http://www.risc.jku.at/projects/stout/software/urau.php.

Web interface explanation. The input form of the web page of the first-order rigid unranked anti-unification algorithm consists of five rows:

Anti-unification problem: (Use the semicolon to separate the equations of the system. Hedge equations are allowed.)	(f(a,b,c), g(a)) =^= (f(a,b,a,c), g(a), h(b))
Rigidity function:	Longest common subsequence ⌄
Minimum alignment length:	1
Iterate all possibilities:	☑
Output format:	Simple ⌄
Submit	

In the first row, the anti-unification problem should be given. It consists of some anti-unification equations, separated by semicolons. Each anti-unification equation consists of two hedges, with =^= in between. The second row contains a drop-down menu to chose a rigidity function. Currently, the only two possibilities are longest common subsequence and longest common substring.

Furthermore, in the third row, one can specify the minimal alignment length l. We define $\mathcal{R}_l(\tilde{s}, \tilde{q}) := \{a : |a| \geqslant l, a \in \mathcal{R}(\tilde{s}, \tilde{q})\}$ as the rigidity function which corresponds to a given rigidity function $\mathcal{R}$ satisfying the length restriction. The implementation uses $\mathcal{R}_l$ and for any $\mathcal{R}$ holds $\mathcal{R}_0 = \mathcal{R}$. By unchecking the check-box from the fourth row, the user can specify to only compute the $\mathcal{R}_\mathsf{T}$-generalization for the first alignment which is returned by the rigidity function $\mathcal{R}_l$ (nondeterministically).

In the last row, the output format can be specified. One can choose form a drop-down box between simple, verbose and progress. The first choice only shows some basic facts and the computed $\mathcal{R}_\mathsf{T}$-generalizations. The verbose output format shows some additional information, like the differences at the input hedges. By choosing the progress output format, all the debug information will be shown to the user.

How to use. We assume that there are two data sources `in1` and `in2` available in form of `Reader` instances, each of them containing one of the hedges to be generalized. Moreover, the variable `eqSys` is of appropriate type and there is a Boolean variable `iterateAll` which corresponds to the option "Iterate all possibilities" of the web interface. We explain the usage of the library on a code fragment:

```
1   RigidityFnc rFnc=new RigidityFncSubsequence().setMinLen(3);
2   eqSys = new EquationSystem<AntiUnifyProblem>() {
3       public AntiUnifyProblem newEquation() {
4           return new AntiUnifyProblem();
5       } };
6   new InputParser<AntiUnifyProblem>(eqSys)
7           .parseHedgeEquation(in1, in2);
8   new AntiUnify(rFnc, eqSys, DebugLevel.SILENT) {
9       public void callback(AntiUnifySystem res, Variable var)
            {
10          System.out.println(res.getSigma().get(var));
11      }; }.antiUnify(iterateAll, null);
```

In the first line a certain rigidity function is instantiated and the minimum alignment size is set to the value 3. There are two rigidity functions available from the library. The one which is used in the code fragment computes longest common subsequence alignments. The other one is called `RigidityFncSubstring` and computes longest common substring alignments. It is easy to implement a different rigidity function. One simply has to extend the base class `RigidityFnc` which is provided by the library.

The lines 2 to 5 show the instantiation of an equation system which is of type `AntiUnifyProblem`. It is used in line 6 to instantiate a parser instance.

In line 7, the mentioned input sources are used to create one equation of two hedges, which is added to the equation system. One could add more equations to the system by just calling the method `parseHedgeEquation(in3, in4)` again.

After specifying the rigidity function and parsing the equation system, the main algorithm `AntiUnify` is invoked using this data (line 8). There is one additional argument, which specifies the debug level. For production use we want to silently compute all the generalizations and process them by a callback function, which is defined in the lines 9 to 11. For debugging, one must also specify a print stream at line 11 instead of `null`. The callback function is invoked for each generalization and it provides two arguments for the implementation. The first one is of type `AntiUnifySystem` and contains all the data which has been collected during the run: The substitution `getSigma`, the store `getStore` and some additional information. The second argument is the generalization variable. The computed generalization is the value which is associated with this variable in the substitution. Line 10 prints this generalization.

During the anti-unification process, fresh variables are introduced. They are named by a sequence number which is put between a prefix and a suffix. The counter for generating the number sequence is static and can be reset by calling the function `Node Factory.resetCounter`. The prefix and the suffix for fresh term variables and also for fresh hedge variables can be specified by the user. Therefore the class `Node Factory` offers four static variables, named `PREFIX_FreshTermVar`, `SUFFIX_FreshTermVar`, `PREFIX_FreshHedgeVar` and `SUFFIX_FreshHedgeVar`.

4   Unranked Second-Order Anti-unification

The language used in section 3 does not permit higher-order variables. This imposes a natural restriction on solutions: The computed lggs do not reflect similarities between input hedges, which are located under distinct heads or at different depths. For instance, $f(a, b)$ and $g(h(a, b))$ are generalized by a single variable, although both terms contain a and b and a more natural generalization could be, e.g., $\overset{\circ}{X}(a, b)$, where $\overset{\circ}{X}$ is a higher-order variable. In applications, it is often desirable to detect these similarities. Therefore, in [5], an anti-unification algorithm has been developed where second-order power is gained by using context variables to generalize vertical differences at the input hedges. Hedge variables are used to generalize horizontal differences.

Definitions.   Given pairwise disjoint countable sets of unranked function symbols $\mathcal{F}$ (typically $a, b, c, f, g, \dots$), hedge variables $\mathcal{V}_H$ (typically $X, Y, \dots$), unranked context variables $\mathcal{V}_C$ (typically $\overset{\circ}{X}, \overset{\circ}{Y}, \dots$), and a special symbol $\circ$ (the hole), *terms* t, *hedges* $\tilde{s}$, and *contexts* $\tilde{c}$ are defined by the following grammar:

$$t ::= X \mid f(\tilde{s}) \mid \overset{\circ}{X}(\tilde{s}) \qquad \tilde{s} ::= t_1, \dots, t_n \qquad \tilde{c} ::= \tilde{s}_1, \circ, \tilde{s}_2 \mid \tilde{s}_1, f(\tilde{c}), \tilde{s}_2 \mid \tilde{s}_1, \overset{\circ}{X}(\tilde{c}), \tilde{s}_2$$

where $X \in \mathcal{V}_H$, $f \in \mathcal{F}$, $\overset{\circ}{X} \in \mathcal{V}_C$, and $n \geqslant 0$.

A context $\tilde{c}$ can apply to a hedge $\tilde{s}$, denoted by $\tilde{c}[\tilde{s}]$, obtaining a hedge by replacing the hole in $\tilde{c}$ with $\tilde{s}$. For example, $(\overset{\circ}{X}(X), f(f(\circ), b))[a, \overset{\circ}{X}(a)] = (\overset{\circ}{X}(X), f(f(a, \overset{\circ}{X}(a)), b))$. Application of a context to a context is defined similarly.

A substitution is a mapping from hedge variables to hedges and from context variables to contexts. When substituting a context variable $\overset{\circ}{X}$ by a context, the context will be applied to the argument hedge of $\overset{\circ}{X}$. The definition of positions and all the relations defined on positions, as well as the definition of an alignment are taken from section 3.

We only give an informal definition of *admissible alignments*. A necessary and sufficient condition for alignments to be admissible, as well as the exact definitions can be found in [5]. An alignment $\mathfrak{a}$ of two hedges $\tilde{s}$ and $\tilde{q}$ is called *admissible* iff there exists a generalization $\tilde{g}$ of $\tilde{s}$ and $\tilde{q}$ which contains all the corresponding symbols from $\mathfrak{a}$.

We call such a $\tilde{g}$ a *supporting generalization* of $\tilde{s}$ and $\tilde{q}$ with respect to $\mathfrak{a}$.

Least general supporting generalizations might not be unique. For instance, for (a, b, a) and (b, c) with the admissible alignment $b\langle 2, 1 \rangle$, we have two supporting least general generalizations (X, b, X, Y) and (X, b, Y, X). Therefore, we are interested in a special class of supporting generalizations, which we call $\mathcal{R}_C$-generalizations.

Given two variable-disjoint hedges $\tilde{s}, \tilde{q}$ and their admissible alignment $\mathfrak{a}$, a hedge $\tilde{g}$ is called an $\mathcal{R}_C$-*generalization* of $\tilde{s}$ and $\tilde{q}$ with respect to $\mathfrak{a}$, if $\tilde{g}$ is a supporting generalization of $\tilde{s}$ and $\tilde{q}$ with respect to $\mathfrak{a}$ such that the following conditions are fulfilled:

1. There exist substitutions σ, ϑ with $\tilde{g}\sigma = \tilde{s}$ and $\tilde{g}\vartheta = \tilde{q}$ such that all the contexts in σ and ϑ are singleton contexts.
2. No context variable in $\tilde{g}$ applies to the empty hedge.
3. $\tilde{g}$ doesn't contain horizontal consecutive hedge variables.
4. $\tilde{g}$ doesn't contain vertical chains of variables.
5. $\tilde{g}$ doesn't contain context variables with a hedge variable as the first or the last argument (i.e., no subterms of the form $\overset{\circ}{X}(X, \dots)$ and $\overset{\circ}{X}(\dots, X)$).

The implemented anti-unification algorithm has $O(n^2)$ time complexity and $O(n)$ space complexity, where n is the size of the input. It solves the following problem:

Given: Two variable-disjoint hedges $\tilde{s}$ and $\tilde{q}$ and their admissible alignment $\mathfrak{a}$.

Find: A least general $\mathcal{R}_C$-generalization of $\tilde{s}$ and $\tilde{q}$ with respect to $\mathfrak{a}$.

For instance, $\mathring{X}(a, b)$ is an $\mathcal{R}_C$-generalization of $f(g(a, b, c))$ and (a, b) with respect to $\mathfrak{a}\langle 1 \cdot 1 \cdot 1, 1 \rangle b\langle 1 \cdot 1 \cdot 2, 2 \rangle$, while $\mathring{X}(a, b, X)$ and $\mathring{X}(\mathring{Y}(a, b))$ are not.

Web page. The implementation of the algorithm is available from
`http://www.risc.jku.at/projects/stout/software/urauc.php`.

Web interface explanation. The input form of the web page of unranked second-order anti-unification consists of five rows, where the first, the fourth and the last row are equal to those of the unranked first-order anti-unification web interface.

Anti-unification problem: (Use the semicolon to separate the equations of the system. Hedge equations are allowed.)	`f(c), f(f(g(a, a)), a, a) =^= c, f(g(b, b, b), b, b, b)`
Alignment computation:	Input an alignment by hand ⌄ `f<2.1, 2> g<2.1.1, 2.1>`
Justify computed generalization:	☑ By obtaining substitutions from the store...
Iterate all possibilities:	☑ Compute generalizations for all admissible alignments...
Output format:	Simple ⌄
Submit	

In the second row, the alignment computation can be chosen. The only two possibilities are longest admissible alignments and the input of an alignment by hand. If the user selects the computation of longest admissible alignments, then the program automatically generates the set of all admissible alignments with maximum length, and the corresponding supporting generalizations are computed. Otherwise, the user has to specify an alignment in the input box next to the drop-down menu.

In the third row one can specify, whether or not to justify the computed $\mathcal{R}_C$-generalization. For justification of a generalization $\tilde{g}$, the recorded differences of the input hedges $\tilde{s}, \tilde{q}$ are used to obtain two substitutions σ, ϑ. Then the program tests whether $\tilde{g}\sigma = \tilde{s}$ and $\tilde{g}\vartheta = \tilde{q}$ holds. The justification fails if this is not the case.

How to use. The usage of this algorithm is very similar to the one we explained in section 3. Instead of a rigidity function there is an alignment computation function. The library offers two such functions: The first one, called `AlignFncLAA`, computes longest admissible alignments. The other one is `AlignFncInput` and can be used to specify a certain admissible alignment. The admissibility test for this alignment has to be done in advance. Therefore the `Alignment`-class offers a method `isAdmissible` which returns `true` iff an alignment is admissible. Alignment computation functions have the common base class `AlignFnc`. This base class can be used to implement other alignment computation functions.

5 Higher-Order Pattern Anti-unification

The higher-order anti-unification algorithm described in [6] works on simply typed λ-terms: It takes as input two such terms of the same type, in η-long β-normal form, and returns their least general pattern generalization. Patterns here mean higher-order patterns à la Miller [19]. (Note that it is not required the input to be patterns.) Such a generalization always exists, is unique modulo α-equivalence and variable renaming, and can be computed in cubic time within linear space with respect to the size of the input, see [6].

Definitions. Simple types are constructed from *basic types* δ with the help of the type constructor $\rightarrow$ by the grammar $\tau := \delta \mid \tau \rightarrow \tau$. *Variables* and *constants* have an assigned type. Then λ-*terms* t are built using the grammar:

$$t ::= x \mid c \mid \lambda x.t \mid (t_1 \, t_2) \quad \text{where } x \text{ is a typed variable and } c \text{ is a typed constant.}$$

Terms like $(\ldots (h \, t_1) \ldots t_m)$, where h is a constant or a variable, are written as $h(t_1, \ldots, t_m)$, and terms of the form $\lambda x_1. \cdots . \lambda x_n.t$ as $\lambda x_1, \ldots, x_n.t$. Substitutions map variables to terms of the same type, and can be extended to arbitrary terms as usual. A *higher-order pattern (HOP)* is a λ-term, in which, when written in η-long β-normal form, all free variables apply to pairwise distinct bound variables. For instance, if we use capital letters for free variables, $\lambda x.f(X(x), Y)$, $f(c, \lambda x.x)$ and $\lambda x, y.X(\lambda z.x(z), y)$ are patterns, while $\lambda x.f(X(X(x)), Y)$, $f(X(c), c)$ and $\lambda x, y.X(x, x)$ are not.

Given two variable-disjoint λ-terms t_1 and t_2, we say that a λ-term t that generalizes both t_1 and t_2 is their *higher-order pattern generalization*, if t is an HOP. The HOP anti-unification (HOPAU) algorithm solves the following problem:

Given: Higher-order terms t_1 and t_2 of the same type in η-long β-normal form.
Find: A least general higher-order pattern generalization of t_1 and t_2.

For instance, if $t_1 = \lambda x, y.f(h(x, x, y), h(x, y, y))$ and $t_2 = \lambda x, y.f(g(x, x, y), g(x, y, y))$, then $t = \lambda x, y.f(X(x, y), Y(x, y))$ is a higher-order pattern lgg of t_1 and t_2.

Web page. The implementation of the HOPAU algorithm is available from
`http://www.risc.jku.at/projects/stout/software/hoau.php`.

Web interface explanation. The implementation slightly differs from the theoretical algorithm: In addition to simply-typed terms, it can also take untyped input. It has an advantage that the user does not necessarily have to supply types, but has a disadvantage that the terms may not be typeable or normalizable. The input form of the Web interface to HOPAU algorithm consists of four rows shown below:

Anti-unification problem: (Use the semicolon to separate the equations of the system.)	`\x,y.f(x,y) =^= \x,y.f(y,x)`
Maximum reduction recursion:	`100`
Justify computed generalization:	☑ (An error will occure if the justification fails.)
Output format:	Simple ☑ User friendly: ☑
Submit	

In the first row, the anti-unification problem should be given. The problems consist of one or more anti-unification equations, separated by semicolon. Each such equation consists of two λ-terms, with $=\hat{}\,=$ in between. The backslash \ is used instead of λ.

In the second row, the maximum recursion depth of the β-reduction can be specified. This is to avoid infinite chain of reductions for terms like $(\lambda x.(x\ x))(\lambda x.(x\ x))$.

As in Sect. 4, one can choose to justify the computed lgg in the third row.

In the last row, the output format can be specified. One can choose form a drop-down box between simple, verbose, progress, and progress-origin. The first three of them are like those described in Sect. 3. By choosing the output format progress-origin, all the debug information will be shown to the user, but the original names of bound variables are used. This is useful for debugging, as all the bound variables are renamed by the parser, giving them unique names.

5.1   Deciding α-equivalence

The HOPAU algorithm performs a constructive α-equivalence test to see whether different terms can be abstracted by the same variable. It is needed to ensure that the computed generalization is least general. Such a problem arises, e.g., in the course of generalization of the terms $t_1 = \lambda x, y, z.f(x(y, z), x(z, y))$ and $t_2 = \lambda x, y, z.f(X(y, \lambda u.u), X(z, \lambda v.v))$. To see if the same variable can be used in the generalization of the arguments of t_1 and t_2, we have to check whether there exists a bound variable renaming ρ such that $x(y, z)\rho = x(z, y)$ and $X(y, \lambda u.u)\rho \overset{\triangle}{=} X(z, \lambda v.v)$.

The algorithm that performs such a test is integrated in the HOPAU implementation, but we provide access to it separately as well, due to the fact that the problem is interesting, may appear in various contexts, and having a tool to solve it is useful. The algorithm solves the following problem (in linear time and space):

> *Given:* A set of equations of the form $t \Rightarrow s$ where t and s are λ-terms, and two sets of variables, the domain D and the range R.
>
> *Find:* A variable renaming substitution $\rho : D \rightarrow R$, such that $t\rho$ is α-equivalent to s for all equations $t \Rightarrow s$, if it exists. Otherwise report failure.

The generalization problem for t_1 and t_2 above creates the set of equations $\{x(y, z) \Rightarrow x(z, y), X(y, \lambda u.u) \Rightarrow X(z, \lambda v.v)\}$, the domain $D = \{x, y, z\}$ and the range $R = \{x, y, z\}$. Then the α-equivalence decision algorithm returns the renaming $\rho = \{x \mapsto x, y \mapsto z, z \mapsto y\}$. Afterwards, this renaming can be used to answer the original question of generalization of t_1 and t_2, obtaining the lgg $\lambda x, y, z.f(Y(x, y, z), Y(x, z, y))$ where, indeed, the variable Y appears twice.

Web page. The α-equivalence decision algorithm is available from
http://www.risc.jku.at/projects/stout/software/hoequiv.php.

Web interface explanation. The input form of the Web interface to the α-equivalence algorithm consists of four rows shown below:

Equivariance problem set: (Use the semicolon to separate the equations of the system.)	`f(x,y) = f(y,x)`		
Domain:	u, v, w, x, y, z	Range:	u, v, w, x, y, z
Maximum reduction recursion:	100		
Output format:	Simple ∨	User friendly: ☑	
Submit			

The first, the third and the fourth row are equivalent, respectively, to the first, the second and the fourth ones in the HOPAU interface, described above. (The terms of an equivariance equation are separated by = instead of =^=.) In the second row, the two sets of variables which specify the domain and the range should be given.

How to use. We explain the usage on a code fragment and assume that there are two data sources `in1` and `in2` available in form of `Reader` instances, each of them contains one of the λ-terms. There is also an integer variable `maxReduce` which specifies the maximum recursion depth of β-reduction.

```
1  Set<Variable> ran = DataStructureFactory.$.newSet();
2  ran.add(new Variable("x", null));
3  ran.add(new Variable("y", null));
4  Map<Variable,Variable> permutation = new PermEquiv(eqSys,
         dom, ran).compute(DebugLevel.SILENT, null);
5  System.out.println(permutation);
```

The lines 1–3 show how range variables used in the mapping are specified. The second parameter of the `Variable`-constructor specifies the type of the variable. (`null` is used for untyped variables.) To obtain a new set, `DataStructureFactory.$` is used, which is a singleton instance of type `DataStructureFactory`. The user can change the behavior by simply assigning another implementation of this type to `$`. We assume that a set `dom` of domain variables is available and the set of equations `eqSys` exists (e.g., it can be created in a similar way as in unranked anti-unification above). In line 4, after specifying the domain and the range and parsing the equation system, the main algorithm `PermEquiv` is invoked using this data. It silently computes the renaming permutation, which is represented as a mapping from variables to variables.

6   Nominal Anti-unification

Nominal techniques have been introduced in [12, 13] to formally represent and study systems with binding. The nominal anti-unification (NAU) algorithm developed in [7] takes as input two terms-in-contexts (pairs of a freshness constraint and a nominal term) and tries to compute a generalization term-in-context. Under the assumption that the set of atoms permitted in generalizations is finite, there is a unique lgg modulo variable renaming and α-equivalence. The algorithm has $O(n^4)$ time complexity and $O(n^2)$ space complexity, where n is the size of the input.

Definitions. Nominal terms contain *variables* and *atoms*. Variables can be instantiated and atoms can be bound. We have *sorts of atoms* ν and *sorts of data* δ as disjoint sets. *Atoms* $(a, b, \ldots)$ have one of the sorts of atoms. *Variables* $(X, Y, \ldots)$ have a sort of atom or data. Nominal function symbols $(f, g, \ldots)$ have an arity of the form $\tau_1 \times \cdots \times \tau_n \to \delta$, where δ is a sort of data and τ_i are sorts given by the grammar $\tau ::= \nu \mid \delta \mid \langle \nu \rangle \tau$. Abstractions have sorts of the form $\langle \nu \rangle \tau$. A *swapping* $(a\,b)$ is a pair of atoms of the same sort. A *permutation* π is a sequence of swappings. It can apply to terms and cause swapping the names of atoms. *Nominal terms* t are given by the grammar below, where $a.t$ is abstraction (it binds a) and $\pi \cdot X$ is called suspension:

$$t ::= f(t_1, \ldots, t_n) \mid a \mid a.t \mid \pi \cdot X$$

Suspensions suspend application of the permutation π to X until X is instantiated. Substitutions are defined in the standard way, and their application allows atom capture, for instance, $a.X\{X \mapsto a\} = a.a$.

A *freshness context* ∇ is a finite set of pairs of the form $a \# X$ stating that the instantiation of X cannot contain free occurrences of a. A *term-in-context* is a pair $\langle \nabla, t \rangle$ of a freshness context ∇ and a term t. A term-in-context $\langle \nabla, t \rangle$ is *based* on a set of atoms A, if all the atoms which occur in t and ∇ are elements of A. The NAU algorithm solves the following problem:

Given: Two nominal terms t_1 and t_2 of the same sort, a freshness context ∇, and a *finite* set of atoms A such that $\langle \nabla, t_1 \rangle$ and $\langle \nabla, t_2 \rangle$ are based on A.
Find: A term-in-context $\langle \Gamma, t \rangle$ which is also based on A, such that $\langle \Gamma, t \rangle$ is a least general generalization of $\langle \nabla, t_1 \rangle$ and $\langle \nabla, t_2 \rangle$.

For instance, for $t_1 = f(b, a)$, $t_2 = f(X, (a\,b) \cdot X)$, $\nabla = \{b \# X\}$, and $A = \{a, b\}$, the NAU algorithm computes the lgg of $\langle \nabla, t_1 \rangle$ and $\langle \nabla, t_2 \rangle$, which is $\langle \varnothing, f(Y, (a\,b) \cdot Y) \rangle$.

Web page. The nominal anti-unification algorithm is available from
http://www.risc.jku.at/projects/stout/software/nau.php.

Web interface explanation. The input form of the Web interface to the NAU algorithm consists of five rows shown below, where the first, the fourth and the fifth row are similar to the first, third and fifth explained in section 4.

Anti-unification problem: (Use the semicolon to separate the equations of the system.)	f(a,b) =^= f(b,c)
Freshness context:	e.g. a#X, b#Y
Extra atoms:	(Atoms from the problem…
Justify computed generalization:	☑ (An error will occure if the justification fails.)
Output format:	Simple ∨
Submit	

All the anti-unification equations share the same freshness context ∇, which can be specified in the second row. The computed term-in-context is a generalization of $\langle \nabla, t \rangle$ and $\langle \nabla, s \rangle$ for every anti-unification equation t =^= s.

As all the terms-in-context $\langle \nabla, t \rangle$ and $\langle \nabla, s \rangle$ obtained by anti-unification equations t =ˆ= s have to be based on the same set of atoms A, all the atoms which appear in the anti-unification problem as well as those from ∇ are assumed to be elements of A. In the third row, the user may specify some additional atoms which are in A.

How to use. To explain the library usage on a code example, we again assume the existence of two Reader instances in1 and in2 which contain the nominal terms to be generalized. Furthermore, we assume that there is a Reader instance inA for reading atoms and inN for the freshness context. Both of them are assumed to be comma separated sets, e.g., inN = {a#X,b#Y,...} and inA = {c,d,...}, where the braces are optional. The data source inA only specifies extra atoms, which do nor appear in in1, in2 and inN.

```
1  final NodeFactory factory = new NodeFactory();
2  eqSys = new EquationSystem<AntiUnifyProblem>() {
3      public AntiUnifyProblem newEquation(NominalTerm t,
            NominalTerm s) {
4          return new AntiUnifyProblem(t, s, factory);
5      } };
6  FreshnessCtx nablaIn = new InputParser(factory)
7          .parseEquationAndCtx(in1, in2, inA, inN, eqSys);
8  new AntiUnify(eqSys, nablaIn, DebugLevel.SILENT, factory) {
9      public void callback(AntiUnifySystem res, Variable var)
            {
10              System.out.println(res.getNablaGen());
11              System.out.println(res.getSigma().get(var));
12      }; }.antiUnify(false, null);
```

In contrast to the other libraries, an instance of NodeFactory is needed, which we create in line 1. The lines 2 to 5 demonstrate the creation of an equation system.

All the input sources are parsed in line 7. The new equation is added to eqSys and the parsed freshness context is returned. Moreover, the factory instance remembers all the parsed atoms regardless of the input source they come from. More equations may be added eqSys by calling the method parseEquation(in1, in2, eqSys) from InputParser. Atoms and freshness contexts can also be parsed separately.

Line 10 shows that, additionally to the substitution and store, the generated freshness context is provided by the instance res of the class AntiUnifySystem.

Again, one can specify how fresh variables and fresh atoms are named. In contrast to the other three libraries, this functionality is implemented by private instance variables of NodeFactory and appropriate getter and setter methods.

6.1 Deciding Equivariance

The nominal equivariance algorithm checks whether two terms differ from each other only by a permutation and bound atom renaming, i.e., if they are equivariant. Equivariance problem arises, for instance, in the course of generalization of the terms-in-contexts $p_1 = \langle \varnothing, f(a, b) \rangle$ and $p_2 = \langle \varnothing, f(b, c) \rangle$, where the atoms permitted in the generalization are a, b, and c, then the term-in-context $\langle \{c\#X, a\#Y\}, f(X, Y)\rangle$ generalizes p_1 and p_2, but it is not least general. To compute the latter, we need to reflect the fact that generalizations of the atoms are related to each other: One can be obtained from the other by the permutation $(b\,c)(c\,a)$. This leads to a least general generalization $\langle \{c\#X\}, f(X, (b\,c)(c\,a)\cdot X)\rangle$.

The equivariance decision algorithm solves the following problem (in quadratic time and space):

> *Given:* A set of equations of the form $t \Rightarrow s$, a freshness context ∇, and a finite set of atoms A such that all $\langle \nabla, t\rangle$ and $\langle \nabla, s\rangle$ are based on A.
>
> *Find:* A permutation π of variables from A such that for all equations $t \Rightarrow s$, $\pi \cdot t$ is α-equivalent to s with respect to ∇, if such a π exists. Otherwise report failure.

For instance, in the example above, the permutation $(b\,c)(c\,a)$ was computed by the equivariance algorithm for $\{a \Rightarrow b, b \Rightarrow c\}$, $A = \{a, b, c\}$, and $\nabla = \varnothing$.

Web page. The equivariance decision algorithm is available from
`http://www.risc.jku.at/projects/stout/software/nequiv.php`.

Web interface explanation. The input form is nearly the same as the one for NAU:

Equivariance problem set: (Use the semicolon to separate the equations of the system.)	f(a,b) = f(b,c)
Freshness context:	e.g. a#X, b#Y
Justify computed permutation:	☑ (An error will occure if the justification fails.)
Output format:	Simple ⌄
Submit	

There are two differences: The row to specify extra atoms is missing, because the computed permutation must only permute atoms which appear in the problem set and further on, terms of an equivariance equation are separated by = instead of =^=.

How to use. We assume to have data sources for two nominal terms `in1` and `in2`, and another one for a freshness context, called `inN`, similarly to the NAU algorithm. Moreover, we assume that an equation system `eqSys` has already been instantiated and that a `NodeFactory` instance, called `factory`, exists. We explain the usage of the library on the following code fragment:

```
1  InputParser parser = new InputParser(factory);
2  parser.parseEquation(in1, in2, eqSys);
3  FreshnessCtx nablaIn = parser.parseNabla(inN);
4  Collection<? extends Atom> atomSet = factory
5          .getAllByType(factory.classAtom);
6  Permutation pi = new Equivariance(eqSys, atomSet, nablaIn)
7          .compute(factory, false, DebugLevel.SILENT, null);
8  System.out.println(pi);
```

In line 1 the parser instance is created, which afterwards is used to parse the equation and the freshness context from the input sources. The lines 4 and 5 demonstrate how one can obtain the collected set of atoms from the `NodeFactory` instance.

Later in line 6 this set is needed to instantiate a class named `Equivariance`, which encapsulates the computation of a permutation `pi`. The computation returns `null`, if no permutation exists for the input. The class `Permutation` contains two mappings from atoms to atoms (`Map<Atom, Atom>`): The permutation itself can be obtained by calling `getPerm` and the inverse permutation, which can be obtained by `getInverse`. Furthermore the class `Permutation` provides some methods to work with permutations and swappings.

Acknowledgments. This research has been supported by the Austrian Science Fund (FWF) under the project SToUT (P 24087-N18).

References

[1] Alpuente, M., Escobar, S., Espert, J., Meseguer, J.: ACUOS: Order-sorted modular ACU generalization (2013), http://safe-tools.dsic.upv.es/acuos/

[2] Alpuente, M., Escobar, S., Meseguer, J., Espert, J.: A modular order-sorted equational generalization algorithm. Information and Computation 235, 98–136 (2014)

[3] Armengol, E., Plaza, E.: Bottom-up induction of feature terms. Machine Learning 41(3), 259–294 (2000)

[4] Baader, F.: Unification, weak unification, upper bound, lower bound, and generalization problems. In: Book, R.V. (ed.) RTA 1991. LNCS, vol. 488, pp. 86–97. Springer, Heidelberg (1991)

[5] Baumgartner, A., Kutsia, T.: Unranked second-order anti-unification. In: Kohlenbach, U. (ed.) WoLLIC 2014. LNCS, vol. 8652, pp. 66–80. Springer, Heidelberg (2014)

[6] Baumgartner, A., Kutsia, T., Levy, J., Villaret, M.: A variant of higher-order anti-unification. In: Van Raamsdonk, F. (ed.) RTA. LIPIcs, vol. 21, pp. 113–127. Schloss Dagstuhl - Leibniz-Zentrum fuer Informatik (2013)

[7] Baumgartner, A., Kutsia, T., Levy, J., Villaret, M.: Nominal anti-unification. In: Kutsia, T., Ringeissen, C. (eds.) Proc. 28th International Workshop on Unification, UNIF 2014. RISC Technical Report Series, vol. (14-06) (2014)

[8] Bulychev, P.E., Kostylev, E.V., Zakharov, V.A.: Anti-unification algorithms and their applications in program analysis. In: Pnueli, A., Virbitskaite, I., Voronkov, A. (eds.) PSI 2009. LNCS, vol. 5947, pp. 413–423. Springer, Heidelberg (2010)

[9] Burghardt, J.: E-generalization using grammars. Artif. Intell. 165(1), 1–35 (2005)

[10] De Souza Alcantara, T., Ferreira, J., Maurer, F.: Interactive prototyping of tabletop and surface applications. In: Forbrig, P., Dewan, P., Harrison, M., Luyten, K. (eds.) EICS, pp. 229–238. ACM (2013)

[11] Delcher, A.L., Kasif, S.: Efficient parallel term matching and anti-unification. J. Autom. Reasoning 9(3), 391–406 (1992)

[12] Gabbay, M., Pitts, A.M.: A new approach to abstract syntax with variable binding. Formal Asp. Comput. 13(3-5), 341–363 (2002)

[13] Gabbay, M.J.: A Theory of Inductive Definitions with alpha-Equivalence. PhD thesis, University of Cambridge, UK (2000)

[14] Huet, G.: Résolution d'équations dans des langages d'ordre 1,2,...,ω. PhD thesis, Université Paris VII (September 1976)

[15] Krumnack, U., Schwering, A., Gust, H., Kühnberger, K.-U.: Restricted higher-order anti-unification for analogy making. In: Orgun, M.A., Thornton, J. (eds.) AI 2007. LNCS (LNAI), vol. 4830, pp. 273–282. Springer, Heidelberg (2007)

[16] Kutsia, T., Levy, J., Villaret, M.: Anti-unification for unranked terms and hedges. J. Autom. Reasoning 52(2), 155–190 (2014)

[17] Li, H., Thompson, S.: Similar code detection and elimination for Erlang programs. In: Carro, M., Peña, R. (eds.) PADL 2010. LNCS, vol. 5937, pp. 104–118. Springer, Heidelberg (2010)

[18] Lu, J., Mylopoulos, J., Harao, M., Hagiya, M.: Higher order generalization and its application in program verification. Ann. Math. Artif. Intell. 28(1-4), 107–126 (2000)

[19] Miller, D.: A logic programming language with lambda-abstraction, function variables, and simple unification. J. Log. Comput. 1(4), 497–536 (1991)

[20] Pfenning, F.: Unification and anti-unification in the calculus of constructions. In: LICS, pp. 74–85. IEEE Computer Society (1991)

[21] Plotkin, G.D.: A note on inductive generalization. Machine Intel. 5(1), 153–163 (1970)

[22] Reynolds, J.C.: Transformational systems and the algebraic structure of atomic formulas. Machine Intel. 5(1), 135–151 (1970)

[23] Schmid, U.: Inductive Synthesis of Functional Programs. LNCS (LNAI), vol. 2654. Springer, Heidelberg (2003)

The D-FLAT System for Dynamic Programming on Tree Decompositions

Michael Abseher, Bernhard Bliem, Günther Charwat,
Frederico Dusberger, Markus Hecher, and Stefan Woltran

Institute of Information Systems 184/2
Vienna University of Technology
Favoritenstrasse 9–11, 1040 Vienna, Austria
{abseher,bliem,gcharwat,dusberg,hecher,woltran}@dbai.tuwien.ac.at

Abstract. Complex reasoning problems over large amounts of data pose
a great challenge for computer science. To overcome the obstacle of high
computational complexity, exploiting structure by means of tree decompositions has proved to be effective in many cases. However, the implementation of suitable efficient algorithms is often tedious. D-FLAT is a
software system that combines the logic programming language Answer
Set Programming with problem solving on tree decompositions and can
serve as a rapid prototyping tool for such algorithms. Since we initially
proposed D-FLAT, we have made major changes to the system, improving its range of applicability and its usability. In this paper, we present
the system resulting from these efforts.

Keywords: Answer Set Programming, tree decompositions, treewidth.

1 Introduction

Complex reasoning problems over large amounts of data arise in many application domains for computer science and pose a great challenge to push methods
from Artificial Intelligence toward practical use. For formalizing complex problems, *declarative approaches* often lead to readable and maintainable code. A
more and more popular candidate for such an approach is Answer Set Programming (ASP) [11,17], for which highly efficient solvers are available that offer rich
languages for modeling the problems at hand.

In order to overcome performance problems on large problem instances, structural features need to be exploited. A prominent means for this endeavor is the
concept of tree decompositions (see, e.g., [9]). Many problems can be efficiently
solved with dynamic programming (DP) algorithms on tree decompositions if
the structural parameter "treewidth" is bounded, which means, roughly, that
the graph resembles a tree to a certain extent. With such an approach, the
runtime explosion can be confined to only this parameter instead of input size.
Consequently, if the treewidth is bounded, even huge instances of many complex
problems can efficiently be solved.

E. Fermé and J. Leite (Eds.): JELIA 2014, LNAI 8761, pp. 558–572, 2014.
© Springer International Publishing Switzerland 2014

We focus here on *a combination of ASP and problem solving via DP on tree decompositions*. For this, we have implemented a free software system called D-FLAT[1] [4], for rapid prototyping of DP algorithms in ASP. Since ASP is well suited for a lot of problems, it is often also well suited for parts of such problems, making it an appealing candidate to work on decomposed problem instances. The key feature of D-FLAT is that the user is only required to write an encoding of the DP algorithm on a tree decomposition in the ASP language, and the system takes care of tedious tasks that are not related to the problem.

The initial prototype of D-FLAT [4] stored partial solutions in tables. It became clear, however, that for problems higher in the polynomial hierarchy than NP a more general data structure is required. We have shown in [5] that using a tree-shaped data structure instead greatly increases applicability.

In this paper we present the D-FLAT system resulting from the major changes since its initial presentation in [4]. Our main contributions are:

1. We introduce *item trees* as the central data structure in D-FLAT algorithms.
2. We show how item trees allow problems to be solved in the style of Alternating Turing Machines while also taking decomposition into account.
3. We present the special predicates used for communication between the system and the user's encoding.
4. Finally, we show how the system interprets the answer sets of the user's program for constructing item trees and eventually solving the problem.

This work is structured as follows. In Section 2, we provide background on Answer Set Programming, tree decompositions and the original prototype of D-FLAT. In Section 3, we present the current version of D-FLAT and describe its components in detail. Finally, we give a conclusion and an outlook in Section 4.

An extended version of this paper can be found in the technical report [1].

2   Background

Answer Set Programming Answer Set Programming (ASP) is a declarative language where a *program* Π is a set of *rules*

$$a_1 \vee \cdots \vee a_k \leftarrow b_1, \ldots, b_m, \text{not } b_{m+1}, \ldots, \text{not } b_n.$$

The constituents of a rule $r \in \Pi$ are $h(r) = \{a_1, \ldots, a_k\}$, $b^+(r) = \{b_1, \ldots, b_m\}$ and $b^-(r) = \{b_{m+1}, \ldots, b_n\}$. We call r a *fact* if $b^+(r) = b^-(r) = \emptyset$, and we omit the $\leftarrow$ symbol in this case. Intuitively, a rule r states that if an answer set contains all of $b^+(r)$ and none of $b^-(r)$, then it contains some element of $h(r)$. A set of atoms I satisfies a rule r if $I \cap h(r) \neq \emptyset$ or $b^-(r) \cap I \neq \emptyset$ or $b^+(r) \setminus I \neq \emptyset$. I is a *model* of a set of rules if it satisfies each rule. I is an *answer set* of a program Π if it is a subset-minimal model of the program $\Pi^I = \{h(r) \leftarrow b^+(r) \mid r \in \Pi, b^-(r) \cap I = \emptyset\}$ [18].

[1] http://dbai.tuwien.ac.at/research/project/dflat/ (including download link)

ASP programs can be viewed as succinctly representing problem solving spec-ifications following the *Guess & Check* principle. A "guess" can, for example, be performed using disjunctive rules which non-deterministically open up the search space. Constraints (i.e., rules r with $h(r) = \emptyset$), on the other hand, amount to a "check" by imposing restrictions that solutions must obey.

In this paper, we use the language of the grounder *Gringo* [15,16] (version 4) where programs may contain variables that are instantiated by ground terms (elements of the Herbrand universe, i.e., constants and compound terms con-taining function symbols) before a solver computes answer sets according to the propositional semantics stated above.

Example 1. The following program solves the 3-COLORABILITY problem for graphs that are given as facts using the predicates `vertex` and `edge`.

```
color(red;grn;blu).
1 { map(X,C) : color(C) } 1 ← vertex(X).
← edge(X,Y), map(X,C;Y,C).
```

Informally, the first rule is shorthand for the three facts `color(red)`, `color(grn)` and `color(blu)`. The second rule states that any vertex from the input graph shall be mapped to one color. The colon controls the instantiation of the variable C such that it is only instantiated with arguments of the predicate `color`. The third rule checks that adjacent vertices never receive the same color. In this rule, `map(X,C;Y,C)` stands for `map(X,C)`, `map(Y,C)`.

Tree Decompositions Tree decompositions and treewidth, originally defined in [21], are well-known tools for tackling computationally hard problems. Infor-mally, treewidth is a measure of the cyclicity of a graph, and many NP-hard prob-lems become tractable if the treewidth is bounded. There are several overviews of this topic, such as [8,6,3,20]. The intuition behind tree decompositions is ob-taining a tree from a (potentially cyclic) graph by subsuming multiple vertices under one node and thereby isolating the parts responsible for the cyclicity. The definition of tree decompositions can also be extended to hypergraphs, but in this paper we will only consider graphs for the sake of presentation.

Definition 1. *A* tree decomposition *of a graph* $G = (V, E)$ *is a pair* (T, χ) *where* $T = (N, F)$ *is a (rooted) tree and* $\chi : N \to 2^V$ *assigns to each node a set of vertices (called the node's bag), such that the following conditions are met:*

1. *For every vertex* $v \in V$, *there exists a node* $n \in N$ *such that* $v \in \chi(n)$.
2. *For every edge* $e \in E$, *there exists a node* $n \in N$ *such that* $e \subseteq \chi(n)$.
3. *For every* $v \in V$, *the subtree of* T *induced by* $\{n \in N \mid v \in \chi(n)\}$ *is connected.*

We call $\max_{n \in N} |\chi(n)| - 1$ *the* width *of the decomposition. The* treewidth *of a graph is the minimum width over all its tree decompositions.*

Figure 1 shows a graph together with a tree decomposition of it that has width 2. This decomposition is optimal because the graph contains a cycle and thus its treewidth is at least 2. (A graph is a tree iff it has treewidth 1.)

Constructing an optimal tree decomposition is intractable [2]. However, when considering treewidth as a parameter, the problem is fixed-parameter tractable (FPT) [14], i.e., solvable in time $\mathcal{O}(f(w) \cdot n^c)$, where c is a constant, n is the size of the input, w is its treewidth and $f(w)$ depends only on w [7]. Moreover, there are efficient heuristics that produce good tree decompositions [10,13,19].

Tree decompositions are prominently used for solving problems with dynamic programming algorithms. These algorithms generally start at the leaf nodes and traverse the tree decomposition to the root. At each node, partial solutions for the subgraph induced by the vertices encountered so far are computed and stored in a data structure corresponding to that tree decomposition node. Typically, the size of each such data structure only depends on the width of the tree decomposition, and the number of tree decomposition nodes is linear in the size of the input graph. Thus, when the width is bounded by a constant, the search space for each subproblem remains constant as well, and the number of subproblems only grows by a linear factor for larger instances.

Example 2. To solve the 3-COLORABILITY problem with a bottom-up traversal of the tree decomposition in Figure 1, we can first compute all proper 3-colorings of the subgraphs induced by $\{a, b, c\}$ and $\{c, e\}$, respectively. In the node with bag $\{b, c, d\}$ we proceed similarly but now only look for colorings (i) which are consistent combinations of some coloring from each child node, and (ii) where the "new" vertex d is colored consistently with respect to its neighbors (b and c). Here we can disregard the colors of a and e because condition 3 from Definition 1 guarantees that these vertices will never appear again in the bottom-up traversal.

The D-FLAT System D-FLAT [1,4] is a framework for solving computational problems by dynamic programming on a tree decomposition of the input. It proceeds as follows.

1. D-FLAT parses a representation of the problem instance and automatically constructs a tree decomposition of it using heuristic methods which are proposed in [13]. For details, we refer to [1].
2. It provides a data structure suitable for storing partial solutions for many problems. The programmer only needs to specify (using ASP) how to populate the data structure associated with a tree decomposition node.
3. D-FLAT traverses the tree decomposition in post-order and calls an ASP system at each tree decomposition node for computing the data structure corresponding to that node by means of the user-specified program.
4. The framework automatically combines the partial solutions and prints all complete solutions. Alternatively, it is also possible to solve decision, counting and optimization problems.

In our presentation of the initial D-FLAT prototype [4] we were able to successfully apply it to several problems, and we showed in [5] which modifications could further extend its applicability. In the current paper we present the new version of D-FLAT that results from these extensions.

3   The Extended D-FLAT System

This section gives an overview of D-FLAT with the emphasis on the extensions made since [4] for solving any problem expressible in monadic second-order logic in FPT time [5]. This includes many problems in PSPACE.

3.1   Item Trees

D-FLAT equips each tree decomposition node with an *item tree*. This is the data structure that shall contain information about (candidates for) partial solutions. At each node during D-FLAT's bottom-up traversal of the tree decomposition, the problem-specific algorithm can store data in the item tree of that node.

Each node in an item tree contains an *item set*. The elements of this set, called *items*, are arbitrary ground ASP terms. An item tree node also contains additional information about the item set as well as data required for putting together complete solutions, which will be described later in this section.

Item trees are similar to computation trees of Alternating Turing Machines (ATMs) [12]. Like in ATMs, a branch can be seen as a computation sequence, and branching amounts to non-deterministic guesses. We will repeatedly come back to the ATM analogy in the course of this section.

Usually we want to restrict the information within an item tree to information about the current decomposition node's bag elements. The reason is that when the maximum size of an item tree only depends on the bag size, and if the decomposition width is bounded by a constant, the size of each item tree is also bounded. This allows us to achieve FPT algorithms.

Each branch in an item tree may be associated with a cost value, which allows for optimization problems to be solved. If costs are given, D-FLAT automatically only reports optimal solutions. Details on this are found in [1].

Example 3. Figure 1 shows a graph, one of its tree decompositions and, for each decomposition node, the corresponding item tree that could result from an algorithm for 3-COLORABILITY. Each item tree node at depth 1 encodes a coloring of the vertices in the respective bag. The meaning of the symbols $\vee$, $\top$ and $\perp$ will be explained later in this section.

Extension Pointers. For solving a complete problem instance, it is usually necessary to combine information from different item trees. For example, in order to find out if a proper coloring of a graph exists, we not only have to check if a proper coloring of each subgraph induced by a bag exists but also if, for each bag, we can pick a local coloring in such a way that each vertex is never colored differently by two chosen local colorings.

For this reason each item tree node has a (non-empty) set of *extension pointer tuples*. The elements of such a tuple are called *extension pointers* and reference item tree nodes from children of the respective decomposition node. Roughly, an extension pointer specifies that the information in the source and target nodes can reasonably be combined.

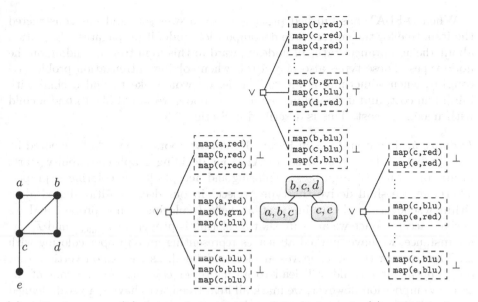

(a) A 3-col-orable graph

(b) A tree decomposition of the instance in (a) with item trees for 3-COLORABILITY (not showing extension pointers)

Fig. 1. Item trees for a decomposition of a 3-COLORABILITY instance

Example 4. Consider Figure 1b again. In the following examples, let $\mathcal{I}_S$ denote the item tree of the node whose bag is S. In $\mathcal{I}_{\{a,b,c\}}$ and $\mathcal{I}_{\{c,e\}}$, all nodes have the same set of extension pointer tuples: the set consisting of the empty tuple, as those decomposition nodes have no children. The set of extension pointer tuples at the root of $\mathcal{I}_{\{b,c,d\}}$ consists of a single binary tuple – one element references the root of $\mathcal{I}_{\{a,b,c\}}$, the other references the root of $\mathcal{I}_{\{c,e\}}$. For a node ν at depth 1 of $\mathcal{I}_{\{b,c,d\}}$, the set of extension pointer tuples consists of all tuples (ν_1, ν_2) such that ν_1 and ν_2 are nodes at depth 1 of $\mathcal{I}_{\{a,b,c\}}$ and $\mathcal{I}_{\{c,e\}}$, respectively. Moreover, if an element of the current bag $\{b, c, d\}$ is assigned a color in ν_1 or ν_2, then ν colors it in the same way.

Item Tree Node Types. Like states of ATMs, item tree nodes in D-FLAT can have one of the four types: "or", "and", "accept" or "reject". Unlike ATMs, however, the mapping in D-FLAT is partial, i.e., a node's type may be undefined. The problem-specific algorithm determines which item tree node is mapped to which type. The following conditions must be fulfilled for an item tree $\mathcal{I}$.

- If a non-leaf node of $\mathcal{I}$ has been mapped to a type, it is either "or" or "and".
- If a leaf of $\mathcal{I}$ has been mapped to a type, it is either "accept" or "reject".
- If a node of $\mathcal{I}$ extends a node with defined type, it must be mapped to the same type.

When D-FLAT has finished processing all answer sets and has constructed the item tree for the current tree decomposition node, it propagates information about the acceptance status of nodes upward in this item tree depending on the node types. These types also play a role when solving optimization problems – roughly, when something is an "or" node, we would like to find a child with minimum cost, and if something is an "and" node, we would like to find a child with maximum cost. This is described in Section 3.3.

Example 5. The item trees in Figure 1b all have roots of type "or", denoted by the symbol $\vee$. This is because an ATM for deciding graph corolability starts in an "or" state, then guesses a coloring and accepts if this coloring is proper. Therefore, we shall derive the type "reject" in our decomposition-based algorithm whenever we determine that a guessed coloring is not proper, and we derive "accept" once we are sure that a coloring is proper. In $\mathcal{I}_{\{a,b,c\}}$ and $\mathcal{I}_{\{c,e\}}$, for instance, we have marked all leaves representing an improper coloring with $\perp$. The types of the other leaves are left undefined, as guesses on vertices that only appear later could still lead to an improper coloring. At the root of the tree decomposition however, we mark all item tree leaves having a yet undefined type with $\top$ because all vertices have been encountered.

3.2   D-FLAT's Interface for ASP

D-FLAT invokes an ASP solver at each node during a bottom-up traversal of the tree decomposition. The user-defined, problem-specific encoding is augmented with input facts describing the current bag as well as the bags and item trees of child nodes. Additionally, the original problem instance is supplied as input. The answer sets of this ASP call specify the item tree that D-FLAT shall construct for the current decomposition node. D-FLAT provides facts about the tree decomposition and child item trees according to Table 1. We have omitted some less frequently used predicates for clarity. A complete list is given in [1].

Each answer set corresponds to a branch in the new item tree. The predicates for specifying this branch are described in Table 2. One should keep in mind, however, that D-FLAT may merge subtrees as described in Section 3.3. Therefore, after merging, one branch in the item tree may comprise information from multiple answer sets.

Example 6. A possible encoding for the 3-COLORABILITY problem is shown in Listing 1.1. We use colors to highlight input and output predicates. Note that it would be more convenient (and faster) to encode this problem using the simplified ASP interface for problems in NP described in [1], which we omit from this paper for space reasons.

Line 1 specifies that each answer set declares a branch of length 1, whose root node has the type "or". Line 2 guesses a color for each current vertex. The "reject" node type is derived in line 3 if this guessed coloring is improper. Lines 4 and 5 guess a branch for each child item tree. Due to line 6, the guessed combination of predecessor branches only leads to an answer set if it does not

Table 1. The most commonly used input predicates describing the tree decomposition and item trees of child nodes in the decomposition

Input predicate	Meaning
final	The current tree decomposition node is the root.
current(V)	V is an element of the current bag.
introduced(V)	V is a current vertex but was in no child node's bag.
removed(V)	V was in a child node's bag but is not in the current one.
root(S)	S is the root of an item tree from a child of the current node.
sub(R, S)	R is an item tree node with child S.
childItem(S, I)	The item set of item tree node S contains I.
childCost(S, C)	C is the cost value corresponding to the item tree leaf S.
childOr(S)	The type of the item tree node S is "or".
childAnd(S)	The type of the item tree node S is "and".
childAccept(S)	The type of the item tree leaf S is "accept".
childReject(S)	The type of the item tree leaf S is "reject".

Table 2. The most commonly used output predicates for constructing the item tree of the current decomposition node

Output predicate	Meaning
item(L, I)	The item set of the node at level L of the current branch shall contain the item I.
extend(L, S)	The node at level L of the current branch shall extend the child item tree node S.
cost(C)	The leaf of the current branch shall have a cost value of C.
length(L)	The current branch shall have length L.
or(L)	The node at level L of the current branch shall have type "or".
and(L)	The node at level L of the current branch shall have type "and".
accept	The leaf of the current branch shall have type "accept".
reject	The leaf of the current branch shall have type "reject".

```
1  length(1). or(0).
2  1 { item(1,map(X,red;X,grn;X,blu)) } 1 ← current(X).
3  reject ← edge(X,Y), item(1,map(X,C;Y,C)).
4  extend(0,S) ← root(S).
5  1 { extend(1,S) : sub(R,S) } 1 ← root(R).
6  ← item(1,map(X,C1)), childItem(S,map(X,C2)),
         extend(_,S), C1 ≠ C2.
7  reject ← childReject(S), extend(_,S).
8  accept ← final, not reject.
```

Listing 1.1. D-FLAT encoding for 3-COLORABILITY

```
1   length(2). or(0). and(1).
2   1 { item(L,map(X,red;X,grn;X,blu)) } 1 ← current(X),
        L = 1..2.
3   ← edge(X,Y), item(L,map(X,C;Y,C)).
4   ← item(2,map(V,red)), not item(1,map(V,red)).
5   extend(0,S) ← root(S).
6   1 { extend(L+1,S) : sub(R,S) } 1 ← extend(L,R),
        L = 0..1.
7   ← item(L,map(X,C1)), childItem(S,map(X,C2)),
        extend(L,S), C1 ≠ C2.
8   item(2,fail) ← item(1,map(V,red)),
        not item(2,map(V,red)).
9   item(2,fail) ← extend(2,S), childItem(S,fail).
10  reject ← final, item(2,fail).
11  accept ← final, not reject.
```

Listing 1.2. D-FLAT for a subset-minimization variant of 3-COLORABILITY

contradict the coloring guessed in line 2. This makes sure that only branches are joined that agree on all common vertices, as each vertex occurring in two child nodes must also appear in the current node due to the connectedness condition of tree decompositions. If a guessed predecessor branch has led to a conflict (denoted by a "reject" node type), this information is retained in line 7. Finally, line 8 derives the "accept" node type if no conflict has occurred.

Example 7. For a more involved example, consider a variant of the 3-COLOR-ABILITY problem: Given an input graph, we now want to compute only those proper 3-colorings whose red vertices are minimal (w.r.t. set inclusion) among all proper 3-colorings. A D-FLAT encoding for this problem is shown in Listing 1.2.

Item trees now have height 2, again with the root being an "or" node, but its children now being "and" nodes (line 1). Each item tree node at depth 1 encodes a proper coloring of the current bag elements (lines 2 and 3). Let R denote the set of vertices assigned "red" by this coloring. The children of this item set node encode all proper colorings whose red vertices R' are a subset of R (lines 2–4). If $R' \subset R$, the item "fail" is put into the respective item set (lines 8 and 9). In case a coloring at depth 2 containing "fail" survives until the final decomposition node, the respective leaf of the item tree is set to the type "reject" (line 10). As this leaf witnesses, its parent encodes a proper coloring whose red vertices are not minimal. Since this parent is an "and" node, it becomes rejecting, too. What remains at depth 1 after pruning rejecting nodes are exactly those nodes that can be extended (via the extension pointers) to proper 3-colorings whose red vertices are minimal in the sense we required.

3.3   D-FLAT's Handling of Item Trees

Every time the ASP solver reports an answer set for the current tree decomposition node, D-FLAT creates a new branch in the current item tree, which results in a so-called *uncompressed item tree*. Subsequently D-FLAT prunes subtrees of that tree that can never be part of a solution in order to avoid unnecessary computations in future decomposition nodes. For optimization problems, D-FLAT then propagates information about the optimization values upward in the uncompressed item tree. The item tree so far is called uncompressed because it may contain redundancies that are eliminated in the final step.

Constructing an Uncompressed Item Tree from the Answer Sets. In an answer set, all atoms using extend, item, or and and with the same depth argument, as well as accept and reject, constitute what we call a *node specification*. To determine where branches from different answer sets diverge, D-FLAT uses the following recursive condition: Two node specifications coincide (i.e., describe the same item tree node) iff (1) they are at the same depth in the item tree; (2) their item sets, extension pointers and node types are equal; and (3) both are at depth 0, or their parent node specifications coincide. In this way, an (uncompressed) item tree is obtained from the answer sets.

Propagation of Acceptance Statuses and Pruning of Item Trees. In Section 3.1 we have defined the different node types that an item tree node can have. When D-FLAT has processed all answer sets and constructed the uncompressed item tree, these types come into play. That is to say, D-FLAT then prunes subtrees from the uncompressed item tree.

First of all, if the current tree decomposition node is the root, D-FLAT prunes from the uncompressed item tree any subtree rooted at a node whose type is still undefined. Then, regardless of whether the current decomposition node is the root, D-FLAT prunes subtrees of the uncompressed item tree depending on the *acceptance status* of its nodes. The acceptance status of a node can either be "undefined", "accepting" or "rejecting", which we define now.

A node in an item tree is *accepting* if (a) its type is "accept", (b) its type is "or" and it has an accepting child, or (c) its type is "and" and all children are accepting. A node is *rejecting* if (a) its type is "reject", (b) its type is "or" and all children are rejecting, or (c) its type is "and" and it has a rejecting child. The acceptance status of nodes that are neither accepting nor rejecting is *undefined*.

After having computed the acceptance status of all nodes in the current item tree, D-FLAT prunes all subtrees rooted at a rejecting node, as we can be sure that these nodes will never be part of a solution.

Note that in case the current decomposition node is the root, there are no nodes with undefined acceptance status because D-FLAT has pruned all subtrees rooted at nodes with undefined type. Therefore, in this case, the remaining tree consists only of accepting nodes. For decision problems, we can thus conclude that the problem instance is positive iff the remaining tree is non-empty. For enumeration problems, we can follow the extension pointers down to the leaves of the tree decomposition in order to obtain complete solutions by combining all item sets along the way. This is described in more detail in Section 3.4. Recursively extending all item sets in this way would yield a (generally very big) item tree that usually corresponds to the accepting part of a computation tree that an ATM would have when solving the complete problem instance. (But of course D-FLAT does not materialize this entire tree in memory.)

Example 8. Consider again Figure 1b. Because $\mathcal{I}_{\{b,c,d\}}$ is the final item tree in the decomposition traversal, D-FLAT would subsequently remove all nodes with undefined types (but there are none in this case). Then it would prune all rejecting nodes and conclude that the root of $\mathcal{I}_{\{b,c,d\}}$ is accepting because it has an accepting child. Therefore the problem instance is positive. At the decomposition root, we are then left with an item tree having only six leaves, each encoding a proper coloring of the vertices b, c and d, and storing extension pointers that let us extend the respective coloring of these vertices to proper colorings of all the other vertices, too.

Propagation of Optimization Values in Item Trees. For optimization problems, after an uncompressed item tree has been computed, an additional step is done. Each leaf in the item tree stores an optimization value (or "cost") that has been specified by the user's program. D-FLAT now propagates these optimization values from the leaves toward the root of the current uncompressed item tree such that the optimization value of a leaf node is its cost, and the optimization value of an "or" or "and" node is the minimum or maximum, respectively, among the optimization values of its children.

Compressing the Item Tree. The uncompressed item tree obtained in the previous step may contain redundancies that must be eliminated in order to avoid an explosion of memory and runtime. The following situations can arise:

- There are two isomorphic sibling subtrees where all corresponding nodes have equal item sets, node types and (when solving an optimization problem) optimization values. In this case, D-FLAT merges these subtrees into one and unifies their sets of extension pointers.
- An optimization problem is being solved and there are two isomorphic sibling subtrees where all corresponding nodes have equal item sets and node types, but the root of one of these subtrees is "better" than the root of the other. In this context, a node n_1 is "better" than one of its siblings, n_2, if the parent of n_1 and n_2 either has type "or" and the cost of n_1 is less than that of n_2, or their parent has type "and" and the cost of n_1 is greater than that of n_2. In this case, D-FLAT retains only the subtree rooted at the "better" node.

For problems in NP, this redundancy elimination can be done on the fly [1].

3.4   Materializing Complete Solutions

After all item trees have been computed, it remains to materialize complete solutions. We first describe how D-FLAT does this for enumeration problems.

In the item tree at the root of the decomposition there are only accepting nodes left after the pruning described in Section 3.3. Starting with the root of this item tree, D-FLAT extends each of the nodes recursively as follows.

To obtain a complete extension of an item tree rooted at a node n, we recursively extend the item set of n by unifying it with all items of nodes reachable via extension pointers. For each child n' of n we also perform this procedure and add each possible extension of n' to the children to the current extension of n. When extending n' in this way, however, D-FLAT takes care to only pick an extension pointer tuple of n' if every node that is being pointed to in this tuple is a child of a node that is used for the current extension of n.

For optimization problems, D-FLAT only materializes optimal solutions. That is, if n is an "or" node with optimization value c, D-FLAT only extends those children of n that actually have the value c. Due to D-FLAT's propagation of optimization values (cf. Section 3.3), the optimization value of an "or" node is the minimum of the values of its children. For "and" nodes this is symmetric.

D-FLAT allows the depth until which the final item tree is to be extended to be limited by the user. This is useful if, e.g., only existence of a solution shall be determined. In such a case, we could limit the materialization depth to 0. This would lead to only the root of the final item tree being extended. If D-FLAT yields an extension, a solution in fact exists. This is because the final item tree would have no root in case no solutions existed (cf. Section 3.3). Limiting the materialization depth can thus save us from potentially materializing exponentially many solutions for decision problems.

Moreover, limiting the materialization depth is also helpful for counting problems. If the user limits this depth to d and in the final item tree there is a node at depth d having children, D-FLAT prints for each extension of this node how many extended children would have been materialized. For the most common case, where the materialization depth is limited to 0, D-FLAT is able to calculate the number of possible extensions while doing the main bottom-up traversal of the decomposition for computing the item trees. Hence, for classical counting problems, D-FLAT offers quite efficient counting.

3.5   Debugging Support

Since it can be hard to find the cause of erroneous results of D-FLAT encodings, we have developed a debugging tool that visualizes the generated tree decomposition and the computed item trees. It allows to inspect how certain solutions came to be and thus greatly simplifies debugging. We refer to [1] for details.

3.6   Experiments

In [4] we have experimentally evaluated the prototype of D-FLAT. In the current paper, we additionally consider the MAXIMUM INDEPENDENT SET problem with

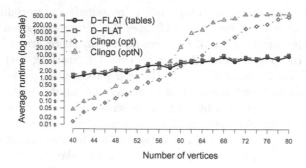

Fig. 2. Comparison of runtimes on the MAXIMUM INDEPENDENT SET problem

the new version of D-FLAT. For each number of vertices in $\{40, 42, \ldots, 80\}$, we have generated 20 random instances that admit a tree decomposition of width 12. On each instance we have executed D-FLAT 1.0.0 (with an encoding using the simplified ASP interface and the default implementation for join nodes of weakly normalized decompositions [1]) as well as the ASP system Clingo 4.3.0. The experiments were run on a system with 48 GB of RAM and 2 Intel Xeon 64-bit CPUs (each with 4 cores) at 2.33 GHz using only a single core.

Figure 2 shows that the runtime of Clingo 4.3.0 increases exponentially, both for finding just a single optimal solution (denoted by "opt" in the figure) as well as counting the number of optimal solutions ("optN"). Note that especially for "optN" the curve seems to flatten toward the right side of the figure, but this is because timeouts (> 10 minutes) were counted as 10 minutes. The runtime of D-FLAT increases linearly and it outperforms Clingo on the larger instances.

4 Conclusion

In this paper we have presented the D-FLAT system for solving problems by means of dynamic programming on a tree decomposition of the instance. The key feature is that D-FLAT allows the user to specify the problem-specific computations in the logic programming language of Answer Set Programming.

We have discussed the most significant changes made since the initial publication of D-FLAT in [4]. In particular, these extensions allow D-FLAT to solve any problem expressible in monadic second-order logic [5]. This significantly extends its range of applicability. For instance, D-FLAT can thus solve Quantified Boolean Formulas or compute subset-minimal models of propositional theories. Furthermore, we provide a debugging tool that facilitates development of algorithms for D-FLAT.

Future work. We will analyze which features of tree decompositions have the most influence on the runtime of D-FLAT. Moreover, we will investigate for which fragments of ASP we can automatically generate a dynamic programming algorithm for tree decompositions from a "traditional" encoding.

Acknowledgments. This work is supported by the Austrian Science Fund (FWF) projects P25518, P25607 and Y698, and by the Vienna University of Technology special fund "Innovative Projekte" (9006.09/008).

References

1. Abseher, M., Bliem, B., Charwat, G., Dusberger, F., Hecher, M., Woltran, S.: D-FLAT: Progress report. Technical Report DBAI-TR-2014-86, Vienna University of Technology (2014)
2. Arnborg, S., Corneil, D.G., Proskurowski, A.: Complexity of finding embeddings in a k-tree. SIAM J. Algebraic Discrete Methods 8(2), 277–284 (1987)
3. Aschinger, M., Drescher, C., Gottlob, G., Jeavons, P., Thorstensen, E.: Structural decomposition methods and what they are good for. In: Proc. STACS. LIPIcs, vol. 9, pp. 12–28. Schloss Dagstuhl – Leibniz-Zentrum für Informatik (2011)
4. Bliem, B., Morak, M., Woltran, S.: D-FLAT: Declarative problem solving using tree decompositions and answer-set programming. TPLP 12(4-5), 445–464 (2012)
5. Bliem, B., Pichler, R., Woltran, S.: Declarative dynamic programming as an alternative realization of courcelle's theorem. In: Gutin, G., Szeider, S. (eds.) IPEC 2013. LNCS, vol. 8246, pp. 28–40. Springer, Heidelberg (2013)
6. Bodlaender, H.L.: A tourist guide through treewidth. Acta Cybern. 11(1-2), 1–22 (1993)
7. Bodlaender, H.L.: A linear-time algorithm for finding tree-decompositions of small treewidth. SIAM J. Comput. 25(6), 1305–1317 (1996)
8. Bodlaender, H.L.: Discovering treewidth. In: Vojtáš, P., Bieliková, M., Charron-Bost, B., Sýkora, O. (eds.) SOFSEM 2005. LNCS, vol. 3381, pp. 1–16. Springer, Heidelberg (2005)
9. Bodlaender, H.L., Koster, A.M.C.A.: Combinatorial optimization on graphs of bounded treewidth. Comput. J. 51(3), 255–269 (2008)
10. Bodlaender, H.L., Koster, A.M.C.A.: Treewidth computations I. Upper bounds. Inf. Comput. 208(3), 259–275 (2010)
11. Brewka, G., Eiter, T., Truszczyński, M.: Answer set programming at a glance. Commun. ACM 54(12), 92–103 (2011)
12. Chandra, A.K., Kozen, D., Stockmeyer, L.J.: Alternation. J. ACM 28(1), 114–133 (1981)
13. Dermaku, A., Ganzow, T., Gottlob, G., McMahan, B., Musliu, N., Samer, M.: Heuristic methods for hypertree decomposition. In: Gelbukh, A., Morales, E.F. (eds.) MICAI 2008. LNCS (LNAI), vol. 5317, pp. 1–11. Springer, Heidelberg (2008)
14. Downey, R.G., Fellows, M.R.: Parameterized Complexity. Monographs in Computer Science. Springer (1999)
15. Gebser, M., Kaminski, R., Kaufmann, B., Ostrowski, M., Schaub, T., Thiele, S.: A user's guide to gringo, clasp, clingo, and iclingo. Preliminary Draft (2010), http://potassco.sourceforge.net
16. Gebser, M., Kaminski, R., Kaufmann, B., Schaub, T.: Answer Set Solving in Practice. Synthesis Lectures on Artificial Intelligence and Machine Learning. Morgan & Claypool Publishers (2012)
17. Gelfond, M., Leone, N.: Logic programming and knowledge representation – the A-Prolog perspective. Artif. Intell. 138(1-2), 3–38 (2002)
18. Gelfond, M., Lifschitz, V.: Classical negation in logic programs and disjunctive databases. New Generation Comput. 9(3/4), 365–386 (1991)

19. Gottlob, G., Leone, N., Scarcello, F.: Hypertree decompositions and tractable queries. J. Comput. Syst. Sci. 64(3), 579–627 (2002)
20. Niedermeier, R.: Invitation to Fixed-Parameter Algorithms. Oxford Lecture Series in Mathematics and its Applications. Oxford University Press (2006)
21. Robertson, N., Seymour, P.D.: Graph minors. III. Planar tree-width. J. Comb. Theory, Ser. B 36(1), 49–64 (1984)

ACUOS: A System for Modular ACU Generalization with Subtyping and Inheritance[*]

María Alpuente[1], Santiago Escobar[1], Javier Espert[1], and José Meseguer[2]

[1] DSIC-ELP, Universitat Politècnica de València, Spain
{alpuente,sescobar,jespert}@dsic.upv.es
[2] University of Illinois at Urbana-Champaign, USA
meseguer@illinois.edu

Abstract. Computing generalizers is relevant in a wide spectrum of automated reasoning areas where analogical reasoning and inductive inference are needed. The ACUOS system computes a complete and minimal set of semantic generalizers (also called "anti-unifiers") of two structures in a typed language *modulo* a set of equational axioms. By supporting types and any (modular) combination of associativity (A), commutativity (C), and unity (U) algebraic axioms for function symbols, ACUOS allows reasoning about typed data structures, e.g. lists, trees, and (multi-)sets, and typical hierarchical/structural relations such as *is_a* and *part_of*. This paper discusses the modular ACU generalization tool ACUOS and illustrates its use in a classical artificial intelligence problem.

1 Introduction

Generalization is the dual of unification [14]. Roughly speaking, in this work the generalization problem for two expressions t_1 and t_2 means finding their *least general generalization* (lgg), i.e., the least general expression t such that both t_1 and t_2 are instances of t under appropriate substitutions. For instance, the expression father(X,Y) is a generalizer of both father(john,sam) and father(tom,sam), but their least general generalizer, also known as *most specific generalizer* (msg) and *least common anti–instance* (lcai), is father(X,sam). Applications of generalization arise in many artificial intelligence areas, including case-based reasoning, analogy making, web and data mining, ontology learning, machine learning, theorem proving, and inductive logic programming, among others [5,12,13,16].

While ordinary, syntactic generalization is useful for some applications, it has two important limitations. First, it cannot generalize common data structures such as records, lists, trees, or (multi-)sets, which satisfy specific premises such as the order among the elements in a set being irrelevant. For instance, let us

---

[*] This work has been partially supported by the EU (FEDER) and the Spanish MINECO under grants TIN 2010-21062-C02-02 and TIN 2013-45732-C4-1-P, by Generalitat Valenciana PROMETEO2011/052, and by NSF Grant CNS 13-10109. J. Espert has also been supported by the Spanish FPU grant FPU12/06223.

E. Fermé and J. Leite (Eds.): JELIA 2014, LNAI 8761, pp. 573–581, 2014.

introduce the constants john, sam, peter, tom, mary, chris, and joan, and consider the predicate symbols twins, ancestors, spouses, and children that establish several relations among (a selection of) such constants. Since twins is a symmetric relation, we would like the pair "john and sam" to be in the relation twins if the pair "sam and john" is in the relation twins. For the time being, let us introduce a new *tuple constructor* symbol (;) to satisfy commutativity and an overloaded use of twins as a unary symbol such that the expressions twins((john;sam)) and twins((sam;john)) are equivalent *modulo* the commutativity of the (;) operator. Then, we can generalize twins((john;sam)) and twins((sam;tom)) as twins((X;sam)), whereas without equational attributes the least general (or most specific) generalizer of twins(john,sam) and twins(sam,tom) is twins(X,Y).

Similarly, we can express the relation given by the ancestors of a person by means of a list using the *list concatenation* operator (.). We assume that a person's name is automatically coerced into a singleton list. Due to the associativity of list concatenation, i.e.,(x.y).z = x.(y.z), we can use the flattened list (john.sam.mary.peter) as a very compact and convenient representation for the congruence class modulo associativity whose members are the different parenthesized list expressions, e.g., ((john.sam).mary).peter, john.(sam.mary).peter, john.(sam.(mary.peter)), etc. Then, for the expressions ancestors(chris,(john.sam.mary.peter)) and ancestors(joan, (tom.mary.john)), the least general generalizer is ancestors(X,(Y.mary.Z)), which reveals that mary is the only common ancestor of chris and joan. Note that ancestors(chris,(john.sam.mary.peter)) is an instance (modulo A) of ancestors(X,(Y.mary.Z)) by the substitution {X/chris, Y/(john.sam), Z/peter}.

Due to the equational axioms, in general there can be more than one least general generalizer of two expressions. For instance, let us record the marriage history of a person using a list, e.g. sam.sam.tom.peter for the marriage history of mary, where she divorced sam and married him again. Then, the expressions spouses(mary,(sam.sam.tom.peter)) and spouses(joan,(tom.tom.john)) have two incomparable least general generalizers: (a) spouses(X, (Y.tom.Z)) and (b) spouses(U, (V.V.W)), respectively meaning that both mary and joan have married tom, and they both repeated marriage (consecutively) with their first husband. Note that the two generalizers are least general and incomparable, since neither one is an instance (modulo associativity) of the other.

Furthermore, if we consider the set of children of a person, this set should be recognized irrespectively of the order in which the children's names are written in the set. Let us introduce a new symbol (&) that satisfies associativity, commutativity, and unit element ∅; i.e., X & ∅ = X and ∅ & X = X. Then, we can use the flattened multiset (john & mary & peter & sam) (with a total order on elements given, e.g., by the lexicographic order) as a very compact and convenient representation for the congruence class modulo associativity, commutativity, and unit element (written ACU) whose members are the different parenthesized expressions with all permutations of the elements and as many occurrences of ∅ as needed, due to

unity [6]. Working modulo ACU, the expressions (i) `children(chris,(john &`
`sam & mary & peter))` and (ii) `children(joan,(tom & sam & john))` can be generalized as `children(P,(john & sam & X))` but they can also be generalized as
`children(P',(john & sam & X' & Y))` since `children(joan,(tom & sam & john))`
is an instance (modulo ACU) of `children(P',(john & sam & X' & Y))` by the substitution `{P'/joan, X'/tom, Y/∅}`. Actually, for every least general generalizer t,
the set of all ACU generalizers that are equivalent to t *modulo* ACU-renaming[1] is
infinite, i.e.,

```
children(P0, (john & sam & X0)),
children(P1, (john & sam & X1 & Y1)),
children(P2, (john & sam & X2 & Y2 & Z2)), ...
```

yet we can choose one of them, typically the smallest one, as the class representative. Note that `children(P,(john & sam & X))` is an instance (modulo
ACU) of `children(P',(john & sam & X' & Y))` by the substitution `{X'/X,`
`Y/∅}` but also `children(P',(john & sam & X' & Y))` is an instance (modulo
ACU) of `children(P,(john & sam & X))` by the substitution `{X/(X' & Y)}`.

The second problem with ordinary generalization is that it does not cope with
types and subtypes, which can lead to more specific generalizers. For instance, assume that the constants `john`, `sam`, `peter`, and `tom` belong to type Male and that
`mary`, `joan`, and `chris` belong to type Female. Let us introduce another type People for the typed version of the ACU (multi-)set structures on which the relation
`children` described above is defined. The Male and Female types can be considered as subtypes of a common type Person, which is itself a subtype of People
representing a singleton set. Subtyping implies automatic coercion. Note that the
empty set, denoted by ∅, belongs to People. Then, the above expressions (i) and
(ii) have one typed ACU least general generalizer `children(P:Female,(john`
`& sam & X:Male & Y:People))` that we choose as the representative of the infinite ACU congruence class. Note that `children(P':Female,(john & sam &`
`X':People))` is not a least general generalizer since it is strictly more general; it
suffices to see that the class representative is an instance of it with substitution
`{P':Female/P:Female,X':People/(X:Male & Y:People)}`.

This work presents ACUOS, a mature and highly developed implementation of
the order-sorted ACU least general generalization algorithm that we formalized
in [1]. ACUOS has been written in the high-performance language Maude [11]
that supports reasoning modulo algebraic properties and reflection. To the best
of our knowledge, this is the first generalization system that is able to compute
least general generalizers in order-sorted theories modulo equational axioms.

In Section 2, we describe the system and discuss how it can be used to address
artificial intelligence problems that need a form of ACU generalization. This is
done by focusing on a simple and classical artificial intelligence problem that
is known as the Rutherford analogy [8,9], proving that our system fulfills the
objective to recognize that atoms resemble tiny solar systems. Experimental

---

[1] i.e., the equivalence relation $\approx_{ACU}$ induced by the relative generality (subsumption)
preorder $\leq_{ACU}$: $s \approx_{ACU} t$ iff $s \leq_{ACU} t$ and $t \leq_{ACU} s$.

results given in Section 3 show that ACUOS performs efficiently in practice. For a discussion of the related literature, we refer to [2,3,1,4,10]

2   Use Case: Extracting Analogies

In this section, we analyze and extract structural commonalities between two representative sets of physical assertions, one of which regards the electromagnetic forces in the atom while the other one considers gravitational forces in the solar system. First, we provide a functional representation for the solar system and the Rutherford model for the atom and then we use ACUOS to automatically extract a precise correspondence between them. Note that this is a classical example of *higher-order generalization* [8], in the sense that function symbols themselves are generalized by using function variables. We explain how higher-order reasoning can be achieved within our first-order setting by using reflection through the Maude meta-programming capabilities [7].

2.1   Problem Representation

Let us introduce a meta-representation for models by introducing the HModel sort (or type) that is defined in Figure 1, using (sub-)sorts HTerm and HOperator. The generic Maude implementation given in Figure 1 is then used in Figure 2 to specify the operators that describe the two considered systems (i.e., the domain relations). Each relation r such as mass, charge, or attraction is represented by an HTerm that is rooted by a suitable operator that is given appropriate equational axioms, similarly to the operators[2] (;), (.), and (&) discussed in Section 1. In other words, the semantic information concerning each domain is encoded using appropriate equational attributes for the relation r itself (e.g., the action-reaction principle of gravitational forces is captured by the commutativity property of the attraction operator). In Maude syntax, this can be done by declaring the equational attributes of any given symbol through the use of special tags. Not only is this concise, it is also efficient because it takes advantage of the powerful optimizations included in the Maude interpreter [6].

Maude syntax is almost self-explanatory, using explicit keywords such as fmod, sort, and op to introduce a module, sort, and operator, respectively. The declaration subsort A1 ... An < B denotes that A1 ... An are subsorts of B and implies automatic coercion. The keywords assoc and comm respectively specify associativity and commutativity axioms for an operator. The keyword prec establishes the precedence of an operator. Module inclusion is denoted by inc. Using this representation, our knowledge of each domain can simply be encoded as a first-order term of sort HTerm, as shown in Figure 3, which depicts the two terms that respectively encode the gravitational solar system and the Rutherford model for the atom.

---

[2] Notice the *mixfix* notation [6] in the definition of the operators (e.g., op _;_ : HModel HModel -> HModel), which uses underscores _ to indicate that each argument of the function will replace one of the underscores (e.g., the term (x;y)).

```
fmod HIGHER-ORDER-metarepresentation is
  sorts HModel HTerm HOperator HVariable .
  sorts HTermList HTermPair HConj HRule .
  subsort HOperator HVariable < HTerm .
  subsort HTerm < HTermList HConj HModel .
  subsort HRule < HTerm .
  op _[_]  : HOperator HTermList -> HTerm [prec 10] .
  op __    : HOperator HTermPair -> HTerm [prec 10] .
  op _,_   : HTermList HTermList -> HTermList [assoc prec 20] .
  op <_,_> : HTerm HTerm -> HTermPair [comm prec 20] .
  op _/\_  : HConj HConj -> HConj [assoc comm prec 30] .
  op _=>_  : HConj HTerm -> HRule [prec 40] .
  op _;_   : HModel HModel -> HModel [assoc comm prec 50] .
endfm
```

Fig. 1. Generic higher-order meta-representation

```
fmod DOMAIN-OPERATORS is inc HIGHER-ORDER .
  ops mass sun planet gravity : -> HOperator .
  ops charge coulomb electron nucleus : -> HOperator .
  ops attraction distant : -> HOperator [comm] .
  ops x y : -> HVariable .
endfm
```

Fig. 2. Signature of the analogy domain operators

Solar System
mass[sun] ;
mass[planet] ;
distant⟨sun,planet⟩ ;
mass[x] ∧ mass[y] ⇒ gravity[x,y] ;
gravity[x,y] ⇒ attraction[x,y]

Rutherford Atom Model
charge[y] ∧ charge[x] ⇒ coulomb[x,y] ;
charge[electron] ;
charge[nucleus] ;
distant⟨electron,nucleus⟩ ;
coulomb[x,y] ⇒ attraction[x,y]

Fig. 3. Analogy problem representation

After feeding the ACUOS generalization tool with the Maude specification given in Figures 1 and 2, together with the two input terms of Figure 3, we obtain the least general ACU generalizer shown in Figure 4. For clarity, we omit the sorting information in the results and summarize it as an annotation at the bottom of the figure.

Generalization of Solar System and Rutherford Atom
P[X] ;
P[Y] ;
distant⟨X,Y⟩ ;
P[x] ∧ P[y] ⇒ Q[x,y] ;
Q[x,y] ⇒ attraction[x,y]

where variables P, Q belong to sort HOperator and variables X, Y to sort HTerm; note that P,Q encode higher-order variables in our first-order setting.

Fig. 4. ACU generalization of the analogy problem

2.2   Further Generalization Capabilities

The analogy extracted so far relates a planet in the solar system with an electron in the atom, and the Sun with the atom nucleus. The related entities planet and electron are the only argument of the relations mass and charge, respectively. However, they both appear as arguments of the relations gravity and coulomb, though in different order. Also, the order of appearance of the definitions for the relations coulomb and gravity differs in both models. Therefore, the correspondence between the two models would have been hard to establish without considering the commutativity and associativity of the operators (_∧_) and (_;_).

We must often extract analogies from large deductive databases that, unlike our previous example, contain irrelevant information with respect to the analogies that we intend to extract. Let us further illustrate the advantages of our order-sorted, equational generalization approach by slightly modifying our example with the introduction of irrelevant knowledge. Specifically, suppose that we add the assertions positive(nucleus) and negative(electron) into the Rutherford Atom description and the assertion heavier-than(sun,planet) into the solar system model. Figure 5 below shows the extended domain representation together with the recomputed least general generalization result; the only difference is the addition of a variable Z (of sort HModel), which can be thought of as a container for the unnecessary pieces of information that are automatically disregarded in this case.

Extended Solar System
mass[sun] ; mass[planet] ;
distant⟨sun,planet⟩ ;
mass[x] ∧ mass[y] ⇒ gravity[x,y] ;
gravity[x,y] ⇒ attraction[x,y] ;
heavier-than[sun,planet]

Extended Rutherford Atom Model
charge[y] ∧ charge[x] ⇒ coulomb[x,y] ;
charge[electron] ; charge[nucleus] ;
distant⟨electron,nucleus⟩ ;
coulomb[x,y] ⇒ attraction[x,y] ;
positive[nucleus] ; negative[electron]

Generalization of Extended Solar System and Extended Rutherford Atom
Z ; P[X] ; P[Y] ; distant⟨X,Y⟩ ; P[x] ∧ P[y] ⇒ Q[x,y] ; Q[x,y] ⇒ attraction[x,y] ;

Fig. 5. ACU generalization of the extended analogy problem

3   The ACU Generalization System ACUOS

The ACUOS backend consists of about 1000 lines of Maude code that essentially implement the algorithm of [1], making heavy use of the Maude metaprogramming capabilities based on reflection. The algorithm is formalized as an inference system in the style of [14], with specific rules for solving and decomposing constraints (i.e., generalization subproblems) involving symbols that obey equational axioms, such as ACU and their combinations. The number of independent, order-sorted least general generalizers modulo E-renaming, where E consists of any combination of associativity, commutativity, and unity axioms of two expressions, is always finite [1], and our algorithm terminates for every generalization problem, while computing a complete and minimal generalization set (that is, a set covering all independent generalizations).

The implementation of [1] in ACUOS has been optimized as follows. First, we identify many generalization subproblems that are equal modulo (equational) variable renaming, which enables the use of Maude memoization thus leading to exponential speed-ups for common generalization problems. Second, we delay adding any *sort* information for new variables until needed, which avoids repeated computation of subsorts for the same terms. Finally, those computations that are deterministic are encoded as Maude equations (instead of rules), thereby greatly reducing the search space as well as the memory usage due to the different treatment of rules and equations in Maude [6]. Thanks to these improvements, we can handle terms that are up to 50% larger than the preliminary, naïve implementation reported in [1].

ACUOS is publicly available at `http://safe-tools.dsic.upv.es/acuos` and comes with an intuitive web interface which allows the tool to be used through a Java Web application. Alternatively, ACUOS can also be used without the Web interface, by directly invoking the Maude generalization routine `lggs` that is implemented in the ACUOS backend. This is the preferred approach to integrate ACUOS with third-party software. For convenience, the system is also endowed with a *Full Maude* [6] user-level command allowing the user to harness the full power of the tool while being liberated from ancillary meta-level technicalities.

3.1   Experiments

In this section, we report on some experiments we have conducted with the ACUOS system. When computing modulo equational axioms, the size of the equivalence classes of the least general generalizers gives a measure of the complexity of the problem (see [15] for some theoretical results on the complexity of generalization). We use three symbols for denoting the different sizes: 0 when there is no generalizer for two terms (unlike the case of syntactical generalization, in the order-sorted setting the sorts of different *kinds*[3] are incompatible and then the terms of these sorts have no generalization, not even a variable); ω when there is a finite number of elements in the equivalence classes of the generalizers; and ∞ when the equivalence classes (w.r.t. $\approx_{ACU}$) can have an infinite number of ACU-equivalent generalizers. Any combinations of the A and C axioms are in the ω class. The introduction of the U axiom leads to size ∞ (even if the number of ACU least general generalizers is still finite).

We have tested our tool with several representative generalization problems taken from the literature that can be found online and in the distribution package. The benchmarks used for the analysis are: (i) `incompatible types`, a problem without any generalizers; (ii) `twins`, `ancestors`, `spouses`, `siblings`, and `children`, as described in the introduction; (iii) `only-U`, a generalization problem modulo (just) unity axioms, i.e., without A and C; (iv) `synthetic`, an involved example mixing A, C, and U axioms for different symbols; (v) `multiple inheritance`, which uses a classic example of multiple subtyping from [6] to

---

[3] Each connected component in the poset of sorts has a top sort that is called the *kind*.

illustrate the interaction of advanced type hierarchies with order-sorted generalization; (vi) `rutherford`, the example of Section 2; (vii) and `chemical`, a variant of the case-based reasoning problem for chemical compounds discussed in [5].

Table 1. Experimental results

Test	G	#	N	ms.
incompatible types	0	2	0	16
twins (C)	ω	6	1	16
ancestors (A)	ω	22	5	40
spouses (A)	ω	16	3	16
spouses (AU)	∞	16	6	360
siblings (AC)	ω	14	2	80
children (ACU)	∞	12	1	288
only-U (U)	∞	10	1	16
synthetic	ω	20	2	20
multiple inheritance	ω	10	4	28
rutherford	ω	54	1	462
chemical	ω	20	2	240

Table 1 shows our experimental results. For each problem, we show its generalization class (G), the size (number of symbols) of the input terms (#), the number of least general generalizers for each problem (N), and the total computation time (ms). As mentioned in Section 3, we achieve a dramatic improvement w.r.t. the preliminary tool reported in [1], where only the incompatible types and the twins benchmarks can be run with comparable performance; the rest of the examples time out for AC or ACU terms with more than six symbols, with the computation times surpassing one minute. Table 1 reflects that the runtimes of our algorithm do not just depend on the equational attributes given to each symbol and the size of the input terms but also on the actual shape of the terms (in particular, whether there are repeated subterms or not). This demonstrates the effectivity of the memoization mechanism that we introduced as an improvement in Section 3. Actually, we achieve up to 90% of reduction in the size of the search space w.r.t. the coarse search space generated without the improvements discussed in Section 3.

Considering the high combinatorial complexity of the ACU generalization problem, our implementation is reasonably time efficient. For example, most of the examples discussed in Section 1 took on the order of 10 ms on standard hardware (3.30 GHz Intel Xeon E3-1240 with 8Gb of RAM memory).

References

1. Alpuente, M., Escobar, S., Espert, J., Meseguer, J.: A Modular Order-sorted Equational Generalization Algorithm. Information and Computation 235, 98–136 (2014)
2. Alpuente, M., Escobar, S., Meseguer, J., Ojeda, P.: A Modular Equational Generalization Algorithm. In: Hanus, M. (ed.) LOPSTR 2008. LNCS, vol. 5438, pp. 24–39. Springer, Heidelberg (2009)

3. Alpuente, M., Escobar, S., Meseguer, J., Ojeda, P.: Order–Sorted Generalization. ENTCS 246, 27–38 (2009)
4. Alpuente, M., Espert, J., Escobar, S., Meseguer, J.: ACUOS: A System for Modular ACU Generalization with Subtyping and Inheritance. Tech. rep., DSIC-UPV (2013), http://riunet.upv.es/handle/10251/38854
5. Armengol, E.: Usages of Generalization in Case-Based Reasoning. In: Weber, R.O., Richter, M.M. (eds.) ICCBR 2007. LNCS (LNAI), vol. 4626, pp. 31–45. Springer, Heidelberg (2007)
6. Clavel, M., Durán, F., Eker, S., Lincoln, P., Martí-Oliet, N., Meseguer, J., Talcott, C. (eds.): All About Maude - A High-Performance Logical Framework. LNCS, vol. 4350. Springer, Heidelberg (2007)
7. Clavel, M., Durán, F., Eker, S., Lincoln, P., Martí-Oliet, N., Meseguer, J., Talcott, C.L.: Reflection, metalevel computation, and strategies. In: All About Maude [6], pp. 419–458
8. Gentner, D.: Structure-Mapping: A Theoretical Framework for Analogy*. Cognitive Science 7(2), 155–170 (1983)
9. Krumnack, U., Schwering, A., Gust, H., Kühnberger, K.-U.: Restricted higher order anti unification for analogy making. In: Orgun, M.A., Thornton, J. (eds.) AI 2007. LNCS (LNAI), vol. 4830, pp. 273–282. Springer, Heidelberg (2007)
10. Kutsia, T., Levy, J., Villaret, M.: Anti-Unification for Unranked Terms and Hedges. Journal of Automated Reasoning 520, 155–190 (2014)
11. Meseguer, J.: Conditioned rewriting logic as a united model of concurrency. Theor. Comput. Sci. 96(1), 73–155 (1992)
12. Muggleton, S.: Inductive Logic Programming: Issues, Results and the Challenge of Learning Language in Logic. Artif. Intell. 114(1-2), 283–296 (1999)
13. Ontañón, S., Plaza, E.: Similarity measures over refinement graphs. Machine Learning 87(1), 57–92 (2012)
14. Plotkin, G.: A note on inductive generalization. In: Machine Intelligence, vol. 5, pp. 153–163. Edinburgh University Press (1970)
15. Pottier, L.: Generalisation de termes en theorie equationelle: Cas associatif-commutatif. Tech. Rep. INRIA 1056, Norwegian Computing Center (1989)
16. Schmid, U., Hofmann, M., Bader, F., Häberle, T., Schneider, T.: Incident Mining using Structural Prototypes. In: García-Pedrajas, N., Herrera, F., Fyfe, C., Benítez, J.M., Ali, M. (eds.) IEA/AIE 2010, Part II. LNCS, vol. 6097, pp. 327–336. Springer, Heidelberg (2010)

Drawing Euler Diagrams from Region Connection Calculus Specifications with Local Search

François Schwarzentruber[1] and Jin-Kao Hao[2]

[1] ENS Rennes, Campus de Ker lann, Av Robert Schumann, 35170 Bruz, France
[2] LERIA, Université d'Angers, 2 Bd Lavoisier, 49045 Angers Cedex 01, France

Abstract. This paper describes a local search based approach and a software tool to approximate the problem of drawing Euler diagrams. Specifications are written using **RCC-8**-constraints and radius constraints. Euler diagrams are described as set of circles.

1 Introduction

Euler diagrams are pictures to understand relations between concepts. Sets (= concepts) are represented as regions in the plane and inclusions or intersections of those regions depict inclusions or intersections of the corresponding sets. Euler diagrams are a very general tool that is used in a wide range of application areas. For instance, Figure 1 shows an Euler diagram representing the relations of the complexity classes as many computer scientists may believe they are. Generally speaking, the user may want to generate automatically Euler diagrams from a knowledge base expressed in description logic [20].

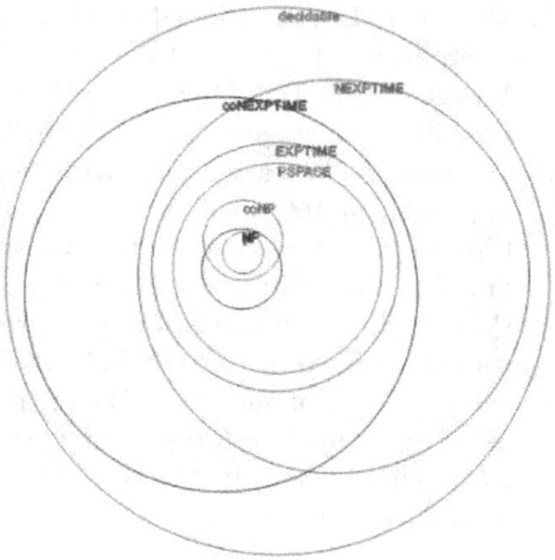

Fig. 1. Euler diagram drawn by our tool

This paper presents a proof-of-concept software tool for drawing Euler diagrams by constraint solving with local search available here: http://www.irisa.fr/prive/fschwarz/constrainteddrawing.

Given a set of geometrical objects and a set of constraints over these objects, the objective is to find a drawing that contains the geometrical objects and satisfies the set of given constraints. In this work, objects are circles and our first aim is to draw Euler diagrams from constraints given as an input.

As discussed in Section 6 on related work, there are different approaches to solve this problem of drawing Euler diagrams. One prominent work is to use algorithms coming from graph theory [17]. Nevertheless, when we deal with drawing

E. Fermé and J. Leite (Eds.): JELIA 2014, LNAI 8761, pp. 582–590, 2014.
© Springer International Publishing Switzerland 2014

generation, there is a need which seems essential: the user should be offered the possibility of interacting with the generated drawing. For instance, the user should be allowed to move or resize a circle in the current Euler diagram. Then the system should be able to take into account the input of the user and correct the drawing with respect to the constraints. With the graph theory approach, it seems difficult and even impossible to correct Euler diagrams interactively. That is why, we claim that the local search approach, thanks to its high flexibility, is a suitable method for this problem. Local search both takes into account the input of the user and corrects the picture in order to always satisfy the constraints.

Concerning the constraint specification language, we decided to start from **RCC-8** constraints [11], where **RCC** stands for 'Region connection calculus'. Indeed, **RCC-8** is a desirable formalism for constraint specifications of Euler diagrams. It provides constraints that describe pure set theory concepts. For instance, the proposition 'a and b are disjoint' is expressed as the circles representing the relation 'a and b are disconnected' (DC). This information may come from a knowledge base where the description logic formula $a \sqcap b = \neg \top$ is inferred [20].

Moreover, this tool may be used to draw Euler diagrams representing sets in a topological space (for instance this tool may be used by a math teacher in an introductory course in topology). And **RCC-8** also provides topological concepts. As in illustration, if a and b are sets in a topological space such that interiors of a and b are disjoint and closures of a and b are not disjoint, we may express that the circles representing a and b are externally connected (EC) (see Figure 2).

The paper is organized as follows. In section 2 we describe the language we consider. Section 3 gives the semantics. Section 4 is dedicated to the local search procedure. Section 5 presents the implementation. Section 6 reviews related work. Perspectives are provided in the concluding section. Proofs and experimental results are in [16].

2   Syntax

The syntax of the language $\mathcal{L}$ of constraints is defined by the following rule:

$$\varphi \; ::= \; R(a,b) \; \mid \; radius(a) = r \; \mid \; (\varphi \vee \varphi)$$

where a and b range over a set of constant symbols, r is a rational number and R ranges over the symbol predicates of **RCC-8**. Intuitive meanings of **RCC-8**-relations are given in table 1 and figure 2 gives them in pictures $\mathbb{REL}_{RCC-8}$.

3   Semantics

Usually in logic, semantics is given in terms of truth values. A formula φ is either true or false in a given model. But, for the local search algorithm, we need the semantics to be soft and we measure how much a formula φ is true (or false).

Table 1. Intuitive meanings of **RCC-8**-relations

Construction	Intuitive meaning
$DC(a,b)$	a and b are disconnected
$EC(a,b)$	a and b are externally connected
$PO(a,b)$	a and b partially overlap
$TPP(a,b)$	a is a tangential proper part of b
$TPP^{-1}(a,b)$	b is a tangential proper part of a
$NTPP(a,b)$	a is a non-tangential proper part of b
$NTPP^{-1}(a,b)$	b is a non-tangential proper part of a
$EQ(a,b)$	a and b are equal
$radius(a) = r$	the radius of the circle a is r
$(\varphi \vee \psi)$	φ or ψ

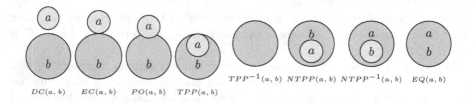

Fig. 2. The eight **RCC-8**-relations in pictures

First we define the hard semantics of our language $\mathcal{L}$. Second we define the soft semantics and we make a correspondence between them.

Models are pairs $\mathcal{M} = \langle C, i \rangle$ where:

- C is a non-empty set of circles of non-zero radius in the plane (for all $c \in C$, we respectively denote $c.x$, $c.y$ and $c.r > 0$ the abscissa, the ordinate and the radius of the circle c ; we note $c.c$ the center of c);
- i assigns to each constant symbol an element in C.

To ease the readability, a constant symbol a also designates $i(a)$, that is the circle represented by a in a model $\mathcal{M}$.

3.1 Hard Semantics

Let us define the truth conditions as follows.

Definition 1. *Let* $\mathcal{M} = \langle C, i \rangle$ *a model. We define the relation* $\mathcal{M} \models \varphi$ *by induction on* $\varphi \in \mathcal{L}$ *as follows:*

$$\mathcal{M} \models DC(a,b) \qquad \textit{iff } d(a.c, b.c) > a.r + b.r;$$
$$\mathcal{M} \models EC(a,b) \qquad \textit{iff } d(a.c, b.c) = a.r + b.r;$$
$$\mathcal{M} \models PO(a,b) \qquad \textit{iff } d(a.c, b.c) \in]|a.r - b.r|, a.r + b.r[;$$
$$\mathcal{M} \models TPP(a,b) \qquad \textit{iff } d(a.c, b.c) = b.r - a.r \;(\textit{and } a.r \leq b.r);$$
$$\mathcal{M} \models TPP^{-1}(a,b) \quad \textit{iff } d(a.c, b.c) = a.r - b.r \;(\textit{and } b.r \leq a.r);$$
$$\mathcal{M} \models NTPP(a,b) \quad \textit{iff } d(a.c, b.c) < b.r - a.r \;(\textit{and } a.r < b.r);$$
$$\mathcal{M} \models NTPP^{-1}(a,b) \; \textit{iff } d(a.c, b.c) < a.r - b.r \;(\textit{and } a.r > b.r);$$
$$\mathcal{M} \models EQ(a,b) \qquad \textit{iff } a.c = b.c \textit{ and } a.r = b.r;$$
$$\mathcal{M} \models radius(a) = r \;\; \textit{iff } i(a).r = r;$$
$$\mathcal{M} \models (\varphi \vee \psi) \qquad \textit{iff } \mathcal{M} \models \varphi \textit{ or } \mathcal{M} \models \psi.$$

The problem we tackle here is defined as follows:

- input: a finite set $I = \langle \varphi_1, \ldots, \varphi_n \rangle$ of constraints in $\mathcal{L}$;
- output: a model $\mathcal{M}$ such that for all $i \in \{1, \ldots, n\}$, $\mathcal{M} \models \varphi_i$.

The corresponding decision problem $\mathcal{L}$-SAT takes the same input and outputs yes, iff there exists a model $\mathcal{M}$ such that for all $i \in \{1, \ldots, n\}$, $\mathcal{M} \models \varphi_i$.

Proposition 1. *$\mathcal{L}$-SAT is NP-hard and in PSPACE.*

3.2   Soft Semantics

φ	Objective functions $obj(\varphi)$
$DC(a,b)$	$max(0, 2^{(a.r+b.r)-d(a.c,b.c)} - 0.0001)$
$EC(a,b)$	$\lvert d(a.c, b.c) - (a.r + b.r) \rvert$
$PO(a,b)$	$\lvert d(a.c, b.c) - max(a.r, b.r) \rvert$
$TPP(a,b)$	$\lvert d(a.c, b.c) - (b.r - a.r) \rvert$
$TPP^{-1}(a,b)$	constraint of $TPP(b,a)$
$NTPP(a,b)$	$\lvert d(a.c, b.c) - \frac{(b.r - a.r)}{2} \rvert + max\left(0,0001 + \frac{a.r - b.r}{b.r}\right)$
$NTPP^{-1}(a,b)$	constraint of $NTPP(b,a)$
$EQ(a,b)$	$d(a.c, b.c) + \lvert a.r - b.r \rvert$
$radius(a) = r$	$\lvert a.r - r \rvert$
$\varphi \vee \psi$	$min(obj(\varphi), obj(\psi))$

Fig. 3. Objective functions

Now, a formula is evaluated according to an objective function $obj : \mathcal{L} \to \mathbb{R}$, defined by induction on φ as given in figure 3. Now we interpret obj over models $\mathcal{M}$. We note $obj(\varphi)_{\mathcal{M}}$ the value obtained in $\mathcal{M}$.

Proposition 2. *If $obj(\varphi)_{\mathcal{M}} = 0$, then $\mathcal{M} \models \varphi$.*

Note that one could have chosen other objective functions than proposition 2. Those objective functions have been chosen experimentally so that the local search algorithm described in the next section works.

4   Local Search

Given a problem instance $I = \langle \varphi_1, \ldots, \varphi_n \rangle$, we use a local search approach to determine an Euler diagram respecting the constraints of I. Generally speaking, local search constitutes a simple optimization approach which improves iteratively the current solution based on a neighborhood relation [10]. In our case, the local search algorithm explores the search space Ω of possible drawings $\mathcal{M}$ of a set of circles with the purpose of finding a feasible drawing satisfying the predicates (constraints) of the given formula. The pseudo-code is defined as follows:

$$\mathcal{M} := \text{generate randomly a drawing}$$
$$\textbf{while true do}$$
$$\quad \mathcal{M}_{new} := getSolutionInNeighborhood(\mathcal{M})$$
$$\quad \textbf{if } \mathcal{M}_{new} \text{ is better than } \mathcal{M} \textbf{ then}$$
$$\quad\quad \mathcal{M} := \mathcal{M}_{new}$$

The algorithm never stops and keeps improving the current solution $\mathcal{M}$. To represent a model $\mathcal{M}$ (i.e. a drawing), $\mathcal{M}$ is considered as a vector, where indices are constant symbols a and each element $\mathcal{M}[a]$ is a circle represented by its center $(\mathcal{M}[a].x, \mathcal{M}[a].y)$ and its radius $\mathcal{M}[i].r$.

The function $getSolutionInNeighborhood(\mathcal{M})$ returns a new solution $\mathcal{M}_{new}$, where for all constant symbols a, $\mathcal{M}_{new}[a].x$, $\mathcal{M}_{new}[a].y$, $\mathcal{M}_{new}[a].r$ are respectively obtained by adding randomly chosen numbers in an interval $[-\epsilon, \epsilon]$ to respectively $\mathcal{M}[a].x$, $\mathcal{M}[a].y$, $\mathcal{M}[a].r$. That is, a new drawing is obtained by moving every circle center from its current position to a new position and modifying slightly each radius (this move operator defines thus the neighborhood relation of our local search algorithm).

Solutions are compared with the following total order.

Definition 2. *Given two candidate solutions (drawings) $\mathcal{M}, \mathcal{M}_{new} \in \Omega$, $\mathcal{M}_{new}$ is better than $\mathcal{M}$ if $\sum_{i=1}^{n} obj(\varphi_i)_{\mathcal{M}_{new}} \leq \sum_{i=1}^{n} obj(\varphi_i)_{\mathcal{M}}$, where $obj(\varphi_i)_{\mathcal{M}}$ and $obj(\varphi_i)_{\mathcal{M}_{new}}$ are the values of the objective function $obj(\varphi_i)$ that corresponds to the ith constraint φ_i for respectively $\mathcal{M}_{new}$ and $\mathcal{M}$.*

5   Implementation

Our local search algorithm available as a web application written in Javascript can be found here: http://www.irisa.fr/prive/fschwarz/constrainteddrawing.

5.1   Syntax Used in The Software

The user can add circles and constraints by clicking on the appropriate buttons in the palette. Let us describe the syntax we use in the software to define circles and constraints. In the left part of the screen, the user adds a circle by writing `circle(name);` where name is a string for the name of the circle. Constraints are created with functions. For instance `TPP(name1, name2)` creates a *TPP* constraints between the circle named name1 and the circle named name2. The construction or(constraint1, constraint2) returns a constraint that represents the disjunction of constraint1 and constraint2. The construction addConstraint(constraint) adds the constraint constraint in the set of constraints.

5.2   Interaction

The user may *assist* the local search. During the local search, the user can move the circles by drag and drop and modify the radius of each circle. When the user makes a modification in the drawing, she directly modifies the current model $\mathcal{M}$. Those modifications are directly taken in account in real-time by the local search algorithm.

6   Related Work

6.1   Region Connection Calculus

RCC-8 [11] is a first order logic for spatial reasoning. Contrary to the version we adopt in this article, variables are interpreted by regions of an abstract topological space. The satisfiability problem of a first order formula given in **RCC-8** is undecidable, more precisely not recursively enumerable [7].

Nevertheless, the satisfiability problem, called RSAT, of a formula of the form $\exists x_1, \ldots \exists x_n, \bigwedge_{i,j \in \{1, \ldots n\}} \bigvee_{R \in C(i,j)} R(x_i, x_j)$ where n is a positive integer, $C(i,j)$ a subset of $\mathbb{REL}_{\textbf{RCC-8}}$, is NP-complete [12].

The satisfiability problem for **RCC-8** formulas over *disc-homeomorphs* is NP-complete [14,13]. We should have emphasized that the problem addressed in our paper is not about disc-homeomorphs but about discs. We here tackle the satisfiability problem for **RCC-8** formulas over *discs* its exact complexity is still an open problem (see proposition 1). An extension of **RCC-8** with Boolean operations over sets has been studied in [6]. Soft semantics for **RCC-8** are also given in [15,18].

6.2   Constrained Graph Drawing

Drawing with Constraint. Constraints have long been used for graph drawing. Generally, the positions of constrained objects to draw can be computed in polynomial time. For instance, in drawing software like Geogebra, one may state, for example, that Δ_1 contains point A and is orthogonal to line Δ_2 [5]. Similarly, in a graphical user interface library, the layout is computed from easily solvable constraints as 'the window is horizontally separated in two parts. The first part is a textbox. The second contains three buttons displayed vertically'. For these systems, various layout algorithms have been studied [2,8]. Finally, there exist tools to compute nice graphical representations of graphs [1,3]. Displaying graphs consists in solving constraints such as two connected nodes are close and two different edges do not cross.

Bottom-Up Approach for Drawing Euler Diagrams. The visualization tool Tulip integrates a functionality for Euler diagrams [17]. The input of this system is given by an extensive description of the elements of sets. For instance, the following can be a possible input:

$$P := \{path, linearprog\}$$
$$NP := \{path, linearprog, intlinearprog, sat\}$$
$$coNP := \{path, linearprog, intlinearprog, valid\}$$

Tulip is a 'bottom-up' approach. It considers the elements (in the example, elements are *path*, *linearprog*, etc.) as nodes in a graph constrained by the set-theoretical relations (in the example, $P \subseteq NP$, etc.). Tulip displays the graph and extracts an Euler diagram from it. The shape of a region corresponding to a set (for instance P) is delimited by the positions of the elements in that set (for instance, *path* and *linearprog*). Thus, the shape can be arbitrary and the diagram may be difficult to read. A similar approach can be found in [21].

On the contrary, our approach is 'top-down'. The shape of the region are circles. We do not specify elements that are in sets. Furthermore, contrary to Tulip, our framework can be extended to capture constraints as 'the radius of the disc representing NP is $10cm$'.

Other top-down Approaches for Euler Diagrams. The authors of [4] describe a software tool for Euler diagrams which are made up of circles (see the site: http://www.eulerdiagrams.com/software.htm). Their algorithm is based on the theory of piercings [19] and is able to draw nice diagrams. Yet, their approach does not capture topological constraints as TPP (circle a is a tangential proper part of b) and the size of circles are not easily adjustable. Very recently, another interesting tool is presented in [9] which is able to draw not only circles, but also ellipses.

Compared to these tools, our approach distinguishes itself by some interesting features. First, our tool is based on the **RCC-8** language which enables both precise and rich constraint specifications. For instance, our tool allows the specification of topological constraints. Second, one can specify the radius of circles, and our system can then adjust dynamically these radius for a better visualization. Last but not least, in our approach, the user can always modify the drawing by moving and resizing circles and the system will adjust the drawing accordingly and adaptively.

7   Conclusion

This study makes the bridge between logical framework **RCC-8**, generation of Euler diagrams (and more generally drawings under constraints), as well as heuristic search.

A first extension is to add a large collection of elements in addition of circles (rectangles, splines, etc.). Then an interesting perspective is to combine constraints that do not require search (for instance constraints of Geogebra, or tractable fragments of **RCC-8** [12]) and constraints that require search. That is, the tool should be able to choose how to solve the constraints by detecting which method to apply and on which part of the drawing.

Another perspective is to improve the graphical interface. From a better graphical interface, we can start to make the tool tested by users and do experimental validations (can users write constraints they need? do users feel as if the tool understands their constraints?).

Finally, it would be interesting to integrate default reasoning in the tool. For instance the sole constraint P TPP NP (tangential proper part) should avoid the radius of P to be too small. This may be solved by using default reasoning: *by default*, P TPP NP implies that the radius of P is approximately the half of the radius of NP.

Another interesting research problem concerns the axiomatization. Is there an axiomation of **RCC-8** where objects are circles? Having an axiomatization may help us to improve the software so that it could give explanations for the generated drawings.

References

1. Auber, D.: Tulip a huge graph visualization framework. In: Graph Drawing Software, pp. 105–126. Springer (2004)
2. Borning, A., Marriott, K., Stuckey, P.J., Xiao, Y.: Solving linear arithmetic constraints for user interface applications. In: ACM Symposium on User Interface Software and Technology, pp. 87–96 (1997)
3. Ellson, J., Gansner, E.R., Koutsofios, E., North, S.C., Woodhull, G.: Graphviz and dynagraph static and dynamic graph drawing tools. In: Graph Drawing Software, pp. 127–148. Springer (2004)
4. Flower, J., Howse, J.: Generating euler diagrams. In: Hegarty, M., Meyer, B., Narayanan, N.H. (eds.) Diagrams 2002. LNCS (LNAI), vol. 2317, pp. 61–75. Springer, Heidelberg (2002)
5. Hohenwarter, M., Preiner, J.: Dynamic mathematics with geogebra. Journal of Online Mathematics and its Applications, 7 (2007)
6. Kontchakov, R., Nenov, Y., Pratt-Hartmann, I., Zakharyaschev, M.: On the decidability of connectedness constraints in 2d and 3d euclidean spaces. In: IJCAI Proceedings-International Joint Conference on Artificial Intelligence, vol. 22, p. 957 (2011)
7. Lutz, C., Wolter, F.: Modal logics of topological relations. Logical Methods in Computer Science 2, 1–14 (2006)
8. Marriott, K., Moulder, P., Stuckey, P.J.: Solving disjunctive constraints for interactive graphical applications. In: Walsh, T. (ed.) CP 2001. LNCS, vol. 2239, pp. 361–376. Springer, Heidelberg (2001)
9. Micallef, L., Rodgers, P.: Drawing area-proportional venn-3 diagrams using ellipses. In: 2012 Grace Hopper Celebration of Women in Computing, ACM Student Research Competition and Poster Session. ACM Press (2012)
10. Papadimitriou, C.H.: Computational complexity. John Wiley and Sons Ltd. (2003)
11. Randell, D.A., Cui, Z., Cohn, A.G.: A spatial logic based on regions and connection. KR 92, 165–176 (1992)
12. Renz, J., Nebel, B.: On the complexity of qualitative spatial reasoning: A maximal tractable fragment of the region connection calculus. Artificial Intelligence 108(1), 69–123 (1999)
13. Schaefer, M., Sedgwick, E., Štefankovič, D.: Recognizing string graphs in np. Journal of Computer and System Sciences 67(2), 365–380 (2003)
14. Schaefer, M., Stefankovic, D.: Decidability of string graphs. In: Proceedings of the Thirty-Third Annual ACM Symposium on Theory of Computing, pp. 241–246. ACM (2001)
15. Schockaert, S., De Cock, M., Kerre, E.E.: Spatial reasoning in a fuzzy region connection calculus. Artificial Intelligence 173(2), 258–298 (2009)
16. Schwarzentruber, F., Hao, J.-K.: Drawing euler diagrams from region connection calculus specifications. Technical report
17. Simonetto, P., Auber, D., Archambault, D.: Fully automatic visualisation of overlapping sets. In: Computer Graphics Forum, vol. 28, pp. 967–974. Wiley Online Library (2009)

18. Sridhar, M., Cohn, A.G., Hogg, D.C.: From video to rcc8: exploiting a distance based semantics to stabilise the interpretation of mereotopological relations. In: Egenhofer, M., Giudice, N., Moratz, R., Worboys, M. (eds.) COSIT 2011. LNCS, vol. 6899, pp. 110–125. Springer, Heidelberg (2011)
19. Stapleton, G., Zhang, L., Howse, J., Rodgers, P.: Drawing euler diagrams with circles: The theory of piercings. IEEE Trans. Vis. Comput. Graph. 17(7), 1020–1032 (2011)
20. Van Harmelen, F., Lifschitz, V., Porter, B.: Handbook of knowledge representation, vol. 1. Elsevier (2008)
21. Verroust, A., Viaud, M.-L.: Ensuring the drawability of extended euler diagrams for up to 8 sets. In: Blackwell, A.F., Marriott, K., Shimojima, A. (eds.) Diagrams 2004. LNCS (LNAI), vol. 2980, pp. 128–141. Springer, Heidelberg (2004)

Probabilistic Abstract Dialectical Frameworks

Sylwia Polberg[1],* and Dragan Doder[2],**

[1] Vienna University of Technology, Institute of Information Systems
Favoritenstraße 9-11, 1040 Vienna, Austria
[2] University of Luxembourg, Computer Science and Communications
Rue Richard Coudenhove-Kalergi 6, L-1359 Luxembourg

Abstract. Although Dung's frameworks are widely approved tools for abstract argumentation, their abstractness makes expressing notions such as support or uncertainty very difficult. Thus, many of their generalizations were created, including the probabilistic argumentation frameworks (PrAFs) and the abstract dialectical frameworks (ADFs). While the first allow modeling uncertain arguments and attacks, the latter can handle various dependencies between arguments. Although the actual probability layer in PrAFs is independent of the chosen semantics, new relations pose new challenges and new interpretations of what is the probability of a relation. Thus, the methodology for handling uncertainties cannot be shifted to more general structures without any further thought. In this paper we show how ADFs are extended with probabilities.

Keywords: Abstract argumentation, abstract dialectical frameworks, probabilistic argumentation frameworks.

1 Introduction

Within the last decade, argumentation has emerged as a central field of Artificial Intelligence [1]. One of its subfields is the abstract argumentation, at the heart of which lies the Dung's argumentation framework (AF) [2]. Although quite powerful, for many applications Dung's AFs appear too abstract in order to conveniently model all aspects of an argumentation problem. This has led to the development of their numerous enrichments [3]. One of AF's shortcomings is the insufficient handling of the levels of uncertainty [4], an aspect which typically occurs in domains, where diverging opinions are raised. This calls for augmenting AFs with probabilities [4,5]. They serve as a basis to generate AF–subgraphs, which naturally represent the possible situations induced by the uncertainties in a given probabilistic framework (PrAF). From them we obtain extensions and their associated uncertainty coming from the subgraphs. Consequently, the uncertainty layer is independent of the underlying semantics and of the framework itself, which is considered one of its greatest strengths.

* The author is supported by the Vienna PhD School of Informatics and the FWF project I1102. We would also like to thank Stefan Woltran for his valuable comments.
** The author is supported by the National Research Fund (FNR) of Luxembourg through project PRIMAT.

E. Fermé and J. Leite (Eds.): JELIA 2014, LNAI 8761, pp. 591–599, 2014.

Argument and attack uncertainties had proved to be a useful concept. There-fore, it is not unreasonable that an AF enrichment should also incorporate them [6]. Due to the independency of the probability layer, it was claimed that it can be done easily [5]. However, it is natural to expect that the probability of a positive relation between the arguments may be interpreted in different ways. While we may doubt if e.g. a positive interaction between a and b will be carried out, we can also question whether b requires a (or only a) to hold. Thus, the con-ditions for accepting an argument might be uncertain. Those two interpretations of relation probabilities are modeled in exactly the opposite way. Assuming that the relation does not occur, in the first case b would not be acceptable, while in the latter it would not be a problem. Generating the subgraphs in the usual manner would allow us to model only one of the scenarios at a time. Thus, new relations pose new challenges and this research should not be dismissed so easily.

Unfortunately, AFs permit only binary conflict. Among the most general structures addressing this issue [3] are abstract dialectical frameworks (ADFs) [7]. They assign acceptance conditions to arguments, which can be seen as a Boolean functions stating if its "owner" can be accepted or not w.r.t. given ar-guments. Although various other frameworks that can handle positive relations were proposed [8–10], our preliminary findings show that they can be expressed within ADFs. Thus, ADFs make a good base for probabilistic frameworks that would allow us to model various uncertain relations, not limited to attack or support only. In this paper we create a framework joining both the uncertainty and the relation research – the probabilistic abstract dialectical framework. We show that it generalizes ADFs as well as PrAFs. Our goal is to model situations when the requirements to accept an argument might be uncertain. We achieve it by assigning not a single acceptance condition to an argument, but a number of them. We then adopt the subgraph approach to our new setting. Consequently, we are able to generalize the methodology introduced by PrAFs to handle dif-ferent interpretations of probability. Finally, we discuss other possible methods of augmenting ADFs with uncertainties and give pointers for future work.

2   Dung's Framework and its Probabilistic Extensions

Definition 1. *A* ***Dung's argumentation framework*** *(AF) is a pair* $F = \langle A, R \rangle$ *where* A *is a set of arguments and* $R \subseteq A \times A$ *is the attack relation.*

An argument $a \in A$ *is* ***defended*** *(in F) by* $S \subseteq A$ *if* $\forall b \in A$ *s.t.* $(b, a) \in R$, $\exists c \in S$ *s.t.* $(c, b) \in R$. *A set* $S \subseteq A$ *is:*
- ***conflict–free***, *if there are no* $a, b \in S$, *such that* $(a, b) \in R$.
- ***stable***, *if it is conflict–free and for all* $a \in A \setminus S$, $\exists b \in S$, *s.t.*$(b, a) \in R$;
- ***admissible***, *if it is conflict–free and each* $a \in S$ *is defended (in F) by* S;
- ***complete***, *if it is admissible and each* a *defended (in F) by* S *is in* S;
- ***grounded***, *if it is the least w.r.t.* $\subseteq$ *complete;*
- ***preferred***, *if it is maximal w.r.t.* $\subseteq$ *admissible.*

By $\sigma(F)$ *we will denote the extensions of* F *under semantics* σ *listed above.*

For an AF $F = (A, R)$ and a set $A' \subseteq A$, by $R_{A'}$ we denote the restriction of R to $A' \times A'$, i.e. $R_{A'} = \{(a, b) \in R \mid a, b \in A'\}$.

We will now recall the probabilistic frameworks [5]. In this setting, instead of asking if a set of arguments is an extension of a given semantics, one now expects to analyze the probability that it is. This is addressed by the idea of subgraphs, which express the possible interpretations of the original probabilistic framework F_{PR} in terms of AFs, whereby it is not sure that all arguments or attacks in F_{PR} actually appear in a given AF. The collection of such graphs represents the possible scenarios induced by the probabilities in the initial structure.

Definition 2. *A **probabilistic argumentation framework** (PrAF) F_{PR} is a tuple $\langle A, R, P_A, P_R \rangle$, where $\langle A, R \rangle$ is a Dung's framework, $P_A : A \longrightarrow (0,1]$ and $P_R : R \longrightarrow (0,1]$ are the probabilities of arguments and attacks.*

Definition 3. *Let $F_{PR} = (A, R, P_A, P_R)$ be a PrAF. A **subgraph** [1] G of F_{PR} (denoted $G \sqsubseteq F_{PR}$) is a pair (A', R') s.t. 1) $A' \subseteq A$ and $\{a \in A \mid P_A(a) = 1\} \subseteq A'$, and 2) $R' \subseteq R_{A'}$ and $\{(a,b) \in R \mid a,b \in A', P_A(a) = P_A(b) = 1, P_R(a,b) = 1\} \subseteq R'$. $s(F_{PR}) = \{G \mid G \sqsubseteq F_{PR}\}$ denotes the set of all subgraphs of F_{PR}.*

Given a semantics σ and its potential extension E, we determine the subgraphs of an F_{PR} that have E as their AF σ–extension. The sum of the probabilities of such subgraphs gives us the final probability that E is a σ–extension of F_{PR}.

Definition 4 ([5]). *Let $F_{PR} = \langle A, R, P_A, P_R \rangle$ be a PrAF and let $G = \langle A', R' \rangle \sqsubseteq F_{PR}$. Then the probability of G is:*

$$p_{F_{PR}}(G) = (\prod_{a \in A'} P(a))(\prod_{a \in A \setminus A'} (1 - P(a)))(\prod_{r \in R'} P_R(r))(\prod_{r \in R_{A'} \setminus R'} (1 - P_R(r))). \quad (1)$$

Theorem 1 ([5]). *The function $p_{F_{PR}}$ is a probabilistic distribution on the set $s(F_{PR})$, i.e., a nonnegative function s.t. $\sum_{G \sqsubseteq F_{PR}} p_{F_{PR}}(G) = 1$.*

Definition 5. *Let $F_{PR} = \langle A, R, P_A, P_R \rangle$ be a PrAF, $E \subseteq A$ a set of arguments, and $\sigma \in \{conflict\text{-}free, admissible, complete, preferred, stable, grounded\}$ a semantics. The set of subgraphs of F_{PR} for which E is a σ-extension is $Q^{\sigma}_{F_{PR}}(E) = \{G \in s(F_{PR}) \mid E \in \sigma(G)\}$. The probability that $E \subseteq A$ is in $\sigma(F_{PR})$ is defined as:*[2]

$$P^{\sigma}_{F_{PR}}(E) = \sum_{G \in Q^{\sigma}_{F_{PR}}(E)} p_{F_{PR}}(G). \quad (2)$$

3 Abstract Dialectical Frameworks

Abstract dialectical frameworks have been defined in [7] and further developed in [11–16]. Their main goal is to be able to express arbitrary relations, which is achieved by the use of acceptance conditions. They define what sets of arguments related to a given argument should be present for it to be accepted or rejected.

---

[1] In [5], subgraphs are called AFs induced from F_{PR}

[2] The definition from [5] is more general, it computes the probability that a set is a subset of a σ extension.

Definition 6. *An **abstract dialectical framework** (ADF) as a tuple $\langle S, L, C \rangle$, where S is a set of **arguments** (nodes), $L \subseteq S \times S$ is a set of **links** (edges) and $C = \{C_s\}_{s \in S}$ is a set of **acceptance conditions**, one condition per each argument. An **acceptance condition** is given by a total function $C_s : 2^{par(s)} \rightarrow \{in, out\}$, where $par(s) = \{p \in S \mid (p, s) \in L\}$ is the set of **parents** of s.*

One can also use the propositional representation, i.e. with $C = \{\varphi_s\}_{s \in S}$ where φ_s is a propositional formula over the parents of s. Since the links no longer define the nature of the connections between the arguments and can be easily extracted from the conditions, we can use shortened notation $D = \langle S, C \rangle$.

Instead of returning sets of accepted arguments, the semantics of ADFs from [11] produce three–valued interpretations in which arguments are assigned truth–values from $\{\mathbf{t}, \mathbf{f}, \mathbf{u}\}$. The values are compared w.r.t. precision (information) ordering $\leq_i$, defined as $\mathbf{u} \leq_i \mathbf{t}$ and $\mathbf{u} \leq_i \mathbf{f}$. It can be extended to interpretations: given two interpretations v and v' on S, $v \leq_i v'$ iff $\forall_{s \in S} v(s) \leq_i v'(s)$. In case v is three and v' two–valued (i.e. has only $\mathbf{f}$ and $\mathbf{t}$ mappings), we say that v' *extends* v. The set of all two–valued interpretations extending v is denoted $[v]_2$. The pair $(\{\mathbf{t}, \mathbf{f}, \mathbf{u}\}, \leq_i)$ forms a complete meet–semilattice with the meet operation $\sqcap$ defined as: $\mathbf{t} \sqcap \mathbf{t} = \mathbf{t}$, $\mathbf{f} \sqcap \mathbf{f} = \mathbf{f}$ and $\mathbf{u}$ in all other cases. $\sqcap$ can also be defined for interpretations: for interpretations v and v' on S, $v \sqcap v' = v''$ where $\forall_{s \in S} v''(s) = v(s) \sqcap v'(s)$. Meet simply checks whether two interpretations agree on assignments or not. Finally, we will use v^x to denote a set of arguments mapped to x by v, where $x \in \{\mathbf{t}, \mathbf{f}, \mathbf{u}\}$. We can now recall the ADF semantics from [11], which are based on the notion of a characteristic operator:

Definition 7. *Let $D = \langle S, L, C \rangle$ with $C = \{\varphi_s\}_{s \in S}$ be an ADF, V_S the set of all three–valued interpretations defined on S, $s \in S$ and v an interpretation in V_S. The **three–valued characteristic operator** of D is a function $\Gamma_D : V_S \rightarrow V_S$ s.t. $\Gamma_D(v) = v'$ with $v'(s) = \bigsqcap_{w \in [v]_2} C_s(par(s) \cap w^{\mathbf{t}})$. We say that v is:*

- *— **admissible** iff $v \leq_i \Gamma_D(v)$;*
- *— **complete** iff $v = \Gamma_D(v)$;*
- *— **preferred** iff it is $\leq_i$–maximal admissible;*
- *— **grounded** iff it is the least fixpoint of Γ_D.*

The stable semantics is a slightly different case, as formally we receive a set, not an interpretation. However, stability leaves nothing undecided, and we can just map arguments not in the set to $\mathbf{f}$. The definition uses the concept of a reduct. Reduction of an acceptance condition simply means that the occurrences of rejected arguments are replaced by $\mathbf{f}$ (one can also use $\bot$).

Definition 8. *Let $D = \langle S, C \rangle$ with $C = \{\varphi_s\}_{s \in S}$ be an ADF. We say that $M \subseteq S$ is a **model** of D iff $\forall m \in M, C_m(S \cap par(m)) = in$ and $\forall s \in S, C_s(M \cap par(s)) = in$ implies $s \in M$. A **reduct** of D w.r.t. M is $D^M = (M, C^M)$, where for $m \in M$ we set $C_m^M = \varphi_m[b/\mathbf{f} : b \notin M]$. Let gv be the grounded model of D^M. Model M is **stable** iff $M = gv^{\mathbf{t}}$.*

Finally, we recall that ADFs properly generalize AFs [11].

Definition 9. *For an $F = \langle A, R \rangle$, the associated ADF is $D_F = \langle A, R, \{\varphi_a\}_{a \in A} \rangle$ with $\varphi_a = \bigwedge_{b:(b,a) \in R} \neg b$ for $a \in A$. For an interpretation v, the set $E_v = \{a \in A \mid v(a) = \mathbf{t}\}$ defines the unique extension associated with v.*

Theorem 2. *Let F be an AF and D_F its associated ADF. An extension E is in $\sigma(F)$, where $\sigma \in \{admissible, complete, preferred, stable, grounded\}$, iff it is in $\sigma(D_F)$.*

4 Probabilistic Abstract Dialectical Frameworks

The probability of a positive interaction between arguments can be interpreted in several ways. First of all, it can happen that a given argument is actually supporting another one only with a certain probability, which can have its source in e.g. ambiguity or incompletion. However, it is also possible that the requirements to accept a given argument change. This brings us to the idea of ADFs in which the acceptance conditions are assigned a level of uncertainty. In order to grasp the probabilities of different scenarios, instead of a single condition, an argument receives a block of acceptance conditions. Each member of the block is assigned a probability in a way that they all sum up to 1. The uncertainty of a condition should be understood as the uncertainty of the argument's requirements for acceptance. This also means that at a given point, only a single condition of a block can "happen". However, it does not mean that only one relation targeted at this argument can occur. If we consider an AF and its associated ADF (Definition 9), both augmented with probabilities, it is not the case that every condition and its probability would correspond to one attack and its probability in the original framework. ADF conditions provide a bigger point of view and express the general requirements of an argument to hold. Given an argument attacked by two others (with some probabilities), ADFs would model the situation with four conditions – when both, none, and only one of the attacks occur.

The idea of our method of determining the probability of an extension is similar to the one in PrAFs. Just like in PrAFs we generated AF subgraphs, in probabilistic ADFs we will create ADFs. This brings us to another reason why the total probability of a condition block has to be 1. In PrAFs, if we knew that a attacks b with a chance 0.3, then we also knew that a does not attack b with a chance 0.7. In ADFs, should a given acceptance condition be used with probability 0.3, what condition should occur with 0.7? The state of an argument is always defined by the condition, thus on any occasion one has to be assigned. Consequently, it is important that the total probability of a block is 1.

Let us now describe our party example and introduce the framework. We can observe that ADFs can express relations between arguments (see argument d) which go beyond the usual understanding of attack or support and that cannot, to the best of our knowledge, be conveniently modeled in any other framework.

Example 1. Julia is throwing a dinner party and is deciding with her husband Mark which of their friends – Anne, Bernard, Cecilia and David – to invite. Bernard and Cecilia are taking care of their sick mother and the two of them will not be able to come at the same time. Mark was told that Anne had to reject one of Bernard's projects at work and he might not want to meet with her now. Julia believes that David is still angry at Cecilia for their bad break up and will not come if she is invited unless Anne, who is his current girlfriend, also shows up. However, Mark thinks that David is fine with it now and Cecilia's presence should not be a problem, but he might prefer to come with Anne anyway since she is leaving for a business trip soon. Finally, they both agree that even though Anne would like to come, she might not be able to due to the travel preparations. We now construct arguments a, b, c and d representing Anne, Bernard, Cecilia and David coming to the dinner, and their possible acceptance conditions. The condition of a is just $\top$, since Anne's decision does not depend on anyone else. However, since she is busy, a is assigned a probability of 0.5. The condition of b might be just $\neg c$ – since Bernard cannot come together with Cecilia – but it can also be $\neg a \wedge \neg c$ due to issues with Anne. We give both of them a 0.5 chance. Similarly, c is assigned $\neg b$. Finally, we have that condition of d might be $a \vee \neg c$, reflecting Davids problem with Cecilia, or just a in case he sorted it out and just wants time with Anne. We assign to them probabilities 0.7 and 0.3 respectively.

Definition 10. *A **probabilistic abstract dialectical framework** (PrADF) is a tuple $D_{PR} = \langle A, \{C_a\}_{a \in A}, P_A, \{P_{C_a}\}_{a \in A}\rangle$, where A is a set of **arguments**, $C_a = \{\varphi_{a,i} \mid i = 1, \ldots, n_a\}$ is a set of possible **acceptance conditions** of a, $P_A : A \to (0, 1]$ is the **probability of arguments** and $P_{C_a} : C_a \to (0, 1]$ s.t. $\sum_{\varphi_{a,i} \in C_a} P_C(\varphi_{a,i}) = 1$, is the **probability of acceptance conditions**.*

We can now continue with the definition of a subframework in our new setting. We first choose an arbitrary subset of arguments – the only restriction is that it contains the ones that are certain to happen. We then assign each argument an acceptance condition from its block and thus obtain our subframework. However, it can happen that an argument occurring in the condition no longer appears in our set. Therefore, what needs to be performed is the reduction of the conditions (see Definition 8). This brings us to the definition of a subframework:

Definition 11. *Let $D_{PR} = \langle A, \{C_a\}_{a \in A}, P_A, \{P_{C_a}\}_{a \in A}\rangle$ be a PrADF and $A' \subseteq A$ a set of arguments s.t. $\{a \in A \mid P_A(a) = 1\} \subseteq A'$. Given a collection of indices $\{i_a\}_{a \in A'}$, the induced **subframework** is $D' = \langle A', \{\varphi_{a,i_a}^{A'}\}_{a \in A'}\rangle$. The set of all subframeworks of D_{PR} is denoted by $s(D_{PR})$.*

Note that it is possible that two acceptance conditions of an argument a that are initially different in a PrADF, i.e. $\varphi_{a,i} \neq \varphi_{a,j}$ for some $j \neq i$, become equivalent in some subframework $D' = \langle A', \{\varphi_{a,i}^{A'}\}_{a \in A'}\rangle$ (i.e. $\varphi_{a,i}^{A'} = \varphi_{a,j}^{A'}$ [3]). Thus, the definition of the probability of D' has to take this situation into account.

Definition 12. *Let $D_{PR} = \langle A, \{C_a\}_{a \in A}, P_A, \{P_{C_a}\}_{a \in A}\rangle$ be a PrADF and $D' = \langle A', \{\varphi_{a,i_a}^{A'}\}_{a \in A'}\rangle$ its subframework. The probability of D' is defined as:*

$$p_{D_{PR}}(D') = \Big(\prod_{a \in A'} P_A(a)\Big)\Big(\prod_{a \in A \setminus A'} (1 - P_A(a))\Big)\Big(\prod_{a \in A'} \sum_{j : \varphi_{a,j}^{A'} = \varphi_{a,i}^{A'}} P_{C_a}(\varphi_{a,j})\Big). \quad (3)$$

---

[3] We identify the equivalent formulas, since they induce the same acceptance functions.

Theorem 3. *Given a PrADF $D_{PR} = \langle A, \{C_a\}_{a \in A}, P_A, \{P_{C_a}\}_{a \in A}\rangle$, the function $p_{D_{PR}}$ is a probabilistic distribution on the set $s(D_{PR})$, i.e., a nonnegative function s.t. $\sum_{D' \in s(D_{PR})} p_{D_{PR}}(D') = 1$.*

We will now proceed with PrADF semantics, focusing on the extensions associated with ADF interpretations.

Definition 13. *Let $D_{PR} = \langle A, \{C_a\}_{a \in A}, P_A, \{P_{C_a}\}_{a \in A}\rangle$ be a PrADF and $E \subseteq A$. The set of all subframeworks D' of D_{PR} s.t. E is a σ extension of D_{PR}, where $\sigma \in \{admissible, complete, preferred, stable, grounded\}$, is:*

$$Q_{D_{PR}}^\sigma(E) = \{D' \sqsubseteq D_{PR} \mid \exists v \in \sigma(D') \text{ s.t. } v^t = E\}. \tag{4}$$

The probability that E is a σ-extension of D_{PR} is defined as:

$$P_{D_{PR}}^\sigma(E) = \sum_{D' \in Q_{D_{PR}}^\sigma(E)} p_{D_{PR}}(D'). \tag{5}$$

Example 2. Let us now construct a PrADF D for our scenario from Example 1. Our arguments are $\{a, b, c, d\}$, where $P_A(a) = 0.5$ and since there are no reasons against, $P_A(b) = P_A(c) = P_A(d) = 1$. As discussed before, $\varphi_a = \top$. This is the only condition of a and thus $P_{C_a}(\varphi_a) = 1$. For b we have $\varphi_{b_1} = \neg c$ and $\varphi_{b_2} = \neg a \wedge \neg c$ with probabilities $P_{C_b}(\varphi_{b_1}) = P_{C_b}(\varphi_{b_2}) = 0.5$. In the case of c, $\varphi_c = \neg b$ and has chance of 1 just like a. Finally, for d we have $\varphi_{d_1} = a \vee \neg c$ and $\varphi_{d_2} = a$ with chances $P_{C_d}(\varphi_{d_1}) = 0.7$ and $P_{C_d}(\varphi_{d_2}) = 0.3$. We obtain 6 possible subframeworks: $D_{G_1} = \langle\{a, b, c, d\}, \{\varphi_a = \top, \varphi_b = \neg c, \varphi_c = \neg b, \varphi_d = a\}\rangle$, $D_{G_2} = \langle\{a, b, c, d\}, \{\varphi_a = \top, \varphi_b = \neg a \wedge \neg c, \varphi_c = \neg b, \varphi_d = a\}\rangle$, $D_{G_3} = \langle\{b, c, d\}, \{\varphi_b = \neg c, \varphi_c = \neg b, \varphi_d = \neg c\}\rangle$, $D_{G_4} = \langle\{a, b, c, d\}, \{\varphi_a = \top, \varphi_b = \neg a \wedge \neg c, \varphi_c = \neg b, \varphi_d = a \vee \neg c\}\rangle$, $D_{G_5} = \langle\{a, b, c, d\}, \{\varphi_a = \top, \varphi_b = \neg c, \varphi_c = \neg b, \varphi_d = a \vee \neg c\}\rangle$, and $D_{G_6} = \langle\{b, c, d\}, \{\varphi_b = \neg c, \varphi_c = \neg b, \varphi_d = \bot\}\rangle$. Their probabilities and extension are listed in Table 1. Note D_{G_3} and D_{G_6} can be induced in two ways, as reducing φ_{b_1} and φ_{b_2} w.r.t. $\{b, c, d\}$ leads to equivalent formulas.

As expected, there is no possibility of inviting everyone. The next options in which we get the most friends are extensions $\{a, b, d\}$ and $\{a, c, d\}$. The first one has probability $p_D(D_{G_1}) + p_D(D_{G_5}) = 0.25$ if we assume preferred or complete semantics, but 0 in case of grounded. The other set occurs in $D_{G_1}, D_{G_2}, D_{G_4}$ and D_{G_5}, which yields probability 0.25 w.r.t. grounded semantics and 0.5 otherwise. Inviting just Anne and David, i.e. $\{a, d\}$, would have a chance of 0.5 in admissible semantics ($D_{G_1}, D_{G_2}, D_{G_4}$ and D_{G_5}), 0.25 in complete and grounded (D_{G_1} and D_{G_5}), and would not be possible at all in preferred and stable cases. Going just for the manly team - $\{b, d\}$ would give us 0 probability in the grounded case, 0.52 in admissible and 0.35 in any other.

Note that by setting argument probability to 1 and using single element acceptance condition blocks, we easily retrieve ADFs from PrADFs. We close this section by showing that PrADFs properly generalize PrAFs.

Table 1. Subframeworks of D and their extensions

$s(D)$	p_D	stb	grd	adm	prf	com
D_{G_1}	0.075	{a, b, d}, {a, c, d}	{a, d}	∅, {a}, {b}, {c},{a, b}, {a, c}, {a, d}, {a, b, d}, {a, c, d}	{a, b, d}, {a, c, d}	{a, d}, {a, b, d}, {a, c, d}
D_{G_2}	0.075	{a, c, d}	{a, c, d}	∅, {a}, {c}, {a, c}, {a, d}, {a, c, d}	{a, c, d}	{a, c, d}
D_{G_3}	0.35	{c}, {b, d}	∅	∅, {b}, {c}, {b, d}	{c}, {b, d}	∅, {c}, {b, d}
D_{G_4}	0.175	{a, c, d}	{a, c, d}	∅, {a}, {c}, {a, c}, {a, d}, {a, c, d}	{a, c, d}	{a, c, d}
D_{G_5}	0.175	{a, b, d}, {a, c, d}	{a, d}	∅, {a}, {b}, {c}, {a, b}, {a, c}, {a, d}, {b, d}, {a, b, d}, {a, c, d}	{a, b, d}, {a, c, d}	{a, d}, {a, b, d}, {a, c, d}
D_{G_6}	0.15	{b}, {c}	∅	∅, {b}, {c}	{b}, {c}	∅, {b}, {c}

Definition 14. *The PrADF associated to the PrAF* $F_{PR} = \langle A, R, P_A, P_R \rangle$ *is* $D_{F_{PR}} = \langle A, \{C_a\}_{a \in A}, P_A, \{P_{C_a} \mid a \in A\} \rangle$, *where:*
- $C_a = \{\bigwedge_{(b,a) \in R'} \neg b \mid R' \subseteq R\}$
- $P_{C_a}(\bigwedge_{(b,a) \in R'} \neg b) = (\prod_{(b,a) \in R'} P_R((b,a)))(\prod_{(b,a) \in R \setminus R'} (1 - P_R((b,a))))$

Theorem 4. *Let* $F_{PR} = \langle A, R, P_A, P_R \rangle$ *be a PrAF and let* $D_{F_{PR}}$ *be its associated PrADF. Then* $P^\sigma_{F_{PR}}(E) = P^\sigma_{D_{F_{PR}}}(E)$.

5 Discussion and Future Work

One of the most interesting observations we have made in our research is the fact that the probabilities of acceptance conditions allow us to express the probabilities of arguments. This method is unique to ADFs and is possible thanks to the fact that we can have a $\varphi_s = \bot$ condition, which is simply interpreted as s *does not exist*. Consequently, an argument–based PrADF can be transformed into an acceptance condition based one. Given an argument a assigned probability arg_1 and conditions $C_1, ..., C_n$ with probabilities $p_1, ..., p_n$, we can shift the argument uncertainty into a condition. We produce an additional formula $C_{n+1} = \bot$ with probability $1 - arg_1$ and alter the probabilities of existing conditions by multiplying them by arg_1. Consequently, PrADFs can be improved and that a simpler, cleaner formulation can be created. We would like to fully develop this idea in our future work and create an approach without the independency assumption.

A particular line of research in abstract argumentation concerns the formalization of argumentation semantics in terms of logics. A uniform logical formalization for PrAFs using probabilistic logic was already developed in [17]. We believe that this approach may be further extended in order to logically formalize PrADFs. Finally, we would like to study the complexity of PrADFs and their semantics and possibly provide an implementation.

References

1. Bench-Capon, T.J.M., Dunne, P.E.: Argumentation in artificial intelligence. Artificial Intelligence 171, 619–641 (2007)
2. Dung, P.M.: On the acceptability of arguments and its fundamental role in nonmonotonic reasoning, logic programming and n-person games. Artificial Intelligence 77, 321–358 (1995)
3. Brewka, G., Polberg, S., Woltran, S.: Generalizations of Dung frameworks and their role in formal argumentation. IEEE Intelligent Systems 29, 30–38 (2014)
4. Hunter, A.: A probabilistic approach to modelling uncertain logical arguments. International Journal of Approximate Reasoning 54, 47–81 (2013)
5. Li, H., Oren, N., Norman, T.J.: Probabilistic argumentation frameworks. In: Modgil, S., Oren, N., Toni, F. (eds.) TAFA 2011. LNCS, vol. 7132, pp. 1–16. Springer, Heidelberg (2012)
6. Li, H., Oren, N., Norman, T.J.: Relaxing independence assumptions in probabilistic argumentation. In: Proceedings of ArgMAS 2013 (2013) (forthcoming)
7. Brewka, G., Woltran, S.: Abstract dialectical frameworks. In: Lin, F., Sattler, U., Truszczyński, M. (eds.) Proceedings of the 12th International Conference on Principles of Knowledge Representation and Reasoning (KR 2010), pp. 780–785. AAAI Press (2010)
8. Cayrol, C., Lagasquie-Schiex, M.C.: Bipolarity in argumentation graphs: Towards a better understanding. International Journal of Approximate Reasoning 54, 876–899 (2013)
9. Nouioua, F.: AFs with necessities. Further semantics and labelling characterization. In: Liu, W., Subrahmanian, V.S., Wijsen, J. (eds.) SUM 2013. LNCS, vol. 8078, pp. 120–133. Springer, Heidelberg (2013)
10. Polberg, S., Oren, N.: Revisiting support in abstract argumentation systems. In: Proceedings of COMMA 2014 (forthcoming, 2014)
11. Brewka, G., Ellmauthaler, S., Strass, H., Wallner, J.P., Woltran, S.: Abstract dialectical frameworks revisited. In: Proceedings of IJCAI 2013, pp. 803–809. AAAI Press (2013)
12. Polberg, S., Wallner, J.P., Woltran, S.: Admissibility in the abstract dialectical framework. In: Leite, J., Son, T.C., Torroni, P., van der Torre, L., Woltran, S. (eds.) CLIMA XIV 2013. LNCS, vol. 8143, pp. 102–118. Springer, Heidelberg (2013)
13. Strass, H.: Approximating operators and semantics for abstract dialectical frameworks. Artificial Intelligence 205, 39–70 (2013)
14. Strass, H.: Instantiating knowledge bases in abstract dialectical frameworks. In: Leite, J., Son, T.C., Torroni, P., van der Torre, L., Woltran, S. (eds.) CLIMA XIV 2013. LNCS, vol. 8143, pp. 86–101. Springer, Heidelberg (2013)
15. Strass, H., Wallner, J.P.: Analyzing the computational complexity of abstract dialectical frameworks via approximation fixpoint theory. In: Proceedings of KR 2014, Vienna, Austria (forthcoming, 2014)
16. Polberg, S.: Extension–based semantics of abstract dialectical frameworks. Technical Report DBAI-TR-2014-85, Institute for Information Systems, Technical University of Vienna (2014)
17. Doder, D., Woltran, S.: Probabilistic argumentation frameworks – A logical approach. In: Straccia, U., Cali, A. (eds.) SUM 2014. LNCS, vol. 8720, pp. 134–147. Springer, Heidelberg (2014)

Argumentative Aggregation of Individual Opinions

Cosmina Croitoru

MPII Saarbrücken, Germany

Abstract. Over a new abstract model of aggregating individual issues – *abstract debates* – we introduce an entire class of *aggregating operators* by borrowing ideas from *Abstract Argumentation* to *Social Choice Theory*. The main goal was to introduce *rational* aggregation methods which do not satisfy the commonly used *independence condition* in Social Choice Theory. This type of *context dependent aggregation* is very natural, could be useful in many real world decision making scenarios, and the present paper provides the first theoretical investigation of it.

1 Introduction

Comparing and assessing different points of view in order to obtain *fair and rational* collective aggregation of them is the main research topic of *Social Choice Theory* (SCT) [4] having major philosophical, economic, and political significance. The most important methodological tool in SCT is the axiomatic method, pioneered by Arrow [3], and consisting in formulating normatively desirable properties of aggregation rules as *postulates* or *axioms*, in order to obtain precise characterizations of the aggregation rules that satisfy these properties. The AI developments, especially in the area of collective decision making in *Multiagent Systems*, have lead to the emergence of a new research area called *Computational Social Choice* (CSC), mainly concerned with the design and analysis of collective decision making mechanisms. If in classical SCT the objects of aggregation belong to *preferential knowledge* [5], recent developments apply the same methodology to other types of information: *beliefs* [14], *judgments* [16], *ontologies* [19], *graphs* [1, 13], and *argumentation frameworks* [8, 12].

Argumentation is a powerful mechanism for automating the decision making process of autonomous agents. Several recent works have studied the problem of accommodating ideas from CSC to Argumentation [17, 22, 20, 21, 7, 12]. Most of them rely on Dung's *Argumentation Frameworks* and their acceptability semantics [10].

In this paper, we go beyond what we have done in [9] by borrowing ideas from Abstract Argumentation Frameworks to CSC, hence in the converse direction of the above line of research on this subject. Inspired by Dung's admissibility based semantics, we consider a new interpretation of the *collective rationality*. More precisely, we introduce a novel framework for aggregating individual *opinions* expressed as pairs of disjoint sets of positive and negative positions on a given finite set of *facts*. Each opinion having a negative position on some fact *attacks* all other opinions having positive positions on this fact. The attack digraph obtained, viewed as an argumentation framework, gives rise to rational coalition formations, whose collective opinions are viewed as aggregate opinions of the society. This represents a novel *qualitative approach* to the aggregation

E. Fermé and J. Leite (Eds.): JELIA 2014, LNAI 8761, pp. 600–608, 2014.

of individual opinions contrasting the usual quantitative voting methods.Let us consider a simple mundane choice situation. The table in Figure 1 presents the available pizza toppings, $F = \{pepperoni, salami, ham, onion, olive, pineapple\}$, and the opinions on F of a group of five friends, $S = \{Anne, Bob, Cara, Dan, Elly\}$.

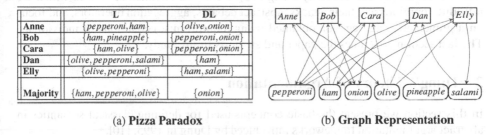

	L	DL
Anne	$\{pepperoni, ham\}$	$\{olive, onion\}$
Bob	$\{ham, pineapple\}$	$\{pepperoni, onion\}$
Cara	$\{ham, olive\}$	$\{pepperoni, onion\}$
Dan	$\{olive, pepperoni, salami\}$	$\{ham\}$
Elly	$\{olive, pepperoni\}$	$\{ham, salami\}$
Majority	$\{ham, pepperoni, olive\}$	$\{onion\}$

(a) **Pizza Paradox**   (b) **Graph Representation**

Fig. 1. A debate and its bipartite digraph representation

As we can see, *Anne* likes (agrees) *pepperoni* and *ham* but dislikes (disagrees) *olive* and *onion*. Similarly, we can read the opinions of the other members of *S*. The table is entitled **Pizza Paradox** since if we consider the *majority opinion* (obtained by including each fact in one of the two sets of liked and disliked facts using the majority rule) as output, then this has the unpleasant property that **each** *individual dislikes a topping in the collective output*: $(\{ham, pepperoni, olive\}, \{onion\})$. Note that this happens despite the majority rule gives a consistent opinion, i.e. a disjoint pair of subsets of F.

The basic idea of the *argumentative aggregation of individual opinions* is to consider *collective opinions* by merging the opinions of non-conflicting coalitions of individuals. A coalition is conflict-free if the individual's opinions in the coalition does not attack each other. Such a coalition is called an *autarky* if, in addition, has the property that the collective opinion counterattacks any attack of the opinion of an individual not in coalition. This property offers a rational justification for the output opinion.
In our example, such an autarky is $\mathscr{C}_1 = \{Bob, Cara\}$ giving the output opinion $O_{\mathscr{C}_1} = (\{ham, pineapple, olive\}, \{pepperoni, onion\})$. $O_{\mathscr{C}_1}$ attacks the opinions of *Anne*, *Dan* or *Elly* (on *pepperoni*) in response of their attacks (on *olive*, or *ham*). Another autarky is $\mathscr{C}_2 = \{Elly\}$ with her vegetarian opinion $O_{\mathscr{C}_2} = (\{olive, pepperoni\}, \{ham, salami\})$.

This kind of explanatory selection of the output opinion arises in more important choice situations, where the facts could be: ethical values; drugs to be administrated to a patient; meanings of a discourse; actions, goals, propositions in political practice.

We introduce different types of autarkies, corresponding to the admissible based extensions in abstract argumentation. In fact, we show that *any argumentation framework can be viewed as a particular abstract debate*. This implies that the time complexity of the decision problems on the abstract debates is high, often beyond NP.

In the new framework, a natural way of elimination the conflicts in a coalition gives rise to *compromise autarkies* and their collective opinions enlarge the set of opinions returned by the argumentative aggregation operators. It is proved that the argumentative aggregation operators satisfy appropriate *unanimity* and *anonymity* conditions but not the analogue of Arrow's *independence condition*. This shows that the argumentative aggregation is strongly dependent on the context: *the position of the collective opinion on a fact depends not only on the positions of individual opinions on this fact, but also depends on their position on other facts*. The rest of the paper is organized as follows. The next section presents a brief description of argumentation frameworks and their semantics, as introduced by Dung [10]. It follows the main section in which we introduce opinions and their attacks, abstract debates, aggregation operators, and focus on argumentative aggregation obtained using (compromise) coalitions of individuals. The last section concludes the paper and suggests future study.

2   Dung's Theory of Argumentation

In this section we present the basic concepts used for defining classical semantics in abstract argumentation frameworks introduced by Dung in 1995, [10].

Definition 1. An *Argumentation Framework* is a digraph $AF = (A, D)$, where A is a finite and nonempty set; the vertices in A are called *arguments*, and if $(a, b) \in D$ is a directed edge, then *argument a defeats (attacks) argument b*.

Let $AF = (A, D)$ be an argumentation framework. For each $a \in A$ we denote $a^+ = \{b \in A | \ (a, b) \in D\}$ the set of all arguments *attacked* by a, and $a^- = \{b \in A | \ (b, a) \in D\}$ the set of all arguments *attacking* a. These notations can be extended to sets of arguments. The set of all arguments *attacked by* $S \subseteq A$ is $S^+ = \bigcup_{a \in S} a^+$, and the set of all arguments *attacking* S is $S^- = \bigcup_{a \in S} a^-$. We also have $\emptyset^+ = \emptyset^- = \emptyset$.

The set S of arguments *defends* an argument $a \in A$ if $a^- \subseteq S^+$ (i.e. any a's attacker is attacked by an argument in S). The set of *all arguments defended by* a set S of arguments is denoted by $F(S)$. For $\mathbb{M} \subseteq 2^A$, $\mathbf{max}(\mathbb{M})$ denotes the set of maximal (w.r.t. set-inclusion) members of $\mathbb{M}$ and $\mathbf{min}(\mathbb{M})$ denotes the set of its minimal members.

Definition 2. Let $AF = (A, D)$ be an argumentation framework.

– A *conflict-free set* in AF is a set $S \subseteq A$ with property $S \cap S^+ = \emptyset$ (i.e. there are no attacking arguments in S). We will denote $\mathbf{cf}(AF) = \{S \subseteq A | S$ is conflict-free set $\}$.
– An *admissible set* in AF is a set $S \in \mathbf{cf}(AF)$ with property $S^- \subseteq S^+$ (i.e. defends its elements). We will denote $\mathbf{adm}(AF) = \{S \subseteq A | S$ is admissible set $\}$.
– A *complete extension* in AF is a set $S \in \mathbf{cf}(AF)$ with property $S = F(S)$. We will denote $\mathbf{comp}(AF) = \{S \subseteq A | S$ is complete extension $\}$.
– A *preferred extension* in AF is a set $S \in \mathbf{max}(\mathbf{comp}(AF))$. $\mathbf{pref}(AF) := \mathbf{max}(\mathbf{comp}(AF))$.
– A *grounded extension* in AF is a set $S \in \mathbf{min}(\mathbf{comp}(AF))$. $\mathbf{gr}(AF) := \mathbf{min}(\mathbf{comp}(AF))$.
– A *stable extension* in AF is a set $S \in \mathbf{cf}(AF)$ with the property $S^+ = A - S$. We will denote $\mathbf{stab}(AF) = \{S \subseteq A | S$ is stable extension $\}$.

3   Abstract Debates

In this section we introduce our new framework of aggregating individual opinions, consider its relationship with argumentation frameworks in order to define the argumentative aggregation operators.

Let $F \neq \emptyset$ be a finite set of *facts (items)*. An *opinion on F* (shortly, *F-opinion*) is a pair $O = (L, DL)$ of disjoint sets of facts: $L, DL \subseteq F$ and $L \cap DL = \emptyset$. L is the set of *liked (agreed, accepted) facts* in O and DL is the set of *disliked (disagreed, rejected) facts* in O (the facts in $F - (L \cup DL)$ are not the subject of opinion O). $\mathcal{O}(F)$ denotes the set of all *F-opinions*. $O = (L, DL) \in \mathcal{O}(F)$ is a *full opinion* if $L \cup DL = F$, and a *single-minded opinion* if $|L| = 1$. An *Abstract Debate* is a tuple $AD = (F, S, \{O_s\}_{s \in S})$, where: S, the *society*, is a finite non-empty set of *individuals (agents, persons)*; $O_s \in \mathcal{O}(F)$ is the *F-opinion* of individual $s \in S$. We denote by $\mathscr{AD}(F, S)$ the set of all abstract debates of S over F. The *graph representation* of the abstract debate $AD = (F, S, \{O_s\}_{s \in S})$ is the bipartite digraph $G_{AD} = (F, S; E)$, where $(f, s) \in E$ if and only if $f \in L_s$ and $(s, f) \in E$ if and only if $f \in DL_s$. The graph representation of the debate in the introduction is depicted in Figure 1 b). This is an intuitive and concise representation of a debate.

Note that our abstract debates correspond to *profiles* in SCT and to *agendas* in the Judgment Aggregation area. In fact, our framework is equivalent to judgment aggregation with atomic propositions only (and their negations) and with the standard requirement of *completeness* dropped. Also, note that if in the bipartite digraph G_{AD} a node $f^* \in F$ with $f^* = \arg\max_{f \in F}(|f^+| - |f^-|)$ is selected, then we obtain the well-known *dis&approval* voting procedure characterized axiomatically in [2].

Our approach is based on the following relationship between abstract debates and argumentation frameworks.

Definition 3. (Abstract Debates vs Argumentation Frameworks)
(i) Let $O_1 = (L_1, DL_1), O_2 = (L_2, DL_2) \in \mathcal{O}(F)$. O_1 *agrees with* O_2 on $f \in F$ if $f \notin L_1 \cap DL_2 \cup DL_1 \cap L_2$. O_1 *attacks* O_2 on $f \in F$ if $f \in DL_1 \cap L_2$. O_1 *agrees with* O_2 if O_1 agrees with O_2 on every $f \in F$. O_1 *attacks* O_2 if there is $f \in F$ such that O_1 attacks O_2 on f. The *argumentation framework associated to* $AD = (F, S, \{O_p\}_{p \in S}) \in \mathscr{AD}(F, S)$ is $AF(AD) = (S, D)$ in which the arguments are the individuals and an individual s_1 attacks an individual s_2 if and only if O_{s_1} attacks O_{s_2}.

(ii) Let $AF = (A, D)$ be an argumentation framework such that $(a, a) \notin D, \forall a \in A$. The *abstract debate assocsiated to* AF is $AD_{AF} = (F_{AF}, S_{AF}, \{O_s\}_{s \in S_{AF}})$, where $F_{AF} = \{f_a | a \in A\}$, $S_{AF} = \{s_a | a \in A\}$, and for each $a \in A$, $O_{s_a} = (\{f_a\}, \{f_b | b \in a^+\})$.

In Figure 2 i) is illustrated the attack digraph of the argumentation framework associated to the pizza topping debate in the Introduction. Note that we labelled each attack with the set of facts on which the corresponding opinions attacks each other (h=ham, p=pepperoni, s=salami, o=olive). In Figure 2 ii) we have the attack digraph of a simple argumentation framework AF, and the bipartite digraph representation of its associated abstract debate AD_{AF}, is depicted in Figure 2 iii). Note that in AD_{AF} each fact f_a is liked by exactly one individual s_a, and all individual's opinions are single minded.

The argumentation framework $AF(AD)$ can be used to consider particular sets of compatible individuals such that their merged collective opinion defends itself against the attacks of the opinions of individuals outside these sets.
A *coalition* in $AD = (F, S, \{O_p\}_{p \in S})$ is any subset $\mathscr{C} \subseteq S$. $\mathscr{C}$ is *opinion-closed* if

$$O_{\mathscr{C}} = (L_{\mathscr{C}}, DL_{\mathscr{C}}) = \left(\bigcup_{p \in \mathscr{C}} L_p, \bigcup_{p \in \mathscr{C}} DL_p \right) \in \mathcal{O}(F). \qquad O_{\mathscr{C}} \text{ is the collective}$$

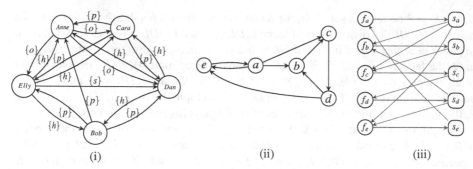

Fig. 2. Abstract Debates vs Argumentation Frameworks

opinion of the coalition $\mathscr{C}$. Note that a coalition $\mathscr{C}$ is opinion-closed if and only if $\mathscr{C}$ is a conflict-free set in $AF(AD)$. It follows that each admissible based extension in $AF(AD)$ gives rise to a collective opinion in $\mathscr{O}(F)$ and the semantics in $AF(AD)$ can be transferred to the abstract debate AD.

Definition 4. Let $AD = (F, S, \{O_p\}_{p \in S}) \in \mathscr{A}\mathscr{D}(F, S)$ an abstract debate.

– A coalition $\mathscr{C}$ is an *autarky* in AD if $\mathscr{C}$ is an admissible set in $AF(AD)$, i.e. if it is opinion-closed and for each $p \in S - \mathscr{C}$, if O_p attacks $O_{\mathscr{C}}$ then $O_{\mathscr{C}}$ attacks O_p.
– A coalition $\mathscr{C}$ is a *strong autarky* in AD if $\mathscr{C}$ is a complete extension in $AF(AD)$, i.e. if it is an autarky, and, for each $p \notin \mathscr{C}$ such that O_p is not attacked by $O_{\mathscr{C}}$, there is $s \notin \mathscr{C}$ such that O_s attacks O_p and $O_{\mathscr{C}}$ does not attack O_s. A *minimal strong autarky* (*maximal strong autarky*) is a strong autarky such that there is no strong autarky strictly contained in it (stricly containing it).
– A coalition $\mathscr{C}$ is a *stable coalition* in AD if $\mathscr{C}$ is a stable extension in $AF(AD)$, i.e. if it is opinion-closed and $O_{\mathscr{C}}$ attacks the opinion O_p of any individual p outside $\mathscr{C}$.

Example 1. Let AD be the topping pizza debate in the introduction. The only non-empty opinion-closed coalitions are singletons and $\mathscr{C}_1 = \{Bob, Cara\}$. We can observe that $O_{\mathscr{C}_1} = \{Bob, Cara\} = (\{ham, pineapple, olive\}, \{pepperoni, onion\})$ attacks O_{Anne}, O_{Dan}, and O_{Elly}. It follows that $\mathscr{C}_1 = \{Bob, Cara\}$ is a stable coalition (hence it is an autarky, a strong autarky, and a maximal strong autarky). We can also easily see that $\{Anne\}$ and $\{Dan\}$ are not autarkies but $\mathscr{C}_2 = \{Elly\}$ is a stable coalition.

Example 2. Let AD be the abstract debate represented in the Figure 3 below.

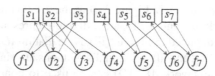

Fig. 3. Bipartite digraph representation of debate in Example 2

$\mathscr{C}_1 = \{s_5, s_7\}$ is an autarky. Indeed, $O_{\mathscr{C}_1} = (\{f_5, f_7\}, \{f_4, f_6\})$. $O_{s_4} = (\{f_4\}, \{f_5\})$ attacks $O_{\mathscr{C}_1}$ but this counterattacks O_{s_4}; $O_{s_6} = (\{f_6\}, \{f_7\})$ attacks $O_{\mathscr{C}_1}$ but this counterattacks O_{S_7}; no other O_{S_i} attacks $O_{\mathscr{C}_1}$, for $i \in \{1,2,3\}$. $\mathscr{C}_1$ is also a strong autarky, but it is not a maximal strong autarky since $\mathscr{C}_2 = \{s_1, s_3, s_5, s_7\}$ is also a strong autarky as we can easily verify. Note that $\mathscr{C}_2$ is also a stable coalition.

For the debate AD_{AF} associated to an argumentation framework AF, the above different type of coalitions translate to the corresponding admissible based extensions in AF. Hence the decision problems on argumentation frameworks can be polynomially transformed into instances on abstract debates. Two typical examples are given below.

Cred$_{msa}$: Given an abstract debate $AD = (F, S, \{O_p\}_{p \in S})$, and a fact $f \in F$. Is f contained in the liked facts set $L_{\mathscr{C}}$ of some maximal strong autarky $\mathscr{C}$ in AD?

Skept$_{msa}$: Given an abstract debate $AD = (F, S, \{O_p\}_{p \in S})$, and a fact $f \in F$. Is f contained in the liked facts set $L_{\mathscr{C}}$ of each maximal strong autarky $\mathscr{C}$ in AD?

Using the time complexity results on the corresponding decision problems for argumentation frameworks [11], and the above remark we obtain the following Theorem.

Theorem 5. **Cred$_{msa}$** *is NP-complete and* **Skept$_{msa}$** *is* Π_2^P*-complete.*

Coalitions are very restrictive when the opinions of individuals are full-opinions (in this case, the only nonempty opinion-closed coalitions are singletons). Inspired by political practice, we consider a strategical way of coalition formation: some members of a coalition renounces at some liked facts for making the coalition opinion-closed.

Definition 6. Let $\mathscr{C}$ be a coalition in $AD = (F, S, \{O_s\}_{s \in S})$. A $\mathscr{C}$-*compromise* is a function $\alpha : \mathscr{C} \to 2^F$ such that for every $s \in \mathscr{C}$ we have $\alpha(s) \neq \emptyset$, $\alpha(s) \subset L_s$ and

$$O_{\mathscr{C};\alpha} = (L_{\mathscr{C};\alpha}, DL_{\mathscr{C}}) = \Big(\bigcup_{p \in \mathscr{C}} \alpha(p), \bigcup_{p \in \mathscr{C}} DL_p \Big) \in \mathscr{O}(F).$$

If α a $\mathscr{C}$-compromise, the pair $(\mathscr{C}, \alpha)$ is a *compromise* σ for $\sigma \in \{$ *autarky, strong autarky, minimal strong autarky, maximal strong autarky, stable coalition*$\}$ if $\mathscr{C}$ is a σ in the abstract debate $AD_{|\mathscr{C};\alpha} = (F, S, \{O'_s\}_{s \in S})$, where $DL'_s = DL_s$ for every $s \in S$, and $L'_s = L_s$ if $s \in S - \mathscr{C}$ and $L'_s = \alpha(s)$ if $s \in \mathscr{C}$.

Example. Let us consider again the pizza topping debate, and $\sigma =$ stable coalition. Clearly $\mathscr{C}_3 = \{Anne, Dan\}$ is not opinion-closed. But, we can obtain a $\mathscr{C}_3$-compromise by taking $\alpha_3(Anne) = \{pepperoni\}$ and $\alpha_3(Dan) = \{pepperoni, salami\}$. Then $(\mathscr{C}_3, \alpha_3)$ is a stable coalition with $O_{\mathscr{C}_3;\alpha_3} = (\{pepperoni, salami\}, \{olive, onion, ham\})$.

Note that in debates $AD = (F, S, \{O_s\}_{s \in S})$ with $L_p \neq \emptyset, \forall p \in S$, if $\mathscr{C}$ is σ then $\mathscr{C}$ is also a *compromise* σ (by taking $\alpha_0(s) = L_s$ for each $s \in \mathscr{C}$). Also, in the debates AD with $|L_p| = 1, \forall p \in S$, a coalition $\mathscr{C}$ is compromise σ if and only if $\mathscr{C}$ is σ.

We define now our argumentative aggregation operators.

Definition 7. An *argumentative aggregation operator* for abstract debates is a function $\mathbb{A}_\sigma : \mathscr{AD}(F, S) \to 2^{\mathscr{O}(F)}$ such that for any $AD \in \mathscr{AD}(F, S)$,

$$\mathbb{A}_\sigma(AD) = \{O_{\mathscr{C};\alpha} | (\mathscr{C}, \alpha) \text{ is a compromise } \sigma\}.$$

In the terminology of SCT, our argumentative aggregation operators, $\mathbb{A}_\sigma$, are *(irreso-lute) social functions*. We can reduce the set of aggregate opinions by an appropriate choosing of σ. Another possibility is to keep in $\mathbb{A}_\sigma(AD)$ only the opinions with a maximal (w.r.t. inclusion) set of liked facts. This would eliminate the trivial opinion $(\emptyset, \emptyset)$ for $\sigma =$ autarky. Other strategy of reducing the set $\mathbb{A}_\sigma(AD)$ is to retain only the opinions at minimum distance to the entire set of individuals opinion (after defining appropriate distance functions).

We now turn to conditions one may wish to impose on an aggregation operator as usually done in SCT. Let $\mathbb{A}_\sigma : \mathscr{AD}(F,S) \to 2^{\mathscr{O}(F)}$ be an argumentative aggregation operator for $\sigma \in \{$ *autarky, strong autarky, minimal strong autarky, maximal strong autarky, stable coalition*$\}$. We begin with the uncontroversial requirement that, if all individuals have the same opinion, this should be the collective one **(Unanimity)**. Clearly, if in an abstract debate $AD = (F,S,\{O_s\}_{s\in S})$ we have $O_s = O \in \mathscr{O}(F)$ for every $s \in S$, then the grand coalition S is σ and its collective opinion is $O_S = O$. Hence every $\mathbb{A}_\sigma$ satisfies the unanimity condition. Another basic democratic requirement of an aggregation operator is **Anonymity:** for every two abstract debates $AD = (F,S,\{O_s\}_{s\in S})$ and $AD' = (F,S,\{O'_s\}_{s\in S})$ such that there is a permutation $\pi : S \to S$ with $O'_s = O_{\pi(s)}$, we have $\mathbb{A}_\sigma(AD) = \mathbb{A}_\sigma(AD')$. Clearly, if $\pi : S \to S$ is a permutation, then a coalition $\mathscr{C}$ is σ if and only if $\pi(\mathscr{C}) = \{\pi(s)|s \in \mathscr{C}\}$ is σ. Hence every $\mathbb{A}_\sigma$ satisfies the anonymity condition. Similarly, we can easily argue that every $\mathbb{A}_\sigma$ satisfies **Neutrality**: the set of aggregate opinions returned by $\mathbb{A}_\sigma$ for a debate obtained by renaming the facts in a debate is obtained by renaming the facts in each aggregate opinion returned by $\mathbb{A}_\sigma$ for that debate. Also, by the definition, every $\mathbb{A}_\sigma$ satisfies **Compatibility** (each returned opinion agrees with at least one individual opinion), introduced in [18].

The main tool used in SCT to change the argument of an aggregation operator without changing the output is the *Arrow's independence of irrelevant alternatives*. $\mathbb{A}_\sigma$ satisfies **Independence** if for every $f \in F$, $AD^1 = (F,S,\{O^1_p\}_{p\in S})$, $AD^2 = (F,S,\{O^2_p\}_{p\in S})$,

if O^1_s agrees with O^2_s on f for all $s \in S$, then for every opinion $O_1 \in \mathbb{A}(AD_1)$ there is a nontrivial opinion $O_2 \in \mathbb{A}(AD_2)$ such that O_1 agrees with O_2 on f.

Since the operators $\mathbb{A}_\sigma$ are not "fact wise" and are strongly dependent on the context of the debate on which they are applied, we have the following theorem.

Theorem 8. *Argumentative aggregation operators $\mathbb{A}_\sigma$ do not satisfy independence.*

Proof. Let $F = \{f,g,h\}$ be the set of facts and let $S = \{s_1,s_2,s_3\}$. Let $AD^1 = (F,S,\{O^1_p\}_{p\in S})$ be the abstract debate in which $O^1_{s_1} = (\{f\},\{g\})$, $O^1_{s_2} = (\{g\},\{f\})$, $O^1_{s_3} = (\{h\},\{g\})$. Since all opinions in AD^1 are single minded, we have no compromise σ in the debate AD^1. The coalition $\mathscr{C} = \{s_1,s_3\}$ is an autarky with $O_{\mathscr{C}} = (\{f,h\},\{g\})$. There is no autarky containing s_2 and other member of S since by adding s_1 or s_3 to $\{s_2\}$ the resulting coalition is not opinion-closed. The coalition $\mathscr{C}' = \{s_2\}$ is not an autarky since $O_{\mathscr{C}'} = (\{g\},\{f\})$ does not defend against the attack of $O^1_{s_3} = (\{h\},\{g\})$. It follows that $\mathbb{A}_\sigma(AD^1) = \{(\{f,h\},\{g\})\}$. Let $AD^2 = (F,S,\{O^2_p\}_{p\in S})$ be the abstract debate in which $O^2_{s_1} = (\{f\},\{h\})$, $O^2_{s_2} = (\{g\},\{f,h\})$, $O^2_{s_3} = (\{h\},\emptyset)$. All opinions in AD^2 are single minded, hence we have no compromise σ in the debate AD^2. The only autarky is

$\mathscr{C} = \{s_2\}$, therefore $\mathbb{A}_\sigma(AD^2) = \{(\{g\},\{f,h\})\}$. Hence no opinion in $\mathbb{A}_\sigma(AD^1)$ agrees with an opinion in $\mathbb{A}_\sigma(AD^2)$ on f. But, O_s^1 agrees with O_s^2 on f, $\forall s \in S$. $\square$

4 Discussion

In spite of its proximity to the field of judgment aggregation (JA), in our approach the "facts" in F are not a priory logically related. However, it is possible to discuss problems related to "logical consistency" by considering *opinion spaces*, in which an opinion $O = (L,DL)$ is *consistent* if and only if $\overline{L} \cap DL = \emptyset$, where $\overline{L}$ is the set of facts entailed by L under a predefined entailment relation on F. The opinion attack digraph is defined now by considering that an opinion $O = (L,DL)$ attacks any opinion $O' = (L',DL')$ if and only if $DL \cap \overline{L'} \neq \emptyset$. In this way, we meet questions related to logically based AF's ([6]), since opinion-closed coalitions are not simply conflict-free sets (as we obtained for the particular case $\overline{X} = X$). However, using specific rules from judgment aggregation field (see [15] and its references), could be worthwhile, when these are applied to our set $\mathbb{A}_\sigma(AD)$ of aggregate opinions. Of course, our incipient study of the properties of argumentative operators must be developed. Most of the properties studied in SCT or JA are quantitative in nature and require introducing a structure on the set of abstract debates in order to replace the independence property as a vehicle for passing from a profile (debate) to another one to obtain impossibility or non-manipulability results.

References

[1] Airiau, S., Endriss, U., Grandi, U., Porello, D., Uckelman, J.: Aggregating dependency graphs into voting agendas in multi-issue elections. In: Proc. of IJCAI 2011 (2011)

[2] Alcantud, J., Laruelle, A.: Dis&approval voting: A characterization. Social Choice and Welfare, 1–10 (2013)

[3] Arrow, K.: A difficulty in the concept of social welfare. Journal of Political Economy, 328–346 (1950)

[4] Arrow, K.: Social Choice and Individual Values. Wiley (1963)

[5] Arrow, K., Sen, A., Suzumura, K.: Handbook of Social Choice and Welfare. Elsevier (2002)

[6] Caminada, M., Amgoud, L.: On the evaluation of argumentation formalisms. Artificial Intelligence 171, 286–310 (2007)

[7] Caminada, M., Pigozzi, G.: On judgment aggregation in abstract argumentation. Autonomous Agents and Multi-Agent Systems 22, 64–102 (2011)

[8] Coste-Marquis, S., Devred, C., Konieczny, S., Lagasquie-Schiex, M.C., Marquis, P.: On the merging of Dung's argumentation systems. Journal of Artificial Intelligence 171, 730–753 (2007)

[9] Croitoru, C.: Abstract debates. In: Proc. of ICTAI 2013 (2013)

[10] Dung, P.M.: On the acceptability of arguments and its fundamental role in nonmonotonic reasoning, logic programming and n-person games. Artificial Intelligence 77, 321–357 (1995)

[11] Dunne, P., Bench-Capon, T.: Coherence in finite argument systems. Artificial Intelligence 141, 187–203 (2002)

[12] Dunne, P., Marquis, P., Wooldridge, M.: Argument aggregation: Basic axioms and complexity results. In: Proc. of COMMA 2012 (2012)

[13] Endriss, U., Grandi, U.: Graph aggregation. In: Proc. of COMSOC 2012 (2012)

[14] Konieczny, S., Pérez, R.P.: Merging information under constraints: A logical framework. Journal of Logic and Computation 12, 773–808 (2002)

[15] Lang, J., Pigozzi, G., Slavkovik, M., van der Torre, L.: Judgment aggregation rules based on minimization. In: Proc. of TARK 2011, pp. 238–246 (2011)

[16] List, C., Puppe, C.: Judgment aggregation: A survey, ch. 19, pp. 158–190. Oxford University Press (2009)

[17] Pigozzi, G.: Belief merging and the discursive dilemma: An argument-based account to paradoxes of judgment aggregation. Synthese 152, 285–298 (2006)

[18] Pigozzi, G., Grandi, U.: On compatible multi-issue group decisions. In: Proc. of LOFT 2012 (2012)

[19] Porello, D., Endriss, U.: Ontology merging as social choice. In: Leite, J., Torroni, P., Ågotnes, T., Boella, G., van der Torre, L. (eds.) CLIMA XII 2011. LNCS, vol. 6814, pp. 157–170. Springer, Heidelberg (2011)

[20] Rahwan, I., Larson, K., Tohme, F.: A characterisation of strategy-proofness for grounded argumentation semantics. In: Proc. of IJCAI 2009, pp. 251–256 (2009)

[21] Rahwan, I., Tohme, F.: Collective argument evaluation as judgement aggregation. In: Proc. of AAMAS 2010 (2010)

[22] Tohmé, F.A., Bodanza, G.A., Simari, G.R.: Aggregation of attack relations: A social-choice theoretical analysis of defeasibility criteria. In: Hartmann, S., Kern-Isberner, G. (eds.) FoIKS 2008. LNCS, vol. 4932, pp. 8–23. Springer, Heidelberg (2008)

Measuring Dissimilarity between Judgment Sets

Marija Slavkovik and Thomas Ågotnes

University of Bergen, PB. 7802, 5020 Bergen, Norway
{marija.slavkovik,thomas.agotnes}@infomedia.uib.no

Abstract. Distances and scores are widely used to measure (dis)similarity between objects of information such as preferences, belief sets, judgment sets, etc. Typically, measures are directly imported from information theory or topology, with little consideration for adequacy in the context of comparing logically related information. We propose a set of desirable properties for measures used to aggregate (logically related) *judgments*, and show which of the measures used for this purpose satisfy them.

1 Introduction

The aggregation of sets of logically related information is a problem that occurs in at least four disciplines with intersecting areas of interest with multiagent systems and artificial intelligence: judgement aggregation [3], belief revision [11], social choice [3] and abstract argumentation [2]. Many approaches to aggregating sets of information are based on comparing the information sets and measuring how similar they are. Furthermore, studies of complexity of various forms of manipulation, see for example [9,8,1], extensively rely on similarity comparisons. For an effective comparison, information sets cannot be viewed as inseparable units that are either entirely the same or entirely different from each other.

Simply counting the number of units on which collections of information differ, namely using the Hamming distance [10], is adequate only when these units are logically independent [12,7,2]. Although the Hamming distance is extensively used to aggregate them [12,8,11,16,17], in general, neither sets of beliefs, arguments labelings, votes, preferences, nor sets of judgments contain exclusively logically unrelated elements. How should logically related information sets be compared, namely, which properties should be satisfied by the (dis)similarity measures used?

We focus on sets of judgments and their comparison for the purpose of aggregation. Since judgment aggregation has known relations with belief merging [17], preference aggregation [15], voting [13], and aggregation of labelings within abstract argumentation [4,2], dissimilarity measures for sets of judgments can also be applied in these disciplines. In this paper we focus on three tasks: a) identifying a set of properties common to all dissimilarity measures used in the literature; b) defining desirable properties of dissimilarity measures that are apt for comparing sets containing logically related information; c) showing that there exist measures that satisfy both sets of properties.

In Section 2 we give the necessary preliminaries, while in Section 3 we first discuss related work and then we attend to tasks a) and b). In Section 4 we concern ourselves with task c). In Section 5 we draw conclusions and outline directions for future work.

E. Fermé and J. Leite (Eds.): JELIA 2014, LNAI 8761, pp. 609–617, 2014.

2 Preliminaries

Judgment aggregation problems are typically represented using a set $\mathcal{L}$ of well-formed propositional logic formulas, including $\top$ (tautology) and $\bot$ (contradiction). An *issue* is a pair of formulas $\{\varphi, \neg\varphi\} \subset \mathcal{L}$ where φ is neither a tautology nor a contradiction. For simplicity, we often abuse notation and write only the positive formula when we discuss issues. An *agenda* $\mathcal{A}$ is a finite set of issues, $\mathcal{A} = \{\varphi_1, \neg\varphi_1, \ldots, \varphi_m, \neg\varphi_m\}$. A sub-agenda $Y \subset \mathcal{A}$ is a subset of issues from $\mathcal{A}$, e.g., $Y = \{p, \neg p\}$ is a sub-agenda for $\mathcal{A} = \{p, \neg p, q, \neg q\}$. A *judgment* on an issue $\{\neg\varphi, \varphi\} \in \mathcal{A}$ is one of φ or $\neg\varphi$.

A *judgment set* J is a subset of $\mathcal{A}$, *complete* iff for each $\{\neg\varphi, \varphi\} \in \mathcal{A}$ either $\varphi \in J$ or $\neg\varphi \in J$, and incomplete otherwise. A judgment set J is consistent iff it is a consistent set of formulas. For a given agenda $\mathcal{A}$, the set of all consistent nonempty judgment sets is $\mathcal{D}(\mathcal{A})$, while $\mathbb{D}(\mathcal{A}) \subset \mathcal{D}(\mathcal{A})$ is the set of all consistent and complete judgement sets. Judgment sets $J_1, J_2 \in \mathbb{D}(\mathcal{A})$ are *complementary* when for every $\varphi \in \mathcal{A}$, $\varphi \in J_1$ iff $\neg\varphi \in J_2$.

A *profile* $P \subset \mathbb{D}(\mathcal{A})^n$ is a tuple $P = \langle J_1, \ldots, J_n \rangle$ of judgment sets for agents $1, \ldots, n$. An (irresolute) judgment aggregation rule is a correspondence $F : \mathbb{D}(\mathcal{A})^n \to 2^{\mathbb{D}(\mathcal{A})} \backslash \varnothing$. Namely, a judgment aggregation rule associates a set of complete and consistent judgment sets for an agenda $\mathcal{A}$, called *collective judgment sets*, to a profile of judgments for the same $\mathcal{A}$. Two very basic properties for judgment aggregation rules are *unanimity*, for every $P \in \mathbb{D}(\mathcal{A})^n$ s.t. $P = \langle J, J, \ldots, J \rangle$, $F(P) = \{J\}$, and *anonymity* for every permutation σ of P and every $P \in \mathbb{D}(\mathcal{A})^n$, $F(P) = F(\sigma(P))$.

Two existing classes of judgment aggregation rules make use of similarity or dissimilarity measures, respectively, selecting collective judgment sets: *scoring rules* [6], which here we refer to using F_s, and *distance-based rules* [7,8,16,17], here denoted with $F_{d,\odot}$. We give the respective definitions for these two classes of rules using our notation. For any $\mathcal{A}, P \in \mathbb{D}(\mathcal{A})^n$, $P = \langle J_1, \ldots, J_n \rangle$:

$$F_s(P) = \operatorname*{argmax}_{J \in \mathbb{D}(\mathcal{A})} \sum_{i \in [1,n]} \sum_{\varphi \in J \cap J_i} s(J_i, \varphi), \quad F_{d,\odot}(P) = \operatorname*{argmin}_{J \in \mathbb{D}(\mathcal{A})} \odot (d(J_1, J), \ldots, d(J_n, J)).$$

In the definition of F_s, s is a *scoring function* of type $s : \mathbb{D}(\mathcal{A}) \times \mathcal{A} \to \mathbb{R}$. Scoring functions assign judgment set-dependent scores for each possible judgment that can be cast. One set J is more similar to a given J_i than another j set J', if the sum of scores of the judgments in J, according to the J_i-respective scoring, is higher than that sum of the scores assigned to judgments in J'.

In the definition of $F_{d,\odot}$, two functions are used to determine the collective judgment sets. The function $\odot : \mathbb{R}^n \to \mathbb{R}$ is an n-ary aggregation function that assigns a unique value to an n-ary vector of values. E.g., the function Σ in definition of F_s is an n-ary aggregation function; other examples include max, min, and Π. The second function used in the definition of $F_{d,\odot}$ is the dissimilarity function d, defined for every $\mathcal{A} \subset \mathcal{L}$, as $d : \mathbb{D}(\mathcal{A}) \times \mathbb{D}(\mathcal{A}) \to \mathbb{R}$, which assigns a higher number the more different J_i is from J.

Dissimilarity measures are typically defined as functions that take as arguments two sequences of equal length: for every $\mathcal{A} \in \mathcal{L}$, $d : \mathcal{A}^m \times \mathcal{A}^m \to \mathbb{R}$. Observe that d is being defined for all agendas; we stipulate that d compares judgment sets that are complete and consistent judgment sets for the *same* agenda.

Although scores and dissimilarity measures appear to be different functions, we show that for every scoring function s there exists a corresponding dissimilarity function d_s, and as a result, we show that the F_s rules are a special case of the $F_{d,\odot}$ rules.

Definition 1. *For every agenda $\mathcal{A} \subset \mathcal{L}$ and scoring function $s : \mathbb{D}(\mathcal{A}) \times \mathcal{A} \to \mathbb{R}$, for every $J, J' \in \mathbb{D}(\mathcal{A})$ we define $S(J, J') = \sum_{\varphi \in J \cap J'} s(J, \varphi)$. A dissimilarity measure $d_s : \mathbb{D}(\mathcal{A}) \times \mathbb{D}(\mathcal{A}) \to \mathbb{R}$ corresponds to a scoring function $s : \mathbb{D}(\mathcal{A}) \times \mathcal{A} \to \mathbb{R}$ iff, for every $J, J', J'' \in \mathbb{D}(\mathcal{A})$, $d_s(J, J') > d_s(J, J'')$ iff $S(J, J') < S(J, J'')$ and $d_s(J, J') = d_s(J, J'')$ iff $S(J, J') = S(J, J'')$.*

Proposition 1. *For every finite agenda $\mathcal{A} \subset \mathcal{L}$, for every scoring function s there exists a corresponding dissimilarity measure d_s.*

Proof. Observe that $S(J, J')$ gives a J-dependent score that measures *similarity* to a judgement set J' by summing the scores of all the judgments in $J \cap J'$. If instead we sum the scores for the judgments in $J \backslash J'$, we obtain a dissimilarity measure. For each s we can define a d_s as: $d_s(J, J') = \sum_{\varphi \in J \backslash J'}^{s} (J, \varphi)$. To show that d_s is corresponding to s, it is sufficient to observe that the judgment sets are finite, hence the maximal value that s can obtain for a given J is $S(J, J)$ and that $d_s(J, J') = S(J, J) - S(J, J')$. □

It is now easy to show that Proposition 2 holds. The proof of the proposition consists in observing that, for each F_s, and $P \in \mathbb{D}(\mathcal{A})^n$, $F_s(P) = F_{d_s, \Sigma}(P)$.

Proposition 2. *For every scoring rule F's there exists a rule $F_{d,\odot}$ such that for every $P \in \mathbb{D}(\mathcal{A})^n$, $F_s(P) = F_{d,\odot}(P)$.*

Due to Propositions 1 and 2 it is sufficient to consider dissimilarity measures when looking for desirable properties for both similarity and dissimilarity measures in judgment aggregation.

3 Measuring Dissimilarity between Judgment Sets

We first discuss related work on measuring dissimilarity between judgment sets and then what can be considered general requirements for such measures, before discussing how sensitivity to logic relations can be expressed as their property. The general requirements we outline are weak properties that most of the dissimilarity measures in use should satisfy. Although most are obvious, we do need to have them to show that they can be consistent with properties of sensitivity to the logic relations.

Given that it is obvious that a different (dis)similarity measure, even for the same aggregator $\odot$, yields a judgment aggregation rule with different properties, it is surprising that not even very general requirements on the d_s functions induced from scoring rules are required or discussed, meaning that anything goes as long as the scoring rule fits the signature $\mathbb{D}(\mathcal{A}) \times \mathbb{D}(\mathcal{A}) \to \mathbb{R}$. The situation appears to be better when the dissimilarity functions d are used directly in the distance-based rules, whereupon it is usually required that the function d is a pseudo-distance[1] or a distance [5]. It can be observed that the judgment aggregation rule $F_{d,\odot}$ works with any dissimilarity measure. The (pseudo-)distance requirements have been imported from the literature of belief merging [11], from where the $F_{d,\odot}$ rules originate, however the necessity of these requirements in judgment aggregation has never been justified.

The requirement of triangular inequality is easy to drop, since it is not required in belief merging either and no justification for it has been offered in judgment aggregation. The need for the symmetry property is not so clear. Five out of the six scoring functions presented in [6] give rise to d_s that is not symmetric, as it is simple to verify by looking at the examples in [6]. The exception is the simple scoring rule which corresponds to the Hamming distance. When one is measuring a distance, symmetry is necessary, but dissimilarity can be meaningful without symmetry as the scoring rules demonstrate. We therefore consider symmetry desirability to be context-dependent.

In [19] it has been identified that the non negativity and identity of indiscernibles properties of a pseudo-distance are necessary for the $F_{d,\odot}$ rule to satisfy unanimity. It was also established that the anonymity of $F_{d,\odot}$ does not depend on the function d, but on whether the aggregation function $\odot$ is commutative or not. As a consequence, all scoring rules will satisfy anonymity, however only those for which d_s is non-negative will satisfy unanimity.

Let us consider the sensitivity to logic relations for a similarity measure at this point before considering some more properties of measures from the literature. In [7] it is argued that if for an agenda $\mathcal{A}$ two agents cannot disagree on one issue without disagreeing on another issue, then these two disagreements in their judgment sets should not be counted as two disagreements, as the Hamming distance does, but only as one. In [7], this requirement is captured by Axiom 5. A $J_2 \in \mathbb{D}(\mathcal{A})$ is in-between $J_1, J_3 \in \mathbb{D}(\mathcal{A})$, $J_1 \neq J_2 \neq J_3$, if $J_1 \backslash J_2 \subset J_1 \backslash J_3$. Axiom 5 states that if $J_1, J_2 \in \mathbb{D}(\mathcal{A})$ are such that there exists no in-between $J \in \mathbb{D}(\mathcal{A})$, then $d(J_1, J_2) = 1$. Implicitly, in [7] it is advocated that similarity measures should consider the logical relations among issues and not only count disagreements. Here, we make explicit the logic relation sensitivity hinted on in [12,7,2] by defining it as a set of properties for measures.

An agenda $\mathcal{A}$ cannot contain tautologies or contradictions, but we may add arbitrarily many issues to it that are logically equivalent to existing agenda issues. Consider for example two hiring committee members that do not agree that "a candidate is good for the open position" (φ). Adding the issue "the candidate is not bad for the open position" ($\neg\neg\varphi$) to the agenda should not increase the quantity of disagreement between the positions of the agents. Regardless of how many times an issue is cloned in the agenda, the disagreement quantity should not increase, namely, a measure that is sensitive of the logic relations among issues should be *insensitive to agenda clones*.

A property called *disagreement monotonicity*, is considered in [2], for aggregation of labelings in argumentation, but applicable to judgment sets as well. A dissimilarity

---

[1] A pseudo-distance f is a function that (for every x, y, z in its codomain) satisfies $f(x,y) \geq 0$ (nonnegativity), $f(x,y) = 0$ iff $x = y$ (identity of indiscernibles) and $f(x,y) = f(y,x)$(symmetry). A distance additionally satisfies $f(x,y) + f(y,z) \geq f(x,z)$ (triangular inequality).

measure is *disagreement monotonic* if for all $J_1, J_2, J_3 \in \mathbb{D}(\mathcal{A})$ s.t. J_2 is in-between J_1 and J_3, $d(J_1, J_2) < d(J_1, J_3)$. Requiring that the amount of disagreement is strictly increasing with the number of judgments on which two judgment sets differ is not compatible with the insensitivity to agenda clones requirement. Indeed when a clone is added to the agenda, the number of issues on which two judgment sets disagree will increase, but the amount of disagreement will not. Therefore we propose weak disagreement monotonicity, requiring that the amount of disagreement between judgment sets does not decrease with an increase in the number of disagreeing issues in the sets.

In addition to Axiom 5, another requirement was considered in [7], the Axiom 4. Axiom 4 states that, if J_2 is in-between J_1 and J_3, then $d(J_1, J_3) = d(J_1, J_2) + d(J_2, J_3)$. Axiom 4 is strictly stronger than the disagreement monotonicity requirement of [2], namely, in-between together with non-negativity implies disagreement monotonicity, but the implication in the other direction does not hold. In judgment aggregation, disagreement monotonicity is easy to justify, however requiring Axiom 5, that for every judgment set there exists a judgment set at distance 1, is arbitrary outside of the scope of the [7], where this property is needed to characterise the introduced distance. In addition, forcing Axiom 5 limits the domain of the dissimilarity measure to natural numbers. We therefore consider only disagreement monotonicity to be a basic requirement.

The insensitivity to clones requirements can be made stronger. Assume that two committee members agree "not to hire any more academic staff until 2015" ($\neg\varphi'$) but do not agree on "increasing the number of administrative staff" (ψ). The committee members have no need to vote regarding the issue of "increase the number of academic staff and hire John for a lecturer position" ($\varphi' \wedge \varphi''$) as agreeing on $\neg\varphi'$ also means an agreement on $\neg(\varphi' \wedge \varphi'')$. Removing an implied judgment from the judgment sets should not change the amount of disagreement between them. This property we call *insensitivity to consequents*.

Definition 2. *Let* $d : \mathbb{D}(\mathcal{A}) \times \mathbb{D}(\mathcal{A}) \to \mathbb{R}$ *be a dissimilarity measure defined for every* $\mathcal{A} \subset \mathcal{L}$. *The function* d *is an adequate dissimilarity measure for judgment aggregation if, for every* $J_1, J_2, J_3 \in \mathbb{D}(\mathcal{A})$, *properties (p1)-(p3) hold, and an adequate dissimilarity measure for logically related sets of formulas if properties (p1)-(p5) hold. Desirability of (p6) is context-dependent.*

Nonnegativity:	$d(J_1, J_2) \geqslant 0$.	**(p1)**
Identity of indiscernibles:	$d(J_1, J_2) = 0$ *iff* $J_1 = J_2$.	**(p2)**
Agreement monotonicity:	*For every* $J_1 \neq J_2 \neq J_3$, *if* $J_3 \backslash J_2 \subset J_3 \backslash J_1$, *then* $d(J_2, J_3) \leqslant d(J_1, J_3)$.	**(p3)**
Insensitivity to clones:	*If there are* $\psi, \varphi \in \mathcal{A}$ *s.t.* $\psi \equiv \varphi$, *then for every* $J_1, J_2 \in \mathbb{D}(\mathcal{A})$ *it holds that* $d(J_1, J_2) = d(J_1 \backslash \{\varphi, \neg\varphi\}, J_2 \backslash \{\varphi, \neg\varphi\})$.	**(p4)**
Insensitivity to consequents:	*If there exist* $S \subset J_1$ *and* $\varphi \in J_1$ *s.t.* $J_1 \in \mathbb{D}(\mathcal{A})$, $S \vdash \varphi$, *and there is no* $S' \subset S$ *s.t.* $S' \vdash \varphi$, *then for every* $J_2 \in \mathbb{D}(\mathcal{A})$, *it holds that* $d(J_1, J_2) = d(J \backslash \{\varphi, \neg\varphi\}, J' \backslash \{\varphi, \neg\varphi\})$.	**(p5)**
Symmetry:	$d(J_1, J_2) = d(J_2, J_1)$.	**(p6)**

Clearly when comparing $d(J_1, J_2)$ and $d(J_1 \backslash \{\varphi, \neg\varphi\}, J_2 \backslash \{\varphi, \neg\varphi\})$, the sets J_1 and $J_1 \backslash \{\varphi, \neg\varphi\}$ are not complete and consistent judgment sets for the same agenda: $J_1 \in \mathbb{D}(\mathcal{A})$ and $J_1 \backslash \{\varphi, \neg\varphi\} \in \mathbb{D}(\mathcal{A} \backslash \{\varphi, \neg\varphi\})$. However, these two sets do not need to be from the same agenda, we are only comparing two rational numbers. Also observe that while (p4) is a property that refers to issues (that are pairs of judgments), the (p5) property refers to judgments. Lastly, we mention two obvious relationships.

Proposition 3. *If d satisfies insensitivity to consequents, then it also satisfies insensitivity to agenda clones. The reverse does not hold. If d satisfies Axiom 4 as defined in [7], then it also satisfies agreement monotonicity.*

4   Compliance

In this section we analyse existing (dis)similarity measures from the literature and identify which satisfy the desirable properties we outlined. We demonstrate that there does exist a measure that satisfies all (p1)-(p6). We found the following measures: the Hamming and drastic distances d_H and d_D, see *e.g.*, [16], defined respectively as $d_H(J_1, J_2) = |J_2 \backslash J_1| (= |J_1 \backslash J_2|)$ and $d_D(J_1, J_2)$ is 0 iff $J_2 \backslash J_1 = \varnothing$ and 1 otherwise; the five scoring rules from [6]: reversal scoring, entailment scoring, disjoint entailment scoring, minimal entailment scoring and irreducible entailment scoring, giving rise to d_{rv}, d_{et}, d_{ds}, d_{md}, and d_{ir} respectively; the critical subsets distance d_{CS} from [2] and the minimal prime implicant measures introduced in [18], definitions follow. We omit here the definitions of the five scoring functions from [6], and resulting distances, due to space restrictions. These are fairly simple to retrieve from the original work [6], and the proofs involving them are straightforward. We give the definitions of the rest.

We repeat the concept of prime implicants of judgment sets introduced in [18]. Consider an agenda $\mathcal{A}$ and $J \in \mathcal{D}(\mathcal{A})$ with a subset $I \subseteq J$. The set I is an implicant of J if for every $\varphi \in J$ it holds that $I \vdash \varphi$. I is a *prime J-implicant* if I is an implicant of J and there is no $I' \subset I$ s.t. $I' \vdash \varphi$ for every $\varphi \in J$. Intuitively, the prime J-implicant is a set of judgments which when known, all the judgments in J can be known as well. We assume that $PI(\varnothing) = \varnothing$. The minimal prime J-implicant is defined as that prime J-implicant that, among all of the prime J-implicants, has the minimal cardinality. We denote the set of prime implicants for J with $PI(J)$ and the minimal prime J-implicant with $MPI(J)$: $MPI(J) = \underset{I \in PI(J)}{\mathrm{argmin}} |I|$. The Minimal sum prime implicant measure is defined as $d_{msp}(J_1, J_2) = |MPI(J_2 \backslash J_1)| + |MPI(J_1 \backslash J_2)|$.

A *critical set* for an agenda $\mathcal{A}$ is a sub-agenda $Y \subseteq \mathcal{A}$, s.t. for every $J \in \mathbb{D}(\mathcal{A})$, $J \cap Y \vdash \bigwedge J$ and there exists no sub-agenda $Y' \subset Y$ s.t. $J \cap Y' \vdash \bigwedge J$. E.g., for the agenda $\mathcal{A} = \{p, \neg p, q, \neg q, p \wedge q), \neg(p \wedge q)\}$, there is one critical set $Y = \{p, \neg p, q, \neg q, \}$. For a critical subset $Y \subset \mathcal{A}$, $d_{CS}(J_1, J_2) = d_H(J_1 \cap Y, J_2 \cap Y)$.

We also consider the Duddy-Piggins distance d_{DP} from [7]. Let $G = \langle V, E \rangle$ be a graph in which the set of vertices is $V = \mathbb{D}(\mathcal{A})$ and there exists an edge, in the set of edges $E \subseteq \mathbb{D}(\mathcal{A}) \times \mathbb{D}(\mathcal{A})$, between two judgement sets J_1 and J_2 iff there exists no $J_3 \in \mathbb{D}(\mathcal{A})$ in-between J_1 and J_2. For any $J_1, J_2 \in \mathbb{D}(\mathcal{A})$, $d_{DP}(J_1, J_2)$ is the minimal number of edges between J_1 and J_2.

Proposition 4. *The compliance of the dissimilarity measures d_D, d_{msp}, d_{DP}, d_{CS}, d_H, d_{rv}, d_{et}, d_{ds}, d_{md}, and d_{ir} with properties (p1)-(p6) is as in Table 1.*

Proof. We prove only the non-obvious entries.

Table 1. Compliance of existing distances with proposed properties

	(p1)	(p2)	(p3)	(p4)	(p5)	(p6)
d_D, d_{msp}	✓	✓	✓	✓	✓	✓
d_{DP}, d_{CS}	✓	✓	✓	✓	✗	✓
d_H	✓	✓	✓	✗	✗	✓
$d_{rv}, d_{et}, d_{ds}, d_{md}, d_{ir}$	✓	✓	✓	✗	✗	✗

Measures d_{CS} and d_{msp} are agreement monotonic.
Consider $J_1, J_2, J_3 \in \mathbb{D}(\mathcal{A})$, $J_1 \neq J_2 \neq J_3$ s.t. J_2 is in-between J_1 and J_3. For d_{CS}, observe that if J_2 is in-between J_1 and J_3, then also $J_2 \cap Y$ is in-between $J_1 \cap Y$ and $J_3 \cap Y$. Consequently d_{CS} behaves as Hamming distance and is as such agreement monotonic.

For d_{msp} we show that when J_2 is in-between J_1 and J_3 (and $J_1 \neq J_2 \neq J_3$) it holds that $MPI(J_3 \backslash J_2) \subset MPI(J_3 \backslash J_1)$. Observe that when J_2 is in-between J_1 and J_3 we can represent the sets J_1, J_2, J_3 as a union of mutually exclusive sets $S_1, S_2, S_3, \overline{S_2}, \overline{S_3}$: $J_1 = S_1 \cup \overline{S_2} \cup \overline{S_3}$, $J_2 = S_1 \cup S_2 \cup \overline{S_3}$, $J_3 = S_1 \cup S_2 \cup S_3$, where $S_1 = J_1 \cap J_2 \cap J_3$, $S_2 = J_3 \cap J_2$, $\overline{S_3} = \{\neg\varphi \mid \varphi \in S_3\}$, and $\overline{S_3} = J_2 \cap J_1$, $S_2 = \{\neg\varphi \mid \varphi \in S_2\}$. We have that $J_3 \backslash J_1 = S_2 \cup S_3$ and $J_3 \backslash J_2 = S_3$. Since S_2 is consistent with both S_3 and $\overline{S_3}$, clearly neither of these subsets implies the other. Therefore the $MPI(J_3 \backslash J_1) = MPI(J_3 \backslash J_2) \cup MPI(S_2)$ and $MPI(J_3 \backslash J_2) \subset MPI(J_3 \backslash J_1)$. Observe further that $MPI(J_1 \backslash J_3) = MPI(J_2 \backslash J_3) \cup MPI(\overline{S_2})$. Consequently $MPI(J_2 \backslash J_3) \subset MPI(J_1 \backslash J_3)$.

We now have that $d_{msp}(J_2, J_3) = |MPI(S_3)| + |MPI(\overline{S_3})|$ and $d_{msp}(J_1, J_3) = |MPI(S_3)| + |MPI(S_2)| + |MPI(\overline{S_3})| + |MPI(\overline{S_2})|$.

From this proof it also follows that d_{msp} satisfies the Axiom 4 of [7]: observe that $MPI(J_3 \backslash J_2) = MPI(J_3 \backslash J_2) \cup MPI(S_2) = MPI(J_3 \backslash J_2) \cup MPI(J_2 \backslash J_1)$.

The measures d_{DP}, d_{CS} and d_{msp} are insensitive to clones.
Let $\mathcal{A}' = \mathcal{A} \cup \{\varphi, \neg\varphi\}$ where $\varphi \equiv \varphi_i$ for some $\varphi_i \in \mathcal{A}$. Observe that there exists an isomorphism between $\mathbb{D}(\mathcal{A})$ and $\mathbb{D}(\mathcal{A}')$. For every $J \in \mathbb{D}(\mathcal{A})$ there exists exactly one $J' \in \mathbb{D}(\mathcal{A}')$, furthermore $J' = J \cup \{\varphi\}$ iff $\varphi \in J$ and $J' = J \cup \{\neg\varphi\}$ iff $\neg\varphi \in J$. Consequently, there is an edge between J_1 and J_2 in the graph G built for $\mathcal{A}$ iff there is an edge between the corresponding J_1' and J_2' in the graph G' built for $\mathcal{A}'$. Hence for every $J_1, J_2 \in \mathbb{D}(\mathcal{A})$ and corresponding J_1', J_2', $d_{DP}(J_1, J_2) = d_{DP}(J_1', J_2')$.

For d_{CS}, observe that a logically equivalent issue (to some agenda issue) would never be part of the critical set. The insensitivity to clones of d_{msp} is obtained as a consequence of its insensitivity to consequents; proof follows.

The d_{DP} and the d_{CS} are not insensitive to consequents.
As a counter example for d_{DP}, consider an $\mathcal{A} = \{p, \neg p, p \wedge q, \neg(p \wedge q)\}$ and $J_1, J_2 \in \mathbb{D}(\mathcal{A})$ s.t. $J_1 = \{p, p \wedge q\}$ and $J_2 = \{\neg p, \neg(p \wedge q)\}$. Observe that $\{\neg p\} \vdash \neg(p \wedge q)$. We have that $d_{DP}(J_1, J_2) = 2$, because $J_3 = \{p, \neg(p \wedge q)\}$ is in between J_1 and J_2 ($\mathbb{D}(\mathcal{A}) = \{J_1, J_2, J_3\}$). However $d_{DP}(J_1 \backslash \{p \wedge q\}, J_2 \backslash \{\neg(p \wedge q)\}) = 1$, since $J_3 \backslash \{p \wedge q\} = J_2 \backslash \{\neg(p \wedge q)\}$ and these two points in the graph for $\mathcal{A}$ collapse into one point in the graph for $\mathcal{A} \backslash \{p \wedge q, \neg(p \wedge q)\}$.

As a counter example for d_{CS} consider $\mathcal{A} = \{p, \neg p, p \lor q, \neg(p \lor q)\}$. Observe that the critical set $Y = \mathcal{A}$. Consider $J_1 = \{\neg p, \neg(p \lor q)\}$ and $J_2 = \{p, p \lor q\}$. We have $\{p\} \vdash p \lor q$. We have that $d_{CS}(J_1, J_2) = 2$ and $d_{CS}(J_1 \setminus \{p \lor q, \neg(p \lor q)\}, J_2 \setminus \{p \lor q, \neg(p \lor q)\}) = 1$.

The d_{msp} is insensitive to consequents.
Let $\mathcal{A}$ be s.t. $S \subset \mathcal{A}$, $\varphi \in \mathcal{A}$ and $S \vdash \varphi$. Let $\mathcal{A}' = \mathcal{A} \setminus \{\varphi, \neg\varphi\}$ be a sub-agenda of $\mathcal{A}$. Consider a $J_1, J_2 \in \mathbb{D}(\mathcal{A})$ with $S \subset J_2$ and corresponding $J_1' = J_1 \cap \mathcal{A}'$ and $J_2' = J_2 \cap \mathcal{A}'$. There are two possible cases: (a) $\varphi \in J_1$ and (b) $\varphi \notin J_1$. If (a) is the case, then $J_2 \setminus J_1 = J_2' \setminus J_1'$ (also $J_1 \setminus J_2 = J_1' \setminus J_2'$) and thus $d_{msp}(J_1, J_2) = d_{msp}(J_1', J_2')$. If (b) is the case, then $S \not\subset J_1$. We have that $\varphi \notin MPI(J_2 \setminus J_1)$, thus $MPI(J_2 \setminus J_1) = MPI(J_2' \setminus J_1')$. If there exists an $MPI(J_1 \setminus J_2)$ s.t. $\neg\varphi \notin MPI(J_1 \setminus J_2)$, then $|MPI(J_1 \setminus J_2)| = |MPI(J_1' \setminus J_2')|$. If for all $MPI(J_1 \setminus J_2)$, $\neg\varphi \in MPI(J_1 \setminus J_2)$, then there will be exactly one element of S not in $MPI(J_1 \setminus J_2)$ because S minimally entails φ, thus $|MPI(J_1 \setminus J_2)| = |MPI(J_1' \setminus J_2')|$.

5   Summary

Functions are used to quantify the (dis)similarity between different types of information collections, in *e.g.*, belief merging, judgment aggregation, preference aggregation and abstract argumentation. This is the first work to consider the assembly of desirable properties for dissimilarity measures in judgment aggregation, as well as defining properties that identify measures sensitive to the logic relations among judgments.

It is straightforward to show that neither of the scoring distances d_H, d_{rv}, d_{et}, d_{ds}, d_{md}, and d_{ir} are insensitive to clones. Any scoring function s can be transformed into a clone insensitive version s_{ci} using $s_{ci}(J_i, \varphi) = \frac{s(J, \varphi)}{|S_\varphi|}$, where $S_\varphi = \{\psi \mid \psi \in \mathcal{A}, \psi \equiv \varphi\}$. It remains to be explored whether the clone insensitive scores still generalise known voting rules, as studied in [6,13].

Interesting future work arises from looking into how the "logic relation sensitivity" properties of a measure interact with the properties of a judgment aggregation operator that uses them. The first obvious property to investigate is the property of majority-preservation. A profile is majority-consistent when the majoritarian set is consistent. The majoritarian set is the judgment set in which each judgment is supported by a majority in the profile. A judgment aggregation rule is majority-preserving when it selects as a unique collective judgment set the majoritarian set whenever the profile is majority-consistent. Can a distance-based rule using a logic relation sensitive dissimilarity measure be majority-preserving? It can be shown that neither the Duddy-Piggins distance, nor the d_{msp} combined with the sum yield a majority-preserving rule. We conjecture that this result scales to all sensitive measures and aggregators. Other possible dependencies between the judgment aggregation rule and the constituting d, such as agenda separability [14] are likely to exist.

Acknowledgment. We are grateful to Jérôme Lang for his valuable comments on various versions of this paper.

References

1. Baumeister, D., Erdélyi, G., Erdélyi, O.J., Rothe, J.: Computational aspects of manipulation and control in judgment aggregation. In: Perny, P., Pirlot, M., Tsoukiàs, A. (eds.) ADT 2013. LNCS, vol. 8176, pp. 71–85. Springer, Heidelberg (2013)
2. Booth, R., Caminada, M., Podlaszewski, M., Rahwan, I.: Quantifying disagreement in argument-based reasoning. In: Proceedings of the 11th International Conference on Autonomous Agents and Multiagent Systems, AAMAS 2012, Richland, SC, pp. 493–500. International Foundation for Autonomous Agents and Multiagent Systems (2012)
3. Brandt, F., Conitzer, V., Endriss, U.: Computational social choice. In: Weiss, G. (ed.) Multiagent Systems, pp. 213–283. MIT Press (2013)
4. Caminada, M., Pigozzi, G.: On judgment aggregation in abstract argumentation. Autonomous Agents and Multi-Agent Systems 22(1), 64–102 (2011)
5. Deza, M.M., Deza, E.: Encyclopedia of Distances. Springer (2009)
6. Dietrich, F.: Scoring rules for judgment aggregation. Social Choice and Welfare, 1–39 (2013)
7. Duddy, C., Piggins, A.: A measure of distance between judgment sets. Social Choice and Welfare 39(4), 855–867 (2012)
8. Endriss, U., Grandi, U., Porello, D.: Complexity of judgment aggregation. Journal Artificial Intelligence Research (JAIR) 45, 481–514 (2012)
9. Everaere, P., Konieczny, S., Marquis, P.: The strategy-proofness landscape of merging. Journal of Artificial Intelligence Research (JAIR) 28, 49–105 (2007)
10. Hamming, R.W.: Error detecting and error correcting codes. Bell System Technical Journal 29(2), 147–160 (1950)
11. Konieczny, S., Pino Pérez, R.: Logic based merging. Journal of Philosophical Logic 40(2), 239–270 (2011)
12. Lafage, C., Lang, J.: Propositional distances and compact preference representation. European Journal of Operational Research 160(3), 741–761 (2005)
13. Lang, J., Slavkovik, M.: Judgment aggregation rules and voting rules. In: Perny, P., Pirlot, M., Tsoukiàs, A. (eds.) ADT 2013. LNCS, vol. 8176, pp. 230–243. Springer, Heidelberg (2013)
14. Lang, J., Slavkovik, M., Vesic, S.: A weakening of independence in judgment aggregation: agenda separability (extended abstract). In: Schaub, T. (ed.) Proceedings of the 21st European Conference on Artificial Intelligence, page forthcoming (2014)
15. List, C., Puppe, C.: Judgment aggregation: A survey. In: Anand, P., Puppe, C., Pattanaik, P. (eds.) Oxford Handbook of Rational and Social Choice. Oxford (2009)
16. Miller, M.K., Osherson, D.: Methods for distance-based judgment aggregation. Social Choice and Welfare 32(4), 575–601 (2009)
17. Pigozzi, G.: Belief merging and the discursive dilemma: an argument-based account to paradoxes of judgment aggregation. Synthese 152(2), 285–298 (2006)
18. Slavkovik, M., Agotnes, T.: A judgment set similarity measure based on prime implicants. In: Proceedings of the 13th International Conference on Autonomous Agents and Multiagent Systems, AAMAS, page forthcoming (2013)
19. Slavkovik, M., Jamroga, W.: Distance-based rules for weighted judgment aggregation (extended abstract). In: Proceedings of AAMAS, pp. 1405–1406 (2012)

Exploiting Answer Set Programming for Handling Information Diffusion in a Multi-Social-Network Scenario

Giuseppe Marra[1], Francesco Ricca[2], Giorgio Terracina[2], and Domenico Ursino[1,*]

[1] DIIES, University Mediterranea of Reggio Calabria, Via Graziella, Località Feo di Vito, 89122 Reggio Calabria, Italy
[2] Dipartimento di Matematica, University of Calabria, Via Pietro Bucci, 89136 Rende (CS), Italy

Abstract. In this paper we apply Answer Set Programming for analyzing properties of social networks, and we consider Information Diffusion in Social Network Analysis. This problem has been deeply investigated for single social networks, but we focus on a new setting where many social networks coexist and are strictly connected to each other, thanks to those users who join more social networks. We present some experiments allowing us to conclude that the way of spreading information in a Multi-Social-Network scenario is completely different from that of a Single-Social-Network context.

1 Introduction

Answer Set Programming (ASP)[2,14,18,30,31] is a powerful programming paradigm for knowledge representation and declarative problem-solving. The idea of ASP is to represent a given computational problem by a logic program such that its answer sets correspond to solutions, and then, use an answer set solver to find such solutions. The high knowledge-modeling power [2,14] of ASP and the availability of efficient ASP systems [11], make ASP a suitable choice for implementing applications where there is the need of representing and manipulating complex knowledge. Nowadays, ASP counts applications in several fields, ranging from Artificial Intelligence [1,3,4,17,32] to Knowledge Management [2,5], Information Integration [8,7,28,29], and it was also exploited in industrial applications [21,22]. In this paper we apply ASP in a further field, namely Social Network Analysis [12,16]. In particular, we focus on one of the most relevant problems in this field, called Information Diffusion [13,19,20,24,25,26].

Information Diffusion problem has been investigated in the past for a Single-Social-Network context. According to [24], this problem can be divided into three main issues, namely: *(i) modeling diffusion process*, which implies to determine how (i.e., through which paths) information is spread, *(ii) detecting influential*

---

* This work was partially supported by Aubay Italia S.p.A. and by the project BA2Kno (Business Analytics to Know) funded by MIUR.

E. Fermé and J. Leite (Eds.): JELIA 2014, LNAI 8761, pp. 618–627, 2014.

nodes, which requires to identify those nodes of the network that play important roles in the spreading process, and *(iii) analyzing the most diffused topics*, which concerns the detection of the most popular pieces of information within the network and those appearing the most relevant for a given node.

As for the *diffusion process modeling*, a basic predictive model is the *Linear Threshold* (LT) one [20]; it assumes the existence of a static graph (representing the social network) through which the diffusion process proceeds. LT requires the definition of an influence degree on each edge and of a threshold on each node. The diffusion process iteratively proceeds by starting from a set of initially *activated* nodes. Inactive nodes are activated only if the sum of the degrees of the edges directly connected to active nodes is higher than to the corresponding node threshold. An alternative predictive model is the *Independent Cascade* (IC) one [19]. In this model only edge weights play a role in the Information Diffusion process. Indeed, once activated, a node has a unique chance to activate an inactive neighbor node; this chance is directly proportional to the weight of the edge connecting them. More recent models [23,33] improve these seminal ones, allowing, for instance, the relaxation of the synchronicity assumption, previously mandatory.

As for the *detection of influential nodes*, in the past, a variety of approaches facing it in a single social network have been proposed. For instance, Kempe et al. [25,26] propose an approach that exploits both LT and IC to face the *influence maximization* problem. This problem was first introduced in [13]. Given a parameter k, it aims at finding the k maximally influential nodes (i.e., the k best early adopters). Indeed, thanks to a correct choice of them, it is possible to trigger a large Influence Cascade within the network. Furthermore, found solutions can be used to extract some general features characterizing them (i.e., a sort of their "identikit"). We call this side-problem *influential node characterization* and its extension (and next solution) from a Single-Social-Network Context to a MSNS is one of the main contributions of this paper.

Information Diffusion has been largely investigated in the past on single social networks. However, the current scenario is Multi-Social-Network [6,9,10]. Here, many social networks coexist and are strictly connected to each other, thanks to those users who join more social networks, acting as bridges among them. But, what happens to the Information Diffusion problem when passing to this new scenario? New aspects must be taken into account and new considerations are in order. However, to the best of our knowledge, no investigation about this issue has been made in the past. When starting this task, several new questions arise, such as: *(i)* What is the role of bridges for Information Diffusion in a Multi-Social-Network Scenario (MSNS, for short)? *(ii)* Are there other kind of nodes (such as power user or bridge's direct neighbors) that play a key role in Information Diffusion? *(iii)* What is the "identikit" of the most influential nodes? *(iv)* How this identikit varies when the number of social networks of the MSNS increases? In this paper, we exploit ASP to give an answer to these questions and, more in general, to face the Information Diffusion problem in an MSNS.

2   Answer Set Programming

ASP is a declarative programming paradigm based on nonmonotonic reasoning. Its main advantage consists in its declarativity, combined with a relatively high expressive power. In ASP, a *(disjunctive) rule r* has the following form:

$$a_1 \vee \ldots \vee a_n :- b_1, \ldots, b_k, \text{not } b_{k+1}, \ldots, \text{not } b_m.$$

where $a_1, \ldots, a_n, b_1, \ldots, b_m$ are atoms, and $n, k, m \geq 0$. A literal is either an atom a or its negation $\text{not } a$. The disjunction $a_1 \vee \ldots \vee a_n$ is the *head* of r, while the conjunction $b_1, \ldots, b_k, \text{not } b_{k+1}, \ldots, \text{not } b_m$ is its *body*. Rules with empty body are called *facts*. Those with empty head are called *strong constraints*. A rule is *safe* if every variable occurs in some positive literal of the body. An ASP program is a set of safe rules. An atom, a literal, a rule, or a program is *ground* if no variables appear in it. Let P be an ASP program. The *Herbrand universe* U_P and the *Herbrand base* B_P of P, are defined as usual. The ground instantiation G_P of P is the set of all the ground instances of rules of P, that can be obtained by substituting variables with constants from U_P. An *interpretation* I for P is a subset I of B_P. A ground literal ℓ (resp. $\text{not } \ell$) is true w.r.t. I if $\ell \in I$ (resp. $\ell \notin I$), and false (resp. true) otherwise. A ground rule r is *satisfied* by I if at least one atom in the head is true w.r.t. I whenever all literals in the body of r are true w.r.t. I. A model is an interpretation that satisfies all the rules of a program. Given a ground program G_P and an interpretation I, the *reduct* [15] of G_P w.r.t. I is the subset G_P^I of G_P obtained by deleting from G_P the rules in which a body literal is false w.r.t. I. An interpretation I for P is an *answer set* (or stable model [18]) for P if I is a minimal model (under subset inclusion) of G_P^I (i.e., I is a minimal model for the program G_P^I) [15]. Optimal answer sets can be specified by weak constraints. An ASP program with weak constraints is $\Pi = <R, W>$, where R is a program and W is a set of weak constraints. In detail, a *weak constraint* ω is of the form:

$$:\sim b_1, \ldots, b_k, \text{not } b_{k+1}, \ldots, \text{not } b_m.[w@l]$$

where w and l are the weight and level of ω. The semantics of Π extends from the basic case defined above, thus we assume that R and W are ground in the following. A constraint ω is violated by an interpretation I if all literals in ω are true w.r.t. I. An *optimal answer set O* for P is an answer set of R that minimizes the sum of the weights of the violated weak constraints in a prioritized way.

A complete description of the ASP language is out of the scope of this paper; we refer the reader to [2] for a textbook on Answer Set Programming and to [27] for a complete description of the language implemented by DLV, the ASP implementation used for our analysis, which also supports aggregate atoms [15] to easily encode aggregate functions as the ones available in SQL.

3   Modeling a Multi-Social-Network Scenario

A Multi-Social-Network Scenario models a context where several social networks coexist and are strictly connected to each other, thanks to those users who join more social networks. Indeed, when a user joins more social networks, her multiple accounts allow these networks to be connected. We call *bridge user* each user joining more social networks, *bridge (node)* each account of such a user and *me edge* each edge connecting two bridges.

A Multi-Social-Network Scenario Ψ, consisting of n social networks $\{S_1, S_2, \ldots, S_n\}$, can be modeled by a pair $\langle G, T \rangle$. Here, T is a list $\{t_1, t_2, \ldots, t_p\}$ of topics of interest for the users of Ψ. It is preliminarily obtained by performing the union/reconciliation of the topics related to the social networks of Ψ. G is a graph and can be represented as $G = \langle V, E \rangle$. V is the set of nodes. A node $v_i \in V$ represents a user account in a social network of Ψ. $E = E_f \cup E_m$ is a set of edges. E_f is the set of friendship edges; E_m is the set of me edges. An edge $e_j \in E$ is a triplet $\langle v_s, v_t, L_j \rangle$. v_s and v_t are the source and the target nodes of e_j, whereas L_j is a list of p pairs $\langle t_{j_k}, w_{j_k} \rangle$, where t_{j_k} is a topic and w_{j_k} is a real number between 0 and 1 representing the corresponding weight. This weight depends on both t_{j_k} and the ability of the user associated with v_t to propagate, to the user associated with v_s, the information related to t_{j_k}.

4 Formalizing the Information Diffusion Problem in a Multi-Social-Network Scenario

As previously pointed out, to extend the information diffusion problem from a single social network to an MSNS, it is necessary to consider the peculiarities of this scenario. As for the first issue of the Information Diffusion problem (i.e., the *diffusion process model*), we chose to exploit the Linear Threshold model. Our updated version of this model in MSNS works as the traditional one, except for me edges. In fact, as said before, a me edge links two accounts of the *same* user (i.e. bridge nodes) belonging to different social networks. Thus, it makes no sense to talk of *influence degree* for these edges, since a user cannot influence herself. Actually, we can still define a degree for me edges but it depends on the probability of a bridge user to share the content in other social networks joined by her (i.e., to spread the information from a social network to another one). This probability is a function of both the habits of the bridge user and the features of the two social networks she joins. Moreover, as for the activation rule of bridge nodes, the definition of a threshold is misleading. Indeed, given a me edge and a bridge, if this last does not activate the corresponding bridge at the moment of its own activation, it's unrealistic that it will do this task in a second time. As a consequence, it is reasonable to adopt an activation policy for me edges similar to the one suggested by the Independent Cascade model. This means that, at the time of its activation, given a me edge and a bridge, this last has a single chance proportional to the probability defined for the edge, to activate the corresponding bridge. On the basis of this reasoning, our diffusion process model (called MSNS-DP model) is as follows.

MSNS-DP model. Consider an Information Diffusion task in an MSNS and assume that at the jth step some nodes have already been activated. At the $(j+1)^{th}$ step an inactive node n is activated if: *(i)* the sum of the degrees of friendship edges directly connecting n to already active neighbors is higher than the threshold associated with n, and/or *(ii)* a random number uniformly extracted in the interval $[0, 1]$ is lower than the diffusion probability of a me edge connecting n to a bridge activated at the jth step.

As for the second issue of the Information Diffusion problem (i.e., *the detection and characterization of influential spreaders*), we start from the influence maximization problem introduced in the Introduction. However, even in this case, some modifications are in order. In fact, when passing from a single social network to an MSNS, it could happen that the optimal solution found by classical approaches maximizes the diffusion in a single network leaving uncovered the remaining ones. In order to take the peculiarities of the MSNS into account, a slightly different definition of the influence maximization problem (called MSNS-IM problem) is required.

MSNS-IM Problem. Given in input:
- A Multi-Social-Network Scenario Ψ, made of n social networks $\{S_1, \ldots, S_n\}$.
- A list D of n elements. The generic element D_h of D consists of a tuple $\langle S_h, p_h, c_h \rangle$. Here, S_h is a social network of Ψ. c_h is the minimum desired coverage for S_h, i.e., the minimum number of nodes of S_h which must be reached by the information to spread throughout Ψ. p_h denotes the priority of S_h, it is an integer from 1 to n, where 1 (resp., n) is the maximum (resp., minimum) priority. The social network with the maximum (resp., minimum) priority will the first (resp., the last) to have its coverage requirements satisfied.
- A list τ of q elements. The generic element $\tau[k]$ of τ is a pair $\langle t_k, \omega_k \rangle$. Here, t_k corresponds to the kth element of the set of topics T of Ψ. ω_k is a real number, belonging to the interval $[0, 1]$ and indicating the weight of t_k in the information to spread throughout Ψ.

The MSNS-IM problem in Ψ requires to find the minimum set of the nodes of Ψ allowing the maximization of the coverage of the social networks of Ψ, taking into account the minimum required network coverage, the network priorities (as expressed in D), and the topics characterizing the information to spread (as expressed in τ). Observe that this version of the problem is quite different from the one specified for single social networks in the past. Indeed, it does not fix the parameter k but asks to find the minimum set of nodes (i.e., minimizing k) that are able to trigger a diffusion process that guarantees, at least, the coverage requirements represented in D. In this way, the optimization task is transferred to the number of earlier starters, whereas the maximization of the overall coverage is not considered, since it makes no sense in an MSNS. Clearly, the solution of MSNS-IM problem, along with a next study of returned nodes, leads to the detection and characterization of influential spreaders and, therefore, to face the second issue of the Information Diffusion problem. Finally, in our definition, topics (i.e., the third issue of the Information Diffusion problem - see the Introduction) can be handled by means of the list τ given in input. In this way, once the topics of interest of each node have been determined, it is possible to state how much a node is important in the Information Diffusion process into consideration.

5   Handling Information Diffusion in a MSNS with ASP

The MSNS-IM problem described in the previous section is extremely complex. The adoption of ASP has been a strategic choice to allow an easy modeling and a fast set-up of the approach implementation. Interestingly, the elegant modeling of the problem in ASP is associated with acceptable performances of the implementation.

First, let us define the input format of the problem. Let starting_node(V) be the set of nodes from which initially *activated* nodes must be chosen. Let edge(V1,V2,K) be the relation containing the edges from V1 to V2, where K specifies the edge kind (i.e., me or friendship). Let edge_topic(V1,V2,T,W) be the set of topics/weights associated with the edge from v_1 to v_2. Let node(V,Sn) represent the set of nodes in the social network S_n. Finally, let D(Sh,Ph,Ch) identify the desiderata for coverage and priority and tau(T,W) the set of topics, with the corresponding weights, of the information to spread.

The logic program designed to solve our problem is as follows

```
 1. in(V) v out(V) :- starting_node(V).
 2. :- D(Sh,Ph,Ch), #count{V:active(V),node(V,Sh)}<=Ch.
 3. active(V) :- in(V).
 4. active(V) :- active(V1),edge(V,V1,me).
 5. active(V) :- node(V,Sn), #sum{W: edge(V,V1,friendship), active(V1),
                  edge_topic(V,V1,T,W), tau(T,Wb) }>=Tw
 6. :~ in(V). [1@4]
 7. :~ node(V,Sn), not active(V). [1@3]
 8. :~ D(S1,P1,C1), D(S2,P2,C2), P1<P2,
            nactive(S1,N1), nactive(S2,N2), N1<N2. [1@2]
 9. nactive(Sn,N) :- node(V,Sn), #count{W: active(W), node(W,Sn)}=N.
10. :~ tau(Ta,Wa), tau(Tb,Wb), active(V1), active(V2), Wa>Wb,
            edge_topic(V1,V2,Ta,W1), edge_topic(V1,V2,Tb,W2), W1<W2. [1@1]
```

where, rule 1. guesses a subset of starting nodes sufficient for the optimization purposes. To discard non admissible solutions, constraint 2. is exploited. In order to compute the nodes activated by the current choice, rules 3. to 5. are applied. Rules 3. and 4. state that a node is active if either it is a starting one, or it reaches an active node through a me edge. In rule 5., Tw is a fixed threshold indicating the minimum weight that must be totalized through the topics of the edges connected to V to activate it. In our experimental campaign we performed some simplifications about this activation policy. In particular, we assumed that all the topics of Ψ have the same weight.It follows that all the friendship edges in Ψ have the same weight (we assign a weight equal to 1 to them). We also assumed that me edges always propagate the information to spread. This means assigning a weight equal to 1 to all me edges. Finally, we assumed also that a node is activated when at least two edges, outgoing from it, are pointing to already activated nodes. This corresponds to set the threshold Tw to 2. Under these assumptions, rules 3.-5. can be simplified.

Returning to the examination of our approach, we point out that the optimization step consisting of the choice of the best models among the consistent ones, is carried out by a number of weak constraints. Specifically, the weak constraint 6. imposes that the number of nodes *in* the consistent solutions must be minimum. The weak constraint 7. imposes the minimization of non-active nodes, whereas the weak constraint 8. states that the best solution must be such that the order of Social Networks in terms of activated nodes must follow what specified in the desiderata or, at least, the number of violations of this order must be minimized. Rule 9. is an auxiliary one, counting the number of active nodes for each social network. Analogously, weak constraint 10. minimizes the number of selected arcs whose list of topics does not comply with the topic classification specified in `tau`. Observe that all the weak constraints have the same weight, but different priorities. This guarantees that, for instance, the minimum sets of nodes providing consistent solutions are identified first, and, among them, the ones minimizing non-active nodes are selected.

6   Experimental Campaign

To test our Information Diffusion approach we performed an experimental campaign on an MSNS consisting of four social networks, namely LiveJournal, Flickr, Twitter and YouTube. We chose these networks because they are the ones allowing an easier access to their own data. Our MSNS has 93177 nodes and 146957 edges. The dataset can be downloaded from: `www.ursino.unirc.it/DiffusionJELIA.html`. The password the Reader must specify is "85749236".

We performed a large number of runs of our ASP program using DLV [27]. In these runs we considered many configurations of the starting nodes. They differed in the number of nodes (ranging from 25 to 100 with a step of 25), the percentage of bridges (ranging from 0 to 100 with a step of 10), and the number of the social networks to cover (ranging from 2 to 4). To reduce the influence of possible outliers, for each configuration we considered four different sets of starting nodes randomly constructed by following the guidelines discussed in Section 4. For each set of starting nodes we considered 10 different network coverage requirements (ranging from 10% to 100% of each social network with a step of 10%). The whole number of runs we have performed was 5280. Due to space limitations, in the following we report only some of obtained results.

As a first experiment we measured the average percentage of bridges in the optimal solutions. For this purpose, we computed the variation of the average percentage of bridges present in the optimal solutions against the variation of the average percentage of bridges present in the sets of starting nodes. Obtained results are shown in Figure 1. Observe that the percentage of bridges in the optimal solutions is generally higher, or much higher, than the percentage of bridges in the sets of starting nodes. This information is precious for drawing an identikit of the most influential nodes for Information Diffusion in an MSNS. Indeed, it suggests that bridges certainly play a key role in Information Diffusion in an MSNS. Therefore, a first feature of influential nodes is that they are generally bridges. Observe that, while it is straightforward that bridges are important for spreading information from a social network to another of an MSNS, it is not so

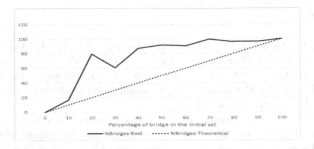

Fig. 1. Average percentage of bridges in the optimal solutions

obvious that starting nodes are generally bridges. Indeed, in principle, it could happen that starting nodes are non-bridges, and bridges are reached only in a second time. The fact that starting nodes are generally bridges is an important result of our paper and indicates that bridges allow the minimization of the set of nodes necessary for spreading information in an MSNS.

As a second experiment we analyzed which kind of nodes generally compose the optimal solutions. For this purpose, we computed the following statistics (we first report the parameters and, then, in parentheses, the obtained value): *(i)* average percentage of bridges (87%); *(ii)* average percentage of the direct neighbors of bridges (13%); *(iii)* average percentage of power users (83%); *(iv)* average percentage of the direct neighbors of power users (7%); *(v)* average percentage of nodes being both bridges and power users (77%); *(vi)* average percentage of nodes being bridges or power users (93%); *(vii)* average percentage of nodes being bridges but not power users (6%); *(viii)* average percentage of nodes being power users but not bridges (7%); *(ix)* average percentage of nodes being neither bridges nor power users (10%); *(x)* average Jaccard coefficient[1] of bridges and power users (82%). From the analysis of these values we can observe that 100% of the nodes in the optimal solutions are either bridges or direct neighbors of bridges. Analogously, 90% of the nodes in the optimal solutions are either power users or direct neighbors of power users. Furthermore, the majority of the bridges involved in the optimal solutions are power users, and vice versa. Finally, only a little fraction of the nodes present in the optimal solutions are neither bridges nor power users. These results allow us to conclude that almost all the bridges in the optimal solutions are power users. It tells also that if an influential node is not a bridge, it is surely a direct neighbor of a bridge. We think that the capability of our approach of finding solutions with a low number of node, as emerged in the first test, is due to the double nature of influential nodes: as bridges they can start the Information Diffusion process among the social networks of our MSNS; as power users they can favor the in-depth diffusion of the same information.

---

[1] We recall that the Jaccard Coefficient $J(A, B)$ between two sets A and B is defined as $J(A, B) = \frac{A \cap B}{A \cup B}$.

References

1. Balduccini, M., Gelfond, M., Watson, R., Nogueira, M.: The USA-Advisor: A Case Study in Answer Set Planning. In: Eiter, T., Faber, W., Truszczyński, M. (eds.) LPNMR 2001. LNCS (LNAI), vol. 2173, pp. 439–442. Springer, Heidelberg (2001)
2. Baral, C.: Knowledge Representation, Reasoning and Declarative Problem Solving. Cambridge University Press (2003)
3. Baral, C., Gelfond, M.: Reasoning Agents in Dynamic Domains. In: Logic-Based Artificial Intelligence, pp. 257–279. Kluwer Academic Publishers (2000)
4. Baral, C., Uyan, C.: Declarative Specification and Solution of Combinatorial Auctions Using Logic Programming. In: Eiter, T., Faber, W., Truszczyński, M. (eds.) LPNMR 2001. LNCS (LNAI), vol. 2173, pp. 186–199. Springer, Heidelberg (2001)
5. Bardadym, V.A.: Computer-Aided School and University Timetabling: The New Wave. In: Burke, E., Ross, P. (eds.) PATAT 1995. LNCS, vol. 1153, pp. 22–45. Springer, Heidelberg (1996)
6. Berlingerio, M., Coscia, M., Giannotti, F., Monreale, A., Pedreschi, D.: The pursuit of hubbiness: Analysis of hubs in large multidimensional networks. Journal of Computational Science 2(3), 223–237 (2011)
7. Bertossi, L., Hunter, A., Schaub, T. (eds.): Inconsistency Tolerance. LNCS, vol. 3300. Springer, Heidelberg (2005)
8. Bravo, L., Bertossi, L.: Logic programming for consistently querying data integration systems. In: Proc. of the International Joint Conference on Artificial Intelligence (IJCAI 2003), Acapulco, Mexico, pp. 10–15 (2003)
9. Buccafurri, F., Lax, G., Nocera, A., Ursino, D.: Discovering Links among Social Networks. In: Flach, P.A., De Bie, T., Cristianini, N. (eds.) ECML PKDD 2012, Part II. LNCS, vol. 7524, pp. 467–482. Springer, Heidelberg (2012)
10. Buccafurri, F., Lax, G., Nocera, A., Ursino, D.: Moving from social networks to social internetworking scenarios: The crawling perspective. Information Sciences 256, 126–137 (2014)
11. Calimeri, F., Ianni, G., Ricca, F.: The third open answer set programming competition. TPLP 14(1), 117–135 (2014)
12. Carrington, P., Scott, J., Wasserman, S.: Models and Methods in Social Network Analysis. Cambridge University Press (2005)
13. Domingos, P., Richardson, M.: Mining the network value of customers. In: Proc. of the ACM SIGKDD International Conference on Knowledge Discovery and Data Mining (KDD 2001), pp. 57–66. ACM, San Francisco (2001)
14. Eiter, T., Gottlob, G., Mannila, H.: Disjunctive Datalog. ACM Transactions on Database Systems 22(3), 364–418 (1997)
15. Faber, W., Leone, N., Pfeifer, G.: Recursive aggregates in disjunctive logic programs: Semantics and complexity. In: Alferes, J.J., Leite, J. (eds.) JELIA 2004. LNCS (LNAI), vol. 3229, pp. 200–212. Springer, Heidelberg (2004)
16. Freeman, L.: The Development of Social Network Analysis. Empirical Press (2006)
17. Garro, A., Palopoli, L., Ricca, F.: Exploiting agents in e-learning and skills management context. AI Communications – The European Journal on Artificial Intelligence 19(2), 137–154 (2006)
18. Gelfond, M., Lifschitz, V.: Classical Negation in Logic Programs and Disjunctive Databases. New Generation Computing 9, 365–385 (1991)
19. Goldenberg, J., Libai, E., Muller, E.: Talk of the network: A complex systems look at the underlying process of word-of-mouth. Marketing Letters 12(3), 211–223 (2001)

20. Granovetter, M.: Threshold models of collective behavior. American Journal of Sociology 83(6), 1127–1138 (1978)
21. Grasso, G., Iiritano, S., Leone, N., Lio, V., Ricca, F., Scalise, F.: An asp-based system for team-building in the gioia-tauro seaport. In: Carro, M., Peña, R. (eds.) PADL 2010. LNCS, vol. 5937, pp. 40–42. Springer, Heidelberg (2010)
22. Grasso, G., Iiritano, S., Leone, N., Ricca, F.: Some DLV Applications for Knowledge Management. In: Erdem, E., Lin, F., Schaub, T. (eds.) LPNMR 2009. LNCS, vol. 5753, pp. 591–597. Springer, Heidelberg (2009)
23. Guille, A., Hacid, H.: A predictive model for the temporal dynamics of information diffusion in online social networks. In: Proc. of the International World Wide Web Conference (WWW 2012) - Companion Volume, pp. 1145–1152. ACM, Lyon (2012)
24. Guille, A., Hacid, H., Favre, C., Zighed, D.: Information Diffusion in Online Social Networks: A Survey. SIGMOD Record 42(2), 17–28 (2013)
25. Kempe, D., Kleinberg, J., Tardos, É.: Maximizing the spread of influence through a social network. In: Proc. of the ACM SIGKDD International Conference on Knowledge Discovery and Data Mining (KDD 2003), pp. 137–146. ACM, Washington, DC (2003)
26. Kempe, D., Kleinberg, J., Tardos, É.: Influential Nodes in a Diffusion Model for Social Networks. In: Caires, L., Italiano, G.F., Monteiro, L., Palamidessi, C., Yung, M. (eds.) ICALP 2005. LNCS, vol. 3580, pp. 1127–1138. Springer, Heidelberg (2005)
27. Leone, N., Pfeifer, G., Faber, W., Eiter, T., Gottlob, G., Perri, S., Scarcello, F.: The DLV System for Knowledge Representation and Reasoning. ACM Transactions on Computational Logic 7(3), 499–562 (2006)
28. Leone, N., Gottlob, G., Rosati, R., Eiter, T., Faber, W., Fink, M., Greco, G., Ianni, G., Kałka, E., Lembo, D., Lenzerini, M., Lio, V., Nowicki, B., Ruzzi, M., Staniszkis, W., Terracina, G.: The INFOMIX System for Advanced Integration of Incomplete and Inconsistent Data. In: Proceedings of the 24th ACM SIGMOD International Conference on Management of Data (SIGMOD 2005), pp. 915–917. ACM Press, Baltimore (2005)
29. Manna, M., Ricca, F., Terracina, G.: Consistent query answering via ASP from different perspectives: Theory and practice. Theory and Practice of Logic Programming 13(2), 277–252 (2013)
30. Marek, V.W., Truszczyński, M.: Stable models and an alternative logic programming paradigm. CoRR cs.LO/9809032 (1998)
31. Niemelä, I.: Logic Programs with Stable Model Semantics as a Constraint Programming Paradigm. In: Niemelä, I., Schaub, T. (eds.) Proceedings of the Workshop on Computational Aspects of Nonmonotonic Reasoning, Trento, Italy, pp. 72–79 (May/June 1998)
32. Nogueira, M., Balduccini, M., Gelfond, M., Watson, R., Barry, M.: An A-Prolog Decision Support System for the Space Shuttle. In: Ramakrishnan, I.V. (ed.) PADL 2001. LNCS, vol. 1990, pp. 169–183. Springer, Heidelberg (2001)
33. Saito, K., Ohara, K., Yamagishi, Y., Kimura, M., Motoda, H.: Learning diffusion probability based on node attributes in social networks. In: Kryszkiewicz, M., Rybinski, H., Skowron, A., Raś, Z.W. (eds.) ISMIS 2011. LNCS, vol. 6804, pp. 153–162. Springer, Heidelberg (2011)

Reasoning about Dynamic Normative Systems

Max Knobbout, Mehdi Dastani, and John-Jules Ch. Meyer

Utrecht University, Department of Information and Computing Sciences
PO Box 80.089, 3508 TB Utrecht, The Netherlands

Abstract. The use of normative systems is widely accepted as an effective approach to control and regulate the behaviour of agents in multi-agent systems. When norms are added to a normative system, the behaviour of such a system changes. As of yet, there is no clear formal methodology to model the dynamics of a normative system under addition of various types of norms. In this paper we view the addition of a norm as an update of a normative system, and we provide update semantics to model this process.

1 Introduction

The use of normative systems is widely accepted as an effective approach to control and regulate the behavior of agents in multi-agent systems [12]. Normative systems are generally considered as systems that specify the standards of behaviours for the agents, such as which actions or which states should be achieved or avoided [11,10,1].

A lot of research has focused on deciding (or proving) correctness of a normative system. A normative system is correct if, after implementing it, the objectives of the system designer are satisfied [11]. This might include restrictions like robustness of defection [3,7] or rationality to comply [2,4]. However, these approaches do not cope with the fact that the behaviour of a system may change over time. When norms are added to a normative system, it may for example be that certain actions become forbidden, or certain states become allowed. As of yet, there is no clear formal methodology to model the dynamics of a normative system under addition of various types of norms.

In this paper we provide update semantics for norm addition which allows us to characterize the dynamics of norm addition in a formal way. The view we adopt is that normative systems can be modelled by pointed labelled transition systems, which show which normative (institutional) facts become true under execution of which actions. A norm is a closed operation on these models: they transform normative systems into new normative systems such that the resulting system is aligned with the norm. In this paper we explore how these operations work, and how we can use these operations to prove various properties of a normative system in a dynamic environment.

In the first part of this paper we provide our model of normative systems. We then give a language to construct norms, show how we can update normative systems with these norms and finally show how we can reason with these updates.

E. Fermé and J. Leite (Eds.): JELIA 2014, LNAI 8761, pp. 628–636, 2014.

2   Framework

This section defines the models we use for normative systems, and defines the language we use to express properties of these systems. A normative system in this paper is viewed as an entity which characterizes all the normative facts which are currently true and can become true under execution of certain actions. It is important to note that a normative system does not encode (brute) facts about the environment of the agents. A state in the normative system determines the normative facts which are applicable at the current moment. These normative facts constitute the prohibitions and obligations the agents have at the current moment. Whenever an action occurs in the brute system, the normative system (possibly) progresses from one normative state to another, in which new normative facts might hold. Thus, like in Searle's work [9], even though the brute facts and institutional facts exist in different dimensions, there exists some relation between the two. An example might be a library which lends out books to customers. When a customer borrows a book, the library asserts that it is normatively/legally the case that the customer is holding a book. This proposition might very well correspond to a brute proposition (fact), but they have a different meaning in a normative context. In this paper, we are merely interested in normative systems, and only assume the existence of some actions which may occur in the brute system. Formally, we assume we have an action alphabet Act which denotes the set of possible actions that can occur in a brute system. When a certain action $\alpha \in Act$ occurs in the brute system and a normative system is in a certain state q, we might progress to a different normative state q' in which different normative facts might hold. Formally, a normative system frame F is a tuple $(Q, Act, \rightarrow, \Pi, V)$ such that:

- Q is a non-empty finite set of normative states.
- Act is a finite action alphabet from the brute system.
- $\rightarrow \subseteq Q \times Act \times Q$ is a relation between states with actions, such that for all $q \in Q$ and $\alpha \in Act$ there exists exactly one $q' \in Q$ such that $(q, \alpha, q') \in \rightarrow$. Since the relation is functional, we write $q[\alpha]$ to denote the state q' for which it holds that $(q, \alpha, q') \in \rightarrow$.
- Π is a finite set of normative propositions.
- $V \subseteq \Pi$ is a finite set of violation propositions.

Note that we distinguish between general normative propositions (i.e. "The customer is holding a book") and violations, since it is often useful to talk about forbidden states. As a convention, we write p to denote an element from the set Π and v as an element from V. We define a tuple of the form $N = (F, \mu)$ as a *normative system*, where F is a normative system frame and μ a valuation function mapping a $q \in Q$ to an element from $\mathcal{P}(\Pi)$. A pointed normative system is a pair (N, q) such that N is a normative system, and $q \in Q$ a normative state from N. The language of propositional logic with action modality, written in this paper as $\mathbf{L_{modal}}$, consists of formulas φ built by the following (standard) grammar:

$$\varphi ::= p \mid \neg\varphi \mid \varphi_1 \vee \varphi_2 \mid \Box_\alpha\varphi \qquad (p \in \Pi, \alpha \in Act)$$

Along a pointed normative system (N, q), we can evaluate formulas of $\mathbf{L_{modal}}$ in the following (standard) way:

- $N, q \models p$ iff $p \in \mu(q)$
- $N, q \models \neg\varphi$ iff $N, q \not\models \varphi$
- $N, q \models \varphi_1 \vee \varphi_2$ iff $N, q \models \varphi_1$ or $N, q \models \varphi_2$.
- $N, q \models \Box_\alpha\varphi$ iff $N, q[\alpha] \models \varphi$

Given a pointed normative system (N, q), we say that a sequence of actions $\alpha_1...\alpha_n$ *brings about* normative state of affairs φ if and only if $N, q \models \Box_{\alpha_1}...\Box_{\alpha_n}\varphi$. As is standard, we say that $N \models \varphi$ holds whenever for all $q \in Q$ it holds that $N, q \models \varphi$, and we say that $\models \varphi$ holds (alternatively, "φ is valid") whenever for all normative systems N we have $N \models \varphi$. Whenever we refer to the language $\mathcal{L}_{prop}$ we refer to language of propositional logic, which is the fragment of this language without the modalities of $\Box_\alpha$. We will now briefly discuss an example normative system of a library which lends out books to customers. This will show how we can evaluate formula's from our logic on pointed normative system. This example will also function as a running example throughout this paper to demonstrate how various norms may alter the behaviour of the system.

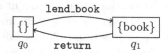

Fig. 1. Normative system N_{library}

Running Example. Consider the normative system N_{library} in Figure 1, which is a very simple example of a library that lends out books to customers. As a convention in this paper, whenever we draw a normative system we omit the reflexive arrows. Here 'book' denotes a normative proposition that a customer is borrowing a book. The library can either be in state q_0 or state q_1, and depending on the performed actions can switch between these states. An example of a formula that holds in this system is $N_{\text{library}}, q_1 \models \Box_{\text{return}} \neg book$, although the behaviour of this system is currently very limited. We will see how the addition of norms allows the system to show more interesting and complex behaviour.

3   Language for Norm Updates

In this section we begin our first step into developing a simple model and language of normative update that is still able to capture a broad variety of different kinds of norms. The kinds of norms we consider in this section are of the 'to-do' variant: A norm of this type, when added to the system, ensures that after execution of a certain action in certain states, certain normative facts are true or false. For example, the library from our example might add a norm stating that lending a book is now forbidden (i.e., after execution of the 'lend_book' action a violation will start to hold). To extend the expressiveness of these kinds of norms even further, we also optionally allow the addition of a 'repair' action. For example, the library may state that lending a book causes a violation, until a fee is paid which removes the violation. Although we often think about the addition of a norm as the addition of a prohibition (i.e. something becomes forbidden), it is also easy to imagine that a norm can enable normative facts to become true which are related to things such as policy updates. For example, the library may update their policy by allowing the lending of magazines, i.e. after the performance of a lend_mag ("lend magazine") action the library will assert that the proposition *magazine* is true, until a return_mag ("return magazine") action is performed. It is important to note that the addition of these norms are not 'physical' actions of the brute system: They come from outside the system (i.e. a designer) and are not triggered by brute actions. In more realistic scenarios, this might very well be the case, as for example the signing of a contract might very well instantiate certain norms to come into effect.

In the remainder of this section, we give a language to construct these kinds of norms, we show how we can update a normative system using these norms and finally we show some interesting properties of this update.

3.1   Language and Update

Given a normative system, we construct the language of norms $\mathbf{L_{norm}}$ in the following way:

$$\nu ::= (Act_T, \varphi, +p, Act_R)|(Act_T, \varphi, -p, Act_R)$$

Where:

$$\varphi \in \mathcal{L}_{prop},\; p \in \Pi,\; Act_T, Act_R \subseteq Act$$

Intuitively, an update of the form $(Act_T, \varphi, +v, Act_R)$ should be interpreted as meaning that whenever an action from Act_T has been taken (the set of trigger actions), to be in a φ-state causes violation v until an action from Act_R has been taken (the set of repair actions). Whenever a repair action occurs, the normative state of affairs are equivalent to what they were before the update. Note that the set Act_R can be empty, which implies that the update is permanent, i.e. it will from then on always be the case that for every φ-state the proposition p is true. The set Act_T can also be empty, but this implies that the update does nothing, since the norm can never be triggered. Some examples:

- $(\{\texttt{speeding}\}, \top, +v, \{\texttt{pay\_fine}\})$: After speeding, a violation occurs which persists for any possible state ($\top$ is valid for all states) until a fine is payed.
- $(\{\texttt{smoking}\}, \texttt{restaurant}, +v, Act)$: It is forbidden to smoke in a restaurant. More specifically, after smoking, to be in a *'restaurant'*-state causes violation v. No specific repair action has to be performed such as paying a fee, since any action (besides again smoking) is a repair action.

- ({drunk_driving}, ⊤, −license, {driving_test}): After drunk driving, the drivers license is revoked for any possible state, until a driving test has been performed.

These updates work on pointed normative systems. This means that these norms both update the normative system itself and the current state. However, given the nature of the kind of norms we consider in this paper, the normative state of affairs of the current state is not altered since a trigger action has to occur first. In this paper we want to give a clear semantic interpretation to how a pointed normative system should behave when a norm from our language is added to the system. This is why we introduce the notion of *norm-aligned*: We say that an updated system is norm-aligned if the resulting system implements the new restrictions of the added norm. Formally:

Definition 1 (Norm-Aligned Update). *Given a pointed normative system* (N, q) *updated with norm* $(Act_T, \varphi, +p, Act_R)$, *we say that the resulting pointed normative system is* norm-aligned *iff for every atomic normative proposition* p' *and every (possibly empty) sequence of actions* $\alpha_1...\alpha_n$, *we have that* $\alpha_1...\alpha_n$ *brings about* p' *if ...*

1. *...it was the case that* $\alpha_1...\alpha_n$ *brought about* p' *in the original system (i.e.* $N, q \models \Box_{\alpha_1}...\Box_{\alpha_n} p'$*), or if ...;*
2. *...* $p' = p$, $\alpha_1...\alpha_n$ *brought about* φ *before the update* $(N, q \models \Box_{\alpha_1}, ..., \Box_{\alpha_n} \varphi)$, *and the norm was triggered but not repaired, that is* $\exists i : \alpha_i \in Act_T, \forall j > i : \alpha_j \notin Act_R$*).*

This definition gives exact restrictions to what a 'correct' update of a pointed normative system ought to be and we can in a similar manner define this for an update of the form $(Act_T, \varphi, -p, Act_R)$. Although these norms may appear at first quite limited in expressiveness, more complex norms can be expressed by combining a multitude of these simpler norms. For example, a complex norm which states that it should always be the case that before entering the train, a ticket needs to be bought, can be encoded with the following two norms in their respective order: (buy_ticket, ⊤, +ticketBought, leave_train) and (enter_train, ¬ticketBought, +v, leave_train). Here *ticketBought* is a normative proposition to denote that a ticket has been bought.

We will now show how we can update a pointed normative system to a new pointed normative system which is norm-aligned. Given a pointed normative system (N, q) and a norm $(Act_T, \varphi, +p, Act_R)$, we write $(N, q)[(Act_T, \varphi, +p, Act_R)]$ to denote the updated system. Formally, given $N = ((Q, Act, \to, \Pi, V), \mu)$ and $\nu = (Act_T, \varphi, +p, Act_R)$, we let $(N, q)[\nu] = (N[\nu], q[\nu]) = (N', q')$ such that:

- Normative system $N' = ((Q', Act, \to', \Pi, V), \mu')$, where:
  - $Q' = \{q^r, q^a \mid q \in Q\}$
    That is, for every state $q \in Q$ we create two copies in the updated system; one in which the norm is active (q^a) and one in which it is repaired (q^r);

$$\rightarrow' = \{(q_i^r, \alpha, q_j^r) \mid q_i[\alpha] = q_j \text{ and } \alpha \notin Act_T\} \bigcup$$
$$\{(q_i^r, \alpha, q_j^a) \mid q_i[\alpha] = q_j \text{ and } \alpha \in Act_T\} \bigcup$$
$$\{(q_i^a, \alpha, q_j^a) \mid q_i[\alpha] = q_j \text{ and } \alpha \notin Act_R \backslash Act_T\} \bigcup$$
$$\{(q_i^a, \alpha, q_j^r) \mid q_i[\alpha] = q_j \text{ and } \alpha \in Act_R \backslash Act_T\}$$

Whenever we are in a repaired state (q_i^r) and a trigger action has been performed, we go to an active state (q_j^a). Whenever we are in an active state (q_i^a) and a repair action has been performed which is not also a trigger action, we go to a repaired state (q_j^r). If no trigger or repair action is performed, we remain in an active (or repaired) state. Note that we write q_i and q_j to simply denote that these states might possibly be different; we attach no further meaning to this indexing;

- For every $q \in Q$:

$$\mu'(q^r) = \mu(q) \text{ and } \mu'(q^a) = \begin{cases} \mu(q) \cup \{p\} & \text{if } N, q \models \varphi \\ \mu(q) & \text{otherwise} \end{cases}$$

That is, all active states (q^a) are updated with atomic proposition p.

- State $q' = q^a$

Alternatively, for an update with $-p$, the updated valuation function μ' becomes:

$$\mu'(q^r) = \mu(q) \text{ and } \mu'(q^a) = \begin{cases} \mu(q) \backslash \{p\} & \text{if } N, q \models \varphi \\ \mu(q) & \text{otherwise} \end{cases}$$

The way this update works is that it makes a copy of every state q in which either the newly added norm is active (q^a to denote that it is active) or in which the added norm is repaired (q^r to denote that it is repaired). Moreover, the transitions between active and repaired states are analogous to the transitions of the original system except for any action that triggers or repairs the norm.

3.2   Running Example

We return to the running example of the library visualized in figure 1. As discussed in the beginning of this section, suppose that the library now updates their policy such that they now also allow customers to borrow magazines. They do this by adding the following norm:

$$\nu_0 = (\{\texttt{lend\_mag}\}, \top, +\texttt{magazine}, \{\texttt{return}\})$$

This norm states that the library (normatively) asserts that a customer has a magazine if he borrows a magazine, and retracts this fact when a customer returns the borrowed items (here, the action **return** is seen as either returning a book or a magazine, or both). By following the rules of the update, we see in Figure 2 how we go from system N_{library} to $N_{\text{library}}[\nu_0]$, and states q_0 and q_1 to q_0^r and q_1^r respectively. We have the following:

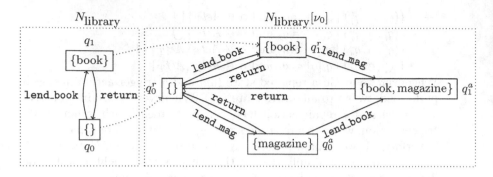

Fig. 2. System N_{library} together with $N_{\text{library}}[\nu_0]$

1. In the initial system, after performance of the lend_mag action the library did not assert that 'magazine' was the case (i.e. the policy was not yet implemented):

$$N_{\text{library}}, q_0 \models \Box_{\text{lend\_mag}}(\neg book \wedge \neg magazine)$$

2. After the addition of this norm, this is the case:

$$(N_{\text{library}}, q_0)[\nu_0] \models \Box_{\text{lend\_mag}}(\neg book \wedge magazine)$$

3. After the addition of this norm, if the customer returns the magazine, the library no longer asserts that the customer is holding a magazine:

$$(N_{\text{library}}, q_0)[\nu_0] \models \Box_{\text{lend\_mag}}\Box_{\text{return}}(\neg book \wedge \neg magazine)$$

Now, if we would consider the most simple normative system as a system consisting of only a single state with an empty valuation (call this the minimal system), it is not hard to see that N_{library} is in fact the minimal system updated with the norm (lend_book, ⊤, +book, return_book). So we see that by combining these norms in meaningful ways we are able to express a wide variety of different complex normative behaviour.

3.3 Properties

The norm update we provided governs interesting logical properties, which we briefly want to touch upon in this section. As mentioned earlier, when we update a pointed normative system the valuation of the current state remains unchanged. This is exactly characterized by the property that for any pointed normative system (N, q) and norm $\nu \in \mathbf{L_{norm}}$ we have that:

$$N, q \models \varphi \text{ iff } (N, q)[\nu] \models \varphi$$

Moreover, we mentioned that whenever a norm $\nu = (Act_T, \varphi, +p, Act_R)$ is not triggered, the normative state of affairs of the system remains as it was before the update. This is characterized by:

$$N, q \models \Box_{\alpha_1}...\Box_{\alpha_n}\varphi \text{ and } \alpha_1, ..., \alpha_n \notin Act_T \text{ implies } (N,q)[\nu] \models \Box_{\alpha_1}...\Box_{\alpha_n}\varphi$$

Finally, for any sequence of actions $\alpha'_1...\alpha'_n$ in which norm ν was triggered but not repaired (i.e. $\exists i : \alpha'_i \in Act_T, \forall j > i : \alpha'_j \notin Act_R$) we have the property that:

$$N, q \models \Box_{\alpha_1}...\Box_{\alpha_n}\varphi \text{ implies } (N,q)[\nu] \models \Box_{\alpha_1}...\Box_{\alpha_n}p$$

And for the norm $\nu' = (Act_T, \varphi, -p, Act_R)$ we have:

$$N, q \models \Box_{\alpha_1}...\Box_{\alpha_n}\varphi \text{ implies } (N,q)[\nu] \models \Box_{\alpha_1}...\Box_{\alpha_n}\neg p$$

Which corresponds to the fact that triggering a norm can indeed change the normative state of affairs. That is to say, whenever after a sequence of actions $\alpha'_1...\alpha'_n$ that triggered the norm it is the case that φ holds, and we updated with a norm stating that for all φ states it is the case that $+p$ (alternatively $-p$), then the update indeed ensures this. Certainly more interesting properties exist, but lay beyond the scope of this paper.

4   Conclusions and Future Research

In this paper we provided update semantics to characterize the dynamics of norm addition of various types of norms. This allows us to provide exact semantics for computational systems that incorporate norm-update. Moreover, this line of work can provide a natural progression to the development of norm-based programming languages, which currently is an important topic within the agent community [5]. From a practical point of view, this framework can be useful for a designer/legislator that has to decide whether or not to introduce a new norm to a system. The new norm may have various effects and non-effects on the behaviour of a system which might initially be overlooked. With a formal and rigid framework like the one provided in this paper, we can verify exactly what these effects are. From a theoretical point of view, it also makes sense to view a normative system as a dynamic entity. For example, in the field of deontic logic [6] (i.e. the logic that concerns itself with what is obligatory and prohibited), we often find that viewing a normative system as a static entity may result in several paradoxes, such as is the case with contrary-to-duty obligations [8].

For future research, we would like to study how different kinds of norms lead to different kinds of possible updates (e.g. norms of the 'to-be' variant, or norms with deadlines). Moreover, it would be very useful and interesting to develop a dynamic logic to reason about these properties. If a sound and complete axiomatization can be given, we can use automated theorem provers to prove several properties of normative systems in a dynamic environment. We can also apply this framework to other well known frameworks of normative systems, such as the coloured systems considered in [10]. Lastly, the relation between the current framework of dynamic normative systems and the established theory of deontic logic needs to be explored further.

References

1. Ågotnes, T., van der Hoek, W., Rodríguez-Aguilar, J.A., Sierra, C., Wooldridge, M.: On the logic of normative systems. In: Proceedings of the Twentieth International Joint Conference on Artificial Intelligence (IJCAI 2007), pp. 1175–1180 (2007)
2. Ågotnes, T., van der Hoek, W., Wooldridge, M.: Normative system games. In: Proceedings of the 6th International Joint Conference on Autonomous Agents and Multiagent Systems (AAMAS 2007), pp. 881–888 (2007)
3. Ågotnes, T., van der Hoek, W., Wooldridge, M.: Robust normative systems and a logic of norm compliance. Logic Journal of the IGPL 18(1) (2010)
4. Bulling, N., Dastani, M.: Verifying normative behaviour via normative mechanism design. In: Proceedings of the Twenty-Second International Joint Conference on Artificial Intelligence (IJCAI 2011), pp. 103–108 (2011)
5. Dastani, M.: 2apl: A practical agent programming language. Autonomous Agents and Multi-Agent Systems 16(3), 214–248 (2008)
6. John-Jules, C., Meyer, R.W.: Deontic Logic in Computer Science: Normative System Specification. Wiley (1994)
7. Knobbout, M., Dastani, M.: Reasoning under compliance assumptions in normative multiagent systems. In: Proceedings of the 11th International Joint Conference on Autonomous Agents and Multiagent Systems (AAMAS 2012), pp. 331–340 (2012)
8. Prakken, H., Sergot, M.J.: Contrary-to-duty obligations. Studia Logica 57(1), 91–115 (1996)
9. Searle, J.: The Construction of Social Reality. The Free Press, New York (1995)
10. Sergot, M.J.: Action and agency in norm-governed multi-agent systems. In: Artikis, A., O'Hare, G.M.P., Stathis, K., Vouros, G.A. (eds.) ESAW 2007. LNCS (LNAI), vol. 4995, pp. 1–54. Springer, Heidelberg (2008)
11. Shoham, Y., Tennenholtz, M.: On the synthesis of useful social laws for artificial agent societies. In: Proceedings of the Tenth National Conference on Artificial Intelligence (AAAI 1992), pp. 276–281 (1992)
12. Wooldridge, M.J.: An Introduction to MultiAgent Systems, 2nd edn. John Wiley and Sons (2009)

A Modal Logic of Knowledge, Belief, and Estimation

Costas D. Koutras[1], Christos Moyzes[2], and Yorgos Zikos[2]

[1] Department of Informatics and Telecommunications
University of Peloponnese
end of Karaiskaki Street, 22 100 Tripolis, Greece
ckoutras@uop.gr
[2] Graduate Programme in Logic, Algorithms and Computation (MPLA)
Department of Mathematics, University of Athens
Panepistimiopolis, 157 84 Ilissia, Greece
cmoyzes@yahoo.gr, zikos@sch.gr

Abstract. We introduce **KBE**, a modal epistemic logic for reasoning about *Knowledge*, *Belief* and *Estimation*, three attitudes involved in an agent's decision-making process. In our logic, *Knowledge* and *Belief* are captured by S4.2, a modal logic holding a distinguished position among the epistemic logics investigated in AI and Philosophy. The *Estimation* operator of **KBE** is a kind of generalized '*many*' or '*most*' quantifier, whose origins go back to the work of J. Burgess and A. Herzig, but its model-theoretic incarnation ('weak filters') has been introduced by K. Schlechta and V. Jauregui. We work with *complete weak filters* ('*weak ultrafilters*') as we are interested in situations where an estimation can be always reached. The axiomatization of **KBE** comprises 'bridge' axioms which reflect the intuitive relationship of '*estimation*' to '*knowledge*' and '*belief*', several introspective properties are shown to hold and it comes out that *believing* φ can be equivalently defined in **KBE** as '*estimating that φ is known*', an interesting fact and an indication of the intuitive correctness of the introduced *estimation* operator. The model theory of **KBE** comprises a class of frames combining relational Kripke frames with Scott-Montague semantics, in which neighborhoods are collections of 'large' sets of possible worlds. Soundness and completeness is mentioned and a tableaux proof procedure is sketched.

1 Introduction

The various logics of *Knowledge* and *Belief* have found very important applications in *Knowledge Representation*, *Distributed Computing*, *Security* and *Cryptography*, *Game Theory* and *Economics*. On the other hand, it is natural to ask *whether knowledge and belief suffice* to guide the decision-making process of an agent acting in a complex environment. Given the fact that an agent typically reasons in terms of incomplete information, it is natural to consider that its epistemic state is incomplete; the same for its belief set. In the absence of knowledge, the agent can proceed to an estimation on the truth (or falsity) of a certain fact, in view of the available evidence and in several situations where a decision *has* to be taken at any rate, the estimation should necessarily be accomplished. The **interaction** of **Knowledge**, **Belief** and **Estimation** crops all over, implicitly or explicitly.

E. Fermé and J. Leite (Eds.): JELIA 2014, LNAI 8761, pp. 637–646, 2014.

In our logic, **estimation** is intended to capture the intuition that the agent can estimate that φ is true (in the sense that she 'bets' on its truth rather than its falsity) in the case φ is true in '*many*' alternative situations to the one the agent is situated in. The axiomatization of **KBE** comprises four '*bridge*' axioms that pin down the relationship of estimation to knowledge and belief, as suggested by our intuition on what '*estimation*' actually means. We insist on estimation being consistent and complete, if it is to be really useful in the decision-making process. We prove some 'introspective' properties of estimation and **it turns out that, in KBE, belief can be equivalently defined in terms of estimation and knowledge**: believing that φ is true amounts exactly to the agent estimating that she knows φ. This is clearly close to our intuition on '*estimation*' as a weak version of belief, which traditionally comes in many facets and many variants. Regarding the model theory of **KBE**, we work with a class of frames which combine a subclass of **S4.2** relational frames (those with a *final* cluster), endowed with Scott-Montague semantics. Due to space limitations, proofs of the results and full presentation of the tableaux proof procedure, is left for the full report [20].

The logic **KBE** resembles the approach of J. Burgess in [4], where a 'probably' operator is added to **S5**. In [15], Andreas Herzig employs the same operator, providing an axiomatization which is very close to the 'most' modality underlying our estimation operator. However, our approach is the first to combine such a generalized quantifier with a normal modal system, providing a full completeness proof both for the Hilbert-style axiomatization and the tableaux proof procedure introduced; see [20].

2   Background Material

We assume that the reader is well acquainted with the notation and the terminology of Modal Logic; we refer to [16,7,3] for Modal Logic and to [11] for a tour in epistemic logic (see also [24,2,26]). In particular, we assume that the reader is readily aware of the epistemic interpretation of the widely used modal axioms. We will work with **S4.2**, which is the normal modal logic **KT4G**, assuming Lenzen's approach [23,22] in which belief can be defined through knowledge: see ('abbreviation') **DB** in Section 3.1 and [20] for details. It is well-known that **S4.2** is determined by the class of reflexive, transitive and directed relational frames; in [18] (and independently in [21]) it is proved that **S4.2** is also determined by the subclass of frames which possess a non-empty *final* (*terminal*) *cluster*, intuitively, a non-empty universally-related set of worlds 'seen' by every world in the frame.

The interpretation of estimation as a '*many*' ('*most*') quantifier requires a model-theoretic interpretation of this notion. In classical Model Theory, it is the notion of '*filter*' (*non-empty* collection of sets, *upwards closed* and *closed under intersection*) that captures the 'large' subsets of the universe. For various reasons this notion is not entirely appropriate for our purposes and we work with the '*weak filters*' (non-empty collections of pairwise-disjoint sets, upwards closed) introduced in [25,17]. Actually, we work with '*weak ultrafilters*' introduced in [1], requiring further that either a set or its complement (but not both) is a '*large*' set. The reader is referred to [19], in which it is shown that the notion of '*weak ultrafilter*' is non-trivial and that every 'consistent' weak filter can be extended to a weak ultrafilter. It is worth noting that similar notions of generalized quantification have been introduced earlier by W. Carnielli et al. in [5,6].

Definition 1. *Consider sets* $W \neq \emptyset$, $Z \subseteq W$, $F \subseteq \mathcal{P}(W)$ *and the following properties:*

(**wf1**) $W \in F$

(**wf2**) $(\forall X \in F)(\forall Y \subseteq W)(X \subseteq Y \Longrightarrow Y \in F)$

(**wf3**) $(\forall X \subseteq W)(X \in F \Longrightarrow W \setminus X \notin F)$

(**wuf**) $(\forall X \subseteq W)(X \notin F \Longrightarrow W \setminus X \in F)$

(**inZ**) $(\forall A, D \in F)(A \cap D \cap Z \neq \emptyset)$

If (wf1) *to* (wf3) *hold for* F, *then it is called a* **weak filter over** W *[25,17]. If* (wuf) *holds for weak filter* F, *then it is called a* **weak ultrafilter over** W. *If* (inZ) *holds for a weak filter* F *then it is called* **weak filter over** W **with intersections in** Z.

3 The Logic KBE

The logic **S4.2** has been advocated by W. Lenzen as the 'correct' logic of knowledge, as it contains practically every one of the 'plausible' principles governing knowledge, belief and their interaction. In the full report [20] we discuss in detail the epistemic importance of **S4.2** and the work of W. Lenzen and R. Stalnaker. We proceed to enrich **S4.2** with *estimation*; see [20] for the rationale of the axioms.

3.1 Axiomatization of KBE

We consider the propositional bimodal language $\mathcal{L}_{KBE}$ with the propositional variables $\Phi = \{p_0, p_1, \ldots\}$, the *falsum* $\bot$, the implication connective $\supset$ and the modal operators K and E. The intended interpretation is that $K\varphi$ is read as '*the agent* ***knows*** φ', $B\varphi$ (it is an abbreviation) is read as '*the agent* ***believes*** φ', $E\varphi$ is read as '*the agent* ***estimates*** *that* φ *is true*'. We proceed now to list the axioms of **KBE**, including the abbreviation for belief.

Abbreviation

DB. $B\varphi \equiv \neg K \neg K\varphi$ *Belief definition.*

Axioms

K. $K\varphi \wedge K(\varphi \supset \psi) \supset K\psi$
Knowledge is closed under logical consequence.

T. $K\varphi \supset \varphi$
Only true things are known.

4. $K\varphi \supset KK\varphi$
Positive introspection, with respect to knowledge.

CB. $B\varphi \supset \neg B\neg\varphi$
Belief is consistent.

BE. $B\varphi \supset E\varphi$

Beliefs are estimations.

CCE. $E\varphi \equiv \neg E\neg\varphi$
Estimation is consistent and complete.

EK. $E\varphi \wedge K(\varphi \supset \psi) \supset E\psi$
Estimation can be inferred, only through knowledge.

PIE. $E\varphi \supset KE\varphi$
Introspection with respect to estimation.

Definition 2. **KBE** *is the propositional bimodal logic axiomatized by* **K, T, 4, CB, BE, CCE, EK, PIE** *and closed under rule* **RN$_K$**. $\dfrac{\varphi}{K\varphi}$

The next result, whose proof consists of formal **KBE** derivations (see [20]) clarifies some properties of the logic, of 'introspective' nature.

Proposition 1.

i. *Positive 'Introspection' wrt estimation is valid in all three epistemic 'degrees':*
   $E\varphi \supset KE\varphi,\ E\varphi \supset BE\varphi,\ E\varphi \supset EE\varphi \in$ **KBE**

ii. *So is the negative 'Introspection' wrt estimation:*
   $\neg E\varphi \supset K\neg E\varphi,\ \neg E\varphi \supset B\neg E\varphi,\ \neg E\varphi \supset E\neg E\varphi \in$ **KBE**

iii. *Non-estimation implies introspection wrt ignorance and 'lack of certainty':*
   $\neg E\varphi \supset K\neg K\varphi,\ \neg E\varphi \supset B\neg K\varphi,\ \neg E\varphi \supset E\neg K\varphi \in$ **KBE**
   $\neg E\varphi \supset K\neg B\varphi,\ \neg E\varphi \supset B\neg B\varphi,\ \neg E\varphi \supset E\neg B\varphi \in$ **KBE**

iv. $KE\varphi \equiv E\varphi \in$ **KBE**

v. $EK\varphi \equiv B\varphi \in$ **KBE**

Remark 1. Note that, by the last item of Prop. 1 above, belief can be equivalently defined as '*estimation that the agent knows*'. Defining knowledge in terms of belief and vice versa, is a very interesting topic in epistemic logic (see [14]). In that respect, it is interesting that belief can be equivalently defined in an **S4.2** framework, in a rather intuitive way, through an 'estimation' operator. In the same fashion, item (iv) says that knowledge about estimation amounts exactly to estimation itself.

3.2   The Possible-Worlds Models of KBE

In this section, we define the frames and models of **KBE**. These structures properly mix an interesting subclass of **S4.2**-frames (the reflexive, transitive, with a final cluster FC) with Scott-Montague semantics [7, *neighborhood semantics*], in which each neighborhood is a *complete collection of large sets* on the epistemic alternatives of the world at hand - a weak ultrafilter. In the following definition, the properties (**cce**) and (**ek**) are essentially (**wf2**), (**wf3**) and (**wuf**) of Definition 1 of weak ultrafilters, properly stated, as we define **weak ultrafilters** on $\mathcal{R}(w)$.

Definition 3. *Consider the triple* $\mathfrak{F} = \langle W, \mathcal{R}, \mathcal{N} \rangle$, *where* W *is a non-empty set,* $\mathcal{R} \subseteq W \times W$, $\mathcal{N} : W \to \mathcal{P}(\mathcal{P}(W))$ *and*

- $\mathcal{R}$ *is reflexive, transitive and has a nonempty* final cluster
  $FC = \{v \in W \mid (\forall w \in W)\ w\mathcal{R}v\}$.
- $\mathcal{N}$ *is such, that* $\forall w \in W$

    (**nr**) $\mathcal{N}(w) \subseteq \mathcal{P}(\mathcal{R}(w))$

    (**be**) $FC \in \mathcal{N}(w)$

    (**pie**) $\forall X \subseteq \mathcal{R}(w)\ \forall u \in W\ \left(X \in \mathcal{N}(w)\ \&\ w\mathcal{R}u \Longrightarrow X \cap \mathcal{R}(u) \in \mathcal{N}(u) \right)$

    (**cce**) $\forall X \subseteq \mathcal{R}(w)\ \left(X \in \mathcal{N}(w) \Longleftrightarrow \mathcal{R}(w) \setminus X \notin \mathcal{N}(w) \right)$

    (**ek**) $\forall X, Y \subseteq \mathcal{R}(w)\ \left(X \in \mathcal{N}(w)\ \&\ Y \supseteq X \Longrightarrow Y \in \mathcal{N}(w) \right)$

$\mathfrak{F}$ is called a **kbe-frame**. $\mathfrak{M} = \langle \mathfrak{F}, V \rangle$ is called a **kbe-model**, if it is based on a kbe-frame and $V : \Phi \to \mathcal{P}(W)$ is a valuation. It is not hard to show that the class of kbe-frames is nonempty [20]. Given a model $\mathfrak{M} = \langle W, \mathcal{R}, \mathcal{N}, V \rangle$ for the language $\mathcal{L}_{KBE}$, the valuation $V : \Phi \to \mathcal{P}(W)$ can be extended to all formulae of $\mathcal{L}_{KBE}$ in a straightforward way. In [20] the following result is proved.

Theorem 1. (Soundness & Completeness) KBE *is sound and strongly complete w.r.t. the class of all kbe-frames.*

Using Theorem 1 we can show that various 'introspective' principles are not **KBE**-axioms. Having in mind that 'estimation' is conceived as a weak form of a belief-like attitude, the fact that $E\varphi \supset B\varphi$ is not a **KBE**-theorem is consistent with our intuition. Among the formulae of Fact 2.(iii), $E\varphi \supset EK\varphi$ deserves a comment. The fact that it is not a theorem of **KBE** is welcomed; otherwise, given that $EK\varphi \supset B\varphi \in$ **KBE** (Prop. 1.(v)) and **BE**, estimation would collapse to belief ($E\varphi \equiv B\varphi$ would be a theorem of **KBE**) and this would immediately invalidate our attempt to define estimation as a weak form of belief. In the same fashion, it is really good news that $EK\varphi \supset K\varphi$ is not a **KBE**-theorem. This formula introduces a strong form of the '*infallibility argument*' or else the '*paradox of the perfect believer*' (see [11]): in view of axiom **T**, it finally requires that something is true whenever our agent estimates that she knows it.

Fact 2.   i. $E\varphi \supset B\varphi \notin$ **KBE**

  ii. $\neg B\neg \varphi \supset B\varphi \notin$ **KBE**

iii. $E\varphi \supset KK\varphi$, $E\varphi \supset KB\varphi \notin$ **KBE**
     $E\varphi \supset BK\varphi$, $E\varphi \supset BB\varphi \notin$ **KBE**
     $E\varphi \supset EK\varphi$, $E\varphi \supset EB\varphi \notin$ **KBE**

iv. $EK\varphi \supset K\varphi \notin$ **KBE**

 v. $E\varphi \wedge E(\varphi \supset \psi) \supset E\psi \notin$ **KBE**

4   Tableaux for KBE

In this section we sketch a tableau system for **KBE** using *prefixed formulas*. A reminder on terminology is in order: a *prefix* is a finite sequence of natural numbers, separated by periods. A *prefixed formula* is an expression of the form $\sigma \ \varphi$, where σ is a prefix and φ is a formula. A tableau branch is *closed* if it contains both $\sigma \ \varphi$ and $\sigma \ \neg\varphi$ for some prefix σ and formula φ. A tableau is *closed* if all of its branches are closed. A tableau or branch is *open* if it is not closed. The terminology and most of the techniques we use, draw from [8,9].

The intention for the prefixes is that they name worlds in a model, and the world named by $\sigma.n$ is accessible from the world named by σ. The worlds of a kbe-model either belong to its final cluster or not, so we will be using two kinds of prefixed formulas; of the form $0.n, n \in \mathbb{N}$ to represent the first, and of the form $1.\sigma$ to represent the latter. Prefixes of the form $0.n$ do not allow tracking of some accessibility relation, but are sufficient for the final cluster, exactly because it is a cluster, i.e. relation $\mathcal{R}$ is universal in it.

4.1   Tableaux Rules

Before presenting the rules themselves we need a notion of *accessibility* between prefixes, proper for kbe-models. For the alphabet of our tableaux, we assume $B\varphi, \langle K \rangle \varphi$, $\langle E \rangle \varphi, \varphi \supset \psi, \varphi \equiv \psi$ are abbreviations for $\neg K \neg K \varphi, \neg K \neg \varphi, \neg E \neg \varphi, \neg \varphi \vee \psi, (\varphi \supset \psi) \wedge (\psi \supset \varphi)$ respectively, thus no corresponding rules have to be specified.

Definition 4. *A prefix σ' is accessible from a prefix σ if and only if σ is an initial segment of σ' (proper or otherwise), or σ' is of the form $0.n, n \in \mathbb{N}$.*

Definition 5. *A kbe-tableau for a formula φ is a tableau that starts with the prefixed formulas $1 \ \neg\varphi$ and $0.1 \ \top$ and is extended using any of the rules below.*

A few words on the rules that follow: **KBE** is normal with respect to K, and our rules for K (and $\neg$K) state what they should, regarding semantics. What makes the rules appropriate for an **S4.2**-*frame,* is that we introduce at least a prefix for the final cluster with $0.1\top$, and reflexivity, transitivity and that the final cluster is both 'final' and a cluster, is integrated into our notion of prefix *accessibility.* Regarding [**CCE**-rule] and [**PIE**-rule], as their name suggests, they exist to tend to axioms **CCE** and **PIE**. Axiom **CCE** is in fact an equivalence, but we decide to transform all $\langle E \rangle$ into E and have no use for the other direction. Axiom **PIE** is also not exactly what our rule implies, but for the sake of shortening proofs, one can observe the only applicable rule to a formula $KE\varphi$ is [Kν-rule]; we do it outright. Finally, regarding modality E, **KBE** is monotonic with respect to it. The proper rule, is that for any pair $\langle E \rangle \ \varphi$, $E\psi$ there is a world such that φ, ψ hold (see [9] regarding the Logic **U**, and specifically Chapter 6.13 for a tableau for **U**). In our case, $\langle E \rangle$ has turned into E, and not just any world will do, but one accessible with respect to $\mathcal{R}$; [E-rule] is created accordingly. Also note that φ can be the same as ψ.

For prefixes σ of the form $1.\sigma'$:

[Double negation rule] $\dfrac{\sigma \; \neg\neg\varphi}{\sigma \; \varphi}$

[Conjunctive rules] $\dfrac{\sigma \; \varphi \wedge \psi}{\begin{array}{c}\sigma \; \varphi \\ \sigma \; \psi\end{array}} \quad \dfrac{\sigma \; \neg(\varphi \vee \psi)}{\begin{array}{c}\sigma \; \neg\varphi \\ \sigma \; \neg\psi\end{array}}$

[Disjunctive rules] $\dfrac{\sigma \; \varphi \vee \psi}{\sigma \; \varphi \,|\, \sigma \; \psi} \quad \dfrac{\sigma \; \neg(\varphi \wedge \psi)}{\sigma \; \neg\varphi \,|\, \sigma \; \neg\psi}$

[Kν-rule] $\dfrac{\sigma \; K\varphi}{\sigma' \; \varphi}$ for all σ' accessible from σ and already existing on the branch.

[Kπ-rule] $\dfrac{\sigma \; \neg K\varphi}{\sigma.n \; \neg\varphi}$ for any prefix $\sigma.n$ new to the branch.

[CCE-rule] $\dfrac{\sigma \; \neg E\varphi}{\sigma \; E\neg\varphi}$

[PIE-rule] $\dfrac{\sigma \; E\varphi}{\sigma' \; E\varphi}$ for all σ' accessible from σ and already existing on the branch.

[E-rule] $\dfrac{\begin{array}{c}\sigma \; E\varphi \\ \sigma \; E\psi\end{array}}{\begin{array}{c}\sigma.n \; \varphi \\ \sigma.n \; \psi\end{array}}$ for any prefix $\sigma.n$ new to the branch.

For prefixes $0.n$ we have, in essence, the same rules, but the exact notation for rules introducing a new world is:

[Kπ-rule] $\dfrac{0.n \; \neg K\varphi}{0.m \; \neg\varphi}$ for any prefix $0.m$ new to the branch.

[E-rule] $\dfrac{\begin{array}{c}0.n \; E\varphi \\ 0.n \; E\psi\end{array}}{\begin{array}{c}0.m \; \varphi \\ 0.m \; \psi\end{array}}$ for any prefix $0.m$ new to the branch.

Definition 6. *A closed kbe-tableau for a formula φ is a **kbe-tableau proof** for φ.*

Let us see an example from Prop. 1.

$$EKp \equiv \neg K \neg Kp$$
1 $\neg((\neg EKp \vee \neg K \neg Kp) \wedge (\neg \neg K \neg Kp \vee EKp))$ 1.
0.1 $\top$ 2.

1 $\neg(\neg EKp \vee \neg K \neg Kp)$ 3.   1 $\neg(\neg \neg K \neg Kp \vee EKp)$ 10.
1 $\neg \neg EKp$ 4.   1 $\neg \neg \neg K \neg Kp$ 11.
1 $\neg \neg K \neg Kp$ 5.   1 $\neg EKp$ 12.
1 EKp 6.   1 $\neg K \neg Kp$ 13.
1 $K \neg Kp$ 7.   1 $E \neg Kp$ 14.
1.1 Kp 8.   1.1 $\neg \neg Kp$ 15.
1.1 $\neg Kp$ 9.   1.1 Kp 16.
                                               0.1 $E \neg Kp$ 17.
                                               0.2 $\neg Kp$ 18.
                                               0.3 $\neg p$ 19.
                                               0.3 p 20.

Item 1 is the negation of the formula we want to prove expressed in the tableaux language and item 2 is standard. Items 3 and 10 are from 1 by [Disjunctive Rule]. Items 4 and 5 are from 3 by a [Conjunctive Rule]. Items 6 and 7 are from 4 and 5 respectively by [Double negation rule]. Item 8 is from 6 by [E-rule]. Item 9 is from 7 by [Kν-rule]. Item 11 and 12 are from 10 by a [Conjunctive rule]. Item 13 is from 11 by [Double negation rule]. Item 14 is from 12 by [CCE-rule]. Item 15 is from 13 by [Kπ-rule]. Item 16 is from 15 by [Double negation rule]. Item 17 is from 14 by [**PIE**-rule]. Item 18 is from 17 by [E-rule]. Item 19 is from 18 by [Kπ-rule] and item 20 is from 16 by [Kν-rule]. In the full report [20] we develop a systematic tableaux-based procedure and prove finite model property and decidability of **KBE**.

5   Conclusions

To the best of our knowledge (belief and estimation) our work is the first to provide a modal treatment of (qualitative) estimation, with respect to its interaction with knowledge and belief. The analysis of **KBE** is in line with the tradition of possible-worlds analysis in epistemic logic and sheds light on the nature of belief as '*estimation that φ is known*'. There exist similar approaches, involving the notion of *certainty*. The relation *of knowledge, belief* and *certainty* has been investigated by Halpern [13], Lenzen [22] and other authors. *Certainty* is also called '*robust belief*' by some authors, as opposed to '*strong belief*'; belief is a delicate interesting notion with a lot of useful variants.

As far as future research is concerned, we believe that the most important question is the identification of the computational properties of **KBE**. Moreover, it seems very challenging to try to embed a similar modal 'estimation' operator in first-order modal epistemic logic. This is bound to raise several technical and philosophical issues, but it seems a very promising and interesting problem.

Acknowledgments. We wish to thank the anonymous JELIA 2014 referees for many useful and insightful comments on the philosophical aspects of *knowledge, belief* and *estimation*, along with many useful pointers to the literature. Some of the comments and the questions asked, will certainly find their way in the final, full version of this work.

References

1. Askounis, D., Koutras, C.D., Zikos, Y.: Knowledge means 'all', belief means 'most'. In: del Cerro, L.F., Herzig, A., Mengin, J. (eds.) JELIA 2012. LNCS, vol. 7519, pp. 41–53. Springer, Heidelberg (2012)
2. Aucher, G.: Principles of knowledge, belief and conditional belief. In: Rebuschi, M., Batt, M., Heinzmann, G., Lihoreau, F., Musiol, M., Trognon, A. (eds.) Dialogue, Rationality, and Formalism. Logic, Argumentation & Reasoning, vol. 3, Springer (2014)
3. Blackburn, P., de Rijke, M., Venema, Y.: Modal Logic. Cambridge Tracts in Theoretical Computer Science, vol. (53). Cambridge University Press (2001)
4. Burgess, J.P.: Probability logic. J. Symb. Log. 34(2), 264–274 (1969)
5. Carnielli, W.A., Sette, A.M.: Default operators. In: Workshop on Logic, Language, Information and Computation, WOLLIC 1994, UFPE, Recife (1994)
6. Carnielli, W.A., Veloso, P.A.S.: Ultrafilter logic and generic reasoning. In: Gottlob, et al. (eds.) [12], pp. 34–53
7. Chellas, B.F.: Modal Logic, an Introduction. Cambridge University Press (1980)
8. Fitting, M., Mendelsohn, R.L.: First-Order Modal Logic. Synthése Library, vol. 277. Kluwer Academic Publishers (1998)
9. Fitting, M.C.: Proof Methods for Modal and Intuitionistic Logics. D. Reidel Publishing Co., Dordrecht (1983)
10. Gabbay, D.M., Woods, J. (eds.): Logic and the Modalities in the Twentieth Century. Handbook of the History of Logic, vol. 7. North-Holland (2006)
11. Gochet, P., Gribomont, P.: Epistemic logic. Gabbay and Woods [10], vol. 7, pp. 99–195 (2006)
12. Gottlob, G., Leitsch, A., Mundici, D. (eds.): KGC 1997. LNCS, vol. 1289. Springer, Heidelberg (1997)
13. Halpern, J.: The relationship between knowledge, belief and certainty. Annals of Mathematics and Artificial Intelligence 4, 301–322 (1991)
14. Halpern, J., Samet, D., Segev, E.: Defining knowledge in terms of belief: The modal logic perspective. Review of Symbolic Logic (to appear)
15. Herzig, A.: Modal probability, belief, and actions. Fundamenta Informaticae 57(2-4), 323–344 (2003)
16. Hughes, G.E., Cresswell, M.J.: A New Introduction to Modal Logic. Routledge (1996)
17. Jauregui, V.: Modalities, Conditionals and Nonmonotonic Reasoning. PhD thesis, Department of Computer Science and Engineering, University of New South Wales (2008)
18. Kaminski, M., Tiomkin, M.L.: The modal logic of cluster-decomposable kripke interpretations. Notre Dame Journal of Formal Logic 48(4), 511–520 (2007)
19. Koutras, C.D., Moyzes, C., Nomikos, C., Zikos, Y.: On the 'in many cases' modality: tableaux, decidability, complexity, variants. In: Likas, A., Blekas, K., Kalles, D. (eds.) SETN 2014. LNCS, vol. 8445, pp. 207–220. Springer, Heidelberg (2014)
20. Koutras, C.D., Moyzes, C., Zikos, Y.: A modal logic of Knowledge, Belief and Estimation. Technical report, Graduate Programme in Algorithms and Computation (2014) (available through the authors' webpages)
21. Koutras, C.D., Zikos, Y.: A note on the completeness of S4.2. Technical report, 2013, Graduate Programme in Logic, Algorithms and Computation (December 2013)
22. Lenzen, W.: Recent Work in Epistemic Logic. North-Holland (1978)

23. Lenzen, W.: Epistemologische Betrachtungen zu [S4,S5]. Erkenntnis 14, 33–56 (1979)
24. Pacuit, E.: Dynamic epistemic logic I: Modeling knowledge and belief. Philosophy Compass 8(9), 798–814 (2013)
25. Schlechta, K.: Defaults as generalized quantifiers. Journal of Logic and Computation 5(4), 473–494 (1995)
26. Stalnaker, R.: On logics of knowledge and belief. Philosophical Studies 128(1), 169–199 (2006)

A Logic for Belief Contraction

Konstantinos Georgatos*

Department of Mathematics and Computer Science
John Jay College
City University of New York
524 West 59th Street
New York, NY 10019
U.S.A.
kgeorgatos@jjay.cuny.edu

Abstract. We introduce a logical system in which we can define a belief contraction modal connective. The logic is based on a combination of Moss-Parikh subset space logic and temporal logic. The semantics is the system of spheres used in conditional logic and the belief contraction connective encodes minimization of the distance between two spheres. We prove completeness and decidability and show that the belief contraction connective satisfies most of the AGM postulates when those are translated into statements of the logic.

1 Introduction

The operation of belief contraction and its companion belief revision was originally defined for deductively closed sets of sentences. This choice is justified because beliefs may first be thought of as sentences and logical omniscience, although somewhat impractical, is convenient and ubiquitous.

Nevertheless, research on belief change was soon extended to belief change of objects representing beliefs other than theories. There is base revision where the beliefs are represented by a usually finite but not deductively closed set of sentences. Another popular view of belief revision is that of an operation on propositions such as the one in [1] or an operation on a more general propositional epistemic state (for example [2]). A more abstract view of belief change as a set theoretic or algebraic operator has also been explored ([3,4,5]). In all the above cases, belief change was explored in metalanguage.

In this paper, we will study belief contraction as a (definable modal) connective in a logical system that is not in metalanguage but in the object language. We will use a belief contraction connective, denoted by $\ominus$, to form sentences in a language of the form $a \ominus b$. It is important to notice that contraction here is neither represented indirectly through a conditional nor as an operator within a modality. The meaning (extension) of the sentence $a \ominus b$ will be all epistemic states (the notion of epistemic state will be defined later) that can be reached by

* Support for this project was provided by a PSC-CUNY Award, jointly funded by The Professional Staff Congress and The City University of New York.

E. Fermé and J. Leite (Eds.): JELIA 2014, LNAI 8761, pp. 647–656, 2014.

a contraction with the belief b from some epistemic state where a was believed. This is a natural view of the meaning of the contraction of a belief a with the belief b when a is not all we believe (a theory).

There are a few advantages in our approach:

- expressing contraction into an object language makes contraction amenable to a study using a wide variety of formal logic techniques and semantics,
- proofs in the logical system amount to an algorithm of constructing the contracted belief set, that is, this representation is constructive with respect to the original formulation of contraction postulates,
- expressive power is increased as we can form arbitrary nestings and therefore successive application of the contraction connective, resulting in a more comprehensive treatment of contraction which includes iteration.

The logical system we employ is a combination of linear temporal logic and the subset space logic introduced by Moss and Parikh ([6]). The basic combining system and semantics have been introduced by Heinemann ([7]). Our contribution is to alter the meaning of until, define contraction, and adjust completeness and decidability results.

In the next section, we present the language of our logical system, the semantics, the axiomatization and the definition of contraction (Definition 2). Then, we study the properties of the contraction connective, compare the results with related work and conclude with a discussion of the ways this research can be extended.

2   Syntax and Semantics

Definition 1. *The language of belief contraction logic will be the language of subset space logic augmented with the* next *operator* $\bigcirc$ *and an* until *operator* U, *i.e. the least set such that* Atom, *a set of atomic propositions, is a subset of* $\mathcal{L}$ *and closed under the following rules:*

$$\frac{\phi, \psi \in \mathcal{L}}{\phi \wedge \psi, \phi U \psi \in \mathcal{L}} \qquad \frac{\phi \in \mathcal{L}}{\neg \phi, \bigcirc \phi, \Box \phi, \mathsf{K} \phi \in \mathcal{L}}.$$

We will write $\bigodot a$ for $\neg \bigcirc \neg a$, $\Diamond a$ for $\neg \Box \neg a$ and $\mathsf{L} a$ for $\neg \mathsf{K} \neg a$. We will also assume that unary bind stronger that binary connectives, so for example $\bigodot a U b$ stands for $(\bigodot a) U b$. The next operator is needed to describe the sequential contraction, that is, next is one-step contraction and not strictly temporal as it is in [8],[9], or [10]. For general contraction we need the following

Definition 2. *The* contraction $a \ominus b$ *of a with b is the formula*

$$\mathsf{L} \neg b \wedge (\bigodot b U a).$$

Definition 2 is the cornerstone of this paper and will be explained in detail after the presentation of semantics.

We modify the original subset semantics using a sequence of decreasing subsets which we will call a system of spheres. This is a slight variation of Heinemann finite descending chains in [7].

Definition 3. *Let X be a set, then a system of spheres S is a sequence of decreasing subsets $\{U_i\}_{i=1}^{\infty}$ of X, i.e. $U_{i+1} \subseteq U_i$ such that if $U_i = U_j$ for some $j > i$, then $U_i = U_k$ for all $k \geqslant i$. If $U_i = U_j$ holds for some $i \neq j$ then the system will be called* finite *and, otherwise,* infinite. *Let S be a system of spheres, then a* model *is a triple $\langle X, S, v \rangle$, where v is the initial interpretation.*

The satisfaction relation $\models_{\mathcal{M}}$, where $\mathcal{M}$ is the model $\langle X, S, v \rangle$, is a subset of $(X \overset{\cdot}{\times} S) \times \mathcal{L}$ defined recursively by:

$$x, U_i \models_{\mathcal{M}} A \qquad \text{iff } x \in v(A), \text{ where } A \in \text{Atom}$$
$$x, U_i \models_{\mathcal{M}} \phi \wedge \psi \text{ iff } x, U_i \models_{\mathcal{M}} \phi \text{ and } x, U_i \models_{\mathcal{M}} \psi$$
$$x, U_i \models_{\mathcal{M}} \neg\phi \qquad \text{iff } x, U_i \not\models_{\mathcal{M}} \phi$$
$$x, U_i \models_{\mathcal{M}} \bigcirc\phi \qquad \text{iff } x \in U_{i+1} \text{ and } x, U_{i+1} \models_{\mathcal{M}} \phi.$$
$$x, U_i \models_{\mathcal{M}} \square\phi \qquad \text{iff for all } j \geqslant i \; x, U_j \models_{\mathcal{M}} \phi.$$
$$x, U_i \models_{\mathcal{M}} \mathsf{K}\phi \qquad \text{iff for all } y \in U_i, \; y, U_i \models_{\mathcal{M}} \phi$$
$$x, U_i \models_{\mathcal{M}} \phi\mathsf{U}\psi \quad \text{iff there exists } j \geqslant i \text{ and } y \in U_j \text{ such that } y, U_j \models_{\mathcal{M}} \mathsf{K}\psi$$
$$\text{and for all } i \leqslant k < j \; y, U_k \models_{\mathcal{M}} \mathsf{K}\phi.$$

If $x, U_i \models_{\mathcal{M}} \phi$ for all (x, U_i) belonging to $X \overset{\cdot}{\times} S$ then ϕ is valid *in $\mathcal{M}$, denoted by $\mathcal{M} \models \phi$.*

We describe the process of reasoning when the epistemic state expands to encompass other possibilities. This is also the central idea behind the system-of-spheres semantics for conditional logic. Knowing a proposition on a given epistemic state is modeled using necessity. This correspondence allows us to express the minimization of the distance of an epistemic state, where the antecedent is consistent, for the interpretation of contraction. Since we look at the state we came from, indices in our models describe the opposite of expansion and increase as the states get smaller. Observe that satisfaction does not depend on the index but rather on the subset:

Lemma 1. *Let $x \in X$ and $U_i = U_j$ with $i \neq j$ then, for all $\phi \in \mathcal{L}$*

$$x, U_i \models \phi \quad \text{iff} \quad x, U_j \models \phi.$$

The axiom system **CL** consists of axiom schemes 1 through 16 and rules of table 1 (see page 650). We will write $\vdash_{\mathbf{CL}} \phi$ (or just $\vdash$) iff ϕ is a theorem of **CL**.

Axiom 2 stipulates that the non-epistemic facts true in the world of an agent will remain true as the only change we allow is epistemic. The actual state of an agent remains always the same although the agent's view may change. Axioms 3 to 8 is just the axiomatization of LTL (linear temporal logic) with next and always (accounting for points that do not have a successor). Axioms 9 to 12 are the axioms of the modal logic **S5**. Axiom 13 is the Cross Axiom of the original logic of subsets; the "perfect recall" of [11] for a single modality. The effect of this axiom is that the sequence of subsets is non-increasing. Axioms 15 and 16 are the axioms for until. Axiom 15 says that the until connective implies the existence of the future state where ψ is believed. Axiom 16 is the inductive definition of the until, akin to the inductive definition of until in linear temporal

Table 1. Axioms for CL

Axioms

1. All propositional tautologies
2. $(A \rightarrow \bigcirc A) \wedge (\neg A \rightarrow \bigcirc \neg A)$, for all $A \in$ Atom
3. $\bigcirc(\phi \rightarrow \psi) \rightarrow (\bigcirc\phi \rightarrow \bigcirc\psi)$
4. $\bigcirc\phi \rightarrow \bigcirc\phi$
5. $\Box(\phi \rightarrow \psi) \rightarrow (\Box\phi \rightarrow \Box\psi)$
6. $\Box\phi \rightarrow \phi$
7. $\Box\phi \rightarrow \bigcirc\Box\phi$
8. $\Box(\phi \rightarrow \bigcirc\phi) \rightarrow (\phi \rightarrow \Box\phi)$
9. $K(\phi \rightarrow \psi) \rightarrow (K\phi \rightarrow K\psi)$
10. $K\phi \rightarrow \phi$
11. $K\phi \rightarrow KK\phi$
12. $\phi \rightarrow KL\phi$
13. $K\bigcirc\phi \rightarrow \bigcirc K\phi$
14. $\bigcirc K\phi \rightarrow K\bigcirc\phi$
15. $\phi U\psi \rightarrow \Diamond K\psi$
16. $\phi U\psi \leftrightarrow K\psi \vee (K\phi \wedge \bigcirc(\phi U\psi))$

Rules

$$\frac{\phi \rightarrow \psi, \phi}{\psi} \text{ MP}$$

$$\frac{\phi}{K\phi} \text{ K-Necessitation} \qquad \frac{\phi}{\Box\phi} \text{ } \Box\text{-Necessitation} \qquad \frac{\phi}{\bigcirc\phi} \text{ } \bigcirc\text{-Necessitation}$$

---

logic. Observe that satisfaction of aUb at the pair x, U_i does not depend on x but on U_i due to the use of K modalities in the truth condition. This means that aUb is a *knowledge* formula, that is, it is equivalent to a formula of the form Ka or $\neg Ka$ and the following is a theorem (follows from Axioms 15 and 16)

$$aUb \quad \leftrightarrow \quad K(aUb).$$

This means that if aUb is true the agent believes it. Obviously this definition of until is not standard. The reason we chose to treat until formulas as knowledge formulas, instead of employing the standard definition of until is technical as it simplifies greatly the completeness proof. In particular, this version of until is deterministic just like in linear temoral logic and allows us to reuse parts of the completeness of that logic. The extension $ex(a)$ of all knowledge formulas a can be identified with a set of subsets

$$ex(a) = \{U_i : y, U_i \models a\}.$$

Therefore, the meaning of the epistemic until $ex(aUb)$ is contextual as it depends on the epistemic view of the agent. Also, spheres will represent the belief state of the agent as they determine the satisfaction of knowledge formulas.

Heinemann has combined the logic of subsets and linear temporal logic in several papers. He studied the temporal logic of decreasing subsets in [8] and added a pointwise *until* in [12]. He then studied the temporal logic of increasing subset [13] without next and a combination of alternating increasing and decreasing subsets in [14]. Combinations of epistemic and temporal logic is naturally a useful combination and several other approaches combining those two exist in the literature ([15,16,9]).

We now turn to the semantics of contraction. The until formula aUb, as defined, allows us to define a minimization procedure among subsets of X. To see that, suppose that $(\odot \neg b)Ua$ holds in a state x, U_i. This means that $\odot b$ is believed in all states smaller than U_i until we reach a state U_j where a is believed. In particular, b is believed in all epistemic states between U_i and U_j (including U_j and excluding U_i). If we specify that $\neg b$ is a possibility in U_i then U_i is the minimum epistemic state that contains U_j where $\neg b$ is a possibility. In this sense, the conditional U may act as a minimization operator.

The same basic idea lies behind belief contraction: contracting the belief b at a state, where a and b is believed, means to expand this state with a *possibility* of $\neg b$ and doing it in a minimal way. In other words, we seek to reach the minimum state where $\neg b$ is a possibility. Now, it easy to express all the above syntactically and define: the *contraction* $a \ominus b$ of a with b with the formula

$$L \neg b \wedge (\odot b U a).$$

Observe that $\odot$ is necessary in $\odot b U a$ as if it was omitted then Kb would be true in the current state and would contradict $L \neg b$. Here is an example that illustrates the above procedure. The model consists of a set $X = \{x, y, z\}$, $S = \{\{x\}, \{x, y\}, \{x, y, z\}\}$ and an initial valuation on three atomic formulas $v(a) = \{x\}$, $v(b) = \{x, y\}$ and $v(c) = \{x, y, z\}$. We have $x, \{x\} \models K(a \wedge b \wedge c)$, $x, \{x, y\} \models L \neg a \wedge K(b \wedge c)$ and $x, \{x, y, z\} \models L \neg a \wedge L \neg b \wedge Kc$. We have $x, \{x\} \models \neg(a \ominus b)$, $x, \{x, y\} \models a \ominus a \wedge \neg(a \ominus b)$ and $x, \{x, y, z\} \models \neg(a \ominus a) \wedge (a \ominus b) \wedge \neg(a \ominus c)$. We also have $ex(a \ominus a) = \{\{x, y\}\}$, $ex(a \ominus b) = \{\{x, y, z\}\}$, and $ex(a \ominus c) = \{\emptyset\}$.

The following holds:

Theorem 1. *The axioms and rules of* **CL** *are sound with respect to systems of spheres.*

Proof. The proof is straightforward and we show only soundness for Axiom 16. Suppose $x, U_i \models aUb$ and let $j \geq i$ be the least such that $y, U_j \models Kb$ and for all $i \leq k < j$, $x, U_k \models Ka$. If $i = j$ then $x, U_i \models Kb$. If $j > i$ then $j \geq i + 1$, therefore $x, U_i \models Ka$ and $x, U_{i+1} \models aUb$. The other direction is similar.

The proof of completeness runs along the lines of the linear temporal logic. Unfortunately, we cannot make full use of Heinemann's completeness theorem as it is not obvious how some definitions could apply to our framework (for example the satisfaction of U in the canonical model, see page 79 in [7]).

Theorem 2. *The axioms and rules of* **CL** *are complete with respect to systems of spheres.*

Theorem 3. **CL** *has the finite model property and therefore it is decidable.*

3   Properties of the Contraction Connective

We will now explore to some extent the properties that the contraction connective satisfies. We cannot always compare directly the contraction defined with the vast number of properties introduced for the theory contraction operators. Sometimes properties of theory operators do not correspond to some property for contraction between formulas. Other times, theory contraction postulates have two or more possible translations.

Recall that the contraction $a \ominus b$ of a with b is defined by

$$\mathsf{L}\neg b \wedge (\bigcirc b \mathsf{U} a).$$

We shall use this last form to illustrate the correspondence with the traditional AGM postulates.

The Closure postulate only concerns theory contractions.

Inclusion translates to

$$\mathsf{K}a \rightarrow a \ominus b.$$

This is not a theorem of our logic and a model counterexample is easy to find: let $X = \{x, y\}$, $S = \{\{x\}, \{x, y\}\}$ and $v(a) = \{x\}$. We have $x, \{x\} \models \mathsf{K}a$, and $x, \{x, y\} \models a \ominus a$, but $x, \{x, y\} \models \mathsf{L}\neg a$. At first sight, as this counterexample shows, the source of the failure of inclusion is that the framework is more expressive: we can express belief consistency. In the state we reach after contraction, we believe in the consistency of $\neg a$, which contradicts the belief in a where we started from. In other words, contraction with a is not achieved by the removal of a, but the addition of the possibility of $\neg a$.

Notice that if we contract with a proposition b whose negation $\neg b$ is consistent with a, then inclusion is valid if we restrict formulas to those without an occurrence of the contraction operator. The additional expressive power of referring to contraction within the language allows us to express iterated contractions. In particular, we can define a model where $x, U_i \models a \ominus b$ and $x, U_j \models a \ominus b \ominus c$ for some $U_j \supsetneq U_i$, i.e., we need to reach some $U_j \supsetneq U_i$ to contract with c. This provides another counterexample of inclusion because $x, U_i \models \neg (a \ominus b) \ominus c$.

We now turn to Vacuity that translates to

$$(a \wedge \mathsf{L}\neg b) \ominus b \leftrightarrow a \wedge \mathsf{L}\neg b.$$

This is a theorem in our logic and follows from the axioms of temporal logic. (Use $\bigcirc a \mathsf{U} b \rightarrow b \vee \bigcirc a \mathsf{U}(b \wedge a)$.)

Consistency is guaranteed by Classical logic and the definition of contraction: if b is a theorem then so is $\neg(a \ominus b)$.

Extensionality corresponds to the provable rule

$$b \leftrightarrow c \quad \text{then} \quad a \ominus b \leftrightarrow a \ominus c.$$

Recovery translates to

$$a \ominus b \wedge \mathsf{K}b \to \mathsf{K}a,$$

which is a theorem because the following

$$a \ominus b \to \mathsf{L}\neg b$$

is a theorem. It seems that Recovery is upheld for the wrong reason, as the Inclusion case presented earlier, namely the ability to express consistency. So we might opt for the following pointwise translation of recovery:

$$a \ominus b \wedge b \to a.$$

This is not a theorem, which makes the $\ominus$ a case of Makinson's withdrawal operator ([17]), and this can be shown with a three element model. Let $X = \{x, y, z\}$ and $S = \{\{x\}, \{x, y, z\}\}$. Also let $v(a) = \{x, y\}$ and $v(b) = \{x, z\}$. We have $x, \{x\} \models \mathsf{K}a$, and $z, \{x, y, z\} \models a \ominus b \wedge b$ but $z, \{x, y, z\} \not\models \neg a$.

We now turn to the last two postulates that have been proved to correspond to linear structures.

Intersection is directly translated to

$$a \ominus (b \wedge c) \to a \ominus b \vee a \ominus c.$$

One can show that it follows from the axioms of temporal logic (using the theorem $(a \wedge b)\mathsf{U}c \to a\mathsf{U}b \wedge a\mathsf{U}c$.)

Conjunction translates to the rule

$$\text{if} \quad a \ominus (b \wedge c) \to \mathsf{L}\neg b \quad \text{then} \quad a \ominus b \to a \ominus (b \wedge c).$$

The rule is provable in the logic using the contrapositive of the antecedent and the fact that until formulas are knowledge formulas.

4   Comparison with Other Work

This work should be thought of as part of a considerable amount of work that tries to establish links between object language representations of belief change operations. Herzig in [18] studied belief change operators in the object language. The results include both update operators and conditionals but for the representation results a restriction to non nested update operators was required. Giordano et al ([19,20]) take a different approach where conditionals are in object language but the operators are in metalanguage. The correspondence is established by a representation result based on Ramsey test. Again some of the axioms involve non nested fragments.

A similar approach is that of Dynamic Doxastic logic ([21]) and the more recent Dynamic Epistemic Logic that use action modalities corresponding to belief change operators much like dynamic logic (see [22,23,24]—and more recently in combination with temporal logic [25]). Such formulas correspond to conditionals and similarly they are restricted to the boolean fragment of the language. This work is complementary: we believe that the results of the present paper can be translated to Dynamic Epistemic Logic, therefore systems based on this logic can be equipped with a temporal-like contraction operator.

Bonanno ([10]) used a different approach involving temporal logic and two operators that of Belief and Receiving Information to axiomatize logical systems that describe the process of revision. Belief revision operators are still kept in the metalanguage and the correspondence is done at the semantical level much like Giordano's approach.

5   Conclusion

We showed that it is possible to incorporate assertions about belief contraction within the language. We are able to axiomatize those assertion with the help of temporal logic and Moss-Parikh subset space logic. We also show that the logic is complete with respect to models made out of linearly ordered decreasing subsets, much like the models used in conditional logic as well as the systems-of-spheres used to model belief change.

This research suggests an interesting direction; namely, a wider class of models. Although linearly ordered subsets is a simple semantical framework and bonds well with previous research, it is natural to ask if this work can be generalized to more permissive structures. It has been shown that belief revision and nonmonotonic logic fare well with partially ordered subsets ([26]) or even metric spaces and graphs ([4]).

A relaxation of the semantical framework is useful for another reason. If we simply model expansion with conjunction, we can express a belief revision connective $a * b$ defined by contraction via the Levi identity:

$$(a \ominus \neg b) \wedge b.$$

Revision is defined using the primary connectives with

$$a * b \quad \leftrightarrow \quad b \wedge (\odot \neg b \mathsf{U} a).$$

Although we may nest the above definition, the resulting formulas do not correspond to successive revisions because a system of linearly ordered subsets is simply *not* closed under revision. Closure under other forms of belief change, apart from contraction, requires a richer semantical framework.

References

1. Katsuno, H., Mendelzon, A.O.: Propositional knowledge base revision and minimal change. Artificial Intelligence 52, 263–294 (1991)
2. Lehmann, D.: Belief revision, revised. In: Proceedings of the Fourteenth International Joint Conference of Artificial Intelligence (IJCAI 1995), pp. 1534–1540 (1995)

3. Pais, J.: Revision algebra semantics for conditional logic. Studia Logica 51(2), 279–316 (1992)
4. Georgatos, K.: Geodesic revision. Journal of Logic and Computation 19(3), 447–459 (2009), doi:10.1093/logcom/exn008
5. Georgatos, K.: Iterated contraction based on indistinguishability. In: Artemov, S., Nerode, A. (eds.) LFCS 2013. LNCS, vol. 7734, pp. 194–205. Springer, Heidelberg (2013)
6. Dabrowski, A., Moss, L.S., Parikh, R.: Topological reasoning and the logic of knowledge. Annals of Pure and Applied Logic 78(1-3), 73–110 (1996)
7. Heinemann, B.: A modal logic for discretely descending chains of sets. Studia Logica 76(1), 67–90 (2004)
8. Heinemann, B.: Topological nexttime logic. In: Kracht, M., de Rijke, H.W., Zakharyaschev, M. (eds.) Advances in Modal Logic 1996, pp. 99–113. Center for the Study of Language and Information, Stanford (1998)
9. Battigalli, P., Bonanno, G.: The logic of belief persistence. Economics and Philosophy 13(01), 39–59 (1997)
10. Bonanno, G.: Axiomatic characterization of the agm theory of belief revision in a temporal logic. Artificial Intelligence 171(2-3), 144–160 (2007)
11. Schmidt, R.A., Tishkovsky, D.: On combinations of propositional dynamic logic and doxastic modal logics. Journal of Logic, Language and Information 17(1), 109–129 (2008)
12. Heinemann, B.: Temporal aspects of the modal logic of subset spaces. Theoretical Computer Science 224(1-2), 135–155 (1999)
13. Heinemann, B.: On sets growing continuously. In: Pandu Rangan, C., Raman, V., Sarukkai, S. (eds.) FST TCS 1999. LNCS, vol. 1738, pp. 420–431. Springer, Heidelberg (1999)
14. Heinemann, B.: Extending topological nexttime logic. In: Proceedings of the Seventh International Workshop on Temporal Representation and Reasoning (TIME 2000), pp. 87–94. IEEE Computer Society, Washington, DC (2000)
15. Kraus, S., Lehmann, D.: Knowledge, belief and time. Theoretical Computer Science 58(1-3), 155–174 (1988)
16. Fagin, R., Halpern, J.Y., Moses, Y., Vardi, M.Y.: Reasoning About Knowledge. MIT Press (1995)
17. Makinson, D.: On the status of the postulate of recovery in the logic of theory change. Journal of Philosophical Logic 16, 383–394 (1987)
18. Herzig, A.: Logics for belief base updating. In: Handbook of Defeasible Reasoning and Uncertainty Management, vol. 3, pp. 189–231. Kluwer Academic Publishers, Belief Change (1998)
19. Giordano, L., Gliozzi, V., Olivetti, N.: Iterated belief revision and conditional logic. Studia Logica 70(1), 23–47 (2002)
20. Giordano, L., Gliozzi, V., Olivetti, N.: Weak AGM postulates and strong Ramsey test: A logical formalization. Artificial Intelligence 168(1-2), 1–37 (2005)
21. Segerberg, K.: Belief revision from the point of view of doxastic logic. Logic Journal of IGPL 3(4), 535–553 (1995)
22. de Rijke, M.: Meeting some neighboursa dynamic modal logic meets theories of change and knowledge representation. In: van Eijck, J., Visser, A. (eds.) Logic and Information Flow, pp. 170–195. MIT Press, Cambridge (1994)
23. van Ditmarsch, H.P.: Prolegomena to dynamic logic for belief revision. In: Uncertainty, Rationality, and Agency, pp. 175–221. Springer, Netherlands (2006)

24. van Benthem, J.: Dynamic logic for belief revision. Journal of Applied Non-Classical Logics 17(2), 129–155 (2007)
25. van Ditmarsch, H.P., van der Hoek, W., Ruan, J.: Connecting dynamic epistemic and temporal epistemic logics. Logic Journal of the IGPL 21(3), 380–403 (2013)
26. Georgatos, K.: To preference via entrenchment. Annals of Pure and Applied Logic 96(1-3), 141–155 (1999)

Logic Foundations of the OCL Modelling Language

Enrico Franconi[1], Alessandro Mosca[1,2],
Xavier Oriol[3], Guillem Rull[4], and Ernest Teniente[3]

[1] KRDB Research Centre, Free University of Bozen-Bolzano, Italy
[2] SIRIS Academic, Spain
[3] Universitat Politècnica de Catalunya, Spain
[4] Universitat de Barcelona, Spain

Abstract. In this paper we define *the* first-order fragment of the Object Constraint Language (OCL), the declarative language for describing rules that apply to conceptual schemas in the Unified Modelling Language (UML). This fragment covers the whole of OCL without arithmetic operators, aggregation functions, iterators, and recursion. We give the set theoretical formal syntax and semantics in an elegant, concise, and clear way. This fragment has the same expressivity as domain-independent first-order logic (*aka* relational algebra), in the sense that any relational algebra expression can be reformulated as a logically equivalent OCL expression, and vice-versa.

1 Introduction

Graphical modelling languages like UML, ORM or ER, provide a general and intuitive idea of the concepts of the domain being modelled and the associations among them. However, these languages are not expressive enough to allow defining all the relevant information of the domain.

For example, consider the class diagram in Fig. 1 about employees and their departments. The diagram captures all the necessary concepts (i.e. *Employee*, *JuniorEmployee* and *Department*) together with their associations (i.e. *WorksIn* and *Manages*), thus providing an intuitive idea of the specified domain. Nevertheless, the schema as such is not expressive enough to encode further relevant

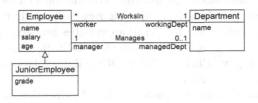

Fig. 1. Class diagram of employees and departments

E. Fermé and J. Leite (Eds.): JELIA 2014, LNAI 8761, pp. 657–664, 2014.
© Springer International Publishing Switzerland 2014

characteristics of the domain, e.g., that junior employees cannot manage a department or that the salary of the manager of a department must be the highest one among the salaries of the workers of that department.

For this reason, the usage of graphical modelling languages is usually complemented with some textual languages that allow defining such additional information in a precise and unambiguous way. The OCL language (Object Constraint Language) [1] is one of the most well-known textual languages used for this purpose. OCL is a declarative language that allows defining conditions that the schema states should satisfy. Although OCL may be used to define structural as well as behavioural conditions, in this paper we will consider just the structural ones, i.e., OCL integrity constraints that any class diagram state should always satisfy. Examples of OCL integrity constraints over the above UML schema are:

context Employee **inv** ManagerIsOlder:
    self.age **<= self**.workingDept.manager.age

context JuniorEmployee **inv** GradeStudentSalary:
    self.grade='degree' **implies self**.salary > 15000

context JuniorEmployee **inv** JuniorIsNotManager:
    self.managedDept->**isEmpty()**.

Intuitively, *ManagerIsOlder* states that no employee in a department can be older than its manager. *GradeStudentSalary* ensures that junior employees with a degree must earn a salary greater than 15000. *JuniorIsNotManager* guarantees that no junior employee manages a department.

It is conjectured that there is a relationship between OCL and the Relational Algebra (RA). This relationship is important since RA is at the heart of the SQL query and constraint language for relational databases, and SQL could be used to check the validity of OCL constraints over actual data. However, up to our knowledge, nobody has succeeded in formally establishing the exact nature of such a relationship. For instance, [2] and [3] argue that OCL does not capture RA because there is no possibility to translate some relational algebra operations into OCL. However, such a strong claim remains unproved in [3], where the authors simply ground their argument on some presumably hard OCL cases. On the other hand, [4] proposes an approach to simulate relational algebra queries over UML by using OCL constraints and operations: it is not clear whether this approach can work with nested relational algebra operations like, for instance, a cartesian product after a selection. [5] provides an informal translation without any claim of even soundness. An informal translation in first order logic with heavy usage of primitive functions also for most of the first order expressible constructs is introduced in [6]. Practical approaches implementing a translation from OCL to SQL have problems too: MySQL4OCL [7] relies on some MySQL procedures which clearly falls out of RA; OCL2SQL [8] lacks a theoretical basis and has an unsound translation.

The main contribution of this paper is the identification by formal means of the first-order fragment of OCL having the same expressivity relational algebra

```
OCL-Bool ::= OCL-Bool BoolOp OCL-Bool |
             not OCL-Bool |
             OCL-Set = OCL-Set |
             OCL-Set <> OCL-Set |
             OCL-Set ->includesAll(OCL-Set) |
             OCL-Set ->excludesAll(OCL-Set) |
             OCL-Set ->forAll(Var | OCL-Bool) |      OCL-Value ::= Constant |
             OCL-Set ->exists(Var | OCL-Bool) |                   Var(.fRole)*.attr
             OCL-Set ->isEmpty() |             BoolOp  ::= and | or | xor | implies
             OCL-Set ->notEmpty() |           CompOp  ::= < | <= | = | >= | > | <>
             OCL-Set ->size() CompOp Integer | Var     ::= ⟨a variable name⟩
             OCL-Set ->one(Var | OCL-Bool) |   Class   ::= ⟨a class name⟩
             Var = Var |                       Assoc   ::= ⟨an association name⟩
             Var <> Var |                      role    ::= ⟨a role name⟩
             Var.oclIsKindOf(Class) |          fRole   ::= ⟨a functional role name⟩
             OCL-Value CompOp OCL-Value        attr    ::= ⟨an attribute name⟩
OCL-Set  ::= OCL-Set ->union(OCL-Set) |        Integer ::= ⟨an integer number⟩
             OCL-Set ->intersection(OCL-Set) | Constant ::= ⟨a constant name⟩
             OCL-Set - OCL-Set |
             OCL-Set ->select(Var | OCL-Bool) |
             OCL-Set ->reject(Var | OCL-Bool) |
             OCL-Set.role [ [role] ] |
             Var.role [ [role] ] |
             Class.allInstances()
```

Fig. 2. Syntax of OCL$_{FO}$

(i.e. any RA expression can be reformulated as an equivalent OCL expression of our fragment, and vice-versa). For this purpose, we exploit the connection between the domain-independent fragment of first-order logic and RA. As stated in the following sections, this fragment covers the expressive power of OCL without arithmetic operations, aggregation functions, iteration, recursion, and other non first order features. We provide the formal syntax and semantics to this fragment in an elegant, concise, and clear way since we base the semantics on set theoretical constructs.

The OCL constraints mentioned before could be expressed as follows in RA:

1. $\pi_s \sigma_{o1 < o2}((\text{Emp} \bowtie_{s=s} \text{EmpAge}) \bowtie_{s=s}$
$(\text{Emp} \bowtie_{s=worker} \text{WorksIn} \bowtie_{dept=mDept} \text{Manages} \bowtie_{manager=s} \text{EmpAge})) = \emptyset$

2. $\pi_s((\text{JuniorEmp} \bowtie_{s=s} \text{JuniorEmpGrade}) \bowtie_{s=s} \{\text{degree}\}) \setminus$
$\pi_s(\sigma_{o>15000}(\text{Emp} \bowtie_{s=s} \text{EmpSalary})) = \emptyset$

3. $\text{JuniorEmp} \cap \pi_s(\text{JuniorEmp} \bowtie_{s=manager} \text{Manages}) = \emptyset$

2   The OCL$_{FO}$ Fragment of OCL

This section introduces the syntax and the semantics of boolean statements in OCL$_{FO}$, the first-order fragment of OCL. The OCL$_{FO}$ fragment contains all the first-order features of OCL, and it leaves out arithmetic operators, aggregation functions, iterators, and recursion. We will show in the following section that OCL$_{FO}$ is equally expressive as the domain-independent fragment of first-order logic. Figure 2 defines all the legal boolean statements in OCL$_{FO}$, built from a signature including class names, role names (among them, functional role names), association names, attribute names, and constant names. The signature specifies to which association name each role name is attached to, via the function ass : role ↦ Assoc; the function comp : role ↦ role, defined only for roles of binary associations, returns the complementary role of a given role. The signature is given according to an associated UML class diagram. As expected, boolean statements are composed by simpler boolean statements, and make use of set descriptions obtained by composition of simpler sets or by navigation along classes and roles.

Notice that an OCL constraint begins by declaring at top level the class from which the navigation starts, and that the *special* variable name **self** – denoting objects from that class – may occur within the OCL constraint. In our formalisation we assume a simplified equivalent form of OCL constraints, where the top-level class declaration is replaced by bounding the **self** variable with a universal quantification ranging over all the elements of the declared class. So, the OCL constraint:

context top-class **inv** invariant-label: ϕ

is automatically transformed into the equivalent boolean statement:

top-class.**allInstances()->forAll(self** | ϕ).

Note that unbound variables – i.e., variables not in the scope of **forAll**, **exists**, **one**, **select**, **reject** quantifiers – are disallowed in boolean statements. Moreover, the core of OCL$_{FO}$ excludes obvious cases which could be easily be encoded in the language. This is the case of multiple variables, the iterator operator **->isUnique**, the non-iterator operators **includes** and **excludes**, and the instance operators **oclIsTypeOf** and **oclIsKindOf**.

The semantics of an OCL$_{FO}$ boolean statement is given by means of the interpretations satisfying the statement. An *interpretation* is a relational structure, namely a pair $\mathcal{I} = \langle \Delta^{\mathcal{I}}, \cdot^{\mathcal{I}} \rangle$ with a non-empty set $\Delta^{\mathcal{I}}$—the *domain* of the interpretation of object identifiers and values—and an *interpretation function* $\cdot^{\mathcal{I}}$—defined over the signature of the OCL constraints, namely class names, role/association names, attribute names, and constant names. Interpretations do not distinguish between object identifiers and values, since the evaluation of OCL constraints does not depend on this distinction, due to the strict syntactic requirements for the appearance of attributes within boolean statements. A class name is interpreted as a set of domain elements, a role name is interpreted as a set of pairs of domain elements, an attribute name is interpreted as a function from domain elements to domain elements, and constant names are interpreted as domain elements with the same name (standard name assumption). Intuitively, an interpretation represents a *state* (or *snapshot*) of the system, namely a complete description of an instance of the modelled system: it indicates the classes object identifiers belong to, the inter-relations between object identifiers via association's roles, and the values objects have via their attributes. An interpretation $\mathcal{I}$ *satisfies* a set of OCL constraints – i.e., it is a *model* for it, written $\mathcal{I} \models \Phi$ – if and only if the interpretation function $\cdot^{\mathcal{I}}$, extended over arbitrary boolean statements as specified in the inductive definition of Figure 3, evaluates to TRUE for each constraint in the set of boolean statements. Models represent the *legal* states of the constraints.

OCL-Bool^I	$\in \{$TRUE, FALSE$\}$
(OCL-Bool$_1$ BoolOp OCL-Bool$_2$)^I	$\equiv$ OCL-Bool$_1{}^I$ BoolOp OCL-Bool$_2{}^I$
(**not** OCL-Bool)^I	$\equiv \neg$OCL-Bool^I
(OCL-Set$_1$ = OCL-Set$_2$)^I	$\equiv$ OCL-Set$_1{}^I$ = OCL-Set$_2{}^I$
(OCL-Set$_1$ <> OCL-Set$_2$)^I	$\equiv$ OCL-Set$_1{}^I \neq$ OCL-Set$_2{}^I$
(OCL-Set$_1$->**includesAll**(OCL-Set$_2$))^I	$\equiv$ OCL-Set$_1{}^I \supseteq$ OCL-Set$_2{}^I$
(OCL-Set$_1$->**excludesAll**(OCL-Set$_2$))^I	$\equiv$ (OCL-Set$_1{}^I \cap$ OCL-Set$_2{}^I$) $= \emptyset$
(OCL-Set->**forAll**(Var | OCL-Bool))^I	$\equiv$ (OCL-Set$^I \setminus$ (OCL-Set$^I \cap$ OCL-Bool$^{I,\text{Var}}$)) $= \emptyset$
(OCL-Set->**exists**(Var | OCL-Bool))^I	$\equiv$ (OCL-Set$^I \cap$ OCL-Bool$^{I,\text{Var}}$) $\neq \emptyset$
(OCL-Set->**isEmpty**())^I	$\equiv$ OCL-Set$^I = \emptyset$
(OCL-Set->**notEmpty**())^I	$\equiv$ OCL-Set$^I \neq \emptyset$
(OCL-Set->**size**() CompOp n)^I	$\equiv$ $\|$OCL-Set$^I\|$ CompOp n
(OCL-Set->**one**(Var | OCL-Bool))^I	$\equiv$ $\|$OCL-Set$^I \cap$ OCL-Bool$^{I,\text{Var}}\| = 1$
(v_1 = v_2)^I	$\equiv$ ($v_1 = v_2$)
(v_1 <> v_2)^I	$\equiv$ ($v_1 \neq v_2$)
(v.**oclIsKindOf**(Class))^I	$\equiv v \in$ Class^I
(OCL-Value$_1$ CompOp OCL-Value$_2$)^I	$\equiv$ OCL-Value$_1{}^I$ CompOp OCL-Value$_2{}^I$
OCL-Bool$^{I,\text{Var}}$	$= \{v \in \Delta^I \mid$ (OCL-Bool$_{[\text{Var}/v]}$)^I = TRUE$\} \subseteq \Delta^I$
OCL-Set^I	$\subseteq \Delta^I$
(OCL-Set$_1$->**union**(OCL-Set$_2$))^I	$=$ OCL-Set$_1{}^I \cup$ OCL-Set$_2{}^I$
(OCL-Set$_1$->**intersection**(OCL-Set$_2$))^I	$=$ OCL-Set$_1{}^I \cap$ OCL-Set$_2{}^I$
(OCL-Set$_1$ − OCL-Set$_2$)^I	$=$ OCL-Set$_1{}^I \setminus$ OCL-Set$_2{}^I$
(OCL-Set->**select**(Var | OCL-Bool))^I	$=$ OCL-Set$^I \cap$ OCL-Bool$^{I,\text{Var}}$
(OCL-Set->**reject**(Var | OCL-Bool))^I	$=$ OCL-Set$^I \setminus$ OCL-Bool$^{I,\text{Var}}$ OCL-Set$_2{}^I$
(OCL-Set•role)^I	$= \pi_{\text{role}}($OCL-Set$^I \bowtie_{\text{comp(role)}}$ ass(role)^I)
(v•role)^I	$= \pi_{\text{role}} \sigma_{\text{comp(role)}=v}$ ass(role)^I
(OCL-Set•role$_d$[role$_s$])^I	$= \pi_{\text{role}_d}($OCL-Set$^I \bowtie_{\text{role}_s}$ ass(role$_s$)^I)
(v•role$_d$[role$_s$])^I	$= \pi_{\text{role}_d} \sigma_{\text{role}_s=v}$ ass(role$_s$)^I
(Class.**allInstances**())^I	$=$ Class^I
OCL Value^I	$\in \Delta^I$
Constant^I	$= v_{\text{Constant}}$
(v•fRole$_1$•$\cdots$•fRole$_n$•attr)^I	$=$ attr^I(fRole$_n^I(\cdots($fRole$_1^I(v))))$

Fig. 3. Semantics of OCL$_{\text{FO}}$

For example, the OCL constraint:

context JuniorEmployee **inv** GradeStudentsSalary:
  self.grade='degree' **implies** **self**.salary > 15000

is satisfied in the following interpretation $\mathcal{I}_0$, namely in the state where all the junior employees with a degree have a salary above 15000:

$\Delta^{\mathcal{I}_0} = \{john, mary, melissa, degree, diploma, 16000, 22000, 8000, \ldots\}$
JuniorEmployee$^{\mathcal{I}_0} = \{john, mary\}$
grade$^{\mathcal{I}_0} = \{john \mapsto degree, mary \mapsto degree, melissa \mapsto diploma\}$
salary$^{\mathcal{I}_0} = \{john \mapsto 16000, mary \mapsto 22000, melissa \mapsto 8000\}$

In other words, $\mathcal{I}_0 \models$ GradeStudentsSalary. In fact, it is easy to see that the following holds:

(JuniorEmployee$^{\mathcal{I}_0} \setminus$
  (JuniorEmployee$^{\mathcal{I}_0} \cap$
    $\{v \in \Delta^{\mathcal{I}_0} \mid$ grade$^{\mathcal{I}_0}(v) =$ degree$^{\mathcal{I}_0} \to$ salary$^{\mathcal{I}_0}(v) > 15000^{\mathcal{I}_0}\}$)) $= \emptyset$.

3   Equivalence of OCL$_{FO}$ with Relational Algebra

We show in this section that OCL$_{FO}$ and Relational Algebra are equally expressive. The notion of *equal expressivity* is captured by the following two theorems.

Theorem 1 (Completeness for RA). *Let q be an arbitrary n-ary RA expression, $q(\mathcal{I})$ the evaluation of q over an interpretation $\mathcal{I}$, and t an arbitrary n-tuple. Then there exists a set of OCL$_{FO}$ boolean statements Φ, such that for any interpretation $\mathcal{I}$:*

$$t \in q(\mathcal{I}) \quad \textbf{if and only if} \quad \mathcal{I} \models \Phi.$$

Theorem 2 (Soundness). *Let ϕ be an arbitrary OCL$_{FO}$ boolean statement. Then there exist finitely many RA expressions $p_1, \ldots, p_m, q_1, \ldots, q_n$ – with $\sum_{i=1}^{m} |p_i| + \sum_{i=1}^{n} |q_i| \leq k \cdot |\phi|$ for some k – such that for any interpretation $\mathcal{I}$:*

$$\mathcal{I} \models \phi \quad \textbf{if and only if} \quad \bigwedge_{i=1}^{m} p_i(\mathcal{I}) = \emptyset \wedge \bigwedge_{i=1}^{n} q_i(\mathcal{I}) \neq \emptyset.$$

There exists a reduction from the membership problem of a tuple in the answer of a RA expression over a database instance to the satisfiability problem of a set of OCL constraints over the same database (*completeness*); and there exists a reduction from the satisfiability problem of an OCL constraint over a database instance to (non-)emptiness problem of the answer of a sequence RA expressions (whose total size is linearly bounded by the size of the original OCL constraint) over the same database (*soundness*). We sketch below the proofs of the theorems.

In [2], Mandel and Cengarle conclude that OCL is incomplete for RA: "In order to achieve completeness OCL should just include a concept of tuple functions (or creation of virtual classes) and a mechanism for creating instances of any type or class. These instances are of course not meant to be included to the current model of the class diagram but to allow navigation on a higher level of abstraction." Indeed, in order to prove the completeness for RA of OCL$_{FO}$, for each association in the signature we create an *association* class whose instances represent *exactly* the tuples of the association. That is, a tuple identifier represents the same tuple in any association class, and any tuple is represented by a unique tuple identifier in any association class. Tuple identifiers and tuple components are related by means of binary relations corresponding to the roles. A global correspondence between roles of a n-ary association and positions of a n-ary relation has to be globally established in the signature. This encoding is called *global reification*. An association class R is created out of the roles $r_1, \cdots, r_n$ of an n-ary association as follows:

```
R.allInstances() ->forAll(id_A | R.allInstances() ->forAll(id_B |
   (id_A.r₁ = id_B.r₁ and ... and id_A.r_n = id_B.r_n) implies id_A = id_B)) ,
```

where $r_1, \cdots, r_n$ are n attributes of the association class, homonym with the n roles of the n-ary association. The above constraint guarantees that instances of the association class are in one-to-one correspondence with n-tuples identified via its attributes. The association class is the *reified* (aka *objectified*) version of the association. In addition to that we need to guarantee that two instances of distinct association classes are globally the same whenever they identify the same n-tuple; the OCL constraints needed to guarantee global reification are inspired by the work in [9]. Once we have association classes and access to their components defined by a set of OCL$_{FO}$ constraints, it is easy to write additional constraints in OCL$_{FO}$ encoding the basic constructs of RA.

Let us consider now the association class R of arity 4 with attributes a, b, c, d obtained by joining two association classes R1 and R2 of arity 3 by R1.a = R2.a and R1.b = R2.b. We can formalise this with the following OCL constraints, in addition to the reification constraints mentioned above for the three relations.

($\rightarrow$) For any pair of instances in R1 in R2 with the same value for a and b, there must exist an instance in R that represents its join:

```
R1.allInstances() ->forAll(id₁ | R2.allInstances() ->forAll(id₂ |
    id₁.a = id₂.a and id₁.b = id₂.b implies
        R.allInstances() ->exists(id |
            id.a = id₁.a and id.b = id₁.b and id.c = id₁.c and id.d = id₂.d))).
```

($\leftarrow$) Any instance of R should come from the join of two instances of R1 and R2 respectively:

```
R.allInstances() ->forAll(r |
    R1.allInstances() ->exists(id₁ |
        id₁.a = r.a and id₁.b = r.b and id₁.c = r.c) and
    R2.allInstances() ->exists(id₂ |
        id₂.a = r.a and id₂.b = r.b and id₂.d = r.d)).
```

In order to prove soundness, we reduce OCL$_{FO}$ boolean statements to formulas in the *domain-independent* fragment of first-order logic with the Standard Name Assumption. Due to the known equivalence of domain-independent first-order logic and RA, then for each OCL$_{FO}$ boolean statement there exists an equivalent RA expression. A formula is domain-independent if whenever it is satisfiable in an interpretation with a given domain, then it is satisfiable in a *compatible* interpretation. Two interpretations are compatible if they differ only for their domain. We observe that all the constraints representing the meaning of OCL$_{FO}$ are all domain-independent and reducible to emptiness checks, and they are all encodable as first-order logic formulas.

4 Conclusions

OCL is a formal language for defining constraints that serves as a complement for graphical modelling languages such as UML. Although it was known that a relationship between OCL and RA should exist, this relationship had not been formally proved before. In this paper, we have identified OCL$_{FO}$, the first-order fragment of OCL, which covers the entire of OCL except for its non first-order features (aggregation, recursion, etc.), and we have proved that OCL$_{FO}$ has the same expressivity as RA, that is, any RA expression can be rewritten into an equivalent OCL_{FO} one, and vice-versa. This paper extends [10] by considering an extended fragment of OCL and proving the equivalence with RA. On the other hand, [10] provides computational means for reasoning in OCL-lite.

Acknowledgements. This work has been partly supported by Ministerio de Ciencia e Innovación under project TIN2011-24747 and by the FI grant from the Secreteria d'Universitats i Recerca of the Generalitat de Catalunya.

References

1. Object Management Group: OMG object constraint language (OCL). Technical Report formal/2012-01-01, Object Management Group, Inc. (2012)
2. Mandel, L., Cengarle, M.V.: On the expressive power of the object constraint language OCL. In: Wing, J.M., Woodcock, J. (eds.) FM 1999. LNCS, vol. 1708, pp. 854–874. Springer, Heidelberg (1999)
3. Balsters, H.: Modelling database views with derived classes in the UML/OCL-framework. In: Stevens, P., Whittle, J., Booch, G. (eds.) UML 2003. LNCS, vol. 2863, pp. 295–309. Springer, Heidelberg (2003)
4. Queralt, A., Teniente, E.: Verification and validation of UML conceptual schemas with OCL constraints. ACM Trans. Softw. Eng. Methodol. 21(2), 13 (2012)
5. Clavel, M., Egea, M., de Dios, M.A.G.: Checking unsatisfiability for OCL constraints. In: Proceedings of the Workshop The Pragmatics of OCL and Other Textual Specification Languages, vol. 24. ECEASST (2009)
6. Beckert, B., Keller, U., Schmitt, P.H.: Translating the object constraint language into first-order predicate logic. In: Proceedings of VERIFY, Workshop at Federated Logic Conferences, FLoC (2002)
7. Egea, M., Dania, C., Clavel, M.: MySQL4OCL: A stored procedure-based MySQL code generator for OCL. Electronic Communications of the EASST 36 (2010)
8. Demuth, B., Wilke, C.: Model and object verification by using Dresden OCL. In: Proceedings of the Russian-German Workshop Innovation Information Technologies: Theory and Practice, Ufa, Russia, pp. 687–690 (2009)
9. Franconi, E., Mosca, A.: Towards a core ORM2 language (research note). In: Demey, Y.T., Panetto, H. (eds.) OTM 2013 Workshops 2013. LNCS, vol. 8186, pp. 448–456. Springer, Heidelberg (2013)
10. Queralt, A., Artale, A., Calvanese, D., Teniente, E.: OCL-Lite: finite reasoning on UML/OCL conceptual schemas. Data & Knowledge Engineering 73, 1–22 (2012)
11. Demuth, B., Hussmann, H.: Using UML/OCL constraints for relational database design. In: France, R.B. (ed.) UML 1999. LNCS, vol. 1723, pp. 598–613. Springer, Heidelberg (1999)
12. Clavel, M., Egea, M., García de Dios, M.A.: Building an efficient component for OCL evaluation. Electronic Communications of the EASST 15 (2008)
13. Akehurst, D.H., Bordbar, B.: On querying UML data models with OCL. In: Gogolla, M., Kobryn, C. (eds.) UML 2001. LNCS, vol. 2185, pp. 91–103. Springer, Heidelberg (2001)

Constraint-Based Algorithm
for Computing Temporal Invariants

Jussi Rintanen

Department of Information and Computer Science
Aalto University, Helsinki, Finland*

Abstract. Automatically identified invariants are an important part of reductions of state-space reachability problems to SAT and related formalisms as a method of pruning the search space. No general algorithms for computing temporal invariants have been proposed before. Earlier algorithms restrict to unconditional actions and at-most-one invariants. We propose a powerful inductive algorithm for computing invariants for timed systems, showing that a wide range of timed modeling languages can be handled uniformly. The algorithm reduces the computation of timed invariants to a sequence of temporal logic consistency tests.

1 Introduction

Invariants are facts that hold in all reachable states of a transition system. In search methods other than explicit state space search, including symbolic search with SAT [9] and backward chaining search, the search space includes (partial) states that are not reachable from the initial states. For these search methods invariants help pruning the search space. Additionally, as an approximate upper-bound for the set of all reachable states, invariants can help in analyzing properties of the state space, with applications in planning, verification, diagnosis, and other forms of reasoning about transition systems.

The leading methods for computing invariants for untimed/asynchronous systems can be viewed as approximations of exact symbolic methods for computing the set of all reachable states, such as those based on binary decision diagrams [2]. These methods inductively compute a sequence of sets of states reachable with a given number of actions. Upon reaching a fixpoint, the computation terminates. Most works on invariants have adopted the inductive construction [10,6,7,11,12] which is well understood in the context of untimed/asynchronous systems.

The conceptual difficulties about reasoning with partial *temporal* states, as well as the concurrency of actions, have hampered attempts to apply the inductive construction in the timed setting. The main challenges in the timed setting are, first, identifying the form of induction suitable for timed systems with several concurrent and temporally overlapping actions, and, second, developing sufficiently powerful and efficient temporal reasoning methods for handling complex timed transition system models. We present solutions to both of these problems.

* Also affiliated with Griffith University, Brisbane, Australia, and the Helsinki Institute of Information Technology, Finland. This work was funded by the Academy of Finland (Finnish Centre of Excellence in Computational Inference Research COIN, 251170).

E. Fermé and J. Leite (Eds.): JELIA 2014, LNAI 8761, pp. 665–673, 2014.

The structure of the paper is as follows. After formal preliminaries in Section 2, the new algorithm is presented in Section 3. A core component of the algorithm, temporal consistency tests, is presented in Section 4. Experiments with the algorithm are summarized in Section 5 before concluding the paper in Section 6.

2   Problem Definition

Formulas x and $\neg x$ for $x \in X$ are *literals*. The *complement* $\bar{l}$ of a literal l is defined by $\bar{x} = \neg x$ and $\overline{\neg x} = x$. We define actions as pairs consisting of a precondition (a propositional formula) and an effect which indicates how and when state variables change. Effects are conditional on values of state variables at the time instant the action is taken.

Definition 1 (Actions). *Let X be a finite set of (Boolean) state variables. An* action *over X is a pair (p, e) where p is a propositional formula over X and e is a set of rules $\phi \rhd l@t$, where ϕ is a propositional formula over X, l is a literal over X, and $t > 0$ is a rational number. Effect l takes place after time t has passed provided that ϕ was true.*

Definition 2 (Transition systems). *A transition system is a 3-tuple $\langle X, I, A \rangle$ where X is a finite set of (Boolean) state variables, $I : X \rightarrow \{0, 1\}$ is the initial state (a total function from state variables to 0 and 1), and A is a set of actions.*

Above we have left out one important component of timed systems, dependencies between actions that prevent some combinations of actions being taken. Actions may use the same (implicitly represented) resources, and hence cannot temporally overlap. Several alternative definitions of this kind of exclusions between actions are possible [13,8,4], and here we only assume that exclusions can be factored to binary relations between actions: if a given action a_1 is taken at time t, then another action a_2 cannot be taken during the interval $[t + t_1, t + t_2]$ for some t_1 and t_2 such that $0 \le t_1 \le t_2$.

Plans are finite sets $P \subseteq A \times \mathbb{Q}+$ that schedule actions so that action exclusions are respected: if $a_1 \in A$ is exclusive of $a_2 \in A$ being taken at $[t_1, t_2]$, and $(a_1, t) \in P$, then $(a_2, t') \in P$ for no t' such that $t + t_1 \le t' \le t + t_2$.

Definition 3 (Plans and executions). *Given a transition system $\langle X, I, A \rangle$, an* execution *for a plan P is a mapping $v : \mathbb{Q} \times X \rightarrow \{0, 1\}$ from time points and state variables to 0 and 1 such that*

1. *$v(0, x) = I(x)$ for all $x \in X$,*
2. *$v(t, p) = 1$ if $(a, t) \in P$ and $a = (p, e)$, where $v(t, p)$ denotes the obvious generalization of the values $v(t, x), x \in X$ to arbitrary Boolean formulas p,*
3. *if $(a, t) \in P$ and $\phi \rhd l@t' \in a$, then $v(t + t', l) = 1$,*
4. *state variables not changed by actions retain their values: for any t_l and t_u such that $t_l < t_u$, if*
   - *$v(t_l, x) = 1$, and*
   - *there is no $(a, t') \in P$ such that $\phi \rhd \neg x@t'' \in e$ (where $a = (p, e)$) and $t_l \le t' + t'' \le t_u$*
   then $v(t_i, x) = 1$ for all t_i such that $t_l < t_i \le t_u$. (Analogously for $v(t_l, x) = 0$.)

For a given transition system $T = \langle X, I, A \rangle$, propositional formulas ϕ such that $v(t, \phi) = 1$ for every execution v of T and every $t \in \mathbb{Q}$ are *invariants*. Later we use a generalization of this notion to temporal logic formulas.

2.1 Temporal Logic Representations

We use a linear temporal logic for reasoning about actions and invariants, with both actions and invariants represented as formulas in the logic.

Definition 4. *Let* $\Sigma = \{x_1, \ldots, x_n\}$ *be a set of atomic propositions. Then our temporal language consists of exactly those formulas that are obtained with the following inductive definition.*

1. *x is a formula for every $x \in \Sigma$.*
2. *Formulas with $\neg$, $\vee$ and $\wedge$ are defined in the usual way.*
3. *$[t_0, t_1]\phi$ is a formula if ϕ is a formula and t_0 and t_1 are rational numbers such that $t_0 \leq t_1$. This is a metric temporal modal operator saying that ϕ holds at all time points t such that $t_{now} + t_0 \leq t \leq t_{now} + t_1$ where t_{now} is the time point in which the formula is evaluated. The formula $[t]\phi$ is defined as an abbreviation for $[t, t]\phi$.*
4. *$\phi_1 \mathcal{U} \phi_2$ is a formula if ϕ_1 and ϕ_2 are formulas. This is the temporal operator* until, *which says that if ϕ_1 is true in all time points until ϕ_2 is true.*

Boolean connectives $\rightarrow$ and $\leftrightarrow$ are defined by $\phi \rightarrow \psi \equiv_{def} \neg\phi \vee \psi$ and $\phi \leftrightarrow \psi \equiv_{def} (\phi \rightarrow \psi) \wedge (\psi \rightarrow \phi)$.

2.2 Semantics for Temporal Formulas

Temporal formulas are evaluated with respect to linear temporal models $v : \mathbb{Q} \times \Sigma \rightarrow \{0, 1\}$ that assign a truth value to every rational time point and atomic proposition. Consequently, we can identify executions with linear temporal models. Formulas have a standard semantics, with the truth of formulas at time point t denoted by $v \models_t \phi$.

Definition 5. *The truth of a temporal formula ϕ at time point t in a given model v is recursively defined as follows.*

1. *$v \models_t b$ iff $v(t, b) = 1$, for atomic propositions $b \in \Sigma$.*
2. *Truth with truth-functional $\neg$, $\vee$ and $\wedge$ is as usual.*
3. *$v \models_t \phi \mathcal{U} \psi$ iff $v \models_{t'} \phi$ for all $t' \geq t$ such that $v \not\models_{t''} \psi$ for all t'' such that $t \leq t'' \leq t'$.*
4. *$v \models_t [t_1, t_2]\phi$ iff $v \models_{t'} \phi$ for all t' such that $t_1 \leq t' \leq t_2$.*

We also use half-open and open intervals with the operators $]t_1, t_2]$, $[t_1, t_2[$, and $]t_1, t_2[$, which are defined analogously. The operator $\square$ is identified with $]-\infty, \infty[$.

2.3 Representation of Actions

We translate action descriptions into this temporal language. The atomic propositions are $a_1, \ldots, a_n$ where $1, \ldots, n$ is some indexing of the $n = |A|$ actions in a transition system $\langle X, I, A \rangle$, and $x_1, \ldots, x_m$ for the $m = |X|$ state variables in X. Actions (p, e) with index i are formalized as follows.

$$a_i \rightarrow p \tag{1}$$

$$(\phi \wedge a_i) \rightarrow [t]l \text{ for all } (\phi \rhd l@t) \in e \tag{2}$$

Depending on the planning language used, there are *action exclusion* constraints preventing an action from being taken if some other action has been taken recently. Main forms of such constraints can be translated into formulas

$$a_i \rightarrow [t_0, t_1] \neg a_j \tag{3}$$

where t_0 and t_1 are rational numbers such that $t_0 \leq t_1$. The working of our invariant algorithm is independent of how these constraints are derived. Representative definitions of action exclusion can be found in literature [13,8,4].

Frame axioms indicate when a fact remains unchanged. For every $x \in X$ we have

$$x \rightarrow (x \mathcal{U} c) \tag{4}$$

where c is the disjunction of all formulas $[-t](a_i \wedge \phi)$ such that $(\phi \rhd \neg x@t) \in e$ for the action (p, e) with index i. There is an analogous axiom $\neg x \rightarrow (\neg x \mathcal{U} c^{\neg})$ indicating the conditions $c^{\neg}$ for change from true to false.

We denote the set of all formulas above by $\alpha_{X,A}$.

3   The Algorithm

Standard invariant algorithms [10,5,3,6,7,11,12] are not applicable in the timed setting where multiple actions can be taken concurrently. For classical planning, the basic induction step in invariant computation is determining, for a given action, which true facts remain true after the action has been taken. With timed models, this basic step must cover the possibility of other actions being taken concurrently. For example, two actions both with precondition a and respectively effects $\neg a, b$ and $\neg a, c$ individually cannot falsify candidate invariant $\neg(b \wedge c)$, but taken simultaneously they will.

The inductive algorithm for deriving invariants for timed systems is given in Figure 1, with the subprocedure *weaken* explained later.

```
 1:  PROCEDURE temporalinvariants(X, I, A);
 2:  C := {x ∈ X | I ⊨ x} ∪ {¬x | x ∈ X, I ⊭ x};
 3:  REPEAT
 4:      C_old := C;
 5:      FOR EACH a ∈ A and c ∈ C such that φ ▷ l@t is an effect of a and l̄ occurs in c DO
 6:          S_a,c := the formula given in Lemma 1;
 7:          IF S_a,c is consistent THEN
 8:              C := C\{c};
 9:              C := C ∪ weaken_{S_a,c}(c);
10:  UNTIL C = C_old;
11:  RETURN C;
```

Fig. 1. Algorithm for computing timed invariants

The induction follows the idea of constructing a schedule of temporal actions step by step. We consider the construction of such schedules in a specific form. Instead of an inductive step that allows adding an arbitrary action in an arbitrary location of a schedule, we only add actions in the end of the schedule so that no other action is taken later, and no actions with a smaller index (according to an arbitrary ordering $<$) can be taken at the same last time point.

Assuming that all schedules of $i - 1$ actions satisfy a certain set C of candidate invariants, we consider schedules of i actions to test which of the candidate invariants are still satisfied. The passage from $i - 1$ to i actions corresponds to adding an action $a \in A$ to a schedule with $i - 1$ actions.

The base case of the induction is the execution with 0 actions with I as the initial state at some unspecified time point and at all preceding and succeeding time points.

For the inductive cases, we can over-approximate executions with $i - 1$ actions that satisfy candidate invariants C_{old} with the following formula.

$$S = \{\Box\phi \mid \phi \in \alpha_{X,A}\}\cup$$
$$\{[-\infty, 0[\phi \mid \phi \in C_{old}\}$$

This formula says that all changes during the execution correspond to some actions (as formalized by $\alpha_{X,A}$) and that all candidate invariants hold until 0.

For a given action a and candidate invariant c that could be falsified by an effect $\phi \triangleright l@t$ we extend this set further. Now a will be taken at time point 0 as the last action at (the arbitrarily chosen) time point 0, no actions are taken after 0, and no action with index smaller than a's is taken at 0. Hence we have

$$S_{a,c} = S \cup \{[0]a, [0]\phi, [t]\neg c\}$$
$$\cup\{]0, \infty[\neg a' \mid a' \in A\}$$
$$\cup\{[0]\neg a' \mid a' \in A, d(a') < d(a)\}$$

for executions with some $i - 1$ actions extended with the ith action a.

The important properties of $S_{a,c}$ are stated in the next lemma. Section 4 provides an efficient incomplete procedure for the consistency tests. Although we have fixed 0 to be the time point where a is taken in $S_{a,c}$, this choice does not lose generality and the result holds for an arbitrary time points.

Lemma 1. *Let $\alpha_{X,A}$ be the translation of actions A into temporal logic as given earlier, $a \in A$ an action with effect $\phi \triangleright \bar{l}@t$, C_{old} a set of candidate invariants, and c a candidate invariant with occurrence of the literal l. Let*

$$S_{a,c} = \{\Box\phi \mid \phi \in \alpha_{X,A}\}$$
$$\cup\{[-\infty, 0[\phi \mid \phi \in C_{old}\}$$
$$\cup\{[0]a, [0]\phi, [t]\neg c\}$$
$$\cup\{]0, \infty[\neg a' \mid a' \in A\}$$
$$\cup\{[0]\neg a' \mid a' \in A, d(a') < d(a)\}.$$

If $S_{a,c}$ is inconsistent, then there is no execution with actions from A such that 1. action a is taken at some time point t', 2. formulas in C_{old} are true until t' (excluding t'), 3. no action is taken after t', 4. no lower index action is taken at t', and 5. action a makes one of the literals in c is false at $t' + t$.

After an attempt to prove that a candidate invariant remains true has failed, it will be replaced by logically weaker candidate invariants. The new candidate invariants either add a new disjunct, or replace a disjunct $[t_0, t_1]l$ by a weaker one $[t'_0, t'_1]l$ such that $t_0 \leq t'_0 \leq t'_1 \leq t_1$ and either $t_0 < t'_0$ or $t'_1 < t_1$.

Our algorithm is general and is not limited to any particular form of (candidate) invariants. For performance reasons, our implementation (Section 5) limits to (candidate) invariants of forms l and $l_1 \vee [-t, 0]l_2, t \geq 0$.

We define $\text{weaken}_{S_{a,c}}(\phi)$ as the set of all maximal weakenings of ϕ as read from the partial assignment that satisfied $S_{a,c}$ (see Section 4), with maximality defined in terms of inclusion of intervals $[t, t']l$.

Lemma 2. $\text{weaken}_{S_{a,c}}(\phi) \not\models \phi$, and $\phi \models \phi'$ for all $\phi' \in \text{weaken}_{S_{a,c}}(\phi)$.

In the main loop of the algorithm, line 5 tests whether the effects of action a mention a state variable occurring in a candidate invariant c. If not, c cannot be possibly falsified by a. Otherwise, a more thorough test is performed in the form of the consistency test on line 7. If $S_{a,c}$ is inconsistent then a cannot possibly falsify c. If $S_{a,c}$ is consistent, then it may be possible that c is falsified by a, and c has to be weakened or eliminated. This consistency test for the linear temporal logic is approximated as described in Section 4.

Only candidate invariants that pass all tests and cannot therefore be falsified by any action in any reachable state will remain in the set C until the algorithm reaches a fixpoint. Therefore all such formulas are invariants. However, due to the approximate consistency test and syntactic restrictions on the form of the invariants, not all invariants are always found.

Theorem 1. *If the algorithm temporalinvariants(X, I, A) returns C, then all formulas in C are true everywhere in every execution of $\langle X, I, A \rangle$.*

Proof. The proof is by induction on i, the number of iterations of the outermost repeat-until loop on lines 3-10. The proof is based on identifying the number of iterations with the number of action occurrences in an execution. Let C_i be the value of the variable C in the beginning of each iteration of the loop (with iterations numbered as 0,1,...).

Induction hypothesis: $v \models_t c$ for every t and every $c \in C_i$ and every execution v of $\langle X, I, A \rangle$ with i actions.

Base case $i = 0$: By construction, C_0 consists of formulas true in the initial state, and hence in all states that precede or follow, as no actions are taken anywhere.

Inductive case $i \geq 1$: For any $c \in C_i$ it must be that $S_{a,c}$ is inconsistent for every $a \in A$ (otherwise c would have been eliminated between lines 7 and 9.)

Hence by Lemma 1 there is no execution with i actions in which that "last" action would make c false (with C_{old} representing all executions with $i - 1$ actions.) Assume there is an execution v with i actions in which some other than the "last" action would make c false. We could remove a from this execution to obtain an execution with $i - 1$ actions that still falsifies c, and hence by induction hypothesis we would have $c \notin C_{i-1}$. Since C_i is logically weaker than C_{i-1} (due to formulas being replaced by strictly weaker ones (Lemma 2)), we could not have $c \in C_i$. Hence there is no execution with i actions with c false at some time point.

4 Approximate Consistency Tests

We now present an efficient and sound but incomplete approximation of temporal logic consistency based on constraint networks, as required in the consistency tests of $S_{a,c}$ in the preceding section. A constraint network is constructed for a set of temporal logic formulas. Every subformula is represented as a node in the constraint network and associated with two sets of intervals, one for *true* and another for *false*. Each rule infers intervals for a node given its neighbors. The neighbors are the immediate subformulas, the parent formula, and sibling formulas. The rules are of the form

$$\frac{(g_1 : i_1)\phi_1, \ldots, (g_n : i_n)\phi_n}{(g : i)\phi}$$

where $\phi_1, \ldots, \phi_n$ and ϕ are formulas respectively with tags $(g_j : i_j), j \in \{1, \ldots, n\}$ and $(g : i)$, where each g_j is either $\top$ or $\bot$ to express truth or falsity, and i_j is a set (union) of intervals where ϕ_j has the specified truth value. A rule is applied by first selecting a node for a formula of the form of the consequent ϕ. Then the tags $(g_j : i_j)$ for $\phi_1, \ldots, \phi_n$ (in some rules only a single interval) are retrieved. Finally the tag $(g : i)$ for the consequent is computed and the new intervals i added to the old intervals of ϕ.

The rules for truth-functional connectives are obvious. Next we list some of the more interesting propagation rules. The rules for the interval operator are the following.

$$\frac{(\top : [t_0, t_0'])\phi}{(\mathsf{I} : [t_0 - t, t_0' - t'])[t, t']\phi} \quad (5) \qquad \frac{(\mathsf{I} : [t_0, t_0'])[t, t']\phi}{(\top : [t_0 + t, t_0' + t'])\phi} \quad (7)$$

$$\frac{(\bot : [t_0, t_0'])\phi}{(\bot : [t_0 - t', t_0' - t])[t, t']\phi} \quad (6)$$

In the first rule, the interval $[t_0 - t, t_0' - t']$ is empty if $t_0' - t' < t_0 - t$. In the first two rules, intervals with infinite end-points are handled specially, as subtraction of ∞ or $-\infty$ from itself is not well-defined. We define finite additions and subtractions to the infinities by $\infty + r = \infty$ and $-\infty + r = -\infty$. In rule (5), if both the interval starting point t_0 of ϕ and the operator starting point t are $-\infty$, then the starting point for $[t, t']\phi$ is $-\infty$ as well. Similarly for end points ∞.

The rules for the *until* operator are the following.

$$\frac{(\bot : i_0)\phi_0, (\bot : i_1)\phi_1}{(\bot : i_0 \cap i_1)\phi_0 \mathcal{U} \phi_1} \tag{8}$$

$$\frac{(\top : [t, t'])\phi_0 \mathcal{U} \phi_1, (\bot : [t_1, t_1'])\phi_1}{(\top : [\max(t, t_1), t_1'])\phi_0} \text{ if } \begin{matrix} [t, t_9'] \cap \\ [t_1, t_1'] \end{matrix} \neq \emptyset \tag{9}$$

In all of the rules above we have used *closed* intervals only. The rules can be adapted to open and half-open intervals as well as to interval operators with such intervals.

Initially, all nodes are labelled with $(\top : \emptyset)$ and $(\bot : \emptyset)$ with $\top$ denoting *true* and $\bot$ *false*, and with the empty set of intervals $\emptyset$ indicating that no truth or falsity is known for any time interval. We detect a contradiction when $i_1 \cap i_2 \neq \emptyset$ for $(\top : i_1)\phi$ and $(\bot : i_2)\phi$ and some ϕ, that is, ϕ has to be both true and false in at least one time point.

The constraint propagation procedure does not terminate for all formula sets. However, for all sets $S_{a,c}$ we have tried the procedure quickly terminates.

5   Experiments

We have experimented with the algorithm and problem instances featured in the temporal planning tracks of the 2008 and 2011 planning competitions (IPC), modeled in timed PDDL. Table 1 summarizes runtimes and other statistics.

Table 1. Statistics for a number of IPC domains. We give the runtimes (in seconds) for the easiest and hardest instance in each domain, the number of instances for which the computation terminated in under 10 minutes, the numbers of invariants found, and the numbers of actions.

problem	runtime			invariants		actions	
	min.	max.	< 600 s	min.	max.	min.	max.
crewplanning	1.33	83.34	30/30	225	2925	27	1393
elevators	7.85	> 14400	25/30	740	$\geq$ 23934	1672	141384
elevators/numeric	2.79	7311.33	22/30	704	$\geq$ 31620	448	10734
openstacks/adl	1.45	283.16	30/30	86	1508	45	2074
openstacks/numeric	0.64	5.13	30/30	104	960	15	102
openstacks/numeric/adl	0.68	7.16	30/30	66	638	15	102
openstacks/strips	1.52	384.80	30/30	124	1830	45	2074
parcprinter	2.57	> 14400	24/30	656	$\geq$ 17530	61	3979
pegsol	0.62	3.61	30/30	40	986	76	76
sokoban	5.40	> 14400	19/30	1682	$\geq$ 40274	280	28240
transport/numeric	1.08	> 14400	16/30	124	$\geq$ 57240	66	22869
floortile	2.10	19.33	20/20	264	2610	148	606
matchcellar	0.43	1.03	10/10	2	10	3	210
parking	3.94	392.60	20/20	653	6991	726	7406
storage	27.96	> 14400	10/20	2430	$\geq$ 18684	3400	130480
tms	1.79	> 14400	5/20	774	$\geq$ 5664	133	12141
turnandopen	4.36	805.85	18/20	704	10354	464	12216

6   Conclusion

We have, for a first time, presented a general algorithm for computing a large class of invariants for timed systems, with the analysis of such systems and speeding up reasoning with them as the main applications. Earlier works on timed invariants in planning have limited to narrow classes of invariants or narrow classes of timed models [13,1]. Our framework is applicable to a wide range of timed models and forms of invariants.

Similarly to the strongest earlier algorithms for untimed or asynchronous systems, our algorithm is based on a fixpoint iteration which starts from a set of candidate invariants characterizing the initial state, and weakens this set to cover all reachable states of the system. Iteration N of the algorithm corresponds to reachability by schedules of N timed actions, with the fixpoint corresponding to schedules with any number of actions.

Due to the generality of our algorithm, its scalability for large action sets and high number of state variables is not as good as with simpler algorithms. Future work will focus on finding interesting performance vs. generality trade-offs.

References

1. Bernardini, S., Smith, D.E.: Automatic synthesis of temporal invariants. In: Proceedings of the Ninth Symposium on Abstraction, Reformulation, and Approximation, SARA 2011, Parador de Cardona, Cardona, Catalonia, Spain, July 17-18. AAAI Press (2011)
2. Burch, J.R., Clarke, E.M., Long, D.E., MacMillan, K.L., Dill, D.L.: Symbolic model checking for sequential circuit verification. IEEE Transactions on Computer-Aided Design of Integrated Circuits and Systems 13(4), 401–424 (1994)
3. Edelkamp, S., Helmert, M.: Exhibiting knowledge in planning problems to minimize state encoding length. In: Biundo, S., Fox, M. (eds.) ECP 1999. LNCS (LNAI), vol. 1809, pp. 135–147. Springer, Heidelberg (2000)
4. Fox, M., Long, D.: PDDL2.1: An extension to PDDL for expressing temporal planning domains. Journal of Artificial Intelligence Research 20, 61–124 (2003)
5. Gerevini, A., Schubert, L.: Inferring state constraints for domain-independent planning. In: Proceedings of the 15th National Conference on Artificial Intelligence (AAAI 1998) and the 10th Conference on Innovative Applications of Artificial Intelligence (IAAI 1998), pp. 905–912. AAAI Press (1998)
6. Gerevini, A., Schubert, L.K.: Discovering state constraints in DISCOPLAN: Some new results. In: Proceedings of the 17th National Conference on Artificial Intelligence (AAAI 2000) and the 12th Conference on Innovative Applications of Artificial Intelligence (IAAI 2000), pp. 761–767. AAAI Press (2000)
7. Haslum, P., Geffner, H.: Admissible heuristics for optimal planning. In: Chien, S., Kambhampati, S., Knoblock, C.A. (eds.) Proceedings of the Fifth International Conference on Artificial Intelligence Planning Systems, pp. 140–149. AAAI Press (2000)
8. Haslum, P., Geffner, H.: Heuristic planning with time and resources. In: Cesta, A. (ed.) Recent Advances in AI Planning, Sixth European Conference on Planning (ECP 2014), pp. 107–112. AAAI Press (2014)
9. Kautz, H., Selman, B.: Pushing the envelope: planning, propositional logic, and stochastic search. In: Proceedings of the 13th National Conference on Artificial Intelligence and the 8th Innovative Applications of Artificial Intelligence Conference, pp. 1194–1201. AAAI Press (1996)
10. Rintanen, J.: A planning algorithm not based on directional search. In: Cohn, A.G., Schubert, L.K., Shapiro, S.C. (eds.) Principles of Knowledge Representation and Reasoning: Proceedings of the Sixth International Conference (KR 1998), pp. 617–624. Morgan Kaufmann (1998)
11. Rintanen, J.: An iterative algorithm for synthesizing invariants. In: Proceedings of the 17th National Conference on Artificial Intelligence (AAAI-2000) and the 12th Conference on Innovative Applications of Artificial Intelligence (IAAI-2000), pp. 806–811. AAAI Press (2000)
12. Rintanen, J.: Regression for classical and nondeterministic planning. In: Ghallab, M., Spyropoulos, C.D., Fakotakis, N. (eds.) ECAI 2008: Proceedings of the 18th European Conference on Artificial Intelligence, pp. 568–571. IOS Press (2008)
13. Smith, D.E., Weld, D.S.: Temporal planning with mutual exclusion reasoning. In: Dean, T. (ed.) Proceedings of the 16th International Joint Conference on Artificial Intelligence, pp. 326–337. Morgan Kaufmann Publishers (1999)

Answer Set Solver Backdoors

Emilia Oikarinen[1] and Matti Järvisalo[2]

[1] HIIT and Department of Information and Computer Science, Aalto University, Finland
[2] HIIT and Department of Computer Science, University of Helsinki, Finland

Abstract. Backdoor variables offer a generic notion for providing insights to the surprising success of constraint satisfaction solvers in solving remarkably complex real-world instances of combinatorial problems. We study backdoors in the context of answer set programming (ASP), and focus on studying the relative size of backdoors in terms of different state-of-the-art answer set solving algorithms. We show separations of ASP solver families in terms of the smallest existing backdoor sets for the solvers.

1   Introduction

Answer set programming (ASP) [28,4] offers an expressive rule-based declarative language for conveniently modelling hard combinatorial problems, together with highly efficient solver technology for finding solutions (answer sets) to the rule-based constraint models. Answer set solver technology [21,30,31,2,19,26,22,15,1] builds on the success of Boolean satisfiability (SAT) [3] solving techniques (DPLL [8,7], CDCL [6,27]) and implements additional inference mechanisms for native reasoning over answer set programs, most notably, well-foundedness checking. While advances in ASP and SAT solvers have improved our ability to efficiently solve and reason over a remarkably wide range of important real-world problems, our understanding for the fundamental reasons for this success is still somewhat lacking. The concept of backdoor variables, as introduced originally in [32], offers a generic notion for providing insights to the surprising success of constraint satisfaction solvers in solving remarkably large and complex real-world instances of combinatorial problems. Informally, a backdoor B is a subset of the variables in a problem instance, such that a systematic search procedure needs to nondeterministically assign values (branch) only on the variables in B in order to decide the instance. Given that a search procedure has a small backdoor to a problem instance, the procedure can in principle decide the instance efficiently.

In this paper, we study backdoors in the context of ASP. While several other extensions of backdoors have been studied [9,10,29], there has only recently been work on backdoors in the context of ASP, and mainly from the parameterized complexity perspective [13]. In contrast, we focus on studying the relative size of backdoors in terms of *practical* state-of-the-art answer set solving algorithms. As the underlying motivation, we aim at further understanding structural properties of answer set programs in terms of to what extent specific search techniques (subsolvers) can potentially discover "hidden structure", characterized by small backdoors, in the programs. Closely following the techniques implemented in different solvers, we formalize different solver variants in terms of three dimensions: (i) *well-foundedness*, (ii) *conflict-learning*, and

E. Fermé and J. Leite (Eds.): JELIA 2014, LNAI 8761, pp. 674–683, 2014.

(iii) *branching*, reflecting algorithmic choices in answer set solvers. Different choices along the three dimensions allow for a more fine-grained analysis than that possible in the context of SAT solvers [10], especially due to the fact that dimensions (i) and (iii) do not have direct counterparts in SAT solving. As the basis of our analysis, we define *answer set solver backdoors* extending related backdoor concepts from SAT along the three dimensions, opening a new point of view to analyzing the effectiveness of different answer set solving techniques in terms of problem structure. As the main results, we show up to *exponential* separations of the ASP solver families characterized by different choices along the three dimensions in terms of the smallest existing backdoor sets for the solvers, both on satisfiable and unsatisfiable families of answer set programs.

2 Preliminaries

Answer Set Semantics. A normal logic program (or an *answer set program* in this context) Π over a finite set $\mathcal{P}$ of atoms consists of a finite set of *rules* of the form r : $h \leftarrow p_1, \ldots, p_m, \sim p_{m+1}, \ldots, \sim p_n$, where $0 < m \leq n$, $h \in \mathcal{P} \cup \{\bot\}$ (where $\bot$ stands for falsity), and, for each $i = 1..n$, $p_i \in \mathcal{P}$. A rule r consists of a *head*, head$(r) = h$, and a *body*, body$(r) = \{p_1, \ldots, p_m, \sim p_{m+1}, \ldots, \sim p_n\}$. The symbol "$\sim$" is *default negation*. A *default literal* is an atom p or its default negation $\sim p$. The set of atoms appearing in program Π is denoted by atom(Π). The set of bodies (resp. heads) in Π is body$(\Pi) = \{$body$(r) \mid r \in \Pi\}$ (resp. head$(\Pi) = \{$head$(r) \mid r \in \Pi\}$). For each atom $p \in$ head(Π), let body$(p) = \{$body$(r) \mid r \in \Pi,$ head$(r) = p\}$ to represent the set of rules bodies that share the same head p. For a rule r, let body$(r)^+ = \{p_1, \ldots, p_m\}$ and body$(r)^- = \{p_{m+1}, \ldots, p_n\}$ denote the sets of positive and negative (default negated) atoms in body(r), respectively.

In ASP, we are interested in *stable models* [17] (or *answer sets*) of a given program Π. A truth assignment for an answer set program Π is a function τ that maps atoms in Π to $\{0, 1\}$. An assignment τ extends implicitly to default literals by requiring that $\tau(\sim p) = 1 - v$ for each atom p such that $\tau(p) = v \in \{0, 1\}$. An assignment τ can be extended over a set of literals β: $\tau(\beta) = 1$ if $\tau(p) = 1$ for all $p \in \beta^+$ and $\tau(p) = 0$ for each $p \in \beta^-$; otherwise $\tau(\beta) = 0$. τ satisfies a rule $r \in \Pi$ iff $\tau($body$(r)) = 1$ implies $\tau($head$(r)) = 1$. An assignment τ that satisfies all rules of a program Π is an answer set of Π if and only if there is no complete assignment τ' distinct from τ such that (i) $\tau(p) = 0$ implies $\tau'(p) = 0$, and (ii) τ' satisfies each rule in the program

Relation to Boolean Satisfiability (SAT). For a Boolean variable x, there are two *literals*, the positive literal x and the negative literal $\neg x$. A *clause* is a disjunction of literals and a CNF formula a conjunction of clauses. A truth assignment for a CNF formula F is a function τ that maps variables in F to $\{0, 1\}$. An assignment τ extends implicitly to literals by requiring that $\tau(\neg x) = 1 - v$ for each variable x such that $\tau(x) = v \in \{0, 1\}$. A clause C is satisfied by τ if $\tau(l) = 1$ for some literal $l \in C$. An assignment τ satisfies F if it satisfies every clause in F.

Clark [5] defines the completion of a given answer set program Π, mapping Π to a CNF formula comp(F) as follows. For a body $\beta = \{p_1, \ldots, p_m, \sim p_{m+1}, \ldots, \sim p_n\} \in$ body(Π), let $B(\beta)$ stand for $\beta \leftrightarrow p_1 \wedge \cdots \wedge p_m \wedge \neg p_{m+1} \wedge \cdots \wedge \neg p_n$ interpreted as a CNF formula where β and all p_i's are viewed as Boolean variables; we will liberally refer to atoms and Boolean variables interchangeably.

$B(\beta)$ characterizes that (i) the body of a rule is 1 if all its literals are 1, and (ii) some literal in the body must be 0 if the head is 0 For an atom $p \in \text{head}(\Pi)$ with body$(p) = \{\beta_1, \ldots, \beta_k\}$, $H(p)$ stands for $p \leftrightarrow \beta_1 \vee \cdots \vee \beta_k$, characterizing that (i) a head atom must be 0 if all of the bodies of the rules defining it are 0, and (ii) the head atom must be 1 if there is a rule such that the body is 1. The completion of Π is then the CNF formula $\text{comp}(\Pi) = \bigwedge_{\beta \in \text{body}(\Pi)} B(\beta) \wedge \bigwedge_{p \in \text{head}(\Pi)} H(p)$. For any Π, the satisfying assignments of $\text{comp}(\Pi)$ capture the *supported models* of Π. In general, every answer set of Π is also a supported model. However, the supported models coincide with answer sets only when Π is *tight* [12,11], is which case an assignment τ satisfying $\text{comp}(\Pi)$ corresponds to the answer set $A_\tau(p) = \tau(p)$ if and only if $p \in \text{atom}(\Pi)$ of Π, obtained basically by restricting τ to $\text{atom}(\Pi)$.

In case Π is non-tight, A_τ might not be an answer set of Π, due to *loops* in Π that induce cyclic support among atoms assigned to 1 in τ. *Loop formulas* can be used to prohibit such cyclic support. For a given program Π and a set $U \subseteq \text{atom}(\Pi)$ of atoms, the set of *external bodies* of U in Π, denoted by $EB(U, \Pi)$, is $\{\text{body}(r) \mid r \in \Pi, \text{head}(r) \in U, \text{body}(r)^+ \cap U = \emptyset\}$. The loop formula induced by U for Π, where $EB(U, \Pi) = \{\beta_1, \ldots, \beta_k\}$, is $L(U, \Pi) = \bigwedge_{p \in U}(p \to \beta_1 \vee \cdots \vee \beta_k)$. For any non-tight program Π and satisfying truth assignment τ for $\text{comp}(\Pi)$, we know that A_τ is an answer set of Π if and only if τ satisfies the loop formulas induced by each non-empty $U \subseteq \text{atom}(\Pi)$, i.e., all loop formulas for Π: $L(\Pi) = \bigwedge_{\emptyset \subset U \subseteq \text{atom}(\Pi)} L(U, \Pi)$. There is an exponential number of loop formulas in the worst-case [24], which makes the direct approach of answer set solving Π by satisfiability checking $\text{comp}(\Pi) \wedge L(U, \Pi)$ infeasible in practice.

3   Search for Answer Sets

We now describe formalizations of answer set solver variants which we analyze in terms of the relative size of backdoors, based on the fact that, for any program Π, the answer sets of Π correspond to the satisfying assignments for $\text{comp}(\Pi) \wedge L(\Pi)$. Indeed, the various answer set solvers available today can be characterized as implementing variants of the classical the Davis–Putnam–Logemann–Loveland (DPLL) procedure [8,7] or the *conflict-driven clause learning* (CDCL) algorithm [6,27], with additional propagation techniques for performing well-foundedness checks over $L(\Pi)$.

DPLL implements a standard backtracking depth-first search for satisfiability, with *unit propagation* over clauses for extending deterministically the current partial assignment τ making decisions (branching) on variables. Unit propagation over F and τ refers to applying the following rules until fixpoint: if there is a clause $(l \vee l_1 \vee \cdots \vee l_k)$ such that $\tau(l_i) = 0$ for all $i = 1..k$, let $\tau(l) = 1$. Unit propagation on the completion $\text{comp}(\Pi)$ and loop formulas $L(\Pi)$ of an answer set program Π is tightly connected with native propagation rules [16,14] on the level of the answer set program. While CDCL also makes decisions and employs unit propagation, in contrast to DPLL it does not implement standard backtracking, but rather uses a conflict analysis scheme for learning *conflict clauses* from seen conflicting assignments, and performs *non-chronological backtracking* after learning a conflict clause to erase more than one decision from the current assignment. For detailed accounts on conflict-driven answer set solving, see [23,15], and e.g. [18,20] for accounts on the relation of ASP and SAT solving.

Concretely, given a program Π as input, our formalizations of answer set solvers differ in three dimensions:
(1) whether well-foundedness checks over the loop formulas $L(\Pi)$ are performed *eagerly* (**EWF**) after each decision during search under the current partial assignment τ, or *lazily* (**LWF**) after reaching a satisfying assignment for $\mathrm{comp}(\Pi)$;
(2) whether a form of *conflict learning* is employed (**CL**), in analogy with CDCL, or not (**noCL**), in analogy with DPLL; and
(3) whether the solver makes decisions on all atoms in $\mathrm{comp}(\Pi)$ (**B**), or only on atoms in $\mathrm{atom}(\Pi)$ (**noB**), i.e., *not* on the atoms of the form β, which would correspond to making decision on the bodies of rules), yielding eight solver variants $\{(X, Y, Z)\}$ where $X \in \{\mathbf{EWF}, \mathbf{LWF}\}$, $Y \in \{\mathbf{CL}, \mathbf{noCL}\}$, and $Z \in \{\mathbf{B}, \mathbf{noB}\}$. The different variants are closely related to techniques implemented in state-of-the-art answer set solvers. For examples, the DLV [21] and Smodels [30] systems relate with $(\mathbf{EWF}, \mathbf{noCL}, \mathbf{noB})$; Nomore++ [2] with $(\mathbf{EWF}, \mathbf{noCL}, \mathbf{B})$; Smodels$_{cc}$ [31] (a conflict-learning variant of Smodels) with $(\mathbf{EWF}, \mathbf{CL}, \mathbf{noB})$; the SAT-based answer set solvers ASSAT [25], Cmodels [19], and SUP [22], incorporating variants of **LWF**, relate with $(\mathbf{LWF}, \mathbf{CL}, \mathbf{B})$; and finally, Clasp [15] relates most closely with $(\mathbf{EWF}, \mathbf{CL}, \mathbf{B})$, together with WASP [1] and SAG [26], both of which employ forms of (partial) **EWF**.

4 Backdoors

We continue by defining backdoors in the context of answer set solving. In general, backdoors are defined in terms of tractable (polynomial-time decidable) subclasses which may be either syntactically-defined classes such as Horn programs or 2-SAT, or, more closely related to solvers, subclasses defined via *subsolvers*, such as unit propagation in the context of SAT. Here our focus is on the latter type. Due to the page limit, we omit the technical definitions of *(traditional) strong unit-propagation backdoors* [32] and *learning-sensitive backdoors (wrt unit propagation)* [10] in the context of SAT. As natural counterparts of these definitions, we now define $(X, \mathbf{noCL}, Z)$-backdoors and $(X, \mathbf{CL}, Z)$-backdoors, respectively, in the context of ASP. We start with $(X, \mathbf{noCL}, Z)$-backdoors, which serve as the counterparts of strong backdoors. Similarly as for CNF formulas, $\Pi|_\tau$ denotes the simplified program obtained by assigning values to atoms according to τ.

Definition 1. *Given an answer set program Π, a subset $B \subseteq \mathrm{atom}(\Pi) \cup \mathrm{body}(\Pi)$ is a $(X, \mathbf{noCL}, Z)$-backdoor, where $X \in \{\mathbf{EWF}, \mathbf{LWF}\}$ and $Z \in \{\mathbf{B}, \mathbf{noB}\}$, if the following conditions hold:*

- *If $X = \mathbf{EWF}$, then for every truth assignment $\tau : B \to \{0, 1\}$, unit propagation on $\mathrm{comp}(\Pi) \wedge L(\Pi)$ and τ returns a satisfying assignment for $\Pi|_\tau$ or concludes that $\Pi|_\tau$ is unsatisfiable.*
- *If $X = \mathbf{LWF}$, then for every truth assignment $\tau : B \to \{0, 1\}$, unit propagation on $\mathrm{comp}(\Pi)$ and τ returns a satisfying assignment for $\mathrm{comp}(\Pi)$ or concludes that $\Pi|_\tau$ is unsatisfiable.*

- *If $Z = noB$, then $B \subseteq$ atom(Π).*

Since comp(Π) over-approximates the answer sets of Π, in the case $X = \mathbf{LWF}$, unit propagation can be restricted to comp(Π) without loss of generality: If unit propagation on comp(Π) and τ determines that comp$(\Pi)|_\tau$ is unsatisfiable, then $\Pi|_\tau$ is also unsatisfiable. If unit propagation on comp(Π) and τ returns a satisfying assignment for comp(Π), we know that the assignment is either an answer set of Π, or unit propagation on comp$(\Pi) \wedge L(\Pi)$ and τ concludes unsatisfiability.

We continue by defining $(X, \mathbf{CL}, Z)$-backdoors as natural counterparts of learning-sensitive backdoors in SAT.

Definition 2. *Given an answer set program Π, a subset $B \subseteq$ atom$(\Pi) \cup$ body(Π) is a $(X, \mathbf{CL}, Z)$-backdoor for Π if there exists a search tree exploration order for the $(X, \mathbf{CL}, Z)$-solver such that the following conditions hold:*

- *The solver branches only on the variables in B.*
- *The solver uses unit propagation on comp$(\Pi) \wedge L(\Pi)$ when all variables in B are assigned.*
- *The solver either finds a satisfying assignment for Π or proves Π unsatisfiable.*
- *If $X = \mathbf{LWF}$, then the solver uses $L(\Pi)$ for unit propagation only when the current assignment is complete over atom$(\Pi) \cup$ body(Π).*
- *If $Z = noB$, then $B \subseteq$ atom(Π).*

Notice that, in contrast to $(X, \mathbf{noCL}, Z)$-backdoors, here the additional unit propagation enabled by $L(\Pi)$ can play a critical role in terms of causing a conflict, which would then allow the solver to learn from the conflict. Thus, in connection with the lazy well-foundedness checking employed in SAT-based ASP solvers which employ CDCL SAT-solvers, in case $X = \mathbf{LWF}$ unit propagation on $L(\Pi)$ is postponed until a complete assignment is reached on comp(Π) alone.

5   Analysis

As the main results of this paper, we will now analyze the relative size of (X, Y, Z)-backdoors that exist for different answer set solver variants. We begin with relatively simple observations.

Theorem 1. *The following claims hold for any program Π, $B \subseteq$ atom$(\Pi) \cup$ body(Π), and $X \in \{\mathbf{EWF}, \mathbf{LWF}\}$, $Y \in \{\mathbf{CL}, \mathbf{noCL}\}$, $Z \in \{B, \mathbf{noB}\}$.*

(a) If B is a $(\mathbf{LWF}, Y, Z)$-backdoor for Π, then it is a $(\mathbf{EWF}, Y, Z)$-backdoor for Π.
(b) If B is a $(X, \mathbf{noCL}, Z)$-backdoor, then it is a $(X, \mathbf{CL}, Z)$-backdoor for Π.
(c) If B is a $(X, Y, \mathbf{noB})$-backdoor, then it is a (X, Y, B)-backdoor for Π.

Theorem 2. *For any tight program Π, $B \subseteq$ atom$(\Pi) \cup$ body(Π), and $Y \in \{\mathbf{CL}, \mathbf{noCL}\}$, $Z \in \{B, \mathbf{noB}\}$, it holds that B is a $(\mathbf{LWF}, Y, Z)$-backdoor for Π if and only if B is a $(\mathbf{EWF}, Y, Z)$-backdoor for Π.*

In many cases, bounds on the sizes of backdoors in SAT can be mapped into bounds on the sizes of backdoors in ASP. For this, we use a straightforward encoding cnf2asp(F) of a CNF formula F as

$$\{\bot \leftarrow {\sim}x_1, \ldots, {\sim}x_m, x_{m+1}, \ldots, x_n \mid (x_1 \vee \ldots \vee x_m \vee \neg x_{m+1} \vee \ldots \vee \neg x_n) \in F\} \cup$$
$$\{x \leftarrow {\sim}\hat{x} \mid \text{variable } x \text{ occurs in } F\} \cup \{\hat{x} \leftarrow {\sim}x \mid \text{variable } x \text{ occurs in } F\},$$

where the first set of rules encode the clauses in F, and the latter two enforce the classical semantics over the variables (atoms) using a new atom $\hat{x}$ for each x.

Theorem 3. *Let F be a CNF formula and B a subset of variables in F.*

(a) If B is a strong backdoor for F, then B is a $(X, \boldsymbol{noCL}, Z)$-backdoor for cnf2asp($F$) for any $X \in \{\boldsymbol{EWF}, \boldsymbol{LWF}\}$ and $Z \in \{\boldsymbol{B}, \boldsymbol{noB}\}$.
(b) If B is a learning-sensitive backdoor for F, then B is a $(X, \boldsymbol{CL}, Z)$-backdoor for cnf2asp(F) for any $X \in \{\boldsymbol{EWF}, \boldsymbol{LWF}\}$ and $Z \in \{\boldsymbol{B}, \boldsymbol{noB}\}$.

Theorem 4. *For any CNF formula F, if the smallest strong (resp. learning-sensitive) backdoors for F are of size k, then the smallest $(X, \boldsymbol{noCL}, Z)$-backdoors (resp. $(X, \boldsymbol{CL}, Z)$-backdoors) for cnf2asp(F) are of size at least k for any $X \in \{\boldsymbol{EWF}, \boldsymbol{LWF}\}$ and $Z \subset \{\boldsymbol{B}, \boldsymbol{noB}\}$.*

In addition to being able to carry over results from SAT to ASP, in particular cases—especially, when conflict-learning is not enabled—results for unsatisfiable programs carry over to satisfiable programs, using the following transformation:

$$\text{trsat}(\Pi) = \{e \leftarrow {\sim}d\} \cup \{d \leftarrow {\sim}e\} \cup \{\text{head}(r) \leftarrow \text{body}(r), {\sim}d \mid r \in \Pi\}.$$

This translation essentially encodes an exclusive-or choice between d and e, and each of the rules in Π is conditioned on ${\sim}d$.

Theorem 5. *For any unsatisfiable program Π for which the smallest $(X, \boldsymbol{noCL}, Z)$-backdoors are of size k, it holds that (i) trsat(Π) has an answer set, and that (ii) the smallest $(X, \boldsymbol{noCL}, Z)$-backdoors for trsat($\Pi$) are at least of size k, for any $X \in \{\boldsymbol{EWF}, \boldsymbol{LWF}\}$ and $Z \in \{\boldsymbol{B}, \boldsymbol{noB}\}$.*

Proof. (sketch) The assignment τ such that $\tau(d) = 1$ and $\tau(a) = 0$ for all $a \in$ atom(trsat(Π)) $\setminus \{d\}$ is the unique answer set of trsat(Π). Furthermore, the smallest $(X, \boldsymbol{noCL}, Z)$-backdoors for trsat($\Pi$) can be shown to be at least of size k. $\square$

We will next focus on the effects of different choices for $X \in \{\boldsymbol{EWF}, \boldsymbol{LWF}\}$ and $Y \in \{\boldsymbol{CL}, \boldsymbol{noCL}\}$ on the relative sizes of (X, Y, Z)-backdoors. We begin by focusing on unsatisfiable programs. First, we exploit a result from [10] for backdoors in SAT via the connections between backdoors in SAT and ASP we established in Sect. 5.

Theorem 6. *[10] There are unsatisfiable CNF formulas for which the smallest learning-sensitive backdoor are exponentially smaller than the smallest strong backdoors.*

Theorem 7. *There are unsatisfiable programs for which the smallest $(\boldsymbol{LWF}, \boldsymbol{CL}, \boldsymbol{noB})$-backdoors are exponentially smaller than the smallest $(\boldsymbol{EWF}, \boldsymbol{noCL}, \boldsymbol{B})$-backdoors.*

Proof. Take any witness of Theorem 6. By Theorem 3, a smallest learning-sensitive backdoor B for F is any $(\mathbf{LWF}, \mathbf{CL}, \mathbf{noB})$-backdoor for cnf2asp($F$). By Theorems 6 and 4, the smallest $(\mathbf{EWF}, \mathbf{noCL}, \mathbf{B})$-backdoors are exponentially larger than B. □

To compare the differences between lazy and eager propagation, we need to consider non-tight programs, thus involving a more fine-grained analysis than what is possible in the context of SAT. Interestingly, there are programs which have *exponentially* smaller $(\mathbf{EWF}, \mathbf{noCL}, \mathbf{noB})$-backdoors than $(\mathbf{LWF}, \mathbf{CL}, \mathbf{noB})$-backdoors; that is, lazy well-foundedness checking can cause an exponential blow-up in the size of backdoor.

Theorem 8. *There are unsatisfiable programs for which the smallest* $(\mathbf{EWF}, \mathbf{noCL}, \mathbf{noB})$ *-backdoors are exponentially smaller than the smallest* $(\mathbf{LWF}, \mathbf{noCL}, \mathbf{B})$*-backdoors.*

Proof. (sketch) Consider the unsatisfiable program

$$
\begin{aligned}
\Pi_n = \{&f \leftarrow \sim f, \sim p_{i,1}, \ldots, \sim p_{i,n-1} \mid i = 1..n\} \cup \\
\{&f \leftarrow \sim f, p_{i,k}, p_{j,k}i, j = 1..n, k = 1..n-1, i \neq j\} \cup \\
\{&p_{i,k} \leftarrow p_{i,k} \mid i = 1..n, k = 1..n-1\},
\end{aligned}
$$

from [18], where $n = 2^m$ for some m. Notice that there is no external support for atoms $p_{i,k}$ (the only rule with an atom $p_{i,k}$ in the head is a self-loop). This and the first rule cause the unsatisfiability of the program. Now $\{f\}$ is a $(\mathbf{EWF}, \mathbf{noCL}, \mathbf{noB})$-backdoor for Π_n (note that $\tau(p_{i,j}) = 0$ for all i, j can directly be propagated with $\mathbf{EWF}$). However, for a $(\mathbf{LWF}, \mathbf{CL}, \mathbf{B})$-backdoor, in order to check the loops of the form $p_{i,k} \leftarrow p_{i,k}$, one must first have a complete truth assignment, which can be shown to require assigning at least n atoms. Thus, a $(\mathbf{LWF}, \mathbf{noCL}, \mathbf{B})$-backdoor has to be at least of size n. □

We now turn our attention to backdoors for satisfiable programs.

Theorem 9. *[10] There are satisfiable CNF formulas for which there are learning-sensitive backdoors that are smaller than the smallest strong backdoors.*

Theorem 10. *There are satisfiable programs for which there are* $(\mathbf{LWF}, \mathbf{CL}, \mathbf{noB})$*-backdoors that are smaller than the smallest* $(\mathbf{EWF}, \mathbf{noCL}, \mathbf{B})$*-backdoors.*

Proof. Like Theorem 7, follows from Theorems 9, 3, and 4. □

Theorem 11. *There are satisfiable programs for which the smallest* $(\mathbf{EWF}, \mathbf{noCL}, \mathbf{noB})$*-backdoors are exponentially smaller than the smallest* $(\mathbf{LWF}, \mathbf{CL}, \mathbf{noB})$*-backdoors.*

Proof. (sketch) Consider the program $\Pi_n = P_0 \cup P_1 \cup \cdots \cup P_n$ such that $P_0 = \{d \leftarrow \sim d, c\}$ and $P_i = \{a_i \leftarrow b_i.\ b_i \leftarrow a_i.\ e_i \leftarrow \sim a_i, \sim b_i, \sim c\}$ for all $i = 1..n$, where $n = 2^m$ for some m. The assignment $\tau(e_i) = 1$ for all $i = 1..n$ and $\tau(a) = 0$ for all $a \in \mathrm{atom}(\Pi_n) \setminus \{e_1, \ldots, e_n\}$ is the unique answer set of Π_n. Now, $\{d\}$ is a $(\mathbf{EWF}, \mathbf{noCL}, \mathbf{noB})$-backdoor for Π_n. However, the smallest $(\mathbf{LWF}, \mathbf{noCL}, \mathbf{noB})$-backdoors and $(\mathbf{LWF}, \mathbf{CL}, \mathbf{noB})$-backdoors can be shown to be of size $n + 1$. □

By a simple modification, we have an analogous results for unsatisfiable programs.

Theorem 12. *There are unsatisfiable programs for which the smallest* (**EWF**, **noCL**, **noB**)*-backdoors are exponentially smaller than the smallest* (**LWF**, **CL**, **noB**)*-backdoors.*

Proof. Consider the program $\Pi'_n = \Pi_n \cup \{\bot \leftarrow e_1, \ldots, e_n, {\sim}a_1, \ldots, {\sim}a_n, {\sim}b_1, \ldots,$ ${\sim}b_n, {\sim}c, {\sim}d\}$. The additional rule disallows in a naive way exactly the only satisfying assignment for Π_n, being equivalent with the clause $\bigvee_{i=1}^{n} \neg e_i \vee \bigvee_{i=1}^{n} a_i \vee \bigvee_{i=1}^{n} b_i \vee c \vee d$. This rule has $3n + 2$ atoms in the body. Hence under any assignment over no more than $3n$ atoms, unit propagation cannot derive anything based on the rule. It follows that the arguments in the proof of Theorem 11 are valid also for Π'_n. $\qquad\square$

Finally, we look at the question of whether allowing solvers to branch on the bodies of rules (i.e., on the β variables in $\text{comp}(\Pi)$), or put another way, whether restricting solvers to branch only on atoms, has an effect on the size of smallest backdoors.

Theorem 13. *There are unsatisfiable programs for which the smallest* (**LWF**, **noCL**, **B**)*-backdoors are exponentially smaller than the smallest* (**EWF**, **noCL**, **noB**)*-backdoors.*

Proof. (sketch) Consider the tight program $\Pi_k^n = \{f \leftarrow {\sim}f\} \cup P_1^n \cup \cdots \cup P_k^n$, where

$$P_i^n = \{f \leftarrow B_i \mid B_i = \{{\sim}a_{i,1}, \ldots, {\sim}a_{i,n}\}\} \cup \{a_{i,j} \leftarrow B_{i,j} \mid B_{i,j} = B_i \setminus \{{\sim}a_{i,j}\}, j = 1..n\}$$

and $n = 2^k$. There are (**LWF**, **noCL**, **B**)-backdoors of size k for Π_k^n: Consider any set $\{f, B_1, \ldots, B_{j-1}, B_{j+1}, B_k\}$ that contains f and all except one bodies B_i from Π_k^n. On the other hand, it can be shown that the smallest (**EWF**, **noCL**, **noB**)-backdoor are of size at least $(k-1) \cdot (n-1) + 1$. $\qquad\square$

Additionally, we establish that in connection with eager well-foundedness checking, conflict-learning even when restricting branching on atoms can have exponentially smaller backdoors than without conflict-learning.

Theorem 14. *There are unsatisfiable programs for which the smallest* (**LWF**, **CL**, **noB**)*-backdoors are exponentially smaller than the smallest* (**EWF**, **noCL**, **B**)*-backdoors.*

Proof. Consider the CNF formula F_3 from [10, Proof of Theorem 3] with $k + 3 \cdot 2^k$ variables, having a learning-sensitive backdoor of size k. Now, by Theorem 3 the translation $\text{cnf2asp}(F_3)$, which is a tight program, has a (**LWF**, **CL**, **noB**)-backdoor of size k. On the other hand, as shown in [10, Proof of Theorem 3], the smallest strong backdoors for F_3 are at least of size $2^k + k$. Thus, by Theorem 4 the smallest (**EWF**, **noCL**, **B**)-backdoors of $\text{cnf2asp}(F_3)$ are at least of size $2^k + k$. $\qquad\square$

6   Conclusions

Closely following the techniques implemented in different solvers, we introduced *answer set solver backdoors* defined with respect to three dimensions of answer set solving techniques. As the main results, we showed up to exponential separations of the resulting notions of answer set solver backdoors, which we believe to highlight intrinsic differences of the solver variants in terms of their behavior w.r.t. problem structure.

Acknowledgements. Work funded by Academy of Finland, grants 251170 (Centre of Excellence in Computational Inference Research), 250518 (EO), and 276412 (MJ).

References

1. Alviano, M., Dodaro, C., Faber, W., Leone, N., Ricca, F.: WASP: A native ASP solver based on constraint learning. In: Cabalar, P., Son, T.C. (eds.) LPNMR 2013. LNCS (LNAI), vol. 8148, pp. 54–66. Springer, Heidelberg (2013)
2. Anger, C., Gebser, M., Linke, T., Neumann, A., Schaub, T.: The nomore++ system. In: Baral, C., Greco, G., Leone, N., Terracina, G. (eds.) LPNMR 2005. LNCS (LNAI), vol. 3662, pp. 422–426. Springer, Heidelberg (2005)
3. Biere, A., Heule, M., van Maaren, H., Walsh, T. (eds.): Handbook of Satisfiability. Frontiers in Artificial Intelligence and Applications, vol. 185. IOS Press (2009)
4. Brewka, G., Eiter, T., Truszczynski, M.: Answer set programming at a glance. Commun. ACM 54(12), 92–103 (2011)
5. Clark, K.: Negation as failure. In: Readings in Nonmonotonic Reasoning, pp. 311–325. Morgan Kaufmann Publishers (1987)
6. Darwiche, A., Pipatsrisawat, K.: Complete algorithms. In: Biere et al [3], pp. 99–130
7. Davis, M., Logemann, G., Loveland, D.: A machine program for theorem proving. Communications of the ACM 5(7), 394–397 (1962)
8. Davis, M., Putnam, H.: A computing procedure for quantification theory. Journal of the ACM 7(3), 201–215 (1960)
9. Dilkina, B.N., Gomes, C.P., Malitsky, Y., Sabharwal, A., Sellmann, M.: Backdoors to combinatorial optimization: Feasibility and optimality. In: van Hoeve, W.-J., Hooker, J.N. (eds.) CPAIOR 2009. LNCS, vol. 5547, pp. 56–70. Springer, Heidelberg (2009)
10. Dilkina, B.N., Gomes, C.P., Sabharwal, A.: Tradeoffs in the complexity of backdoors to satisfiability: Dynamic sub-solvers and learning during search. Ann. Math. Artif. Intell. 70(4), 399–431 (2014)
11. Erdem, E., Lifschitz, V.: Tight logic programs. Theory and Practice of Logic Programming 3(4-5), 499–518 (2003)
12. Fages, F.: Consistency of Clark's completion and existence of stable models. Journal of Methods of Logic in Computer Science 1, 51–60 (1994)
13. Fichte, J.K., Szeider, S.: Backdoors to normality for disjunctive logic programs. In: Proc. AAAI. AAAI Press (2013)
14. Gebser, M., Schaub, T.: Characterizing ASP inferences by unit propagation. In: ICLP Workshop on Search and Logic: Answer Set Programming and SAT, Seattle, pp. 41–56 (August 16, 2006)
15. Gebser, M., Kaufmann, B., Schaub, T.: Conflict-driven answer set solving: From theory to practice. Artif. Intell. 187, 52–89 (2012)
16. Gebser, M., Schaub, T.: Tableau calculi for logic programs under answer set semantics. ACM Trans. Comput. Log. 14(2), 15 (2013)
17. Gelfond, M., Lifschitz, V.: The stable model semantics for logic programming. In: Proc. ICLP/SLP 1988, pp. 1070–1080. MIT Press (1988)
18. Giunchiglia, E., Leone, N., Maratea, M.: On the relation among answer set solvers. Ann. Math. Artif. Intell. 53(1-4), 169–204 (2008)
19. Giunchiglia, E., Lierler, Y., Maratea, M.: Answer set programming based on propositional satisfiability. Journal of Automated Reasoning 36(4), 345–377 (2006)
20. Järvisalo, M., Oikarinen, E.: Extended ASP tableaux and rule redundancy in normal logic programs. Theory and Practice of Logic Programming 8(5-6), 691–716 (2008)
21. Leone, N., Pfeifer, G., Faber, W., Eiter, T., Gottlob, G., Perri, S., Scarcello, F.: The DLV system for knowledge representation and reasoning. ACM Transactions on Computational Logic 7(3), 499–562 (2006)

22. Lierler, Y.: Abstract answer set solvers. In: Garcia de la Banda, M., Pontelli, E. (eds.) ICLP 2008. LNCS, vol. 5366, pp. 377–391. Springer, Heidelberg (2008)
23. Lierler, Y.: Abstract answer set solvers with backjumping and learning. TPLP 11(2-3), 135–169 (2011)
24. Lifschitz, V., Razborov, A.: Why are there so many loop formulas? ACM Transactions on Computational Logic 7(2), 261–268 (2006)
25. Lin, F., Zhao, Y.: ASSAT: Computing answer sets of a logic program by SAT solvers. Artificial Intelligence 157(1–2), 115–137 (2004)
26. Lin, Z., Zhang, Y., Hernandez, H.: Fast SAT-based answer set solver. In: Proc. AAAI, pp. 92–97. AAAI Press (2006)
27. Marques-Silva, J.P., Lynce, I., Malik, S.: Conflict-driven clause learning SAT solvers. In: Biere et al [3], pp. 131–153
28. Niemelä, I.: Logic programs with stable model semantics as a constraint programming paradigm. Annals of Mathematics and Artificial Intelligence 25(3-4), 241–273 (1999)
29. Samer, M., Szeider, S.: Backdoor sets of quantified boolean formulas. In: Marques-Silva, J., Sakallah, K.A. (eds.) SAT 2007. LNCS, vol. 4501, pp. 230–243. Springer, Heidelberg (2007)
30. Simons, P., Niemelä, I., Soininen, T.: Extending and implementing the stable model semantics. Artificial Intelligence 138(1–2), 181–234 (2002)
31. Ward, J., Schlipf, J.: Answer set programming with clause learning. In: Lifschitz, V., Niemelä, I. (eds.) LPNMR 2004. LNCS (LNAI), vol. 2923, pp. 302–313. Springer, Heidelberg (2003)
32. Williams, R., Gomes, C.P., Selman, B.: Backdoors to typical case complexity. In: Proc. IJCAI, pp. 1173–1178. Morgan Kaufmann (2003)

Incremental SAT-Based Method with Native Boolean Cardinality Handling for the Hamiltonian Cycle Problem

Takehide Soh[1], Daniel Le Berre[2], Stéphanie Roussel[2],
Mutsunori Banbara[1], and Naoyuki Tamura[1]

[1] Kobe University 1-1, Rokko-dai, Nada, Kobe, Hyogo 657-8501 Japan
{soh@lion.,tamura@,banbara@}kobe-u.ac.jp
[2] CNRS - Université d'Artois, Rue Jean Souvraz, SP-18, F-62307, Lens, France
{leberre,sroussel}@cril.univ-artois.fr

Abstract. The Hamiltonian cycle problem (HCP) is the problem of
finding a spanning cycle in a given graph. HCP is NP-complete and has
been known as an important problem due to its close relationship to the
travelling salesman problem (TSP), which can be seen as an optimization variant of finding a minimum cost cycle. In a different viewpoint,
HCP is a special case of TSP. In this paper, we propose an incremental
SAT-based method for solving HCP. The number of clauses needed for
a CNF encoding of HCP often prevents SAT-based methods from being
scalable. Our method reduces that number of clauses by relaxing some
constraints and by handling specifically cardinality constraints. Our approach has been implemented on top of the SAT solver Sat4j using Scarab.
An experimental evaluation is carried out on several benchmark sets and
compares our incremental SAT-based method against an existing eager
SAT-based method and specialized methods for HCP.

1 Introduction

The Hamiltonian cycle problem (HCP) is the problem of finding a spanning
cycle, called *Hamiltonian cycle*, in a given graph. HCP is listed in Karp's 21
NP-complete problems [24] and has been known as an important problem due
to its close relationship to the travelling salesman problem (TSP). On the one
hand, HCP is a special case of TSP. On the other hand, TSP can be seen as
an optimization variant of HCP and the development of an effective method for
TSP would have a significant impact in computer science.

HCP has been theoretically studied in graph theory [16,17]. Besides, HCP
is tackled in Operations Research (OR). For instance, Jäger and Zhang [21]
shows a method based on the Hungarian algorithm and Karp-Steele patching
for solving HCP on directed graphs. More recently, Eshragh *et. al.* shows a
hybrid algorithm and a Mixed Integer Programming (MIP) model for HCP on
undirected graphs [12].

HCP also has been studied in Artificial Intelligence using propositional satisfiability (SAT). In SAT-based methods, the main issue for solving HCP is how

E. Fermé and J. Leite (Eds.): JELIA 2014, LNAI 8761, pp. 684–693, 2014.

to encode connectivity constraints. Those constraints can also be seen as permutation constraints which have been studied in Constraint Programming [18]. An encoding method was proposed in 90's by [20,19] named later *absolute encoding*. Following that, in 2003, Prestwich proposed the *relative encoding* [28] which requires fewer clauses than the absolute encoding. In 2009, Velev and Gao further improve the relative encoding by merging encoding variables and applying triangulation to a given graph [32] which achieved indeed 4 orders of magnitude speedup on satisfiable structured graphs from the DIMACS graph coloring instances compared to the one by Prestwich [28]. However, the number of clauses in the encoding is increasing by $O(n^3)$ and it is still difficult to solve graph instances which consist in over 1,000 nodes.

In this paper, we escape the current limitations of SAT-based methods using an abstraction/refinement approach and by natively handling Boolean cardinality constraints. Note that we consider in our encoding for undirected graphs as in [28,32].

- **Incremental HCP Solving.** The encoding of the connectivity constraints often causes the generation of a huge amount of clauses which prevent SAT-based methods from being scalable. Our method thus relaxes the connectivity constraints to reduce the number of clauses and incrementally refines the encoding by adding new clauses when sub-cycles are detected.

- **Native Boolean Cardinality Handling.** Another issue when translating HCP to SAT is to express Boolean Cardinality (BC) constraints, for which various encoding into CNF exists. In addition to using those existing BC encodings, we propose to use a solver with native support for BC constraints, called *Native BC*. The Native BC has the advantages to reduce encoding time and memory usage. Native BC is provided as a specific constraint in the SAT solver Sat4j [27].

Implementation on a System Tightly Integrated with SAT Solvers. Since SAT solvers are necessary to invoke many times in incremental HCP solving, communication cost is not negligible. We thus implement the first version of our method on Scarab [31] which is tightly integrated with Sat4j.

We carried out experiments on three benchmark sets. One is color04 which is used in [32] and comes from DIMACS graph coloring instances [1]. The second one is knight which is a set of knight's tour instances used in [12]. The third one is tsplib which is the whole set of HCP instances in TSPLIB [4]. On those benchmark sets, we compare the proposed incremental SAT-based methods against the previous eager SAT-based method by Velev and Gao [32], a HCP solving method by Eshragh et al. [12], and the state-of-the-art TSP solver LKH. The latter provided the best answers for instances with unknown optima from DIMACS TSP Challenge [2] and provides an interface for HCP. In our experiments, we used the latest version 2.0.7 of LKH, whose performance on HCP is improved from previous versions [3]. All benchmark, programs, experimental results explained in this paper are available in: http://kix.istc.kobe-u.ac.jp/~soh/scarab/jelia2014/

2   Hamiltonian Cycle Problems

The Hamiltonian cycle problem (HCP) is the problem of finding a spanning cycle in a given graph. Let $G = (V, E)$ be a graph where V is a set of n nodes and E is a set of edges. A set of auxiliary arcs $A = \{(i, j),\ (j, i) \mid \{i, j\} \in E\}$ is also introduced for simple modeling. Let $x_{ij}(i \neq j)$ be a Boolean variable for each arc $(i, j) \in A$, which is equal to 1 when (i, j) is used in a solution cycle. Then, a direct modeling of HCPs would be using the following constraints.

$$\sum_{(i,j)\in A} x_{ij} = 1 \qquad\qquad \text{for each node } i = 1, \ldots, n. \qquad \text{(out-degree)}$$

$$\sum_{(i,j)\in A} x_{ij} = 1 \qquad\qquad \text{for each node } j = 1, \ldots, n. \qquad \text{(in-degree)}$$

$$\sum_{i,j\in S} x_{ij} \leq |S| - 1, \qquad\qquad S \subset V,\ 2 \leq |S| \leq n - 2 \qquad \text{(connectivity)}$$

The *out-degree* and *in-degree* constraints force that, for each node, in-degree and out-degree are respectively exactly one in a solution cycle. The *connectivity* constraint prohibits the formation of sub-cycles, i.e., cycles on proper subsets of n nodes. HCPs have been tackled by SAT-based methods. In [28], transitive relations for all possible permutations of three nodes are used to represent the connectivity constraint, which however results in $O(n^3)$ clauses. Velev and Gao follow this encoding, i.e., it basically needs $O(n^3)$ clauses, but they practically reduce the number of clauses by a triangulation for a given graph [32]. Besides, they also improve encoding by merging ordering variables. As a result, their SAT-based method achieves 4 orders of magnitude speedup on satisfiable structured graphs from the DIMACS graph coloring instances. However, it struggles to find a Hamiltonian cycle when the graph has over 1,000 nodes.

3   Proposal

3.1   Incremental HCP Solving

Previous SAT-based methods encode all constraints of HCP into SAT and compute its solution using a single execution of the SAT solver: we call those methods "eager". The main drawback of those eager methods for HCP is the encoding of connectivity constraints which results basically in $O(n^3)$ clauses.

To solve large HCPs, instead of encoding connectivity constraints into CNF and run a SAT solver once, we relax those constraints and incrementally execute the SAT solver on an abstraction of the problem. If the solution found contains sub-cycles, we prevent them in the new abstraction by adding new clauses. As such, we generate the clauses encoding the connectivity constraints "on demand", or "lazily". Such approach correspond to a *Counterexample-Guided Abstraction Refinement* (CEGAR) loop for HCP which was originally proposed in the context of model checking [9] and depicted in Fig. 1.

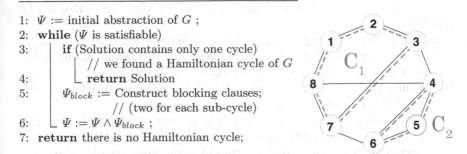

1:   $\Psi :=$ initial abstraction of G ;
2:   **while** (Ψ is satisfiable)
3:       **if** (Solution contains only one cycle)
            // we found a Hamiltonian cycle of G
4:         **return** Solution
5:      $\Psi_{block} :=$ Construct blocking clauses;
          // (two for each sub-cycle)
6:      $\Psi := \Psi \wedge \Psi_{block}$;
7:   **return** there is no Hamiltonian cycle;

Fig. 1. CEGAR Iteration for Solving HCP   **Fig. 2.** Counter Example

The initial abstraction is built by omitting the connectivity constraint. That is, cardinality constraints corresponding to in/out-degree constraints are encoded. We also encode $x_{ij} + x_{ji} \leq 1$ for each edge $\{i, j\} \in E$ to prevent sub-cycles between two nodes. Those encoding results in a CNF formula Ψ (Line 1), which represents an abstract HCP constraint model. It ensures that every node must belong to some cycle but it does not ensure that the cycle is a Hamiltonian cycle. Fig. 2 shows such a case: every node belongs to a cycle but there is more than one cycle. SAT solving is then executed and the CEGAR iteration starts (Line 2). Whenever the formula is unsatisfiable, the iteration ends and it is decided that there is no Hamiltonian cycle (Line 8). If the formula is satisfiable and its model contains a single cycle then it must be a Hamiltonian cycle (Line 4). Otherwise, the solution consists of multiple sub-cycles which represent counter examples. To refine the constraints, some blocking clauses are added to Ψ to block each sub-cycle clockwise and counterclockwise (Line 6 and 7). This procedure is iterated until a Hamiltonian cycle is found or Ψ becomes unsatisfiable. Blocking clauses are generated to prevent the sub-cycles to appear again. In the case of Fig. 2, the following four clauses are generated: $\neg x_{12} \vee \neg x_{23} \vee \neg x_{37} \vee \neg x_{78} \vee \neg x_{81}$ to block C_1 clockwise. $\neg x_{87} \vee \neg x_{73} \vee \neg x_{32} \vee \neg x_{21} \vee \neg x_{18}$ to block C_1 counterclockwise. $\neg x_{46} \vee \neg x_{65} \vee \neg x_{54}$ to block C_2 clockwise. $\neg x_{45} \vee \neg x_{56} \vee \neg x_{64}$ to block C_2 counter-clockwise. Note that, even in the worst case, we do not always need to block all sub-cycles in a given graph since in/out-degree constraints ensure that every node belongs to some cycle. For instance, in Fig. 2, it is not necessary to block a sub-cycle $(1, 2, 3, 4, 8)$ since the remaining nodes $\{5, 6, 7\}$ cannot construct any sub-cycles.

3.2 Native Boolean Cardinality Handling

By the relaxation of connectivity constraints, we may reduce considerably the number of clauses compared to eager SAT-based methods [19,28,32]. This section discusses how to encode the remaining in/out-degree constraints, which form Boolean cardinality (BC) constraints $\sum_{i=1}^{m} x_i \, \# \, k$ where $x_i \in \{0, 1\}$ are Boolean variables, m is an integer represents the number of variables, the relational operator $\#$ is one of $\{\leq, \geq, =\}$, k is an integer represents the degree (threshold) of the constraint.

Boolean cardinality encoding into CNF has been actively studied [30,6,29,13]. When we use *binomial encoding*, $\binom{m}{k}$ clauses are needed. It is improved by using *Totalizer* $(O(m^2))$ [6], or *Sequential Counter* $(O(m \cdot k))$ [30]. However, even when using the Sequential Counter for encoding the BC constraints in HCP, $O(n^2)$ clauses are needed for graph instances consisting of n nodes.

One way to avoid generating those clauses is to support natively a specific representation of those cardinality constraints in the SAT solver. It is expected that such specialized SAT-based systems could benefit from avoiding the time of CNF encoding, and reducing the number of constraints in the solver, which reduces the amount of memory used.

The Sat4j library [27] started in 2004 as an implementation in Java of the original Minisat specification [11]. In contrast with recent versions of Minisat, and most SAT solvers, the underlying SAT solver is still designed to work with custom constraints, not just clauses. Sat4j has a native representation of BC constraints, denoted *Native BC* in the rest of the paper. It currently emulates a BC constraint $\sum_{i=1}^{n} x_i \geq k$. This specific constraints generates clauses of size $n - k + 1$ when it detects a conflict with the current assignment. In addition, whenever it detects that $n - k$ variables are already assigned to 0, it forces the remaining variables to be 1 using the $n - k$ falsified literals as an explanation for those propagation. One can consider that such constraint generates "on demand" or lazily the clauses of the binomial encoding.

4   Experimental Results

This section provides experimental results to evaluate the effectiveness of the incremental HCP solving, Native BC, and their implementation on Scarab. We also have a comparison with other specialized methods. The following systems are used:

- Eager SAT-based method (referred to as Velev) is our implementation of the previous SAT-based method by Velev and Gao [32]. It runs with Minisat2.2.
- HCP/TSP Solver LKH is the state-of-the-art TSP solver which provided the best answers for instances with unknown optima from DIMACS TSP Challenge [2] and provides an interface for HCP. In our experiments, we used the latest version 2.0.7 of LKH, whose performance on HCP is improved from previous versions [3].
- Incremental HCP Solving (referred to as S4J-S, S4J-N) is the proposed methods implemented on Scarab. Two versions are prepared to measure the effectiveness of using Sequential Counter or Native BC, respectively. We have also tested another encoding method Totalizer in all instances but omit their results since they are similar (or slightly inferior) to Sequential Counter. Readers can check the results of Totalizer in the supplemental web page. Note that learned clauses are cleared after each iteration since keeping them

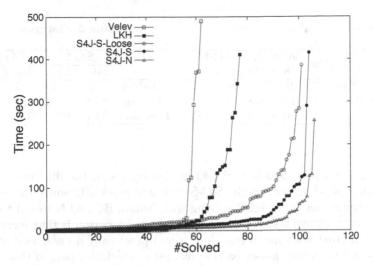

Fig. 3. Cactus Plot on `color04`, `knight`, and `tsplib`

across calls did not accelerate searches but other heuristic values are kept through all iterations.

— We also prepared, S4J-S-Loose, a variant of S4J-S, which is implemented on loosely integrated system to measure the implementation difference.

All experiments are carried out on Intel Xeon 2.93 GHz within the timelimit of 500 seconds. 4GB heap memory is allowed in the Java virtual machine settings (-Xms4g -Xmx4g). Sat4j with the prebuilt solver "Glucose21" is used for incremental HCP solving, which gave the best overall results from the available solvers of the library on the benchmarks used. Benchmark sets are selected from the literature of the previous eager SAT-based method [32] and a HCP solving method by Eshragh et al. [12]: `color04` comes from DIMACS graph coloring instances [1] used in the eager SAT-based method [32]. It consists of 119 instances whose number of nodes ranges from 11 to 10,000. `knight` is a set of knight's tour instances used in [12]. In the literature, only 3 instances of sizes 8x8, 12x12, 20x20 are used. In the experiments, we additionally use 8 instances of sizes 30x30, 40x40, ..., and 100x100 for wider comparisons. `tsplib` is the whole set of HCP instances of TSPLIB [4]. Similar to `knight`, two of them are used in [12] and we additionally use the remaining 7 instances for wider comparisons.

Fig. 3 shows a cactus plot denoting all results of compared systems: Velev, LKH, S4J-S, S4J-N, and S4J-S-Loose. In the result, the eager SAT-based method Velev solved 60 instances but slows down in early stage. A reason is the number of encoded clauses which explodes to over 100 million even when #nodes of the input graph is 500. It is obviously closed to the limit of SAT solvers. For instance, it generates 194,186,195 clauses for `DSJC500.5` (#nodes is 500) and could not encode `latin_square` (#nodes is 900) within 500 seconds. LKH solved 81 instances, which is more than Velev but less than the incremental HCP solving

Table 1. #Solved per Graph-Size

Graph Size	#Ins.	Velev [32] #S	(%)	S4J-N #S	(%)
$n \leq 200$	54	45	(83)	48	(89)
$200 < n \leq 2000$	63	15	(23)	49	(78)
$2000 < n$	21	0	(0)	8	(38)

Table 2. Statistics

	S4J-S #Ite.	S4J-S #Cyc.	S4J-N #Ite.	S4J-N #Cyc.
Median	10	48	7	20
Average	60.0	311.8	37.9	310.5
Maximum	3332	9188	761	7604

methods: S4J-S-Loose, S4J-S, and S4J-N. Among them, the difference of S4J-S-Loose and S4J-S is not small: S4J-S is faster especially until 100 seconds. Consequently, incremental HCP solving with Native BC S4J-N solved the most instance – it is always faster than other methods. A reason is that incremental methods can start with much less clauses and practically do not need so many iterations and blocking clauses as is explained in the latter part of this section. We also have a literature-based comparison with results provided by Eshragh *et. al.* [12]. They carried experiments on knight's tour problems of 8x8, 12x12, and 20x20, and TSPLIB problems of alb1000 and alb2000. Runtimes of S4J-N range from 1 second to 8 seconds while runtimes of their method range from 2 seconds to 165,600 seconds.

Table 1 shows the distribution of the number of solved instances for the number n of nodes on Velev and S4J-N. In case of $n \leq 200$, both Velev and S4J-N solved more than 80% of instances. However, in case of $200 < n \leq 2000$, Velev could solve only 23% of instances while S4J-N solves 78% of instances. Moreover, even the case of $2000 < n$, S4J-N still solves 38% of instances. With regard to the number of nodes of graphs, the largest satisfiable instance solved by Velev is 1-Insertions_6 ($n = 607$), one by S4J-N is alb5000 ($n = 5,000$) [1]. In the literature [7,32], triangulation techniques are proposed to reduce the number of transitivity constraints and they are supposed to be effective for sparse graphs. If we select graph instances whose density are less than 0.03 and number of nodes are less than 2000 (33 out of 138), the difference between Velev and S4J-N becomes smaller but S4J-N still solves 25 instances while Velev solves 16 instances.

Table 2 shows the median, average, and maximum numbers of iterations and cycles for all satisfiable instances solved by each of S4J-S and S4J-N. We can read the followings from this table. The maximum number of cycles found for one instance is less than 10 thousands, that is, we need at most 20 thousands clauses in addition to the base clauses for solving those instances. Also, the median numbers of cycles show that we generally need much less additional clauses. The median numbers of iterations and cycles are almost stable in two encoding methods. In some cases, from the maximum numbers of iterations, we need to launch the SAT solver over thousands times. Considering that the given time limit is 500 seconds, the cost of the invocation of SAT solving procedure is preferred to be low in incremental HCP solving.

---

[1] S4J-N solved qg.order100 ($n = 10,000$) with 512 seconds a bit longer than timelimit.

In addition to above experiments and analyses, readers can find further experiments and comparisons (e.g. using other SAT solvers) in:
http://kix.istc.kobe-u.ac.jp/~soh/scarab/jelia2014/.

5   Related Work

In 2000, Clarke *et al.* proposed Counterexample-Guided Abstraction Refinement (CEGAR) in the context of model checking [9], which receives a program text and abstract functions are extracted from it. Following their work, there are some applications of CEGAR to Presburger Arithmetic [25], deciding the theory of Arrays [14], and the RNA-folding problem [15]. Recently, the use of CEGAR was proposed to solve QBF [23], Circumscription [22] and argumentation inference [10]. We believe that such approach can be applied to even more cases in Artificial Intelligence.

In the context of solving TSP, there is a traditional OR technique proposed in 80's which translates TSP into the assignment problem [8,26]. Jäger and Zhang [21] apply this OR technique to HCP on directed graphs by using the Hungarian algorithm and Karp-Steele patching. Though only for a small proportion of instances, a SAT approach is used in their rare last step (14 out of 4266 instances) to guarantee completeness. It is described in the literature [21] that their method is less effective to undirected graphs, in particular, in the case that a given graph have no Hamiltonian cycle their method will enumerate all sub-cycles in the main step which cause a long running time. In our method, the SAT approach is central and part of a CEGAR loop, which practically performs well on undirected graphs for both SAT/UNSAT problems. Comprehensive experiments are carried by using several encoding/solvers. Our work provides some hints on the importance of (not) encoding cardinality constraints into CNF.

6   Conclusion

In this paper, we proposed an incremental SAT-based method with Native BC for solving HCP. It overcomes other methods by reducing the cost of full encoding of connectivity constraints and CNF encoding of BC constraints. Our work gives analyses for encoded clauses and iterations, and also points out that pre-processing affects the convergence of CEGAR iterations for solving HCP. Recently, Abío *et. al.* presented an approach which balance the use of encoding and the use of custom propagators within SMT [5]. In our work, a custom propagator is used for BC while a lazy encoding of the combination constraints is performed using CEGAR. It is another kind of balance between encoding and propagation.

Acknowledgements. This work was partially funded by JSPS KAKENHI Grant Numbers 24300007 and 25730042.

References

1. DIMACS Graph Coloring, http://mat.gsia.cmu.edu/COLOR/instances.html
2. DIMACS TSP Challnege, http://dimacs.rutgers.edu/Challenges/TSP/
3. LKH, http://www.akira.ruc.dk/~keld/research/LKH/
4. TSPLIB, http://comopt.ifi.uni-heidelberg.de/software/TSPLIB95/.
5. Abío, I., Nieuwenhuis, R., Oliveras, A., Rodríguez-Carbonell, E., Stuckey, P.J.: To encode or to propagate? The best choice for each constraint in SAT. In: Schulte, C. (ed.) CP 2013. LNCS, vol. 8124, pp. 97–106. Springer, Heidelberg (2013)
6. Bailleux, O., Boufkhad, Y., Roussel, O.: A translation of pseudo boolean constraints to SAT. Journal on Satisfiability, Boolean Modeling and Computation 2(1-4), 191–200 (2006)
7. Bryant, R.E., Velev, M.N.: Boolean satisfiability with transitivity constraints. ACM Trans. Comput. Log. 3(4), 604–627 (2002)
8. Carpeneto, G., Toth, P.: Some new branching and bounding criteria for the asymmetric travelling salesman problem. Management Science 26(7), 736–743 (1980)
9. Clarke, E.M., Grumberg, O., Jha, S., Lu, Y., Veith, H.: Counterexample-guided abstraction refinement. In: Emerson, E.A., Sistla, A.P. (eds.) CAV 2000. LNCS, vol. 1855, pp. 154–169. Springer, Heidelberg (2000)
10. Dvorák, W., Järvisalo, M., Wallner, J.P., Woltran, S.: Complexity-sensitive decision procedures for abstract argumentation. Artif. Intell. 206, 53–78 (2014)
11. Eén, N., Sörensson, N.: An extensible SAT-solver. In: Giunchiglia, E., Tacchella, A. (eds.) SAT 2003. LNCS, vol. 2919, pp. 502–518. Springer, Heidelberg (2004)
12. Eshragh, A., Filar, J.A., Haythorpe, M.: A hybrid simulation-optimization algorithm for the Hamiltonian cycle problem. Annals OR 189(1), 103–125 (2011)
13. Frisch, A.M., Giannaros, P.A.: SAT encodings of the at-most-k constraint: Some old, some new, some fast, some slow. In: Proceedings of the The 9th International Workshop on Constraint Modelling and Reformulation, ModRef 2010 (2010)
14. Ganesh, V., Dill, D.L.: A decision procedure for bit-vectors and arrays. In: Damm, W., Hermanns, H. (eds.) CAV 2007. LNCS, vol. 4590, pp. 519–531. Springer, Heidelberg (2007)
15. Ganesh, V., O'Donnell, C.W., Soos, M., Devadas, S., Rinard, M.C., Solar-Lezama, A.: Lynx: A programmatic SAT solver for the rna-folding problem. In: Cimatti, A., Sebastiani, R. (eds.) SAT 2012. LNCS, vol. 7317, pp. 143–156. Springer, Heidelberg (2012)
16. Gould, R.J.: Advances on the Hamiltonian problem - a survey. Graphs and Combinatorics 19(1), 7–52 (2003)
17. Gould, R.J.: Recent advances on the Hamiltonian problem: Survey III. Graphs and Combinatorics 30(1), 1 46 (2014)
18. Hnich, B., Walsh, T., Smith, B.M.: Dual modelling of permutation and injection problems. J. Artif. Intell. Res (JAIR) 21, 357–391 (2004)
19. Hoos, H.H.: SAT-encodings, search space structure, and local search performance. In: Proceedings of the 16th International Joint Conference on Artificial Intelligence (IJCAI 1999), pp. 296–303 (1999)
20. Iwama, K., Miyazaki, S.: SAT-variable complexity of hard combinatorial problems. In: Proceedings of the IFIP 13th World Computer Congress, pp. 253–258 (1994)
21. Jäger, G., Zhang, W.: An effective algorithm for and phase transitions of the directed Hamiltonian cycle problem. J. Artif. Intell. Res (JAIR) 39, 663–687 (2010)

22. Janota, M., Grigore, R., Marques-Silva, J.: Counterexample guided abstraction refinement algorithm for propositional circumscription. In: Janhunen, T., Niemelä, I. (eds.) JELIA 2010. LNCS (LNAI), vol. 6341, pp. 195–207. Springer, Heidelberg (2010)
23. Janota, M., Klieber, W., Marques-Silva, J., Clarke, E.: Solving qbf with counterexample guided refinement. In: Cimatti, A., Sebastiani, R. (eds.) SAT 2012. LNCS, vol. 7317, pp. 114–128. Springer, Heidelberg (2012)
24. Karp, R.M.: Reducibility among combinatorial problems. In: Complexity of Computer Computations, pp. 85–103 (1972)
25. Kroning, D., Ouaknine, J., Seshia, S.A., Strichman, O.: Abstraction-based satisfiability solving of presburger arithmetic. In: Alur, R., Peled, D.A. (eds.) CAV 2004. LNCS, vol. 3114, pp. 308–320. Springer, Heidelberg (2004)
26. Laporte, G.: The traveling salesman problem: An overview of exact and approximate algorithms. European Journal of Operational Research 59(2), 231–247 (1992)
27. Le Berre, D., Parrain, A.: The Sat4j library, release 2.2. Journal on Satisfiability, Boolean Modeling and Computation 7, 59–64 (2010)
28. Prestwich, S.D.: SAT problems with chains of dependent variables. Discrete Applied Mathematics 130(2), 329–350 (2003)
29. Marques-Silva, J., Lynce, I.: Towards robust CNF encodings of cardinality constraints. In: Bessière, C. (ed.) CP 2007. LNCS, vol. 4741, pp. 483–497. Springer, Heidelberg (2007)
30. Sinz, C.: Towards an optimal CNF encoding of boolean cardinality constraints. In: van Beek, P. (ed.) CP 2005. LNCS, vol. 3709, pp. 827–831. Springer, Heidelberg (2005)
31. Soh, T., Tamura, N., Banbara, M.: Scarab: A rapid prototyping tool for SAT-based constraint programming systems. In: Järvisalo, M., Van Gelder, A. (eds.) SAT 2013. LNCS, vol. 7962, pp. 429–436. Springer, Heidelberg (2013)
32. Velev, M.N., Gao, P.: Efficient SAT techniques for relative encoding of permutations with constraints. In: Nicholson, A., Li, X. (eds.) AI 2009. LNCS (LNAI), vol. 5866, pp. 517–527. Springer, Heidelberg (2009)

Revisiting Reductants in the Multi-adjoint Logic Programming Framework*

Pascual Julián-Iranzo[1], Jesús Medina[2], and Manuel Ojeda-Aciego[3]

[1] University of Castilla-La Mancha. Dept. of Information Technologies and Systems, Ciudad Real, Spain
[2] Universidad de Cádiz. Dept. de Matemáticas, Cádiz, Spain
[3] Universidad de Málaga. Dept. de Matemática Aplicada, Málaga, Spain

Abstract. In this work, after revisiting the different notions of reductant arisen in the framework of multi-adjoint logic programming and akin frameworks, we introduce a new, more adequate, notion of reductant in the context of multi-adjoint logic programs. We study some of its properties and its relationships with other notions of reductants.

Keywords: Fuzzy Logic Programming, Multi-adjoint Logic Programming, Reductants.

1 Introduction

Fuzzy extensions of the logic programming paradigm have been investigated since the late eighties and the decade of the nineties [1, 4, 7, 9, 20]; later, some general frameworks were introduced and their interrelationships were studied [2, 5, 10, 12, 17, 19]; currently, one can still find papers on the subject of fuzzy logic programming, some of them even from the perspective of category theory, which address important issues in this topic [3, 11, 15]. This work focuses on multi-adjoint logic programming [13] and, specifically, on the most adequate notion of reductant for a logic program.

Multi-adjoint logic programming is a flexible framework combining fuzzy logic and logic programming. Roughly speaking, a multi-adjoint logic program can be seen as a set of implicational rules annotated by a truth degree (a value of a complete lattice). One of the main features of the multi-adjoint framework is its flexibility, in that rules need not be written with common implications, and the most suitable one can be used instead; another important feature is that it works even when the conjunctors used in the body of the rules are neither commutative or associative.

Reductancts were first introduced in the context of generalized annotated logic programming [9] in order to deal with problems related to incompleteness. The multi-adjoint logic programming paradigm has to deal with a similar problem of incompleteness that may arise when programs are interpreted in a

---

* Partially supported by the Spanish MICINN projects TIN2012-39353-C04-01, TIN2012-39353-C04-04 and the Spanish Ministry of Economy and Competition under grant TIN2013-45732-C4-2-P.

E. Fermé and J. Leite (Eds.): JELIA 2014, LNAI 8761, pp. 694–702, 2014.

non-linear lattice. Specifically, it might be not possible to compute the greatest correct answer (for a given goal and program) due to the existence of incomparable elements in $(L, \preceq)$, see [13]. As a result, multi-adjoint programs need to incorporate a special kind of rules, called *reductants*, in order to preserve the (approximate) completeness property, and this introduces severe penalties in the implementation of efficient multi-adjoint logic programming systems, since not only the size of programs increases but also their execution time. Moreover, the original definitions of reductants often produce infinitely many reductants for some programs. Therefore, if we want to develop complete and efficient implementation systems for the multi-adjoint logic framework, it is essential to define more accurate notions of reductants and methods for optimizing their computation. In this work, after revisiting different notions of reductant proposed for multi-adjoint programs, we define a new, more adequate, notion of reductant and we study some of its formal properties.

2 Syntax and Semantics of Multi-adjoint Logic Programs

We will work with a first order language, $\mathcal{L}$, containing variables, function symbols, predicate symbols, constants, the classical quantifiers ($\forall$ and $\exists$), and several (arbitrary) connectives in order to increase language expressiveness.

In our fuzzy setting, we assume a number of implication connectives ($\leftarrow_i$) together with other connectives, so-called "aggregators" (usually denoted $@_j$), used to build the bodies of the rules. The general definition of aggregation operators subsumes conjunctive operators (denoted by $\&_k$), disjunctive operators ($\vee_l$), and average and hybrid operators. The truth function for an n-ary aggregation operator[1] $@ : L^n \to L$ is required to be monotone and fulfill $@(\top, \ldots, \top) = \top$, $@(\bot, \ldots, \bot) = \bot$. The underlying set of truth-values is assumed to be a complete lattice L together with a collection of adjoint pairs intended to produce the evaluation of *modus ponens* [6].

A *rule* is a formula $H \leftarrow_i \mathcal{B}$, where H is an atomic formula (usually called the *head*) and $\mathcal{B}$ (which is called the *body*) is a formula built from atomic formulas $B_1, \ldots, B_n$, $n \geq 0$, truth values of L and aggregation operators. Rules whose body is $\top$ are called *facts* (usually, we will represent a fact as a rule with an empty body). A *goal* is a body submitted as a query to the system. Variables in a rule are assumed to be universally quantified. Roughly speaking, a multi-adjoint logic program is a set of pairs $\langle \mathcal{R}; \alpha \rangle$, where $\mathcal{R}$ is a rule and α is a *weight*, usually assigned by an expert.

Formulas are interpreted on a multi-adjoint lattice. In this framework, it is sufficient to consider Herbrand interpretations, in order to define a declarative semantics. See [13] for a formal characterization of a *fuzzy interpretation*, $\mathcal{I}$, as a mapping from the Herbrand base, $B_{\mathcal{L}}$, into the multi-adjoint lattice of truth values L and a notion of evaluation and satisfiability of formulas.

---

[1] Note that, as no confusion arises, we use the same notation for a formal function symbol and its semantic meaning.

The procedural semantics can be formalized as an operational phase followed by an interpretive one. The operational phase uses a residuum-based generalization of *modus ponens* [6] that, given an atomic goal A and a program rule $\langle H \leftarrow_i \mathcal{B}; v \rangle$, if there is a most general unifier substitution $\theta = mgu(\{A = H\})$ the atom A is substituted by the expression $(v \&_i \mathcal{B})\theta$. In the following, we write $\mathcal{C}[A]$ to denote a formula where A is a sub-expression (usually an atom) occuring in the—possibly empty—context $\mathcal{C}[]$. Moreover, $\mathcal{C}[A/H]$ means the replacement of A by H in context $\mathcal{C}[]$. Also we use $Var(s)$ for referring to the set of variables occurring in the syntactic object s, whereas $\theta[Var(s)]$ denotes the substitution obtained from θ by restricting its domain, $Dom(\theta)$, to $Var(s)$.

Definition 1 (Admissible Steps). *Let $\mathcal{Q}$ be a goal and let σ be a substitution. The pair $\langle \mathcal{Q}; \sigma \rangle$ is a state and we denote by $\mathcal{E}$ the set of states. Given a program $\mathcal{P}$, an* admissible computation *is formalized as a state transition system, whose transition relation $\leadsto_{AS} \subseteq (\mathcal{E} \times \mathcal{E})$ is the smallest relation satisfying the following* admissible rules *(where we consider that A is the selected atom in $\mathcal{Q}$):*

1) $\langle \mathcal{Q}[A]; \sigma \rangle \leadsto_{AS} \langle (\mathcal{Q}[A/v\&_i\mathcal{B}])\theta; \sigma\theta \rangle$ *if $\theta = mgu(\{H = A\})$, $\langle H \leftarrow_i \mathcal{B}; v \rangle$ in $\mathcal{P}$.*
2) $\langle \mathcal{Q}[A]; \sigma \rangle \leadsto_{AS} \langle (\mathcal{Q}[A/\bot]); \sigma \rangle$ *if there is no rule in $\mathcal{P}$ whose head unifies A.*

Formulas involved in admissible computation steps are renamed apart before being used. The symbols $\leadsto_{AS}^{+}$ and $\leadsto_{AS}^{*}$ denote, respectively, the transitive closure and the reflexive, transitive closure of $\leadsto_{AS}$.

Definition 2. *Let $\mathcal{P}$ be a program and let $\mathcal{Q}$ be a goal. An* admissible derivation *is a sequence $\langle \mathcal{Q}; id \rangle \leadsto_{AS}^{*} \langle \mathcal{Q}'; \theta \rangle$. When $\mathcal{Q}'$ is a formula not containing atoms, the pair $\langle \mathcal{Q}'; \sigma \rangle$, where $\sigma = \theta[Var(\mathcal{Q})]$, is called an* admissible computed answer *(a.c.a.) for that derivation.*

If we exploit all atoms of a goal, by applying admissible steps as much as needed during the operational phase, then it becomes a formula with no atoms which can be then directly interpreted in the multi-adjoint lattice L.

Definition 3 (Interpretive Step). *Let $\mathcal{P}$ be a program, $\mathcal{Q}$ a goal and σ a substitution. We formalize the notion of* interpretive computation *as a state transition system, whose transition relation $\leadsto_{IS} \subseteq (\mathcal{E} \times \mathcal{E})$ is the smallest one satisfying: $\langle Q[@(r_1, \ldots, r_n)]; \sigma \rangle \leadsto_{IS} \langle Q[@(r_1, \ldots, r_n)/v]; \sigma \rangle$, where v is the truth value obtained after evaluating $@(r_1, \ldots, r_n)$ in the lattice $\langle L, \preceq \rangle$ associated with $\mathcal{P}$.*

Definition 4. *Let $\mathcal{P}$ be a program and $\langle Q; \sigma \rangle$ an a.c.a., that is, $\mathcal{Q}$ is a goal not containing atoms. An* interpretive derivation *is a sequence $\langle Q; \sigma \rangle \leadsto_{IS}^{*} \langle Q'; \sigma \rangle$. When $Q' = r \in L$, $\langle L, \preceq \rangle$ being the lattice associated with $\mathcal{P}$, the state $\langle r; \sigma \rangle$ is called a* fuzzy computed answer *(f.c.a.) for that derivation.*

We denote by $\leadsto_{IS}^{+}$ and $\leadsto_{IS}^{*}$ the transitive closure and the reflexive, transitive closure of $\leadsto_{IS}$, respectively. Also note that, sometimes, when it is not important to pay attention on the substitution component of a f.c.a. $\langle r; \theta \rangle$ (maybe, because $\theta = id$) we shall refer to the value component r as the "f.c.a.".

3 Different Notions of Reductant

In this section we survey the different notions of reductants raised over the last years in the field of fuzzy logic programming, describing some of their features which are important for the present work.

The original notion of reductant appeared in the framework of generalized annotated logic programming [9] was initially adapted to the multi-adjoint logic programming framework in the following terms [13]:

Definition 5 (Reductant). *Let $\mathcal{P}$ be a program, A a ground atom, and the (non empty) set of rules $\{\langle C_i \leftarrow_i \mathcal{B}_i; v_i \rangle \mid 1 \leq i \leq n\}$ in $\mathcal{P}$ whose head matches with A (i.e., for each C_i there exists a θ_i such that $A = C_i \theta_i$). A reductant for A in $\mathcal{P}$ is a rule $\langle A \leftarrow @(\mathcal{B}_1, \ldots, \mathcal{B}_n)\theta; \top \rangle$ where $\theta = \theta_1 \cdots \theta_n$, the connective $\leftarrow$ is any implication with an adjoint conjunctor, and the truth function for the intended aggregator $@$ is defined as $@(b_1, \ldots, b_n) = sup\{v_1 \&_1 b_1, \ldots, v_n \&_n b_n\}$.*

This notion was introduced as a valuable theoretical tool for proving the (approximate) completeness property of the multi-adjoint logic programming framework. It is worth to note that, contrariwise to the original definition of a reductant in [9], which is uniquely linked with a program, this one is linked to a ground atom and a program.

In order to preserve the approximate completeness property, it is necessary to construct the "completion" of a program, extending it with all their reductants. So, if one has to compute all the reductants associated with a program, all the atoms of the Herbrand base of that program, which might be infinite, should be taken into account. Hence, although this notion of reductant is theoretically valuable may easily turn impractical because of its potential non-termination. Therefore, it was soon clear that if we wanted to implement complete systems we needed a new notion of reductant leading to finite completions and producing reductants able to be executed more efficiently.

As a step further in the path of trying to avoid the proliferation of an infinite number of reductants, in [14, 15], a new notion named G-reductant was introduced. The aim was that a single generalized reductant was required to cover all the (possibly infinite) calls to atoms headed by a specific predicate symbol defined in a program.

Definition 6 (G-Reductant). *Given a program $\mathcal{P}$ and a definite predicate p in $\mathcal{P}$, a G-reductant for the predicate p in $\mathcal{P}$ is a rule*

$$\langle p(X_1, \ldots, X_m) \leftarrow @(\hat{\theta}_1 \& \mathcal{B}_1, \ldots, \hat{\theta}_n \& \mathcal{B}_n); \top \rangle$$

where

- *$\{\langle C_i \leftarrow_i \mathcal{B}_i; v_i \rangle \mid 1 \leq i \leq n\}$ is the non-empty set of rules such that every C_i is an instance of $p(X_1, \ldots, X_m)$ via the substitution $\theta_i = \{X_1/t_{i1}, \ldots, X_m/t_{im}\}$;*
- *$\hat{\theta}_i \equiv (X_1 \approx t_{i1} \& \cdots \& X_m \approx t_{im})$ with $\approx$ being a unification operator defined by the rule $R_\approx \equiv \langle X \approx X; \top \rangle$, which is considered to be included in every multi-adjoint program;*
- *the connective $\leftarrow$ is any implication with an adjoint conjunction $\&$, and the truth function for the intended aggregator $@$ is the same as in Definition 5.*

Observe that, although only finitely many G-reductants are generated for a given program (just one for each definite predicate in the program), due to the fact that they are built in a non-evaluated form, computing with this kind of reductants becomes inefficient. By this reason, in [16], unfolding-based techniques were applied for simplifying general reductants: the idea was to perform computational steps on the body of G-reductants, at transformation time, in order to improve their efficiency at execution time.

Despite the accomplishments obtained by these transformation techniques, the overall process is little intuitive and, what is worst, it does not guarantee the approximate completeness of a multi-adjoint logic programming framework.

4   A New Notion of Reductant: Sets of Critical Rules

In this section we propose a new notion of reductant, once again in the line of [9], aiming at solving the aforementioned problems inherent to the other notions of reductant. We seek a new notion of reductant such that:

1. is not attached to a certain kind of goals for its computation,
2. can be computed efficiently, and
3. there is no need to consider infinitely many of them.

To begin with, we will informally discuss the underlying idea, and then proceed with the formal definition. Firstly, note that the need of using reductants arises when for a program $\mathcal{P}$ and an atom A (with or without variables) launched as a goal, there exist different derivations leading to fuzzy computed answers with the same computed substitution but leading to incomparable truth-values: $\langle v_1; \theta \rangle, \ldots, \langle v_n; \theta \rangle$. In this case, $\langle \sup\{v_1, \ldots, v_n\}; \theta \rangle$ can be proven to be a fuzzy correct answer which is not computed by the operational mechanism. In general, this problem may occur when there exist sets of rules in a program whose heads unify. We shall say that such sets are "sets of critical rules".

Definition 7 (Critical Rules). *Let $\mathcal{P}$ be a program, and $\mathcal{R}_1 \equiv \langle H_1 \leftarrow B_1, v_1 \rangle$, and $\mathcal{R}_2 \equiv \langle H_2 \leftarrow B_2, v_1 \rangle$ two rules in $\mathcal{P}$ that are renamed apart. The rules $\mathcal{R}_1$ and $\mathcal{R}_2$ are said to be* critical *iff H_1 and H_2 unify, that is, there exists a substitution $\theta = mgu\{H_1, H_2\} \not\equiv fail$.*

A set of rules in $\mathcal{P}$, is a set of critical rules *iff the set of their heads unify.*

Note that a set of critical rules is composed by a subset of rules defining a certain predicate p in $\mathcal{P}$.

Example 1. Let $\mathcal{P} = \{\mathcal{R}_1 : \langle p(a, g(Z)) \leftarrow_1; v_1 \rangle, \mathcal{R}_2 : \langle p(Y, g(Y)) \leftarrow_2; v_2 \rangle\}$ be a program. The rules $\mathcal{R}_1$ and $\mathcal{R}_2$ are critical rules, since $mgu\{p(a, g(Z)), p(Y, g(Y))\} = \{Y/a, Z/a\} \not\equiv fail$.   □

Now we can introduce the new notion of reductant.

Definition 8 (Critical Reductant). *Let $\mathcal{P}$ be a program and $\{\langle H_i \leftarrow_i \mathcal{B}_i; v_i \rangle \mid 1 \leq i \leq n\}$ a set of critical rules in $\mathcal{P}$ with $\theta = mgu\{H_1, \ldots, H_n\}$. Then, the* *rule* $\langle H_1\theta \leftarrow @_{sup}(v_1 \&_1 \mathcal{B}_1, \ldots, v_n \&_n \mathcal{B}_n)\theta; \top\rangle$ *is a critical reductant of* $\mathcal{P}$, *where the connective* $\leftarrow$ *is any implication with an adjoint conjunctor, and the truth function for the aggregator* $@_{sup}$ *is the supremum operator.*

It is worth to recall that we are assuming an extended language where truth degrees and adjoint conjunctions are allowed in the body of program rules.

Observe that for programs with finitely many rules there always exist finitely many critical reductants. If $\mathcal{P}_p$ is the set of rules defining a predicate p, the elements in the powerset of $\mathcal{P}_p$ (excluding the empty set and the singletons) are the candidates to generate critical reductants, but only those which form sets of critical rules truly generate them. The sets of critical rules ordered by inclusion form a partially ordered set. The critical reductants obtained from the maximal elements of that set of sets will be called *maximal reductants*.

Example 2. For the program $\mathcal{P}$ of Example 1 there exists just one reductant, namely $\langle p(a, g(a)) \leftarrow sup\{v_1, v_2\}; \top\rangle$, which is obtained from the maximal set of critical rules $\{\mathcal{R}_1, \mathcal{R}_2\}$. Therefore, this is a maximal reductant.

5   Formal Properties of Critical Reductants

In this section we establish some important properties of critical reductants which are substantive for the correctness of the multi-adjoint logic programming framework. The first result is a technical lemma, which will be used later.

Lemma 1. *Let* $\mathcal{A}$ *be a formula,* $\mathcal{I}$ *an interpretation and* θ *a substitution. Then* $\mathcal{I}(\mathcal{A}) \leq \mathcal{I}(\mathcal{A}\theta)$.

Proposition 1. *If* $\mathcal{R}$ *is a critical reductant of a multi-adjoint program* $\mathcal{P}$, *then every interpretation* $\mathcal{I}$ *which is a model of* $\mathcal{P}$ *is also a model of the critical reductant* $\mathcal{R}$, *that is,* $\mathcal{P} \models \mathcal{R}$.

The converse result is not true in general; in fact, the natural requirement for it to be true is very restrictive, as we will show in Proposition 2.

Given a program $\mathcal{P}$, the set of the critical reductants of $\mathcal{P}$ will be denoted as $\mathcal{P}_R$, and the following result shows a procedure in order to obtain a model from $\mathcal{P}_R$.

Proposition 2. *Given a multi-adjoint program* $\mathcal{P}$ *and a model* $\mathcal{I}$ *of* $\mathcal{P}_R$, *if* $\mathcal{I}(A) = \inf\{\mathcal{I}(A\theta) \mid \langle A\theta \leftarrow @_{sup}(v_1 \&_1 \mathcal{B}_1, \ldots, v_n \&_n \mathcal{B}_n)\theta; \top\rangle$ *is a critical reductant*$\}$ *then* $\mathcal{I}$ *is a model of* $\mathcal{P}$.

The following proposition relates the notion of critical reductant and the G-reductant developed in [14,15]. We claim the equivalence between maximal critical reductants of a multi-adjoint program $\mathcal{P}$ and the G-reductants of $\mathcal{P}$, after a sequence of unfolding steps.

In the context of logic programs, "unfolding" means to transform a program rule by replacing it by the set of rules obtained after application of a computation step (in all its possible forms) on the body of the selected rule [18]. Unfolding was defined for the multi-adjoint framework in [8].

Let $\mathcal{P}$ be a program and $\mathcal{R} \equiv \langle A \leftarrow B; v \rangle \in \mathcal{P}$ a program rule. Then, the fuzzy unfolding of program $\mathcal{P}$ with respect to rule $\mathcal{R}$ is the new program $\mathcal{P}' = (\mathcal{P} \smallsetminus \{\mathcal{R}\}) \cup \mathcal{U}$ such that: $\mathcal{U} = \{\langle A\sigma \leftarrow B'; v \rangle \mid \langle B; id \rangle \leadsto_{AS} \langle B'; \sigma \rangle\}$. Note that the set $\mathcal{U}$ may be a singleton when the unfolding step is performed on an atom of the body with a predicate at the root which is defined deterministically by just one rule. Unfolding is a program transformation technique which preserves semantics.

Proposition 3. *Any G-reductant of a multi-adjoint program $\mathcal{P}$ can be transformed into a maximal critical reductant of $\mathcal{P}$ after a sequence of unfolding steps.*

An important question, given a multi-adjoint program, is to know how many reductants are necessary to take into account in order to preserve the approximate completeness of the framework. We focus now on this question, and drive the discussion by means of one small but significative example.

Example 3. Given the program

$$\mathcal{P} = \{\mathcal{R}_1 : \langle p(a, Y, Z) \leftarrow; v_1 \rangle, \mathcal{R}_2 : \langle p(X, b, Z) \leftarrow; v_2 \rangle, \mathcal{R}_3 : \langle p(X, Y, c) \leftarrow; v_3 \rangle\}$$

one can compute the following reductants, according to the corresponding sets of critical rules:

- Set of critical rules $\{\mathcal{R}_1, \mathcal{R}_2\}$: $Red_1 \equiv \langle p(a, b, Z) \leftarrow sup\{v_1, v_2\}; \top \rangle$,
- Set of critical rules $\{\mathcal{R}_1, \mathcal{R}_3\}$: $Red_2 \equiv \langle p(a, Y, c) \leftarrow sup\{v_1, v_3\}; \top \rangle$,
- Set of critical rules $\{\mathcal{R}_2, \mathcal{R}_3\}$: $Red_3 \equiv \langle p(X, b, c) \leftarrow sup\{v_2, v_3\}; \top \rangle$,
- Set of critical rules $\{\mathcal{R}_1, \mathcal{R}_2, \mathcal{R}_3\}$: $Red_4 \equiv \langle p(a, b, c) \leftarrow sup\{v_1, v_2, v_3\}; \top \rangle$. Note that this is a maximal reductant.

Some derivations that can be performed with the original program $\mathcal{P}$ and the goal $p(a, b, Z)$ are:

- $\langle p(a, b, Z); id \rangle \overset{\mathcal{R}_1}{\leadsto}_{AS} \langle v_1; \{Y_1/b, Z/Z_1\} \rangle$ with fca1 $\langle v_1; \{Z/Z_1\} \rangle$,
- $\langle p(a, b, Z); id \rangle \overset{\mathcal{R}_2}{\leadsto}_{AS} \langle v_2; \{X_1/a, Z/Z_1\} \rangle$ with fca2 $\langle v_2; \{Z/Z_1\} \rangle$,
- $\langle p(a, b, Z); id \rangle \overset{\mathcal{R}_3}{\leadsto}_{AS} \langle v_3; \{X_1/a, Y_1/b, Z/c\} \rangle$ with fca3 $\langle v_3; \{Z/c\} \rangle$.

It is worth to state that the fuzzy computed answers fca1 and fca2 are problematic, because they compute the same answer substitution but different truth degrees. From this, by soundness, it can be inferred that $\langle v_1; \{Z/Z_1\} \rangle$ and $\langle v_2; \{Z/Z_1\} \rangle$ are correct answers and, therefore, the existence of a correct answer $\langle sup\{v_1, v_2\}; \{Z/Z_1\} \rangle$ which is better than the preceding correct answers, but cannot be computed by the operational mechanism. In order to solve this problem it is necessary to complete $\mathcal{P}$ with the reductant Red_1. Now the following derivation is possible: $\langle p(a, b, Z); id \rangle \overset{Red_1}{\leadsto}_{AS} \langle sup\{v_1, v_2\}; \{Z/Z_1\} \rangle$, that computes the missing fuzzy computed answer.

On the other hand, note that just including the unique maximal reductant Red_4 (disregarding the other reductants of $\mathcal{P}$) does not solve the problem. The only leading derivation in this case is: $\langle p(a, b, Z); id \rangle \overset{Red_4}{\leadsto}_{AS} \langle \sup\{v_1, v_2, v_3\}; \{Z/c\} \rangle$, computing the fuzzy computed answer $\langle \sup\{v_1, v_2, v_3\}; \{Z/c\} \rangle$ but not the correct answer $\langle \sup\{v_1, v_2\}; \{Z/Z_1\} \rangle$.

Finally, if we consider the goal $p(a, b, c)$ and the program $\mathcal{P}$, it is possible to obtain the following one step derivations:

- $\langle p(a, b, c); id \rangle \overset{\mathcal{R}_1}{\leadsto}_{AS} \langle v_1; \{Y_1/b, Z_1/c\} \rangle$ with fca4 $\langle v_1; id \rangle$,
- $\langle p(a, b, c); id \rangle \overset{\mathcal{R}_2}{\leadsto}_{AS} \langle v_2; \{X_1/a, Z_1/c\} \rangle$ with fca5 $\langle v_2; id \rangle$,
- $\langle p(a, b, c); id \rangle \overset{\mathcal{R}_3}{\leadsto}_{AS} \langle v_3; \{X_1/a, Y_1/b\} \rangle$ with fca6 $\langle v_3; id \rangle$.

The fuzzy computed answers fca4, fca5 and fca6 are correct answers as well, and this leads, by definition, to the existence of the correct answer $\langle \sup\{v_1, v_2, v_3\}; id \rangle$. This makes the extension of $\mathcal{P}$ with the reductant Red_4, in order to compute it, necessary: $\langle p(a, b, c); id \rangle \overset{Red_4}{\leadsto}_{AS} \langle \sup\{v_1, v_2, v_3\}; id \rangle$,   □

The previous example shows that all reductants of a program (associated with the different sets of critical rules) are necessary for preserving the (approximate) completeness of the multi-adjoint logic programming framework. Also, it can be seen as a counter-example to the statement claiming that, "it is only necessary to extend a multi-adjoint program with a significative subset of its reductants to preserve completeness".

6   Conclusions

We have revisited the concept of a reductant in the framework of multi-adjoint logic programming. After presenting a summary of the different notions of reductant appeared in this field, we have defined the concept of a set of critical rules and a new notion of reductant. Significantly, the new notion of reductant allows for recovering approximate completeness by including just finitely many critical reductants; contrariwise to that happens with the previous notions proposed in the literature, which generate infinitely many of them. We have studied some of the formal properties of the new notion of reductant and its relationships with other notions of reductant. Specifically, we have proved that, as expected, any model of $\mathcal{P}$ is also a model of their critical reductants. However, the converse property does not hold in general, but under very restrictive conditions. We have proved that any G-reductant can be transformed into a maximal critical reductant by using unfolding transformations. Also we have shown, by means of a small but significative example, that it is necessary to compute all the reductants associated with a multi-adjoint logic program (and not only a significative subset of them: e.g., its maximal critical reductants). These reductants must be attached to the program in order to preserve the approximate completeness property of the multi-adjoint logic programming framework.

References

1. Baldwin, J.F., Martin, T.P., Pilsworth, B.W.: Fril- Fuzzy and Evidential Reasoning in Artificial Intelligence. John Wiley &; Sons, Inc. (1995)
2. Cao, T.H., Noi, N.V.: A framework for linguistic logic programming. International Journal of Intelligent Systems 25(6), 559–580 (2010)
3. Eklund, P., Galán, M.Á., Helgesson, R., Kortelainen, J., Moreno, G., Vázquez, C.: Towards categorical fuzzy logic programming. In: Masulli, F. (ed.) WILF 2013. LNCS (LNAI), vol. 8256, pp. 109–121. Springer, Heidelberg (2013)
4. Eklund, P., Klawonn, F.: Neural fuzzy logic programming. IEEE Transactions on Neural Networks 3(5), 815–818 (1992)
5. Guadarrama, S., Muñoz, S., Vaucheret, C.: Fuzzy prolog: A new approach using soft constraints propagation. Fuzzy Sets and Systems 144(1), 127–150 (2004)
6. Hájek, P.: Metamathematics of fuzzy logic, vol. 4. Springer (1998)
7. Ishizuka, M., Kanai, N.: Prolog-ELF Incorporating Fuzzy Logic. In: Joshi, A.K. (ed.) Proc. of the 9th International Joint Conference on Artificial Intelligence (IJ-CAI 1985), Los Angeles, CA, USA, pp. 701–703. Morgan Kaufmann (1985)
8. Julián, P., Moreno, G., Penabad, J.: On Fuzzy Unfolding. A Multi-adjoint Approach. Fuzzy Sets and Systems, Elsevier 154, 16–33 (2005)
9. Kifer, M., Subrahmanian, V.: Theory of generalized annotated logic programming and its applications. Journal of Logic Programming 12, 335–367 (1992)
10. Krajči, S., Lencses, R., Vojtáš, P.: A comparison of fuzzy and annotated logic programming. Fuzzy Sets and Systems 144(1), 173–192 (2004)
11. Kuhr, T., Vychodil, V.: Fuzzy logic programming reduced to reasoning with attribute implications. Fuzzy Sets and Systems (in press 2014)
12. Le, V.H., Liu, F., Tran, D.K.: Fuzzy linguistic logic programming and its applications. Theory and Practice of Logic Programming 9, 309–341 (2009)
13. Medina, J., Ojeda-Aciego, M., Vojtáš, P.: Similarity-based unification: A multi-adjoint approach. Fuzzy Sets and Systems 146(1), 43–62 (2004)
14. Morcillo, P., Moreno, G.: A practical approach for ensuring completeness of multi-adjoint logic computations via general reductants. In: Lucio, G.M.P., Peña, R. (eds.) Proc. of IX Jornadas sobre Programación y Lenguajes, PROLE 2009, San Sebastián, Spain, September 8-11, pp. 355–363. Universidad del País Vasco (2009) ISBN 978-84-692-4600-9
15. Morcillo, P., Moreno, G.: Improving completeness in multi-adjoint logic computations via general reductants. In: Proc. of 2011 IEEE Symposium on Foundations of Computational Intelligence, Paris, France, April 11-15, pp. 138–145. IEEE (2011)
16. Morcillo, P., Moreno, G.: Simplifying general reductants with unfolding-based techniques. In: Arenas, P., Gulías, V., Nogueira, P. (eds.) Proc. of XI Jornadas sobre Programación y Lenguajes, PROLE 2011, A Coruña, Spain, September 5-7, pp. 154–168 (sección de trabajos en progreso). Universidade da Coruña (2011) ISBN 978-84-9749-487-8
17. Moreno, G., Pascual, V.: A hybrid programming scheme combining fuzzy-logic and functional-logic resources. Fuzzy Sets and Systems 160(10), 1402–1419 (2009), Special Issue: Fuzzy Sets in Interdisciplinary Perception and Intelligence
18. Pettorossi, A., Proietti, M.: Rules and Strategies for Transforming Functional and Logic Programs. ACM Computing Surveys 28(2), 360–414 (1996)
19. Vojtáš, P.: Fuzzy Logic Programming. Fuzzy Sets and Systems 124(1), 361–370 (2001)
20. Yasui, H., Hamada, Y., Mukaidono, M.: Fuzzy prolog based on Lukasiewicz implication and bounded product. In: Proc. of IEEE Symp on Fuzzy Systems FUZZ-IEEE, pp. 949–954 (1995)

Author Index